Mitsubishi - Pajero
Vehicle Repair Manual

Also sold as Mitsubishi - Montero and Shogun

Petrol/Gasoline and Diesel models

NM - 2000 t

NP 2004 to 2006 (Exceed - Luxury model)

NS - NT 2007 to 2010

This repair and maintenance manual has been published to help provide Mitsubishi Pajero owners and enthusiasts with an invaluable, comprehensive and thorough guide in all aspects of restoration, maintenance and mechanical repair work.

The manual is published from the latest information obtained by the publishers. Where extensive research is undertaken to obtain the information for the benefit of people who purchase this manual.

DISCLAIMER

Every endeavour has been made to ensure all information in this manual is accurate. Mistakes and omissions can always occur, and the publisher does not assume any duty or care, or legal responsibility in relation to the content of this book.

Maintenance, repair and tune-up are essential for safe and reliable use of all motor vehicles. These operations should be undertaken in such a manner as to eliminate the possibility of personal injury or in such a way that could damage the vehicle or compromise the safety of the vehicle, driver, passenger or a third party.

Published By:
Renniks Publications Pty Ltd,
Unit 3
37-39 Green Street,
Banksmeadow
NSW, 2019
Australia.

Phone: 61 2 9695 7055
Fax::   61 2 9695 7355

www.ellery.com.au   www.renniks.com

© Copyright 2009

Copyright
This publication is copyright. Other than for the purposes of and subject to the conditions prescribed under the Copyright Act, no part of it may in any form or by any means (electronic, mechanical, microcopying, photocopying, recording or otherwise) be reproduced, stored in a retrieval system or transmitted without prior written permission. Enquiries should be addressed to the Publisher.

National Library of Australia Card number and ISBN

ISBN 1 87672021 2

INDEX

CONTENTS	PAGE

GENERAL INFORMATION ... 7
- Vehicle Identification ... 7
- General Specifications (Australian Vehicles) ... 8
- Official Recall Information ... 10

ENGINE TUNE-UP and MAINTENANCE ... 11
- Petrol / Gasoline Engines ... 16
- Diesel Engines ... 19
- Jacking & Lifting Points ... 21

V6 ENGINE MAINTENANCE & REBUILD 3.0L, 3.5L, & 3.8L SOHC M.P.I. ... 22
- Engine Maintenance ... 23
- Engine Rebuild ... 40
- Problem Diagnosis ... 51
- Specifications ... 52

V6 ENGINE MAINTENANCE AND REBUILD (3.5L) DOHC GDI ... 56
- Engine Maintenance ... 58
- Engine Rebuild ... 74
- Problem Diagnosis ... 84
- Specifications ... 85

2.8 litre DIESEL SOHC (4M40) ENGINE MAINTENANCE AND REBUILD ... 88
- Engine Maintenance ... 90
- Engine Rebuild ... 108
- Problem Diagnosis ... 121
- Specifications ... 122

3.2 litre, incl COMMON RAIL - DOHC (4M41) DIESEL ENGINE MAINTENANCE AND REBUILD ... 124
- Engine Maintenance ... 126
- Engine Rebuild ... 142
- Problem Diagnosis ... 156
- Specifications ... 157

ENGINE ELECTRICAL ... 161
General Maintenance (Battery) ... 162
Alternator System ... 163
- Removal and Installation ... 168
- Component Checking ... 169
- Specifications ... 172

Starter System ... 168
- Removal and Installation ... 168
- Repairs ... 169
- Specifications ... 172

COOLING SYSTEM ... 173
- Maintenance ... 174
- Water Pumps and Fittings ... 173
- Cooling Fans ... 180
- Radiator ... 181
- Problem Solving and Diagnosis ... 183

CONTENTS	PAGE
IGNITION, FUEL & EMISSION SYSTEMS (Petrol)	**184**
On Vehicle Inspection	185
Emission System	196
Ignition System	201
Fuel System	203
GLOW, FUEL & EMISSION SYSTEMS (Diesel)	**212**
On Vehicle Inspection	213
Glow System	218
Diesel Fuel System	220
Emission System	229
Turbo System	231
EXHAUST SYSTEM	**235**
CLUTCH	**239**
Maintenance	239
Major Repairs	240
Problem Solving and Diagnosis	244
MANUAL TRANSAXLE V5M31	**246**
Maintenance	247
Major Repairs and Rebuild	248
Transmission Assembly	250
Specifications	256
MANUAL TRANSAXLE V5MT1	**257**
Maintenance	257
Major Repairs and Rebuild	258
Specifications	264
AUTOMATIC TRANSAXLE - V5A51	**265**
Maintenance	266
Minor Repairs	270
Minor Repairs	271
Transmission Assembly	273
Specifications	282
TRANSFER	**285**
Maintenance	286
Minor Repairs	287
Transmission Assembly	290
Specifications	299
STEERING	**301**
Minor Maintenance	302
Rack & Pinion Gear	304
Power Steering Pump	307
Steering Column	313
Problem Solving	315
Specifications	316

CONTENTS	PAGE
FRONT SUSPENSION, AXLE & DRIVESHAFTS	**317**
Wheel Alignment	318
Front Suspension	320
Front Axle Assembly	323
Front Hub Assembly	324
Front Driveshafts	325
Differential Assembly	329
Problem Diagnosis	332
Specifications	334
REAR SUSPENSION, AXLE & DRIVESHAFTS	**335**
Wheel Alignment	336
Suspension	337
Rear Hub Assembly	342
Rear Propeller Shaft	344
Rear Axle Assembly	346
Differential Assembly	349
Specifications	353
BRAKE SYSTEMS	**354**
Routine Maintenance	355
Master Cylinder & Booster (no ABS)	359
Hydraulic Brake Booster (HBB)	361
Load Proportioning Valve	364
Front Brake Assembly	365
Rear Brake Assembly	367
Park Brake Assembly	369
ABS Components	372
Specifications	378
FUEL TANK and EFI FUEL PUMP	**380**
General Information	380
Service Operations	381
Specifications	386
BODY	**387**
Dash/Instrument Panel	388
Back Door / Tail Gate	392
Front and Rear Door Assemblies	395
Stationary Glass	404
Headlining and Trim	404
Seats and Seat Belt Assemblies	405
Front Sheet Metal	409
Bumper Bars & Front Grille	411
Windscreen Wipers & Washers	415
HEATING, AIR CONDITIONING and AUTOMATIC CLIMATE CONTROL	**418**
General Information / Maintenance	419
Compressor	420
Condenser Assembly	421
Evaporator / Receiver Drier	422
Front Heater & Blower Assembly	422

CONTENTS	PAGE

HEATING, AIR CONDITIONING and AUTOMATIC CLIMATE CONTROL Continued.
- Heating Component Inspection 424
- Rear Heater & Air Conditioner 430
- Automatic Climate Control 433
- Problem Diagnosis 435

BODY ELECTRICAL 438
- Service Operations - Instrument Cluster 439
- Radio - Stereo Systems 442
- Switches, Components & Keyless Entry 445
- SRS - Supplemental Restraint System 448
- Horn Assembly 451
- Cruise Control 451
- Lights & Switches 454
- Specifications 461

DIAGNOSTICS 463
- General Information 464
- MPI 3.5 & 3.8 (pre 2004) SOHC Diagnostics 465
- MPI 3.8 (post 2004) SOHC Diagnostics 471
- GDI DOHC Diagnostics 481
- 4M41 3.2L DOHC Diagnostics 488
- 4M41 3.2L DOHC Common Rail Diagnostics 495
- Cruise Control 502
- Automatic Transmission 503
- Automatic Climate Control 507
- ABS Diagnostics 508
- SRS Diagnostics 510

ELECTRICAL 513
- Fuses & Relays 513
- Wiring Colour Codes 515
- Wiring Diagrams 515

GENERAL INFORMATION

VIN - Vehicle Identification Number
The vehicle identification number is stamped on the bulkhead in the engine compartment.

Compliance Plate
The compliance plate certifies that your vehicle complies to the Country design rules at the time of manufacture.

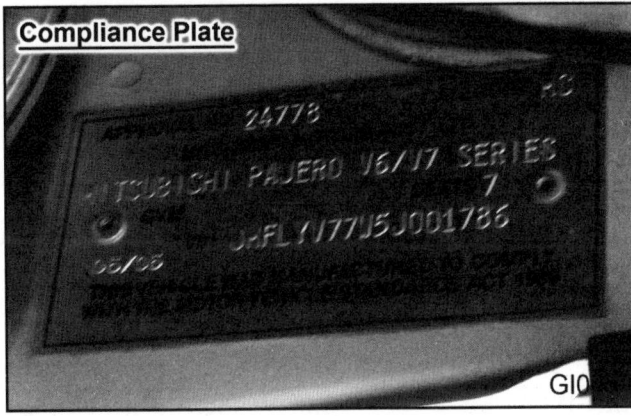

Vehicle Information Code Plate
The vehicle information code plate displays the model code, engine model, transmission model, body colour code, interior code, option code and exterior code.

Vehicle Data Plate
The vehicle date plate gives the vehicle information, this should be used to assist when purchasing parts etc, to ensure the correct components are used.

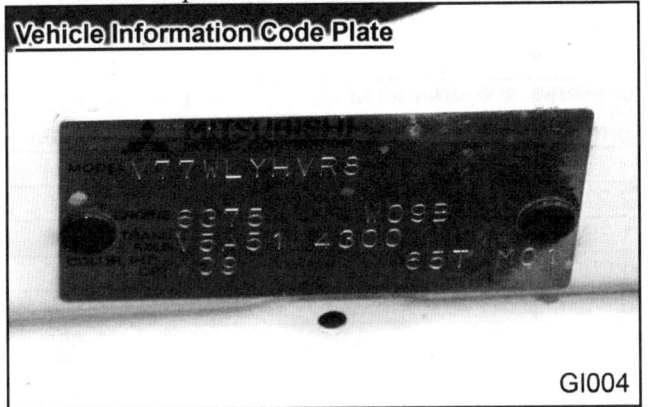
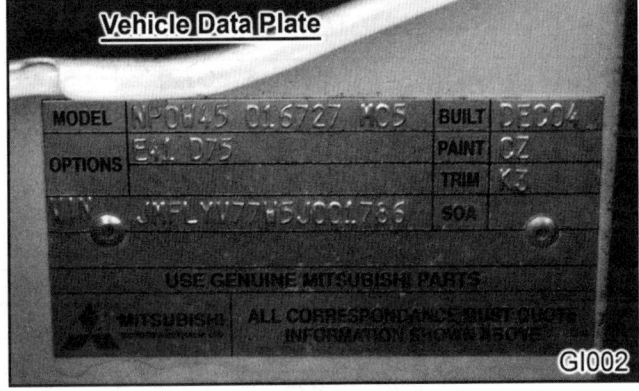

Engine Identification Number
The engine identification number is stamped on the engine cylinder block. (refer to appropriate engine chapter for location of engine number).

Tyre Placard
The tyre placard is located inside the drivers side door jam and indicates the correct tyre inflation pressures for your vehicle.

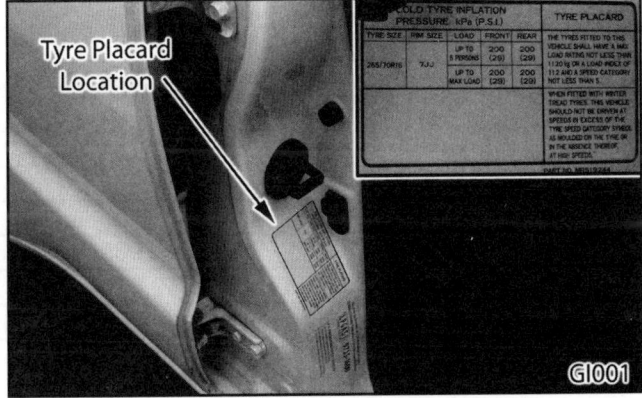

7

GENERAL MODEL SPECIFICATIONS (Australia)

Note: All general information specifications in this section are for Australian release vehicles unless otherwise specified. Specifications for vehicles in other countries may vary slightly.

ENGINE DATA

ENGINE	3.0L V6 (6G72)	3.5L V6 (6G74 MPI)	3.5L V6 (6G74 GDI)	3.8L V6 (6G75)
Displacement (cc)	2,972	3,497	3,496	3,828 cc
Bore x Stroke (mm)	91.1 x 76.0	93.0 x 85.8	93.0 x 85.8	95.0 x 90.0
Compression Ratio	9.0:1	9.0:1	9.5 / 10.4:1	9.5:1
Max Power KW@rpm	109kW @ 5000rpm	140kW @ 5000rpm	153kW @ 5000rpm	150kW @ 5000rpm
Max Torque Nm@rpm	234Nm @ 4000rpm	303Nm @ 3500rpm	300Nm @ 3000rpm	314Nm @ 3250rpm
Firing Order	1-2-3-4-5-6	1-2-3-4-5-6	1-2-3-4-5-6	1-2-3-4-5-6

ENGINE	3.8L V6 (6G75)(NS)	2.8L (4M40)	2.8L (4M40) Turbo Intercooled	3.2L (4M41)
Displacement (cc)	3.828 cc	2,835 cc	2,835 cc	3200 cc
Bore x Stroke (mm)	95.0 x 90.0	95.0 x 100.0	95.0 x 100.0	98.5 x 105.0
Compression Ratio	9.5:1	21.0:1	21.0:1	17.0:1
Max Power KW@rpm	175kW @ 5500rpm	71kW @ 4000rpm	92kW @ 4000rpm	121kW @ 3800rpm
Max Torque Nm@rpm	329Nm @ 2750rpm	198Nm @ 2000rpm	292Nm @ 2000rpm	373Nm @ 2000rpm
Firing Order	1-2-3-4-5-6			

TRANSMISSION DATA

PETROL ENGINE	3.0L V6 (6G72)		3.5L V6 (6G74 MPI)		3.5L V6 (6G74 GDI)		3.8L V6 (6G75)	
RATIO	Auto	Manual	Auto	Manual	Auto	Manual	Auto	Manual
1st	2.826	3.918	3.789	4.234	2.804	3.952	3.789	4.234
2nd	1.493	2.261	2.057	2.238	1.531	2.238	2.057	2.238
3rd	1.000	1.395	1.421	1.398	1.000	1.398	1.421	1.398
4th	0.730	1.000	1.000	1.000	0.705	1.000	1.000	1.000
5th		0.829		0.731	0.819		0.761	0.731	0.819
Reverse	2.703	3.952	3.865	3.553	2.393	3.952	3.865	3.553
Transfer								
- low	1.925	1.925	1.900	1.900	1.900	1.900	1.900	1.900
- high	1.000	1.000	1.000	1.000	1.000	1.000	1.000	1.000
Final Gear	4.875	4.875	4.300	4.300	4.636	4.636	4.300	4.300

DIESEL ENGINE	2.8L (4M40)		2.8L (4M40) Turbo		3.2L (4M41)	
RATIO	Auto	Manual	Auto	Manual	Auto	Manual
1st	-	3.967	-	3.952	3.789	4.234
2nd	-	2.136	-	2.238	2.057	2.238
3rd	-	1.360	-	1.398	1.421	1.398
4th	-	1.000	-	1.000	1.000	1.000
5th	-	0.856	-	0.761	0.731	0.761
Reverse	-	3.578	-	3.952	3.865	3.553
Transfer						
- low		1.900		1.900	1.900	1.900
- high		1.000		1.000	1.000	1.000
Final Gear		4.875		4.875	3.917	4.100

GENERAL INFORMATION

ELECTRICAL

PETROL ENGINE	3.0L V6 (6G72)	3.5L V6 (6G74 MPI)	3.5L V6 (6G74 GDI)	3.8L V6 (6G75)
Battery	48AH/5 HR	48AH/5 HR	48AH/5 HR	48AH/5 HR
Alternator	75 Amp	90 Amp	90 Amp	90 Amp

DIESEL ENGINE	2.8L (4M40)	2.8L (4M40) Turbo	3.2L (4M41)
Battery	64AH/5 HR	64AH/5 HR	64AH/5 HR
Alternator	65 Amp	65 Amp	65 Amp

FUEL TANK

	NM SWB	NM LWB	NP SWB	NP LWB	NS - NT SWB	NS - NT LWB
Capacity (L)	75 / 45	90	65	90	69	88

TOWING CAPACITY

	3.5L (V6)	3.5L (V6)	3.8L (V6)	2.8L (diesel)	3.2L (diesel)
Without Trailer Brakes (kg)	750	750	750	750	750
With Trailer Brakes (kg)	2500	2500	2500	2500	2500
Max Tow Ball Weight (kg)	250	250	250	250	250

DIMENSIONS

	NM SWB	NM LWB	NP SWB	NP LWB	NS - NT SWB	NS - NT LWB
Overall Length (mm)	4260	4775 / 4795	4315	4810 / 4830	4385	4900
Overall Width (mm)	1845	1845	1895[1]	1895[1]	1875	1875
Overall Height (mm)	1845	1855	1845[2]	1855[2]	1880	1900
Front Track (mm)	1560	1560	1560	1560	1560	1570
Rear Track (mm)	1560	1560	1560	1560	1560	1570
Wheel Base (mm)	2545	2780	2545	2780	2545	2780
Front overhang (mm)	710	710	745	745	765	765
Rear overhang (mm)	1005	1285 / 1305	1025	1285 / 1305	1075	1355
Gross Vehicle Mass (kg)	2510	2760	2510	2810 / 2760	2550/2660	2920
Max Approach Angle	42°	42°	39°	39°	36.7°	36.6°
Max Departure Angle	33.5°	24°	33.5°	24°	34.8°	25.0°
Turning Circle (m)					10.6	11.4

[1] Without wheelhouse mouldings (flares)
[2] Without roof rails

WHEELS & TYRES (NM/NP)

Wheel Type	Wheel Size	Rim Offset (mm)	Tyre Size	Wheel Runout (mm) Radial	Lateral
Steel	16 x 6JJ	46 mm	235/80R16 109S	1.2 or less	1.2 or less
Aluminum	16 x 7JJ	46 mm	265/70R16 112S	1.0 or less	1.0 or less
	17 x 7.5JJ	46 mm	265/70R17 112H	1.0 or less	1.0 or less

WHEELS & TYRES (NS)

Wheel Type	Wheel Size	Rim Offset (mm)	Tyre Size	Wheel Runout (mm) Radial	Lateral
Aluminum	17 x 7.5JJ	46 mm	265/65R17 112H	1.0 or less	1.0 or less
	18 x 7.5JJ	46 mm	265/60R18 110H	1.0 or less	1.0 or less

OFFICIAL MODEL RECALL INFORMATION (Australia)

DATE & CAMPAIGN NUMBER	MODEL & YEARS	DETAILS
31/08/2001 #010008	NM Pajero February 2000 to June 2001	Accumulator diaphragm on the booster may have been assembled incorrectly and if it fails will reduce the power assistance.
24/10/2001 #010009	NM Pajero (parts manufactured b/w 7th July 2000 and 20th September 2001)	Tow bar tongues susceptible to embrittlement that may cause the tongue to break in service under certain circumstances.
24/07/2007 #010036	NS Pajero (automatic) 21st November 2006 and 23rd March 2007	Possibility the bolt welded to the manual control lever may develop a crack when shift cable attaching nut is tightened. May result in incorrect gear selection than that shown on the selector lever.
28/11/2007 #010037	NS Pajero 20th August 2007 and 23rd August 2007	Incorrect nuts used to retain the front right hand drive shaft and both the front propeller shafts.
18/09/2008 #JKG2008-GC28-33	NM & NP Pajero (ABS vehicles) February 2000 to 28th July 2003	Potential for the accumulator fitted to the hydraulic brake booster to lose pressure.

ENGINE TUNE-UP & MAINTENANCE

Description	Page
Check Oil Level	12
Check Oil Pressure	12
Oil Filter	12
Replacement	12
Checking and Filling Cooling System	13
Inspect and Replace Air Filter	13
Compression Check	14
6G7 - Petrol Vehicles	14
4M4 - Diesel Vehicles	14
Compression Test Results	14
Drive Belts	14
Inspection	14
Stages of Belt Wear	15
Drive Belt Tension - 6G7	15
Belt Replacement - 6G7	15
Drive Belt Tension - 4M4	15
Alternator Belt Tension & Adjustment - 4M4	15
A/C Compressor Belt Tension & Adjustment - 4M4	16
PETROL / GASOLINE ENGINES	16
Inspection Of Spark Plugs	16
Intake Manifold Vacuum Check - 6G7	16

Description	Page
Inspection & Adjustment - Ignition Timing	17
6G7-MPI	17
6G7-GDI	17
Idle Speed Inspection - 6G7	17
Vehicles with catalytic converter	17
Idle Mixture Inspection - 6G7	17
Vehicles with catalytic converter	17
Idle Speed & Mixture Adjustment - 6G7	17
Vehicles without catalytic converter	17
Lash Adjuster Inspection - 6G7	18
Bleeding Lash Adjuster System	18
Valve Clearance Check & Adjust	18
Petrol V6 3.0, 3.5 & 3.8 SOHC	18
MIVEC Variable Valve Timing 3.8 SOHC	18
DIESEL ENGINES	19
Fuel Filter and Water Trap	19
Bleeding Air from Fuel System	19
Valve Clearance Check & Adjust	20
4M40	20
4M41	20
MAINTENANCE HINTS	21
JACKING AND LIFTING POINTS	21

ENGINE TUNE-UP & MAINTENANCE

CHECK OIL LEVEL

The oil level should be between the L & F marks on the level gauge. Inspect for leakage, and fill oil up to the F mark if level is low.

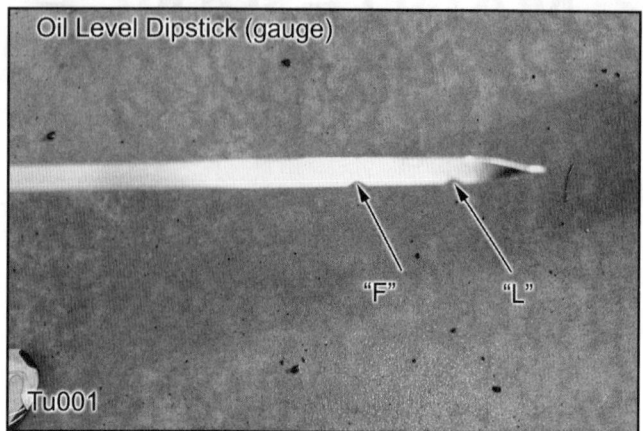

Petrol Engines
Oil Capacity
3.5 litre
  SOHC MPI - Without oil filter.................4.0 L
              - With oil filter.....................4.3 L
3.8 litre
  SOHC MPI - Without oil filter.................4.3 L
              - With oil filter.....................4.3 L

  DOHC GDI - Without oil filter.................4.6 L
              - With oil filter.....................4.9 L

Oil Classification
  SAE Grade .... 0W-30, 5W-30 or 10W- 30*
  API Grade ....SG or Higher
* any of these SAE grades providing API grade is correct.

Diesel Engines
  4M4:   - Without oil filter.................8.8 L
              - With oil filter.....................9.8 L
Oil Classification
  SAE Grade .... 0W-30, 5W-30 or 10W- 30*
  API Grade ....CD or Higher
* any of these SAE grades providing API grade is correct.

CHECKING ENGINE OIL PRESSURE

1. Ensure that engine is at operating temperature and disconnect wiring harness connector from oil pressure sender unit.
2. Loosen and remove oil pressure sender unit.
3. Install a suitable oil pressure gauge assembly into oil pressure sender unit hole.
4. Start engine and check oil pressure reading with engine running under no load.

Oil Pressure: Idle 29kPa
                  3500 rpm 294-686kPa

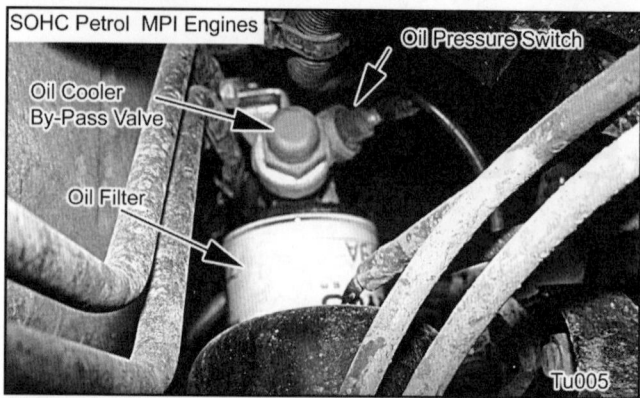

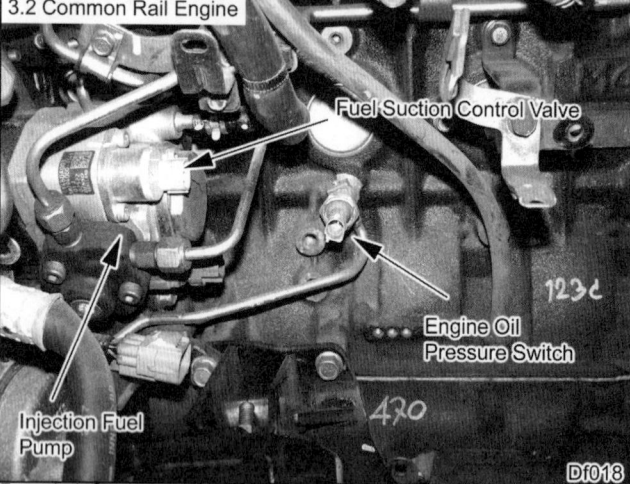

5. a) After completing test, apply LOCTITE 243 sealant or equivalent to sender unit threads.
   b) Install and torque sender unit.
   Oil sender unit..9-11 Nm
   c) Install wiring harness connector, start engine and check for oil leaks.

OIL FILTER

* The oil filter should be replaced every 10,000 Kilometres or 6 months whichever occurs first. It is common practice for the oil filter and engine oil to be replaced together.

Petrol V6 3.0, 3.5 & 3.8 SOHC Engine

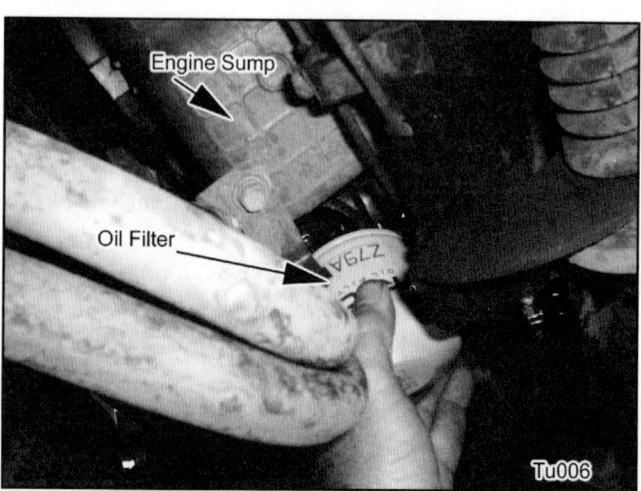

12

ENGINE TUNE-UP & MAINTENANCE

Petrol V6 GDI 3.5 DOHC Engine

Diesel 4M40 2.8 SOHC & 4M41 3.2 DOHC Engine

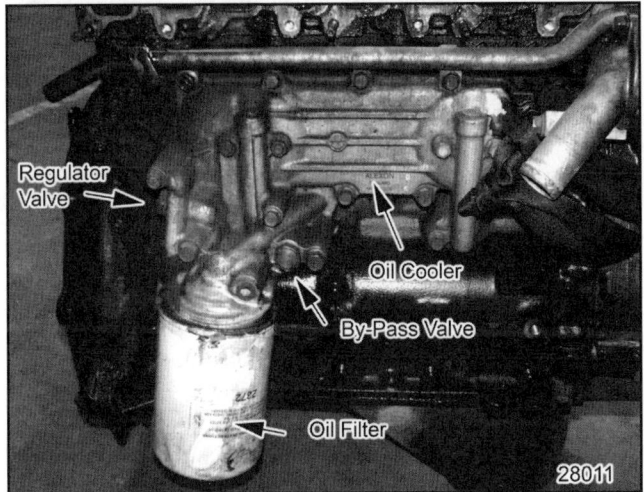

Replacement

1. Ensure engine is at operating temperature and switched off. (Hot oil is thinner, therefore drains better).
2. Place a drain try under the vehicle, remove the sump plug, draining the engine oil.
3. Unscrew oil filter with a suitable oil filter wrench, then remove and discard.
4. Smear some clean engine oil over filter seal and screw filter into place only tightening by hand.
5. Ensure the sump plug is tightened then fill engine with required oil.
6. Start engine and run until the oil pressure light goes out, then switch off and check oil level.
7. Top up as required and check for any oil leaks.

CHECKING & FILLING COOLING SYSTEM

If the cooling system needs to be drained, the following instructions should be obeyed when refilling the cooling system to ensure that the block is drained fully.

1. Adjust heater control to maximum.
2. Have a coolant mixture such as Tectaloy coolant on hand to fill system.
   * *Do not combine different types of antifreeze or corrosion inhibitors as they may be incompatible. If a different type is to be used, firstly flush the system with clean water.*
3. Remove radiator/coolant system cap and fill system with coolant mixture.

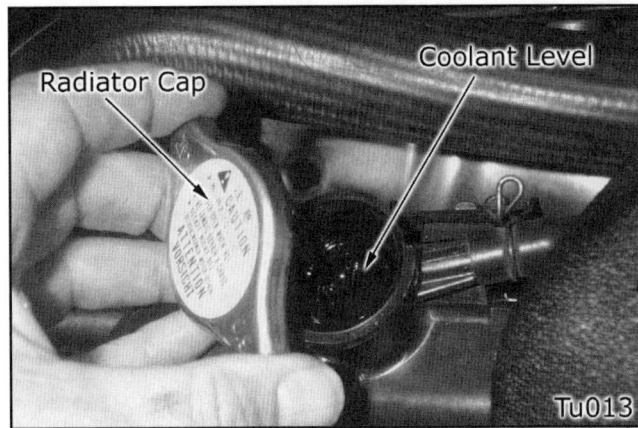

4. Remove top from coolant reservoir and top up system.
5. When the coolant is cold the coolant level should be at the FULL mark. Depending on the engine temperature the level will vary.
   Coolant Capacity .... 9.5 litres
6. Start engine and run it at 2000 rpm for 5 minutes to open thermostat and purge air from system. Ensure to have the heater turned on.
7. Ensure radiator is full then fill supply tank to "FULL/MAX" mark.

INSPECT and REPLACE AIR FILTER

1. Inspect the air cleaner element to ensure it is not excessively damaged, dirty or oily.
2. Clean the element with compressed air.

13

COMPRESSION CHECK - 6G7 (Petrol)

1. Make sure of the following:
   a) Engine is at operating temperature.
   b) Battery is at (or near) full charge.
   c) Spark plugs are removed.
   e) Disconnect the electrical connector to the crank angle sensor, then to the starter solenoid connect a remote control starter.

2. a) Install a suitable compression tester into spark plug hole, then crank engine several times to obtain highest reading.
   b) Read compression gauge indication.
3. Check remaining cylinders.
   MPI - Compression @ 250-400rpm ......1275 kPa
   - Min. @ 250-400rpm ....980.7 kPa
   GDI - Compression @ 250-400rpm ......1177 kPa
   - Min. @ 250-400rpm ....875 kPa
   Max. Variation b/w cylinders.....................98 kPa
* If cylinder compression in 1 or more cylinders is low, pour a small amount of engine oil into the cylinders through the spark plug holes and test compression.

COMPRESSION CHECK - 4M4 (Diesel)

1. Make sure of the following.
   a) Engine is at operating temperature.
   b) Battery is at (or near) full charge.
   c) Glow plugs are removed.
   d) Disconnect the electrical connector to fuel cut solenoid valve.
2. a) Install a suitable compression tester into glow plug hole, then crank engine several times to obtain highest reading.
   b) Read compression gauge indication.
3. Check remaining cylinders.
   4M40 - Compression @ 280rpm ....2843 kPa
   - Min. @ 280rpm..........................2256 kPa
   4M41 - Compression @ 240rpm ....2844 kPa
   - Min. @ 240rpm..........................2256 kPa
   Max. variation b/w cylinders ....294 kPa
* If cylinder compression in 1 or more cylinders is low, pour a small amount of engine oil into the cylinders through the spark plug holes and test compression.

Compression Test Results

Normal — Compression builds up quickly and evenly on each cylinder.

Piston Rings — Low on 1st stroke, tending to build up on following strokes, but does not reach normal. Improves considerably with addition of oil.

Valves — Low on 1st stroke and does not tend to build up on following strokes. Does not improve much with addition of oil.

Head Gasket — If compression in any 2 adjacent cylinders is low (and if adding oil does not help compression), cylinder head gasket has blown out.

DRIVE BELTS

Drive belts must be checked often to ensure that they are still in good operating condition, also pulley misalignment should be checked to reduce belt wear. Damaged belts should be replaced.

Incorrectly adjusted drive belts will cause belt squeal and components will not be driven. Belts that are over tightened can damage component bearings. Belts that are tensioned correctly reduce noise and extend the life of the belt. Belt's that have operated for 10-15 minutes are treated as a used belt, and adjusted to used belt specification.

Inspection

* Some belt squeal when the engine is started or stopped is normal and has no effect on durability of drive belt.
* Condition of the belt is best judged by twisting the belt so as to see the surfaces.

ENGINE TUNE-UP & MAINTENANCE

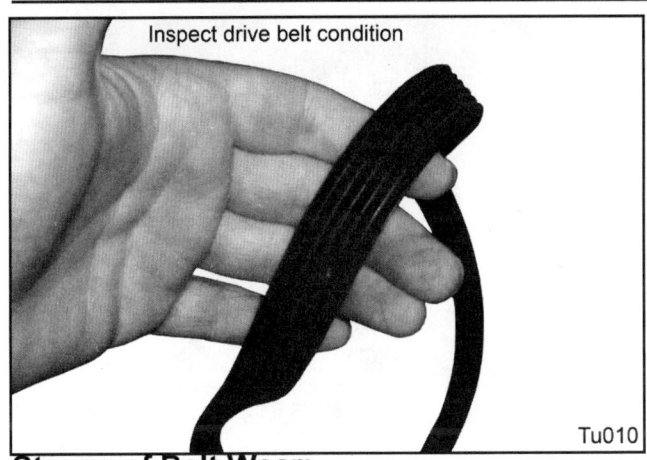

Inspect drive belt condition

Tu010

Stages of Belt Wear:

New Belt — No Cracks or chunks.

Moderately Used — Minor cracks; some wear on surfaces. Replacement not required.

Severely Used — Several cracks per inch. Should be replaced before chunking occurs.

Failed Belt — Separation of belt material from backing (chunking). Replace belt immediately.

DRIVE BELT TENSION CHECK and REPLACEMENT - Petrol V6 Engines

The vehicles are fitted with a self adjusting tensioner, which means they will never need adjusting for the life of the belt. They have a wear mark indicator on the auto tensioner which gives an indication of when the belt needs replacing.

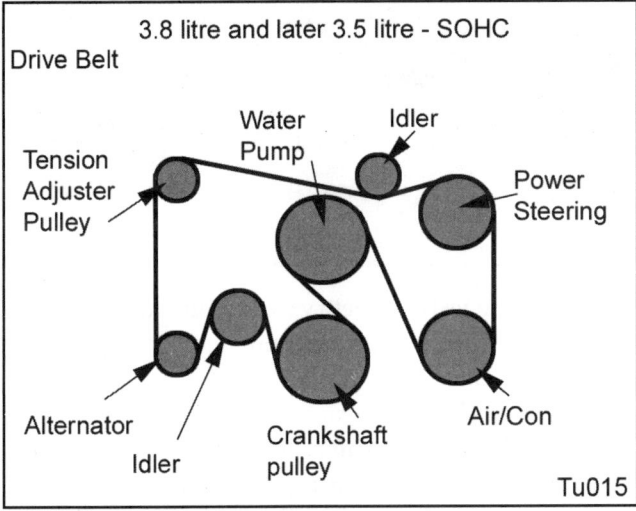

3.8 litre and later 3.5 litre - SOHC
Tu015

Belt Replacement

1. Use a 3/8" drive socket bar to the auto tensioner and rotate clockwise to release tension on drive belt.
2. Align the two holes on the tensioner and insert a 5mm Allen key to hold tensioner in position.

Tu016

3. Remove drive belt from pulleys and remove from vehicle.
4. Install new belt ensuring the belt is routed correctly.
   Note: Correct routing of the serpentine belt is shown on the bonnet label.
5. Release the tensioner and check the tensioner markings are in the correct position.

DRIVE BELT TENSION & ADJUSTMENT - Diesel Engines

Alternator Drive Belt Tension & Adjustment

1. Apply a force of approximately 100N to the drive belt as show in diagram and measure the belt deflection.
   Belt Deflection - Inspection .... 8-11 mm
                       - Adjustment .... 10-11 mm
                       - Replacement .... 8-9 mm
2. If tension is not to specification adjust as follows.
   a) Loosen the alternator and pivot bolt and the adjuster lock bolt.

Tu009

   b) Adjust the belt deflection by turning the adjusting bolt.
   c) Tighten lock bolt and pivot bolt to specification.

15

ENGINE TUNE-UP & MAINTENANCE

3. Crank the engine forward at least one turn and then recheck belt tension.

A/C Compressor Drive Belt Tension & Adjustment

1. Apply a force of approximately 100N to the drive belt as shown in diagram and measure the belt deflection.
   Belt Deflection - Inspection .... 7 - 8 mm
                      - Adjustment .... 7 - 8 mm
                      - Replacement .... 6 - 6.5 mm
2. If tension is not to specification adjust as follows.
   a) Loosen the tensioner pulley lock bolt.
   b) Use adjusting bolt to adjust the belt deflection.
   c) Tighten lock bolt to specification.
   Lock Bolt .... 44 Nm
3. Recheck belt tension.

PETROL / GASOLINE ENGINES

FIRING ORDER

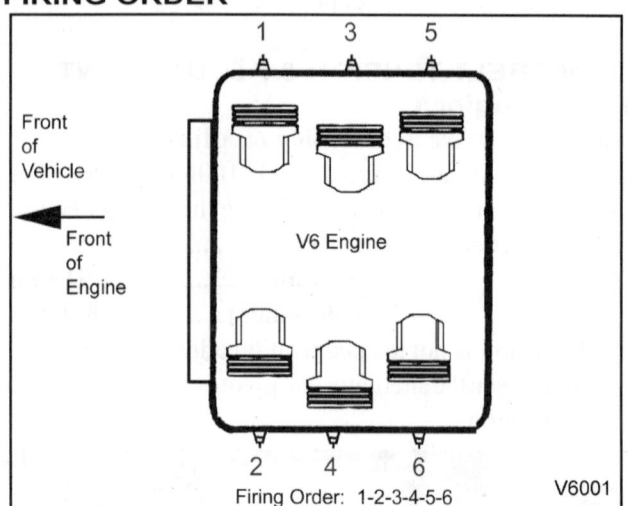

Firing Order: 1-2-3-4-5-6

6 Cylinder Engines 1-2-3-4-5-6

Inspection of Spark Plugs

1. Remove, Clean & Inspect Spark Plugs.
   a) Clean spark plugs with a plug cleaner or wire brush.
   b) Examine the spark plugs for electrode wear, thread damage and insulator damage. Replace the plugs if worn or damaged.
2. Adjust Electrode Gap. Gently bend the outer electrode to obtain the correct electrode gap.
   Electrode gap
   Australia 1.0-1.1 mm (pre-gaped), service 1.3mm
   General Export 0.7-0.8mm
   Australia Type .... NGK - PFR5J-11
   General Export Type .... NGK - BKR5E

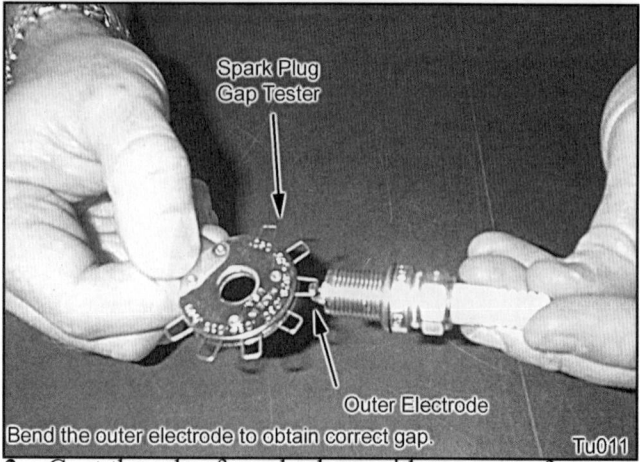

Bend the outer electrode to obtain correct gap.

3. Coat threads of spark plugs with a smear of grease, this is to help prevent the plugs binding. Especially important with alloy head engines.
4. Install and tighten spark plugs.
   Spark Plug Torque Specification .... 20-28 Nm

INTAKE MANIFOLD VACUUM CHECK (6G7)

1. Ensure engine is at normal operating temperature, then switch ignition off (lock position).
2. Connect a tachometer to the engine.

3. **MPI Vehicles:** Connect a vacuum gauge to the vacuum hose between the fuel pressure regulator and the air intake plenum.
4. **GDI Vehicles:**
   a) From the PCV valve disconnect the ventilation hose and connect to a vacuum gauge.
   From the PCV valve disconnect the ventilation hose and connect to a vacuum gauge.
   b) Plug the PCV valve.
5. Start the engine and run at idle for at least 4 minutes then check to ensure the idle speed is to specification.
   Idle Speed .... 700 +/- 100 rpm
6. Check the intake manifold vacuum using the vacuum gauge.
   Vacuum (minimum) .... 60 kPa

ENGINE TUNE-UP & MAINTENANCE

7. Turn off engine, remove vacuum gauge and tachometer.

INSPECTION & ADJUSTMENT IGNITION TIMING (SOHC-MPI)

1. Ensure engine is at normal operating temperature, transaxle is in neutral (manual) or park (auto) and all lighting and accessories are off.
2. Ensure the ignition is switched off fully, then connect the MUT-II to the diagnostic connector.
3. Start engine and idle then check to ensure the idle speed is to specification.
   Idle Speed .... 700 +/- 50 rpm
4. Select #17 of the MUT-II actuator test, and check basic ignition timing is to specification.
   Basic Ignition Timing .... 5° BTDC +/-3°
5. If basic ignition timing is not within specification, inspect and troubleshoot fuel system.
6. Press the clear key on the MUT-II tester to release the actuator test.
7. Inspect ignition timing is to specification.
   Ignition Timing - 6G72 .... 15° BTDC
                    - 6G74 .... 10° BTDC
                    - 6G75 .... 10° BTDC

INSPECTION & ADJUSTMENT IGNITION TIMING (DOHC-GDI)

1. Ensure engine is at normal operating temperature, transaxle is in neutral (manual) or park (auto) and all lighting and accessories are off.
2. Ensure the ignition is switched off fully, then connect the MUT-II to the diagnostic connector.
3. To terminal 7 of the ignition coil intermediate connector, connect a timing light.
4. Start engine and idle then check to ensure the idle speed is to specification.
   Idle Speed .... 700 +/- 100 rpm
   Note: 600 +/- 100rpm, when idling condition has been operating for less than 4 minutes.
5. Select #17 of the MUT-II actuator test, and check basic ignition timing is to specification.
   Basic Ignition Timing .... 5° BTDC +/-3°
6. If basic ignition timing is not within specification inspect and troubleshoot fuel system.
7. Press the clear key on the MUT-II tester to release the actuator test.
8. Inspect ignition timing is to specification.
   Ignition Timing .... 12° BTDC
9. Fully turn off ignition then disconnect the tachometer and MUT-II tester.

IDLE SPEED INSPECTION (6G7) (vehicles with catalytic converter)

* Idle speed adjustment is controlled automatically by the ISC system.

1. Ensure engine is at normal operating temperature, transaxle is in neutral (manual) or park (auto) and all lighting and accessories are off.
2. Ensure the ignition is switched off fully, then connect the MUT-II to the diagnostic connector.
3. Start engine, select #17 of the MUT-II actuator test, and check basic ignition timing is to specification.
   Basic Ignition Timing .... 5° BTDC +/-3°
4. Press the clear key on the MUT-II tester to release the actuator test.
5. Run the engine at idle for at least 2 minutes, select #22 of the MUT-II tester to check idle speed.
   Idle Speed .... 700 +/- 100 rpm
   Note: GDI vehicles idle speed will be 600 +/- 100rpm, when idling condition has been operating for less than 4 minutes.
6. If idle speed is not to specification inspect and troubleshoot fuel system.

IDLE MIXTURE INSPECTION (6G7)
(vehicles with catalytic converter)

1. Ensure engine is at normal operating temperature, transaxle is in neutral (manual) or park (auto) and all lighting and accessories are off.
2. Ensure the ignition is switched off fully, then connect the MUT-II to the diagnostic connector.
3. Start engine, select #17 of the MUT-II actuator test, and check basic ignition timing is to specification.
   Basic Ignition Timing .... 5° BTDC +/-3°
4. Press the clear key on the MUT-II tester to release the actuator test.
5. Race engine at 2,500 rpm for 2 minutes, connect a CO and HC tester and check the contents.
   CO contents   - MPI........................... 0.5% or less
                 - GDI........................... 0.1% or less
   HC contents .... 100ppm or less
6. If the reading is not within acceptable range inspect the following items.
   a) Diagnostic output.
   b) Compression Pressure.
   c) Injectors.
   d) Ignition coil, ignition leads and spark plugs.
   e) Evaporative emission control system.
7. If CO contents are not within specification replace the three way catalyst.

IDLE SPEED & MIXTURE ADJUSTMENT (6G7-MPI) (vehicles without catalytic converter) [Export to South Africa and GCC]

Important: *Idle speed adjustment is controlled automatically by the ISC motor system.*

1. Ensure engine is at normal operating temperature, transaxle is in neutral (manual) or park (auto) and all

ENGINE TUNE-UP & MAINTENANCE

lighting and accessories are off.
2. Ensure the ignition is switched off fully, then connect the MUT-II to the diagnostic connector.
3. Start engine and check the basic ignition timing.
   Basic Ignition Timing .... **5° BTDC +/-3°**
4. Run the engine at idle for at least 2 minutes, select #22 of the MUT-II tester to check idle speed.
   Idle Speed .... **700 +/- 100 rpm**
5. If idle speed is not to specification inspect and troubleshoot fuel system.
6. Connect a CO tester then start engine and race at 2,500 rpm for 10 seconds.
7. At idle check the CO content.
   CO contents ....**1.5% +/- 0.5%**
8. If not to specification, use the mixture adjusting screw to adjust idle mixture to specification.
   The mixing adjustment screw is located along side the Air flow sensor.

LASH ADJUSTER and INSPECTION (6G7)
A malfunctioning lash adjuster sounds like a clattering noise and is present immediately after starting engine.

Bleeding Lash Adjuster System
1. Check engine oil to ensure it is at the correct level and is in good condition. Adjust oil level as required.
2. Run the engine at idle for 2-3 minutes.
3. With engine at idle increase engine speed to approximately 3000rpm over a 15 second interval then release accelerator pedal and allow engine speed to drop to idle, hold for 15 seconds and repeat procedure approximately 30 times.
4. Once noise is eliminated repeat at least five more times.
   Note: *The noise should be eliminated after 10-30 times.*
5. Run engine at idle for 2-3 minutes to ensure noise is eliminated.
6. If noise is not eliminated perform Simple Lash adjuster check to ensure the noise is caused by a faulty lash adjuster and not another problem.

Petrol V6 3.0, 3.5 & 3.8 SOHC MPI Engine.
There is no adjustment only an inspection and replace faulty parts if required.

Simple Lash Adjuster Check
1. With the engine turned off remove the rocker cover and set cylinder No1. to TDC on compression stroke.
2. Refer to illustrations and check the "small arrow" marked rocker arms as follows:
   a) Attempt to push the rocker arm down at the point directly above the lash adjuster.
   b) If the rocker arm is easily pushed down the lash

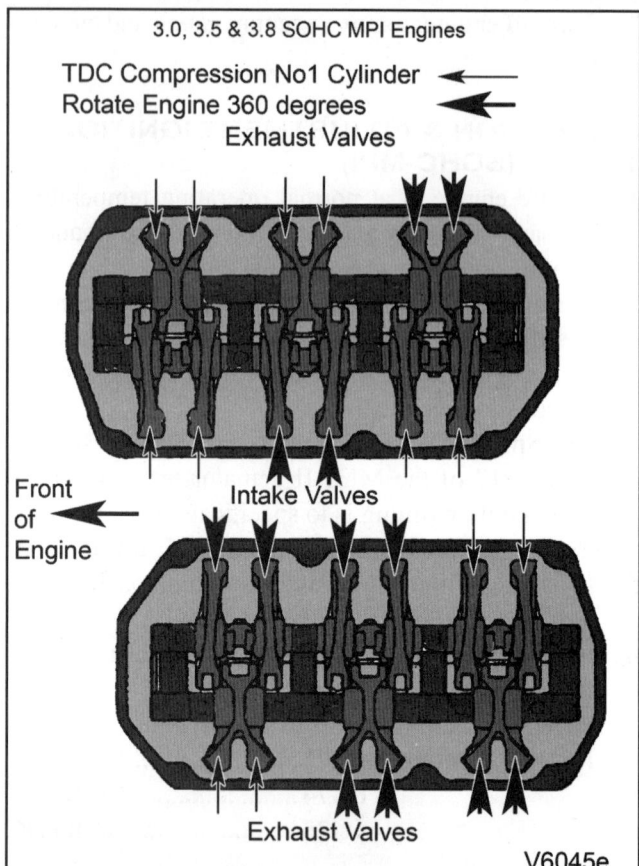

adjuster is defective, if the rocker arm is stiff and hard to press down then the lash adjuster is in good order.
3. If the lash adjusters are all in good order investigate other possible causes of the abnormal noise.
4. Rotate the engine crankshaft 360° and test "large arrow" marked rocker arms shown.

MIVEC Variable Valve Timing - 3.8 SOHC
Exhaust There is no adjustment only an inspection and replace faulty parts if required.

Lash Adjuster Check
1. Remove spark plugs to allow easier rotation of engine.
2. Turn engine by hand so the groove on the crankshaft pulley is aligned with the "T" timing mark. Check for the notches on the camshafts as described in the SOHC Engine Chapter.
3. Remove the rocker covers and check the slackness of the rocker arms for cylinder numbers 1 and 4.
   Note: *See illustration on next page.*
4. Check valve clearance of the intake valves, if not as specified, loosen the lock nut of the adjuster. Turn adjuster to obtain correct valve clearance, tighten lock nut of the adjuster.
   MIRVEC Intake Valve Clearance:
   (Cold) ....**0.10 mm**
5. Check the valve clearance of all valves as per illustration on next page.

ENGINE TUNE-UP & MAINTENANCE

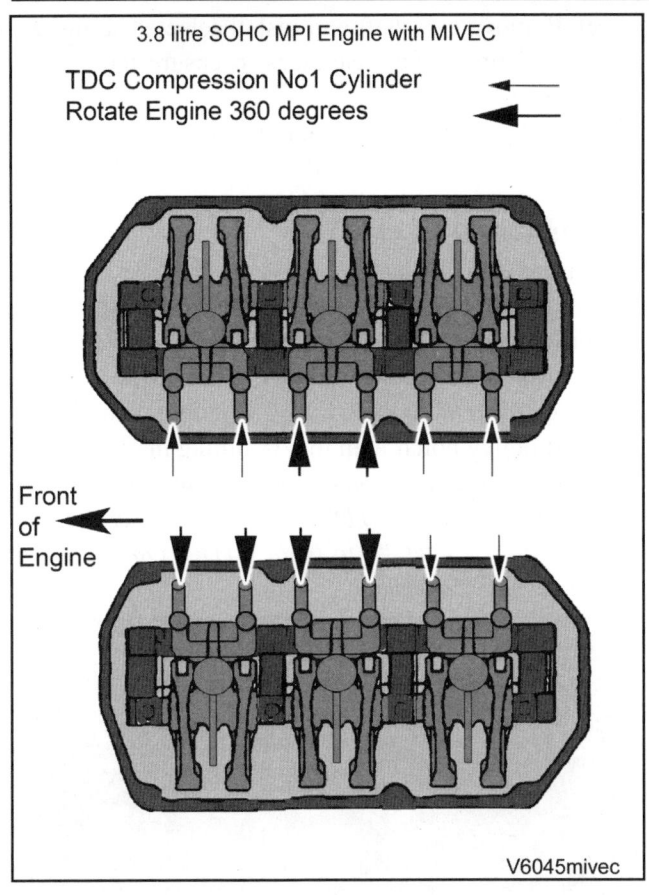

3.8 litre SOHC MPI Engine with MIVEC
TDC Compression No1 Cylinder
Rotate Engine 360 degrees

Front of Engine

V6045mivec

DIESEL ENGINES

FUEL FILTER and WATER TRAP
Discard Water
1. Loosen water sensor nut at bottom of filter.
2. Operate hand pump at top of filter, until all water is removed.

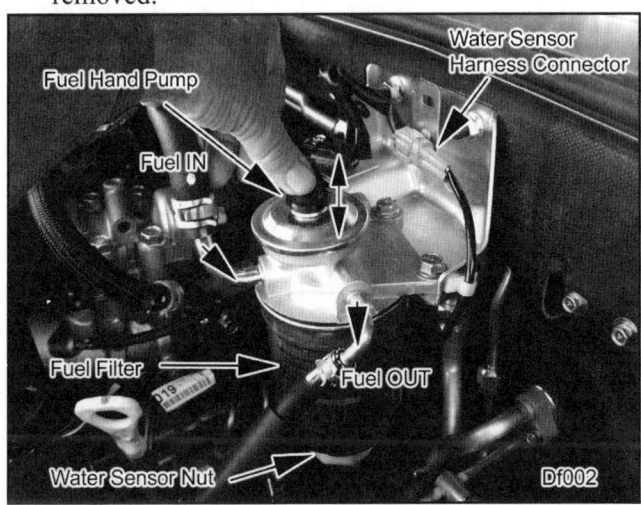

3. Tighten water sensor nut at bottom of filter.

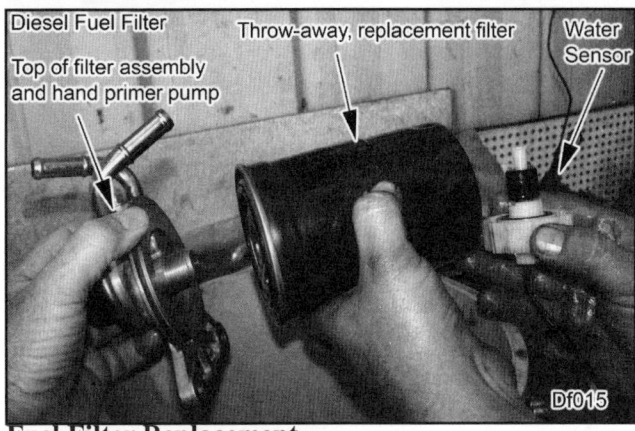

Fuel Filter Replacement
1. Loosen and remove water sensor nut at bottom of filter.
2. Remove and replace fuel filter canister, make sure "O" ring is in correct position.
3. Fit and tighten water sensor nut at bottom of filter.
4. Bleed air from the fuel filter as described below.

BLEED AIR from FUEL SYSTEM
Air needs to bleed from the fuel system after filter replacement, fuel nozzle disconnected, fuel injection pump removed and fuel lines replaced.
Fuel pipes, injection pump and pipes in fuel system after fuel filter need to have air bleed from where ever disconnected

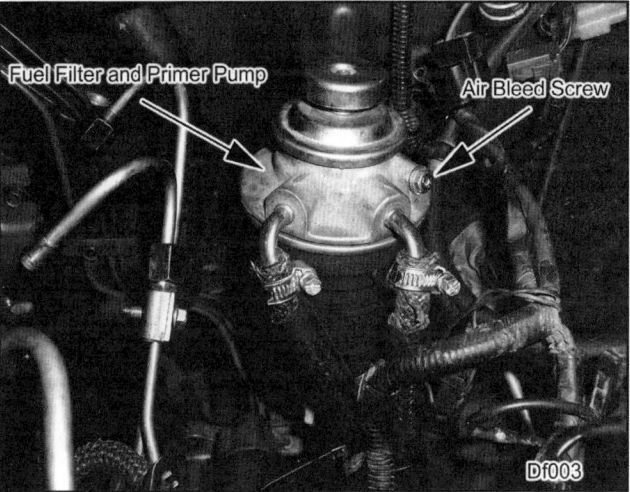

1*. Loosen air bleeder screw at top of filter.
2. Operate hand primer pump on top of fuel filter until all signs of air are removed, the pressure of the hand pump will increase.
3*. Tighten air bleeder screw at top of filter.
* *1. Loosen fuel pipe to fuel nozzle or fuel injection pump or fuel pipe replaced.*
   3. Tighten fuel pipe to fuel nozzle or fuel injection pump or fuel pipe replaced.

19

ENGINE TUNE-UP & MAINTENANCE

VALVE CLEARANCE CHECK & ADJUSTMENT - 4M40 - 2.8 litre

1. Ensure engine is at normal operating temperature.
2. Remove the rocker cover and then remove all the glow plugs. (refer to engine or fuel system chapters for assistance).
3. Set cylinder #1 or #4 to CTDC by aligning the crankshaft pulley notch with the '0' timing mark.
   Note: *If camshaft notch is facing directly upwards, cylinder #1 is at CTDC, then turn the crankshaft once for cylinder #4 to be at CTDC. Only turn the crankshaft clockwise.*
4. Use a feeler gauge to measure the clearance between the top of the lifter shim and the base circle diameter of the camshaft.
5. At TDC compression cylinder No1 adjust the valves indicated below.

Cylinder	1	2	3	4
Intake	X	X		
Exhaust	X		X	

At TDC compression cylinder No4 adjust the valves indicated below.

Cylinder	1	2	3	4
Intake			X	X
Exhaust		X		X

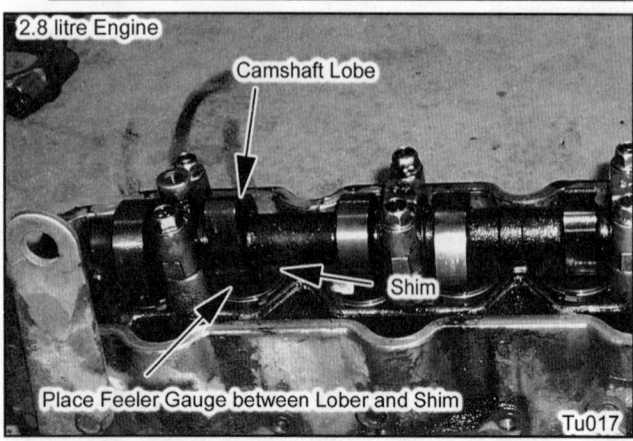

6. Check for specification clearance.
   Valve Clearance (Cold)
   Intake .... 0.2 mm
   Exhaust .... 0.3 mm
   a) Use a thickness gauge to measure the valve clearances.
      Standard Value - Intake .... 0.25 mm
                     - Exhaust .... 0.35 mm
   b) Note any locations which are not to specification, then use the following formula to select the correct adjustment shims.
      S = IS + MV - SV
      S = Adjustment Shim
      IS = Installed Shim
      MV = Measured Value
      SV = Standard Value

   c) Remove camshaft and install selected shims, re-measure valve clearances to ensure they are to specification.
7. Repeat procedure for remaining valve clearances.

VALVE CLEARANCE CHECK & ADJUSTMENT - 4M41

1. Ensure engine is cold.
2. Remove the rocker cover and then remove all the glow plugs. (refer to engine or fuel system chapters for assistance).
3. Set cylinder #1 or #4 to CTDC by aligning the crankshaft pulley notch with the '0' timing mark.
   Note: *If camshaft notch is facing directly upwards, cylinder #1 is at CTDC, then turn the crankshaft once for cylinder #4 to be at CTDC. Only turn the crankshaft clockwise.*

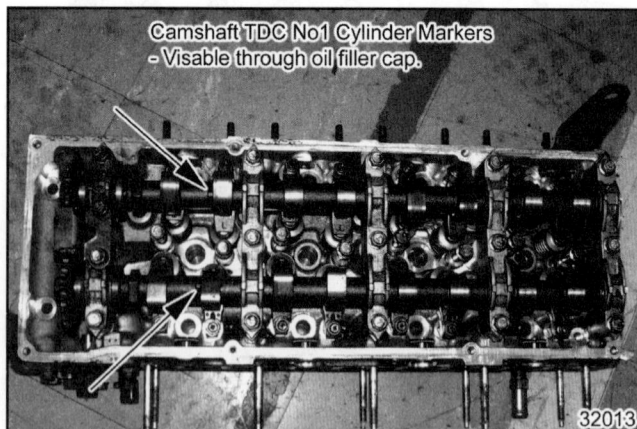

4. Check and adjust valve clearances as follows, referring to the diagram.
5. At TDC compression cylinder No1 adjust the valves indicated below.

Cylinder	1	2	3	4
Intake	X	X		
Exhaust	X		X	

At TDC compression cylinder No4 adjust the valves indicated below.

Cylinder	1	2	3	4
Intake			X	X
Exhaust		X		X

6. Use a feeler gauge to measure the clearance between the top of the rocker arm and the base circle diameter of the camshaft.
7. If clearance is not to specification loosen the lock nut, adjust the adjuster with a feeler gauge inserted, then tighten lock nut.
   a) Use a thickness gauge to measure the valve clearances.

20

ENGINE TUNE-UP & MAINTENANCE

Standard Value - Intake .... 0.10 mm
                - Exhaust .... 0.15 mm

b) If not to specification loosen the locknut, then use the adjusting screw to adjust so the gauge passes with a slight drag.
c) Tighten lock nut to specification and recheck valve clearance.
   Lock Nut .... 9.5 Nm
8. Repeat procedure for remaining valve clearances.

MAINTENANCE HINTS

1. a) When any internal engine parts are serviced, care and cleanliness are important.
   b) An engine is a combination of many machined, honed, polished and lapped surfaces with tolerances that are measured in thousandths of a millimetre.
   c) Friction areas should be coated liberally with engine oil during assembly to protect and lubricate the surfaces on initial operation.
   d) Proper cleaning and protection of machined surfaces and friction areas is part of the repair procedure and is considered standard workshop practice.
2. When valve train components are removed for service, they should be kept in order and should be installed in the same locations (with the same mating surfaces) as when removed.
3. Battery terminals should be disconnected before any major work is begun. If not, damage to wiring harnesses or other electrical components could result.
4. When raising or supporting the engine for any reason, do not use a jack under the oil pan. There are small clearances between the oil pan and the suction pipe screen, so jacking may cause the oil pan to be bent against the screen, causing damage to oil suction pipe assembly.

Problem Diagnosis

See ENGINE, FUEL and EMISSION Chapters for additional Problem Diagnosis.

Jacking And Lifting Points

The following points are recommended for jacking or supporting to prevent damage to the vehicle. Never leave the vehicle supported on a floor jack only, always use axle stands to minimise the chances of personal harm.

AXLE STANDS

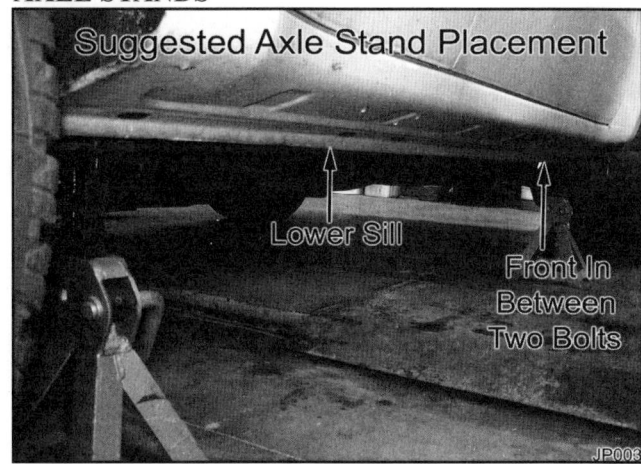

FLOOR JACK
Front

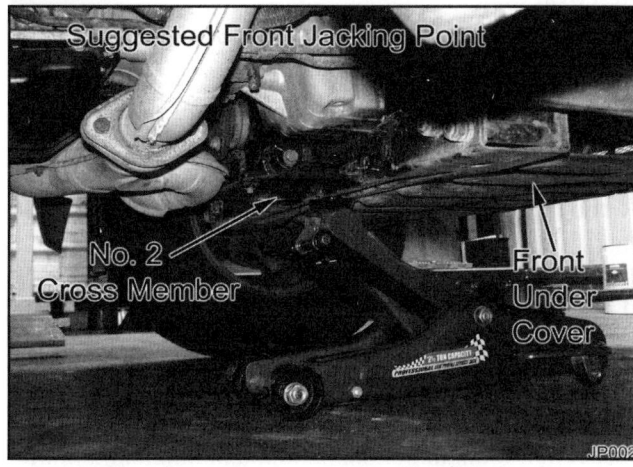

Rear

21

V6 ENGINE MAINTENANCE & REBUILD 3.0L, 3.5L & 3.8L SOHC M.P.I.

Subject	Page
GENERAL DESCRIPTION	23
Engine Serial Number	23
ENGINE MAINTENANCE	23
Intake Plenum & Intake Manifold Assembly	24
Removal	24
Installation	24
Exhaust Manifolds	25
Remove	25
Installation	26
Crankshaft Balancer	26
Remove	26
Install	26
Rocker Covers and/or Seals	26
Remove	26
Installation	27
MIVEC Variable Valve Timing	27
MIVEC Rocker Arm Piston	28
Inspection	28
Timing Belt Cover, Timing Belt And Gears	28
Remove	28
Timing Belt Inspection	29
Install	29
Crankshaft Oil Seal	31
Replace	31
Cylinder Heads, Valves & Camshafts	31
Remove	32
Cylinder Head Reconditioning	32
Dismantle	32
Clean	33
Inspection	33
Valve Guides	34
Clearance Checks	34
Guide Replacement	34
Valve Seats	34
Replacing Valve Seat	35

Subject	Page
Valve Stem Oil Seals	35
Replacement	35
Valve Springs	35
Valves	36
Camshafts	37
Inspection	37
Assemble Cylinder Head	37
Install Cylinder Head	37
Oil Pump	38
Removal	38
Dismantle	38
Inspection	38
Assembly	39
Installation	39
Flywheel/Drive Plate	39
Remove	39
Inspection	39
Install	39
Ring Gear	39
Replacement	39
Replacement Techniques	40
Rear Main Oil Seal	40
Replace	40
Spigot Bearing	40
Replacement	40
ENGINE REBUILD	40
Engine Assembly	40
Removal	40
Dismantle	41
Assembly	41
Oil Pan (Sump)	41
Remove	41
Installation	41

V6 ENGINE MAINTENANCE & REBUILD 3.0L, 3.5L & 3.8L SOHC M.P.I.

Subject	Page
Oil Pump Suction Pipe, Screen and Baffle	41
Removal	41
Installation	42
Piston and Connecting Rod Assembly	42
Remove	42
Dismantle	42
Inspection	43
Assembly & Installation	43
Piston Rings	44
Installation	44
Connecting Rod Bearings	45
Inspection & Replacement	45
Crankshaft	46
Removal	46
Inspection	47
Installation	47
Main Bearings	48
Inspection and Installation	48
Cylinder Block	49
Inspection	49
Cylinder Reconditioning & Piston Fitting	50
PROBLEM DIAGNOSIS	51
SPECIFICATIONS	52
TORQUE WRENCH SPECIFICATIONS	55

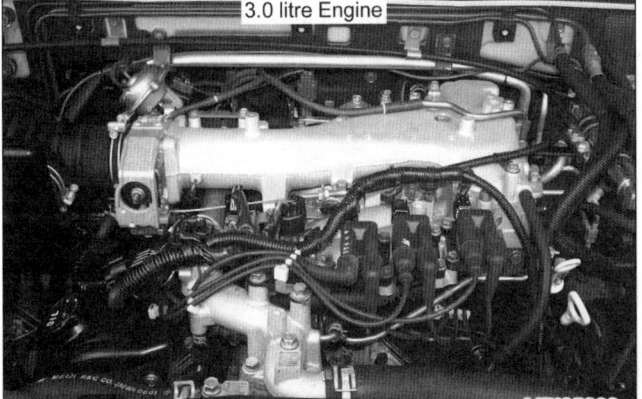

GENERAL DESCRIPTION

The 6G72 (3.0L), 6G74 (3.5L) and 6G75 (3.8L) engine is a 60° V6 cylinder overhead camshaft unit, there is one camshaft mounted in each aluminium cylinder head.

The cylinder block is made of cast iron, the 3.0 litre has standard bore of 91.1 mm and stroke of 76.0 mm, displacement is 2972cc. The 3.5 litre has standard bore of 93.0 mm and stroke of 85.8 mm, displacement is 3497cc. The 3.8 litre has standard bore of 95.0 mm and stroke of 90.0 mm, displacement is 3828cc.

The 3.0 and 3.5 litre engines have a compression ratio of 9.0:1, 3.8 litre engines compression ratio is 9.5:1 and 9.8:1, with variable valve timing on some models 2008 on.

The cylinder numbering is as illustrated. Firing order is 1-2-3-4-5-6.

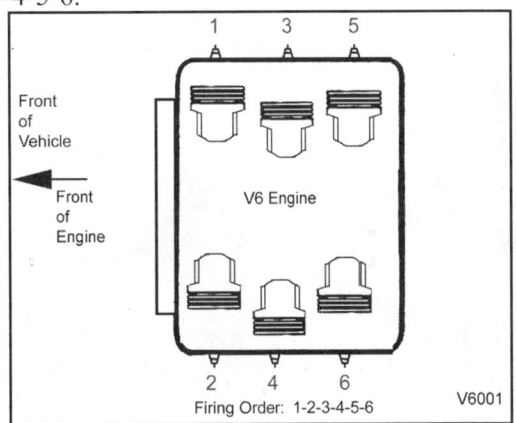

MIVEC - Variable valve timing was an option for the 3.8 litre engine in 2008, this option increased power by approximately 23%.

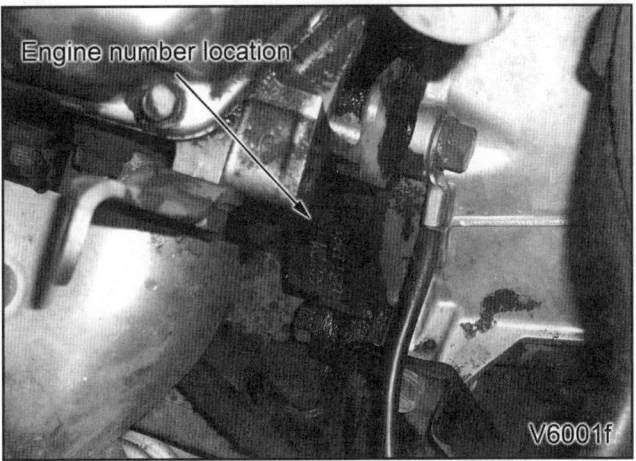

ENGINE SERIAL NUMBER
Engine No. Location: On the rear, right-hand side engine block casting, just in front of bell housing.

ENGINE MAINTENANCE

* **For general maintenance procedures such as oil change and drive belt inspection refer to the "Tune-up & Maintenance Chapter".**

V6 ENGINE MAINTENANCE & REBUILD 3.0L, 3.5L & 3.8L SOHC M.P.I.

INTAKE PLENUM & INTAKE MANIFOLD ASSEMBLY

Remove

1. Detach the battery earth lead from the battery, then release the lower radiator hose and drain the cooling system.
2. Release the air intake tube from the throttle body and air cleaner housing, then withdraw the tube.
3. Release and withdraw the engine top dress-up cover from the engine, if fitted.
4. [3.5] Release the accelerator cable from the throttle body assembly.
   [3.8] Release the accelerator electrical connector from the throttle body assembly.

5. a) Release the brake booster hose, other vacuum hoses and PCV hose from the intake plenum assembly.
   b) Release the fuel union from the injector, loosen union slow, as there may still be fuel pressure.
   c) Release the earth straps from the manifold assembly.
6. Release the EGR pipe retaining bolts from the intake plenum and the exhaust manifold, then withdraw the EGR pipe from the engine assembly.
7. Release the bolts retaining the intake plenum support to the intake plenum and cylinder head, withdraw the bracket.
8. Release and withdraw the hydraulic pressure pipe.
9. Mark all vacuum hoses to assist in assembly, then withdraw the vacuum hoses required to withdraw the intake chamber.
10. a) Release the water bypass hoses from the intake plenum assembly.
    b) Release and withdraw the wiring loom connectors from the intake assembly, position them to one side.
11. Release the intake plenum retaining bolts from the intake manifold assembly, then withdraw the intake plenum from the intake manifold and gasket.

12. Disconnect and remove the fuel rail and injectors.
13. Remove the bolts attaching the intake manifold, remove intake manifold and gasket.

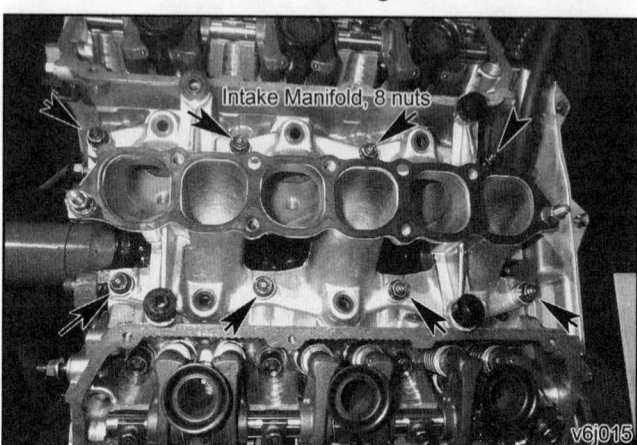

Install

1. a) Clean the intake plenum to manifold surface, ensure that all the old gasket is removed from the surface.
   b) Clear the manifold to intake plenum surface, ensure that all the old gasket is removed from the surface.
2. Install the intake manifold with new gaskets, then install bolts tightening left and right bank to 5-8Nm. Then tighten to specification.

24

V6 ENGINE MAINTENANCE & REBUILD 3.0L, 3.5L & 3.8L SOHC M.P.I.

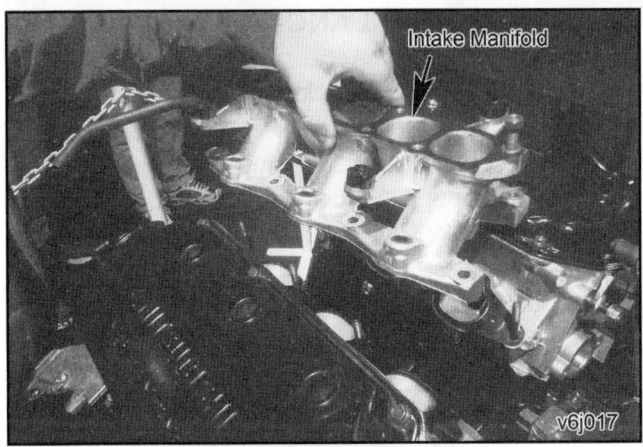

Intake Manifold Bolts: **22Nm**

3. Install the fuel injectors and fuel rail, using new "O-rings.

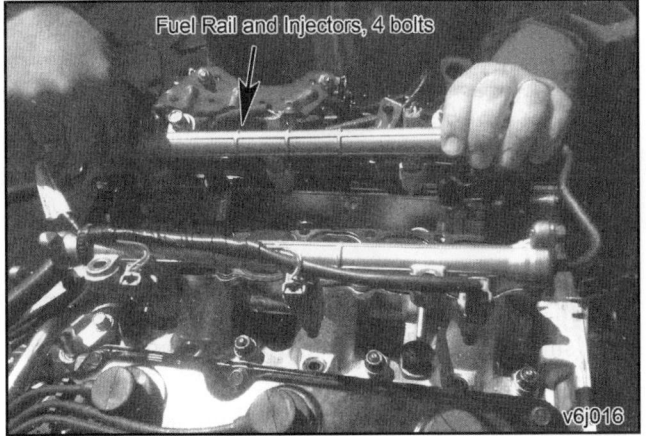

4. a) Fit the wiring loom connectors to there corresponding components on the intake chamber.
   b) Fit the water bypass hoses to the intake manifold, then secure the hoses in place using the hose clamps.
5. a) Fit the new intake plenum to manifold gasket, then lower the intake plenum into place on the manifold.

   b) Fit the intake plenum retaining bolts and nuts, then tension the retaining nuts to specification.

   Intake Plenum **18Nm**
   Intake Plenum Stay - M8 .... **18Nm**
   Intake Plenum Stay - M10 .... **35Nm**

6. Fit the vacuum hoses to the intake plenum, ensuring that the marks on the intake plenum and hoses are matching.
7. a) Fit the intake plenum support bracket to the cylinder head and intake chamber.
   b) With the support bracket in place, fit the retaining bolts, then tension the retaining bolts to specification.

   Intake Plenum Support .... **37 Nm**

8. Fit the EGR pipe to the EGR valve and exhaust manifold, then tension the retaining bolts to specifications.

   EGR Pipe To EGR Valve .... **18 Nm**
   EGR Pipe to Manifold **25Nm**

9. a) Secure the earth strap to the intake chamber assembly.
   b) Fit the fuel union to the cold start injector, tension the retaining bolt, then fit the wiring connector to the injector terminal.
   c) Fit the brake booster hose, PS air hose, IACV vacuum hose and PCV hose to the intake chamber assembly.
10. Fit the intake manifold plenum cover to the engine assembly, then secure it into position.
11. [3.5] Install the accelerator cable to the throttle body assembly.

    [3.8] Connect the accelerator electrical connector to the throttle body assembly.
12. Fit the air intake tube to the air cleaner assembly, then to the throttle body, tighten the retaining clamps to specifications.
13. a) Ensure the lower radiator hose is fitted, then proceed to fill the cooling system.
    b) Connect the battery terminal to the battery, then run the vehicle and check for signs of leaks, then road test the vehicle.

EXHAUST MANIFOLDS
Remove
1. Remove the oil level dip stick and tube.

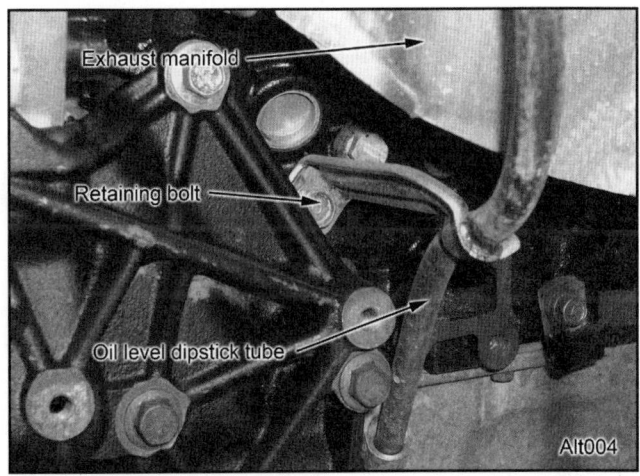

25

2. Remove the heat shields from both exhaust manifolds.

3. Remove the bolts attaching the exhaust pipe to the exhaust manifolds.
4. As required remove any fittings from the manifolds such as EGR pipe.
5. Remove the nuts attaching each manifold to the cylinder head and remove manifolds.

Install

1. Using new gaskets install the exhaust manifolds to the engine and tighten retaining bolts to specification.
   Exhaust Manifold Nuts: 12 Valve............ 18 Nm
   24 Valve............ 44 Nm

2. Tighten the manifold flange to exhaust pipe nuts to specification.
   Manifold to Exhaust Pipe Bolts................. 35Nm
3. Install the EGR pipe using new gaskets, tighten to specification.
   EGR Pipe to Manifold................. 25Nm
4. Install the heat shields to the exhaust manifolds, tightening to specification, then install the oil level dipstick and tube.
   Heat Shield Retaining Nuts...................... 14 Nm

CRANKSHAFT BALANCER
Remove

1. Disconnect battery earth lead and remove drive belts as shown in the Belt Drive section.
2. It may be an advantage to remove air cleaner and air intake tube, fan, radiator shroud and radiator.
3. Pull park brake fully on, chock rear wheel and transmission in gear.
4. Loosen and remove balancer retaining bolt.
5. Remove balancer from crankshaft with pulley puller.

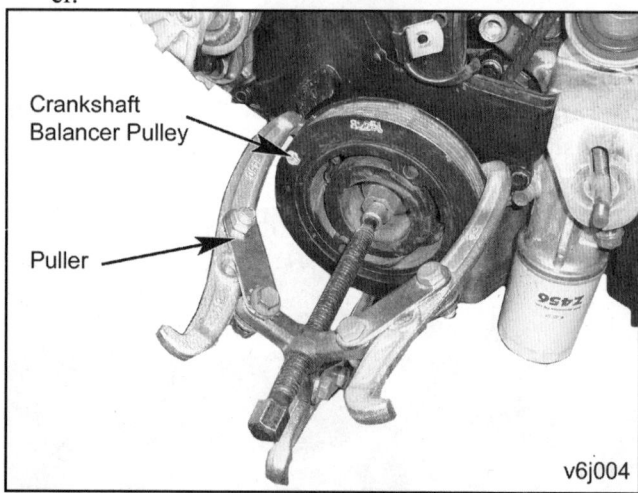

Install

1. Using engine oil, lubricate front seal surface of balancer.
2. Install balancer, engaging key on crankshaft with slot in balancer.
   Crankshaft Balancer................................ 182 Nm
3. Install the crankshaft pulley, tighten attaching bolt to specification.
4. Install and inspect drive belt operation.
5. Install air cleaner and air intake tube, fan, radiator shroud and radiator if removed.

ROCKER COVERS AND/OR SEALS
Remove

1. Remove the spark plug leads from the left side spark plugs.
2. Disconnect the breather hose between rocker covers and PCV valve form left side rocker cover.
3. Left bank rocker cover.
   a) Unscrew rocker cover to cylinder head fasteners and remove rocker cover from cylinder head.
   b) If replacing rocker cover seal, remove seal from recess in rocker cover to cylinder head.
4. Remove the intake plenum assembly as previously described in this chapter.
5. Remove the spark plug leads form the right side spark plugs.
6. a) Unscrew rocker cover to cylinder head fasteners and remove rocker cover from cylinder head.

V6 ENGINE MAINTENANCE & REBUILD 3.0L, 3.5L & 3.8L SOHC M.P.I.

b) If replacing rocker cover seal, remove seal from recess in rocker cover to cylinder head.

7. Remove spark plug tube top rubber seals if seals are damaged or rubber has become to hard to form a good seal to the rocker cover.

Install

1. a) If required install new seals to top of spark plug tubes.
    b) If necessary, install seal to rocker cover recess.
    c) Install rocker cover fastener and seal assemblies.
    Note: Make sure seal is correctly installed in rocker cover.
2. Install rocker cover to cylinder head and torque bolts to specification.
   Rocker Cover Bolts:.....................3.4Nm
3. Secure the wiring looms to the rocker covers, then clip the wiring loom connectors to there corresponding components.
4. Fit the intake chamber as previously described.

MIVEC Variable Valve Timing

MIVEC engines have a different (larger) rocker cover to accommodate the altered rocker arms

2008 Mitsubishi introduced variable valve timing to the Pajero, 3.8 MPI engine increasing the maximum power to 184kW while still retaining low rpm power and torque. The MIVEC system has a piston in each intake rocker arm which is activated by engine rpm and oil pressure, this piston in each rocker arm is held in position by a spring. With increased oil pressure the piston moves out and pushes a "T" lever against the rocker arm. This then results in a high and longer valve lift at a higher engine rpm, giving the cylinder heads a higher air flow hence more power.

At low rpm with the piston in the retracted position the "T" lever freely floats and does not effect the normal

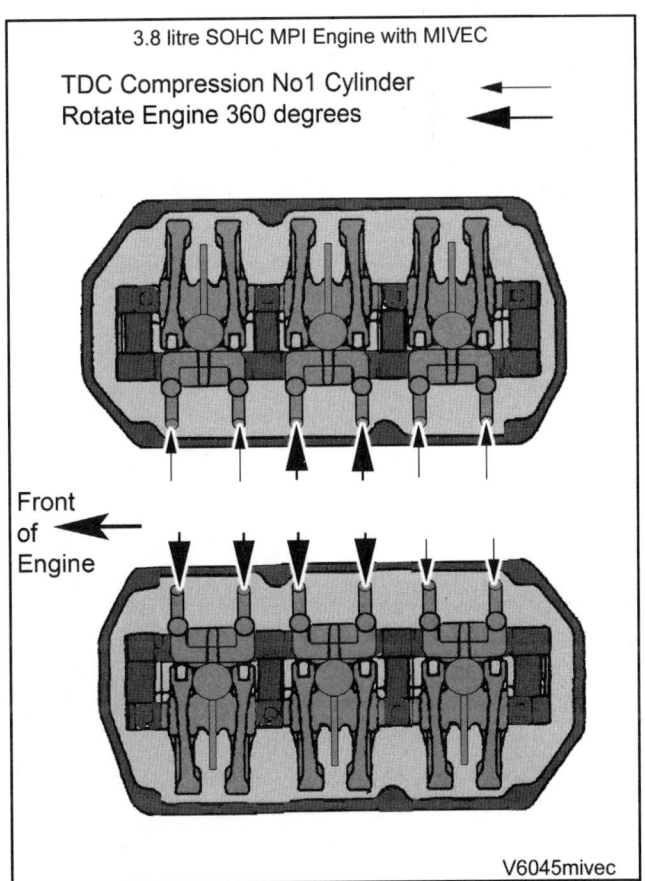

V6 ENGINE MAINTENANCE & REBUILD 3.0L, 3.5L & 3.8L SOHC M.P.I.

action of the rocker arm. Without the extra valve lift the engine retains the properties od good idling, low rpm power and torque.

MIVEC - ROCKER ARM PISTON
Inspection
1. Remove spark plugs to allow easier rotation of engine.
2. turn engine by hand so the groove on the crankshaft pulley is aligned with the "T" timing mark. Check for the notches on the camshafts as described earlier in this chapter.
3. Remove the oil pressure feeder control valve.
4. Remove the oil pressure switch.

5. Remove the rocker covers and check the slackness of the rocker arms for cylinder numbers 1 and 4.
6. Place your finger over the oil passage hole at the depth of the oil control valves installation hole.
   Use compressed air (more than 620 kPa) at the oil pressure switch installation hole, check that the rocker arm piston can move.
7. Check all rocker arm pistons for movement action.

TIMING BELT COVER, TIMING BELT and GEARS (CAMSHAFT OIL SEALS)
** *Timing belts do have a life span, and the average life of a timing belt under normal driving conditions is 100,000 kilometres, (approx. 62,000 mile).*

Remove
1. Detach the battery cables, remove the battery and cover.
2. Remove the air cleaner and air intake tubing.
3. Remove the engine protection skid panel from under the vehicle.
4. Drain the engine coolant.
5. Remove the radiator shroud.
6. Set the drive belt automatic tensioner as previously described. Remove drive belt.
7. Remove top timing belt cover, bolts and gasket.
8. a) Rotate the crankshaft so the crankshaft is at TDC/compression on number 1 cylinder.
   b) Check that TDC indicator mark align on the camshaft sprocket gears and cylinder head.
   Note: *Never rotate the crankshaft anti-clockwise.*
9. a) Use an oil based crayon, place alignment marks on the timing belt and camshaft gears and crankshaft gear.
   b) Also draw an arrow showing direction of rotation of timing belt, if the belt is to reinstalled on the engine.

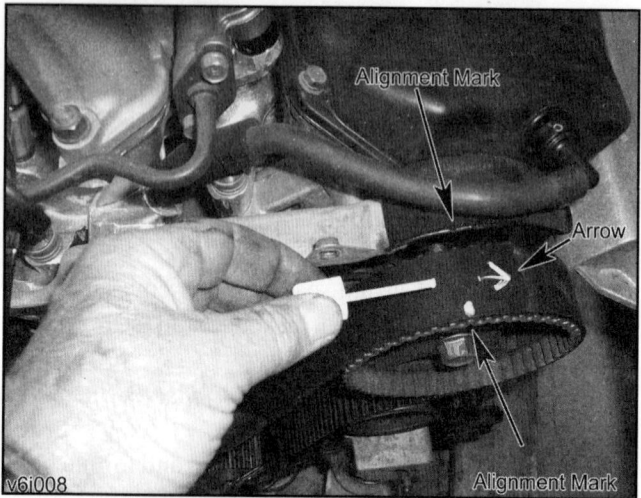

10. Remove the crankshaft pulley.
11. Remove the fan then fan pulley.
12. Remove the drive belt automatic tensioner.
13. Detach the power steering pump and tie to one side.
14. Unbolt the air conditioner compressor and tie to one side.
15. Remove the air conditioner compressor bracket.
16. Remove the accessory mount bracket from the front of the engine.
17. Remove the timing indicator, 1 bolt.

V6 ENGINE MAINTENANCE & REBUILD 3.0L, 3.5L & 3.8L SOHC M.P.I.

18. Remove the lower timing belt cover.
19. Check that TDC indicator mark align on the crankshaft sprocket and timing indicator on oil pump cover.

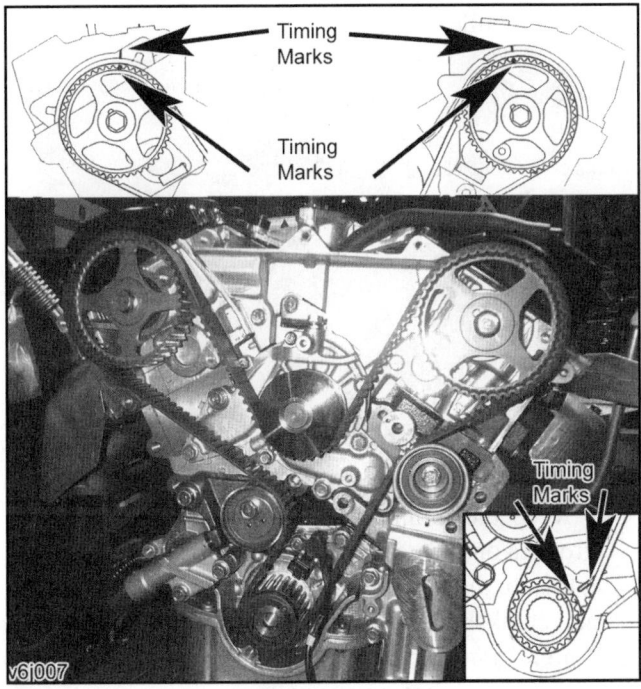

20. Remove crankshaft sensor, move to one side.
21. Only use this step if removing camshaft gears. - Loosen the bolts attaching the camshaft gears to the camshafts.
22. Insert a 1.4mm hex key into tensioner, it may require a little leverage with a large screw driver. This will stop the tensioner rod from moving out once the belt

is removed.
23. Loosen the idler tensioner pulley bolt and remove the idler tension pulley.
24. Remove the timing pulley belt from the pulleys.
25. Remove the bolts attaching the camshaft gears to the camshafts.
26. Remove camshaft seals with a screw driver or seal remover if required.
27. Remove tensioner attaching bolts.

Inspection

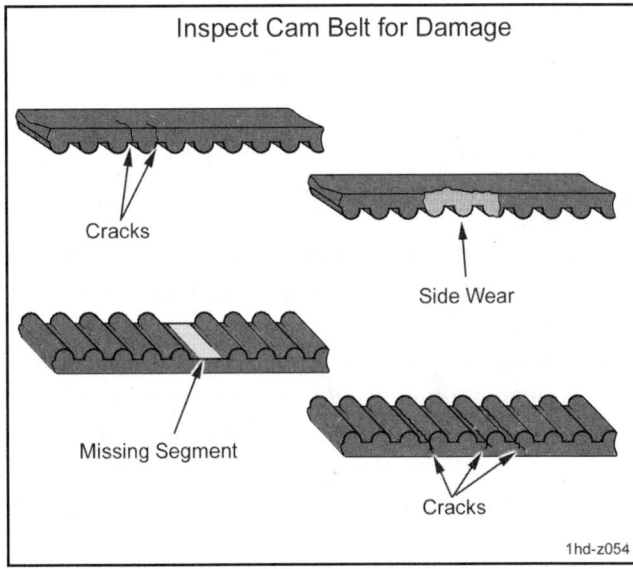

1. Condition of the belt ribs is best judged as the belt is bent one of the idler pulleys.
   Even if a belt is relatively new "replace if any sign of wear is obvious".
   Check for cracks or chunks missing, wear on ribs and in grooves, separation of rib material from backing.
2. Check the auto tensioner rod protrusion for specification, and pressure for movement, if not with in specification replace.
   1) Measure protrusion of push rod with no force:
   2) Apply 98-196Nm force and measure protrusion of push rod:
   3) Deduct measurement 2 from 1:
   Tensioner Rod Protrusion Variation: 1mm or less
   Note: If tensioner has plug on end place a washer on end to protect plug.

Install

1. If you do not have a key in the tensioner and rod, as per step 22 in "Remove".
   Compress the auto tensioner by placing tensioner in a vice, press the protrusion rod in until a setting pin such as 1.4 mm wire or small hex Allen key can be inserted through the tensioner body and protrusion rod to hold protrusion rod in place.
   Note: *If tensioner has plug on end place a washer on*

end to protect plug.
Install timing belt auto tensioner and tighten bolt to specification.
Timing Belt Auto Tensioner Bolts: 23Nm

2. Install tensioner pulley.
   a) Fit the timing belt tensioner to the engine, then fit the mounting bolt.
   b) Lever the tensioner so it is released (two small holes horizontal below the bolt) and tighten the tensioner retaining bolt.
   Tensioner Idler Retaining bolt: 44Nm
3. Install new camshaft seals if required, apply a little amount of oil to seal lips, this will allow the seals to be installed without being damaged.
4. Install the camshaft sprockets and bolts attaching the camshaft sprockets, if the bolts are not tightened to specification tighten later when timing belt is installed.
   Camshaft Sprocket Bolt 88Nm
5. a) Position the crankshaft sprocket 3 teeth away from TDC No1 piston.
   Note: *This allows the camshafts to be turned without hitting the the top of the pistons.*
   b) The TDC alignment marks of the camshaft sprockets should be aligned. (V33V timing marks are different to the V63W and V73W series engines, see description at front of chapter)
   c) Align TDC marks of the crankshaft sprocket.
6. Install crankshaft sensor.

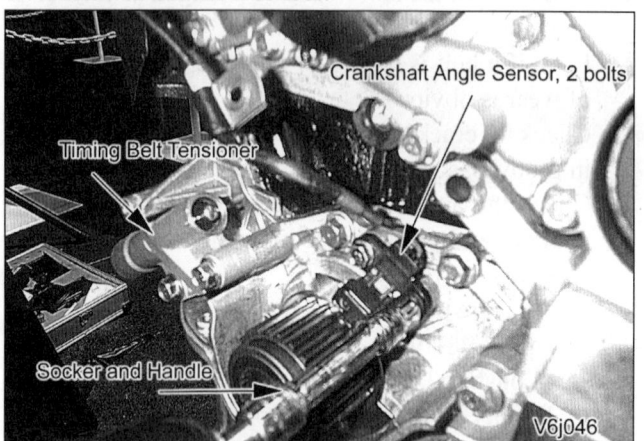

7. Install the timing belt to the original position aligning the timing marks made when removing the timing belt. Taking note that the belt is rotating the same direction as previously, check for direction of arrow made when removing belt.
   * **New Timing Belt:** (a) Position the camshaft gears and crankshaft gear into the correct position.
   * Camshaft gear marks are to be aligned with the marks.
   * Install timing belt onto the lower section of the crankshaft gear, around the inside of the idler pulley, over the left camshaft gear, under top pulley (water

pump), over the right bank camshaft gear, inside idler tension pulley.

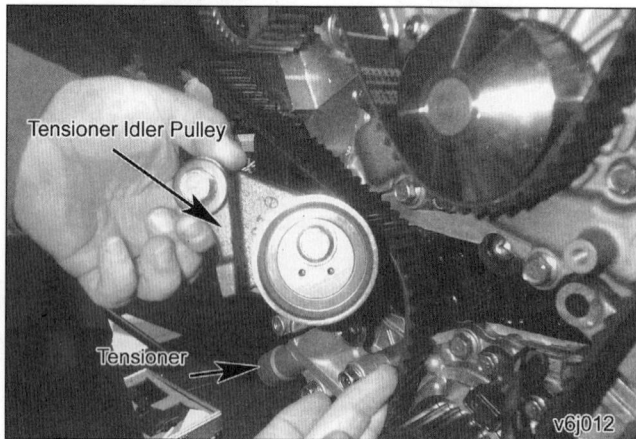

* Keep the timing belt tight and meshed into the grooves on the gears.
* Ensure the alignment marks on the camshaft gears and crankshaft pulley are aligned.
Note: *Right side camshaft sprocket can turned with little force, do not jam your fingers during installation of belt.*

8. Tighten the camshaft sprockets to specification if not tightened.
   Camshaft Sprocket Bolt 88Nm
9. Apply anti-clockwise force to camshaft sprocket, so the timing belt on the tension side is stretched. Check all timing alignment marks are still aligned.
10. Loosen tensioner pulley bolt, hold the tensioner pulley against the timing belt and temporarily tighten the tension pulley bolt, make sure the timing belt alignment marks are all aligned.
    Note: *V33V series engines the 2 holes are below the bolt, lever tensioner pulley anti-clockwise to put tension on belt.*
    V63W and V73W series engines the 2 holes are above the bolt, lever tensioner pulley clockwise to put tension on belt.
11. Use a socket and breaker bar, rotate engine backwards 1/4 of a turn, then clockwise to check all timing marks are aligned.

V6 ENGINE MAINTENANCE & REBUILD 3.0L, 3.5L & 3.8L SOHC M.P.I.

12. Loosen tensioner bolt, rotate the tensioner pulley so that the 2 small holes are horizontal above the tensioner pulley bolt, tighten tensioner pulley bolt to specification.
    Tensioner Pulley Bolt:............................ 44Nm
13. Rotate engine 2 turns clockwise and leave to let belt tension to settle for approx 15 minutes. Check the wire or key in the timing belt auto tensioner is not jammed tight. If it is Rotate the crankshaft 90° clockwise then rotate the crankshaft 90° clockwise. The wire should be able to be removed freely.
14. Check length of the protrusion of the auto tensioner rod.
    Timing Belt Auto Tensioner Rod Assembled Protrusion:..3.8-5.0 mm
15. Fit the lower timing belt cover to the engine, then secure it in place with the retaining bolts.
16. a) Fit the crankshaft balancer to the engine, then fit the retaining bolt to the crankshaft damper.
    b) While securing the crankshaft balancer, tighten the damper retaining bolt, ensure it's tensioned to specification.
    Crankshaft Balancer ....182 Nm
17. Fit the upper timing belt covers to the engine, then fit and tighten the cover retaining bolts.

18. Install accessory mount assembly, note bolts lengths and torque.

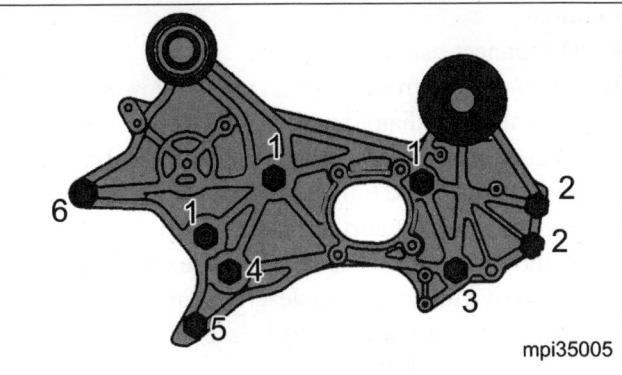

Bolt	Dia & Length	Torque Nm
1	10 x 100	41
2	10 x 30	41
3	10 x 100	44
4	12 x 100	74
5	8 x 30	22
6	10 x 106	44

19. Install air conditioner compressor bracket and compressor.
20. Install the power steering pump.
21. Install front drive belt automatic tensioner pulley.
    Automatic Tensioner Bolt........................... 24 Nm
22. Install the drive belt and release the automatic tensioner as previously described.
23. Install fan pulley and fan, then the radiator shroud.
24. Top up coolant level.
25. Install air cleaner and air intake tubing.
26. Install the engine protection skid panel to under the vehicle.
27. Fit the battery cable to the battery, then run the vehicle and check that everything is operating correctly.

CRANKSHAFT FRONT OIL SEAL
Replace
1. Remove timing belt and crankshaft sprocket as described in this manual.
2. a) Remove the crankshaft sensor blade, and crankshaft spacer.
   b) Remove old seal with a screw driver or seal remover.
   c) Install new seal with a seal installer, ensure the seals lips are not pulled back or crooked.
   d) Replace the crankshaft spacer and crankshaft sensor blade.
3. Replace timing belt and crankshaft sprocket as described in this manual.

CYLINDER HEAD, VALVES & CAMSHAFTS
Make sure that all valve train components are kept in order so they can be installed in their original locations.

V6 ENGINE MAINTENANCE & REBUILD 3.0L, 3.5L & 3.8L SOHC M.P.I.

Remove
1. Disconnect battery earth lead.
2. Drain coolant from engine at radiator lower hose and remove top radiator hose.
3. Rotate crankshaft so engine is at TDC compression No1 cylinder, the timing mark of the crankshaft balancer is aligned with the "T" on the timing belt cover. Remove crankshaft balancer bolt, use a pulley remover to remove the pulley, as described in this chapter.
4. a) Remove the upper timing belt cover bolts and cover as previously described.
   b) Remove the lower timing belt cover bolts and cover as previously described.
5. Check for alignment mark on camshaft gear in line with cylinder head / back of camshaft gear cover.
6. Use an oil based crayon, place alignment marks the timing belt and cam shaft gear, injection pump gear and crankshaft gear. Also draw an arrow showing direction of rotation of timing belt, if the belt is to be reinstalled on the engine.
7. Remove crankshaft sensor, move to one side.
8. Loosen the bolts attaching the camshaft gears to the camshafts.
9. Insert a 1.4mm hex key into tensioner, it may require a little leverage with a large screw driver. This will stop the tensioner rod from moving out once the belt is removed
10. Remove the timing pulley belt from the pulleys.
11. Remove the bolts attaching the camshaft gears to the camshafts.
12. Remove alternator.
    a) Remove nuts from alternator adjuster bracket studs and remove engine harness earth wire connection and wiring harness retainer bracket.
    b) Remove alternator, remove alternator support bolts, then remove support assembly.
13. Remove the attaching oil dipstick tub support bolt.
14. Remove the intake manifold as described in this chapter. # Main points listed below.
    a) Remove air cleaner to intake plenum tube.
    b) Remove the manifold top cover or heat shield if fitted.
    c) Remove vacuum hoses, auxiliary air hose, accelerator cable, accelerator return spring and the kick down cable (auto) from the throttle body.
    d) Detach the cold start injector pipe, water pass hose.
    e) Separate the air intake plenum from the lower intake manifold 2 bolts and 2 nuts.
    f) Remove the fuel rails and injectors.
    g) Remove the bolts and nuts attaching the intake manifold, remove v6 manifold and gaskets.
15. Remove the engine lifting bracket.
16. Remove the exhaust manifolds as described in this chapter.
    * If you wish you may leave the exhaust manifolds attached to the exhaust pipe. Disconnect the exhaust pipes, then allow the manifolds to move to one side allowing you access to remove the cylinder heads.
17. Remove the bolts securing the rocker covers, rocker cover and gasket as previously described in this chapter.
18. Loosen the cylinder head bolts in the order, working from the front and rear of the engine to the centre of the assembly. Loosen a little each pass until the bolts are loose. Remove cylinder head bolts.
19. Lift the cylinder heads and gaskets from engine block.

CYLINDER HEAD RECONDITIONING
* Make sure that all valve train components are kept together and identified so that they can be installed in their original locations.

Dismantle
1. Remove the bolts securing the each rocker arm shaft to the head, loosen gradually and in order from the ends to the middle.
   (Install brackets [Part No E9M40-2] to hold lash adjusters to rocker arms for convenience.)
   Remove the rocker arm shafts, rocker arms and bolts with lash adjusters.

2. Compress valve springs in turn with a conventional spring compressor and remove valve collets.

V6 ENGINE MAINTENANCE & REBUILD 3.0L, 3.5L & 3.8L SOHC M.P.I.

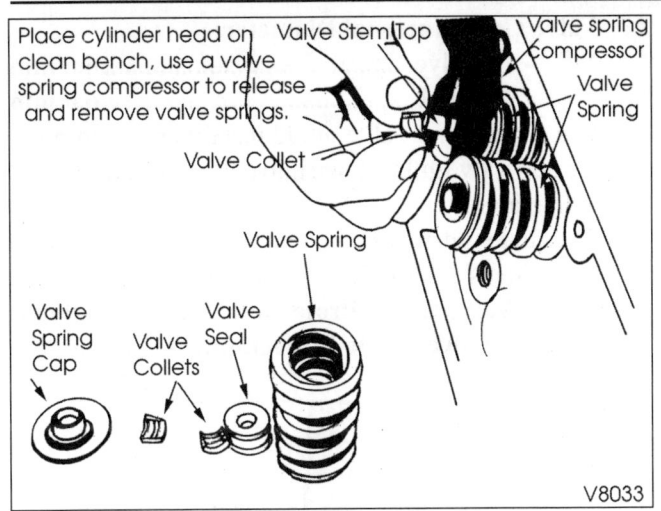

3. Remove the following:
   a) Valve spring caps, springs, valve stem oil seals and valve spring seats.
   b) Valves from cylinder head.
      Caution: *Do not force valves out of guides, as mushroomed valve ends due to lifter wear or dirt in the guide, will damage guide. Remove burrs by chamfering valve stem with an oil stone or file.*

4. Remove the camshaft end cap, 2 bolts.
5. Slide the camshafts from the heads. The right head camshaft is removed from the distributor hole, at the rear of the head. The left side head the camshaft is removed from the camshaft thrust case at the rear of the head.
   Note: The right side camshaft has a 4mm slot for the distributor drive.

Clean
1. a) Clean all carbon from combustion chambers, valve ports, etc, with a rotary-type carbon removing wire brush.
      * Do not use a wire brush on any gasket sealing surface.
   b) Clean cylinder head gasket surface.
2. Thoroughly clean valve guides with a suitable cleaning solvent or a wire brush.

3. Clean valve heads with a drill and wire brush.
   * Do not scratch the valve stem.
4. Wash all components in a suitable cleaning solvent and air dry with dry compressed air.

Cylinder Head Inspection
1. Cylinder heads should be inspected for cracks in valve seats and combustion chambers, and for external cracks to water jackets.
2. Check cylinder head deck surface for corrosion.
3. Using a straight edge and feeler gauge, check cylinder head deck, intake and exhaust manifold surfaces for distortion. Check cylinder head deck surface diagonally, longitudinally and transversely.

These surfaces may be refaced once only by parallel grinding.
* Head to block surface if more than 0.15mm (0.0059in) must be removed from any surface, replace cylinder head.
* Head to manifold surface if more than 0.10mm (0.004in) must be removed from any surface, replace cylinder head.
4. Inspect the following:
   a) Cylinder head for cracks, especially between valve seats or exhaust ports.

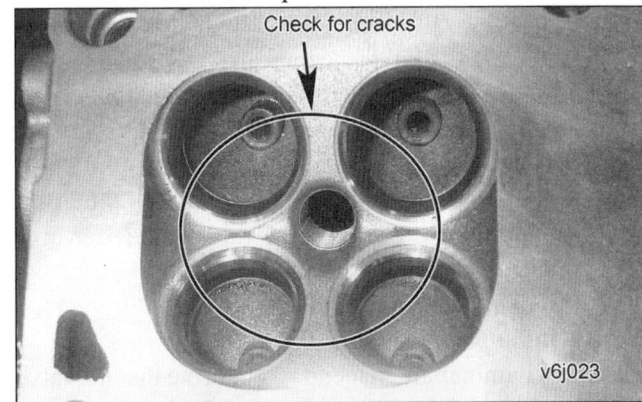

   b) Cylinder head deck surface for corrosion, casting sand inclusions or blow holes.
   c) Cylinder block valve seats and valve guide holes.

33

12 Valve
Inlet valve seat insert hole diameter
- 0.3 mm Oversize ....44.30 - 44.33 mm
- 0.6 mm Oversize ....44.60 - 44.63 mm

Exhaust valve seat insert hole diameter
- 0.3 mm Oversize ....38.30 - 38.33 mm
- 0.6 mm Oversize ....38.60 - 38.63 mm

Valve guide hole diameter ....13.00 - 13.02 mm
- 0.05 mm Oversize ....13.05 - 13.07 mm
- 0.25 mm Oversize ....13.25 - 13.27 mm
- 0.50 mm Oversize ....13.50 - 13.52 mm

Camshaft/camshaft bearing clearance .0.06-0.10 mm

24 Valve
Inlet valve seat insert hole diameter
- 0.3 mm Oversize ....34.30 - 34.33 mm
- 0.6 mm Oversize ....34.60 - 34.63 mm

Exhaust valve seat insert hole diameter
- 0.3 mm Oversize ....31.80 - 31.83 mm
- 0.6 mm Oversize ....32.10 - 32.13 mm

Valve guide hole diameter ....11.00 - 11.02 mm
- 0.05 mm Oversize ....11.05 - 11.07 mm
- 0.25 mm Oversize ....11.25 - 11.27 mm
- 0.50 mm Oversize ....11.50 - 11.52 mm

Camshaft/camshaft bearing clearance .0.06-0.10 mm

VALVE GUIDES
Clearance Checking

1. Excessive valve stem to guide bore clearance will cause lack of power, rough idling and noisy valve operation.
2. Insufficient clearance will result in noisy and sticking of the valve and will interfere with smoothness of operation of engine.
3. Measure inside diameter with an ID micrometer, also measure the valve stem, then use the following sum to calculate the guide clearance.
   ** Guide diameter - stem diameter = clearance **
   Valve stem to guide clearance
   - Inlet ....0.02 - 0.05 mm
   - Exhaust ....0.04 - 0.07 mm
4. If it is necessary to replace the valve guide see valve guide replacement in this chapter.

Valve Guide Replacement

1. Use a hammer and flat end rod to drive the old valve guide down into the port area of the head, at room temperature.
   Note: Remove the snap ring from the exhaust valve guides.
2. Measure guide hole, if over specified ID rebore to fit the over size valve guide.
   Valve Guide OD sizes ....0.05, 0.25 & 0.50mm
3. Valve guides ID specifications.

Valve Guide Internal Diameter:
- 12 Valve .... 6.6 mm
- 24 Valve .... 6.0 mm

4. Use a press and valve guide installing die to press the new valve guide down into cylinder head, at room temperature.
5. The guide is driven down into the cylinder head until the guide is at specified height from head.
   Intake Valve Guide Projection: .... 14.0 mm
   Exhaust Valve Guide Projection: .... 14.0 mm

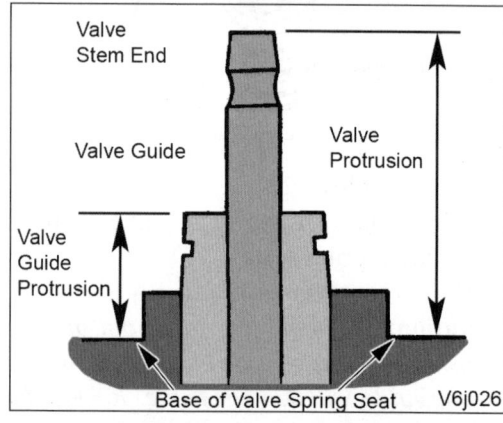

6. Ream bush out with a 6mm reamer to obtain specified diameter.

VALVE SEATS

1. Reconditioning the valve seats is very important because the seating of the valves must be perfect for the engine to deliver the power and performance its develops.
2. Another important factor is the cooling of the valve head. Good contact between each valve and its seat in the head is imperative to ensure that the heat in the valve head will be properly carried away.
3. Several different types of equipment are available for reconditioning valve seats. The recommendations of the manufacturer of the equipment being used should be carefully followed to attain proper results.
4. Check valve seats for any evidence of pitting or damage at valve contact surface. If pitting is evident, the valve seats will need to be reconditioned.

* Because the valve guide serves to support and centre the valve seat grinder, it is essential that the valve guide is serviced before reconditioning the valve seats.
5. If the seat is too wide after grinding, it may be narrowed by using a 30° or 65° grinding stone. The 30° stone will lower the seat and the 65° stone will raise the seat.
6. If the valves seats are reconditioned, the valves must also be reconditioned (refer VALVES) or replace valves as necessary.

REPLACING VALVE SEAT

1. Using a lathe, turn down the out side diameter of a valve head so it fill fit neatly into inside of the valve seat.
2. Cover the head that surrounds the valve seat with an inflammable paste, such as soap paste. This will stop damage from weld spatter.
3. Weld a continuous run of weld around the edge of the valve, so it is welded to the inside of the valve seat.
4. Lift the head so the top of the valve can be tapped to free the valve seat.
5. Slide the machined valve and valve seat out of the head.
6. Machine the head as the new valve seat is over size by 0.38mm diameter and depth.
7. The new valve seat should not to be hit or forced into the head as this will cause damage to the seat and head.
8. Place the new valve seat in liquid nitrogen or dry ice so the seat will shrink in size.
9. Carefully place the valve seat into position with an old valve (converted into a special tool as shown in diagram) positioned through the seat into the valve guide. Gently tap the special tool to position and centre the valve seat

VALVE STEM OIL SEALS
Replacement
1. Disconnect battery earth lead.
2. Remove the following:
   a) Spark plug leads from spark plugs.
   b) Spark plug from relevant cylinder and screw air adaptor into spark plug hole.
   c) Rocker cover as previously described in this chapter.
   d) Timing belt and covers as described in this chapter.
   e) Camshaft that belongs to the relevant cylinder.
3. Apply air pressure via a special fitting that screws into the spark plug hole, to hold valves in closed position.
4. a) Compress valve spring with valve spring compressor.
   b) Remove valve collets.
   * Before installing valve spring compressor, it may be necessary to tap top of valve cap with a soft-faced hammer to overcome the binding of the valve collets in the valve spring cap.
5. a) Remove spring cap, spring and valve compressor as an assembly.
   b) Remove and discard old valve stem oil seal.
6. Install new valve stem oil seal and make sure the seal fully seats on top of the valve guide.
   * Make sure the correct type of seal is fitted to the appropriate valve, based on part No. and package description.
7. a) Install spring, cap and valve compressor as an assembly on the valve stem.
   b) Install valve collets and slowly release spring compressor, then remove spring compressor.
   c) Disconnect air line to special tool.
8. Install the following:
   a) Camshaft as previously described in this Chapter.
   b) Replace timing belt and covers as described in this chapter.
   c) Rocker cover as previously described in this Chapter.
9. Remove special tool and install and torque spark plug.
10. Install spark plug leads and battery earth lead.
11. Start engine and check for oil leaks and valve train noise.

VALVE SPRINGS

1. Inspect valve spring surfaces on valve seat and valve cap for wear or gouging. Replace components as necessary.
2. a) Check spring ends. If they are not parallel, the spring is bent.
   b) Replace valve springs that do not meet specification.
3. a) Check valve spring load with a spring tester.
   b) Springs should be compressed to the specified height and checked against specifications.
   c) Replace any valve spring if not to specification.

12 Valve   - Free length 49.8mm
            - Free length Minimum... 48.8mm
24 Valve   - Free length 51.0mm
            - Free length Minimum... 50.0mm

d) Measure installed load/height of valve spring.

Spring Load/Installed Height:
- 12 Valve 323/40.4
- 24 Valve 216/44.2

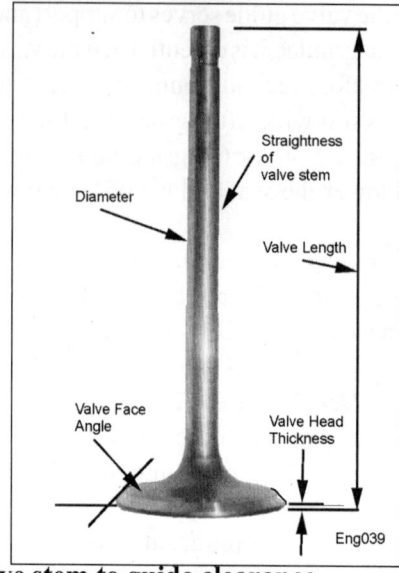

VALVES

1. a) Inspect valve stem for burrs and scratches. (Burrs and minor scratching may be removed with an oil stone.)
   b) Valves with excessive stem wear or that are warped should be replaced.
   c) Inspect valve stem tip for wear. The valve tip may be reconditioned by grinding.
   d) Follow the grinder manufacturers instructions. Make sure the new tip surface is at right-angles to the valve stem.
   e) Do not grind valve below minimum specified length.
2. Inspect valve stem collet groove for damage.
3. a) Check valve face for burning or cracking.
   b) If pieces have broken off, inspect corresponding piston and cylinder head area for damage.
4. a) Inspect valve stem for straightness and valve head for bending or distortion using 'V' blocks.
   b) Bent or distorted valves must be replaced.
5. Valves with pitted or grooves faces can be reconditioned with a valve refacing machine, ensuring correct relationship between head and stem.
   * If pitting or grooving is so deep that refacing would result in a 'knife' edge at the valve head, the valve must be replaced.
   * Measure valve margin after refacing valves. If margin is less than minimum specified, the valve must be replaced.
6. Lightly lap reconditioned valves into valve seat.
   * New valves must not be lapped. Lapping destroys the protective coating on the valve face.
7. Measure valves for specification.

12 Valve Engines:
Valve height   - Inlet .... 102.97 mm
                  - Inlet wear limit .... 102.47 mm
                  - Exhaust .... 102.67 mm
                  - Exhaust wear limit. 102.17 mm
Stem diameter   - Inlet .... 6.6 mm
                  - Exhaust .... 6.6 mm
Head Thickness   - Inlet .... 1.2 to 0.07 mm
                  - Exhaust .... 2.0 to 1.5 mm
Valve face angle .... 43.5° - 44.0°
Valve seat contact width .... 0.90 - 1.30 mm
Valve stem to guide clearance
                  - Inlet .... 0.03 - 0.06 mm
                  - Inlet wear limit .... 0.10 mm
                  - Exhaust .... 0.05 - 0.09 mm
                  - Exhaust wear limit .... 0.15 mm

24 Valve Engines:
Valve height   - Inlet .... 112.30 mm
                  - Inlet wear limit .... 111.80 mm
                  - Exhaust .... 114.11 mm
                  - Exhaust wear limit. 113.61 mm
Stem diameter   - Inlet .... 6.0 mm
                  - Exhaust .... 6.0 mm
Head Thickness   - Inlet .... 1.0 to 0.5 mm
                  - Exhaust .... 1.2 to 0.7 mm
Valve face angle .... 43.5° - 44.0°
Valve seat contact width .... 0.90 - 1.30 mm
Valve stem to guide clearance
                  - Inlet .... 0.02 - 0.05 mm
                  - Inlet wear limit .... 0.10 mm
                  - Exhaust .... 0.04 - 0.06 mm
                  - Exhaust wear limit .... 0.15 mm

8. After refacing or installing a new valve, check for correct seating as follows.
   a) Lightly coat valve face with bearing blue.
   b) Insert valve and rotate about 1/6 of a revolution.
   c) Remove valve and check for full contact with seat.
      i) If partial contact is indicated, insert valve again and turn through a full revolution.
      ii) If blue on seat indicates full contact, reface valve.
      iii) If partial contact is still indicated, re-grind cylinder head valve seat.
      iv) Measure valve assembled protrusion from valve spring seat surface for specification.
   12 Valve
   Valve Assembled Protrusion 41.65mm
   Maximum 42.15mm

24 Valve
Valve Assembled Protrusion 49.30mm
Maximum 49.80mm

d) Clean all traces of bearing blue from valves and seats.

CAMSHAFTS
Inspection.
1. Check camshaft bearing journals and lobes for overheating, damage or wear (discolouration).
2. Inspect camshaft journal diameter with micrometer. Replace camshaft if journals are not within specifications.

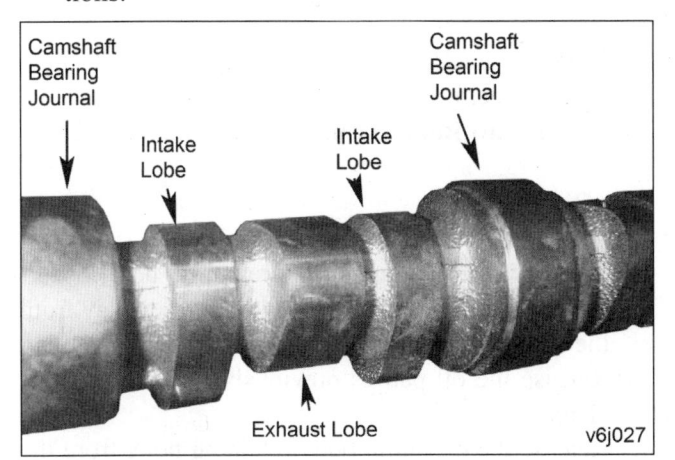

Camshaft Journal diameter:
12 Valve .... 34.5 mm
24 Valve .... 45.0 mm
Bearing clearance .... 0.01 - 0.04 mm

3. Position camshaft on 'V' blocks and check the camshaft run-out using a dial gauge.
   Camshaft Run-out .... 0.06 mm
4. Inspect the camshaft lobe heights, using a micrometer, record all the results.
   Height of cam lobe
   SOHC - Inlet .... 37.58 mm
           - Exhaust .... 36.95 mm
   wear limit - Inlet .... 37.08 mm
              - Exhaust .... 36.45 mm

ASSEMBLE CYLINDER HEAD
1. Dry and clean all components thoroughly.
2. Using clean engine oil, lubricate valve stems and valve guides thoroughly.
3. Install valves in corresponding guides.
4. Make sure that seals fully seat on top of guide, install new valve stem oil seals. The original seals may not be the same colour as the replacement seals.
5. Install the valve spring seat over the valve guide onto the cylinder head.
6. Place valve springs and cap over valve stem.
7. Using a suitable spring compressor, compress valve springs.

* Excess compression could cause spring cap to damage valve stem oil seal, ensure to compress valve springs only enough to install valve collets.

8. Install valve collets, making sure that they locate accurately in groove in top end of valve stem. Release the valve spring compressor slowly ensuring that the collets sit properly. Grease may be used to hold collets in place.
9. Lubricate the camshaft journals and lobes with molybdenum grease. Slide the camshafts into the heads. The right camshaft has the camshaft position sensor ring attached by one bolt, bolt is tightened at
   Camshaft Position Sensor Ring Bolt 22Nm
10. Replace the rocker arm shafts, rocker arms and bolts with lash adjusters.
    Install rocker arm shaft bolts, however do not tighten enough for the valve springs to be compressed.
    Install rocker arm shaft spring clips, install from top down then rotate position as shown.

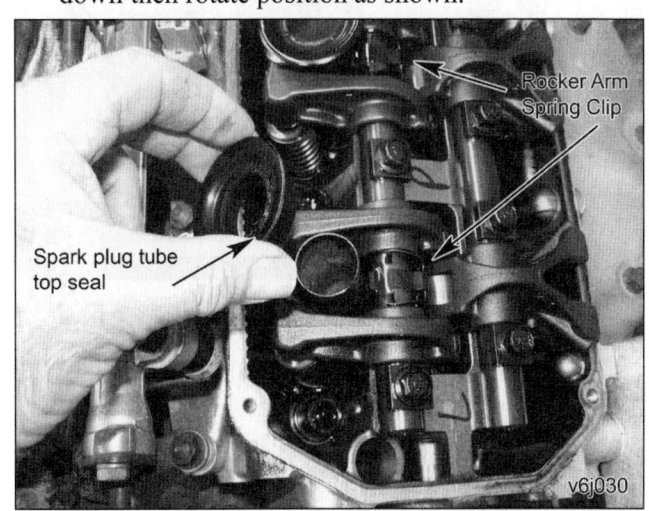

Tighten the bolts to specification in order from the middle to the end.
(Install brackets [Part No E9M40-2] to hold lash adjusters to rocker arms for convenience.)
Rocker Arm - Rocker Shaft 32Nm

INSTALL CYLINDER HEAD
1. Place dowel pins into block, place head gasket in position over dowel pins on cylinder block.

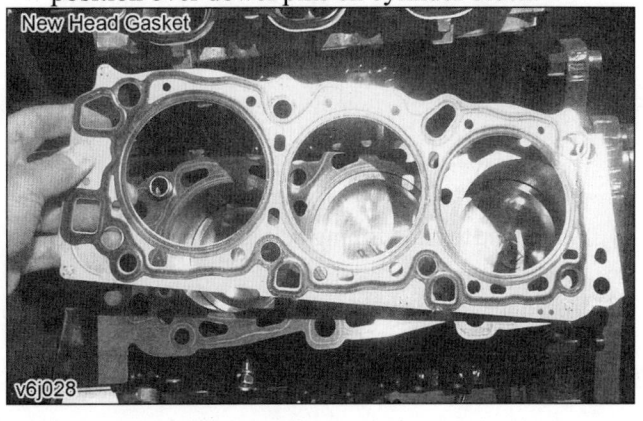

V6 ENGINE MAINTENANCE & REBUILD 3.0L, 3.5L & 3.8L SOHC M.P.I.

Note: The cylinder head gasket has an identification mark, the identification mark faces up.

2. a) Carefully guide cylinder head into place over dowel pins and gasket.
   b) Place cylinder head and tighten with finger, remove dowel pins during this procedure.
3. Tighten the head bolts to the following sequence and in the order shown.

```
Head Bolt Tightening Sequence
← Engine Front
Right Bank
  6        2        3        7
  5        1        4        8
Left Bank
  8        4        1        5
  5        1        4        8
```

Cylinder Head Bolts
Step 1:
Cylinder head bolts - Cold - in 3 stages.......108Nm
Step 2
Loosen bolts
Step 3
Cylinder head bolts - Cold - in 3 stages.......108Nm
* It is important to follow the given procedure to avoid head gasket failure and possible engine damage.

4. Turn the engine over so the crankshaft is at TDC/compression on number 1 cylinder.
5. Install new spark plug tube seals.
6. Install new oil seals at the front of the camshafts.
7. Install the camshaft gears and bolts, tightening to specification.
   Camshaft Sprocket Bolt 88Nm
8. Install rocker covers and gaskets.
9. The No1. piston should be at TDC as described in point number 4.
10. Align the camshaft gear alignment marks with the rocker cover marks as described in timing belt section.
11. Adjust the tension timing belt idler pulley to help belt installation.
12. Install the timing belt to the original position aligning the timing marks made when removing the timing belt. Taking not that the belt is rotating the same direction as previously, check for direction arrow made when removing belt.

** Timing belts do have a life span, and the average life of a timing belt should be 100,000 kilometres, 62,000 mile for normal driving conditions.
See Timing Belt section.

13. Check the timing belt runs correctly and that the timing marks on the camshaft gears, and crankshaft gear are in the correct position at TDC compression on No 1 cylinder.
14. a) Install timing belt lower and upper front covers and tighten the bolts to specification.
    b) Install front drive belt pulley and bracket, tighten to specification.
15. Install the crankshaft balancer pulley, tighten attaching bolt to specification.
    Crankshaft Balancer bolt.......................... 182Nm

OIL PUMP
Remove
1. Withdraw the timing belt as previously described.
2. Remove the crankshafts sprocket and key way from the crankshaft.
3. Release the oil pan as previously described in this chapter.
4. Release the oil pump body retaining bolts from the oil pump body, then tap the inside of the oil pump body assembly to release it from the cylinder block.

Dismantle
1. Remove the oil pump body cover retaining screws, then remove cover plate.
2. Withdraw the inner and outer rotors from the front pump body.
3. Release the relief valve retaining cir-clip from the rear housing body, then withdraw the retainer, spring and piston.
4. Tap the crankshaft seal from the pump body, then dispose of the seal.

Inspection
1. Wash and dry all parts, then lay out parts on a clean bench.

V6 ENGINE MAINTENANCE & REBUILD 3.0L, 3.5L & 3.8L SOHC M.P.I.

2. Check for damage and wear to the outer race to pump housing.
3. Check for damage and wear to the rotor to outer race.
   Inner Rotor tip clearance .... **0.06 - 0.18mm**
   Outer rotor to pump clearance ...... **0.10 - 0.18mm**
   Max **0.35mm**
4. Check the cover surface for damage by rotor and rotor clearance (use a straight edge).
   Rotor side clearance to pump .... **0.04 - 0.10mm**
   If components are to be replaced, replace as a complete unit.

5. Visually inspect relief valve for smoothness of surfaces, check when assembling that the spring will keep the valve closed when the cap is fitted.

Assemble
1. Install a new crankshaft seal to the pump housing.
2. Fit the relief valve piston, spring and retainer into the rear pump body, then secure in place with the cir-clip.
3. Fit the rotor shaft seal to the front housing, when tapping it into place be careful not to damage the seal.
4. Fit the inner rotor into the front pump body, do not damage the shaft seal, then fit the outer rotor to front pump body.
5. Fit a new gasket to the front pump body and install pump cover.

Install
1. With a new gasket fitted the cylinder block, position the oil pump assembly, then fit and tension the oil pump assembly retaining bolts to specifications.
   Oil Pump Assembly **9.3Nm**
2. Fit the oil pan as previously described in this chapter.
3. Fit the crankshaft key-way and sprocket to the crankshaft.
4. Fit the timing belt as previously described in this chapter.

FLYWHEEL/DRIVEPLATE
Remove
Before removal of flywheel/driveplate take note of the location of paint aligning marks on flywheel and pressure plate, before removing clutch pressure plate, the driveplate and torque converter also have paint aligning marks.
If not visible, scribe aligning marks on all parts.

1. To remove transmission refer to Manual Transmission or Automatic Transmission in this manual.
2. Vehicles with manual transmission:
   Remove the clutch pressure plate and driven plate as per Clutch section in this manual.
3. Block flywheel driveplate from turning, using a screwdriver or suitable locking tool. Remove flywheel/driveplate crankshaft bolts and flywheel/driveplate.

Inspection.
The flywheel and flexplate are purposely out of balance and no attempt should be made to balance these as an individual unit.
1. Check flywheel/driveplate ring gear for badly worn, damaged or cracked teeth.
   If needed, replace flywheel ring gear or driveplate, for details refer to "ring gear" section in this chapter.
   Check starter motor pinion gear for damage, if ring gear teeth are damaged replace pinion gear, for details refer to "Starting System chapter".
2. Inspect crankshaft and flywheel/driveplate matching surfaces for burrs. Using a fine mill file remove burrs if present.

Install
1. Install flywheel/driveplate to crankshaft, and tighten bolts to the correct specification.
   Flywheel / Driveplate Bolts **74Nm**
2. Mount a dial indicator on the rear of cylinder block for vehicles with automatic transmission. Inspect flexplate Run-out at the torque converter mounting bolt holes. Run-out should not exceed the following specifications.
   Try to correct by tapping high side with a mallet if Run-out exceeds specification. Replace driveplate if this condition can not be corrected.
3. Inspect starter motor operation.

RING GEAR
Replacement
The ring gear is welded to the driveplate and is serviced only as an assembly for vehicles with automatic transmission. Therefore must be replaced as a complete unit.
For vehicles with manual transmission, the ring gear is a shrink fit on the flywheel flange, and if damaged, can be removed and replaced.

V6 ENGINE MAINTENANCE & REBUILD 3.0L, 3.5L & 3.8L SOHC M.P.I.

Replacement Techniques

1. To remove flywheel refer to Flywheel/ Driveplate section in this manual for details.
2. To remove ring gear drill a hole between two ring gear teeth and split gear at this point using a chisel.
3. Make sure that there are no foreign matter or burrs on new ring gear and flywheel matching surface. Remove burrs using a fine mill file (if present).
4. Heat and shrink a new gear in place as follows:
   a) Using an emery cloth, polish several spots on ring gear.
   b) Using a hot plate or a slow moving torch, heat ring gear until the polished spots turn blue (approximately 320 degrees Celsius).
   * Heating the ring gear in excess of 427 degrees Celsius will destroy ring gear heat treatment.
   c) Quickly place ring gear in position against shoulder of flywheel using 2 pairs of pliers. Allow ring gear to cool slowly until it contracts and is firmly held in place.
5. To install flywheel refer to Flywheel/Driveplate section in this manual. Tighten bolt to specification.

REAR MAIN OIL SEAL
Replace

1. Remove flywheel/driveplate, as described in "Flywheel/driveplate" in this manual.
2. Remove old seal with a screw driver or seal remover.
3. Install new seal with a seal installer, ensure the seals lips are not pulled back or crooked.

4. Clean flywheel/drive plate attaching bolt threads in rear of crankshaft using a thread tap.
   Install new flywheel/flexplate and attaching bolts, tighten bolts to the correct torque specification.
   Flywheel/flexplate bolt tensioning 74Nm
5. Reinstall transmission, check engine and transmission lubricant levels.
6. Road test vehicle and check for lubrication leaks.

SPIGOT BEARING
Before removing plate, take note of the position of the paint aligning marks on flywheel and pressure plate. If marks are not visible, scribe aligning marks on both parts.

Replacement

1. To remove transmission refer to Manual Transmission section in this manual for details.
2. To remove clutch pressure plate and driven plate refer to Clutch section in this manual.
3. To remove spigot bearing use a Slide hammer.
4. Use a piloted screwdriver to replace spigot bearing. Place new bearing on pilot of tool with radius in bore of bearing next to shoulder on tool. Drive bearing into crankshaft to the dimension as shown in the diagram. Use thin film of SAE 90 Gear Oil to lubricate the bearing.
5. To install clutch assembly and transmission refer to Clutch and Manual Transmission sections in this manual.

ENGINE REBUILD.

ENGINE ASSEMBLY.
Remove

1. Discharge fuel system as described in Fuel chapter and then disconnect the battery.
2. Disconnect battery leads
3. a) Remove bottom radiator hose from the radiator, and drain the cooling system, then remove the top and bottom radiator hoses from the engine.
   b) Remove the fan assembly and radiator as outlined in Cooling chapter.
4. Mark the position of the bonnet hinge brackets on the bonnet, then release and withdraw the bonnet from the vehicle.
5. Remove the air cleaner assembly.
6. Drain engine oil sump.
7. Disconnect the left and right exhaust pipes to exhaust manifolds, see exhaust system chapter.
8. Disconnect the accelerator cable / electrical connector and then disconnect the vacuum hoses including the booster vacuum hose.
9. Disconnect heater hoses.
10. Disconnect the electrical connections for throttle position sensor, ignition coils, etc.
11. Disconnect the connector for the coolant temperature gauge and the coolant temperature sensor.
12. Disconnect main wiring harness from engine and battery harness.
13. Remove intake plenum and throttle body to have access to injector loom.
14. Unclip engine harness from the starter, alternator, oil

V6 ENGINE MAINTENANCE & REBUILD 3.0L, 3.5L & 3.8L SOHC M.P.I.

pressure sensor and fuel injectors and place to side of engine bay, ensure the wiring harness is labelled.

15. Remove front drive belt, slacken off idler tension.
16. Disconnect the high pressure fuel hose and the fuel return hose.
17. Remove the power steering and A/C drive belt if not already removed.
18. Remove the power steering pump and A/C compressor, leaving the hoses and pipes connected and position out of the way.
    Note: *Do not allow them to hang, they must be tied up.*
19. Remove the starter motor heat shield then remove the starter motor.
20. Support engine with engine crane then release the engine mounts and remove engine from vehicle.
21. Loosen bolt nuts at engine mountings.
22. Remove bolts from the engine including sump to the transaxle.
23. Raise engine slightly to take weight off mounts by attaching an appropriate lifting hook and chain to engine lifting brackets if fitted. Otherwise care must be taken not to damage engine components with rope or chain while lifting engine.
24. Remove bolts from engine mountings.
25. Raise engine with front tilted upwards.
    * Do not allow engine to swing backwards or forward and damage any of the components.
26. Separate engine and transmission assemblies if necessary. Refer to Manual Transmission or Automatic Transmission for details.

Dismantle.
1. Mount engine assembly in an appropriate engine stand.
2. Remove the following parts as previously described or about to be described, in this chapter.
   a) Intake manifold.
   b) Rocker Covers.
   c) Exhaust manifolds.
   d) Oil filter.
   e) Crankshaft balancer.
   f) Timing belt covers.
   g) Timing belt, camshaft gears.
   h) Camshafts.
   i) Cylinder heads
   j) Engine sump.
   k) Oil pump suction pipe and baffle.
   l) Flywheel/flexplate.
   m) Engine rear end plate.
   n) Crankshaft.
   o) Piston and connecting rod assemblies.

Assembly.
Assembly techniques for each part are outlined in this section under there particular headings.

1. Make sure that all bolts and nuts are tightened as specified in this section.
2. Use specified engine lubricant and coolant when refilling.
3. Inspect transmission fluid level, add lubricant as required.
4. Inspect for fuel, coolant, oil and exhaust leaks. Repair as required.
5. Check engine hood alignment.

OIL PAN (SUMP)
Remove
1. Drain oil from oil pan.
2. Remove the dip stick.
3. Remove the small left side cover, 2 bolts.
4. Remove oil pan bolts, oil pan and seal, dispose of oil seal.

Install
1. Clean all matching surfaces of oil pan and cylinder block thoroughly.
2. Apply sealant to the oil pan surface groove and around the bolt holes.
3. Install oil pan and seal to crankcase, and tighten as specified.
   Take care with 2 bolts to transaxle, as they could easily miss the hole and go to the side of the transaxle housing.
   Oil Pan to Engine .... 6 Nm
   Oil Pan to Transaxle .... 37 Nm
   Oil Pan Small Cover left side, bolt 11Nm
4. Make sure oil pan drain plug is tightened as specified, use a new drain plug seal.
   Oil pan drain plug.. 39Nm
5. Replace dip stick.
6. Refill oil pan with the correct amount of engine oil as specified.
7. Start engine and inspect for oil leaks. Repair as required.
8. Stop engine and check oil level on dip stick.

OIL PUMP SUCTION PIPE AND BAFFLE
Remove
1. Remove the oil pan from the engine as previously described in this chapter.
2. Release the suction pipe and bracket retaining bolt from the assembly.

V6 ENGINE MAINTENANCE & REBUILD 3.0L, 3.5L & 3.8L SOHC M.P.I.

3. Remove the suction pipe from the engine.
4. Remove the suction pipe gasket from the engine, dispose of the gasket.

Install

1. Fit a new suction pipe gasket to the engine, then fit the suction pipe and baffle into place. 
2. Fit the suction pipe and baffle retaining nuts, then tension the nuts to specifications.
   Oil suction pipe and screen .... 19 Nm
   Oil suction pipe bracket .... 9 Nm
3. Fit the oil pan to the engine.

PISTON AND CONNECTING ROD ASSEMBLY.

Both piston and cylinder bore condition must be considered together when fitting new pistons. Production and service pistons have the same nominal weight and can be intermixed without affecting engine balance. If needed, used pistons may be fitted selectively to any cylinder of the engine, providing they are in good condition.
Piston pin assemblies and ring sets are available in oversize.
Note: It will be an advantage to remove the main bearing cradle before removing pistons and connecting rods.

Remove

1. Remove cylinder heads as described in Cylinder Head section.
2. To remove oil pan (sump), oil suction pipe and screen.
3. Inspect cylinder bores above piston ring travel. If bores are worn so that a ridge or similar exists. Turn crankshaft so that piston is at bottom of stroke and cover piston with a cloth to collect cuttings. Remove the ridge with a ridge remover, this is to be done for each cylinder.
4. Using an etching marker or felt tipped pen, mark all connecting rods, caps and pistons to indicate cylinder identification, if not marked. 
5. Remove rod assemblies and piston as follows,
   a) With connecting rod crankshaft journal straight down (Bottom Dead Centre), remove connecting rod cap bolts and remove cap with bearing shell.
   b) Push piston and connecting rod from cylinder using a long guide. Remove guides and install cap and bolts to connecting rod.
6. Remove all other piston and connecting rod assemblies using the same procedure.

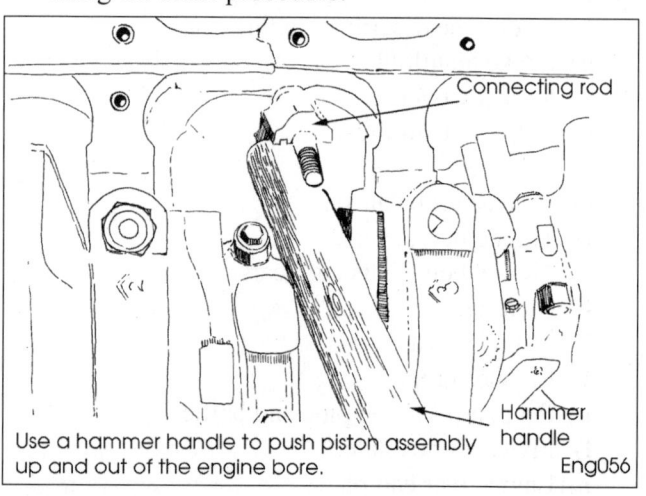

Dismantle.

1. Expand and slide piston rings off to remove and dispose of them.
   Worn rings may have sharp edges ensure to take care

42

V6 ENGINE MAINTENANCE & REBUILD 3.0L, 3.5L & 3.8L SOHC M.P.I.

when removing piston rings.
2. Piston pin can now be removed as follows:
Press piston pin from piston with a mandrel and press, until piston pis free.
Press in load 7,350-17,200N

Inspection.
1. Thoroughly clean carbon from piston heads and from ring grooves using a suitable tool and remove any gum or varnish from piston skirts using a suitable cleaning solvent.
2. Check cylinder walls for ridges, roughness or scoring which indicates excessive wear. Inspect cylinder bores for taper and out-of-round using an accurate cylinder gauge at top, middle and bottom of bore, both parallel and at right angles to centre line of engine. Refer to Cylinder Block section for details.
3. Examine piston skirt thoroughly for scored or rough surfaces, cracks in skirt or crown, chipping, broken ring lands or uneven wear which would cause rings to seat improperly or have excessive clearance in ring grooves. Pistons should be replaced if faulty or damaged.
Pistons are cam ground, which means that the diameter at right angles to the piston pin is greater than the diameter parallel to the piston pin. When a piston is checked for size, it must be done at points 90° to the piston bore.

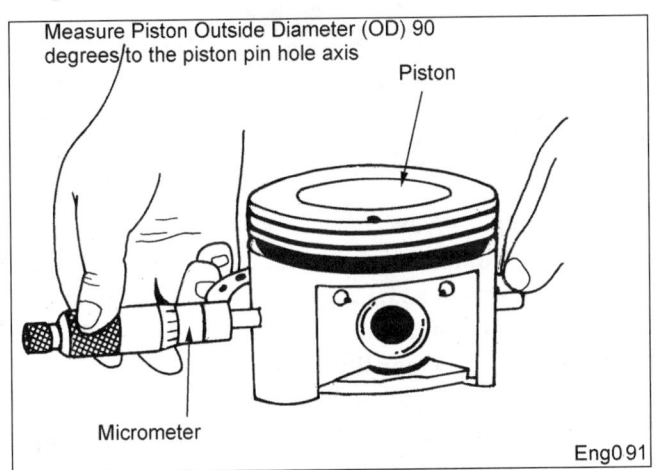

Piston diameter
6G72 .... 91.1 mm
6G74 .... 93.0 mm
6G75 .... 95.0 mm
Piston to bore clearance .... 0.02 - 0.04 mm
Piston oversize ...... 0.50 mm, 0.75 mm, 1.00 mm

4. Check piston pin bores and piston pins for wear. Piston pins and piston pin bores must be free of scuffing or varnish when being measured. Use a micrometer to measure the piston pin, and a dial bore gauge or an inside micrometer to measure piston pin bore.
Piston pin hole diameter .... 22.0 mm

Piston and pin should be replaced if not as specified.
5. Remove bearing shells from connecting rod, install cap and bolts. Tighten bolts as specified.
Connecting Rod Cap Bolt:
12 Valve 51Nm
24 Valve .... 34Nm plus 90 degree turn
6. Place connecting rod assembly on a checking fixture and inspect rod for twist or bend.
Replace if twisted or bent, do not attempt to straighten rod.
Inspect new connecting rods using the same procedure before using them.
Connecting rod - bend .... 0.05 mm
- twist .... 0.1 mm
7. Check outside of connecting rod bearing shells and internal diameter of connecting rod big end for wear indicating high spots in the rod big end.
8. Remove cap bolts and inspect bolts for stretching by comparing them with a new bolt, if stretched, replace.

Assembly and Installation.
1. Using engine oil, lubricate piston pin and piston pin bore.
2. Install piston pin on mandrel.
3. Assemble installer guide and piston support to base.
4. Install piston and connecting rod over guide.
Note: *The front mark on the piston must be facing up so pin is pressed in from piston front mark side.*

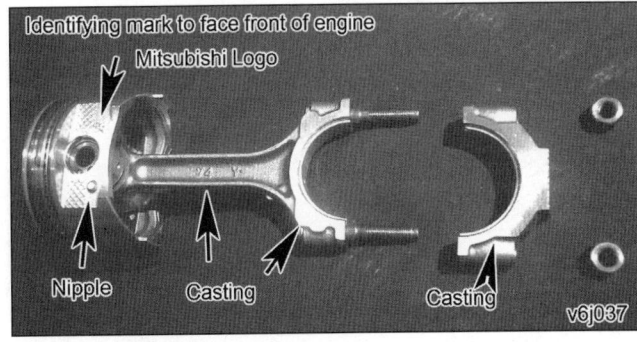

5. Press piston pin into place with a mandrel, until piston pin bottoms.
Press in load 7,350-17,200N
6. To install piston rings refer to Piston Rings section.
7. Make sure connecting rod bearing shells, pistons, cylinder bores and crankshaft journals are totally clean, then, using clean engine oil, coat cylinder bores and all bearing surfaces.
8. Position the crankpin straight down before installation of a piston and rod assembly in its bore.
9. Remove cap, and with bearing upper shell seated in connecting rod, install the 'short' guide tool into inner bolt hole. Install 'long' guide tool into the other bolt

hole.

Guides hold upper bearing shell in place and protects crankshaft journal from damage during installation of connecting rod and piston assembly.

10. Make sure piston ring gaps are separated as described in Piston Rings section.
11. Using clean engine oil, lubricate piston and rings. With a suitable ring compressor, compress rings. Install each piston and connecting rod assembly into its cylinder bore.
12. Lightly tap piston into its bore, using a hammer handle, while holding ring compressor firmly against cylinder block until all piston rings have entered bore.
13. Push piston down bore until connecting rod seats against crankshaft journal.
14. Remove connecting rod guides. Install bearing cap and lower bearing shell assembly. Install cap bolts and tighten and then loosen one full turn. Then tighten again as specified.

Connecting Rod Cap Bolt:
12 Valve.................................... 51Nm
24 Valve...............34Nm plus 90 degree turn

15. Turn crankshaft to make sure crankshaft and connecting rod can move freely. If crankshaft binds, check bearing cap to rod orientation again and bearing clearance or connecting rod alignment.
16. Measure side clearance between crankshaft journal and connecting rod.

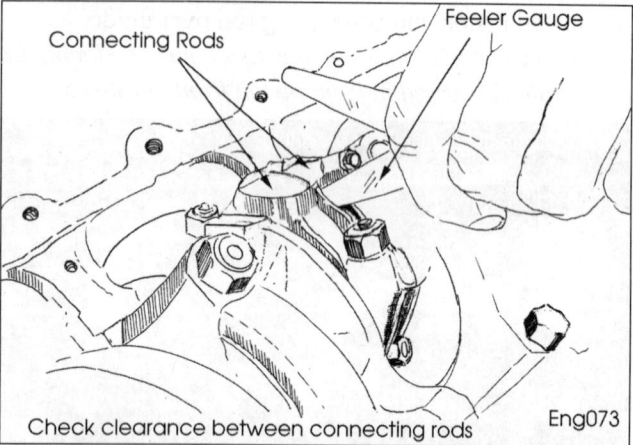

Connecting Rod side clearance.....0.10 - 0.25 mm
- service limit (main/big end)........... 0.4 mm

If side clearance is not as specified, to check bearing clearance refer to Connecting Rod Bearing section, or connecting rod alignment.

Connecting Rod bearing clearance 0.02 - 0.05mm
- service limit (main/big end)........... 0.1 mm

17. Install remaining piston and connecting rod assemblies using the same procedure.

PISTON RINGS.
Install

The pistons have three rings (two compression rings and one oil ring). The top ring is a molybdenum filled, balanced section, barrel lapped type. The second ring is an inverted torsional taper faced type. The oil ring is of three piece design, comprising two segments and a spacer.

1. Using a set of rings comparable in size to the piston being used install compression ring in relevant cylinder bore, then using the head of a piston, press ring down into the bore.
   Using a piston in this manner will place ring square with cylinder wall.
   Ensure not to distort the ring during this operation, or it may bind in the piston ring groove. Fit each ring separately to the cylinder in which it is going to be installed.
2. Using a feeler gauge, measure gap between ends of ring.

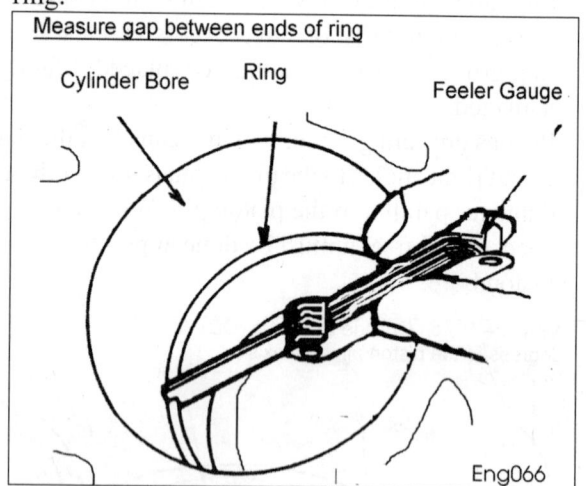

Ring gap - New
- Compression.......................0.30 - 0.45 mm
- Scraper...............................0.45 - 0.60 mm
- Oil ring...............................0.10 - 0.35 mm

Ring gap - Wear limit
- Compression.................................. 0.8 mm
- Scraper.. 0.8 mm
- Oil ring.. 1.0 mm

Remove ring and try another, if the gap between the ends of a compression ring is below specification. The ring gap may be enlarged by filing.

3. Inspect gap between ends of each oil control ring segment.

Oil Ring Steel Rail Gap Specification:
- Oil ring ....0.10 - 0.35 mm

4. Carefully remove all traces of carbon from ring grooves in piston and check grooves for any chips or burrs that might cause ring to bind when fitting.
5. Slip outer surface of each compression ring in respective piston ring groove and roll ring entirely around

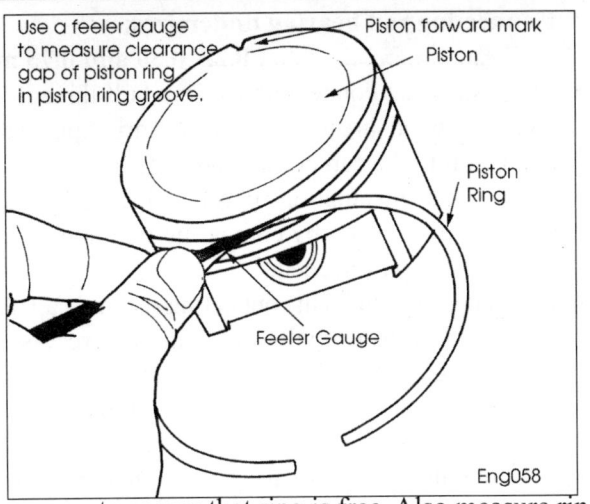

V6 ENGINE MAINTENANCE & REBUILD 3.0L, 3.5L & 3.8L SOHC M.P.I.

groove to ensure that ring is free. Also measure ring to piston groove side clearance.

Side clearance
- **Compression** .... 0.03 - 0.07 mm
- **Scraper** .... 0.02 - 0.06 mm

Try another ring if it is too tight. If no ring can be found That fits the specification, the ring may be ground to size using emery paper placed on a piece of glass.
If using a new piston, try another piston.

* High spots in the ring groove may be cleaned up with careful use of a fine file, do not try to cut the piston ring groove.

6. Install oil ring spacer in bottom piston ring groove. The ends of the spacer butt against each other.
7. Install one steel segment from top of piston downward into oil ring groove and install remaining steel segment from bottom of piston skirt upwards into the oil ring groove.
8. Install compression rings in first and second grooves of each piston.
   Make sure the correct compression ring are installed in the first and second grooves, and the correct way up.
9. Do a final test of ring fit in piston grooves. Separate ends as illustrated.

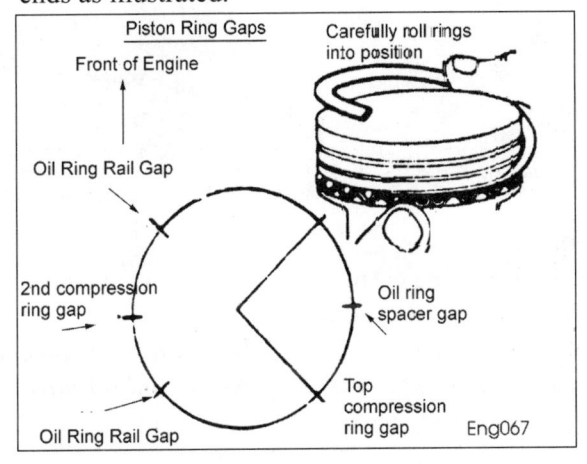

* Do not install piston with ring gaps in line, as this will allow compression leakage at this point.

CONNECTING ROD BEARINGS

Each connecting rod bearing consists of 2 bearing halves or shells which are interchangeable in the rod and cap. When the shells are in place, the ends extend slightly beyond the parting surfaces of the rod and cap. When the rod bolts are tightened, the shells are tightly clamped in place to ensure positive seating and to prevent rotation. The connecting rod bearings are of the precision insert type and do not use shims for adjustment. The ends of the bearing shells must never be filed flush with parting surface of rod or cap.

Inspection and Replacement.
Connecting rod bearings can be replaced without removing the rod and piston assembly from the engine.

1. Using an etching marker or felt tipped pen, mark connecting rods and caps to indicate cylinder number and orientation of cap.
2. Remove connecting rod cap securing nuts and remove cap and lower bearing shell. 
3. Push piston and connecting rod up cylinder bore, so that connecting rod is free from crankshaft journal. Remove bearing shell from connecting rod.
4. Clean crankshaft journal and measure for out of round or taper using a micrometer. Replace crankshaft, if not as specified in CRANKSHAFT section.
   Crankshaft Connecting Rod Bearing Journal Diameter
5. Wipe oil from both inner and outer surfaces of bearing shells.
6. Inspect inner surface of bearing shells for gouges, wear or embedded foreign matter.
   If foreign matter is found, determine its nature and source.
   Inspect outer surface of bearing shell for surface wear (indicates movement of shell or high spot in surrounding material), looseness or turning (flattened tangs and wear grooves), or overheating (discolouration). The crankshaft may be bent or have tapered bearing journals if uneven side to side wear is found. If needed, remove crankshaft, refer to CRANKSHAFT section

V6 ENGINE MAINTENANCE & REBUILD 3.0L, 3.5L & 3.8L SOHC M.P.I.

and inspect crankshaft for bend or journal taper.
* Bearing failure, other than normal wear, must be examined carefully.

7. Install bearing shells in original positions in connecting rod and cap if inspection reveals that crankshaft is OK.
8. Pull connecting rod down onto crankshaft so that upper bearing is seated against crankshaft journal.
9. Place a piece of plastigage across width of bearing journal, parallel to crankshaft centre line.
* Make sure plastigage is not placed across oil hole in journal.
10. Install connecting rod cap in original position as described in step 4. Tighten bolts as specified. Make sure that crankshaft does not rotate with plastigage installed.

Connecting Rod Cap Bolt:
   12 Valve................................. 51Nm
   24 Valve...............34Nm plus 90 degree turn

11. Remove connecting rod cap bolts, and cap. Inspect for flattened plastigage sticking to either crankshaft or bearing shell in cap.
12. Determine bearing clearance by comparing width of flattened plastigage at widest point with graduation on plastigage envelope. The number within the graduation on the envelope indicates the clearance.
Clearance between connecting rod bearings and crankshaft should not exceed specification.
If a bearing is being fitted to an out of round journal, ensure to fit plastigage to the maximum diameter of the journal. If the bearing is fitted to the minimum diameter, and the journal is out of round 0.008mm, interference between the bearing and journal will result in rapid bearing failure.

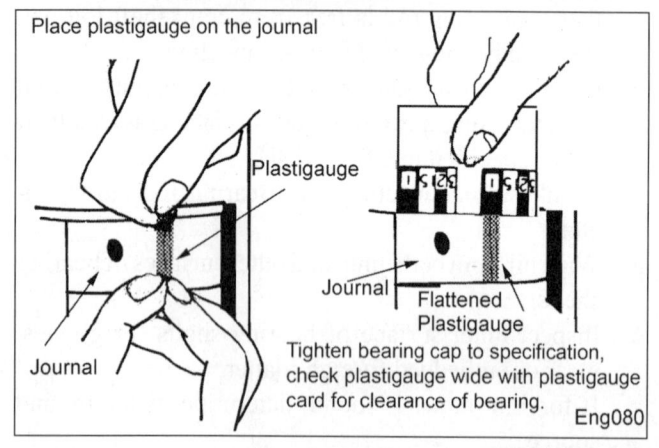

Connecting Rod side clearance.....0.10 - 0.25 mm
   - service limit (main/big end)........... 0.4 mm

If side clearance is not as specified, to check bearing clearance refer to Connecting Rod Bearing section, or connecting rod alignment.

Connecting Rod bearing clearance 0.02 - 0.05mm
   - service limit (main/big end)........... 0.1 mm

Connecting rod bearing undersizes:
   ....0.25, 0.50 and 0.75 mm

13. Make sure that connecting rod cap bolt threads and connecting rod threads are clean and dry. Apply some engine oil to the cap bolt threads.
Before final installation of cap bolts, determine if bolts have stretched by comparing with a new bolt. Replace bolt/s as needed.
14. Install bearing shells in connecting rod and cap making sure notches in shells match up with recesses in connecting rod and cap.
Inspect clearance of new bearing with plastigage as previously described.
15. Remove all remains of plastigage after measuring. Using clean engine oil lubricate bearing shells and journal. Install connecting rod cap in original position, tighten bolts as specified.

Connecting Rod Cap Bolt:
   12 Valve................................. 51Nm
   24 Valve...............34Nm plus 90 degree turn

16. With bearing shells installed and cap bolts tightened, it should be possible to move connecting rod backwards and forwards on crankshaft journal as allowed by end clearance. Also, the crankshaft should turn without binding.

Connecting Rod bearing clearance 0.02 - 0.05mm
   - service limit (main/big end)........... 0.1 mm

If connecting rod binds on crankshaft journal, loosen and tighten bearing cap bolts.
If rod still cannot be moved or crankshaft binds, inspect bearing cap to rod orientation, bearing clearance or connecting rod alignment.

CRANKSHAFT.

Remove

To check bearing clearance before removing crankshaft from crankcase as described.

Note: 6G74 engines (3.5 and 3.8 litre) have a 4 bolt main bearing type cradle, 6G72 engines (3.0 litre) have a 2 bolt main bearing type cradle.

1. When engine is removed from vehicle and mounted in a suitable stand and remove oil pan.

V6 ENGINE MAINTENANCE & REBUILD 3.0L, 3.5L & 3.8L SOHC M.P.I.

2. Remove flywheel/driveplate and engine end plate, rear seal retainer.
3. Remove oil pump suction pipe and screen.
4. Remove timing belt and crankshaft sprocket refer to Timing Belt section.
5. Using an etching marker or felt tipped pen to mark connecting rod caps to indicate cylinder number and orientation of cap.
6. Remove connecting rod caps and bolts and push connecting rods away from crankshaft.
7. Remove main bearing cap cradle bolts in order as shown and cradle.

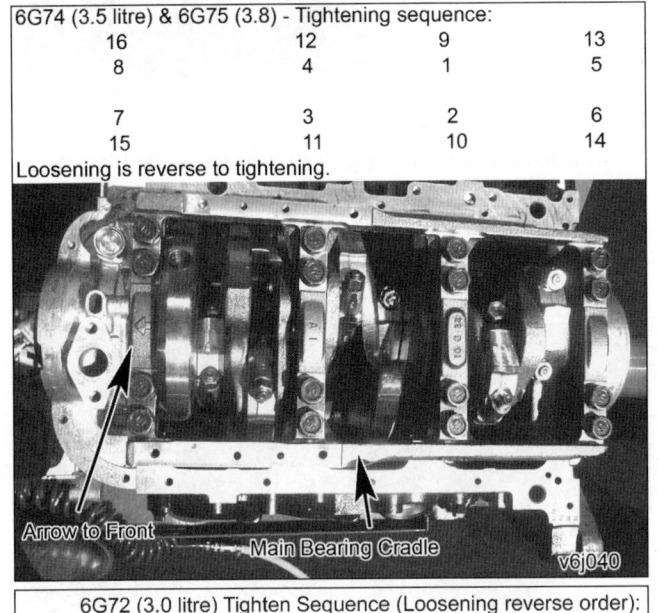

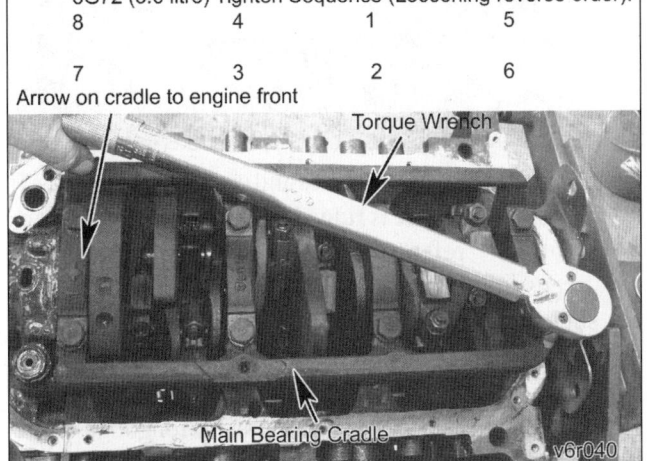

6G74 (3.5 litre) & 6G75 (3.8) - Tightening sequence:
```
16      12      9      13
 8       4      1       5

 7       3      2       6
15      11     10      14
```
Loosening is reverse to tightening.

6G72 (3.0 litre) Tighten Sequence (Loosening reverse order):
```
 8       4      1       5

 7       3      2       6
```
Arrow on cradle to engine front

Use a soft faced hammer tap the cradle to break cradle to crankcase seal.

8. Lift crankshaft from cylinder block.
9. Remove key from front end of crankshaft, if needed, using a suitable punch and hammer.

Inspection.

1. Using a suitable cleaning solvent, wash crankshaft and dry with compressed air.
2. Check crankshaft oil passages for obstructions.
3. Check all bearing journals and thrust surfaces for: Gouges, overheating (discolouration), cracks, grooving chips or roughness

   The crankshaft must be machined or replaced if it has any burned spots, cracks or sever gouging. Slight roughness may be removed using a fine polishing cloth soaked in clean engine oil. Burrs may also be removed using a fine oil stone.
4. Check connecting rod and main bearing shells for embedded foreign material and determine its source.
5. Using a micrometer measure bearing journals for taper, excessive wear or out-of-round.

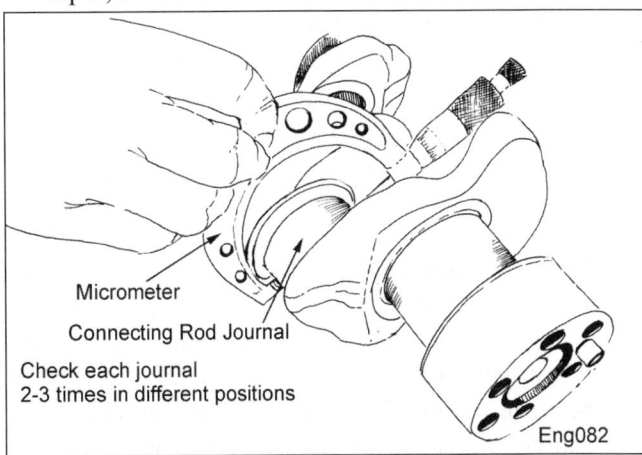

Check each journal 2-3 times in different positions

Main bearing journals diameter
6G72 .... 60.0 mm
6G74 .... 64.0 mm
Connecting Rod Journal diameter
6G72 .... 50 mm
6G74 .... 55 mm
End float controlled by .... No.3 bearing
Connecting Rod journal diameter .... 50.0 mm
- max. allowable ovality .... 0.03 mm
- max. allowable taper .... 0.005 mm
Main bearing clearance .... 0.02 - 0.048 mm
- service limit .... 0.1 mm

6. Inspect crankshaft for run-out by supporting front and rear main bearing journals in 'V' blocks and checking journals with a dial gauge.
7. Place a dial gauge indicator at crankshaft rear flange and inspect rear flange Run-out. During this inspection, make sure that crankshaft is thrust forward on 'V' blocks so that there is no possibility of crankshaft end float affecting dial gauge reading.

Crankshaft Rear Flange Run-out ... 0.05-0.25 mm
Wear Limit 0.4mm

8. If not as specified, replace crankshaft.

Installation.

1. Inspect main bearing clearance, if needed, refer to MAIN BEARINGS section for details.
2. Using a clean engine oil lubricate all crankshaft journals and main bearing upper shells in crankcase.
3. Sit crankshaft in place in main bearing upper shells

47

in crankcase. Ensure not to damage crankshaft thrust washers at No.3 main bearing. Also ensure not to contact connecting rod journals with connecting rod and install main bearing caps.

Using a thin film of Loctite 515 Gasket Eliminator or equivalent apply to rear main bearing cap to crankcase mating surface. Keep sealant out of bolt holes and use sparingly.

*Make sure that the bearing caps are installed onto the crankcase in the correct manner.
Tighten the bolts finger tight.

4. It will be necessary to line up thrust washers with No.3 bearing shells, before tightening main bearing cap bolts.
Move crankshaft fore and aft the length of its travel several times (last movement forward) to do this.

5. Ensure all main bearing cap bolts are tightened as specified.
   Main Bearing Cradle Bolts:
   12 Valve...93Nm
   24 Valve...74Nm

6. Use a feeler gauge to measure crankshaft end float between front of No.3 main bearing thrust washer and crankshaft thrust faces, you will need to force crankshaft forward to do this.
   **Crankshaft Rear Flange Run-out...0.05-0.25 mm
   Wear Limit 0.4mm**
   Replace No.3 main bearing thrust washers if clearance is excessive.

7. Turn crankshaft to make sure crankshaft and connecting rods have free movement. Inspect orientation of bearing caps, correct fitting of bearing cradle (mains and connecting rods) or fitting of bearing shells or bearing clearance, if crankshaft binds.

8. Install the rear main oil seal and retainer.

9. To install flywheel/driveplate as described.

MAIN BEARINGS.

Each crankshaft main bearing journal has 2 bearing halves or shells which are not the same and not interchangeable in the bearing cap or crankcase. The upper (crankcase) shell is grooved to supply oil to the connecting rod bearing, while the lower (bearing cap) shell is not grooved. The 2 bearing shells must not be interchanged. The No.3 bearing has thrust washers to take end thrust.
Standard size upper shells are used in the crankcase with 0.25mm under sized or standard size shells in the bearing caps, depending on bearing clearance.
When shells are placed in crankcase and bearing cap, the end extends slightly beyond the parting surfaces so that when cradle bolts are tightened, the shells clamp tightly in place to ensure positive seating and to prevent turning. The ends of the bearing shells must never be filed flush with parting surfaces of crankcase or bearing cradle.

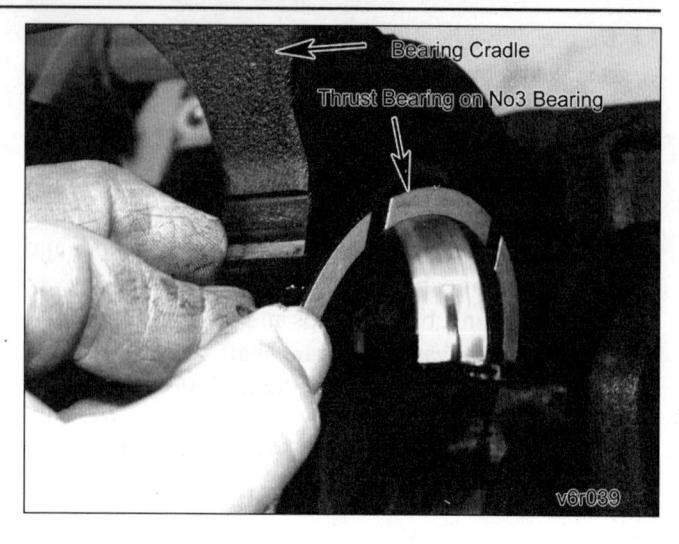

Inspection

1. Remove main bearing cradle bolts from bearing to be inspected, and remove cradle and lower bearing shell.
   * Tap main bearing cradle to break cradle to crankcase seal to remove.

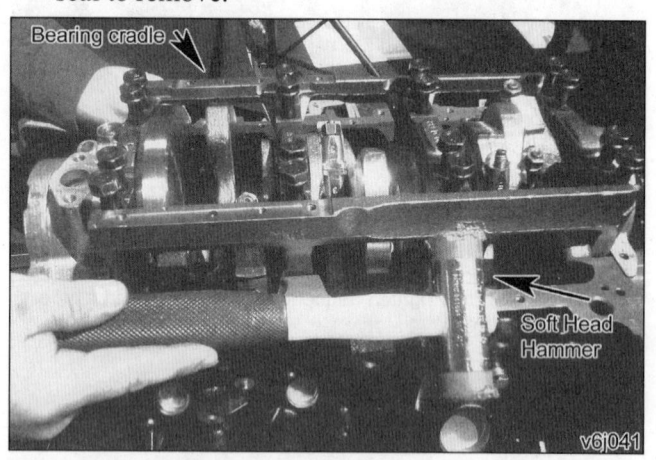

2. Check lower bearing shells and crankshaft journals. If the journal surface is ridged or heavily scored, replace crankshaft, refer to Crankshaft section for details.
To ensure satisfactory engine operation, new bearing shells must be installed as described in Main Bearing section and if necessary Connecting Rod Bearings section.
Inspect inner surface of bearing shells for gouges, wear or embedded foreign material. If foreign material is found, determine its nature and source. Inspect outer surface of bearing shells for surface wear (indicates movement of shell or high spot in surrounding material), looseness, rotation (flattened tangs and wear grooves), and overheating (discolouration).
Inspect thrust surfaces of thrust washers for grooving or wear. Grooves are caused by irregularities in the crankshaft thrust surfaces or dirt as described in Crankshaft section.
If condition of lower bearing shells and crankshaft journals is satisfactory, inspect bearing clearance as

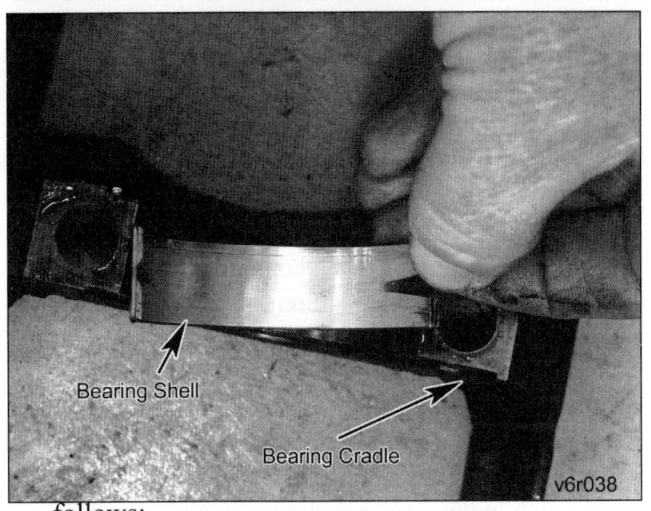

follows:

3. Wipe oil from crankshaft journal and inner and outer surfaces of lower bearing shell.
   Install bearing shell in original position in bearing cap.
4. Place a piece of plastigage across full width of crankshaft journal, parallel to crankshaft centre line.
   * Make sure plastigage will not seat across oil hole in journal.
5. Install bearing cap and bolts into cylinder block.
   * Install bearing caps by loosely installing cap bolts and then lightly tap bearing cap into position, in order to prevent the possibility of cylinder block and or main bearing cap damage.
   * Do not pull the bearing cradle into place with the bearing cradle bolts.
6. Tighten bearing cradle bolts as specified.
   * Ensure that crankshaft does not rotate with plastigage installed.
   Main Bearing Cradle Bolts:
   12 Valve.. 93Nm
   24 Valve.. 74Nm
7. Remove bearing cradle bolts and cradle. Look for flattened plastigage sticking to either crankshaft or bearing shell in bearing cradle. 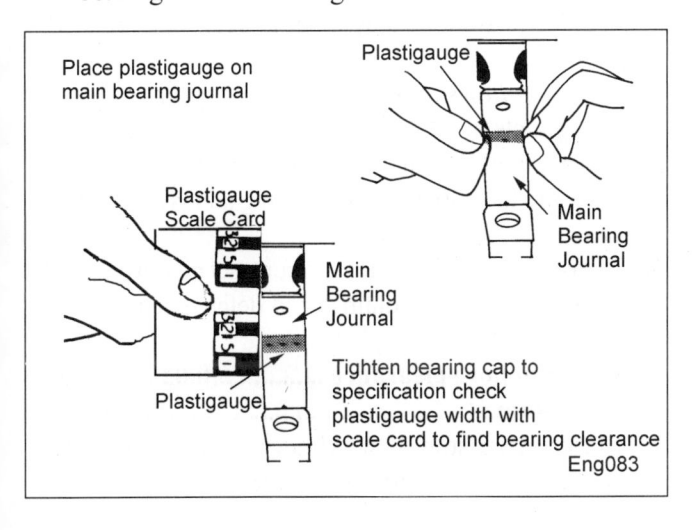
8. Check bearing clearance by comparing width of flattened plastigage at widest point with graduation on plastigage envelope. The number within the graduation on the envelope indicates the clearance.
   Main bearing and crankshaft journal clearance should not exceed specification.
   Main Bearing Clearance: .... 0.02 - 0.048 mm
   - service limit .... 0.1 mm
   This method of checking main bearing clearance does not give any indication of crankshaft journal taper or out of round.
   To measure taper, out of round or undersized, the crankshaft must be removed from the cylinder block as described in CRANKSHAFT section.
9. It is advisable to install new bearing shells if bearing clearance exceeds specification and check clearance as previously described.
   If lower bearing is standard size, install a 0.25 mm undersized shell and check clearance again.
   Replace crankshaft as described in "Crankshaft" section if clearance is still not as specified.
10. Make sure that main bearing cradle bolt threads and crankcase threads are clean and dry.
    * Before final installation of cradle bolts, determine if bolts have stretched by comparing with new one. Replace bolts and tighten.
    Main Bearing Cradle Bolts:
    12 Valve.. 93Nm
    24 Valve.. 74Nm

CYLINDER BLOCK.
Inspection.
1. When engine is removed from vehicle and mounted in a suitable engine stand, remove all parts as outlined under the particular part heading in this section.
2. Clean all cylinder block gasket surfaces.
3. Remove all coolant jacket welsh plugs and oil gallery screw plugs.
4. Clean cylinder block thoroughly using a suitable cleaning solution. Flush with clean water or steam. Spray or wipe cylinder bores and machined surfaces using engine oil.
   Caustic cleaning solutions destroy all bearing and alloy materials. All bearing and alloy parts if not removed before cleaning must be replaced.
   Do not use caustic solutions to clean bearing material or alloy parts.
5. Check all oil passages for obstructions.
6. Using a straight edge and feeler gauge, inspect cylinder block deck surface for flatness.
   If any distortion or irregularity is less than specified, cylinder block surface may be machined.
   Flatness of gasket surface .... less than 0.05 mm
   Flatness of gasket surface - maximum ... 0.10 mm

V6 ENGINE MAINTENANCE & REBUILD 3.0L, 3.5L & 3.8L SOHC M.P.I.

Grinding limit -
combined block and cylinder head..........0.20 mm
Cylinder Block Height:
    6G72 .... 210 mm
    6G74 .... 228 mm
Replace cylinder block if irregularity or distortion is more than specified.

7. Check oil pan and oil pump body area for burrs or damage. Minor damage may be cleaned up with a fine mill file.
8. If needed, clean all threaded holes using a suitable threaded tap or drill out and install thread insert.
9. Measure cylinder bore walls for taper, excessive ridging, oversize and out-of-round.

Max. bore oversize .... 1.00 mm
Max. diameter difference b/n cylinders: ...... 0.02 mm
Max. bore wear (before rebore) .... 0.02 mm
Max ovality and taper (before rebore) .... 0.02 mm

Cylinder Reconditioning and Piston Fitting.
It will be necessary to smooth bores to fit new pistons, if one or more cylinder bores are scored, rough or worn beyond limits.

It will not be necessary to rebore all cylinders to the same oversize order to maintain engine balance if few bores require correction, since all oversize service pistons are held to the same weight as standard size pistons.

Do not try to machine oversize pistons to fit cylinder bores, this will destroy the surface treatment and affect the weight. The smallest possible oversize service pistons should be used and the cylinder bores should be honed to size for proper clearances.

Measure all new pistons at right angles to the piston pin bore, before the honing or reboring operation is started.

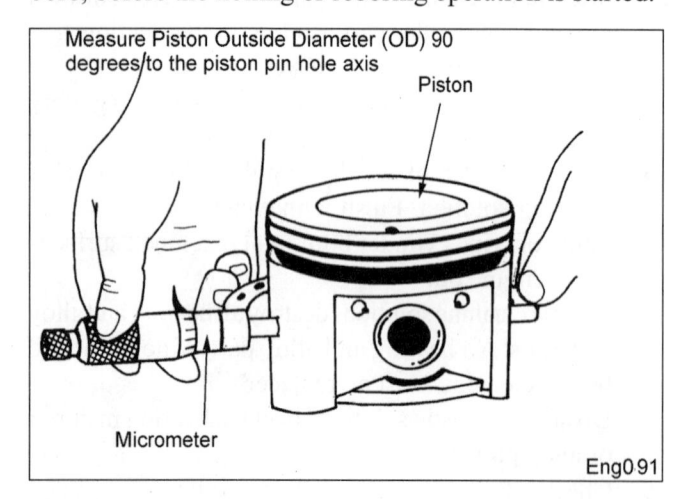

Measure Piston Outside Diameter (OD) 90 degrees to the piston pin hole axis
Piston
Micrometer
Eng091

Piston diameter
    6G72 .... 91.1 mm
    6G74 .... 93.0 mm
Piston to bore clearance .... 0.02 - 0.04 mm
Piston oversize .... 0.50 mm, 0.75 mm, 1.00 mm
Honing is recommended for trueing bore if cylinder bore wear does not exceed specification. The bore should be trued up by boring and then hone finished, if wear or out-of-round exceeds specification.

All crankshaft bearing caps must be in place and tightened as specified when reboring cylinder bores, to prevent distortion of bores in final assembly.

Leave 0.025 mm on the diameter for final honing to give the specified clearance when taking the final cut.

Follow the Hone Manufacturers recommendations for the use of the hone and cleaning and lubrication during honing. Noting the following points.

Pass the hone through the entire length of the cylinder bore at the rate of approximately 60 cycles per minute when finished honing. This should produce the desired 45° cross hatch pattern on cylinder walls which will ensure minimum oil consumption and maximum ring life.

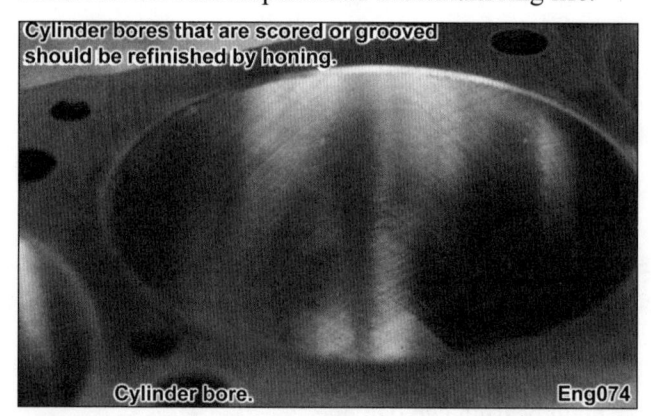

Cylinder bores that are scored or grooved should be refinished by honing.
Cylinder bore. Eng074

Each piston must be fitted individually to the bore in which it will be installed and marked to ensure correct assembly during the final honing. After the final honing and before the piston is inspected for fit, each cylinder bore must be washed and dried thoroughly to remove all traces of abrasive and then allowed to cool. Apply clean engine oil to cylinder bores. The pistons and cylinder block must be at a common temperature before inspecting.

The glazed cylinder walls should be slightly dulled when new piston rings are installed without reboring cylinders, but without increasing the bore diameter, by means of the finest grade of stone in a cylinder hone.

Proceed as follows to inspect piston to cylinder bore.
1. Using a clean cloth wipe cylinder walls and pistons and apply clean engine oil to cylinder bores.
2. Measure the bore accurately using an inside micrometer.
3. Measure piston diameter and subtract piston diameter from cylinder bore diameter to determine piston-to-bore clearance.

Piston to bore clearance .... 0.02 - 0.04 mm
Maximum .... 0.085 mm

4. Mark each piston with cylinder number to which it will be fitted and proceed to hone cylinders and fit pistons.

50

Handle the pistons with care and do not attempt to force them through the cylinder until cylinder has been honed to the correct size, as pistons can be damaged through careless handling.

Assemble parts as described under the correct heading in this section. If coolant and oil gallery plugs were removed when dismantling, install using specified sealant.

Problem Diagnosis.

Problems and Possible Causes.
Problems should be corrected, when proper diagnosis is made, by repair, adjustment or part replacement as needed. Refer to the correct section in this manual.

High Oil Loss
1) Tighten bolts and/or replace gaskets and seals as required for external leaks.
2) Check oil with car on a level surface and allow adequate drain down time to ensure a correct reading of dipstick.
3) Severe usage such as towing or continuous high speed driving will normally cause oil consumption to increase.
4) PCV system failure.
5) Use recommended S.A.E viscosity for current temperatures. Refer to Lubrication Section for details on incorrect oil viscosity.
6) Valve guides and/or valve stem seals worn, or seals omitted. Ream guides and install oversize service valves and/or new valve stem seals.
7) Allow enough time for the piston rings to seat. Replace worn or broken rings as needed, if rings have been incorrectly installed, worn or broken, or not seated.
8) Piston incorrectly installed or mis-fitted.

Gaskets.
1) Incorrectly tightened fasteners or damaged/dirty threads.
2) Worn or damaged gasket (cracking or porosity).
3) Fluid pressure/level too high.
4) Incorrect sealant used (when required)

Inspection of Seals.
1) Damaged seal bore (burred, nicked, scratched)
2) Worn or loose bearing causing excessive seal wear.
3) Worn or damaged seal or incorrect installation.
4) Fluid pressure/level too high.

Oil Leak Investigation
Oil leaks are easily located and repaired by visually finding the leak and replacing or repairing the required parts.
1) Determine whether the fluid is transmission lubricant, engine oil, power steering fluid etc.
2) Run the car at normal operating temperature and park the car over a large sheet of paper. After a few minutes, you should be able to find the approximate location of the leak by drippings on the paper.
3) Use a degreaser or steam to clean the area of the leak, drive the car for a few kilometres. Then visually inspect the suspected part for signs of an oil leak.

Black Light and Dye Method.
There are many dye and light kits available for finding leaks.
a) Pour required amount of dye into leaking part.
b) Operate the car under normal operating conditions as instructed in the kit.
c) Shine the light in the suspected area. The dyed fluid will appear as a yellow path leading to the problem.

Low Oil Pressure
1) Blocked oil filter.
2) Incorrect oil viscosity for expected temperature, or oil diluted with moisture or unburned fuel mixtures.
3) Excessive bearing clearance.
4) If the oil level is low, fill to mark on dipstick.
5) Oil pump dirty/worn, or oil pump suction pipe screen blocked, or hole in oil pump suction pipe.
6) Incorrect or failing oil pressure sender.

ENGINE KNOCKS
When Engine Cold And Continues Knocking For Two Or Three Minutes
Increases with torque
1) Tighten or replace as required if drive pulleys or balancer are loose or broken.
2) Replace piston if clearance from piston to bore is excessive. (Cold engine piston knock usually disappears when the cylinder is grounded out. Cold engine piston knock which disappears in 1.5 min. can be considered acceptable.)
3) Connecting rod bent.

Heavy Knock With Torque Applied
1) Replace parts as required of pulley hub or balancer broken.
2) Loose torque converter to flexplate bolts.
3) Check if exhaust system contacting underbody.
4) Cracked flexplate/flywheel.
5) Main bearing clearance or connecting rod bearing clearance excessive.

Light Knock while Hot
1) Inspect fuel quality if preignition or spark knock.
2) Loose torque converter to flexplate bolts.
3) Connecting rod clearing clearance excessive.

Knocks On First Start-up Only Lasting Few Seconds

1) Incorrect oil viscosity. Install correct oil viscosity for expected temperatures.
2) Hydraulic lifter bleed down.
   Some valves will be open when the engine is stopped. Spring force against lifters will tend to bleed lifter down. Only if the problem is consistent should repairs be attempted.
3) Replace crankshaft thrust bearing shells if excessive crankshaft end float.
4) Replace worn parts if front main bearing clearance is excessive.

SPECIFICATIONS

GENERAL
Type - 6G72, 6G74 & 6G75 .... V6 OHC/OHV
No. of Cylinders .... Six
Displacement:
6G72 .... 2972 cc
6G74 .... 3497 cc
6G75 .... 3828 cc
Compression ratio:
3.0 and 3.5 engines 9.0:1
3.8 engines .... 9.5:1 and 9.8:1
Bore and Stroke (nominal):
6G72: .... 91.1 x 76.0
6G74: .... 93.0 x 85.8
6G75: .... 95.0 x 90.0
Firing Order 1-2-3-4-5-6
Fuel requirements .... Unleaded

CYLINDER BLOCK
Material .... Alloy cast iron
Flatness of gasket surface .... less than 0.05 mm
Flatness of gasket surface - maximum .... 0.10 mm
Grinding limit -combined block and cylinder head .0.20 mm
Cylinder bore diameter:
6G72 .... 91.1 mm
6G74 .... 93.0 mm
6G75 .... 95.0 mm
Max. bore oversize .... 1.00 mm
Max. diameter difference between cylinders: .. 0.02 mm
Max. bore wear (before reconditioning) .... 0.02 mm
Max ovality and taper (before reconditioning) 0.02 mm
Cylinder Block Height:
    6G72 .... 210 mm
    6G74 .... 228 mm

CYLINDER HEAD
Material .... Aluminium alloy
Type .... Compact hemispherical
Max. allowable distortion - head surface .... 0.2 mm
Grinding limit .... 0.2 mm
Max. allowable distortion - intake surface .... 0.2 mm
Max. allowable distortion - exhaust surface ...... 0.3 mm
6G75 .... 120mm

12 Valve
Inlet valve seat insert hole diameter
    - 0.3 mm Oversize .... 44.30 - 44.33 mm
    - 0.6 mm Oversize .... 44.60 - 44.63 mm
Exhaust valve seat insert hole diameter
    - 0.3 mm Oversize .... 38.30 - 38.33 mm
    - 0.6 mm Oversize .... 38.60 - 38.63 mm
Valve guide hole diameter .... 13.00 - 13.02 mm
    - 0.05 mm Oversize .... 13.05 - 13.07 mm
    - 0.25 mm Oversize .... 13.25 - 13.27 mm
    - 0.50 mm Oversize .... 13.50 - 13.52 mm
Camshaft/camshaft bearing clearance ...... 0.06-0.10 mm
24 Valve
Inlet valve seat insert hole diameter
    - 0.3 mm Oversize .... 34.30 - 34.33 mm
    - 0.6 mm Oversize .... 34.60 - 34.63 mm
Exhaust valve seat insert hole diameter
    - 0.3 mm Oversize .... 31.80 - 31.83 mm
    - 0.6 mm Oversize .... 32.10 - 32.13 mm
Valve guide hole diameter .... 11.00 - 11.02 mm
    - 0.05 mm Oversize .... 11.05 - 11.07 mm
    - 0.25 mm Oversize .... 11.25 - 11.27 mm
    - 0.50 mm Oversize .... 11.50 - 11.52 mm
Camshaft/camshaft bearing clearance ...... 0.06-0.10 mm

VALVES
12 Valve Engines:
    Valve height   - Inlet .... 102.97 mm
                       - Inlet wear limit .... 102.47 mm
                       - Exhaust .... 102.67 mm
                       - Exhaust wear limit ... 102.17 mm
    Stem diameter   - Inlet .... 6.6 mm
                       - Exhaust .... 6.6 mm
    Head Thickness   - Inlet .... 1.2 to 0.07 mm
                       - Exhaust .... 2.0 to 1.5 mm
    Valve face angle .... 43.5° - 44.0°
    Valve seat contact width .... 0.90 - 1.30 mm
    Valve stem to guide clearance
                       - Inlet .... 0.03 - 0.06 mm
                       - Inlet wear limit .... 0.10 mm
                       - Exhaust .... 0.05 - 0.09 mm
                       - Exhaust wear limit .... 0.15 mm
    Valve Stem Assembled Protrusion 41.65mm
                       Maximum 42.15mm

24 Valve Engines:
- Valve height
  - Inlet .... 112.30 mm
  - Inlet wear limit .... 111.80 mm
  - Exhaust .... 114.11 mm
  - Exhaust wear limit .... 113.61 mm
- Stem diameter
  - Inlet .... 6.0 mm
  - Exhaust .... 6.0 mm
- Head Thickness
  - Inlet .... 1.0 to 0.5 mm
  - Exhaust .... 1.2 to 0.7 mm
- Valve face angle .... 43.5° - 44.0°
- Valve seat contact width .... 0.90 - 1.30 mm
- Valve stem to guide clearance
  - Inlet .... 0.02 - 0.05 mm
  - Inlet wear limit .... 0.10 mm
  - Exhaust .... 0.04 - 0.06 mm
  - Exhaust wear limit .... 0.15 mm
- Valve Stem Assembled Protrusion 49.30mm
  - Maximum 49.80mm
- Hydraulic lash adjuster dry clearance .... 0.5 - 1.3 mm

MIVEC Engine
- Valve height
  - Inlet .... 109.33 mm
  - Inlet wear limit .... 108.83 mm
  - Exhaust .... 113.50 mm
  - Exhaust wear limit .... 113.00 mm
- Stem diameter
  - Inlet .... 6.0 mm
  - Exhaust .... 6.0 mm
- Head Thickness
  - Inlet .... 1.0 to 0.5 mm
  - Exhaust .... 1.2 to 0.7 mm
- Valve face angle .... 43.5° - 44.0°
- Valve seat contact width .... 0.90 - 1.30 mm
- Valve stem to guide clearance
  - Inlet .... 0.02 - 0.047 mm
  - Inlet wear limit .... 0.10 mm
  - Exhaust .... 0.035 - 0.062 mm
  - Exhaust wear limit .... 0.15 mm
- Valve Stem Assembled Protrusion 49.30mm
  - Maximum 49.80mm
- Hydraulic lash adjuster dry clearance .... 0.5 - 1.3 mm

VALVE GUIDES
- Valve Guide OD sizes
  - 0.05, 0.25 & 0.50mm available
- Valve Guide ID
  - 12 Valve: Valve Guide Internal Diameter: ... 6.6 mm
  - 24 Valve: Valve Guide Internal Diameter: ... 6.0 mm
- Valve Guide projection
  - Intake Valve Guide Projection: .... 14.0 mm
  - Exhaust Valve Guide Projection: .... 14.0 mm

VALVE SPRINGS
- Spring Length
  - 12 Valve
    - Free length .... 49.8 mm
    - Free length Minimum .... 48.8 mm
  - 24 Valve
    - Free length .... 51.0 mm
    - Free length Minimum .... 50.0 mm
  - MIVEC Engine
    - Free length .... 56.19 mm
    - Free length Minimum .... 55.19 mm

- Installed load/height of valve spring.
  - 12 Valve
    - Spring Load/Installed Height 323/40.4
  - 24 Valve
    - Spring Load/Installed Height 216/444.2

CAMSHAFT
- Material .... Cast iron
- Camshaft bearings .... Aluminium alloy
- Bearing clearance .... 0.01 - 0.04 mm
- Camshaft Journals
  - 12 Valve
    - Camshaft Journal diameter .... 34.5 mm
  - 24 Valve
    - Camshaft Journal diameter .... 45.0 mm
- Camshaft Run-out
  - Camshaft Run-out .... 0.06 mm
- Camshaft Lobe Heights
  - Height of cam lobe
    - SOHC
      - Inlet .... 37.58 mm
      - Exhaust .... 36.95 mm
    - wear limit
      - Inlet .... 37.08 mm
      - Exhaust .... 36.45 mm
    - MIVEC Engine
      - Inlet Low Speed .... 36.228 mm
      - Inlet High Speed .... 37.209 mm
      - Exhaust .... 37.874 mm
    - wear limit
      - Inlet Low Speed .... 35.728 mm
      - Inlet High Speed .... 36.709 mm
      - Exhaust .... 37.874 mm

PISTONS
- Material .... Aluminium alloy
- Type .... Auto thermic type
- Piston pin hole diameter .... 22.0 mm
- Piston diameter
  - 6G72 .... 91.1 mm
  - 6G74 .... 93.0 mm
  - 6G75 .... 95.0 mm
- Piston to bore clearance .... 0.02 - 0.04 mm
- Piston oversize .... 0.50 mm, 0.75 mm, 1.00 mm

PISTON PIN
Type.............................Press fit in connecting rod
Material.. Alloy steel
Diameter.. 22.0 mm
Offset in piston... 0.3 mm
Press in load 7,350-17,200N

PISTON RINGS
Number 3
Ring gap - New - Compression .... 0.30 - 0.45 mm
                - Scraper .... 0.45 - 0.60 mm
                - Oil ring .... 0.10 - 0.35 mm
Service limit   - Compression .... 0.8 mm
                - Scraper .... 0.8 mm
                - Oil ring................................ 1.0 mm
Side clearance - Compression .... 0.03 - 0.07 mm
                - Scraper .... 0.02 - 0.06 mm

CONNECTING ROD
Material............................ Forged carbon steel
Small end bore diameter .... 22 mm
Big end bore diameter
6G72... 50 mm
6G74... 55 mm
6G75... 55 mm
Connecting Rod bearing clearance .... 0.02 - 0.05 mm
    - service limit (main/big end) .... 0.1 mm
Connecting rod bearing undersizes................. 0.25 mm
                        .... 0.50 mm
                        .... 0.75 mm
Connecting rod
    - bend... 0.05 mm
    - twist... 0.1 mm
Connecting rod side clearance on journal......................
    0.10 - 0.25 mm
    - service limit .... 0.4 mm
Bearing material............................... Aluminium alloy

CRANKSHAFT
No. of main bearings..4
Main bearing journals diameter
    - 6G72 .... 60.0 mm
    - 6G74 .... 64.0 mm
    - 6G75 .... 64.0 mm
Connecting Rod Journal diameter
    - 6G72 .... 50.0 mm
    - 6G74 .... 55.0 mm
    - 6G75 .... 55.0 mm
End float controlled by..............................No.3 bearing
End play .... 0.05 - 0.25 mm
    - limit .... 0.4 mm

Connecting Rod journal
    - max. allowable ovality .... 0.03 mm
    - max. allowable taper .... 0.005 mm
Main bearing clearance .... 0.02 - 0.048 mm
    - service limit .... 0.1 mm
Connecting Rod bearing clearance .... 0.02 - 0.05 mm
    - service limit .... 0.1 mm

Oil Pump
Inner Rotor tip clearance......................... 0.06 - 0.18mm
Side clearance of rotor to pump housing 0.04 - 0.10mm
Outer rotor to pump housing clearance... 0.10 - 0.18mm
        Max... 0.35mm

SEALANT
Camshaft Position Sensor ....
Mitsubishi 970389 or equilivant (a semi drying type)
Oil Pan ....
Mitsubishi 970389 or equilivant (a semi drying type)

TORQUE SPECIFICATION

Description	Nm
Alternator bracket M8	48
Alternator bracket M10	23
Alternator pivot nut	44
Camshaft Position Sensor Ring	22
Camshaft Sprocket Bolt	88
Camshaft Sprocket Bracket	23
Camshaft thrust case	12
Connecting Rod Cap Bolt:	
12 Valve	51
24 Valve	34Nm plus 90 degree turn
Coolant temperature gauge unit	11
Coolant temperature sensor	29
Crankshaft bolt	182
Crank Angle Sensor	9
Cylinder Head Bolts	
Step 1:	
Cylinder head bolts - Cold - in 3 stages	108Nm
Step 2	
Loosen bolts	
Step 3	
Cylinder head bolts - Cold - in 3 stages	108Nm
Dipstick mounting bolt	13
Drive belt tension pulley nut	49
Drive belt tension nut	35-55
Drive plate bolt	74
Exhaust heat protector bolt	14
Exhaust manifold nut	44
Flywheel mounting bolt	74
Heater pipe bolt	11
Intake Manifold	22
Intake Plenum	18
Intake Plenum Stay - M8	18
- M10	35
Main Bearing Cradle Bolts:	
12 Valve	93Nm
24 Valve	74Nm
Oil filter - bracket bolt - M8	23
- M10	41
Oil pan lower	11
Oil pan cover	11
Oil pan upper	6
Oil pan Baffle - M8	11
- M6	9
Oil suction pipe and screen	11
Oil relief plug	44
Oil pan drain plug	39
Oil pressure switch	10
Oil pump cover	10
Oil pump case	14
Rear oil seal retainer plate	11
Rocker cover bolt	3.9
Rocker arm - rocker shaft	31
Timing Belt cover bolt - M6	11
- M8	13
Timing Belt rear upper cover, left	10-12
Timing Belt Auto Tensioner bolt	23
Timing Belt Tensioner Pulley bolt	48
Timing Belt Tensioner Arm	44
Timing Belt Idler Pulley Bolt	44
Timing Belt Rear Cover	13
Thermostat Housing bolts	18
Throttle Body	11
Thermo switch	6-9
Water inlet fitting bolt	18
Water outlet fitting bolt	18
Water pipe bolt	9
Water pump bolts - M8	14
- M6	5

V6 ENGINE MAINTENANCE & REBUILD (3.5L) DOHC G.D.I.

Subject	Page
GENERAL DESCRIPTION	**57**
Engine Serial Number	57
Maintenance Hints	57
GENERAL MAINTENANCE	**58**
Intake Plenum & Intake Manifold Assembly	**58**
Removal	58
Installation	59
Exhaust Manifolds	**60**
Remove	60
Installation	60
Crankshaft Balancer	**60**
Remove	60
Install	60
Rocker Covers and/or Seals	**61**
Remove	61
Installation	61
Timing Belt Cover, Timing Belt And Gears	**61**
Remove	62
Timing Belt Inspection	63
Install	63
Cylinder Head, Valves & Camshaft	**65**
Remove	65
Cylinder Head Reconditioning	**66**
Dismantle	66
Clean	67
Inspection	67
Valve Guides	**67**

Subject	Page
Clearance Checks	67
Guide Replacement	68
Valve Seats	**68**
Replacing Valve Seat	68
Valve Stem Oil Seals	**68**
Replacement	68
Valve Springs	**69**
Valves	**69**
Camshafts	**70**
Inspection	70
Assemble Cylinder Head	**70**
Install Cylinder Head	**71**
Oil Pump	**72**
Removal	72
Dismantle	72
Inspection	72
Assembly	72
Installation	72
Flywheel/Drive Plate	**73**
Remove	73
Inspection	73
Install	73
Ring Gear	**73**
Replacement	73
Replacement Techniques	73
Rear Main Oil Seal	**73**
Replace	73
Spigot Bearing	**74**
Replacement	74
ENGINE REBUILD	**74**
Engine Assembly	**74**
Removal	74
Dismantle	75
Assembly	75

V6 ENGINE MAINTENANCE & REBUILD 3.5L DOHC G.D.I.

Subject	Page
Oil Pan (Sump)	75
Removal	75
Installation	75
Oil Pump Suction Pipe, Screen and Baffle	75
Remove	75
Installation	76
Piston and Connecting Rod Assembly	76
Remove	76
Dismantle	76
Inspection	76
Assembly & Installation	77
Piston Rings	78
Install	78
Connecting Rod Bearings	79
Inspection & Replacement	79
Crankshaft	80
Remove	80
Inspection	81
Installation	81
Main Bearings	82
Inspection and Installation	82
Rear Main Oil Seal	83
Replace	83
Cylinder Block	83
Inspection	83
Cylinder Reconditioning & Piston Fitting	84
PROBLEM DIAGNOSIS	84
SPECIFICATIONS	85
TORQUE WRENCH SPECIFICATIONS	87

GENERAL DESCRIPTION

The 6G74 - 3.5 litre engine is a V6 cylinder double overhead camshaft unit, there are two camshafts mounted in each aluminium cylinder head.

V6 GDI came in either 12 or 24 valves and has a 4 bolt main bearing type cradle that supports the crankshaft.

The cylinder block made of cast iron with a standard bore of 93.0 mm and stroke of 85.8 mm, displacement is 3496 cc.

The cylinder numbering is as illustrated, from the front of the engine, right side 1-3-5 and left side 2-4-6. Firing order is 1-2-3-4-5-6.

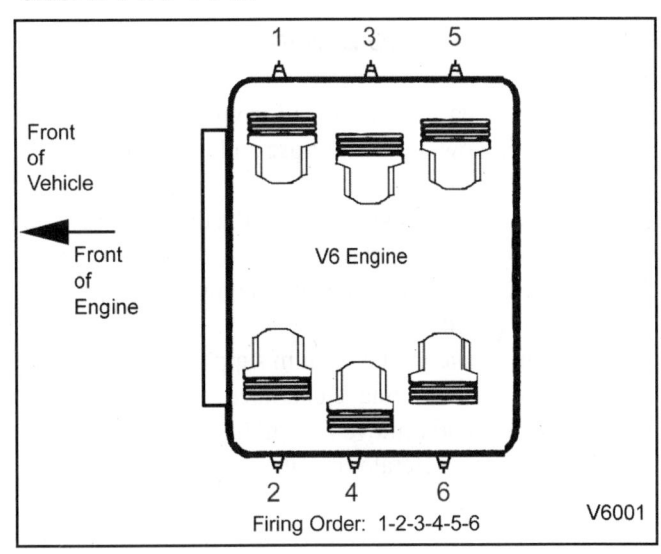

Firing Order: 1-2-3-4-5-6 — V6001

ENGINE SERIAL NUMBER

Engine No. Location: On left-hand side engine block casting, above the oil filter.

MAINTENANCE HINTS

1. **a)** When any internal engine parts are serviced, care and cleanliness are important.
   b) An engine is a combination of many machined, honed, polished and lapped surfaces with tolerances that are measured in thousandths of a millimetre.
   c) Friction areas should be coated liberally with engine oil during assembly to protect and lubricate the surfaces on initial operation.
   d) Proper cleaning and protection of machined surfaces and friction areas is part of the repair procedure and is considered standard workshop practice.

2. When valve train components are removed for service, they should be kept in order and should be installed in the same locations (with the same mating surfaces) as when removed.

3. Battery terminals should be disconnected before any major work is begun. If not, damage to wiring harnesses or other electrical components could result.

V6 ENGINE MAINTENANCE & REBUILD 3.5L DOHC G.D.I.

4. When raising or supporting the engine for any reason, do not use a jack under the oil pan. There are small clearances between the oil pan and the suction pipe screen, so jacking may cause the oil pan to be bent against the screen, causing damage to oil suction pipe assembly.

GENERAL MAINTENANCE

* For general maintenance procedures such as oil change and drive belt inspection refer to the "Tune-up & Maintenance Chapter".

INTAKE MANIFOLD and FUEL RAIL
Remove

1. Detach the battery earth lead from the battery, then release the lower radiator hose and drain the cooling system.
2. Remove the air intake tube from the throttle body and air cleaner housing, then withdraw the tube.
3. Release and withdraw the engine top dress-up cover from the engine, if fitted.
4. a) Remove the intake plenum support bracket to the cylinder head and intake chamber.
5. Disconnect and remove the ignition coil pack.
6. Release the accelerator pedal sensor connector from the throttle body assembly.
   Disconnect the following connectors and harnesses ignition fail sensor, throttle position sensor, injector harness connector, control harness and ignition coil harness connectors, fuel pressure sensor, camshaft position sensor, purge solenoid valve sensor, oxygen sensor, crankshaft angle sensor, water temperature gauge unit, engine coolant temperature sensor, throttle control servo connector.

7. a) Release the vacuum hose, 5 PCV hoses and purge hose from the intake manifold assembly.
   Mark all vacuum to assist in assembly.
   b) Release the fuel union from the injector, loosen union slow, as there may still be fuel pressure.
   c) Release the earth straps from the manifold assembly.

8. a) Release the water outlet fitting.
   b) Remove the purge control solenoid valve.
9. Disconnect the EGR pipe to the intake manifold remove gasket, it is not necessary to remove EGR pipe from exhaust manifold you may wish to loosen nut.
10. Remove the upper intake manifold bolts and remove the intake chamber and gasket.

Tip: *Place a cloth over the opening for the intake manifold to stop any object from falling down into the engine.*

V6 ENGINE MAINTENANCE & REBUILD 3.5L DOHC G.D.I.

11. Disconnect and remove the water out-let pipe and fitting.

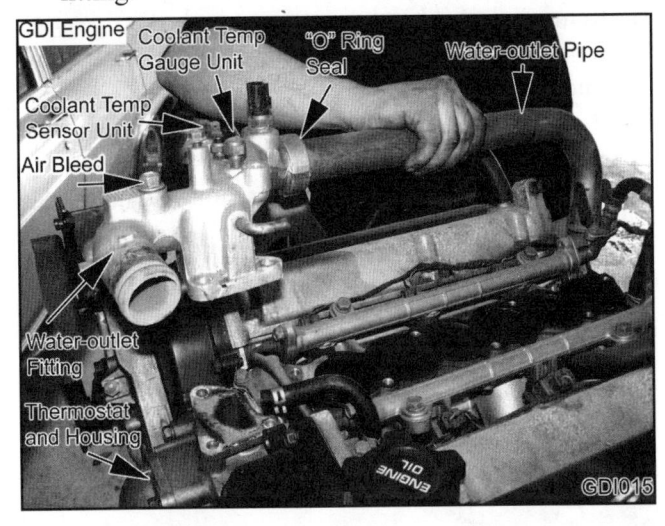

12. Disconnect and remove the fuel rail and injectors.

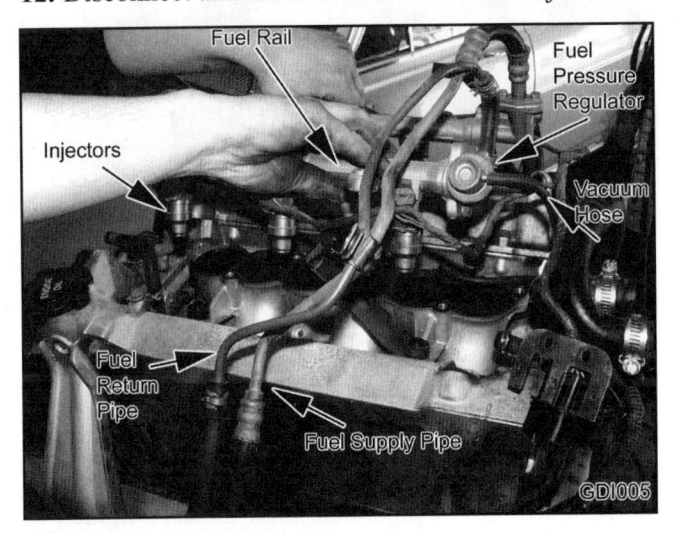

13. Disconnect the intake manifold nuts and remove the intake manifold and gasket.

14. The knock sensor is now accessible if required to remove.

Install

1. Clean the manifold to cylinder heads surface, esure all the old gasket is removed from both sufaces.
2. Install the intake manifold with new gaskets, install nuts tighten in sequence as described.

Inside nuts of each bank first:
Step 1: Right nuts 6Nm
Step 2: Left nuts 22Nm
Step 3: Right nuts 22Nm
Step 4: Left nuts 22Nm

3. Install the fuel injectors and fuel rail, use new O-rings.
   Fuel Rail bolts 12Nm
4. a) Fit the wiring loom connectors to there corresponding components on the intake chamber.
   b) Install the pipe from the fuel rail to the high pressure fuel pump.
   Bolt to Fuel Rail 12Nm
   Bolt to High Pressure Pump 19Nm
   c) Fuel rail end feed pipe.
   Fuel Rail Feed Pipe 19Nm
   d) Fuel pressure sensor flange and bolts.
   Fuel Pressure Sensor Flange Bolts 23Nm
5. Install the water out-let pipe and fitting, use new

59

V6 ENGINE MAINTENANCE & REBUILD 3.5L DOHC G.D.I.

gaskets and "O" ring.

6. Install the upper intake manifold with new gaskets, install bolts tighten in sequence as described.
   Inside nuts of each bank first:
   Step 1: Right bolts 6Nm
   Step 2: Left bolts 22Nm
   Step 3: Right bolts 22Nm
   Step 4: Left bolts 22Nm

7. a) Install the purge control solenoid valve, reconnect hoses to valve.
   b) Fuel pressure sensor flange and bolts.
   Fuel Pressure Sensor Flange Bolts 23Nm

8. Reconnect the accelerator pedal sensor connector to the throttle body assembly.
   Connect the following connectors and harnesses ignition fail sensor, throttle position sensor, injector harness connector, control harness and ignition coil harness connectors, fuel pressure sensor, camshaft position sensor, purge solenoid valve sensor, oxygen sensor, crankshaft angle sensor, water temperature gauge unit, engine coolant temperature sensor, throttle control servo connector.

9. Fit the vacuum hoses to the intake manifold and accessories, ensuring that the marks on the intake plenum and hoses are matching.

10. Install the EGR pipe using new gaskets, tighten to specification.
    EGR Pipe to Intake Manifold 14Nm
    EGR Pipe to Exhaust Manifold Nut 44Nm

11. a) Fit the intake plenum support bracket to the cylinder head and intake chamber.
    b) With the support bracket in place, fit the retaining bolts, then tension the retaining bolts to specification.
    Intake Plenum Support .... 37 Nm

12. a) Secure the earth strap to the intake chamber assembly.
    b) Connect the brake booster hose, IACV vacuum hose and 5 PCV hoses to the intake manifold assembly.

13. Install and connect the ignition coil pack.

14. Fit the intake manifold cover to the engine assembly, then secure it into position.

15. Fit the air intake tube to the air cleaner assembly, then to the throttle body, tighten the retaining clamps to specifications.

16. a) Ensure the lower radiator hose is fitted, then proceed to fill the cooling system.
    b) Connect the battery terminal to the battery, then run the vehicle and check for signs of leaks, then road test the vehicle.

EXHAUST MANIFOLDS
Remove
1. Remove the oil level dip stick and tube.
2. Remove the heat shields from both exhaust manifolds.
3. Remove the bolts attaching the exhaust pipe to the exhaust manifolds.
4. As required remove any fittings from the manifolds such as EGR pipe.
5. Remove the nuts attaching each manifold to the cylinder head and remove manifolds.

Install
1. Using new gaskets install the exhaust manifolds to the engine and tighten retaining bolts to specification.
   Exhaust Manifold Nuts: .... 44 Nm
2. Tighten the manifold flange to exhaust pipe nuts to specification.
   Manifold to Exhaust Pipe Bolts 35Nm
3. Install the EGR pipe using new gaskets, tighten to specification.
   EGR Pipe to Intake Manifold 14Nm
   EGR Pipe to Exhaust Manifold Nut 44Nm
4. Install the heat shields to the exhaust manifolds, tightening to specification, then install the oil level dipstick and tube.
   Heat Shield Retaining Bolts .... 18 Nm

CRANKSHAFT BALANCER
Remove
1. Disconnect battery earth lead and remove drive belts as shown in the Belt Drive section.
2. Pull park brake fully on, chock rear wheel and transmission in gear.
3. Loosen and remove balancer retaining bolt.
4. Remove balancer from crankshaft with pulley puller.

Install
1. Using engine oil, lubricate front seal surface of balancer.

V6 ENGINE MAINTENANCE & REBUILD 3.5L DOHC G.D.I.

2. Install balancer, engaging key on crankshaft with slot in balancer.
3. Install the crankshaft pulley, tighten attaching bolt to specification.
   Crankshaft Balancer Bolt .... **182 Nm**
4. Install and inspect drive belt operation.

ROCKER COVERS AND/OR SEALS
Remove
1. Remove the spark plug leads from the left side spark plugs.

2. Disconnect the breather hose between rocker covers and PCV valve form left side rocker cover.
3. Left bank rocker cover.
   a) Unscrew rocker cover to cylinder head fasteners and remove rocker cover from cylinder head.
   b) If replacing rocker cover seal, remove seal from recess in rocker cover to cylinder head.
4. Remove the intake manifold assembly as previously described in this chapter.
5. Remove the spark plug leads form the right side spark plugs.
6. a) Unscrew rocker cover to cylinder head bolts, note front bolt, remove rocker cover from cylinder head.
   b) If replacing rocker cover seal, remove seal from recess in rocker cover to cylinder head.
7. Remove spark plug tube top rubber seals if seals are damaged or rubber has become to hard to form a good seal to the rocker cover.

Install
1. a) If required install new seals to top of spark plug tubes.
   b) If necessary, install seal to rocker cover recess.
   c) Install rocker cover fastener and seal assemblies.
   Note: Make sure seal is correctly installed in rocker cover.
2. Install rocker cover to cylinder head and torque bolts to specification.
   Rocker Cover Bolts: **3.4Nm**

3. Secure the wiring looms to the rocker covers, then clip the wiring loom connectors to there corresponding components.
4. Fit the intake chamber as previously described.

TIMING BELT COVER, TIMING BELT and GEARS (CAMSHAFT OIL SEALS)
** *Timing belts do have a life span, and the average life of a timing belt under normal driving conditions is 100,000 kilometres, (approx. 62,000 mile).*

V6 ENGINE MAINTENANCE & REBUILD 3.5L DOHC G.D.I.

Remove

1. Detach the battery cables, remove the battery and cover.
2. Remove the air cleaner and air intake tubing.
3. Remove the engine protection skid panel from under the vehicle.
4. Drain the engine coolant.
5. Remove the radiator shroud.
6. Set the drive belt automatic tensioner as previously described, in Maintenance and Tune-up chapter. Remove drive belt.
7. Remove top timing belt covers, bolts and gasket.
8. a) Rotate the crankshaft so the crankshaft is at TDC/compression on number 1 cylinder.

   b) Check that TDC indicator mark align on the camshaft sprocket gears and cylinder head.

   Note: *Never rotate the crankshaft anti-clockwise.*

9. a) Use an oil based crayon, place alignment marks on the timing belt and camshaft gears and crankshaft gear.

   b) Also draw an arrow showing direction of rotation of timing belt, if the belt is to reinstalled on the engine.

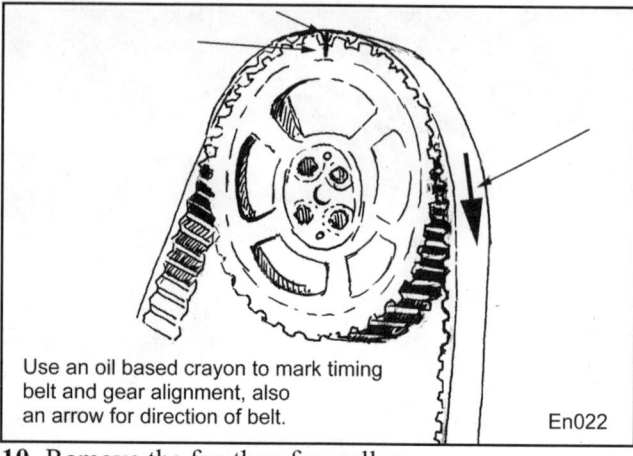

Use an oil based crayon to mark timing belt and gear alignment, also an arrow for direction of belt.

10. Remove the fan then fan pulley.
11. Remove the crankshaft pulley.
12. Remove the drive belt automatic tensioner.
13. Detach the power steering pump and tie to one side.
14. Unbolt the air conditioner compressor and tie to one side.
15. Remove the air conditioner compressor bracket.
16. Remove the accessory mount bracket from the front of the engine.
17. Remove the lower timing belt cover. 
18. Check that TDC indicator mark align on the crankshaft sprocket and timing indicator on oil pump cover.

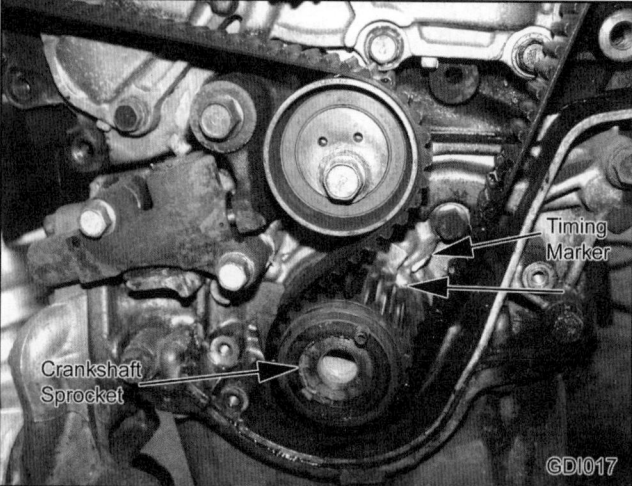

62

V6 ENGINE MAINTENANCE & REBUILD 3.5L DOHC G.D.I.

19. Remove crankshaft sensor, move to one side.
20. Only use this step if removing camshaft gears. - Loosen the bolts attaching the camshaft gears to the camshafts.
21. Insert a 1.4mm hex key into tensioner, it may require a little leverage with a large screw driver. This will stop the tensioner rod from moving out once the belt is removed.

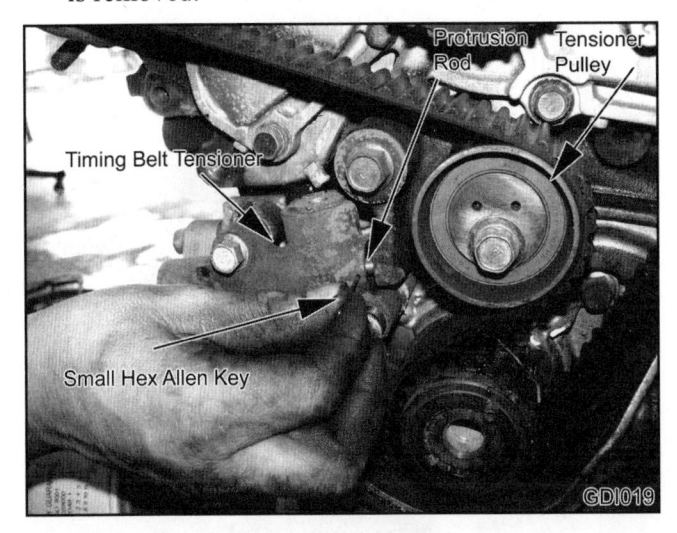

22. Loosen the idler tensioner pulley bolt and remove the idler tension pulley.
23. Remove the timing pulley belt from the pulleys.
24. Remove the bolts attaching the camshaft gears to the camshafts.

25. Remove camshaft seals with a screw driver or seal remover if required. It is advisable to remove rocker cover and front camshaft bearing and seal cap to replace seals.
26. Remove tensioner attaching bolts.

Inspection

1. Condition of the belt ribs is best judged as the belt is bent one of the idler pulleys.
   Even if a belt is relatively new "replace if any sign of wear is obvious".
   Check for cracks or chunks missing, wear on ribs and in grooves, separation of rib material from backing.
2. Check the auto tensioner rod protrusion for specification, and pressure for movement, if not with in specification replace.
   1) Measure protrusion of push rod with no force:
   2) Apply 98-196Nm force and measure protrusion of push rod:
   3) Deduct measurement 2 from 1:
   Tensioner Rod Protrusion Variation: 1mm or less
   Note: If tensioner has plug on end place a washer on end to protect plug.

Install

1. If you do not have a key in the tensioner and rod, as per step 22 in "Remove".
   Compress the auto tensioner by placing tensioner in a vice, press the protrusion rod in until a setting pin such as 1.4 mm wire or small hex Allen key can be inserted through the tensioner body and protrusion rod to hold protrusion rod in place.
   Note: If tensioner has plug on end place a washer on end to protect plug.
   Install timing belt auto tensioner and tighten bolt to specification.
   Timing Belt Auto Tensioner Bolts: 23Nm
2. Install tensioner pulley.
   a) Fit the timing belt tensioner to the engine, then fit the mounting bolt.
   b) Lever the tensioner until it is released (two small holes horizontal below the bolt) and tighten the tensioner retaining bolt.
   Tensioner Idler Retaining bolt: 44Nm
3. Install new camshaft seals if required, apply a little amount of oil to seal lips, this will seals to be installed

without damaging the seal.
4. Install the camshaft sprockets and bolts attaching the camshaft sprockets, if the bolts are not tightened to specification tighten later when timing belt is installed.
   Camshaft Sprocket Bolt 88Nm
5. a) Position the crankshaft sprocket 3 teeth away from TDC No1 piston.
   Note: This allows the camshafts to be turned without hitting the top of the pistons.
   b) The TDC alignment marks of the camshaft sprockets should be aligned. (V33V timing marks are different to the V63W and V73W series engines, see description at front of chapter)
   c) Alignment the TDC marks of the crankshaft sprocket.
6. Install the timing belt to the original position aligning the timing marks made when removing the timing belt. Taking not that the belt is rotating the same direction as previously, check for direction arrow made when removing belt.
   * **New Timing Belt:** (a) Position the camshaft gears and crankshaft gear into the correct position.
   * Camshaft gear marks are to aligned with the marks.
   * Install timing belt onto the lower section of the crankshaft gear, around the inside of the idler pulley, over the left bank camshaft sprockets place a paper clip on each sprocket and belt to hold belt in place. Under top pulley (water pump), over the right bank camshaft sprockets place paper clips on each sprocket and belt to hold belt in place, inside idler tension pulley.
   * Keep the timing belt tight and meshed into the grooves on the gears.
   * Ensure the alignment marks on the camshaft gears and crankshaft pulley are aligned.
   Note: Right side camshaft sprocket can turn with little force, do not jam your fingers during installation of belt.
7. Tighten the camshaft sprockets to specification if not tightened.
   Camshaft Sprocket Bolt 88Nm
8. Apply anti-clockwise force to camshaft sprocket, so the timing belt on of the tension side is stretched. Check all timing alignment marks are still aligned.
9. Loosen tensioner bolt, hold the tensioner pulley against the timing belt and temporarily tighten the tension pulley bolt, make sure the timing belt alignment marks are all aligned.
   Note: The 2 holes are above the bolt, lever tensioner pulley clockwise to put tension on belt.
10. Use a socket and breaker bar, rotate engine backwards 1/4 of a turn, then clockwise to check all timing marks are aligned.
11. Loosen tensioner bolt, rotate the tensioner pulley so that the 2 small holes are horizontal above the tensioner pulley bolt, tighten tensioner pulley bolt to specification. The belt tension should be 4.4Nm
    Tensioner Pulley Bolt: 44Nm
12. Rotate engine 2 turns clockwise and leave to let belt tension to settle for approx 15 minutes. Check the wire or key in the timing belt auto tensioner is not jammed tight. If it is Rotate the crankshaft 90° clockwise then rotate the crankshaft 90° clockwise. The wire should be able to be removed freely.

13. Check length of the protrusion of the auto tensioner rod.
    Timing Belt Auto Tensioner Rod Assembled Protrusion: .... 3.8-5.0 mm
14. Install crankshaft sensor.

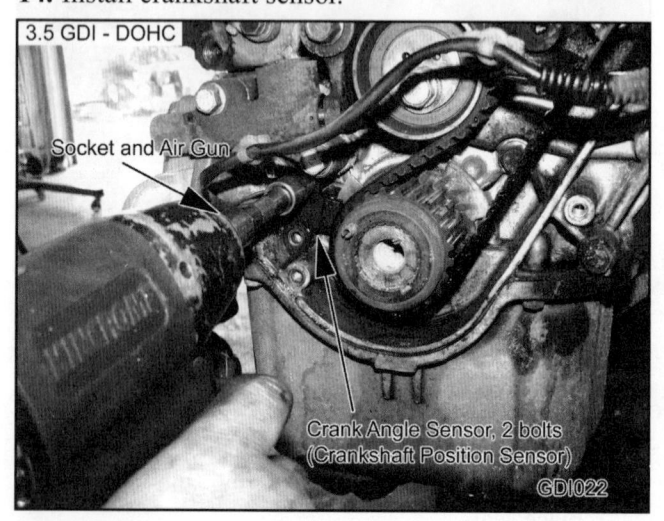

15. Fit the lower timing belt cover to the engine, then secure it in place with the retaining bolts.
16. a) Fit the crankshaft balancer to the engine, then fit the retaining bolt to the crankshaft damper.
    b) While securing the crankshaft balancer, tighten the damper retaining bolt, ensure it's tensioned to specifications.

Crankshaft Balancer ....182 Nm

17. Fit the upper timing belt covers to the engine, then fit and tighten the cover retaining bolts.
18. Install accessory mount assembly, note bolts lengths and torque.

Bolt	Dia & Length	Torque Nm
1	10 x 100	41
2	10 x 30	41
3	10 x 100	44
4	12 x 100	74
5	8 x 30	22
6	10 x 106	44

19. Install air conditioner compressor bracket, compressor.
20. Install the power steering pump.
21. Install front drive belt automatic tensioner pulley.

Automatic Tensioner Bolt..........................24 Nm

22. Install the drive belt and release the automatic tensioner as previously described.
23. Install fan pulley and fan, radiator shroud.
24. Top up coolant level.
25. Install air cleaner and air intake tubing.
26. Fit and tension the drive belts to the air conditioner, alternator and power steering pulleys.
27. Fit the battery cable to the battery, lower the vehicle from the safety stands, then run the vehicle and check that everything is operating correctly.

CYLINDER HEAD, VALVES & CAMSHAFTS

Make sure that all valve train components are kept in order so they can be installed in their original locations.

Remove

1. Disconnect battery earth lead.
2. Drain coolant from engine at radiator lower hose and remove top radiator hose.
3. Rotate crankshaft so engine is at TDC compression No1 cylinder, the timing mark of the crankshaft balancer is aligned with the "T" on the timing belt cover. Remove crankshaft balancer bolt, use a pulley remover to remove the pulley, as described in this chapter.
4. a) Remove the upper timing belt cover bolts and covers as previously described.
   b) Remove the lower timing belt cover bolts and cover as previously described.
5. Check for alignment mark on camshaft gear in line with cylinder head / back of camshaft gear cover.
6. Use an oil based crayon, place alignment marks the timing belt and cam shaft gear, injection pump gear and crankshaft gear. Also draw an arrow showing direction of rotation of timing belt, if the belt is to be reinstalled on the engine.
7. Remove crankshaft sensor, move to one side.
8. Loosen camshaft gear bolt.
9. Insert a 1.4mm hex key into tensioner, it may require a little leverage with a large screw driver. This will stop the tensioner rod from moving out once the belt is removed
10. Remove the timing pulley belt from the pulleys.
11. Remove the bolts attaching the camshaft gears to the camshafts.
12. Remove alternator.
    a) Remove nuts from alternator adjuster bracket studs and remove engine harness earth wire connection and wiring harness retainer bracket.
    b) Remove alternator, remove alternator support bolts, then remove support assembly.
13. Remove the attaching oil dipstick tub support bolt.
14. Remove the intake manifold as described in this chapter. # Main points listed below.
    a) Remove the manifold top cover or heat shield if fitted
    b) Remove air cleaner to intake manifold tube.
    c) Remove vacuum hoses, auxiliary air hose, accelerator position sensor connector and other connectors from the intake manifold.
    d) Detach the EGR pipe, water pass hose.
    e) Remove water out let and fittings.

Right Cylinder Head Water Pipe Fitting, 2 bolts

    f) Remove the intake manifold and gasket from the engine.
    g) Remove the fuel rails and injectors.
15. Remove the engine lifting brackets.
16. Remove the exhaust manifolds as described in this chapter.
    * If you wish you may leave the exhaust manifold attached to the exhaust pipe. Disconnect the exhaust pipe front bracket, then allow the manifolds to move to one side allowing you access to remove the cylinder heads.
17. Remove the bolts securing the camshaft holders (bearing caps), remove the camshafts.
    Note: *Mark camshafts IN and EX, plus which cylinder*

V6 ENGINE MAINTENANCE & REBUILD 3.5L DOHC G.D.I.

head, (mark at 12 0'clock) before removing to help assembly.

Note: *Do not mix the camshaft holders, they must be assembled to the original position they were removed from.*

18. Remove the roller rocker arms, keep them in order of removal.

19. Remove the lash adjusters, keep them in order of removal.

20. Loosen the cylinder head bolts in the order, working from the front and rear of the engine to the centre of the assembly. Loosen a little each pass until the bolts are loose. Remove cylinder head bolts.

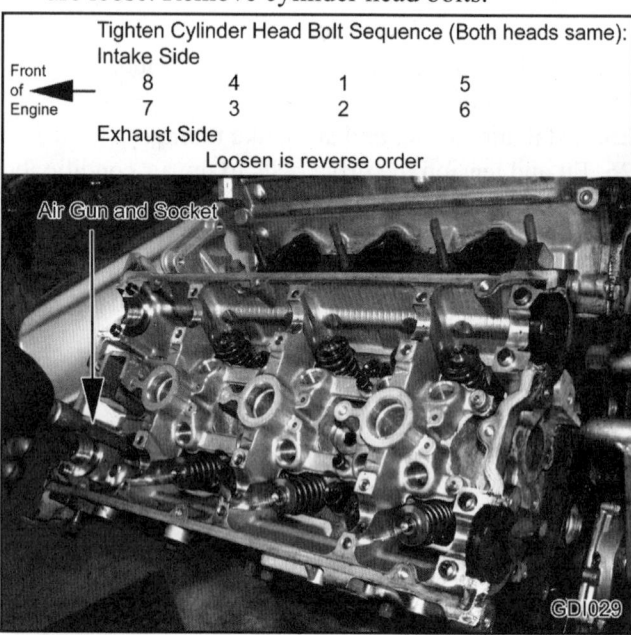

```
Tighten Cylinder Head Bolt Sequence (Both heads same):
         Intake Side
Front      8      4      1      5
of
Engine     7      3      2      6
         Exhaust Side
         Loosen is reverse order
```

21. Lift the cylinder heads and gaskets from engine block.

CYLINDER HEAD RECONDITIONING

* Make sure that all valve train components are kept together and identified so that they can be installed in their original locations.

Dismantle

1. Compress valve springs in turn with a conventional spring compressor and remove valve collets.
2. Remove the following:
   a) Valve spring caps, springs, valve stem oil seals and valve spring seats.
   b) Valves from cylinder head.
      Caution: *Do not force valves out of guides, as mushroomed valve ends due to lifter wear or dirt*

in the guide, will damage guide. Remove burrs by chamfering valve stem with an oil stone or file.

Clean

1. a) Clean all carbon from combustion chambers, valve ports, etc, with a rotary wire brush.
   * Do not use wire brush on gasket sealing surfaces.
   b) Clean cylinder head gasket surface of cylinder head.
2. Thoroughly clean valve guides with a suitable cleaning solvent or a wire brush.
3. Clean valve heads with a drill and wire brush.
   * Do not scratch the valve stem.
4. Wash all components in a suitable cleaning solvent and air dry with dry compressed air.

Cylinder Head Inspection

1. Cylinder heads should be inspected for cracks in valve seats and combustion chambers, and for external cracks to water jackets. 
2. Check cylinder head deck surface for corrosion.
3. Using a straight edge and feeler gauge, check cylinder head deck, intake and exhaust manifold surfaces for distortion. Check cylinder head deck surface diagonally, longitudinally and transversely.

These surfaces may be refaced once only by parallel grinding.
* Head to block surface if more than 0.20mm (0.0059in) must be removed from any surface, replace cylinder head.
* Head to manifold surface if more than 0.20mm (0.004in) must be removed from any surface, replace cylinder head.

4. Inspect the following:
   a) Cylinder head for cracks, especially between valve seats or exhaust ports.
   b) Cylinder head deck surface for corrosion, casting sand inclusions or blow holes.
   c) Inspect cylinder head for:

Inlet valve seat insert hole diameter
   - 0.3 mm Oversize .... 36.30 - 36.33 mm
   - 0.6 mm Oversize .... 36.60 - 36.63 mm

Exhaust valve seat insert hole diameter
   - 0.3 mm Oversize .... 33.30 - 33.33 mm
   - 0.6 mm Oversize .... 33.60 - 33.63 mm

Valve guide hole diameter .... 12.00 - 12.02 mm
   - 0.05 mm Oversize .... 12.05 - 12.07 mm
   - 0.25 mm Oversize .... 12.25 - 12.27 mm
   - 0.50 mm Oversize .... 12.50 - 12.52 mm

Camshaft/camshaft bearing clearance 0.06-0.10 mm

VALVE GUIDES

Clearance Checking

1. Excessive valve stem to guide bore clearance will cause lack of power, rough idling and noisy valve operation.
2. Insufficient clearance will result in noisy and sticking of the valve and will interfere with smoothness of operation of engine.
3. Measure inside diameter with an ID micrometer, also measure the valve stem, then use the following sum to calculate the guide clearance.
   ** Guide diameter - stem diameter = clearance **

Valve stem to guide clearance
   - Inlet .... 0.02 - 0.05 mm
   - Exhaust .... 0.04 - 0.07 mm

4. If it is necessary to replace the valve guide see valve

V6 ENGINE MAINTENANCE & REBUILD 3.5L DOHC G.D.I.

guide replacement in this chapter.

Valve Guide Replacement
1. Use a hammer and flat end rod to drive the old valve guide down into the port area of the head, at room temperature.
   Note: *Remove the snap ring from the exhaust valve guides.*
2. Measure guide hole, if over specified ID rebore to fit the over size valve guide.
   Valve Guide OD sizes
   - 0.05, 0.25 & 0.50mm available
3. Valve guides ID specifications.
   Valve Guide Internal Diameter: ....6.0 mm
4. Use a press and valve guide installing die to press the new valve guide down into cylinder head, at room temperature.
5. The guide is driven down into the cylinder head until the guide is at specified height from head.

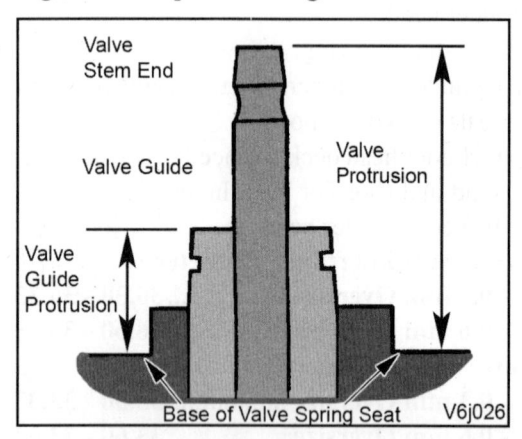

Installed dimension .... 14.00 +/- 0.30 mm
6. Ream bush out with a 6mm reamer to obtain specified diameter.

VALVE SEATS
1. Reconditioning the valve seats is very important because the seating of the valves must be perfect for the engine to deliver the power and performance its develops.
2. Another important factor is the cooling of the valve head. Good contact between each valve and its seat in the head is imperative to ensure that the heat in the valve head will be properly carried away.
3. Several different types of equipment are available for reconditioning valve seats. The recommendations of the manufacturer of the equipment being used should be carefully followed to attain proper results.
4. Check valve seats for any evidence of pitting or damage at valve contact surface. If pitting is evident, the valve seats will need to be reconditioned.
   * Because the valve guide serves to support and centre the valve seat grinder, it is essential that the valve guide

is serviced before reconditioning the valve seats.
5. If the seat is too wide after grinding, it may be narrowed by using a 30° or 65° grinding stone. The 30° stone will lower the seat and the 65° stone will raise the seat.
6. If the valves seats are reconditioned, the valves must also be reconditioned (refer VALVES) or replace valves as necessary.

REPLACING VALVE SEAT
1. Using a lathe, turn down the out side diameter of a valve head so it fill fit neatly into inside of the valve seat.
2. Cover the head that surrounds the valve seat with an inflammable paste, such as soap paste. This will stop damage from weld spatter.
3. Weld a continuous run of weld around the edge of the valve, so it is welded to the inside of the valve seat.
4. Lift the head so the top of the valve can be tapped to free the valve seat.
5. Slide the machined valve and valve seat out of the head.
6. Machine the head as the new valve seat is over size by 0.38mm diameter and depth.
7. The new valve seat should not to be hit or forced into the head as this will cause damage to the seat and head.
8. Place the new valve seat in liquid nitrogen or dry ice so the seat will shrink in size.
9. Carefully place the valve seat into position with an old valve (converted into a special tool as shown in diagram) positioned through the seat into the valve guide. Gently tap the special tool to position and centre the valve seat

VALVE STEM OIL SEALS
Replacement
1. Disconnect battery earth lead.
2. Remove the following:
   a) Spark plug leads from spark plugs.
   b) Spark plug from relevant cylinder and screw air adaptor into spark plug hole.
   c) Rocker cover as previously described in this chapter.
   d) Timing belt and covers as described in this chapter.
   e) Camshaft that belongs to the relevant cylinder.
3. Apply air pressure via a special fitting that screws into the spark plug hole, to hold valves in closed position.
4. a) Compress valve spring with valve spring compressor.
   b) Remove valve collets.
      * Before installing valve spring compressor, it

may be necessary to tap top of valve cap with a soft-faced hammer to overcome the binding of the valve collets in the valve spring cap.

5. a) Remove spring cap, spring and valve compressor as an assembly.
   b) Remove and discard old valve stem oil seal.

6. Install new valve stem oil seal and make sure the seal fully seats on top of the valve guide.

* Make sure the correct type of seal is fitted to the appropriate valve, based on part No. and package description.
  Intake valve seals ....gray colour
  Exhaust valve seals .... grayish green colour

7. a) Install spring, cap and valve compressor as an assembly on the valve stem.
   b) Install valve collets and slowly release spring compressor, then remove spring compressor.
   c) Disconnect air line to special tool.

8. Install the following:
   a) Camshaft as previously described in this Chapter.
   b) Replace timing belt and covers as described in this chapter.
   c) Rocker cover as previously described in this Chapter.

9. Remove special tool and install and torque spark plug.

10. Install spark plug leads and battery earth lead.

11. Start engine and check for oil leaks and valve train noise.

VALVE SPRINGS

1. Inspect valve spring surfaces on valve seat and valve cap for wear or gouging. Replace components as necessary.

2. a) Check spring ends. If they are not parallel, the spring is bent.
   b) Replace valve springs that do not meet specification.

3. a) Check valve spring load with a spring tester.
   b) Springs should be compressed to the specified height and checked against specifications.
   c) Replace any valve spring if not to specification.
   Free length............................47.2 mm
   Free length Minimum........................46.2 mm
   d) Measure installed load/height of valve spring.
   Spring Load/Installed Height N/mm..230/37.9

VALVES

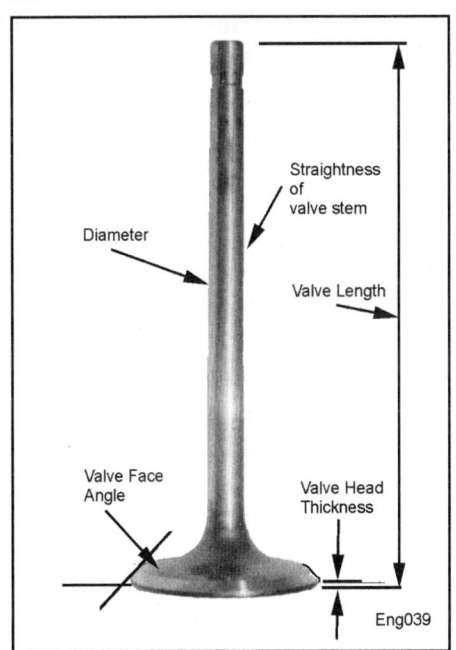

1. a) Inspect valve stem for burrs and scratches. (Burrs and minor scratching may be removed with an oil stone.)
   b) Valves with excessive stem wear or that are warped should be replaced.
   c) Inspect valve stem tip for wear. The valve tip may be reconditioned by grinding.
   d) Follow the grinder manufacturers instructions. Make sure the new tip surface is at right-angles to the valve stem.

e) Do not grind valve below minimum specified length.
2. Inspect valve stem collet groove for damage.
3. a) Check valve face for burning or cracking.
   b) If pieces have broken off, inspect corresponding piston and cylinder head area for damage.
4. a) Inspect valve stem for straightness and valve head for bending or distortion using 'V' blocks.
   b) Bent or distorted valves must be replaced.
5. Valves with pitted or grooves faces can be reconditioned with a valve refacing machine, ensuring correct relationship between head and stem.
   * If pitting or grooving is so deep that refacing would result in a 'knife' edge at the valve head, the valve must be replaced.
   * Measure valve margin after refacing valves. If margin is less than minimum specified, the valve must be replaced.
6. Lightly lap reconditioned valves into valve seat.
   * New valves must not be lapped. Lapping destroys the protective coating on the valve face.
7. Measure valves for specification.

   Valve height - Inlet .... 102.28 mm
   - Inlet wear limit .... 101.78 mm
   - Exhaust .... 101.40 mm
   - Exhaust wear limit .100.90 mm
   Stem diameter - Inlet .... 6.6 mm
   - Exhaust .... 6.6 mm
   Head Thickness - Inlet .... 1.0 to 0.05 mm
   - Exhaust .... 1.5 to 1.0 mm
   Valve face angle 43.5° - 44.0°
   Valve seat contact width .... 0.90 - 1.30 mm
   Valve stem to guide clearance
   - Inlet .... 0.02 - 0.05 mm
   - Inlet wear limit .... 0.10 mm
   - Exhaust .... 0.04 - 0.07 mm
   - Exhaust wear limit ..... 0.15 mm

8. After refacing or installing a new valve, check for correct seating as follows.
   a) Lightly coat valve face with bearing blue.
   b) Insert valve and rotate about 1/6 of a revolution.
   c) Remove valve and check for full contact with seat.
      i) If partial contact is indicated, insert valve again and turn through a full revolution.
      ii) If blue on seat indicates full contact, reface valve.
      iii) If partial contact is still indicated, re-grind cylinder head valve seat.
      iv) Measure valve assembled protrusion from valve spring seat surface for specification.
      Intake
      Valve Assembled Protrusion 47.10mm
      Maximum 47.60mm
      Exhaust
      Valve Assembled Protrusion 46.60mm
      Maximum 47.10mm
   d) Clean all traces of bearing blue from valves and seats.

CAMSHAFTS
Inspection.
1. Check camshaft bearing journals and lobes for overheating, damage or wear (discolouration).

2. Inspect camshaft journal diameter with micrometer. Replace camshaft if journals are not within specifications.
   Camshaft Journal diameter .... 26.0 mm
   Bearing clearance .... 0.01 - 0.04 mm
3. Position camshaft on 'V' blocks and check the camshaft run-out using a dial gauge.
   Camshaft Run-out .... 0.06 mm
4. Inspect the camshaft lobe heights, using a micrometer, record all the results.
   Height of cam lobe
   DOHC   - Inlet (Europe) .... 35.20 mm
   - Inlet (Hong Kong) .... 34.85 mm
   - Exhaust .... 34.91 mm

   Wear limit - Inlet (Europe) .... 34.70 mm
   - Inlet (Hong Kong) .... 34.35 mm
   - Exhaust .... 34.41 mm

ASSEMBLE CYLINDER HEAD
1. Dry and clean all components thoroughly.
2. Using clean engine oil, lubricate valve stems and valve guides thoroughly.
3. Install valves in corresponding guides.
4. Make sure that seals fully seat on top of guide, install new valve stem oil seals. The original seals may not be the same colour as the replacement seals.
5. Install the valve spring seat over the valve guide onto the cylinder head.
6. Place valve springs and cap over valve stem.

V6 ENGINE MAINTENANCE & REBUILD 3.5L DOHC G.D.I.

7. Using a suitable spring compressor, compress valve springs.
   * Excess compression could cause spring cap to damage valve stem oil seal, ensure to compress valve springs only enough to install valve collets.

8. Install valve collets, making sure that they locate accurately in groove in top end of valve stem. Release the valve spring compressor slowly ensuring that the collets sit properly. Grease may be used to hold collets in place.

9. Lubricate the camshaft journals and lobes with molybdenum grease. Slide the camshafts into the heads. The right camshaft has the camshaft position sensor ring attached by one bolt, bolt is tightened at
   Camshaft Position Sensor Ring Bolt 22Nm

INSTALL CYLINDER HEAD

1. Place dowel pins into block, place head gasket in position over dowel pins on cylinder block.
   Note: *The cylinder head gasket has an identification mark, the identification mark faces up.*

2. a) Carefully guide cylinder head into place over dowel pins and gasket.

   b) Place cylinder head and tighten with finger, remove dowel pins during this procedure.

3. Tighten the head bolts to the following sequence and in the order shown.

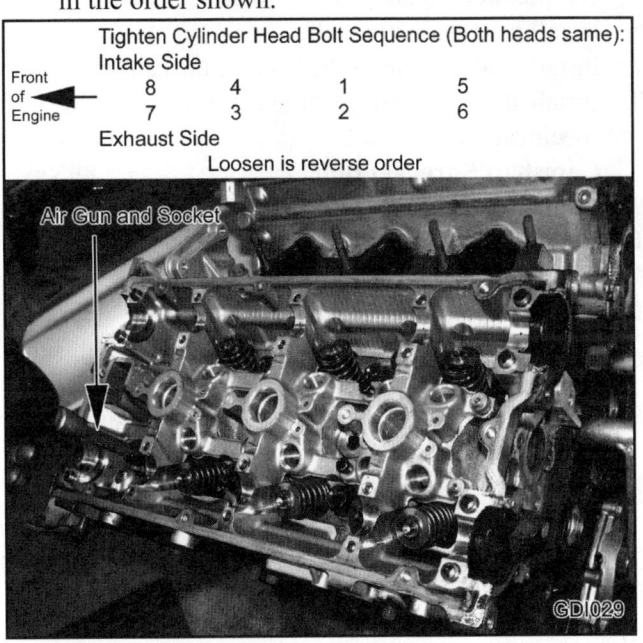

   Tighten Cylinder Head Bolt Sequence (Both heads same):
   Intake Side
   Front of Engine
   8   4   1   5
   7   3   2   6
   Exhaust Side
   Loosen is reverse order

   Step 1:
   Cylinder head bolts - Cold - in 3 stages .. 108Nm
   Step 2
   Loosen bolts
   Step 3
   Cylinder head bolts - Cold - in 3 stages .. 108Nm
   * It is important to follow the given procedure to avoid head gasket failure and possible engine damage.

4. Install the camshafts and camshaft bearing caps (camshaft holders), tighten to specification in the order shown.

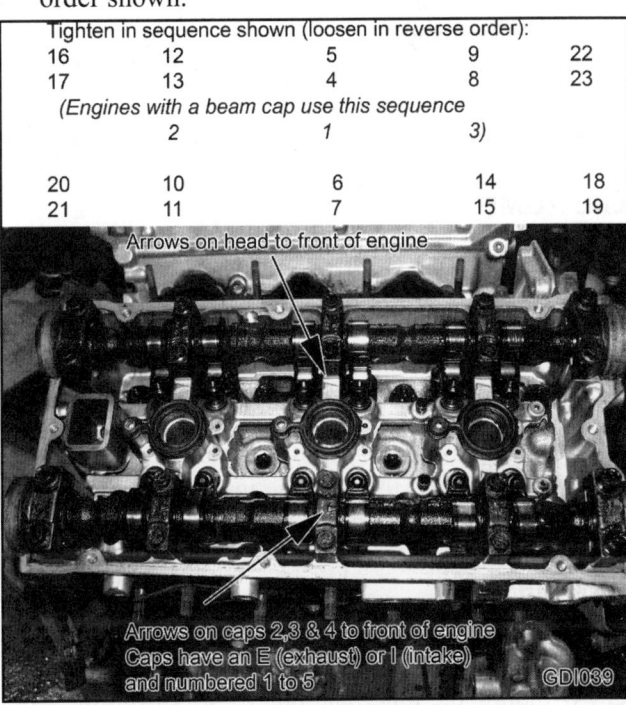

   Tighten in sequence shown (loosen in reverse order):
   16   12   5   9   22
   17   13   4   8   23
   (Engines with a beam cap use this sequence
        2   1   3)
   20   10   6   14   18
   21   11   7   15   19

   Note: *Also see "TIMING BELT COVER, TIMING BELT and GEARS (CAMSHAFT OIL*

71

SEALS)" for further information.

5. Turn the engine over so the crankshaft is at TDC/compression on number 1 cylinder.
6. Install new spark plug tube seals.
7. Install new oil seals at the front of the camshafts.
8. Install the camshaft gears and bolts, tightening to specification.
   Camshaft Sprocket Bolt 88Nm
9. Install rocker covers and gaskets.
10. The No1. piston should be at TDC as described in point number 4.
11. Align the camshaft gear alignment marks with the rocker cover marks as described in timing belt section.
12. Adjust the tension timing belt idler pulley to help belt installation.
13. Install the timing belt to the original position aligning the timing marks made when removing the timing belt. Taking not that the belt is rotating the same direction as previously, check for direction arrow made when removing belt.
    ** *Timing belts do have a life span, and the average life of a timing belt should be 100,000 kilometres, 62,000 mile for normal driving conditions.*
    See Timing Belt section.
14. Check the timing belt runs correctly and that the timing marks on the camshaft gears, and crankshaft gear are in the correct position at TDC compression on No 1 cylinder.
15. a) Install timing belt lower and upper front covers and tighten the bolts to specification.
    b) Install front drive belt pulley and bracket, tighten to specification.
16. Install the crankshaft balancer pulley, tighten attaching bolt to specification.
    Crankshaft Balancer bolt 182Nm

OIL PUMP
Remove
1. Remove the timing belt as previously described.
2. Remove the crankshafts sprocket and key way from the crankshaft.
3. Release the oil pan as previously described in this chapter.
4. Release the oil pump body retaining bolts from the oil pump body, then tap the inside of the oil pump body assembly to release it from the cylinder block.

Dismantle
1. Remove the oil pump body cover retaining screws, then remove cover plate.
2. Withdraw the inner and outer rotors from the front pump body.
3. Release the relief valve retaining cir-clip from the rear

housing body, then withdraw the retainer, spring and piston.
4. Tap the crankshaft seal from the pump body, then dispose of the seal.

Inspection
1. Wash all parts and dry, lay out parts on a clean bench.
2. Check for damage and wear to the outer race to pump housing.
3. Check for damage and wear to the rotor to outer race.
   Inner Rotor tip clearance .... 0.03 - 0.08mm
   Outer rotor to pump clearance ...... 0.10 - 0.18mm
   Max 0.35mm
4. Check the cover surface for damage by rotor and rotor clearance (use a straight edge).
   Rotor side clearance to pump .... 0.04 - 0.10mm
   If components are to be replaced, replace as a complete unit.
5. Visually inspect relief valve for smoothness of surfaces, check when assembling that the spring will keep the valve closed when the cap is fitted.

Assemble
1. Install a new crankshaft seal to the pump housing.
2. Fit the relief valve piston, spring and retainer into the rear pump body, then secure in place with the cir-clip.
3. Fit the rotor shaft seal to the front housing, when tapping it into place be careful not to damage the seal.
4. Fit the inner rotor into the front pump body, do not damage the shaft seal, then fit the outer rotor to front pump body.
5. Fit a new gasket to the front pump body and install pump cover.

Install
1. With a new gasket fitted the cylinder block, position the oil pump assembly, then fit and tension the oil pump assembly retaining bolts to specifications.

Oil Pump Assembly **9.3Nm**

2. Fit the oil pan as previously described in this chapter.
3. Fit the crankshaft key-way and sprocket to the crankshaft.
4. Fit the timing belt as previously described in this chapter.

FLYWHEEL/DRIVEPLATE
Remove
Before removal of flywheel/driveplate take note of the location of paint aligning marks on flywheel and pressure plate, before removing clutch pressure plate, the driveplate and torque converter also have paint aligning marks. If not visible, scribe aligning marks on all parts.

1. To remove transmission refer to Manual Transmission or Automatic Transmission in this manual.
2. Vehicles with manual transmission:
   Remove the clutch pressure plate and driven plate as per Clutch section in this manual.
3. Block flywheel driveplate from turning, using a screwdriver or suitable locking tool. Remove flywheel/driveplate crankshaft bolts and flywheel/driveplate.

Inspection.
The flywheel and flexplate are purposely out of balance and no attempt should be made to balance these as an individual unit.

1. Check flywheel/driveplate ring gear for badly worn, damaged or cracked teeth.
   If needed, replace flywheel ring gear or driveplate, for details refer to "ring gear" section in this chapter.
   Check starter motor pinion gear for damage, if ring gear teeth are damaged replace pinion gear, for details refer to "Starting System chapter".
2. Inspect crankshaft and flywheel/driveplate matching surfaces for burrs. Using a fine mill file remove burrs if present.

Install
1. Install flywheel/driveplate to crankshaft, and tighten bolts to the correct specification.
   Flywheel / Driveplate Bolts **74Nm**
2. Mount a dial indicator on the rear of cylinder block for vehicles with automatic transmission. Inspect flexplate Run-out at the torque converter mounting bolt holes. Run-out should not exceed the following specifications.
   Try to correct by tapping high side with a mallet if Run-out exceeds specification. Replace driveplate if this condition can not be corrected.
3. Inspect starter motor operation.

RING GEAR
Replacement
The ring gear is welded to the driveplate and is serviced only as an assembly for vehicles with automatic transmission. Therefore must be replaced as a complete unit.
For vehicles with manual transmission, the ring gear is a shrink fit on the flywheel flange, and if damaged, can be removed and replaced.

Replacement Techniques
1. To remove flywheel refer to Flywheel/ Driveplate section in this manual for details.
2. To remove ring gear drill a hole between two ring gear teeth and split gear at this point using a chisel.
3. Make sure that there are no foreign matter or burrs on new ring gear and flywheel matching surface. Remove burrs using a fine mill file (if present).
4. Heat and shrink a new gear in place as follows:
   a) Using an emery cloth, polish several spots on ring gear.
   b) Using a hot plate or a slow moving torch, heat ring gear until the polished spots turn blue (approximately 320 degrees Celsius).
      * Heating the ring gear in excess of 427 degrees Celsius will destroy ring gear heat treatment.
   c) Quickly place ring gear in position against shoulder of flywheel using 2 pairs of pliers. Allow ring gear to cool slowly until it contracts and is firmly held in place.
5. To install flywheel refer to Flywheel/Driveplate section in this manual. Tighten bolt to specification.

REAR MAIN OIL SEAL
Tip: It is advisable to remove seal retainer to fit the new oil seal, see later in this chapter.
Replace
1. Remove flywheel/driveplate, as described in "Flywheel/driveplate" in this manual.
2. Remove old seal with a screw driver or seal remover.

V6 ENGINE MAINTENANCE & REBUILD 3.5L DOHC G.D.I.

Image labels: Spigot Bearing Location (Manual transmission); Rear Oil Seal Retainer, 5 bolts if removing retainer; Rear Oil Seal; GDI042

3. Install new seal with a seal installer, ensure the seals lips are not pulled back or crooked.
4. Clean flywheel/drive plate attaching bolt threads in rear of crankshaft using a thread tap.
   Install new flywheel/flexplate and attaching bolts, tighten bolts to the correct torque specification.
   Flywheel/flexplate bolt tensioning 74Nm
5. Reinstall transmission, check engine and transmission lubricant levels.
6. Road test vehicle and check for lubrication leaks.

SPIGOT BEARING

Before removing plate, take note of the position of the paint aligning marks on flywheel and pressure plate. If marks are not visible, scribe aligning marks on both parts.

Replacement
1. To remove transmission refer to Manual Transmission section in this manual for details.
2. To remove clutch pressure plate and driven plate refer to Clutch section in this manual.
3. To remove spigot bearing use a Slide hammer.
4. Use a piloted screwdriver to replace spigot bearing. Place new bearing on pilot of tool with radius in bore of bearing next to shoulder on tool. Drive bearing into crankshaft to the dimension as shown in the diagram. Use thin film of SAE 90 Gear Oil to lubricate the bearing.
5. To install clutch assembly and transmission refer to Clutch and Manual Transmission sections in this manual.

ENGINE REBUILD.

ENGINE ASSEMBLY.
Remove
1. Discharge fuel system as described in Fuel chapter and then disconnect the battery.
2. Disconnect battery leads

3. a) Remove bottom radiator hose from the radiator, and drain the cooling system, then remove the top and bottom radiator hoses from the engine.
   b) Remove the fan assembly and radiator as outlined in Cooling chapter.
4. Mark the position of the bonnet hinge brackets on the bonnet, then release and withdraw the bonnet from the vehicle.
5. Remove the air cleaner assembly.
6. Drain engine oil sump.
7. Disconnect the left and right exhaust pipes to exhaust manifolds, see exhaust system chapter.
8. Disconnect the accelerator cable and then disconnect the vacuum hoses including the booster vacuum hose.
9. Disconnect heater hoses.
10. Disconnect the electrical connections for throttle position sensor, ignition coils, etc.
11. Disconnect the connector for the coolant temperature gauge and the coolant temperature sensor.
12. Disconnect main wiring harness from engine and battery harness.
13. Remove intake plenum and throttle body to have access to injector loom.
14. Unclip engine harness from the starter, alternator, oil pressure sensor and fuel injectors and place to side of engine bay, ensure the wiring harness is labelled.
15. Remove front drive belt, slacken off idler tension.
16. Disconnect the high pressure fuel hose and the fuel return hose.
17. Remove the power steering and A/C drive belt if not already removed.
18. Remove the power steering pump and A/C compressor, leaving the hoses and pipes connected and position out of the way.
    Note: *Do not allow then to hang, they must be tied up.*
19. Remove the starter motor heatsheild then remove the starter motor.
20. Support engine with engine crane then release the engine mounts and remove engine from vehicle.
21. Loosen bolt nuts at engine mountings.
22. Remove bolts from the engine including sump to the transaxle.
23. Raise engine slightly to take weight off mounts by attaching an appropriate lifting hook and chain to engine lifting brackets if fitted. Otherwise care must be taken not to damage engine components with rope or chain while lifting engine.
24. Remove bolts from engine mountings.
25. Raise engine with front tilted upwards.
    * Do not allow engine to swing backwards or forward and damage any of the components.
26. Separate engine and transmission assemblies if nec-

V6 ENGINE MAINTENANCE & REBUILD 3.5L DOHC G.D.I.

essary. Refer to Manual Transmission or Automatic Transmission for details.

Dismantle.
1. Mount engine assembly in an appropriate engine stand.
2. Remove the following parts as previously described or about to be described, in this chapter.
   a) Intake manifold.
   b) Rocker Covers.
   c) Exhaust manifolds.
   d) Oil filter.
   e) Crankshaft balancer.
   f) Timing belt covers.
   g) Timing belt, camshaft gears.
   h) Camshafts.
   i) Cylinder heads.
   j) Engine sump.
   k) Oil pump suction pipe and baffle.
   l) Flywheel/flexplate.
   m) Engine rear end plate.
   n) Crankshaft.
   o) Piston and connecting rod assemblies.

Assembly.
Assembly techniques for each part are outlined in this section under there particular headings.
1. Make sure that all bolts and nuts are tightened as specified in this section.
2. Use specified engine lubricant and coolant when refilling.
3. Inspect transmission fluid level, add lubricant as required.
4. Inspect for fuel, coolant, oil and exhaust leaks. Repair as required.
5. Check engine hood alignment.

OIL PAN (SUMP)
Remove
1. Drain oil from oil pan.
2. Remove the dip stick.
3. Remove the small left side cover, 2 bolts.
4. Remove oil pan bolts, oil pan and seal, dispose of oil seal.

Install
1. Clean all matching surfaces of oil pan and cylinder block thoroughly.
2. Apply sealant to the oil pan surface groove and around the bolt holes.
3. Install oil pan and seal to crankcase, and tighten as specified.
   Take care with 2 bolts to transaxle, as they could easily miss the hole and go to the side of the transaxle

housing.
Oil Pan .... 11 Nm
Oil Pan to Rear Oil Seal Retainer .... 6 Nm
Oil Pan to Transaxle .... 37 Nm
Oil Pan small cover left side, transaxle bolt ....
.. 11 Nm

4. Make sure oil pan drain plug is tightened as specified, use a new drain plug seal.
Oil pan drain plug.. 39Nm
5. Replace dip stick.
6. Refill oil pan with the correct amount of engine oil as specified.
7. Start engine and inspect for oil leaks. Repair as required.
8. Stop engine and check oil level on dip stick.

OIL PUMP SUCTION PIPE AND BAFFLE
Remove
1. Remove the oil pan from the engine as previously described in this chapter.
2. Release the suction pipe and bracket retaining bolt from the assembly.
3. Remove the suction pipe from the engine.
4. Remove the suction pipe gasket from the engine, dispose of the gasket.

V6 ENGINE MAINTENANCE & REBUILD 3.5L DOHC G.D.I.

Install

1. Fit a new suction pipe gasket to the engine, then fit the suction pipe and baffle into place.
2. Fit the suction pipe and baffle retaining nuts, then tension the nuts to specifications.
   Oil suction pipe and screen .... **19 Nm**
   Oil suction pipe bracket .... **9 Nm**
3. Fit the oil pan to the engine.

PISTON AND CONNECTING ROD ASSEMBLY.

Both piston and cylinder bore condition must be considered together when fitting new pistons. Production and service pistons have the same nominal weight and can be intermixed without affecting engine balance. If needed, used pistons may be fitted selectively to any cylinder of the engine, providing they are in good condition.
Piston pin assemblies and ring sets are available in oversize.
Note: Remove the main bearing cradle before removing pistons and connecting rods.

Remove

1. Remove cylinder heads as described in Cylinder Head section.
2. To remove oil pan (sump), oil suction pipe and screen.
3. To remove the main bearing cradle as described in this chapter.
4. Inspect cylinder bores above piston ring travel. If bores are worn so that a ridge or similar exists. Turn crankshaft so that piston is at bottom of stroke and cover piston with a cloth to collect cuttings. Remove the ridge with a ridge remover, this is to be done for each cylinder.
5. Using a stamp and hammer or etching marker, mark all connecting rods, caps and pistons to indicate cylinder identification.
6. Remove rod assemblies and piston as follows,
   a) With connecting rod crankshaft journal straight down (Bottom Dead Centre), remove connecting rod cap bolts and remove cap with bearing shell.

   b) Push piston and connecting rod from cylinder using a long guide. Remove guides and install cap and bolts to connecting rod.
7. Remove all other piston and connecting rod assemblies using the same procedure.

Dismantle.

1. Expand and slide piston rings off to remove and dispose of them.
   Worn rings may have sharp edges ensure to take care when removing piston rings.
2. Piston pin can now be removed as follows:
   Press piston pin from piston with a mandrel and press, until piston pis free.
   Press in load **7,350-17,200N**

Inspection.

1. Thoroughly clean carbon from piston heads and from ring grooves using a suitable tool and remove any gum or varnish from piston skirts using a suitable cleaning solvent.
2. Check cylinder walls for ridges, roughness or scoring which indicates excessive wear. Inspect cylinder bores for taper and out-of-round using an accurate cylinder gauge at top, middle and bottom of bore, both parallel and at right angles to centre line of engine. Refer to Cylinder Block section for details.
3. Examine piston skirt thoroughly for scored or rough surfaces, cracks in skirt or crown, chipping, broken ring lands or uneven wear which would cause rings to seat improperly or have excessive clearance in ring grooves. Pistons should be replaced if faulty or damaged.
   Pistons are cam ground, which means that the diameter at right angles to the piston pin is greater than the

diameter parallel to the piston pin. When a piston is checked for size, it must be done at points 90° to the piston bore.

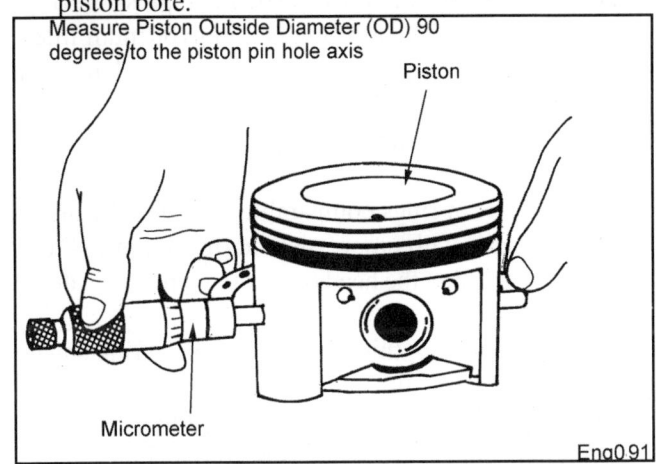

Measure Piston Outside Diameter (OD) 90 degrees to the piston pin hole axis

Piston diameter .... 93.0 mm
Piston to bore clearance .... 0.02 - 0.04 mm
Piston oversize ...... 0.50 mm, 0.75 mm, 1.00 mm

4. Check piston pin bores and piston pins for wear. Piston pins and piston pin bores must be free of scuffing or varnish when being measured. Use a micrometer to measure the piston pin, and a dial bore gauge or an inside micrometer to measure piston pin bore.
Piston pin hole diameter .... 22.0 mm
Piston and pin should be replaced if not as specified.

5. Remove bearing shells from connecting rod, install cap and bolts. Tighten bolts as specified.
Connecting Rod Cap Bolt:
    .... 34Nm plus 90 degree turn

6. Place connecting rod assembly on a checking fixture and inspect rod for twist or bend.
Replace if twisted or bent, do not attempt to straighten rod.
Inspect new connecting rods using the same procedure before using them.
Connecting rod   - bend .... 0.05 mm
                        - twist .... 0.1 mm

7. Check outside of connecting rod bearing shells and internal diameter of connecting rod big end for wear indicating high spots in the rod big end.

8. Remove cap bolts and inspect bolts for stretching by comparing them with a new bolt, if stretched, replace.

Assembly and Installation.
Note: *Take note of identification marks for correct orientation during assembly.*

1. Using engine oil, lubricate piston pin and piston pin bore.
2. Install piston pin on mandrel.
3. Assemble installer guide and piston support to base.

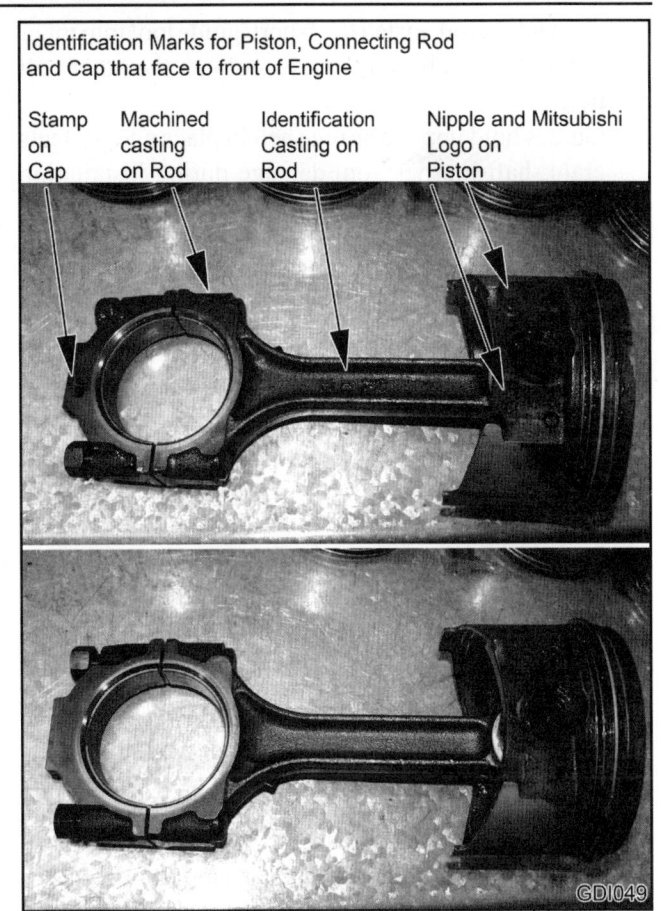

Identification Marks for Piston, Connecting Rod and Cap that face to front of Engine

| Stamp on Cap | Machined casting on Rod | Identification Casting on Rod | Nipple and Mitsubishi Logo on Piston |

4. Install piston and connecting rod over guide.
Note: *The front mark on the piston must be facing up so pin is pressed in from piston front mark side.*

Piston Front Mark, this mark faces towards the front of the engine

5. Press piston pin into place with a mandrel, until piston pin bottoms.
Press in load 7,350-17,200N

6. To install piston rings refer to Piston Rings section.
7. Make sure connecting rod bearing shells, pistons, cylinder bores and crankshaft journals are totally clean, then, using clean engine oil, coat cylinder bores and all bearing surfaces.
8. Position the crankpin straight down before installation of a piston and rod assembly in its bore.
9. Remove cap, and with bearing upper shell seated in

connecting rod, install the 'short' guide tool into inner bolt hole. Install 'long' guide tool into the other bolt hole.

Guides hold upper bearing shell in place and protects crankshaft journal from damage during installation of connecting rod and piston assembly.

10. Make sure piston ring gaps are separated as described in Piston Rings section.
11. Using clean engine oil, lubricate piston and rings. With a suitable ring compressor, compress rings. Install each piston and connecting rod assembly into its cylinder bore.
12. Lightly tap piston into its bore, using a hammer handle, while holding ring compressor firmly against cylinder block until all piston rings have entered bore.
13. Push piston down bore until connecting rod seats against crankshaft journal.
14. Remove connecting rod guides. Install bearing cap and lower bearing shell assembly. Install cap bolts and tighten and then loosen one full turn. Then tighten again as specified.
    Connecting Rod Cap Bolt:
    .... **34Nm plus 90 degree turn**
15. Turn crankshaft to make sure crankshaft and connecting rod can move freely. If crankshaft binds, check bearing cap to rod orientation again and bearing clearance or connecting rod alignment.
16. Measure side clearance between crankshaft journal and connecting rod.

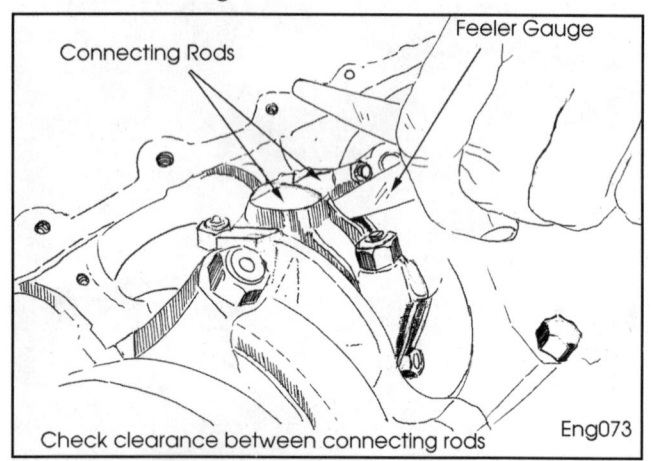

Check clearance between connecting rods

Connecting Rod side clearance.....0.10 - 0.25 mm
 - service limit (main/big end)..........0.4 mm

If side clearance is not as specified, to check bearing clearance refer to Connecting Rod Bearing section, or connecting rod alignment.
Connecting Rod bearing clearance 0.02 - 0.05mm
 - service limit (main/big end)..........0.1 mm

17. Install remaining piston and connecting rod assemblies using the same procedure.

PISTON RINGS.
Install
* The pistons have three rings (two compression rings and one oil ring). The top ring is a molybdenum filled, balanced section, barrel lapped type. The second ring is an inverted torsional taper faced type. The oil ring is of three piece design, comprising two segments and a spacer.

1. Using a set of rings comparable in size to the piston being used install compression ring in relevant cylinder bore, then using the head of a piston, press ring down into the bore.
   Using a piston in this manner will place ring square with cylinder wall.
   Ensure not to distort the ring during this operation, or it may bind in the piston ring groove. Fit each ring separately to the cylinder in which it is going to be installed.
2. Using a feeler gauge, measure gap between ends of ring.

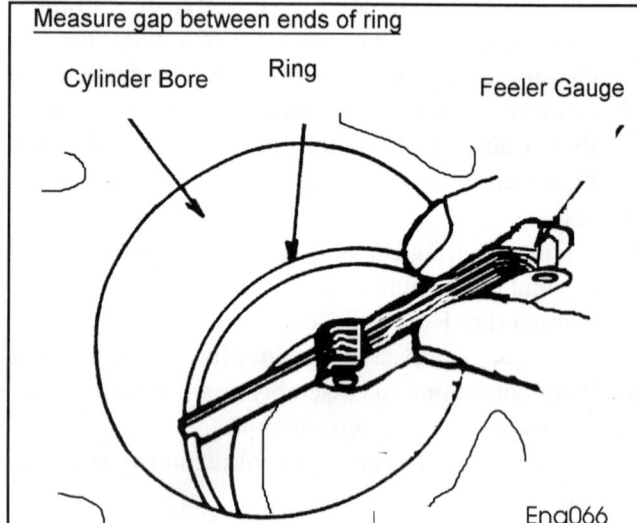

Measure gap between ends of ring

Ring gap   - New
 - Compression.......................0.30 - 0.45 mm
 - Scraper...............................0.45 - 0.60 mm
 - Oil ring...............................0.10 - 0.35 mm
Ring gap   - Wear limit
 - Compression..................................0.8 mm
 - Scraper..0.8 mm
 - Oil ring..1.0 mm

Remove ring and try another, if the gap between the ends of a compression ring is below specification. The ring gap may be enlarged by filing.

3. Inspect gap between ends of each oil control ring segment.
   Oil Ring Steel Rail Gap Specification:
    - Oil ring ....0.10 - 0.35 mm
4. Carefully remove all traces of carbon from ring grooves in piston and check grooves for any chips or burrs that might cause ring to bind when fitting.

V6 ENGINE MAINTENANCE & REBUILD 3.5L DOHC G.D.I.

5. Slip outer surface of each compression ring in respective piston ring groove and roll ring entirely around groove to ensure that ring is free. Also measure ring to piston groove side clearance.

   Side clearance
   - **Compression** .... 0.03 - 0.07 mm
   - **Scraper** .... 0.02 - 0.06 mm

   Try another ring if it is too tight. If no ring can be found That fits the specification, the ring may be ground to size using emery paper placed on a piece of glass. If using a new piston, try another piston.

   * High spots in the ring groove may be cleaned up with careful use of a fine file, do not try to cut the piston ring groove.

6. Install oil ring spacer in bottom piston ring groove. The ends of the spacer butt against each other.

7. Install one steel segment from top of piston downward into oil ring groove and install remaining steel segment from bottom of piston skirt upwards into the oil ring groove.

8. Install compression rings in first and second grooves of each piston.
   Make sure the correct compression ring are installed in the first and second grooves, and the correct way up.

9. Do a final test of ring fit in piston grooves. Separate ends as illustrated.

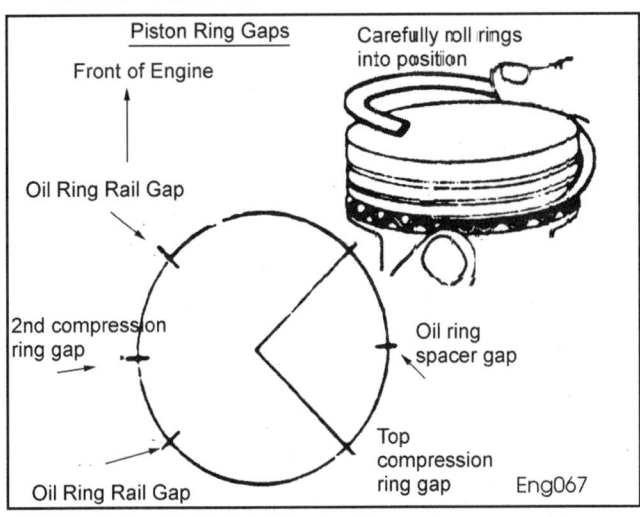

Figure: Piston Ring Gaps — Front of Engine, Oil Ring Rail Gap, 2nd compression ring gap, Oil Ring Rail Gap, Oil ring spacer gap, Top compression ring gap. Carefully roll rings into position. Eng067

* Do not install piston with ring gaps in line, as this will allow compression leakage at this point.

CONNECTING ROD BEARINGS

Each connecting rod bearing consists of 2 bearing halves or shells which are interchangeable in the rod and cap. When the shells are in place, the ends extend slightly beyond the parting surfaces of the rod and cap. When the rod bolts are tightened, the shells are tightly clamped in place to ensure positive seating and to prevent rotation. The connecting rod bearings are of the precision insert type and do not use shims for adjustment. The ends of the bearing shells must never be filed flush with parting surface of rod or cap.

Inspection and Replacement.
Connecting rod bearings can be replaced without removing the rod and piston assembly from the engine.

1. Using a stamp and hammer or etching marker, mark all connecting rods, caps and pistons to indicate cylinder identification and orientation of cap.
2. Remove connecting rod cap securing nuts and remove cap and lower bearing shell.
3. Push piston and connecting rod up cylinder bore, so that connecting rod is free from crankshaft journal. Remove bearing shell from connecting rod.
4. Clean crankshaft journal and measure for out of round or taper using a micrometer. Replace crankshaft, if not as specified in CRANKSHAFT section.
   Crankshaft Connecting Rod Bearing Journal Diameter
5. Wipe oil from both inner and outer surfaces of bearing shells.
6. Inspect inner surface of bearing shells for gouges, wear or embedded foreign matter.
   If foreign matter is found, determine its nature and source.
   Inspect outer surface of bearing shell for surface wear

Photo: Connecting Rod Cap and Bearing Shell. GDI048

Photo: Connecting Rod Bearing. Note: Damage to bearing shell and crankshaft journal. GDI046

79

V6 ENGINE MAINTENANCE & REBUILD 3.5L DOHC G.D.I.

(indicates movement of shell or high spot in surrounding material), looseness or turning (flattened tangs and wear grooves), or overheating (discolouration). The crankshaft may be bent or have tapered bearing journals if uneven side to side wear is found. If needed, remove crankshaft, refer to CRANKSHAFT section and inspect crankshaft for bend or journal taper.

* Bearing failure, other than normal wear, must be examined carefully.

7. Install bearing shells in original positions in connecting rod and cap if inspection reveals that crankshaft is OK.
8. Pull connecting rod down onto crankshaft so that upper bearing is seated against crankshaft journal.
9. Place a piece of plastigage across width of bearing journal, parallel to crankshaft centre line.

* Make sure plastigage is not placed across oil hole in journal.

10. Install connecting rod cap in original position as described in step 4. Tighten bolts as specified. Make sure that crankshaft does not rotate with plastigage installed.

    Connecting Rod Cap Bolt:
    .... 34Nm plus 90 degree turn

11. Remove connecting rod cap bolts, and cap. Inspect for flattened plastigage sticking to either crankshaft or bearing shell in cap.
12. Determine bearing clearance by comparing width of flattened plastigage at widest point with graduation on plastigage envelope. The number within the graduation on the envelope indicates the clearance. Clearance between connecting rod bearings and crankshaft should not exceed specification. If a bearing is being fitted to an out of round journal, ensure to fit plastigage to the maximum diameter of the journal. If the bearing is fitted to the minimum diameter, and the journal is out of round 0.008mm, interference between the bearing and journal will result in rapid bearing failure.

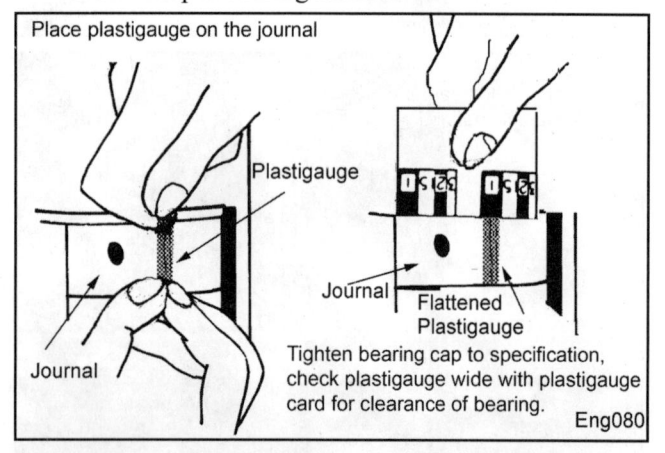

Place plastigauge on the journal

Plastigauge
Journal
Flattened Plastigauge
Tighten bearing cap to specification, check plastigauge wide with plastigauge card for clearance of bearing.
Eng080

Connecting Rod side clearance.....0.10 - 0.25 mm
- service limit (main/big end)...........0.4 mm

If side clearance is not as specified, to check bearing clearance refer to Connecting Rod Bearing section, or connecting rod alignment.

Connecting Rod bearing clearance 0.02 - 0.05mm
- service limit (main/big end)............ 0.1 mm
Connecting rod bearing undersizes:
...................................0.25, 0.50 and 0.75 mm

13. Make sure that connecting rod cap bolt threads and connecting rod threads are clean and dry. Apply some engine oil to the cap bolt threads. Before final installation of cap bolts, determine if bolts have stretched by comparing with a new bolt. Replace bolt/s as needed.
14. Install bearing shells in connecting rod and cap making sure notches in shells match up with recesses in connecting rod and cap. Inspect clearance of new bearing with plastigage as previously described.
15. Remove all remains of plastigage after measuring. Using clean engine oil lubricate bearing shells and journal. Install connecting rod cap in original position, tighten bolts as specified.

    Connecting Rod Cap Bolt:
    .... 34Nm plus 90 degree turn

16. With bearing shells installed and cap bolts tightened, it should be possible to move connecting rod backwards and forwards on crankshaft journal as allowed by end clearance. Also, the crankshaft should turn without binding.

    Connecting Rod bearing clearance 0.02 - 0.05mm
    - service limit (main/big end)........... 0.1 mm

    If connecting rod binds on crankshaft journal, loosen and tighten bearing cap bolts.
    If rod still cannot be moved or crankshaft binds, inspect bearing cap to rod orientation, bearing clearance or connecting rod alignment.

CRANKSHAFT.
Remove

To check bearing clearance before removing crankshaft from crankcase as described.

Note: 6G74 engines (3.5 litre) have a 4 bolt main bearing type cradle, 6G72 engines (3.0 litre) have a 2 bolt main bearing type cradle.

1. When engine is removed from vehicle and mounted in a suitable stand and remove oil pan.
2. Remove flywheel/driveplate and engine end plate, rear seal retainer. .... Remove oil pump suction pipe and screen.
4. Remove timing belt and crankshaft sprocket refer to Timing Belt section.
5. Using a stamp and hammer or etching marker, mark all connecting rods, caps and pistons to indicate cylinder identification and orientation of cap.

V6 ENGINE MAINTENANCE & REBUILD 3.5L DOHC G.D.I.

6. Remove main bearing cap cradle bolts in order as shown and cradle.

```
Main Bearing Cradle Bolts
Tighten Sequence:
14    10    11    15
 6     2     3     7

 5     1     4     8
13     9    12    16

Loosen in Reverse Order

        Front of Engine →
        Arrow faces front of engine
```

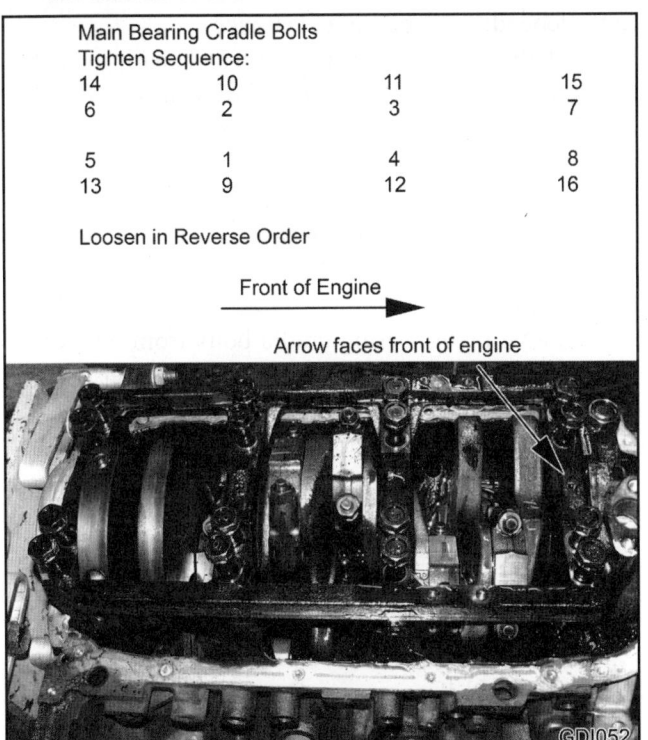

Use a soft faced hammer tap the cradle to break cradle to crankcase seal.

Main Bearing 4 Bolts per Journal Cradle

7. Remove connecting rod caps and bolts and push connecting rods away from crankshaft.
8. Lift crankshaft from cylinder block.
9. Remove key from front end of crankshaft, if needed, using a suitable punch and hammer.

Inspection.

1. Using a suitable cleaning solvent, wash crankshaft and dry with compressed air.
2. Check crankshaft oil passages for obstructions.
3. Check all bearing journals and thrust surfaces for: Gouges, overheating (discolouration), cracks, grooving chips or roughness.

The crankshaft must be machined or replaced if it has any burned spots, cracks or sever gouging. Slight roughness may be removed using a fine polishing cloth soaked in clean engine oil. Burrs may also be removed using a fine oil stone.

4. Check connecting rod and main bearing shells for embedded foreign material and determine its source.
5. Using a micrometer measure bearing journals for taper, excessive wear or out-of-round.

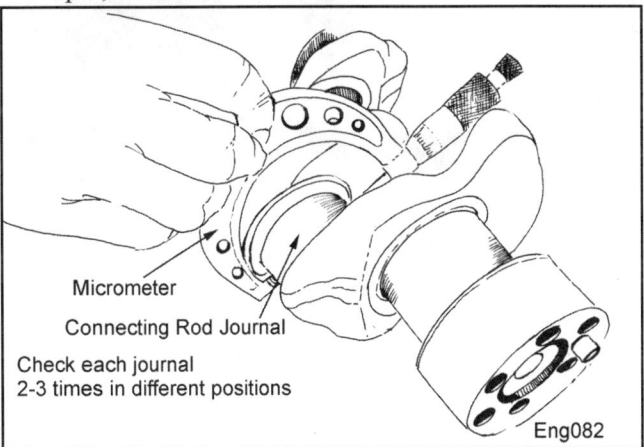

Micrometer
Connecting Rod Journal
Check each journal 2-3 times in different positions

Main bearing journals diameter............. 64.0 mm
Connecting Rod Journal diameter .... 55 mm
End float controlled by .... No.3 bearing
Connecting Rod journal diameter.......... 50.0 mm
    - max. allowable ovality.................. 0.03 mm
    - max. allowable taper .... 0.005 mm
Main bearing clearance............... 0.02 - 0.048 mm
- service limit .... 0.1 mm

6. Inspect crankshaft for run-out by supporting front and rear main bearing journals in 'V' blocks and checking journals with a dial gauge.
7. Place a dial gauge indicator at crankshaft rear flange and inspect rear flange Run-out. During this inspection, make sure that crankshaft is thrust forward on 'V' blocks so that there is no possibility of crankshaft end float affecting dial gauge reading.
Crankshaft Rear Flange Run-out... 0.05-0.25 mm
    Wear Limit 0.4mm
8. If not as specified, replace crankshaft.

Installation.

1. Inspect main bearing clearance, if needed, refer to MAIN BEARINGS section for details.
2. Using a clean engine oil lubricate all crankshaft journals and main bearing upper shells in crankcase.
3. Sit crankshaft in place in main bearing upper shells in crankcase. Ensure not to damage crankshaft thrust washers at No.3 main bearing. Also ensure not to contact connecting rod journals with connecting rod and install main bearing caps.

V6 ENGINE MAINTENANCE & REBUILD 3.5L DOHC G.D.I.

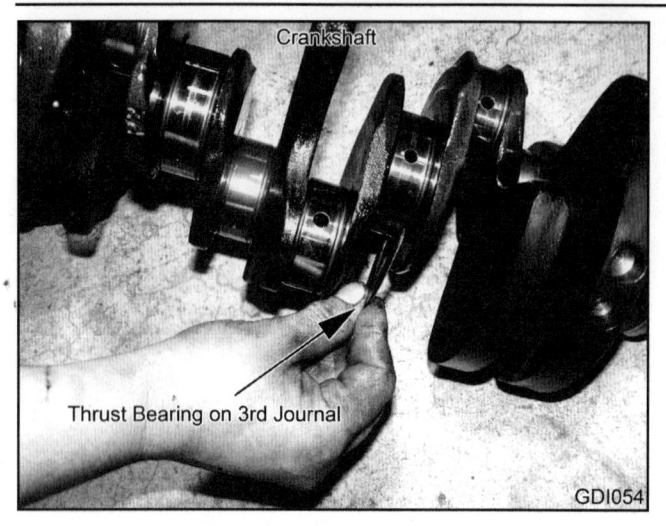

Thrust Bearing on 3rd Journal

Using a thin film of Loctite 515 Gasket Eliminator or equivalent apply to rear main bearing cap to crankcase mating surface. Keep sealant out of bolt holes and use sparingly.

*Make sure that the bearing caps are installed onto the crankcase in the correct manner.
Tighten the bolts finger tight.

4. It will be necessary to line up thrust washers with No.3 bearing shells, before tightening main bearing cap bolts.
   Move crankshaft fore and aft the length of its travel several times (last movement forward) to do this.
5. Ensure all main bearing cap bolts are tightened as specified.
   Main Bearing Cradle Bolts 74Nm
6. Use a feeler gauge to measure crankshaft end float between front of No.3 main bearing thrust washer and crankshaft thrust faces, you will need to force crankshaft forward to do this.
   **Crankshaft Rear Flange Run-out...0.05-0.25 mm
   Wear Limit 0.4mm**
   Replace No.3 main bearing thrust washers if clearance is excessive.
7. Turn crankshaft to make sure crankshaft and connecting rods have free movement. Inspect orientation of bearing caps, correct fitting of bearing cradle (mains and connecting rods) or fitting of bearing shells or bearing clearance, if crankshaft binds.
8. Install the rear main oil seal and retainer.
9. To install flywheel/driveplate as described.

MAIN BEARINGS.

Each crankshaft main bearing journal has 2 bearing halves or shells which are not the same and not interchangeable in the bearing cap or crankcase. The upper (crankcase) shell is grooved to supply oil to the connecting rod bearing, while the lower (bearing cap) shell is not grooved. The 2 bearing shells must not be interchanged. The No.3. bearing has thrust washers to take end thrust.

Standard size upper shells are used in the crankcase with 0.25mm under sized or standard size shells in the bearing caps, depending on bearing clearance.

When shells are placed in crankcase and bearing cap, the end extends slightly beyond the parting surfaces so that when cradle bolts are tightened, the shells clamp tightly in place to ensure positive seating and to prevent turning. The ends of the bearing shells must never be filed flush with parting surfaces of crankcase or bearing cradle.

Inspection

1. Remove main bearing cradle bolts from bearing to be inspected, and remove cradle and lower bearing shell.
   * Tap main bearing cradle to break cradle to crankcase seal to remove.
2. Check lower bearing shells and crankshaft journals. If the journal surface is ridged or heavily scored, replace crankshaft, refer to Crankshaft section for details.
   To ensure satisfactory engine operation, new bearing shells must be installed as described in Main Bearing section and if necessary Connecting Rod Bearings section.
   Inspect inner surface of bearing shells for gouges, wear or embedded foreign material. If foreign material is found, determine its nature and source. Inspect outer surface of bearing shells for surface wear (indicates movement of shell or high spot in surrounding material), looseness, rotation (flattened tangs and wear grooves), and overheating (discolouration).

Main Bearing Shell
Bearing Cradle

Inspect thrust surfaces of thrust washers for grooving or wear. Grooves are caused by irregularities in the crankshaft thrust surfaces or dirt as described in Crankshaft section.

If condition of lower bearing shells and crankshaft journals is satisfactory, inspect bearing clearance as follows:

3. Wipe oil from crankshaft journal and inner and outer surfaces of lower bearing shell.

82

V6 ENGINE MAINTENANCE & REBUILD 3.5L DOHC G.D.I.

Install bearing shell in original position in bearing cap.

4. Place a piece of plastigage across full width of crankshaft journal, parallel to crankshaft centre line.
   * Make sure plastigage will not seat across oil hole in journal.
5. Install bearing cap and bolts into cylinder block.
   * Install bearing caps by loosely installing cap bolts and then lightly tap bearing cap into position, in order to prevent the possibility of cylinder block and or main bearing cap damage.
   * Do not pull the bearing cradle into place with the bearing cradle bolts.
6. Tighten bearing cradle bolts as specified.
   * Ensure that crankshaft does not rotate with plastigage installed.
   Main Bearing Cradle Bolts: **74Nm**
7. Remove bearing cradle bolts and cradle. Look for flattened plastigage sticking to either crankshaft or bearing shell in bearing cradle.
8. Check bearing clearance by comparing width of flattened plastigage at widest point with graduation on plastigage envelope. The number within the graduation on the envelope indicates the clearance.
   Main bearing and crankshaft journal clearance should not exceed specification.
   Main Bearing Clearance: .... **0.02 - 0.048 mm**
   - service limit .... **0.1 mm**
   This method of checking main bearing clearance does not give any indication of crankshaft journal taper or out of round.
   To measure taper, out of round or undersized, the crankshaft must be removed from the cylinder block as described in CRANKSHAFT section.
9. It is advisable to install new bearing shells if bearing clearance exceeds specification and check clearance as previously described.
   If lower bearing is standard size, install a 0.25 mm undersized shell and check clearance again.
   Replace crankshaft as described in "Crankshaft" section if clearance is still not as specified.
10. Make sure that main bearing cradle bolt threads and crankcase threads are clean and dry.
    * Before final installation of cradle bolts, determine if bolts have stretched by comparing with new one. Replace bolts and tighten.
    Main Bearing Cradle Bolts: **74Nm**

REAR MAIN OIL SEAL
Replace
1. Remove flywheel/driveplate, as described in "Flywheel/driveplate" in this manual.
2. a) Remove the oil seal retainer bolts and remove the oil seal retainer.

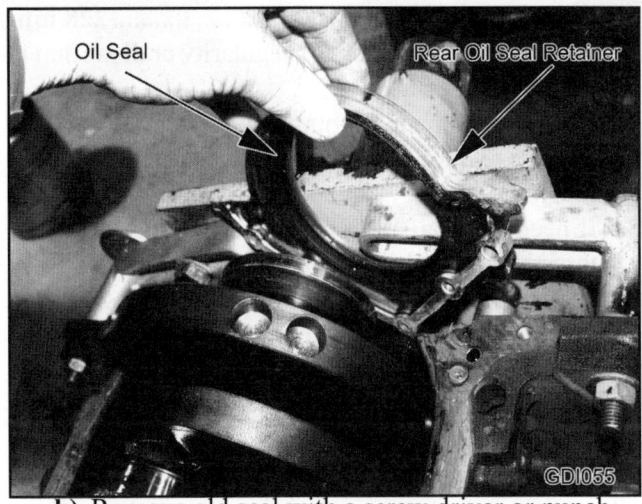

   b) Remove old seal with a screw driver or punch.
   c) Install new seal with a seal installer, ensure the seals lips are not pulled back or crooked.
3. Install rear seal retainer to rear of engine block.
   Rear oil seal retainer plate **11Nm**
4. Clean flywheel/drive plate attaching bolt threads in rear of crankshaft using a thread tap.
   Install new flywheel/flexplate and attaching bolts, tighten bolts to the correct torque specification.
   Flywheel/flexplate bolt tensioning **98Nm**
5. Reinstall transmission, check engine and transmission lubricant levels.
6. Road test vehicle and check for lubrication leaks.

CYLINDER BLOCK.
Inspection.
1. When engine is removed from vehicle and mounted in a suitable engine stand, remove all parts as outlined under the particular part heading in this section.
2. Clean all cylinder block gasket surfaces.
3. Remove all coolant jacket welsh plugs and oil gallery screw plugs.
4. Clean cylinder block thoroughly using a suitable cleaning solution. Flush with clean water or steam. Spray or wipe cylinder bores and machined surfaces using engine oil.
   Caustic cleaning solutions destroy all bearing and alloy materials. All bearing and alloy parts if not removed before cleaning must be replaced.
   Do not use caustic solutions to clean bearing material or alloy parts.
5. Check all oil passages for obstructions.
6. Using a straight edge and feeler gauge, inspect cylinder block deck surface for flatness.
   If any distortion or irregularity is less than specified, cylinder block surface may be machined.
   Flatness of gasket surface .... **less than 0.05 mm**
   Flatness of gasket surface - maximum ... **0.10 mm**
   Grinding limit -
   Combined block and cylinder head .... **0.20 mm**

Cylinder Block Height: .... 228 mm
Replace cylinder block if irregularity or distortion is more than specified.
7. Check oil pan and oil pump body area for burrs or damage. Minor damage may be cleaned up with a fine mill file.
8. If needed, clean all threaded holes using a suitable threaded tap or drill out and install thread insert.
9. Measure cylinder bore walls for taper, excessive ridging, oversize and out-of-round.

Max. bore oversize .... 1.00 mm
Max. diameter difference b/w cylinders: ..... 0.02 mm
Max. bore wear (before rebore) .... 0.02 mm
Max ovality and taper (before rebore) .... 0.02 mm

Cylinder Reconditioning and Piston Fitting.
It will be necessary to smooth bores to fit new pistons, if one or more cylinder bores are scored, rough or worn beyond limits.
It will not be necessary to rebore all cylinders to the same oversize order to maintain engine balance if few bores require correction, since all oversize service pistons are held to the same weight as standard size pistons.
Do not try to machine oversize pistons to fit cylinder bores, this will destroy the surface treatment and affect the weight. The smallest possible oversize service pistons should be used and the cylinder bores should be honed to size for proper clearances.
Measure all new pistons at right angles to the piston pin bore, before the honing or reboring operation is started.
Piston diameter .... 93.0 mm
Piston to bore clearance .... 0.02 - 0.04 mm
Piston oversize .... 0.50 mm, 0.75 mm, 1.00 mm
Honing is recommended for trueing bore if cylinder bore wear does not exceed specification. The bore should be trued up by boring and then hone finished, if wear or out-of-round exceeds specification.
All crankshaft bearing caps must be in place and tightened as specified when reboring cylinder bores, to prevent distortion of bores in final assembly.
Leave 0.025 mm on the diameter for final honing to give the specified clearance when taking the final cut.
Follow the Hone Manufacturers recommendations for the use of the hone and cleaning and lubrication during honing. Noting the following points.
Pass the hone through the entire length of the cylinder bore at the rate of approximately 60 cycles per minute when finished honing. This should produce the desired 45° cross hatch pattern on cylinder walls which will ensure minimum oil consumption and maximum ring life.
Each piston must be fitted individually to the bore in which it will be installed and marked to ensure correct assembly during the final honing. After the final honing and before the piston is inspected for fit, each cylinder bore must be washed and dried thoroughly to remove all traces of abrasive and then allowed to cool. Apply clean engine oil to cylinder bores. The pistons and cylinder block must be at a common temperature before inspecting.
The glazed cylinder walls should be slightly dulled when new piston rings are installed without reboring cylinders, but without increasing the bore diameter, by means of the finest grade of stone in a cylinder hone.

Proceed as follows to inspect piston to cylinder bore.
1. Using a clean cloth wipe cylinder walls and pistons and apply clean engine oil to cylinder bores.
2. Measure the bore accurately using an inside micrometer.
3. Measure piston diameter and subtract piston diameter from cylinder bore diameter to determine piston-to-bore clearance.
   Piston to bore clearance .... 0.02 - 0.04 mm
   Maximum .... 0.085 mm
4. Mark each piston with cylinder number to which it will be fitted and proceed to hone cylinders and fit pistons.
   Handle the pistons with care and do not attempt to force them through the cylinder until cylinder has been honed to the correct size, as pistons can be damaged through careless handling.
   Assemble parts as described under the correct heading in this section. If coolant and oil gallery plugs were removed when dismantling, install using specified sealant.

Problem Diagnosis.

Problems and Possible Causes.
Problems should be corrected, when proper diagnosis is made, by repair, adjustment or part replacement as needed. Refer to the correct section in this manual.

High Oil Loss
1) Tighten bolts and/or replace gaskets and seals as required for external leaks.
2) Check oil with car on a level surface and allow adequate drain down time to ensure a correct reading of dipstick.
3) Severe usage such as towing or continuous high speed driving will normally cause oil consumption to increase.
4) PCV system failure.
5) Use recommended S.A.E viscosity for current temperatures. Refer to Lubrication Section for details on incorrect oil viscosity.
6) Valve guides and/or valve stem seals worn, or seals omitted. Ream guides and install oversize service valves and/or new valve stem seals.

7) Allow enough time for the piston rings to seat. Replace worn or broken rings as needed, if rings have been incorrectly installed, worn or broken, or not seated.
8) Piston incorrectly installed or mis-fitted.

Gaskets.
1) Incorrectly tightened fasteners or damaged/dirty threads.
2) Worn or damaged gasket (cracking or porosity).
3) Fluid pressure/level too high.
4) Incorrect sealant used (when required)

Inspection of Seals.
1) Damaged seal bore (burred, nicked, scratched)
2) Worn or damaged seal or incorrect installation.
3) Fluid pressure/level too high.

Oil Leak Investigation
Oil leaks are easily located and repaired by visually finding the leak and replacing or repairing the required parts.
1) Determine whether the fluid is transmission lubricant, engine oil, power steering fluid etc.
2) Run the car at normal operating temperature and park the car over a large sheet of paper. After a few minutes, you should be able to find the approximate location of the leak by drippings on the paper.
3) Use a degreaser or steam to clean the area of the leak, drive the car for a few kilometres. Then visually inspect the suspected part for signs of an oil leak.

Black Light and Dye Method.
There are many dye and light kits available..
a) Pour required amount of dye into leaking part.
b) Operate the car under normal operating conditions as instructed in the kit.
c) Shine the light in the suspected area. The dyed fluid will appear as a yellow path leading to the problem.

Low Oil Pressure
1) Blocked oil filter.
2) Incorrect oil viscosity for expected temperature, or oil diluted with moisture or unburned fuel mixtures.
3) Excessive bearing clearance.
4) If the oil level is low, fill to mark on dipstick.
5) Oil pump dirty/worn, or oil pump suction pipe screen blocked, or hole in oil pump suction pipe.
6) Incorrect or failing oil pressure sender.

ENGINE KNOCKS
When Engine Cold And Continues Knocking For Two Or Three Minutes
Increases with torque
1) Tighten or replace as required if drive pulleys or balancer are loose or broken.

2) Replace piston if clearance from piston to bore is excessive. (Cold engine piston knock usually disappears when the cylinder is grounded out. Cold engine piston knock which disappears in 1.5 min. can be considered acceptable.)
3) Connecting rod bent.

Heavy Knock With Torque Applied
1) Replace parts as required of pulley hub or balancer broken.
2) Loose torque converter to flexplate bolts.
3) Check if exhaust system contacting underbody.
4) Cracked flexplate/flywheel.
5) Main bearing clearance or connecting rod bearing clearance excessive.

Knocks On First Start-up Only Lasting Few Seconds
1) Incorrect oil viscosity. Install correct oil viscosity for expected temperatures.
2) Hydraulic lifter bleed down.
   Some valves will be open when the engine is stopped. Spring force against lifters will tend to bleed lifter down. Only if the problem is consistent should repairs be attempted.
3) Replace crankshaft thrust bearing shells if excessive crankshaft end float.
4) Replace bearings if bearing clearance is excessive.

SPECIFICATIONS

GENERAL
Type - 6G74 .... V6 DOHC
No. of Cylinders .... Six
Displacement: .... 3497 cc
Compression ratio: 9.5:1
Bore and Stroke (nominal): .... 93.0 x 85.8
Firing Order 1-2-3-4-5-6
Fuel requirements .... Unleaded

CYLINDER BLOCK
Material .... Alloy cast iron
Flatness of gasket surface .... less than 0.05 mm
Flatness of gasket surface - maximum............ 0.10 mm
Grinding limit -combined block and cylinder head .0.20 mm
Cylinder bore diameter: .... 93.0 mm
Max. bore oversize .... 1.00 mm
Max. diameter difference between cylinders: .. 0.02 mm
Max. bore wear (before reconditioning) .... 0.02 mm
Max ovality and taper (before reconditioning) 0.02 mm
Cylinder Block Height: .... 228 mm

CYLINDER HEAD
Material .... Aluminium alloy
Type .... Compact hemispherical
Max. allowable distortion - head surface .... 0.2 mm
Grinding limit .... 0.2 mm
Max. allowable distortion - intake surface .... 0.2 mm
Max. allowable distortion - exhaust surface ...... 0.3 mm
Inlet valve seat insert hole diameter
    - 0.3 mm Oversize .... 36.30 - 36.33 mm
    - 0.6 mm Oversize .... 36.60 - 36.63 mm
Exhaust valve seat insert hole diameter
    - 0.3 mm Oversize .... 33.30 - 33.33 mm
    - 0.6 mm Oversize .... 33.60 - 33.63 mm
Valve guide hole diameter .... 12.00 - 12.02 mm
    - 0.05 mm Oversize .... 12.05 - 12.07 mm
    - 0.25 mm Oversize .... 12.25 - 12.27 mm
    - 0.50 mm Oversize .... 12.50 - 12.52 mm
Camshaft/camshaft bearing clearance...... 0.06-0.10 mm

VALVES
Valve height   - Inlet .... 102.28 mm
                    - Inlet wear limit .... 101.78 mm
                    - Exhaust .... 101.40 mm
                    - Exhaust wear limit ... 100.90 mm
Stem diameter   - Inlet .... 6.6 mm
                      - Exhaust .... 6.6 mm
Head Thickness - Inlet .... 1.0 to 0.05 mm
                      - Exhaust .... 1.5 to 1.0 mm
Valve face angle .... 43.5° - 44.0°
Valve seat contact width .... 0.90 - 1.30 mm
Valve stem to guide clearance
                    - Inlet .... 0.02 - 0.05 mm
                    - Inlet wear limit .... 0.10 mm
                    - Exhaust .... 0.04 - 0.07 mm
                    - Exhaust wear limit .... 0.15 mm
Valve Assembled Height
    Intake
        Valve Assembled Protrusion 47.10mm
        Maximum 47.60mm
    Exhaust
        Valve Assembled Protrusion 46.60mm
        Maximum 47.10mm
Note: Intake valve seals .... gray colour
        Exhaust valve seals .... greyish green colour
Hydraulic lash adjuster dry clearance .... 0.5 - 1.3 mm

VALVE GUIDES
Valve stem to guide clearance
    - Inlet .... 0.02 - 0.05 mm
    - Exhaust .... 0.04 - 0.07 mm
Valve Guide ID
    Valve Guide Internal Diameter: .... 6.6 mm
Valve Guide OD sizes
    - 0.05, 0.25 & 0.50mm available

Valve Guide projection
    Intake Valve Guide Projection: .... 14.0 mm
    Exhaust Valve Guide Projection: .... 14.0 mm

VALVE SPRINGS
Free length .... 47.2 mm
Free length Minimum .... 46.2 mm
Spring Load/Installed Height N/mm 230/37.9

CAMSHAFT
Material .... Cast iron
Camshaft bearings .... Aluminium alloy
Bearing clearance .... 0.01 - 0.04 mm
Camshaft Journals
Camshaft Journal diameter .... 26.0 mm
    Camshaft Run-out .... 0.06 mm
Height of cam lobe
    DOHC   - Inlet (Europe) .... 35.20 mm
                    - Inlet (Hong Kong) .... 34.85 mm
                    - Exhaust .... 34.91 mm
    wear limit   - Inlet (Europe) .... 34.70 mm
                    - Inlet (Hong Kong) .... 34.35 mm
                    - Exhaust .... 34.41 mm

PISTONS
Material .... Aluminium alloy
Type .... Auto thermic type
Piston pin hole diameter .... 22.0 mm
Piston diameter .... 93.0 mm
Piston to bore clearance .... 0.02 - 0.04 mm
Piston oversize .... 0.50 mm, 0.75 mm, 1.00 mm

PISTON PIN
Type .... Press fit in connecting rod
Material .... Alloy steel
Diameter .... 22.0 mm
Offset in piston .... 0.3 mm
Press in load 7,350-17,200N

PISTON RINGS
Number 3
Ring gap - New - Compression .... 0.30 - 0.45 mm
                            - Scraper .... 0.45 - 0.60 mm
                            - Oil ring .... 0.10 - 0.35 mm
Service limit   - Compression .... 0.8 mm
                    - Scraper .... 0.8 mm
                    - Oil ring .... 1.0 mm
Side clearance - Compression .... 0.03 - 0.07 mm
                    - Scraper .... 0.02 - 0.06 mm

CONNECTING ROD
Material .... Forged carbon steel
Small end bore diameter .... 22 mm
Big end bore diameter .... 55 mm

V6 ENGINE MAINTENANCE & REBUILD 3.5L DOHC G.D.I.

Connecting Rod bearing clearance .... 0.02 - 0.05 mm
- service limit (main/big end) .... 0.1 mm
Connecting rod bearing undersizes .... 0.25 mm
.... 0.50 mm
.... 0.75 mm
Connecting rod
- bend.. 0.05 mm
- twist.. 0.1 mm
Connecting rod side clearance on journal . 0.10-0.25mm
- service limit .... 0.4 mm
Bearing material .... Aluminium alloy

CRANKSHAFT

No. of main bearings..4
Main bearing journals diameter .... 64.0 mm
Connecting Rod Journal diameter...................... 55 mm
End float controlled by.............................. No.3 bearing
End play .... 0.05 - 0.25 mm
- limit .... 0.4 mm
Connecting Rod journal
- max. allowable ovality .... 0.03 mm
- max. allowable taper .... 0.005 mm
Main bearing clearance .... 0.02 - 0.048 mm
- service limit .... 0.1 mm
Connecting Rod bearing clearance .... 0.02 - 0.05 mm
- service limit .... 0.1 mm

Oil Pump

Inner Rotor tip clearance..................... 0.03 - 0.08mm
Side clearance of rotor to pump housing 0.04 - 0.10mm
Outer rotor to pump housing clearance... 0.10 - 0.18mm
Max.. 0.35mm

SEALANT

Camshaft Position Sensor ....
Mitsubishi 970389 or equivalent (a semi drying type)
Oil Pan ....
Mitsubishi 970389 or equivalent (a semi drying type)

TORQUE SPECIFICATION

Description	Nm
Alternator bracket M8	48
Alternator bracket M10	23
Alternator pivot nut	44
Camshaft Position Sensor Ring	22
Camshaft Sprocket Bolt	88
Camshaft Sprocket Bracket	23
Camshaft thrust case	12
Connecting Rod Cap Bolt:	34Nm plus 90 degree turn
Coolant temperature gauge unit	11
Coolant temperature sensor	29
Crankshaft bolt	182
Crank Angle Sensor	9
Cylinder Head Bolts	
Step 1: Cylinder head bolts - Cold - in 3 stages	108Nm
Step 2 Loosen bolts	
Step 3 Cylinder head bolts - Cold - in 3 stages	108Nm
Dipstick mounting bolt	13
Drive belt tension pulley nut	49
Drive belt tension nut	35-55
Drive plate bolt	74
Exhaust heat protector bolt	14
Exhaust manifold nut	44
Flywheel mounting bolt	74
Heater pipe bolt	11
Intake Manifold	22
Intake Plenum	18
Intake Plenum Stay - M8	18
- M10	35
Main Bearing Cradle Bolts:	74Nm
Oil filter - bracket bolt - M8	23
- M10	41
Oil pan lower	11
Oil pan cover	11
Oil pan upper	6
Oil pan Baffle - M8	11
- M6	9
Oil suction pipe and screen	11
Oil relief plug	44
Oil pan drain plug	39
Oil pressure switch	10
Oil pump cover	10
Oil pump case	14
Rear oil seal retainer plate	11
Rocker cover bolt	3.9
Rocker arm - rocker shaft	31
Timing Belt cover bolt - M6	11
- M8	13
Timing Belt rear upper cover, left	10-12
Timing Belt Auto Tensioner bolt	23
Timing Belt Tensioner Pulley bolt	48
Timing Belt Tensioner Arm	44
Timing Belt Idler Pulley Bolt	44
Timing Belt Rear Cover	13
Thermostat Housing bolts	18
Throttle Body	11
Thermo switch	6-9
Water inlet fitting bolt	18
Water outlet fitting bolt	18
Water pipe bolt	9
Water pump bolts - M8	14
- M6	5
Water pump bolts - M10	41

ENGINE MAINTENANCE & REBUILD
2.8 litre DIESEL SOHC (4M40)

Subject	Page
GENERAL DESCRIPTION	**89**
Engine Serial Number	89
Maintenance Hints	89
ENGINE MAINTENANCE	**90**
Intercooler	**90**
Removal	90
Installation	90
Intake & Exhaust Manifold Assemblies	**90**
Removal	90
Installation	91
Crankshaft Balancer	**92**
Remove	92
Install	92
Rocker Cover and/or Seal	**92**
Remove	92
Install	93
Timing Chain Cover, Timing Chain And Gears	**93**
Remove	93
Install	95
Cylinder Head, Valves & Camshaft	**96**
Removal	96
Cylinder Head Reconditioning	**98**
Dismantle	98
Clean	98
Inspection	98
Valve Guides	**99**
Clearance Checks	99
Guide Replacement	99
Valve Seats	**99**
Replacing Valve Seat	99
Valve Stem Oil Seals	**100**
Replacement	100
Valve Springs	**100**
Valves	**100**

Subject	Page
Camshaft	**101**
Inspection	101
Assemble Cylinder Head	**101**
Valve Clearance and Shim Selection	102
Cylinder Head Gasket Selection	103
Install Cylinder Head	**103**
Vacuum Pump	**104**
Remove	104
Install	105
Oil Pump / Right Balance Shaft	**105**
Removal	105
Dismantle	105
Inspection	105
Assembly	106
Installation	106
Left Balance Shaft	**106**
Remove	106
Install	106
Flywheel/Drive Plate	**107**
Remove	107
Inspection	107
Install	107
Ring Gear	**107**
Replacement	107
Replacement Techniques	107
Spigot Bearing	**107**
Replacement	107
ENGINE REBUILD	**108**
Engine Assembly	**108**
Removal	108
Dismantle	108
Assembly	108
Oil Pan (Sump)	**109**
Removal	109
Installation	109

2.8 litre DIESEL SOHC (4M40) ENGINE MAINTENANCE & REBUILD

Subject	Page
Oil Pump Suction Pipe, Screen and Baffle	109
Removal	109
Installation	109
Piston and Connecting Rod Assembly	109
Removal	110
Dismantle	110
Inspection	110
Assembly & Installation	111
Piston Rings	112
Installation	112
Connecting Rod Bearings	113
Inspection & Replacement	113
Crankshaft	115
Removal	115
Inspection	115
Installation	116
Main Bearings	117
Inspection and Installation	117
Rear Main Oil Seal	118
Replace	118
Oil Cooler and Element	118
Remove	118
Dismantle	118
Clean and Test	119
Assemble	119
Install	119
Oil Cooler and Element	119
Remove	119
Cylinder Block	119
Inspection	119
Cylinder Reconditioning & Piston Fitting	120

PROBLEM DIAGNOSIS **121**

SPECIFICATIONS **122**

TORQUE WRENCH SPECIFICATIONS .. **123**

GENERAL DESCRIPTION

The 4M40 (2.80L) engine is an in line 4 cylinder SOHC overhead camshaft unit, there is one camshaft mounted in the aluminium cylinder head. 4M40 engines have a 26 bolt main bearing type cradle.

The cylinder block made of cast iron and has a standard bore of 95 mm and stroke of 100 mm, displacement is 2835cc with a compression ratio of 21:1.

The cylinder numbering is as illustrated, from the front of the engine, 1 to 4.

ENGINE SERIAL NUMBER

Engine No. Location: On left-hand side Cylinder Head, the type of engine is cast into the block, above the oil filter.

MAINTENANCE HINTS

1. **a)** When any internal engine parts are serviced, care and cleanliness are important.
   b) An engine is a combination of many machined, honed, polished and lapped surfaces with tolerances that are measured in thousandths of a millimetre.
   c) Friction areas should be coated liberally with engine oil during assembly to protect and lubricate the surfaces on initial operation.
   d) Proper cleaning and protection of machined surfaces and friction areas is part of the repair procedure and is considered standard workshop practice.
2. When valve train components are removed for service, they should be kept in order and should be installed in the same locations (with the same mating surfaces) as when removed.
3. Battery terminals should be disconnected before any major work is begun. If not, damage to wiring harnesses or other electrical components could result.
4. When raising or supporting the engine for any reason, do not use a jack under the oil pan. There are small clearances between the oil pan and the suction pipe screen, jacking may cause the oil pan to be bent against the screen, causing damage to oil suction pipe assembly.

ENGINE MAINTENANCE

* For general maintenance procedures such as oil change and drive belt inspection refer to the "Tune-up & Maintenance Chapter".

Intercooler
Removal
1. Remove the air cleaner assembly, then from the underside of the vehicle remove the skid plate and covers.
2. Remove the radiator shroud, refer to cooling chapter if required.
3. Disconnect the air hoses from the intercooler.
4. Remove intercooler retaining bolts and remove intercooler from vehicle.
5. If required remove the bolts retaining the deflector plate to the intercooler assembly.

Inspection
1. Inspect intercooler fins for damage and foreign material.
2. Inspect intercooler air hoses for cracks, damage or wear, replace if required.

Installation
1. If removed, install the deflector plate to the intercooler assembly and tighten retaining bolts to specification.
   Deflector Plate Bolts.................................. 12 Nm
2. Install intercooler into position and tighten retaining bolts to specification.
   Intercooler Bolts.. 12 Nm
3. Reconnect the intercooler air hoses, tightening clamps to specification.
   Air Hose Clamps .... 6 Nm
   Air Pipe Retaining Bolt .... 9 Nm
4. Install the radiator shroud, refer to cooling chapter if required.
5. Install the air cleaner assembly, then install the skid plate and covers to the underside of the vehicle.

INTAKE and EXHAUST MANIFOLD ASSEMBLIES
Remove
1. Detach the battery earth lead from the battery, then release the lower radiator hose and drain the cooling system.
2. Remove the engine top dress-up cover from the engine, if fitted.
3. Remove the heat shields from exhaust manifold and turbocharger.

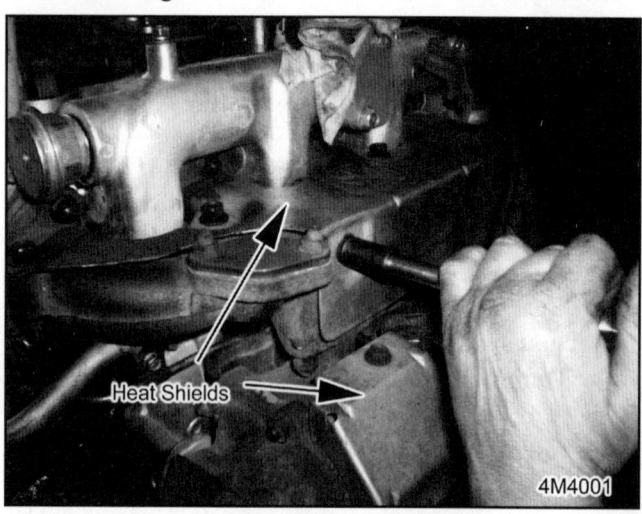

4. a) Remove the intercooler water hoses.
   b) Remove the air tube between the intercooler and air cleaner box.
   c) Remove the intercooler from the engine.
5. a) Remove the air intake tube to the intake manifold body from the turbocharger, remove intake tube.
   b) Remove the air intake tube between the intercooler and turbocharger.
6. Release the accelerator cable from the throttle body assembly.
7. Remove the bolts attaching the exhaust pipe to the turbo-charger.
8. Release the brake booster hose, the vacuum hose and breather hose from the rocker cover.
9. [If fitted] Release the EGR pipe retaining bolts from the intake and the exhaust manifold, then withdraw the EGR pipe from the engine assembly.
10. a) Remove the oil pipe to the turbocharger.
    b) Remove the oil return pipe and hose from the turbocharger.
    c) Disconnect the waste gate hose.
11. Remove the nuts turbocharger, remove turbocharger and gasket, if not removing exhaust manifold and turbo as one unit.
12. Remove the bolts attaching the exhaust manifold, remove exhaust manifold and gasket.

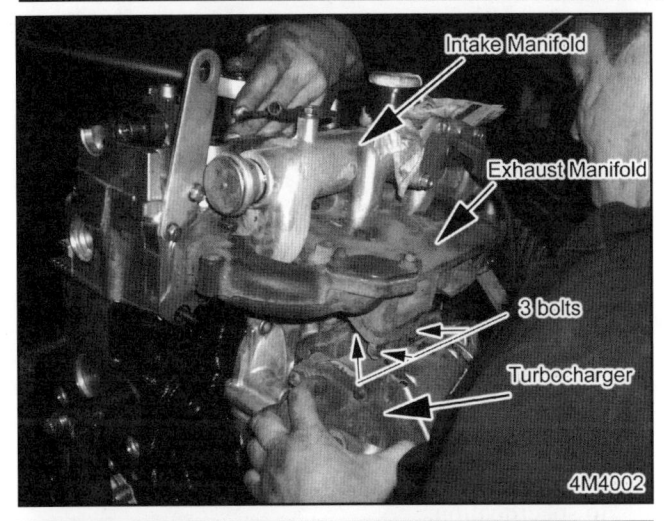

2.8 litre DIESEL SOHC (4M40) ENGINE MAINTENANCE & REBUILD

Intake Manifold Bolts: **21Nm**

3. Install the exhaust manifold with new gaskets, install bolts tighten to specification.

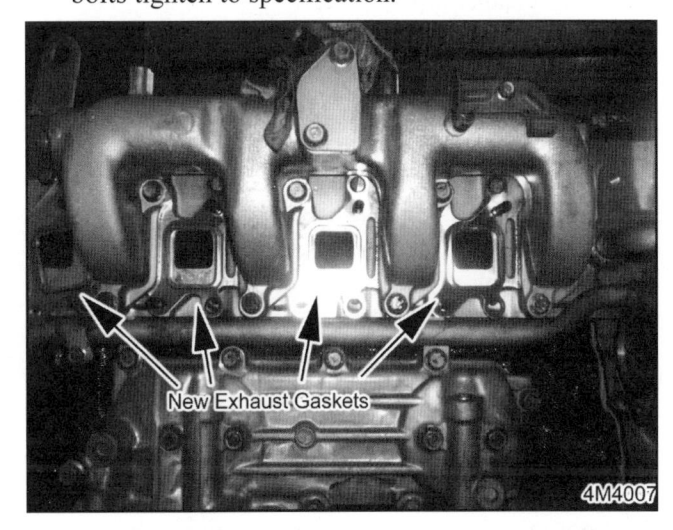

Exhaust Manifold Bolts and Nuts: .... **30 Nm**

4. Install the turbocharger with new gasket, install bolts tighten to specification.
   Turbocharger Nuts: .... **50 Nm**
   Turbocharger Bolts: .... **55 Nm**
5. a) Replace the oil pipe to the turbocharger.
   b) Replace the oil return pipe and hose from the turbocharger.
   c) Connect the waste gate hose.

13. Remove the bolts attaching the intake manifold, remove intake manifold and gasket.

Install

1. a) Clean the intake manifold surface, ensure that all the old gasket is removed from the surface.
   b) Clear the exhaust manifold surface, ensure that all the old gasket is removed from the surface.

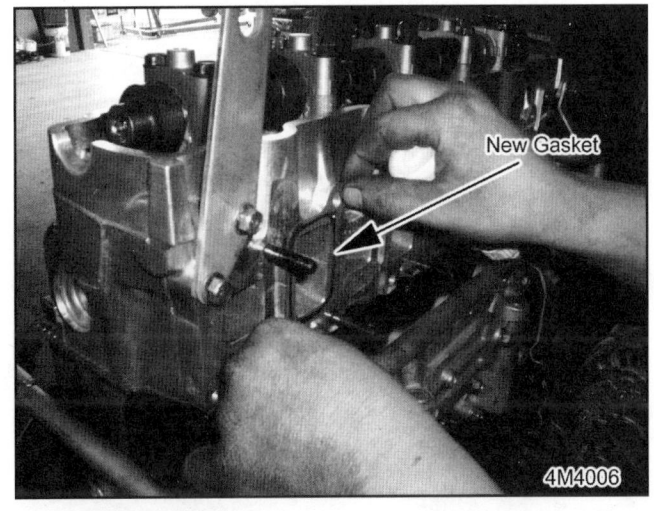

2. Install the intake manifold with new gaskets, install bolts tighten to specification.

91

2.8 litre DIESEL SOHC (4M40) ENGINE MAINTENANCE & REBUILD

6. [If fitted] Install the EGR pipe retaining bolts and fittings to the intake and the exhaust manifolds.
7. Install the exhaust pipe to the turbo-charger, tighten nuts to specification.
   Exhaust Pipe Nuts: .... **49 Nm**
8. Reconnect the brake booster hose, the vacuum hose and breather hose to the rocker cover.
9. Connect the accelerator cable from the throttle body assembly.
10. a) Replace the air intake tube to the intake manifold body from the turbocharger.
    b) Replace the air intake tube between the intercooler and turbocharger.
11. a) Install the intercooler to the engine.
    b) Replace the air tube between the intercooler and air cleaner box.
    c) Replace the intercooler water hoses
12. Install the heat shields from exhaust manifold and turbocharger.
13. Replace the engine top dress-up cover from the engine, if fitted.
14. Connect the battery earth lead from the battery, connect the lower radiator hose and top up the cooling system coolant.

CRANKSHAFT BALANCER
Remove
1. Disconnect battery earth lead, remove drive belts.
2. Pull park brake fully on, chock rear wheel and transmission in gear.
3. Loosen and remove balancer retaining bolt.
4. Remove crankshaft balancer with pulley puller.

Install
1. Using engine oil, lubricate front seal surface of balancer.
2. Install balancer, engaging key on crankshaft with slot in balancer.
3. Install the crankshaft pulley, tap onto crankshaft with a soft head hammer if required, tighten attaching bolt to specification.
4. Install and inspect drive belt operation.

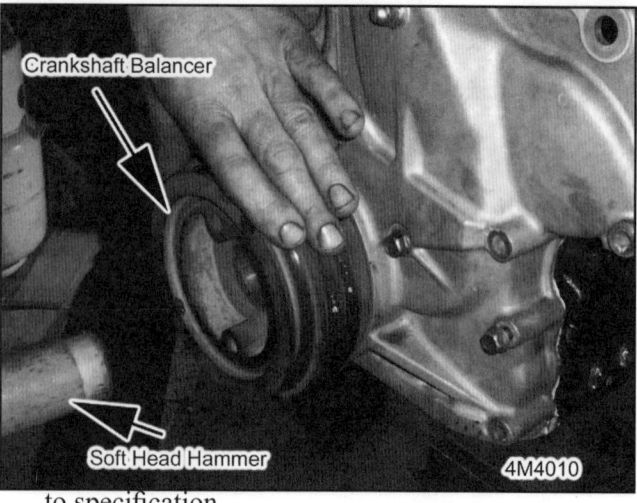

ROCKER COVERS AND/OR SEALS
Remove
1. Remove intercooler as described in this chapter.
2. Disconnect the breather hose between rocker covers and PCV valve from left side rocker cover.
3. Rocker cover.

   a) Unscrew rocker cover to cylinder head fasteners and remove rocker cover from cylinder head.
   b) If replacing rocker cover seal, remove seal from recess in rocker cover.

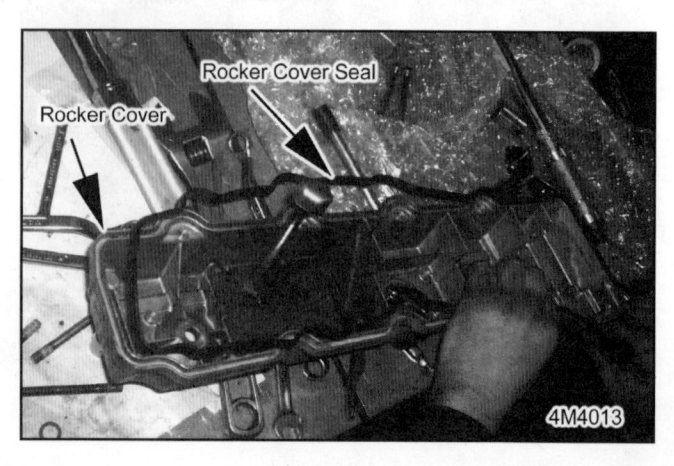

2.8 litre DIESEL SOHC (4M40) ENGINE MAINTENANCE & REBUILD

Install

1. a) If necessary, install seal to rocker cover recess.
   Note: Make sure seal is correctly installed in rocker cover.
   b) Apply sealant to cylinder head on rocker cover contact area, this will help a create a good oil tight seal.

2. Install rocker cover to cylinder head and torque bolts to specification.
   Rocker Cover Bolts:................................. **3.4Nm**

3. Connect the breather hose between rocker covers and PCV valve form left side rocker cover

4. Install the intercooler as previously described.

TIMING CHAIN COVER, TIMING CHAIN and GEARS

Tip: *If you are removing cylinder head, the camshaft gear will rest on to top of the timing chain guide.*

Remove

1. Detach the battery cables, remove the battery shroud.
2. Remove the inter cooler as previously described.
3. Remove the rocker cover as previously described.
4. Detach belts from the alternator, power steering, air conditioner etc.
5. Remove the fan and water pump. 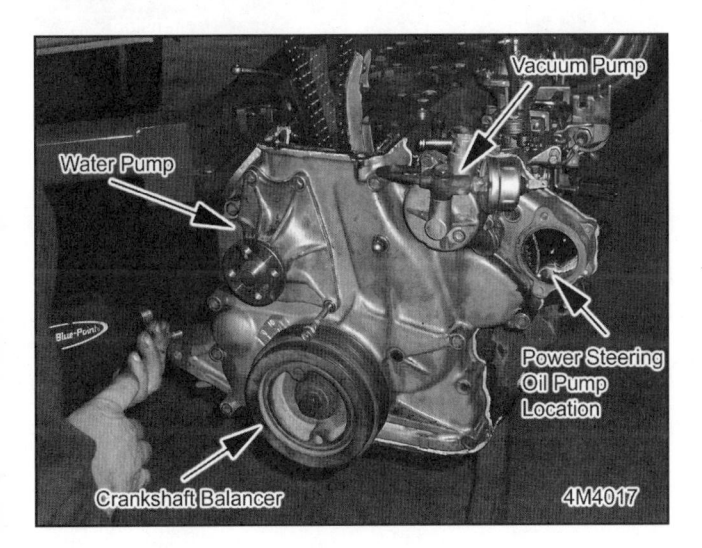
6. Remove the vacuum pump power steering pump. 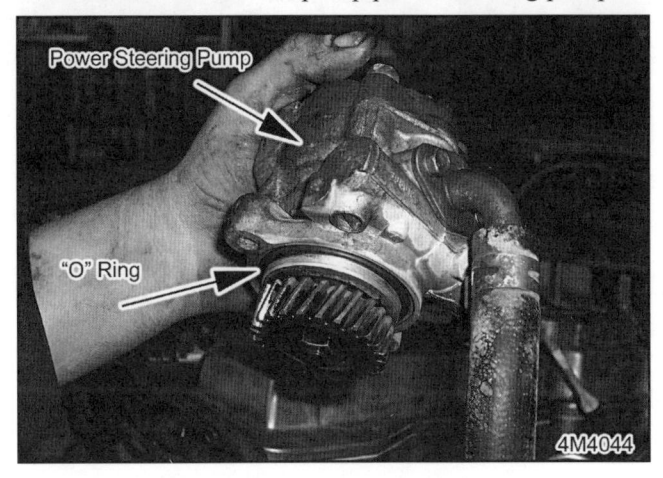
7. Rotate the crankshaft so the crankshaft is at TDC/compression on number 1 cylinder. 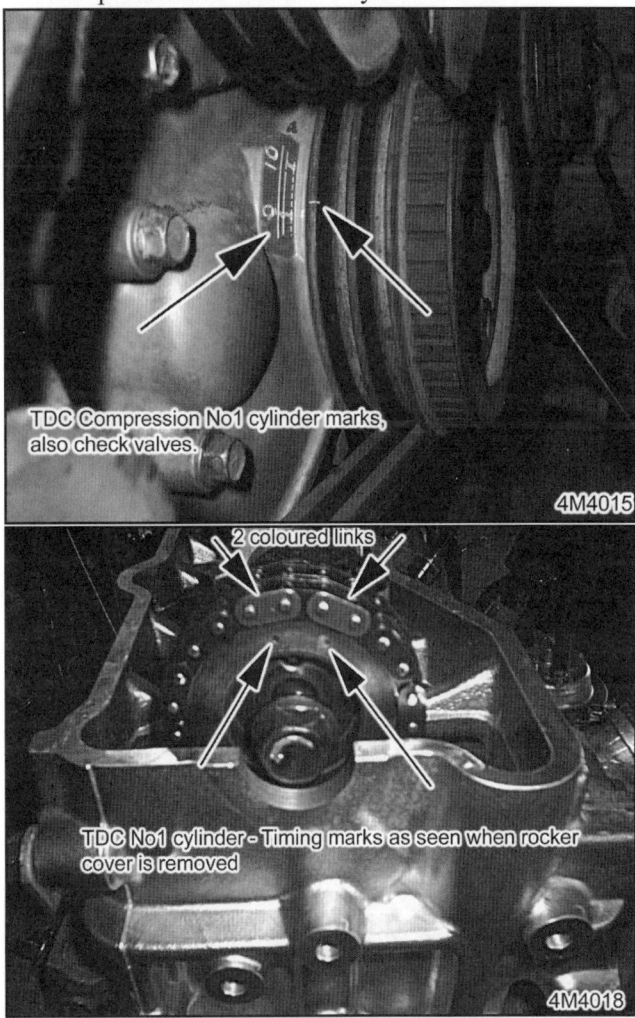
8. Remove the crankshaft pulley.
9. Remove the air conditioner compressor, tie back away from engine to keep pressure off the air conditioner hoses.
10. Remove the air conditioner compressor bracket / adjust / idler pulley.
11. Remove the tensioner cover, loosen the tensioner on the timing chain.

93

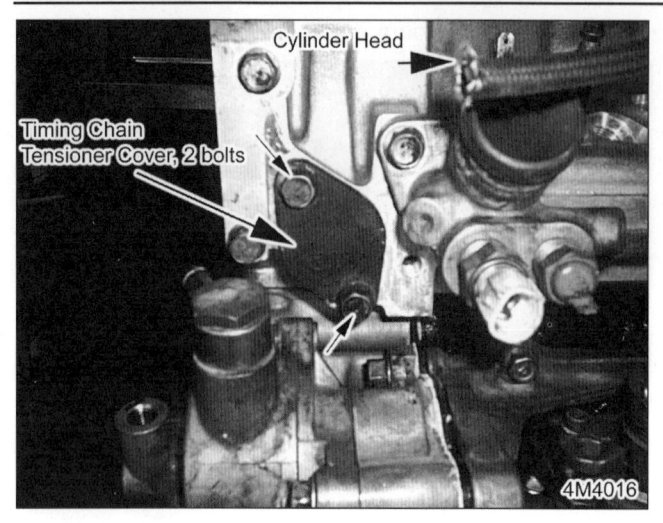

2.8 litre DIESEL SOHC (4M40) ENGINE MAINTENANCE & REBUILD

12. Remove the front timing gear case, bolts and gasket.
13. a) Check that the two alignment marks on the camshaft gear are aligned with the two coloured chain links.
    b) Check that the two alignment marks on the idler gear are either side of the mark on the crankshaft sprocket.
14. Remove the timing chain tensioner cover, relieve the tension on the timing chain. 
15. Loosen the bolt attaching the camshaft gear to the camshaft, hold the camshaft on the hex surface with a spanner.
    Note: The camshaft sprocket bolt is reverse thread.
16. Remove the timing chain tension lever bolt, remove tension lever. 
17. Remove the camshaft gear bolt and gear, plus the timing chain.

18. Remove the timing chain guide, two bolts.

Install

1. Engine at TDC compression number 1 cylinder.
2. Install the chain guides, tighten bolts to specification.
   Timing Chain Guide Bolts: **23Nm**
3. Install timing chain.
   Check that the two alignment marks on the idler gear are either side of the mark on the crankshaft sprocket.
   Place timing chain around idler gear, aligning the timing mark and the coloured link.
   Position the camshaft with the camshaft gear pinj at 12.00 o'clock.
   Hold the camshaft gear, approximately in position to be installed to the camshaft. Install chain onto the camshaft gear, making sure the two alignment marks on the camshaft gear are aligned with the two coloured chain links.
   Fit the camshaft gear onto the camshaft, making sure that all alignment marks and links stay aligned. Install the bolt for the camshaft gear, tighten bolt just more than finger tight, making sure the gear is firmly attached to the camshaft, over the pin.

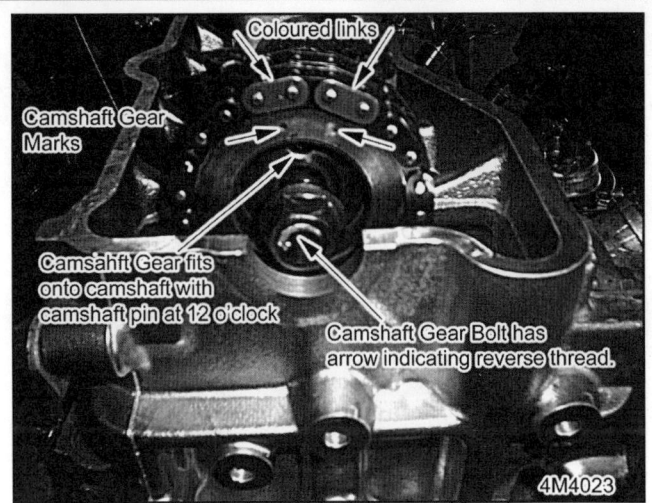

   Tighten camshaft gear bolt to specification.
   Camshaft Gear Bolt: **90Nm**
4. Install the timing chain tensioner, tighten bolt to specification.
   Timing Chain Guide Bolts: **40Nm**
5. Replace the front timing cover oil seal, smear some engine oil on the lips of the seal before installing the timing cover.

6. Apply sealant to the reverse side of the timing cover as indicated

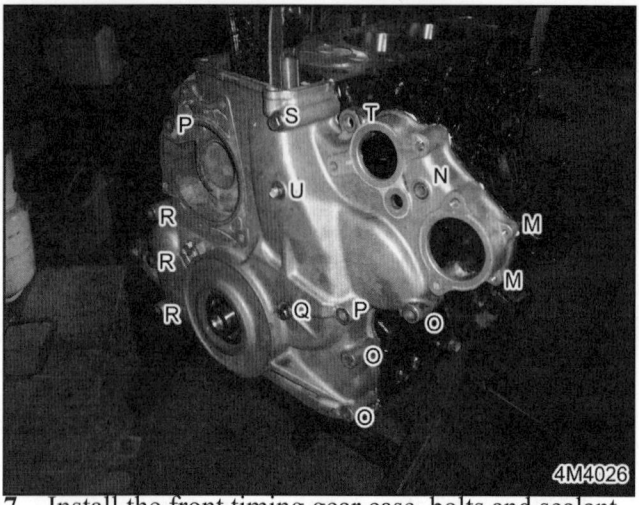

2.8 litre DIESEL SOHC (4M40) ENGINE MAINTENANCE & REBUILD

the chain by a ratchet, if the engine is rotated anti-clockwise it will release the tensioner, then if the engine is started it could damage the camshaft, valves or pistons.

If the engine is rotated anti-clockwise by accident, remove the tensioner and re-install the tensioner correctly to reset it.

11. Install the crankshaft pulley, tighten bolt to specification.
    Crankshaft Pulley Bolt .... 323 Nm
12. Install the two packing blocks at the front and rear of the camshaft. Apply a 2mm bead of sealant all around each packing block.

7. Install the front timing gear case, bolts and sealant. Tighten bolts and nut to specification.

Identification	Bolt / Nut	Torque Nm
M	6 x 16	10
N	8 x 50	23
O	8 x 60	23
P	8 x 75	23
Q	8 x 80	23
R	8 x 85	23
S	8 x 90	23
T	10 x 35	25
U	Nut	23

8. Install the air conditioner compressor bracket / adjust / idler pulley.
9. Install the air conditioner compressor.
10. Tension the timing chain and install the tensioner cover.
    a) Install the (force by hand) plunger into the tensioner.
    Note: The plunger must be installed into tensioner otherwise the tension on the chain will be to great and damage the chain.
    b) Lock the plunger into position with the hook.
    c) Install the tensioner.
    Note: The tensioner automatically keeps tension on

13. Install rocker cover, gasket and bolts.
14. Install the fan and water pump.
15. Install belts for the alternator, power steering, air conditioner etc.
16. Install the inter cooler as previously described.
17. Connect the battery cables, replace the battery shroud.

CYLINDER HEAD, VALVES & CAMSHAFT

*Make sure that all valve train components are kept in order so they can be installed in their original locations.

Remove
1. Disconnect battery earth lead.
2. Remove the inter cooler as previously described.
3. Drain coolant from engine at radiator lower hose and remove top radiator hose.
4. Disconnect glow plug harness connector.
5. Remove alternator.
    a) Remove nuts from alternator adjuster bracket studs and remove engine harness earth wire connection and wiring harness retainer bracket.
    b) Remove alternator, remove alternator support bolts, then remove support assembly.
6. Remove the attaching oil dipstick tub support bolt.
7. Remove the intake and exhaust manifolds as described

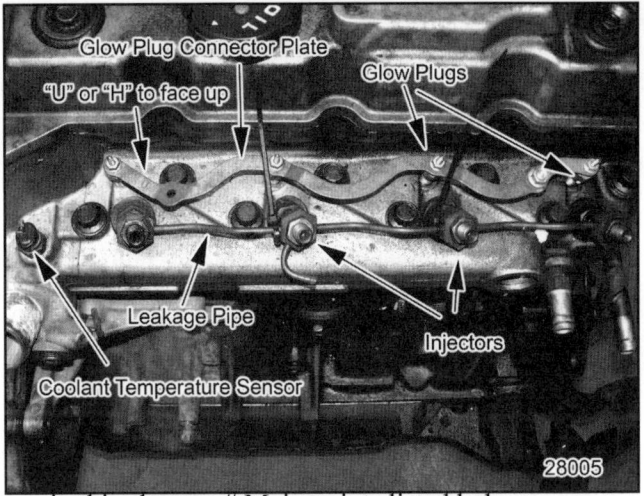

2.8 litre DIESEL SOHC (4M40) ENGINE MAINTENANCE & REBUILD

in this chapter. # Main points listed below.

8. Remove the bolts attaching the exhaust pipe to the turbo-charger.
9. Release the brake booster hose, the vacuum hose and breather hose from the rocker cover.
10. [If fitted] Release the EGR pipe retaining bolts from the intake and the exhaust manifold, then withdraw the EGR pipe from the engine assembly.
11. Remove the fuel injector pipes. 
12. Rotate crankshaft so engine is at TDC compression No1 cylinder, the timing mark of the crankshaft balancer is aligned with the "marker" on the timing chain cover.
    Remove crankshaft balancer bolt, use a pulley remover to remove the pulley, as described in this chapter.
13. Remove the rocker cover as described.
14. Loosen the timing chain tensioner situated on the side of the cylinder head.
15. Loosen and remove the camshaft gear. Tie off timing chain and camshaft gear to the timing chain guide.
    a) Check that the two alignment marks on the camshaft gear are aligned with the two coloured chain links.
    b) Loosen camshaft gear bolt (it has a reverse thread) the arrow on the bolt indicates tightening direction.

Use a shifter or spanner on the camshaft hexagonal section to hold camshaft.

Note: Do not use timing chain to take tension of loosening or tightening camshaft gear bolt.

c) Hold the camshaft gear and chain, while you remove the camshaft gear bolt, ensure the chain does not move on the gear while this happens. Slightly lower the camshaft gear to slacken the chain, use some strong tie wire and tie the chain to the gear. Tie the camshaft gear and chain to the timing chain guide support.

d) Always keep slight tension on chain to make sure it does not jump any teeth on the idler gear.

16. Loosen the cylinder head bolts in the order, working from the front and rear of the engine to the centre of the assembly. Loosen a little each pass until the bolts are loose. Remove cylinder head bolts.

Cylinder Head Bolts									
Loosen									
2		10		18		15		7	
	6		14		20		11		3
	4		12		19		13		5
1		8		16		17		9	
Tighten									
19		11		3		6		14	
	15		7		1		10		18
	17		9		2		8		16
20		13		5		4		12	

17. Lift the cylinder head and gasket from engine block.

Position the camshaft gear and chain so it does not drop behind front timing cover, tie it to the cover.

97

CYLINDER HEAD RECONDITIONING

* Make sure that all valve train components are kept together and identified so that they can be installed in their original locations.

Dismantle

1. Remove the water director located near each combustion tablet
2. Remove the bolts securing the camshaft holders (bearing caps), loosen gradually and in order from the cylinder head ends to the middle. (as shown in this chapter)
   Remove the camshaft.
3. Remove the lifter shims and valve lifters, keeping them in order of removal.
4. Compress valve springs in turn with a suitable spring compressor and remove valve collets.
5. Remove the following:
   a) Valve spring caps, springs, valve spring seats. and valve stem oil seals.
   b) Valves from cylinder head.
   Caution: *Do not force valves out of guides, as mushroomed valve ends due to lifter wear or dirt in the guide, will damage guide. Remove burrs by chamfering valve stem with an oil stone or file.*
6. Remove the glow plugs from the cylinder head.

7. If required remove the combustion tablets.
   a) Heat the cylinder head to allow the cylinder head expansion from the combustion jet, helping removal.
   b) Use a rod inserted through the glow plug hole and tap with a hammer to free the combustion jet.
   Tip: *The combustion chambers are ceramic and will break if hit to hard.*

Clean

1. a) Clean all carbon from combustion chambers, valve ports, etc, with a rotary-type carbon removing wire brush.
   * Do not use a wire brush on any gasket sealing surface.
   b) Clean cylinder head gasket surface of cylinder head.
2. Thoroughly clean valve guides with a suitable cleaning solvent or a wire brush.
3. Clean valve heads with a drill and wire brush.
   * Do not scratch the valve stem.
4. Wash all components in a suitable cleaning solvent and air dry with dry compressed air.

Cylinder Head Inspection

1. Cylinder heads should be inspected for cracks in valve seats and combustion chambers, and for external cracks to water jackets.
2. Check cylinder head deck surface for corrosion.
3. Using a straight edge and feeler gauge, check cylinder head deck, intake and exhaust manifold surfaces for distortion. Check cylinder head deck surface diagonally, longitudinally and transversely.

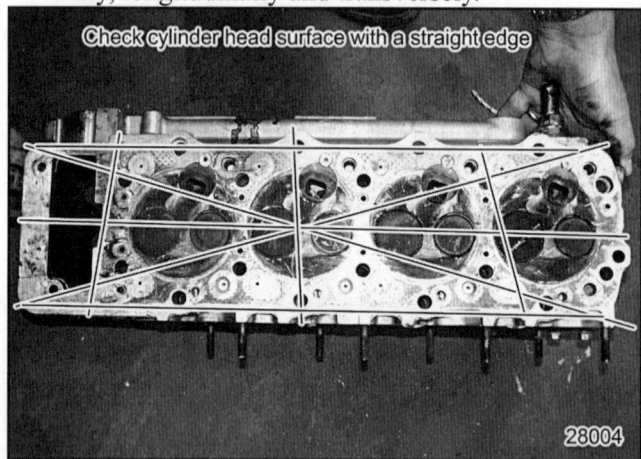

These surfaces may be refaced once only by parallel grinding.
* Head to block surface if more than 0.20 mm must be removed from any surface, replace cylinder head.
4. Inspect the following:
   a) Cylinder head for cracks, especially between valve seats or exhaust ports.

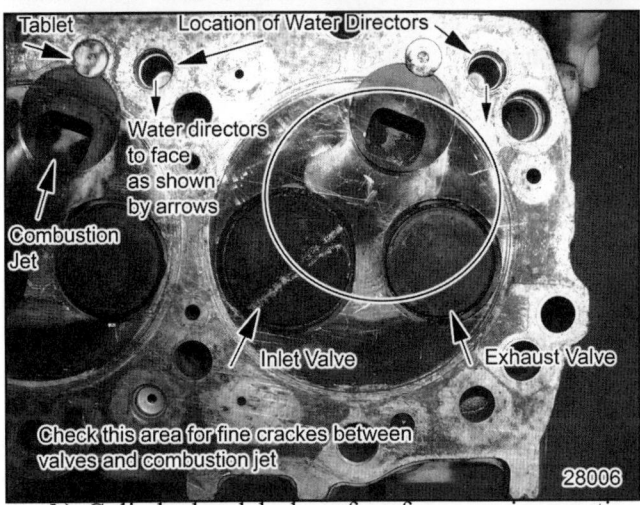

2.8 litre DIESEL SOHC (4M40) ENGINE MAINTENANCE & REBUILD

b) Cylinder head deck surface for corrosion, casting sand inclusions or blow holes.

c) Cylinder block deck surface with a suitable straight edge.

VALVE GUIDES
Clearance Checking

1. Excessive valve stem to guide bore clearance will cause lack of power, rough idling and noisy valve operation.

2. Insufficient clearance will result in noisy and sticking of the valve and will interfere with smoothness of operation of engine.

3. Measure inside diameter with an ID micrometer, also measure the valve stem, then use the following sum to calculate the guide clearance.

   ** Guide diameter - stem diameter = clearance **

   Valve stem to guide clearance
   - Inlet .... 0.03 - 0.05 mm
   - Exhaust .... 0.05 - 0.08 mm

4. If it is necessary to replace the valve guide see valve guide replacement in this chapter.

Valve Guide Replacement

1. Use a hammer and flat end rod to drive the old valve guide down into the port area of the head, at room temperature.

2. Measure guide hole, if over specified ID rebore to fit the over size valve guide.
   Valve guide OD .... 13.06 - 13.018 mm
   - 0.05, 0.25 and 0.50mm Oversize available

3. Valve guides are different length, exhaust valve guide is longer than intake valve guide.

4. Use a press and valve guide installing die to press the new valve guide down into cylinder head, at room temperature.

5. The guide is driven down into the cylinder head until the guide is at specified height from valve spring seat surface.
   Valve Guide Installed Height ..14.00 +/- 0.30 mm

6. Ream bush out with a reamer to obtain specified diameter.

VALVE SEATS

1. Reconditioning the valve seats is very important because the seating of the valves must be perfect for the engine to deliver the power and performance its develops.

2. Another important factor is the cooling of the valve head. Good contact between each valve and its seat in the head is imperative to ensure that the heat in the valve head will be properly carried away.

3. Several different types of equipment are available for reconditioning valve seats. The recommendations of the manufacturer of the equipment being used should be carefully followed to attain proper results.

4. Check valve seats for any evidence of pitting or damage at valve contact surface. If pitting is evident, the valve seats will need to be reconditioned.

   * Because the valve guide serves to support and centre the valve seat grinder, it is essential that the valve guide is serviced before reconditioning the valve seats.

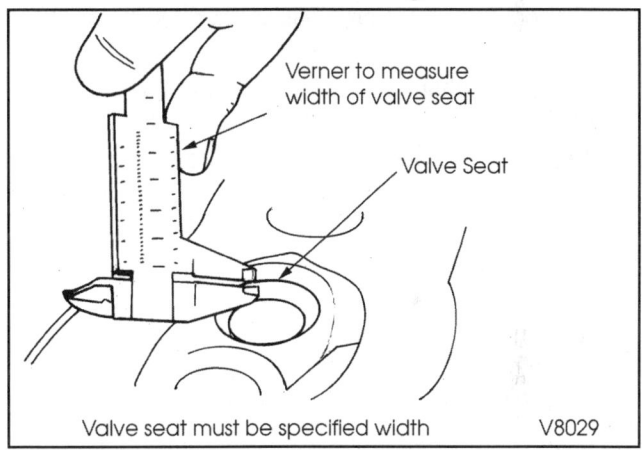

5. If the seat is too wide after grinding, it may be narrowed by using a 30° or 65° grinding stone. The 30° stone will lower the seat and the 65° stone will raise the seat.

6. If the valves seats are reconditioned, the valves must also be reconditioned (refer VALVES) or replace valves as necessary.

REPLACING VALVE SEAT

1. Using a lathe, turn down the out side diameter of a valve head so it fill fit neatly into inside of the valve seat.

2. Cover the head that surrounds the valve seat with an inflammable paste, such as soap paste. This will stop damage from weld spatter.

3. Weld a continuous run of weld around the edge of the valve, so it is welded to the inside of the valve seat.

4. Lift the head so the top of the valve can be tapped to free the valve seat.

5. Slide the machined valve and valve seat out of the head.
6. Machine the head as the new valve seat is over size by 0.38mm diameter and depth.
7. The new valve seat should not to be hit or forced into the head as this will cause damage to the seat and head.
8. Place the new valve seat in liquid nitrogen or dry ice so the seat will shrink in size.
9. Carefully place the valve seat into position with an old valve (converted into a special tool as shown in diagram) positioned through the seat into the valve guide. Gently tap the special tool to position and centre the valve seat

VALVE STEM OIL SEALS
Replacement
1. Disconnect battery earth lead.
2. Remove the following:
   a) Glow plug harness wiring.
   b) Glow plug from relevant cylinder and screw air adaptor into glow plug hole.
   c) Rocker cover as previously described in this chapter.
   d) Timing chain gear as described in this chapter.
   e) Camshaft.
3. Apply air pressure via a special fitting that screws into the glow plug hole, to hold valves in closed position.
4. a) Compress valve spring with valve spring compressor.
   b) Remove valve collets.
      * Before installing valve spring compressor, it may be necessary to tap top of valve cap with a soft-faced hammer to overcome the binding of the valve collets in the valve spring cap.
5. a) Remove spring cap, spring and valve compressor as an assembly.
   b) Remove and discard old valve stem oil seal.
6. Install new valve stem oil seal and make sure the seal fully seats on top of the valve guide.
   * Make sure the correct type of seal is fitted to the appropriate valve, based on part No. and package description.
7. a) Install spring, cap and valve compressor as an assembly on the valve stem.
   b) Install valve collets and slowly release spring compressor, then remove spring compressor.
   c) Disconnect air line to special tool.
8. Install the following:
   a) Camshaft as previously described in this Chapter.
   b) Replace camshaft gear as described in this chapter.
   c) Rocker cover as previously described in this Chapter.
9. Remove special tool and install and torque glow plug.
10. Install glow plug harness and battery earth lead.
11. Start engine and check for oil leaks and valve train noise.

VALVE SPRINGS
1. Inspect valve spring surfaces on valve seat and valve cap for wear or gouging. Replace components as necessary.
2. a) Check spring ends. If they are not parallel, the spring is bent.
   b) Replace valve springs that do not meet specification.
3. a) Check valve spring load with a spring tester.
   b) Springs should be compressed to the specified height and checked against specifications.
   c) Replace any valve spring if not to specification.
   Free length .... 48.8 mm
   Free length Minimum .... 47.8 mm
   d) Measure installed height of valve between spring seat and top of valve.
   Valve Installed Height 38.67mm

VALVES
1. a) Inspect valve stem for burrs and scratches. (Burrs and minor scratching may be removed with an oil stone.)
   b) Valves with excessive stem wear or that are warped should be replaced.
   c) Inspect valve stem tip for wear. The valve tip may be reconditioned by grinding.
   d) Follow the grinder manufacturers instructions. Make sure the new tip surface is at right-angles to the valve stem.

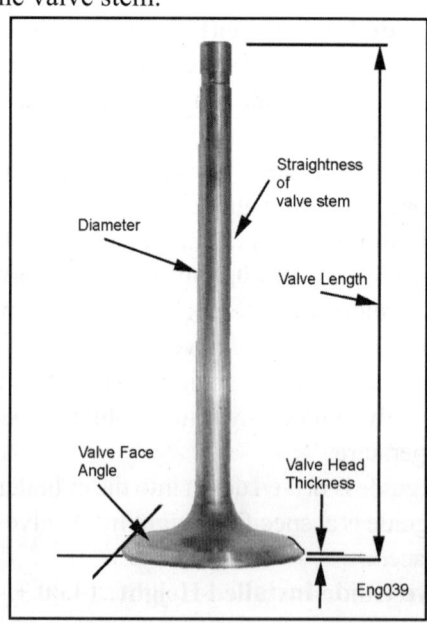

e) Do not grind valve below minimum specified length.
2. Inspect valve stem collet groove for damage.
3. a) Check valve face for burning or cracking.
   b) If pieces have broken off, inspect corresponding piston and cylinder head area for damage.
4. a) Inspect valve stem for straightness and valve head for bending or distortion using 'V' blocks.
   b) Bent or distorted valves must be replaced.
5. Valves with pitted or grooves faces can be reconditioned with a valve refacing machine, ensuring correct relationship between head and stem.
   * If pitting or grooving is so deep that refacing would result in a 'knife' edge at the valve head, the valve must be replaced.
   * Measure valve margin after refacing valves. If margin is less than minimum specified, the valve must be replaced.
6. Lightly lap reconditioned valves into valve seat.
   * New valves must not be lapped. Lapping destroys the protective coating on the valve face.
7. Measure valves for specification.
   Stem diameter - Inlet ....7.96-7.97 mm
                  - Min ....7.85 mm
                  - Exhaust ....7.93-7.95 mm
                  - Min ....7.85 mm
   Valve face angle ....45° - 45.5°
   Valve seat width ....2.0 - 2.8 mm
8. After refacing or installing a new valve, check for correct seating as follows.
   a) Lightly coat valve face with bearing blue.
   b) Insert valve and rotate about 1/6 of a revolution.
   c) Remove valve and check for full contact with seat.
      i) If partial contact is indicated, insert valve again and turn through a full revolution.
      ii) If blue on seat indicates full contact, reface valve.
      iii) If partial contact is still indicated, re-grind cylinder head valve seat.
      iv) Measure calve assembled protrusion from valve spring seat surface for specification.
   d) Clean all traces of bearing blue from valves and seats.

CAMSHAFT
Inspection.
1. Check camshaft bearing journals and lobes for overheating, damage or wear (discolouration).
2. Inspect camshaft journal diameter with micrometer.
3. Position camshaft on 'V' blocks and check the camshaft run-out using a dial gauge.
   Camshaft Run-out ....0.06 mm
4. Inspect the camshaft lobe heights, using a micrometer,

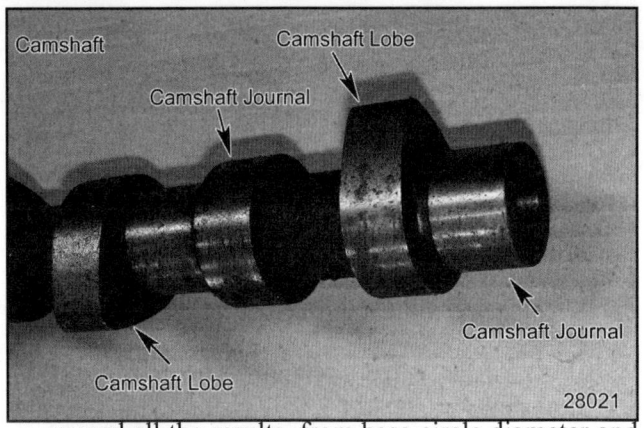

record all the results, from base circle diameter and lobe height.
Height of cam lobe
   - Inlet   2000 model ....9.89 mm
             2001 on ....9.29 mm
   - Exhaust ....10.19 mm

ASSEMBLE CYLINDER HEAD
1. Dry and clean all components thoroughly.
2. Using clean engine oil, lubricate valve stems and valve guides thoroughly.
3. Install valves in corresponding guides.
4. Make sure that seals fully seat on top of guide, install new valve stem oil seals. The original seals may not be the same colour as the replacement seals.
5. Install the valve spring seat over the valve guide onto the cylinder head.
6. Place valve springs and cap over valve stem.

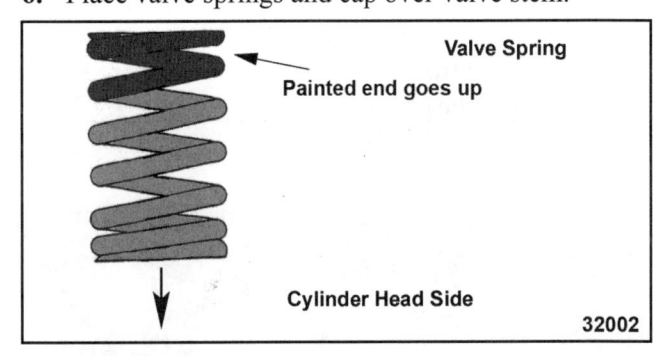

Note: *The pink painted end of valve spring goes to the top.*

7. Using a suitable spring compressor, compress valve springs.
   * Excess compression could cause spring cap to damage valve stem oil seal, ensure to compress valve springs only enough to install valve collets.
8. Install valve collets, making sure that they locate accurately in groove in top end of valve stem. Release the valve spring compressor slowly ensuring that the collets sit properly. Grease may be used to hold collets in place.

2.8 litre DIESEL SOHC (4M40) ENGINE MAINTENANCE & REBUILD

9. Lubricate the valve lifters and install, position the lifter shims on top of the valve lifters.
10. Lubricate the camshaft journals and lobes with molybdenum grease. Position the camshaft onto the head.
11. Lubricate and install the camshaft holders (bearing caps) into place. The camshaft holders have arrows facing to the front of the engine and numbered from the front of the engine.

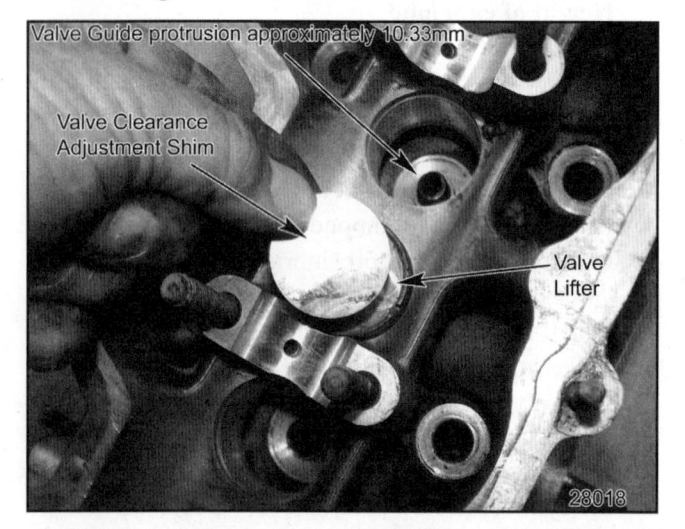

Loosen Camshaft Holder Bolts in order shown:

1	5	9	7	3
2	6	10	8	4

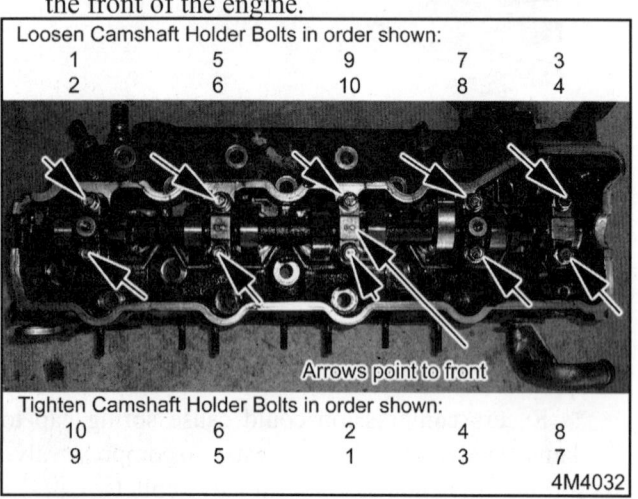

Tighten Camshaft Holder Bolts in order shown:

10	6	2	4	8
9	5	1	3	7

Tighten the camshaft holder bolts to specification in order shown from the middle to the end.
Camshaft Holder Bolts:..............................20 Nm

12. Install the water director, install so the director faces straight across the cylinder head, and to a depth of 5.5mm.

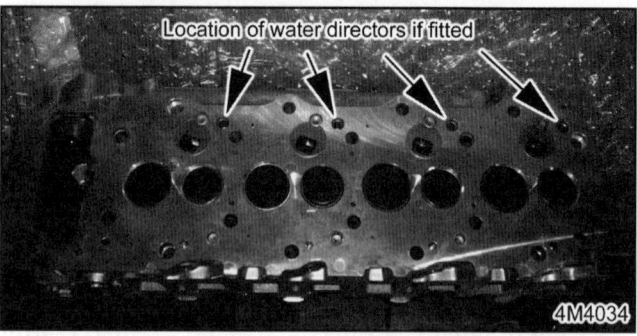

VALVE CLEARANCE - SHIM SELECTION

1. **Timing chain removed** - use a spanner on the hex section of the camshaft to rotate the camshaft so the camshaft lobe base of the circle diameter is on top of the lifter shim you are require to measure clearance.
   Timing chain not removed - rotate the engine with a socket and breaker bar on the crankshaft pulley bolt, rotate engine in a clockwise direction only. Rotate so the camshaft lobe base of the circle diameter is on top of the lifter shim you are require to measure clearance.
2. Use a feeler gauge to measure the clearance between the top of the lifter shim and the base circle diameter of the camshaft.
3. At TDC compression cylinder No1 adjust the valves indicated below.

Cylinder	1	2	3	4
Intake	X	X		
Exhaust	X		X	

At TDC compression cylinder No4 adjust the valves indicated below.

Cylinder	1	2	3	4
Intake			X	X
Exhaust		X		X

4. Check for specification clearance.
   Valve Clearance (Cold)
   Intake .... 0.2 mm
   Exhaust .... 0.3 mm
5. If clearance is not to specification replace the shim

with a shim to give you the correct specified clearance.
6. To replace the shim, use a tool to compress the lifter / valve spring allowing the shim to be removed / installed with a magnetic rod.
7. Install combustion jet to the surface of the cylinder head combustion chamber.
Install the tablet, press tablet down until the surface is below the cylinder head surface.

CYLINDER HEAD GASKET SELECTION

1. Use a dial gauge on top of the cylinder block, rotate the engine so the piston is at the highest position, record the distance of protrusion. This must be carried out and recorded for all pistons.
2. Using the average piston protrusion measurement, use the chart below to select the gasket thickness required.

Note: *If the highest protrusion is more than 0.03mm use the next thickest gasket.*

Piston Protrusion	Head Gasket
Av piston protrusion	Grade & notches
0.475 +/- 0.028 mm	A - 1 notches
0.532 +/- 0.028 mm	B - 2 notches
0.589 +/- 0.028 mm	C - 3 notches
0.646 +/- 0.028 mm	D - 4 notches

INSTALL CYLINDER HEAD

1. Select the correct the correct head gasket grade as described above.
2. Place dowel pins into block, place head gasket in position over dowel pins on cylinder block.

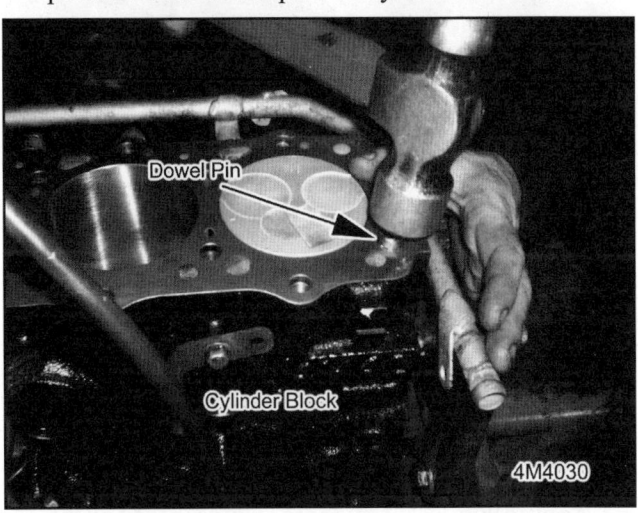

3. Apply sealant at the joining areas of the front timing gear cover the cylinder block.

4. a) Carefully guide cylinder head into place over dowel pins and gasket.
   b) Place cylinder head and tighten with finger, remove dowel pins during this procedure.
   Note: *If the camshaft gear is tied to the timing chain, the cylinder head is lowered over the the camshaft gear and chain while the cylinder head while it is*

103

2.8 litre DIESEL SOHC (4M40) ENGINE MAINTENANCE & REBUILD

being installed. When handling the camshaft gear and timing chain always keep slight tension on chain to make sure it does not jump any teeth on the idler gear.

5. Apply a thin coat of engine to cylinder head bolt thread. Tighten the head bolts to the following sequence and in the order shown.

```
Cylinder Head Bolts
Loosen
 2        10      18      15      7
      6       14      20      11      3
           4      12      19      13      5
 1        8       16      17      9
Tighten
 19       11      3       6       14
     15       7       1       10      18
          17      9       2       8       16
 20       13      5       4       12
```

M12 Bolts - Cold in 5 stages
Cylinder head bolts - Cold - in sequence . 100Nm
Loosen in reverse order
Cylinder head bolts - Cold - in sequence ...50Nm
Rotate .... 90 degrees
Rotate .... 90 degrees
M8 Bolts - Cold in 3 stages
Cylinder head bolts - Cold - in 3 stages 24Nm
* It is important to follow the given procedure to avoid head gasket failure and possible engine damage.

6. Turn the engine over so crankshaft is at TDC/compression on number 1 cylinder.
7. Install new oil seals at the front of the camshafts.
8. Install the water pipe into the head, screw in so it is firm, then turn until it is on the correct angle, however do not tighten over 7Nm.
   Cylinder Head Water Pipe:.........................7Nm
9. Install the camshaft gear and bolt, tightening to specification. If the timing chain is tied to camshaft gear, ensure the chain does not move on the gear.
   Camshaft Gear Bolt (Left hand thread) 90Nm
10. Install the timing chain tensioner, apply sealant to the gasket. See procedure under "Timing Chain Cover, Timing Chain and Gears"
11. Install rocker cover and gasket.
12. The No1. piston should be at TDC as described in point number 5.
13. Install glow plugs and tighten to specification.

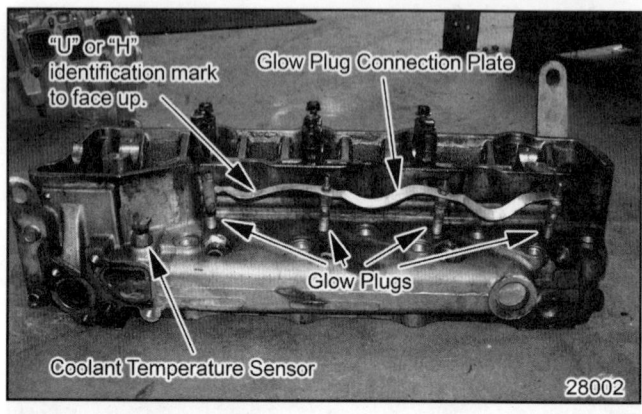

Glow Plug 10Nm
Install connection plate with "U" or "H" facing up.

14. Install the crankshaft pulley, tighten attaching bolt to specification.
    Crankshaft Balancer Pulley bolt 323Nm

VACUUM PUMP
Remove
1. Remove the vacuum hose.
2. Remove the oil pipe and fittings.
3. Remove the oil pressure gauge unit / switch.
4. Remove the vacuum pump bolts, vacuum pump.

Install

1. Clean all matching surfaces of timing cover and vacuum pump thoroughly, .
2. Fit seal and install vacuum pump and bolts. Tighten to specification.
3. Install the oil pressure gauge unit / switch.
4. Install the oil pipe and fittings.
5. Install the vacuum hose.

OIL PUMP / RIGHT BALANCE SHAFT

Remove

1. Remove the front timing cover as described under Timing Chain section. Engine at TDC No 1 cylinder.
2. Check on alignment marks of gears. 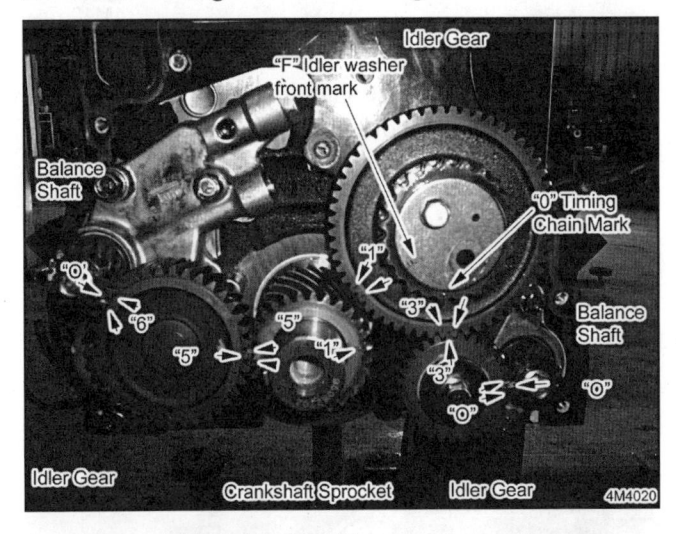
3. Remove the right side idler gear bolt and gear.
4. Remove the right side balance shaft and oil pump assembly, and bolts.

Dismantle

1. Remove the balance shaft gear bolt, washer, balance shaft gear and thrust washer. Remove the balance shaft.
2. Remove the oil pump body cover retaining screws, then remove cover plate.
3. Withdraw the two rotors from the pump body.  
4. Release the relief valve retaining cir-clip from the rear housing body, then withdraw the retainer, spring and piston.

Inspection

1. Wash all parts and dry, lay out parts on a clean bench.
2. Check for damage and wear to the outer race to pump housing.
3. Check for damage and wear to the gear tooth and crest and to pump case.
   Gear tip to Body clearance............0.15 - 0.27mm
   Gear to Pump Cover Clearance.....0.05 - 0.10mm
       Max 0.15mm
   Shaft to oil pump case and cover clearance.........
       ...0.03 - 0.05mm
4. Check the cover surface for damage by gearr and gear clearance (use a straight edge).
   Shaft to oil pump case and cover clearance.........
       ...0.03 - 0.05mm

2.8 litre DIESEL SOHC (4M40) ENGINE MAINTENANCE & REBUILD

If components are to be replaced, replace as a complete unit.

5. Visually inspect relief valve for smoothness of surfaces, check when assembling that the spring will keep the valve closed when the cap is fitted.

Assemble

1. Fit the relief valve piston, spring and retainer into the rear pump body, then secure in place with the cir-clip.
2. Fit the gear and cresent into the pump body.
3. Fit a new gasket to the pump body and install oil pump cover.
4. Install the balance shaft, thrust washer, balance shaft gear, washer and bolt, tighten bolt to specification.
   Balance Shaft Gear Bolt 37Nm

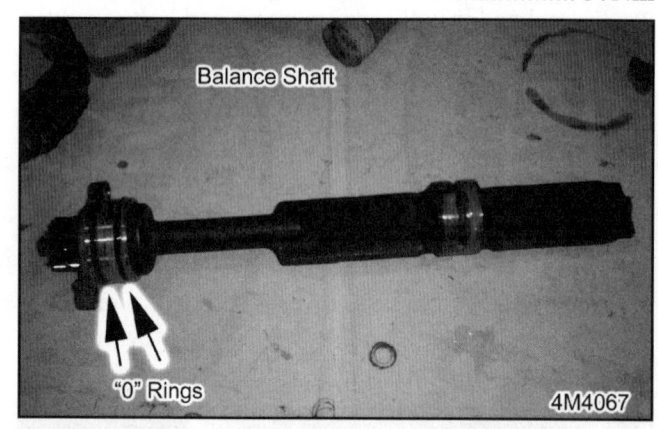

Install

1. Install the oil pump and balance shaft to the engine, position on location pins. Install bolt and tighten.
2. Install the crankshaft key-way and sprocket to the crankshaft.

3. Install the timing chain as previously described in this chapter.

LEFT BALANCE SHAFT

Remove

1. Remove the front timing cover as described under Timing Chain section. Engine at TDC No 1 cylinder.
2. Check on alignment marks of gears. (See earlier illustration)
3. Remove the left side idler gear bolt and gear.
4. Remove the left side balance shaft.

Inspection

1. Wash all parts and dry, lay out parts on a clean bench.
2. Check for damage and wear to the balance shaft bearing journals.

3. Check for damage and wear to the gear teeth.
4. If balance shaft gear has been removed, install the balance shaft thrust washer, balance shaft gear on key, washer and bolt, tighten bolt to specification.
   Balance Shaft Gear Bolt 37Nm

Install

1. Install the left balance shaft to the engine with 2 new "O" rings. Install bolts and tighten.
2. Install the left balance shaft idler gear to the engine. Install bolt and tighten.

3. Install the timing chain cover as previously described in this chapter.

106

FLYWHEEL/DRIVEPLATE

Remove

Before removal of flywheel/driveplate take note of the location of paint aligning marks on flywheel and pressure plate, before removing clutch pressure plate, the driveplate and torque converter also have paint aligning marks. If not visible, scribe aligning marks on all parts.

1. To remove transmission refer to Manual Transmission or Automatic Transmission in this manual.
2. Vehicles with manual transmission:
   Remove the clutch pressure plate and driven plate as per Clutch section in this manual.
3. Block flywheel driveplate from turning, using a screwdriver or suitable locking tool. Remove flywheel/driveplate crankshaft bolts and flywheel/driveplate.

Inspection.

The flywheel and flexplate are purposely out of balance and no attempt should be made to balance these as an individual unit.

1. Check flywheel/driveplate ring gear for badly worn, damaged or cracked teeth.

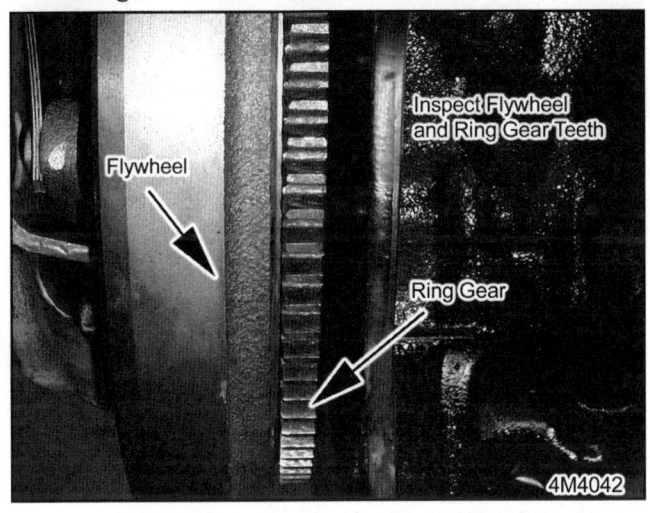

If needed, replace flywheel ring gear or driveplate, for details refer to "ring gear" section in this chapter. Check starter motor pinion gear for damage, if ring gear teeth are damaged replace pinion gear, for details refer to "Starting System chapter".

2. Inspect crankshaft and flywheel/driveplate matching surfaces for burrs. Using a fine mill file remove burrs if present.

Install

1. Install flywheel/driveplate to crankshaft, and tighten bolts to the correct specification.
   Flywheel Bolts 125Nm
   Drive Plate rubber spacer bolts 48Nm
2. Mount a dial indicator on the rear of cylinder block for vehicles with automatic transmission. Inspect flexplate Run-out at the torque converter mounting bolt holes. Run-out should not exceed the following specifications.
   Try to correct by tapping high side with a mallet if Run-out exceeds specification. Replace driveplate if this condition can not be corrected.
3. Inspect starter motor operation.

RING GEAR

Replacement

The ring gear is welded to the driveplate and is serviced only as an assembly for vehicles with automatic transmission. Therefore must be replaced as a complete unit.
For vehicles with manual transmission, the ring gear is a shrink fit on the flywheel flange, and if damaged, can be removed and replaced.

Replacement Techniques

1. To remove flywheel refer to Flywheel/ Driveplate section in this manual for details.
2. To remove ring gear drill a hole between two ring gear teeth and split gear at this point using a chisel.
3. Make sure that there are no foreign matter or burrs on new ring gear and flywheel matching surface. Remove burrs using a fine mill file (if present).
4. Heat and shrink a new gear in place as follows:
   a) Using an emery cloth, polish several spots on ring gear.
   b) Using a hot plate or a slow moving torch, heat ring gear until the polished spots turn blue (approximately 320 degrees Celsius).
      * Heating the ring gear in excess of 427 degrees Celsius will destroy ring gear heat treatment.
   c) Quickly place ring gear in position against shoulder of flywheel using 2 pairs of pliers. Allow ring gear to cool slowly until it contracts and is firmly held in place.
5. To install flywheel refer to Flywheel/Driveplate section in this manual. Tighten bolt to specification.

SPIGOT BEARING

Before removing plate, take note of the position of the paint aligning marks on flywheel and pressure plate. If marks are not visible, scribe aligning marks on both parts.

Replacement

1. To remove transmission refer to Manual Transmission section in this manual for details.
2. To remove clutch pressure plate and driven plate refer to Clutch section in this manual.
3. To remove spigot bearing use a Slide hammer.
4. Use a piloted screwdriver to replace spigot bearing. Place new bearing on pilot of tool with radius in bore of bearing next to shoulder on tool. Drive bearing into crankshaft to the dimension as shown in the diagram.

2.8 litre DIESEL SOHC (4M40) ENGINE MAINTENANCE & REBUILD

Use thin film of SAE 90 Gear Oil to lubricate the bearing.
5. To install clutch assembly and transmission refer to Clutch and Manual Transmission sections in this manual.

ENGINE REBUILD.

ENGINE ASSEMBLY.
Remove
1. Depressurise fuel system remove as described in Fuel chapter and then disconnect the battery.
2. Disconnect battery leads
3. a) Remove bottom radiator hose from the radiator, and drain the cooling system, then remove the top and bottom radiator hoses from the engine.
   b) Remove the fan assembly and radiator as outlined in Cooling chapter.
4. Mark the position of the bonnet hinge brackets on the bonnet, then release and withdraw the bonnet from the vehicle.
5. Remove the air cleaner assembly.
6. Drain engine oil sump.
7. Disconnect the front exhaust pipe, refer to exhaust system chapter.
8. Disconnect the accelerator cable and then disconnect the vacuum hoses including the booster vacuum hose.
9. Disconnect heater hoses.
10. Disconnect the electrical connections for throttle position sensor, ISC servo.
11. Disconnect the connector for the coolant temperature gauge and the coolant temperature sensor.
12. Disconnect main wiring harness from engine and battery harness.
13. Unclip engine harness from the starter, alternator and oil pressure sensor, ensure the wiring harness is labelled.
14. Remove front drive belts, slacken off idler tension.
15. Disconnect the pressure fuel hose and the fuel return hose.
16. Remove the A/C drive belt if not already removed.
17. Remove the power steering pump and A/C compressor, leaving the hoses and pipes connected and position out of the way.
    Note: *Do not allow then to hang, they must be tied up.*
18. Remove the starter motor.
19. Connect an engine crane to the engine and lightly take the weight of the engine. Loosena nd remove the bolts from the engine to the clutch housing. Loosen the engine mount bolts.
20. Raise engine slightly to take weight off mounts by attaching an appropriate lifting hook and chain to engine lifting brackets if fitted. Otherwise care must be taken not to damage engine components with rope or chain while lifting engine.

Support engine with engine crane then release the engine mounts and remove engine from vehicle.
21. Raise engine with front tilted upwards.
    * Do not allow engine to swing backwards or forward and damage any of the components.
22. Separate engine and transmission assemblies if necessary.

Dismantle.
1. Mount engine assembly in an appropriate engine stand.
2. Remove the following parts as previously described or about to be described, in this chapter.
   a) Intake manifold.
   b) Rocker Cover.
   c) Exhaust manifold and turbocharger.
   d) Oil filter.
   e) Vacuum pump.
   f) Crankshaft balancer.
   g) Front timing cover.
   h) Timing chain, camshaft gear.
   i) Camshaft.
   j) Cylinder head
   k) Engine sump.
   l) Oil pump suction pipe and baffle.
   m) Flywheel/flexplate.
   n) Engine rear end plate.
   o) Crankshaft.
   p) Piston and connecting rod assemblies.

Assembly.
Assembly techniques for each part are outlined in this section under there particular headings.
1. Make sure that all bolts and nuts are tightened as specified in this section.
2. Use specified engine lubricant and coolant when refilling.

2.8 litre DIESEL SOHC (4M40) ENGINE MAINTENANCE & REBUILD

3. Inspect transmission fluid level, add lubricant as required.
4. Inspect for fuel, coolant, oil and exhaust leaks. Repair as required.
5. Check engine hood alignment.

OIL PAN (SUMP)
Remove
1. Drain oil from oil pan.
2. Remove the dip stick.
3. Disconnect oil level sensor.
4. Remove oil pan bolts, oil pan and seal, dispose of oil seal.

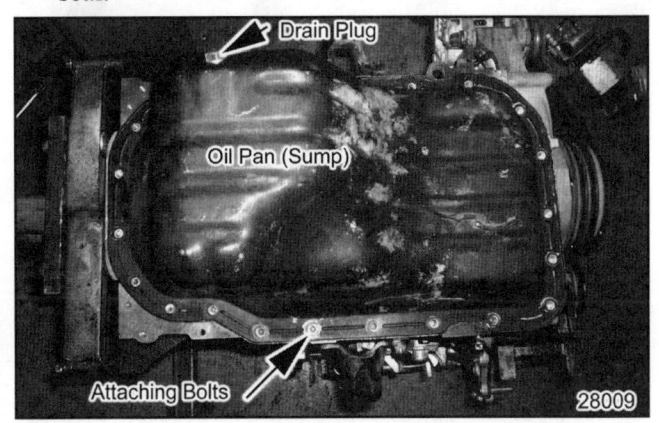

Install
1. Clean all matching surfaces of oil pan and cylinder block thoroughly.
2. Apply sealant to the meeting surface of the front timing cover and engine block.
   Apply 3.5mm bead of sealant to the oil pan surface groove and around the bolt holes.
3. Install oil pan and seal to crankcase, and tighten as specified.
   Oil pan 11Nm
4. Make sure oil pan drain plug is tightened as specified, use a new drain plug seal.
   Oil pan drain plug.................................. 49Nm
5. Replace dip stick.
6. Re-connect oil level sensor.
7. Refill oil pan with the correct amount of engine oil as specified.
8. Start engine and inspect for oil leaks. Repair as required.
9. Stop engine and check oil level on dip stick.

OIL PUMP SUCTION PIPE AND BAFFLE
Remove
1. Withdraw the oil pan from the engine as previously described in this chapter.
2. Release the suction pipe retaining bolts from the engine.
3. Remove the suction pipe, the suction pipe "O ring" from the engine, dispose of the gasket.

Install
1. Fit a new suction pipe "O ring" to the engine, then fit the suction pipe into place.
2. Fit the suction pipe retaining bolts, then tension the nuts to specifications.
   Oil suction pipe and screen 11Nm
3. Fit the oil pan to the engine.

PISTON AND CONNECTING ROD ASSEMBLY.
If the cylinder bore requires machining, remove piston and connecting rod, replace pistons and rings in oversize sets.

Both piston and cylinder bore condition must be considered together when fitting new pistons. Production and service pistons have the same nominal weight and can be

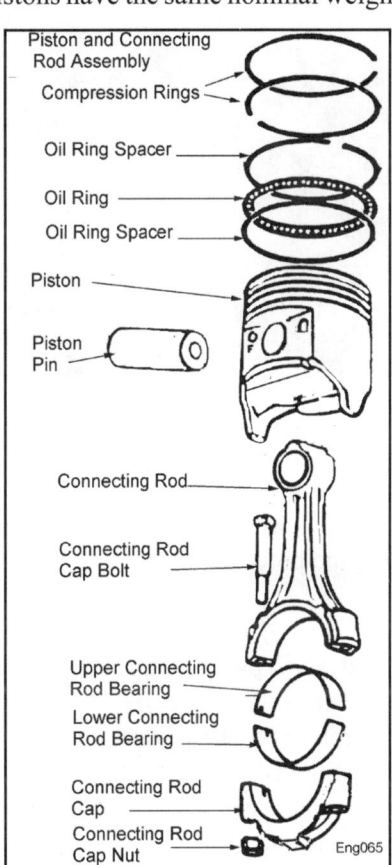

109

intermixed without affecting engine balance. If needed, used pistons may be fitted selectively to any cylinder of the engine, providing they are in good condition.

Piston pin assemblies and ring sets are available in oversize.

Remove

1. Remove cylinder heads as described in Cylinder Head section.
2. To remove oil pan (sump), oil suction pipe and screen.
3. Remove the main bearing cradle as described in this chapter.
4. Inspect cylinder bores above piston ring travel. If bores are worn so that a ridge or similar exists. Turn crankshaft so that piston is at bottom of stroke and cover piston with a cloth to collect cuttings. Remove the ridge with a ridge remover, this is to be done for each cylinder.
5. Use a stamp and hammer or etching marker, mark all connecting rods, caps to indicate cylinder identification.
6. Remove rod assemblies and piston as follows,
   a) With connecting rod crankshaft journal straight down (Bottom Dead Centre), remove connecting rod cap bolts and remove cap with bearing shell.

   b) Push piston and connecting rod from cylinder using a long guide. Remove guides and install cap and bolts to connecting rod.
7. Remove all other piston and connecting rod assemblies using the same procedure.

Dismantle.

1. Expand and slide piston rings off to remove and dispose of them.
   Worn rings may have sharp edges ensure to take care when removing piston rings.
2. Piston pin can now be removed as follows:
   Remove the cir-clip.

Press piston pin from piston with a mandrel and press, until piston pin free. Heat the piston over a heater or with boiling water, will help remove the pin.

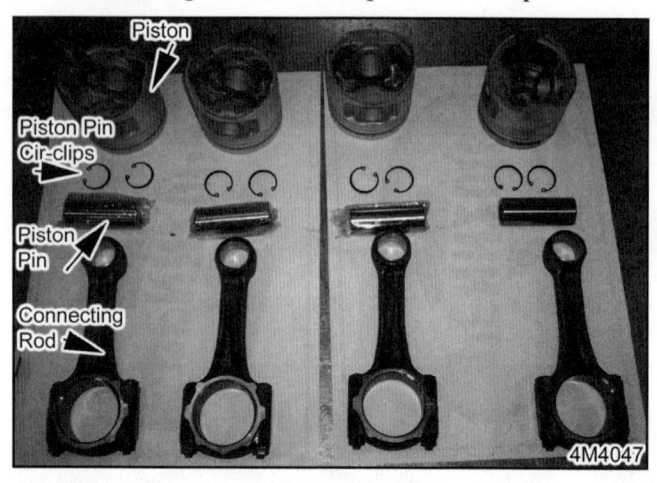

Inspection.

1. Thoroughly clean carbon from piston heads and from ring grooves using a suitable tool and remove any gum or varnish from piston skirts using a suitable cleaning solvent.
2. Check cylinder walls for ridges, roughness or scoring which indicates excessive wear. Inspect cylinder bores for taper and out-of-round using an accurate cylinder gauge at top, middle and bottom of bore, both parallel and at right angles to centre line of engine. Refer to Cylinder Block section for details.
3. Examine piston skirt thoroughly for scored or rough surfaces, cracks in skirt or crown, chipping, broken ring lands or uneven wear which would cause rings to seat improperly or have excessive clearance in ring grooves. Pistons should be replaced if faulty or damaged.

Pistons are cam ground, which means that the diameter at right angles to the piston pin is greater than the diameter parallel to the piston pin. When a piston is checked for size, it must be done at points 90° to the piston bore.

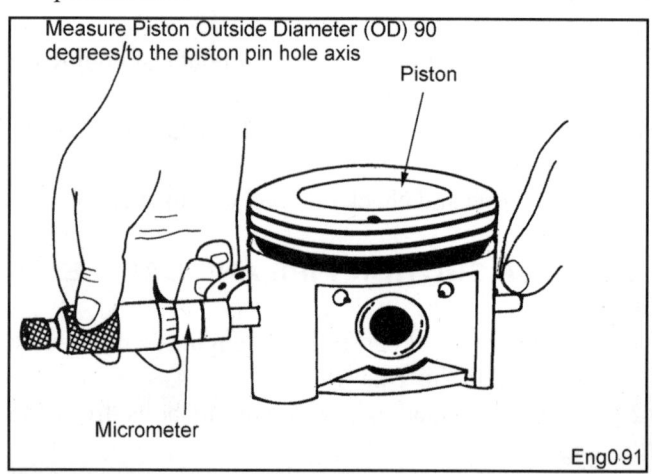

Piston diameter ....94.95 - 94.97 mm
Piston diameter (Turbo) ....94.92 - 94.97 mm
Piston to bore clearance ....0.04 - 0.05 mm
Piston to bore clearance (Turbo) ..0.07 - 0.08 mm
Piston oversizes .....0.50 mm, 0.75 mm, 1.00 mm

4. Check piston pin bores and piston pins for wear. Piston pins and piston pin bores must be free of scuffing or varnish when being measured. Use a micrometer to measure the piston pin, and a dial bore gauge or an inside micrometer to measure piston pin bore.
Piston pin to Piston Clearance.....0.007-0.021mm
Piston and pin should be replaced if not as specified.
5. Remove bearing shells from connecting rod, install cap and bolts. Tighten nuts as specified.
Connecting Rod Cap Bolt: 50Nm
6. Place connecting rod assembly on a checking fixture and inspect rod for twist or bend.
Replace if twisted or bent, do not attempt to straighten rod.
Inspect new connecting rods using the same procedure before using them.
Connecting rod   - bend..........................0.05 mm
                          - twist............................0.05 mm
7. Check outside of connecting rod bearing shells and internal diameter of connecting rod big end for wear indicating high spots in the rod big end.
8. Remove cap bolts and inspect bolts for stretching by comparing them with a new bolt, if stretched, replace.

Assembly and Installation.
1. Using engine oil, lubricate piston pin and piston pin bore.
2. Install piston pin on mandrel. Heat the piston over a heater or with boiling water, will help remove the pin.
3. Assemble installer guide and piston support to base.
4. Install piston and connecting rod over guide.

Note: The front mark on the piston must be facing up so pin is pressed in from piston front mark side.
5. Press piston pin into place with a mandrel, until piston pin bottoms.
Heat the piston over a heater or with boiling water, will help remove the pin.
Install cir-clip.
6. To install piston rings refer to Piston Rings section.
7. Make sure connecting rod bearing shells, pistons, cylinder bores and crankshaft journals are totally clean, then, using clean engine oil, coat cylinder bores and all bearing surfaces.

8. Position the crankpin straight down before installation of a piston and rod assembly in its bore.
9. Remove cap, and with bearing upper shell seated in connecting rod, install the 'short' guide tool into inner bolt hole. Install 'long' guide tool into the other bolt hole.
Guides hold upper bearing shell in place and protects crankshaft journal from damage during installation of connecting rod and piston assembly.
10. Make sure piston ring gaps are separated as described in Piston Rings section.
11. Using clean engine oil, lubricate piston and rings. With a suitable ring compressor, compress rings. Install each piston and connecting rod assembly into its cylinder bore.

111

12. Lightly tap piston into its bore, using a hammer handle, while holding ring compressor firmly against cylinder block until all piston rings have entered bore.

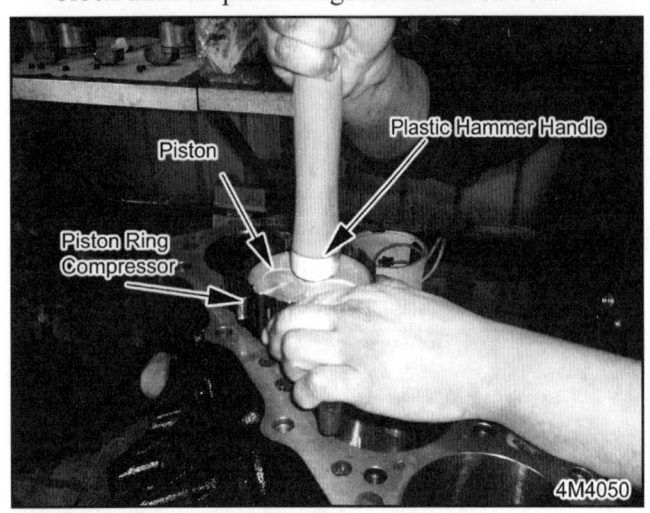

13. Push piston down bore until connecting rod seats against crankshaft journal.
14. Remove connecting rod guides. Install bearing cap and lower bearing shell assembly. Install cap bolts and tighten and then loosen one full turn. Then tighten again as specified.

    Connecting Rod Cap Bolt - 4 steps:
    Step 1 .... 30Nm
    Step 2 .... 50Nm
    Step 3 .... rotate a further 45 degrees
    Step 4 .... rotate a further 45 degrees

15. Turn crankshaft to make sure crankshaft and connecting rod can move freely. If crankshaft binds, check bearing cap to rod orientation again and bearing clearance or connecting rod alignment.
16. Measure side clearance between crankshaft journal and connecting rod.
    If side clearance is not as specified, to check bearing clearance refer to Connecting Rod Bearing section, or connecting rod alignment.

    Connecting Rod bearing clearance 0.03- 0.05 mm
    - service limit (main/big end) .... 0.1 mm
17. Install remaining piston and connecting rod assemblies using the same procedure.

PISTON RINGS.
Install

* *The pistons have three rings (two compression rings and one oil ring). The top ring is a molybdenum filled, balanced section, barrel lapped type. The second ring is an inverted torsional taper faced type. The oil ring is of three piece design, comprising two segments and a spacer.*

1. Using a set of rings comparable in size to the piston being used install compression ring in relevant cylinder bore, then using the head of a piston, press ring down into the bore.

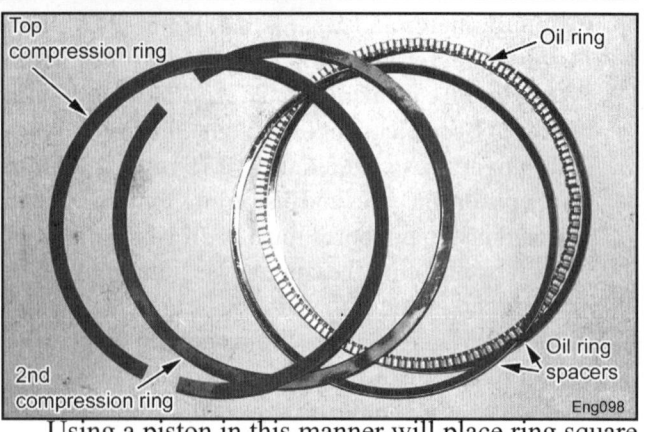

Using a piston in this manner will place ring square with cylinder wall.
Ensure not to distort the ring during this operation, or it may bind in the piston ring groove. Fit each ring separately to the cylinder in which it is going to be installed.

2. Using a feeler gauge, measure gap between ends of ring.

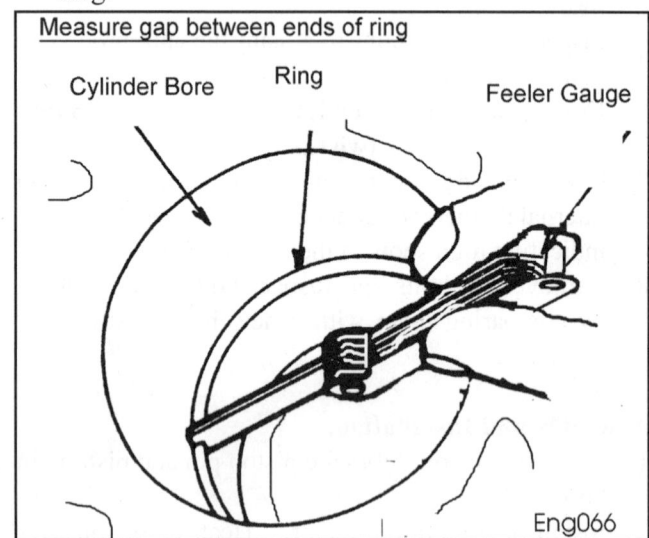

Ring gap	- New
	- Compression .... 0.30 - 0.45 mm
	- Max .... 0.80 mm
2000 model	- Scraper .... 0.30 - 0.45 mm
	- Max .... 0.80 mm
2001 on	- Scraper .... 0.40 - 0.55 mm
	- Max .... 0.80 mm

Remove ring and try another, if the gap between the ends of a compression ring is below specification. The ring gap may be enlarged by filing.

3. Inspect gap between ends of each oil control ring segment.

    Oil Ring Steel Rail Gap Specification:
    - Oil ring - None Turbo .... 0.30 - 0.50 mm
    - Max .... 0.80 mm
    - Oil ring - Turbo .... 0.25 - 0.45 mm
    - Max .... 0.80 mm

4. Carefully remove all traces of carbon from ring grooves in piston and check grooves for any chips or burrs that might cause ring to bind when fitting.
5. Slip outer surface of each compression ring in respective piston ring groove and roll ring entirely around groove to ensure that ring is free. Also measure ring to piston groove side clearance.

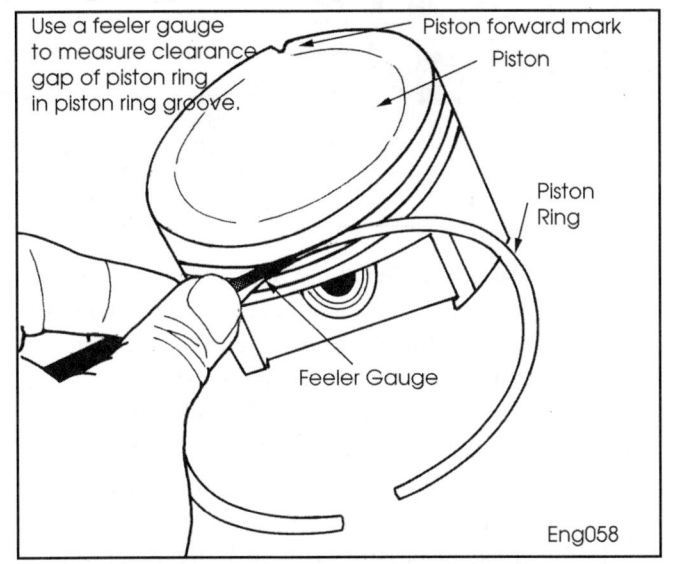

Use a feeler gauge to measure clearance gap of piston ring in piston ring groove.

Eng058

Side clearance
Compression - None Turbo .. 0.06 - 0.11 mm
- Max .... 0.15 mm
Compression - Turbo .... 0.03 - 0.08 mm
- Max .... 0.15 mm
Scraper - None Turbo .... 0.05 - 0.08 mm
- Max .... 0.15 mm
Scraper - Turbo .... 0.07 - 0.10 mm
- Max .... 0.15 mm
Oil Ring .... 0.03 - 0.06 mm
- Max .... 0.15 mm

Try another ring if it is too tight. If no ring can be found that fits the specification, the ring may be ground to size using emery paper placed on a piece of glass. If using a new piston, try another piston.

* High spots in the ring groove may be cleaned up with careful use of a fine file, do not try to cut the piston ring groove.

6. Install oil ring spacer in bottom piston ring groove. The ends of the spacer butt against each other.
7. Install one steel segment from top of piston downward into oil ring groove and install remaining steel segment from bottom of piston skirt upwards into the oil ring groove.
8. Install compression rings in first and second grooves of each piston.
Make sure the correct compression ring are installed in the first and second grooves, and the correct way up.
9. Do a final test of ring fit in piston grooves. Separate ends as illustrated.

* Do not install piston with ring gaps in line, as this will allow compression leakage at this point.

CONNECTING ROD BEARINGS

Each connecting rod bearing consists of 2 bearing halves or shells which are interchangeable in the rod and cap. When the shells are in place, the ends extend slightly beyond the parting surfaces of the rod and cap. When the rod bolts are tightened, the shells are tightly clamped in place to ensure positive seating and to prevent rotation. The connecting rod bearings are of the precision insert type and do not use shims for adjustment. The ends of the bearing shells must never be filed flush with parting surface of rod or cap.

Inspection and Replacement.
Connecting rod bearings can be replaced without removing the rod and piston assembly from the engine.
1. Remove the main bearing cradle as described in this chapter.
2. Use a stamp and hammer or etching marker, mark all connecting rods, caps to indicate cylinder identification.

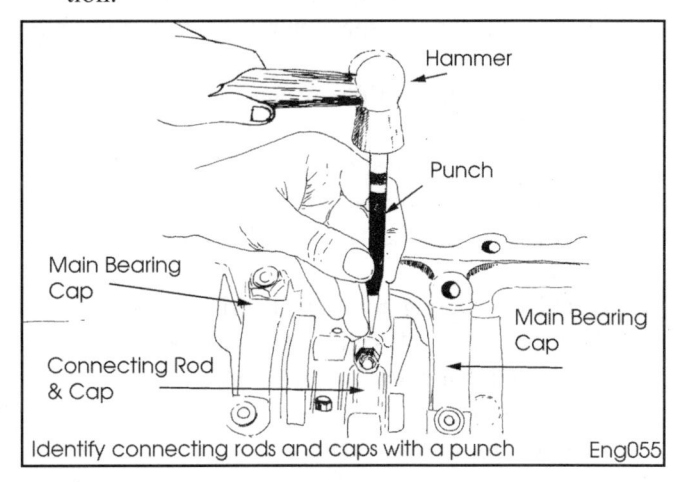

Identify connecting rods and caps with a punch

Eng055

3. Remove connecting rod cap securing nuts and remove cap and lower bearing shell.
4. Push piston and connecting rod up cylinder bore, so that connecting rod is free from crankshaft journal. Remove bearing shell from connecting rod.
5. Clean crankshaft journal and measure for out of round or taper using a micrometer. Replace crankshaft, if not as specified in CRANKSHAFT section.
Crankshaft Connecting Rod Bearing Journal Diameter
6. Wipe oil from both inner and outer surfaces of bearing shells.
7. Inspect inner surface of bearing shells for gouges, wear or embedded foreign matter.
If foreign matter is found, determine its nature and source.

Inspect outer surface of bearing shell for surface wear (indicates movement of shell or high spot in surrounding material), looseness or turning (flattened tangs and wear grooves), or overheating (discolouration).

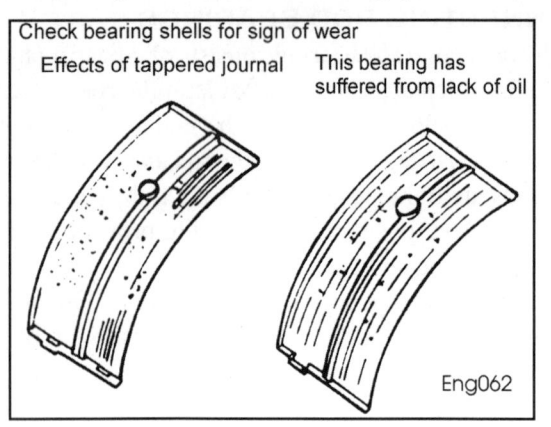

The crankshaft may be bent or have tapered bearing journals if uneven side to side wear is found. If needed, remove crankshaft, refer to CRANKSHAFT section and inspect crankshaft for bend or journal taper.
* Bearing failure, other than normal wear, must be examined carefully.
8. Install bearing shells in original positions in connecting rod and cap if inspection reveals that crankshaft is OK.
9. Pull connecting rod down onto crankshaft so that upper bearing is seated against crankshaft journal.
10. Place a piece of plastigage across width of bearing journal, parallel to crankshaft centre line.
* Make sure plastigage is not placed across oil hole in journal.
11. Install connecting rod cap in original position as described in step 4. Tighten bolts as specified.
Make sure that crankshaft does not rotate with plastigage installed.
Connecting Rod Cap Bolt: 50Nm
12. Remove connecting rod cap bolts, and cap. Inspect for flattened plastigage sticking to either crankshaft or bearing shell in cap.
13. Determine bearing clearance by comparing width of flattened plastigage at widest point with graduation on plastigage envelope. The number within the graduation on the envelope indicates the clearance.
Clearance between connecting rod bearings and crankshaft should not exceed specification.
If a bearing is being fitted to an out of round journal, ensure to fit plastigage to the maximum diameter of the journal. If the bearing is fitted to the minimum diameter, and the journal is out of round 0.008mm, interference between the bearing and journal will result in rapid bearing failure.

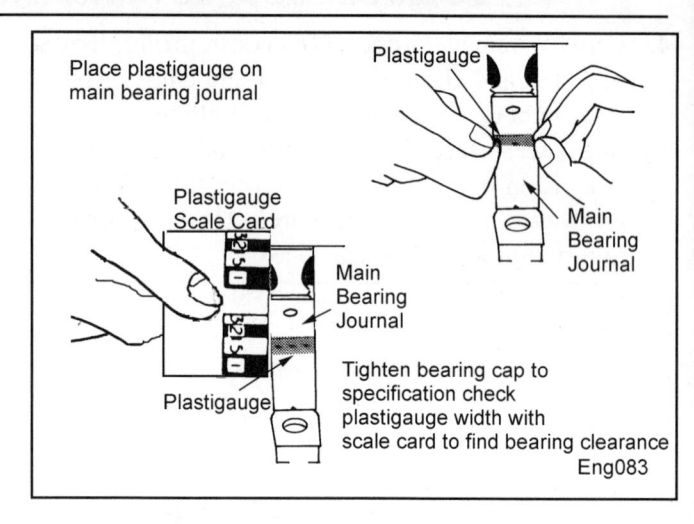

Connecting Rod Bearing Clearance:
.... 0.03 - 0.05 mm
- service limit (main/big end) .... 0.1 mm
Connecting rod bearing undersizes:
.... 0.25, 0.50 and 0.75 mm

14. Make sure that connecting rod cap bolt threads and connecting rod threads are clean and dry. Apply some engine oil to the cap bolt threads.
Before final installation of cap bolts, determine if bolts have stretched by comparing with a new bolt. Replace bolt/s as needed.
15. Install bearing shells in connecting rod and cap making sure notches in shells match up with recesses in connecting rod and cap.
Inspect clearance of new bearing with plastigage as previously described.
16. Remove all remains of plastigage after measuring. Using clean engine oil lubricate bearing shells and journal. Install connecting rod cap in original position, tighten bolts as specified.

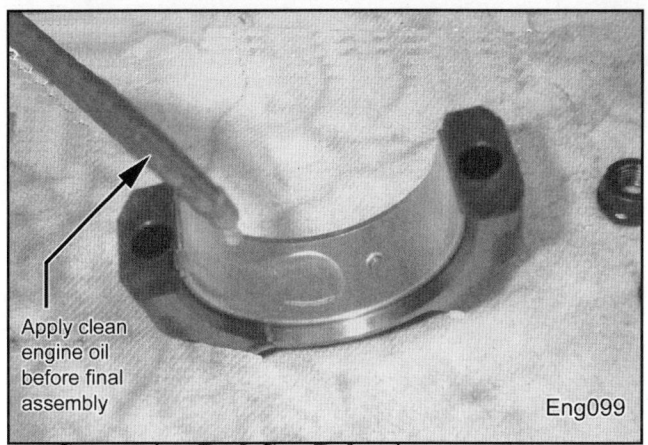

2.8 litre DIESEL SOHC (4M40) ENGINE MAINTENANCE & REBUILD

Apply clean engine oil before final assembly

Connecting Rod Cap Bolt - 4 steps:
Step 1 .... 30Nm
Step 2 .... 50Nm
Step 3 .... rotate a further 45 degrees
Step 4 .... rotate a further 45 degrees

17. With bearing shells installed and cap bolts tightened, it should be possible to move connecting rod backwards and forwards on crankshaft journal as allowed by end clearance. Also, the crankshaft should turn without binding.

Connecting Rod to crankshaft end clearance:
.... 0.15 - 0.45 mm
- service limit .... 0.6 mm

If connecting rod binds on crankshaft journal, loosen and tighten bearing cap bolts.

If rod still cannot be moved or crankshaft binds, inspect bearing cap to rod orientation, bearing clearance or connecting rod alignment.

CRANKSHAFT.

The crankshaft is held into position by a main bearing cradle / lower cylinder bock section with 26 bolts.

Remove

To check bearing clearance before removing crankshaft from crankcase as described.

1. When engine is removed from vehicle and mounted in a suitable stand and remove oil pan.
2. Remove flywheel/driveplate and engine end plate, rear seal retainer.
3. Remove oil pump suction pipe and screen.
4. Remove crankshaft sprocket.
5. Use a stamp and hammer or etching marker, mark all connecting rods, caps to indicate cylinder identification.
6. Remove connecting rod caps and bolts and push connecting rods away from crankshaft.
7. Remove main bearing caps / cradle bolts in order as shown and remove cradle.
    a) Loosen bolts (a little at a time) 1 to 16 in the order shown.

Loosen Bolts as described in text - in the order shown

b) Loosen bolts (a little at a time) 17 to 26 in the order shown.
Use a soft faced hammer tap the cradle to break cradle to crankcase seal.

8. Lift crankshaft from cylinder block.
9. Remove key from front end of crankshaft, if needed, using a suitable punch and hammer.

Inspection.

1. Using a suitable cleaning solvent, wash crankshaft and dry with compressed air.
2. Check crankshaft oil passages for obstructions.
3. Check all bearing journals and thrust surfaces for: Gouges, overheating (discolouration), cracks, grooving chips or roughness
   The crankshaft must be machined or replaced if it has any burned spots, cracks or sever gouging. Slight roughness may be removed using a fine polishing cloth soaked in clean engine oil. Burrs may also be removed using a fine oil stone.
4. Check connecting rod and main bearing shells for embedded foreign material and determine its source.
5. Using a micrometer measure bearing journals for taper, excessive wear or out-of-round.

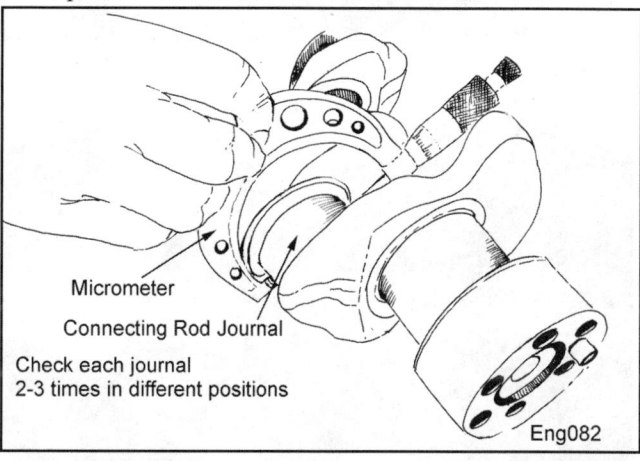

Micrometer / Connecting Rod Journal / Check each journal 2-3 times in different positions

Main bearing journals diameter .... 68.0 mm
End float controlled by .... No.3 bearing

115

Connecting Rod journal diameter.......... 54.0 mm
- max. allowable ovality................. 0.01 mm
- max. allowable taper .... 0.006 mm
Main bearing clearance 1,2,4&5...0.04 - 0.06 mm
- service limit .... 0.1 mm
Main bearing clearance brg 3 .... 0.06 - 0.08 mm
- service limit .... 0.1 mm

6. Inspect crankshaft for run-out by supporting front and rear main bearing journals in 'V' blocks and checking journals with a dial gauge.
7. Place a dial gauge indicator at crankshaft rear flange and inspect rear flange Run-out. During this inspection, make sure that crankshaft is thrust forward on 'V' blocks so that there is no possibility of crankshaft end float affecting dial gauge reading.
Crankshaft Rear Flange Run-out........... 0.06 mm
8. If not as specified, replace crankshaft.

Installation.
1. Inspect main bearing clearance, if needed, refer to MAIN BEARINGS section for details.
2. Using a clean engine oil lubricate all crankshaft journals and main bearing upper shells in crankcase.
3. Sit crankshaft in place in main bearing upper shells in cylinder block. Ensure not to damage crankshaft thrust washers at No.5 main bearing. Also ensure not to contact connecting rod journals with connecting rod and install main bearing caps.

Using a thin film of Loctite 515 Gasket Eliminator or equivalent apply to rear main bearing cradle to cylinder block mating surface. Keep sealant out of bolt holes and use sparingly.
Tighten the bolts finger tight.
4. It will be necessary to line up thrust washers with No.5 bearing shells, before tightening main bearing cap bolts.
Move crankshaft fore and aft the length of its travel several times (last movement forward) to do this.
5. Ensure all main bearing cradle bolts are tightened as specified.

Lower Crankcase Bolts (Nos 1 to 16) 25Nm
Main Bearing Cradle Bolts (Nos 17 to 26) steps:
Step 1 .... 20Nm
Step 2 .... rotate a further 90 degrees
Step 3 .... rotate a further 90 degrees

6. Use a feeler gauge to measure crankshaft end float between front of No.5 main bearing thrust washer and crankshaft thrust faces, you will need to force crankshaft forward to do this.
End play .... 0.10 - 0.28 mm
- limit .... 0.4 mm
Replace No.5 main bearing thrust washers if clearance is excessive.
7. Turn crankshaft to make sure crankshaft and connect-

ing rods have free movement. Inspect orientation of bearing caps, correct fitting of bearing cradle (mains and connecting rods) or fitting of bearing shells or bearing clearance, if crankshaft binds.

8. Install the rear main oil seal and retainer.
9. To install flywheel/driveplate as described.

MAIN BEARINGS.

Each crankshaft main bearing journal has 2 bearing halves or shells which are not the same and not interchangeable in the bearing cap or crankcase. The upper (crankcase) shell is grooved to supply oil to the connecting rod bearing, while the lower (bearing cap) shell is not grooved. The 2 bearing shells must not be interchanged. The No.3. bearing has thrust washers to take end thrust.

Standard size upper shells are used in the crankcase with 0.25mm undersized or standard size shells in the bearing caps, depending on bearing clearance.

When shells are placed in crankcase and bearing cap, the end extends slightly beyond the parting surfaces so that when cradle bolts are tightened, the shells clamp tightly in place to ensure positive seating and to prevent turning. The ends of the bearing shells must never be filed flush with parting surfaces of crankcase or bearing cradle.

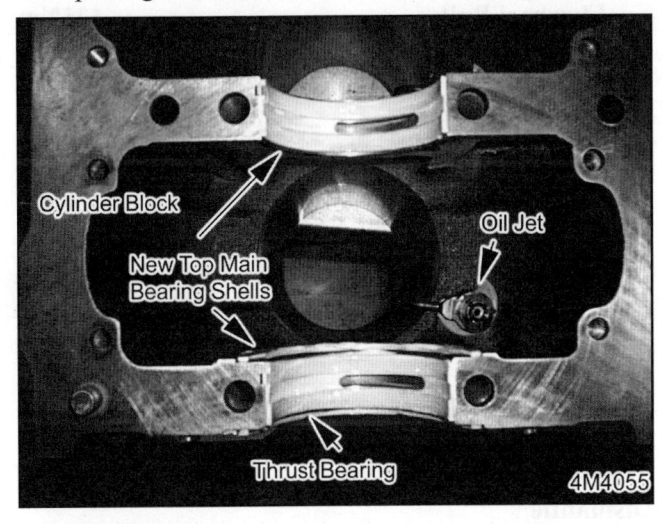

Inspection

1. Remove main bearing cradle bolts, and remove cradle and lower bearing shell.
   * Tap main bearing cradle to break cradle to crankcase seal to remove.
2. Check lower bearing shells and crankshaft journals. If the journal surface is ridged or heavily scored, replace crankshaft, refer to Crankshaft section for details.
   To ensure satisfactory engine operation, new bearing shells must be installed as described in Main Bearing section and if necessary Connecting Rod Bearings section.
   Inspect inner surface of bearing shells for gouges, wear or embedded foreign material. If foreign material is found, determine its nature and source. Inspect outer surface of bearing shells for surface wear (indicates movement of shell or high spot in surrounding material), looseness, rotation (flattened tangs and wear grooves), and overheating (discolouration).
   Inspect thrust surfaces of thrust washers for grooving or wear. Grooves are caused by irregularities in the crankshaft thrust surfaces or dirt as described in Crankshaft section.
   If condition of lower bearing shells and crankshaft journals is satisfactory, inspect bearing clearance as follows:
3. Wipe oil from crankshaft journal and inner and outer surfaces of lower bearing shell.
   Install bearing shell in original position in bearing cap.
4. Place a piece of plastigage across full width of crankshaft journal, parallel to crankshaft centre line.
   * Make sure plastigage will not seat across oil hole in journal.
5. Install bearing cap and bolts into cylinder block.
   * Install bearing caps by loosely installing cap bolts and then lightly tap bearing cap into position, in order to prevent the possibility of cylinder block and or main bearing cap damage.
   * Do not pull the bearing cradle into place with the bearing cradle bolts.
6. Tighten bearing cradle bolts as specified.
   * Ensure that crankshaft does not rotate with plastigage installed.
   See previous illustration for tightening sequence
   Lower Crankcase Bolts (Nos 1 to 16).......... 25Nm
   Main Bearing Cradle Bolts (Nos 17 to 26) steps:
   Step 1 .... 20Nm
   Step 2 .... **rotate a further 90 degrees**
   Step 3 .... **rotate a further 90 degrees**
7. Remove bearing cradle bolts and cradle. Look for flattened plastigage sticking to either crankshaft or bearing shell in bearing cradle.
8. Check bearing clearance by comparing width of flattened plastigage at widest point with graduation on plastigage envelope. The number within the graduation

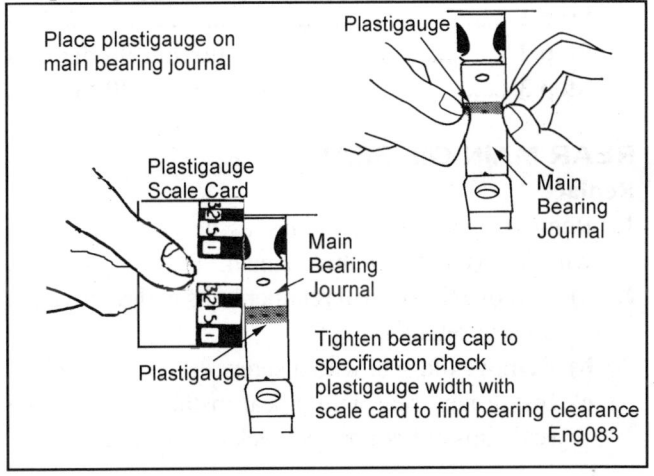

2.8 litre DIESEL SOHC (4M40) ENGINE MAINTENANCE & REBUILD

on the envelope indicates the clearance.
Main bearing and crankshaft journal clearance should not exceed specification.

Main bearing clearance 1,2,4&5...0.04 - 0.06 mm
- service limit .... 0.1 mm
Main bearing clearance brg 3........0.06 - 0.08 mm
- service limit .... 0.1 mm

This method of checking main bearing clearance does not give any indication of crankshaft journal taper or out of round.

To measure taper, out of round or undersized, the crankshaft must be removed from the cylinder block as described in CRANKSHAFT section.

9. It is advisable to install new bearing shells if bearing clearance exceeds specification and check clearance as previously described.

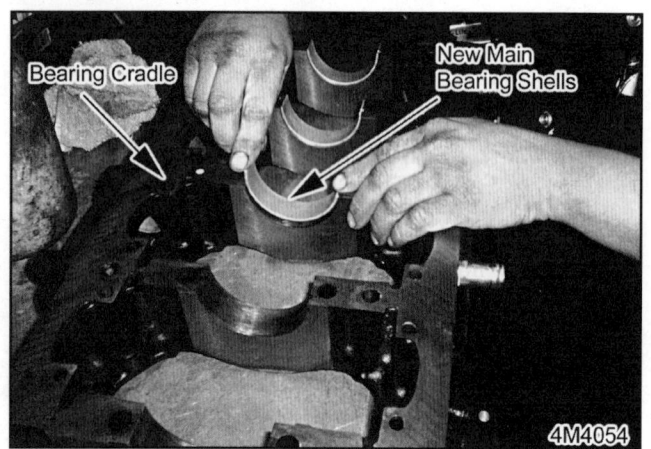

If lower bearing is standard size, install a 0.25 mm undersized shell and check clearance again.
Replace crankshaft as described in "Crankshaft" section if clearance is still not as specified.

10. Make sure that main bearing cradle bolt threads and crankcase threads are clean and dry.
* Before final installation of cradle bolts, determine if bolts have stretched by comparing with new one. Replace bolts and tighten.
See previous illustration for tightening sequence.

Lower Crankcase Bolts (Nos 1 to 16) 25Nm
Main Bearing Cradle Bolts (Nos 17 to 26) steps:
Step 1 .... 20Nm
Step 2 .... rotate a further 90 degrees
Step 3 .... rotate a further 90 degrees

REAR MAIN OIL SEAL
Replace
1. Remove flywheel/driveplate, as described in "Flywheel/driveplate" in this manual.
2. a) Remove the oil seal retainer bolts and remove the oil seal retainer.
   b) Remove old seal with a screw driver or punch.
   c) Install new seal with a seal installer, ensure the seals lips are not pulled back or crooked.

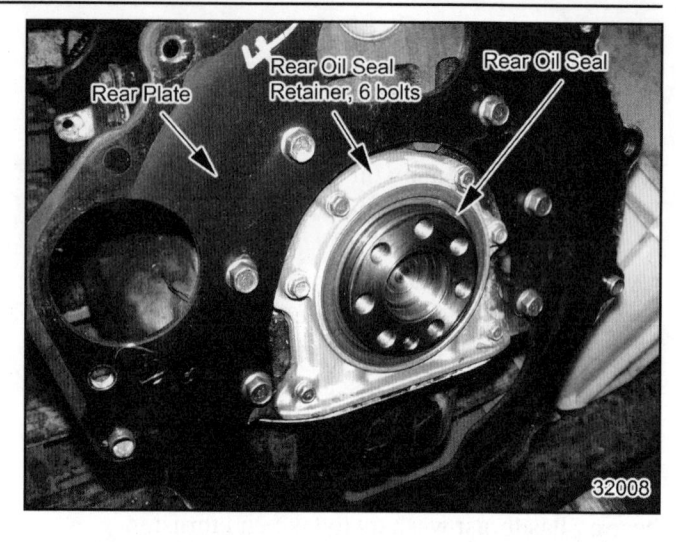

3. Apply a thin coat of oil to the lips of the oil seal.
4. Apply a 3mm bead of sealant around the circumference of the seal retainer, install within 3 minutes.
5. Install rear seal retainer to rear of engine block.
   Rear oil seal retainer plate 11Nm
6. Clean flywheel/drive plate attaching bolt threads in rear of crankshaft using a thread tap.
   Install new flywheel/flexplate and attaching bolts, tighten bolts to the correct torque specification.
   Flywheel Bolts 125Nm
   Drive Plate rubber spacer bolts 48Nm
7. Reinstall transmission, check engine and transmission lubricant levels.
8. Road test vehicle and check for lubrication leaks.

OIL COOLER and ELEMENT
Remove
1. Remove the oil filter.
2. Remove the bolts attaching the cooler to the cylinder block.
3. Remove the cooler assembly and gasket plus 3 "O" rings. Dispose of gasket and "O" rings.

Dismantle
1. Remove the element, 4 nuts.

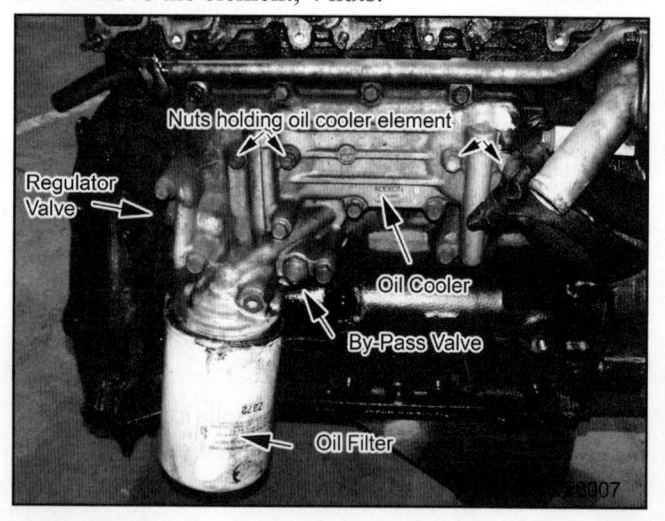

2.8 litre DIESEL SOHC (4M40) ENGINE MAINTENANCE & REBUILD

2. Remove the regulator valve plug, washer, spring and plunger.
3. Remove the bypass plug, washer, spring and plunger.
4. Remove the water / coolant drain plug and washer.

Clean and Test
1. Wash the springs, plungers and element in kerosine to remove any sludge or build up in the element.
2. Dry with compressed air.
3. Test element for leakage:
   a) Apply an air hose to the oil inlet hole, plug the oil outlet hole.
   b) Submerse element in a container of water, apply upto 1470 kPa of air pressure to element and check for air bubbles.
   c) If element is leaking air, replace element.

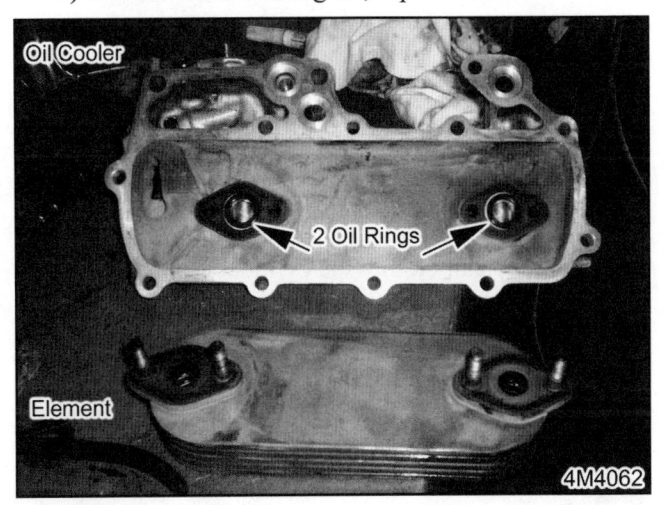

Assemble
1. Replace the water / coolant drain plug and washer.
2. Replace the bypass plug, washer, spring and plunger.
3. Replace the regulator valve plug, washer, spring and plunger.
4. Install the element with new gaskets and washer, 4 nuts.

Oil Cooler Element Nuts: 20Nm

Install
1. Install the cooler assembly with new gasket plus 3 "O" rings. Install 4 bolts and tighten.
2. Install a new oil filter.
3. Top up oil level.

OIL JETS
To help during assembly, take note of the direction the oil jet points too for lubrication.

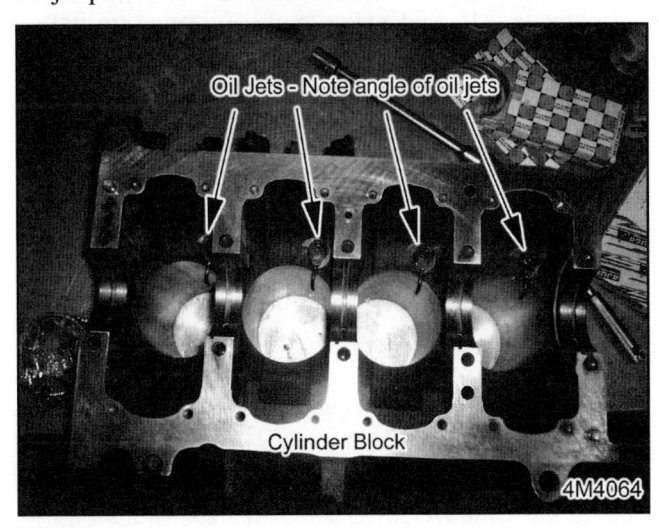

Replace
1. Remove crankshaft as described.
2. Unscrew the union holding the oil jet and remove the oil jet.
3. Clean the oil jet if required.
4. Install the oil jet with a new "O" ring if one was fitted. Tighten oil jet union to specification.
   Note: *Make sure jet faces the correct direct.*
   Oil Jet Union 33Nm
5. Replace crankshaft as described.
6. Install engine oil pan (sump).

CYLINDER BLOCK.
Inspection.
1. When engine is removed from vehicle and mounted in a suitable engine stand, remove all parts as outlined under the particular part heading in this section.
2. Clean all cylinder block gasket surfaces.
3. Remove all coolant jacket welsh plugs and oil gallery screw plugs.
4. Clean cylinder block thoroughly using a suitable cleaning solution. Flush with clean water or steam. Spray or wipe cylinder bores and machined surfaces using engine oil.
   Caustic cleaning solutions destroy all bearing and alloy materials. All bearing and alloy parts if not removed before cleaning must be replaced.
   Do not use caustic solutions to clean bearing material or alloy parts.
5. Check all oil passages for obstructions.

6. Using a straight edge and feeler gauge, inspect cylinder block deck surface for flatness.
   If any distortion or irregularity is less than specified, cylinder block surface may be machined.
   Flatness of gasket surface........ less than 0.05 mm
   Flatness of gasket surface - maximum ... 0.10 mm
   Replace cylinder block if irregularity or distortion is more than specified.
7. Check oil pan and oil pump body area for burrs or damage. Minor damage may be cleaned up with a fine mill file.
8. If needed, clean all threaded holes using a suitable threaded tap or drill out and install thread insert.
9. Measure cylinder bore walls for taper, excessive ridging, oversize and out-of-round.

Cylinder Reconditioning and Piston Fitting.

It will be necessary to smooth bores to fit new pistons, if one or more cylinder bores are scored, rough or worn beyond limits.

It will not be necessary to rebore all cylinders to the same oversize order to maintain engine balance if few bores require correction, since all oversize service pistons are held to the same weight as standard size pistons.

Do not try to machine oversize pistons to fit cylinder bores, this will destroy the surface treatment and affect the weight. The smallest possible oversize service pistons should be used and the cylinder bores should be honed to size for proper clearances.

Measure all new pistons at right angles to the piston pin bore, before the honing or reboring operation is started.

Piston diameter.................................94.95 - 94.97 mm
Piston diameter (Turbo) ....94.92 - 94.97 mm
Piston to bore clearance......................0.04 - 0.05 mm
Piston to bore clearance (Turbo) ....0.07 - 0.08 mm
Piston oversizes............0.50 mm, 0.75 mm, 1.00 mm

Honing is recommended for truing bore if cylinder bore wear does not exceed specification. The bore should be trued up by boring and then hone finished, if wear or out-of-round exceeds specification.

All crankshaft bearing caps must be in place and tightened as specified when reboring cylinder bores, to prevent distortion of bores in final assembly.

Leave 0.025 mm on the diameter for final honing to give the specified clearance when taking the final cut.

Follow the Hone Manufacturers recommendations for the use of the hone and cleaning and lubrication during honing. Noting the following points.

Pass the hone through the entire length of the cylinder bore at the rate of approximately 60 cycles per minute when finished honing. This should produce the desired 45° cross hatch pattern on cylinder walls which will ensure minimum oil consumption and maximum ring life.

Each piston must be fitted individually to the bore in which it will be installed and marked to ensure correct assembly during the final honing. After the final honing and before the piston is inspected for fit, each cylinder bore must be washed and dried thoroughly to remove all traces of abrasive and then allowed to cool. Apply clean engine oil to cylinder bores. The pistons and cylinder block must be at a common temperature before inspecting.

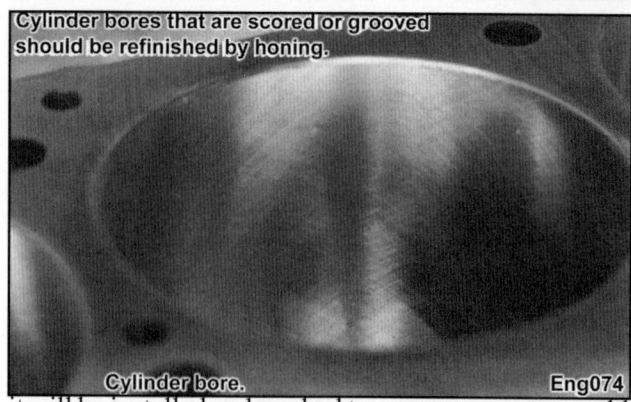

The glazed cylinder walls should be slightly dulled when new piston rings are installed without reboring cylinders, but without increasing the bore diameter, by means of the finest grade of stone in a cylinder hone.

Proceed as follows to inspect piston to cylinder bore.

1. Using a clean cloth wipe cylinder walls and pistons and apply clean engine oil to cylinder bores.

2. Measure the bore accurately using an inside micrometer.
3. Measure piston diameter and subtract piston diameter from cylinder bore diameter to determine piston-to-bore clearance.
4. Mark each piston with cylinder number to which it will be fitted and proceed to hone cylinders and fit pistons.

Handle the pistons with care and do not attempt to force them through the cylinder until cylinder has been honed to the correct size, as pistons can be damaged through careless handling.

Assemble parts as described under the correct heading in this section. If coolant and oil gallery plugs were removed when dismantling, install using specified sealant.

Problem Diagnosis.

Problems and Possible Causes.
Problems should be corrected, when proper diagnosis is made, by repair, adjustment or part replacement as needed. Refer to the correct section in this manual.

High Oil Loss
1) Tighten bolts and/or replace gaskets and seals as required for external leaks.
2) Check oil with car on a level surface and allow adequate drain down time to ensure a correct reading of dipstick.
3) Severe usage such as towing or continuous high speed driving will normally cause oil consumption to increase.
4) PCV system failure.
5) Use recommended S.A.E viscosity for current temperatures. Refer to Lubrication Section for details on incorrect oil viscosity.
6) Valve guides and/or valve stem seals worn, or seals omitted. Ream guides and install oversize service valves and/or new valve stem seals.
7) Allow enough time for the piston rings to seat. Replace worn or broken rings as needed, if rings have been incorrectly installed, worn or broken, or not seated.
8) Piston incorrectly installed or mis-fitted.

Gaskets.
1) Incorrectly tightened fasteners or damaged/dirty threads.
2) Worn or damaged gasket (cracking or porosity).
3) Fluid pressure/level too high.
4) Incorrect sealant used (when required)

Inspection of Seals.
1) Damaged seal bore (burred, nicked, scratched)
2) Worn or loose bearing causing excessive seal wear.
3) Worn or damaged seal or incorrect installation.
4) Fluid pressure/level too high.

Oil Leak Investigation
Oil leaks are easily located and repaired by visually finding the leak and replacing or repairing the required parts.
1) Determine whether the fluid is transmission lubricant, engine oil, power steering fluid etc.
2) Run the car at normal operating temperature and park the car over a large sheet of paper. After a few minutes, you should be able to find the approximate location of the leak by drippings on the paper.
3) Use a degreaser or steam to clean the area of the leak, drive the car for a few kilometres. Then visually inspect the suspected part for signs of an oil leak.

Black Light and Dye Method.
Use a dye and light kits available for finding leaks.
   a) Pour required amount of dye into leaking part.
   b) Operate the car under normal operating conditions as instructed in the kit.
   c) Shine the light in the suspected area. The dyed fluid will appear as a yellow path leading to the problem.

Low Oil Pressure
1) Blocked oil filter.
2) Incorrect oil viscosity for expected temperature, or oil diluted with moisture or unburnt fuel mixtures.
3) Excessive bearing clearance.
4) If the oil level is low, fill to mark on dipstick.
5) Oil pump dirty/worn, or oil pump suction pipe screen blocked, or hole in oil pump suction pipe.
6) Incorrect or failing oil pressure sender.

ENGINE KNOCKS

When Engine Cold And Continues Knocking For Two Or Three Minutes (Increases with torque)
1) Tighten or replace as required if drive pulleys or balancer are loose or broken.
2) Replace piston if clearance from piston to bore is excessive. (Cold engine piston knock usually disappears when the cylinder is grounded out. Cold engine piston knock which disappears in 1.5 min. can be considered acceptable.)
3) Connecting rod bent.

Heavy Knock With Torque Applied
1) Check for a broken pulley hub or balancer.
2) Loose torque converter to flexplate bolts.
3) Check if exhaust system contacting underbody.
4) Cracked flexplate/flywheel.
5) Main bearing clearance or connecting rod bearing clearance excessive.

Light Knock while Hot
1) Inspect fuel quality if pre-ignition knock.
2) Loose torque converter to flexplate bolts.
3) Connecting rod clearing clearance excessive.

Knocks On First Start-up, Lasting a Few Seconds
1) Incorrect oil viscosity. Install correct oil viscosity for expected temperatures.
2) Hydraulic lifter bleed down.
Some valves will be open when the engine is stopped. Spring force against lifters will tend to bleed lifter down. Only if the problem is consistent should repairs be attempted.
3) Replace crankshaft thrust bearing shells if excessive crankshaft end float.
4) Check for excessive main bearing clearance.

SPECIFICATIONS

GENERAL
Type - 4M40 .... Inline 4 SOHC
No. of Cylinders .... Four
Displacement: 2835cc
Compression ratio: 21:1
Bore and Stroke (nominal): .... 95.0 x 100.0
Fuel requirements .... Diesel

CYLINDER BLOCK
Material .... Alloy cast iron
Flatness of gasket surface .... **less than 0.05 mm**
Flatness of gasket surface - maximum .... **0.10 mm**
Piston diameter .... 94.95 - 94.97 mm
Piston diameter (Turbo) .... 94.92 - 94.97 mm
Piston to bore clearance .... 0.04 - 0.05 mm
Piston to bore clearance (Turbo) .... 0.07 - 0.08 mm
Piston oversizes .... 0.50 mm, 0.75 mm, 1.00 mm
Max. bore wear (before reconditioning) .... 0.02 mm
Max ovality and taper (before reconditioning) 0.02 mm
Overall Height .... 210.4 - 210.6 mm

CYLINDER HEAD
Material .... Aluminium alloy
Type .... Swirl Combustion Chamber
Max. allowable distortion - head surface .... 0.2 mm
Grinding limit .... 0.2 mm
Max. allowable distortion - intake surface .... 0.2 mm
Max. allowable distortion - exhaust surface ...... 0.3 mm
Inlet valve seat insert hole diameter 43mm
- 0.3 mm Oversize .... 43.30 - 43.33 mm
- 0.6 mm Oversize .... 43.60 - 43.63 mm
Exhaust valve seat insert hole diameter 37mm
- 0.3 mm Oversize .... 37.30 - 37.33 mm
- 0.6 mm Oversize .... 37.60 - 37.63 mm
Valve guide hole diameter .... 13.00 - 13.0007 mm
- 0.05 mm Oversize .... 13.05 - 13.0507 mm
- 0.25 mm Oversize .... 13.25 - 13.2507 mm
- 0.50 mm Oversize .... 13.50 - 13.5007 mm
Camshaft/camshaft bearing clearance ...... 0.06-0.10 mm

Cylinder Head Selection

Piston Protrusion	Head Gasket
Av piston protrusion	Grade & notches
0.475 +/- 0.028 mm	A - 1 notches
0.532 +/- 0.028 mm	B - 2 notches
0.589 +/- 0.028 mm	C - 3 notches
0.646 +/- 0.028 mm	D - 4 notches

VALVES
Valve Clearance (Cold)
    Intake .... 0.2 mm
    Exhaust .... 0.3 mm
Sinkage from cylinde rhead bottom
    - Inlet .... 0.75-1.25mm - max 1.5mm
    - Exhaust .... 0.95-1.45mm - max 1.7mm
Stem diameter - Inlet .... 7.96-7.97mm - min 7.85mm
    - Exhaust.. 7.93-7.95mm - min 7.85mm
Valve face angle .... 45° - 45.5°
Valve face angle .... 45° - 45.5°
Valve seat width .... 2.0 - 2.8 mm
Valve stem to guide clearance
    - Inlet .... 0.03 - 0.05 mm
    - Exhaust .... 0.05 - 0.08 mm

VALVE GUIDES
Valve guide OD .... 13.06 - 13.018 mm
    - 0.05, 0.25 and 0.50mm Oversize available
Valve Guide Installed Height .... 14.00 +/- 0.30 mm
Valve stem to guide clearance
    - Inlet .... 0.03 - 0.05 mm
    - Exhaust .... 0.05 - 0.08 mm

VALVE SPRINGS
Number 8
Free length .... 48.8 mm
Free length Minimum .... 47.8 mm
Valve Installed Height 38.67mm

CAMSHAFT
Material .... Cast iron
Bearing clearance .... 0.01 - 0.04 mm
Height of cam lobe
- Inlet
    2000 model .... 9.89 mm
    2001 on .... 9.29 mm
- Exhaust 10.19 mm

PISTONS
Material .... Aluminium alloy
Type .... Auto thermic type
Piston diameter .... 94.95 - 94.97 mm
Piston diameter (Turbo) .... 94.92 - 94.97 mm
Piston to bore clearance .... 0.04 - 0.05 mm
Piston to bore clearance (Turbo) .... 0.07 - 0.08 mm
Piston oversizes .... 0.50 mm, 0.75 mm, 1.00 mm
Piston pin to Piston Clearance 0.007-0.021mm

PISTON PIN
Type .... Press fit in connecting rod
Material .... Alloy steel
Piston pin to Piston Clearance 0.007-0.021mm

PISTON RINGS

Number 3
Ring gap   - New
               - Compression .... 0.30 - 0.45 mm
               - Max .... 0.80 mm
2000 model   - Scraper .... 0.30 - 0.45 mm
               - Max .... 0.80 mm
2001 on   - Scraper .... 0.40 - 0.55 mm
               - Max .... 0.80 mm
Oil Ring Steel Rail Gap Specification:
    - Oil ring - None Turbo .... 0.30 - 0.50 mm
    - Max .... 0.80 mm
    - Oil ring - Turbo .... 0.25 - 0.45 mm
    - Max .... 0.80 mm
Side clearance
    Compression - None Turbo .... 0.06 - 0.11 mm
    - Max .... 0.15 mm
    Compression - Turbo .... 0.03 - 0.08 mm
    - Max .... 0.15 mm
    Scraper - None Turbo .... 0.05 - 0.08 mm
    - Max .... 0.15 mm
    Scraper - Turbo .... 0.07 - 0.10 mm
    - Max .... 0.15 mm
    Oil Ring .... 0.03 - 0.06 mm
    - Max .... 0.15 mm

CONNECTING ROD

Material .... Forged carbon steel
Connecting Rod bearing clearance .... 0.03 - 0.05 mm
    - service limit (main/big end) .... 0.1 mm
Connecting rod bearing undersizes .... 0.25 mm
    .... 0.50 mm
    .... 0.75 mm
Connecting rod   - bend .... 0.05 mm
                     - twist .... 0.05 mm
Bearing material .... Aluminium alloy
Connecting Rod to crankshaft end clearance:
    .... 0.15 - 0.45 mm
    - service limit .... 0.6 mm

CRANKSHAFT

No. of main bearings 5
Main bearing journals diameter .... 68.0 mm
End float controlled by .... No.3 bearing
Connecting Rod journal diameter .... 54.0 mm
    - max. allowable ovality .... 0.01 mm
    - max. allowable taper .... 0.006 mm
Main bearing clearance 1,2,4&5 .... 0.04 - 0.06 mm
    - service limit .... 0.1 mm
Main bearing clearance brg 3 .... 0.06 - 0.08 mm
    - service limit .... 0.1 mm
End float controlled by .... No.3 bearing
End play 0.10 - 0.28 mm
    - limit .... 0.4 mm

OIL PUMP

Gear tip to Body clearance .... 0.15 - 0.27mm
Gear to Pump Cover Clearance .... 0.05 - 0.10mm
    Max 0.15mm
Shaft to oil pump case and cover clearance ....
    .... 0.03 - 0.05mm
Shaft to oil pump case and cover clearance ....
    0.03 - 0.05mm

TORQUE SPECIFICATION

Description	Nm
Alternator bracket M8	48
Alternator bracket M10	23
Alternator pivot nut	44
Camshaft Gear Bolt:	90Nm
Connecting Rod Cap Bolt - 4 steps:	
Step 1	30Nm
Step 2	50Nm
Step 3	rotate a further 45 degrees
Step 4	rotate a further 45 degrees
Coolant temperature gauge unit	11
Coolant temperature sensor	29
Crankshaft Balancer bolt	323Nm
Crankshaft:	
Lower Crankcase Bolts (Nos 1 to 16)	25Nm
Main Bearing Cradle Bolts (Nos 17 to 26) steps:	
Step 1	20Nm
Step 2	rotate a further 90 degrees
Step 3	rotate a further 90 degrees
Crank Angle Sensor	9
Cylinder head bolts	
M12 Bolts - Cold in 5 stages	
Cylinder head bolts - Cold - in sequence	100
Loosen in reverse order	
Cylinder head bolts - Cold - in sequence	50
Rotate	90 degrees
Rotate	90 degrees
M8 Bolts - Cold in 3 stages	
Cylinder head bolts - Cold - in 3 stages	24
Cylinder Head Water Pipe:	7
Exhaust Manifold Bolts and Nuts:	30
Exhaust Pipe Nuts:	49
Flywheel mounting bolt	125
Glow Plug	10
Intake Manifold	21
Turbocharger nuts	50
Turbocharger bolts	55
Oil Jet Union	33
Camshaft Holder Bolts:	20
Rocker Cover Bolts:	3.4

3.2 litre, incl COMMON RAIL - DOHC (4M41) DIESEL ENGINE MAINTENANCE & REBUILD

Subject	Page	Subject	Page
GENERAL DESCRIPTION	125	Clearance Checks	134
Engine Serial Number	125	Guide Replacement	134
Maintenance Hints	125	**Valve Seats**	135
		Replacing Valve Seat	135
GENERAL MAINTENANCE	126	**Valve Stem Oil Seals**	135
Intercooler	126	Replacement	135
Removal	126	**Valve Springs**	136
Installation	126	**Valves**	136
Intake Manifold	126	**Camshafts**	137
Removal	126	Inspection	137
Installation	127	**Assemble Cylinder Head**	137
Exhaust Manifolds	127	**Valve Clearance Adjustment**	138
Remove	127	**Install Cylinder Head**	138
Installation	127	**Vacuum Pump**	139
Water Pump	128	Remove	139
Removal	128	Install	139
Installation	128	**Oil Pump and Right Balance Shaft**	140
Crankshaft Balancer	128	Removal	140
Remove	128	Dismantle	140
Install	128	Inspection	140
Rocker Covers and/or Seals	128	Assembly	140
Remove	128	Installation	140
Installation	128	**Flywheel/Drive Plate**	140
Timing Chain, Gear Cover, Timing Gears, Balance Shafts and Oil Pump	129	Remove	140
Remove	129	Inspection	141
Inspection	131	Install	141
Install	131	**Ring Gear**	141
Cylinder Head, Valves & Camshafts	132	Replacement	141
Removal	132	Replacement Techniques	141
Cylinder Head Reconditioning	133	**Spigot Bearing**	141
Dismantle	133	Replacement	141
Clean	134	**ENGINE REBUILD**	142
Inspection	134	**Engine Assembly**	142
Valve Guides	134	Removal	142
		Dismantle	142

Subject	Page
Assembly	143
Oil Pan (Sump)	**143**
Removal	143
Installation	143
Oil Pump Suction Pipe, Screen and Baffle	**143**
Removal	143
Installation	143
Piston and Connecting Rod Assembly	**143**
Removal	144
Dismantle	144
Inspection	144
Assembly & Installation	145
Piston Rings	**147**
Installation	147
Connecting Rod Bearings	**148**
Inspection & Replacement	148
Crankshaft	**150**
Removal	150
Inspection	150
Installation	150
Main Bearings	**152**
Inspection and Installation	152
Rear Main Oil Seal	**153**
Replace	153
Oil Cooler and Element	**154**
Removal	154
Dismantle	154
Clean and Tests	154
Assembly	155
Installation	155
Cylinder Block	**155**
Inspection	155
Cylinder Reconditioning & Piston Fitting	155
PROBLEM DIAGNOSIS	**156**
SPECIFICATIONS	**157**
TORQUE WRENCH SPECIFICATIONS	**160**

GENERAL DESCRIPTION

The 4M41 (3.2L) engine is an in line 4 cylinder overhead camshaft unit, there are two camshafts (DOHC) mounted in the aluminium cylinder head. 4M41 engines have a 26 bolt main bearing type cradle.

The cylinder block made of cast iron and has a standard bore of 98.5 mm and stroke of 105 mm, displacement is 3200cc with a compression ratio of 17:1.

The cylinder numbering is as illustrated, from the front of the engine, 1 to 4.

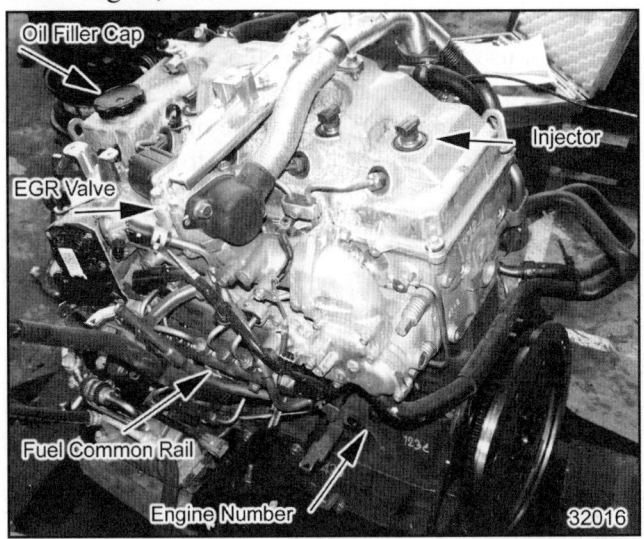

ENGINE SERIAL NUMBER

Engine No. Location: On left-hand side engine block casting, above the starter motor.

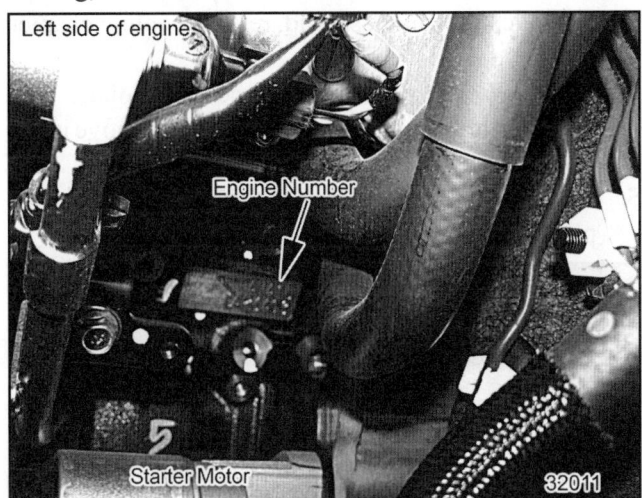

MAINTENANCE HINTS

1. a) When any internal engine parts are serviced, care and cleanliness are important.
    b) An engine is a combination of many machined, honed, polished and lapped surfaces with tolerances that are measured in thousandths of a millimetre.
    c) Friction areas should be coated liberally with engine oil during assembly to protect and lubricate the surfaces on initial operation.

d) Proper cleaning and protection of machined surfaces and friction areas is part of the repair procedure and is considered standard workshop practice.
2. When valve train components are removed for service, they should be kept in order and should be installed in the same locations (with the same mating surfaces) as when removed.
3. Battery terminals should be disconnected before any major work is begun. If not, damage to wiring harnesses or other electrical components could result.
4. When raising or supporting the engine for any reason, do not use a jack under the oil pan. There are small clearances between the oil pan and the suction pipe screen, so jacking may cause the oil pan to be bent against the screen, causing damage to oil suction pipe assembly.

GENERAL MAINTENANCE

* For general maintenance procedures such as oil change and drive belt inspection refer to the "Tune-up & Maintenance Chapter".

Intercooler
Removal
1. Remove the air cleaner assembly, then from the underside of the vehicle remove the skid plate and covers.
2. Remove the radiator shroud, refer to cooling chapter if required.
3. Disconnect the air hoses from the intercooler.
4. Remove intercooler retaining bolts and remove intercooler from vehicle.
5. If required remove the bolts retaining the deflector plate to the intercooler assembly.

Inspection
1. Inspect intercooler fins for damage and foreign material.
2. Inspect intercooler air hoses for cracks, damage or wear, replace if required.

Installation
1. If removed, install the deflector plate to the intercooler assembly and tighten retaining bolts to specification.
   Deflector Plate Bolts.................................. 12 Nm
2. Install intercooler into position and tighten retaining bolts to specification.
   Intercooler Bolts.. 12 Nm
3. Reconnect the intercooler air hoses, tightening clamps to specification.
   Air Hose Clamps .... 6 Nm
   Air Pipe Retaining Bolt .... 9 Nm
4. Install the radiator shroud, refer to cooling chapter if required.
5. Install the air cleaner assembly, then install the skid plate and covers to the underside of the vehicle.

INTAKE MANIFOLD
Remove
1. Detach the battery earth lead from the battery, then release the lower radiator hose and drain the cooling system.
2. Remove the engine top dress-up cover from the engine, if fitted.
3. Remove the side cover from the intake manifold.
4. a) Remove the intercooler water hoses.
   b) Remove the air tube between the intercooler and air cleaner box.
   c) Remove the intercooler from the engine.
5. a) Remove the air intake tube to the intake manifold body from the turbocharger, remove intake tube.
   b) Remove the air intake tube between the intercooler and turbocharger.
6. Release the accelerator electrical connector from the throttle body assembly.
7. [If fitted] Release the EGR pipe retaining bolts from the intake and the exhaust manifold, then withdraw

the EGR pipe from the engine assembly.
8. Remove the bolts attaching the intake manifold, remove intake manifold and gasket.

Install

1. Clean the intake manifold surface, ensure that all the old gasket is removed from the surface. Ensure the old gasket is removed from the surface.
2. Install the intake manifold with new gaskets, install nuts tighten to specification.
   Intake Manifold Nuts: 30Nm
3. [If fitted] Install the EGR pipe retaining bolts and fittings to the intake and the exhaust manifolds.
4. Connect the accelerator cable from the throttle body assembly.
5. a) Replace the air intake tube to the intake manifold body from the turbocharger.
   b) Replace the air intake tube between the intercooler and turbocharger.
6. a) Install the intercooler to the engine.
   b) Replace the air tube between the intercooler and air cleaner box.
   c) Replace the intercooler water hoses
7. Install the side cover to the intake manifold.
8. Replace the engine top dress-up cover from the engine, if fitted.
9. Connect the battery earth lead from the battery, connect the lower radiator hose and top up the cooling system coolant.

EXHAUST MANIFOLD

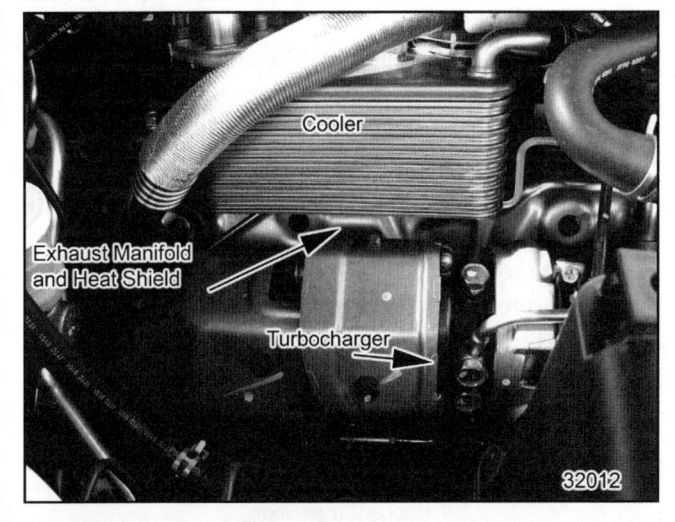

Remove

1. Detach the battery earth lead from the battery, then release the lower radiator hose and drain the cooling system.
2. Remove the engine top dress-up cover from the engine, if fitted.
3. Remove the heat shields from exhaust manifold and turbocharger. 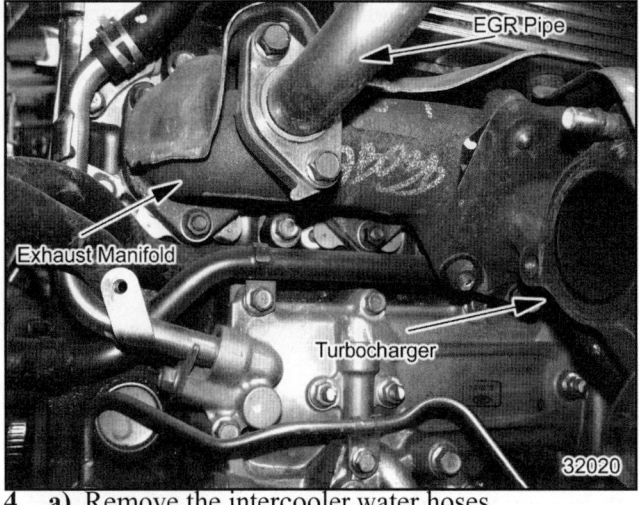
4. a) Remove the intercooler water hoses.
   b) Remove the air tube between the intercooler and air cleaner box.
   c) Remove the intercooler from the engine.
5. a) Remove the air intake tube to the intake manifold body from the turbocharger, remove intake tube.
   b) Remove the air intake tube between the intercooler and turbocharger.
6. Remove the bolts attaching the exhaust pipe to the turbo-charger, if you require to separate them at this stage.
7. Release the EGR pipe retaining bolts from the intake and the exhaust manifold, then withdraw the EGR pipe from the engine assembly.
8. a) Remove the oil pipe to the turbocharger.
   b) Remove the oil return pipe and hose from the turbocharger.
   c) Disconnect the waste gate hose.
9. a) Remove the coolant pipe to the turbocharger.
   b) Remove the coolant return pipe and hose from the turbocharger.
10. Remove the turbocharger nuts, remove turbocharger and gasket.
11. Remove the bolts attaching the exhaust manifold, remove exhaust manifold and gasket.

Install

1. Clear the exhaust manifold surface, ensure that all the old gasket is removed from the surface.
2. Install the exhaust manifold with new gasket, install bolts tighten to specification.
   Exhaust Manifold Bolts and Nuts: ....30 Nm
3. Install the turbocharger with new gasket, install bolts tighten to specification.
   Turbocharger Nuts: ....50 Nm
   Turbocharger Bolts:....................................55 Nm
4. a) Replace the oil pipe to the turbocharger.
   b) Replace the oil return pipe and hose from the turbocharger.
   c) Connect the waste gate hose.

3.2 Litre, incl COMMON RAIL - DOHC (4M41) Diesel Engine Maintenance & Rebuild

5. a) Replace the coolant pipe to the turbocharger.
   b) Replace the coolant return pipe and hose from the turbocharger.
6. [If fitted] Install the EGR pipe retaining bolts and fittings to the intake and the exhaust manifolds.
7. Install the exhaust pipe to the turbo-charger, tighten nuts to specification.
   Exhaust Pipe Nuts: .... **30 Nm**
8. a) Install the intercooler to the engine.
   b) Replace the air tube between the intercooler and air cleaner box.
   c) Replace the intercooler water hoses
9. Install the heat shields from exhaust manifold and turbocharger.
10. Replace the engine top dress-up cover from the engine, if fitted.

WATER PUMP

Remove

1. Slacken off the alternator / water pump drive belt and remove.
2. Remove the fan, and bolts.
3. Remove the thermo fan and coupling, and bolts from the water pump belt pulley.
4. Remove the water pump bolts, water pump and gasket.

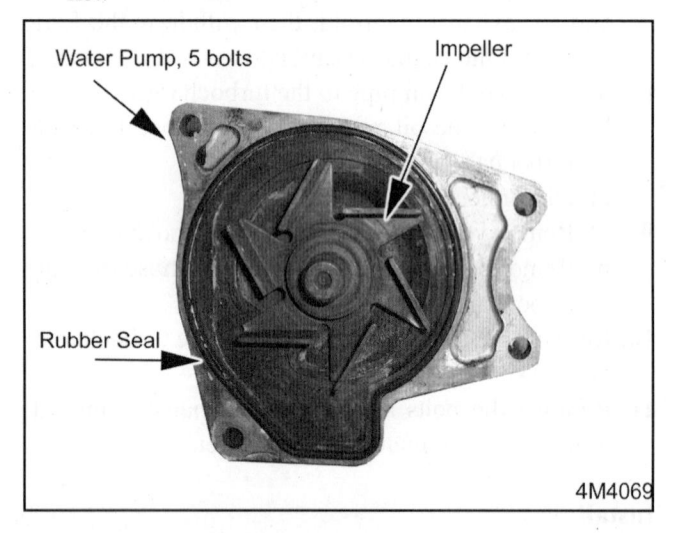

Install

1. Remove old gasket and clean gasket surfaces. Install a new gasket.
2. Install water pump and bolts, tighten to specification.
   Water Pump Bolts: .... **24 Nm**
3. Install thermo fan coupling, and adapter plate to water pump pulley, tighten bolts to specification.
   Thermo Fan Coupling Bolts: .... **24 Nm**
4. Install plastic fan to thermo coupling, tighten bolts to specification.
   Plastic Fan to Thermo Coupling Bolts: ..... **10 Nm**
5. Install and tighten drive belt.

CRANKSHAFT BALANCER

Remove

1. Disconnect battery earth lead and remove drive belts as shown in the Belt Drive section.
2. Pull park brake fully on, chock rear wheel and transmission in gear.
3. Loosen and remove balancer retaining bolt.
4. Remove balancer from crankshaft with pulley puller.

Install

1. Using engine oil, lubricate front seal surface of balancer.
2. Install balancer, engaging key on crankshaft with slot in balancer.
3. Install the crankshaft pulley, tighten attaching bolt to specification.
   Crankshaft Balancer Bolt: **323Nm**
4. Install and inspect drive belt operation.

ROCKER COVERS AND/OR SEALS

Remove

1. Remove intercooler as described in this chapter.
2. Disconnect the breather hose from the rocker cover
3. Rocker cover.
   a) Unscrew rocker cover to cylinder head fasteners and remove rocker cover from cylinder head.
   b) If replacing rocker cover seal, remove seal from recess in rocker cover to cylinder head.

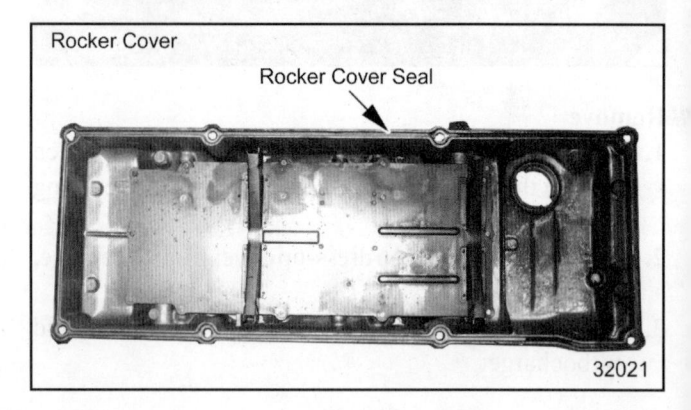

3.2 Litre, incl COMMON RAIL - DOHC (4M41) DIESEL ENGINE MAINTENANCE & REBUILD

Install

1. If necessary, install seal to rocker cover recess.
   Note: Make sure seal is correctly installed in rocker cover.
2. Install rocker cover to cylinder head and torque bolts to specification.
   Rocker Cover Bolts:.....................................**3.4Nm**
3. Connect the breather hose to the rocker cover.
4. Install the intercooler as previously described.

TIMING CHAIN and GEAR COVER, TIMING GEARS, BALANCE SHAFTS and OIL PUMP

Remove

1. Detach the battery cables, remove the battery shroud.
2. Remove the rocker cover as previously described.
3. Detach belts from the alternator and air conditioner.
4. Remove the fan and water pump. 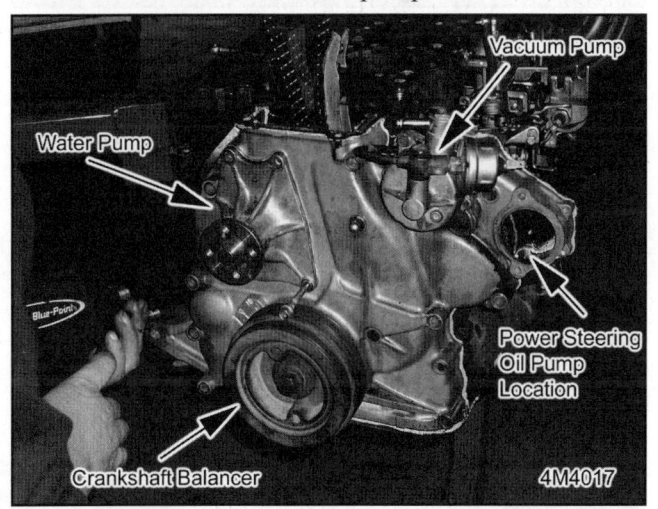
5. Remove the vacuum pump and 3 - "O" rings.
6. Remove the power steering pump and "O" ring. 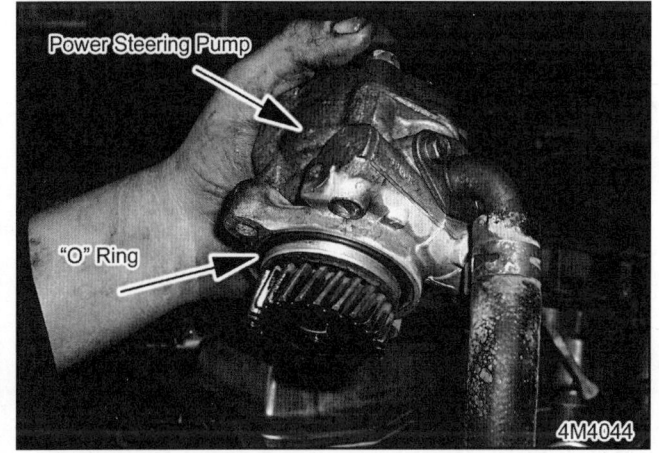
7. Rotate the crankshaft so the crankshaft is at TDC/compression on number 1 cylinder.
8. Remove the crankshaft pulley, use a pulley puller.
9. Remove the air conditioner compressor, tie back away from engine to keep pressure off the air conditioner hoses. 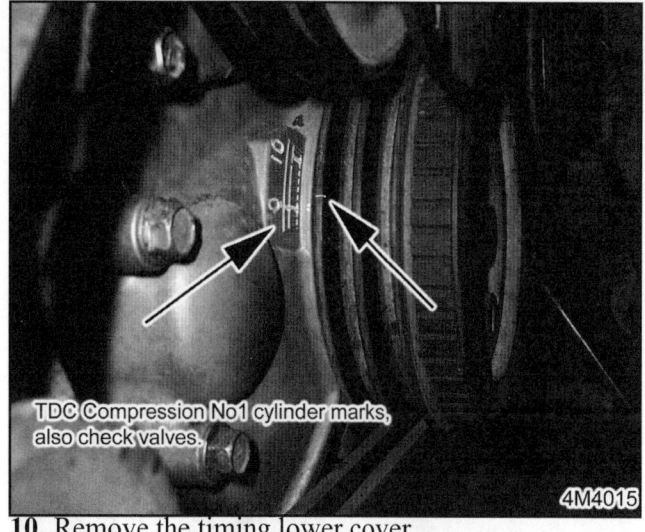
10. Remove the timing lower cover.
11. Remove the bearing block and 2 - "O" rings.
12. Remove the front timing gear case, 2 cap nuts and bolts.
13. a) Check that the two alignment marks on the camshaft gears are aligned with the two coloured chain links.
    b) Check that the two alignment marks on the crankshaft sprocket are aligned.
14. Remove the timing chain upper guide plate.
15. Loosen the camshaft gear bolts, hold the camshaft on the hex surface with a spanner.

3.2 Litre, incl COMMON RAIL - DOHC (4M41) Diesel Engine Maintenance & Rebuild

16. Remove the left side timing chain tension guide lower bolt.
17. Remove the left side timing chain tension guide and shaft.
18. Remove the timing chain lower left guide plate.
19. Remove the timing chain.
20. Remove the camshaft gears.
21. Check that all alignment marks on the gears are aligned as shown.

22. Check gear back lash for excessive wear, replace components that do not meet specification.

Gear back lash check

Crankshaft gear to Idler gear 0.04-0.018mm
    Max 0.3mm
Idler gear to idler gear left side 0.04-0.19mm
    Max 0.3mm
Idler gear left side to left side balance shaft gear
    .... 0.04-0.22mm
    Max 0.4mm
Idler gear to injection pump gear ... 0.04-0.21mm
    Max 0.4mm
Oil pump to right side balance shaft
    .... 0.04-0.19mm
    Max 0.3mm
Oil pump to crankshaft gear 0.04-0.18mm
    Max 0.3mm

23. Remove the right side guide assembly, (bolts, plate and guide).
24. Remove right side balance shaft and oil pump assembly, 3 - "O" rings.

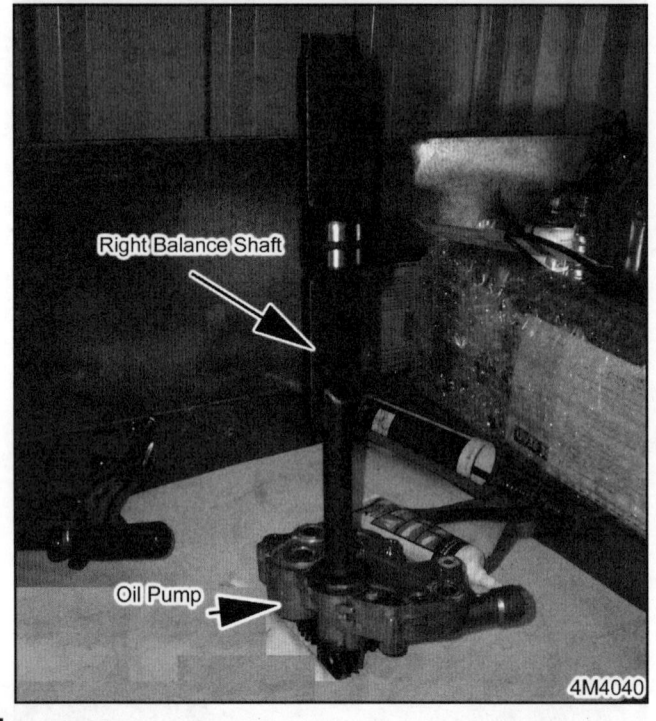

25. Remove the timing chain lower right guide plate.
26. Remove left side idler gear assembly, (bolt, washer gear, gear bush and shaft).
27. Remove left side balance shaft assembly, 2 bolts to remove, 2 "O" rings.
    (If dismantle - bolt, washer, gear, thrust spacer, washer, thrust plate, "O" rings and balance shaft with key).
    Note: *Take note of thrust washer orientation to gear for assembly.*

3.2 Litre, incl COMMON RAIL - DOHC (4M41) DIESEL ENGINE MAINTENANCE & REBUILD

28. Remove the idler gear assembly, (bush, idler gear/sprocket and shaft)

Inspection
1. Check gears for marked teeth.
2. Check bushes for uneven wear marks.
3. Inspect the timing chain tension lever surface for cracks or excessive wear, replace if required.
4. Inspect the timing chain guide surface for cracks or excessive wear, replace if required.

Install
1. Engine at TDC compression number 1 cylinder.
2. Install the idler gear assembly, (bush, idler gear/sprocket and shaft, align idler "1" with crankshaft gear "c" mark.
3. Install left side balance shaft assembly, 2 bolts to remove, 2 "O" rings.
   (Assemble if dismantled - bolt, washer, gear, thrust spacer, washer, thrust plate, "O" rings and balance shaft with key).
   Left Side Balance Shaft Bolts: 12Nm
   Note: *Take note of thrust washer orientation to gear during assembly from dismantle.*

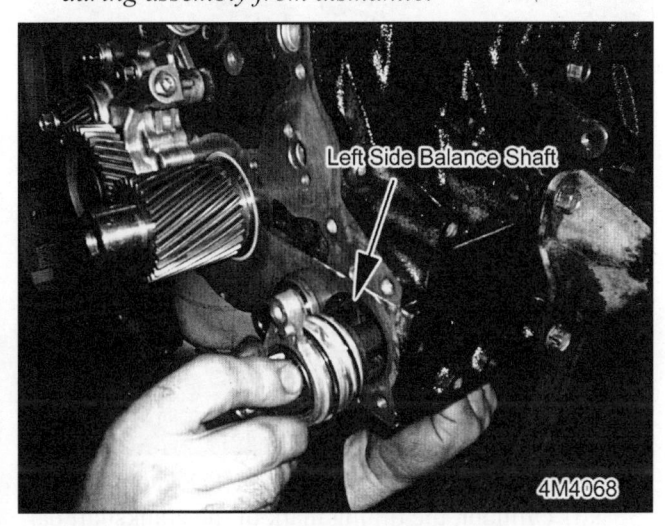

4. Install left side idler gear assembly, (bolt, washer gear, gear bush and shaft). Washer has "F" to front.
   Align idler "3" and "0" with same markings on idler gear and sprocket assembly and balance shaft gear.
5. Install the timing chain lower right guide plate.
6. Install right side balance shaft and oil pump assembly, 3 - "O" rings.
   Oil Pump/Right Side Balance Shaft Bolts: 12Nm
   Align balance shaft gear "0" with right side idler gear "6" mark.
   Align right side idler gear "5" with crankshaft gear "5" mark.

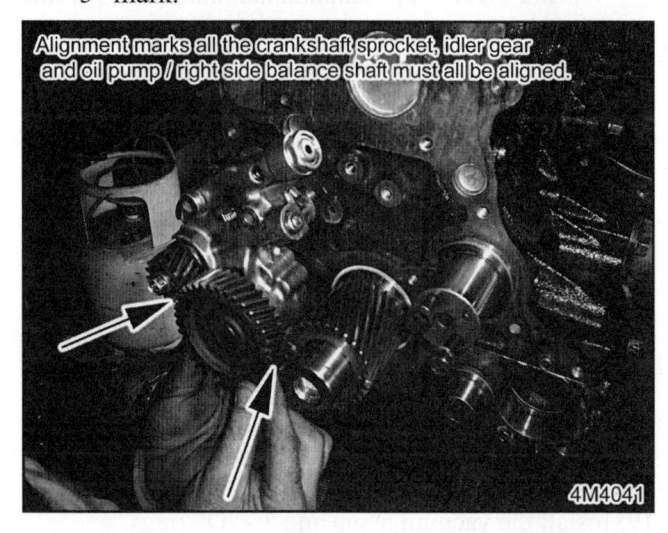

7. Check gear back lash for excessive wear, replace components that do not meet specification.
   See under "Remove step No 21"
8. Install the camshaft gears, while holding the hex section of the camshaft with a spanner. Tighten camshaft gear bolts to specification.
   Camshaft Gear Bolts: 88Nm
9. Install the timing chain.
   a) Check that the alignment marks "1" on the idler gear sprocket and crankshaft gear are aligned.
   b) Check that the camshaft gears are position as:
      - left side "0" at approx 1 o'clock.
      - right side "0" at approx 11 o'clock.
   c) The timing chain has one white link to be aligned with the idler gear sprocket and two lots of two white links to be aligned with the "0" marks of each camshaft gear.
   d) Install timing chain over both camshaft gears aligning white links with "0" marks on camshaft gears. Then install idler gear sprocket with timing chain white link on the "0".
10. Install the right side guide assembly, (bolts, plate and guide).
    Right Side Tension Guide Bolts: 33Nm
11. Install the left side timing chain tension guide and shaft.
12. Install the left side timing chain tension guide lower bolt.
    Left Side Tension Guide Bolt: 40Nm
13. Install the timing chain upper guide plate.

131

3.2 Litre, incl COMMON RAIL - DOHC (4M41) DIESEL ENGINE MAINTENANCE & REBUILD

14. Check timing chain adjustment and wear.
    a) Set the lines on adjusting plate so the lines on the plate and nut align.
    b) Push the tension lever in by hand firmly and measure the distance between the two timing chain surfaces at the narrowest gap.
    c) If not within specification replace timing chain.
    Standard Gap:...................................**16.5mm**
    Max Wear Gap.................................**9.0mm**
15. Install the timing chain lower left guide plate.
16. Replace the front oil seal in the timing case cover.
    a) Remove front seal with a seal remover or screw driver.
    b) Install a new seal with a seal insertion tool.
17. Install the front timing gear case, 2 cap nuts and bolts.
    a) Apply engine oil to the oil seal lips.
    b) Apply a 2.5 - 3.0mm bead of sealant to the surface of the timing case cover.
    Mitsubishi Sealant Part No:...........**MD970389**
    c) Install timing gear case, 2 cap nuts and bolts.
    Timing Cover Cap Nuts:.........................**23 Nm**
18. Install the bearing block and 2 - "O" rings.
19. Install the vacuum pump and 3 - "O" rings.
20. Install the timing lower cover.
21. Install the power steering pump and "O" ring.
22. Install the crankshaft pulley.
    Crankshaft Balancer Bolt:........................**323mm**
23. Tension the timing chain and install the tensioner cover.
    a) Install the (force by hand) plunger into the tensioner.
    Note: The plunger must be installed into tensioner otherwise the tension on the chain will be to great and damage the chain.
    b) Lock the plunger into position with the hook.
    c) Install the tensioner.
    Note: The tensioner automatically keeps tension on the chain by a ratchet, if the engine is rotated anti-clockwise it will release the tensioner, then if the engine is started it could damage the camshaft, valves or pistons.
    If the engine is rotated anti-clockwise by accident, remove the tensioner and re-install the tensioner correctly to reset it.
24. Install the fan and water pump.
25. Install the rocker cover as previously described.
26. Install the air conditioner compressor, tie back away from engine to keep pressure off the air conditioner hoses
27. Install belts from the alternator and air conditioner
28. Install the battery shroud, connect the battery cables.

CYLINDER HEAD, VALVES & CAMSHAFTS

Make sure that all valve train components are kept in order so they can be installed in their original locations.

Remove

1. Disconnect battery earth lead.
2. Remove the inter cooler as previously described.
3. Drain coolant from engine at radiator lower hose and remove top radiator hose.
4. Remove alternator.
    a) Remove nuts from alternator adjuster bracket studs and remove engine harness earth wire connection and wiring harness retainer bracket.
    b) Remove alternator, remove alternator support bolts, then remove support assembly.
5. Remove the attaching oil dipstick tub support bolt.
6. Remove the exhaust manifold as described in this chapter. Main points listed below.
7. Remove the bolts attaching the exhaust pipe to the turbo-charger.
8. Release the brake booster hose, the vacuum hose and breather hose from the rocker cover.
9. [If fitted] Release the EGR pipe retaining bolts from the intake and the exhaust manifold, then withdraw the EGR pipe from the engine assembly.
10. Remove the intake manifold as described.
11. Disconnect glow plug harness connector, where glow plugs are fitted.
12. [Direct Injection]
    a) Remove the fuel delivery pipe.
    [Common Rail]
    a) Remove the fuel delivery pipes between the injectors and the common rail.
    b) Remove the fuel return pipe and fittings.
    c) Remove the injector harness.
13. Rotate crankshaft so engine is at TDC compression No1 cylinder, the timing mark of the crankshaft balancer is aligned with the "T" on the timing belt cover. Remove crankshaft balancer bolt, use a pulley remover to remove the pulley, as described in this chapter.

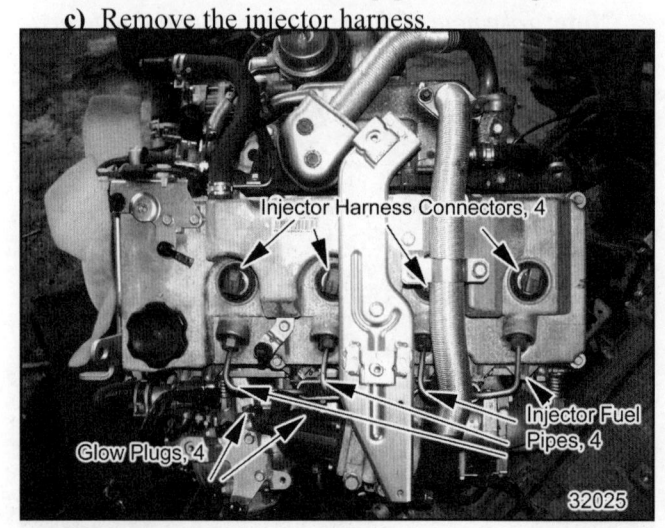

3.2 Litre, incl COMMON RAIL - DOHC (4M41) DIESEL ENGINE MAINTENANCE & REBUILD

14. [Direct Injection]
    a) Disconnect the fuel pipes from the injectors.
    b) Remove the fuel injectors, 2 bolts each.
    [Common Rail]
    a) Disconnect the fuel pipes from the injectors.
    b) Remove the fuel injector supporters and bolts.
    c) Remove the fuel injectors and gaskets.
15. Remove the rocker cover as described.
16. Loosen the timing chain tensioner situated on the side of the cylinder head.
17. Tie off timing chain is it possible with 2 gears.
    a) Remove the front seal to gain access for the spanner to camshaft gear bolt.
    b) The timing chain has two lots of two coloured links that are aligned with two "0" marks of each camshaft gear.
    c) Loosen camshaft gear bolts (it has a reverse thread) the arrow on the bolt indicates tightening direction. Use a shifter or spanner on the camshaft hexagonal section to hold camshaft.

    Note: Do not use timing chain to take tension of loosening or tightening camshaft gear bolt.

    d) Hold the camshaft gears and chain, while you remove the camshaft gears bolts, ensure the chain does not move on the gears while this happens. Slightly lower the camshaft gears to slacken the chain, not slack enough for the , use some strong tie wire to tie the chain to the gears. Tie the camshaft gears and chain to the cylinder head at this stage so the gears and chain will not drop down behind the front timing cover.

    e) Always keep slight tension on chain to make sure it does not jump any teeth on the idler gear.
18. Remove the camshaft holders (bearing caps) into place. Take note that the camshaft holders have arrows facing to the front of the engine and numbered from the front of the engine.
    Loosen the camshaft holder bolts in order shown.

3.2 litre Direct Injection
Camshaft Holders
Loosen:
5	11	14	8	2
6	12	15	9	3
4	10	13	7	1

Tighten:
11	5	2	8	14
10	4	1	7	13
12	6	3	9	15

19. Loosen the cylinder head bolts in the order shown, loosen a little each pass until the bolts are loose. Remove cylinder head bolts.

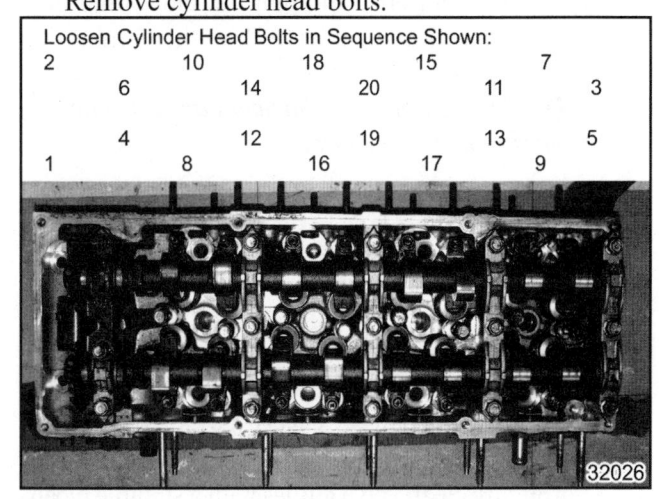

Loosen Cylinder Head Bolts in Sequence Shown:
2		10		18		15		7
	6		14		20		11		3
	4		12		19		13		5
1		8		16		17		9

20. Lift the cylinder head and gasket from engine block.
    Position the camshaft gears and chain so it does not drop behind front timing cover, tie it to the cover.

CYLINDER HEAD RECONDITIONING
* Make sure that all valve train components are kept together and identified so that they can be installed in their original locations.

Dismantle
1. Remove the fuel injectors.
2. Remove the bolts securing the camshaft bearing caps and camshaft holders, loosen gradually and in order from the ends to the middle.
   Remove the camshaft.
3. Remove the roller rockers, keeping them in order of

133

removal as there are short and long roller rockers. The roller rockers are marked with a "S" for short and "L" for long rocker covers.

4. Measure the sinkage of the valves from the cylinder head bottom.
   Standard Valve Sinkage: .... 0.05 - 0.55 mm
   Max .... 0.80 mm
5. Compress valve springs in turn with a suitable spring compressor and remove valve collets.
6. Remove the following:
   a) Valve spring caps, springs, valve spring seats. and valve stem oil seals.
   b) Valves from cylinder head.
      Caution: Do not force valves out of guides, as mushroomed valve ends due to lifter wear or dirt in the guide, will damage guide. Remove burrs by chamfering valve stem with an oil stone or file.
7. Remove the glow plugs from the cylinder head.
8. If required remove the combustion chambers.
   a) Heat the cylinder head to allow the cylinder head expansion from the combustion chamber, helping removal.
   b) Use a rod inserted through the glow plug hole and tap with a hammer to free the combustion chamber.
   Tip: The combustion chambers are ceramic and will break if hit to hard.

Clean

1. a) Clean all carbon from combustion chambers, valve ports, etc, with a rotary-type carbon removing wire brush.
      * Do not use a wire brush on any gasket sealing surface.
   b) Clean cylinder head gasket surface of cylinder head.
2. Thoroughly clean valve guides with a suitable cleaning solvent or a wire brush.
3. Clean valve heads with a drill and wire brush.
   * Do not scratch the valve stem.
4. Wash all components in a suitable cleaning solvent and air dry with dry compressed air.

Cylinder Head Inspection

1. Cylinder heads should be inspected for cracks in valve seats and combustion chambers, and for external cracks to water jackets.
2. Check cylinder head deck surface for corrosion.
3. Using a straight edge and feeler gauge, check cylinder head deck, intake and exhaust manifold surfaces for distortion. Check cylinder head deck surface diagonally, longitudinally and transversely.
   These surfaces may be refaced once only by parallel grinding.

Cylinder Head Distortion: .... less than 0.05 mm
   - Max .... 0.20 mm
* Head to block surface if more than 0.20 mm must be removed from any surface, replace cylinder head.
4. Inspect the following:
   a) Cylinder head for cracks, especially between valve seats or exhaust ports.

   b) Cylinder head deck surface for corrosion, casting sand inclusions or blow holes.
   c) Cylinder block deck surface with a suitable straight edge.

VALVE GUIDES

Clearance Checking

1. Excessive valve stem to guide bore clearance will cause lack of power, rough idling and noisy valve operation.
2. Insufficient clearance will result in noisy and sticking of the valve and will interfere with smoothness of operation of engine.
3. Measure inside diameter with an ID micrometer, also measure the valve stem, then use the following sum to calculate the guide clearance.
   ** Guide diameter - stem diameter = clearance **
   Valve stem to guide clearance
      - Inlet .... 0.02 - 0.06 mm
      - Exhaust .... 0.05 - 0.09 mm
4. If it is necessary to replace the valve guide see valve guide replacement in this chapter.

Valve Guide Replacement

1. Use a hammer and flat end rod to drive the old valve guide down into the port area of the head, at room temperature.
2. Measure guide hole, if over specified ID rebore to fit the over size valve guide.
   Valve guide hole OD .... 12.00 mm
      - 0.05, 0.25 and 0.50mm Oversize available
3. Valve guides different lengths, the intake valve guide

3.2 Litre, incl COMMON RAIL - DOHC (4M41) Diesel Engine MAINTENANCE & REBUILD

is longer than the exhaust vale guide.
4. Use a press and valve guide installing die to press the new valve guide down into cylinder head, at room temperature.
5. The guide is driven down into the cylinder head until the guide is at specified height from valve spring seat surface. Intake and exhaust valve guides are installed to the same specified height.
   Valve Guide Installed Height ....16.50 mm
6. Ream bush out with a reamer to obtain specified diameter.

VALVE SEATS

1. Reconditioning the valve seats is very important because the seating of the valves must be perfect for the engine to deliver the power and performance its develops.
2. Another important factor is the cooling of the valve head. Good contact between each valve and its seat in the head is imperative to ensure that the heat in the valve head will be properly carried away.
3. Several different types of equipment are available for reconditioning valve seats. The recommendations of the manufacturer of the equipment being used should be carefully followed to attain proper results.
4. Check valve seats for any evidence of pitting or damage at valve contact surface. If pitting is evident, the valve seats will need to be reconditioned.
   * Because the valve guide serves to support and centre the valve seat grinder, it is essential that the valve guide is serviced before reconditioning the valve seats.
5. If the seat is too wide after grinding, it may be narrowed by using a 30° or 65° grinding stone. The 30° stone will lower the seat and the 65° stone will raise the seat.
   Valve seat width................................. 1.8 - 2.2 mm
   **   - Min ....2.8 mm**
6. If the valves seats are reconditioned, the valves must also be reconditioned (refer VALVES) or replace valves as necessary.

REPLACING VALVE SEAT

1. Using a lathe, turn down the out side diameter of a valve head so it fill fit neatly into inside of the valve seat.
2. Cover the head that surrounds the valve seat with an inflammable paste, such as soap paste. This will stop damage from weld spatter.
3. Weld a continuous run of weld around the edge of the valve, so it is welded to the inside of the valve seat.
4. Lift the head so the top of the valve can be tapped to free the valve seat.
5. Slide the machined valve and valve seat out of the head.
6. Machine the head as the new valve seat is over size by 0.30mm diameter and depth.
   Valve Seat Inserts Standard Size:
     Intake 35.0mm
     Exhaust 33.0mm
   Over size Valve Seat Insert are in 0.30 and 0.60mm oversize
7. The new valve seat should not to be hit or forced into the head as this will cause damage to the seat and head.
8. Place the new valve seat in liquid nitrogen or dry ice so the seat will shrink in size.
9. Carefully place the valve seat into position with an old valve (converted into a special tool as shown in diagram) positioned through the seat into the valve guide. Gently tap the special tool to position and centre the valve seat

VALVE STEM OIL SEALS

Replacement with cylinder head on, steps 4 to 8 with cylinder head off.

1. Disconnect battery earth lead.
2. Remove the following:
   a) Glow plug harness wiring.
   b) Glow plug from relevant cylinder and screw air adaptor into glow plug hole.
   c) Rocker cover as previously described in this chapter.
   d) Timing chain gear as described in this chapter.
   e) Camshaft.
3. Apply air pressure via a special fitting that screws into the glow plug hole, to hold valves in closed position.
4. a) Compress valve spring with valve spring compressor.
   b) Remove valve collets.
   * Before installing valve spring compressor, it may be necessary to tap top of valve cap with a soft-faced hammer to overcome the binding of the valve collets in the valve spring cap.
5. a) Remove spring cap, spring and valve compressor as an assembly.
   b) Remove and discard old valve stem oil seal.
6. Install new valve stem oil seal and make sure the seal fully seats on top of the valve guide.
   * Make sure the correct type of seal is fitted to the appropriate valve, based on part No. and package description.
7. a) Install spring, cap and valve compressor as an assembly on the valve stem.
   b) Install valve collets and slowly release spring compressor, then remove spring compressor.
   c) Disconnect air line to special tool.
8. Install the following:

a) Camshaft as previously described in this Chapter.
b) Replace camshaft gear as described in this chapter.
c) Rocker cover as previously described in this Chapter.
9. Remove special tool and install and torque glow plug.
10. Install glow plug harness and battery earth lead.
11. Start engine and check for oil leaks and valve train noise.

VALVE SPRINGS

1. Inspect valve spring surfaces on valve seat and valve cap for wear or gouging. Replace components as necessary.
2. a) Check spring ends. If they are not parallel, the spring is bent.
   b) Replace valve springs that do not meet specification.
3. Check spring for squareness, use a square stand valve spring along side, if not within specification replace spring.
   Valve Spring Out of Square Angle ....2 degree
   Max ....4 degree

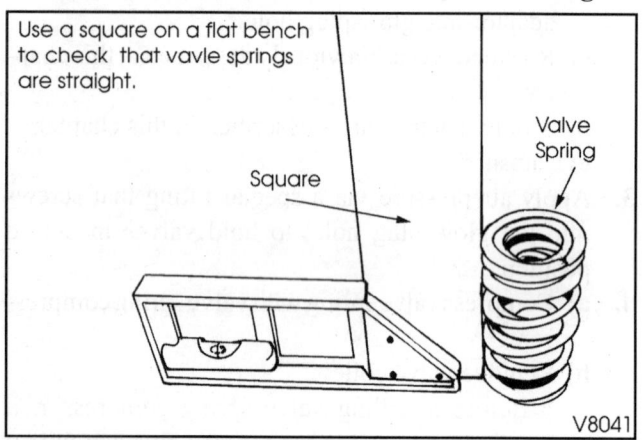

4. a) Check valve spring load with a spring tester.
   b) Springs should be compressed to the specified height and checked against specifications.
   c) Replace any valve spring if not to specification.
   Free length ....51.3 mm
   Compress valve spring and check height at give pressure, replace if not as specified.
   Compressed length at 255N .... 39.5 mm
   d) Measure installed height of valve spring between spring seat and top of valve.
   Valve Installed Height 39.5mm

VALVES

1. a) Inspect valve stem for burrs and scratches. (Burrs and minor scratching may be removed with an oil stone.) 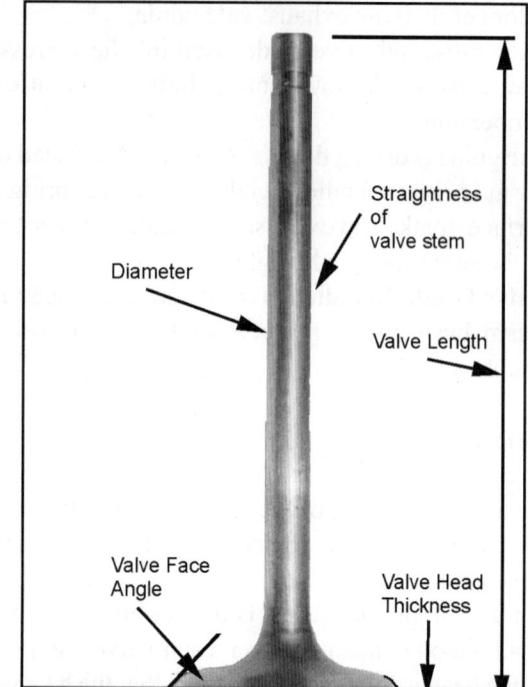
   b) Valves with excessive stem wear or that are warped should be replaced.
   c) Inspect valve stem tip for wear. The valve tip may be reconditioned by grinding.
   d) Follow the grinder manufacturers instructions. Make sure the new tip surface is at right-angles to the valve stem.
   e) Do not grind valve below minimum specified length.
2. Inspect valve stem collet groove for damage.
3. a) Check valve face for burning or cracking.
   b) If pieces have broken off, inspect corresponding piston and cylinder head area for damage.
4. a) Inspect valve stem for straightness and valve head for bending or distortion using 'V' blocks.
   b) Bent or distorted valves must be replaced.
5. Valves with pitted or grooves faces can be reconditioned with a valve refacing machine, ensuring correct relationship between head and stem.
   * If pitting or grooving is so deep that refacing would result in a 'knife' edge at the valve head, the valve must be replaced.
   * Measure valve margin after refacing valves. If margin is less than minimum specified, the valve must be replaced.
6. Lightly lap reconditioned valves into valve seat.
   * New valves must not be lapped. Lapping destroys the protective coating on the valve face.
7. Measure valves for specification.
   Stem diameter   - Inlet .... 6.560 - 6.575 mm
   **   - Min ....6.45 mm**
   **   - Exhaust .... 6.53 - 6.55 mm**
   **   - Min ....6.45 mm**
   Valve face angle 45° +/- 15'

3.2 Litre, incl COMMON RAIL - DOHC (4M41) DIESEL ENGINE MAINTENANCE & REBUILD

Valve Head Thickness: ....1.0 mm
            - Min ....0.8 mm
Valve seat width.............................. 1.8 - 2.2 mm
            - Min ....2.8 mm
Valve stem to guide clearance
            - Inlet .... 0.02 - 0.06 mm
            - Exhaust .... 0.05 - 0.09 mm

8. After refacing or installing a new valve, check for correct seating as follows.
   a) Lightly coat valve face with bearing blue.
   b) Insert valve and rotate about 1/6 of a revolution.
   c) Remove valve and check for full contact with seat.
      i) If partial contact is indicated, insert valve again and turn through a full revolution.
      ii) If blue on seat indicates full contact, reface valve.
      iii) If partial contact is still indicated, re-grind cylinder head valve seat.
   d) Clean all traces of bearing blue from valves and seats.

CAMSHAFTS
Inspection.
1. Check camshaft bearing journals and lobes for overheating, damage or wear (discolouration).
2. Inspect camshaft journal diameter with micrometer. Replace camshaft if journals are not within specifications.
   Camshaft Journal diameter ..... 44.93 - 44.94 mm
3. Position camshaft on 'V' blocks and check the camshaft run-out using a dial gauge.
   Camshaft Run-out ....0.015 mm
          Max: 0.03mm
4. Inspect the camshaft lobe lift, using a micrometer, record all the results, measure the base circle diameter, measure the lobe height, subtract the base circle diameter from the lobe height to obtain the lift.
   Height of cam lobe lift
   Inlet
       - Front .... 6.16 mm
       - Min.................................... 6.11 mm
       - Rear................................... 6.10 mm
       - Min.................................... 6.05 mm

   Exhaust
       - Front .... 5.91 mm
       - Min.................................... 5.86 mm
       - Rear................................... 6.16 mm
       - Min.................................... 6.11 mm

ASSEMBLE CYLINDER HEAD
1. Dry and clean all components thoroughly.
2. Using clean engine oil, lubricate valve stems and valve guides thoroughly.
3. Install valves in corresponding guides.
4. Make sure that seals fully seat on top of guide, install new valve stem oil seals. The original seals may not be the same colour as the replacement seals.
5. Install the valve spring seat over the valve guide onto the cylinder head.
6. Place valve springs and cap over valve stem.
   Note: The blue painted end of valve spring goes to the top.

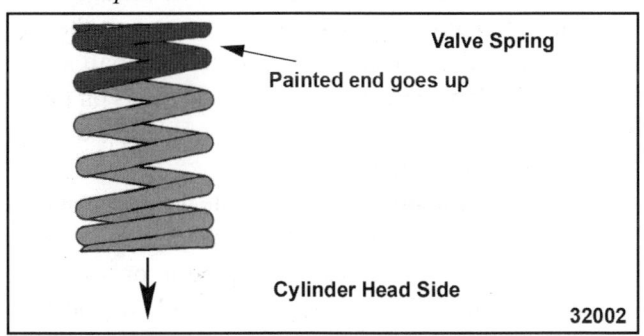

7. Using a suitable spring compressor, compress valve springs.
   * Excess compression could cause spring cap to damage valve stem oil seal, ensure to compress valve springs only enough to install valve collets.
8. Install valve collets, making sure that they locate accurately in groove in top end of valve stem. Release the valve spring compressor slowly ensuring that the collets sit properly. Grease may be used to hold collets in place.
9. Install the lower section of the camshaft holders (bearing caps) into place.
10. Lubricate the roller rockers and install in position, take note of the position of the short "S" and the long "L" roller rockers.

11. Lubricate the camshaft journals and lobes with molybdenum grease. Position the camshaft onto the head.
12. Lubricate and install the camshaft holders (bearing caps) into place. The camshaft holders have arrows facing to the front of the engine and numbered from

137

3.2 Litre, incl COMMON RAIL - DOHC (4M41) Diesel Engine MAINTENANCE & REBUILD

the front of the engine.
Tighten the camshaft holder bolts to specification in order previously shown from the middle to the end.
Camshaft Holder Bolts: .... **20 Nm**

13. Install the glow plugs, tighten to specification.
    Glow Plugs: .... **18 Nm**
14. Install the glow plug wiring bar and tighten glow plug top screws.

VALVE CLEARANCE - ADJUSTMENT

1. **Timing chain removed** - use a spanner on the hex section of the camshaft to rotate the camshaft so the camshaft lobe base of the circle diameter is on top of the rocker arm. The rocker arm should have a slight amount of movement.
   Timing chain not removed - rotate the engine with a socket and breaker bar on the crankshaft pulley bolt, rotate engine in a clockwise direction only. Rotate so the camshaft lobe base of the circle diameter is on top of the lifter shim you are require to measure clearance.
2. At TDC compression cylinder No1 adjust the valves indicated below.

Cylinder	1	2	3	4
Intake	X	X		
Exhaust	X		X	

At TDC compression cylinder No4 adjust the valves indicated below.

Cylinder	1	2	3	4
Intake			X	X
Exhaust		X		X

3. Use a feeler gauge to measure the clearance between the top of the rocker arm and the base circle diameter of the camshaft.
4. Check for specification clearance.
   Valve Clearance (Cold)
   Intake .... **0.1 mm**
   Exhaust .... **0.15 mm**
5. If clearance is not to specification loosen the lock nut, adjust the adjuster with a feeler gauge inserted, then tighten lock nut.

CYLINDER HEAD GASKET SELECTION

1. Use a dial gauge on top of the cylinder block, rotate the engine so the piston is at the highest position, record the distance of protrusion. This must be carried out and recorded for all pistons.
2. Using the average piston protrusion measurement, use the chart below to select the gasket thickness required.

Measure Piston Protrusion for Cylinder Head Gasket Selection

Piston Protrusion	Head Gasket
max piston protrusion	Grade & notches
+ 0.03 - + 0.11 mm	A - 1 notches
- 0.05 - -0.03 mm	B - 2 notches
- 0.13 - - 0.05 mm	C - 3 notches
- 0.23 - - 0.15 mm	D - 4 notches

INSTALL CYLINDER HEAD

1. Select the correct the correct head gasket grade as described above.
2. Place dowel pins into block, place head gasket in position over dowel pins on cylinder block.
3. Apply sealant at the joining areas of the front timing gear cover the cylinder block.
4. a) Carefully guide cylinder head into place over dowel pins and gasket.
   b) Place cylinder head and tighten with finger, remove dowel pins during this procedure.
   Note: *If the camshaft gears are tied to the timing chain, the camshaft gears and chain must be feed up through the cylinder head while it is being installed. Then the camshaft gears must be tied to the cylinder head. Always keep slight tension on chain to make sure it does not jump any teeth on the idler gear.*
5. Apply a thin coat of engine to cylinder head bolt thread and seat section.
   Note: *Cylinder head bolts stretch.*
   Note: *Cylinder head bolts should not be tightened more than twice, there fore it is good practise to mark each cylinder head bolt with a punch each time the head is installed. If the bolts have 2 punch marks, replace them with new bolts.*
   Note: *Cylinder head bolt washers are installed with rounded edge up.*
   Tighten the head bolts to the following sequence and in the order shown.
   M12 Bolts - Cold in 5 stages
   Cylinder head bolts - Cold - in sequence ... 98Nm
   Loosen in reverse order
   Cylinder head bolts - Cold - in sequence ...49Nm
   Rotate .... **90 degrees**
   Rotate .... **90 degrees**

138

3.2 Litre, incl COMMON RAIL - DOHC (4M41) DIESEL ENGINE MAINTENANCE & REBUILD

Two front M10 bolts - Cold in 3 stages
Cylinder head bolts - Cold - in 3 stages 24Nm
* It is important to follow the given procedure to avoid head gasket failure and possible engine damage.

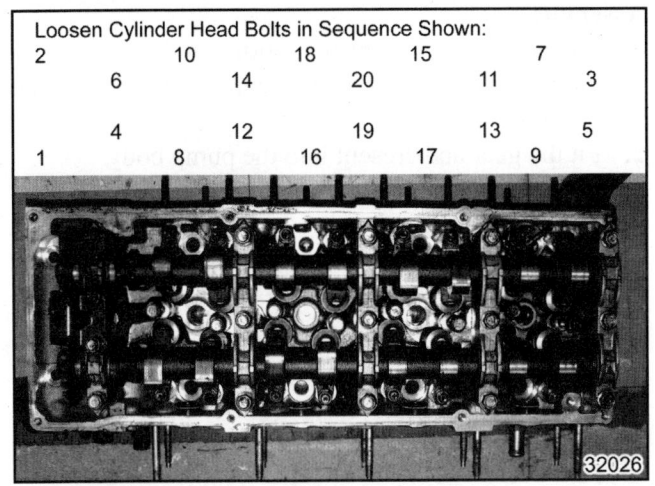

Loosen Cylinder Head Bolts in Sequence Shown:
```
2         10        18        15        7
    6         14        20        11        3
    4         12        19        13        5
1         8         16        17        9
```

6. Turn the engine over so the crankshaft is at TDC/ compression on number 1 cylinder.
   Note: *Steps 7 to 11 if camshaft and valve assemblies are not already installed.*
7. Install the lower section of the camshaft holders (bearing caps) into place.
8. Lubricate the roller rockers and install in position, take note of the position of the short "S" and the long "L" roller rockers.
9. Lubricate the camshaft journals and lobes with molybdenum grease.
   Position the camshafts onto the head, position the camshaft TDC marks at 12 o'clock, see previous illustrations.
10. Lubricate and install the camshaft holders (bearing caps) into place. The camshaft holders have arrows facing to the front of the engine and numbered from the front of the engine.
    Tighten the camshaft holder bolts to specification in order shown from the middle to the end.
    Camshaft Holder Bolts: .... 20 Nm
11. Install the camshaft gears and bolts, tightening to specification. If the timing chain is tied to camshaft gear, ensure the chain does not move on the gears. Ensure the alignment marks are alinged as per directions under "**TIMING CHAIN and GEAR COVER, TIMING GEARS, BALANCE SHAFTS and OIL PUMP**"
    Camshaft Gear Bolt (Left hand thread) 88Nm
12. Adjust the roller rockers as described under "Valve Clearance - Adjustment" in "Maintenance and Tune-up" chapter.
13. [Direct Injection]
    Install the injectors and fuel pipe, tighten bolts to specification.
    Fuel Injector Bolts: .... 21 Nm

[Common Rail]
a) Tighten the support bolts to specified torque.
   Fuel Injector Supporter Bolts: .... 21 Nm
b) Install the injector gaskets and injectors.
c) Coat the bearing surface and injector supporter holder bolts with clean engine oil.
d) Install injector supporters.
e) Install fuel leakage pipe and gaskets to injectors.
f) Tighten the eye bolts at the injector side first then the eye bolts at the cylinder head side next.
   Fuel Injector Assembly Eye Bolts......... 15 Nm
g) Tighten the leakage pipe attaching bolt to specified torque.
   Injector Fuel Leakage Pipe Bolt........... 24 Nm
h) Tighten the injector holder bolts to specified torque, steps 1 & 2:
   Fuel Injector Supporter Bolts............... 10 Nm
   tighten a further 80 deg
* if tightened further than 85 deg, loosen and repeat steps 1 & 2.
14. Install the timing gear upper cover.
15. Install the timing chain tensioner situated on the side of the cylinder head, apply sealant to the gasket. See under "**TIMING CHAIN and GEAR COVER, TIMING GEARS, BALANCE SHAFTS and OIL PUMP**"
16. Install rocker cover and gasket.
17. [Direct Injection]
    a) Install the fuel delivery pipe.
    [Common Rail]
    a) Install the fuel delivery pipes between the injectors and the common rail.
    b) Install the fuel return pipe and fittings.
    c) Replace and connect the injector harness.
18. Install the front timing cover as described.
19. Install the crankshaft pulley, tighten attaching bolt to specification.
    Crankshaft bolt 323Nm

VACUUM PUMP
Remove
1. Remove the vacuum hose.
2. Remove the oil pipe and fittings.
3. Remove the oil pressure gauge unit / switch.
4. Remove the vacuum pump bolts, vacuum pump.

Install
1. Clean all matching surfaces of timing cover and vacuum pump thoroughly.
   Vacuum Pump Cover Bolts 5.4Nm
2. Fit seal and install vacuum pump and bolts. Tighten to specification.
   Vacuum Pump Eye Bolt 20Nm
3. Install the oil pressure gauge unit / switch.

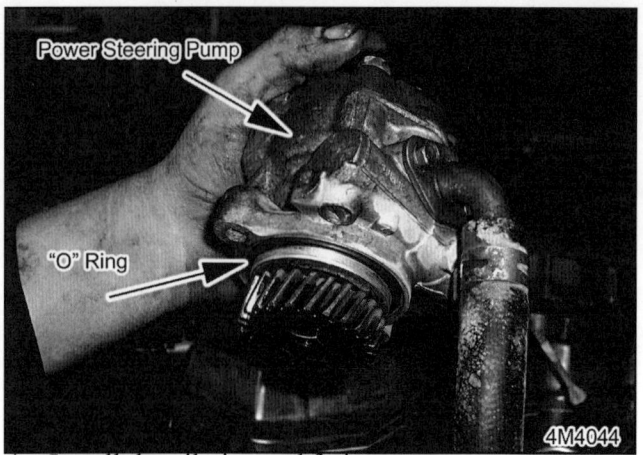

3.2 Litre, incl COMMON RAIL - DOHC (4M41) Diesel Engine Maintenance & Rebuild

4. Install the oil pipe and fittings.
5. Install the vacuum hose.

OIL PUMP / RIGHT BALANCE SHAFT

Also see under "Timing Chain and Gear Cover, Timing Gears, Balance Shafts and Oil Pump" in this chapter

Remove
1. Remove the front timing cover as described under Timing Chain section.
2. Remove the right side balance shaft and oil pump assembly, and bolts.

Dismantle
1. Remove the balance shaft gear bolt, washer, balance shaft gear and thrust washer. Remove balance shaft.
2. Remove the oil pump body cover retaining screws, then remove cover plate.
3. Withdraw the inner and outer rotors from the front pump body.
4. Release the relief valve retaining cir-clip from the rear housing body, then withdraw the retainer, spring and piston.

Inspection
1. Wash all parts and dry, lay out on a clean bench.
2. Check for damage and wear to the outer race to pump housing.
3. Check for damage and wear to the gear tooth and crest and to pump case.
   Inner Gear tip to Crest clearance..0.15 - 0.27mm
   Gear to Pump Cover Clearance....0.05 - 0.10mm
   Max 0.15mm
   Shaft to oil pump case and cover clearance.........
   .. 0.03 - 0.05mm
4. Check the cover surface for damage by gear and gear clearance (use a straight edge).
   Shaft to oil pump case and cover clearance.........
   .. 0.03 - 0.05mm
   If components are to be replaced, replace as a complete unit.

5. Visually inspect relief valve for smoothness of surfaces, check when assembling that the spring will keep the valve closed when the cap is fitted.

Assemble
1. Fit the relief valve piston, spring and retainer into the rear pump body, then secure in place with the cir-clip.
2. Fit the gear and cresent into the pump body.
3. Fit a new gasket to the pump body and install oil pump cover.
4. Install the balance shaft, thrust washer, balance shaft gear, washer and bolt, tighten bolt to specification.
   Balance Shaft Gear Bolt 37Nm

Install
1. Install the oil pump and balance shaft to the engine, position on location pins. Install bolt and tighten.
2. Install the crankshaft key-way and sprocket to the crankshaft.
3. Install the timing chain as previously described in this chapter.

FLYWHEEL/DRIVEPLATE

Remove
Before removal of flywheel/driveplate take note of the location of paint aligning marks on flywheel and pressure plate, before removing clutch pressure plate, the driveplate and torque converter also have paint aligning marks. If not visible, scribe aligning marks on all parts.

1. To remove transmission refer to Manual Transmission or Automatic Transmission in this manual.
2. Vehicles with manual transmission:
   Remove the clutch pressure plate and driven plate as per Clutch section in this manual.
3. Block flywheel driveplate from turning, using a screwdriver or suitable locking tool. Remove flywheel/driveplate crankshaft bolts and flywheel/driveplate.

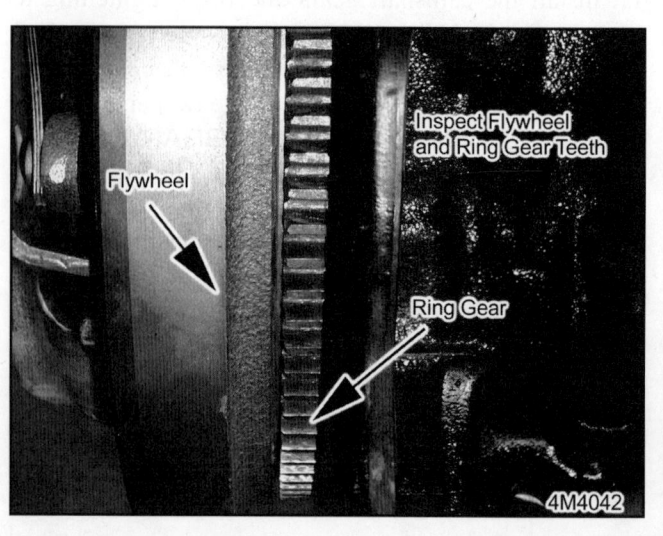

3.2 Litre, incl COMMON RAIL - DOHC (4M41) Diesel Engine MAINTENANCE & REBUILD

Inspection.
The flywheel and flexiplate are purposely out of balance and no attempt should be made to balance these as an individual unit.

1. Check flywheel/driveplate ring gear for badly worn, damaged or cracked teeth.
   If needed, replace flywheel ring gear or driveplate, for details refer to "ring gear" section in this chapter.
   Check starter motor pinion gear for damage, if ring gear teeth are damaged replace pinion gear, for details refer to "Starting System chapter".
2. Inspect crankshaft and flywheel/driveplate matching surfaces for burrs. Using a fine mill file remove burrs if present.

Install
1. Install flywheel/driveplate to crankshaft, and tighten bolts to the correct specification.
   Flywheel / Drive Plate Bolts 123Nm
2. Mount a dial indicator on the rear of cylinder block for vehicles with automatic transmission. Inspect flexiplate Run-out at the torque converter mounting bolt holes. Run-out should not exceed the following specifications.
   Try to correct by tapping high side with a mallet if Run-out exceeds specification. Replace driveplate if this condition can not be corrected.
3. Inspect starter motor operation.

RING GEAR
Replacement
The ring gear is welded to the driveplate and is serviced only as an assembly for vehicles with automatic transmission. Therefore must be replaced as a complete unit.
For vehicles with manual transmission, the ring gear is a shrink fit on the flywheel flange, and if damaged, can be removed and replaced.

Replacement Techniques
1. To remove flywheel refer to Flywheel/ Driveplate section in this manual for details.
2. To remove ring gear drill a hole between two ring gear teeth and split gear at this point using a chisel.
3. Make sure that there are no foreign matter or burrs on new ring gear and flywheel matching surface. Remove burrs using a fine mill file (if present).
4. Heat and shrink a new gear in place as follows:
   a) Using an emery cloth, polish several spots on ring gear.
   b) Using a hot plate or a slow moving torch, heat ring gear until the polished spots turn blue (approximately 320 degrees Celsius).
      * Heating the ring gear in excess of 427 degrees Celsius will destroy ring gear heat treatment.
   c) Quickly place ring gear in position against shoulder of flywheel using 2 pairs of pliers. Allow ring gear to cool slowly until it contracts and is firmly held in place.
5. To install flywheel refer to Flywheel/Driveplate section in this manual. Tighten bolt to specification.

SPIGOT BEARING
Before removing plate, take note of the position of the paint aligning marks on flywheel and pressure plate. If marks are not visible, scribe aligning marks on both parts.

Replacement
1. To remove transmission refer to Manual Transmission section in this manual for details.
2. To remove clutch pressure plate and driven plate refer to Clutch section in this manual.
3. To remove spigot bearing use a Slide hammer.
4. Use a piloted screwdriver to replace spigot bearing. Place new bearing on pilot of tool with radius in bore of bearing next to shoulder on tool. Drive bearing into crankshaft to the dimension as shown in the diagram. Use thin film of SAE 90 Gear Oil to lubricate the bearing.
5. To install clutch assembly and transmission refer to Clutch and Manual Transmission sections in this manual.

3.2 Litre, incl COMMON RAIL - DOHC (4M41) DIESEL ENGINE MAINTENANCE & REBUILD

ENGINE REBUILD.

ENGINE ASSEMBLY.
Remove
1. Discharge fuel system, Remove fuel pump relay, start and idle engine until it stalls, replace relay. Disconnect the battery.

2. Disconnect battery leads
3. a) Remove bottom radiator hose from the radiator, and drain the cooling system, then remove the top and bottom radiator hoses from the engine.
   b) Remove the fan assembly and radiator as outlined in Cooling chapter.
4. Mark the position of the bonnet hinge brackets on the bonnet, then release and withdraw the bonnet from the vehicle.
5. Remove the air cleaner assembly.
6. Drain engine oil sump.
7. Disconnect the front exhaust pipe, refer to exhaust system chapter.
8. Disconnect the accelerator cable / accelerator wiring harness connector, and then disconnect the vacuum hoses including the booster vacuum hose.
9. Disconnect heater hoses.
10. Disconnect the electrical connections for throttle position sensor, ISC servo.
11. Disconnect the connector for the coolant temperature gauge and the coolant temperature sensor.
12. Disconnect main wiring harness from engine and battery harness.
13. Unclip engine harness from the starter, alternator and oil pressure sensor, ensure the wiring harness is labelled.
14. Remove front drive belts, slacken off idler tension.
15. Disconnect the pressure fuel hose and the fuel return hose.
16. Remove the power steering and A/C drive belt if not already removed.
17. Remove the power steering pump and A/C compressor, leaving the hoses and pipes connected and position out of the way.
    Note: *Do not allow then to hang, they must be tied up.*
18. Remove the starter motor heatsheild then remove the starter motor.
19. Remove centre bolt from engine mount at transmission.
20. Raise engine slightly to take weight off mounts by attaching an appropriate lifting hook and chain to engine lifting brackets if fitted. Otherwise care must be taken not to damage engine components with rope or chain while lifting engine.
    Support engine with engine crane then release the engine mounts and remove engine from vehicle.
21. Raise engine with front tilted upwards.
    * Do not allow engine to swing backwards or forward and damage any of the components.
22. Separate engine and transmission assemblies if necessary.

Dismantle.
1. Mount engine assembly in an appropriate engine stand.
2. Remove the following parts as previously described or about to be described, in this chapter.
   a) Intake manifold.
   b) Rocker Cover.
   c) Exhaust manifold and turbocharger.
   d) Oil filter.
   e) Vacuum pump.
   f) Power steering pump.
   g) Crankshaft balancer.
   h) Front timing cover.
   i) Timing chain, camshaft gears.
   j) Camshafts.
   k) Cylinder head
   l) Engine sump.
   m) Oil pump suction pipe and baffle.

n) Flywheel/flexiplate.
o) Engine rear end plate.
p) Crankshaft.
q) Piston and connecting rod assemblies.

Assembly.

Assembly techniques for each part are outlined in this section under there particular headings.

1. Make sure that all bolts and nuts are tightened as specified in this section.
2. Use specified engine lubricant and coolant when refilling.
3. Inspect transmission fluid level, add lubricant as required.
4. Inspect for fuel, coolant, oil and exhaust leaks. Repair as required.
5. Check engine hood alignment.

OIL PAN (SUMP)

Remove

1. Drain oil from oil pan.
2. Remove the dip stick.
3. Disconnect oil level sensor.
4. Remove oil pan bolts, oil pan and seal, dispose of oil seal.

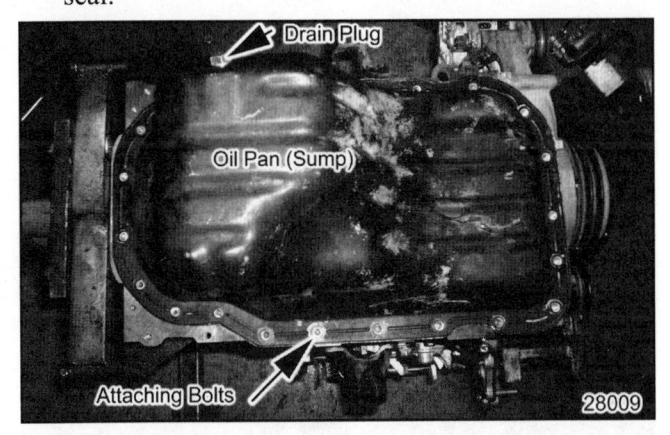

Install

1. Clean all matching surfaces of oil pan and cylinder block thoroughly.
2. Apply sealant to the meeting surface of the front timing cover and engine block.
   Apply 3.5mm bead of sealant to the oil pan surface groove and around the bolt holes.
3. Install oil pan and seal to crankcase, and tighten as specified.
   Oil pan 11Nm
4. Make sure oil pan drain plug is tightened as specified, use a new drain plug seal.
   Oil pan drain plug 49Nm
5. Replace dip stick.
6. Re-connect oil level sensor.
7. Refill oil pan with the correct amount of engine oil as specified.
8. Start engine and inspect for oil leaks. Repair as required.
9. Stop engine and check oil level on dip stick.

OIL PUMP SUCTION PIPE AND BAFFLE

Remove

1. Withdraw the oil pan from the engine as previously described in this chapter.
2. Release the suction pipe retaining bolts from the engine.
3. Remove the suction pipe, the suction pipe "O ring" from the engine, dispose of the gasket.

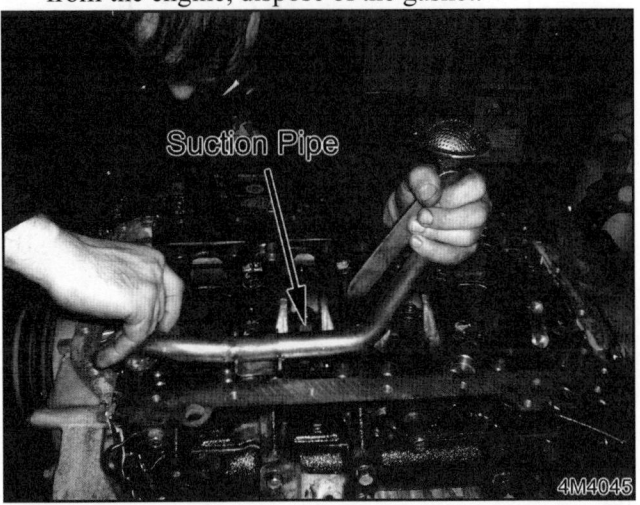

Install

1. Fit a new suction pipe "O ring" to the engine, then fit the suction pipe into place.
2. Fit the suction pipe retaining bolts, then tension the nuts to specifications.
   Oil suction pipe and screen 11Nm
3. Fit the oil pan to the engine.

PISTON AND CONNECTING ROD ASSEMBLY.

If the cylinder bore requires machining, remove piston and connecting rod, replace pistons and rings in oversize sets.

Both piston and cylinder bore condition must be considered together when fitting new pistons. Production and service pistons have the same nominal weight and can be intermixed without affecting engine balance. If needed, used pistons may be fitted selectively to any cylinder of the engine, providing they are in good condition.

Piston pin assemblies and ring sets are available in oversize.

Note: Connecting rod bolts stretch.

Note: Connecting rod bolts should not be tightened more than twice, there fore it is good practise to mark each connecting rod nut with a punch each time the connecting rod cap is removed. If the nuts have 2 punch marks, replace them with new bolts and nuts.

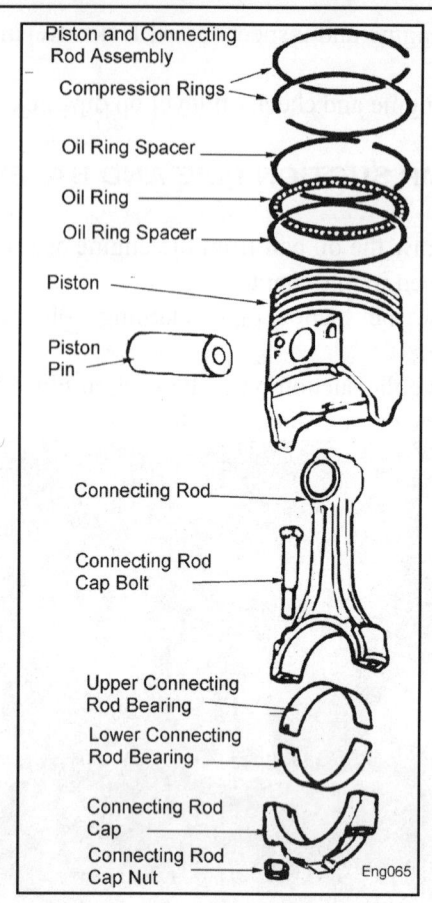

3.2 Litre, incl COMMON RAIL - DOHC (4M41) Diesel Engine Maintenance & Rebuild

Piston and Connecting Rod Assembly (diagram labels): Compression Rings, Oil Ring Spacer, Oil Ring, Oil Ring Spacer, Piston, Piston Pin, Connecting Rod, Connecting Rod Cap Bolt, Upper Connecting Rod Bearing, Lower Connecting Rod Bearing, Connecting Rod Cap, Connecting Rod Cap Nut. Eng065

Remove

1. Remove cylinder heads as described in Cylinder Head section.
2. To remove oil pan (sump), oil suction pipe and screen.
3. Remove the main bearing cradle as described in this chapter.
4. Inspect cylinder bores above piston ring travel. If bores are worn so that a ridge or similar exists.
   Turn crankshaft so that piston is at bottom of stroke and cover piston with a cloth to collect cuttings.
   Remove the ridge with a ridge remover, this is to be done for each cylinder.
5. Use a stamp and hammer or etching marker, mark all connecting rods, caps to indicate cylinder identification, if not marked.

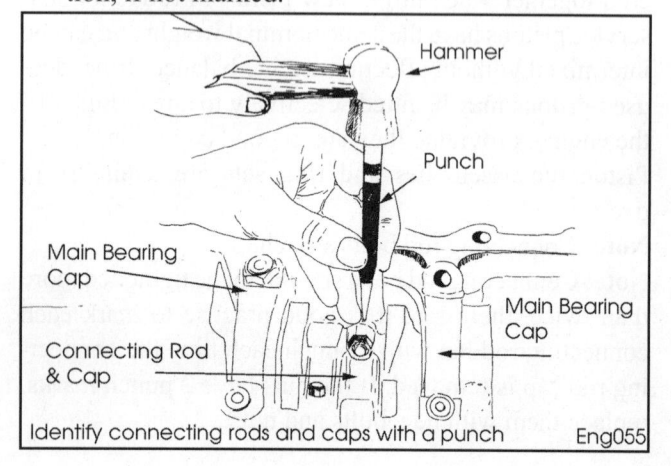

Identify connecting rods and caps with a punch — Hammer, Punch, Main Bearing Cap, Connecting Rod & Cap, Main Bearing Cap. Eng055

6. Remove rod assemblies and piston as follows,
   a) With connecting rod crankshaft journal straight down (Bottom Dead Centre), remove connecting rod cap bolts and remove cap with bearing shell.

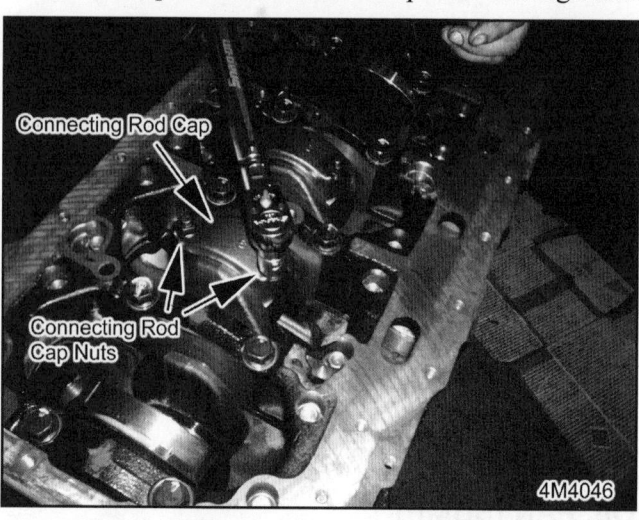

(Photo labels: Connecting Rod Cap, Connecting Rod Cap Nuts. 4M4046)

   b) Push piston and connecting rod from cylinder using a long guide. Remove guides and install cap and bolts to connecting rod.
7. Remove all other piston and connecting rod assemblies using the same procedure.

Dismantle.

1. Expand and slide piston rings off to remove and dispose of them.
   Worn rings may have sharp edges ensure to take care when removing piston rings.
2. Piston pin can now be removed as follows:
   Remove the cir-clip.
   Press piston pin from piston with a mandrel and press, until piston pin free. Heat the piston over a heater or with boiling water, will help remove the pin.

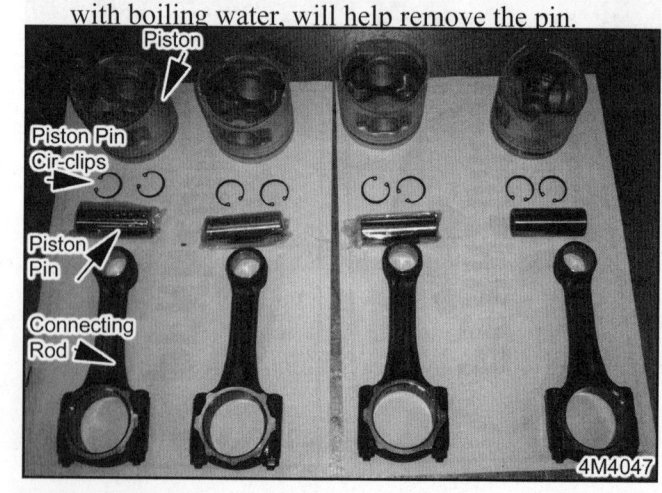

(Photo labels: Piston, Piston Pin Cir-clips, Piston Pin, Connecting Rod. 4M4047)

Inspection.

1. Thoroughly clean carbon from piston heads and from ring grooves using a suitable tool and remove any gum or varnish from piston skirts using a suitable cleaning solvent.
2. Check cylinder walls for ridges, roughness or scoring

144

which indicates excessive wear. Inspect cylinder bores for taper and out-of-round using an accurate cylinder gauge at top, middle and bottom of bore, both parallel and at right angles to centre line of engine. Refer to Cylinder Block section for details.

3. Examine piston skirt thoroughly for scored or rough surfaces, cracks in skirt or crown, chipping, broken ring lands or uneven wear which would cause rings to seat improperly or have excessive clearance in ring grooves. Pistons should be replaced if faulty or damaged.

Pistons are cam ground, which means that the diameter at right angles to the piston pin is greater than the diameter parallel to the piston pin. When a piston is checked for size, it must be done at points 90° to the piston bore.

Note: *Match piston sizes with sizes stamped onto the top of the cylinder block, A, B or C.*

Piston to bore clearance .... 0.04 - 0.05 mm
Piston to bore clearance (Turbo) . 0.07 - 0.08 mm
Piston oversizes .... 0.50 mm, 0.75 mm, 1.00 mm

4. Check piston pin bores and piston pins for wear. Piston pins and piston pin bores must be free of scuffing or varnish when being measured. Use a micrometer to measure the piston pin, and a dial bore gauge or an inside micrometer to measure piston pin bore.

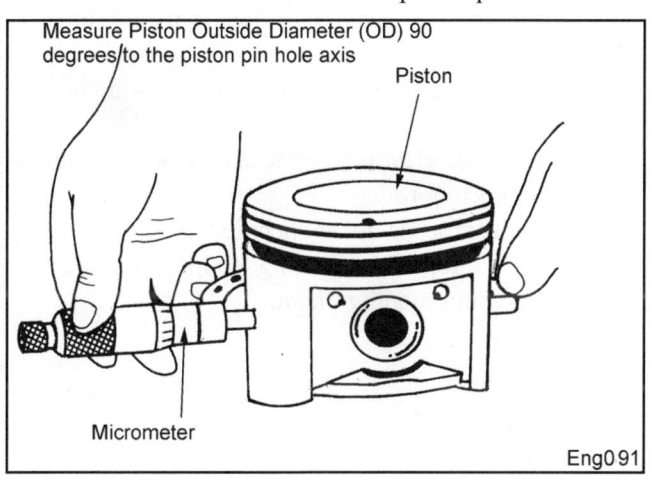

Piston pin to Piston Clearance ... 0.007-0.021 mm
Max .... 0.05 mm
Piston pin to Connecting Rod Bush Clearance
.... 0.03-0.05 mm
Max .... 0.1 mm

Piston and pin should be replaced if not as specified.

5. Remove bearing shells from connecting rod, install cap and bolts. Tighten nuts as specified.
Connecting Rod Cap Nut: 50Nm

6. Place connecting rod assembly on a checking fixture and inspect rod for twist or bend.
Replace if twisted or bent, do not attempt to straighten rod.
Inspect new connecting rods using the same procedure before using them.
Connecting rod - bend .... 0.05 mm
- twist .... 0.05 mm

7. Check outside of connecting rod bearing shells and internal diameter of connecting rod big end for wear indicating high spots in the rod big end.

8. Remove cap bolts and inspect bolts for stretching by comparing them with a new bolt, if stretched, replace.

Assembly and Installation.
Note: *Piston and connecting rod front marks must be to the front of the engine.*

1. Using engine oil, lubricate piston pin and piston pin bore.
2. Install piston pin on mandrel. Heat the piston over a heater or with boiling water, will help remove the pin.
3. Assemble installer guide and piston support to base.
4. Install piston and connecting rod over guide.
Note: *The front mark on the piston must be facing up so pin is pressed in from piston front mark side.*
5. Press piston pin into place with a mandrel, until piston pin bottoms.

Heat the piston over a heater or with boiling water, will help remove the pin.
Install cir-clip.

6. To install piston rings refer to Piston Rings section.
7. Make sure connecting rod bearing shells, pistons, cylinder bores and crankshaft journals are totally clean, then, using clean engine oil, coat cylinder bores and all bearing surfaces.
8. Position the crankpin straight down before installation of a piston and rod assembly in its bore.
9. Remove cap, and with bearing upper shell seated in connecting rod, install the 'short' guide tool into inner bolt hole. Install 'long' guide tool into the other bolt hole.
Guides hold upper bearing shell in place and protects crankshaft journal from damage during installation of connecting rod and piston assembly.
10. Make sure piston ring gaps are separated as described in Piston Rings section.
11. Using clean engine oil, lubricate piston and rings. With a suitable ring compressor, compress rings. Install each piston and connecting rod assembly into its cylinder bore.
12. Lightly tap piston into its bore, using a hammer handle, while holding ring compressor firmly against cylinder block until all piston rings have entered bore. 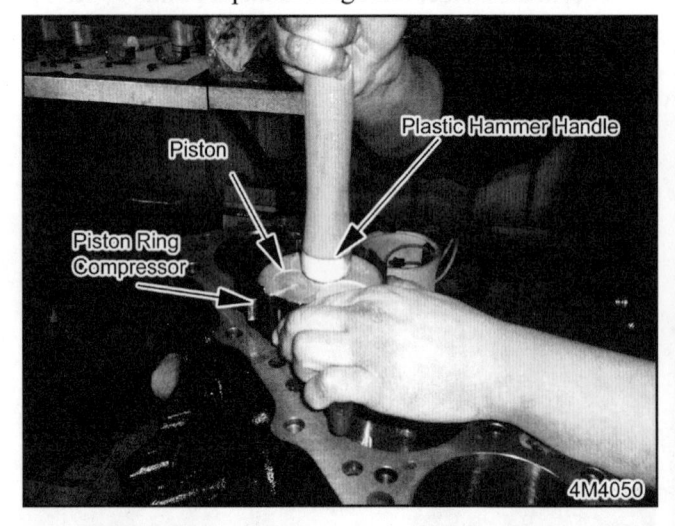
13. Push piston down bore until connecting rod seats against crankshaft journal.
14. Remove connecting rod guides. Install bearing cap and lower bearing shell assembly. Install cap bolts and tighten and then loosen one full turn. Then tighten again as specified.

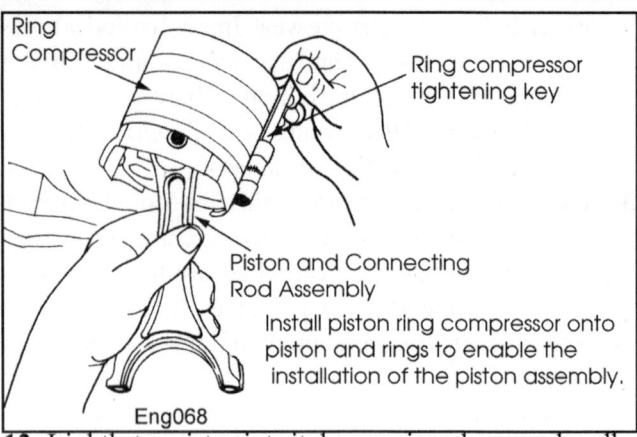

Connecting Rod Cap Bolt - 4 steps:
Step 1 .... 29Nm
Step 2 .... 49Nm
Step 3 .... rotate a further 45 degrees
Step 4 .... rotate a further 45 degrees

15. Turn crankshaft to make sure crankshaft and connecting rod can move freely. If crankshaft binds, check bearing cap to rod orientation again and bearing clearance or connecting rod alignment.
16. Measure side clearance between crankshaft journal and connecting rod.
If side clearance is not as specified, to check bearing clearance refer to Connecting Rod Bearing section, or connecting rod alignment.

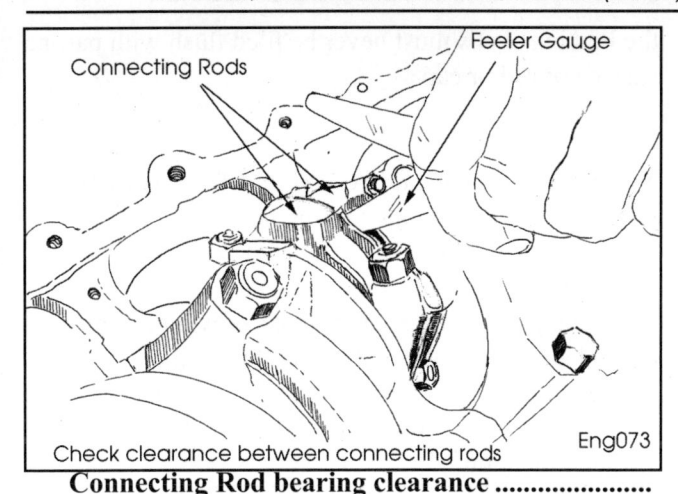

3.2 Litre, incl Common Rail - DOHC (4M41) DIESEL ENGINE MAINTENANCE & REBUILD

Connecting Rod bearing clearance ....
....0.03 - 0.05 mm
- service limit (main/big end) ....0.1 mm

17. Install remaining piston and connecting rod assemblies using the same procedure.

PISTON RINGS.
Install
* The pistons have three rings (two compression rings and one oil ring). The top ring is a molybdenum filled, balanced section, barrel lapped type. The second ring is an inverted torsional taper faced type. The oil ring is of three piece design, comprising two segments and a spacer.

1. Using a set of rings comparable in size to the piston being used install compression ring in relevant cylinder bore, then using the head of a piston, press ring down into the bore.
   Using a piston in this manner will place ring square with cylinder wall.
   Ensure not to distort the ring during this operation, or it may bind in the piston ring groove. Fit each ring separately to the cylinder in which it is going to be installed.

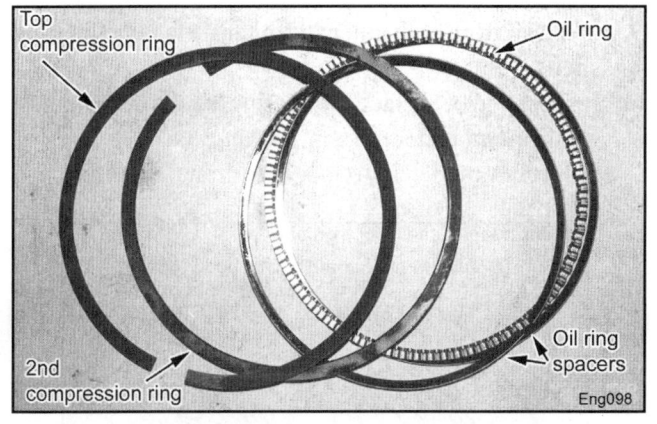

2. Using a feeler gauge, measure gap between ends of ring.

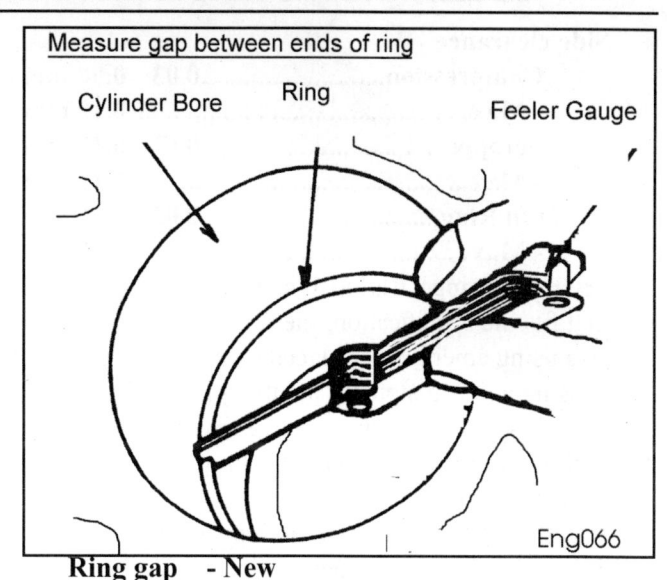

Ring gap - New
- Compression ....0.30 - 0.45 mm
- Max...............................0.80 mm
- Scraper ....0.40 - 0.55 mm
- Max...............................0.80 mm

Remove ring and try another, if the gap between the ends of a compression ring is below specification. The ring gap may be enlarged by filing.

3. Inspect gap between ends of each oil control ring segment.

Oil Ring Steel Rail Gap Specification:
- Oil ring ....0.30 - 0.50 mm
- Max................................0.80 mm

4. Carefully remove all traces of carbon from ring grooves in piston and check grooves for any chips or burrs that might cause ring to bind when fitting.

5. Slip outer surface of each compression ring in respective piston ring groove and roll ring entirely around groove to ensure that ring is free. Also measure ring to piston groove side clearance.

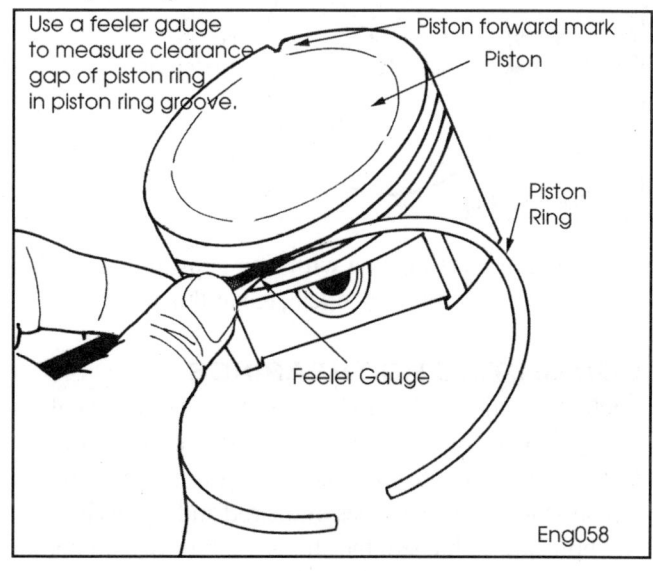

147

3.2 Litre, incl COMMON RAIL - DOHC (4M41) Diesel Engine Maintenance & Rebuild

Side clearance
Compression..........................0.03 - 0.08 mm
- Max..0.15 mm
Scraper................................0.07 - 0.10 mm
- Max..0.15 mm
Oil Ring..............................0.03 - 0.06 mm
- Max..0.15 mm

Try another ring if it is too tight. If no ring can be found that fits the specification, the ring may be ground to size using emery paper placed on a piece of glass.
If using a new piston, try another piston.

* High spots in the ring groove may be cleaned up with careful use of a fine file, do not try to cut the piston ring groove.

6. Install oil ring spacer in bottom piston ring groove. The ends of the spacer butt against each other.
7. Install one steel segment from top of piston downward into oil ring groove and install remaining steel segment from bottom of piston skirt upwards into the oil ring groove.
8. Install compression rings in first and second grooves of each piston.
Make sure the correct compression ring are installed in the first and second grooves, and the correct way up.
9. Do a final test of ring fit in piston grooves. Separate ends as illustrated.

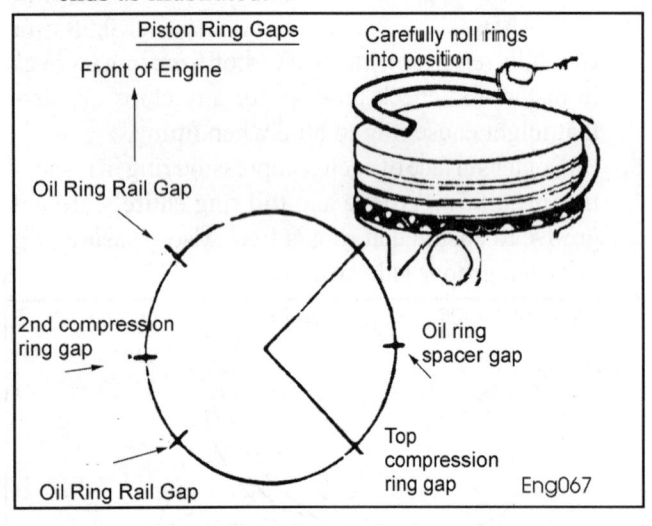

* Do not install piston with ring gaps in line, as this will allow compression leakage at this point.

CONNECTING ROD BEARINGS

Each connecting rod bearing consists of 2 bearing halves or shells which are interchangeable in the rod and cap. When the shells are in place, the ends extend slightly beyond the parting surfaces of the rod and cap. When the rod bolts are tightened, the shells are tightly clamped in place to ensure positive seating and to prevent rotation. The connecting rod bearings are of the precision insert type and do not use shims for adjustment. The ends of the bearing shells must never be filed flush with parting surface of rod or cap.

Note: *See charts under "Crankshaft" section for connecting rod, journal and bearing information.*

Inspection and Replacement.
Connecting rod bearings can be replaced without removing the rod and piston assembly from the engine.

1. Use a stamp and hammer or etching marker, mark all connecting rods and caps to indicate cylinder identification.

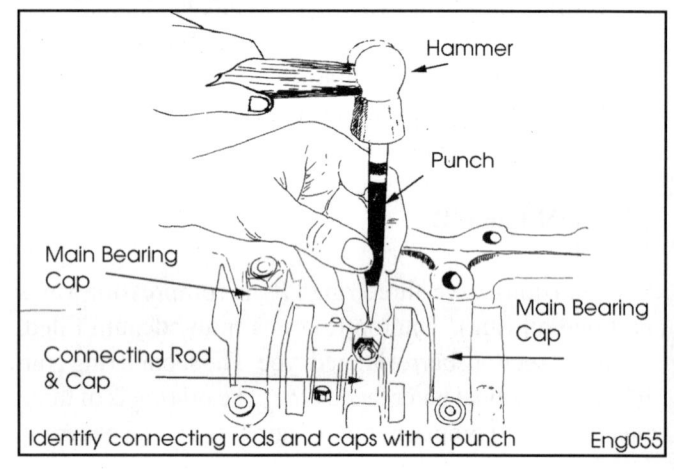

2. Remove connecting rod cap securing nuts and remove cap and lower bearing shell.
3. Push piston and connecting rod up cylinder bore, so that connecting rod is free from crankshaft journal. Remove bearing shell from connecting rod.
4. Clean crankshaft journal and measure for out of round or taper using a micrometer. Replace crankshaft, if not as specified in CRANKSHAFT section.
Crankshaft Connecting Rod Bearing Journal Diameter
5. Wipe oil from both inner and outer surfaces of bearing shells.
6. Inspect inner surface of bearing shells for gouges, wear or embedded foreign matter.
If foreign matter is found, determine its nature and source.

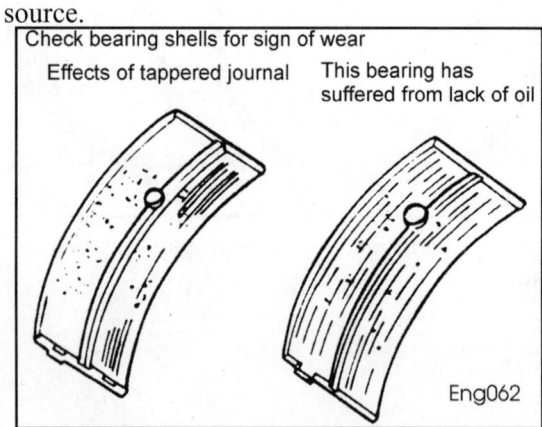

Inspect outer surface of bearing shell for surface wear (indicates movement of shell or high spot in surrounding material), looseness or turning (flattened tangs and wear grooves), or overheating (discolouration). The crankshaft may be bent or have tapered bearing journals if uneven side to side wear is found. If needed, remove crankshaft, refer to CRANKSHAFT section and inspect crankshaft for bend or journal taper.

* Bearing failure, other than normal wear, must be examined carefully.

7. Install bearing shells in original positions in connecting rod and cap if inspection reveals that crankshaft is OK.
8. Pull connecting rod down onto crankshaft so that upper bearing is seated against crankshaft journal.
9. Place a piece of plastigage across width of bearing journal, parallel to crankshaft centre line.

* Make sure plastigage is not placed across oil hole in journal.

10. Install connecting rod cap in original position as described in step 4. Tighten bolts as specified. Make sure that crankshaft does not rotate with plastigage installed.

Connecting Rod Cap Bolt: **50Nm**

11. Remove connecting rod cap bolts, and cap. Inspect for flattened plastigage sticking to either crankshaft or bearing shell in cap.
12. Determine bearing clearance by comparing width of flattened plastigage at widest point with graduation on plastigage envelope. The number within the graduation on the envelope indicates the clearance.

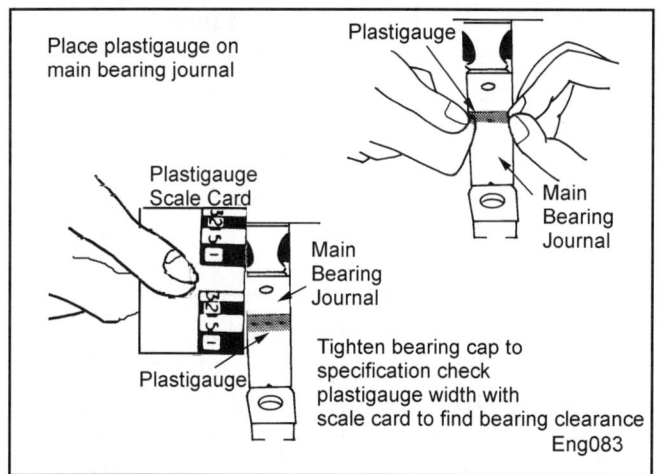

Clearance between connecting rod bearings and crankshaft should not exceed specification.

If a bearing is being fitted to an out of round journal, ensure to fit plastigage to the maximum diameter of the journal. If the bearing is fitted to the minimum diameter, and the journal is out of round 0.008mm, interference between the bearing and journal will result in rapid bearing failure.

Connecting Rod Bearing Clearance:
....0.03 - 0.05 mm
- service limit (main/big end)............0.1 mm
Connecting rod bearing undersizes:
....0.25, 0.50 and 0.75 mm

13. Make sure that connecting rod cap bolt threads and connecting rod threads are clean and dry. Apply some engine oil to the cap bolt threads.
Before final installation of cap bolts, determine if bolts have stretched by comparing with a new bolt. Replace bolt/s as needed.
14. Install bearing shells in connecting rod and cap making sure notches in shells match up with recesses in connecting rod and cap.
Inspect clearance of new bearing with plastigage as previously described.
15. Remove all remains of plastigage after measuring. Using clean engine oil lubricate bearing shells and journal. Install connecting rod cap in original position, tighten bolts as specified.

Connecting Rod Cap Bolt - 4 steps:
Step 1 .... 30Nm
Step 2 .... 50Nm
Step 3 .... **rotate a further 45 degrees**
Step 4 .... **rotate a further 45 degrees**

16. With bearing shells installed and cap bolts tightened, it should be possible to move connecting rod backwards and forwards on crankshaft journal as allowed by end clearance. Also, the crankshaft should turn without binding.

Connecting Rod to crankshaft end clearance:
....0.15 - 0.45 mm
- service limit ....0.6 mm

If connecting rod binds on crankshaft journal, loosen and tighten bearing cap bolts.
If rod still cannot be moved or crankshaft binds, inspect bearing cap to rod orientation, bearing clearance or connecting rod alignment.

CRANKSHAFT.

The crankshaft is held in place by a main bearing cradle / lower cylinder block section with 26 bolts.

Note: Main bearing cradle bolts stretch.

Note: Main bearing cradle bolts should not be tightened more than twice, there fore it is good practise to mark each bolt with a punch each time the cradle is removed. If the bolts have 2 punch marks, replace them with new bolts.

Remove

To check bearing clearance before removing crankshaft from crankcase as described.

1. When engine is removed from vehicle and mounted in a suitable stand and remove oil pan.
2. Remove flywheel/driveplate and engine end plate, rear seal retainer.
3. Remove oil pump suction pipe and screen.
4. Remove crankshaft sprocket.
5. Remove main bearing cradle and bolts in order as shown and remove cradle.
   a) Loosen bolts (a little at a time) 1 to 16 in the order shown.
   b) Loosen bolts (a little at a time) 17 to 26 in the order shown.
      Use a soft faced hammer tap the cradle to break cradle free of the crankcase seal.
6. Use a stamp and hammer or etching marker, mark all connecting rods and caps to indicate cylinder identification.
7. Remove connecting rod caps and bolts and push connecting rods away from crankshaft.
8. Lift crankshaft from cylinder block.
9. Remove key from front end of crankshaft, if needed, using a suitable punch and hammer.

Inspection.

1. Using a suitable cleaning solvent, wash crankshaft and dry with compressed air.
2. Check crankshaft oil passages for obstructions.
3. Check all bearing journals and thrust surfaces for: Gouges, overheating (discolouration), cracks, grooving chips or roughness
   The crankshaft must be machined or replaced if it has any burned spots, cracks or sever gouging. Slight roughness may be removed using a fine polishing cloth soaked in clean engine oil. Burrs may also be removed using a fine oil stone.
4. Check connecting rod and main bearing shells for embedded foreign material and determine its source.
5. Using a micrometer measure bearing journals for taper, excessive wear or out-of-round.

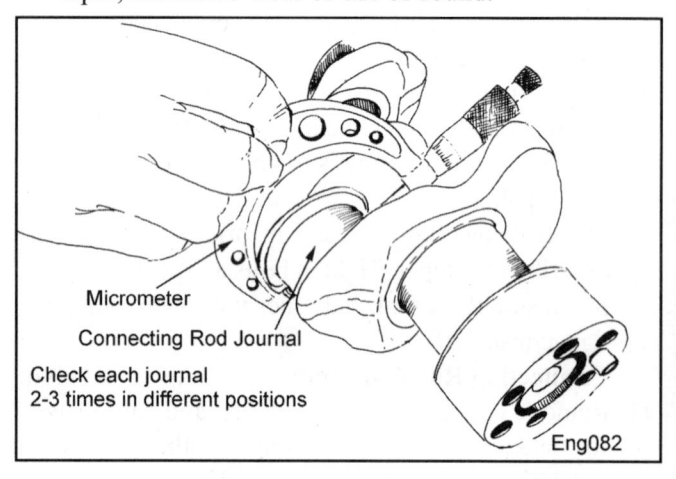

Crankshaft Main Journal		Cyl. Block Stamp	Main Bearing Colour mark
Colour mark	Journal OD mm		
None	67.970 - 67.798	A	Blk/Blk
		B	Blu/Blu
Blue	67.961 - 67.970	A	Yell/Yell
		B	Blk/Blk

Crankshaft Connecting Rod Journal OD mm	Connecting rod big end Int. Dia.	Connecting rod bearing Colour mark
53.980 - 53.988	58.010 - 58.019	None
	58.000 - 58.010	Blue
53.971 - 53.980	58.010 - 58.019	Yellow
	58.000 - 58.010	Black

3.2 Litre, incl COMMON RAIL - DOHC (4M41) Diesel Engine Maintenance & Rebuild

Crankshaft connecting rod journal identification	Connecting rod identification	Connecting rod bearing - Colour mark
None "1"	None	Blue
	Blue	None
Blue "2"	None	None
	Blue	Blue

Main bearing journals diameter .... as above
End float controlled by .... No.3 bearing
Connecting Rod journal diameter .... as above
   - max. allowable ovality .... 0.01 mm
   - max. allowable taper .... 0.006 mm
Main bearing clearance 1,2,4 & 5 ... 0.04 - 0.06 mm
   - service limit .... 0.1 mm
Main bearing clearance brg 3 .... 0.06 - 0.08 mm
   - service limit .... 0.1 mm

6. Inspect crankshaft for run-out by supporting front and rear main bearing journals in 'V' blocks and checking journals with a dial gauge.
7. Place a dial gauge indicator at crankshaft rear flange and inspect rear flange Run-out. During this inspection, make sure that crankshaft is thrust forward on 'V' blocks so that there is no possibility of crankshaft end float affecting dial gauge reading.
Crankshaft Rear Flange Run-out .... 0.06 mm
8. If not as specified, replace crankshaft.

Installation.

1. Inspect main bearing clearance, if needed, refer to MAIN BEARINGS section for details.
2. Using a clean engine oil lubricate all crankshaft journals and main bearing upper shells in crankcase.
3. Sit crankshaft in place in main bearing upper shells in crankcase. Ensure not to damage crankshaft thrust washers at No.5 main bearing. Also ensure not to contact connecting rod journals with connecting rod and install main bearing caps.
Using a thin film of Loctite 515 Gasket Eliminator or equivalent apply to rear main bearing cap to crankcase mating surface. Keep sealant out of bolt holes and use sparingly.

*Make sure that the bearing caps are installed onto the crankcase in the correct manner.
Tighten the bolts finger tight.
4. It will be necessary to line up thrust washers with No.5 bearing shells, before tightening main bearing cap bolts.
Move crankshaft fore and aft the length of its travel several times (last movement forward) to do this.
5. Ensure all main bearing cradle bolts are tightened as specified.

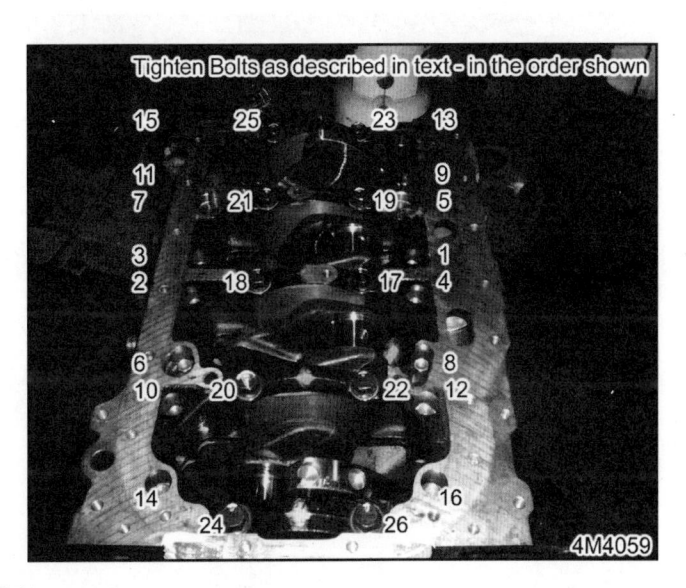

151

Main Bearing Bolts - 4 steps:
Step 1 - bolts 17 to 26 .... 20Nm
Step 2 .... rotate a further 90 degrees
Step 3 .... rotate a further 90 degrees
Step 4 - tighten bolts 1 to 16......................... 25Nm

6. Use a feeler gauge to measure crankshaft end float between front of No.5 main bearing thrust washer and crankshaft thrust faces, you will need to force crankshaft forward to do this.
   End play..0.10 - 0.28 mm
   - limit .... 0.4 mm
   Replace No.3 main bearing thrust washers if clearance is excessive.
7. Turn crankshaft to make sure crankshaft and connecting rods have free movement. Inspect orientation of bearing caps, correct fitting of bearing cradle (mains and connecting rods) or fitting of bearing shells or bearing clearance, if crankshaft binds.
8. Install the rear main oil seal and retainer.
9. To install flywheel/driveplate as described.

MAIN BEARINGS.

Each crankshaft main bearing journal has 2 bearing halves or shells which are not the same and not interchangeable in the bearing cradle or crankcase. The upper (crankcase) shell is grooved to supply oil to the connecting rod bearing, while the lower (bearing cap) shell is not grooved. The 2 bearing shells must not be interchanged. The No.5. bearing has thrust washers to take end thrust.

Standard size upper shells are used in the crankcase with 0.25mm undersized or standard size shells in the bearing caps, depending on bearing clearance.

When shells are placed in crankcase and bearing cap, the end extends slightly beyond the parting surfaces so that when cradle bolts are tightened, the shells clamp tightly in place to ensure positive seating and to prevent turning. The ends of the bearing shells must never be filed flush with parting surfaces of crankcase or bearing cradle.

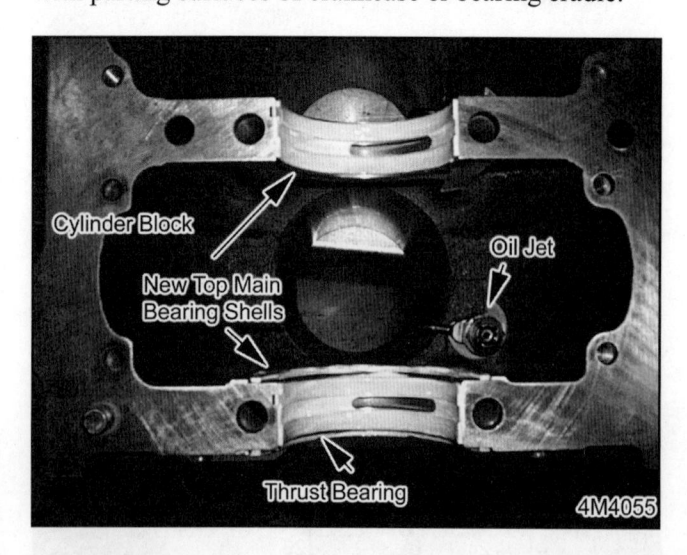

Inspection

1. Remove main bearing cradle bolts, and remove cradle and lower bearing shell.
   * Tap main bearing cradle to break cradle to crankcase seal to remove.
2. Check lower bearing shells and crankshaft journals. If the journal surface is ridged or heavily scored, replace crankshaft, refer to Crankshaft section for details.
   To ensure satisfactory engine operation, new bearing shells must be installed as described in Main Bearing section and if necessary Connecting Rod Bearings section.
   Inspect inner surface of bearing shells for gouges, wear or embedded foreign material. If foreign material is found, determine its nature and source. Inspect outer surface of bearing shells for surface wear (indicates movement of shell or high spot in surrounding material), looseness, rotation (flattened tangs and wear grooves), and overheating (discolouration).
   Inspect thrust surfaces of thrust washers for grooving or wear. Grooves are caused by irregularities in the crankshaft thrust surfaces or dirt as described in Crankshaft section.
   If condition of lower bearing shells and crankshaft journals is satisfactory, inspect bearing clearance as follows:
3. Wipe oil from crankshaft journal and inner and outer surfaces of lower bearing shell.
   Install bearing shell in original position in bearing cap.
4. Place a piece of plastigage across full width of crankshaft journal, parallel to crankshaft centre line.
   * Make sure plastigage will not seat across oil hole in journal.
5. Install bearing cradle and bolts into cylinder block.
   * Install bearing cradle by loosely installing cradle bolts and then lightly tap bearing cap into position, in order to prevent the possibility of cylinder block and or main bearing cradle damage.
   * Do not pull the bearing cradle into place with the bearing cradle bolts.
6. Tighten bearing cradle bolts as specified.
   * Ensure that crankshaft does not rotate with plastigage installed.
   Main Bearing Bolts - 4 steps:
   Step 1 - bolts 17 to 26 .... 20Nm
   Step 2 .... rotate a further 90 degrees
   Step 3 .... rotate a further 90 degrees
   Step 4 - tighten bolts 1 to 16......................... 25Nm
7. Remove bearing cradle bolts and cradle. Look for flattened plastigage sticking to either crankshaft or bearing shell in bearing cradle.
8. Check bearing clearance by comparing width of flattened plastigage at widest point with graduation on

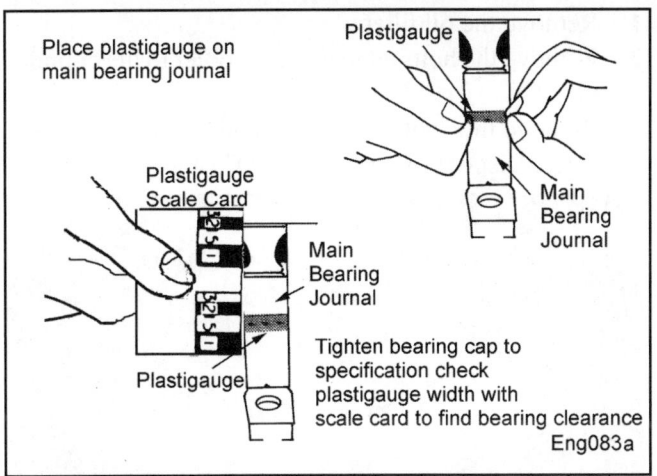

plastigage envelope. The number within the graduation on the envelope indicates the clearance.

Main bearing and crankshaft journal clearance should not exceed specification.

Main bearing clearance 1,2,4&5...0.04 - 0.06 mm
- service limit .... 0.1 mm
Main bearing clearance brg 3 .... 0.06 - 0.08 mm
- service limit .... 0.1 mm

This method of checking main bearing clearance does not give any indication of crankshaft journal taper or out of round.

To measure taper, out of round or undersized, the crankshaft must be removed from the cylinder block as described in CRANKSHAFT section.

9. It is advisable to install new bearing shells if bearing clearance exceeds specification and check clearance as previously described.

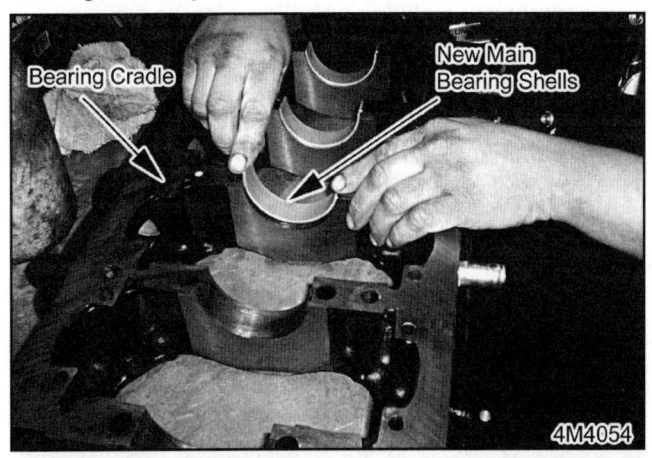

If lower bearing is standard size, install a 0.25 mm undersized shell and check clearance again.

Replace crankshaft as described in "Crankshaft" section if clearance is still not as specified.

10. Make sure that main bearing cradle bolt threads and crankcase threads are clean and dry.

* Before final installation of cradle bolts, determine if bolts have stretched by comparing with new one. Replace bolts and tighten, in order shown in previous illustration.

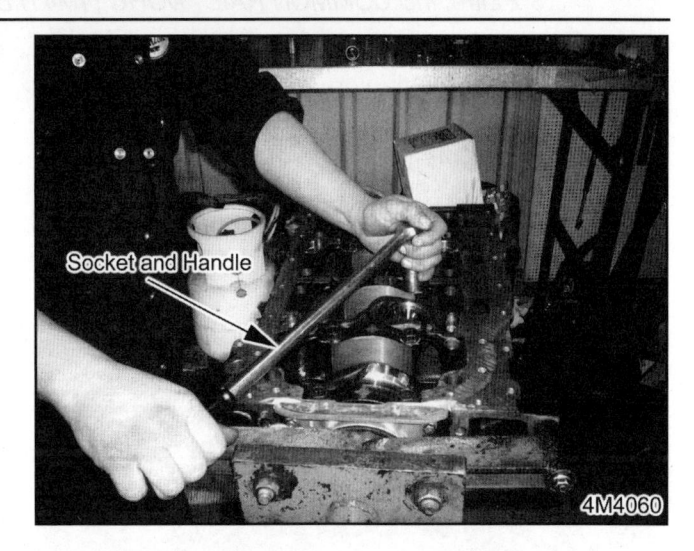

Main Bearing Bolts - 4 steps:
Step 1 - bolts 17 to 26 .... 20Nm
Step 2 .... rotate a further 90 degrees
Step 3 .... rotate a further 90 degrees
Step 4 - tighten bolts 1 to 16 .... 25Nm

REAR MAIN OIL SEAL
Replace

1. a) Remove flywheel/driveplate, as described in "Flywheel/driveplate" in this manual.
   b) Remove rear plate.
2. a) Remove the oil seal retainer bolts and remove the oil seal retainer.
   b) Remove old seal with a screw driver or punch.
   c) Install new seal with a seal installer, ensure the seals lips are not pulled back or crooked.
3. Apply a thin coat of oil to the lips of the oil seal.
4. Apply a 3mm bead of sealant around the circumference of the seal retainer, install within 3 minutes.
5. Install rear seal retainer to rear of engine block.

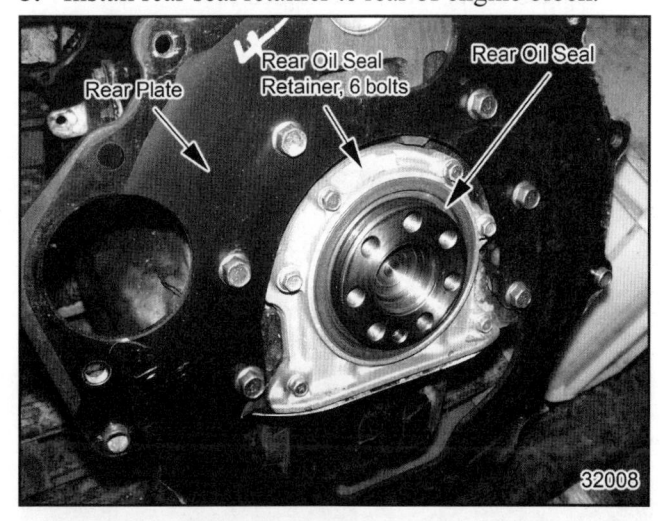

Rear Oil Seal Retainer 11Nm

6. a) Install rear plate and tighten bolts.
   b) Clean flywheel/drive plate attaching bolt threads in rear of crankshaft using a thread tap.

Install new flywheel/flexiplate and attaching bolts, tighten bolts to the correct torque specification.

Flywheel / Drive Plate Bolts **123Nm**

7. Reinstall transmission, check engine and transmission lubricant levels.
8. Road test vehicle and check for lubrication leaks.

OIL JETS

To help during assembly, take note of the direction the oil jet points too for lubrication.

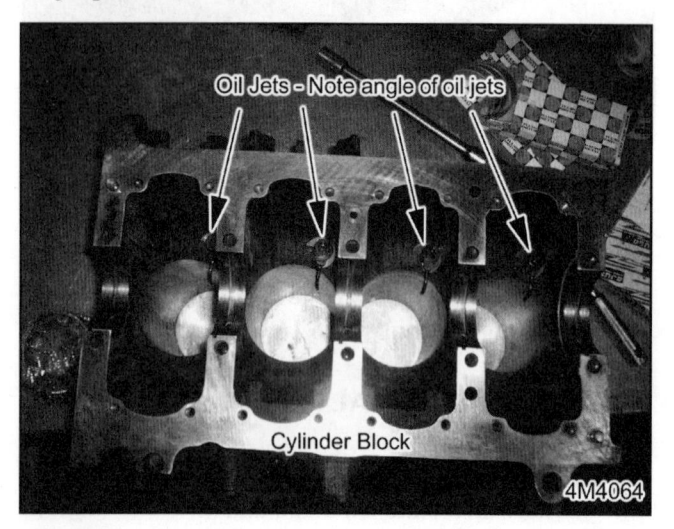

Replace

1. Remove crankshaft as described.
2. Unscrew the union holding the oil jet and remove the oil jet.
3. Clean the oil jet if required.
4. Install the oil jet with a new "O" ring if one was fitted. Tighten oil jet union to specification.
   Note: *Make sure jet faces the correct direct.*
   Oil Jet Union **33Nm**
5. Replace crankshaft as described.
6. Install engine oil pan (sump).

OIL COOLER and ELEMENT
Remove

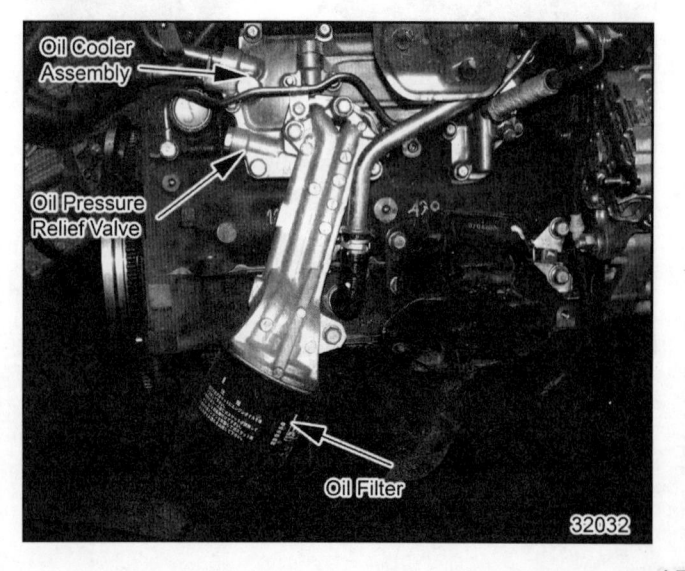

1. Remove the oil filter.
2. Remove the bolts attaching the cooler to the cylinder block.
3. Remove the cooler assembly and gasket plus 3 "O" rings. Dispose of gasket and "O" rings.

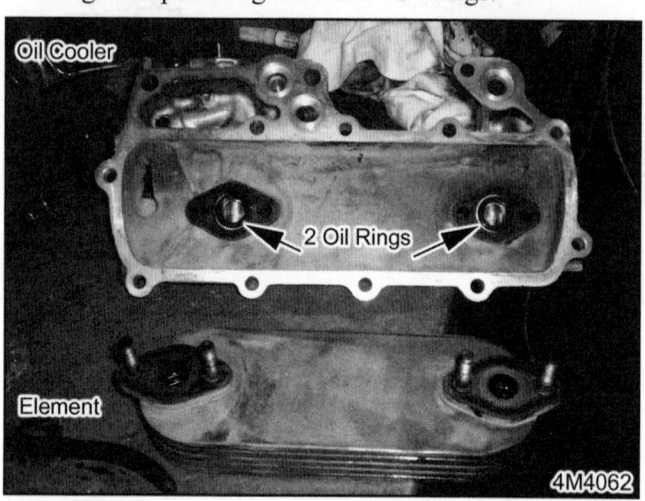

Dismantle

1. Remove the element, 4 nuts.
2. Remove the regulator valve plug, washer, spring and plunger.
3. Remove the bypass plug, washer, spring and plunger.
4. Remove the water / coolant drain plug and washer.

Clean and Test

1. Wash the springs, plungers and element in kerosine to remove any sludge or build up in the element.
2. Dry with compressed air.
3. Test element for leakage:
   a) Apply an air hose to the oil inlet hole, plug the oil outlet hole.
   b) Submerse element in a container of water, apply upto 1470 kPa of air pressure to element and check for air bubbles.
   c) If element is leaking air, replace element.

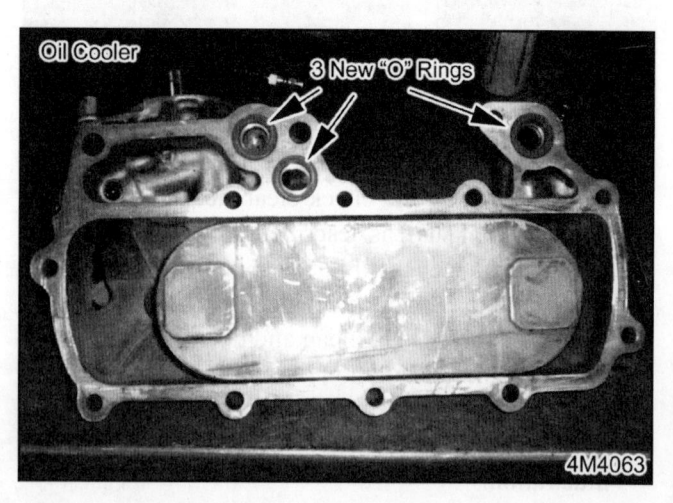

Assemble
1. Instal new gasket and "O" rings, replace the water / coolant drain plug and washer.
2. Replace the bypass plug, washer, spring and plunger.
3. Replace the regulator valve plug, washer, spring and plunger.
4. Install the element with new gaskets and washer, 4 nuts.
   Oil Cooler Element Nuts: 20Nm

Install
1. Install the cooler assembly with new gasket plus 3 "O" rings. Install 4 bolts and tighten.
2. Install a new oil filter.
3. Top up oil level.

CYLINDER BLOCK.
Inspection.
1. When engine is removed from vehicle and mounted in a suitable engine stand, remove all parts as outlined under the particular part heading in this section.
2. Clean all cylinder block gasket surfaces.
3. Remove all coolant jacket welsh plugs and oil gallery screw plugs.
4. Clean cylinder block thoroughly using a suitable cleaning solution. Flush with clean water or steam. Spray or wipe cylinder bores and machined surfaces using engine oil.
   Caustic cleaning solutions destroy all bearing and alloy materials. All bearing and alloy parts if not removed before cleaning must be replaced.
   Do not use caustic solutions to clean bearing material or alloy parts.
5. Check all oil passages for obstructions.
6. Using a straight edge and feeler gauge, inspect cylinder block deck surface for flatness.
   If any distortion or irregularity is less than specified, cylinder block surface may be machined.

Check block surface for flatness.

Flatness of gasket surface........ less than 0.05 mm
Flatness of gasket surface - maximum ... 0.10 mm
Replace cylinder block if irregularity or distortion is more than specified.

7. Check oil pan and oil pump body area for burrs or damage. Minor damage may be cleaned up with a fine mill file.
8. If needed, clean all threaded holes using a suitable threaded tap or drill out and install thread insert.
9. Measure cylinder bore walls for taper, excessive ridging, oversize and out-of-round.

Cylinder Reconditioning and Piston Fitting.
It will be necessary to smooth bores to fit new pistons, if one or more cylinder bores are scored, rough or worn beyond limits.

It will not be necessary to rebore all cylinders to the same oversize order to maintain engine balance if few bores require correction, since all oversize service pistons are held to the same weight as standard size pistons.

Cylinder Standard Bore ID .... 98.50 - 98.53 mm
Cylinder Standard Bore limit .... 98.75 mm

Do not try to machine oversize pistons to fit cylinder bores, this will destroy the surface treatment and affect the weight. The smallest possible oversize service pistons should be used and the cylinder bores should be honed to size for proper clearances.

Measure all new pistons at right angles to the piston pin bore, before the honing or reboring operation is started. The standard piston to bore clearance is required when rebuilding an engine

Piston to bore clearance .... 0.04 - 0.05 mm
Piston oversizes .... 0.50 mm and 1.00 mm

Honing is recommended for truing bore if cylinder bore wear does not exceed specification. The bore should be trued up by boring and then hone finished, if wear or out-of-round exceeds specification.

All crankshaft bearing caps must be in place and tightened as specified when reboring cylinder bores, to prevent distortion of bores in final assembly.

Leave 0.025 mm on the diameter for final honing to give the specified clearance when taking the final cut.

Follow the Hone Manufacturers recommendations for the use of the hone and cleaning and lubrication during honing. Noting the following points.

Pass the hone through the entire length of the cylinder bore at the rate of approximately 60 cycles per minute when finished honing. This should produce the desired 45° cross hatch pattern on cylinder walls which will ensure minimum oil consumption and maximum ring life.

Each piston must be fitted individually to the bore in which it will be installed and marked to ensure correct assembly during the final honing. After the final honing and before the piston is inspected for fit, each cylinder bore must be washed and dried thoroughly to remove all traces of abrasive and then allowed to cool. Apply clean engine oil to cylinder bores. The pistons and cylinder block must be at a common temperature before inspecting.

Cylinder bores that are scored or grooved should be refinished by honing.

Cylinder bore. Eng074

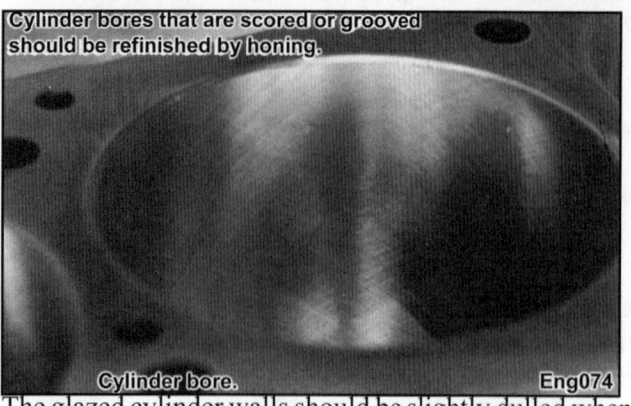

The glazed cylinder walls should be slightly dulled when new piston rings are installed without reboring cylinders, but without increasing the bore diameter, by means of the finest grade of stone in a cylinder hone.

Proceed as follows to inspect piston to cylinder bore.
1. Using a clean cloth wipe cylinder walls and pistons and apply clean engine oil to cylinder bores.

Clean Engine Oil on Cylinder Bores 4M4065

2. Measure the bore accurately using an inside micrometer.
3. Measure piston diameter and subtract piston diameter from cylinder bore diameter to determine piston-to-bore clearance.
4. Mark each piston with cylinder number to which it will be fitted and proceed to hone cylinders and fit pistons.
Handle the pistons with care and do not attempt to force them through the cylinder until cylinder has been honed to the correct size, as pistons can be damaged through careless handling.
Assemble parts as described under the correct heading in this section. If coolant and oil gallery plugs were removed when dismantling, install using specified sealant.

Problem Diagnosis.

Problems and Possible Causes.
Problems should be corrected, when proper diagnosis is made, by repair, adjustment or part replacement as needed. Refer to the correct section in this manual.

High Oil Loss
1) Tighten bolts and/or replace gaskets and seals as required for external leaks.
2) Check oil with car on a level surface and allow adequate drain down time to ensure a correct reading of dipstick.
3) Severe usage such as towing or continuous high speed driving will normally cause oil consumption to increase.
4) PCV system failure.
5) Use recommended S.A.E viscosity for current temperatures. Refer to Lubrication Section for details on incorrect oil viscosity.
6) Valve guides and/or valve stem seals worn, or seals omitted. Ream guides and install oversize service valves and/or new valve stem seals.
7) Allow enough time for the piston rings to seat. Replace worn or broken rings as needed, if rings have been incorrectly installed, worn or broken, or not seated.
8) Piston incorrectly installed or mis-fitted.

Gaskets.
1) Incorrectly tightened fasteners or damaged/dirty threads.
2) Worn or damaged gasket (cracking or porosity).
3) Fluid pressure/level too high.
4) Incorrect sealant used (when required)

Inspection of Seals.
1) Damaged seal bore (burred, nicked, scratched)
2) Worn or loose bearing causing excessive seal wear.
3) Worn or damaged seal or incorrect installation.
4) Fluid pressure/level too high.

Oil Leak Investigation
Oil leaks are easily located and repaired by visually finding the leak and replacing or repairing the required parts.
1) Determine whether the fluid is transmission lubricant, engine oil, power steering fluid etc.
2) Run the car at normal operating temperature and park the car over a large sheet of paper. After a few minutes, you should be able to find the approximate location of the leak by drippings on the paper.
3) Use a degreaser or steam to clean the area of the leak, drive the car for a few kilometres. Then visually inspect the suspected part for signs of an oil leak.

Black Light and Dye Method.
Use a dye and light kit for finding leaks.
a) Pour required amount of dye into leaking part.
b) Operate the car under normal operating conditions as instructed in the kit.
c) Shine the light in the suspected area. The dyed fluid will appear as a yellow path leading to the problem.

Low Oil Pressure
1) Blocked oil filter.
2) Incorrect oil viscosity for expected temperature, or oil diluted with moisture or unburnt fuel mixtures.
3) Excessive bearing clearance.
4) If the oil level is low, fill to mark on dipstick.
5) Oil pump dirty/worn, or oil pump suction pipe screen blocked, or hole in oil pump suction pipe.
6) Incorrect or failing oil pressure sender.

ABNORMAL ENGINE KNOCKS
When Engine Cold And Continues Knocking For Two Or Three Minutes
Increases with torque
1) Tighten or replace as required if drive pulleys or balancer are loose or broken.
2) Replace piston if clearance from piston to bore is excessive. (Cold engine piston knock usually disappears when the cylinder is grounded out. Cold engine piston knock which disappears in 1.5 min. can be considered acceptable.)
3) Connecting rod bent.

Heavy Knock With Torque Applied
1) Replace parts as required of pulley hub or balancer broken.
2) Loose torque converter to flexiplate bolts.
3) Check if exhaust system contacting underbody.
4) Cracked flexiplate/flywheel.
5) Main bearing clearance or connecting rod bearing clearance excessive.

Light Knock while Hot
1) Inspect fuel quality.
2) Loose torque converter to flexiplate bolts.
3) Connecting rod clearing clearance excessive.

Knocks On First Start-up Only Lasting Few Seconds
1) Incorrect oil viscosity. Install correct oil viscosity for expected temperatures.
2) Valve / Roller Rocker Adjustment.
3) Replace crankshaft thrust bearing shells if excessive crankshaft end float.
4) Replace worn parts if front main bearing clearance is excessive.

SPECIFICATIONS

GENERAL
Type - 4M41	Inline 4 DOHC
No. of Cylinders	Four
Displacement:	3200cc
Compression ratio:	21:1
Bore and Stroke (nominal):	98.5 x 105.0
Fuel requirements	Diesel

CYLINDER BLOCK
Material	Alloy cast iron
Flatness of gasket surface	less than 0.05 mm
Flatness of gasket surface - maximum	0.10 mm
Piston diameter	98.45 - 98.47 mm
Piston to bore clearance	0.04 - 0.05 mm
Piston oversizes	0.50 mm and 1.00 mm
Max. bore wear (before reconditioning)	0.02 mm
Max ovality and taper (before reconditioning)	0.02 mm

CYLINDER HEAD
Material	Aluminium alloy
Type	Direct Injection Chamber
Max. allowable distortion - head surface	0.2 mm
Grinding limit	0.2 mm
Max. allowable distortion - intake surface	0.2 mm
Max. allowable distortion - exhaust surface	0.3 mm
Inlet valve seat insert hole diameter	
- 0.3 mm Oversize	35.30 - 35.33 mm
- 0.6 mm Oversize	35.60 - 35.63 mm
Exhaust valve seat insert hole diameter	
- 0.3 mm Oversize	33.3 - 33.325 mm
- 0.6 mm Oversize	33.6 - 33.625 mm
Valve guide hole diameter	12.00 - 12.02 mm
- 0.05 mm Oversize	12.05 - 12.07 mm
- 0.25 mm Oversize	12.25 - 12.27 mm
- 0.50 mm Oversize	12.50 - 12.52 mm
Camshaft/camshaft bearing clearance	0.05-0.09 mm
Max	0.15 mm
Standard Valve Sinkage:	0.05 - 0.55 mm
Max	0.80 mm
Valve seat width	1.8 - 2.2 mm
- Min	2.8 mm
Valve Seat Inserts Standard Size:	
Intake	35mm
Exhaust	33mm

Over size Valve Seat Insert are in 0.30 and 0.60mm oversize

CYLINDER HEAD GASKET SELECTION

Piston Protrusion	Head Gasket
max piston protrusion	Grade & notches
+ 0.03 - + 0.11 mm	A - 1 notches
- 0.05 - -0.03 mm	B - 2 notches
- 0.13 - - 0.05 mm	C - 3 notches
- 0.23 - - 0.15 mm	D - 4 notches

CYLINDER BLOCK

Flatness of gasket surface .... less than 0.05 mm
Flatness of gasket surface - maximum .... 0.10 mm
Cylinder Standard Bore ID .... 98.50 - 98.53 mm
Cylinder Standard Bore limit .... 98.75 mm
Piston to bore clearance .... 0.04 - 0.05 mm
Piston oversizes .... 0.50 mm and 1.00 mm

VALVES / ROLLER ROCKER ADJUSTMENT

Valve Clearance (Cold)
    Intake .... 1.0 mm
    Exhaust .... 1.5 mm

Stem diameter   - Inlet .... 6.560 - 6.575 mm
        - Min .... 6.45 mm
        - Exhaust .... 6.53 - 6.55 mm
        - Min .... 6.45 mm
Valve face angle .... 45° +/- 15'
Valve Head Thickness: .... 1.0 mm
        - Min .... 0.8 mm
Valve seat width .... 1.8 - 2.2 mm
        - Min .... 2.8 mm
Valve stem to guide clearance
        - Inlet .... 0.02 - 0.06 mm
        - Exhaust .... 0.05 - 0.09 mm

VALVE GUIDES

Valve stem to guide clearance
    - Inlet .... 0.02 - 0.06 mm
    - Exhaust .... 0.05 - 0.09 mm
Valve guide hole OD 12.00 mm
    - 0.05, 0.25 and 0.50mm Oversize available
Valve Guide Installed Height .... 16.50 +/- 0.30 mm

VALVE SPRINGS

Number 16
Valve Spring Out of Square Angle .... 2 degree
        Max .... 4 degree
Free length .... 51.3 mm
Compressed length at 255N .... 39.5 mm
Valve Installed Height 39.5mm

CAMSHAFT

Material .... Cast iron
Camshaft Journal diameter .... 44.93 - 44.94 mm

Camshaft journal Oil clearance .... 0.05 - 0.09 mm
    Max .... 0.15 mm
Camshaft Run-out .... 0.015 mm
    Max: 0.03mm
Height of cam lobe lift
    Inlet   - Front .... 6.16 mm
        - Min .... 6.11 mm
        - Rear .... 6.10 mm
        - Min .... 6.05 mm
    Exhaust - Front .... 5.91 mm
        - Min .... 5.86 mm
        - Rear .... 6.16 mm
        - Min .... 6.11 mm

PISTONS

Material .... Aluminium alloy
Type .... Auto thermic type
Piston diameter .... 98.42 - 98.47 mm
(Check size code on top of piston and cylinder block)
    Piston to bore clearance .... 0.04 - 0.05 mm
    Piston to bore clearance (Turbo) .... 0.07 - 0.08 mm
    Piston oversizes .... 0.50 mm, 0.75 mm, 1.00 mm
    Piston pin to Piston Clearance 0.007-0.021mm

PISTON PIN

Type .... Press fit in connecting rod
Material .... Alloy steel
Piston pin to Piston Clearance .... 0.007-0.021 mm
    Max .... 0.05 mm
Piston pin to Connecting Rod Bush Clearance
    .... 0.03-0.05 mm
    Max .... 0.1 mm

PISTON RINGS

Number 3
Ring Gap - New
    - Compression .... 0.30 - 0.45 mm
    - Max .... 0.80 mm
    - Scraper .... 0.40 - 0.55 mm
    - Max .... 0.80 mm
Oil Ring Steel Rail Gap Specification:
    - Oil ring .... 0.30 - 0.50 mm
    - Max .... 0.80 mm
Side clearance
    Compression .... 0.03 - 0.08 mm
    - Max .... 0.15 mm
    Scraper .... 0.07 - 0.10 mm
    - Max .... 0.15 mm
    Oil Ring .... 0.03 - 0.06 mm
    - Max .... 0.15 mm

TIMING CHAIN and GEARS

Gear back lash check
- Crankshaft gear to Idler gear 0.04-0.018mm
- Max 0.3mm
- Idler gear to idler gear left side 0.04-0.19mm
- Max 0.3mm
- Idler gear left side to left side balance shaft gear
- 0.04-0.22mm
- Max 0.4mm
- Idler gear to injection pump gear 0.04-0.21mm
- Max 0.4mm
- Oil pump to right side balance shaft
- 0.04-0.19mm
- Max 0.3mm
- Oil pump to crankshaft gear 0.04-0.18mm
- Max 0.3mm

Timing Chain
- Standard Gap: 16.5mm
- Max Wear Gap 9.0mm

CONNECTING ROD

- Material .... Forged carbon steel
- Connecting rod — bend .... 0.05 mm
- — twist .... 0.05 mm
- Connecting Rod bearing clearance .... 0.03 - 0.05 mm
- — service limit (main/big end) .... 0.1 mm
- Connecting Rod to crankshaft end clearance:
- .... 0.15 - 0.45 mm
- — service limit .... 0.6 mm
- Bearing material .... Aluminium alloy

CRANKSHAFT

- No. of main bearings 5
- End float controlled by .... No.3 bearing
- Main bearing journals diameter .... as below
- End float controlled by .... No.3 bearing
- Connecting Rod journal diameter .... as below
- — max. allowable ovality .... 0.01 mm
- — max. allowable taper .... 0.006 mm
- Main bearing clearance 1,2,4&5 .... 0.04 - 0.06 mm
- — service limit .... 0.1 mm
- Main bearing clearance brg 3 .... 0.06 - 0.08 mm
- — service limit .... 0.1 mm
- End play .... 0.10 - 0.28 mm
- — limit .... 0.4 mm

Crankshaft Main Journal		Cyl. Block	Main Bearing
Colour mark	Journal OD mm	Stamp	Colour mark
None	67.970 - 67.798	A	Blk/Blk
		B	Blu/Blu
Blue	67.961 - 67.970	A	Yell/Yell
		B	Blk/Blk

Crankshaft Connecting Rod Journal OD mm	Connecting rod big end Int. Dia.	Connecting rod bearing Colour mark
53.980 - 53.988	58.010 - 58.019	None
	58.000 - 58.010	Blue
53.971 - 53.980	58.010 - 58.019	Yellow
	58.000 - 58.010	Black

Crankshaft connecting rod journal identification	Connecting rod identification	Connecting rod bearing - Colour mark
None "1"	None	Blue
	Blue	None
Blue "2"	None	None
	Blue	Blue

OIL PUMP

- Inner Gear Tip clearance .... 0.15 - 0.27mm
- Gear to Pump Cover Clearance .... 0.03 - 0.05mm
- Max 0.15mm
- Side Clearance .... 0.05 - 0.10mm
- Max 0.15mm

OIL COOLER

- Bypass Opening Pressure .... 490 +/- 30 kPa
- Regulator Opening Pressure .... 620 +/- 30 kPa

TORQUE SPECIFICATION

Description	Nm
Alternator bracket M8	48
Alternator bracket M10	23
Alternator pivot nut	44
Balance Shaft Left Side Bolts:	12
Camshaft Gear Bolts:	88
Camshaft Holder Bolts:	20
Connecting Rod Cap Bolt - 4 steps:	
Step 1	29
Step 2	49
Step 3	rotate a further 45 degrees
Step 4	rotate a further 45 degrees
Coolant temperature gauge unit	11
Coolant temperature sensor	29
Crankshaft bolt	323
Crank Angle Sensor	9
Cylinder head bolts	
M12 Bolts - Cold in 5 stages	
Cylinder head bolts - Cold - in sequence	98
Loosen in reverse order	
Cylinder head bolts - Cold - in sequence	49
Rotate	90 degrees
Rotate	90 degrees
Two front M10 bolts - Cold in 3 stages	
Cylinder head bolts - Cold - in 3 stages	24
Dipstick mounting bolt	13
Drive belt tension pulley nut	49
Drive belt tension nut	35-55
Engine hanger front	17
Engine hanger exhaust manifold	35
Engine mounting bracket	
- M8	22
- M10	42
- M12	75
Exhaust Manifold Bolts and Nuts:	30
Exhaust Pipe Nuts:	30
Flywheel / Drive Plate Bolts	123
Glow Plug	18
Heater pipe bolt	11
Injector bolts	21
Intake Manifold Nuts:	30
Main Bearing Bolts - 4 steps:	
Step 1 - bolts 17 to 26	20
Step 2	rotate a further 90 degrees
Step 3	rotate a further 90 degrees
Step 4 - tighten bolts 1 to 16	25
Oil Cooler Element Nuts:	20
Oil Jet Union	33
Oil Pan	11
Oil pan drain plug	49
Oil suction pipe and screen	11
Oil relief plug	44
Oil pump cover	10
Oil Pump/Right Side Balance Shaft Bolts:	12
Plastic Fan to Thermo Coupling Bolts:	10
Rear oil seal retainer plate	11
Rocker Cover Bolts:	3.4
Timing Chain Right Side Tension Guide Bolts:	33
Timing Chain Left Side Tension Guide Bolt:	40
Timing Cover Cap Nuts:	23
Thermostat Housing bolts	18
Thermo Fan Coupling Bolts:	24
Thermo switch	6-9
Turbocharger Nuts:	50
Turbocharger Bolts:	55
Water Pump Bolts:	24

ENGINE ELECTRICAL SYSTEM

(Charging & Starting System)

Subject	Page	Subject	Page
BATTERY	**162**	**STARTING SYSTEM**	**168**
General Information	**162**	No Load Test	168
Periodic Maintenance	162	**Starter Motor Removal**	**168**
Testing Battery Electrolyte (Acid)	**162**	6G7	168
Using the Hydrometer	162	4M4	169
Test Result Indications	162	**Starter Motor Dismantle**	**169**
Battery Charging	**163**	**Component Inspection & Testing**	**169**
Fast Charging	163	Clean & Inspect	169
Slow Charging	163	Commutator	169
		Armature Insulation Test	170
ALTERNATOR SYSTEM	**163**	Armature Continuity Test	170
Drive Belt Adjustment	**163**	Armature Short Circuit Test	170
Output Line Voltage Drop Test	**163**	Armature to Commutator Leads	170
Current Output Test	**162**	Over running Clutch	170
Regulated Voltage Test	**164**	Brushes	170
Alternator Removal	**165**	Brush Length	170
6G7 MPI	165	Brush Replacement	170
6G7 GDI	165	-Positive Brushes	170
4M4	165	-Negative Brushes	171
Alternator Overhaul	**165**	Brush Holder Assembly	171
Alternator Installation	**165**	Drive Assembly Check	171
6G7 MPI	165	Bushes	171
6G7 GDI	165	**Starter Motor Assembly**	**171**
4M4	166	**Starter Motor Installation**	**171**
Charging System Diagnosis	**166**	6G7	171
Alternator Disassembly	**166**	4M4	171
Alternator Inspection	**166**		
Rear Bearing	166	**PROBLEM SOLVING & DIAGNOSIS**	**172**
Rotor Check	166		
Brush Check	167	**SPECIFICATIONS**	**172**
Stator Check	167		
Alternator Assembly	167		
PROBLEM SOLVING & DIAGNOSIS	**167**		
SPECIFICATIONS	**168**		

BATTERY

GENERAL INFORMATION
Battery acid is highly corrosive which may on contact, cause personal injury or damage paint surfaces. Any spillage must be immediately diluted and flushed away with clean water.

The battery electrolyte should be maintained at recommended level by topping up with de mineralized water.

Clean the battery terminal and the inside of the cable terminal using a suitable tool.

PERIODIC MAINTENANCE
1. Protect paint finish using suitable covers.
2. Disconnect battery cables at battery (negative first).
3. Remove battery hold down clamp and remove battery from vehicle.
4. Inspect battery carrier for acid damage. If necessary remove corrosion by using a solution of bicarbonate of soda in warm water and scrubbing area with a stiff brush, taking care to avoid spreading corrosion residue, and flush area with clean water. Damaged areas should be repainted to avoid further corrosion.
5. Clean battery cover by same method.
   * Do not allow any cleaning solution or water to enter battery cells as this will dilute electrolyte.
6. Check battery cables for damage and fraying and replace if necessary.
7. Clean Battery terminals. If necessary remove corrosion by using a solution of bicarbonate of soda in warm water and scrubbing area with a stiff brush and flush area with clean water.
8. Check battery case, cover and vents for damage.
9. Install battery and hold down clamp. Do not over tighten hold down clamp as this could crack case.
10. Connect battery cables and tighten to specifications.
    * Ensure battery polarity is not reversed.

TESTING BATTERY ELECTROLYTE (ACID)
A hydrometer should be used to determine the specific gravity of battery electrolyte. The reading obtained indicates amount of unused sulphuric acid remaining in electrolyte and state of charge of battery.

The reading obtained will vary in relation to the temperature of the electrolyte. As the temperature rises the density of the electrolyte decreases and the specific gravity falls. As the temperature falls the density increases and the specific gravity rises.

USING THE HYDROMETER
1. Liquid level of battery cell should be at normal height and electrolyte should be thoroughly mixed with any battery water which may have just been added by charging battery before taking hydrometer readings.
2. Draw electrolyte in and out of hydrometer barrel several times to bring temperature of hydrometer float to that of the acid in the cell.
3. Draw sufficient electrolyte into hydrometer barrel with the pressure bulb fully expanded to lift float so that it does not touch the sides, bottom or top of barrel.
4. Read the hydrometer with the hydrometer in a vertical position.

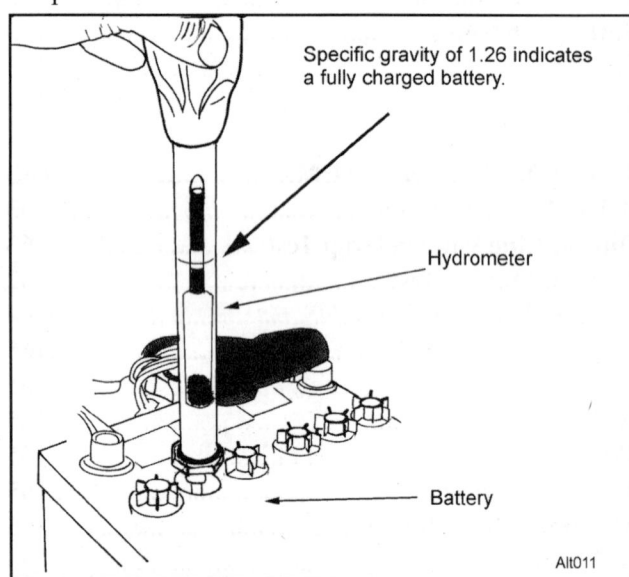

Specific gravity of 1.26 indicates a fully charged battery.

TEST RESULT INDICATIONS

Electrolyte specific gravity	Battery Charge Level
1.240 to 1.260	100%
1.210 to 1.240	75%
1.180 to 1.210	50%
Below 1.130	Completely discharged

A battery should be charged if the specific gravity is less than 1.210. If there is more than 0.25 specific gravity variation between cells then a fault is most likely with the battery itself.

If battery charge is low and battery is serviceable, check alternator operation and all electrical connections.

BATTERY CHARGING

WARNING: *When batteries are being charged explosive gas mixture forms beneath the cover of each cell.*

* Do not smoke near batteries on charge or which have recently been charged.
* Do not break live circuit at terminals of batteries on charge. A spark will occur where the live circuit is broken. Keep all open flames away from battery.

Note: Fast charging will provide sufficient charge after one hour to enable the battery and alternator to carry electrical load however, if possible slow charging is preferable.

FAST CHARGING

Fast charging a battery in the vehicle is not recommended, however if this procedure is used it is most important that the battery is disconnected.

Note: *A battery will be irretrievably damaged if following precautions are not taken.*

1. Battery electrolyte temperature must not exceed 45°C.
   If this temperature is reached, battery should be cooled by reducing charging rate or remove battery from circuit.
2. As batteries approach full charge electrolyte in each cell will begin to gas or bubble. Excessive gassing must not be allowed.
3. Do not fast charge longer than one hour. If battery does not show a significant change in specific gravity after one hour of "FAST" charge, the slow charge method should be used.

SLOW CHARGING

Many discharged batteries can be brought back to good condition by slow charging. Battery should be tested with a hydrometer and a record kept of the readings taken at regular intervals throughout the charge. When a cell has a specific gravity reading that is 0.25 or more below other cells, that cell is faulty and battery should be replaced. Safe slow charging rates can be calculated by allowing one ampere per positive plate per cell (i.e. 4 amperes for a 9 plate battery and 5 amperes for an 11 plate battery). The average time required to charge a battery by the low charge method at normal rates is from 12 to 16 hours, however, when a battery continues to show an increase in specific gravity, battery charge should be continued even if it takes 24 hours or more. Watch the temperature of batteries carefully and if temperature of any one of them reaches 43°C, lower the charging rate.
Battery will be fully charged when it is gassing freely and when there is no further rise in specific gravity after three successive readings taken at hourly intervals. Make sure hydrometer readings are corrected for temperature. Many batteries can be brought back to a useful condition by slow charging at half the normal charging rate from 60 to 100 hours. This long charging cycle is necessary to reconvert crystalline lead sulphate in to active materials.

ALTERNATOR SYSTEM

DRIVE BELT REPLACEMENT & ADJUSTMENT

Refer to the Engine Tune-up and Maintenance chapter for detailed instructions on drive belt removal and adjustment.

ON VEHICLE TESTS

Before carrying out on vehicle tests check:
1. The alternator indicator light is operating.
2. The battery must be fully charged.
3. Engine must be at normal operating temperature.
4. Engine idle must be within specification.

Output Line Voltage Drop Test

1. Make sure all electrical equipment is turned off, and the ignition system is in off position. Disconnect battery earth cable at battery.
2. Detach generator positive lead from the 'B+' generator terminal.
3. Connect positive lead of an ammeter (0-100 Amp scale) to the generator 'B+' terminal, and the negative ammeter lead to the disconnected generator positive lead.
4. Connect positive lead of a voltmeter (0-20 Volt scale minimum) to the generator 'B+' terminal, and negative voltmeter lead to a the battery positive (+ve) lead.
5. Connect a tachometer to the vehicle then connect the negative battery and start the vehicle.
6. With the engine speed running at 2,500 rpm turn the headlights and other lamps on and off to adjust the alternator load so the ammeter reading is slightly above 30A.
7. Gradually decrease the engine speed until the ammeter is reading 30A and then take the reading from the voltmeter.
8. If the voltmeter reading is above the limit value then there is probably a fault in the generator positive read between the "B+" generator terminal and the battery.
   Limit: 0.3V
9. Repair fault in output wiring and re-test.
10. To prevent excessive battery discharge occurring, the engine should be returned and run at idle before switching off engine.
11. Detach battery cable at battery. Remove the voltmeter, ammeter and tachometer, then reconnect the generator positive lead to the generator 'B+' terminal. Connect battery earth cable.

ENGINE ELECTRICAL SYSTEM (charging & starting system)

Current Output Test

1. Make sure all electrical equipment is turned off, and the ignition system is in off position. Disconnect battery earth cable at battery.
2. Detach generator positive lead from the 'B+' generator terminal.
3. Connect positive lead of an ammeter (0-100 Amp scale) to the generator 'B+' terminal, and the negative ammeter lead to the disconnected generator positive lead.
4. Connect positive lead of a voltmeter (0-20 Volt scale minimum) to the generator 'B+' terminal, and negative voltmeter lead to a good earth. Volt meter to alternator B+ , -ve to engine earth should read 12-14 volts

5. Connect a tachometer to the vehicle then connect the negative battery lead and check to ensure the voltmeter reading is equal to the battery voltage.
   Note: *To check voltage reading turn ignition to on position, do not start engine.*
6. Turn on the vehicle headlights and then start the engine.
7. Switch the headlights on to high beam, turn the heater blower onto the highest speed, then increase engine speed to 2,500 rpm. Immediately read the ammeters maximum output value.
8. The ammeter reading should be above the limit value. If it is not above the limit value remove the alternator from the vehicle for further inspection.
   Limit: .... 70% normal current output
   Note: *Refer to Specifications for normal output specification.*
9. To prevent excessive battery discharge occurring, the engine should be returned and run at idle before switching off engine.
10. Detach battery cable at battery. Remove the voltmeter, ammeter and tachometer, then reconnect the generator positive lead to the generator 'B+' terminal. Connect battery earth cable.

Regulated Voltage Test

1. Make sure all electrical equipment is turned off, and the ignition system is in off position. Disconnect battery earth cable at battery.
2. Connect positive lead of a voltmeter (0-20 Volt scale minimum) to the generator 'S' terminal, and negative voltmeter lead to a good earth.
3. Detach generator positive lead from the 'B+' generator terminal.
4. Connect positive lead of an ammeter (0-100 Amp scale) to the generator 'B+' terminal, and the negative ammeter lead to the disconnected generator positive lead.
5. Connect a tachometer to the vehicle then connect the negative battery lead and check to ensure the voltmeter reading is equal to the battery voltage.
   Note: *To check voltage reading turn ignition to on position, do not start engine.*
6. Ensure all lights and accessories are turned off then start engine and increase engine speed to 2,500rpm.
7. When the alternator output current becomes 10A or less read the value on the voltmeter.
8. If voltage reading is within specification the regulator is operating correctly. If the voltage reading is not within specification there is a fault with either the voltage regulator or alternator.

Voltage Regulator Ambient C°	Voltage
-20	14.2 - 15.4
20	13.9 - 14.9
60	13.4 - 14.6
80	13.1 - 14.5

9. To prevent excessive battery discharge, the engine should be run at idle before switching off engine.
10. Detach battery cable at battery. Remove the voltmeter, ammeter and tachometer, then reconnect the generator positive lead to the generator 'B+' terminal. Connect battery earth cable.

ENGINE ELECTRICAL SYSTEM (charging & starting system)

Alternator

Alternator Removal
Petrol - MPI
1. Remove the air cleaner assembly, then remove the undercover from the engine.
2. Remove the drive belt, then disconnect the battery and all wiring from the alternator.
3. Remove the mounting bolts then remove the alternator from vehicle.

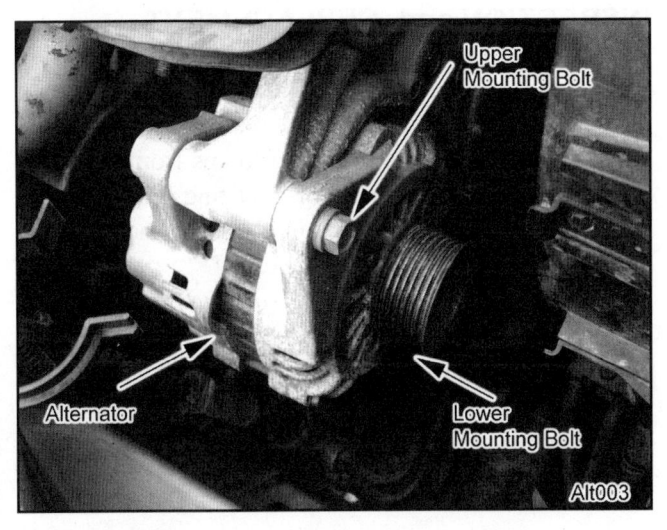

Petrol - GDI
1. Remove the air cleaner assembly from vehicle.
2. Remove the drive belt, then disconnect the battery and all wiring from the alternator.
3. Remove the mounting bolts then remove the alternator from vehicle.

Diesel - 4M4
1. Remove the air cleaner assembly from vehicle.
2. Remove the drive belt, then disconnect the battery and all wiring from the alternator.
3. Remove the mounting bolts then remove the adjusting plate and alternator from vehicle.

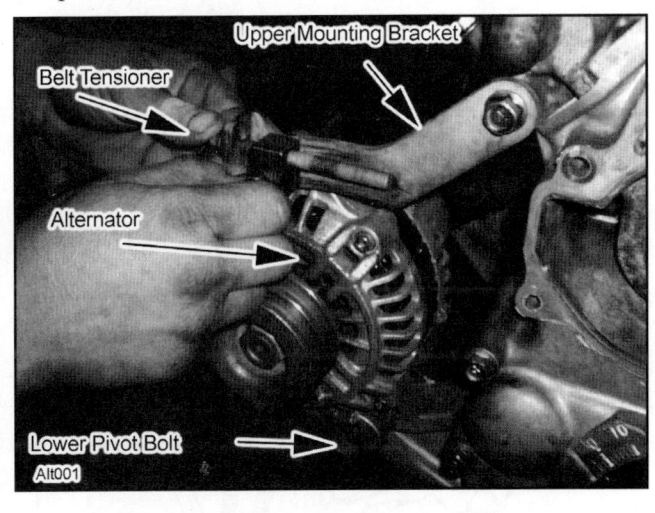

Overhaul
If an alternator is defective it is usually replaced with a new or rebuilt alternator available from an automotive electrician or automotive accessory store. It is generally cheaper to purchase a change over alternator than to try and repair the alternator yourself.

Alternator Installation
Petrol - MPI
1. Install alternator to vehicle.
2. Loosely install the alternator mounting bolts.
3. Install and adjust the alternator belt then tighten alternator bolts to specification.
   Alternator Pivot Bolt .... 44 Nm
   Alternator Adjustment Bolt .... 22 Nm
4. Reconnect the electrical connections to the alternator then reconnect the battery.
5. Install the air cleaner assembly, then install the under cover to the underside of the vehicle.

Petrol - GDI
1. Install alternator to vehicle.
2. Loosely install the alternator mounting bolts.
3. Install and adjust the alternator belt then tighten alternator bolts to specification.
   Alternator Pivot Bolt .... 44 Nm
   Alternator Adjustment Bolt .... 22 Nm
4. Reconnect the electrical connections to the alternator

ENGINE ELECTRICAL SYSTEM (charging & starting system)

then reconnect the battery.

5. Install the air cleaner assembly to the vehicle.

Diesel - 4M4

1. Install the alternator and adjusting plate to vehicle and tighten the alternator mounting bolts to specification.
   Alternator Pivot Bolt .... **49 Nm**
2. Install and adjust the alternator belt.
   Alternator Adjustment Bolt .... **22 Nm**
3. Reconnect the electrical connections to the alternator then reconnect the battery.
4. Install the air cleaner assembly to the vehicle.

CHARGING SYSTEM DIAGNOSIS

Note: Before starting the tests below, ensure that the battery is fully charged, a 30volt voltmeter and suitable test probes are being used.

1. Check that the fusible link is OK and the battery is fully charged.
2. Switch ON the ignition, ensure that the warning lamp is off, disconnect the S&L harness connector and ground the L terminal (harness side).
3. If the warning lamp is OFF in step2, check the condition and/or operation of the warning lamp globe and the fuse for the warning lamp. If faults are found, repair/replace as required.
4. If the warning lamp is ON, check the condition and/or operation of the IC regulator. If faults are found, repair/replace as required.
5. With the ignition switch in the ON position and the warning lamp ON, start the engine, run at 1500RPM and ensure the warning lamp goes OFF. If it does, the system is operating OK.
6. If the warning lamp stays ON after the engine is running at 1500RPN in step5, Check the condition and/or operation of the drive belt, fuse at the S Terminal and/or the condition and/or operation of the S, L Terminal connector. If faults are found, repair/replace as 2required.
7. If no faults are found in step6, let the engine idle, if the warning lamp goes out, the system is OK
8. If the warning lamp still stays ON in step6, (with the engine running at 1500RPM), record the voltage at the alternator terminal B.
9. If the voltage is more than 15v in step8, repair/replace the IC voltage regulator as required.
10. If there is no voltage present in step8, check for an open field circuit. If faults are found, repair/replace as required.
    Please Note: If the test results above are OK, but the system is still showing a fault, check the terminal B connection for tightness.

If the field circuit is open, check the condition of the rotor coil, rotor slip ring and brush. If fault are found, replace any faulty parts found.

Warning Lamp

If there is a fault in the IC Regulator, the warning lamp (Charge) lights up when the alternator is operating.
If this happens, there could be excessive voltage or no voltage being produced

ALTERNATOR REMOVAL, STRIPPING, INSPECTION and REPLACEMENT

1. Start this operation by disconnecting the negative battery terminal and removing the undercover before starting any repairs.
2. Remove the alternator wiring looms from the alternator, loosen the alternator adjusting bracket bolts, remove the alternator fixing bolts and then remove the alternator from the vehicle.
   Note: The rear cover may be difficult to remove because a ring is used to lock the outer race of the rear bearing. To assist in the removal of the rear cover, just heat the bearing box section with a 200w soldering iron. Please do not use a heat gun as it could damage the diode assembly.

INSPECTION

Rear Bearing

Note: If the bearing is removed at any time, do not reuse it again, always replace with a new one. Do not at any time lubricate the rear bearing outer race.

Rotor Check

1. Carry out a resistance check as shown.
   Specified Resistance:
   V6 Petrol, Diesel 2.8 .... 2.0 +/- 0.5 ohms
   Diesel 3.2 .... 3.15 ohms
   If the resistance is not as shown, replace the rotor
2. Carry out an insulator test as shown in the diagram,

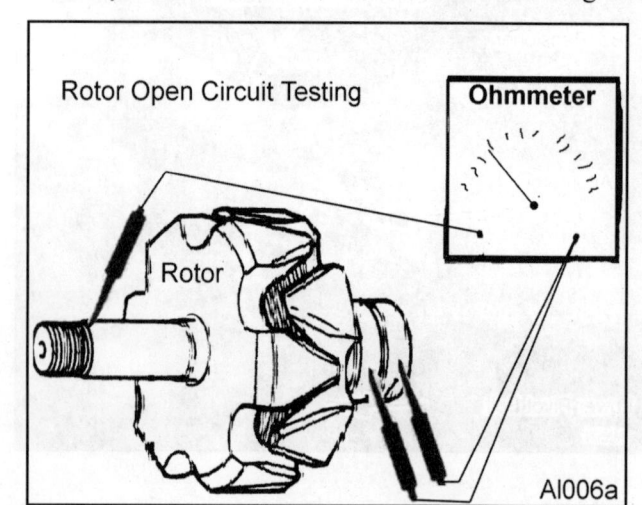

Rotor Open Circuit Testing — Ohmmeter — Rotor

AI006a

166

if continuity exists, replace the rotor.
3. Check the slip rings for wear.

Brush Check
1. Check the brush set and make sure that they move smoothly, if they do not, check the brush holder and clean as required.
2. Check the brush and make sure that it is not worn down to the limit line. If it is, repair/replace as required.

Stator Check
1. Carry out a continuity check on the stator as it is shown in the diagram.
If there is no continuity, replace the stator.

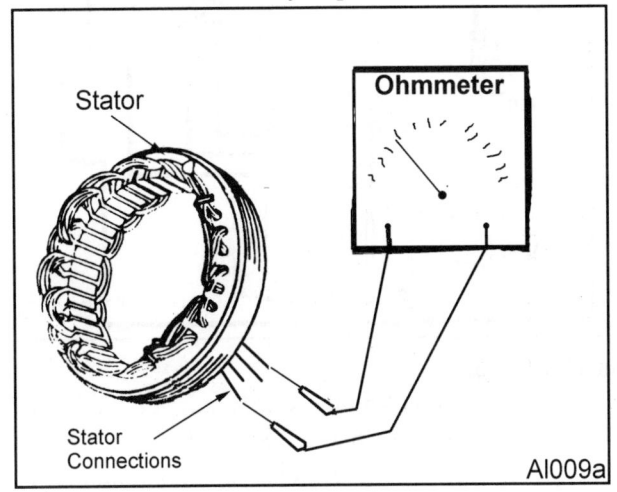

2. Carry out a ground test as shown in the diagram, if continuity exists, replace the stator.

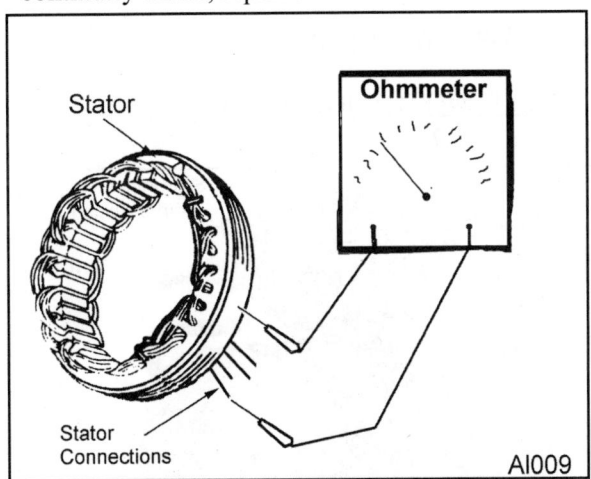

ASSEMBLY
1. Fix the ring into the groove at the rear of the bearing as close to the adjacent area as possible.
   Note: Do not reuse the old bearings at any time.
2. Fit the brush assembly, diode, regulator and stator. Push the brushes up with your fingers and install the rotor
3. Push the brushes up with your fingers and fit them to the rotor.
   Note: Ensure that you do not damage the slip ring/s when carrying out this operation.
4. Carry out the rest of the assembly and refitting procedures in the reverse method of removal.

Problem Solving & Diagnosis

BATTERY WILL NOT CHARGE
* Battery cells not operating
* Battery terminals dirty or loose
* Battery acid level low
* Battery acid specific gravity specification of 1.230
* Loose or corroded connection in charging circuit
* Faulty generator
* Faulty voltage regulator

INDICATOR LIGHT DOES NOT GO ON
* Globe broken or blown
* Defective regulator
* Defective Wiring
  Open circuit in rotor winding

INDICATOR LIGHT STAYS ON
* Positive diode failure
* Defective voltage regulator
* Faulty alternator
* B + cable off or broken
* S cable off or broken
* Battery Overcharged

NOISY ALTERNATOR
* Worn bearings
* Loose alternator drive pulley
* Open or shorted diodes
* Open or shorted Stator winding
* Generator mounting brackets loose
* Worn or frayed drive belt

BATTERY OVERCHARGES
* Battery acid specific gravity not correct
* Shorted battery cell
* Faulty voltage regulator
* Short circuit in rotor winding

ALTERNATOR WILL NOT CHARGE
* Faulty regulator
* Brushes worn or sticking
* Brush springs broken or lost tension
* Faulty rectifiers
* Open circuit in stator wiring, charging circuit or field circuit
* Loose drive belt

ENGINE ELECTRICAL SYSTEM (charging & starting system)

Specifications

Type	Battery Voltage Sensing
Rated output V/A	12/85A
Voltage Regulator	Electronic Built-in type
Number of brushes	2
Brush wear - minimum length	Limit Line
Slip rings to be true within	0.45 mm
Claw poles to be true within	0.50 mm
Resistance - rotor	2.50 +/- 0.13 ohms
V6 Petrol, Diesel 2.8	2.0 +/- 0.5 ohms
Diesel 3.2	3.15 ohms
Regulator output voltage	14.25 - 14.55 V
Output test - 1050 alternator rpm	10 amp
- 1500 alternator rpm	30 amp
- 6000 alternator rpm	85 amp

Alternator output line maximum voltage drop at
30A output   0.3V
Output Current 70% of normal output current

Output Voltage
20 deg C .... 13.9 - 14.9 volts
60 deg C .... 13.4 - 14.6 volts
80 deg C .... 13.1 - 14.5 volts
Rated output volts/amps
  V6 SOHC 12/85
  V6 DOHC 12/85
  Diesel 2.8 .... 12/85
  Diesel 3.2 .... 12/125

TORQUE SPECIFICATION   Nm

Alternator through bolts	4 - 5.4
Adjusting strap to alternator bolt	12 - 15
Alternator pivot bolt	22 - 24
Pulley retaining nut	54 - 68
Alternator through bolts	3.8 - 5.5
B+ terminal to alternator nut	7.5 - 8.5
B+ terminal to rectifier nut	2.7 - 3.8
Regulator retaining screws	1.6 - 3.2
Rectifier fixing screws	2.2 - 3.2
Bearing retaining plate screws	2.1 - 3.0
Capacitor retaining screw	2.7 - 3.8

STARTING SYSTEM

NO LOAD TEST

Check the armature is not seized before performing a NO LOAD TEST. Prise the pinion in a counter clockwise direction with a screwdriver. If the armature will not rotate freely, Do Not perform the No Load Test.

Clamp starter motor securely to test bench and make connections. Close the switch and compare the RPM, current, voltage readings with the following specifications.

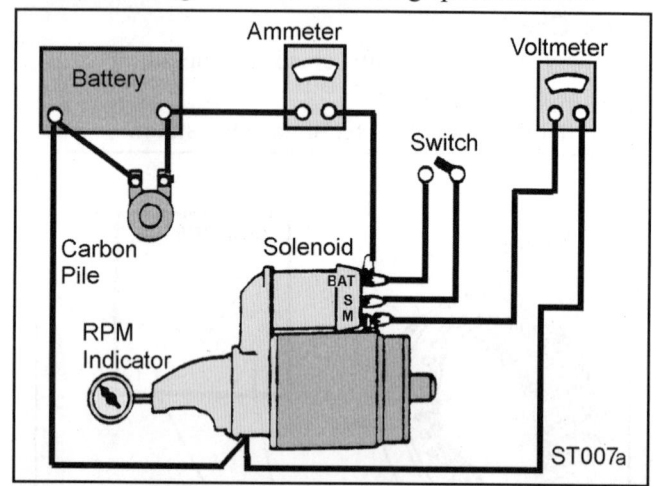

Bosch Starter
- Terminal Voltage .... 12 V
- Current - V6 and 2.8 diesel .... 90 amp
- 3.2 diesel 130
- Minimum Speed .... 5000 rpm or more

Starter Motor

STARTER MOTOR REMOVAL
Removal - 6G7

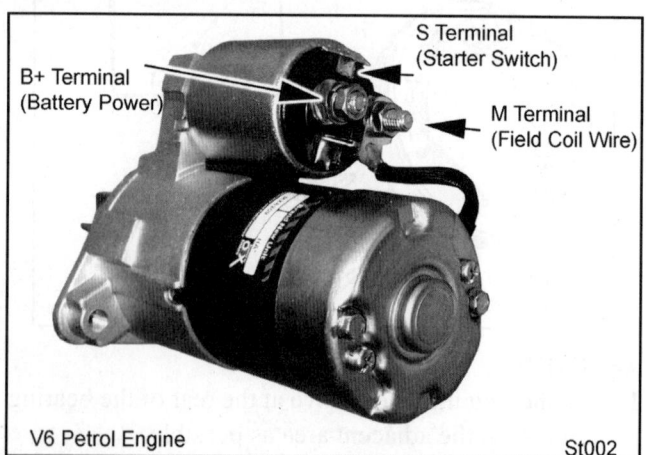

1. From the underside of the vehicle remove the stone guard/cover.
2. Detach battery earth cable at battery and detach the electrical connectors from starter motor solenoid.
3. Loosen the starter motor mounting bolts, support starter motor, remove the mounting bolts and remove

ENGINE ELECTRICAL SYSTEM (charging & starting system)

starter from vehicle.
4. Remove the cover from the starter motor.

Removal - 4M4 Engines

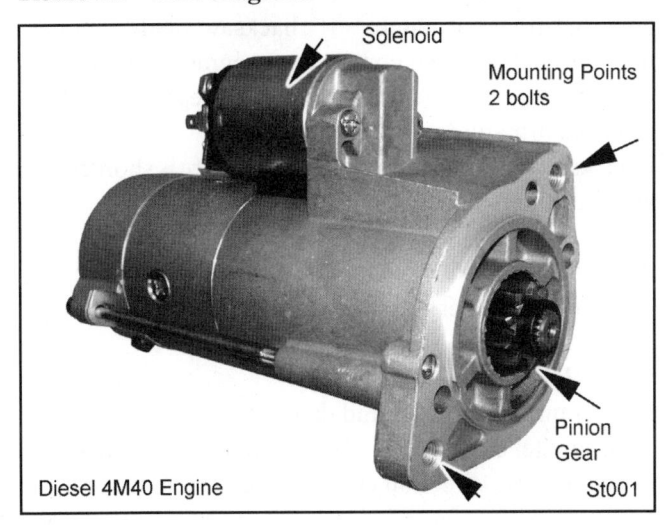

1. Work from the under neath of the vehicle.
2. Detach battery earth cable at battery and detach the electrical connectors from starter motor solenoid. 
3. Loosen the starter motor mounting bolts, support starter motor, remove the mounting bolts and remove starter from vehicle.

STARTER MOTOR DISMANTLE

1. Remove nut and washer from the solenoid field coil terminal, then separate the lead from the terminal and remove the solenoid retaining screws and solenoid.
2. Remove the end cover retaining screws and end cover then remove the C-clip and flat washer.
3. Remove the through bolts retaining the starter motor housing and remove the rear housing.
4. Mark the position of the brush holder in relation to the yoke assembly, then prise back brush retaining lugs and remove brush plate.
5. From assembly remove the armature assembly then remove the yoke assembly.
6. Remove the rubber seal then from the front housing remove the over running clutch, drive pinion assembly and gear set as an assembly.
7. Push the stop ring towards the snap ring using an appropriate sized socket, then remove snap ring, stop ring and over running clutch from shaft.

COMPONENT INSPECTION & TESTING
CLEANING & INSPECTION

With the starter motor completely disassembled, all components should be cleaned and inspected. Wash components except the armature and field coils in a suitable cleaning agent ensuring not to immerse parts to cleaning agent use a brush or cloth.

Caution: *Do not clean armature or field coils with cleaning solvent as damage to the insulation could occur. Clean armature and field coils carefully using compressed air.*

COMMUTATOR

1. Place the armature on a pair of "V" blocks then using a dial indicator check the run-out of the commutator.

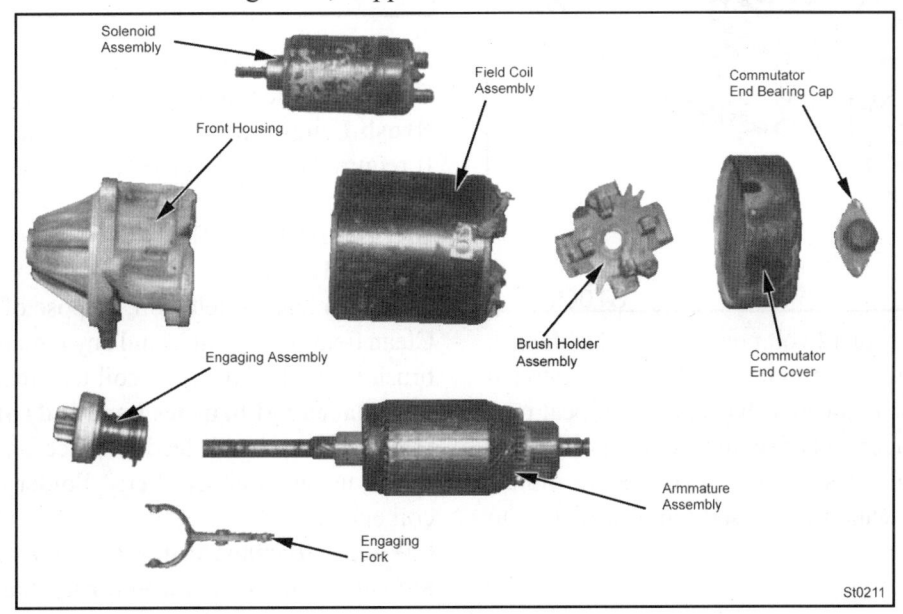

169

ENGINE ELECTRICAL SYSTEM (charging & starting system)

Standard Value..**0.5 mm**
Limit..**0.1 mm**

2. Using vernier callipers check the outside diameter of the commutator.

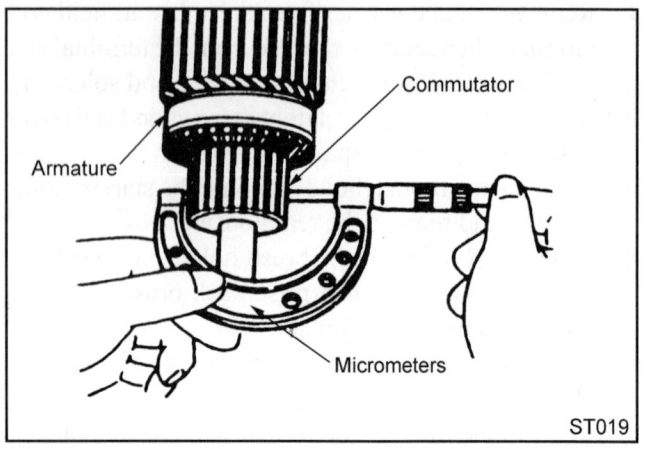

Figure: Commutator, Armature, Micrometers — ST019

Standard Value: - 6G7 ....29.4 mm
                - 4M4 ....32 mm
Limit: - 6G7 ....28.4 mm
                - 4M4 ....31.4 mm

3. Inspect the depth of the undercuts between segments.
Standard Value..**0.5 mm**
Limit..**0.2 mm**

ARMATURE INSULATION TEST
Connect a 240 volt powered test lamp or ohmmeter between the armature core and a commutator segment. If lamp illuminates, armature is grounded and should be replaced. Repeat procedure on the remaining commutator segments.

ARMATURE CONTINUITY TEST

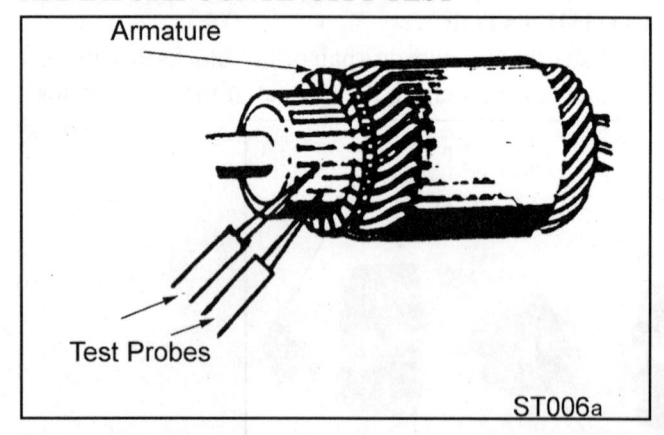

Figure: Armature, Test Probes — ST006a

Using an Ohmmeter (or 12 volt powered DC. test lamp). Touch one probe onto a commutator segment, then touch the remaining probe to an adjacent segment, repeat procedure on each adjacent set of segments. If any adjacent set of segments indicates continuity (test lamp illuminant), the armature windings are shortened, armature to be replaced.

ARMATURE SHORT CIRCUIT TEST
Test armature for short circuits on a growler.
Place armature on growler and switch on growler. Hold a hacksaw blade approximately 6mm above armature core and rotate armature. If hacksaw blade vibrates, undercut between the commutator segments (to a depth of approximately 0.7mm) using a suitable small file, then re-check armature.
If hacksaw blade still vibrates, the armature is short circuit and must be replaced.

ARMATURE TO COMMUTATOR LEADS
Examine, re-solder if required.

OVERRUNNING CLUTCH
Inspect pinion for wear and damage.
Turn counter clock wise and ensure pinion locks then turn in a clockwise direction ensuring movement is smooth.

BRUSHES
Make sure that brushes slide smoothly in their respective holders, brush connections are good and brushes are clean and not chipped.

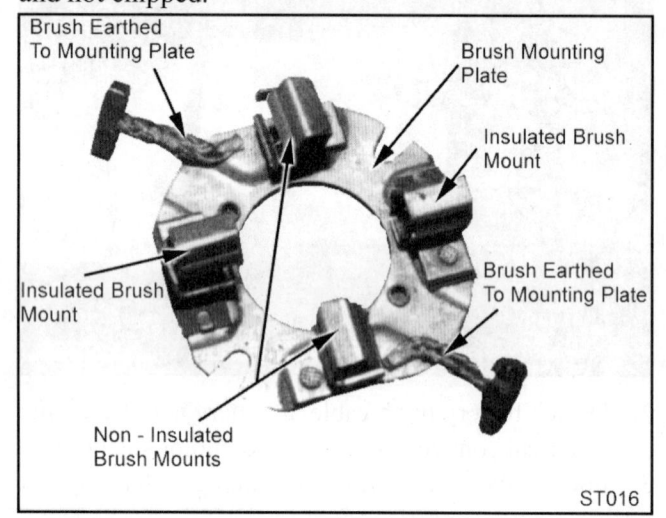

Figure: Brush Earthed To Mounting Plate, Brush Mounting Plate, Insulated Brush Mount, Brush Earthed To Mounting Plate, Insulated Brush Mount, Non - Insulated Brush Mounts — ST016

BRUSH LENGTH
Check brush length is within specification.
Brush Length .... **Wear limit line**
If required replace brushes as follows:

BRUSH REPLACEMENT
Positive Brushes
Cut brush lead at field coil, dispose of brush and spring. Clean field coil terminal and any remaining section of the brush lead, 'Tin' the field coil terminal.
* Replacement brushes have ends of leads 'tinned'.
Hold the new brush lead in place on the field coil terminal, using a pair of pliers. Solder brush lead to field coil end.
* When soldering the new brush lead into place, don't allow the solder to run to far up the lead.

ENGINE ELECTRICAL SYSTEM (charging & starting system)

Negative Brushes

Cut brush lead at the brush holder terminal. Dispose of brush and spring. Clean the brush holder terminal, and any remaining section of the brush lead. Clean remaining brush lead on brush holder. 'Tin' brush holder terminal. Hold new brush lead in place on the brush holder terminal, using a pair of pliers. Solder brush lead to brush holder.

* When soldering the new brush lead into place, do not allow the solder to run to far up the lead.

Test brushes as described in the following information.

BRUSH HOLDER ASSEMBLY

Using an Ohmmeter check the continuity between the brush holder plate and the brush holder. There is to be no continuity.

DRIVE ASSEMBLY CHECK

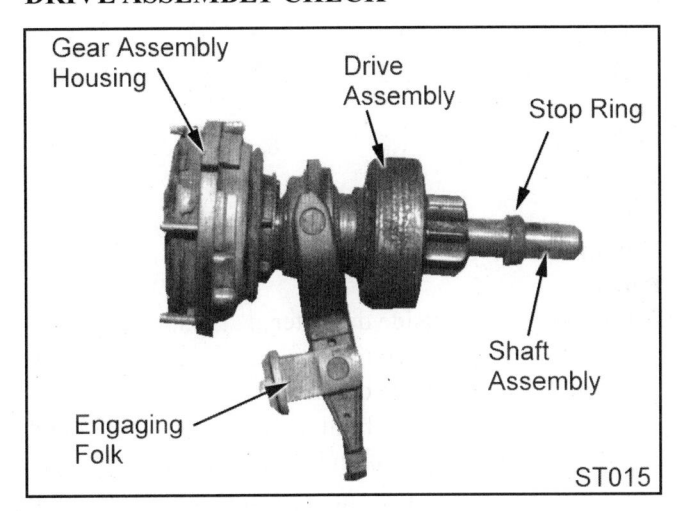

Gear Assembly Housing — Drive Assembly — Stop Ring — Shaft Assembly — Engaging Folk
ST015

Examine pinion gear for burrs and worn or chipped teeth. Check operation of pinion, the pinion gear should rotate free and smooth in relation to the pinion housing when turned in a clockwise direction, but not rotate when turned in a counter clockwise direction.

BUSHES

Check fit of armature shaft in commutator end cover and drive end housing. If bushes are excessively worn, the starter motor is likely to operate inefficiently and/or the armature may foul on field coil poles.

To remove bushes, support the commutator end cover or drive end housing (as appropriate), carefully tap bush out using a suitable mandrel.

* If new bushes are to be installed, they must be soaked in clean engine oil for one hour prior to installation.

To install new bushes, press or tap into place with a suitable shouldered mandrel.

Do not ream bushes after they have been installed as self lubricating qualities of the bush will be diminished.

STARTER MOTOR ASSEMBLY

1. To the planetary gear holder install the over running clutch and stopper ring ensuring the flat side of the stopper ring is towards the over running clutch.
2. Install the snap ring and pull the stop ring over the snap ring with a suitable tool.
3. To the front housing install the over running clutch, drive pinion assembly and gear set assembly ensuring the flat on the gear set housing is aligned with the flat on the front housing.
4. Install rubber seal, then install the yoke assembly followed by the armature assembly.
5. Install brush holder assembly aligning the marks on the yoke assembly made during disassembly.
6. Install rear housing to assembly and then install through bolts tightening to specification.
   Through Bolts .... 8 Nm
7. Install flat washer and C-clip then install the end cover tightening retaining screws to specification.
   End Cover Retaining Screws .... 1.4 - 2.0 Nm
8. Install solenoid assembly and tighten retaining screws to specification, then install lead to the solenoid field terminal and fit washer and retaining nut.
   Solenoid Retaining Screws .... 6 Nm

STARTER MOTOR INSTALLATION

Installation - 6G7

1. Place the starter and cover assembly into position, then install the starter bolts and progressively tighten to specification.
   Starter Motor Retaining Bolts .... 30 Nm
2. Reconnect the starter electrical connections, then connect the battery earth cable.
3. To the underside of the vehicle install the stone guard/cover.

Installation - 4M4

1. Place the starter assembly into position, install the starter bolts and progressively tighten to specification.
   Starter Motor Retaining Bolts .... 30 Nm
2. Reconnect the starter electrical connections, then connect the battery earth cable.
3. To the underside of the vehicle install the stone guard/cover.

PROBLEM DIAGNOSIS

STARTER SYSTEM TROUBLE DIAGNOSIS

1. If the starter does not stop turning, replace the starter solenoid.
2. If the engine does not stop, does the engine turn by cranking?.
3. If the engine in step2 does turn by cranking,, does it turn normally. If it does, check the ignition and fuel system. If faults are found, repair/replace as required.
4. If the engine does not turn normally in step3, (turns slowly), check the battery charging condition, terminal connection and/or terminals for corrosion. If faults are found, repair/replace as required.
5. If the battery condition and operation in step4 is OK in step4, repair/replace the starter motor.
6. If the engine in step2 does not turn by cranking, does the starter motor turn. If it does, does the pinion gear shaft turn. If it does, check the condition and/or operation of the pinion clutch.
7. If the gear shaft in step6 does not turn, check the condition and/or operation of the reduction gear, armature and/or gear shaft. If faults are found, repair/replace as required.
8. If the starter motor in step6 does not turn in step6, check the condition and/or operation of the fuse and fuse links. If faults are found, repair/replace as required.
9. If the fuse links and fuses are OK in step8, check the condition and/or operation of the battery and/or connections. If faults are found, repair/replace as required.
10. If the battery is OK in step9, check the condition and/or operation of the starter system wiring. If faults are found, repair/replace as required.
11. If the system wiring is OK in step10, check the condition and/or operation of the magnetic clutch. If faults are found, repair/replace as required.
12. If the magnetic switch is OK in step11, check the condition and/or operation of the pinion and ring gear mesh. If faults are found, adjust the pinion movement, check the condition and/or operation of the pinion moving mechanism and, or the ring gear. If faults are found, repair/replace as required.
13. If the pinion and ring gear mesh is OK in step12, does the starter turn with a wire from the (+) battery terminal connected to the starter M terminal and a wire from the (-) terminal to the starter body.
14. If the starter in step13 does turn, replace the magnetic switch. If the starter does not turn, repair/replace the starter.

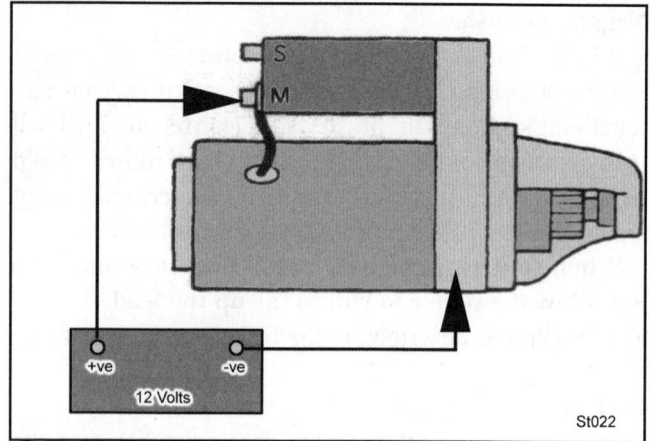

SPECIFICATIONS

All planetary gear reduction type

2001-2007	kW	Pinion teeth
6G7	1.2	8
4M40	2.2	10
4M41	2.2	12
2008 on		
6G7	1.3	8
4M41	2.2	10

Commutator
Petrol
2000-2007 - outside diameter .... 29.4 mm
           - service limit .... 28.8 mm
2008 on   - outside diameter .... 28.35 mm
           - service limit .... 27.35 mm
           - depth of undercut .... 0.5 mm
           - run-out .... 0.2 mm
Brush service limit .... 7 mm
Diesel
2000-2007 - outside diameter .... 32.0 mm
           - service limit .... 31.4 mm
2008 on   - outside diameter .... 32.75 mm
           - service limit .... 31.75 mm
           - depth of undercut .... 0.5 mm
           - run-out .... 0.2 mm
Brush service limit .... 7 mm

TORQUE SPECIFICATIONS

STARTER MOTOR - Diesel engines	Nm
Starter motor to transaxle bolts	27 - 34
Solenoid attaching screws	7.5 - 11
Starter motor through bolts	4.5 - 6
Positive cable attaching nut	6 - 8

STARTER MOTOR - V6 engines	Nm
Starter motor to transaxle bolts	27 - 34
Solenoid attaching screws	6
Starter motor through bolts	8
Positive cable attaching nut	9
Cover Screws	1.4 - 2.0

COOLING SYSTEM

Subject	Page
COOLING SYSTEM	**174**
Coolant	174
GENERAL MAINTENANCE	**174**
Coolant Level Inspection	174
Radiator Cap Pressure Test	174
Anti Freeze Solution	174
Radiator Hose Replacement	174
Coolant Replacement	175
DRIVE BELTS	**175**
Inspection	175
Belt Replacement & Adjustment	175
THERMOSTAT	**175**
Removal - 6G7	175
Removal - 4M4	176
Thermostat test	176
Installation - 6G7	176
Installation - 4M4	176
WATER PUMP	**177**
6 G7 - Petrol	**177**
Removal	177
Installation	177
4D4 - Diesel	**178**
Removal	178
Installation	178
WATER HOSE & PIPE	**178**
6 G7 MPI - Petrol	**178**
Removal	178
Installation	178

Subject	Page
6 G7 GDI - Petrol	**179**
Removal	179
Installation	179
4M40 - Diesel	**179**
Removal	179
Installation	180
4M41 - Diesel	**180**
Removal	180
Installation	180
COOLING FANS	**180**
Mechanical Fan	**180**
Removal - 6G6	180
Removal - 4M4	180
Fan Inspection	180
Fan Clutch Inspection	180
Inspection - 6G6	181
Inspection - 4M4	181
Electric Fan	**181**
Removal	181
Fan Inspection	181
Inspection	181
RADIATOR	**181**
Removal	181
Installation	181
Radiator Inspection	182
Cleaning a Radiator	182
Pressure Test Radiator & Cooling System	182
PROBLEM SOLVING & DIAGNOSIS	**183**
SPECIFICATIONS	**183**

COOLING SYSTEM

Water is circulated by pump through cylinder block, head and then through top hose to top tank of radiator. Water passing down through radiator is cooled by air flow through radiator fins.

Heated water is drawn from cylinder head to inlet manifold and heater unit.

An effective concentration of recommended coolant/inhibitor must be maintained in the cooling system.

The radiator cap is a pressure sealing type. It incorporates two valves; a pressure release valve and a vacuum released valve, and has two functions:
1. To increase pressure in cooling system and thus raise boiling point of coolant.
2. To allow built up pressure to escape when it reaches a certain pressure.

As the coolant is heated it expands and pressure in the system increases. When pressure reaches a predetermined point pressure release valve in radiator cap opens and excess air in the supply tank is forced out of the system.

As the engine cools the coolant contracts thus creating a vacuum in the radiator. The vacuum release valve in the radiator cap opens and allows the air to be drawn back into the supply tank.

Coolant recovery system will not operate if the cooling system has an air leak.

Common misconception is that by removing the thermostat the engine will run cooler, this is incorrect, as it can quite often increase the running temperature and induce overheating. The thermostat acts as a restrictor as well as to stop coolant flow in a cold engine, if you remove the restriction of the coolant flow, fast flowing coolant does not have time to disperse the stored heat from the engine therefore causing the engine to run hotter.

COOLANT

The alloy content of components makes it essential that an effective coolant additive is maintained in the cooling system. Some of the properties of Tectaloy coolant are:
Coolant comes in two different colours Green and Red. Red has a reagent grade indicator dye built into it and as a result should any corrosive acids build up in the cooling system from exhaust gas leaking past the head gasket the coolant will change from red to brilliant yellow. If the coolant does change colour it should be replaced.

As a general rule coolant manufactured by different companies should not be mixed.

Glycol coolant has several properties other than antifreeze, it will help lubricate various valves in the cooling system, thermostat slides and water pump seal surfaces.

Glycol will also raise the boiling point of coolant.

GLYCOL BOILING POINT CHART			
kPa Pressure	**PSI Pressure**	**33% Glycol**	**55% Glycol**
0	0	104.5°C	108.5°C
25	3.7	110.5°C	114.0°C
50	7.4	116.5°C	119.5°C
75	11.0	121.0°C	125.0°C
100	14.7	125.0°C	129.0°C
150	22.1	132.5°C	136.0°C
200	26.4	139.0°C	142.5°C

GENERAL MAINTENANCE

Coolant Level Inspection

The coolant level is inspected by examining the height of the coolant fluid compared to the level marks on the supply tank.

When the coolant is cold the coolant level should be at the FULL mark. Depending on the engine temperature the level will vary. Always ensure the supply tank is kept between the max. and min. lines.

RADIATOR CAP PRESSURE TEST.
1. With cap removed from radiator.
2. Wash cap with clean water before testing, ensure that valves are washed as well, then connect cap to test unit.
3. Increase the pressure applied on the cap until the highest reading of the cap before the pressure valve opens is achieved on the pressure test unit gauge.
4. The reading on the test gauge should be as specified on the radiator cap, also the pressure relief valve should release at its specified reading.
5. Re-test a couple of times and if pressure tester reading is not as cap specification replace cap.

ANTIFREEZE SOLUTION.

Add antifreeze to engine coolant if vehicles are to be driven in districts where the temperature will be under 4°C.

RADIATOR HOSE

Replace

Radiator hoses should be replaced if they show any signs of being split, rotten or badly perished.
1. Drain radiator.
2. Loosen hose clamps at either end of the hose.
3. Slide hose off connections by twisting the hose backwards and forwards at same time.
4. Fit clamps onto hoses and then install the hoses so they do not contact any surfaces that may damage or deteriorate them.
5. Tighten hose clamps.

Note: If installing a used hose, ensure the hose clamp is installed in exactly the same location as it was previously installed to ensure a good seal is obtained.

6. Fill the cooling system with coolant.

COOLANT REPLACEMENT.
DRAIN.
Remove radiator cap and open drain cock on the lower radiator tank.

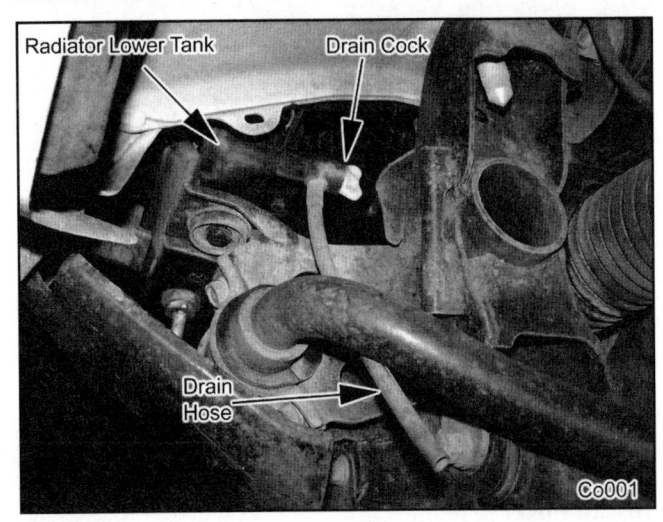

REFILL.
1. Install bottom radiator hose and tighten clamps.
2. Add the specified coolant to the radiator, then fill the system with clean water and install the radiator cap.
3. Turn heater control onto maximum "HOT".
4. Operate engine for 10 minutes or take for 10 minute test drive to allow thermostat to open and bleed air from the system.
5. Top up radiator ensuring it is full then replace cap.
   Note: Care must be taken when removing radiator cap as pressure will be built up in system.
   Note: Bleeding of air from the cooling system must take place, otherwise problems may occur with the cooling system. The Petrol MPI engine has air bleed plugs to allow trapped air from the high points.

DRIVE BELTS
Drive belts must be checked often to ensure that they are still in good operating condition, also pulley misalignment should be checked to reduce belt wear. Damaged belts should be replaced.

Incorrectly adjusted drive belts will cause belt squeal and components will not be driven. Belts that are over tightened can damage component bearings. Belts that are tensioned correctly reduce noise and extend the life of the belt. Belt's that have operated for 10-15 minutes are treated as a used belt, and adjusted to used belt specification.

Inspection
* Some belt squeal when the engine is started or stopped is normal and has no effect on durability of drive belt.
* Condition of the belt is best judged by twisting the belt so as to see the surfaces.

Stages of Belt Wear:
New Belt	No Cracks or chunks.
Moderately Used	Minor cracks; some wear on surfaces. Replacement not required.
Severely Used	Several cracks per inch. Should be replaced before chunking occurs.
Failed Belt	Separation of belt material from backing (chunking). Replace belt immediately.

BELT REPLACEMENT & ADJUSTMENT
Refer to the Engine Tune-up and Maintenance chapter for detailed instructions on drive belt removal and adjustment.

THERMOSTAT
\# The thermostat is situated in the thermostat housing (water inlet fitting) at the front of the engine.

Removal - 6G7
1. Open the coolant drain cock allowing the cooling system to drain.

Cooling System

2. Remove the bolts securing the thermostat housing, then remove the housing, and thermostat.

Removal - 4M4

1. Remove the lower radiator hose allowing the cooling system to drain.
2. Remove the bolts securing the thermostat housing, then remove the housing, and thermostat.

THERMOSTAT TEST.

Used thermostats should be tested before installing.

1. With thermostat removed from vehicle submerge in hot water until it is fully opened and remove.
2. Place a feeler gauge into the opening of the thermostat and place thermostat in cold water to allow it to close on feeler gauge.
3. Place a thermometer and have the thermostat hanging from a feeler gauge in a container of warm water, heat water.
4. When thermostat opens and falls off feeler gauge, record the temperature, this will be the opening temperature of the thermostat.

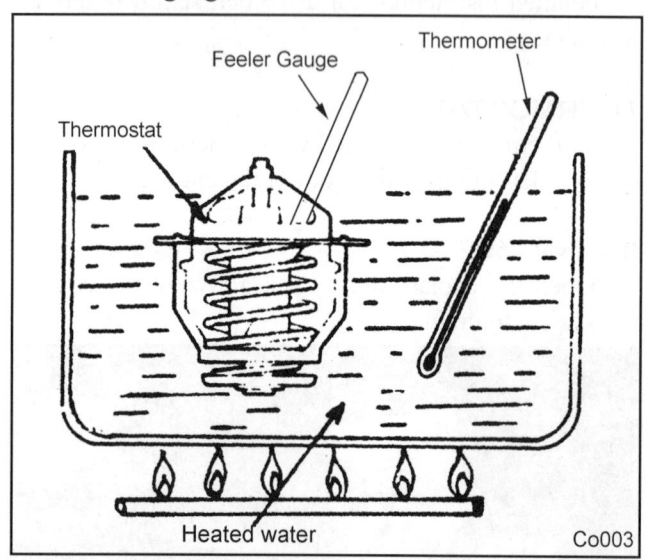

    Opening Temp   - 6G7: .... 88°C +/- 2.0°C
                             - 4D5: .... 82°C +/- 1.5°C
                             - 4M4: .... 86.5°C +/- 2.0°C
    Full Open Temp - 6G7: .... 100°C
                             - 4D5: .... 95°C
                             - 4M4: .... 90°C

Install - 6G7

1. Clean thermostat housing and engine outlet mounting surface to remove all corrosion.
2. Install thermostat with air jiggler to top. Coat new thermostat gasket with water proof sealant and fit to thermostat housing with thermostat already in place.
3. Install thermostat housing to engine outlet mounting surface, tightening bolts to specification.
    Thermostat Cover Bolts - 6G7 .... 12 Nm
4. Reconnect lower radiator hose, then fill and bleed cooling system as previously described.

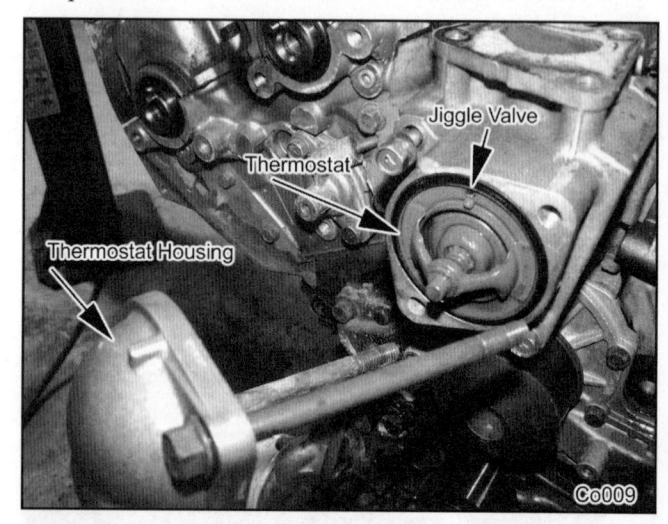

Install - 4M4

1. Clean thermostat housing and engine outlet mounting surface to remove all corrosion.

Cooling System

2. Install thermostat with air jiggler to top. Coat new thermostat gasket with water proof sealant and fit to thermostat housing with thermostat already in place, ensuring thermostat is fitted as shown in diagram.
3. Install thermostat housing retaining bolts and tighten to specification.
   Thermostat Cover Bolts - 4M4 .... 12 Nm
4. Reconnect lower radiator hose, then fill and bleed cooling system as previously described.

WATER PUMP

Remove - 6G7

1. Disconnect the lower radiator hose from the radiator and pump emptying cooling system, then remove hose from the vehicle.
2. Remove the engine timing belt as described in the V6 engine chapter.
3. *GDI models* - Disconnect the temperature sensor electrical connection.
4. From the water pump outlet fitting disconnect the two water hoses, then remove bolts securing the water outlet fitting and bracket
5. Remove the water outlet fitting bracket and fitting, then remove and discard 'O-ring and gasket. 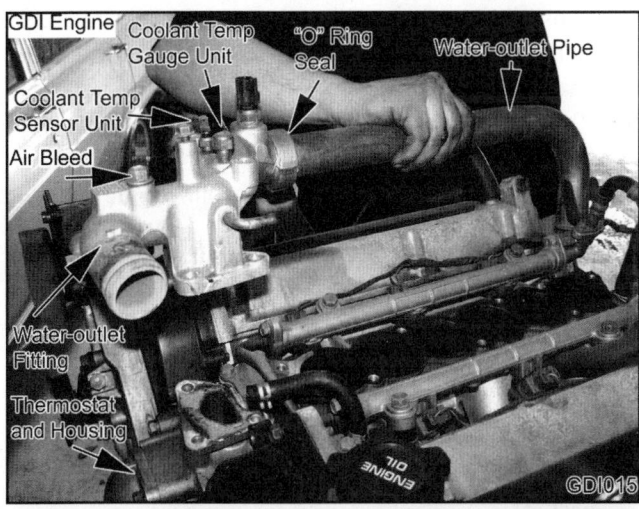  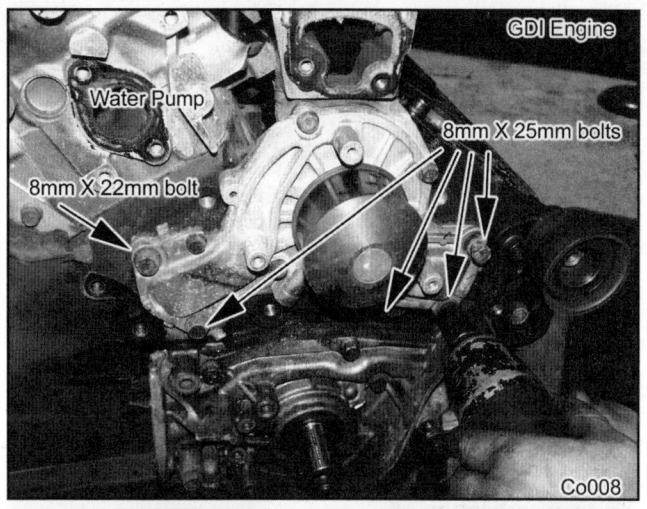 
6. Remove water pump bolts, then remove water pump from front of the engine and discard gasket and 'O-ring.
7. Remove the bolts securing the thermostat case bracket to the water pump then remove bracket and discard gasket.
8. Remove the bolts securing the thermostat case to the bracket, then separate case and bracket, discarding the gasket.

Install - 6G7

1. Using a new gasket, fit the thermostat case to mounting bracket and tighten bolts to specification.
   Bracket to Case Bolts....................9 Nm
2. Using a new gasket, fit the thermostat case assembly to the water pump and tighten retaining bolts to specification.
   Case Assembly to Pump Bolts....................12 Nm
3. Install water pump to front of engine using a new gasket and 'O-ring, then install and tighten retaining bolts to specification.
   Note: See illustration of GDI engine for bolts lengths, the same for MPI engines
   Water Pump Bolts........................24 Nm
4. Using a new gasket and 'O-ring install the water outlet fitting and bracket, then tighten retaining bolts

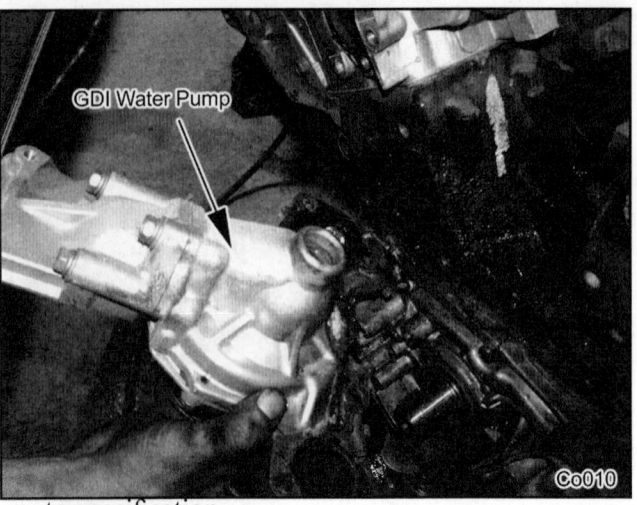

Cooling System

to specification.

Outlet Fitting Bolts .... **12 Nm**
Outlet Fitting Bracket Bolts .... **14 Nm**

5. To the water pump outlet fitting reconnect the two water hoses, then **r**eplace the engine timing belt as described in the V6 engine chapter.
6. Refill cooling system and bleed as previously described in this section.

Remove - 4M4

1. Disconnect lower radiator hose from water pump and radiator, emptying coolant from system.
2. Remove the nuts/bolts securing the fan assembly and remove fan assembly.
3. Remove drive belt, then remove the bolts retaining the coupling plate and remove plate and fan pulley.
4. Remove water pump retaining bolts, then remove water pump from the engine. Remove and discard water pump "O-ring from pump mount if applicable.

Install - 4M4

1. Clean cylinder block pump mounting surface, then fit new "O-ring.
2. Replace water pump on the cylinder block, install bolts and tighten to specification.
Water Pump Bolts .... **14 Nm**

3. Install the fan pulley and coupling plate, tightening bolts/nuts to specification, then install fan belt.
Coupling & Pulley Bolts/Nuts .... **14 Nm**
4. Refill cooling system and bleed as previously described in this section.

WATER HOSE & PIPE

Remove - 6G7 MPI

1. Disconnect the lower radiator hose from the radiator and pump emptying cooling system, then remove hose from the vehicle.
2. Remove the front exhaust pipe and heat shield, refer to exhaust chapter if required.
3. Remove the transmission shift cable bracket, refer to transmission chapter if required.
4. Remove the intake manifold as described in engine chapter.
5. Remove the thermostat as described previously in this chapter.
6. If not already disconnected, disconnect the radiator upper hose from the outlet fitting.
7. From the water pump outlet fitting disconnect and remove the two water hoses.
8. Remove bolts securing the water outlet fitting and thermostat case, remove assembly and discard gasket and O-ring.
9. Remove the bolts securing the thermostat case bracket to the water pump then remove bracket and discard gasket.
10. Disconnect and remove the water hose and water outlet pipe also remove the outlet pipe O-ring.
11. Remove the heater hose and water passage assembly and discard gaskets.

Install - 6G7 MPI

1. Install the heater hose and water passage assembly using new gaskets.
2. Install and connect the water hose and water outlet pipe using new outlet pipe O-rings.
3. Install the thermostat case bracket to water pump using a new gasket and tighten retaining bolts to specification.

Thermostat Case Bracket.......................... 12 Nm
4. Using new gasket and 'O-rings install the water outlet fitting and thermostat case, tightening bolts to specification.
Outlet Fitting & Case Bolts......................... 9 Nm
5. To the water pump outlet fitting connect the two water hoses.
6. Connect the radiator upper hose to the outlet fitting.
7. Install the thermostat as described previously in this chapter.
8. Install the intake manifold as described in engine chapter.
9. Install the transmission shift cable bracket, refer to transmission chapter if required.
10. Install the front exhaust pipe and heat shield, refer to exhaust chapter if required.
11. Refill cooling system and bleed as previously described in this chapter.

Remove- 6G7 GDI
1. Disconnect the lower radiator hose from the radiator and pump emptying cooling system, then remove hose from the vehicle.
2. Remove the thermostat as described previously in this chapter.
3. Remove the intake manifold and injector as described in engine chapter.
4. Remove the high pressure fuel pump, refer to fuel and emission chapter.
5. Remove the bolts securing the water outlet pipe, then disconnect water hose and remove outlet pipe discarding O-rings.
6. Disconnect the heater hose from the water passage assembly, then remove passage retaining bolts and remove assembly, discarding O-rings.
7. Remove the detonation sensor and bracket then disconnect the heater hose.
8. From the water pipe assembly disconnect and remove the water hoses and water pipe.
9. Remove bolts securing water pipe assembly, then remove pipe assembly and discard O-ring.
10. If not already disconnected, disconnect the radiator upper hose from the outlet fitting.
11. From the water pump outlet fitting disconnect and remove the two water hoses.
12. Remove bolts securing the water outlet fitting and thermostat case, remove assembly and discard gasket and O-ring.
13. Remove the bolts securing the thermostat case bracket to the water pump then remove bracket and discard gasket.
14. Remove the bolts securing the left and right fittings, then remove fittings and discard gaskets.

Install - 6G7 GDI
1. Install left and right fittings using new gaskets, tightening bolts to specification.
Fitting Retaining Bolts .... 19 Nm
2. Install the thermostat case bracket to water pump using a new gasket and tighten retaining bolts to specification.
Thermostat Case Bracket............................. 12 Nm
3. Using new gasket and 'O-rings install the water outlet fitting and thermostat case, tightening bolts to specification.
Outlet Fitting & Case Bolts........................... 9 Nm
4. To the water pump outlet fitting connect the two water hoses.
5. Connect the radiator upper hose to the outlet fitting.
6. Install pipe assembly using a new 'O-ring and tighten water pipe retaining bolts to specification.
Water Pipe Bolts... 14 Nm
7. To the water pipe assembly install and connect the water hoses and water pipe.
Water Pipe Bolts... 5 Nm
8. Reconnect heater hose, then install the detonation sensor bracket and sensor.
Detonation Sensor Bracket Bolts............... 28 Nm
Detonation Sensor....................................... 23 Nm
9. Install the water passage assembly using new 'O-rings, tighten retaining bolts to specification and reconnect heater hose.
Water Passage Assembly Bolts.................... 19 Nm
10. Install outlet pipe using new O-rings and tighten retaining bolts to specification, then connect water hose.
Outlet Pipe Bolts.. 14 Nm
11. Install the high pressure fuel pump, refer to fuel and emission chapter.
12. Install the intake manifold and injector as described in engine chapter.
13. Install the thermostat as described previously in this chapter.
14. Refill cooling system and bleed as previously described in this chapter.

Remove - 4M40
1. Drain the cooling system, then remove the intercooler, refer to engine chapter.
2. Disconnect the water hoses and pipe assembly on those vehicles with EGR.
3. Remove the turbocharger and exhaust manifold, refer to engine chapter.
4. Disconnect and remove the bypass pipe, discarding O-rings.
5. Remove the bolts securing the thermostat case then remove case assembly.
6. Remove the bolts securing the heater return pipe, then

Cooling System

remove return pipe and discard O-rings.
7. Remove the vacuum pump pipe, refer to engine chapter if required.
8. Remove the bolts securing the water outlet pipe assembly, then remove assembly and discard gasket.

Install - 4M40
1. Install the water outlet pipe assembly using a new gasket and tighten retaining bolts.
2. Install the vacuum pump pipe, refer to engine chapter if required.
3. Using a new O-ring install the heater return pipe and tighten retaining bolts.
4. Install thermostat case assembly, tightening retaining bolts.
5. Return the bypass pipe using new O-rings, tightening retaining bolts.
6. Install the turbocharger and exhaust manifold, refer to engine chapter.
7. Vehicle with EGR, connect the water hoses and pipe assembly.
8. Refill cooling system and bleed as previously described in this chapter.

Remove - 4M41
1. Drain the cooling system, then remove the air cleaner and EGR cooler, refer to emission and fuel chapter.
2. Disconnect the upper radiator hose from the water outlet pipe assembly.
3. Remove the bolts retaining the outlet pipe assembly, then remove assembly and discard gasket.
4. From the EGR water outlet pipe disconnect the water hose then remove the outlet pipe, discarding O-ring.
5. From the thermostat case remove the bypass pipe, discarding O-rings.
6. From the EGR water inlet pipe disconnect the water hose then remove the inlet pipe, discarding O-ring.
7. Remove the turbocharger water outlet and inlet pipes, then disconnect the heater hose from the heater return pipe.
8. Remove the heater return pipe discarding the O-ring.

Install - 4M41
1. Install the heater return pipe using a new 'O-ring and tighten retaining bolts.
2. Connect the heater hose to the heater return pipe, then install the turbocharger water outlet and inlet pipes using new seal washers.
   Turbocharger Water Outlet Pipe................ 25 Nm
   Turbocharger Water Inlet Pipe.................. 25 Nm
3. Install the EGR water inlet pipe using a new O-ring, then reconnect the water hose to pipe.

4. Install the thermostat case assembly tightening bolts.
5. To the thermostat case install the bypass pipe using new O-rings.
6. Install the EGR water outlet pipe using new O-rings, tightening retaining bolt. Reconnect water hose.
7. Install the outlet pipe assembly using a new gasket, tightening bolts.
8. Reconnect the upper radiator hose to the water outlet pipe assembly.
9. Install the air cleaner and EGR cooler, refer to emission and fuel chapter.
10. Refill cooling system and bleed as previously described in this chapter.

COOLING FANS

MECHANICAL FAN
Removal - 6G7
1. Remove the radiator upper shroud, then remove the drive belt from the vehicle.
2. Remove the bolts securing the fan and clutch assembly, then remove the assembly from the vehicle.

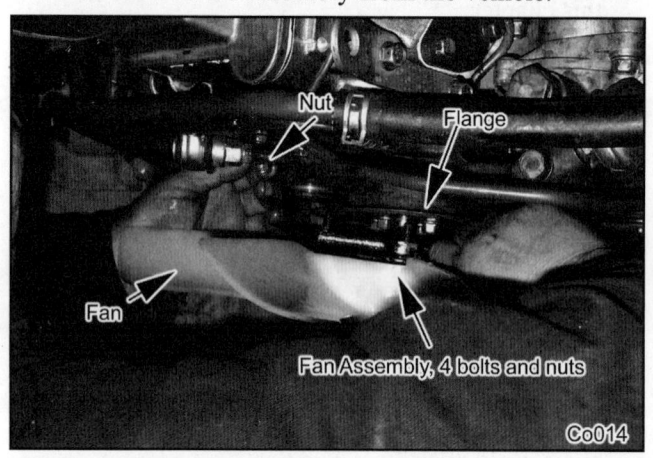

3. Where fitted remove the drive belt pulley.
Removal - 4M4
1. Remove the radiator upper shroud, then remove the drive belt from the vehicle.
2. Remove the bolts securing the fan and clutch assembly, then remove the assembly from the vehicle.

Fan Inspection
1. Inspect the fan blades for any signs of damage or cracks.
2. Inspect the fan hub especially around the bolt holes for signs of damage or cracks.
3. If any damage or cracks are found replace fan.

Fan Clutch Inspection
1. Inspect the fan clutch for any signs of fluid leakage, as loss of fluid will affect the fan speed.

Cooling System

2. With the fan attached to the engine turn the assembly by hand. Some resistance should be felt.
3. If any signs of damage to the clutch assembly or either of the previous two steps failed replace the fan clutch.

Installation - 6G7
1. Where fitted install the drive belt pulley.
2. Install the fan and clutch assembly tightening retaining bolts to specification.
   Fan/Clutch Retaining Bolts............... 11 +/- 1 Nm
3. Install the drive belt then refit the upper radiator shroud.

Installation - 4M4
1. Install the fan and clutch assembly tightening retaining bolts to specification.
   Fan/Clutch Retaining Bolts............... 11 +/- 1 Nm
2. Install the drive belt then refit the upper radiator shroud.

ELECTRIC FAN

Remove
1. Remove the grille as described in Body Chapter
2. Disconnect the electrical harness connector.
3. Remove the bolts securing the fan assembly, then remove the fan from the vehicle.

Fan Inspection
1. Inspect the fan blades for any signs of damage or cracks.
2. Inspect the fan especially around the bolt holes for signs of damage or cracks.
3. If any damage or cracks are found replace fan assembly.

Install
1. Install fan assembly, install the bolts securing the fan assembly.
2. Connect the electrical harness connector.
3. Replace the grille as described in Body Chapter

RADIATOR

Removal
1. Remove the radiator shroud upper and lower covers.
2. Detach lower radiator hose, emptying cooling system, then detach upper radiator hose and place out of the way.
3. Detach transmission oil cooler pipes from radiator tank, on vehicles with automatic transmissions.
4. Detach coolant supply hose from the radiator and remove the reserve tank.
5. Remove the radiator upper insulator assembly. 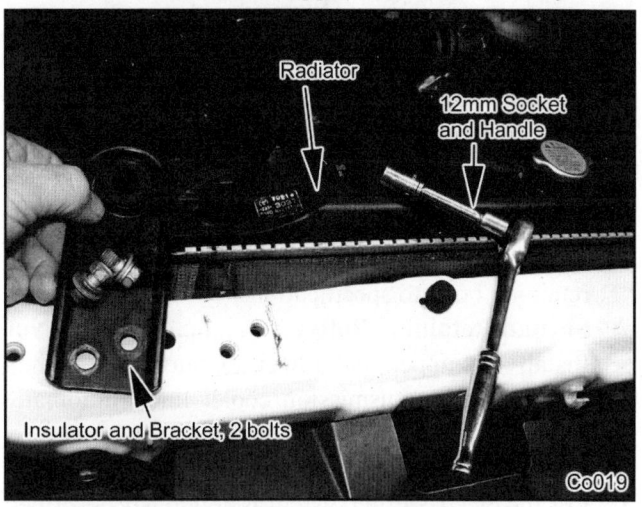
6. Carefully lift the radiator from the vehicle. 
7. Remove the screws retaining the shroud to the radiator then lift shroud from radiator.
8. Remove the lower radiator insulator if required.

Install
1. Ensure the lower radiator insulator is correctly installed, then carefully fit the radiator assembly into the vehicle.
2. Install the upper radiator insulator and tighten the

Cooling System

retaining bolt to specification.

Upper Insulator Bolt .... 10-14 Nm

3. Install the reserve tank into position then reconnect the supply hose to the radiator.
4. Install the radiator shroud into position and tighten retaining bolts to specification.

Shroud Retaining Bolts .... 4-6 Nm

5. Install the upper and lower radiator hoses, then reconnect the transmission cooler lines (automatic models).
6. Install the lower and upper radiator shroud covers.
7. Fill and bleed cooling system as previously described in this chapter.
8. Check the automatic transmission fluid level and top up if required.

RADIATOR INSPECTION

1. Check for damage to fins and core tubes from stones and other projectiles that can cause damage.
2. Clean radiator of any foreign matter that will obstruct air flow and possibly cause over heating problems. Radiator fins can be cleaned with an air hose, blowing air from the back of the radiator or a pressure washer will do the same thing.
3. Check inside the radiator for foreign materials that could block the flow of the coolant through the tubes.

   Blocked radiators are the most common cause of overheating vehicles, as the tubes become blocked with corrosion or fouling caused by incompatible coolants mixed in your cooling system.

CLEANING A RADIATOR

There are two methods of cleaning a blocked radiator.
a) Use a radiator flush.
b) Pull the radiator down by removing the end tanks and clean the tubes by shafting each tube with an appropriate rod.

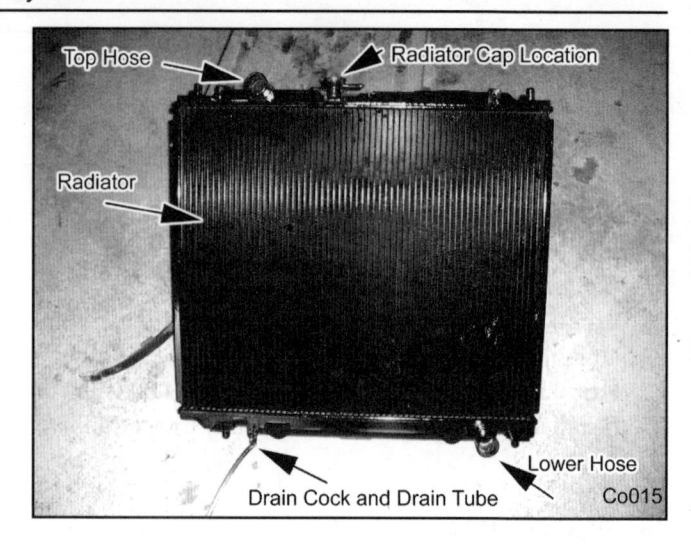

There are two basic types of radiator flush in the market place, one is the strong alkaline type and the other is acid based. Each of these products are suited to different types of cleaning. The acid base flushes are more effective for scale removal but nowhere near as effective as the alkaline flushes in the removal of oils and general organic materials.

Acid based flushes usually have reasonably severe attack rate on the metal components in the cooling system.

The alkaline flushes will attack aluminium components if left in contact at elevated temperatures for extended periods of time. It is most important to strictly follow the manufacture's instructions regarding the time of flush should be left in the cooling system.

Radiator flush should be seen more in the light of preventive maintenance rather than a problem solver.

PRESSURE TEST RADIATOR and COOLING SYSTEM

1. Fill radiator to the full mark or within 10mm of the supply tank neck.
2. Wipe the filler neck sealing surface clean.
3. Using a suitable adaptor, attach pressure tester to filler neck and apply a pressure of 160 kPa to the cooling system.
4. If pressure gauge holds steady, the system is satisfac-

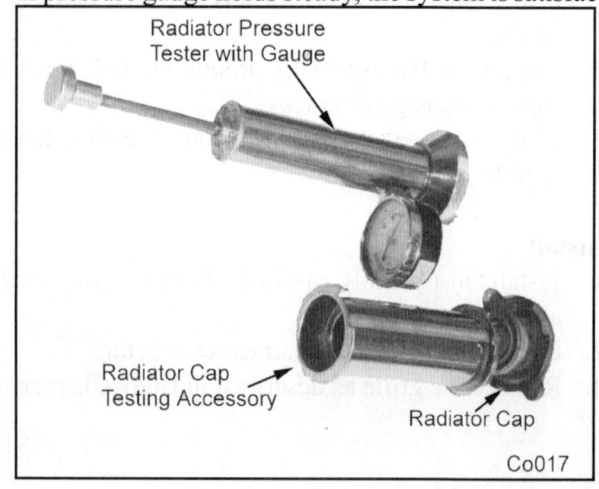

Cooling System

tory. If pressure drops, continue as follows.
5. Check all points for external leaks, if none are evident after gauge shows a drop in pressure, continue test.
6. Remove tester, fit radiator cap and run engine until normal operating temperature is reached, reattach tool, apply recommended pressure and increase engine speed to half throttle. Do not leave tester attached to radiator as this could caused damage to the cooling system because of the excessive pressure.
7. If needle on dial fluctuates, it indicates a combustion leak, generally the head gasket.
8. If needle on dial did not fluctuate in step (6), sharply accelerate the engine several time. If an abnormal amount of water emits from tail pipe it indicates a head gasket leak, cracked block or head.

PROBLEM SOLVING & DIAGNOSIS

PROBLEM: Engine Coolant Temperature High
POSSIBLE CAUSE: & REMEDY'S:
Coolant Level Low - Refill System, pressurize and check for leaks.
Drive Belt Loose - Adjust.
Radiator Fins Blocked - Remove obstruction.
Thermostat Not Operating - Replace Thermostat.
Radiator or Engine Block (blocked by rust, scale or other foreign material) - Flush system.
Water pump faulty - Replace water pump.
Fan clutch faulty - Replace Clutch.
Air trapped in cooling system - bleed air from system

PROBLEM: Engine Coolant Temperature Low.
POSSIBLE CAUSES & REMEDY'S:
Thermostat stuck open - Replace Thermostat.
Thermostat has been removed - Install thermostat
Temperature sending unit inoperative - Replace Unit.
Temperature gauge inoperative - Check installation or replace.

PROBLEM: Low Coolant Level.
POSSIBLE CAUSES & REMEDY'S:
Leaky radiator - Repair or replace radiator.
Cylinder head gasket - Replace head gasket.
Improper tightening of cylinder head bolts - Retighten bolts evenly to specifications, or replace cylinder head bolts.
Cylinder block or head welsh plugs leaking - Repair.
Cracked or warped cylinder head or block - Replace cylinder head or machine surface.
Intake manifold - Replace intake manifold.
Heater hose or radiator hose - Replace hose.
Heater hose or engine hose not sealed correctly - Tighten hose clamps or replace hose clamps.
Air trapped in cooling system - bleed air from system

SPECIFICATIONS

Coolant Capacity
All Engines.. approx. 9.0 litres

Radiator
Type...................................... Vertical flow fin and tube.
Heat rejection capacity
Petrol..203,023 KCal/hr
Diesel 2.8 litre................................251,163 KCal/hr
Diesel 3.2 litre................................232,236 KCal/hr

Radiator Cap
Type.. Pressure vent
Opening pressure:
    All except 6G7:............................. 74 - 103 kPa
    6G7:   upto 2003 .... 74 - 103 kPa
            2003 onwards .... 94 - 122 kPa

Mechanical Fan
Number of blades... 5

Motor
Type.. D.C. Ferrite
Rated voltage ....12 V
Rotation direction................. Clockwise from shaft end.

Water Pump
Type..Centrifugal impeller

Thermostat

	Opening Temperature:	Fully Open
GDI	88+/-2 °C	100 °C
MPI (GCC)	76.5+/-2 °C	90 °C
MPI (except GCC)	82+/-2 °C	95 °C
4M4	76.5+/-2 °C	90 °C

Engine Temp. Gauge Unit Sender
@ 70°C...104 +/- 13.5 Ohm

TORQUE SPECIFICATIONS	Nm
Thermostat housing bolt: - Diesel............................	13
- Petrol.	18
Water pump bolts Petrol.	24
Radiator Mounting Bolts	12

IGNITION, FUEL & EMISSION SYSTEMS - Petrol

Description	Page
3.5 SOHC and DOHC Engines ON VEHICLE INSPECTION	**185**
Inspection Spark Plugs	185
Accelerator Cable Adjustment - MPI	185
Inspection & Adjustment Ignition Timing	185
Firing Order	186
Inspection Of Ignition Coil - MPI	186
Power Transistor Continuity - MPI	187
Inspection of Ignition Lead - MPI	187
Inspection Of Ignition Coil - GDI	187
Primary Coil	187
Secondary Coil	188
Ignition Failure Sensor Check - GDI	188
Throttle Valve Area Cleaning	188
Throttle Position Sensor Adjustment - MPI	188
Throttle Position Sensor Adjustment - GDI	188
Basic Idle Speed Adjustment - MPI	189
Variable Resistor Inspection - MPI	189
Fuel Pump Operation Check (low pressure)	189
Fuel Pressure Test - MPI	189
Fuel Pump Pressure Measurement - GDI	190
b/w Low & High Pressure Pumps	190
b/w High Pressure Pump & Injector	190
Fuel Leak Test - GDI	191
3.8 MPI SOHC Engines ON VEHICLE INSPECTION	**192**
Inspection Spark Plugs	192
Inspection & Adjustment Ignition Timing	192
Firing Order	192
Inspection Of Ignition Coil	192
Primary Coil	192
Secondary Coil	193
Inspection of Ignition Lead	193
Throttle Valve Area Cleaning	193
Basic Idle Speed Adjustment	193
Accelerator Pedal Sensor Adjustment	193
Accelerator Pedal Sensor Check	194
Accelerator Pedal Switch Check	194
Throttle Valve Servo Relay Check	194
Throttle Valve Servo Check	194
Fuel Pump Operation Check (low pressure)	195
Fuel Pressure Test	195
Fuel Leak Test	195
EMISSION SYSTEM	**196**
Vacuum Circuit Inspection	196

Description	Page
Crankcase Emission Control System	196
Positive Crankcase Ventilation System	196
PCV Valve Inspection	196
Evaporative Emission Control System	197
Purge Control System Inspection	197
Purge Port Vacuum Inspection	197
Evaporative Emission Purge Solenoid	197
Emission Canister	198
Removal	198
Installation	198
Exhaust Gas Recirculation System	198
EGR System Inspection - MPI	198
Vacuum Control Valve Inspection	198
EGR Valve Inspection	199
EGR Port Vacuum Inspection	199
EGR Solenoid Inspection	199
EGR Valve Removal / Installation - MPI	199
EGR Valve Inspection - GDI	199
Operation Sound	199
Coil Resistance	199
Operation inspection	199
EGR Valve Removal / Installation - GDI	199
EGR System 3.8 SOHC (except Taiwan)	200
EGR Solenoid Valve Inspection	200
EGR Valve Removal / Installation	200
EGR Pipe Removal / Installation	200
IGNITION SYSTEM	**201**
Ignition Coil - 3.5 V6 SOHC	201
Removal	201
Installation	201
Ignition Coil - 3.5 V6 DOHC	201
Removal	201
Installation	201
Ignition Coil - 3.8 V6 SOHC	201
Removal	201
Installation	201
Crank Angle Sensor	201
Removal	201
Installation	201
Camshaft Position Sensor	202
Removal	202
Installation	202
Detonation Sensor - GDI	202
Removal	202
Installation	202

IGNITION, FUEL & EMISSION SYSTEMS - Petrol Models

Description	Page
FUEL SYSTEM	**203**
Depressurizing Fuel System	203
Accelerator Cable - MPI	203
Removal	203
Installation	203
Intake Manifold - MPI	203
Intake Manifold - GDI	203
Fuel Rail/Injectors - MPI	203
Removal	203
Installation	204
Throttle Body - MPI	204
Removal	204
Disassembly	205
Inspection	205
Assembly	205
Installation	205
Fuel Rail/Injectors - GDI	205
Removal	205
Installation	205
High Pressure Fuel Pump - GDI	206
Removal	206
Installation	206
Throttle Body - GDI	207
Removal	207
Installation	207
Injector Driver - GDI	207
Removal	207
Installation	207
Electronic Control Unit	207
Removal	207
Installation	208
Fuel Gauge Sender/Fuel Pump (in tank)	208
SENSORS	**208**
Intake Air Temperature Sensor	208
Coolant Temperature Sensor	208
Throttle Position Sensor	208
Accelerator Pedal Position Sensor - GDI	209
Accelerator Pedal Position Switch - GDI	209
Oxygen Sensor	209
Control Relay	209
Knock Sensors	210
Injector Check - GDI	210
Idle Speed Control Servo Check - MPI	210
Operation Sound	210
Coil Resistance Check	211
Operational Check	211
Throttle Control Servo - GDI	211
Operational Check	211
Coil Resistance Check	211
Catalyst Temperature Sensor Check - GDI	211
Tachometer Connection	211

3.5 Litre SOHC and DOHC Engines ON VEHICLE INSPECTION

Inspection of Spark Plugs
* Refer to Engine Tune-up & Maintenance Chapter.

Accelerator Cable Adjustment-3.5 litre MPI
1. Ensure the A/C and all lights and lamps are off so that there is no electrical load.
2. Warm up the engine until it reaches normal operating temperature, then check the engine idle speed is to specification.
   Engine Idle Speed .... 700 +/- 100 rpm.
3. Switch off ignition then inspect accelerator cable to ensure there are no sharp bends in the cable and the inner cable play is within specification.
   Inner Cable Play .... 1-2 mm

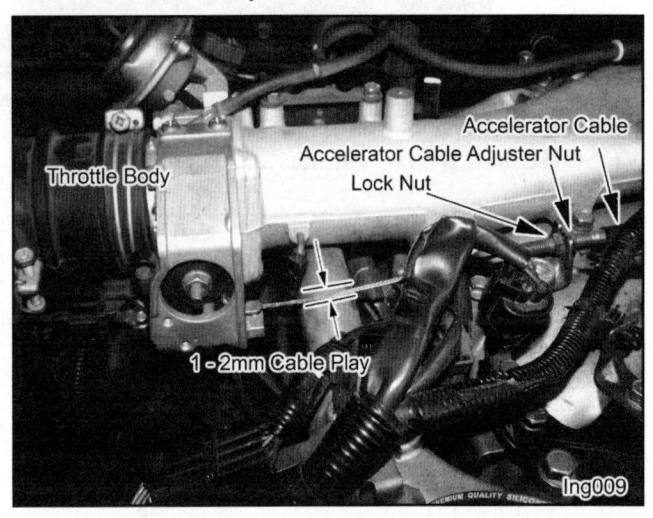

4. If inner cable play is not within specification adjust.
   a) Loosen the lock nut and fully close throttle lever.
   b) Tighten the adjusting nut until just before the throttle lever starts to move.
   c) Loosen adjusting nut one turn, this should bring cable play to within specification, then tighten lock nut.
   Adjustment Bolts .... 12 Nm
5. Ensure the throttle lever is touching the stopper.

INSPECTION & ADJUSTMENT - BASIC IGNITION TIMING
* Refer to Engine Tune-up & Maintenance Chapter.

IGNITION, FUEL & EMISSION SYSTEMS - Petrol Models

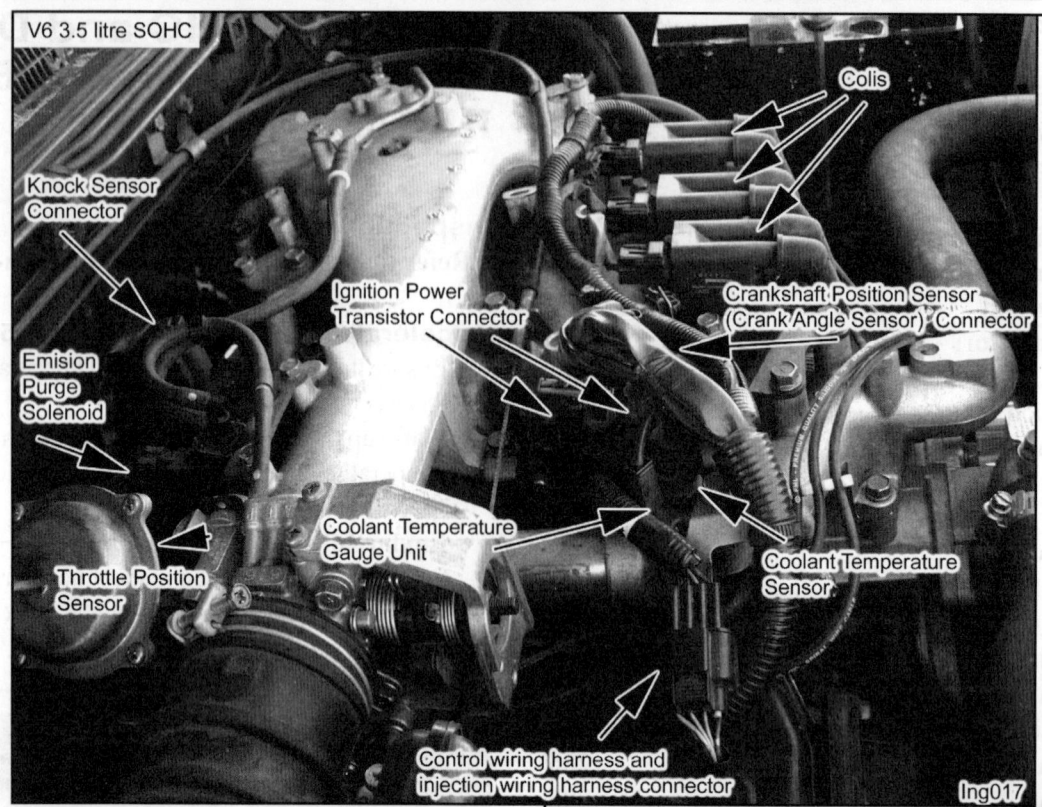

IGNITION SYSTEMS FIRING ORDER
V6 SOHC and DOHC engines **1-2-3-4-5-6**

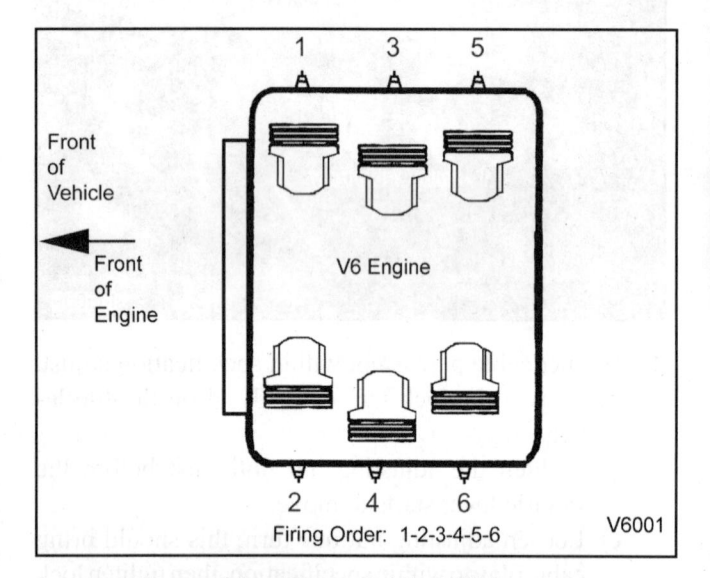

Inspection of Ignition Coil - MPI

1. Measure resistance between terminals for each cylinder. 1-4, 2-5, 3-6 to check the primary coil resistance.

   Primary coil resistance .... **0.74 - 0.90 Ohms**

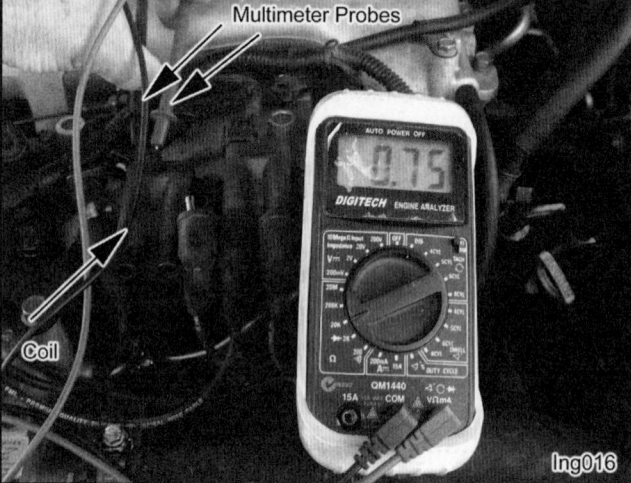

2. Measure resistance between high voltage terminal for each cylinder. 1-4, 2-5, 3-6 to check the secondary coil resistance.

   Secondary coil resistance .... **20.1 - 27.3 kOhms**

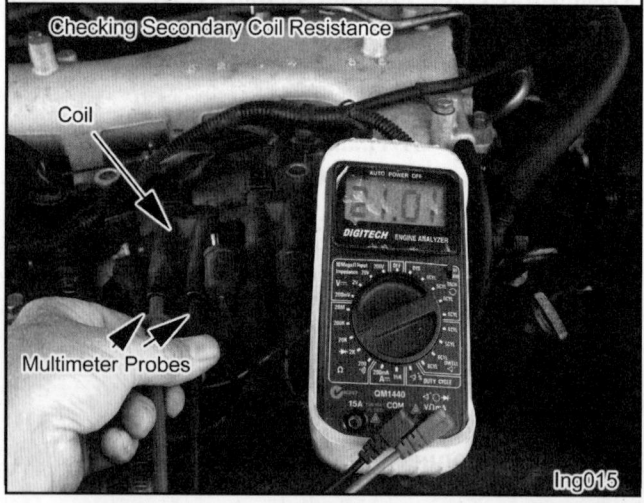

IGNITION, FUEL & EMISSION SYSTEMS - Petrol Models

Power Transistor Continuity Check - MPI
Check for the continuity between the power transistor terminals and replace if defective.
Cylinder #1 - #4 coil side, check continuity between terminals #4 & #13 with 1.5 volts to terminals #3 and #4.

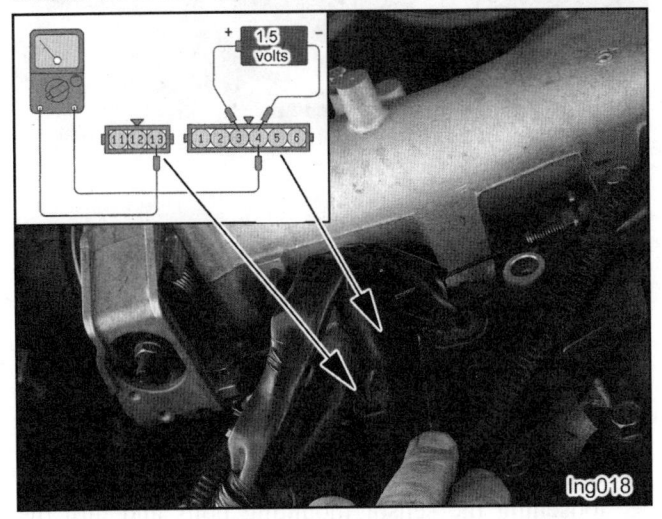

Cylinder #2 - #5 coil side, check continuity between terminals #4 & #12 with 1.5 volts to terminals #2 and #4.

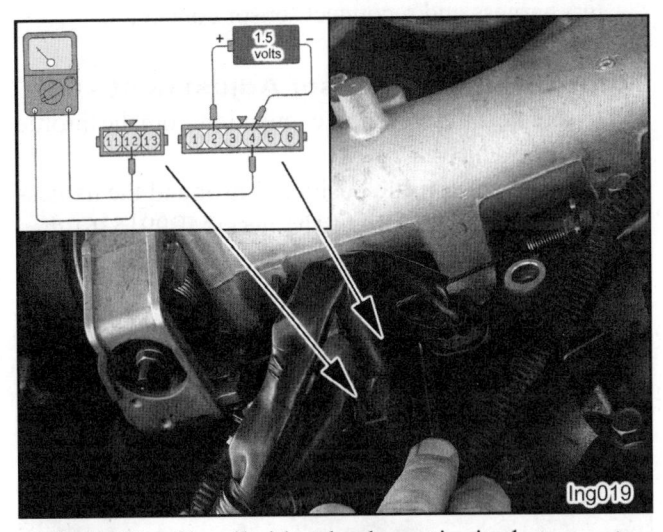

Cylinder#3 - #3 coil side, check continuity between terminals #4 & #11 with 1.5 volts to terminals #1 and #4.

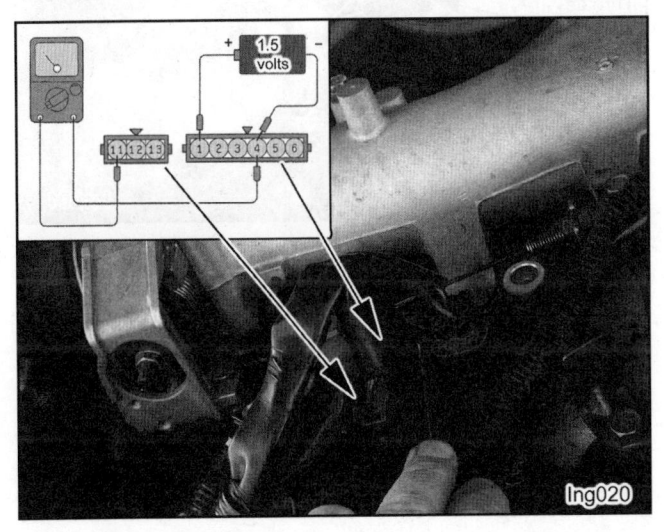

Inspection of Ignition Lead - MPI
1. Inspect the ignition leads to ensure the cap and coating is not cracked or damaged.
2. Measure the resistance of each of the leads to ensure they are withing specification.

Lead Resistance......................... 22 kOhm (limit)

Inspection of Ignition Coil - V6 - DOHC
Primary Coil & Power Transistor Continuity Check
Using an analogue tester, check the continuity of the primary coil and power transistor between terminals 1 and 2.

Note: *Test must be performed within 10 seconds to prevent damage.*

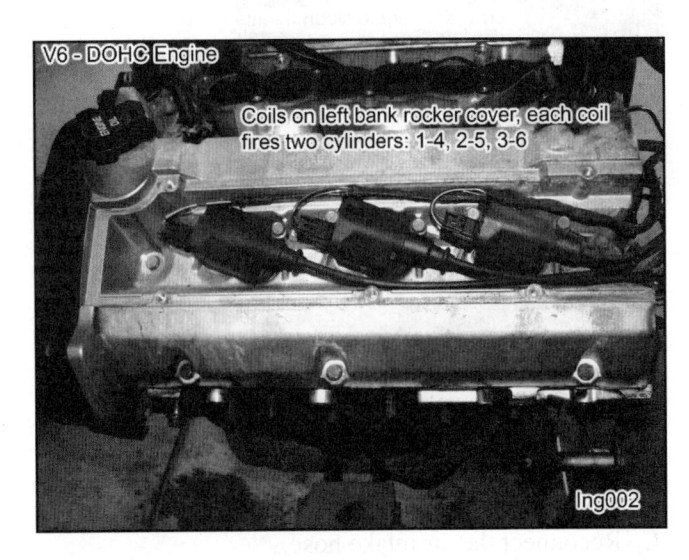

Torch Battery - 1.5 volts	Terminal number		
	1	2	3
1.5 volts - Current applied to terminal 2 and 3	X	X	
No current applied			

187

IGNITION, FUEL & EMISSION SYSTEMS - Petrol Models

Secondary Coil Inspection

1. Disconnect the connector from the ignition coil, remove coil and fit a new spark plug to the ignition coil.
2. Connect the ignition coil connector, earth the spark plug side electrode and crank engine.
3. Check to ensure spark is produced between the spark plug electrodes.
4. Replace ignition coil if no spark is produced and re-check, if again no spark is produced there is a ignition circuit fault.

Ignition Failure Sensor Check - V6 - DOHC

Using an analogue ohmmeter, check the resistance between terminals #3 and #4.

Standard Resistance.......................... 0.1 Ohm or less.

Throttle Valve Area Cleaning

1. Start engine and allow to reach normal operating temperature then switch off.
2. At the throttle body side disconnect the air intake hose.
3. **MPI** - Plug the bypass passage entrance of throttle body.
4. From outside the throttle body spray valve with a carbi cleaner and let it soak for approximately five minutes. 
5. Start and race engine then allow to idle for about one minute and repeat several times.
6. Repeat process a second time to ensure throttle valve area is well cleaned.
7. Reconnect the air intake hose.

Throttle Position Sensor Adjustment - MPI

1. Disconnect the electrical connection from the throttle position sensor.
2. Between the throttle position sensor and the harness connector, connect the test harness (MB991536), then connect a voltmeter to the throttle position sensor between terminals #3 and #1. 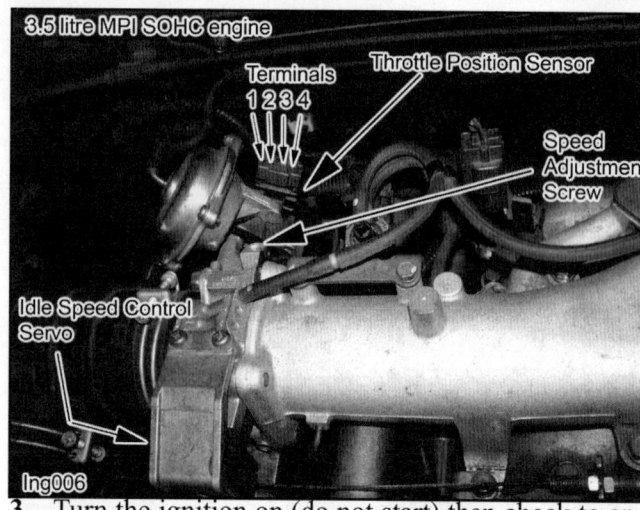
3. Turn the ignition on (do not start) then check to ensure the throttle position sensor output voltage is to specification.

   Output Voltage ....535 - 735 mV

4. If output voltage is not to specification, adjust by loosening the sensor mounting bolts and turn the throttle position sensor.
5. Tighten mounting bolts, switch off ignition, remove test harness and reconnect sensor connector.

Throttle Position Sensor Adjustment - GDI

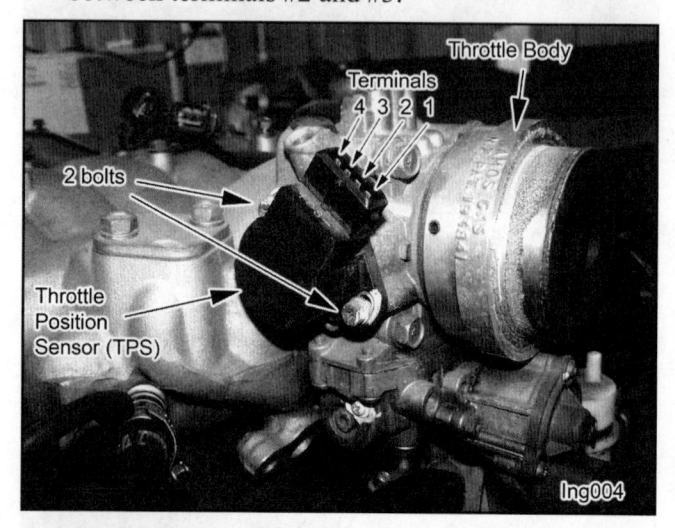

1. Disconnect the electrical connection from the throttle position sensor.
2. Between the throttle position sensor and the harness connector, connect the test harness (MB991536), then connect a voltmeter to the throttle position sensor between terminals #2 and #3.
3. Disconnect the throttle control servo connector then turn the ignition on (do not start).
4. Check to ensure the throttle position sensor 1 output voltage is to specification. While using your finger to fully close the throttle valve.

   Output Voltage .... 0.4 - 0.6 V

5. If output voltage is not to specification, adjust by loosening the sensor mounting bolts and turn the

188

IGNITION, FUEL & EMISSION SYSTEMS - Petrol Models

throttle position sensor.
6. Turn the ignition off, then connect the voltmeter to the throttle position sensor between terminals #4 and #3.
7. Turn the ignition on (do not start) and check to ensure the throttle position sensor 2 output voltage is to specification, while using your finger to fully close the throttle valve.
   Output Voltage .... **4.2 - 4.8 V**
8. If output voltage is not to specification replace the throttle position sensor.
9. Switch off ignition, remove test harness and reconnect sensor connector and throttle control servo connector.

Basic Idle Speed Adjustment - MPI

Important: *Standard idle speed has been adjusted at manufacture by the speed adjusting screw (SAS) and normally does not need adjustment.*

1. Ensure engine is at normal operating temperature, transaxle is in neutral (manual) or park (auto) and all lighting and accessories are off.
2. Ensure the ignition is switched off fully, then connect the MUT-II to the diagnostic connector and earth the diagnostic control terminal.
3. Start engine and idle, select #30 of the MUT-II actuator test, this will hold the ISC servo at the basic step to adjust basic idle speed.
4. Check if idle speed is to specification.
   Idle Speed .... **700 +/- 50 rpm**
5. If idle speed is not to specification remove the cap from the speed adjusting screw and adjust the SAS screw.
6. Press the clear key of the MUT-II to release ISC servo, then turn off engine and disconnect MUT-II.
7. Start engine and idle for ten minutes.

Variable Resistor Inspection - MPI

(mixture adjusting screw) vehicles without catalytic converter.

1. From the variable resistor disconnect the electrical connection, then measure the resistance between terminal #1 and #3 of connector.
   Resistance .... **4 - 6 kOhms**
2. Connect a multimeter between terminals #1 and #2 of the variable resistor and check to ensure the resistance changes smoothly when turning the adjustment screw.
3. Replace assembly if fault is found.

Fuel Pump Operation Check
(Low Pressure)

1. Turn off ignition switch and remove the fuel pump relay.

2. Connect the #2 terminal of the harness side connector to the battery and for sound of fuel pump operation.
   Note: *Removal of the fuel tank filler cap may assist in hearing pump as pump is located in tank.*
3. Pinch fuel hose with fingers to check fuel pressure.

Fuel Pressure Test - MPI

1. Disconnect the fuel pump connector, start engine and allow to run until engine stops.
2. Switch off ignition and reconnect fuel pump connector.
3. At the delivery pipe disconnect the high pressure hose and install a fuel pressure gauge between the delivery pipe and high pressure fuel hose.

4. Using a jumper wire connect the pump drive terminal (2) with the battery +ve terminal to drive the fuel pump and inspect the pressure gauge and connections for fuel leaks under pressure. Fuel pump connector on firewall
5. Stop fuel pump by disconnecting the jumper wire then start engine and run at idle.
6. With engine running at idle measure the fuel pressure.
   Fuel Pressure .... **265 kPa @ idle**
   (vacuum hose connected)

IGNITION, FUEL & EMISSION SYSTEMS - Petrol Models

7. From the fuel pressure regulator disconnect the vacuum hose and block off hose.
8. Measure fuel pressure.
   Fuel Pressure .... 324-343 kPa @ idle
   (vacuum hose disconnected and plugged).
9. Race the engine several times and check to ensure the fuel pressure at idle does not drop.
10. Race the engine several times and hold the fuel return hose lightly in fingers to feel fuel pressure is present.
11. If the fuel pressure in the above procedures is out of specification use the following table to troubleshoot and repair faults.

Problem	Cause	Remedy
Low fuel pressure. Fuel pressure drops	Fuel filter blocked	Replace fuel filter
	Fuel regulator faulty	Replace regulator
	Fuel pump faulty	Replace fuel pump
High fuel pressure	Fuel regulator faulty	Replace fuel regulator
	Blocked fuel return hose	Unblock or replace hose/pipe
Same fuel pressure when vacuum hose is connected or disconnected	Vacuum hose damaged or clogged vacuum nipple on manifold	Replace vacuum hose, unblock vacuum nipple on manifold

12. Stop the engine and check the change in the fuel pressure gauge. If pressure does not drop within 2 minutes it is normal. If it does drop refer to the following table.

Problem	Cause	Remedy
Fuel pressure gradually drops away when engine is stopped	Injector Faulty	Replace injector
	Faulty fuel regulator	Replace fuel regulator
Fuel pressure sharply drops away when engine is stopped	Fuel pump check valve is jammed open	Replace fuel pump

13. Release the fuel line pressure then remove the pressure gauge assembly.
14. Install the high pressure fuel hosing a new 'O-ring which has been coated with clean engine oil.

FUEL PRESSURE MEASUREMENT - GDI

Fuel Pressure Measurement In Line Between Electric Fuel Pump (low-pressure) & Fuel Pump (high-pressure) (GDI)

1. Release the residual pressure from the fuel pipe, then remove the fuel pressure hose from the high pressure fuel pump.
2. Connect a fuel pressure gauge between the pressure hose and fuel pump.
3. Ensure ignition is switch off completely, then connect the MUT-II diagnostic tool to the diagnostic connector.
4. Turn ignition switch on (do not start) from the MUT-II actuator test select #7, and activate the low pressure fuel pump at the fuel tank.
5. Check there are no leaks and either finish the actuator test or switch off ignition.
6. Start engine, run at idle while measuring the fuel pressure.
   Fuel Pressure .... 329 kPa (approx)
7. Race the engine several times and check to ensure the fuel pressure at idle does not drop.
8. If the fuel pressure is not to specification use the following table to troubleshoot and repair faults.

Problem	Cause	Remedy
Low fuel pressure. Fuel pressure drops after racing engine	Fuel filter blocked	Replace fuel filter
	Fuel regulator faulty	Replace regulator
	Low pressure fuel pump faulty	Replace low pressure fuel pump
High fuel pressure	Fuel regulator faulty	Replace fuel regulator
	Blocked fuel return hose	Unblock or replace hose/pipe

9. Stop the engine and check the change in the fuel pressure gauge. If pressure does not drop within 2 minutes it is normal. If it does drop refer to the following table.

Problem	Cause	Remedy
Fuel pressure gradually drops away when engine is stopped	Injector Faulty	Replace injector
	Faulty fuel regulator	Replace fuel regulator
Fuel pressure sharply drops away when engine is stopped	Fuel pump check valve is jammed open	Replace fuel pump

10. Release the fuel line pressure then remove the pressure gauge assembly.
11. Install the high pressure fuel hose using a new 'O-ring which has been coated with clean engine oil.

High Fuel Pressure Measurement Between Fuel Pump (high-pressure) & Injector (GDI)

1. Before carrying out this procedure ensure that the fuel pressure between the low and high pressure fuel pumps is normal.
2. Ensure the ignition is fully turned off (lock) then connect the MUT-II diagnostic tester.
3. Disconnect the intermediate injector harness.
4. Turn the ignition switch on (do not start), then select

IGNITION, FUEL & EMISSION SYSTEMS - Petrol Models

#74 on the MUT-II.

5. Crank the engine without starting for about 2 seconds then check for any fuel leaks. Repair any leaks present.
6. After cranking wait about 20 seconds and check to ensure fuel pressure is 1MPa or more.
   Note: *If pressure is less than 1MPa, leaks may be present around the high pressure fuel pump.*
7. Turn ignition off (lock position) and reconnect the injector intermediate harness connector.
8. Start engine and run at idle and measure the fuel pressure.
   Fuel Pressure @ Idle.......................... 4 - 6.9 MPa
9. Race the engine several times and ensure the idle fuel pressure does not drop. If pressure is not within specification refer to the following table.

Problem	Cause	Remedy
Low fuel pressure.	Fuel regulator faulty	Replace high pressure fuel pump
Fuel pressure drops after racing engine	Low pressure from high pressure fuel pump	Replace high pressure fuel pump
High fuel pressure	Fuel regulator faulty	Replace high pressure fuel pump
	Blocked fuel return hose	Unblock or replace hose/pipe

10. Stop the engine, ensure the ignition is in the fully off position, then disconnect the MUT-II diagnostic tester.

Fuel Leak Test - GDI

1. Disconnect the fuel pump connector, start engine and allow to run until engine stops.
2. Switch off ignition and reconnect fuel pump connector.
3. At the delivery pipe disconnect the high pressure hose and install a fuel pressure gauge between the delivery pipe and high pressure fuel hose.
4. Using a jumper wire connect the pump drive terminal (2) with the battery +ve terminal to drive the fuel pump and inspect the pressure gauge and connections for fuel leaks under pressure.
5. Stop fuel pump by disconnecting the jumper wire then start engine and run at idle.
6. With engine running at idle measure the fuel pressure.
   Fuel Pressure ....265kPa @ idle
   (vacuum hose connected)
7. From the fuel pressure regulator disconnect the vacuum hose and block off hose.
8. Measure fuel pressure.
   Fuel Pressure ....324-343 kPa @ idle
   (vacuum hose disconnected and plugged).
9. Race the engine several times and check to ensure the fuel pressure at idle does not drop.
10. Race the engine several times and hold the fuel return hose lightly in fingers to feel fuel pressure is present.
11. If the fuel pressure in the above procedures is out of specification use the following table to troubleshoot and repair faults.
12. Stop the engine and check the change in the fuel pressure gauge. If pressure does not drop within 2 minutes it is normal. If it does drop refer to the following table.
13. Release the fuel line pressure then remove the pressure gauge assembly.
14. Install the high pressure fuel hosing a new 'O-ring which has been coated with clean engine oil.

IGNITION, FUEL & EMISSION SYSTEMS - Petrol Models

3.8 Litre MPI SOHC Engines ON VEHICLE INSPECTION

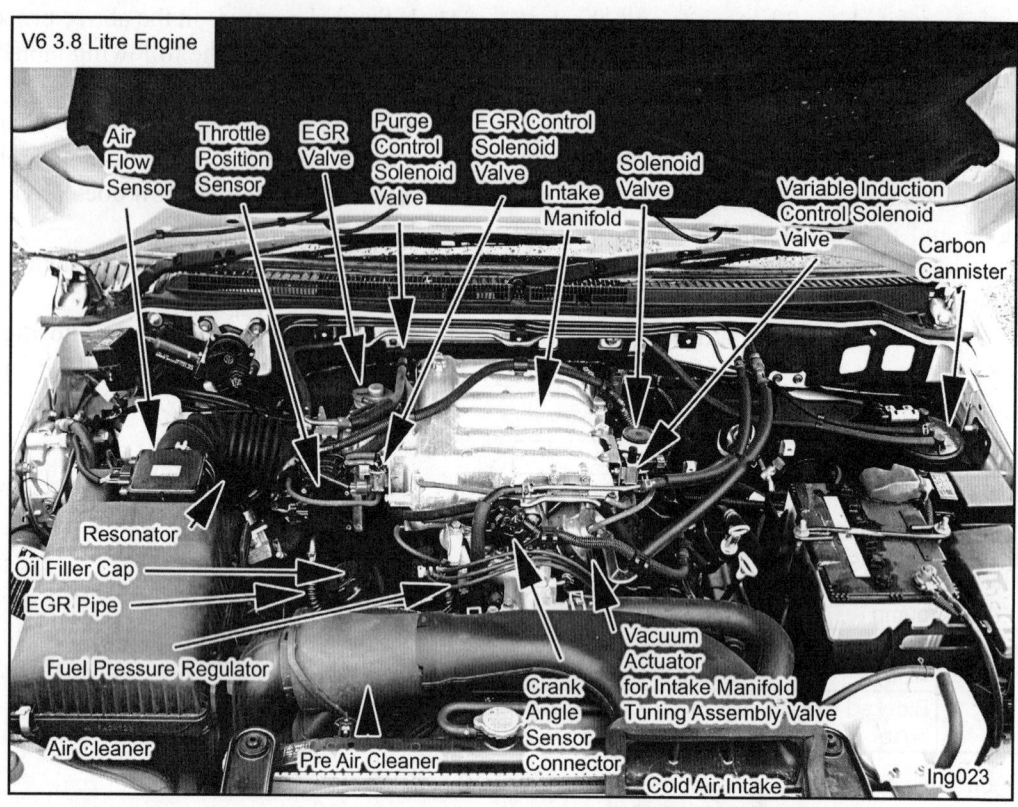

V6 3.8 Litre Engine — labelled components: Air Flow Sensor, Throttle Position Sensor, EGR Valve, Purge Control Solenoid Valve, EGR Control Solenoid Valve, Intake Manifold, Solenoid Valve, Variable Induction Control Solenoid Valve, Carbon Cannister, Resonator, Oil Filler Cap, EGR Pipe, Fuel Pressure Regulator, Air Cleaner, Pre Air Cleaner, Crank Angle Sensor Connector, Vacuum Actuator for Intake Manifold Tuning Assembly Valve, Cold Air Intake.

Inspection of Spark Plugs
* Refer to Engine Tune-up & Maintenance Chapter.

INSPECTION & ADJUSTMENT - BASIC IGNITION TIMING
* Refer to Engine Tune-up & Maintenance Chapter.

IGNITION SYSTEMS .... FIRING ORDER

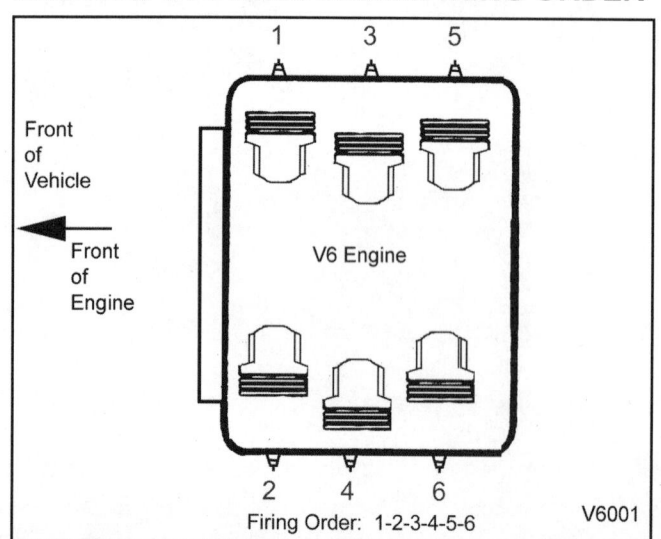

V6 Engine cylinder layout: front of vehicle / front of engine — cylinders 1, 3, 5 (rear bank) and 2, 4, 6 (front bank). Firing Order: 1-2-3-4-5-6.

V6 SOHC and DOHC engines 1-2-3-4-5-6

Inspection of Ignition Coil
Primary Coil & Power Transistor Continuity Check
Using an analogue tester, check the continuity of the primary coil and power transistor between terminals 1 and 2.

Note: *Test must be performed within 10 seconds to prevent damage.*

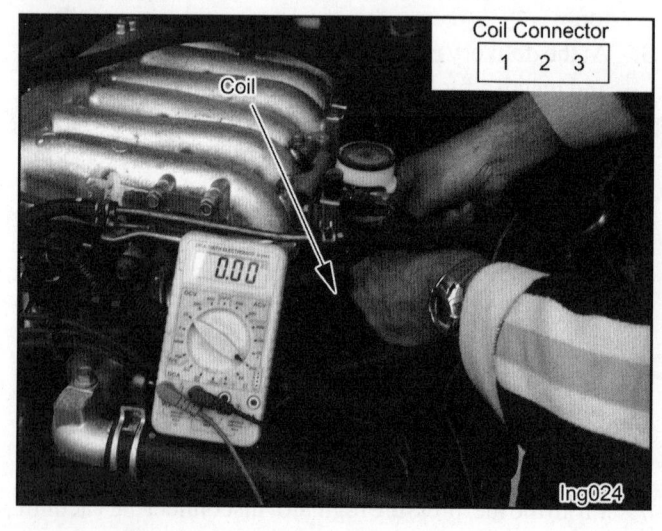

Coil Connector terminals: 1 2 3

IGNITION, FUEL & EMISSION SYSTEMS - Petrol Models

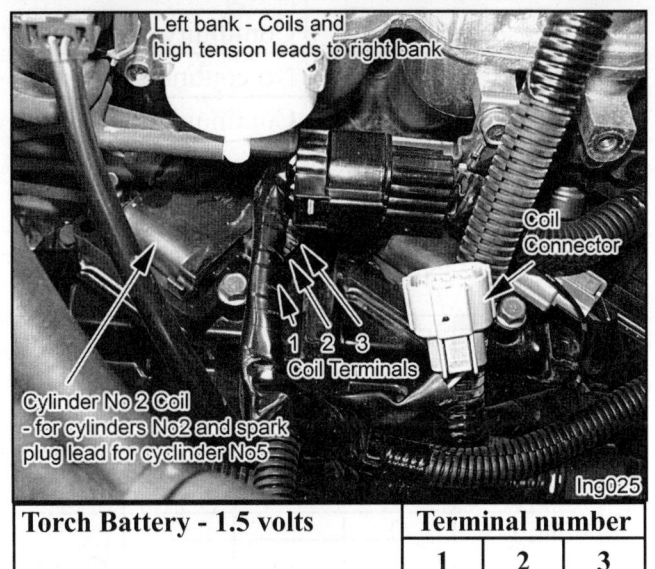

Torch Battery - 1.5 volts	Terminal number		
	1	2	3
1.5 volts - Current applied to terminal 2 and 3	X	X	
No current applied	-	-	

Secondary Coil Inspection

1. Disconnect the connector from the ignition coil, remove coil, 2 bolts.
2. Use a multimeter between the end of the high tension lead and the ignition coil high tension terminal.
   Secondary Coil Resistance .... 8.5 - 11.5 kOhm
3. Replace ignition coil if resistance is not within specification.

Inspection of Ignition Lead

1. Inspect the ignition leads to ensure the coating is not cracked or damaged.

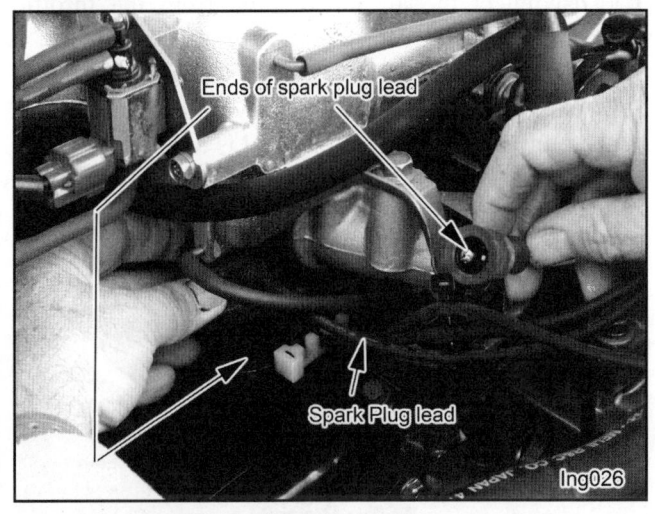

2. Measure the resistance from each the end of the 3 high tension leads to ensure they are withing specification.
   Lead Resistance .... 8.5 kOhm (limit)

Throttle Valve Area Cleaning

1. Start engine and allow to reach normal operating temperature then switch off.
2. At the throttle body side disconnect the air intake hose.
3. Plug the bypass passage entrance of throttle body.
4. From outside the throttle body spray valve with a carbi cleaner and let it soak for approximately five minutes.
5. Start and race engine then allow to idle for about one minute and repeat several times.
6. Repeat process a second time to ensure throttle valve area is well cleaned.
7. Reconnect the air intake hose.

Basic Idle Speed Adjustment

Important: *Standard idle speed has been adjusted at manufacture by the Accelerator Pedal Position Sensor and the Throttle Position Servo*
See following speed adjusting screw (SAS) and normally does not need adjustment.

1. Ensure engine is at normal operating temperature, transaxle is in neutral (manual) or park (auto) and all lighting and accessories are off.
2. Ensure the ignition is switched off fully, then connect the MUT-II to the diagnostic connector and earth the diagnosis control terminal.
3. Start engine and idle, select #30 of the MUT-II actuator test, this will hold the ISC servo at the basic step to adjust basic idle speed.
4. Check if idle speed is to specification.
   Idle Speed .... 700 +/- 50 rpm
5. If idle speed is not to specification remove the cap from the speed adjusting screw and adjust the SAS screw.
6. Press the clear key of the MUT-II to release ISC servo, then turn off engine and disconnect MUT-II.
7. Start engine and idle for ten minutes.

Accelerator Pedal Sensor Adjustment

Note: *Pedal is set in factory during manufacture, only adjust if pedal has been damaged.*

1. Remove accelerator pedal assembly from vehicle.
2. Use a MUT-II tester if possible. However if a tester is not available, connect a voltmeter between terminals 3 of the harness connector and terminal 3 of the accelerator pedal terminal.
3. The accelerator pedal lever has a stopper at the top of the lever. Make sure the top of the lever is against the stopper
   Turn the ignition switch ON but do not start engine, check the voltmeter for specified voltage.

IGNITION, FUEL & EMISSION SYSTEMS - Petrol Models

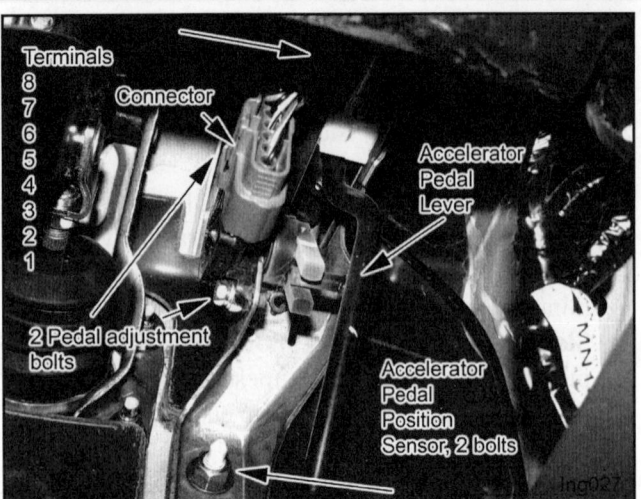

Accelerator Pedal Position Sensor Voltage
....0.0985 - 1.085 volts

4. Loosen the 2 adjustment bolts, adjust the sensor to achieve the specified voltage with the lever against the stopper.
5. Tighten the 2 adjustment bolts, and install accelerator pedal assembly to vehicle.

Accelerator Pedal Sensor Check

Note: Pedal is set in factory during manufacture, only adjust if pedal has been damaged.

1. Disconnect the accelerator pedal connector.
2. Connect a multimeter between terminals 1 and 2 of the accelerator pedal terminals, check for specified resistance. If not replace the sensor.
   Accelerator Pedal Position Resistance
   ....3.5 - 6.5 kOhms
3. Connect a multimeter between terminals 8 and 7 of the accelerator pedal terminals, check for specified resistance. If not replace the sensor.
   Accelerator Pedal Position Resistance
   ....3.5 - 6.5 kOhms
4. a) Connect a multimeter between terminals 2 and 3 of the accelerator pedal terminals, depress the accelerator pedal, the resistance should change smoothly as the accelerator pedal is depressed. If not replace the sensor.
   b) Connect a multimeter between terminals 8 and 6 of the accelerator pedal terminals, depress the accelerator pedal, the resistance should change smoothly as the accelerator pedal is depressed. If not replace the sensor.

Accelerator Pedal Position Switch Check

Note: Pedal is set in factory during manufacture, only adjust if pedal has been damaged.

1. Disconnect the accelerator pedal connector.
2. Connect a multimeter between terminals 4 and 5 of the accelerator pedal terminals, check for specified continuity as in chart.

Released pedal	Continuity
Depressed pedal	No continuity
Released pedal	Continuity

If not replace the sensor.

Throttle Valve Control Servo Relay Check

1. Check relay with a multimeter.

Battery voltage	Terminals			
	1	2	3	4
No voltage		O—|—|—O	
Voltage	O—|—|—O		
		-ve O		O +ve

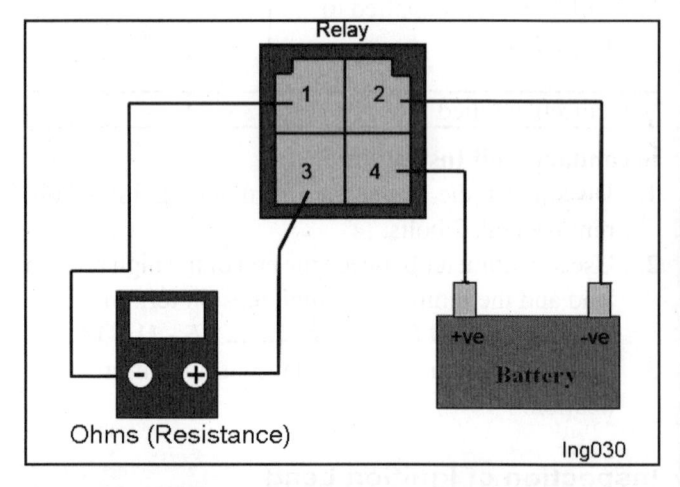

Throttle Valve Control Servo Check

Visual Inspection

1. Disconnect the air intake tube from the throttle body.
2. Turn ignition switch ON do not start engine.
3. Visually check the throttle valve butterfly valve is moving as the accelerator pedal is depressed.

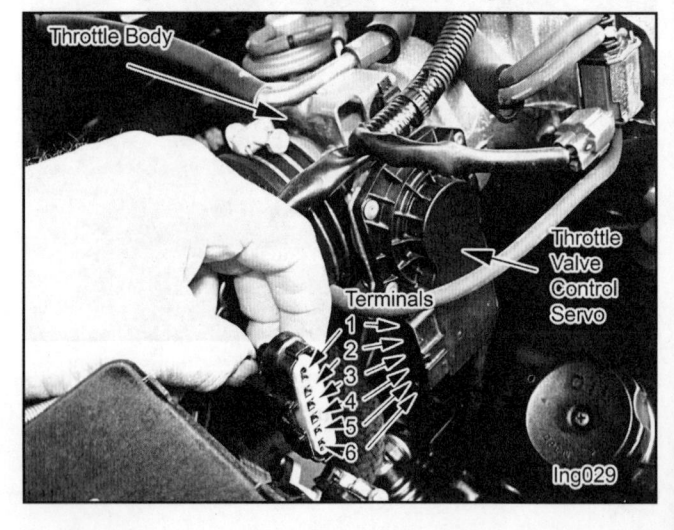

194

IGNITION, FUEL & EMISSION SYSTEMS - Petrol Models

Resistance Check
1. Disconnect the throttle position connector.
2. Connect a multimeter between terminals 5 and 6 of the throttle position servo terminals, check for specified resistance. If not replace the throttle position assembly.
   Throttle Position Servo Resistance at 20° C
   .... 0.3 - 100 Ohms

Fuel Pump Operation Check
(Low Pressure)
1. Turn off ignition switch and remove the fuel pump relay.
2. Connect the #2 terminal of the harness side connector to the battery and for sound of fuel pump operation.
   Note: *Removal of the fuel tank filler cap may assist in hearing pump as pump is located in tank.*
3. Pinch fuel hose with fingers to check fuel pressure.

Fuel Pressure Test
1. Disconnect the fuel pump connector, start engine and allow to run until engine stops.
2. Switch off ignition and reconnect fuel pump connector.
3. At the delivery pipe disconnect the high pressure hose and install a fuel pressure gauge between the delivery pipe and high pressure fuel hose.
4. Using a jumper wire connect the pump drive terminal (2) with the battery +ve terminal to drive the fuel pump and inspect the pressure gauge and connections for fuel leaks under pressure. Fuel pump connector on firewall
5. Stop fuel pump by disconnecting the jumper wire then start engine and run at idle.
6. With engine running at idle measure the fuel pressure.
   Fuel Pressure .... 265 kPa @ idle
   (vacuum hose connected)
7. From the fuel pressure regulator disconnect the vacuum hose and block off hose.
8. Measure fuel pressure.
   Fuel Pressure .... 324-343 kPa @ idle
   (vacuum hose disconnected and plugged).
9. Race the engine several times and check to ensure the fuel pressure at idle does not drop.
10. Race the engine several times and hold the fuel return hose lightly in fingers to feel fuel pressure is present.
11. If the fuel pressure in the above procedures is out of specification use the following table to troubleshoot and repair faults.

Problem	Cause	Remedy
Low fuel pressure. Fuel pressure drops	Fuel filter blocked	Replace fuel filter
	Fuel regulator faulty	Replace regulator
	Fuel pump faulty	Replace fuel pump
High fuel pressure	Fuel regulator faulty	Replace fuel regulator
	Blocked fuel return hose	Unblock or replace hose/pipe
Same fuel pressure when vacuum hose is connected or disconnected	Vacuum hose damaged or clogged vacuum nipple on manifold	Replace vacuum hose, unblock vacuum nipple on manifold

12. Stop the engine and check the change in the fuel pressure gauge. If pressure does not drop within 2 minutes it is normal. If it does drop refer to the following table.

Problem	Cause	Remedy
Fuel pressure gradually drops away when engine is stopped	Injector Faulty	Replace injector
	Faulty fuel regulator	Replace fuel regulator
Fuel pressure sharply drops away when engine is stopped	Fuel pump check valve is jammed open	Replace fuel pump

13. Release the fuel line pressure then remove the pressure gauge assembly.
14. Install the high pressure fuel hosing a new 'O-ring which has been coated with clean engine oil.

Fuel Leak Test - GDI
1. Disconnect the fuel pump connector, start engine and allow to run until engine stops.
2. Switch off ignition and reconnect fuel pump connector.
3. At the delivery pipe disconnect the high pressure hose and install a fuel pressure gauge between the delivery pipe and high pressure fuel hose.
4. Using a jumper wire connect the pump drive terminal (2) with the battery +ve terminal to drive the fuel pump and inspect the pressure gauge and connections for fuel leaks under pressure.
5. Stop fuel pump by disconnecting the jumper wire then start engine and run at idle.
6. With engine running at idle measure the fuel pressure.
   Fuel Pressure .... 265kPa @ idle
   (vacuum hose connected)
7. From the fuel pressure regulator disconnect the vacuum hose and block off hose.
8. Measure fuel pressure.

IGNITION, FUEL & EMISSION SYSTEMS - Petrol Models

Fuel Pressure ....324-343 kPa @ idle (vacuum hose disconnected and plugged).

9. Race the engine several times and check to ensure the fuel pressure at idle does not drop.
10. Race the engine several times and hold the fuel return hose lightly in fingers to feel fuel pressure is present.
11. If the fuel pressure in the above procedures is out of specification use the following table to troubleshoot and repair faults.
12. Stop the engine and check the change in the fuel pressure gauge. If pressure does not drop within 2 minutes it is normal. If it does drop refer to the following table.
13. Release the fuel line pressure then remove the pressure gauge assembly.
14. Install the high pressure fuel hosing a new 'O-ring which has been coated with clean engine oil.

EMISSION SYSTEM

Vacuum Circuit Inspection

1. Check all vacuum hose connections using the pipe diagram as a guide to ensure all connections are properly connected and there are no loose connections.
2. Check to ensure there are no bends, kinks or damaged hoses.

CRANKCASE EMISSION CONTROL SYSTEM

Positive Crankcase Ventilation (PCV) Valve System
Inspection

1. From the positive crankcase ventilation valve remove the ventilation hose.
2. From the rocker cover remove the positive crankcase ventilation valve and reconnect the valve to the ventilation hose.
3. a) Insert a thin rod into the underside of the PCV valve and move the rod in and out to check that the plunger moves.
   b) If plunger does not move there is a restriction in the valve.
   c) Clean or replace valve.
4. Remove the PCV valve, wash in petrol, then shake and you should be able to hear and feel the valve inside move.

DOHC engine, rear of left rocker cover.

5. Start the vehicle and run at idle then using your finger check to ensure that the intake manifold vacuum is felt at the opening of the valve.
6. If no vacuum is felt clean the PCV valve and re-check, replace if required.

196

IGNITION, FUEL & EMISSION SYSTEMS - Petrol Models

SOHC engines, front of left rocker cover.

Purge Port Vacuum
Inspection
1. From the intake manifold disconnect the vacuum hose.
2. Connect a hand vacuum pump to the nipple where the hose was removed.
3. Start the vehicle and race engine, check to ensure the purge vacuum is fairly constant after engine has been raced.
4. If there is a problem with the vacuum inspect the throttle body purge port as it may be clogged and requires cleaning.

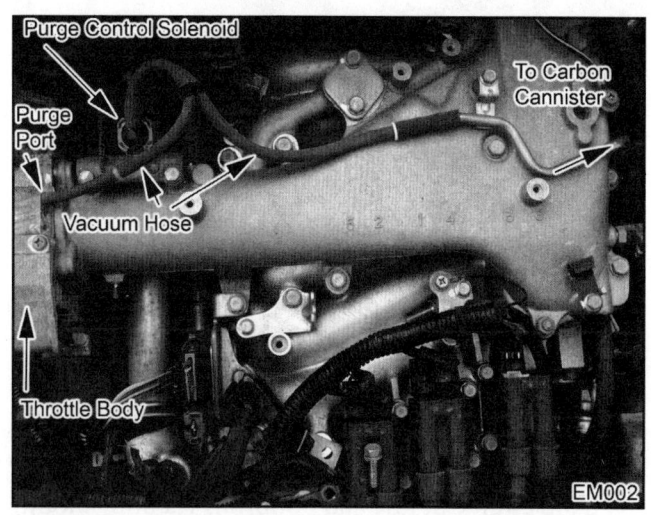

EVAPORATIVE EMISSION CONTROL SYSTEM

Purge Control System
Inspection
1. From the intake manifold disconnect the vacuum hose.
2. Connect a hand vacuum pump to the vacuum hose and plug the nipple where the hose was removed.
3. With the engine idling apply vacuum and check. Apply vacuum when engine is both cold and hot.

Vacuum Pressure.......................... 53kPa

Engine Cold (less than 40°C)	
Status	Condition
3,000 rpm	Vacuum maintained

Engine Hot (higher than 80°C)	
Status	Condition
Idling	Vacuum maintained
3,000rpm	Vacuum will leak for approximately 3min. after engine started.

Evaporative Emission Purge Solenoid
Inspection A
1. Remove engine cover (where fitted), then from the solenoid valve disconnect vacuum hose.
2. Disconnect the electrical connector, then to the nipple (A) of the solenoid valve connect a hand vacuum pump. 
3. Apply voltage direct from battery to solenoid and apply vacuum checking air tightness. Also apply vacuum without voltage and check air tightness.

Voltage Applied .... Vacuum Leaks
No Voltage .... Vacuum Maintained

197

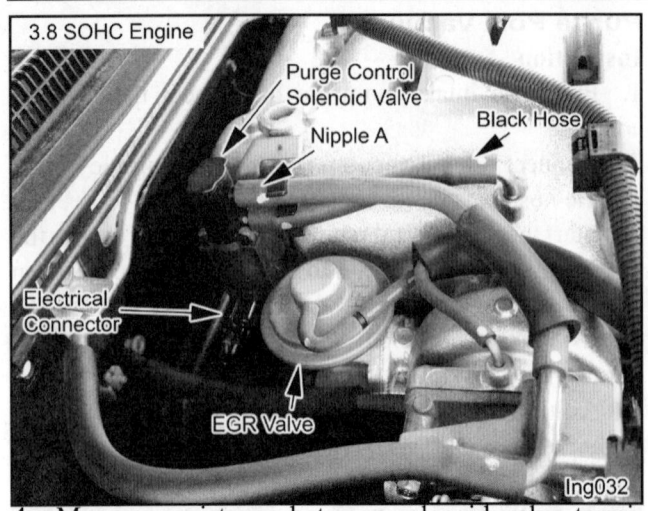

IGNITION, FUEL & EMISSION SYSTEMS - Petrol Models

4. Measure resistance between solenoid valve terminals.
   Standard Value @ 20°C .... 30 - 34 Ohm.

Inspection B
1. Disconnect the black vacuum hose from the intake manifold, block the nipple on the intake manifold.
2. Connect it to a hand vacuum pump.
3. Start the engine and apply a vacuum of 53kPa check below for values.

Vacuum Values

Cold engine at idle and 3000rpm vacuum should hold

Hot engine at idle vacuum should hold

Hot engine at 3000rpm vacuum should diminish

Emission Canister
Removal
1. Remove the air cleaner assembly.
2. Disconnect the hoses from the canister then remove the canister from vehicle.
3. Where fitted disconnect the hoses and electrical connections to the vent solenoid valve and air filter. Remove retaining nuts and remove solenoid and filter. (Taiwan vehicles).
4. Remove the bolts securing the canister bracket and remove bracket.

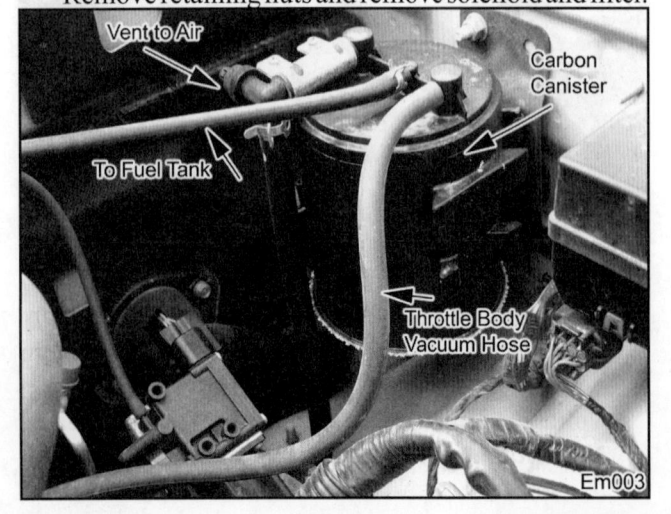

Installation
1. Install canister bracket into vehicle and tighten the retaining bolts.
2. Where fitted install the vent solenoid valve and air filter, then reconnect hoses and electrical connections. (Taiwan vehicles).
3. Install canister into vehicle and reconnect the hoses.
4. Install air cleaner assembly.

EXHAUST GAS RECIRCULATION SYSTEM

Applicable for Europe, UK, South Africa, China, Brazil

Not applicable for Australian NM, NP - 3.5 SOHC vehicles.

Applicable for Australian 3.8 SOHC (countries other than Taiwan) vehicles, see 2 pages further on.

EGR System - MPI
Inspection
1. Remove the engine cover (where fitted), then from the EGR valve disconnect the vacuum hose (green stripe) and install a hand vacuum pump using a "T" connector.
2. Check the vacuum condition when the throttle valve is opened quickly (race engine). Perform this procedure with engine at cold and hot condition.
   Engine Cold (coolant less than 20°C)
   No vacuum generated.
   Engine Hot (coolant greater than 80°C)
   Vacuum will rise over 100mmHg momentarily.
3. Remove the "T" connector and directly connect the pump to the EGR valve.
4. Apply vacuum of 220mmHg or higher and check to see if the engine stalls or idling os unstable.

Vacuum Control Valve - MPI
Inspection
1. From the vacuum control valve disconnect the vacuum hose (white stripe), then connect a hand pump the control valve and plug the vacuum hose.
2. Start the engine, run at idle and check vacuum condition.
   Normal Condition @ Idle.... Approx. 170 mmHg

IGNITION, FUEL & EMISSION SYSTEMS - Petrol Models

EGR Valve - MPI
Inspection
1. Remove the EGR valve, then inspect the valve for carbon deposits, sticking valve, etc.
2. Using a hand vacuum pump, apply 500 mmHg of vacuum and ensure vacuum is maintained.
3. With vacuum applied blow through one side of the EGR passage.
   40 mmHg or less .... **Air is not blown out**
   220 mmHg or more .... **Air is blown out**
4. Install EGR valve using a new gasket and tighten to specification.
   EGR Valve .... **22 Nm**

EGR Port Vacuum - MPI
Inspection
1. From the throttle body EGR vacuum port disconnect the vacuum hose (green stripe), then connect a hand vacuum pump to the port.
2. Ensure vacuum remains fairly constant after raising the engine speed by racing the engine.

EGR Solenoid - MPI
Inspection
1. From the EGR solenoid valve disconnect the vacuum hose (yellow stripe, green stripe), then disconnect the electrical connector.
2. Apply voltage direct from battery to solenoid and apply vacuum checking air tightness. Also apply vacuum without voltage and check air tightness.
   <u>Normal Condition</u>
   With Voltage Applied .... **Vacuum Maintained**
   No Voltage Applied .... **Vacuum Leaks**
3. Measure resistance between solenoid valve terminals.
   Standard Value @ 20°C .... **36-44 Ohm.**

EGR Valve - MPI
Removal
1. Drain the cooling system then remove the engine cover and the air cleaner assembly.
2. From the EGR valve disconnect the water hoses and electrical connection.
3. Remove the bolts securing the EGR pipe to the EGR valve, then unscrew and removal pipe and discard gasket.
4. Remove the bolts securing the EGR valve then remove valve assembly and discard gasket.

Installation
1. Install the EGR valve using a new gasket and tighten retaining bolts to specification.
   EGR Valve Bolts .... **22 Nm**
   Note: *Ensure to install the gasket around the correct way.*
2. Screw in EGR pipe tightening to the correct specification then using a new gasket connect the EGR pipe to the EGR valve, tighten bolts to specification.
   EGR Pipe .... **59 Nm**
   EGR Pipe to Valve Bolts .... **18 Nm**
3. To the EGR valve connect the water hoses and electrical connection.
4. Install the air cleaner assembly, fill cooling system and install engine cover.

EGR Valve Inspection (stepper motor) - GDI
Operation Sound
1. Turn ignition switch on (do not start) and check to ensure the EGR valve stepper motor can be heard.
2. If stepper motor cannot be heard check the motor drive circuit for faults. If circuit is OK probable cause is a malfunction of the stepper motor or ECU.

Coil Resistance
1. Disconnect electrical connector from EGR valve.
2. Measure the resistance between terminals 2 and either terminal 1 or 3.
   Standard Resistance @ 20°C .... **10-20 ohms**
3. Measure the resistance between terminals 5 and either terminal 4 or 6.
   Standard Resistance @ 20°C .... **10-20 ohms**

Operation Inspection
1. Remove the EGR valve, then connect a test harness to the EGR connector.
2. Connect terminal #2 to the positive terminal and connect terminals #1 and #3 to the negative terminal and check if vibration occurs due to the stepper motor operation.
3. Connect terminal #5 to positive battery terminal and connect terminals #4 and #6 to the negative terminal and check if vibration occurs due to the stepper motor operation.
4. If vibration could be felt in the tests the stepper motor is operating normally.

EGR Valve - GDI
Removal
1. Drain the cooling system then remove the engine cover and the air cleaner assembly.
2. From the EGR valve disconnect the water hoses and electrical connection.
3. Remove the bolts securing the EGR pipe to the EGR valve, then unscrew and removal pipe and discard gasket.
4. Remove the bolts securing the EGR valve then remove valve assembly and discard gasket.

Installation

1. Install the EGR valve using a new gasket and tighten retaining bolts to specification.
   EGR Valve Bolts...**22 Nm**
   Note: Ensure to install the gasket around the correct way.
2. Screw in EGR pipe tightening to the correct specification then using a new gasket connect the EGR pipe to the EGR valve, tighten bolts to specification.
   EGR Pipe ....**59 Nm**
   EGR Pipe to Valve Bolts............................**18 Nm**
3. To the EGR valve connect the water hoses and electrical connection.
4. Install the air cleaner assembly, fill cooling system and install engine cover.

EGR System for 3.8 SOHC Countries except Taiwan

EGR Solenoid Valve
Inspection
1. From the EGR solenoid valve disconnect the vacuum hoses, then disconnect the electrical connector.
2. Apply voltage direct from battery to solenoid and apply vacuum to the top nipple (to Throttle Body) checking air tightness. Also apply vacuum without voltage and check air tightness.
   Normal Condition
   With Voltage Applied..........Vacuum Maintained
   No Voltage Applied ....Vacuum Leaks
3. Measure resistance between solenoid valve terminals.
   Standard Value @ 20°C....................**29-34 Ohm**.

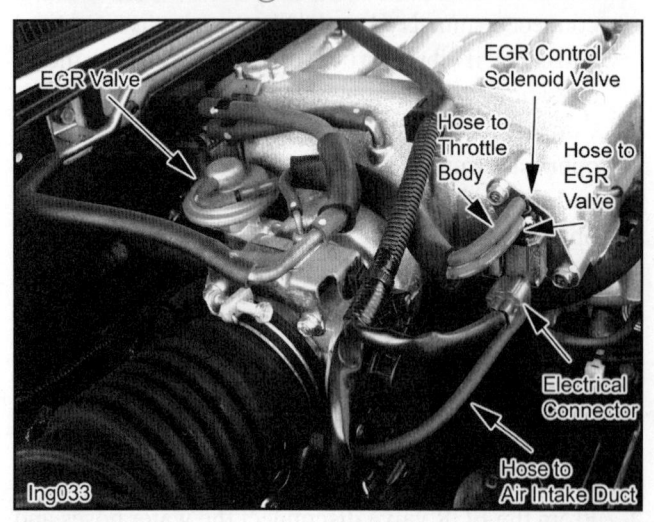

EGR Valve
Removal
1. Disconnect the vacuum hose.
2. Remove the bolts securing the EGR valve then remove valve assembly and discard gasket.

Installation

1. Install the EGR valve using a new gasket and tighten retaining bolts to specification.
   EGR Valve Bolts...**22 Nm**
   Note: Ensure to install the gasket around the correct way.
2. Connect the vacuum hose to the EGR valve.

EGR Pipe

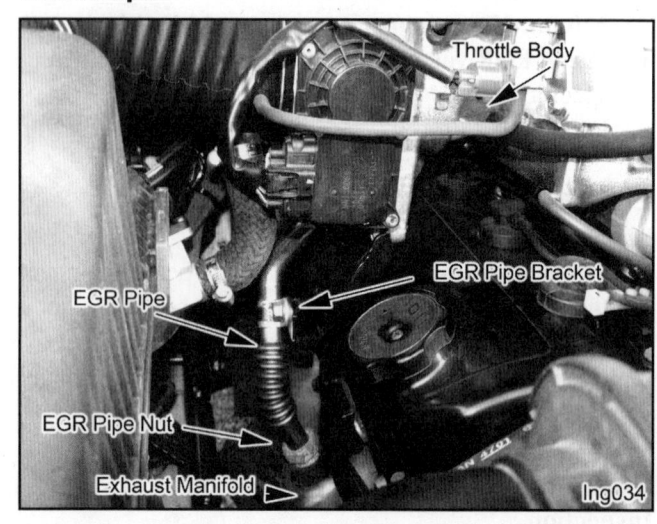

Removal
1. Remove the bracket bolt securing the EGR pipe.
2. Remove the bolts securing the EGR pipe at the exhaust manifold and intake manifold, remove pipe and discard gasket.

Installation
1. Install pipe and gaskets, screw in EGR pipe nut tightening to the correct specification then using a new gasket connect the EGR pipe to the EGR valve, tighten bolts to specification.
   EGR Pipe Nut...**59 Nm**
   EGR Pipe to Valve Bolts............................**18 Nm**
2. Install the bracket bolt securing the EGR pipe.

IGNITION SYSTEM

Ignition Coil - 3.5 V6 SOHC
Removal
1. Disconnect the battery negative cable, then remove the engine cover and remove the air cleaner assembly.
2. Disconnect the electrical connections from the ignition coil then disconnect the ignition leads from the coil pack.
3. Remove the bolts/screws securing the ignition coil and remove coil assembly from vehicle.

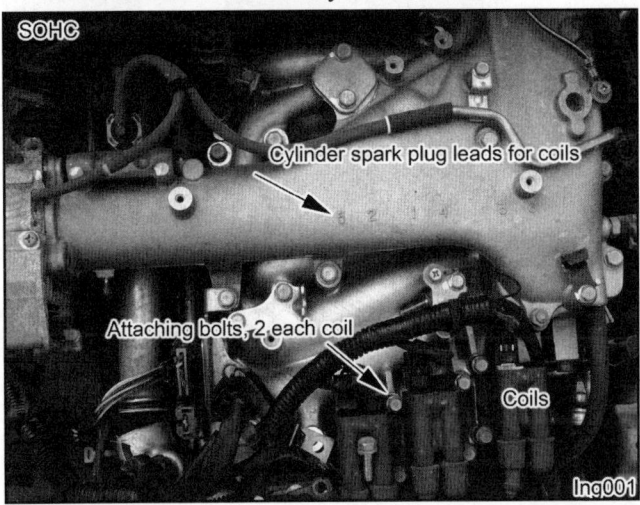

Installation
1. Install the ignition coils and tighten the retaining bolts/screws to specification.
   Ignition Coil Screws/Bolts .... 11 Nm
2. Reconnect the electrical connections to the ignition coil and then reconnect ignition leads to the coil pack.
3. Install the air cleaner assembly and engine cover then reconnect the battery.

Ignition Coil - V6 DOHC
Removal
1. Disconnect the battery negative cable, then remove the engine cover and remove the air cleaner assembly.
2. **Right Bank -** Remove the throttle body as described in this chapter.
3. Remove the bolts securing the ignition coil cover and remove cover.
4. Remove the bolts securing the ignition coil then disconnect electrical connection and remove coil.
5. If required remove spark plugs.

Installation
1. If removed install the spark plugs, tightening to specification.
   Spark Plug .... 25 Nm
   Note: Ensure to smear threads of spark plug with grease to help prevent binding.
2. Install the ignition coil and tighten the retaining bolts/screws then reconnect electrical connection.
   Ignition Coil Screws/Bolts .... 10 Nm
3. Install the ignition coil cover and tighten retaining screws/bolts to specification.
   Cover Screws/Bolts .... 3 Nm
4. **Right Bank -** Install the throttle body as described in this chapter.
5. Install the air cleaner assembly and engine cover then reconnect the battery.

Ignition Coil - 3.8 V6 SOHC
Removal
1. Disconnect the battery negative cable.
2. Disconnect the electrical connection from the ignition coils then disconnect the ignition leads from the coil.
3. Remove the 2 bolts securing each ignition coil and remove coil assemblies from vehicle.

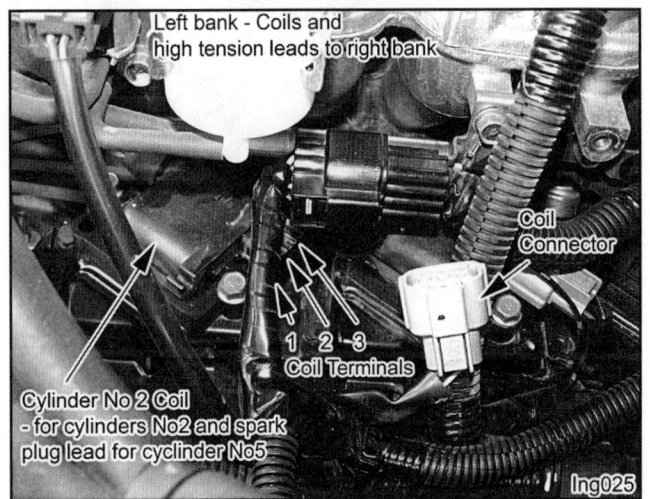

Installation
1. Install the ignition coils and tighten the retaining bolts to specification.
   Ignition Coil Screws/Bolts .... 11 Nm
2. Reconnect the electrical connection to the ignition coil and then reconnect the ignition leads to the coil pack.
3. Reconnect the battery.

Crank Angle Sensor
Removal
1. Remove the timing belt cover as described in the engine chapter.
2. Remove the sensor and cable screws.
3. Disconnect electrical connection and remove sensor assembly from vehicle.

Installation
1. Install crank angle sensor assembly into position in vehicle and reconnect electrical connections.

IGNITION, FUEL & EMISSION SYSTEMS - Petrol Models

3. Remove retaining bolt, then remove sensor and discard 'O-ring.

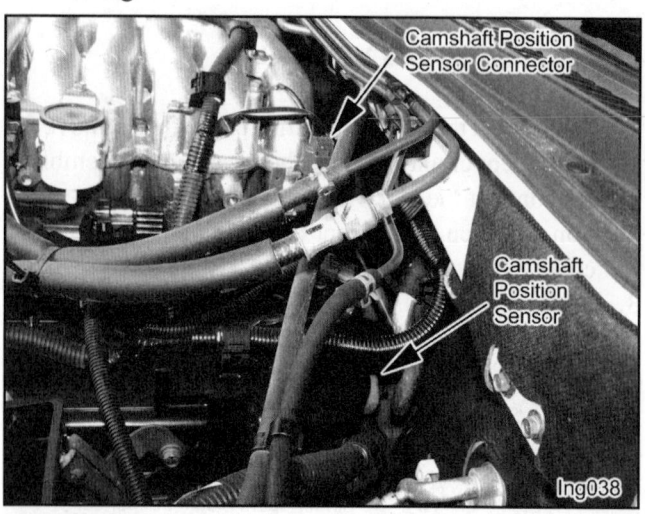

Installation
1. Using a new 'O-ring install the camshaft sensor and tighten retaining bolt to specification.
   Camshaft Position Sensor .... **11 Nm**
2. Reconnect electrical connection then install engine cover if required.

Knock (Detonation) Sensor - 3.8 SOHC and 3.5 GDI DOHC (almost identical)
Removal
1. Remove the intake manifold as described in the engine chapter.
2. Disconnect sensor electrical connection, then unscrew and remove sensor using a special tool to prevent damage to sensor.

Installation
1. Install sensor using special tool and tighten to specification.
   Detonation Sensor .... **23 Nm**
2. Reconnect sensor electrical connection, then install intake manifold as described in engine chapter.

2. Tighten sensor and cable retaining screws/bolts to specification.
   Sensor Bolts .... **8.5 Nm**
   Cable clamp colts .... **11 Nm**
3. Install the timing belt cover as described in the engine chapter.

Camshaft Position Sensor
Removal
1. Remove the engine cover from the engine if fitted.
2. Disconnect the electrical connection from the camshaft position sensor.

FUEL SYSTEM

Depressurising the fuel System

Before removing any of the fuel pipes the following procedure should be followed to prevent fuel spray.

1. Remove the fuel filler cap to release pressure in the tank.
2. The fuel pump relay needs to be removed. On NM - NP models the relay is situated in the engine compartment. On NS and NT models it is located in the fuse box under the steering wheel.

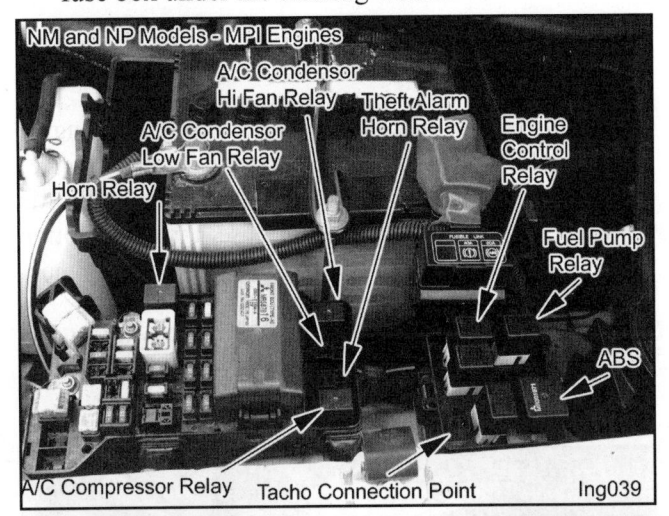

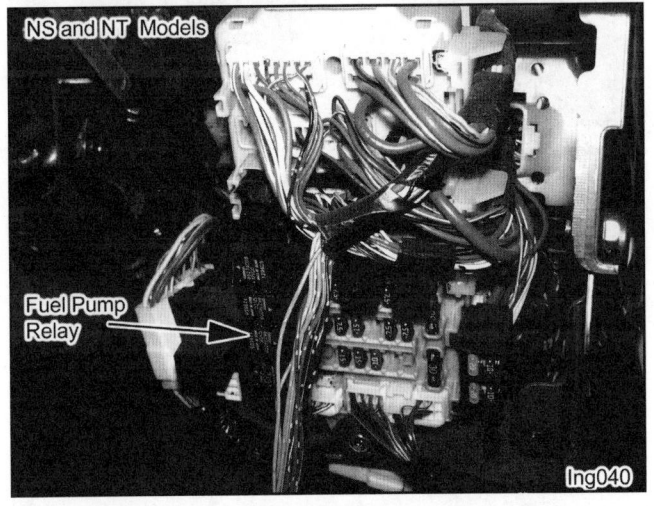

3. On NS and NT models remove the No. 2 fuel pump relay from the fuse panel.
4. Turn the ignition on and crank the engine for at least two seconds.
5. Turn the ignition off and reinstall the fuel pump relay.
6. The vehicle is now ready to be worked on.

Accelerator Cable - MPI
Removal

1. At the throttle body remove the accelerator cable mounting bracket then disconnect the inner cable.
2. Remove the two nuts securing the pedal end of the accelerator cable then disconnect the accelerator cable from the accelerator pedal.
3. Remove cable from vehicle.

Installation

1. Install the accelerator cable to the vehicle, reconnect cable to pedal and tighten cable bracket retaining bolts.
   Cable Bracket Mount ....5 Nm
2. Reconnect the accelerator cable to the throttle body and install mounting bracket and adjustment bolts.
3. Install the cable retaining clamps, tighten retaining bolts to specification.
   Cable Retaining Clamps..............12 Nm
4. Adjust the accelerator cable as described previously in this chapter.
   Accelerator Cable Adjustment Bolts...........5 Nm

Intake Manifold - V6 MPI

See V6 MPI Engine chapter for Intake manifold removal and installation.

Intake Manifold - V6 GDI

See V6 GDI Engine chapter for Intake manifold removal and installation.

FUEL RAIL / INJECTORS - MPI
Removal

1. Discharge the Fuel system as described previously.
2. Disconnect the battery negative cable, then remove the engine cover and remove the air cleaner and intake hose assembly.
3. Remove the upper intake manifold, as described in this chapter.

203

IGNITION, FUEL & EMISSION SYSTEMS - Petrol Models

4. From the fuel pressure regulator disconnect the vacuum hose and fuel return hose.
5. Remove the fuel pressure regulator, then disconnect the fuel pressure hose and discard O-rings.
6. Disconnect the electrical connections for the fuel injectors, then remove the fuel pipe and discard O-rings.
7. Remove the delivery pipe retaining bolts, then remove the delivery pipe and injector assembly along with the insulators, being careful not to drop the injector assembly.
8. Remove the fuel injectors, O-rings and grommets from the delivery pipe.

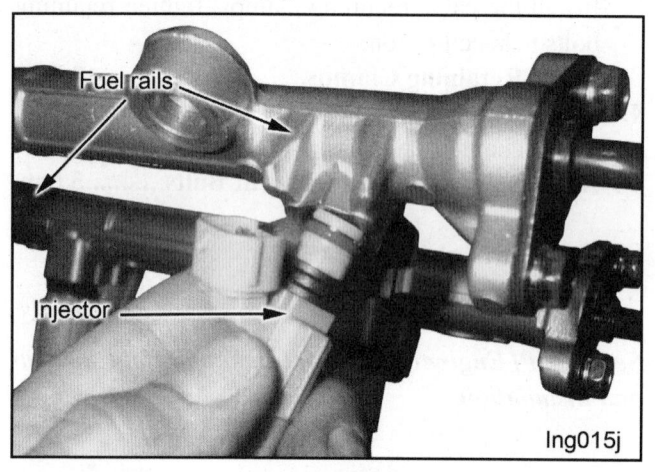

Installation

1. Install grommets and new O-rings to the injectors.
2. Coat the injector O-ring with a small amount of engine oil, then carefully install the injector to the delivery pipe and ensure injector turns smoothly.
   Note: *If injector does not turn smoothly the O-ring may be damaged.*
3. Install delivery pipe and injector assembly with insulators and tighten retaining bolts to specification.
   Fuel Rail/Delivery Pipe Bolts .... 12 Nm
4. Install the fuel pipe ensuring to use new O-rings and tighten the retaining bolts to specification.
   Fuel Pipe Retaining Bolts .... 9 Nm
5. Reconnect the injector electrical connections.
6. Install the fuel pressure hose and the fuel pressure regulator ensuring to use new O-rings and tighten retaining bolts to specification.
   Fuel Pressure Hose Retaining Bolts .... 5 Nm
   Fuel Pressure Regulator Retaining Bolts .... 9 Nm
7. To the fuel pressure regulator connect the vacuum hose and fuel return hose.
8. Install the upper intake manifold, as described in this chapter.
9. Install the air cleaner and intake hose assembly then reconnect the battery.
10. Adjust the accelerator cable as described in this chapter and inspect for any fuel leaks..

THROTTLE BODY - MPI
Removal

1. Drain the cooling system then remove the engine cover and the air cleaner assembly.
2. Disconnect the accelerator cable then from the throttle body disconnect the vacuum hose, throttle position sensor and idle speed control servo electrical connection.
3. Disconnect the water hose from the throttle body then remove the bolts securing the throttle body and remove the throttle body and gasket.

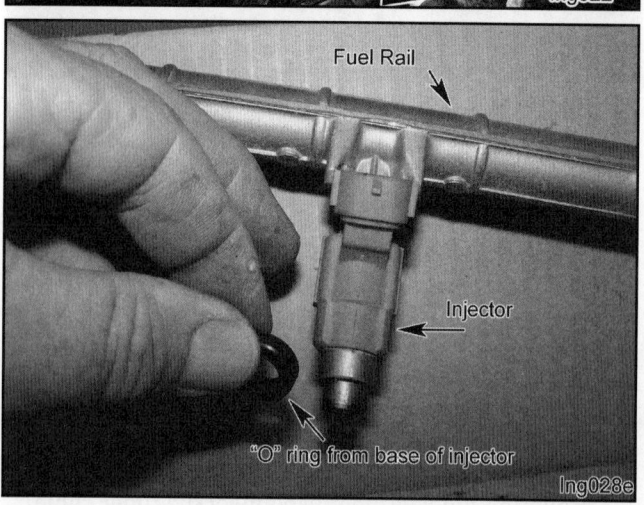

204

IGNITION, FUEL & EMISSION SYSTEMS - Petrol Models

Disassembly

Note: *Only Proceed with disassembly of the throttle body if components require replacement.*

1. Remove the bolts securing the throttle position sensor to the throttle body and remove the throttle position sensor.
2. Cruise control vehicles remove the screws securing the lever assembly and remove.
3. Remove the Idle speed control servo retaining screws and servo, discarding O-ring.
4. Remove the bolts securing the fast idle air valve to the throttle body and then remove assembly and gasket.

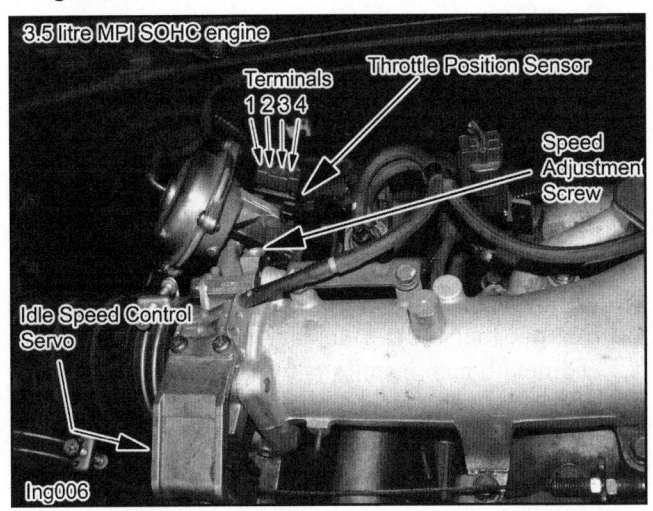

Inspection

1. Clean all throttle body components thoroughly ensuring not to use solvent on the throttle position sensor and the idle speed control servo.
2. Use compressed air to clean vacuum passage to ensure it is not blocked and is free of contaminants.

Assembly

1. Install the fast idle air valve to the throttle body using a new O-ring/gasket and tighten retaining bolts.
   Fast Idle Air Valve........................ 3.4 Nm
2. Install the idle speed control servo using a new O-ring and tighten retaining screws.
3. Cruise control vehicles install the lever assembly tightening retaining screws.
4. To the throttle body install the throttle position sensor as shown and tighten retaining screws to specification.
   Throttle Position Sensor Bolts .... 3.4 Nm
5. Connect a multimeter to terminal #4 and #3 of the connector and check to ensure resistance gradually increases as throttle valve is slowly opened.
   Note: *If not correct replace sensor.*

Installation

1. Install the throttle body using a new gasket then install and tighten retaining bolts to specification.
   Throttle Body Retaining Bolts .... 12 Nm
2. Reconnect the water hose to throttle body, then reconnect the idle speed control servo electrical connection.
3. Reconnect the throttle position sensor, vacuum hose and then reconnect the accelerator cable.
4. Install the air cleaner assembly, fill cooling system and adjust the accelerator cable as described in this chapter.

FUEL RAIL / INJECTORS - GDI

Removal

1. Discharge the Fuel system as described previously.
2. Disconnect the battery negative cable, then remove the engine cover and remove the air cleaner and intake hose assembly.
3. Remove the intake manifold, as described in this chapter.
4. Disconnect the fuel pressure sensor connector, then disconnect the electrical connections from the injectors. 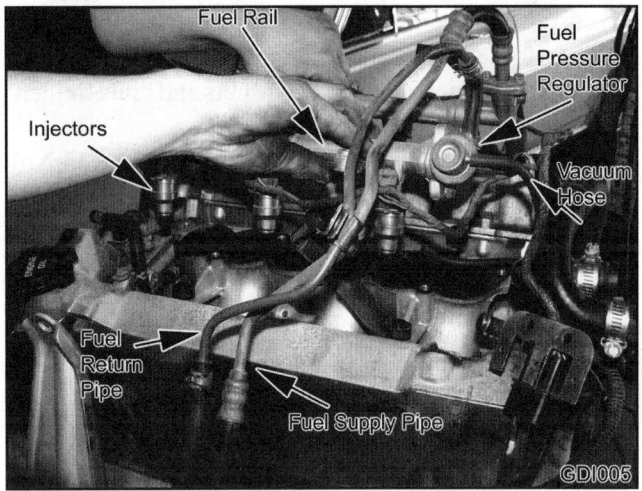
5. Remove the bolts retaining the fuel feed pipes, then remove pipes, backup rings and O-rings.
6. Mark the relation ship of the fuel pressure sensor and flange then remove the flange retaining bolts and remove fuel pressure sensor, O-ring and back-up ring.
7. Remove the injector holders, then remove the fuel rail and injector assembly along with the insulators, being careful not to drop the injector assembly.
8. Remove the fuel injectors, back-up rings and O-rings from the delivery pipe.

Installation

1. To the injectors install the back-up rings and O-rings. As shown in the following diagram.
2. Coat the corrugated washer with petroleum jelly Install the corrugated washer to the injector, ensuring to first coat the washer with petroleum jelly to prevent

205

IGNITION, FUEL & EMISSION SYSTEMS - Petrol Models

it from falling off.

3. Coat the injector O-ring with a small amount of engine oil, then carefully install the injector to the delivery pipe and ensure injector turns smoothly.
   Note: *If injector does not turn smoothly the O-ring may be damaged.*
4. Install the fuel rail spacers to the intake manifold.

5. Install the fuel rail injector assembly to the intake manifold and partially tighten retaining bolts.
6. Install the injector holders, washers and bolts tightening to specification.
   Injector Holder Bolts .... 23 Nm
7. Tighten the fuel rail assembly to specification.
   Fuel Rail/Delivery Pipe Bolts .... 12 Nm
8. To the fuel pressure sensor install the back-up ring and O-ring as shown, then coat the O-ring with clean engine oil.
9. Install the fuel pressure sensor to the delivery pipe, aligning mating marks made on removal.
10. Install the sensor retaining flange and tighten bolts to specification.
    Flange Retaining Bolts .... 23 Nm
    Note: *If sensor requires replacement, the sensor & Flange should be replaced as a set.*
11. To the fuel feed pipes install the back-up rings and O-rings.
12. Coat the O-ring with a small amount of engine oil, then squarely install the fuel feed pipes to delivery pipes and fuel pump, tightening retaining bolts to specification.
    Fuel Feed Pipe Bolts .... 19 Nm
13. Reconnect the fuel pressure sensor connector and the injector connectors.
14. Install the intake manifold, as described in this chapter.
15. Install the air cleaner and intake hose assembly then reconnect the battery.
16. Start and run the engine at 2,000rpm for at least 15 seconds to bleed air from the high-pressure fuel line.
17. Inspect for any fuel leaks then install the engine cover.

HIGH PRESSURE FUEL PUMP - GDI
Removal
1. Discharge the Fuel system as described previously.
2. Disconnect the battery negative cable, then remove the engine cover and remove the air cleaner and intake hose assembly.
3. Remove the intake manifold, as described in this chapter.
4. Disconnect the fuel return hoses from the pump assembly.
5. Remove the bolts retaining the fuel pressure hose, then remove hose and O-ring.
6. Remove the bolts retaining the fuel feed pipe, then remove pipe, backup rings and O-rings.
7. Remove the bolts securing the fuel pump assembly, then remove pump assembly and discard O-ring.

Installation
1. Coat the fuel pump roller and new O-ring with clean engine oil, then install the fuel pump to the cylinder and partially tighten mounting bolts (slightly over finger tight).
2. To the fuel feed pipe install the back-up rings and O-rings.
3. Coat the O-ring with a small amount of engine oil, then squarely install the fuel feed pipe to delivery pipe and fuel pump, tightening retaining bolts to specification.
   Fuel Feed Pipe Bolts .... 19 Nm
4. Tighten the pump mounting bolts in the order shown in two stages.
   Pump Mounting Bolts - Stage 1 .... 5 Nm
   **   - Stage 2 .... 17 Nm**
5. Coat the fuel pressure hose connection O-ring with a small amount of engine oil, then install the pressure hose to the fuel pump and ensure hose turns smoothly.
   Note: *If hose does not turn smoothly the O-ring may be damaged.*
6. Tighten pressure hose retaining bolts to specification.
   Fuel Pressure Hose Bolts .... 5 Nm
7. Connect the fuel return hoses to the pump assembly.
8. Install the intake manifold, as described in this chapter.
9. Install the air cleaner and intake hose assembly then reconnect the battery.
10. Start and run the engine at 2,000rpm for at least 15 seconds to bleed air from the high-pressure fuel

IGNITION, FUEL & EMISSION SYSTEMS - Petrol Models

line.
11. Inspect for any fuel leaks then install the engine cover.

THROTTLE BODY - DOHC - GDI
Removal
1. Drain the cooling system then remove the engine cover and the air cleaner assembly.
2. Remove the bolts securing the throttle body stay and remove stay from engine.
3. Disconnect the electrical connections from the control servo and throttle position sensor.
4. Label and disconnect the water hoses from the throttle body then remove mounting bolts and remove the throttle body and gasket.

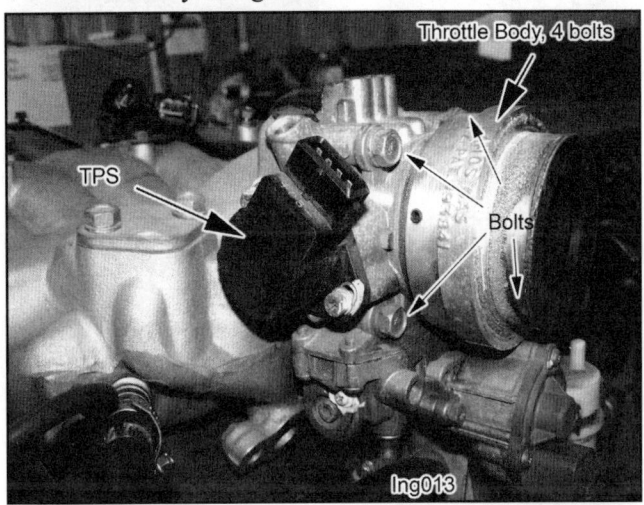

Installation
1. Install the throttle body using a new gasket then install and tighten retaining bolts to specification.
   Throttle Body Retaining Bolts .... 12 Nm
   Note: *If throttle body is replaced, initialize the electronically controlled throttle valve system by turning the ignition switch on then off (lock) within one second. Leave switched off for at least ten seconds.*
2. Reconnect the water hoses to throttle body, then reconnect the control servo and throttle position sensor electrical connections.
3. Install the throttle body stay tightening bolts to specification.
   Stay Retaining Bolts .... 18 Nm
4. Install the air cleaner assembly, then fill cooling system.

Injector Driver - GDI
Removal
1. Disconnect the negative battery terminal then disconnect the electrical harness from the injector driver.
2. Remove the nuts securing the injector driver (located near the fire wall in the engine bay rear left corner), to the mounting bracket and remove assembly.
3. If required remove mounting bracket.

Installation
1. If removed install the mounting bracket.
   Mounting Bracket Bolts .... 21 Nm
2. Install the injector driver to the mounting bracket and tighten retaining nuts to specification.
   Injector Driver Nuts .... 5 Nm
3. Connect the electrical harness to the injector driver, then reconnect the battery earth.

Engine Electronic Control Unit (ECU)
Note: *The engine ECU is located tightly between the heater and left side body panel.*

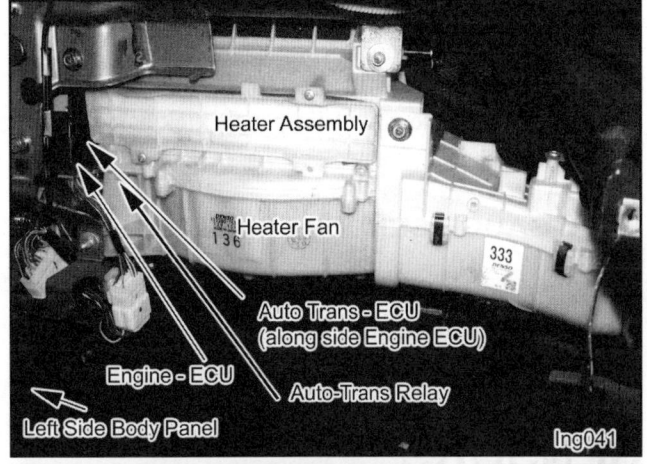

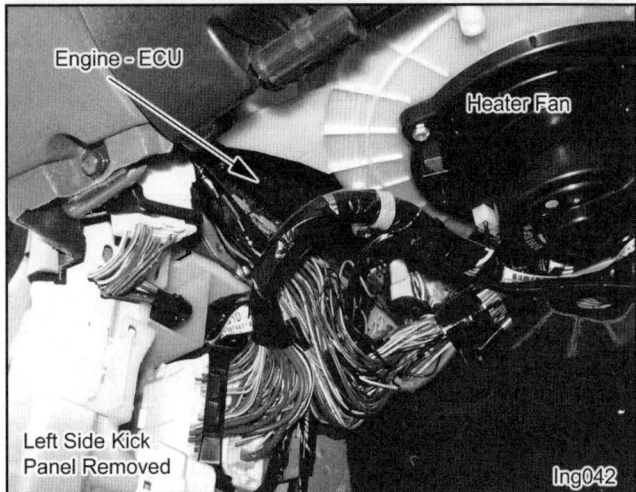

Removal
1. From the passenger side of the vehicle, remove the side cowl trim panel (kick panel).
2. Disconnect the main harness connections, then remove the auto transmission control relay.
3. Disconnect the electrical connections for the auto transmission-ECU, then remove mounting bolts and remove from vehicle.
4. Disconnect the electrical connections for the engine-ECU, then remove mounting bolts and remove ECU from vehicle.
5. If required remove the bolt securing the mounting

IGNITION, FUEL & EMISSION SYSTEMS - Petrol Models

bracket and remove bracket.

Installation
1. If removed install ECU mounting bracket and tighten bolts to specification.
   ECU Mounting Bracket Bolt .... **5 Nm**
2. Install the engine-ECU into position, tighten mounting bolts to specification and reconnect the electrical connection.
   ECU Mounting Nut .... **5 Nm**
3. Install the auto transmission-ECU into position, tighten mounting bolts to specification and reconnect the electrical connection.
   ECU Mounting Nut .... **5 Nm**
4. Install the transmission control relay, the reconnect the main harness connections.
   Auto Trans Control Relay Bolt .... **5 Nm**
5. Replace the side cowl trim panel (kick panel) to the vehicle.

FUEL GAUGE SENDER / FUEL PUMP (in tank)
Refer to fuel tank chapter for instructions on the removal and installation of the fuel pump.

SENSORS

Intake Air Temperature Sensor
* *The intake air temperature sensor is incorporated into the airflow sensor assembly.*

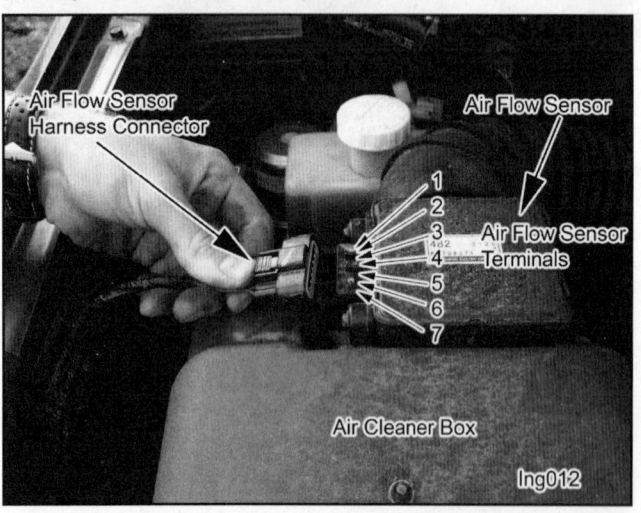

1. At the air cleaner body disconnect the air flow sensor connector.
2. At terminals #4 and #6 measure the resistance, then using a hair drier or heat gun heat the sensor and note the resistance should decrease.

Temperature °C	Resistance kOhms
20	2.30 - 3.00
80	0.30 - 0.42

Coolant Temperature Sensor
1. Drain engine coolant to a level below the inlet manifold then disconnect electrical connector and remove sensor from manifold then connect a multimeter to the sensor.
2. Immerse the sensing portion of the sensor in water then keep note of the resistance reading while heating water.

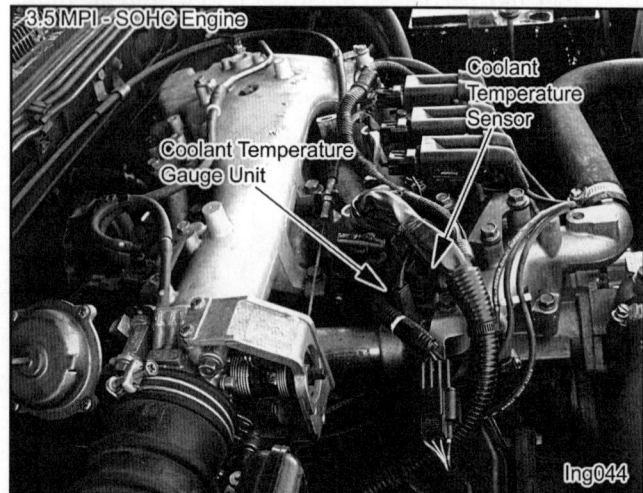

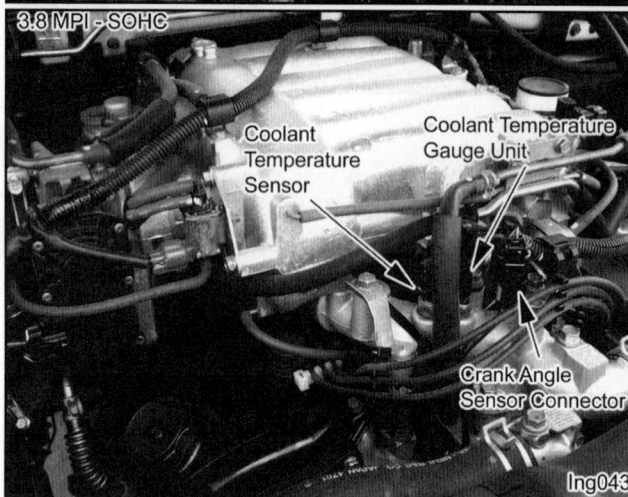

Temperature °C	Resistance kOhms
20	2.10 - 2.70
80	0.26 - 0.36

3. Reinstall the sensor using loctite 242 and tighten to specification.
   Coolant Temperature Sensor .... **29 Nm**

Throttle Position Sensor
1. At the throttle body disconnect the connector for the throttle position sensor, then between terminals #1 and #4 (MPI) or terminals #1 and #3 (GDI) measure the resistance at the throttle position sensor connector.

IGNITION, FUEL & EMISSION SYSTEMS - Petrol Models

Resistance - MPI .... 3.5 - 6.5 kOhms
              - GDI .... 0.9 - 2.5 kOhms

2. a) **MPI** - Measure resistance at the throttle position sensor connector between terminals #1 and #3.

   b) **GDI** - Measure the resistance at the throttle position sensor connector between terminals #1 and #2, and between terminals #1 and #4.

3. Slowly open the throttle valve from idle position to full open position.
4. Resistance should change smoothly in proportion with the throttle valve opening angle.
5. Replace throttle position sensor if not to specification or does not change smoothly.

Accelerator Pedal Position Sensor - GDI

1. At the top of the accelerator pedal disconnect the connector for the pedal position sensor.
2. Measure the resistance at the accelerator pedal position sensor connector between terminals #2 and #1, and between terminals #8 and #7.
   Resistance .... 3.5 - 6.5 kOhms
3. Measure the resistance at the accelerator pedal position sensor connector between terminals #2 and #3, and between terminals #8 and #6.
4. Slowly depress accelerator pedal, the resistance should change smoothly in proportion with pedal travel.
5. Replace throttle position sensor if not to specification or does not change smoothly.

Accelerator Pedal Position Switch - GDI

1. At the top of the accelerator pedal disconnect the connector for the pedal position sensor.
2. Measure the resistance at the accelerator pedal position sensor connector between terminals #4 and #5.

Pedal Position	Continuity
Depress	No Continuity
Release	Continuity

3. Replace throttle position sensor if not to specification.

Oxygen Sensor

1. Disconnect the connector for the oxygen sensor and connect test harness (MB998464) to the connector of the oxygen sensor.
2. Check continuity between terminals #1 and #3 and replace sensor if there is no continuity.

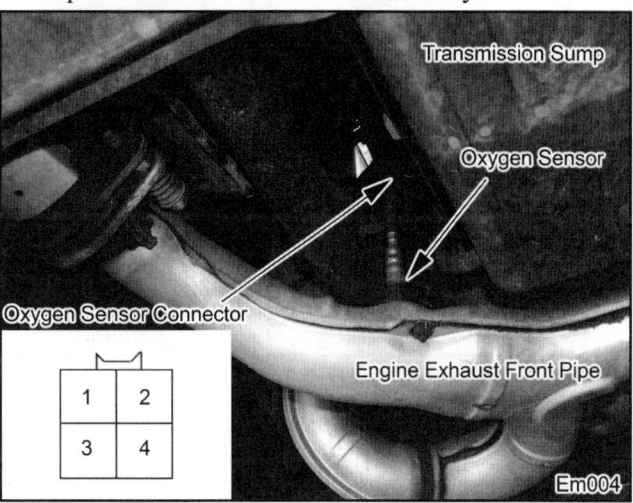

Continuity .... 4.5 - 8.0 Ohm @ 20°C

3. Start engine, warm up the engine coolant to at least 80°C.
4. To the battery positive (+) and negative (-) terminals connect the oxygen sensor terminals #1 and #3 respectively using jumper wires.
5. Across terminals #2 and #4 connect a voltmeter then repeatedly race the engine and measure the oxygen sensor output voltage.
   Engine racing .... 0.6 - 1.0 V

Control Relay
Inspection

1. Remove the control relay for the ECU or Fuel pump.
2. Check the continuity between the relay terminals.

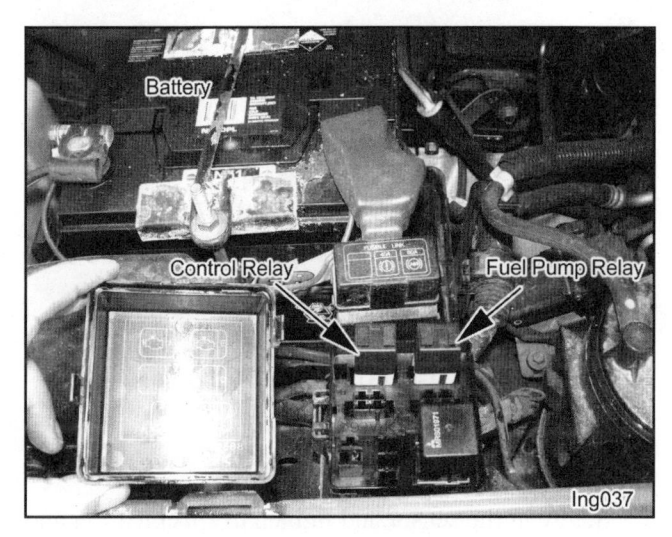

209

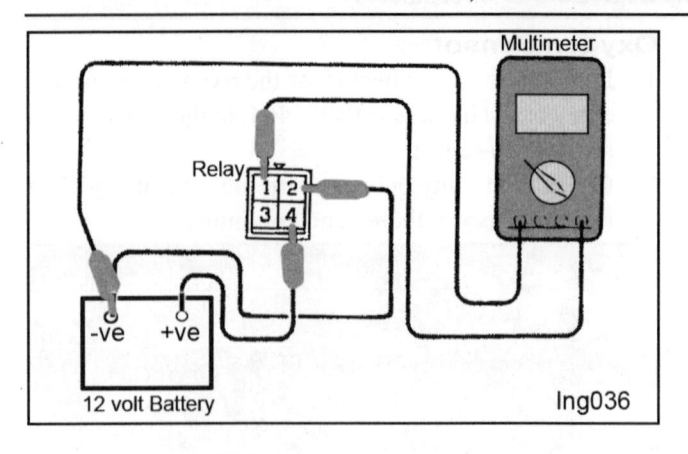

IGNITION, FUEL & EMISSION SYSTEMS - Petrol Models

Terminals	Continuity
2 - 4	Continuity
1 - 3	No Continuity

3. Connect relay terminal #4 to the (+ve) battery terminal and relay terminal #2 to the (-ve) battery terminal.
4. Connect and disconnect the connection to the relay at terminal #2 (-ve) and check the voltage readings at terminal #1 are to specification.

Jumper Wire	Voltage (terminal 1)
Connected	Battery Voltage
Disconnected	0V

5. If control relay is faulty replace.

Knock Sensor
Remove
1. Remove intake manifold and the sensor is located between the 2 cylinder banks of the block for the V6 engines. 
2. Unscrew the sensor to remove and disconnect electrical harness.

Install
1. Screw in the sensor and tighten to specification and connect electrical harness.
   Knock Sensor.. 20-25Nm

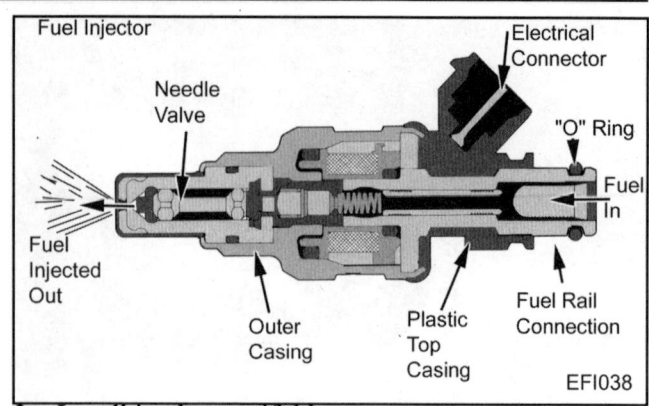

2. Install intake manifold.

Injector Check
1. Disconnect the intermediate harness connector for the injector, then measure the resistance between terminals.

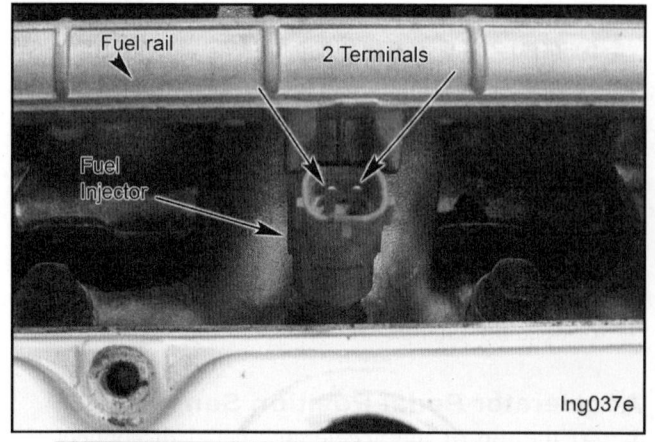

MPI Models

Injector	Terminals	Resistance @20°C
#1	8 - 3	13 - 16 Ohm
#2	5 - 2	13 - 16 Ohm
#3	8 - 1	13 - 16 Ohm
#4	8 - 7	13 - 16 Ohm
#5	8 - 6	13 - 16 Ohm
#6	8 - 5	13 - 16 Ohm

GDI Models

Injector	Terminals	Resistance @20°C
#1	11 - 12	0.9 - 1.1 Ohm
#2	5 - 6	0.9 - 1.1 Ohm
#3	9 - 10	0.9 - 1.1 Ohm
#4	3 - 4	0.9 - 1.1 Ohm
#5	7 - 8	0.9 - 1.1 Ohm
#6	1 - 2	0.9 - 1.1 Ohm

2. Reconnect intermediate harness connector.

Idle Speed Control Servo Check - MPI
(stepper motor)
Operation Sound
1. Ensure the coolant temperature is below 20°C,
2. Switch the ignition on (do not start) and check to

IGNITION, FUEL & EMISSION SYSTEMS - Petrol Models

ensure the operation sound of the stepper motor can be heard.

3. If operation sound can not be heard, check the activation circuit. If circuit is normal a fault exists with the stepper motor or ECU.

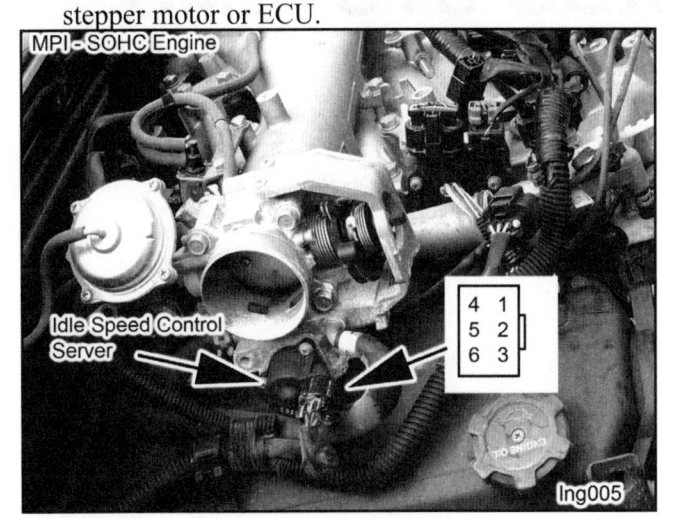

Coil Resistance Check

1. Disconnect the connector from the idle speed control servo and install test harness.
2. Measure the resistance between terminal #2 and either terminal #1 or #3.
   Resistance @ 20°C............................ 28 - 33 Ohm
3. Measure the resistance between terminal 5 and either terminal 6 or 4.
   Resistance @ 20°C............................ 28 - 33 Ohm

Operational Check

1. Remove the throttle body as described in this chapter then remove the stepper motor.
2. Install test harness to the connector of the idle speed control servo, then to the white and green clip of the test harness connect a 6V power supply.
3. As outlined in the following steps connect negative lead of power supply to test harness and check if vibration of the stepper motor activation can be felt.
   a) negative terminal to red and black clip.
   b) negative terminal to blue and black clip.
   c) negative terminal to blue and yellow clip.
   d) negative terminal to red and yellow clip.
   e) negative terminal to red and black clip.
   f) repeat steps e to a in sequence.
4. If vibration can be felt the steeper motor is operating normally.

Throttle Control Servo Check - GDI
Operation Check

1. From the throttle body remove the air intake hose, then turn the ignition to the ON position.
2. Depress the accelerator pedal and the throttle valve should open and close in proportion with the pedal movement.

Coil Resistance Check

Disconnect the throttle control servo connector, then measure the resistance between the terminals.

Terminals	Resistance @20°C
1 - 2	0.6 - 1.0 Ohm
1 - 3	0.6 - 1.0 Ohm
2 - 3	0.6 - 1.0 Ohm

Catalyst Temperature Sensor Check - GDI

1. Disconnect the connector for the catalyst temperature sensor, then measure the resistance between terminals.
   Resistance .... 1MOhm @ 20°C
   Note: *Resistance will be approximately 77kOhm when catalyst surface temperature is 400°C.*
2. If sensor is not within specification replace sensor.

Tachometer Connection

1. Insert a wire or paper clip into the No3 terminal of the Engine RPM harness connector
2. Connect a tachometer to the wire or paper clip.
3. Read the rpm of the engine shown on the tachometer.

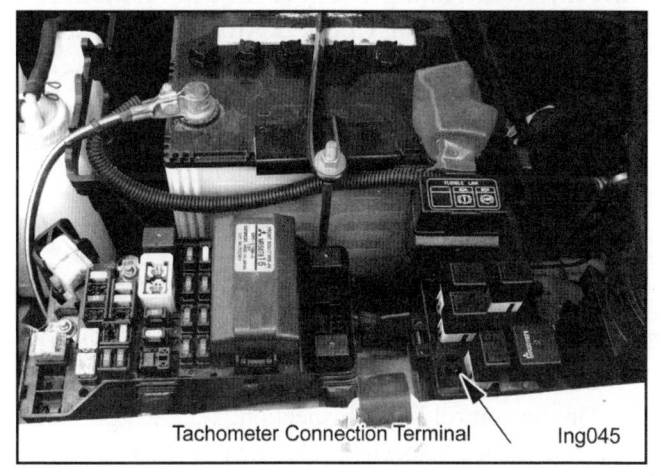

211

DIESEL FUEL, GLOW PLUGS, EMISSION & TURBO SYSTEMS

Description	Page
ON VEHICLE INSPECTION	**213**
Accelerator Cable Adjustment - 4M40	213
Engine Idle Speed Check & Adjust - 4M40	213
Engine Idle Speed Inspection - 4M41	214
Fuel Injection Timing Check & Adjust - 4M40	214
Fuel Injection Timing Check & Adjust - 4M41	215
Fuel Filter Water Evacuation	216
Fuel Line Air Evacuation	216
Fuel Injection Pump Inspection - 4M40	216
Fuel Cut Solenoid Valve Operation	216
Fuel Cut Solenoid Valve Coil Resistance	216
Boost Compensator Check	216
Fuel Injection Pump Inspection - 4M41	216
Fuel Cut Solenoid Valve - 4M41	216
Operation	216
Coil Resistance Inspection	217
Timing control Valve Inspection	217
GE Actuator Inspection (electric governor)	217
Fuel Temperature Sensor Inspection	217
Control Sleeve Position Sensor Inspection	217
Timer Piston Position Sensor Inspection	217
Engine Speed Sensor Inspection (main)	217
Engine Speed Sensor Inspection (backup)	218
Intake Air Restriction Equipment Check-4M41	218
Main/Sub throttle solenoid valve operation	218
Main/Sub throttle solenoid valve resistance	218
GLOW SYSTEM	**218**
Self-Regulating Glow System Inspection	218
Glow Plug Relay Inspection	218
Glow Plug Inspection	219
Glow Plug	219
Removal	219
Installation	219

Description	Page
DIESEL FUEL SYSTEM	**220**
Fuel Discharge Prevention	220
Accelerator Cable - 4M40	220
Removal	220
Installation	220
Accelerator Pedal Position Sensor - 4M41	221
Adjustment	221
Accelerator Pedal Position Switch - 4M41	221
Coolant Temperature Sensor	221
4M40	221
4M41	222
Intake Air Temp. Sensor Inspection - 4M41	222
Intercooler	222
Removal	222
Inspection	222
Installation	222
Fuel Injector Pressure Check	223
Injector Pump & Nozzle - 4M40	223
Removal	223
Installation	224
Injection Nozzle - 4M40	225
Disassembly	225
Inspection	225
Assembly	225
Injection Pump - 4M40	225
Disassembly	225
Assembly	225
Injection Nozzle - 4M41	225
Removal	225
Disassembly	225
Assembly	226
Installation	226
Injection Pump - 4M41	226
Removal	226
Disassembly	227

DIESEL FUEL, GLOW PLUGS, EMISSION & TURBO SYSTEMS - Diesel Models

Description	Page
Injection Pump - 4M41 Con'td	227
Assembly	227
Installation	227
Injection Pump - 4M41 (common Rail)	227
Removal	227
Installation	228
Electronic Control Unit	228
Removal	228
Installation	228
Fuel Gauge Sender/Fuel Pump	228
EMISSION SYSTEM	**229**
Vacuum Circuit Inspection	229
EGR System Inspection	229
4M40	229
4M41	229
EGR Solenoid Valve	229
Operation Inspection	229
Valve Resistance Inspection	229
Lever Position Sensor Adjustment - 4M40	229
Engine Speed Sensor Inspection - 4M40	229
Solenoid Timer Inspection - 4M40	229
EGR Vavle Inspection - 4M41	230
Catalytic Converter	230
TURBO CHARGER	**231**
General Description	231
Turbocharger Operation	231
Waste Gate Operation	231
General Information	231
Waste Gate Actuator Inspection	231
Turbo Charger - 4M40	232
Removal	232
Disassembly	232
Clean/Inspection	232
Assembly	232
Installation	232
Turbo Charger - 4M41	232
Removal	232
Disassembly	232
Clean/Inspection	233
Assembly	233
Installation	233
TurboCharger On Vehicle Inspection	233
Rotor Shaft	233
Turbine Wheel	234
Compressor Wheel	234
Waste Gate Valve	234
Turbo Charger Problem Diagnosis	234

ON VEHICLE INSPECTION

Fuel Filter and Bleeding Fuel System
See under Engine Tune-up and Maintenance

Combustion Firing Order
The combustion order of both diesel engines is as listed.
4M4 1-2-3-4

Accelerator Cable Adjustment - 4M40
1. Ensure the A/C and all lights and lamps are off so that there is no electrical load.
2. Warm the engine until it reaches normal operating temperature, check the engine idle speed specification.
   Engine Idle Speed .... 750 +/- 100 rpm.
3. Switch off ignition then inspect accelerator cable to ensure there are no sharp bends in the cable and the inner cable play is within specification.
   Inner Cable Play .... 1-2 mm

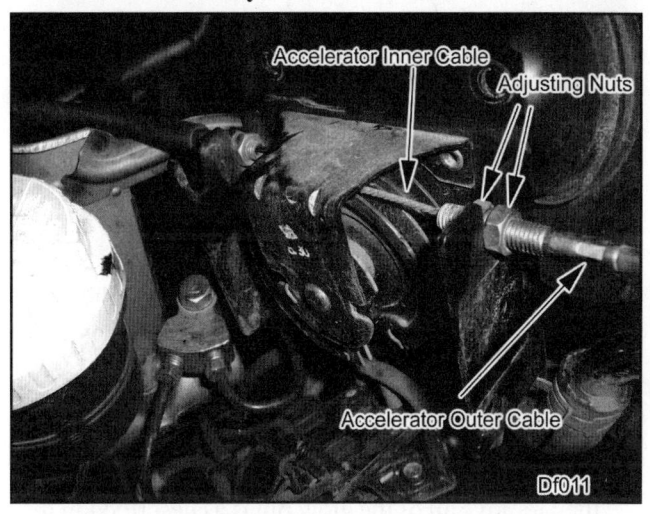

4. If inner cable play is not within specification adjust.
   a) Loosen the lock nut and fully close throttle lever.
   b) Tighten the adjusting nut until just before the throttle lever starts to move.
   c) Loosen adjusting nut one turn, this should bring cable play to within specification, then tighten lock nut.
      Adjustment Bolts .... 12 Nm
5. Ensure the throttle lever is touching the stopper.

Engine Idle Speed Check & Adjust - 4M40
1. Check to ensure injection timing is correct before checking idle speed.
2. Ensure engine is at normal operating temperature, transaxle is in neutral (manual) or park (auto) and all lighting and accessories are off.

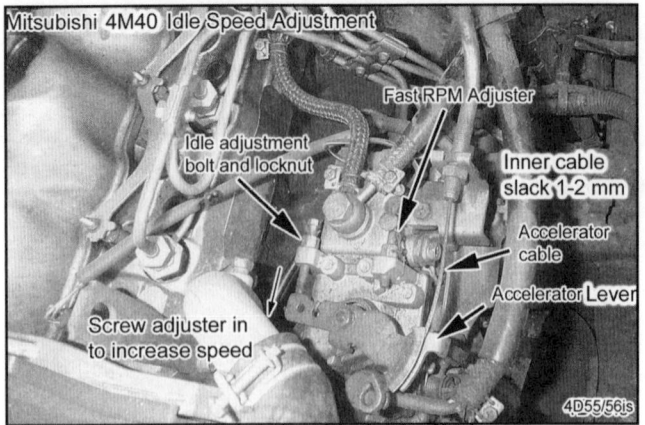

DIESEL FUEL, GLOW PLUGS, EMISSION & TURBO SYSTEMS - Diesel Models

3. Ensure the ignition is switched off, then connect an engine tachometer to the injection nozzle.
4. Start engine and check idle speed.
   Idle Speed .... 750 +/- 100 rpm
5. If idle speed is not within specification loosen the idle adjusting screw lock nut, adjust idle speed to specification and tighten lock nut.

Engine Idle Speed Inspection - 4M41
Idle speed is set by the engine-ECU and cannot be manually adjusted.

1. Ensure engine is at normal operating temperature, transaxle is in neutral (manual) or park (auto) and all lighting and accessories are off.
2. Ensure the ignition is switched to Lock (off), then connect a engine tachometer to the injection nozzle.
3. Start engine and check idle speed.
   Idle Speed .... 750 +/- 20rpm
4. If idle speed is not within specification indicates a fault with the electronically controlled fuel injection system.

Fuel Injection Timing Check & Adjust-4M40

1. Have the engine at normal operating temperature then remove all of the glow plugs as described in this chapter.
2. Set the #1 cylinder to compression top dead centre by aligning the notch of the crankshaft pulley with '0' timing mark. (do <u>not</u> turn crankshaft in anti-clockwise direction)
   Note: *Compression top dead centre is set if the camshaft cam marker (cast knob on camshaft near lobe) is positioned as shown (visible through oil filler hole with cap removed).*
3. Check to ensure the pushrod in the prestroke measuring adapter is protruding by 12mm, then push dial gauge onto adaptor until its needle starts to move then secure with screw.
4. From the injection pump remove the timing check plug and gasket then install the prestroke measuring adapter assembly and hold at a position where the gauge needle starts to move.

5. Turn the crankshaft in a clockwise direction to set #1 cylinder approximately 30° before CTDC.

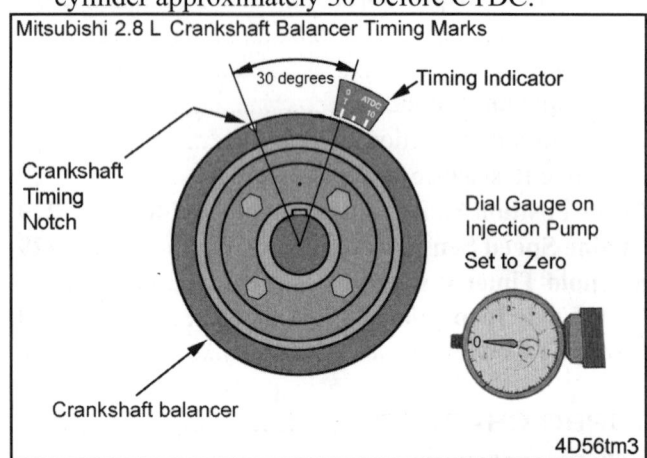

6. Set the dial gauge needle to 0 and check to ensure the needle does not move if the crankshaft is turn slightly in either direction (2 - 3°).

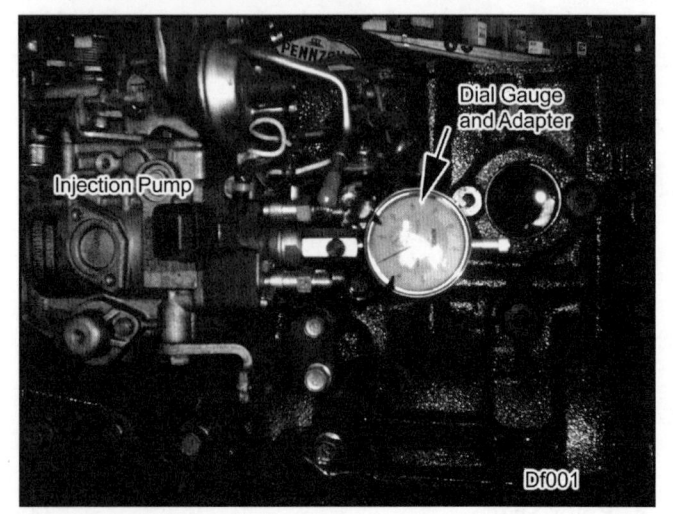

7. Turn crankshaft clockwise to align crankshaft notch to specifications below and check to ensure the dial gauge reading is to specification.
   Turbo with EGR Valve .... 9° ATDC
   Turbo without EGR Valve .... 12° ATDC
   Standard Value Lift on Dial Gauge ....
   .... 1 +/- 0.03 mm

214

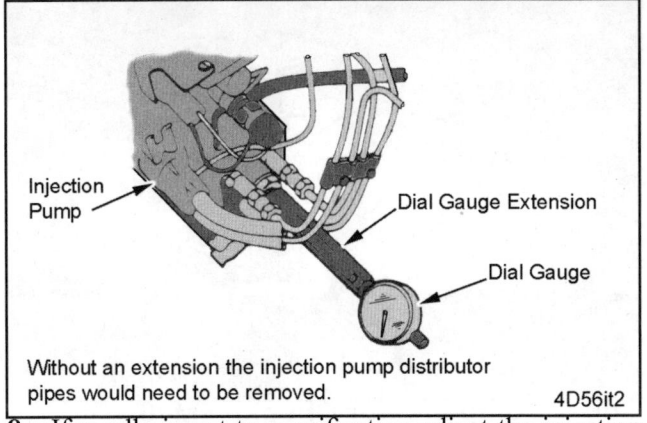

DIESEL FUEL, GLOW PLUGS, EMISSION & TURBO SYSTEMS - Diesel Models

Without an extension the injection pump distributor pipes would need to be removed. 4D56it2

8. If needle is not to specification adjust the injection timing as follows.
   a) Loosen the injection pipe nuts and then loosen the injection pump bolts and nuts.
   Note: *Do not remove bolts and nuts.*
   b) Tilt the pump assembly left and right and adjust gauge needle so display value is uniform.
   c) Tighten the injection pump mounting bolts and nuts, then check adjustment has been made by repeating steps 5 to 7.
   d) Once adjustment has correctly been made, tighten the pump mounting bolts and nuts.
   e) Using two spanners tighten the injection pipe nuts to specification.
   Inject Pipe Nuts........................ 13Nm
9. Remove the pre-stroke measuring adaptor assembly then install the timing check plug using a new gasket.
   Timing Check Plug .... 17 Nm
10. Install the glow plugs as described in this chapter.

Fuel Injection Timing Check & Adjust - 4M41

1. Have the engine at normal operating temperature then remove all of the glow plugs as described in this chapter.
2. Remove the #1 cylinder delivery valve and gasket (with CPV).
3. Install gasket and delivery valve (without CPV) to pump and tighten to specification.
   Delivery Valve............................. 49 Nm
4. Install an old auxiliary injection pipe to the valve and shape pipe as shown.
5. Turn the crankshaft clockwise using an appropriate tool to set the #1 cylinder to compression top dead centre by aligning the notch of the crankshaft pulley with '0' timing mark.
   Note: *Compression top dead centre is set if the camshaft cam lobe is positioned as shown (oil filler cap removed).*

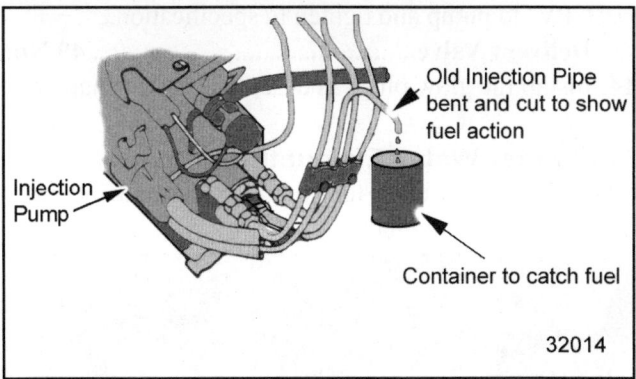

Old Injection Pipe bent and cut to show fuel action
Container to catch fuel 32014

6. Turn the crankshaft in a clockwise direction to set #1 cylinder 30° BTDC of compression stroke.

Camshaft TDC No1 Cylinder Markers - Visable through oil filler cap. 32013

7. Turn the ignition switch to lock (off) position and connect the MUT-II diagnostic tester.
8. Turn ignition switch on and perform the actuator test on MUT-II.
9. Operate the fuel filter hand pump to supply fuel and turn engine clockwise allowing fuel to flow through injection pipe.
10. If fuel flow decreases turn engine slower and stop when fuel flow stops. During this condition check fuel injection timing.
    Injection Timing........................ 4°BTDC
11. If not to specification adjust the injection timing as follows.
    a) Loosen the injection pipe nuts and then loosen the injection pump bolts and nuts.
    Note: *Do not remove bolts and nuts.*
    b) Tilt the pump assembly left or right adjust.
    c) Tighten the injection pump mounting bolts and nuts, then check adjustment has been made by repeating steps 8 to 10.
    d) Once adjustment has correctly been made, tighten the pump mounting bolts and nuts.
    e) Using two spanners tighten the injection pipe nuts to specification.
    Inject Pipe Nuts........................ 13Nm
12. Remove the delivery valve and gasket (without CPV).
13. Using a new gasket install the delivery valve (with

DIESEL FUEL, GLOW PLUGS, EMISSION & TURBO SYSTEMS - Diesel Models

CPV) to pump and tighten to specification.
Delivery Valve.. 49 Nm
14. Install the glow plugs as described in this chapter.

Fuel Filter Water Evacuation
* The illumination of the fuel filter warning lamp indicates there is water in the fuel filter.

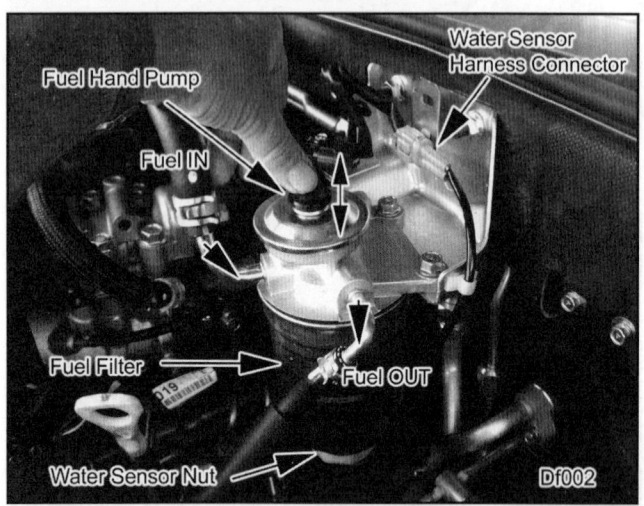

Evacuation
Loosen the water level sensor, pump water from fuel pump using hand pump, then tighten water level sensor to specification.
Water Level Sensor .... 2.5 Nm

Fuel Filter Cartridge Replacement
* Refer to fuel tank and pump chapter.

Fuel Line Air Evacuation
* If any procedure is carried out which allows air to enter the fuel system perform the following procedure.

Procedure
Loosen the air plug on the fuel filter. Cover the air bleed plug with a cloth, then repeatedly pump the hand pump until no bubbles are present. Tighten air plug to specification.
Fuel Filter Air Plug .... 6 Nm
Repeat until operation of the hand pump becomes stiff.

FUEL INJECTION PUMP INSPECTION-M40
Fuel Cut Solenoid Valve Operation-4M40
Using a sound scope, check to ensure the fuel cut solenoid valve is operating when ignition switch is turned to ON.

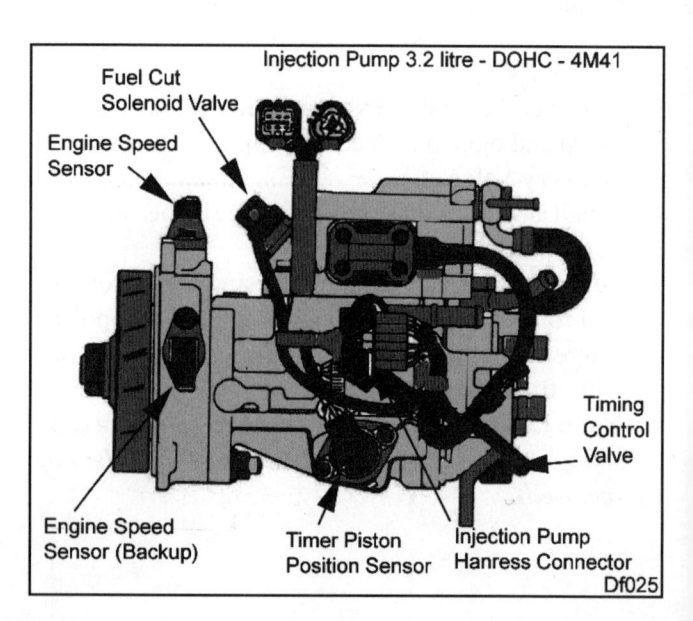

Fuel Cut Solenoid Valve Coil Resistance-4M40
Measure the resistance between terminals #1 and #5 of the fuel cut solenoid valve.
Standard Resistance................................. 8 - 10 Ohms

Boost Compensator Check - 4M40
Remove the hose from the nipple of the boost compensator connect a hand pump and apply a pressure of 30 kPA checking to ensure pressure is maintained.

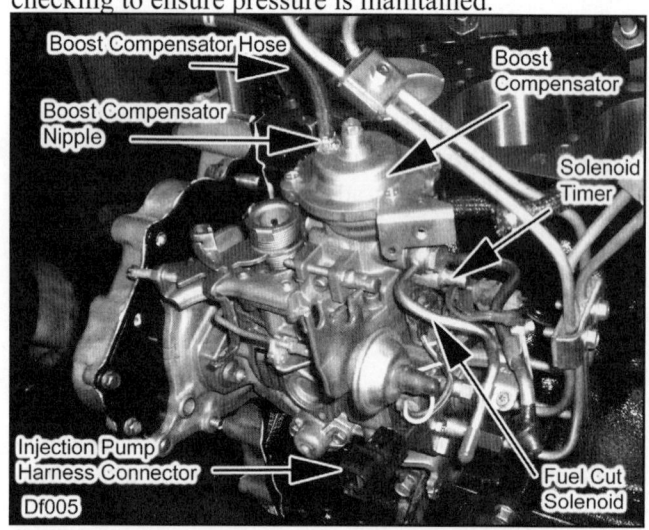

FUEL INJECTION PUMP INSPECTION
FUEL CUT SOLENOID VALVE - 3.2 - 4M41
Operation
Using a sound scope, check to ensure the fuel cut solenoid valve is operating when ignition switch is turned to ON.

216

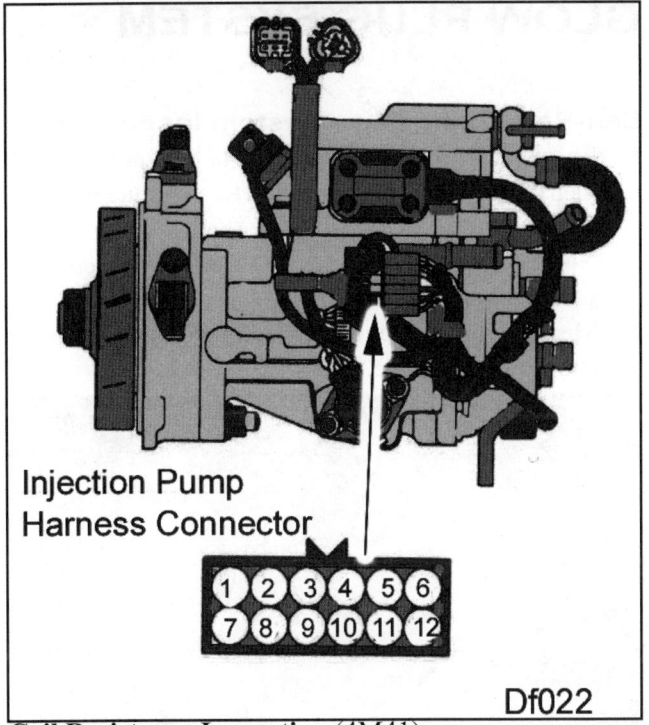

DIESEL FUEL, GLOW PLUGS, EMISSION & TURBO SYSTEMS - Diesel Models

Injection Pump Harness Connector

Df022

Coil Resistance Inspection (4M41)
Disconnect injection pump connector then measure the resistance between terminal #1 and the injection pump body.
Standard Resistance..............................6.8 - 9.2 Ohm

Timing Control Valve Inspection (4M41)
Disconnect injection pump connector then measure the resistance between terminals #5 and #9.
Standard Resistance............................10.8 - 11.2 Ohm

GE Actuator Inspection (electric governor) (4M41)
Disconnect injection pump connector then measure the resistance between terminals #6 and #10.
Standard Resistance............................0.64 - 0.72 Ohm

Fuel Temperature Sensor Inspection (4M41)
Disconnect injection pump connector then measure the resistance between terminals #7 and #11.
Standard Resistance..............................1.4 - 2.6 Ohm

Control Sleeve Position Sensor Inspection (4M41)
Disconnect injection pump connector then measure the resistance between terminals as follows.

Terminals	Resistance
4 and 12	10.8 - 11.2 Ohm
4 and 8	5.6 - 6.2 Ohm
8 and 12	5.6 - 6.2 Ohm

Timer Piston Position Sensor Inspection (4M41)
Disconnect the connector for the timer piston position sensor, then measure the resistance between the following terminals.

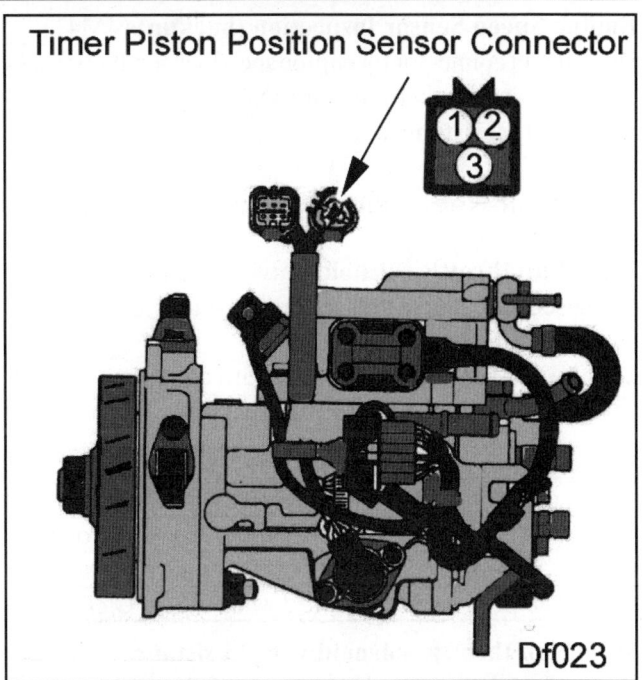

Timer Piston Position Sensor Connector

Df023

Terminals	Resistance
1 and 2	160 - 168 Ohm
1 and 3	80 - 84 Ohm
2 and 3	80 - 84 Ohm

Engine Speed Sensor Inspection (main) (4M41)
Disconnect connector for engine speed sensor, then measure the resistance between terminals #2 and #3.
Standard Resistance..................................2.15 kOhm

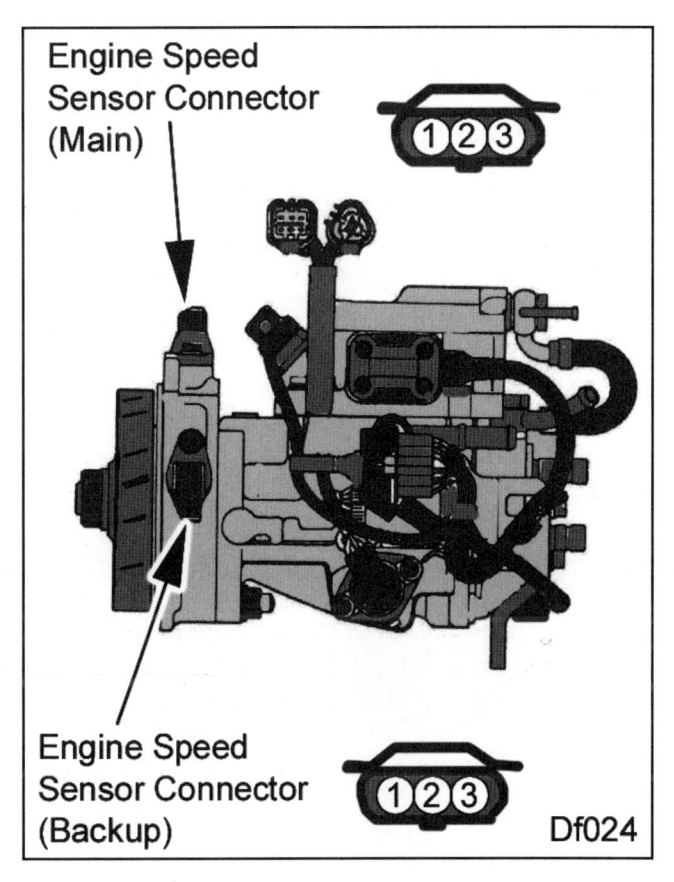

Engine Speed Sensor Connector (Main)

Engine Speed Sensor Connector (Backup)

Df024

217

DIESEL FUEL, GLOW PLUGS, EMISSION & TURBO SYSTEMS - Diesel Models

Engine Speed Sensor Inspection (backup) (4M41)
Disconnect connector for engine speed sensor, then measure the resistance between terminals #2 and #3.
Standard Resistance..................................2.15 kOhm

Intake Air Restriction Equipment Check- 4M41
Main/Sub throttle solenoid valve operation
1. Disconnect the main/sub throttle solenoid valve connector and vacuum hose.
2. Using a hand pump apply negative pressure to each nipple of the solenoid valve assembly.

System Voltage	Condition
current supplied	Leak negative pressure
(negative pressure maintained when nipple A closed)	
Cold	Leak negative pressure
(negative pressure maintained when nipple C closed)	

Main/Sub throttle solenoid valve resistance
Disconnect the intermediate harness connector for main/sub throttle solenoid valve, then measure the coil resistance.

Valve	Terminal	Resistance
Main	2 and 6	36 - 44 Ohm
Sub	1 and 5	36 - 44 Ohm

GLOW PLUG SYSTEM

Self-Regulating Glow System Inspection
1. Ensure that the battery voltage is between 11-13V, then check to ensure the coolant temperature is below 40°C.
   Note: *If coolant temperature is to high disconnect sensor electrical connection.*
2. Measure the resistance between the glow plug body and glow plug plate.

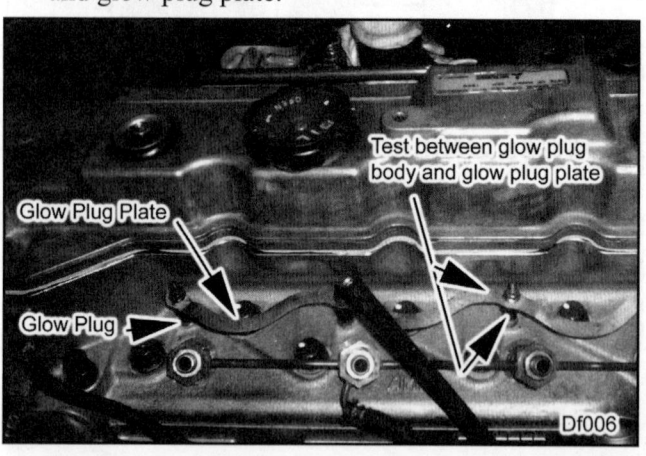

Resistance @ 20°C........................0.05 - 0.07 Ohm

3. Between the glow plug plate and glow plug body connect a voltmeter.
4. Turn ignition switch to ON position (do not start) and immediately measure the voltage. Also check to ensure the indicator lamp illuminates.
   Standard Voltage..9-11 V
   Note: *After 8 seconds voltage drops to 0V.*
5. While cranking the engine measure the voltage.
   Cranking Voltage .... 6V or more
6. Start engine and while engine is warming up measure the voltage.
   Standard Voltage..12 - 15 V
   Note: *If engine coolant temperature reaches 60°C or 180 seconds has passed the voltage reading will return to 0V.*

Glow Plug Relay Inspection
Glow plug relay on side of engine bay near engine bay fuse box
1. Check there is continuity between terminal #1 of the glow plug relay and the bracket (earth).
   Approximately.. 20 Ohms
2. Disconnect the harnesses connected to terminals #2 and #3 of the glow plug relay.
3. Connect terminal 1 of the relay to battery positive terminal and the bracket to the battery negative terminal using jumper cables.
   Note: *If incorrect terminals are connected it will result in damage to the relay.*

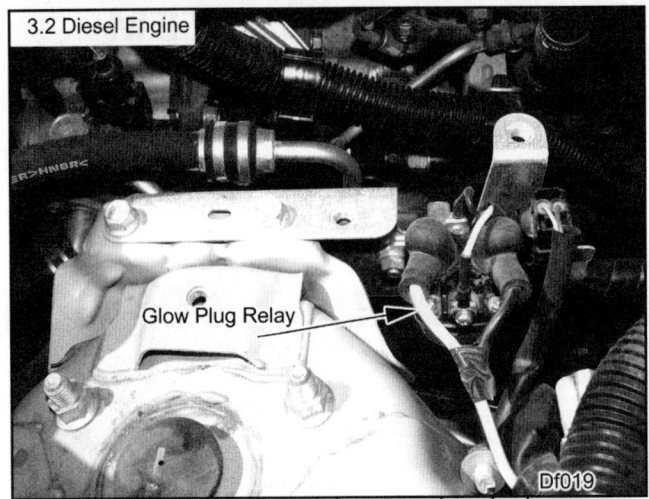

DIESEL FUEL, GLOW PLUGS, EMISSION & TURBO SYSTEMS - Diesel Models

3.2 Diesel Engine

4. While disconnecting and connecting the jumper cable at the battery positive (+) terminal measure the continuity between terminals #2 and #3 of the glow plug relay.

Jumper (+) Cable	Continuity b/w 2 - 3
Connected	0.01 Ohm or less
Disconnected	No continuity

Glow Plug Inspection

1. Remove the glow plug plate, refer to glow plug removal.

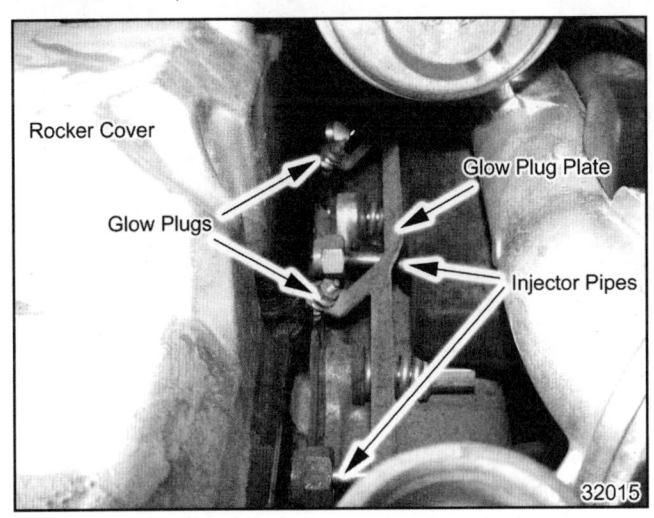

2. Measure the resistance between the glow plug terminals and body.

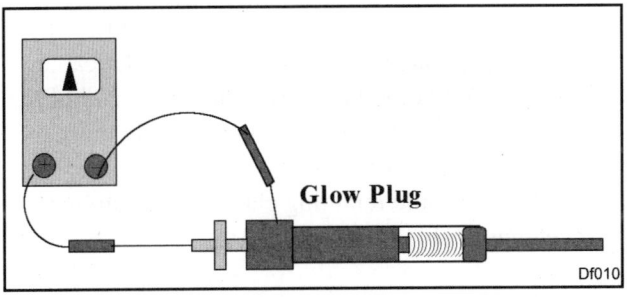

4M40 .... 0.6 Ohm @ 20°C
4M41 .... 1.1 Ohm @ 20°C

3. Apply 12 volts to glow plug and check if the glow plug tip becomes red hot within 15 seconds, if not replace glow plug.

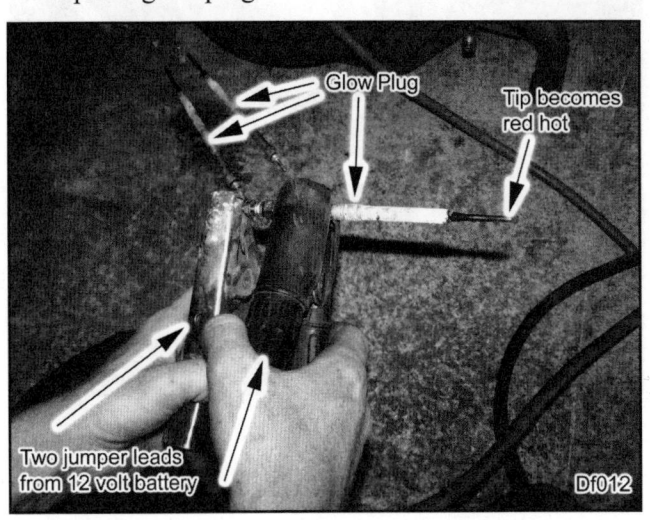

Glow Plug
Removal

1. Remove the intercooler from the vehicle, refer to engine chapter for assistance.
2. Remove the EGR pipe from the vehicle, not really required but will make it easier.
3. Disconnect the glow plug connectors by removing the retaining nuts. 
4. Remove the glow plug plate then unscrew and remove the glow plugs.

Installation

1. Install glow plugs tightening to specification, then install the glow plug plate.
   Glow Plug .... **18 Nm**
2. Connect the glow plug connectors then tighten the retaining nuts to specification.
   Glow Plug Connector Nut .... **1.8 Nm**
3. Install the EGR pipe to the vehicle, refer to engine chapter for assistance.
4. Install the intercooler to the vehicle, refer to engine chapter for assistance.

219

DIESEL FUEL, GLOW PLUGS, EMISSION & TURBO SYSTEMS - Diesel Models

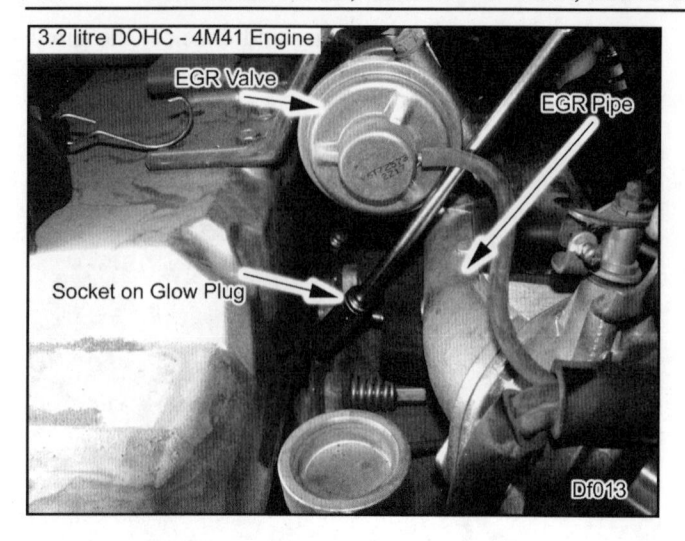

DIESEL FUEL SYSTEM

Fuel Pressure Discharge

1. Disconnect the Suction Control Valve relay located in the engine bay.

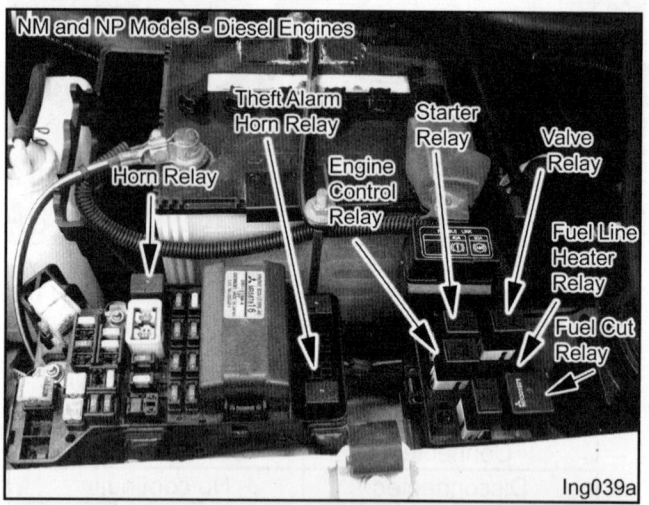

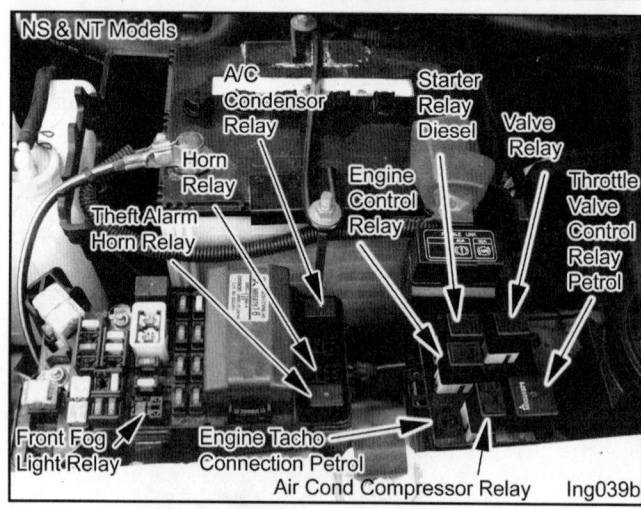

2. Start the engine and allow to run until it stops (cuts out).
3. Turn off the ignition switch and reconnect the fuel pump connector.

Accelerator Cable - 4M40 only
Removal
1. At the injection pump remove the accelerator cable mounting bracket then disconnect the inner cable.
2. Remove the two bolts securing the pedal end of the accelerator cable then disconnect the accelerator cable from the accelerator pedal.
3. Remove the cable retaining clamps then remove the accelerator cable from vehicle.

Installation
1. Install the accelerator cable to the vehicle, reconnect cable to pedal and tighten cable bracket retaining

220

DIESEL FUEL, GLOW PLUGS, EMISSION & TURBO SYSTEMS - Diesel Models

bolts.
Cable Bracket Mount .... 5 Nm
2. Reconnect the accelerator cable to the injection pump and install mounting bracket and adjustment bolts.
3. Install the cable retaining clamps, tighten retaining bolts to specification.
Cable Retaining Clamps............................ 12 Nm
4. Adjust the accelerator cable so there is 1-2 mm of inner cable slackness as described previously in this chapter.
Accelerator Cable Adjustment Bolts........... 5 Nm

Accelerator Pedal Sensor - 4M41

Adjustment
Note: *Pedal is set in factory during manufacture, only adjust if pedal has been damaged.*
1. Remove accelerator pedal assembly from vehicle.
2. Use a MUT-II tester if possible. However if a tester is not available, connect a voltmeter between terminals 3 of the harness connector and terminal 3 of the accelerator pedal terminal.
3. The accelerator pedal lever has a stopper at the top of the lever. Make sure the top of the lever is against the stopper
Turn the ignition switch ON but do not start engine, check the voltmeter for specified voltage.

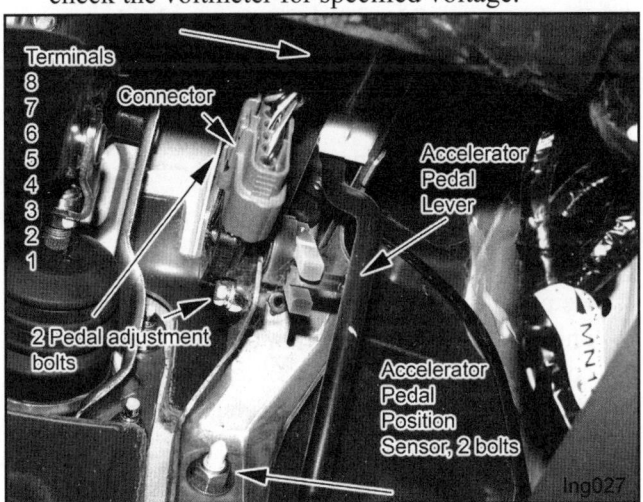

Accelerator Pedal Position Sensor Voltage
...0.0985 - 1.085 volts

4. If Loosen the 2 adjustment bolts, adjust the sensor to achieve the specified voltage with the lever against the stopper.
5. Tighten the 2 adjustment bolts, and install accelerator pedal assembly to vehicle.

Accelerator Pedal Sensor Check
Note: *Pedal is set in factory during manufacture, only adjust if pedal has been damaged.*
1. Disconnect the accelerator pedal connector.
2. Connect a multimeter between terminals 1 and 2 of the accelerator pedal terminals, check for specified resistance. If not replace the sensor.
Accelerator Pedal Position Resistance
...3.5 - 6.5 kOhms
3. Connect a multimeter between terminals 8 and 7 of the accelerator pedal terminals, check for specified resistance. If not replace the sensor.
Accelerator Pedal Position Resistance
...3.5 - 6.5 kOhms
4. a) Connect a multimeter between terminals 2 and 3 of the accelerator pedal terminals, depress the accelerator pedal, the resistance should change smoothly as the accelerator pedal is depressed. If not replace the sensor.
   b) Connect a multimeter between terminals 8 and 6 of the accelerator pedal terminals, depress the accelerator pedal, the resistance should change smoothly as the accelerator pedal is depressed. If not replace the sensor.

Accelerator Pedal Position Switch Check
Note: *Pedal is set in factory during manufacture, only adjust if pedal has been damaged.*
1. Disconnect the accelerator pedal connector.
2. Connect a multimeter between terminals 4 and 5 of the accelerator pedal terminals, check for specified continuity as in chart.
If not replace the sensor.

Released pedal	Continuity
Depressed pedal	No continuity
Released pedal	Continuity

Coolant Temp Sensor Inspection - 4M40
1. Drain engine coolant to a level below the inlet manifold then disconnect electrical connector and remove sensor from manifold then connect a multimeter to the sensor.
2. Immerse the sensing portion of the sensor in water

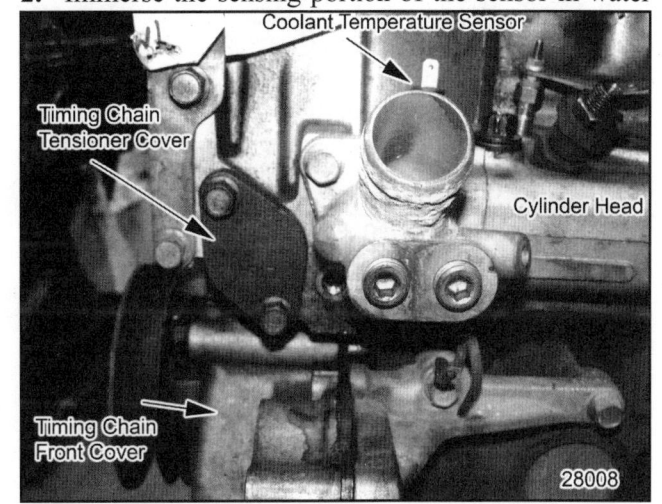

DIESEL FUEL, GLOW PLUGS, EMISSION & TURBO SYSTEMS - Diesel Models

then keep note of the resistance reading while heating water.

Temperature °C	Resistance kOhms
0	7.7 - 9.5
20	2.9 - 3.6
40	1.3 - 1.7
80	0.26 - 0.35

3. Reinstall the sensor using loctite 242 and tighten to specification.
   Coolant Temperature Sensor .... 30 Nm

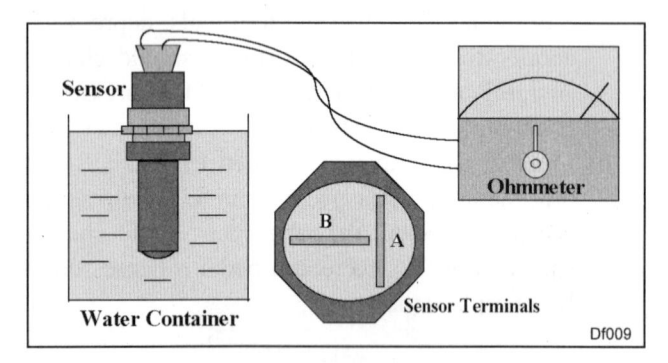

Coolant Temp Sensor Inspection - 4M41

1. Drain engine coolant to a level below the inlet manifold then disconnect electrical connector and remove sensor from manifold then connect a multimeter to the sensor.

2. Immerse the sensing portion of the sensor in water then keep note of the resistance reading while heating water.

Temperature °C	Resistance kOhms
20	2.3 - 2.6
80	0.30 - 0.34

3. Reinstall the sensor using loctite 242 and tighten to specification.
   Coolant Temperature Sensor .... 40 Nm

Intake Air Temp. Sensor Inspection - 4M41
(boost air temp sensor)

1. Remove the boost air temperature sensor.

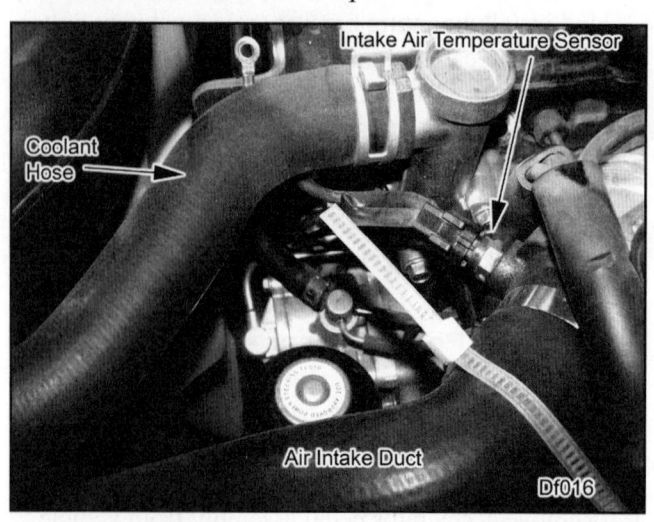

2. Measure the resistance of the sensor at the connector terminals.

Temperature °C	Resistance kOhms
20	2.3 - 2.9
80	0.30 - 0.39

3. Measure the resistance of the sensor as sensor is being warmed using a hair dryer or heat gun. The resistance should decrease as the sensor is heated up.
4. Replace sensor if sensor is not to specification or does not change at all.
5. Install sensor using a new gasket and tighten to specification.
   Boost Air Temp Sensor .... 15 Nm

Intercooler
Removal

1. Remove the air cleaner assembly, then from the underside of the vehicle remove the skid plate and covers.
2. Remove the radiator shroud, refer to cooling chapter if required.
3. Disconnect the air hoses from the intercooler.
4. Remove intercooler retaining bolts and remove intercooler from vehicle.
5. If required remove the bolts retaining the deflector plate to the intercooler assembly.

Inspection

1. Inspect intercooler fins for damage and foreign material.
2. Inspect intercooler air hoses for cracks, damage or wear, replace if required.

Installation

1. If removed, install the deflector plate to the intercooler

DIESEL FUEL, GLOW PLUGS, EMISSION & TURBO SYSTEMS - Diesel Models

assembly and tighten retaining bolts to specification.
Deflector Plate Bolts.................................. 12 Nm
2. Install intercooler into position and tighten retaining bolts to specification.
Intercooler Bolts.. 12 Nm
3. Reconnect the intercooler air hoses, tightening clamps to specification.
Air Hose Clamps.. 6 Nm
Air Pipe Retaining Bolt .... 9 Nm
4. Install the radiator shroud, refer to cooling chapter if required.
5. Install the air cleaner assembly, then install the skid plate and covers to the underside of the vehicle.

FUEL INJECTOR PRESSURE CHECK
Note: When using a nozzle tester, do not allow diesel being sprayed from the nozzle to come into contact with your hands or body. Ensure that you wear goggles to protect your eyes.

1. Install the injector nozzle to the pressure tester and bleed any air from the flare nut.
2. Pump the tester handle slowly (once per second) and watch the pressure gauge (reading the pressure, just as the pressure starts dropping.

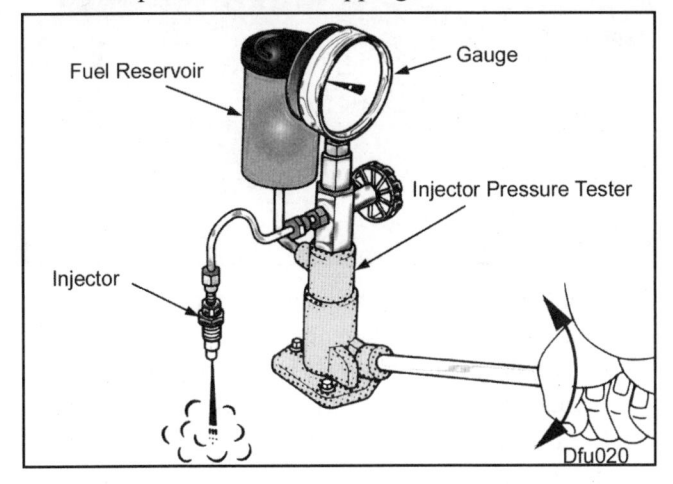

4M40 Engine
Specified Pressure ....14,710 to 156907kPa
4M41 Engine
Specified Pressure .... 17.60 to 18.58mPa
No1 Open Pressure .... 17.60 to 18.58mPa
No2 Open Pressure .... 22.60 to 23.60mPa
Note: Always check the initial injection pressure using a new nozzle.

3. If the pressure needs adjusting, change the adjusting shims. If the thickness of the shim is increased, the pressure will rise. If the thickness is decreased, the pressure will drop.
   [4M40 Engine] A shim thickness of 0.10mm is equal to a difference of 1,177 to 2,157kpa.
4. Carry out leakage test by maintaining the pressure at about:
   [4M40] 12,749 to 13,729kpa
   [4M41] 17.60 to 18.58mPa
   - for 10 seconds, and ensuring that there is no dripping from the nozzle tip or around the body.
5. If there are leaks, clean, overhaul or replace the injection nozzle.
6. Carry out spray pattern check by pumping the tester handle one full stroke per second.
7. Check that the spray angles and pattern are as shown in the diagram in this chapter.
8. If the spray pattern is not OK, clean, overhaul or replace the injection nozzle.

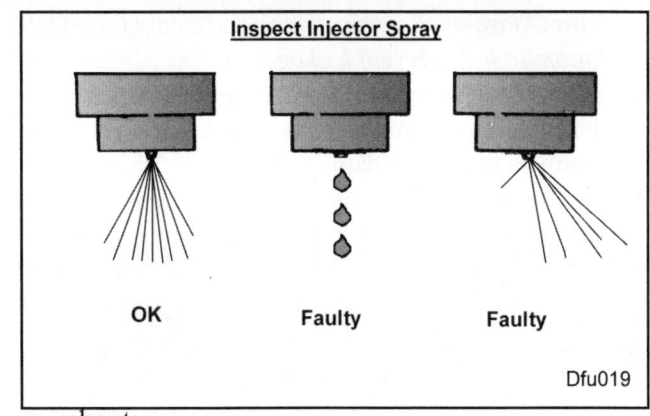

INJECTION PUMP & NOZZLE - 4M40
Removal
1. Disconnect and remove the battery and battery tray, then drain the cooling system.
2. Disconnect the intercooler hose.
3. Disconnect the lever position sensor and lever position switch connections. (auto models).
4. Vehicles fitted with immobilizer system disconnect the connector for the fuel cut valve controller.
5. Disconnect the fuel injection pump wiring connector, then disconnect the accelerator cable.
6. Disconnect the fuel pipe from the pump assembly and plug the hose ends.
7. Vehicle fitted with EGR system remove the water hose connection, then disconnect the water pipe.

DIESEL FUEL, GLOW PLUGS, EMISSION & TURBO SYSTEMS - Diesel Models

Note: *Mark relationship of hose and clamp for installation, to help prevent leakage.*

8. Remove the injection pipe retaining clamps, then disconnect and remove the injection pipes using two spanners to prevent damage.
9. Disconnect the fuel return hose. 
10. Hold the fuel return pipe with a spanner and remove the retaining nut, then remove the fuel return pipe and gaskets.
    Note: *If an attempt is made to loosen the nut without holding the return pipe it is likely to result in a broken pipe.*
11. Using a deep socket unscrew and remove the injector nozzle assembly and discard the holder and nozzle gaskets.
    Important: *Mark cylinder # on injector nozzle and cap the injector nozzle hole to prevent entry of foreign material.*
12. Disconnect the boost hose and remove the stay bracket.
13. Set the #1 cylinder to compression top dead centre by aligning the notch of the crankshaft pulley with '0' timing mark.
    Note: *Compression top dead centre is set if the protrusion on camshaft points directly upwards when the filler cap is removed.*
14. Remove injection pump assembly.

Installation

1. Set the #1 cylinder to compression top dead centre by aligning the notch of the crankshaft pulley with '0' timing mark. (do not turn crankshaft in anti-clockwise direction)
   Note: *Compression top dead centre is set if the camshaft cam marker (cast knob on camshaft near lobe) is positioned as shown (visible through oil filler hole with cap removed). See illustration Df008 in this chapter.* 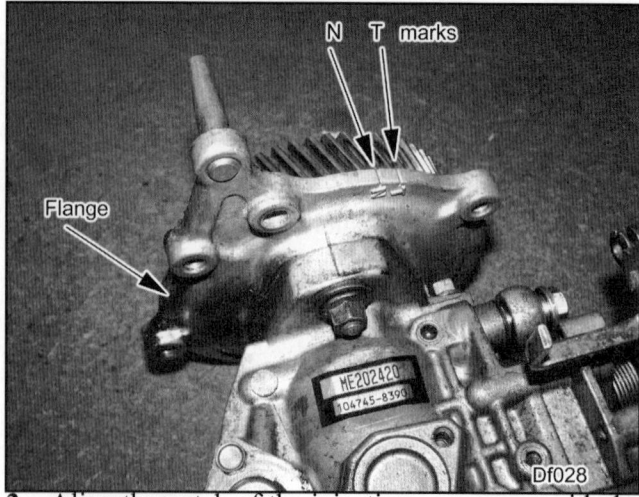
2. Align the notch of the injection pump gear with the 'N' for none-turbo models and "T" for turbo models mating marks on the flange plate, then install injection pump to the timing gear case and install pump. 
3. Install stay bracket and tighten retaining bolts to specification, then reconnect the boost hose.
4. Ensure the injection nozzle hole in the cylinder head is clean, then install new nozzle and holder gaskets.
5. Install injection nozzle assembly to cylinder head tightening to specification.
   Injector Nozzle Assembly .... 54 Nm
6. Install the fuel return pipe using a new gasket, then tighten the retaining nut to specification while holding the return pipe with a second spanner.
   Return Pipe Nut .... 29 Nm
7. Connect the fuel return hose, then install and tighten the injection pipes to specification ensuring to use two spanners.
   Injection Pipes .... 23 Nm
8. Install the injection pipe retaining clamps and tighten bolts.
   Return Pipe Nut .... 29 Nm
9. Connect the water pipe and water hose (where fitted).
10. Reconnect the fuel hoses to the pump assembly, then

DIESEL FUEL, GLOW PLUGS, EMISSION & TURBO SYSTEMS - Diesel Models

reconnect the accelerator cable and fuel injection pump electrical connector.

11. Those vehicles fitted with immobilizer system reconnect the fuel cut valve controller electrical connector.
12. Reconnect the lever position sensor and lever position switch connections. (auto models).
13. Fit the intercooler hose, then install the battery tray and battery.
14. Bleed air from the fuel line as described in this chapter.
15. Fill and bleed cooling system, refer to cooling chapter for assistance.
16. Check and adjust the injection timing, as described in this chapter.
17. Adjust the accelerator cable, as described in this chapter.
18. On automatic vehicles adjust the lever position sensor, as described in this chapter.

INJECTION NOZZLE - 4M40

Disassembly
1. Gently hold the injection nozzle retaining nut in a vice fitted with soft jaws.
2. While holding the retaining nut with a ring spanner loosen the nozzle holder body using a deep socket.
3. Remove assembly from vice and remove the retaining nut.
4. From the assembly remove the nozzle tip, distance piece and retaining pin.
5. Remove the pressure spring and shim from holder body.

Inspection
Remove injectors and test each injector as described under "Fuel Injector Pressure Check" in this chapter.

Assembly
1. To the nozzle body install the shim, pressure spring and the spring retaining pin.
2. Install the distance piece followed by the nozzle tip, then install the retaining nut tightening by hand.
3. Gently hold the injection nozzle retaining nut in a vice fitted with soft jaws.
4. While holding the retaining nut with a ring spanner tighten the nozzle holder body to specification using a deep socket.
   Retaining Nut .... 38 Nm
5. Remove assembly from vice.

INJECTION PUMP - 4M40

Disassembly
1. Loosen the injector pump gear retaining nut, then using a gear puller release the pump gear.
2. Fully remove the retaining nut and injection pump gear.
3. Remove the nuts and washers retaining the flange plate, then remove flange plate.
4. Remove the 'O-ring and key.

Assembly
1. Install a new 'O-ring which has been coated with clean engine oil, then install the key to pump shaft.
2. Install the flange plate tightening the retaining nuts.
3. Fit the injection pump gear to the gear shaft, then tighten retaining nut to specification, ensuring the gear pulls on squarely.
   Gear Retaining Nut...................................... 64 Nm

INJECTION NOZZLE - 4M41

Removal
1. Withdraw the engine oil dipstick then remove the bolts securing the dipstick tube and remove tube from engine.
2. Remove the bolts/nuts from the injection pipe clamps and remove clamps, then remove the injection pipe stay.
3. Disconnect and remove the injection pipes using two spanners to prevent damage, then remove the injection pipe seal.
4. Disconnect the fuel return hose, then remove the bolts securing the fuel return pipe and remove fuel return pipe and gaskets.
5. Remove the rocker cover from the engine.
6. Remove the bolts securing the fuel leak-off pipe, then remove pipe and pipe gaskets.
7. Remove the bolts retaining the injector nozzle assembly then remove nozzle assembly and gasket.
   Important: *Mark cylinder # on injector nozzle and cap the injector nozzle hole to prevent entry of foreign material.*

Disassembly
1. Remove the retaining nut from the injector assembly, then remove the nozzle and needle valve.
2. From the assembly remove the pin, then remove the

spacer and lift piece.
3. Remove the spring seat and shim then remove the second spring and pushrod.
4. Remove the collar, then remove the spring seat, first spring and shim from the nozzle holder.

Assembly
1. To the nozzle holder install the shim, first spring and the spring seat.
2. Install the collar and push rod, then install the second spring, shim and spring seat.
3. Install the lift piece spacer and pin to the assembly.
4. Install the needle valve and nozzle, then install the retaining nut tightening to specification.
   Retaining Nut .... 34 Nm

Installation
1. Install the injector nozzle gasket, then apply a small amount of clean engine oil to the injector nozzle 'O-ring.
2. Ensure the injection nozzle hole in the cylinder head is clean, then install injection nozzle assembly and tighten retaining bolts to specification.
   Injector Nozzle Assembly .... 21 Nm
3. Install the fuel leak-off pipe using new gaskets then tighten retaining bolts to specification.
   Leak-off Pipe Bolts .... 13 Nm
4. Install the rocker cover, refer to engine chapter for assistance.
5. Install the fuel return pipe using new gaskets then tighten retaining bolts to specification and install the fuel return hose.
   Fuel Return Pipe Bolts .... 13 Nm
   Note: *Ensure fuel return hose is install to pipe by at least 15mm.*
6. Coat the new injection pipe seal with a small amount of clean engine oil then carefully install seal.
7. To the injection pipe sealing surface apply a small amount of clean engine oil then connect the injection pipes.
8. Tighten the injection pipe and pipe nut to specification using two spanners as shown.
   Injection Pipe Nut .... 31 Nm
9. Install the injection pipe stay and the retaining clamps, tighten to specification.
   Stay Bolts .... 22 Nm
   Clamps Bolts/Nuts .... 22 Nm
10. Coat the dipstick tube 'O-ring with clean engine oil, then install the dipstick tube, tightening retaining bolts to specification. Install engine oil dipstick.
    Dipstick Tub Bolts 22Nm

INJECTION PUMP - 4M41

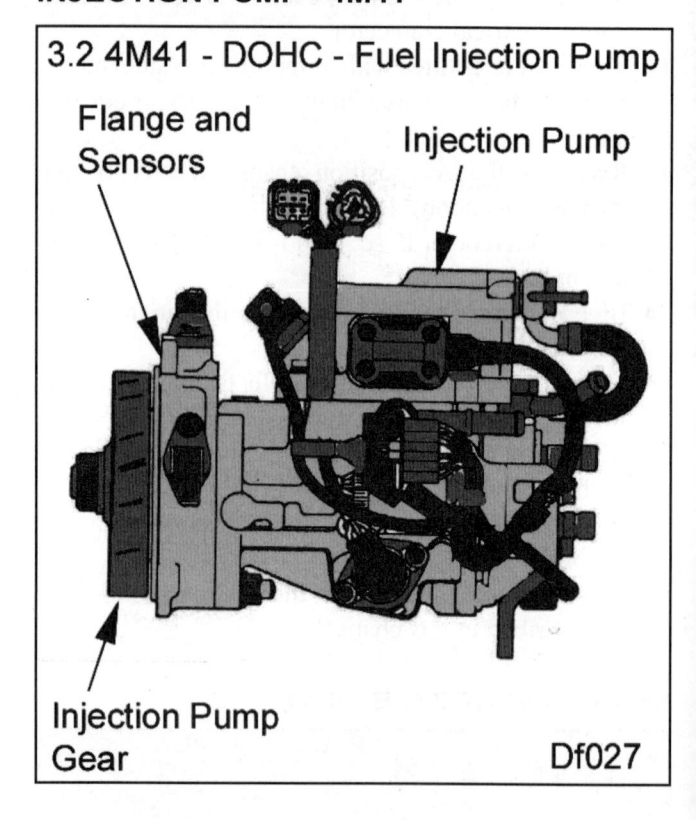

3.2 4M41 - DOHC - Fuel Injection Pump
Flange and Sensors
Injection Pump
Injection Pump Gear
Df027

Removal
1. Remove the engine cover then disconnect and remove the battery and battery tray.
2. Remove the air cleaner assembly from vehicle, refer to engine chapter for assistance.
3. Remove the injection pipe then remove the intercooler hose.
4. Set the #1 cylinder to compression top dead centre by aligning the notch of the crankshaft pulley with '0' timing mark.
   Note: *Compression top dead centre is set if the camshafts cam lobes are positioned as shown (oil filler cap removed).*
   See illustration No32013earlier in this chapter
5. Remove the vacuum pump assembly, refer to engine chapter for assistance.
6. Disconnect the electrical connections for the injection pump and the main speed sensor connector.
7. Disconnect the connections from the speed sensors then remove the sensor retaining bolts and remove sensors from pump assembly.
8. Label and disconnect the fuel return hoses and fuel main hose from the pump assembly and plug the hose ends.
9. Remove the bolts retaining the injection pump stays and remove stays from pump assembly.
10. Remove the bolts securing the injection pump cover and remove cover assembly from pump.
11. Remove injection pump assembly.

DIESEL FUEL, GLOW PLUGS, EMISSION & TURBO SYSTEMS - Diesel Models

Disassembly

1. Remove the injector pump gear retaining nut, then remove the sub gear retaining snap ring.
2. Remove the injection pump sub gear and spring then remove the pump gear using a gear puller.
3. Remove the sensor plate retaining bolts and remove sensor plate.
4. Remove the nuts and washers retaining the flange plate, then remove flange plate.
5. Remove the 'O-ring and key.

Assembly

1. Install a new 'O-ring which has been coated with clean engine oil, then install the key to pump shaft.
2. Install the flange plate tightening the retaining nuts to specification.
   Flange Plate Nuts .... 38 Nm
3. Install the sensor plate and tighten retaining bolts to specification.
   Sensor Plate Bolts .... 1.5 Nm
4. Fit the injection pump gear to the gear shaft, then tighten retaining nut to specification, ensuring the gear pulls on squarely.
   Gear Retaining Nut .... 180 Nm
5. Install the spring followed by the sub gear and secure with snap ring.

Installation

1. Insert bolt as shown to hold gear and sub gear in position. (bolt M6x16)
   Note: If pump assembly or gear assembly has been replaced the bolt should already be installed.
2. Set the #1 cylinder to compression top dead centre by aligning the notch of the crankshaft pulley with '0' timing mark. (do **not** turn crankshaft in anti-clockwise direction)
   Note: Compression top dead centre is set if the camshaft cam marker (cast knob on camshafts near lobe) is positioned as shown (visible through oil filler hole with cap removed).
3. Align the notch of the injection pump gear with the notch of the flange plate, then install injection pump to the timing gear case and install pump bolts.
   (Aligning the match marks allows for the injection pump gear to turn as it is being installed).
   Pump Assembly Bolts .... 54 Nm
4. Remove the holding bolt inserted previously.
5. Install the injection pump cover assembly, then install the retaining bolts along with the insulator and collar.
6. Install the injection pump stays and tighten stay retaining bolts to specification.
   Stay Retaining Bolts .... 18 Nm
7. Connect the fuel return hoses and fuel main hose to the pump assembly, ensuring they are connected to correct locations.
   Note: Ensure hoses are fitted to fittings with an overlap of at least 25mm.
8. Install the speed sensors and tighten retaining bolts to specification, then reconnect electrical connections.
   Engine Speed Sensor Bolts .... 5 Nm
9. Connect the electrical connections for the injection pump and the main speed sensor connector.
10. Install the vacuum pump assembly, refer to engine chapter for assistance.
11. Install the injection pipe then install the intercooler hose.
12. Install the air cleaner assembly to vehicle, refer to engine chapter for assistance.
13. Install the engine cover then install the battery tray and battery.

INJECTION PUMP - 4M41 [Common Rail]

Removal

1. Remove the engine cover then disconnect and remove the battery and battery tray.
2. Remove the air cleaner assembly from vehicle, refer to engine chapter for assistance.
3. Remove the injection pipe then remove the intercooler hose.
4. Set the #1 cylinder to compression top dead centre by aligning the notch of the crankshaft pulley with '0' timing mark.
   Note: Compression top dead centre is set if the camshafts cam lobes are positioned as shown (oil filler cap removed).
   See illustration No32013 earlier in this chapter
5. Disconnect the electrical connections for the injection pump.
6. Label and disconnect the fuel return hoses and fuel main hose from the pump assembly and plug the hose ends.
7. Remove injection pump assembly.

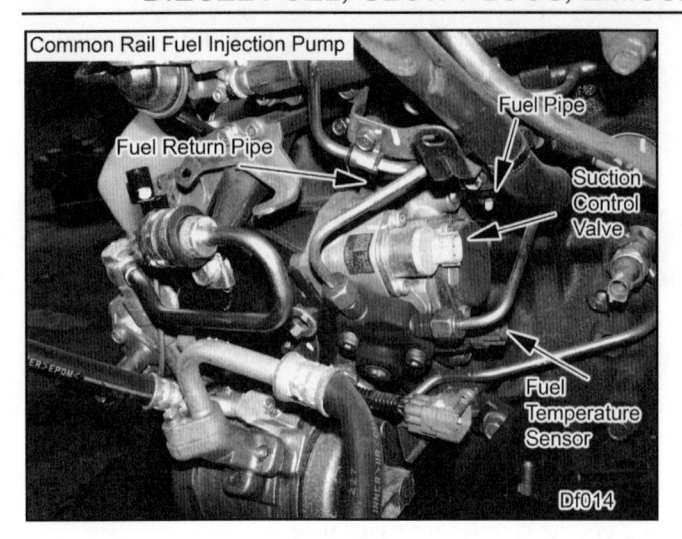

DIESEL FUEL, GLOW PLUGS, EMISSION & TURBO SYSTEMS - Diesel Models

Installation

1. Insert a bolt to hold gear and sub gear in position.
   Note: *If pump assembly or gear assembly has been replaced the bolt should already be installed.*
2. Set the #1 cylinder to compression top dead centre by aligning the notch of the crankshaft pulley with '0' timing mark. (do <u>not</u> turn crankshaft in anti-clockwise direction)
   Note: *Compression top dead centre is set if the camshaft cam marker (cast knob on camshafts near lobe) is positioned as shown (visible through oil filler hole with cap removed).*
3. Align the notch of the injection pump gear with the notch of the flange plate, then install injection pump to the timing gear case and install pump bolts.
   (Aligning the match marks allows for the injection pump gear to turn as it is being installed.
   Pump Assembly Bolts .... 54 Nm
4. Remove the holding bolt inserted previously.
5. Connect the fuel return hoses and fuel main hose to the pump assembly, ensuring they are connected to correct locations.
   Note: *Ensure hoses are fitted to fittings with an overlap of at least 25mm.*
6. Install the speed sensors and tighten retaining bolts to specification, then reconnect electrical connections.
   Engine Speed Sensor Bolts .... 5 Nm
7. Connect the electrical connections for the injection pump and the main speed sensor connector.
8. Install the injection pump cover assembly, then install the retaining bolts along with the insulator and collar.
9. Install the injection pipe then install the intercooler hose.
10. Install the air cleaner assembly to vehicle, refer to engine chapter for assistance.
11. Install the engine cover then install the battery tray and battery.

Engine Electronic Control Unit (ECU)
Removal

1. From the passenger side of the vehicle, remove the side cowl trim panel (kick panel).
2. Disconnect the main harness connections, then remove the auto transmission control relay.
3. Disconnect the electrical connections for the auto transmission-ECU, then remove mounting bolts and remove from vehicle.
4. Disconnect the electrical connections for the engine-ECU, then remove mounting bolts and remove ECU from vehicle.
5. If required remove the bolt securing the mounting bracket and remove bracket.

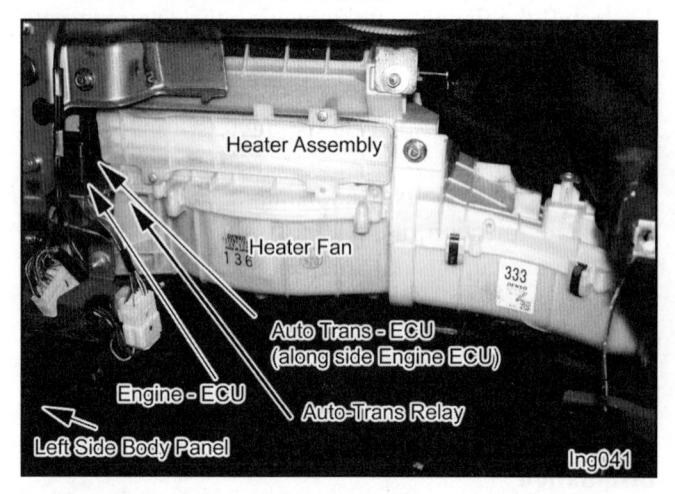

Installation

1. If removed install ECU mounting bracket and tighten bolts to specification.
   ECU Mounting Bracket Bolt .... 5 Nm
2. Install the engine-ECU into position, tighten mounting bolts to specification and reconnect the electrical connection.
   ECU Mounting Nut .... 5 Nm
3. Install the auto transmission-ECU into position, tighten mounting bolts to specification and reconnect the electrical connection.
   ECU Mounting Nut .... 5 Nm
4. Install the transmission control relay, the reconnect the main harness connections.
   Auto Trans Control Relay Bolt .... 5 Nm
5. Replace the side cowl trim panel (kick panel) to the vehicle.

FUEL GAUGE SENDER / FUEL PUMP

Refer to fuel tank chapter for instructions on the removal and installation of the fuel pump.

DIESEL FUEL, GLOW PLUGS, EMISSION & TURBO SYSTEMS - Diesel Models

EMISSION SYSTEM

Vacuum Circuit Inspection

1. Check all vacuum hose connections using the pipe diagram as a guide to ensure all connections are properly connected and there are no loose connections.
2. Check to ensure there are no sharp bends, kinks or damaged hoses.

EGR System Inspection - 4M40

1. Start the engine and allow to reach operating temperature (minimum 65°C)
2. Suddenly depress the accelerator pedal to race engine and check to ensure the EGR valve diaphragm lifts.

EGR System Inspection - 4M41

1. Start the engine and allow to reach operating temperature (minimum 65°C), turn off the A/C switch and place selector lever in P range.
2. Check the operation of the EGR valve.

Engine Condition	EGR Valve Condition
Idling (no load)	Open
Sudden racing	Closed (diaphragm lowers)

EGR Solenoid Valve Operation Inpsection- 4M40

1. Disconnect the solenoid valve connectors and vacuum hoses.
2. To each nipple of the EGR solenoid valve attach a vacuum pump and apply negative pressure.
3. Check to ensure the valve are airtight when voltage is applied to each terminal of the EGR solenoid valves and when voltage is not applied.

EGR Solenoid Valve #1 (4M40)	
Battery Voltage	**Normal Condition**
Current is flowing	Vacuum leaks
(vacuum maintained when nipple B is plugged).	
Current not flowing	Vacuum maintained

EGR Solenoid Valve #1 (4M41)	
Battery Voltage	**Normal Condition**
Current is flowing	Vacuum leaks
(vacuum maintained when nipple A is plugged).	
Current not flowing	Vacuum leaks
(vacuum maintained when nipple B is plugged).	

EGR Solenoid Valve #2 (4M40)	
Battery Voltage	**Normal Condition**
Current is flowing	Vacuum leaks
(vacuum maintained when nipple D is plugged).	
Current not flowing	Vacuum leaks
(vacuum maintained when nipple E is plugged).	

EGR Solenoid Valve #2 (4M41)	
Battery Voltage	**Normal Condition**
Current is flowing	Vacuum leaks
(vacuum maintained when nipple C is plugged).	
Current not flowing	Vacuum maintained

EGR Solenoid Valve Resistance Inspection

Measure the resistance between the terminals of the EGR solenoid valve.

Standard .... 36 - 44Ohms @ 20°C

Lever Position Sensor Adjustment (LPS)- 4M40

1. Run the engine until it reaches normal operating temperature (above 80°C).
2. Sufficiently loosen the accelerator cable and connect test harness to the connector of the lever position sensor.
3. Between terminal #1 (red) and terminal #3 (blue) of the position sensor connect a digital voltmeter.
4. Turn on the ignition switch but do NOT start engine and measure the output voltage.

Lever Condition	Voltage
Idle Position	0.8 - 1.3V
Fully Open	4.1 - 4.9V

5. If not to specification, loosen the sensor mounting screw and turn sensor to adjust. Tighten retaining screw.
   Note: *Turning clockwise will increase voltage.*
6. Turn off ignition switch remove test harness and adjust accelerator cable play.

Engine Speed Sensor Inspection - 4M40

1. Disconnect the electrical connection for the engine speed sensor.
2. Measure the resistance between terminals #2 and #5 of the sensor.
   Sensor Resistance .... 1.3 - 1.9 kOhms

Solenoid Timer Inspection - 4M40

1. Disconnect the connector for the solenoid timer.
2. Apply voltage greater than 8.5V between terminals #2 and #5 of injection pump harness connector.

3. The operating sound should be herd, if not replace solenoid timer.
   (See illustrations Df004 and Df005 in this chapter)

EGR Valve and (DC Motor) Inspection 4M41 - 3.2 Diesel - Common Rail

1. Disconnect the harness connector and remove DC motor.
2. Check the EGR valve is not jammed open, clean carbon build-up from valve.

3. Use voltmeter and a variable voltage supply to check operation of DC motor.
4. Connect the volt meter to terminals No1 and No2.
5. Connect to terminals No3 - 5 volts +ve terminal No2 - 5 volts -ve.
6. Connect to terminals No6 - 5 volts +ve terminal No4 - 5 volts -ve.
   Check that valve is open.
7. Increase both voltage supplies by 1 volt at a time, with 5 second intervals, do so until valve opens, as this is happening check reading of volt meter to be the same as voltage supplied. If the DC motor is faulty.
8. Install DC motor and connect the harness connector. Tighten bolts to specification.
   EGR Valve bolts **48Nm**

Catalytic Converter

For removal and installation of the Catalytic Converter refer to the exhaust system chapter.

DIESEL FUEL, GLOW PLUGS, EMISSION & TURBO SYSTEMS - Diesel Models

TURBO CHARGER

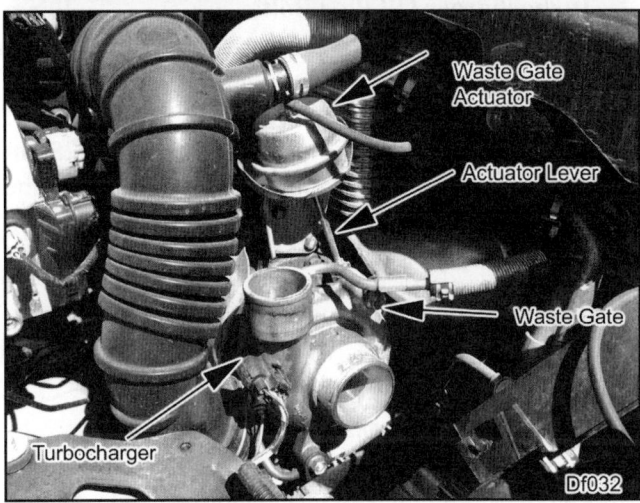

GENERAL DESCRIPTION
The turbocharger is a system that is used to create a large increase in the volume of air sent to the combustion chamber. Due to the increase in available air there is an increase in the engine output, due mainly to a proportional increase in the amount of fuel that can be burned in the combustion chamber.

Turbocharger Operation
The turbocharger housing contains an impeller and a turbine wheel. The turbine wheel is driven by exhaust gas which passes the turbine wheel causing it to rotate, this causes the impeller to also rotate as it is fitted to the same shaft as the turbine wheel. When the impeller rotates air is drawn in through the air cleaner and is compressed, this creates a greater volume of air to be supplied to the combustion chamber. As the engine speed increases so does the volume of exhaust gas supplied to the turbine creating an increase in turbine speed. Due to the increase in turbine speed there is a proportional increase in impeller speed, this creates an increase in the air pressure and an increase in the power output of the engine.

Waste Gate Operation
As the turbine wheel turns faster so does the impeller, this causes a constantly rising air pressure in the combustion chamber. Air pressure from the turbocharger needs to be regulated and not allowed to increase above set values, this is when the 'Waste Gate Valve' comes into operation.
As the air pressure increases in the turbocharger outlet rises to a set value the waste gate valve opens, this causes a reduction in the amount of exhaust gas passing through the turbocharger turbine, this in turn causes the turbine and impeller speeds to drop.
Due to the drop in impeller speed the air pressure also starts to drop, this causes the waste gate valve to now close and in turn allows an increase in exhaust gas through the turbine again. This controls the amount of air pressure being supplied to the combustion chamber to a predetermined value.

GENERAL INFORMATION
The following points should be noted when operating a turbocharged engine or when carrying out any repairs to a turbocharger unit.
Due to the high revolutions that the turbocharger operates at 20,000 -115,000rpm, it is advisable to allow the engine to idle for at least 20-120 seconds before turning the engine off, this allows the turbocharger revolutions to drop to a reasonable speed before the engine is turned off. Once the engine has been turned off there is no longer a pressurised supply of oil for the turbocharger bearings and if the speed of the turbocharger is too great, damage to the bearings may result.
If the turbocharger is faulty and needs replacing take note of the following points to help diagnose fault cause.
1. *Conditions that the vehicle was operated under*
2. *Quality of the engine oil and quantity*
3. *Check oil lines for restriction etc.*

If removing the turbocharger from the engine make sure that the oil inlet, exhaust and intake ports are plugged to prevent entry of foreign material.
"If fitting a new or reconditioned turbocharger to an engine put 20cc (1.2 cu in) of engine oil into the turbocharger oil inlet and turn the impeller by hand to allow oil to coat the bearings before installation of the unit to engine.

Waste Gate Actuator Inspection
1. To the nipple connect a hand pump.
2. Gradually apply pressure and check what pressure begins it activate the waste gate actuator rod.
   Standard Pressure - 4M40 .... 96 kPa
                               - 4M41 .... 161 kPa
   Note: *Do not apply pressure greater than 115kPa for 4M40 or 161kPa for 4M41.*
3. If the pressure is greatly different from the standard specification check the actuator or waste valve and

DIESEL FUEL, GLOW PLUGS, EMISSION & TURBO SYSTEMS - Diesel Models

Waste Gate Actuator — Air Gun — Check The Amount Of Air Pressure Being Applied To Acuator

replace if required.

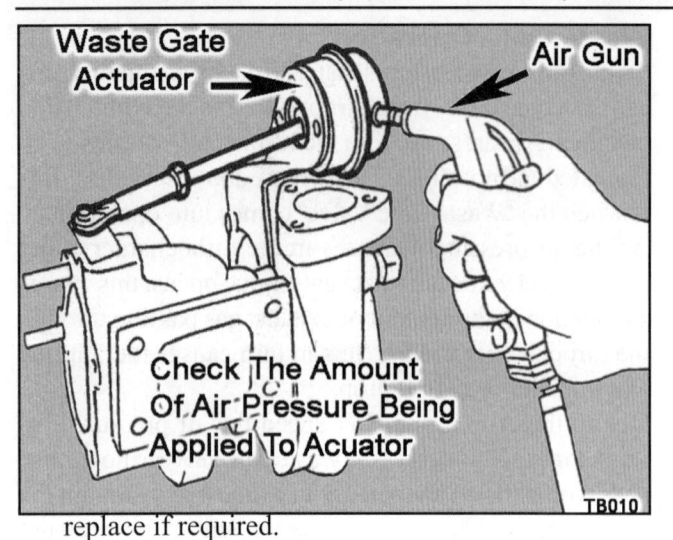

Turbo Charger - 4M40
Removal
1. Remove the air intake and air to throttle body ducting from the turbocharger.
2. Remove the heat shield from the turbocharger and exhaust manifold.
3. Remove the water feed and return pipes from the turbocharger.
4. Remove the oil feed and return pipes from the turbocharger.
5. Remove the wastegate actuator vacuum tube form the wastegate actuator diaphragm.
6. Remove the exhaust pipe mounting bolts from turbocharger.
7. Remove the bolts attaching the turbocharger to the exhaust manifold.
8. Remove the turbocharger.

Disassembly
1. From the turbocharger assembly remove the hose, then remove the actuator.
2. Unscrew and remove the coupling then remove the turbine housing by gentle taping with a rubber mallet.
3. Remove the snap ring securing the cartridge assembly in the compressor cover and remove cover by gently tapping with a rubber mallet.

Cleaning
1. Before cleaning assembly visually inspect for any signs of burning, abrasions or any other flaws. Replace if required.
2. Clean the dismantled parts in a nonflammable cleaning solvent and dry using compressed air.

Assembly
1. Install the cartridge assembly to the compressor cover using a new 'O-ring which has been coated in clean engine oil.
2. Install the snap ring ensuring the tapered surface is facing upwards.
3. Install the turbine housing, securing with coupling and tighten coupling nut to specification.
   Coupling Nut .... **8.1 Nm**
4. To the turbocharger assembly install the actuator and hose.

Installation
1. Install turbocharger to the exhaust manifold, tighten bolts to specification.
   Turbocharger to Exhaust Manifold Bolts: 49Nm
2. Install the oil feed and return pipes from the turbocharger with new gaskets and seals, tighten bolts to specification.
   Turbocharger Oil Pipe Bolts: **20Nm**
3. Install the water feed and return pipes from the turbocharger with new gaskets and seals, tighten bolts to specification.
   Turbocharger Water Pipes Bolts: **25Nm**
4. Replace the wastegate actuator vacuum tube to the wastegate actuator diaphragm.
5. Install the heat shield from the turbocharger and exhaust manifold.
6. Remove the air intake and air to throttle body ducting from the turbocharger.

Turbo Charger - 4M41
Removal
1. Remove the air intake and air to throttle body ducting from the turbocharger.
2. Remove the heat shield from the turbocharger and exhaust manifold.
3. Remove the water feed and return pipes from the turbocharger.
4. Remove the oil feed and return pipes from the turbocharger.
5. Remove the wastegate actuator vacuum tube form the wastegate actuator diaphragm.
6. Remove the exhaust pipe mounting bolts from turbocharger.
7. Remove the bolts attaching the turbocharger to the exhaust manifold. (Remove the exhaust manifold if it easier to work on the turbocharger).
8. Remove the turbocharger.

Disassembly
1. From the turbocharger assembly remove the hose, then remove the actuator.
2. Unscrew and remove the coupling then remove the turbine housing by gentle taping with a rubber mallet.
3. Remove the snap ring securing the cartridge assembly

DIESEL FUEL, GLOW PLUGS, EMISSION & TURBO SYSTEMS - Diesel Models

in the compressor cover and remove cover by gently tapping with a rubber mallet.

Cleaning

1. Before cleaning assembly visually inspect for any signs of burning, abrasions or any other flaws. Replace if required.
2. Clean the dismantled parts in a non-flammable cleaning solvent and dry using compressed air.

Assembly

1. Install the cartridge assembly to the compressor cover using a new 'O-ring which has been coated in clean engine oil.
2. Install the snap ring ensuring the tapered surface is facing upwards.
3. Install the turbine housing, securing with coupling and tighten coupling nut to specification.
   Coupling Nut .... 8.1 Nm
4. To the turbocharger assembly install the actuator and hose.

Installation

1. Install turbocharger to the exhaust manifold, tighten bolts to specification.
   Turbocharger to Exhaust Manifold Bolts.. 49Nm
2. Install the oil feed and return pipes from the turbocharger with new gaskets and seals, tighten bolts to specification.
   Turbocharger Oil Pipe Bolts: 20Nm
3. Install the water feed and return pipes from the turbocharger with new gaskets and seals, tighten bolts to specification.
   Turbocharger Water Pipes Bolts: 25Nm
4. Replace the wastegate actuator vacuum tube to the wastegate actuator diaphragm.
5. Install the heat shield from the turbocharger and exhaust manifold.
6. Remove the air intake and air to throttle body ducting from the turbocharger.

TURBOCHARGER

On Vehicle Inspection

1. Check the air intake ducts between the air cleaner and the turbocharger and between the turbocharger outlet and the intake manifold
   a) Check air filter for blockage or damage replace if faulty
2. Check the exhaust for leakage between the cylinder head and the turbocharger inlet port.

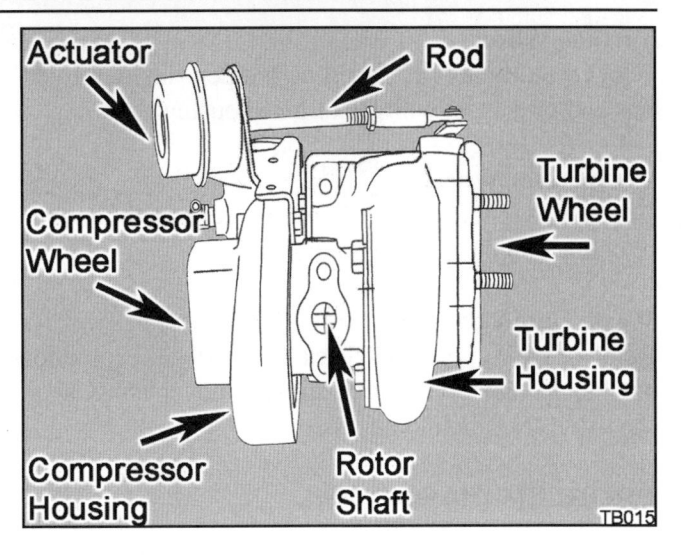

Inspection
Rotor Shaft

1. Check and ensure that the rotor shaft rotates smoothly and that there are no carbon deposits on the rotor shaft.
2. Record the run out on the rotor shaft.
   Specified Run Out 0.056-0.127mm
3. Record the end play on the rotor shaft.
   Specified End Play 0.013-0.097mm

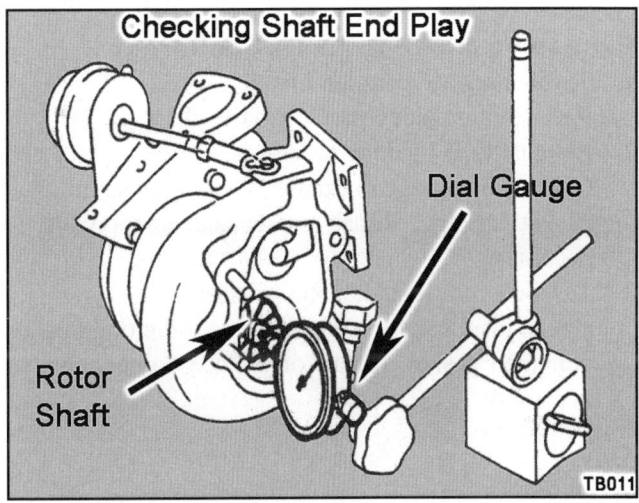

Turbine Wheel
Check the turbine wheel for oil, carbon deposits, deformed fins and/or contact with the turbine housing.

Compressor Wheel
Check the compressor wheel for oil, deformed fins and/or contact on the compressor housing.

Waste Gate Valve
Remove the rod pin and check the wastegate valve for cracks, deformations and/or smooth movement. Check the valve seat for smoothness.

PROBLEM DIAGNOSIS

Poor Acceleration, Lack of Power or Excessive Fuel Consumption:
1. Turbocharging pressure too low:
   Check turbo boost pressure.
   If pressure is below specification, start diagnosis at item 2.
2. Restriction in Intake System:
   Check air cleaner, ducting etc., for restrictions, repair or replace parts as necessary.
3. Leak in Intake System:
   Check all connections on intake system, replace any faulty or suspect gaskets etc.
4. Exhaust System Restriction:
   Check exhaust system side of the turbocharger for any restrictions, repair or replace faulty components.
5. Leak in Exhaust System:
   Check the exhaust system for a leak before the turbine, causing a reduction in the amount of gas flow passed the turbine, repair or replace components as necessary.
6. Turbocharger Operation Erratic:
   Check the following - end float of turbocharger shaft, runout of shaft and check turbine/impeller for freedom of movement, as shown earlier.

Excessive Noise from Turbocharger
1. Turbocharger Operation Erratic:
   Refer to item No. 6 previous fault chart
2. Exhaust Pipe Leaking or Vibrating:
   Check for damage to exhaust system, loose mounts, gasket leakage. Repair or replace components as necessary.
3. Turbocharger Insulator Resonance:
   Check insulator for damage, loose mounting nuts or damaged gasket. Repair or replace components as necessary.

Excessive Oil Consumption or White Smoke
1. Turbocharger Shaft Seal Faulty:
   Check for excessive runout in the turbine / impeller shaft. Replace turbocharger assembly if faulty. Remove the elbow from turbine side of turbocharger and check for excessive carbon deposits in turbine wheel. This is an indication that the oil seal is faulty, replace the turbocharger assembly.

EXHAUST SYSTEM

GENERAL DESCRIPTION

Engines are fitted with a single pipe exhaust system, the engine exhaust manifold or manifolds as in the V6 engine is connected to a front pipe. A single pre-muffler or catalytic converter is located between the engine front pipe and the centre pipe muffler assembly. From there it is connected to the rear main muffler which exits the rear of the vehicle.

The exhaust system is supported by rubber insulators at different sections.

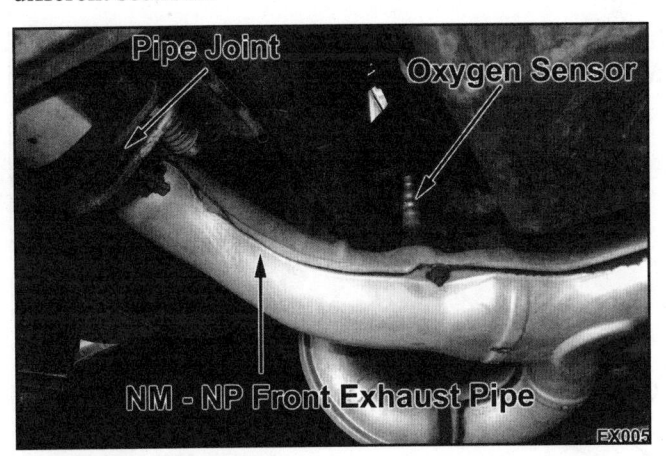

SERVICE NOTES

When installing any exhaust system component, care must be taken to install each component in correct order.

Incorrect assembly of exhaust system components can often be the cause of rattles and 'booms' due to incorrect alignment or clearance from body or suspension parts.

While installing the exhaust system, ensure that the correct assembly, installation, tightening sequence and clearance for the system involved are observed. Generally speaking, fit the components closest to the engine first, and work your way back to the rear of the vehicle.

Many vehicles are fitted with a heat shield over the exhaust manifold and catalytic converter, if these heat shields are fitted they must be reinstalled as there could be danger to the vehicle from excess heat.

When exhaust system service work is required, refer to illustrations for necessary information and proper alignment and arrangement of each component position.

Use exhaust sealer and new gaskets at pipe flanges to ensure a proper seal which will not leak exhaust gases.

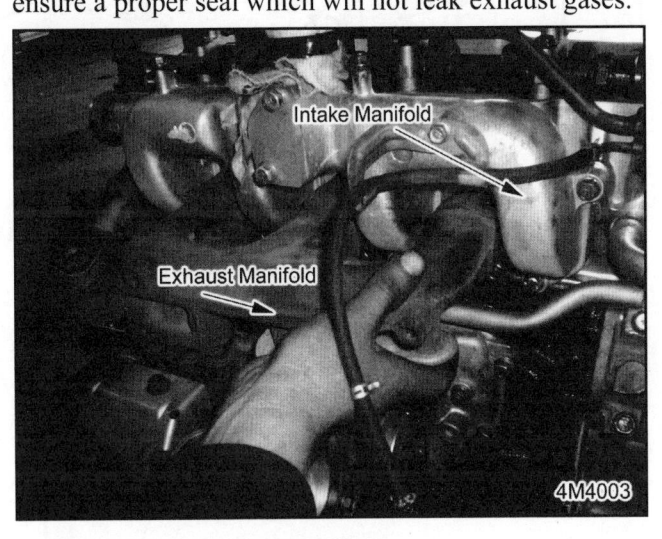

CATALYTIC CONVERTER

The catalytic converter is similar to a muffler in appearance. Inside the steel housing, the converter comprises of ceramic monolith which is surrounded by a mat, this prevents the monolith from contacting the inner casing. The surfaces of the ceramic monolith contain Rhodium, Palladium and Platinum which are exposed to exhaust gases, (this creates the chemical reaction necessary to oxidize carbon monoxide and hydrocarbons to harmless carbon dioxide).

The catalytic converter normally operates at approximately 600°C. The catalytic material is very sensitive to the effects of a rich or lean fuel mixture which causes the temperature of the converter to rise rapidly to the temperature at which the ceramic material melts.

EXHAUST SYSTEM

Caution: *Excessively rich or lean fuel mixture can cause sudden failure of the catalytic converter.*

The catalytic converter is also sensitive to the use of leaded petrol. This causes deposits to form in the converter which restrict the exhaust flow and prevent the catalyst from working.

* The use of unleaded petrol results in black tail pipe deposits rather than the grey colour most people are familiar with. The black colour does not therefore, indicate a state of poor engine tune.

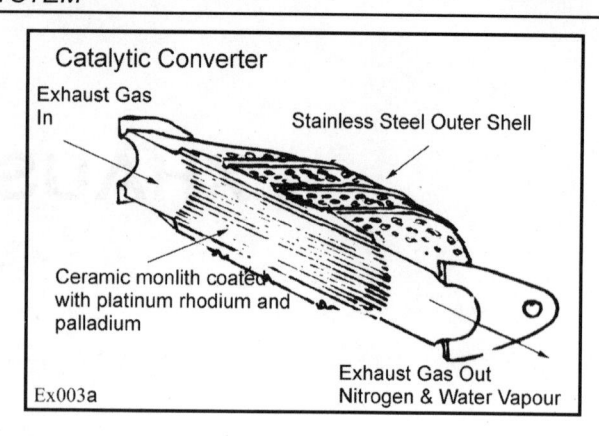

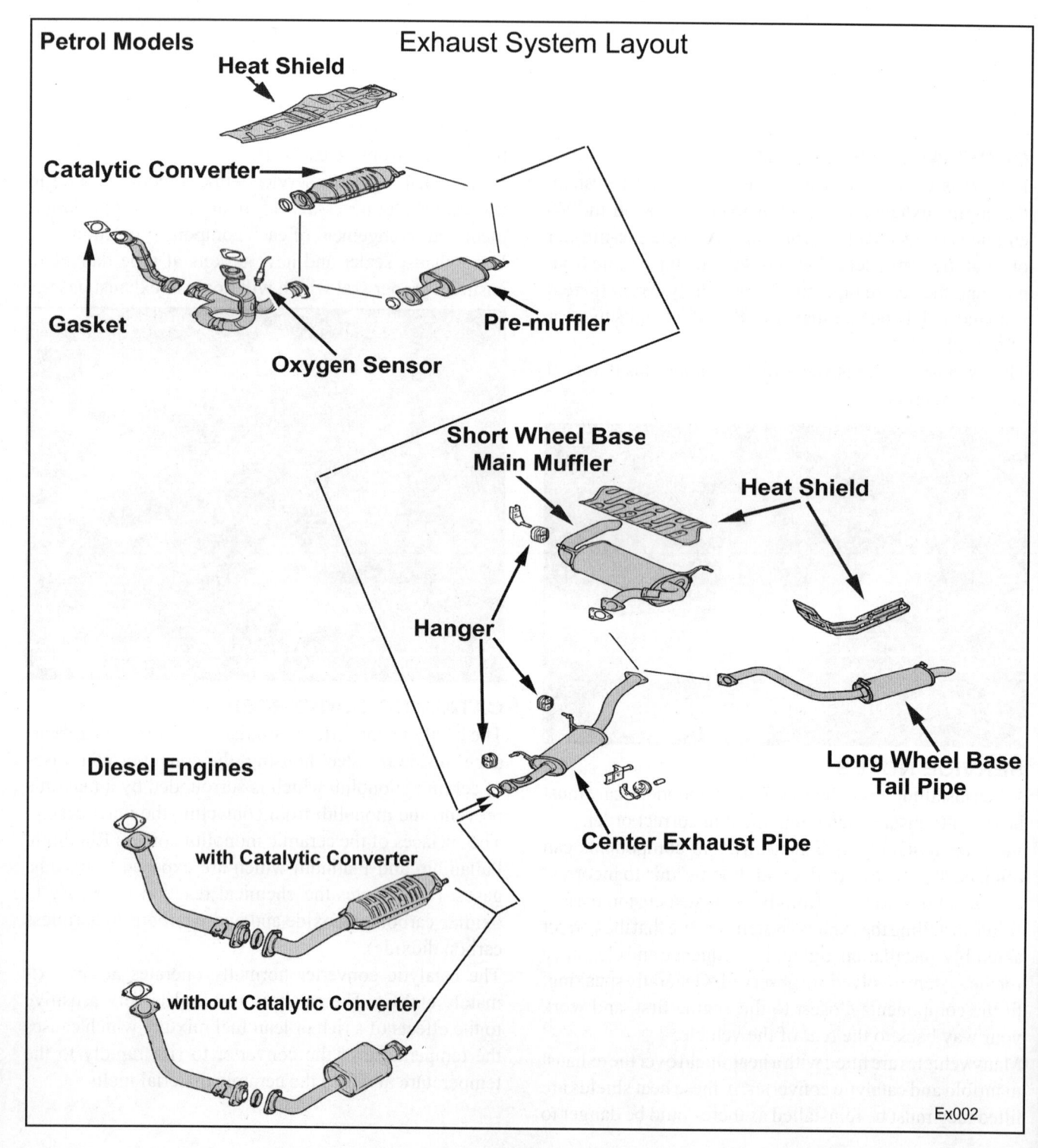

Catalytic Converter
- Exhaust Gas In
- Stainless Steel Outer Shell
- Ceramic monlith coated with platinum rhodium and palladium
- Exhaust Gas Out: Nitrogen & Water Vapour

Ex003a

Exhaust System Layout

Petrol Models
- Heat Shield
- Catalytic Converter
- Gasket
- Oxygen Sensor
- Pre-muffler

- Short Wheel Base Main Muffler
- Heat Shield
- Hanger
- Long Wheel Base Tail Pipe
- Center Exhaust Pipe

Diesel Engines
- with Catalytic Converter
- without Catalytic Converter

Ex002

EXHAUST SYSTEM

PROBLEM DIAGNOSIS

Problem: Leaking exhaust gases!
Possible Cause: Damaged or improperly installed converter gaskets.
Remedy: Replace gasket as necessary.
Possible Cause: Burned or rusted-out exhaust pipe or muffler.
Remedy: Replace component as necessary.

Problem: Exhaust noises!
Possible Causes and Remedies:
Possible Cause: Leaks at manifold or pipe connections.
Remedy: Torque clamps at leaking connections, or replace gasket.
Possible Cause: Burned or blown-out pipe or muffler.
Remedy: Replace pipe/muffler assembly as necessary.
Possible Cause: Exhaust manifold cracked or broken.
Remedy: Replace manifold.
Possible Cause: Leak between manifold and cylinder head.
Remedy: Torque manifold to cylinder head studs.

Problem: Loss of engine power, hesitation, surging, bad fuel economy, stalling / hard starting!
Possible Causes and Remedies:
Possible Cause: Clogged catalytic converter (may result from serious engine malfunction or wrong fuel).
Remedy: Replace catalytic converter.
Possible Cause: Crushed pipe work.
Remedy: Replace pipe work.

Problem: Internal rattling in muffler!
Possible Cause: Dislodged turning tubes and/or baffles in muffler.
Remedy: Replace muffler.
Possible Cause: Catalytic converter monolith has crumbled and pieces blown into muffler.
Remedy: Replace catalytic converter assembly and affected muffler.

EXHAUST SYSTEM

Torque Settings

Description	Nm
Petrol Engines: NM - NT	
Exhaust Hanger Bracket:	
NM - NP	13 +/- 2
NS - NT	20 +/- 5
Oxygen Sensor	44 +/- 5
Centre pipe to Main muffler:	
NM - NP	49 +/- 10
NS - NT	41 +/- 10
Centre Pipe to Catalytic Converter:	
NM - NP	49 +/- 10
NS - NT	49 +/- 10
Centre Pipe to Pre-muffler (w/o Catalytic converter)	
NM - NP	49 +/- 10
Front Exhaust Pipe to Catalytic Converter:	
NM - NP	49 +/- 4
NS - NT	41 +/- 10
Front Pipe to Pre-muffler (w/o catalytic converter):	
NM - NP	49 +/- 4
Front Pipe to Exhaust Manifold:	
NM - NP	49 +/- 5
NS - NT	49 +/- 10
Front Right Hand Pipe to Front Left Hand Pipe:	
NM - NP	25 +/- 4
NS - NT	41 +/- 10
Diesel Engines: NM - NP	
Exhaust Hanger Bracket:	13 +/- 2
Centre Pipe to Main Muffler:	49 +/- 10
Centre Pipe to Catalytic Converter:	49 +/- 10
Centre Pipe to Pre-muffler (w/o catalytic converter):	
NM - NP	49 +/- 10
Front Pipe to Catalytic Converter Pipe:	25 +/- 4
Front Pipe to Pre-muffler Pipe:	25 +/- 4
Front Pipe to Exhaust Manifold:	49 +/- 10
Diesel Engines: NS - NT Manual Transmission	
Exhaust Hanger Bracket:	20 +/- 5
Exhaust Muffler Hanger:	9.5 +/- 3.5
Exhaust Main Muffler to Tail Pipe:	41 +/- 10
Rear Catalytic Converter to Main Muffler:	49 +/- 10
Front Pipe To Rear Catalytic Converter:	41 +/- 10
Front Catalytic Converter to Manifold:	41 +/- 10
Front Catalytic Converter Cover:	7.0 +/- 3.0
Diesel Engines: NS - NT SWB Automatic	
Rear Exhaust Hanger Bracket:	20 +/- 5
Centre Exhaust Pipe to Main Muffler:	41 +/- 10
DPF to Centre Exhaust Pipe:	49 +/- 10
Exhaust Gas Temperature Sensor:	30 +/- 5
Front Exhaust Pipe to Manifold:	41 +/- 10
Front Exhaust Pipe to Catalytic Converter:	41 +/- 10
Catalytic Converter to DPF:	49 +/- 10
Dash Panel Heat Protector:	4.5 +/- 1.5
Exhaust Muffler Hanger:	9.5 +/- 3.5
Diesel Engines: NS - NT SWB Automatic	
Rear Exhaust Hanger Bracket:	20 +/- 5
Main Muffler to Tail Pipe:	41 +/- 10
DPF to Main Muffler:	49 +/- 10
Exhaust Gas Temperature Sensor:	30 +/- 5
Catalytic converter to DPF:	49 +/- 10
Front Pipe to Catalytic Converter:	41 +/- 10
Front Pipe to Manifold:	41 +/- 10
Exhaust Muffler Hanger:	9.5 +/- 3.5

CLUTCH

Subject	Page
MINOR MAINTENANCE	239
Visual Inspection	239
Master Cylinder Inspection	240
Bleeding Hydraulic Clutch System	240
MAJOR REPAIRS	240
CLUTCH MASTER CYLINDER	240
Removal	240
Dismantle	240
Assembly	240
Installation	241
CLUTCH SLAVE CYLINDER.	240
Removal	241
Dismantle	241
Assembly	241
Installation	242
CLUTCH PEDAL	242
Removal	242
Installation	242
Adjustment	242
CLUTCH POSITION SWITCH	243
Removal	243
Check	243
Installation	243
CLUTCH ASSEMBLY	243
Removal	243
Inspection	243
Installation	243
PROBLEM DIAGNOSIS	245
SPECIFICATIONS	245
TORQUE SETTINGS	245

MINOR MAINTENANCE

There are several items which affect good clutch operation, therefore it is necessary before performing any major clutch service, to make preliminary inspections to determine whether the trouble is actually in the clutch.

VISUAL INSPECTION

1. Check condition of the hydraulic lines and ensure that components are assembled correctly, taking note that the lines do not have sharp bends or are rubbing against objects.
2. Check level of fluid in the master cylinder reservoir. Brake fluid will absorb water over time and will need to be replaced periodically.
3. Check clutch master cylinder for leaking seals.
4. Check clutch slave cylinder and lines for leaking seals and unions.
5. Check condition of clutch pedal bushes and shaft.
6. Check clutch pedal height and control rod adjustment, as outlined in this chapter.
7. Check condition of engine and transmission mountings.

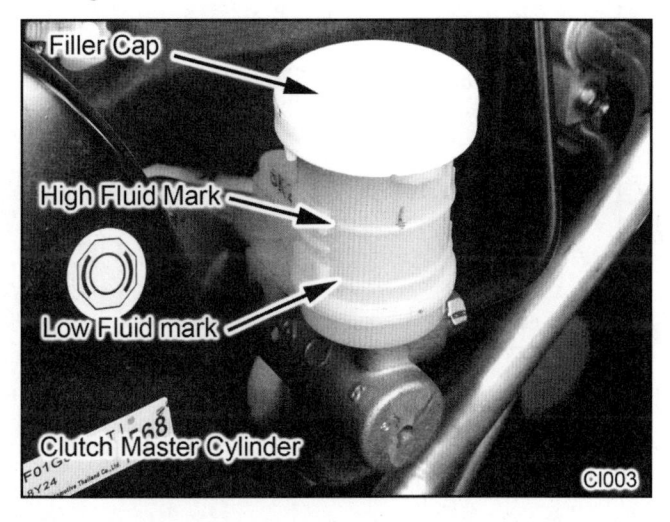

CLUTCH

MASTER CYLINDER INSPECTION

1. Check that the level of brake fluid is within the levels marked on the cylinder reservoir.
2. Refill with specified brake fluid.
   Clutch fluid specified .... Dot 4 brake fluid
   Note: Use only the specified brake fluid, and avoid using a mixture of fluids.
3. Inspect to make sure the air vent in the reservoir cap is clear and air can be blown through it.

BLEEDING HYDRAULIC CLUTCH SYSTEM

1. Fit a tube to the bleed valve located on the slave cylinder with the other end in a container half full of brake fluid. Keep an eye on the reservoir level and top up during the bleeding process if required.
2. With an assistant, push down on the clutch pedal several times. Push down on the pedal while the bleed valve is loosened just enough to allow brake fluid (air if present) to bleed out of the hose attached to the bleed valve.
3. Tighten the bleed valve before the clutch pedal is allowed to return to its normal position.
   Bleed Valve .... 11 +/- 1 Nm
4. Repeat steps 2 & 3 until the system is free of air. This is detected by having a firm feeling clutch pedal when pushed down.
5. Check the fluid level of the master cylinder reservoir. Top up to marked full level if required. Do not reuse fluid bled from the clutch system.
   Specified Clutch fluid................Dot 4 brake fluid

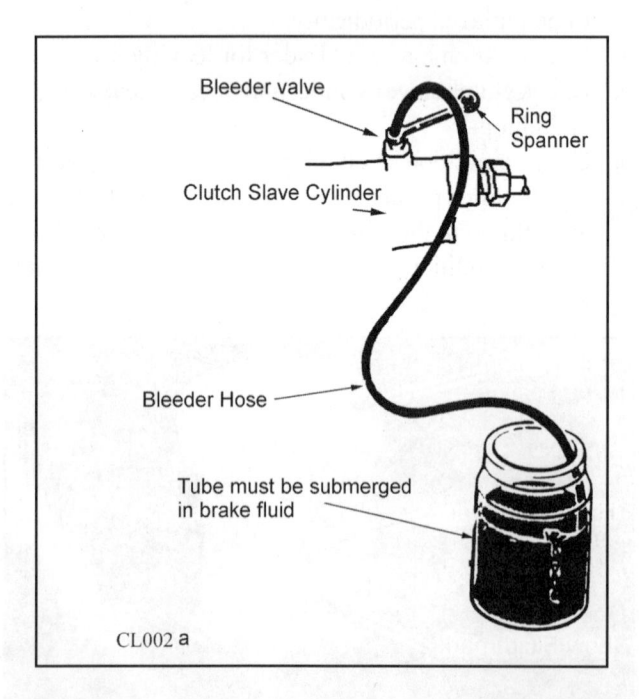

MAJOR REPAIRS

CLUTCH MASTER CYLINDER

Removal

1. Withdraw as much fluid from the master cylinder reservoir as possible, then remove the clutch fluid line from the master cylinder. Be sure to cover the line to stop brake fluid from dripping on painted surfaces.
2. Release the clutch cylinder pushrod from the clutch pedal by removing the clevis pin. Then remove the two securing nuts from within the engine bay. It may be necessary to remove the lower instrument panel to give easier access to the clevis pin.
3. Withdraw the master cylinder from the fire wall.

Dismantle

1. Slide back the boot from the rear of master cylinder assembly to give access to the piston stopper ring. Use cir-clip pliers or a small screwdriver to remove the snap ring.
   Note: It is not necessary to undo the lock nut on the push rod assembly.
2. Withdraw the snap ring and push rod from the clutch cylinder assembly.
3. Withdraw the piston assembly from the clutch cylinder.
4. Using a pin punch remove the spring pin from the assembly to release the reservoir tank and seal.

Assembly

Note: When re-assembling the master cylinder make sure to use a new piston assembly, piston stopper ring and boot.

1. Put the seal into the master cylinder assembly and then secure the reservoir using the spring pin.
2. Coat the piston with clean brake fluid.
3. Install the piston assembly securing it with the new piston stopper.

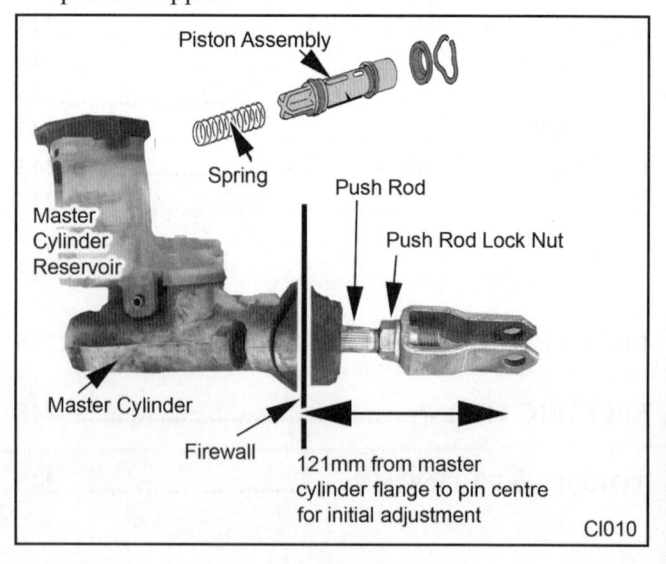

240

CLUTCH

Clutch Slave Cylinder Assemby

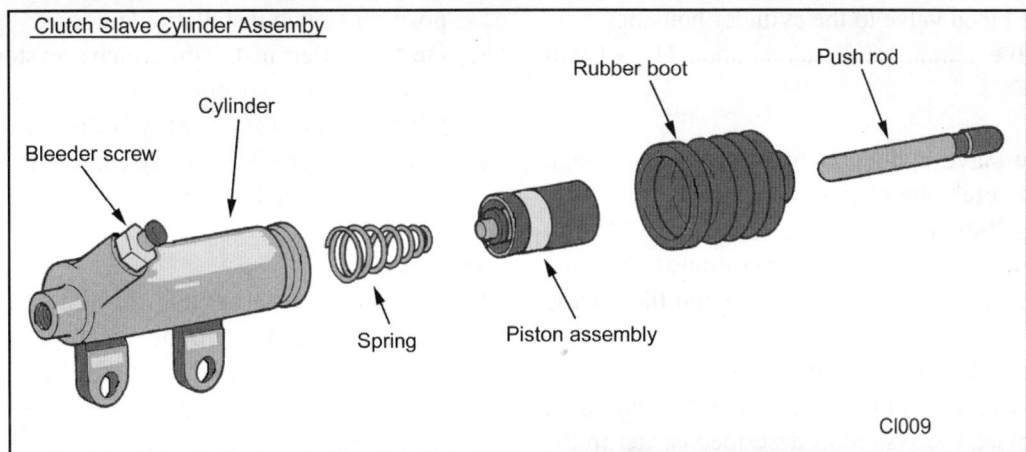

Note: Use rubber grease to lube the contact point of the piston and push rod assembly.

4. Install the push rod with a new rubber protective boot.
5. If the lock nut was removed the standard distance of the push rod will need to be set. The distance is measured from between the mounting holes of the master cylinder and the centre of the clevis pin hole.
   Note: This will help with clutch pedal adjustment later on.
   Pushrod Length.................. 121 +/- 1 mm
   Pushrod Locknut.................13 +/- 2 Nm

Installation

1. Position the master cylinder on to the fire wall of the vehicle ensuring to use the gasket, then secure with the retaining bolts.
   Master Cylinder Retaining Nuts.........13 +/- 2 Nm
2. Attach the clutch cylinder pushrod to the clutch pedal using the clevis pin and snap pin.
   Note: Before installing the clevis pin use rubber grease to lubricate it
3. Connect the clutch pipe to the clutch cylinder, then refill and bleed the clutch system as described earlier in the chapter.
4. Check and adjust the clutch pedal height as required using the sections later in the chapter.

CLUTCH SLAVE CYLINDER

Removal

Note: There is three variations on the way the slave cylinder is mounted to the gear box, depending on motor combinations. The removal procedure is basically the same for all.

1. Drain the fluid from the lines into a suitable container, being careful not to spill any brake fluid onto any painted surface.
2. Remove the banjo union bolt from the slave cylinder.
3. Undo the retaining bolts holding the cylinder and remove from the vehicle.

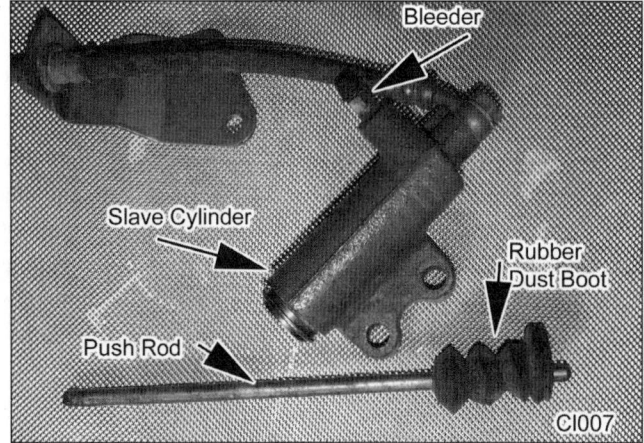

Dismantle

Note: Sometimes it is cheaper to replace the slave cylinder as an assembly rather than try to repair it.

1. Remove the bleed valve from the cylinder body, then remove the push rod and boot.
2. Apply air pressure to the bleed valve hole to push the piston and spring from the cylinder bore. Wrap a towel around the end of the cylinder to prevent the piston from popping out quickly.
3. Remove the piston cup from the piston. Separate the spring from the piston. Inspect piston, seals and spring for wear or damage, also inspect the cylinder bore for scoring or rust.
4. Using a cylinder gauge, measure at three points the diameter of the cylinder. The clearance should not exceed **0.15mm** between the piston and cylinder
   Note: If there is damage to the cylinder replace the whole assembly.

Assembly

1. Fit the new piston cup to the piston, ensuring the seal is seated correctly. Apply rubber grease to the outer surfaces of the piston and cup.
2. Coat the cylinder bore with the specified brake fluid.
3. Slide the spring into the cylinder bore, then the piston. Make sure the spring and piston are seated correctly.
4. Install boot onto the cylinder, then the push rod.

CLUTCH

5. Install the bleed valve to the cylinder housing.
   Bleed Valve .... **11 +/- 1 Nm**

Installation
1. Install the slave cylinder into place on the clutch housing securely, tightening the retaining bolts.
   Retaining Bolts (6G74) .... **35 +/- 6 Nm**
2. It is recommended to put rubber grease onto the contact point of the slave cylinder push rod and the release fork.
3. Connect the fluid line to the slave cylinder, making sure to use new sealing washers, then tighten union bolt and bleed the system as described earlier in the chapter.
   Banjo Union Bolt
   (6G74) .... **23 +/- 2 Nm**
   (4M40) .... **23 +/- 2 Nm**
   (6G72) .... **23 +/- 2 Nm**
   (4M41) .... **25 +/- 5 Nm**

CLUTCH PEDAL
Removal
1. Remove the lower instrument panel as described in the body chapter.
2. Remove the clutch arm stopper stay if fitted.
3. Remove the clutch position switch if fitted, by removing the electrical connector and loosening the lock nut.
   Note: *The switch can be left in place, but on removing the pedal assembly it can be damaged.*
4. Remove the snap pin and the clevis pin for the clutch master cylinder. Undo the retaining nuts for the clutch master cylinder.
5. Undo the pedal assembly mounting bolts and remove the assembly.
6. On models where fitted remove the turnover spring and bushings.

Installation
1. On models where fitted install the turnover spring and bushings.
2. Install the pedal assembly into place and do up the mounting bolts to the specified torque.
   Pedal Assembly Mounting Bolts .... **12 +/- 2 Nm**
3. Install the nuts on the clutch master cylinder and tighten to specification.
   Clutch Master Cylinder Nuts .... **13 +/- 2 Nm**
4. Before installing the clevis pin lubricate it with grease, then push snap pin into place.
5. The clutch pedal needs to be adjusted to the recommended height and free play. As described in the adjustment section.
6. Install the clutch position switch (Vehicles with auto cruise control) referring to the steps in the clutch position switch installation guide.
7. On NS models install the clutch arm stopper stay and tighten bolts to specification.
   Clutch Arm Stopper Stay Bolts .... **12 +/- 2 Nm**
8. Using the steps in the body chapter install the lower instrument panel.

Adjustment
1. Pull back the carpet and underlay from under the clutch pedal. Measure the clutch pedal height from the centre of the pedal pad to the floor pan.

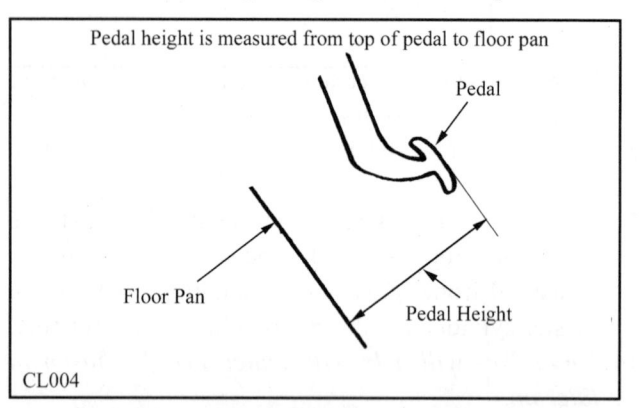

Pedal height is measured from top of pedal to floor pan

CL004

Pedal Height
NM, NP - (left hand drive) .... 202 - 205 mm
NM, NP - (right hand drive) .... 197 - 200 mm
NS - .... 195.7 - 198.7 mm

2. Measure the clutch pedal clevis pin play from the bottom of the pedal pad. The clevis pin needs to be lubricated with grease.
   Clutch Pedal Clevis Pin Free Play .... **1 - 3 mm**
   Note: *Play is measured to when the pedal first has the slightest resistance.*
3. If not within specification adjust as follows:
   a) Loosen the lock nut on the pushrod or the clutch pedal position switch locknut (vehicles with auto cruise control) to adjust the height.
   b) Bring the clutch pedal height into specification by screwing the stopper bolt or pedal switch in or out.
4. Depress the clutch pedal several times then re-check the clutch pedal height and pedal free travel are within specification.
5. If disengaged pedal height or clutch free play are not within specification, check the condition of the master and slave cylinders and the clutch. Also you may need to bleed the clutch system. When all is correct re-check the free play and the disengaged pedal height again.
   Clutch Pedal Free Play NM - NP .... **6 - 13 mm**
   Clutch Pedal Free Play NS - NT .... **4 - 13 mm**
   Disengaged Pedal Height
   NM - NP (LH Drive Vehicle)... 75mm or more
   NM - NP (RH Drive Vehicle)... 70mm or more
   NS - NT .... 120 mm or more

CLUTCH

6. If still not within specification after bleeding the system the pressure and clutch plates should be removed and inspected.

CLUTCH POSITION SWITCH
Note: Before the clutch switch can be checked you will need to adjust the clutch pedal as described earlier.

Removal
1. Remove the lower instrument panel as described in the body chapter.
2. Disconnect the electrical connector.
3. Unscrew the lock nut to release the pressure on the switch. Then unscrew the clutch switch all the way out.

Check
1. Disconnect the electrical terminal. Using a multimeter connect the two probes to the terminals of the clutch switch.

Pedal Position	Specified Condition
Fully depressed	Less than 2 Ohm
Released	Open circuit

2. If the above readings are not achieved the switch is fault and will need to be replaced.

Installation
Note: *Before the clutch switch can be replaced you will need to adjust the clutch pedal as described earlier.*
1. Install the switch so that there is **0.5 - 1.5 mm** clearance between the stopper and the contact point.
2. When that is done do up the lock nut.
   Clutch Switch Lock Nut .... 12 +/- 3 Nm
3. Check the operation of the switch again and if correct replace the electrical connector.
4. Replace the lower panel as described in the body chapter.

CLUTCH ASSEMBLY
Removal
1. Withdraw the transmission from the vehicle as described in the transmission chapter.
2. Place an alignment mark on the clutch cover and flywheel to help with assembly.
3. Release clutch assembly retaining bolts, then lift the assembly (clutch disc & clutch cover) from vehicle.
4. Using special tool (puller with hook) withdraw the spigot bearing, if requiring replacement.
5. To remove the release fork, undo the retaining bolt at the bottom of the release fork shaft.
6. Remove the lower sealing cap to drop out the fork shaft and the two packings.

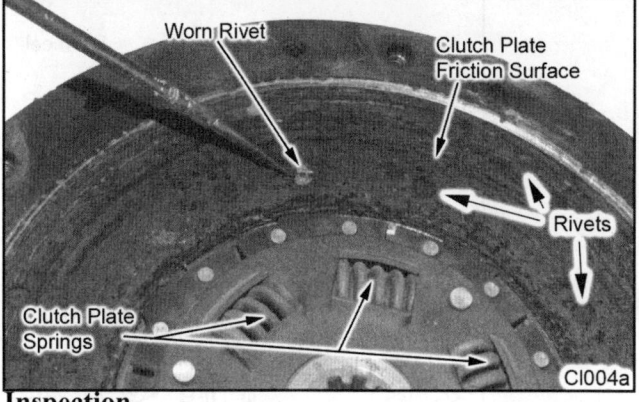

Inspection
1. Check the clutch disc for spring damage and play, uneven contact, loose rivets and rivet sink.
   Rivet Sink Limit .... 0.3 mm
2. The fly wheel needs to be checked for surface damage, like hot spots, cracked surface and glazing, also check for run-out.
3. Inspect the clutch release bearing to ensure its not noisy or rough when spun.
   Note: Be careful not to clean the clutch release bearing with solvent as it is filled with grease.
4. The clutch cover diaphragm spring fingers need to be checked for wear and uneven height. If the limit is exceeded replace the clutch cover.
   Height Limit .... 0.5 mm
5. Inspect the release fork for abnormal wear on the surfaces that contact with the release bearing.
6. If the general condition is in doubt for any component replace as needed. It is recommended to replace the clutch cover and clutch disc as a matched set.

Installation
1. Fit the spigot bearing using the special tool to tap it into place.
2. Install the release fork shaft with the two new packings in place above and below the release fork. Tighten the retaining bolt to specification. Apply the specified grease to the shaft where it contacts the release fork.

CLUTCH

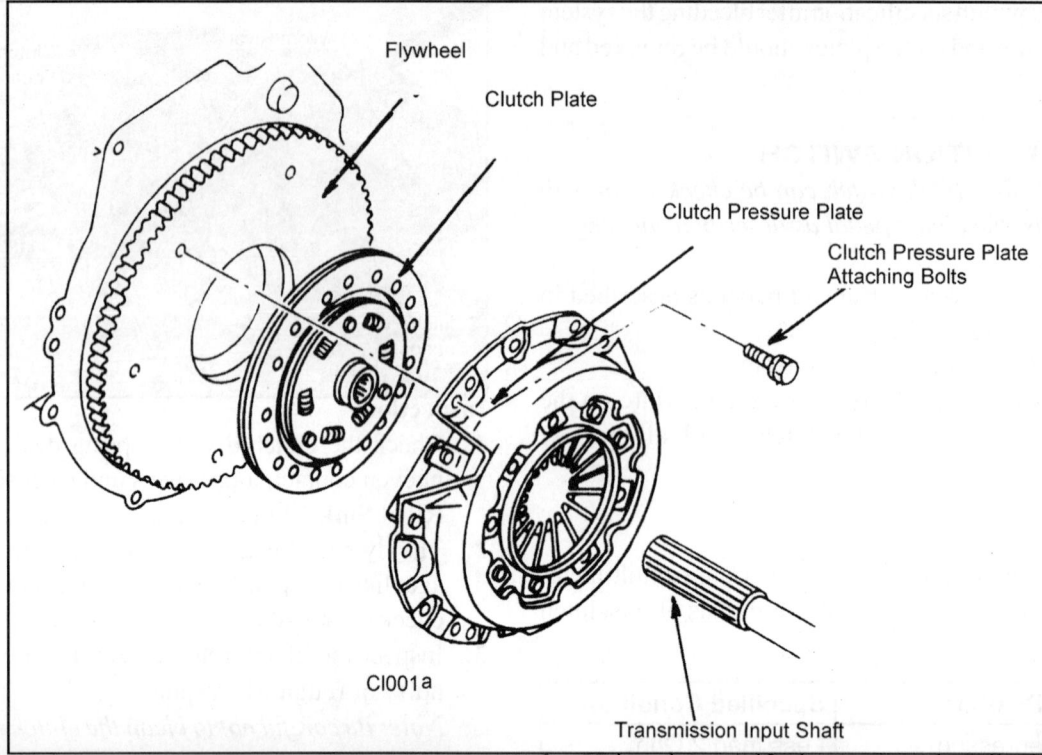

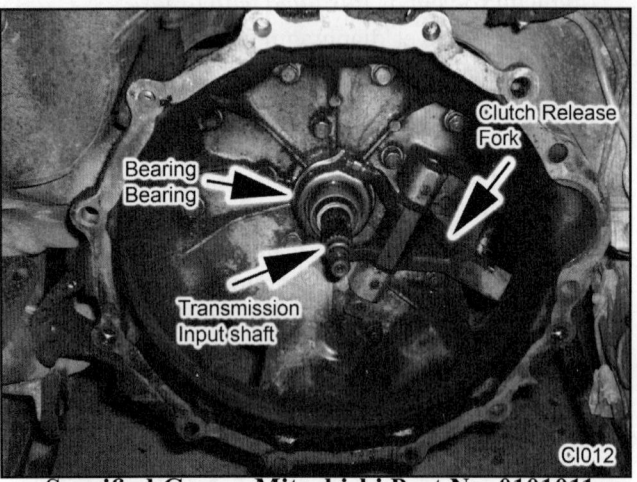

Figure: Flywheel, Clutch Plate, Clutch Pressure Plate, Clutch Pressure Plate Attaching Bolts, Transmission Input Shaft (CI001a)

Figure: Bearing, Clutch Release Fork, Transmission Input shaft (CI012)

Specified Grease Mitsubishi Part No. 0101011 or equivalent.
Release Fork Retaining Bolt .... 12 +/- 1 Nm

3. When the release fork is installed a new sealing cap must be press fitted 2 mm below the gearbox housing surface.
4. If removed replace the release bearing coating the inside of the bearing where it will contact with the input shaft with the specified grease.
5. Using a clutch aligning tool fit the clutch disc into place, then the clutch cover assembly over the top using the alignment marks made on removal as a guide.
6. Fit the clutch cover retaining bolts, nipping them up to hold the clutch plate.
7. Check the clutch assembly is aligned correctly, then tension the retaining bolts to specification. The bolts need to be tightened in a diagonal sequence.

Clutch Cover Bolts............................. 19 +/- 3 Nm

8. Using the specified grease as described earlier coat the splines of the clutch disc.
9. Fit the transmission as described in the transmission chapter. Bleed the clutch slave cylinder as described in this chapter.

PROBLEM DIAGNOSIS

Problem: Clutch fails to release
Possible Cause: Improper pedal travel.
Remedy: Adjust pedal height.
Possible Cause: Faulty clutch disc.
Remedy: Replace clutch disc and cover.
Possible Cause: Release fork & bearing not assembled properly.
Remedy: Install properly.
Possible Cause: Clutch disc warped or bent.
Remedy: Replace clutch disc and cover.
Possible Cause: Insufficient brake fluid.
Remedy: Top up reservoir to correct level.

Problem: Slipping!
Possible Cause: Insufficient pedal free travel.
Remedy: Check and adjust pedal height.
Possible Cause: Oil soaked clutch disc.
Remedy: Replace clutch disc and cover. Correct leak at source.
Possible Cause: Warped clutch disc.
Remedy: Replace clutch disc and cover.
Possible Cause: Weak diaphragm spring.
Remedy: Replace clutch disc and cover.
Possible Cause: Clutch disc overheated.
Remedy: Allow to cool and re-check.

Problem: Grabbing (chattering)!
Possible Cause: Oiled, burned or glazed facing.
Remedy: Replace clutch disc and cover. Correct leak at source.
Possible Cause: Warped clutch disc.
Remedy: Replace clutch disc.

Problem: Rattling - transmission click!
Possible Cause: Release fork loose.
Remedy: Install properly.

Problem: Noisy!
Possible Cause: Fork shaft improperly installed.
Remedy: Install properly & lubricate.

Problem: Pedal stays on floor!
Possible Cause: No brake fluid in master cylinder.
Remedy: Top up reservoir and bleed system.
Possible Cause: Spring wear in clutch disc.
Remedy: Replace clutch disc and cover.

Problem: Hard pedal effort!
Possible Cause: Binding in clutch pedal.
Remedy: Lubricate clevis pin and free up.
Possible Cause: Clutch disc worn.
Remedy: Replace clutch disc and cover.

SPECIFICATIONS

CLUTCH DISC
Type .... Single dry disc plate
Disc Size
    NS (V5M31-E-KD Trans) .... 250x160 mm
    NS (V5M31-E-XC Trans) .... 275x180 mm
Facing Rivet Sink Limit .... 0.3 mm

CLUTCH COVER
Type .... Diaphragm spring
Diaphragm Spring Finger Height Diff .... 0.5 mm

RELEASE BEARING
Type .... Prelubricated, sealed bearing.

SLAVE CYLINDER
Piston to bore clearance service limit .... 0.15 mm

CLUTCH PEDAL
Pedal play (at clevis pin) .... 1 - 3 mm
Pedal free travel (including pedal play)
    NM, NP, - .... 6 - 13 mm
    NS - NT .... 4 - 13 mm
Pedal height (measured at floor)
    NM - NP (LH Drive Vehicles) .... 202-205 mm
    NM - NP (RH Drive Vehicles) .... 197-200 mm
    NS - NT .... 195.7-198.7 mm
Disengaged Pedal Height
    NM - NP (LH Drive Vehicle) ..... 75mm or more
    NM - NP (RH Drive Vehicle) ..... 70mm or more
    NS - NT .... 120 mm or more

RECOMMENDED FLUID
DOT3 or DOT4 Brake fluid.

TORQUE SETTINGS

Description	Nm
Clutch Master Cylinder Pushrod Lock nut	12 +/- 3
Master Cylinder Mounting Nuts	13 +/- 2
Clutch Switch Lock Nut	12 +/- 3
Clutch Pedal Stopper Stay	12 +/- 2
Clutch Pedal Assembly Mounting Bolts	12 +/- 2
Slave Cylinder Banjo Bolt	
6G74	23 +/- 2
4M40	23 +/- 2
6G72	23 +/- 2
4M41	25 +/- 5
Slave Cylinder Retaining Bolts (6G74)	35 +/- 6
Slave Cylinder Bleeder Nipple	11 +/- 1
Clutch Release Fork Retaining Bolt	12 +/- 1
Clutch Cover Mounting Bolts	19 +/- 3

MANUAL TRANSAXLE - V5M31

Subject	Page
MAINTENANCE	247
Oil Level Check	247
Replacing Transmission Oil	247
4WD Detection Switch Check	247
Transmission Controls - Part Time 4WD	247
Remove	247
Install	247
Transmission Controls - SSII 4WD	248
Remove	248
Install	248
MAJOR REPAIRS AND REBUILD	248
Transmission & Transfer Assembly	248
Removal	248
Separation - Part Time 4WD	249
Assembly - Part Time 4WD	249
Separation - Super Select II 4WD	249
Assembly - Super Select II 4WD	250
Installation	250

Subject	Page
TRANSMISSION ASSEMBLY	250
Transmission Disassembly	250
Sub Assemblies	
Main Drive Pinion	252
Disassembly	252
Assembly	252
Countershaft Cluster Gear	252
Disassembly	252
Assembly	252
Main Shaft	253
Disassembly	253
Assembly	253
Transmission Assembly	254
Spacer Selection Main Drive Pinion End Play	254
Assembly	254
SPECIFICATIONS	256
TORQUE WRENCH SPECIFICATIONS	256

MANUAL TRANSMISSION - V5M31

MAINTENANCE

Oil Level Check
1. Remove the transaxle filler plug.

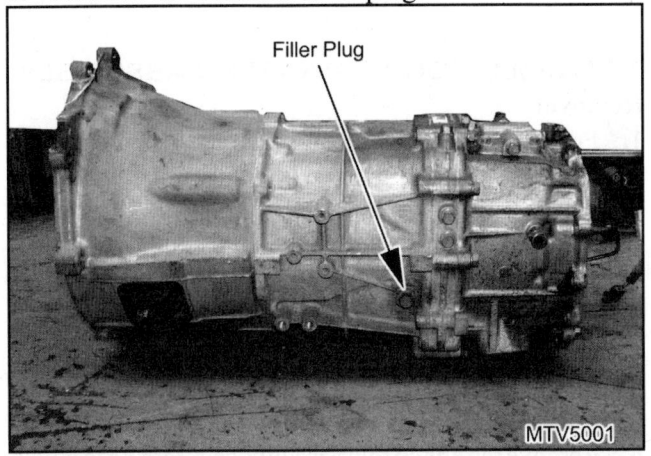

2. Check to ensure the oil level is at the bottom of the filler plug hole and that the oil is in relatively good condition.
3. Replace oil filler plug and tighten plug to specification.
   Filler Plug specified torque .... **32 Nm**

Checking and Replacing Transmission Oil
1. Position an oil catching tray under the transmission, make sure it has the capacity to hold the oil from the transaxle.
2. Remove the drain plug and allow gear oil to grain from transmission.
3. Replace the drain plug and tighten to specification.
   Transmission Drain Plug .... **32 Nm**

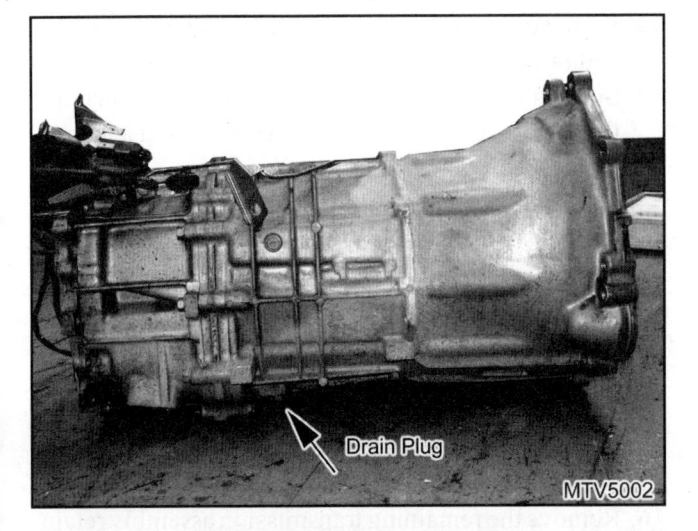

4. Remove the filler plug, fill the transmission to the full level with the specified transmission fluid.
   Full level is at the bottom of the filler plug hole.
   Transmission Oil Capacity .... **3.2 litres**
   Transmission Gear Oil .... **SAE 75W-85W**
   .... **API GL-4**

5. Replace transmission filler plug and tighten plug to specification.
   Transmission Filler Plug .... **32 Nm**

4WD DETECTION SWITCH CHECK (part time 4wd)
Check continuity b/w terminal #1 and #2 of the black connector on the side of the transfer case.

Transfer lever position	Continuity
2H	No Continuity
4H	Continuity

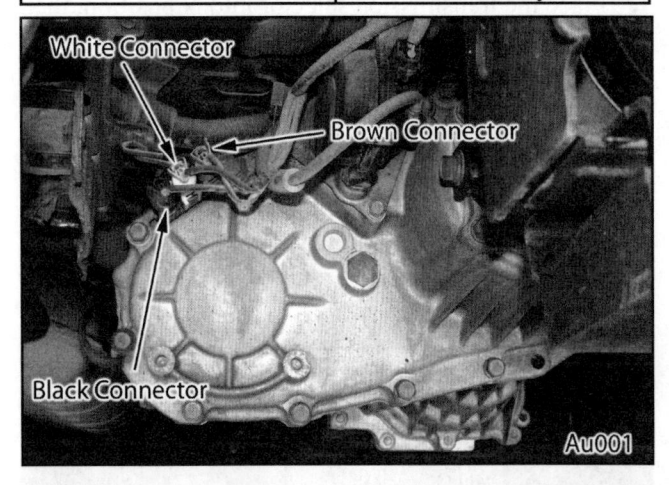

HIGH/LOW DETECTION SWITCH CHECK (part time 4wd)
Check continuity b/w terminal #1 and #2 of the grey connector on the side of the transfer case.

Transfer lever position	Continuity
4H	No Continuity
Between 4H & 4L	Continuity
4L	Continuity

Transmission Controls (part time 4WD)
Removal
1. Place the transmission selector into N position and the transfer selector into 4H position, then remove the selector knobs.
2. From the centre console remove the parking brake lever cover and cup holder, then remove the centre section of the centre console. Refer to body chapter in required.
3. Remove the screws securing the shift control boot retainer, then remove the retainer plate and boot.
4. Remove the snap rings from the transmission control lever and transfer control lever.
5. Remove the transmission control lever assembly and the transfer control lever assembly.

Installation
1. Install the transmission control lever assembly and the transfer control lever assembly into position and

247

MANUAL TRANSMISSION - V5M31

secure with retaining snap rings.
2. Install the shift control boot then install the boot retainer and tighten retaining screws.
3. Install the centre section of the centre console, then install the parking brake lever cover and cup holder. Refer to body chapter in required.
4. Install selector knobs to the selector controls, then check operation of each control lever.

Transmission Controls (super select 4WDII)
Removal
1. Place the transmission selector into N position, then remove the selector knobs.
2. From the centre console remove the parking brake lever cover and cup holder, then remove the centre section of the centre console. Refer to body chapter in required.
3. Disconnect the electrical connection from the transfer select switch assembly, then remove the assembly retaining screws and remove transfer select switch assembly.

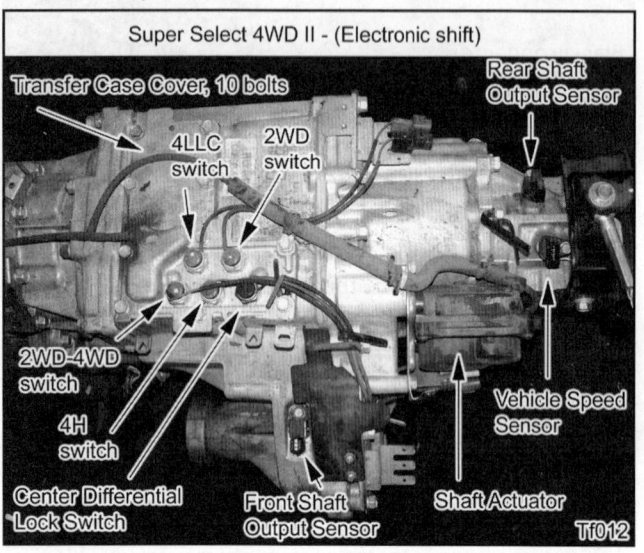

Super Select 4WD II - (Electronic shift)
Transfer Case Cover, 10 bolts; Rear Shaft Output Sensor; 4LLC switch; 2WD switch; 2WD-4WD switch; 4H switch; Center Differential Lock Switch; Front Shaft Output Sensor; Vehicle Speed Sensor; Shaft Actuator. Tf012

4. Remove the screws securing the shift control boot retainer, then remove the retainer plate and boot.
5. Remove the snap ring from the transmission control lever control lever assembly.

Installation
1. Install the transmission control lever assembly into position and secure with retaining snap ring.
2. Install the shift control boot then install the boot retainer and tighten retaining screws.
3. Install the transfer select switch assembly into position tighten retaining bolts to specification.
4. Reconnect the electrical connection the the transfer switch.
5. Install the centre section of the centre console, then install the parking brake lever cover and cup holder. Refer to body chapter in required.

6. Install selector knob to the selector controls and check operation of controls.

MAJOR REPAIR/REBUILD

TRANSMISSION & TRANSFER ASSEMBLY
Removal
1. From under the vehicle remove the skid plates and under cover, then remove the radiator shroud lower cover.
2. Drain the transmission fluid and transfer oil.
3. Remove the front exhaust pipe from vehicle.
4. Remove the front & rear propeller shafts, referring to the rear suspension/axle chapter for assistance.
5. 4M4 - Remove the intercooler from the vehicle, referring to fuel chapter for assistance.
6. Remove the clutch release cylinder, referring to clutch chapter if required.
7. 4M41 - Remove the clutch damper assembly, referring to clutch chapter if required.
8. 4M4 - Remove the exhaust support bracket, disconnect the battery cable connection and then remove the spacer rubber and dust cover.
9. Remove the heater hose retaining bracket, then remove the starter motor, referring to engine electrical chapter for assistance.
10. 6G7 - Remove the bolts retaining the cover, then remove the cover followed by the oil pan retaining bolts.
11. Remove the guard from under the transfer assembly, then remove the dynamic damper from the transfer assembly.
12. Remove the bolts securing the tension wire bracket and remove bracket from transfer assembly.
13. Support transmission on a jack or transmission hoist, then remove the centre transmission mount and insulator.
14. Label and disconnect the electrical connections from the transmission assembly.
15. Disconnect the clutch release bearing using the following procedure.
    a) Remove the clutch housing service hole cover, then operate the release fork and push the release bearing towards the clutch side.
    b) Separate the release bearing using a large flat blade screwdriver.
16. Remove the remaining transmission assembly retaining bolts, slide the transmission back away from the engine then low transmission on jack and remove from vehicle.
17. Disconnect and remove tension wire from transfer assembly.

MANUAL TRANSMISSION - V5M31

Installation
1. Connect the tension wire to the transfer assembly, tightening bolt to specification.
   Tension Wire Bolt: **24Nm**
2. Raise the transmission assembly on the jack and position into place on engine.
3. Install the transmission assembly retaining bolts in their correct locations and tighten to specification.
   Transmission Assembly Bolts:

4M4	A (12 x 25mm)	48 Nm
	B (10 x 45mm)	48 Nm
	C (10 x 50mm)	48 Nm

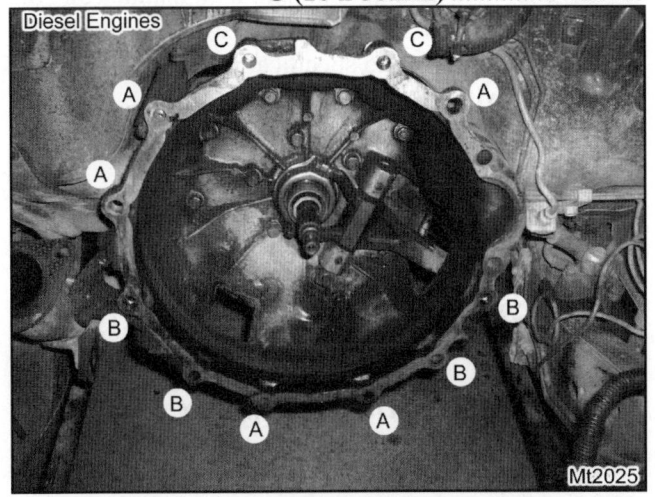

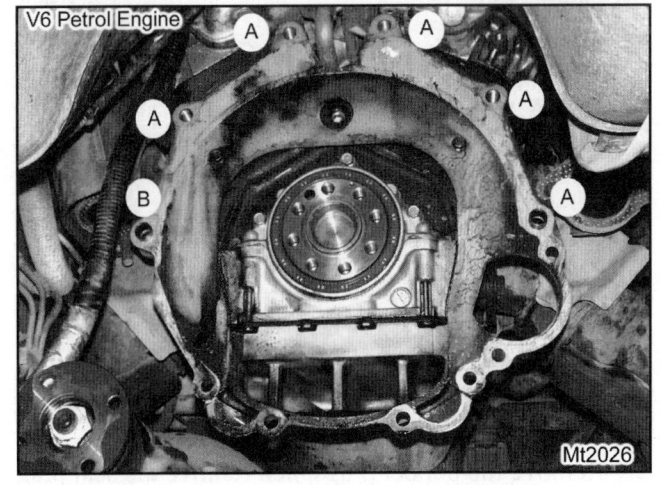

6G7	A (12 x 40mm)	74 Nm
	B (12 x 55mm)	89 Nm

4. Connect the electrical connection for the transmission using the labels made on removal to assist.
5. Install the transmission mount insulator to the transmission centre mount, then install the centre mount.
   Insulator to Mount Bolts .... **44 Nm**
   Crossmember Bolts .... **44 Nm**
   Crossmember Nuts .... **26 Nm**
6. Install the tension wire bracket tightening bolts to specification.
   Tension Wire Bolt .... **24 Nm**
   Tension Wire Bracket Bolts .... **53 Nm**
7. Install the dynamic damper to the transfer assembly and the transfer guard, tighten the retaining bolts to specification.
   Dynamic Damper Bolts .... **35 Nm**
   Transfer Guard Bolts .... **35 Nm**
8. 6G7 - Install the oil pan to transmission retaining bolts then install the cover bolts, tightening to specification.
   Oil Pan to Transmission Bolts .... **36 Nm**
   Cover Bolts .... **6 Nm**
9. Install the starter motor, referring to engine electrical chapter for assistance, then install the heater hose bracket.
   Starter Motor Mounting Bolts .... **30 Nm**
10. 4M4 - Install the dust cover, spacer rubber and then install the exhaust support bracket.
    Exhaust Support Bracket Bolts .... **49 Nm**
11. 4M41 - Install the clutch damper assembly, referring to clutch chapter if required.
12. Install the clutch release cylinder, referring to clutch chapter if required.
13. 4M4 - Install the intercooler to the vehicle, referring to fuel chapter for assistance.
14. Install the front and rear propeller shafts, referring to the rear suspension/axle chapter for assistance.
15. Install the front exhaust pipe to vehicle.
16. Reinstall the radiator shroud lower cover, then install the skid plates and under cover.
17. Refill transmission and transfer assembly as described previously.

TRANSMISSION & TRANSFER ASSEMBLY
Separation - Part Time 4WD
1. With the assembly removed from the vehicle, remove vacuum hose from the assembly.
2. Remove the spring pin securing the change shifter then remove the shifter.
3. Remove the bolts securing the transfer to the transmission assembly and separate the transfer assembly from the transmission.

Assembly
1. Apply a bead of sealant to the transfer case then slide the transfer case onto the transmission assembly and tighten retaining bolts to specification.
   Transfer Retaining Bolts .... **36 Nm**
2. Install the change shifter and secure in position with retaining spring pin, ensuring split in pin faced down the shift rail.
3. Install the vacuum hose to the transmission assembly.

Separation - Super Select II 4WD
1. With the assembly removed from the vehicle, remove vacuum hose from the assembly.

MANUAL TRANSMISSION - V5M31

2. From the top of the transfer case assembly remove the 4LLC switch, gasket and steel ball, then remove the 2WD switch, gasket and steel ball.
3. Remove the centre differential lock switch, gasket and steel ball, then remove the 4H switch gasket and steel ball.
4. Remove the 2WD-4WD switch, gasket and steel ball then remove the control housing retaining bolts and control housing.
5. Remove the spring pin securing the change shifter then remove the shifter.
6. Remove the bolts securing the transfer to the transmission assembly and separate the transfer assembly from the transmission.

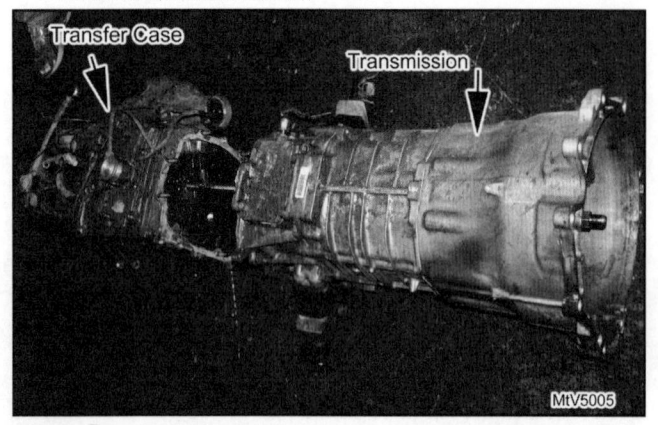

Assembly

1. Apply a bead of sealant to the transmission / transfer case contacting surface then slide the transfer case onto the transmission assembly and tighten retaining bolts to specification.
   Transfer Retaining Bolts .... 36 Nm

2. Install the change shifter and secure in position with retaining spring pin, ensuring split in pin faced down the shift rail.
3. To the control housing apply a bead of sealant, then install the control housing to the transfer assembly, tightening retaining bolts to specification.
   Control Housing Bolts .... 19 Nm

4. Install the steel ball and 2WD-4WD switch using a new gasket and tighten to specification.
   2WD-4D Switch .... 36 Nm
5. Install the steel ball and 4H switch using a new gasket and tighten to specification.
   4H Switch .... 36 Nm
6. Install the steel ball and centre differential lock switch using a new gasket and tighten to specification.
   Centre Differential Lock Switch .... 36 Nm
7. Install the steel ball and 2WD switch using a new gasket and tighten to specification.
   2WD Switch .... 36 Nm
8. Install the steel ball and 4LLC switch using a new gasket and tighten to specification.
   4LLC Switch .... 36 Nm
9. Install the vacuum hose to the transmission assembly.

TRANSMISSION ASSEMBLY

TRANSMISSION DISASSEMBLY

1. Unscrew the reverse light switch from the transfer case adaptor, then remove the gasket and steel ball. 
2. Remove the poppet plugs then remove the seal plug (petrol) or 4WD switch (diesel) from the top of the transfer case adaptor.
3. Remove the bolts securing the upper cover to the transfer case adaptor and remove cover.
4. Remove the plug, resistance spring and steel ball.

MANUAL TRANSMISSION - V5M31

5. Remove the return plunger plug A, then remove the return spring and Neutral return plunger A from the upper cover.
6. Remove the return plunger plug B, then remove the return spring and Neutral return plunger B from the upper cover.
7. Remove the stopper bracket then remove the special bolt from the top of the upper cover.
8. Remove the spring pin securing the control shaft to the control finger, then remove the control shaft followed by the control finger.
9. a) Put the two speed gears into engagement by sliding the two shift forks.
   b) Shift the reverse shift fork and 5th synchronizer sleeve to engage the gears, this will lock the shaft.
   c) Remove the main shaft lock nut, then remove the countershaft cluster gear lock nut.
10. Remove the bolts securing the transfer case adaptor to the transmission assembly, then remove the case adaptor.  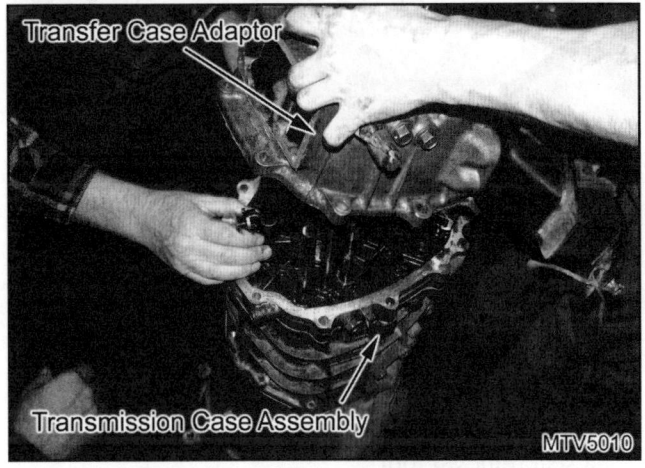
11. From the end of the counter shaft remove the bearing using a suitable bearing puller, then remove the counter reverse gear.
12. Remove the thrust washer from the reverse idler gear then remove the reverse idler gear and needle bearing.
13. From the mainshaft remove the bearing using a suitable bearing puller, then remove the reverse gear and needle bearing.
14. Remove the bolts securing the 5th speed shift lever and remove lever.
15. Remove the spring pin securing the reverse shift fork to the shift rail, then remove the shift fork and reverse synchronizer sleeve.
16. From the transmission case remove the poppet plug 'A', springs and the steel ball.
17. From the transmission case remove the two 'B' poppet plugs, springs and steel balls, then slide the reverse shift rail from the transmission case.
18. Remove snap ring.
19. Remove the 5th speed shift fork and the 5th speed synchronizer sleeve, then slide the shift rail from the transmission case.
20. Remove the reverse gear bearing sleeve, synchronizer

MANUAL TRANSMISSION - V5M31

spring and ring together as an assembly using a suitable puller (tool # MD998020).
21. From the main shaft remove the reverse brake gear followed by the overtop gear.
22. From the countershaft remove the 5th synchronizer hub, ring and spring.
23. From the counter shaft remove the counter 5th speed gear followed by the needle bearings.
24. Remove the reverse idler gear shaft from the assembly.
25. Remove the bolts securing the clutch housing to the transmission case and separate the housing from the case.

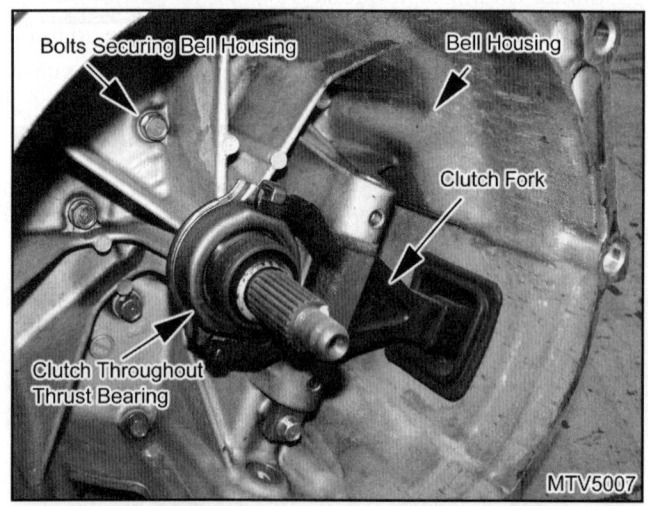

26. From the transmission case remove the oil seal using a seal removal tool.
27. Remove the spacer, then remove the snap ring securing the main drive pinion bearing to the transmission case.
28. Remove the bolts securing the transmission case to the intermediate plate then slide the transmission case from the assembly.

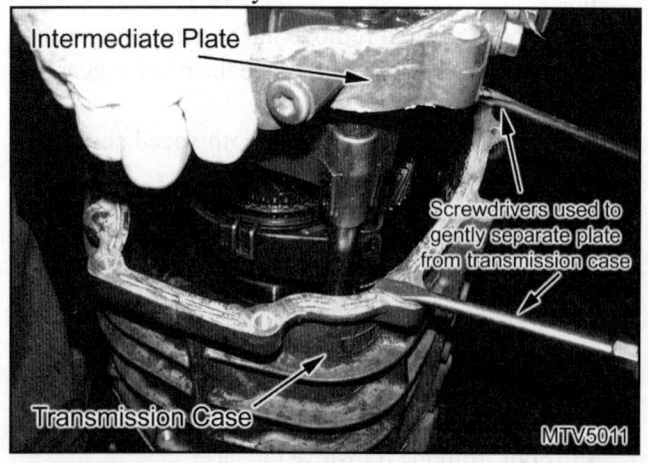

29. Remove the magnet and magnet holder from within the transmission case.
30. Remove the interlock plunger from the 3rd-4th speed shift mechanism.
31. Remove the spring pins from the 3rd-4th and 1st-2nd speed shift forks.
32. From the assembly remove the 3rd-4th speed shift rail followed by the 3rd-4th speed shift fork.
33. Remove the interlock plunger from the 3rd-4th speed shift mechanism.
34. From the assembly remove the 1st-2nd speed shift rail followed by the 1st-2nd speed shift fork.
35. Remove the bolts securing the rear bearing retainer and remove the bearing retainer from the intermediate plate.
36. Push the mainshaft and countershaft assemblies against the intermediate plate, then remove the two retaining snap rings.
37. From the gear assembly remove the intermediate plate.
   Note: *It ma be necessary to hold the main drive pinion and tap the plate free using a rubber mallet.*
38. From the mainshaft assembly remove the main drive pinion, needle bearings, synchronizer ring and spring.

SUB-ASSEMBLIES

Main Drive Pinion
Disassembly
Remove the front bearing snap ring from the main drive pinion then remove the front bearing using a suitable press.

Assembly
Install the bearing to the main drive pinion using a press, then install a snap ring with gives an end play within specification..
Bearing End Play .... 0.0-0.06 mm

Counter Shaft Cluster Gear
Disassembly
1. Remove the snap ring securing the inner race and bearing to the counter shaft assembly.
2. Remove the inner race and bearing from the counter shaft assembly using a suitable press.
3. Remove the snap ring securing the sub gear, then remove the sub gear and spring.
4. Using a suitable press, remove the bearing sleeve from the counter shaft assembly.
5. Remove the inner race and bearing from the counter shaft assembly using a suitable press.

Assembly
1. To the counter shaft assembly install the bearing and inner race using a suitable press, then press the bearing sleeve onto the counter shaft gear assembly.
2. Install the sun gear spring to the countershaft ensuring to insert the long leg of the spring into the shaft.

Photo labels: Intermediate Plate; 3rd/4th Speed Shift Fork; Main Drive Pinion; 1st/2nd Speed Shift Fork; Main Shaft Assembly; Reverse Idler Gear; Counter Cluster Gear

3. Install the sub gear to the counter shaft gear inserting the end of the spring in the small hole of the gear.
4. Turn the sub gear clockwise until the holes in the sub gear align with the holes in the counter shaft gear.
5. Install a 50mm long M5 bolt to the aligned holes and leave in place until the counter shaft gear assembly is installed into the transmission.
6. To the counter shaft assembly install the bearing and inner race using a suitable press, then install the retaining snap ring.

Main Shaft
Disassembly
1. Remove the 3rd-4th speed synchronizer sleeve, then remove the snap ring securing the 3rd-4th speed synchronizer hub.
2. From the main shaft assembly press off the 3rd-4th speed synchronizer hub, then remove the synchronizer spring, outer ring, cone and inner ring.
3. From the mainshaft assembly remove the 3rd speed gear and needle bearings.
4. From the main shaft assembly remove the 5th speed gear, bearing, bearing sleeve and 1st speed gear as an assembly using a suitable bearing removal tool.
5. Remove the needle bearing, then remove the 1st-2nd speed synchronizer sleeve, inner ring, cone, outer ring and spring.
6. From the main shaft assembly remove the 1st-2nd speed synchronizer hub and 2nd speed gear as an assembly using a suitable bearing removal tool.
7. From the main shaft remove the needle bearings.

Assembly
1. To the main shaft install the needle bearing, install the 2nd speed gear to the main shaft.
2. To the 1st-2nd speed synchronizer hub install the synchronizer inner ring, outer ring and cone, then install the hub assembly to the main shaft using a suitable press.
3. To the hub assembly install the synchronizer sleeve, ensuring it is installed in the correct direction and is aligned with the synchronizer hub.
4. To the synchronizer ring install the spring then assemble the synchronizer assembly and install.
5. Install the needle bearing to the main shaft then install the 1st speed gear.
6. Using a suitable press install the bearing sleeve to the assembly then install the bearing.
7. Install the 5th speed gear to the main shaft assembly by pressing into position.
8. To the opposite end of the main shaft install the needle bearing and 3rd speed gear.
9. To the 3rd-4th speed synchronizer hub install the synchronizer inner ring, outer ring and cone, then

install the hub assembly to the main shaft using a suitable press.
10. To the hub assembly install the synchronizer sleeve, ensuring it is installed in the correct direction and is aligned with the synchronizer hub.
11. Install the correct size snap ring to the assembly so the 3rd-4th speed synchronizer hub end play is within specification.
   Synchronizer Hub End Play .... 0-0.08 mm

TRANSMISSION ASSEMBLY
Spacer Selection Main Drive Pinion End Play
1. To the transmission case install the main drive pinion then at the points shown place solder approximately 10mm long by 1.6mm diameter.

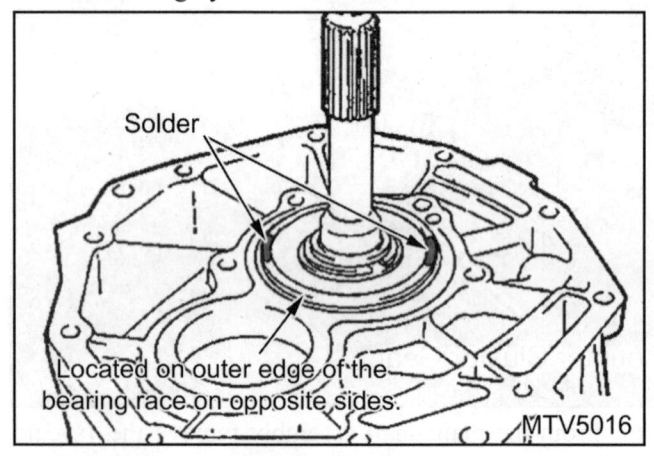

2. Install the clutch housing and tighten bolts to specification.
   Clutch Housing Bolts .... 36 Nm
3. Remove the clutch housing and measure the thickness of the crushed solder. Select a spacer of the measured thickness to obtain specified end play.
   Specified End Play .... 0.00 - 0.1 mm

Assembly
1. To the clutch housing install the main shaft and countershaft cluster as an assembly.
2. Install the intermediate plate to the assembly by gently tapping on using a rubber mallet, then install the two retaining snap rings.
3. Install the rear bearing retainer and tighten retaining bolts to specification.
   Bearing Retainer Bolts .... 19 Nm
4. Install the 1st-2nd shift fork and shift rail, then install the interlock plunger.
5. Install the 3rd-4th shift fork and shift rail, then install the interlock plunger.
6. Install the spring pins with split in the pin facing down the rail.
7. To the transmission case apply a 1.5 mm bead of sealant, then install transmission case to assembly and tighten the retaining bolts to specification.
   Case to Intermediate Plate Bolts .... 36 Nm
8. Install snap ring and then install the spacer selected previously.
9. Install oil seal to the transmission case, then coat the seal lips with grease.
10. Apply a bead of sealant to the transmission case then install the clutch housing to the transmission case and tighten retaining bolts to specification.
    Clutch Housing to Case Bolts .... 36 Nm

11. Install the reverse idler gear shaft.
12. To the counter shaft install the needle bearing, then install the counter 5th speed gear ensuring it is installed facing the correct direction.
13. To the countershaft install the synchronizer ring, spring and 5th synchronizer hub, ensuring the synchronizer hub is installed in the correct direction.
14. To the main shaft install the overtop gear then using a suitable press install the reverse brake gear.
15. Install the synchronizer ring and spring, then install the reverse brake gear.
16. Install the synchronizer ring and spring, then install the reverse gear bearing sleeve using a press.
17. Slide the 5th speed shift rail into position in the transmission case, then install the 5th speed synchronizer sleeve and fork.
18. Install snap ring then install the reverse shift rail, synchronizer sleeve and shift fork, securing in position with spring pin.
    Note: Ensure the split in the spring faces down the shift rail.
19. To the transmission case install the two steel balls, springs and the two 'B' poppet plugs, tightening plugs to specification.
    Poppet Plugs 36Nm
    Note: The small end of the spring goes towards the steel ball.
20. Install the steel ball, spring and poppet plug 'A', tightening plug to specification.
    Poppet Plugs 36Nm
    Note: The small end of the spring goes towards the steel ball.

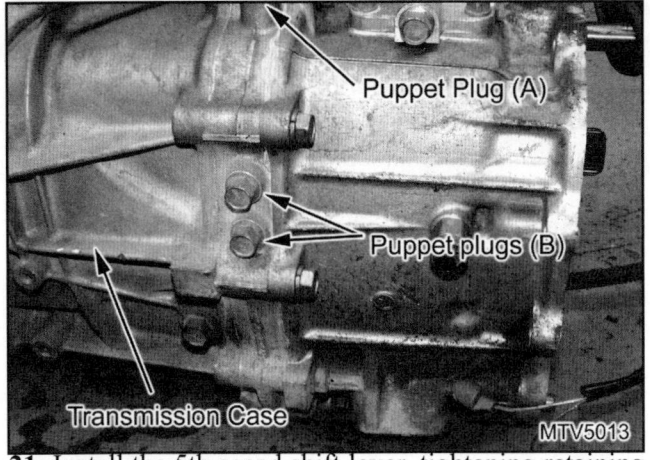

21. Install the 5th speed shift lever, tightening retaining bolts to specification.
    Shift Lever Bolt .... 19 Nm
22. Install the needle bearing followed by the reverse gear, then press the bearing into position using a suitable press.
23. Install the needle bearing followed by the reverse idler gear ensuring to install gear in the correct direction.
24. Install the thrust washer then install the counter reverse gear, ensuring the gear is installed in the correct direction.
25. To the end of the counter shaft install the bearing using a suitable press.
26. To the transfer case adaptor apply a bead of sealant then install the case adaptor to transmission case and tighten retaining bolts to specification.
    Transfer Adaptor to Transmission .... 36Nm 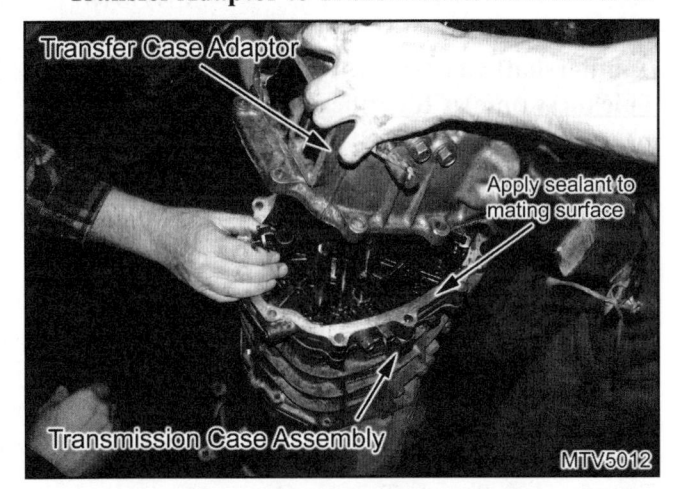
27. Engage the two speed gears by sliding the synchronizer sleeves forward, then shift the reverse shift fork and 5th synchronizer sleeve to engage gears and lock shaft.
28. Install the mainshaft lock nut tightening to specification, then release lock nut and retighten to specification. 
    Main Shaft Lock Nut .... 260 Nm
29. Install the countershaft cluster lock nut tightening to specification, then release lock nut and retighten to specification.
    Countershaft Cluster Lock Nut .... 260 Nm
30. Stake both locknuts using a punch. 
31. Install the control finger into transmission assembly then slide the control shaft into position and secure with spring pin.
    Note: *Split in spring pin should face down the shaft.*
32. To the special bolt apply sealant to the underside of the bolt head and also to the treads of the retaining nut. Then install the special bolt and stopper bracket, tightening bracket nut to specification.
    Stopper Bracket Nut .... 19 Nm
33. Install the neutral return plunger B to the upper cover, then install the return spring and plunger seal bolt.
    Plunger Seal Bolt .... 36 Nm
34. Install the neutral return plunger A to the upper cover, then install the return spring and plunger seal bolt.
    Plunger Seal Bolt .... 36 Nm
35. Install the steel ball and resistance spring, then install the plug which has bean coated with sealant.

Sealant.................................3M ATD Part #8660

36. Apply a bead of sealant to the upper cover, then install the upper cover and tighten retaining bolts to specification.
    Upper Cover Bolts................................19 Nm

37. Install the poppet plugs then install the seal plug (petrol) or 4WD switch (diesel) to the top of the transfer case adaptor.
    Thread sealant..............................3M ATD #8660
    4WD Switch.......................................36 Nm
    Poppet / Seal Plugs............................36 Nm

38. Install the steel ball then screw in the reverse light switch using a new gasket.
    Backup Light Switch ....34 Nm

SPECIFICATIONS

Type .... Manual transmission
Model... V5M31

Transmission:

Gear	4M4	6G7
1st:	3.952:1	4.234:1
2nd:	1.238:1	2.238:1
3rd:	1.398:1	1.398:1
4th:	1.000:1	1.000:1
5th:	0.761:1	0.819:1
Reverse:	3.553:1	3.553:1

Transfer:

Gear		
High	1.000	1.000:1
Low	1.925	1.900:1

Recommended Lubrication ....Hypoid gear oil, SAE 75W-90   API GL-4
Quantity: - Transmission ....3.2 litres
              - Transfer ....2.5 litres

Main drive pinion bearing end play .... 0-0.06 mm
Main drive pinion end play .... 0-0.1 mm
3rd-4th speed synchro hub end play .... 0-0.08 mm
Countershaft cluster gear bearing
end play ....0-0.15 mm

Clearance b/w outer synchronizer ring back surface and gear... 0.3 mm

Main Drive Gear Bearing end-play Snap Ring

Thickness (mm)	Identification	Part No.
2.32	Blue	MB919165
2.37	None	MB919166
2.42	Brown	MB919167
2.47	White	MB919168

Main Drive Gear End Play Spacer

Thickness (mm)	Identification	Part No.
0.68	None	MB919169
0.77	Red	MB919170
0.86	Yellow	MB919171
0.95	Orange	MB919172
1.04	White	MB919173

3rd-4th Speed Synchro Hub End-Play Snap Ring

Thickness (mm)	Identification	Part No.
2.18	Blue	MB919184
2.25	None	MB919185
2.32	Brown	MB919186
2.39	White	MB919187

Countershaft Cluster Gear End-Play Snap Ring

Thickness (mm)	Identification	Part No.
1.48	Blue	MB919176
1.62	None	MB919177

TORQUE SPECIFICATIONS

Description	Nm
Clutch housing - transmission case bolts	36
Transmission Case to Intermediate Plate	36
Intermediate Plate to Transfer Case Adaptor	36
Transfer Case Adaptor to Transfer Case Plate	36
Transfer Case Plate to Transfer Case	36
Mainshaft locking nut	260
Countershaft cluster gear locking nut	260
Rear bearing retainer	19
5th speed gear shift lever	19
Neutral Return Plunger Plugs	36
Upper cover mounting bolt	19
Stopper bracket mounting bolt	19
Poppet Plug	36
Backup Lamp Switch	30

MANUAL TRANSMISSION - V5MT1

Subject	Page
MAINTENANCE	257
Oil Level Check	257
Checking and Replacing Transmission Oil	257
MAJOR REPAIRS AND REBUILD	258
Transmission	258
Removal	258
Installation	258
Transmission & Transfer	259
Separation	259
Assembly	259
Transmission Dismantle	259
Main Shaft	260
Disassembly	260
Inspection	261
Assembly	261
Gear Shift Case	261
Disassembly	261
Assembly	261
Transmission Assembly	262
SPECIFICATIONS	264

MAINTENANCE

Oil Level Check
1. Remove the transaxle filler plug.

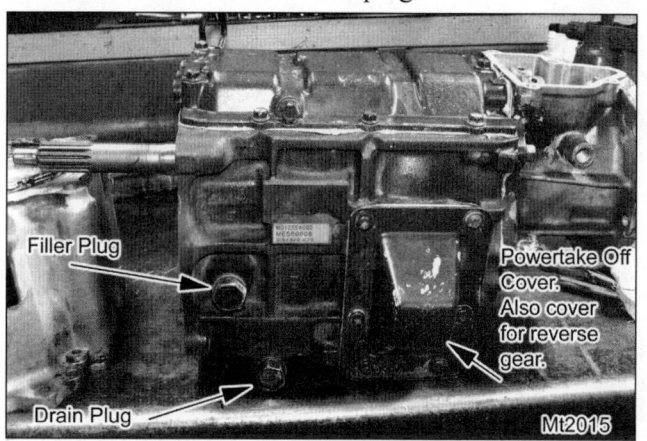

2. Check to ensure the oil level is at the bottom of the filler plug hole and that the oil is in relatively good condition.
3. Replace oil filler plug and tighten to specification.
   Filler Plug specified torque .... 39 Nm

Checking and Replacing Transmission Oil
1. Position an oil catching tray under the transmission, make sure it has the capacity to hold the oil from the transaxle.
2. Remove the drain plug and allow gear oil to grain from transmission.
3. Replace the drain plug and tighten to specification.
   Transmission Drain Plug .... 39 Nm
4. Remove the filler plug, fill the transmission to the full level with the specified transmission fluid.
   Full level is at the bottom of the filler plug hole.
   Transmission Oil Capacity .... 3.2 litres
   Transmission Gear Oil .... SAE 75W-90
   API GL-4

MANUAL TRANSMISSION - V5MT1

5. Replace transmission filler plug and tighten plug to specification.
   Transmission Filler Plug .... 39 Nm

MAJOR REPAIR/REBUILD

Removal

1. From under the vehicle remove the skid plates and under cover, then remove the radiator shroud lower cover.
2. Drain the transmission fluid and transfer oil.
3. Remove the front exhaust pipe from vehicle.
4. Remove the front and rear propeller shaft, referring to the rear suspension/axle chapter for assistance.
5. 4M4 - Remove the intercooler from the vehicle, referring to fuel chapter for assistance.
6. 6G7 - Remove the clutch cylinder heat shield.
7. Remove the clutch release cylinder, referring to clutch chapter if required.
8. 4M41 - Remove the clutch damper assembly, referring to clutch chapter if required.
9. 4M4 - Remove the exhaust support bracket, disconnect the battery cable connection and then remove the spacer rubber and dust cover.
10. Remove the heater hose retaining bracket, then remove the starter motor, referring to engine electrical chapter for assistance.
11. 6G7 - Remove the bolts retaining the cover, then remove the cover followed by the oil pan retaining bolts.
12. Remove the guard from under the transfer assembly, then remove the dynamic damper from the transfer assembly.
13. Remove the bolts securing the tension wire bracket and remove bracket from transfer assembly.
14. Support transmission on a jack or transmission hoist, then remove the centre transmission mount and insulator.
15. Label and disconnect the electrical connections from the transmission assembly.
16. Disconnect the clutch release bearing using the following procedure.
    a) Remove the clutch housing service hole cover, then operate the release fork and push the release bearing towards the clutch side.
    b) Separate the release bearing using a large flat blade screwdriver.
17. Remove the remaining transmission assembly retaining bolts, slide the transmission back away from the engine then low transmission on jack and remove from vehicle.
18. Disconnect and remove tension wire from transfer assembly.

Installation

1. Connect the tension wire to the transfer assembly, tightening bolt to specification.
   Tension Wire Bolt: 24Nm
2. Raise the transmission assembly on the jack and position into place on engine.
3. Install the transmission assembly retaining bolts in their correct locations and tighten to specification.
   Transmission Assembly Bolts:
4M4	A (12 x 25mm)	48 Nm
	B (10 x 45mm)	48 Nm
	C (10 x 50mm)	48 Nm
6G7	A (12 x 40mm)	74 Nm
	B (12 x 55mm)	89 Nm

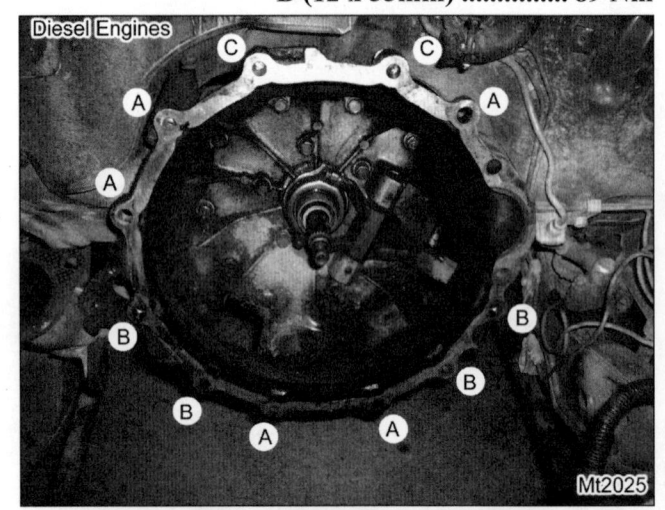

4. Connect the electrical connection for the transmission using the labels made on removal to assist.
5. Install the transmission mount insulator to the transmission centre mount, then install the centre mount.
   Insulator to Mount Bolts .... 44 Nm
   Crossmember Bolts .... 44 Nm
   Crossmember Nuts .... 26 Nm
6. Install the tension wire bracket tightening bolts to specification.
   Tension Wire Bolt .... 24 Nm
   Tension Wire Bracket Bolts .... 53 Nm
7. Install the dynamic damper to the transfer assembly

MANUAL TRANSMISSION - V5MT1

and the transfer guard, tighten the retaining bolts to specification.
Dynamic Damper Bolts .... **35 Nm**
Transfer Guard Bolts................................. **35 Nm**

8. 6G7 - Install the oil pan to transmission retaining bolts then install the cover bolts, tightening to specification.
Oil Pan to Transmission Bolts................... **36 Nm**
Cover Bolts .... **6 Nm**

9. Install the starter motor, referring to engine electrical chapter for assistance, then install the heater hose bracket.
Starter Motor Mounting Bolts................... **30 Nm**

10. 4M4 - Install the dust cover, spacer rubber and then install the exhaust support bracket.
Exhaust Support Bracket Bolts .... **49 Nm**

11. 4M41 - Install the clutch damper assembly, referring to clutch chapter if required.
12. Install the clutch release cylinder, referring to clutch chapter if required.
13. 6G7 - Install the clutch cylinder heat shield.
14. 4M4 - Install the intercooler to the vehicle, referring to fuel chapter for assistance.
15. Install the front and rear propeller shaft, referring to the rear suspension/axle chapter for assistance.
16. Install the front exhaust pipe to vehicle.
17. Reinstall the radiator shroud lower cover, then install the skid plates and under cover.
18. Refill transmission and transfer assembly as described previously.

TRANSMISSION & TRANSFER ASSEMBLY
Separation - Part Time 4WD
1. With the assembly removed from the vehicle, remove vacuum hose from the assembly.
2. Remove the spring pin securing the change shifter then remove the shifter.
3. Remove the bolts securing the transfer to the transmission assembly and separate the transfer assembly from the transmission.

Assembly
1. Apply a bead of sealant to the transfer case then slide the transfer case onto the transmission assembly and tighten retaining bolts to specification.
Transfer Retaining Bolts .... **36 Nm**

2. Install the change shifter and secure in position with retaining spring pin, ensuring split in pin faced down the shift rail.
3. Install the vacuum hose to the transmission assembly.

TRANSMISSION DISASSEMBLY
1. Remove the plug, spring and steel ball from the top of the transmission assembly.
2. Remove the seal plug, neutral return spring and neutral return plunger A from the side of the transmission assembly.

3. Remove the seal plug, neutral return spring and neutral return plunger B from the side of the transmission assembly.

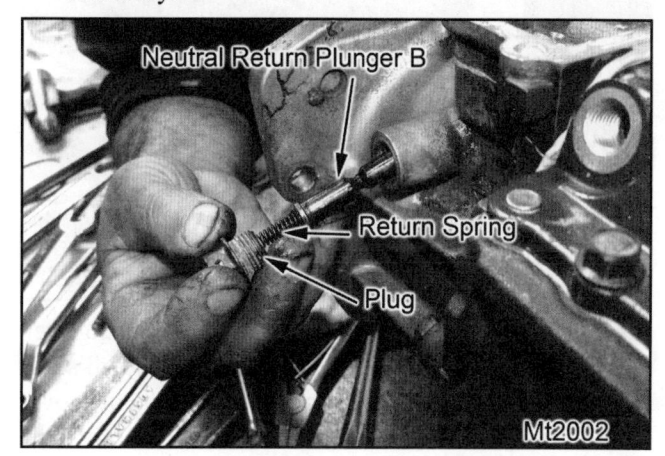

4. Remove the bolts securing the adaptor cover then remove the cover from the transmission case.
5. Remove the spring pin securing the control finger to the control shaft, then slide the control shaft from the transmission.
6. Remove the control finger from transmission assembly, then using a punch remove the three spring pins from the shift jaws.
7. Remove the bolts securing the transfer case adapter, then slide the case adapter from the transmission case.

MANUAL TRANSMISSION - V5MT1

8. From the transfer case adaptor remove the 1st-2nd, 3rd-4th and 5th-reverse gear shift jaws, then remove the three seal rings.
9. Remove the bolts securing the gear shift case, then lift the case assembly from the transmission case.
10. Remove the bolts retaining the clutch housing then remove the clutch housing followed by the oil seal. 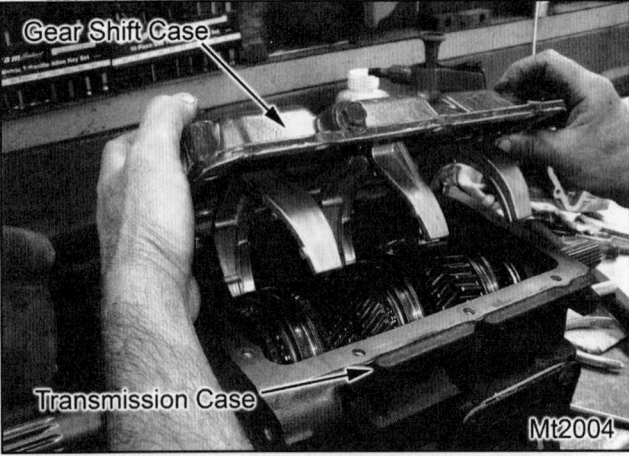
11. Remove the bolts securing the power take off cover to the side of the transmission case, then remove the cover and gasket.
12. From the end of the mainshaft assembly remove the locknut, then reverse shaft lock piece. 
13. Using a slide hammer remove the reverse shaft from the transmission case, then remove the O-ring.
14. From the transmission case remove the two side washers, needle bearings, snap rings, spacers, sub gears, springs and then remove the reverse gear.
15. From the end of the countershaft remove the snap ring retaining the bearing, then remove the bearing using a suitable bearing puller.
16. From the opposite end of the countershaft remove the shaft and bearing snap rings then remove the bearing using a suitable bearing puller.
17. Remove the snap ring from the bearing on the mainshaft, then remove the bearing using a suitable bearing puller.
18. Remove the two snap rings securing the drive pinion and bearing to the transmission case, then remove the bearing using a suitable bearing puller.
19. Pull the drive pinion to the front of the transmission case, then lift the mainshaft assembly from the case.
20. From the transmission case remove the drive pinion, then remove the pilot bearing. 
21. From the transmission case remove the countershaft.

Main Shaft
Disassembly

1. From the main shaft assembly remove the #3 thrust washer, then remove the overdrive gear, needle bearing and synchronizer ring.
2. Remove the snap ring securing the synchronizer hub, then remove the hub and synchronizer sleeve as an assembly.
3. Separate the synchronizer sleeve, hub and springs being careful not to lose the keys.
4. From the mainshaft remove the reverse gear and needle bearing.
5. From the opposite end of the mainshaft remove the synchronizer ring then remove the snap ring securing the synchronizer hub.
6. Using a suitable press, remove the hub and synchronizer sleeve from the shaft as an assembly.
7. Separate the synchronizer sleeve and hub being careful not to lose the springs and keys.

260

8. From the assembly remove the outer synchronizer ring, then remove the synchronizer cone and inner synchronizer ring.
9. From the shaft assembly remove the third gear, needle bearing, #1 thrust washer and steel ball.
10. Remove the snap ring securing the second gear, then remove the #2 thrust washer, second gear and needle bearing.
11. From the mainshaft remove the snap ring, then remove the inner synchronizer ring, synchronizer cone and outer synchronizer ring.
12. Remove the hub and synchronizer sleeve from the shaft as an assembly.
13. Separate the synchronizer sleeve and hub being careful not to lose the springs and keys.
14. Remove the outer synchronizer ring, synchronizer cone and inner synchronizer ring, then remove the first gear and needle bearing from the mainshaft.

Inspection

1. Inspect all gears to ensure the teeth are not worn or damaged.
2. Inspect the synchronizer ring internal surface for damage and also inspect for damage to the teeth.
3. Check for specified clearance for the synchronizer ring to speed gears.
   Clearance .... 0.3 mm (minimum)
4. Check that the synchronizer sleeve and hub slide smoothly and also inspect the sleeve and hub for damage.
5. Inspect the clutch teeth on the speed gears for damage and wear, also inspect the synchronizer cone for damage, wear and rough surface.
6. Inspect the synchronizer springs for breakage and also inspect the key centre protrusion for wear.

Assembly

1. To the main shaft install the needle bearing and first gear.
2. To the synchronizer hub install the synchronizer springs and keys while sliding on the synchronizer sleeve.
3. To the main shaft install the inner synchronizer ring, synchronizer cone and outer synchronizer ring.
4. Slide the synchronizer hub assembly into position on shaft, then install the outer synchronizer ring, cone and inner synchronizer ring.
5. Install retaining snap ring to the mainshaft.
6. To the main shaft install the needle bearing and second gear, then install the #2 thrust washer and snap ring.
7. To the main shaft install the #1 thrust washer, steel ball, needle bearing and third gear.
8. To the synchronizer hub install the synchronizer springs and keys while sliding on the synchronizer sleeve.
9. To the main shaft install the inner synchronizer ring, synchronizer cone and outer synchronizer ring.
10. Slide the synchronizer hub assembly into position on shaft, then install the synchronizer ring and snap ring.
11. To the opposite end of the mainshaft install the needle bearing and reverse gear then install the synchronizer ring.
12. To the synchronizer hub install the three keys and two springs, ensure the springs are touching each of the keys, then slide the synchronizer sleeve onto the assembly.
13. To the main shaft slide on the synchronizer hub assembly, then install the synchronizer ring and retaining snap ring.
14. To the mainshaft install the needle bearing and overdrive gear, then install the #3 thrust washer.

Gear Shift Case
Disassembly

1. From the gear shift case remove the reverse lamp switch.
2. Remove the screw plug from the case then remove the poppet spring and steel ball.
3. Remove the other two screw plugs from the case, then remove the two poppet springs and steel balls.
4. From the end of the case remove the three plugs, then remove the three spring pins securing the shift forks to the shift rails.
5. Remove the 5th-reverse shift rail and the shift fork, then remove the two steel balls.
6. Remove the 3rd-4th shift rail and the shift fork, then remove the two steel balls.
7. Remove the 1st-second shift rail and the shift fork.
8. Inspect the shaft rail bushings and remove if defective.

Assembly

1. If required install new teflon bushing's to the gear shift case as shown.

MANUAL TRANSMISSION - V5MT1

2. Install the 1st-2nd shift rail and shift fork, then install the two steel balls.
3. Install the 3rd-4th shift rail and shift fork, then install the two steel balls.
4. Install the 5th-reverse shift rail and shift fork, then install the three shift fork retaining spring pins.
   Note: *Ensure the spring pin is installed plush and the split in the pin is aligned with the centre line of the shift rail.*
5. To the end of the shift case install the three plugs.
6. To the case install the three steel balls and poppet springs, ensuring the narrow end of the spring is against the steel ball.
7. Install the three screw plugs tightening to specification.
   Poppet Spring Plugs 40Nm
8. Install the reverse light switch to the shift case, tightening to specification.
   Reverse Light Switch ....35 Nm

TRANSMISSION ASSEMBLY

1. To the countershaft gear fit the snap and overdrive gear, but do not insert snap ring in it's groove.
2. Push both the snap ring and overdrive gear towards the reverse gear and install the countershaft assembly into transmission case.
3. Push the overdrive gear back into position and install the snap ring into it's grove.
4. Using an appropriate drift and hammer install the bearing to the drive pinion, then install the bearing snap ring.
5. Install the drive pinion to the transmission case and then install the bearing snap ring.
6. To the rear of the drive pinion install the pilot bearing, then install the mainshaft assembly into the transmission case. 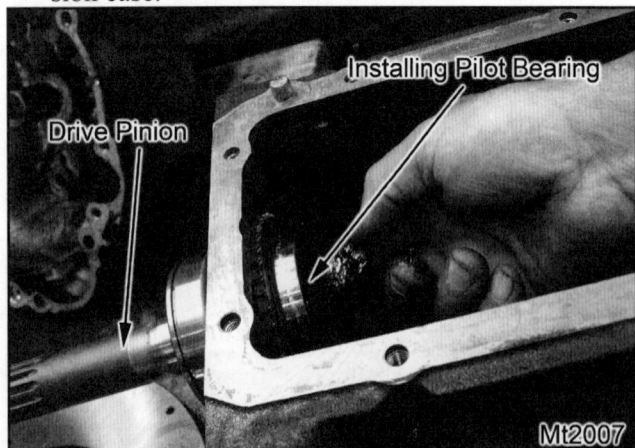
7. While holding the main shaft push in the drive pinion until the bearing snap ring is resting firmly against the transmission case.
8. Install the mainshaft bearing snap ring to the bearing then install the bearing onto the mainshaft using an appropriate drift and hammer.
9. To the countershaft bearing install the snap ring, then support the countershaft assembly using special tool (#MH061405) and install the bearing.
10. Install the snap ring to the end of the countershaft and remove the special tool. 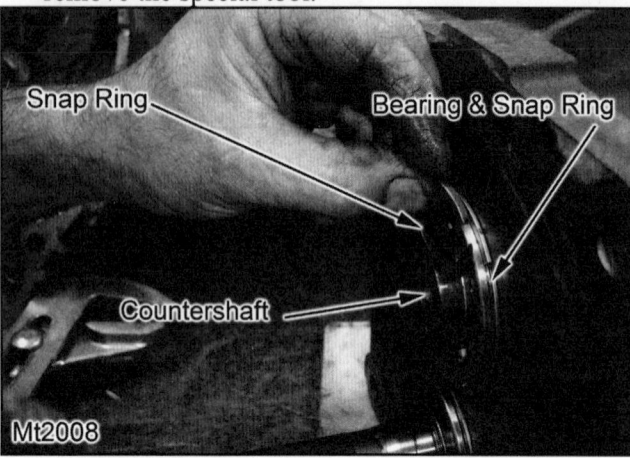
11. Install the bearing, then secure in place using retaining snap ring.
12. a) To the reverse gear install the long ends of the springs, then fit the two sub gears, spacers and secure with snap rings.
    b) Turn the sub gears to line up all the through holes and insert a screwdriver in the holes to hold in position.
13. Install the reverse gear assembly into the transmission case.
14. Install the needle bearings and two side washers, ensuring to install washers in the correct direction.
    Note: *Install washers with tabs facing outwards.*
15. Install the O-ring to the reverse shaft, then install the reverse shaft into the transmission case and secure with lock piece.
    Lock Piece Bolt..41 Nm 
16. a) Slide the 1-2 speed synchronizer sleeve to the 1st speed side and the 5th-reverse synchronizer sleeve to the reverse side. (this prevents the main shaft from turning).

b) Install and tighten the lock nut to specification, then punch the locknut into the two grooves of the main shaft.
Mainshaft Lock Nut.............................. 260 Nm

17. Using a new gasket install the power take off cover to the transmission case and tighten retaining bolts to specification.
Power Take Off Cover .... 19 Nm
18. To the clutch housing install a new oil seal using a seal installation tool and then apply grease to the seal lip. 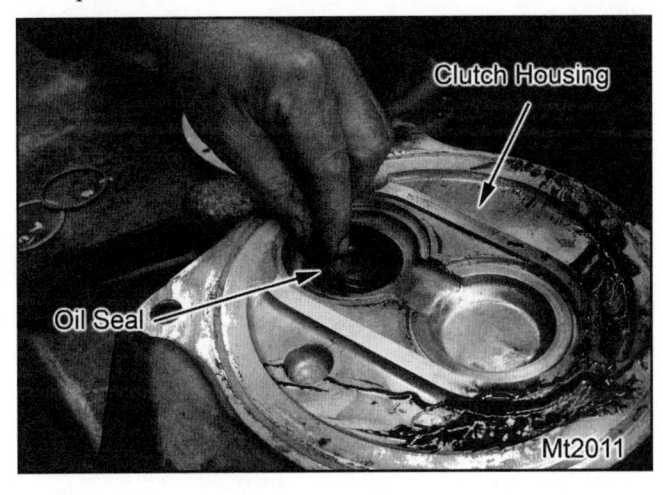
19. To the contact surface of the clutch housing install a bead of sealant, then install the clutch housing to the transmission case and tighten retaining bolts to specification.
Clutch Housing Bolts .... 119 Nm
20. To the gear shift case install a bead of sealant, then install the gear shift case to the transmission case and tighten retaining bolts to specification.
Gear Shift Case Bolts .... 24 Nm
21. To the transfer case adaptor install the three seal rings.
22. To the transfer case adaptor install a bead of sealant, then partially install the transfer adaptor and hold in position with retaining bolts.
Note: *If adaptor is fully installed it will prevent the jaws from being installed.*
23. Install the three shift jaws to there correct shafts, then fully install the case adaptor and tighten bolts to specification.
Transfer Case Adaptor Bolts .... 41 Nm
24. Align the holes of the shift jaws with the holes in the shift rails and install the retaining spring pins, ensuring the pins are flush and the split is aligned with the shaft centre line.
25. To the transfer case adaptor install the control finger followed by the control shaft and secure with spring pin. 
26. To the adaptor cover apply a bead of sealant, then install the adaptor cover and tighten retaining bolts to specification.
Adaptor Cover Bolts .... 24 Nm
27. To the side of the transmission case install the neutral return plunger A, return spring and seal plug.
Note: *Coat contact surface of plunger with grease.*
28. To the side of the transmission case install the neutral return plunger B, return spring and seal plug.
Note: *Coat contact surface of plunger with grease.*
Seal Plug .... 36 Nm
29. To the top of the transmission case install the steel ball, spring and plug, tightening to specification.
Plug .... 48 Nm

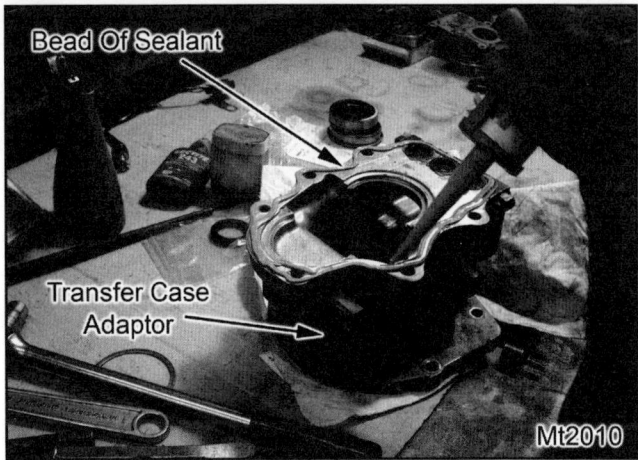

SPECIFICATIONS

Type .... Manual transmission
Model.. V5MT1
Engine Model... Petrol

Transmission	Gear	Ratios
	1st:	3.918:1
	2nd:	2.261:1
	3rd:	1.395:1
	4th:	1.000:1
	5th:	0.829:1
	Reverse:	3.925:1
Transfer:	High	1.000
	Low	1.925

Recommended Lubrication .... Hypoid gear oil, SAE 75W-90 API GL-4

Quantity: - Transmission .... 3.2 litres
 - Transfer .... 2.5 litres

TORQUE SPECIFICATION

Description	Nm
Clutch housing - transmission case bolts	119
Transfer Case Adaptor to Transmission	41
Transfer Case Adaptor to Transfer	36
Gear shift case bolts	24
Power take-off cover	19
Adaptor Cover	24
Mainshaft locking nut	260
Reverse Shaft Lock Piece Bolt	41
Clutch release fork fulcrum	58
Backup Lamp Switch	35
Gear Shift Case Poppet Plugs	40
Neutral Return Plunger Plugs	36
Poppet Plug on Transfer Case Adaptor	48

AUTOMATIC TRANSMISSION

V5A51 & V5A5A

Description	Page
MAINTENANCE	266
Transmission Fluid	266
Fluid Level	266
Fluid Condition	266
Fluid Replacement	266
Inhibitor Switch Adjustment	266
Inhibitor Switch Continuity Check	267
4WD Detection Switch	267
High/Low Detection Switch	267
4L Detection Switch	267
2WD/4WD Switch Continuity	267
4H Switch Continuity	267
Centre Differential Lock Switch Continuity	267
2WD Switch Continuity	268
4LLc Switch Continuity	268
Hydraulic Pressure Adjustments	268
Line Pressure	268
Hydraulic Pressure Tables	268
A/T Fluid Temperature Sensor Check	269
A/T Control Relay Check	269
A/T Control Solenoid Valve Assembly Check	269
Auto Transmission ECU	269
Removal	269
Installation	269
MINOR REPAIRS	270
Oil Cooler	270
Pipe/Hose Inspection	270
Removal - Standalone type	270
Installation - Standalone type	270
Control Cable & Selector Lever	270
Adjustment	270
Remove	270
Install	270
MAJOR REPAIRS	271
Transmission & Transfer Assembly	271
Removal	271
Installation	271
Separation	272
Assembly	272

Description	Page
TRANSMISSION ASSEMBLY	273
Transmission Disassembly	273
Sub Assemblies	274
Transfer Case Adaptor	274
Dismantle	274
Assemble	274
Oil Pump	274
Dismantle	274
Assemble	274
Underdrive Clutch	274
Dismantle	274
Assemble	275
Reverse & Overdrive Clutch	274
Dismantle	275
Assemble	275
Direct Clutch	276
Dismantle	276
Assemble	276
Low/Reverse Annulus Carrier	276
Dismantle	276
Assemble	276
Centre Support	277
Dismantle	277
Installation	277
Second Brake	277
Dismantle	277
Assemble	277
Direct Annulus Gear	277
Dismantle	277
Assemble	277
Output Shaft Support	277
Dismantle	277
Assemble	277
Valve Body Dismantle	277
Main Assembly	277
Upper Valve Body	277
Lower Valve Body	278
Valve Body Assembly	278
Lower Valve Body	278
Upper Valve Body	278
Main Assembly	278
Transmission Assembly	279
SPECIFICATIONS	282

AUTOMATIC TRANSMISSION (V5A51 & V5A5A)

MAINTENANCE

TRANSMISSION FLUID

Fluid Level

1. Ensure vehicle is at normal operating temperature, engine idling then park on a level surface and apply hand brake.
2. With the vehicles brakes applied, shift the transaxle through all the gears, then return to neutral.
3. Withdraw the transaxle dipstick, then clean the existing fluid form the dipstick and refit the dipstick.
4. Withdraw the dipstick again from the transaxle, then read the fluid level indicated on it. 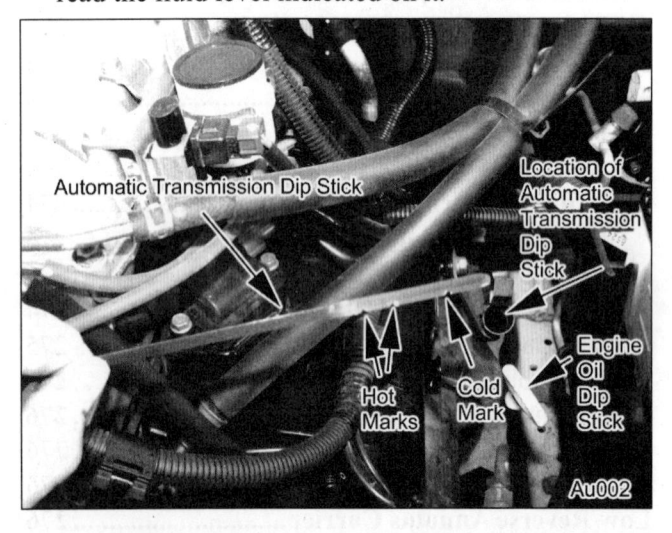
5. Fill the transaxle with the correct fluid until it is within the indicated marks (hot marks) on the dipstick.
6. If fluid is added only add a small amount at a time, this will help to prevent over filling the transaxle.

Fluid Condition

It is necessary to keep the transaxle fluid in good condition, as dirty transaxle fluid may cause damage to the transaxle internal components.
The transaxle fluid will require replacing if the fluid has a burnt smell, or is black and dirty.

Fluid Replacement

1. Raise vehicle and place on jack stands, then position a drain tray under the transaxle oil pan and differential.
2. Remove the drain plugs and allow fluid to drain. 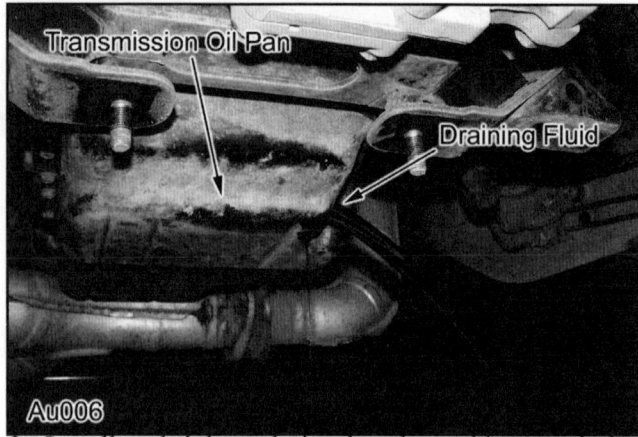
3. Install and tighten drain plug then add transmission fluid, filling to the cold level. Fill through the dipstick tube.
   Drain Plugs................................30-35 Nm
4. Start engine and allow transaxle to reach normal operating temperature, then apply vehicles brakes, shift the transaxle through all the gears, then return to neutral.
5. Recheck fluid level and add sufficient transmission fluid to bring to the correct operating level between the upper and lower hot marks.
6. Inspect to ensure there are no leaks.

INHIBITOR SWITCH ADJUSTMENT

1. Place the selector lever in the "N" position, then loosen the manual control lever adjusting nut.
2. Place the manual control lever in the neutral position, then loosen the inhibitor switch mounting bolts.
3. Turn the switch so that the hole in the end of the control lever and the hole in the inhibitor switch flange are aligned. 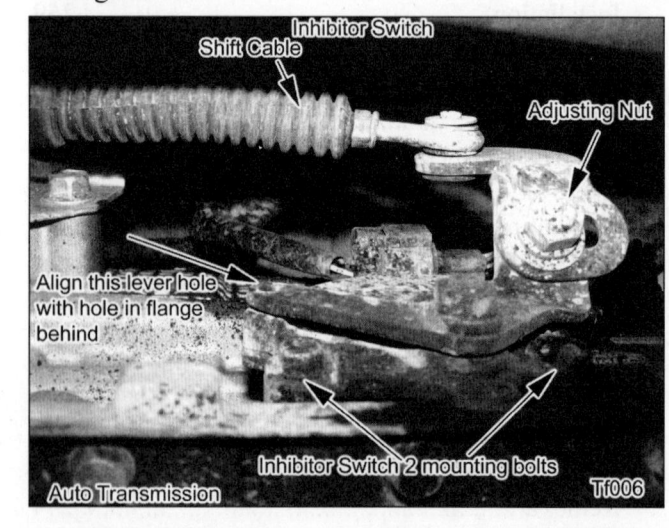
4. Tighten the inhibitor switch bolts to specification.
   Inhibitor Switch Bolts............................10-12 Nm
5. Pull the control cable gently as shown then tighten the manual lever adjusting nut to specification.
   Adjusting Nut................................24 Nm
6. Check to ensure the selector lever is still in the neutral

position and that each position selected with the lever operates and functions properly.

INHIBITOR SWITCH CONTINUITY CHECK

Item	Terminal #	
P	1 - 7	9 - 10
R	7 - 8	
N	2 - 7	9 - 10
D	3 - 7	
3	4 - 7	
2	5 - 7	
L	6 - 7	

Note: Vehicle with sports mode only use four positions P, R, N & D.

HIGH/LOW DETECTION SWITCH CHECK (part time 4wd)

Check continuity b/w terminal #1 and #2 of the grey connector on the side of the transfer case.

Transfer lever position	Continuity
4H	No Continuity
Between 4H & 4L	Continuity
4L	Continuity

4L DETECTION SWITCH CHECK (part time 4wd)

Check continuity b/w the terminal of the white connector on the side of the transfer case and the transfer case.

Transfer lever position	Continuity
4L	Continuity
Other than 4L	No Continuity

2WD/4WD SWITCH CONTINUITY CHECK (super select 4wd II)

Check continuity b/w terminals of the black connector at the left of the transfer case (as shown).

Transfer lever position	Continuity
2H, 4H	Continuity
4HLc, 4LLc	No Continuity

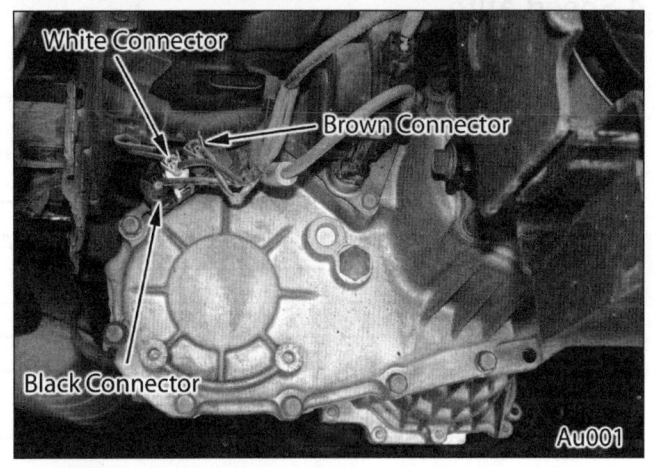

4H SWITCH CONTINUITY CHECK (super select 4wd II)

Check continuity b/w terminals of the white connector at the left of the transfer case (as shown).

Transfer lever position	Continuity
2H, 4LLc	No Continuity
4H, 4HLc	Continuity

CENTRE DIFFERENTIAL LOCK SWITCH CONTINUITY CHECK (super select 4wd II)

Check continuity b/w terminals of the brown connector at the left of the transfer case (as shown).

Transfer lever position	Continuity
2H, 4H	No Continuity
4HLc, 4LLc	Continuity

4WD DETECTION SWITCH CHECK (part time 4wd)

Check continuity b/w terminal #1 and #2 of the black connector on the side of the transfer case.

Transfer lever position	Continuity
2H	No Continuity
4H	Continuity

AUTOMATIC TRANSMISSION (V5A51 & V5A5A)

2WD SWITCH CONTINUITY CHECK (super select 4wd II)

Check continuity b/w terminals of the black connector at the left of the transfer case (as shown).

Transfer lever position	Continuity
2H	Continuity
4H, 4HLc, 4LLc	No Continuity

4LLc SWITCH CONTINUITY CHECK (super select 4wd II)

Check continuity b/w terminals of the brown connector at the left of the transfer case (as shown).

Transfer lever position	Continuity
4LLc	Continuity
2H, 4H, 4HLc	No Continuity

HYDRAULIC PRESSURE TEST

1. Run the engine until the transmission fluid is at a temperature of 70-80°C.
2. Jack up the vehicle so as the wheels will rotate freely.
3. To each pressure discharge port connect an oil pressure gauge.
4. Measure the hydraulic pressure at each port as shown in pressure table and ensure values are within specification.

Line Pressure Adjustment

1. Remove the drain plugs and allow fluid to drain into a container, then remove the oil pan bolts and remove transaxle oil pan.
2. Turn the adjusting screw to adjust the underdrive pressure in "D", 1st or 2nd gear to specification. Refer to diagram.
   Specified Value .... 1010-1050 kPa
   (adjust to middle range of specification)
   Note: *One complete turn of the screw will change line pressure by 38kPa.*
3. Install oil pan to transaxle using a new gasket and tighten bolts to specification.
   Oil Pan Retaining Bolts .... 11 Nm
4. Ensure drain plug is installed and tightened to speci-

STANDARD HYDRAULIC PRESSURE TABLES

4 Speed Auto

Measurement Conditions			Standard Hydraulic Pressure kPa					
Shift Lever Position	Shift Range Position	Engine Speed RPM	Underdrive Clutch Pressure (UD)	Reverse Clutch Pressure (RC)	Overdrive Clutch Pressure (OD)	Low & Brake Pressure (LR)	Second Brake Pressure (2nd)	Torque Converter Pressure (DR)
P	-	2,500	-	-	-	260 - 340	-	500 - 700
R	Reverse	2,500	-	1270 - 1770	-	1270 - 1770	-	500 - 700
N	-	2,500	-	-	-	260 - 340	-	500 - 700
L	1st	2,500	1010 - 1050	-	-	1,010-1,050	-	500 - 700
2	2nd	2,500	1010 - 1050	-	-	-	1010 - 1050	500 - 700
3	3rd	2,500	784 - 882	-	784 - 882	-	-	-
D	4th	2,500	-	-	784 - 882	-	784 - 882	-

5 Speed Auto (sports mode)

Measurement Conditions			Standard Hydraulic Pressure (kPa)						
Shift Lever Position	Shift Range Position	Engine Speed RPM	Underdrive Clutch Pressure (UD)	Reverse Clutch Pressure (RC)	Overdrive Clutch Pressure (OD)	Direct Clutch Pressure (DIR)	Low & Brake Pressure (LR)	Second Brake Pressure (2nd)	Reduction Brake Pressure (RB)	Torque Converter Pressure (DR)
P	-	2,500	-	-	-	-	260-340	-	1010-1050	500-700
R	Reverse	2,500	-	1270-1770	-	-	1270-1770	-	1270-1050	500-700
N	-	2,500	-	-	-	-	260-340	-	260-340	500-700
Sports Mode	1st	2,500	1010-1050	-	-	-	1010-1050	-	1010-1050	500-700
Sports Mode	2nd	2,500	1010-1050	-	-	-	-	1010-1050	1010-1050	500-700
	3rd	2,500	784-882	-	784-882	-	-	-	784-882	450-650
	4th	2,500	784-882	-	784-882	784-882	-	-	-	-
	5th	2,500	784-882	-	784-882	784-882	-	784-882	-	-

AUTOMATIC TRANSMISSION (V5A51 & V5A5A)

fication, then refill transaxle as outlined previously under transaxle fluid replacement.

5. Check line pressure.

A/T FLUID TEMPERATURE SENSOR CHECK

1. Remove the transmission pan from the transmission, ensuring to drain transmission fluid first.
2. Remove the temperature sensor from the transmission.

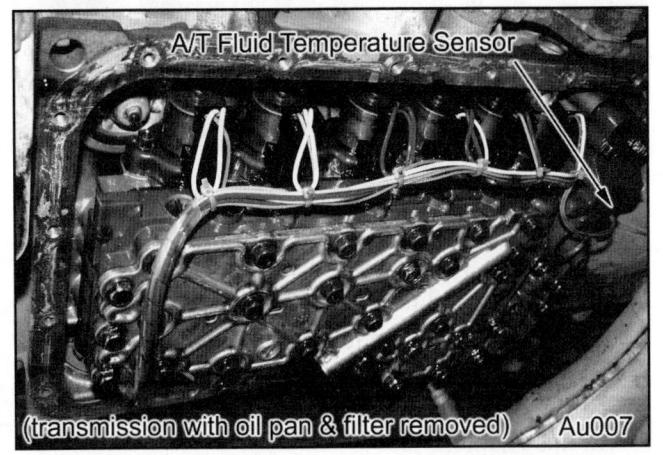

3. Measure the resistance between terminals #1 and #2 of the A/T fluid temperature sensor at the temperatures shown in the following table.

Temp (°C)	Resistance (kOhms)
0	16.7 - 20.5
20	7.3 - 8.9
40	3.4 - 4.2
60	1.9 - 2.2
80	1.0 - 1.2
100	0.57 - 0.69

4. Replace the temperature sensor if not within specified range.

A/T CONTROL RELAY CHECK

1. Remove the control relay from the vehicle.
2. Connect terminal #2 of the relay to the battery (-ve) terminal and terminal #4 to the (+ve) terminal using jump wires.
3. Check continuity between terminals #1 and #3 of the control relay while alternately connecting and disconnecting the jump leads from the battery.

Jump Leads	Continuity
Connected	Continuity
Disconnected	No Continuity

4. Replace the control relay if there is a malfunction.

A/T CONTROL SOLENOID VALVE ASSEMBLY CHECK

1. Drain transmission fluid and remove the transmission oil pan.
2. Disconnect the connectors from the solenoid valves, then measure the resistance between terminal #1 and #2 of each solenoid valve.

Solenoid Valve	Resistance @ 20°C
Damper Clutch Control (DCC)	2.7 - 3.4 kOhms
Low & Reverse (LR)	2.7 - 3.4 kOhms
Second (2nd)	2.7 - 3.4 kOhms
Underdrive (UD)	2.7 - 3.4 kOhms
Overdrive (OD)	2.7 - 3.4 kOhms
Reduction (RED)	2.7 - 3.4 kOhms

3. Replace solenoid if not within specification.

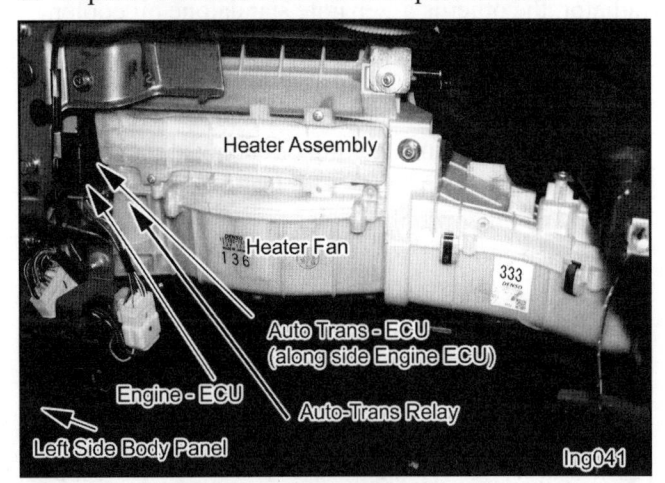

AUTO TRANSMISSION ECU

Note: The Auto Trans - ECU and Engine ECU are located tightly between the heater and left side body panel.

Removal

1. From the passenger side of the vehicle, remove the side cowl trim panel (kick panel).
2. Disconnect the main harness connections, then remove the auto transmission control relay.
3. Disconnect the electrical connections for the auto transmission-ECU, then remove mounting bolts and remove from vehicle.
4. Disconnect the electrical connections for the engine-ECU, then remove mounting bolts and remove ECU from vehicle.
5. If required remove the bolt securing the mounting bracket and remove bracket.

Installation

1. If removed install ECU mounting bracket and tighten bolts to specification.
   ECU Mounting Bracket Bolt .... 5 Nm
2. Install the engine-ECU into position, tighten mounting bolts to specification and reconnect the electrical connection.
   ECU Mounting Nut .... 5 Nm
3. Install the auto transmission-ECU into position, tighten mounting bolts to specification and reconnect

AUTOMATIC TRANSMISSION (V5A51 & V5A5A)

the electrical connection.
ECU Mounting Nut..........................5 Nm

4. Install the transmission control relay, the reconnect the main harness connections.
Auto Trans Control Relay Bolt..................5 Nm

5. Replace the side cowl trim panel (kick panel) to the vehicle.

MINOR REPAIRS

OIL COOLER
Two types of oil coolers are used on is incorporated in the radiator, the other is a separate standalone oil cooler.

Oil Cooler Pipe & Hose Inspection
1. Check the fittings of the cooler pipes and hoses to ensure they are not leaking or damaged.
2. Inspect cooler lines/hoses for leaks, distortion, cracks and any other problems.
3. Replace cooler line pipes and hoses as required.

Removal - Stand Alone Cooler
1. Drain the transmission fluid as outlined previously in this chapter, then remove the skip plate and covers from under the vehicle.
2. Remove the right hand side headlight assembly, refer to body electrical for assistance.
3. From the oil cooler assembly disconnect the two fluid hoses.
4. Remove the bolts securing the oil cooler and bracket assembly to the vehicle and remove the oil cooler assembly.

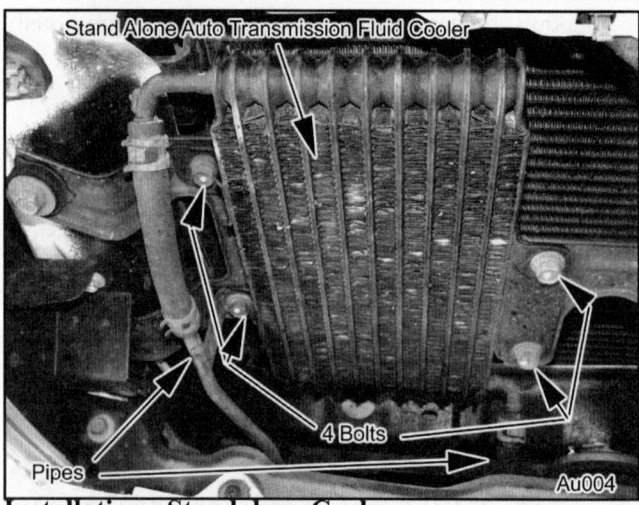

Installation - Standalone Cooler
1. Install the oil cooler and bracket assembly into vehicle and tighten retaining bolts to specification.
Oil Cooler Mounting Bolts..........................12 Nm
2. Reconnect the fluid hoses to the oil cooler assembly.
3. Install headlight assembly, referring to body electrical chapter for assistance.
4. Fill transmission with fluid as described previously in this chapter.
5. Check to ensure there are no fluid leaks, then install the skid plate and under body covers.

CONTROL CABLE & SELECTOR LEVER
Refer to Transfer Chapter for Removal and installation procedure for the control cables and selector levers.

Adjustment
1. Have the control lever in the N position, then loosen the upper control lever adjusting nut.
2. Check to ensure the inhibitor switch is at the N range, then adjust the upper control lever so there is no slackness or excessive tightness in the control cable.
3. Tighten adjusting nut to specification.
Adjusting Nut..................................24 Nm
4. Check that the selector lever corresponds with the transmission range selected.

Removal
1. Remove the centre console from the vehicle, refer to body chapter if required.
2. Disconnect the control cable from the selector lever assembly, then disconnect the electrical connections.
3. Remove the lever assembly retaining bolts and remove assembly from vehicle.

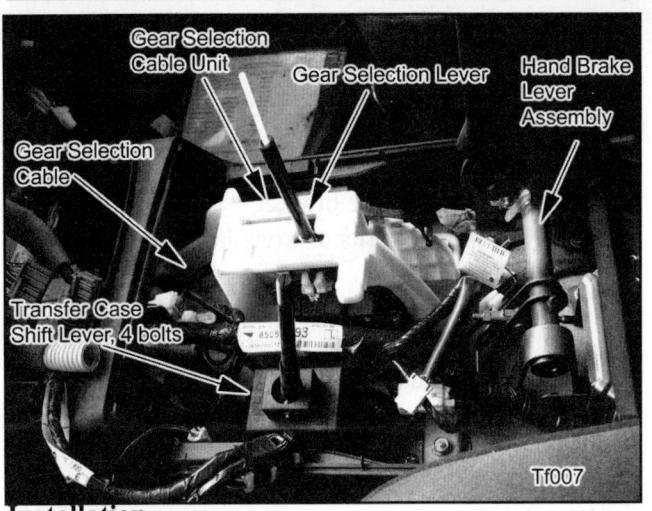

AUTOMATIC TRANSMISSION (V5A51 & V5A5A)

Installation

1. Install the selector lever assembly into position and tighten retaining bolts to specification.
   Selector Lever Retaining Bolts .... 11 Nm
2. Reconnect the control cable to the selector lever assembly, then connect the electrical connections.
3. Install the centre console into the vehicle, refer to body chapter if required.
4. Adjust control cable as previously outlined.

MAJOR REPAIR

TRANSMISSION & TRANSFER ASSEMBLY
Removal

1. From under the vehicle remove the skid plates and under cover, then remove the radiator shroud lower cover.
2. Drain the transmission fluid and transfer oil.
3. Remove the front exhaust pipe from vehicle.
4. Remove the front and rear propeller shaft, referring to the rear suspension/axle chapter for assistance.
5. **4M4** - Remove the intercooler from the vehicle, referring to fuel chapter for assistance.
6. Remove the bolts securing the fluid level dipstick tube and remove the tube from the transmission assembly.
7. Remove the retaining pin from the control cable and disconnect control cable from the transmission.
8. **4M4** - Remove the exhaust support bracket, disconnect the battery cable connection and then remove the spacer rubber and dust cover.
9. Remove the heater hose retaining bracket, then remove the drive plate connection bolts and push the torque converter back towards the transmission.
10. **6G7** - Remove the bolts retaining the cover, then remove the cover.
11. Remove the starter motor and starter motor cover (where fitted), referring to engine electrical chapter for assistance.
12. **6G7** - Remove the oil pan to transmission retaining bolts, then remove the bolt retaining the battery cable connection.
13. Disconnect the oil cooler pipes from the transmission assembly.
14. Remove the bolts securing the dynamic damper, then remove the dynamic damper from the vehicle.
15. Remove the bolts securing the tension wire bracket and remove bracket from transfer assembly.
16. Support transmission on a jack or transmission hoist, then remove the centre transmission mount and insulator. 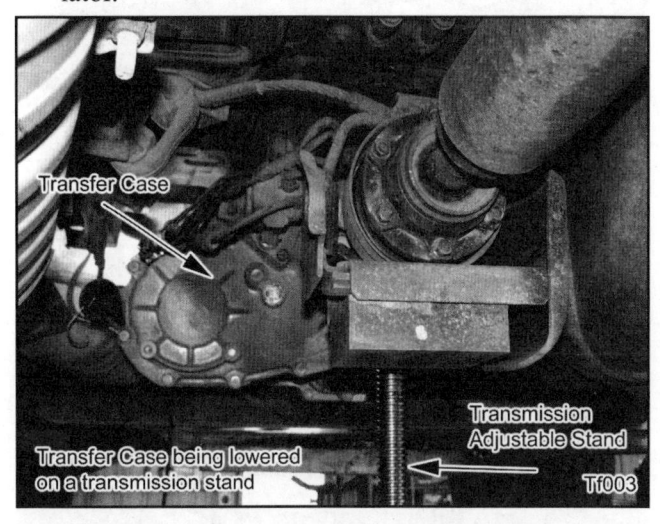
17. Label and disconnect the electrical connections from the transmission assembly.
18. Remove the remaining transmission assembly retaining bolts, slide the transmission back away from the engine then low transmission on jack and remove from vehicle.
19. Disconnect and remove tension wire from transfer assembly.

Installation

1. Connect the tension wire to the transfer assembly, tightening bolt to specification.
   Tension Wire Bolt: 24Nm
2. Raise the transmission assembly on the jack and position into place on engine.
3. Install the transmission assembly retaining bolts in there correct locations and tighten to specification.
   Transmission Assembly Bolts:
       4M4   A (10 x 25mm) .... 48 Nm
                  B (10 x 45mm) .... 48 Nm
                  C (10 x 50mm) .... 48 Nm

AUTOMATIC TRANSMISSION (V5A51 & V5A5A)

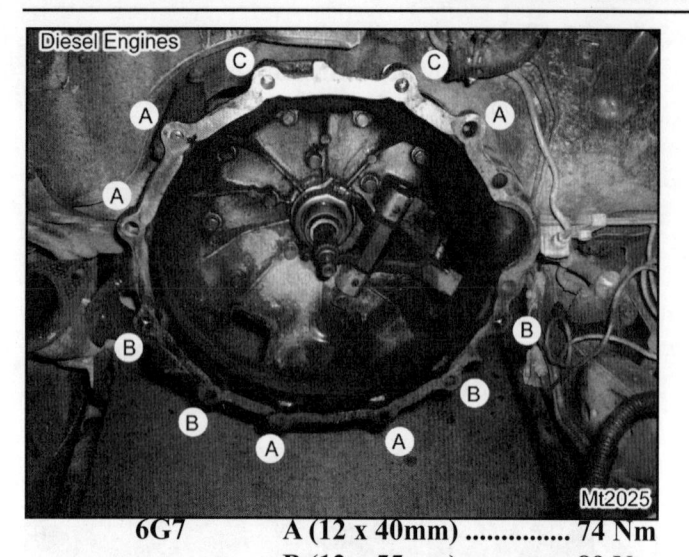

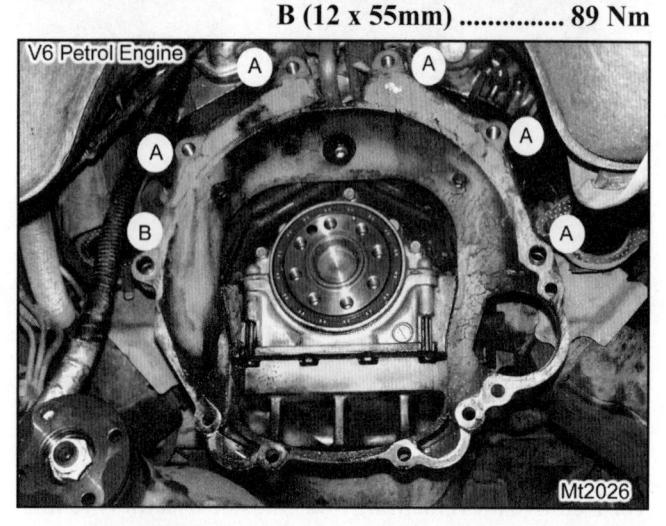

Diesel Engines

6G7   A (12 x 40mm) .... 74 Nm
B (12 x 55mm) .... 89 Nm

V6 Petrol Engine

4. Connect the electrical connection for the transmission using the labels made on removal to assist.
5. Install the transmission mount insulator to the transmission centre mount, then install the centre mount.
   Insulator to Mount Bolts .... 44 Nm
   Cross-member Bolts .... 44 Nm
   Cross-member Nuts .... 26 Nm
6. Install the tension wire bracket tightening bolts to specification.
   Tension Wire Bolt .... 24 Nm
   Tension Wire Bracket Bolts .... 53 Nm
7. Install the dynamic damper to the transfer assembly and tighten the retaining bolts to specification.
   Dynamic Damper Bolts .... 35 Nm
8. Install the oil cooler pipes to the transmission assembly using new gaskets and tighten retaining bolts to specification.
   Oil Cooler Pipe Bolts .... 42 Nm
   Oil Cooler Pipe Bracket Bolts .... 5 Nm
9. 6G7 - Install the oil pan to transmission retaining bolts tightening to specification.
   Oil Pan to Transmission Bolts .... 36 Nm
10. Install the starter motor cover and then install the starter motor, referring to engine electrical chapter for assistance.
    Starter Motor Mounting Bolts .... 30 Nm
11. 6G7 - Install the cover tightening bolts to specification.
    Cover Bolts .... 11 Nm
12. Install the heater hose bracket.
13. Install torque converter to driveplate bolts and tighten bolts to specification.
    Torque Converter Bolts .... 49 Nm
14. 4M4 - Install the dust cover, spacer rubber and then install the exhaust support bracket.
    Exhaust Support Bracket Bolts .... 49 Nm
15. Install the transmission control cable and secure with retaining pin, then install the dipstick tube.
    Dipstick Tube Lower Mounting Bolt .... 44 Nm
    Dipstick Tube Upper Mounting Bolt .... 24 Nm
16. 4M4 - Install the intercooler to the vehicle, referring to fuel chapter for assistance.
17. Install the front and rear propeller shaft, referring to the rear suspension/axle chapter for assistance.
18. Install the front exhaust pipe to vehicle.
19. Reinstall the radiator shroud lower cover, then install the skid plates and under cover.
20. Refill transaxle as described previously.

TRANSMISSION & TRANSFER ASSEMBLY
Separate
1. With the assembly removed from the vehicle, remove the nuts and bolts securing the transfer to the case adaptor and separate the transfer from the assembly.
2. From the transfer case adaptor remove the bolt securing the cable end bracket and remove the bracket.
3. From the transfer case adaptor remove the two harness brackets.
4. Remove the bolts securing the transfer case adaptor to the transmission assembly and separate the adaptor from the transmission.

Assemble
1. To the transfer case adaptor apply a bead of sealant as shown then install the adaptor to the transmission assembly and tighten the retaining bolts to specification.
   Transmission to Transfer Adaptor ...... 48+/-6 Nm
2. To the adaptor install the two harness brackets, then install the cable end bracket.
3. To the transmission assembly install the transfer case and tighten the transfer case to adaptor bolts/nuts to specification.
   Transfer to Transfer Adaptor .... 35+/-6 Nm

AUTOMATIC TRANSMISSION (V5A51 & V5A5A)

TRANSMISSION ASSEMBLY

TRANSMISSION DISASSEMBLY

1. Remove the input shaft and output shaft speed sensors, then remove the manual control lever.
2. Remove the park/neutral switch and then remove the parking gear snap ring and parking gear.
3. Remove the oil pan and gasket from the transaxle assembly. 
4. Remove the screws securing the oil filter and remove the filter and O-ring from transmission. 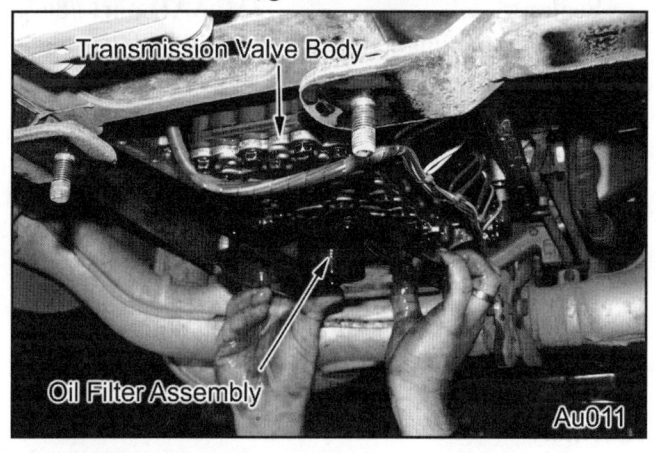
5. Remove the detent spring, then disconnect the electrical connectors from the valve body. 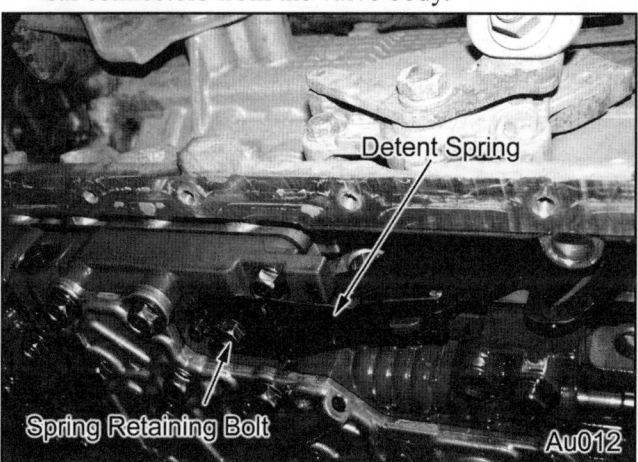
6. Remove the bolts (12) securing the valve body then remove the oil temperature sensor. 
7. Remove the valve body from the transmission, then remove the three O-rings.
8. Remove the snap ring securing the solenoid valve harness, then remove valve harness.
9. Remove two oil seals then remove the oil strainer.
10. Remove the seal ring, then remove the overdrive clutch accumulator piston and spring. (label piston and spring).
11. Remove the seal ring, then remove the second brake accumulator piston and springs. (label piston and springs).
12. Remove the seal ring, then remove the low/reverse brake accumulator piston and springs. (label piston and springs).
13. Remove the seal ring, then remove the underdrive clutch accumulator piston and springs. (label piston and springs).
14. Remove the snap ring securing the reduction brake accumulator cover then remove the cover, spring and piston (label piston and spring).
15. Remove the snap ring securing the direct clutch accumulator cover then remove the cover, spring and piston (label piston and spring).
16. Remove the detent lever spring pin, then remove the pin for the manual control lever.
17. Remove manual control lever shaft, two O-rings, detent lever and roller rod.
18. Remove the bolts securing the torque converter housing, then remove the torque converter housing.
19. From the transmission assembly remove the bolts securing the oil pump.
20. Use special tool (MD998333) installed in holes marked, remove the oil pump then remove the gasket.

AUTOMATIC TRANSMISSION (V5A51 & V5A5A)

Special Tool (for removal of pump)

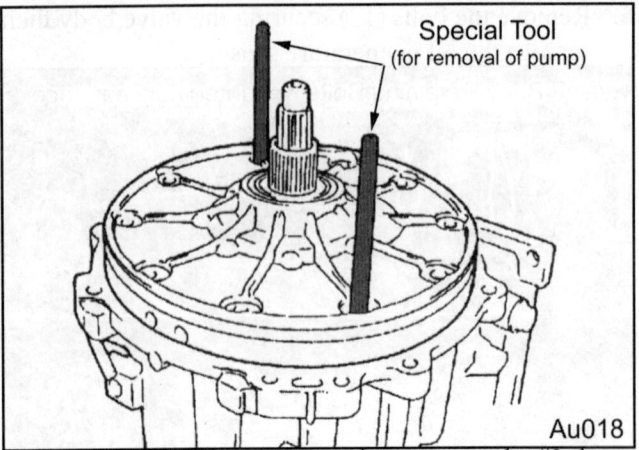

Au018

21. Remove the #1 thrust race then remove the #2 thrust bearing.
22. Remove the reverse and overdrive clutch assembly from the transmission case, then remove the #3 thrust bearing.
23. From the transmission case remove the overdrive clutch hub, then remove the #4 thrust bearing followed by the reverse sun gear.
24. Remove the snap ring securing the second brake, then remove the second brake and return spring.
25. Remove the pressure plate then remove the three brake plates and four brake discs.
26. From the transmission assembly remove the low/reverse annulus gear, then remove the #7 thrust bearing.
27. Remove the snap ring securing the reaction plate then remove the reaction plate and one brake disc.
28. Remove the snap ring securing the brake plates and discs, then remove the five plates and five brake discs.
29. Remove the pressure plate followed by the wave spring.
30. Remove the snap ring retaining the centre support, then remove the centre support, followed by the #8 thrust race and #9 thrust bearing.
31. From the transmission case remove the direct annulus gear, then remove the #12 thrust bearing.
32. Remove the direct planetary carrier from the transmission case, then remove the two seal rings from the planetary carrier.
33. Remove the snap ring securing the reduction brake cover, then remove the cover and O-ring.
34. Remove the snap ring from the reduction brake piston, then remove the piston nut, piston and seal ring.
35. Remove the Reduction brake piston adjusting rod and spring from the transmission assembly.
36. From the transmission assembly remove the direct clutch assembly then remove the #13 thrust bearing.
37. Remove the reduction brake band from the transmission case.
38. From the side of the transmission case remove the anchor plug and O-ring.
39. Remove the bolts (8) securing the output shaft support, then remove the shaft support and gasket.

DISMANTLE SUB ASSEMBLIES

TRANSFER CASE ADAPTER
Dismantle
1. From the transfer case adaptor remove the parking sprag shaft, then remove the parking sprag and spring.
2. Remove the sealing caps from the parking roller support shafts, then remove the shafts followed by the parking roller support.
3. From the transfer case adaptor remove the oil seal using a oil seal remover.

Assemble
1. Install the oil seal to the transfer case adaptor using a seal installation tool.
2. Install the parking roller support into position, then install the roller support shafts.
3. Press the sealing caps into the adaptor to a depth of 1.5mm below surface then apply sealant to the caps.
   Sealant: .... 3M AAD part #8672
4. Install the parking sprag and spring to the adaptor plate, ensuring to have the ends of the spring positioned correctly, then securing in position with the parking sprag shaft.

Oil Pump
Dismantle
1. From the oil pump housing remove the O-ring.
2. Remove the seal rings from the oil pump, then remove the oil seal.

Assembly
1. Install a new oil seal to the pump housing ensure to firstly coat the seal with A.T.F. then install the seal rings.
2. To the oil pump assembly install the O-ring, then coat the outside surface of the O-ring with automatic Transmission fluid.

Underdrive Clutch
Dismantle
1. Compress clutch assembly using appropriate tool, then remove clutch pack retaining snap ring.
2. From assembly remove the clutch reaction plate, clutch discs and clutch plates.
   Clutch Disc 4
   Clutch Plate 4

AUTOMATIC TRANSMISSION (V5A51 & V5A5A)

Reaction Plate..1

3. Compress clutch assembly using appropriate tool, then remove the spring retainer snap ring.
4. Remove the spring retainer, D-ring and return spring.
5. Remove the underdrive clutch piston and the three D-rings.

Inspection
1. Inspect all driving discs to ensure the facing material is in good condition, replace if damaged or if mating surface can be scraped off easily.
2. Inspect splines of driving discs for damage and wear.
3. Inspect the surfaces of the steel plate and pressure plates for burning, scoring and damage, replace if required.
4. Inspect the steel plate lug grooves in the clutch retainer for damage also inspect piston seal ring surfaces of clutch retainer.
5. Inspect inner bore of clutch retainer and clutch retainer bushing for wear.
6. Inspect the piston bore for score marks, also inspect seal ring grooves for damage.
7. Inspect piston spring, retainer and cir-clip for distortion.

Assemble
1. To the clutch retainer install the three D-rings which have first been coated with clean transmission fluid.
2. Install the underdrive clutch piston, then align the two return spring holes with the projections on the underdrive clutch piston.
3. Assemble the return springs then install the D-ring which has firstly been coated with clean transmission fluid.
4. Install the spring retainer then compress assembly and install the snap ring.
5. Soak the clutch discs in Clean transmission fluid prior to installation.
6. Install the clutch plates, clutch discs and the clutch reaction plate.
7. Compress assembly and install retaining snap ring, then check the snap ring clearance is within specification.
   Snap ring clearance ....1.7 +/-0.1 mm

Reverse & Overdrive Clutch
Dismantle
1. From the input shaft remove the two seal rings.
2. Remove the input shaft retaining snap ring then remove the input shaft from the assembly.
3. Remove the clutch pack retaining snap ring, then remove the clutch reaction plate, clutch discs and clutch plates.
   Clutch Disc 2
   Clutch Plate 2
   Reaction Plate 1
4. Compress clutch assembly using appropriate tool, then remove 2nd clutch pack retaining snap ring and then remove the second clutch reaction plate, clutch discs and clutch plates.
   Clutch Disc 5
   Clutch Plate 5
   Reaction Plate 1
5. Compress the assembly and remove the spring retainer snap ring, then remove the spring retainer and D-ring.
6. Remove the return spring, then remove the overdrive clutch piston and D-ring.
7. Remove the reverse clutch piston from the clutch retainer then remove the three D-rings.

Inspection
1. Inspect all driving discs to ensure the facing material is in good condition, replace if damaged or if mating surface can be scraped off easily.
2. Inspect splines of driving discs for damage and wear.
3. Inspect the surfaces of the steel plate and pressure plates for burning, scoring and damage, replace if required.
4. Inspect the steel plate lug grooves in the clutch retainer for damage also inspect piston seal ring surfaces of clutch retainer.
5. Inspect inner bore of clutch retainer and clutch retainer bushing for wear.
6. Inspect the piston bore for score marks, also inspect seal ring grooves for damage.
7. Inspect the piston spring, retainer and cir-clip for distortion.

Assembly
1. To the clutch retainer install the D-rings which have been coated with clean transmission fluid.
2. Install the reverse clutch piston to the clutch retainer aligning the holes of the piston and the retainer.
3. Install the D-ring which has been coated with clean transmission fluid to the overdrive clutch piston then install the overdrive clutch piston.
4. Install the return spring aligning the two return spring holes with the projections on the overdrive clutch piston.
5. Install the D-ring which have been coated in clean transmission fluid to the spring retainer, then install the spring retainer to the assembly.
6. Evenly compress the assembly using the appropriate tool then install the retaining snap ring.

7. Install the clutch plates, clutch discs and the clutch reaction plate, ensuring to firstly soak the clutch discs in clean transmission fluid prior to installation.
8. Compress assembly and install retaining snap ring, then check the snap ring clearance is within specification.
   Snap ring clearance ....2.1 +/-0.1 mm
9. Install the remaining clutch plates and clutch discs as shown, ensuring to soak the clutch discs in clean transmission fluid prior to installation.
10. Install the clutch reaction plate then compress assembly and install retaining snap ring.
11. Install the clutch reaction plate then compress assembly and install retaining snap ring.
12. Check the snap ring clearance is within specification.
    Snap ring clearance ....1.6 +/-0.1 mm

DIRECT CLUTCH
Dismantle
1. Compress clutch assembly using appropriate tool, then remove clutch pack retaining snap ring.
2. From assembly remove the clutch reaction plate, clutch discs and clutch plates.
3. Compress assembly and remove the spring retainer snap ring, then remove the spring retainer, D-ring and return spring.
4. Remove the direct clutch piston and the 2 D-rings from the clutch retainer.

Inspection
1. Inspect all driving discs to ensure the facing material is in good condition, replace if damaged or if mating surface can be scraped off easily.
2. Inspect splines of driving discs for damage and wear.
3. Inspect the surfaces of the steel plate and pressure plates for burning, scoring and damage, replace if required.
4. Inspect the steel plate lug grooves in the clutch retainer for damage also inspect piston seal ring surfaces of clutch retainer.
5. Inspect inner bore of clutch retainer and clutch retainer bushing for wear.
6. Inspect the piston bore for score marks, also inspect seal ring grooves for damage.
7. Inspect the piston spring, retainer and cir-clip for distortion.

Assemble
1. To the clutch retainer first install the D-rings which has first been coated with clean transmission fluid.
2. Install the direct clutch piston, then install the return spring and the D-ring which has firstly been coated with clean transmission fluid.
3. Install the spring retainer then compress assembly and install the snap ring.
4. Soak the clutch discs in Clean transmission fluid prior to installation.
5. Install the clutch plates, clutch discs and the clutch reaction plate.
6. Compress assembly and install retaining snap ring, then evenly press the clutch return spring retainer down by a weight of 49N, and check the snap ring clearance is within specification.
   Snap ring clearance ....1.1 +/-0.1 mm

Low/Reverse Annulus Carrier
Dismantle
1. Remove the snap ring securing the overdrive planetary carrier, then remove planetary carrier and #5 thrust bearing.
2. Remove the underdrive sun gear followed by the #4 thrust bearing.
3. Remove the output planetary carrier from the low/reverse annulus gear.
4. Remove the stopper plate, then remove the one-way clutch and snap ring.

Inspection
1. Thoroughly clean all components.
2. Inspect the thrust surfaces and thrust bearing for damage and wear, replace if required.
3. Inspect the teeth of the planetary gear for wear and chips.
4. Inspect the planet pinion carrier roller bearing for wear, score marks and that it runs freely.

Assembly
1. To the low/reverse annulus gear install the snap ring then install the one-way clutch, ensuring the arrow stamp is facing outwards.
2. Install the stopper plate, ensuring the plate claws are engaged securely in the annulus gear groove.
3. Install the output planetary carrier to the assembly then install the #6 thrust bearing, ensuring it is installed in the correct direction.
   Note: *Use petroleum jelly on thrust bearing to help retain in position.*
4. Install the underdrive sun gear to the assembly, then install the #5 thrust bearing, ensuring it is installed in the correct direction.
   Note: *Use petroleum jelly on thrust bearing to help retain in position.*
5. Install the overdrive planetary carrier to the assembly and secure with the retaining snap ring.

Centre Support
Dismantle
1. Gently compress clutch assembly using appropriate tool, then remove retaining snap ring.
2. From assembly remove the plate followed by the one-way clutch inner race and O-ring.
3. Remove the spring retainer, then remove the return spring followed by the low/reverse brake piston from the centre support.
4. Remove the two D-rings from the piston assembly.

Installation
1. To the low/reverse brake piston install the two D-rings which have firstly been coated with clean transmission fluid.
2. Install the low/reverse brake piston to the centre support, then install the return spring.
3. Install the spring retainer to the assembly, then install the O-ring to the centre support.
4. Install the one-way clutch inner race to the assembly, then install the plate.
5. Gently compress assembly using appropriate tool, then install retaining snap ring.

Second Brake
Dismantle
Remove the second brake retainer from brake piston, then remove the 2 D-rings.

Assembly
To the second brake piston install the D-rings which has first been coated with clean transmission fluid, then install the second brake retainer.

Direct Annulus Gear
Dismantle
1. Remove the snap ring retaining the output flange in the direct annulus gear, then remove the output flange.
2. Remove the #10 thrust bearing, then remove the underdrive clutch hub and #11 thrust bearing.
3. From the direct annulus gear remove the underdrive clutch.

Assembly
1. Install the underdrive clutch to the direct annulus gear, then install the #11 thrust bearing to the underdrive clutch.
   Note: *Use petroleum jelly on thrust bearing to help retain in position.*
2. Install the underdrive clutch hub to the assembly, then install the #10 thrust bearing to the underdrive clutch hub.
   Note: *Use petroleum jelly on thrust bearing to help retain in position.*
3. Install the output flange to the assembly and secure in position using the retaining snap ring.

Output Shaft Support
Dismantle
1. Remove the snap ring securing the one-way clutch to the output shaft support, then remove the one-way clutch.
2. From the Output shaft support remove the two seal rings.

Assembly
1. To the output shaft support install the two seal rings.
2. Install the one-way clutch to the output shaft support, ensuring the identification groove is facing outwards.
3. Secure one-way clutch with snap ring.

Valve Body Assembly
Dismantle
Main Assembly
1. Remove the screws securing the solenoid valve support then remove the valve support and solenoid valves.
   Note: *Before remove ensure to identify each solenoid and its location to ensure correct reassembly. White pant marks or similar work well.*
2. Remove the manual valve pin and the manual valve from the valve body.
3. Remove the bolts securing the cover to the lower valve body then remove the cover and gasket.
4. Remove the bolts securing the upper valve body to the lower valve body.
5. Carefully lift the upper valve body from the lower valve body then remove the upper valve body gasket being careful not to lose the two steel balls and spring.
6. From the upper valve body remove the damping valve and valve spring, then remove the two orifice check balls and spring.
   Note: *Make note of the location of the balls and spring to ensure correct installation.*
7. From the lower valve body assembly carefully remove the separator plate and lower valve body gasket, being carefully not to lose the steel ball and spring.
8. Remove the line relief steel ball and spring from the lower valve body then remove the four knock bushings and dowel pin.

Upper Valve Body
1. Remove the retaining roller pin, then remove the damper clutch control valve sleeve, damper clutch control valve and damper clutch control valve spring.
2. Remove the stopper plate, then remove the stopper plug and switching valve.

3. Remove retaining plate then remove the fail-safe valve A sleeve, fail-safe valve A2, fail-safe valve A spring and the fail-safe valve A1.
4. Remove retaining plate then remove the fail-safe valve B sleeve and fail-safe valve B.
5. Remove the stopper plate, then remove the stopper plug and the torque converter pressure control valve and spring.

Lower Valve Body
1. Remove the retaining roller pin then remove the overdrive clutch pressure control valve sleeve, control valve and valve spring.
2. Remove the retaining roller pin, then remove the underdrive clutch pressure control valve sleeve, valve and spring.
3. Remove the retaining roller pin, then remove the second brake pressure control valve sleeve, valve and spring.
4. Remove retaining roller pin, then remove the reduction brake pressure control valve sleeve, valve and spring.
5. Remove retaining plate then remove the fail-safe valve C sleeve, and valve.
6. Remove retaining roller pin, then remove the low/reverse brake pressure control valve sleeve, control valve and spring.
7. Remove the retaining plate, then remove the regulator valve adjusting screw, valve sleeve, valve spring and valve.
8. Remove retaining roller pin, then remove the torque converter clutch control valve sleeve, control valve and spring.

Inspection
1. Wash all parts in a suitable cleaning solvent then dry with compressed air.
2. Inspect all mating surfaces for damage, distortion or warpage (use a straight edge).
3. Ensure all metering holes in valve body and transfer plate are open.
4. Inspect all valves for burrs, nicks and damage.
5. Inspect all valve springs for damage and distortion.

Assembly
Lower Valve Body
1. Insert the low/reverse brake pressure control valve spring and valve into valve body housing, then install the valve sleeve and secure with retaining roller pin.
2. Insert the fail-safe valve C into valve body housing, then install the valve sleeve and secure with retaining plate.
3. Insert the reduction brake pressure control valve spring and valve into valve body housing, then install the valve sleeve and secure with retaining roller pin.
4. Insert the second brake pressure control valve spring and valve into valve body housing, then install the valve sleeve and secure with retaining roller pin.
5. Insert the underdrive clutch pressure control valve spring and valve into valve body housing, then install the valve sleeve and secure with retaining roller pin.
6. Insert the overdrive clutch pressure control valve spring and valve into valve body housing, then install the valve sleeve and secure with retaining roller pin.
7. Insert the regulator valve, valve spring and valve sleeve into valve body housing, then install the adjusting screw and secure with retaining plate.
8. Insert the torque converter clutch control valve spring and valve into valve body housing, then install the valve sleeve and secure with retaining roller pin.

Upper Valve Body
1. Insert the torque converter pressure control valve spring and valve into valve body housing, then install the plug and secure with retaining plate.
2. Insert the fail-safe valve B into valve body housing, then install the valve sleeve and secure with retaining plate.
3. Insert the fail-safe valve A1, valve A spring and valve A2 into valve body housing, then install the valve sleeve and secure with retaining plate.
4. Install the switching valve to the valve body then install the plug and secure with retaining plate.

Main Assembly
1. Install the four knock bushings and dowel pin to the lower valve body.
   Note: *Ensuring the bushing and dowel pin protrude from the valve body by the correct amount.*

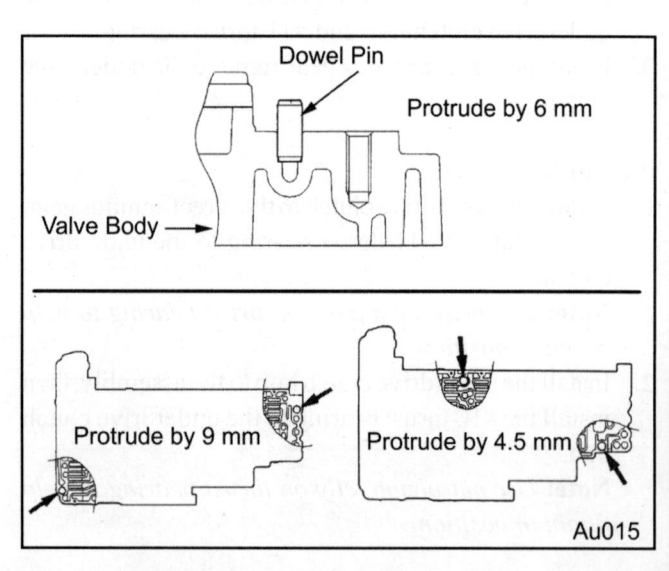

AUTOMATIC TRANSMISSION (V5A51 & V5A5A)

2. Install the line relief steel ball and spring to the lower valve body.
3. To the lower valve body install the gasket, then install the separator plate.
4. To the upper valve body install the damping valve and valve spring, ensuring to use a new seal ring then install the two orifice check balls and spring to their correct locations.
5. Install the upper valve body gasket to the upper valve body, then carefully install lower valve body assembly to the upper valve body and tighten retaining bolts to specification.
   Valve Body Bolts .... 11 Nm
6. Install the cover gasket and cover to the lower valve body and tighten retaining bolts to specification.
   Cover Retaining Bolts.................................. 11 Nm
7. Install the manual valve to the valve body assembly and then install the manual valve pin.
8. Install the solenoid valves to the valve body ensuring to install solenoids in their correct location.
   Note: *Use marks made on disassembly to assist.*
9. Install the solenoid valve support and tighten the retaining screws to specification.
   Solenoid Valve Support Screws .... 6 Nm

TRANSMISSION ASSEMBLY

1. To the transmission case install a new output shaft support gasket, then install the output shaft support and tighten retaining bolts to specification.
   Output Shaft Support.......................... 23+/-3 Nm
2. To the anchor plug fit a new O-ring then install anchor plug and tighten to specification.
   Anchor Plug .... 98+/-15 Nm
3. Install the reduction brake band with the anchor bracket hole fitted onto the anchor plug, then install the apply bracket into the reduction brake piston adjusting rod hole.
4. To the direct clutch retainer install the #13 thrust bearing, ensuring it is installed in the right direction.
5. Carefully install the direct clutch assembly, being careful not to move the reduction brake band.
6. Screw the reduction brake piston adjusting rod into the piston, then install a new seal ring to the piston.
7. Install the reduction brake spring, to the transmission assembly then install the reduction brake piston and secure with retaining snap ring.
8. a) By hand tighten the reduction brake piston adjusting rod, then using special tool (MB991693) hold the brake piston to prevent it from rotating.
   b) Tighten the reduction brake piston adjusting rod to 10Nm then back off, repeat this process.
   c) Tighten adjusting rod to 5 Nm then back off 5 $1/2$ turns.
   d) Remove special tool and tighten the piston nut to specification.
   Piston Lock Nut .... 19+/-3 Nm
9. To the reduction brake piston cover install a new O-ring, then install cover and secure with retaining snap ring.
10. To the direct planetary carrier shaft install two new seal rings, then install two new seal rings to the front of the direct planetary carrier.
11. Install the direct planetary carrier into the output shaft support, then install the #12 thrust bearing to the front of the direct planetary carrier.
    Note: *Use petroleum jelly on thrust bearing to help retain in position.*
12. Install the direct annulus gear to the transmission assembly then install the #9 thrust bearing to the direct annulus gear.
    Note: *Use petroleum jelly on thrust bearing to help retain in position.*
13. Measure and record the thickness of the #8 thrust race, then install the thrust race to the rear side of the centre support.
    Note: *Use petroleum jelly on thrust bearing to help retain in position.*
14. Install the centre support to the transmission case with the oil hole facing the lower side of the transmission.
    Note: *Be careful the #8 thrust race does not fall off centre support.*
15. a) Install special tool (MB991603) to the transmission case using the transfer case adapter bolt., then install a dial gauge to the tool.
    b) Alternately push the direct planetary carrier and the direct annulus gear and measure the end play of the direct planetary carrier.
    Note: *Make sure the centre support does not move when pushing on the direct planetary carrier and use special tool (MD998304) to push direct annulus gear.*
    c) Using the measurement taken in step 13 and the dial gauge reading, select and replace the #8 thrust race with one of suitable thickness to achieve specified end play.
    Specified End Play 0.25-0.55mm
    d) Re-measure end play to ensure it is within specification.
16. a) With the special tool and dial gauge still fitted, install the centre support retaining snap ring.
    b) Alternately push in the direct planetary carrier and the centre support and measure the end play of the centre support.
    Note: *When pushing in the direct planetary carrier, ensure the centre support contacts the snap ring.*
    c) Using the dial gauge reading, select and replace

the centre support retaining snap ring with one of suitable thickness to achieve specified end play.
Specified End Play 0.0-0.16mm
   d) Re-measure end play to ensure it is within specification.
   e) Remove the dial gauge and special tool.
17. a) To the low/reverse brake piston install the wave spring, then install the tool (MB991632) followed by the brake discs, brake plates and snap ring.
   Note: *Tool (MB991632) is installed in replacement of the pressure plate for the low/reverse brake.*
   b) Install the original reaction plate and snap ring, then install tool (MD998913) to dial gauge and move special tool (MB991632) and measure the movement.
   c) Using the dial gauge reading, select and replace the reaction plate retaining snap ring with one of suitable thickness to achieve specified end play.
   Note: *When reassembling with new snap ring leave the tool in place for now.*
   Specified End Play 0.0-0.16mm
   d) Re-measure end play to ensure it is within specification.
18. a) Install the brake discs and brake plates, then install the tool (MB991632) instead of the pressure plate. Then install the return spring, second brake and snap ring.
   Brake Discs..4
   Brake Plates...3
   b) Install dial gauge to tool (MD998913) and move tool (MB991632) and measure the movement.
   b) Refer to table and select appropriate pressure plate.
   Standard End Play.....................1.49-1.95 mm

End play	Thickness	Id code	Part #
1.2 - 1.4	1.6	F	MR336390
1.4 - 1.6	1.8	E	MR336391
1.6 - 1.8	2.0	D	MR336392
1.8 - 2.0	2.2	C	MR336393
2.0 - 2.2	2.4	B	MR336394
2.2 - 2.4	2.6	A	MR336395
2.4 - 2.6	2.8	0	MR336396
2.6 - 2.8	3.0	1	MR336397

19. Remove the snap ring, second brake, return spring and special tool installed during step 18, then install the selected pressure plate and reinstall the return spring, second brake and snap ring.
20. a) Install dial gauge to tool (MD998913) and move tool (MB991632) (installed in step 17) and measure the movement.
   b) Refer to table and select appropriate pressure plate.
   Standard End Play.....................1.65-2.11 mm

End play	Thickness	Id code	Part #
1.5 - 1.7	1.8	E	MD759425
1.7 - 1.9	2.0	D	MD759426
1.9 - 2.1	2.2	C	MD759427
2.1 - 2.3	2.4	B	MD759428
2.3 - 2.5	2.6	A	MD759429
2.5 - 2.7	2.8	0	MD759430
2.7 - 2.9	3.0	1	MD759431

21. Remove all parts installed during steps 17 to 20.
22. Install the #7 thrust bearing to the rear side of the low/reverse annulus gear.
   Note: *Use petroleum jelly on thrust bearing to help retain in position.*
23. Install the low/reverse annulus gear to the transmission assembly being careful so the #7 thrust bearing does not fall off.
24. To the transmission assembly install the reverse sun gear, then install the wave spring to the low/reverse brake piston.
25. Install the pressure plate selected earlier, then install the brake discs and brake plates and secure with retaining snap ring.
26. Install the reaction plate to the transmission assembly, ensuring to install it in the correct direction, then install the snap ring selected previously.
27. Install the brake discs, brake plates and pressure plates selected previously.
28. To the transmission assembly install the return spring and the second brake then secure in position with retaining snap ring.
   Note: *Ensure the return spring is installed with the flat side facing the back of the transmission.*
29. Install #4 thrust bearing to the reverse sun gear, then install the #3 thrust bearing to the overdrive clutch hub and install overdrive clutch hub to transmission.
   Note: *Use petroleum jelly on thrust bearing to help retain in position.*
30. Install the reverse and overdrive clutch to the transmission assembly, then install the #2 thrust bearing to the clutch.
   Note: *Use petroleum jelly on thrust bearing to help retain in position.*
31. To the oil pump install the #1 thrust race, using petroleum jelly to hold thrust race in position.
32. Install the oil pump gasket and pump assembly using alignment tool (MD998412).
33. Tighten the pump retaining bolts to specification.
   Oil Pump Bolts ....20-26 Nm
34. Measure the input shaft end play and select #1 thrust washer to achieve correct end play specification.
   Standard End Play..........................0.25-0.81 mm
35. Remove #1 thrust washer installed in step 31 and replace with newly selected washer and recheck end

AUTOMATIC TRANSMISSION (V5A51 & V5A5A)

play to ensure it is to specification.

36. Install the converter housing and tighten retaining bolts to specification.
    Converter Housing Bolts .... 42-54 Nm
37. To the detent lever install the parking roller, then install two new O-rings to the manual control shaft.
38. To the transmission case install the manual control shaft with the detent lever and parking rod and secure with retaining pin.
39. Install the spring pin so the split in the pin is at right angles to the manual control shaft as shown.
40. To each accumulator piston install a new seal ring.
41. Install the direct clutch accumulator spring, piston and cover, then secure in position with the retaining snap ring.
42. Install the reduction brake accumulator spring, piston and cover, then secure in position with the retaining snap ring.
43. Install the underdrive clutch accumulator spring, piston and cover, then secure in position with the retaining snap ring.
44. Install the low/reverse brake accumulator spring, piston and cover, then secure in position with the retaining snap ring.
45. Install the second brake accumulator spring, piston and cover, then secure in position with the retaining snap ring.
46. Install the overdrive clutch accumulator spring, piston and cover, then secure in position with the retaining snap ring.
47. To the transmission assembly install two new oil seals as shown, then install the oil strainer. 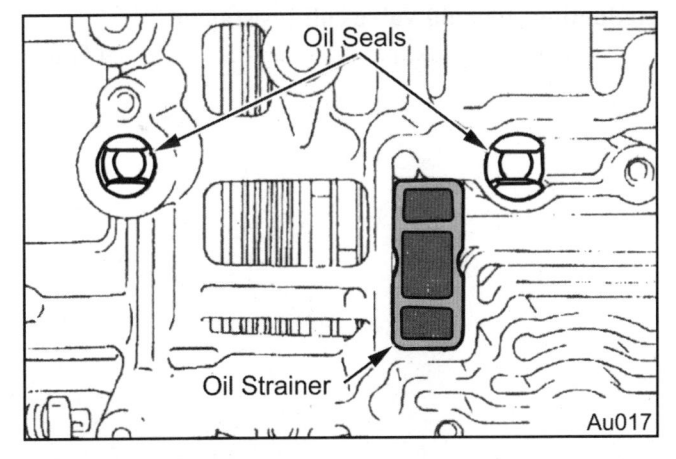
48. Install the solenoid valve harness and secure socket into position with snap ring.
49. To the transmission case install three new O-rings, then install the the valve body, inserting the manual valve pin into the groove of the detent lever.
50. Install the oil temperature sensor to the transmission, then install the valve body bolts as shown in diagram and tighten to specification.
    Valve Body Bolts .... 10-12 Nm

Bolt Locations: A .... 25 mm
B .... 30 mm
C .... 40 mm
D .... 45 mm
E .... 55 mm

51. Connect the electrical connectors to the valve body, then install the detent spring and tighten retaining bolt to specification.
    Detent Spring Bolt .... 5-7 Nm
52. Install the oil filter to the transmission assembly using a new O-ring. 
53. To the oil pan apply a liquid gasket, then install the oil pan to transmission and tighten bolts to specification.
    Oil Pan Bolts .... 10-12 Nm
54. Install the parking gear to the transmission so the side without the spline faces the transmission and secure in position with retaining snap ring
55. To the side of the transmission assembly install the inhibitor switch and manual control lever.
    Inhibitor switch Bolts .... 10-12 Nm
    Manual Control Lever Nut .... 19-25 Nm
56. Install the output shaft speed sensor and the input shaft speed sensor, tighten retaining bolt to specification.
    Output Shaft Speed Sensor Bolt .... 10-12 Nm
    Input Shaft Speed Sensor Bolt .... 10-12 Nm

AUTOMATIC TRANSMISSION (V5A51 & V5A5A)

SPECIFICATIONS

Model: V5A51
.... V5A5A
Type: Electronically controlled 5 speed

Torque Converter:
- stall speed   6G72 .... 2100-2600rpm
                          6G74 .... 2200-2700rpm
                          4M40 .... 2200-2700rpm
                          4M41 .... 2400-2900rpm

Lubrication:
Transmission - type .... ATF SPIII
                - capacity 2001 .... 9.3 litres
                                2002 on .... 9.7 litres

Transfer Case - type .... Hypoid gear oil
                            SAE70W-90 (API GL-4)
                - capacity .... 2.8 litres

Gear Ratios: 1st   3.789
                          2nd   2.057
                          3rd   1.421
                          4th   1.000
                          5th   0.731
                          Reverse 3.865

Transfer: High   1.000
               Low   1.900

TRANSMISSION

Direct planetary carrier .... 0.25-0.55 mm
Brake reaction plate end play .... 0.00 - 0.16 mm
Low-reverse brake end play .... 1.65 - 2.11 mm
Second brake end play .... 1.49 - 1.95 mm
Input shaft end play .... 0.25 - 0.81 mm
Underdrive clutch end play .... 1.60 - 1.80 mm
Overdrive clutch return spring retainer end play
.... 0.0 - 0.09 mm
Overdrive clutch end play .... 2.0 - 2.2 mm
Reverse clutch end play .... 1.5 - 1.7 mm
Centre support end play .... 0 - 0.16 mm
Direct clutch end play .... 1.0 - 1.2 mm

TRANSFER

Input gear bearing end play .... 0.0 - 0.06 mm
Countershaft gear end play .... 0.0 - 0.15 mm
Countershaft gear bearing end play .... 0.0 - 0.08 mm
2-4WD clutch hub end play .... 0.0 - 0.08 mm
H-L clutch hub end play .... 0.0 - 0.08 mm
Rear output shaft preload .... 0.12 - 0.24 mm
Rear output shaft end play .... 0.0 - 0.12 mm
Rear output shaft bearing end play .... 0.0 - 0.08 mm
Rear output shaft annulus gear
end play .... 0.0 - 0.08 mm
Differential lock hub end play .... 0.0 - 0.08 mm
Clearance b/w outer synchro ring &
drive sprocket .... 0.3 mm (limit)

Oil Temperature sensor:
    @0°C .... 16.7 - 20.5 kOhms
    @20°C .... 7.3 - 8.9 kOhms
    @40°C .... 3.4 - 4.2 kOhms
    @60°C .... 1.9 - 2.2 kOhms
    @80°C .... 1.0 - 1.2 kOhms
    @100°C .... 0.57 - 0.69 kOhms

Damper clutch control solenoid valve coil:
    @20°C .... 2.7 - 3.4 Ohms

Low-reverse solenoid valve coil resistance:
    @20°C .... 2.7 - 3.4 Ohms

Second solenoid valve coil resistance:
    @20°C .... 2.7 - 3.4 Ohms

Underdrive solenoid valve coil resistance:
    @20°C .... 2.7 - 3.4 Ohms

Overdrive solenoid valve coil resistance:
    @20°C .... 2.7 - 3.4 Ohms

Reduction solenoid valve coil resistance:
    @20°C .... 2.7 - 3.4 Ohms

AUTOMATIC TRANSMISSION (V5A51 & V5A5A)

TRANSMISSION

Thrust washer selection for adjustment of direct planetary carrier end play:

Thickness (mm)	Identification	Part No.
1.6	None	MR276705
1.8	None	MR276706
2.0	None	MR276707
2.2	None	MR276708
2.3	None	MR276709

Thrust washer selection for adjustment of input shaft end play:

Thickness (mm)	Identification	Part No.
1.4	None	MD723063
1.6	None	MD707267
1.8	None	MD723064
2.0	None	MD707268
2.2	None	MD723065
2.4	None	MD724358
2.6	None	MD754798

Snap ring selection for adjustment of underdrive clutch and overdrive clutch end plays:

Thickness (mm)	Identification	Part No.
1.6	Brown	MD759660
1.7	None	MD759661
1.8	Blue	MD759662
1.9	Brown	MD758892
2.0	None	MD750841
2.1	Blue	MD750842
2.2	Brown	MD750843
2.3	None	MD750844
2.4	Blue	MD750845
2.5	Brown	MD750846
2.6	None	MD750847
2.7	Blue	MD750848
2.8	Brown	MD750849
2.9	None	MD750850
3.0	Blue	MD750851

Snap ring selection for adjustment of centre support & brake reaction plate end play:

Thickness (mm)	Identification	Part No.
2.2	None	MD756784
2.3	Blue	MD756785
2.4	Brown	MD758552
2.5	None	MD758553

Pressure plate selection for adjustment of second brake end play:

Thickness (mm)	Identification	Part No.
1.6	F	MR336390
1.8	E	MR336391
2.0	D	MR336392
2.2	C	MR336393
2.4	B	MR336394
2.6	A	MR336395
2.8	0	MR336396
3.0	1	MR336397

Snap ring selection for adjustment of reverse clutch end play:

Thickness (mm)	Identification	Part No.
1.6	None	MD761088
1.7	Blue	MD761089
1.8	Brown	MD761090
1.9	None	MD758947
2.0	Blue	MD756690
2.1	Brown	MD756691
2.2	None	MD756692
2.3	Blue	MD756693
2.4	Brown	MD756694
2.5	None	MD756695
2.6	Blue	MD756696
2.7	Brown	MD756697
2.8	None	MD756698

Snap ring selection for adjustment of low/reverse brake end play:

Thickness (mm)	Identification	Part No.
1.8	E	MD759425
2.0	D	MD759426
2.2	C	MD759427
2.4	B	MD759428
2.6	A	MD759429
2.8	0	MD759430
3.0	1	MD759431

Snap ring selection for adjustment of overdrive clutch return spring retainer end play:

Thickness (mm)	Identification	Part No.
1.48	Brown	MR336158
1.53	None	MR336159
1.58	Blue	MR336160
1.63	Brown	MR336161

Snap ring selection for adjustment of direct clutch end play:

Thickness (mm)	Identification	Part No.
1.9	Brown	MD758946
2.0	None	MD753397
2.1	Blue	MD753398
2.2	Brown	MD753399
2.3	None	MD753400
2.4	Blue	MD753401
2.5	Brown	MD753402
2.6	None	MD753403
2.7	Blue	MD753404
2.8	Brown	MD753405
2.9	None	MD753406
3.0	Blue	MD753407

VALVE BODY SPRING IDENTIFICATION

Wire Diameter (mm)
Regulator valve spring 1.3
Torque converter pressure control valve spring 1.6
Torque converter clutch control valve spring 0.7
Fail-safe valve A spring 0.7
Damping valve spring 1.0
Line relief valve spring 1.0
Orifice check ball spring 0.5
Pressure control valve spring 0.7

Outside Diameter (mm)
Regulator valve spring 13.3
Torque converter pressure control valve spring 11.2
Torque converter clutch control valve spring 5.9
Fail-safe valve A spring 8.9
Damping valve spring 7.7
Line relief valve spring 7.0
Orifice check ball spring 4.5
Pressure control valve spring 7.6

Free Length (mm)
Regulator valve spring 44.6
Torque converter pressure control valve spring 29.4
Torque converter clutch control valve spring 28.1
Fail-safe valve A spring 21.9
Damping valve spring 35.8
Line relief valve spring 17.3
Orifice check ball spring 15.4
Pressure control valve spring 37.7

Of Loops
Regulator valve spring 10.5
Torque converter pressure control valve spring 9.5
Torque converter clutch control valve spring 19
Fail-safe valve A spring 9.5
Damping valve spring 17
Line relief valve spring 10
Orifice check ball spring 15
Pressure control valve spring 25

Torque Specifications

Description   **Nm**
Transmission
Output shaft support mounting bolt .... 23+/-3
Upper valve body mounting bolt .... 11+/-1
Park/Neutral position switch mounting bolt .... 11+/-1
Anchor plug .... 98+/-15
Oil pan mounting bolt .... 11+/-1
Oil filter mounting bolt .... 6+/-1
Oil pump mounting bolt .... 23+/-3
Cable end bracket mounting bolt .... 48+/-6
Converter housing to
transmission case tightening bolt .... 48+/-6
Output shaft speed sensor mounting bolt .... 11+/-1
Reduction brake piston nut .... 19+/-3
Separating plate mounting bolt .... 6+/-1
Solenoid support mounting bolt .... 6+/-1
Transfer to transfer case adapter
tightening bolt .... 35+/-6
Transmission case to
transfer case adapter tightening bolt .... 48+/-6
Input shaft speed sensor mounting bolt .... 11+/-1
Valve body mounting bolt .... 11+/-1
Detent spring mounting bolt .... 6+/-1
Manual control lever body mounting nut .... 22+/-3
Lower valve body mounting bolt .... 11+/-1
Lower valve body cover mounting bolt .... 11+/-1

TRANSFER

Description	Page
MAINTENANCE	**286**
Transfer Case	**286**
Oil Level	286
Oil Replacement	286
4WD Detection Switch	**286**
High/Low Detection Switch	**286**
4L Detection Switch	**286**
2WD/4WD Switch Continuity	**287**
4H Switch Continuity	**287**
Centre Differential Lock Switch Continuity	**287**
2WD Switch Continuity	**287**
4LLc Switch Continuity	**287**
Transfer Select Switch Check	**287**
MINOR REPAIRS	**287**
Transfer ECU & 4WD Indicator-ECU	**287**
Transfer-ECU Check	287
4WD Indicator-ECU check	287
Removal	287
Installation	287
M-ASTC & M-ATC ECU	**288**
Check	288
Removal	289
Installation	289
Control Cable / Inhibitor Switch	**289**
Adjustment	289
Remove	289
Install	289
Auto Transmission Selector Lever	**289**
Remove	289
Install	289
Transfer Shift Lever (part time 4WD)	**290**
Remove	290
Install	290
Transfer Shift Lever (SSII 4WD)	**290**
Remove	290
Install	290
TRANSFER ASSEMBLY	**290**
Transfer Removal & Installation	**290**

Description	Page
Transfer Disassembly	**291**
SSII 4WD	291
Part Time 4WD	293
Sub Components	**293**
Transfer Case Plate	**293**
Dismantle	293
Assemble	294
Transfer Input Gear	**294**
Dismantle	294
Assemble	294
Countershaft Gear - Part time 4WD	**294**
Dismantle	294
Assemble	294
Countershaft Gear - SSII 4WD	**294**
Dismantle	294
Assemble	294
Rear Output Shaft	**294**
Dismantle	294
Assemble	294
Front Output Shaft	**295**
Dismantle	295
Assemble	295
Transfer Drive Shaft	**295**
Dismantle	295
Assemble	295
H-L Shift Rail - Part Time 4WD	**295**
Dismantle	295
Assemble	295
2-4WD Shift Rail & H-L Shift Rail - SSII 4WD	**295**
Dismantle	295
Assemble	295
Shift Rail Drive Gear - SSII 4WD	**295**
Dismantle	295
Assemble	295
Speedometer Gear - Part Time 4WD	**295**
Dismantle	295
Assemble	295
Transfer Assembly	**296**
SSII 4WD	296
Part Time 4WD	298
SPECIFICATIONS	**299**

TRANSFER

MAINTENANCE

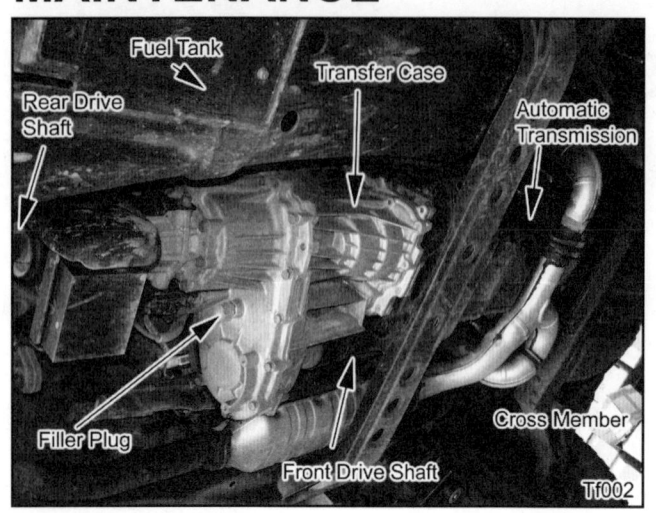

TRANSFER CASE
Oil Level
1. Remove the oil filler plug and check to ensure the oil level is at the bottom of the plug hole.
2. Inspect the oil to ensure it is not excessively dirty, then replace the filler plug and tighten to specification.
   Oil Filler Plug .... 32 Nm

Oil Replacement
1. Position a drain tray under the transfer case, then remove the drain plug and allow oil to drain.
2. Install the drain plug and tighten to specification.
   Oil Drain Plug .... 32 Nm
   Remove the oil filler plug fill the transfer case to the bottom of the filler plug hole.
   Transfer Oil Capacity .... 2.5 litres
   Transfer Gear Oil .... SAE 75W-85W
   API GL-4
3. Replace the filler plug, tightening to specification, then inspect to ensure there are no leaks.
   Oil Filler Plug .... 32 Nm

4WD DETECTION SWITCH CHECK (part time 4wd)
The switch connectors are easily accessed near the rear of the transfer case. If the switches need to be accessed, the transmission and transfer case will need to be lowered to gain access to the detection switches.

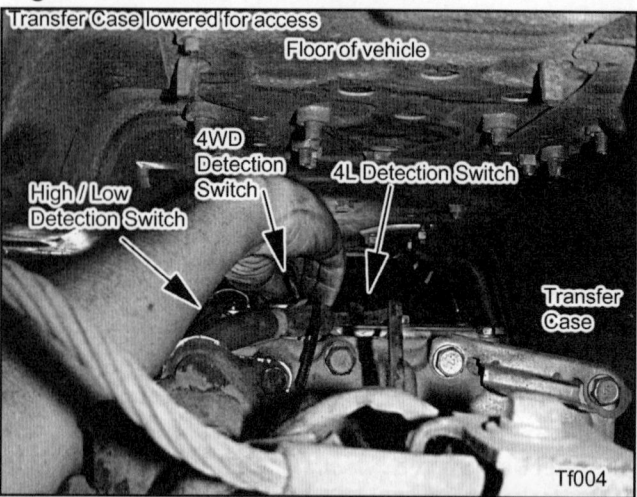

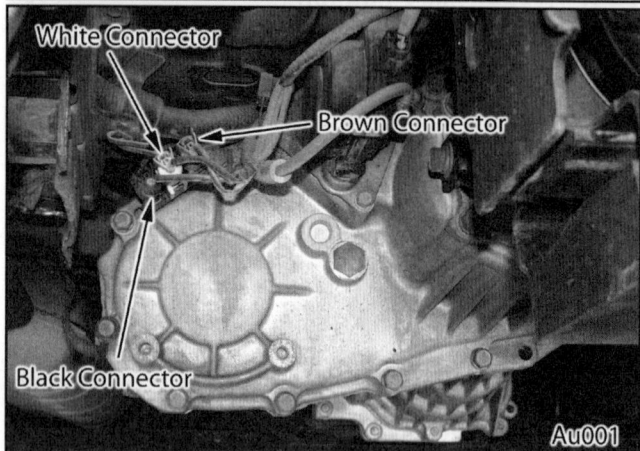

Check continuity b/w terminal #1 and #2 of the black connector on the side of the transfer case.

Transfer lever position	Continuity
2H	No Continuity
4H	Continuity

HIGH/LOW DETECTION SWITCH CHECK (part time 4wd)
Check continuity b/w terminal #1 and #2 of the brown / grey connector on the side of the transfer case.

Transfer lever position	Continuity
4H	No Continuity
Between 4H & 4L	Continuity
4L	Continuity

4L DETECTION SWITCH CHECK (part time 4wd)
Check continuity b/w the terminal of the white connector on the side of the transfer case and the transfer case.

TRANSFER

Transfer lever position	Continuity
4L	Continuity
Other than 4L	No Continuity

2WD/4WD SWITCH CONTINUITY CHECK (super select 4wd II)

Check continuity b/w terminals of the black connector at the left of the transfer case (as shown).

Transfer lever position	Continuity
2H, 4H	Continuity
4HLc, 4LLc	No Continuity

4H SWITCH CONTINUITY CHECK (super select 4wd II)

Check continuity b/w terminals of the white connector at the left of the transfer case (as shown).

Transfer lever position	Continuity
2H, 4LLc	No Continuity
4H, 4HLc	Continuity

CENTRE DIFFERENTIAL LOCK SWITCH CONTINUITY CHECK (super select 4wd II)

Check continuity b/w terminals of the brown connector at the left of the transfer case (as shown).

Transfer lever position	Continuity
2H, 4H	No Continuity
4HLc, 4LLc	Continuity

2WD SWITCH CONTINUITY CHECK (super select 4wd II)

Check continuity b/w terminals of the black connector at the left of the transfer case (as shown).

Transfer lever position	Continuity
2H	Continuity
4H, 4HLc, 4LLc	No Continuity

4LLc SWITCH CONTINUITY CHECK (super select 4wd II)

Check continuity b/w terminals of the brown connector at the left of the transfer case (as shown).

Transfer lever position	Continuity
4LLc	Continuity
2H, 4H, 4HLc	No Continuity

TRANSFER SELECT SWITCH CHECK

1. Vehicle stopped, hand brake on, ignition key ON.
2. The automatic transmission selection lever should be in "N"
3. Move transfer shift lever between 2H, 4H, 4HLc and 4LLc, make sure the dash 4WD indication light illuminates according to the position of the lever. The light should illuminate within 5 seconds of the selection.

Note: *If the vehicle is not stopped or the shift lever was not in "N". the 4WD indication light will flash and the 4WD will not be activated.*

MINOR REPAIRS

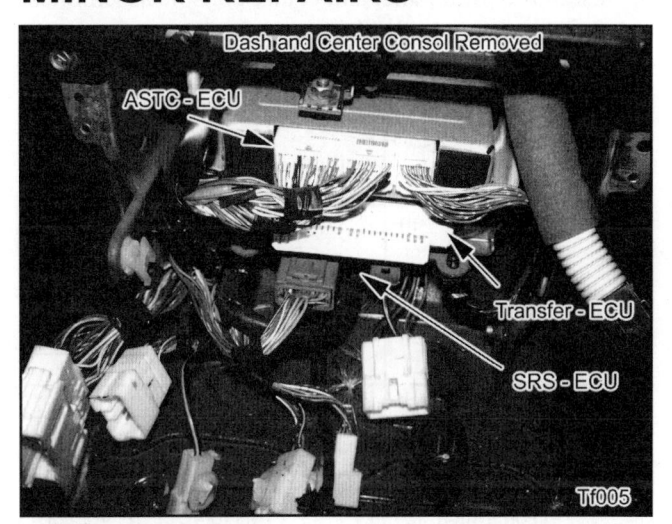

TRANSFER ECU & 4WD INDICATOR-ECU
Transfer-ECU Check

The transfer ECU is located behind the dash centre console unit as shown above.

4WD Indicator-ECU Check

With the control unit and harness still connected, earth the #8 terminal then measure the terminal voltage.

Removal

1. Disconnect the negative cable from the battery.
2. Remove the centre console assembly and front panel assembly as described in the body chapter.
3. Disconnect the electrical connections from the ECU and bracket assembly.
4. Remove the nuts securing the ECU and bracket assembly and remove from vehicle.

Installation

1. Install the ECU and bracket assembly into the vehicle and tighten the retaining nuts to specification.
   Transfer-ECU Mounting Nuts .... 5 Nm
2. Connect the electrical connections to the ECU and bracket assembly.

TRANSFER

Transfer ECu Connector

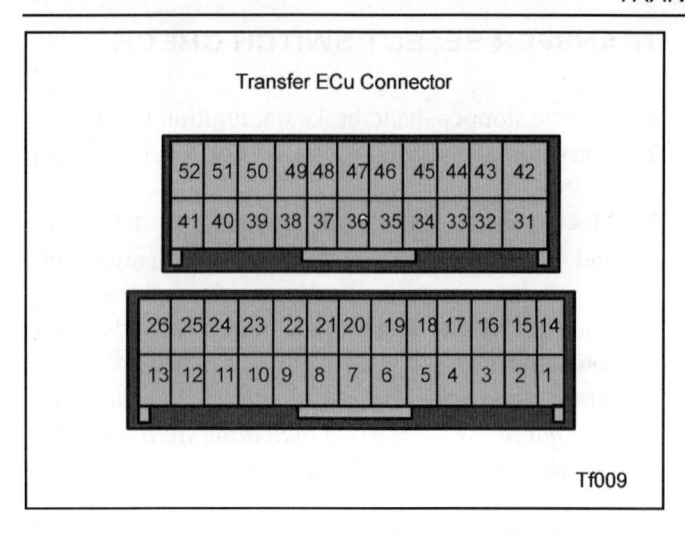

```
52 51 50 49 48 47 46 45 44 43 42
41 40 39 38 37 36 35 34 33 32 31

26 25 24 23 22 21 20 19 18 17 16 15 14
13 12 11 10  9  8  7  6  5  4  3  2  1
```
Tf009

3. Install the front panel and centre console assemblies, referring to the body chapter for assistance.

Terminal #	Inspection Item	Inspection Condition 1. Ignition Switch	Inspection Condition 2. Transfer Lever Position	Terminal Voltage
1	Free wheel engage switch	ON	2H	System Voltage
			4H*1	0V
2	4WD detection switch	ON	2H	System Voltage
			4H, 4L	0V
3	Ignition Switch	OFF	-	0V
		ON	-	System Voltage
6	Hi/Low detection switch	ON	Shifting from 4H to 4L or vice versa	System Voltage
			2H, 4H, 4L	0V
7	Free wheel clutch changeover solenoid valve	ON	4H, 4L	0V
			2H*2	System Voltage
10	4WD indicator lamp	ON	2H	0V
			4H, 4L	System Voltage

*1 - When vehicle has been moved once.
*2 - Shift lever from 4H to 2H and then turn the ignition switch to OFF and then back to ON.

M-ASTC and M-ATC ECU check

2004 on with M-ASTC and M-ATC installed to automatic transmission and 4WD transfer.
The ECU are located as shown for 2000 to 2003 models, with the M-ATC or M-ASTC ECU being the upper ECU.
The ECU connector terminals are the same, as shown for 2000 to 2003 models.
With the control unit and harness still connected, earth the #8 terminal then measure the terminal voltage.

Terminal Number	Inspection Item	Inspection Condition	What is Normal
6	M-ATC-ECU or M-ASTC-ECU signal [FR]	Ignition ON	1 volt or less
8	M-ATC-ECU or M-ASTC-ECU signal [RL]	Ignition ON	1 volt or less
10	M-ATC-ECU or M-ASTC-ECU signal [RR]	Ignition ON	1 volt or less
19	M-ATC-ECU or M-ASTC-ECU signal [FL]	Ignition ON	1 volt or less
37	2WD indication light [RL]	- Auto in N - Transfer lever changing between 4HLc and 4LLc	Voltage alternates around 1 volt or less then stabilizes
		- Auto in N - Transfer lever changing between 2H and 4H and 4HLc	System voltage
38	4WD indication light [FL]	- Auto in N - Transfer lever 2H	1 volt or less
		- Auto in N - Transfer lever other than 2H	Alternating between system voltage and 1 volt or less
48	2WD indication light [RR]	- Auto in N - Transfer lever changing between 4HLc and 4LLc	Voltage alternates around 1 volt or les then stabilizes
		- Auto in N - Transfer lever changing between 2H and 4H and 4HLc	System voltage
49	4WD indication light [FR]	- Auto in N - Transfer lever 2H	1 volt or less
		- Auto in N - Transfer lever other than 2H	Alternating between system voltage and 1 volt or less
52	4LLc indicator light	- Auto in N - Transfer lever 4LLc	1 volt or less
		- Auto in N - Transfer lever other than 2H	System voltage

TRANSFER

M-ASTC and M-ATC ECU
Removal
1. Disconnect the negative cable from the battery.
2. Remove the centre console assembly and front panel assembly as described in the body chapter.
3. Disconnect the electrical connections from the M-ATC or M-ASTC ECU and bracket assembly.
4. Remove the nuts securing the M-ATC or M-ASTC ECU and bracket assembly and remove from vehicle.

Installation
1. Install the M-ATC or M-ASTC ECU and bracket assembly into the vehicle and tighten the retaining nuts to specification.
   Transfer-M-ATC or M-ASTC ECU Mounting Nuts .... 5 Nm
2. Connect the electrical connections to the M-ATC or M-ASTC ECU and bracket assembly.
3. Install the front panel and centre console assemblies, referring to the body chapter for assistance.

CONTROL CABLE / INHIBITOR SWITCH
Adjustment
1. Have the control lever in the N position, the hole in the inhibitor switch lever must be aligned with the hole in the flange behind the lever. Then loosen the upper control lever adjusting nut.
2. Check to ensure the inhibitor switch is at the N range, then adjust the upper control lever so there is no slackness or excessive tightness in the control cable.
3. Tighten adjusting nut to specification.
   Adjusting Nut .... 24 Nm
4. Check that the selector lever corresponds with the transmission range selected.

Removal
1. Remove the centre console from the vehicle, refer to body chapter if required.
2. Disconnect the control cable from the transmission by removing the mounting nut, then disconnect the control cable unit from the selector lever assembly.
3. Remove the control cable from the vehicle.

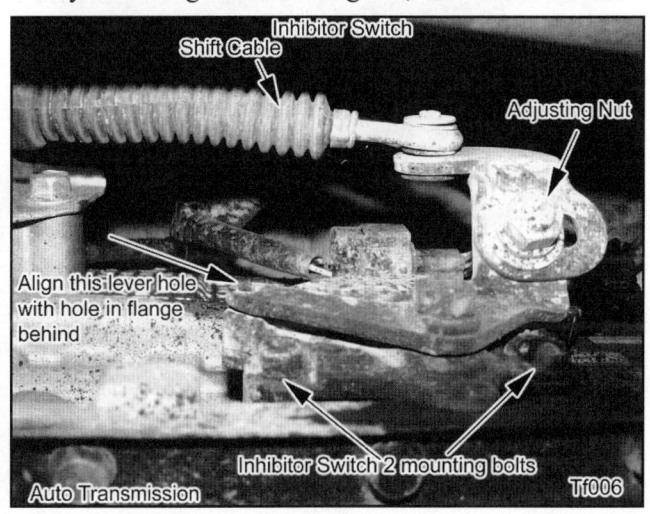

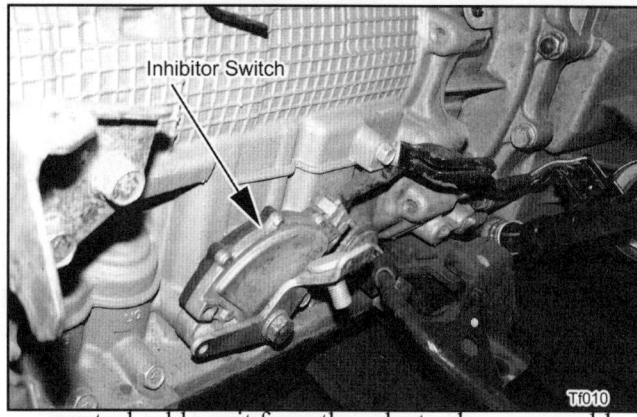

Installation
1. Install the control cable into the vehicle and tighten the bracket retaining screws.
   Fire Wall Bracket Screws .... 12 Nm
2. Reconnect the control cable unit to the selector lever, then connect the control cable to the transmission.
3. Ensure the selector lever is in the neutral position, then loosen cable nut and gently pull control cable in direction shown and tighten retaining nut to specification.
   Control Cable Adjustment Nut .... 13 Nm
4. Check to ensure the selector lever operates and functions properly for each selection.

AUTO TRANS SELECTOR LEVER
Removal
1. Remove the centre console from the vehicle, refer to body chapter if required.
2. Disconnect the control cable from the selector lever assembly, then disconnect the electrical connections.
3. Remove the lever assembly retaining bolts and remove assembly from vehicle.

Installation
1. Install the selector lever assembly into position and tighten retaining bolts to specification.

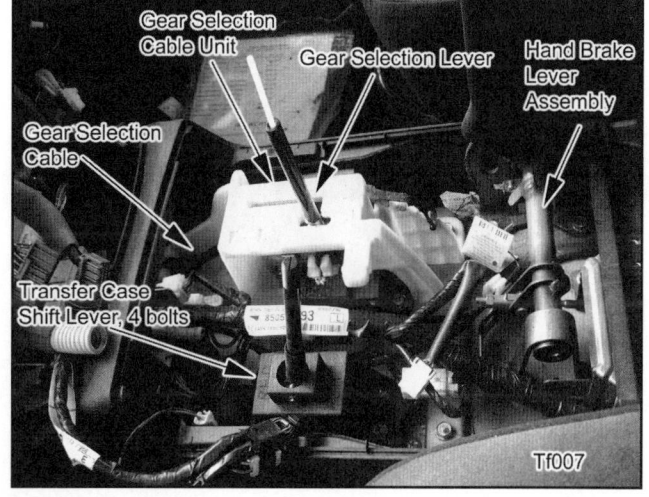

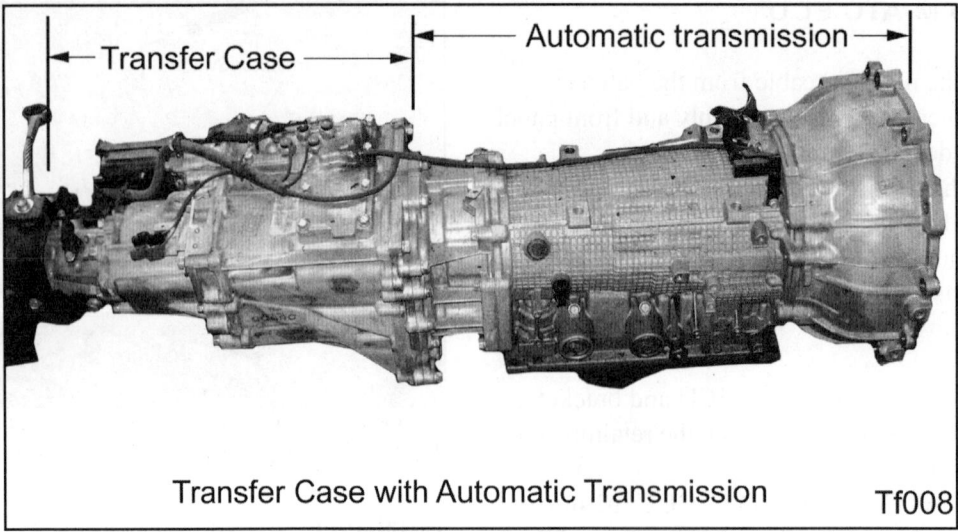

TRANSFER

Transfer Case with Automatic Transmission Tf008

Selector Lever Retaining Bolts .... 11 Nm
2. Reconnect the control cable to the selector lever assembly, then connect the electrical connections.
3. Install the centre console into the vehicle, refer to body chapter if required.
4. Adjust control cable as previously outlined.

TRANSFER SHIFT LEVER (Part Time 4WD)
Removal
1. Remove centre console section around the shift lever from the vehicle, refer to body chapter if required.
2. Unscrew the shift lever knob.
3. Remove the shift lever rubber boot and remove bolts from the support plate from the floor pan.
4. The shift lever is held in the transfer case by a circlip, remove the cir-clip and pull the lever up and out of the transfer case.

Installation
1. Install the shift lever assembly into position and install the cir-clip into the top of the transfer case.

2. Install the shift lever rubber boot and support plate, replace bolts attaching support plate to the floor pan.

3. Screw the shift lever knob into place.
4. Replace the centre console section around the shift lever to the vehicle, refer to body chapter if required.

TRANSFER SHIFT LEVER (Super Select 4WD II - Electronic shift)
Removal
1. Remove the centre console section around the shift lever from the vehicle, refer to body chapter if required.
2. Unbolt the shift lever assembly.
3. Disconnect the electrical harness connectors, remove the shift lever assembly from the vehicle.

Install
1. Place shift lever assembly to the vehicle, connect harness connectors.
2. Install the shift lever and tighten the bolts.

TRANSFER ASSEMBLY

TRANSFER REMOVAL & INSTALLATION
Refer to the appropriate transmission chapter for removal

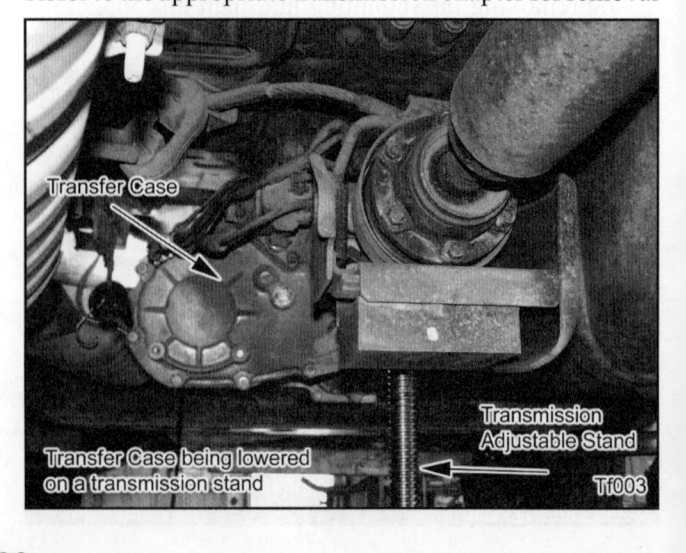

290

TRANSFER

Figure Tf012: Super Select 4WD II - (Electronic shift) — Transfer Case Cover, 10 bolts; 4LLC switch; 2WD switch; Rear Shaft Output Sensor; 2WD-4WD switch; 4H switch; Center Differential Lock Switch; Front Shaft Output Sensor; Shaft Actuator; Vehicle Speed Sensor

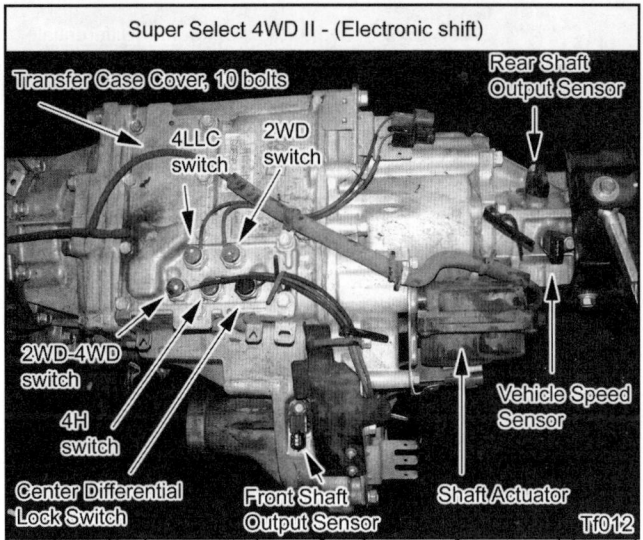

and installation procedures for the transfer assembly and separation from transmission assembly.

TRANSFER DISASSEMBLY - SSII 4WD
Automatic Transmission

1. From the transfer assembly disconnect and remove the vacuum hose.
2. Unscrew the 4LLC switch from the transfer case then remove switch, gasket and steel ball.
3. Unscrew the 2WD switch from the transfer case then remove switch, gasket and steel ball.
4. Unscrew the centre differential lock switch from the transfer case then remove switch, gasket and steel ball.
5. Unscrew the H4 switch from the transfer case then remove switch, gasket and steel ball.
6. Unscrew the 2WD-4WD switch from the transfer case then remove switch, gasket and steel ball.
7. Remove the bolts securing the transfer case cover, then remove the cover from the transfer assembly.

All Transmissions

8. From the transfer assembly remove the two shift rail drive gears.
9. Remove the dust seal guard, then remove the bolts securing the dynamic damper and remove from assembly.
10. Remove the bolt retaining the vehicle speed sensor, then remove the sensor and O-ring.
11. Remove the bolts retaining the rear and front output sensors, then remove the sensors and O-rings.
12. Remove the bolts securing the shift actuator and remove the shift actuator and O-ring, then slide the main shift rail from the assembly.
13. Remove the bolts securing the rear cover then remove rear cover from assembly and then remove the rear cover oil seal.

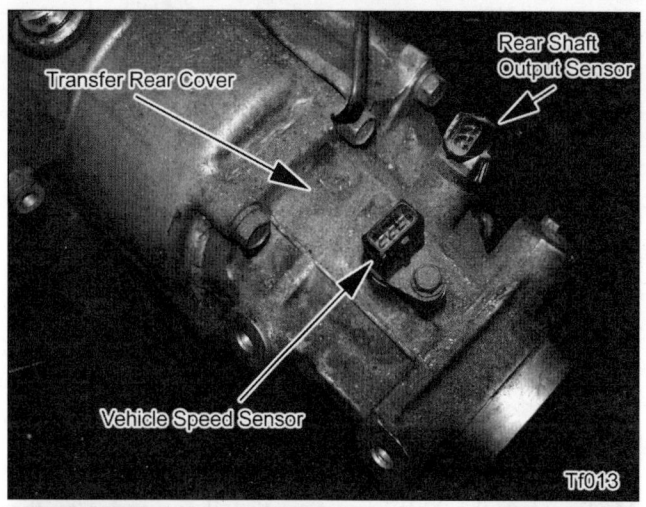

Figure Tf013: Transfer Rear Cover; Rear Shaft Output Sensor; Vehicle Speed Sensor

Figure Tf014: Transfer Rear Cover

14. Remove the snap ring securing the sensor rotor, then remove the sensor rotor, being careful not to loose the steel ball.

Figure Tf015: Sensor Rotor; Snap Ring

15. From the transfer assembly remove the oil guide and the two snap rings, the rear snap ring is the spacer.

TRANSFER

16. Remove the bolts securing the chain cover to the transfer case then remove the cover from the assembly. The cover may require a small amount of leverage to free the front output shaft rear bearing from the rear cover.

17. From the transfer assembly remove the rear output shaft, then remove the O-ring and bearing.

18. Remove the snap ring securing the centre differential planetary carrier, then remove the carrier assembly and viscous coupling.

19. Remove the chain, front output shaft and sun gear together as a set from the transfer case.
20. From the sun gear assembly remove the drive sprocket, bearing and then remove the synchronizer assembly.
21. From the assembly remove the snap ring then remove the 2-4WD clutch hub, clutch sleeve and bearing from the sun gear.
22. Remove the 2-4WD shift fork then remove the wave spring.
23. Remove the spacer being careful not to lose the steel ball.
24. Remove the snap ring retaining the differential lock hub and remove hub.
25. Remove the bolts retaining the transfer case plate and remove the case plate from the transfer case.
26. **Manual Transmission** - Remove the bearing retainer, then remove the input gear.
27. Remove the bearing from the end of the transfer drive shaft, then remove the counter shaft gear and spacer.

292

TRANSFER

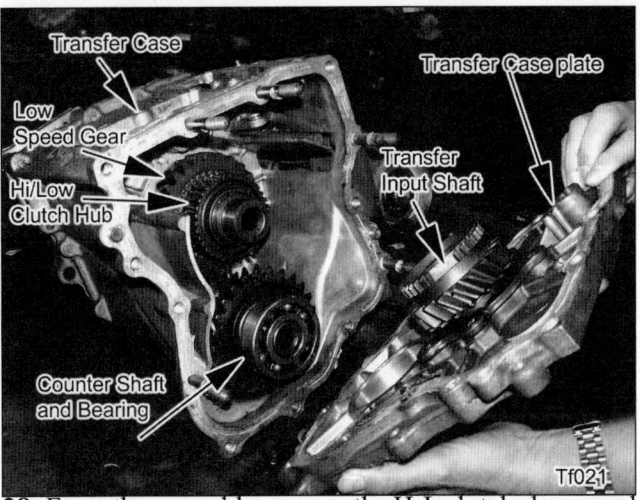

28. From the assembly remove the H-L clutch sleeve and clutch fork.

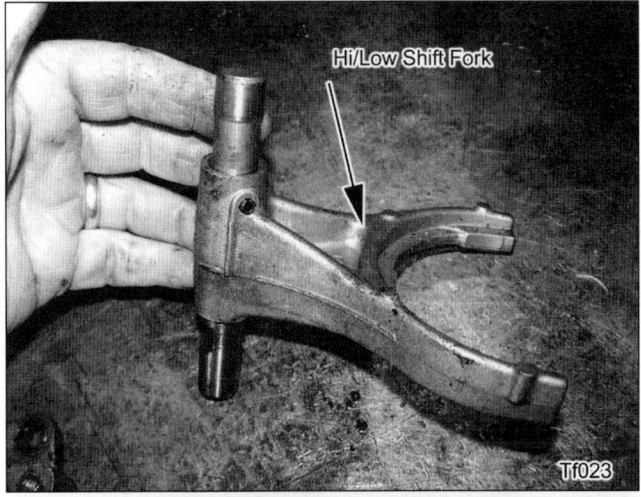

29. Remove the snap ring retaining the H-L clutch hub, then remove the clutch hub, low speed gear and bearing.
30. Remove the bolts retaining the rear bearing retainer, then remove the retainer followed by the transfer drive shaft.
31. From the transfer case remove the dust seal guard then the oil seal.

TRANSFER DISASSEMBLY - Part Time 4WD

1. Unscrew the 4WD switch from the transfer case then remove the transfer switch, gasket and steel ball.
2. Unscrew and remove the three poppet plugs from the transmission case then remove the poppet spring and steal ball.
3. Remove the bolt retaining the vehicle speed sensor, then remove the sensor.
4. Remove the bolts retaining the transfer case plate and remove the plate from the transfer assembly.
5. Remove the needle bearing, countershaft and spacer from the transfer case.
6. Remove the dust seal guard, then remove the bolts securing the dynamic damper and remove from assembly.
7. Remove the bolts securing the rear cover then remove rear cover and spacer from assembly, then remove the oil seal.
8. Remove H-L shift rail plug, then remove the spring pin from the H-L shift fork.
9. Place the H-L shift rail at the high side, then place the 2-4WD shift rail at the 4WD position.
10. Remove the chain cover retaining bolts then remove the chain cover followed by the H-L shift rail.
    Note: *If 2-WD shift rail is placed in 2WD position the chain cover will not be able to be removed.*
11. Remove the H-L shift fork and clutch sleeve from the transfer case.
12. Remove the interlock plunger, then using a punch remove the spring pin for the 2-4WD shift lug.
13. Remove the 2-4WD shift lug and distance piece from the 2-4WD shift rail.
14. Remove the E-clip from the 2-4WD shift assembly, then remove the two spring seats and spring.
15. Remove the 2-4WD shift rail then remove the 2-4WD shift fork.
16. Remove the chain, front output shaft and rear output shaft together as a set from the transfer case.
17. From the transfer case remove the dust seal guard then the oil seal.

SUB COMPONENTS - ALL

TRANSFER CASE PLATE
Dismantle
1. From the transfer case plate remove the bolts securing the bearing retainer.
2. Remove the bearing retainer, then remove the transfer input gear.
3. From the transfer case plate remove the oil seal then remove the baffle plate.

293

TRANSFER

Assembly
1. To the transfer case plate install the baffle plate, then install the oil seal using an appropriate seal installation tool.
2. Install the transfer input gear then install the bearing retainer and tighten retaining bolts to specification.
   Bearing Retainer Bolts .... **20+/-2 Nm**
   Note: If using old bolts firstly coat with thread sealant.

TRANSFER INPUT GEAR
Dismantle
1. From the input gear remove the snap retaining the bearing, then remove the bearing.
2. Remove the cone spring retaining snap ring then remove the cone spring and sub gear.

Assembly
1. To the transfer input gear install sub gear and cone spring, then secure in place with snap ring.
2. Press the bearing to the input gear, then install the retaining snap ring which gives a bearing end play to specification.
   Bearing End Play .... **0 - 0.06 mm**

COUNTERSHAFT GEAR - Part Time 4WD
Dismantle
1. Carefully press bearing from the countershaft gear.
2. Remove the snap ring securing the roller bearing then remove the roller bearing from the countershaft gear.

Assembly
1. To the countershaft gear press on the roller bearing.
2. To the assembly install the thickest snap ring possible and check to ensure the bearing end play is within specification.
   Bearing End Play .... **0-0.08 mm**
3. To the opposite end of the countershaft gear install the bearing using a suitable press.

COUNTERSHAFT GEAR - SSII 4WD
Dismantle
1. Carefully press the bearing from the countershaft gear.
2. Remove the snap ring securing the roller bearing then remove the spacer and roller bearing from the countershaft gear.
3. From the countershaft gear remove the inner race by pressing off.

Assembly
1. To the countershaft gear press on the inner race, then install the roller bearing and spacer.
2. To the assembly install the thickest snap ring possible and check to ensure the bearing end play is within specification.
   Bearing End Play .... **0-0.08 mm**
3. To the opposite end of the countershaft gear install the bearing using a suitable press.

REAR OUTPUT SHAFT
Dismantle
1. From the output shaft remove the snap ring securing the annulus gear and remove the gear.
2. Remove the snap ring from the bearing then press the bearing from the output shaft using a suitable press.

Assembly
1. Install the bearing to the output shaft using an appropriate press, then install the thickest snap ring possible.
2. Check to ensure the output shaft bearing end play is thin specification.
   Output Shaft End Play .... **0-0.08 mm**
3. Install the annulus gear to the assembly, then install the thickest snap ring possible.
4. Check to ensure the annulus gear end play is within specification.
   Annulus Gear End Play .... **0-0.08 mm**

TRANSFER

FRONT OUTPUT SHAFT

Dismantle
1. Support the bearing with appropriate clamp, then press the front output shaft from the bearing.
2. Remove the sensor rotor.
3. Support the bearing with appropriate clamp, then press the front output shaft from the bearing.

Assembly
1. Support the front output shaft with appropriate clamp, then press on the bearing.
2. Install the sensor rotor.
3. Support the front output shaft with appropriate clamp, then press on the bearing.

TRANSFER DRIVE SHAFT

Dismantle
Support the transfer drive shaft with appropriate clamp into a press and then press the bearing from the shaft.

Assembly
Support the transfer drive shaft with appropriate clamp into a press and then press the bearing onto the shaft..

H-L SHIFT RAIL - Part Time 4WD

Dismantle
1. Remove the return spring plug from the plunger boss, then remove the two return springs and select plunger.
2. Remove the plunger boss from the H-L Shift fork.

Assembly
1. To the H-L shift fork install the plunger boss tightening retaining bolts to specification.
   Plunger Boss Bolts .... 19 Nm
2. Install the select plunger and two return springs, then install the plug screwing in until it is flush with the plunger boss.

2-4WD SHIFT RAIL & H-L SHIFT RAIL -SSII 4WD

Dismantle
1. Remove the spring pin from the 2-4WD shift fork, then slide the shift fork from the shift rail and remove the spring.
2. Remove the spring pin from the H-L shift fork, then slide the shift fork from the shift rail.

Assembly
1. Install the H-L shift fork to the shift rail, firstly applying grease to the mating surface of the shift rail.
2. Install the spring pin ensuring the split is facing towards the forward end of the transfer.
3. To the 2-4WD shift rail install the spring and shift fork, firstly applying grease to the mating surface of the shift rail.
4. Install the spring pin ensuring the split is facing towards the forward end of the transfer.

SHIFT RAIL DRIVE GEAR - SSII 4WD

Dismantle
1. Remove the snap ring securing the shift rail drive gear to the shaft and remove the gear.
2. From the shaft remove the bearing, then remove the washer and the second snap ring.

Assembly
1. To the shift rail gear shaft install the snap ring, then install the washer and bearing.
2. Install the drive gear to the assembly with the mark on the gear at the opposite end to the washer.
3. Secure gear to shaft by installing the retaining snap ring.

SPEEDOMETER GEAR - Part Time 4WD

Dismantle
1. Remove the large O-ring from the speedometer gear sleeve.
2. Remove the spring pin securing the driven gear, then remove the driven gear from the assembly.
3. Remove the driven gear O-ring.

Assemble
1. Install a new driven gear O-ring which has been soaked in clean gear oil.
2. Install the driven gear to the sleeve and secure in position with retaining spring pin, ensuring the split in the pin faces outwards.
3. To the speedometer gear sleeve install a new O-ring which has been soaked in clean gear oil.

TRANSFER ASSEMBLY - SSII 4WD
All Models
1. To the transfer case press in a new oil seal using an appropriate seal installation tool, then install the dust seal guard.
2. Install the transfer drive shaft, then install the bearing retainer, tightening bolts to specification.
   Bearing Retainer Bolts .... 20+/-2 Nm
   Note: Before installing bolts coat threads with thread sealer.
3. Install the bearing and low speed gear, then install the H-L clutch hub.
4. Install a snap ring which will give specified end play for the H-L clutch hub.
   H-L Clutch Hub End Play .... 0-0.08 mm
5. To the transfer case install the H-L shift fork and H-L clutch sleeve together, ensuring to firstly coat the inserted portion of the H-L shift fork shaft with grease.
6. a) To the spacer location of the transfer case install two pieces of solder.
   Note: Solder should be approximately 10mm x 1.6mm.
   b) Install the countershaft gear and transfer case plate tightening bolts to specification.
   c) Remove the transfer case plate and countershaft gear then remove the two pieces of solder.
   d) Measure the thickness of the solder and determine the correct size spacer to achieved specified end play.
   Specified End Play   Auto .... 0-0.45 mm
   Manual .... 0-015 mm
7. Install selected spacer then install the counter shaft gear and bearing.

8. **Manual Transmission** - Install the input gear, then install the bearing retainer, tightening bolts to specification.
   Bearing Retainer Bolts .... 19 Nm
9. Apply grease to the transfer case plate at the insertion point of the H-L shift rail, then apply a bead of sealant to the case plate.
10. Ensure the notched portion of the input gear is located at the countershaft gear bearing hole, then install the transfer case plate, tightening retaining bolts to specification.
    Transfer Case Plate Bolts/Nuts .... 36 Nm
11. Install the differential lock hub then select a snap ring which will give a specified end play for the differential lock hub.
    Specified End Play .... 0.0-0.08 mm
12. Install the selected snap ring to the transfer drive shaft, then install the steel ball and spacer, ensuring the spacer oil groove is towards the chain cover.
13. Install the wave spring then install the 2-4WD shift fork.
14. To the sun gear install the bearing, clutch sleeve and 2-4WD clutch hub.
15. Select and install the snap ring to secure the clutch hub which will give the specified end play.
    Specified End Play .... 0-0.08 mm
16. a) Combined the synchronizer outer ring cone and inner ring pressing them against the drive sprocket.
    b) Check the specified limit with a feeler gauge as shown and replace the synchronizer set.
    Specified Limit .... 0.3 mm
    c) To the synchronizer outer and inner ring apply gear oil.
    d) Line up the notched section of the 2-4WD clutch hub with the projecting portion of the synchronizer ring and install synchronizer ring.
17. To the sun gear install the bearing.
18. a) Assembly the drive sprocket, chain and front output shaft, ensuring the chain is meshed correctly.
    b) Install the assembly to the transfer assembly, aligning the holes on the drive sprocket with protrusions of the synchronizer cone.
19. Install the viscous coupling, then install the centre differential planetary carrier and secure with retaining snap ring.
20. To the assembly install the bearing followed by the O-ring which has been coated in grease, then install the rear output shaft.
21. Apply grease to the chain cover at the insertion point of the 2-4WD shift rail, then apply a bead of sealant to the cover.
22. Install the chain cover to the transfer case and tighten the retaining bolts to specification.
    Chain Cover Bolts .... 36 Nm

TRANSFER

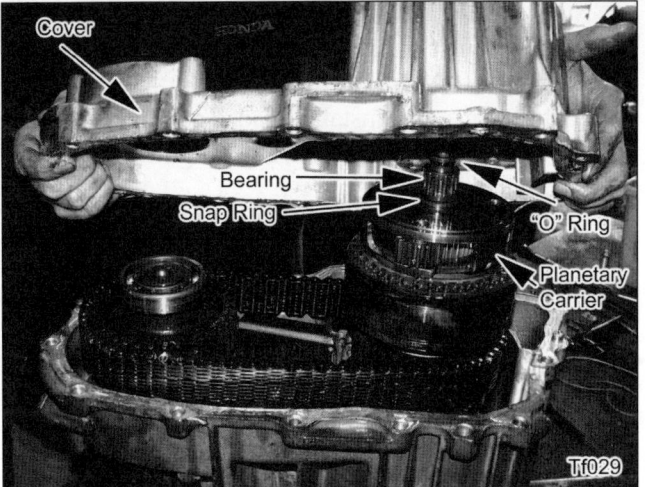

23. a) To the bearing groove of the rear output shaft install the snap ring then with the output shaft pressed against the chain cover measure the clearance between the snap ring and cover.

   b) Select a snap ring which is equal to the measured thickness plus the standard value.
   Standard Value.....................................0.12 mm

   c) Remove the snap ring from the bearing groove then install the selected snap ring.

   d) Reinstall the snap ring to the bearing groove.

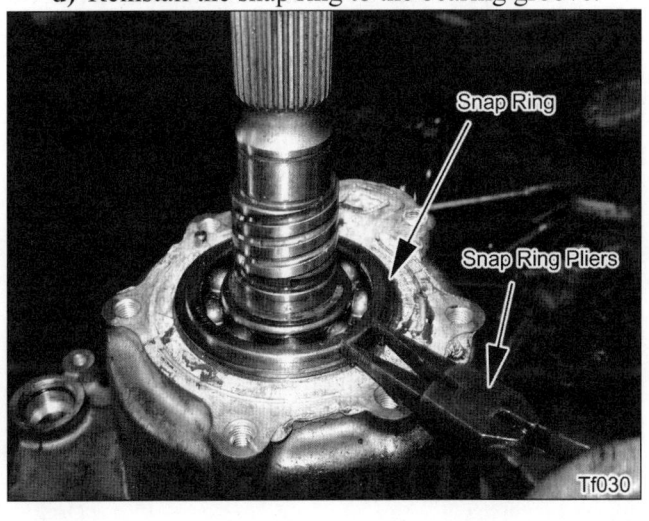

24. a) Press the output shaft against the chain cover measure the clearance between the snap ring and bearing.

   b) Select a snap ring which is equal to the measured thickness plus the standard value.
   Standard Value............................0.12-0.24 mm

   c) Install the snap ring to the bearing groove.

25. Install the oil guide, then install the steel ball and sensor rotor, securing with retaining snap ring.

26. To the rear cover install the oil seal using a seal installation tool, then apply grease to the seal lip.

27. To the rear cover install a bead of sealant to the mating surface, then install the rear cover and tighten retaining bolts to specification.
   Rear Cover Bolts... 36 Nm

28. Coat the O-ring with grease and install to transmission assembly, then partially install the main shift rail.

29. Connect the main shift rail key with the actuator key then install the shift actuator to the transfer case.
   Shift Actuator Bolts .... 11+/-1 Nm

30. Install new O-rings to the front and rear output sensors, then install sensors to the transfer case and tighten retaining bolts to specification.
   Output Sensor Bolts.............................. 11+/-1 Nm

31. Install a new O-ring to the vehicle speed sensor, then install sensor to the transfer case, tighten bolts to specification.
   Speed Sensor Bolt.................................. 11+/-1 Nm

32. To the transfer case install the dynamic damper, tightening retaining bolts to specification then install the dust seal guard.
   Dynamic Damper Bolts ....35+/-6 Nm

33. To the transfer assembly install the two shift rail drive gears, aligning the marked tooth with the third gear groove.

Automatic Transmission

34. To the transfer case cover install a bead of sealant to the mating surface, then install the case cover and tighten retaining bolts to specification.

297

TRANSFER

Transfer Case Cover Bolts .... 19+/-2 Nm

35. Install a new gasket to the 2WD-4WD switch, then install the steel ball and switch to the transfer assembly, tightening to specification.
2WD-4WD Switch .... 35+/-6 Nm
36. Install a new gasket to the 4H switch, then install the steel ball and switch to the transfer assembly, tightening to specification.
4H Switch .... 35+/-6 Nm
37. Install a new gasket to the Centre differential lock switch, then install the steel ball and switch to the transfer assembly, tightening to specification.
Centre Differential Lock Switch .... 35+/-6 Nm
38. Install a new gasket to the 2WD switch, then install the steel ball and switch to the transfer assembly, tightening to specification.
2WD Switch .... 35+/-6 Nm
39. Install a new gasket to the 4LLC switch, then install the steel ball and switch to the transfer assembly, tightening to specification.
4LLC Switch .... 35+/-6 Nm
40. To the transfer assembly install and connect the vacuum hose.

TRANSFER ASSEMBLY - Part Time 4WD
Spacer Selection Countershaft Gear End Play

1. On the transfer case place solder approximately 10mm long by 1.6mm diameter.
2. Install the countershaft gear and transfer case plate tightening bolts to specification.
Transfer Case Plate Bolts .... 36 Nm
3. Remove the remove the case plate and countershaft gear, then measure the thickness of the crushed solder. Select a spacer of the measured thickness to obtain specified end play.
Specified End Play .... 0.00 - 0.15 mm

Assembly

1. To the transfer case press in a new oil seal using an appropriate seal installation tool, then install the dust seal guard.
2. a) Assembly the rear output shaft, chain and front output shaft, ensuring the chain is meshed correctly.
   b) Install the 2-4WD shift fork to the 2-4WD clutch sleeve.
   c) Install the front and rear output shafts while inserting the 2-4WD shift rail in the shift fork hole.
3. To the 2-4WD shift assembly install the two spring seats and spring then secure in position using retaining E-ring.
4. To the 2-4WD shift rail install the distance piece, then install the shift plug and secure with retaining spring pin.

Note: Ensure split in pin faces down the shaft.

5. Install the interlock plunger, then install the H-L clutch sleeve and shift fork.
6. To the chain cover install a bead of sealant to the mating surface, then install the cover tightening bolts to specification.
Chain Cover Bolts .... 36 Nm
7. Install the H-L shift rail into transfer assembly, then align the shift rail and shift fork spring pin holes and install the spring pin.

Note: The split in the spring pin should face the axial centre of the shift rail.

8. Install the H-L shift rail plug.
9. To the rear cover install the oil seal using a seal installation tool, then apply grease to the seal lip.
10. a) Measure the projection of the rear output shaft bearing.
    b) Select a spacer which will obtain a clearance which is within specification and install spacer.
    See illustration Tf026 on previous page.
Specified Clearance .... 0-0.1 mm
11. To the rear cover install a bead of sealant to the mating surface, then install the rear cover and tighten retaining bolts to specification.
Rear Cover Bolts .... 36 Nm
12. To the transfer case install the dynamic damper, tightening retaining bolts to specification then install the dust seal guard.
Dynamic Damper Bolts .... 36 Nm
13. Install the spacer selected in the preassembly procedure, then install the countershaft gear and needle bearing.
14. a) Apply a bead of sealant to the transfer case plate then align one of the sub gear teeth with the notched tooth of the input gear.
    b) Install the transfer plate and input gear as an assembly and tighten transfer plate bolts to specification.
Transfer Plate Bolts .... 36 Nm
15. Install the vehicle speed sensor tightening to specification.
Vehicle Speed Sensor .... 11 Nm
16. Install steel ball and spring then install the three poppet plugs to the transmission case tightening to specification.
Plugs 36Nm

Note: The spring is inserted with the small end against the ball.

Note: If reusing the plug coat with thread sealant.

17. Install the steel ball and transfer switch using a new gasket, then install the 4WD switch.
Transfer Switch .... 35 Nm
4WD Switch .... 35 Nm

SPECIFICATIONS

Lubrication:
Transfer Case - type.....................Hypoid gear oil
SAE70W-90 (API GL-4)
 - capacity ....2.8 litres

Transfer: High........................ 1.000
Low......................... 1.900

Input gear bearing end play .... 0.0 - 0.06 mm
Countershaft gear end play.................... 0.0 - 0.15 mm
Countershaft gear bearing end play..... 0.0 - 0.08 mm
2-4WD clutch hub end play................... 0.0 - 0.08 mm
H-L clutch hub end play....................... 0.0 - 0.08 mm
Rear output shaft preload .... 0.12 - 0.24 mm
Rear output shaft end play.................... 0.0 - 0.12 mm
Rear output shaft bearing end play...... 0.0 - 0.08 mm
Rear output shaft annulus gear
end play.. 0.0 - 0.08 mm
Differential lock hub end play .... 0.0 - 0.08 mm
Clearance b/w outer synchro ring &
drive sprocket.. 0.3 mm (limit)

Oil Temperature sensor:
@0°C..16.7 - 20.5 kOhms
@20°C......................................7.3 - 8.9 kOhms
@40°C......................................3.4 - 4.2 kOhms
@60°C......................................1.9 - 2.2 kOhms
@80°C......................................1.0 - 1.2 kOhms
@100°C....................................0.57 - 0.69 kOhms

Damper clutch control solenoid valve coil:
@20°C...................................2.7 - 3.4 Ohms

Low-reverse solenoid valve coil resistance:
@20°C...................................2.7 - 3.4 Ohms

Second solenoid valve coil resistance:
@20°C...................................2.7 - 3.4 Ohms

Underdrive solenoid valve coil resistance:
@20°C...................................2.7 - 3.4 Ohms

Overdrive solenoid valve coil resistance:
@20°C...................................2.7 - 3.4 Ohms

Reduction solenoid valve coil resistance:
@20°C...................................2.7 - 3.4 Ohms

TRANSFER

Spacer selection for adjustment of input gear bearing end play:

Thickness (mm)	Identification	Part No.
2.30	None	MD704199
2.35	Red	MD704200
2.40	White	MD704201
2.45	Blue	MD704202
2.50	Green	MD704203

Spacer selection for adjustment of countershaft gear end play:

Thickness (mm)	Identification	Part No.
1.77	None	MB896728
1.91	blue	MB896729
2.05	Brown	MB896730
2.19	White	MB896731
2.33	Red	MB896732

Snap ring selection for adjustment of countershaft gear bearing end play:

Thickness (mm)	Identification	Part No.
1.48	Blue	MB919176
1.62	None	MB919177

Snap ring selection for adjustment of H-L clutch hub end play:

Thickness (mm)	Identification	Part No.
2.18	None	MR410928
2.25	None	MR410929
2.32	None	MR410930
2.39	None	MR410931

Snap ring selection for adjustment of differential lock hub end play:

Thickness (mm)	Identification	Part No.
2.56	None	MD738386
2.63	Red	MD738387
2.70	White	MD738388
2.77	Blue	MD738389
2.84	Yellow	MD738390
2.91	Green	MD738391
2.98	Brown	MD738392

Snap ring selection for adjustment of 2-4WD clutch hub end play:

Thickness (mm)	Identification	Part No.
2.56	None	MD738393
2.63	Red	MD738394
2.70	White	MD738395
2.77	Blue	MD738396
2.84	Yellow	MD738397

Snap ring selection for adjustment of rear output shaft bearing end play:

Thickness (mm)	Identification	Part No.
2.26	None	MD734311
2.33	Red	MD734312
2.40	White	MD734313
2.47	Blue	MD734314

Snap ring selection for adjustment of rear output shaft annulus gear end play:

Thickness (mm)	Identification	Part No.
1.90	None	MR305024
1.94	None	MR305025
1.98	None	MR305026
2.02	None	MR305027
2.06	None	MR305028
2.10	None	MR305029

Snap ring selection for adjustment of rear output shaft preload:

Thickness (mm)	Identification	Part No.
1.57	None	MR486340
1.63	None	MR486341
1.69	None	MR486342
1.75	None	MR486343
1.81	None	MR486344
1.87	None	MR486345
1.93	None	MR486346
1.99	None	MR486347
2.05	None	MR477935
2.11	None	MR477936
2.17	None	MR477937
2.23	None	MR477938
2.29	None	MR477939
2.35	None	MR477940
2.41	None	MR477941
2.47	None	MR477942
2.53	None	MR477943
2.59	None	MR477944
2.65	None	MR477945
2.71	None	MR477946

Spacer selection for adjustment of rear output shaft end play:

Thickness (mm)	Identification	Part No.
2.57	None	MR477950
2.63	None	MR477951
2.69	None	MR477952
2.75	None	MR477953
2.81	None	MR477954
2.87	None	MR477955
2.93	None	MR477956
2.99	None	MR477957
3.05	None	MR477958
3.11	None	MR477959
3.17	None	MR477960
3.23	None	MR477961
3.29	None	MR477962
3.35	None	MR477963
3.41	None	MR477964
3.47	None	MR477965
3.53	None	MR477966
3.59	None	MR477967
3.65	None	MR477968
3.71	None	MR486348
3.77	None	MR486349
3.83	None	MR486350
3.89	None	MR486351
3.95	None	MR486352

Torque Specifications

Description	Nm
Dynamic Damper	35+/-6
Transfer case cover tightening bolt	19+/-2
Input gear bearing retainer mounting bolt	20+/-2
Transfer case to chain cover tightening bolt	35+/-6
Rear bearing retainer mounting bolt	20+/-2
Transfer case plate to transfer case tightening bolt and nut	35+/-6
Rear cover to chain cover tightening bolt	35+/-6
Shift actuator mounting bolt	11+/-1
4LLC switch	35+-/6
2WD switch	35+/-6
Centre differential lock switch	35+/-6
4H switch	35+/-6
2WD-4WD switch	35+/-6
Vehicle speed sensor mounting bolt	11+/-1
Front output sensor mounting bolt	11+/-1
Rear output sensor mounting bolt	11+/-1

STEERING

Subject	Page
MINOR MAINTENANCE	**302**
Steering Gear Lubrication	302
Power Steering Fluid Contamination	302
Power Steering Fluid Level	302
Drain Power Steering Fluid	302
Bleeding the System	302
Tie Rod Ball Joint	302
Removal	302
Installation	303
Steering Wheel Free Play Check	303
Stationary Steering Effort Check	303
RACK & PINION STEERING GEAR	**304**
Removal	304
Dismantle	304
Clean and Inspect	305
Assembly	305
Total Pinion Preload Adjustment	306
Tie Rod Swing Torque Check	306
Installation	306
POWER STEERING PUMP	**307**
Oil Pump Pressure Test	307
Oil Pressure Switch Test	308
Power Steering Pump Hoses & Tubes	308
Removal	308
Installation	308

Subject	Page
Power Steering Pump - Petrol	**308**
Removal	308
Dismantle	308
Assembly	309
Installation	309
Power Steering Pump - Diesel	**310**
Removal	310
Dismantle (4M40,4M41)	310
Dismantle (3200)	311
Assembly (4M40,4M41)	311
Assembly (3200)	311
Installation	311
Steering Wheel (airbag & clock spring)	**312**
Removal	312
Installation	312
STEERING COLUMN	**313**
Upper and Lower Cover	**313**
Removal	313
Installation	313
Steering Column	**313**
Removal	313
Dismantle	314
Assembly	314
Installation	314
PROBLEM DIAGNOSIS	**315**
SPECIFICATIONS	**316**
TORQUE SETTINGS	**316**

MINOR MAINTENANCE

STEERING GEAR LUBRICATION
Rack and pinion steering assemblies have a semi-liquid grease, which is included during the rack and pinion assembly. The rack and pinion assembly can not be checked during a vehicle service.

POWER STEERING FLUID CONTAMINATION
If power steering fluid has been contaminated, the power steering lines should be flushed. Also the steering pump, rack and pinion gear must be removed. All must be dismantled and thoroughly cleaned before assembly.

POWER STEERING FLUID LEVEL
Check the fluid level in the reservoir with the vehicle parked on a level surface. Start the engine and turn the steering wheel several times to raise the temperature of the fluid. Check the fluid for foaming or milkiness. The fluid should be between the Min and Max marks.

The fluid level height should not vary by more than 5 mm when the engine is running and when it is stopped. If it varies more than 5 mm the system should be bleed.
Specified Fluid .... Dexron II

DRAIN POWER STEERING FLUID
1. Jack up the front of the vehicle and support on stands.
2. Disconnect the return hose from the power steering reservoir, attach a piece of flexible hose to the return hose and place the end in an empty container.
3. Disconnect the ignition coil or crank angle sensor then intermittently crank the engine while turning the steering wheel from lock to lock. (This will drain all fluid from system).
4. Reattach the return hose, fill the system with specified power steering fluid to correct level.
5. Bleed air from system, check fluid level and top up if required.

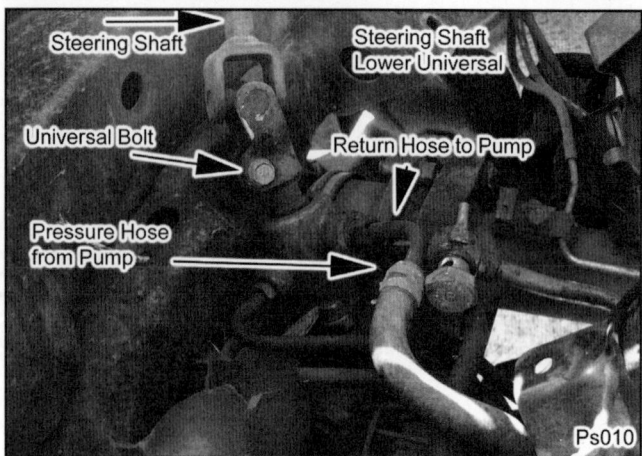

BLEEDING THE SYSTEM
Note: After repairs the system must be bleed of any air, using the following procedures. The bleeding procedure should only be done with the engine cranking. The level in the reservoir should always be kept above the min mark.

1. Jack up front of vehicle and place on safety stands.
2. From the coil disconnect the primary lead or the crank angle sensor to prevent engine starting.
3. Crank engine and turn steering from lock to lock five or six times to circulate the fluid, top up reservoir if needed.
4. Repeat step 3 until the reservoir does not need fluid added.
5. Reconnect the primary coil lead or crank angle sensor and start engine (idle only). Turn the steering wheel from lock to lock until there are no visible air bubbles in the reservoir.
6. Inspect to ensure reservoir is filled to correct level and that the fluid is not milky, then check to ensure there is only minimal change in fluid height when steering is turned from lock to lock.
7. Check the level of fluid from when the engine is running to when it is stopped. The level should not change by more than 5 mm.

Note: If there is a large change in fluid height bleed system again. If the system is not bleed completely it could lessen the life of the pump and other parts.

Tie Rod Ball Joint
Removal
1. Raise vehicle and support on safety stands. Remove the road wheels. Remove split pins and loosen tie rod end retaining nut 1/4 of a turn and break taper bond using a tie rod removal tool.
2. Undo tie rod assembly lock nut.
3. Remove tie rod end from knuckle, and unscrew tie rod end from tie rod.

STEERING

Note: *Take note of how many turns it takes to remove, for use when installing the new one.*

Installation

1. Screw tie rod end onto tie rod, the same amount of turns as the old one took to remove. The recommended distance between the lock nut and boot end is.

   NM - NP .... 57 mm
   NS (SWB) .... 46 mm
   NS (LWB) .... 41 mm

2. Temporarily tighten the lock nut for the tie rod end.

3. Install tie rod end to the knuckle, tighten the nut, and instal a new split pin.

   Tie Rod Ball Joint Lock Nut:
   NM - NP .... 39 +/- 5 Nm
   NS .... 47 +/- 13 Nm

4. Replace the wheels and lower vehicle.

5. Check the toe-in and toe out and if needed adjust. Tighten the lock nut of the tie rod end.

   Tie Rod End Lock Nut:
   NM- NP .... 71 +/- 7 Nm
   NS .... 93 +/- 15 Nm

STEERING WHEEL FREE PLAY CHECK

1. Start the engine, have the wheels facing straight ahead.

2. Measure the distance the steering wheel takes to turn before the wheels start to move.
   Maximum Limit .... 30 mm

3. If the maximum limit is exceeded check the condition of the steering shaft and the linkage connections. Replace or repair as needed

4. If the free play is still above the limit, check the free play with the engine stopped. Make sure the wheels are pointing straight ahead, load 5N to the outside of the steering wheel and check the play.
   Maximum Limit .... 10 mm

5. If still outside the free play limit remove the steering gear and check the total pinion preload as described later in the chapter.

STATIONARY STEERING EFFORT CHECK

1. Have the vehicle idling with the wheels pointing straight ahead, parked on a flat paved area.

2. Attach a spring balance to the outside of the steering wheel and measure the steering force required to turn the wheel from straight ahead position to the left and right (within a range of 1.5 turns). While doing the check make sure that there is no big change in the required effort.
   Steering Effort .... 39.2 N or less
   Allowable Change .... 5.9 N or less

3. If the results are outside the limit check the steering gear, tyre pressure, and all components condition.

303

Rack & Pinion Steering Rack

Note: *Before starting any work the battery should be disconnected and left for at least 90 seconds. Make sure to centre the wheels to avoid damage to the SRS clock spring and air bag module. It is recommended to remove the air bag module and steering wheel.*

Steering Rack Removal

1. On vehicles fitted with the 3200 turbo diesel the stabilizer bar, upper and lower radiator shrouds, and intercooler will need to be removed.
2. Raise the vehicle, position on safety stands and remove wheels, then disconnect tie rod ends from the knuckle. Remove the vehicle under cover. Drain power steering system as described previously.
3. a) On RHD vehicles remove the right hand tie rod end.
   b) On LHD vehicles remove the left hand tie rod end. This will help with removal of the rack in later steps.
4. To make the job easier it is recommended to remove the front propeller shaft. Remove the connector and hose to the free wheel actuator. Undo the bracket for the wheel speed sensor harness.
5. Remove the bolts securing the pressure hose mounting brackets into position, then disconnect and remove the pressure hose and return tube.

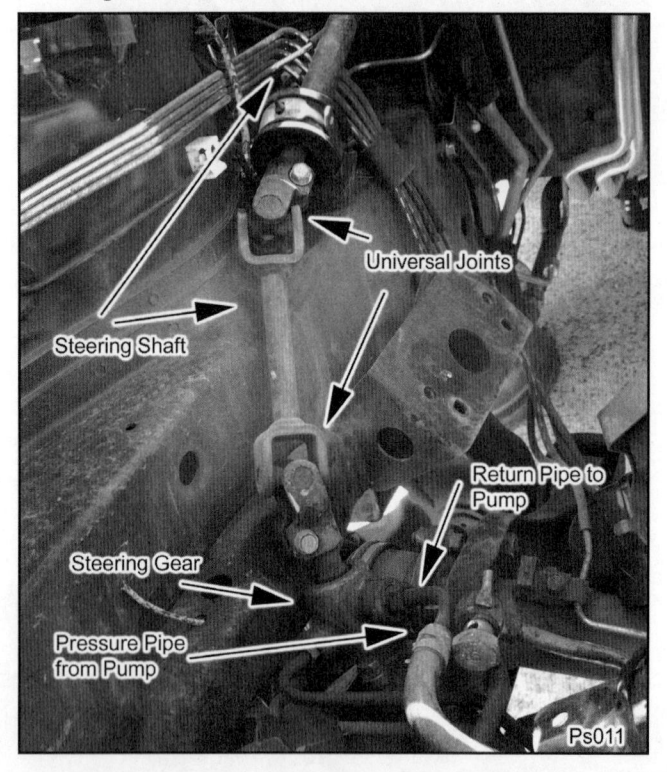

6. a) On RHD vehicles remove the bolts securing the right hand differential mounting bracket to the front frame assembly and the No 2 cross-member.
   b) On LHD vehicles remove the bolts securing the left hand differential mounting bracket to the front frame assembly.
7. Remove the bolt out of steering shaft lower column joint where it connects to the steering rack.
8. Remove the steering rack mounting bracket bolts and bracket. Remove the mounting nuts and washers.
9. a) On RHD vehicles pull the rack as far as possible to the left, then lower the right hand end and remove assembly from vehicle.
   b) On LHD vehicles pull the rack as far as possible to the right, then lower the left hand end and remove assembly from vehicle.

Dismantle

1. Remove the mounting cushion and bushing from the assembly then remove tie rod ends and bellows from each end of the steering gear assembly.
2. Disconnect the feed tubes and remove any remaining fluid from the assembly by slowly moving rack and discard O-rings.
3. Bend back the tab washers securing the tie rods to the rack using a large screwdriver or similar tool.
4. Remove the tie rods from the rack by unscrewing, then remove the tab washer and spring.
5. Remove the lock nut for the rack support cover, then remove the rack support cover, support spring and rack support.
6. From the lower section of the gear housing remove the end plug then from the lower end of the pinion remove the locking nut.
7. Remove the bolts securing the valve housing and remove housing then remove the pinion and lower oil seal from the housing by gently taping with soft hammer.
8. Carefully cut the seal ring from the pinion assembly, then remove the upper bearing and oil seal from the housing with the aid of a socket and soft hammer.
9. Using a pair of circlip pliers in the holes located in the rack stopper (which is in the gear housing) turn the rack stopper in a clockwise direction until the circlip end protrudes through the slot in the rack tube.
10. Turn in the opposite direction and remove clip.
11. From the housing remove the rack stopper, rack bushing and the rack as an assembly. From the rack bushing remove the O-ring.
12. Secure the rack bushing in a vice fitted with soft jaws then using a screw driver prise out the oil seal.
13. From the housing remove the ball bearing, needle bearing and oil seal using a suitable drift.
14. If not already removed, remove the seal rings from the rack piston, pinion and valve assembly using a screwdriver.

STEERING

Power Steering Rack

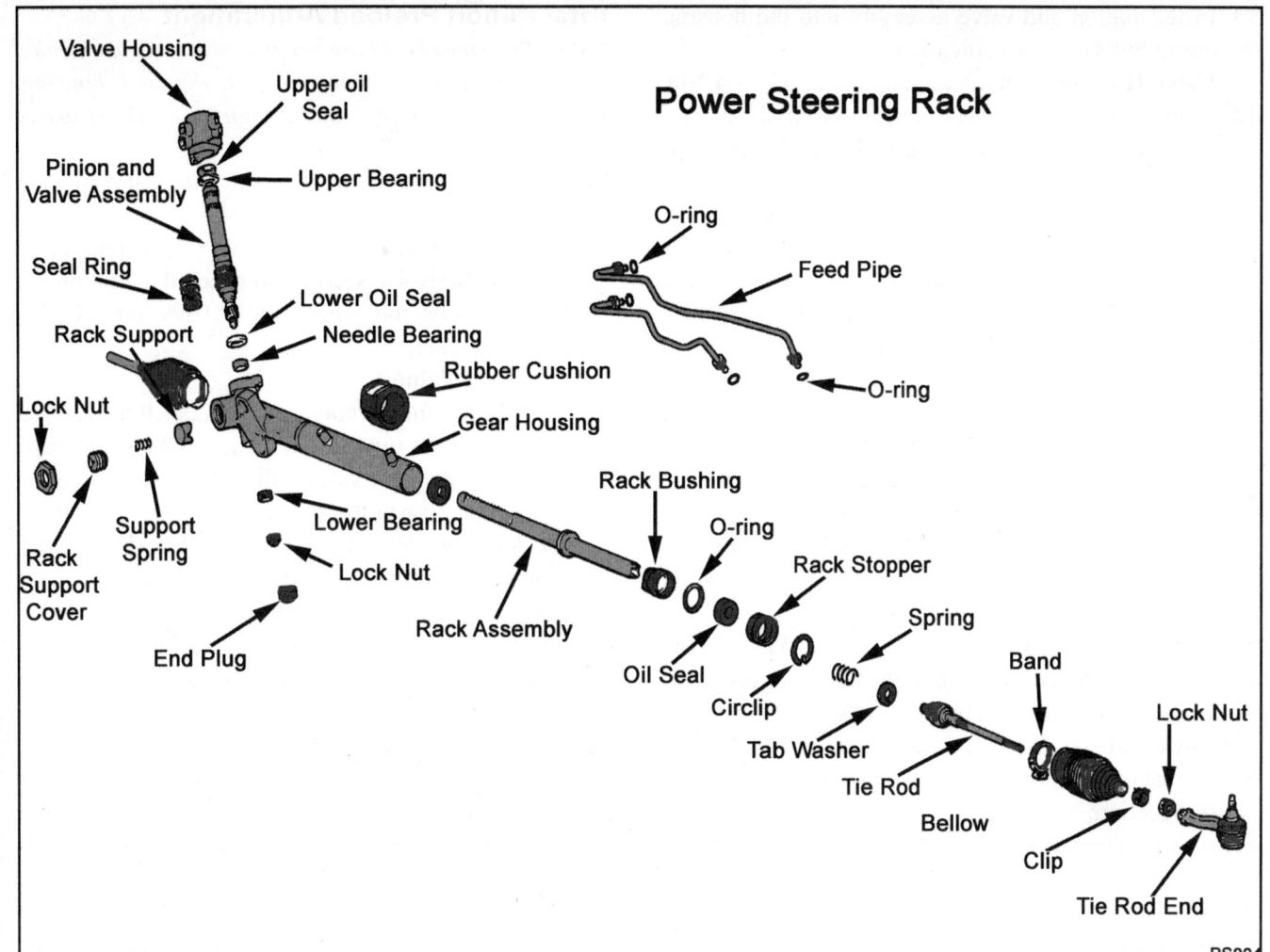

Clean and Inspect.

1. Using suitable cleaning solvent wash parts and dry off with compressed air.
2. Disregard all seals and replace with new ones. Examine rubber boots for damage, replace if necessary.
3. Inspect bearings for signs of binding, damage and wear, examine rack and pinion for wear or faulty teeth, rack bushing, bearing and seal.
4. Check rack housing internal surfaces for scour marks and damage.
5. Check rack pad for wear and damage, examine valve housing and bearing, then valve sleeve for wear or damage.

Assembly

Note: *During assembly ensure to coat all seals, O-rings and bearings with specified power steering fluid. New O-rings and seals should be used on reassembly.*

1. To the gear housing install the needle bearing and lower bearing using the pinion bearing installer tool. Also install the oil seal into the housing tube using the pinion oil seal installer tool.
2. Compress the oil seal and O-ring into the grooves using the pinion seal protector-installer tool.
3. Coat the rack teeth with multipurpose grease being careful not cover over the vent hole, then cover the rack teeth with the rack seal protector ensuring the tool has firstly been coated with power steering fluid.
4. Insert rack into gear housing and remove tool.
5. Install the O-ring then press the rack bushing oil seal into rack bushing.
6. Wrap plastic tape around the end of the rack assembly (to prevent damage) then install the rack bushing and rack stopper to the housing tube.
7. Align the mark on the rack stopper with the slot in the housing tube.
8. Install circlip into anchor hole then turn the tool clockwise to feed the circlip into the tube until it is firm.
9. Press the pinion upper oil seal and then upper bearing into valve housing using the pinion bearing/seal installer.
10. To pinion and valve assembly install the seal ring.
11. Press the lower oil seal into the valve housing. When installed the upper surface of the oil seal should stick out by about 1 mm. If the seal is installed flush with the housing it can result in fluid leaks.
12. To the surfaces of the pinion teeth apply multipurpose grease and power steering fluid to the surfaces of the pinion valve seal ring.

STEERING

13. Install pinion and valve assembly into the housing doing bolts up to specification.
    Valve Housing Bolts .... 22 +/- 4 Nm
14. From underneath the gear housing install a new self locking nut to the pinion assembly and tighten to specification.
    Pinion Self Locking Nut .... 25 +/- 4 Nm
15. Coat the end plug threads with semi-drying sealant then install and tighten plug.
    End Plug .... 59 +/- 10 Nm
16. Use a punch to bend over the tabs on the end plug to lock it into place
17. To the surface of the rack support which contacts the rack, coat with multipurpose grease then to the rack support cover threads apply semi-drying sealant.
18. To the housing install the rack support, spring, support cover. Using the special tool **MB991204** tighten the rack support cover to the specified torque. Then undo the rack support cover by about 10°.
    Rack Support Cover .... 12 +/- 2 Nm
19. Using the special tool to stop the rack support cover from spinning tighten the lock nut to specification.
    Lock Nut .... 59 +/- 10 Nm
20. Adjust total pinion preload as described at the end of this section.
21. Install the springs and new tab washers to the rack assembly. Screw tie rods into the rack assembly.
22. Tighten tie rods to specification then bend over the tab washers into notches on tie rod.
    Tie Rods .... 88 +/- 10 Nm
23. Install feed tubes and new O-ring, then tighten to specification. To the locations where the bellows are retained coat with silicon grease.
    Feed Tubes .... 15 +/- 3 Nm
24. To the housing slide on a new band for the bellows then install bellows and secure with the large band and small outer clip. When the large band has been installed, recommended gap at crimping point is.
    Crimping Gap .... 2.4 - 2.8 mm.
25. To the tie rods install the tie rod ends and adjust both to specified length. If needed replace the tie rod end dust boots.
    Tie Rod Length .... 57 mm
    Tie Rod End Lock Nut:
    NM - NP .... 71 +/- 7 Nm
    NS .... 93 +/- 15 Nm
    Note: Tie rod length is explained earlier in the chapter under tie rod installation.
26. Install the gear housing mounting bushes. The gear mounting rubber should be installed to the housing so that there is a gap of 390 mm between the centres of the gear housing and gear mounting bushes.
27. Before installing the steering assembly the total pinion preload adjustment needs to be performed.

Total Pinion Preload Adjustment

Note: When the checks are being done it is recommended that the bellows are removed from the rack housing. Measure the pinion preload through the whole stroke of the rack.

1. Position rack so tie rods are in the centre of their stroke.
2. Rotate the pinion gear at the rate of one rotation in approximately 4-6 seconds to check the total pinion Preload using the special tool MB991006 (Pinion preload socket).
   Standard Value
   - Total pinion preload .... 0.6 - 1.7 Nm
   - Change in torque .... 0.4 Nm (or less)
3. If outside standard value, adjust by reverse rotating rack support cover to a range within 0 - 30°. Then recheck the total pinion preload. If it can not be adjusted to within recommendations check the rack support cover, spring and rack support. Replace if needed.
4. After adjustment is complete lock rack support cover by tightening lock nut as mentioned earlier.

Tie Rod Assembly Swing Torque Check

1. Place tie rod in a position so it can be swung back and forth 10 times.
2. Measure the tie rod swing torque using a spring balance.
   Swing Torque .... 11-35 N (1.4 - 4.9 Nm)
3. Replace tie rod if measurement is above specification. If torque is below specification and there is no looseness or grinding in ball joint the tie rod is serviceable, otherwise replace.

Steering Rack Installation

1. Place steering rack assembly in position,
   a) On RHD vehicles (with the right hand tie rod removed) install the assembly in from underneath at an angle, then push it to the left as far as possible.
   b) On LHD vehicles (with the left hand tie rod removed) install the assembly in from underneath at an angle, then push it to the right as far as pos-

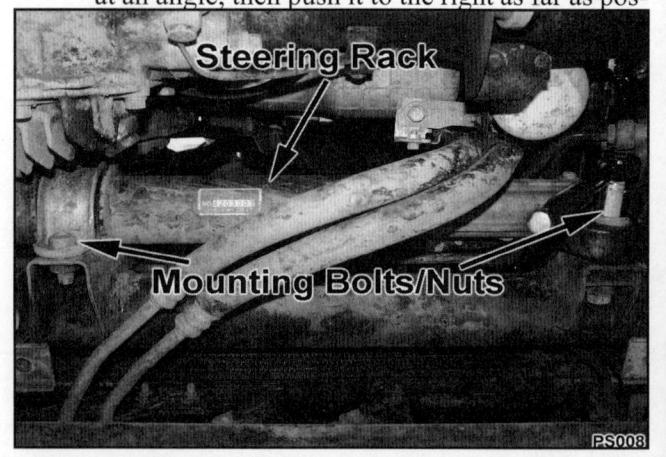

STEERING

sible.
2. Install the mounting bracket and tighten retaining bolts to specification. Install the mounting nuts.
   Steering Rack Mounting Bolts:
   NM - NP .... 69 +/- 9 Nm
   NS 3800 .... 117 +/- 17 Nm
   NS 3200 .... 82 +/- 12 Nm
   Steering Rack Mounting Nuts:
   NM - NP .... 69 +/- 9 Nm
   NS 3800 .... 82 +/- 12 Nm
   NS 3200 .... 117 +/- 17 Nm
3. a) On RHD vehicles position the differential mounting bracket into position and tighten the retaining bolts to specification.
   Diff bracket to front frame .... 69 +/- 9 Nm
   Diff bracket to No.2 crossmember 69 +/- 9 Nm
   b) On LHD vehicles position the differential mounting bracket into position and tighten the retaining bolts to specification.

   Diff bracket to front frame .... 69 +/- 9 Nm
4. Install the steering shaft lower joint to the steering rack and tighten retaining bolt to specification.
   Steering column shaft joint .... 18 +/- 2 Nm
5. a) RHD vehicles install the right hand tie rod end.
   b) LHD vehicles install the left hand tie rod end.
   Note: The recommended distance between lock nut and boot is 57 mm. See earlier in chapter.
6. Install the pressure hose and return tube into position tightening to specification, then install pressure hose retaining brackets and bolts tighten to specification.
   Pressure Hose & Return Tube .... 15 +/- 3 Nm
   Hose & Tube Brackets .... 12 +/- 2 Nm
7. Install tie rod ends to knuckle assembly, tighten retaining nut to specification and install a new split pin.
   Tie Rod End Ball Joint Nut:
   NM - NP .... 39 +/- 5 Nm
   NS .... 47 +/- 13 Nm
8. Install the under cover. Replace wheels and lower vehicle, then refill system and bleed as described previously.
9. Adjust wheel alignment to specification.

POWER STEERING PUMP

Note: Before performing hydraulic circuit test, carefully check drive belt tension, condition of driving pulley and fluid level. The engine should be at normal operating temperature and operating at idle. Front tyres at correct pressure.

Oil Pump Pressure Test
1. Disconnect the pressure hose from the pump assembly and connect the test equipment as shown in diagram.

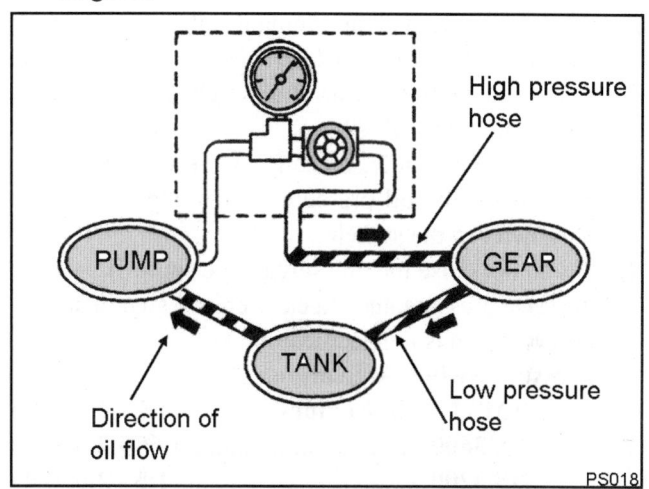

2. Start the vehicle. Turn the steering wheel from lock to lock several times and ensure air is bleed from the system and fluid is at temperature (50-60°C).
3. Have engine idling at approximately 1000rpm.
4. Fully close the pressure gauge shut-off valve and check to ensure oil pump relief pressure is to specification.
   Pump Relief Pressure:
   NM - NP All Engines .... 8.3 - 9.0 MPa
   NS 3800 .... 7.8 - 8.3 Mpa
   NS 3200 .... 8.5 - 9.0 Mpa
   Note: The pressure gauge shut-off valve must not remain closed for longer than 10 seconds.
5. If not to specification rebuild or replace the oil pump assembly then recheck pressure.
6. With valve fully open check to ensure the hydraulic pressure is to specification.
   Pressure Value: -NM - NP Petrol .... 0.34 MPa
                        -NM - NP Diesel .... 0.29 MPa
                        -NS All Engines .... 0.5 MPa
7. If not to specification check for problems with fluid line or steering gear, correct fault and recheck.
8. Fully turn the steering wheel in one direction and check the retention hydraulic pressure is to specification.
   Retention Hydraulic Pressure:
   NM - NP All Engines .... 8.3 - 9.0 MPa
   NS 3800 .... 7.8 - 8.3 MPa
   NS 3200 .... 8.5 - 9.0 MPa

STEERING

9. If below specification rebuild steering gear assembly then recheck pressure. If above specification rebuild oil pump flow control valve then recheck pressure.
10. Remove test equipment, reconnect pressure hose and tighten to specification.
    Pressure Hose Connection.................. 57 +/- 7 Nm
11. Bleed air from the system as described previously.

Oil Pressure Switch Test

1. Disconnect the pressure hose from the pump assembly and connect the test equipment as shown in the diagram in the previous step.
2. Turn the ignition on and remain stationary. Turn the steering wheel from lock to lock several times and ensure air is bleed from the system and fluid is at temperature (50-60°C).
3. With engine at idle, disconnect the electrical connection for the oil pressure switch and connect an ohmmeter to the switch.
4. Gradually close the pressure gauge shut-off valve to increase pressure and check to ensure switch activation pressure is to specification.
   Pressure Switch Activation:
   NM - NP All Engines................ 1.5 - 2.0 MPa
   NS 3800.................................. 1.65 - 2.0 MPa
   NS 3200.................................. 1.5 - 2.0 MPa
5. Reduce the hydraulic pressure by gradually opening the valve and check to ensure the switch deactivating pressure is to specification.
   Pressure Switch Activation:
   NM - NP All Engines................ 1.5 - 2.0 MPa
   NS 3800.............................. 1.2 MPa or more
   NS 3200.................................. 0.5 - 2.0 MPa
6. Remove test equipment, reconnect pressure hose and tighten to specification.
   Pressure Hose Connection.................... 57 +/- 7 Nm
7. Bleed air from the system as described previously.

Power Steering Pump Hoses and Tubes
Removal

1. Remove the under cover from the vehicle.
2. Place drain tray under steering rack, disconnect hoses from rack and plug the rack hose fittings to prevent entry of foreign material.
3. Drain power steering fluid from pump reservoir via hoses.
4. Disconnect hoses from steering pump and remove hoses from vehicle. Ensure to plug the hose fittings to prevent entry of foreign material.

Installation

1. Remove plugs from rack and connect power steering hoses to steering rack.
2. Remove plugs from pump, then connect power steering hoses to power steering pump.
3. Install the under cover to the vehicle.
4. Fill power steering fluid with specified fluid then bleed air from system as described previously.

Power Steering Pump - Petrol
Removal

1. Remove drive belt and drain the power steering fluid as described previously.
2. Remove the battery and battery tray from vehicle.
3. Disconnect pressure switch connector.
4. Disconnect hoses from power steering pump and drain any remaining fluid from pump into drain tray then plug hoses to prevent entry of foreign matter.
5. Remove the mounting bolts securing pump housing to bracket.
6. Remove pump from vehicle, placing it on a clean work bench.

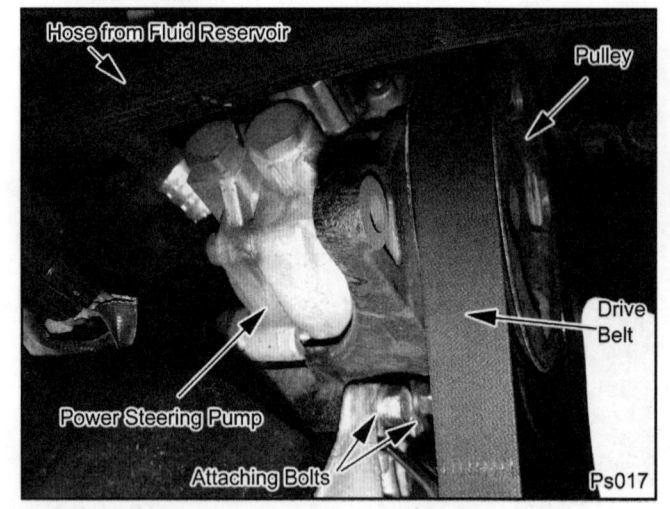

Dismantle - Petrol

1. Remove the pump cover retaining bolts and remove pump cover and O-ring.
2. Remove adaptor ring, then remove the vanes and cam ring.
3. Remove the snap ring from the end of the shaft then remove the pulley and shaft.
4. Remove the rotor then remove the side plate and O-rings.
5. From the pump housing remove the oil seal, then unscrew and remove the terminal assembly along with the two O-rings.
6. Unscrew and remove the inner plug A, then remove the O-ring.
7. Unscrew and remove the inner plug B, then remove the O-ring.
8. From the pump cover unscrew and remove the inner plug C, then remove the O-rings.
9. Remove the pump cover, suction connector retaining screws and connector, then remove O-ring.

STEERING

Petrol Power Steering Pump

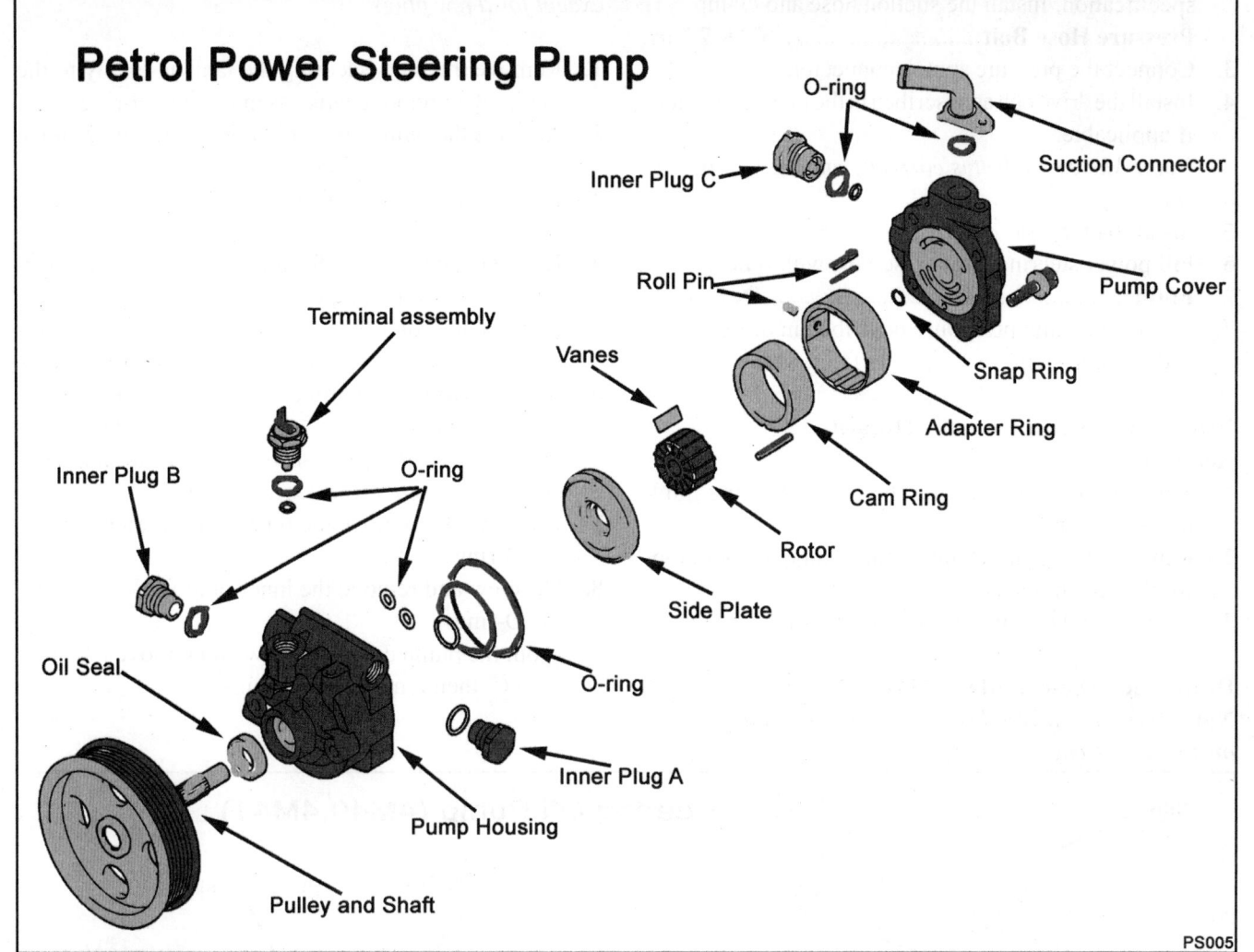

Assembly - Petrol

Important: *During assembly ensure to coat all seals and O-rings with specified power steering fluid and never reuse old O-rings and oil seals.*

Specified Fluid .... Dexron II

1. To the pump cover install the suction connector using a new 'O-ring and tighten retaining bolts to specification.
   Suction Connector Bolts .... 9.9 +/- 2.1 Nm
2. To the pump cover install inner plug 'C' using two new O-rings and tighten to specification.
   Inner Plug 'C' .... 37 +/- 2 Nm
3. To the pump housing install inner plugs 'A' and 'B' using new 'O-rings and tightening to specification.
   Inner Plug 'A' .... 44 +/- 5 Nm
   Inner Plug 'B' .... 35 +/- 4 Nm
4. To the pump housing install the terminal assembly using new 'O-rings and tighten to specification.
   Terminal Assembly .... 28 +/- 2 Nm
   Note: Never pull apart the terminal assembly as it is not able to be serviced.
5. Coat oil seal with power steering fluid, using a suitable tool press the oil seal into the pump housing.
6. To the pump housing install the O-rings then install the side plate.
7. Install the rotor to the pump assembly ensuring the punch mark is facing towards the side plate.
8. Install the pulley and shaft assembly to the pump housing and secure with retaining snap ring.
9. To the pump housing assembly install the cam ring ensuring the identification mark is facing towards the side plate.
10. To the rotor install the vanes, ensuring the round edge is facing towards the outside.
11. To the pump housing install the adaptor ring.
12. Install the pump cover O-ring to the pump housing then install the pump cover, tightening retaining bolts to specification.
    Pump Cover Retaining Bolts .... 24 +/- 2 Nm

Installation

1. Position pump in the mounting bracket, then install retaining bolts and tighten.
   Pump Mounting Bolts:
   - NM - NP .... 22 +/- 4 Nm
   - NS .... 39 +/- 6 Nm
2. Reconnect pressure hose to pump and tighten to

specification. Install the suction hose and clamp.

Pressure Hose Bolt .... **57 +/- 7 Nm**

3. Connect the pressure switch connector.
4. Install the drive belt as described in the tune up chapter. If applicable.
   Note: Make sure belt is correctly engaged on pulley ribs.
5. Install battery tray and battery.
6. Fill power steering pump reservoir with fluid.
   Fluid .... **Dexron II**
7. Follow bleeding procedure described in this chapter and bleed system.

Power Steering Pump - Diesel
Removal
1. Remove the bolts securing the power steering fluid pipes to the pump.
2. Remove the pump retaining bolts and remove pump from front engine cover.
3. Remove and discard the "O" ring from the pump.

Dismantle - Diesel (4M40, 4M41)
Note: There are a couple of power steering pumps used on the diesel engines. They are all basically the same except for a few plugs.

1. Remove the bolts securing the tank assembly to the pump, then remove tank assembly and O-ring.
2. Remove the pump cover retaining bolts and remove pump cover and O-ring.
3. Remove adaptor ring, then remove the vanes and cam ring.
4. Remove the snap ring from the end of the shaft then remove the oil pump gear.
5. Remove the rotor then remove the side plate and O-rings including the O-rings from the pump cover.
6. (4M41) From the pump cover unscrew and remove the terminal assembly along with the two O-rings.
   Note: Never attempt to disassemble the terminal assembly as it is not a serviceable item.
7. Unscrew and remove the inner plug A, then remove the O-ring.
8. Unscrew and remove the inner plug B, then remove the O-ring.
9. From the pump cover unscrew and remove the inner plug C, then remove the O-rings.

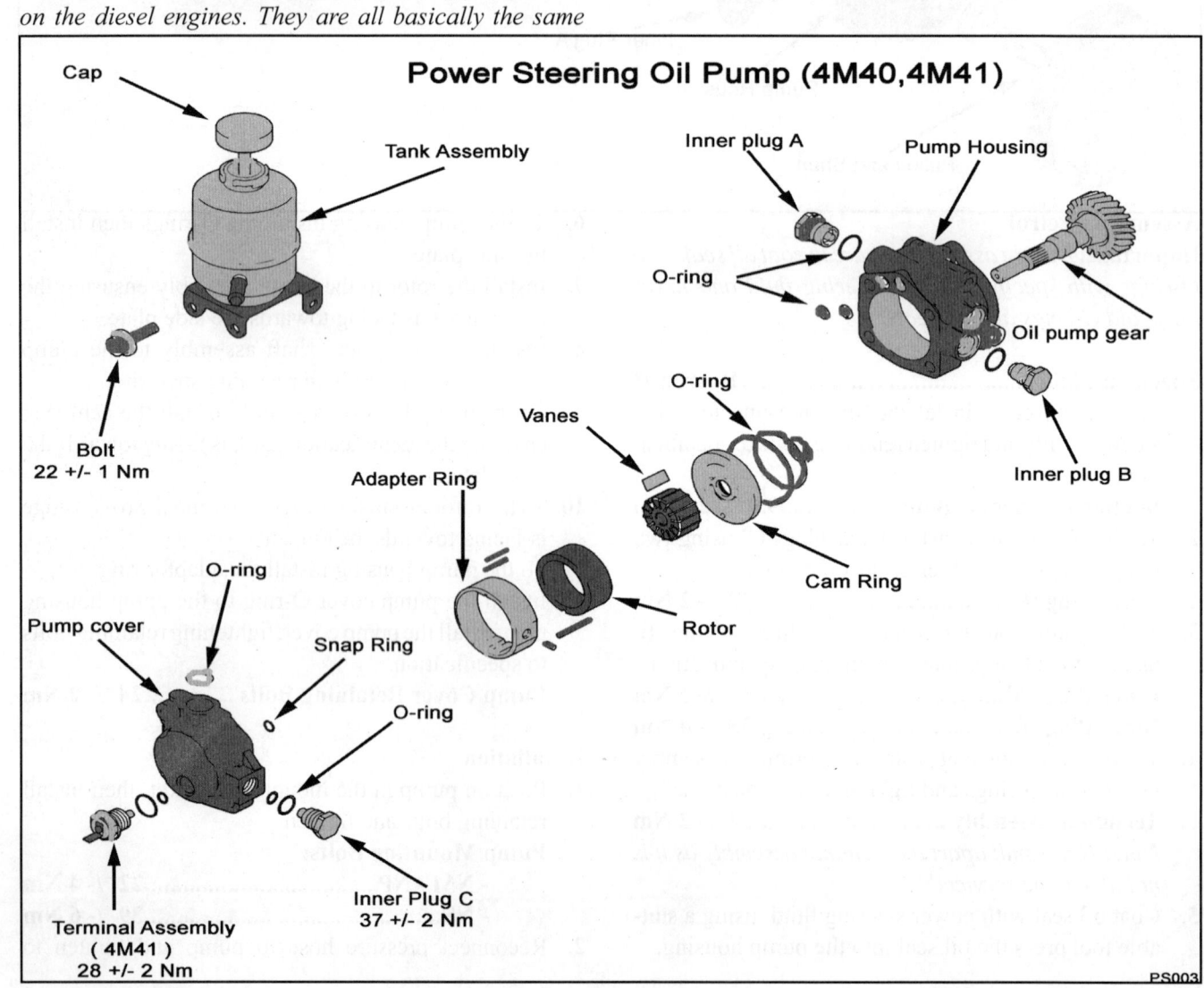

Power Steering Oil Pump (4M40, 4M41)

Labels: Cap, Tank Assembly, Bolt 22 +/- 1 Nm, O-ring, Pump cover, Snap Ring, O-ring, Terminal Assembly (4M41) 28 +/- 2 Nm, Inner Plug C 37 +/- 2 Nm, Adapter Ring, Vanes, O-ring, Rotor, Cam Ring, Inner plug A, Pump Housing, O-ring, Oil pump gear, Inner plug B

STEERING

Dismantle - Diesel (3200)

1. Remove the pump cover retaining bolts and remove pump cover and O-ring.
2. Remove the remove the vanes from the rotor, and then remove the cam ring.
3. Remove the rotor and the side plate and O-rings including the O-rings from the pump cover.
4. Remove the suction connector and O-ring. Unscrew the connector assembly and remove it, also remove the spool, flow control spring and associated O-rings.
5. From the pump cover unscrew and remove the terminal assembly along with the two O-rings.
   Note: Never attempt to disassemble the terminal assembly as it is not a serviceable item.

Assembly - Diesel (4M40, 4M41)

Important: *During assembly ensure to coat all seals and O-rings with specified power steering fluid and never reuse old O-rings.*

Specified Fluid .... **Dexron II**

1. To the pump cover install inner plug 'C' using new O-rings and tighten to specification.
   Inner Plug 'C'..37 +/- 2 Nm
2. To the pump housing install inner plugs 'A' and 'B' using new O-rings and tighten to specification.
   Inner Plug 'A'..44 +/- 5 Nm
   Inner Plug 'B'..35 +/- 4 Nm
3. (4M41) To the pump cover install the terminal assembly using new O-rings and tighten to specification.
   Terminal Assembly ....28 +/- 2 Nm
4. To the pump housing install the O-rings then install the side plate.
5. Install the rotor to the pump assembly ensuring the punch mark is towards the side plate.
6. Install the oil pump gear to the pump housing and secure with retaining snap ring.
7. To the pump housing assembly install the cam ring ensuring the identification mark is towards the side plate.
8. To the rotor install the vanes, ensuring the round edge is towards the outside.
9. To the pump housing install the adaptor ring.
10. Install the pump cover O-ring to the pump housing then install the pump cover tightening retaining bolts to specification.
    Pump cover retaining bolts ....24 +/- 2 Nm
11. Install tank assembly O-ring to the pump assembly then install the tank assembly tightening retaining bolts to specification.
    Tank Assembly Bolts...........................22 +/- 1 Nm

Assembly - Diesel (3200)

Important: *During assembly ensure to coat all seals and O-rings with specified power steering fluid and never reuse old O-rings.*

Specified Fluid .... **Dexron II**

1. To the pump cover install the terminal assembly using new O-rings and tighten to specification.
   Terminal Assembly ....28 +/- 2 Nm
2. To the pump cover install the suction connector and O-ring. Tighten bolts to specification.
   Suction Connector Bolts...................9.8 +/- 2.0 Nm
3. To the pump cover install the flow control spring, spool, O-rings and the two connector assemblies, tightening to specification.
   Connector Assembly ....59 +/- 10 Nm
4. To the pump housing install the O-rings then install the side plate.
5. Install the rotor to the pump assembly ensuring the punch mark is towards the side plate.
6. To the pump housing assembly install the cam ring ensuring the identification mark is towards the side plate.
7. To the rotor install the vanes, ensuring the round edge is towards the outside.
8. Install the pump cover O-ring to the pump housing then install the pump cover tightening retaining bolts to specification.
   Pump cover retaining bolts ....24 +/- 2 Nm

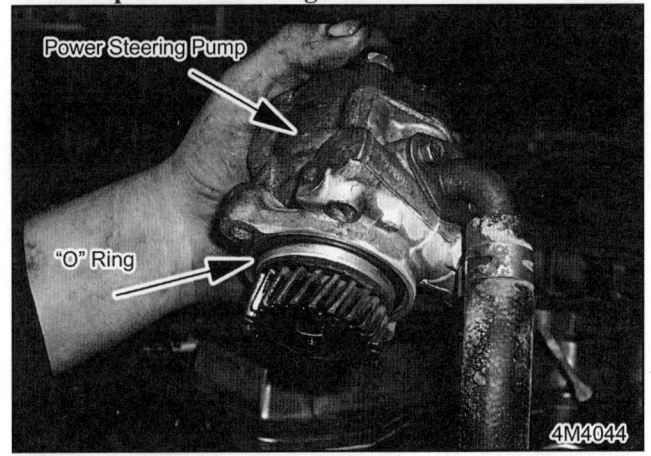

Installation

1. Install a new "O" ring to the power steering pump.
2. Install pump to the front engine cover, ensure the gears mesh as the pump is installed. Tighten bolts.
3. Install the power steering fluid pipes to the pump, install bolts and tighten.

STEERING

STEERING WHEEL

Steering Wheel, Driver Side Airbag & Clock Spring

Note: *For passenger side airbag removal refer to instruments chapter.*

Removal

1. Ensure the wheels are pointing in the straight ahead position then turn the ignition to the lock position and remove key.
2. Disconnect the negative battery terminal and allow to sit for at least 60 seconds before proceeding.
3. **Vehicles without SRS:**
   a) Remove the horn pad from the steering wheel by removing the bolt from underneath.
   b) Remove the steering wheel retaining nut and the two washers.
   c) Remove the steering wheel using a suitable steering wheel puller.

4. **Vehicles with SRS (NM - NP):**
   a) On SRS vehicles remove the cover by inserting special tool (MB990784) or a thin screwdriver in to the small notch from underneath the steering wheel.
   b) Through the hole disconnect electrical connections for airbag module and the horn. 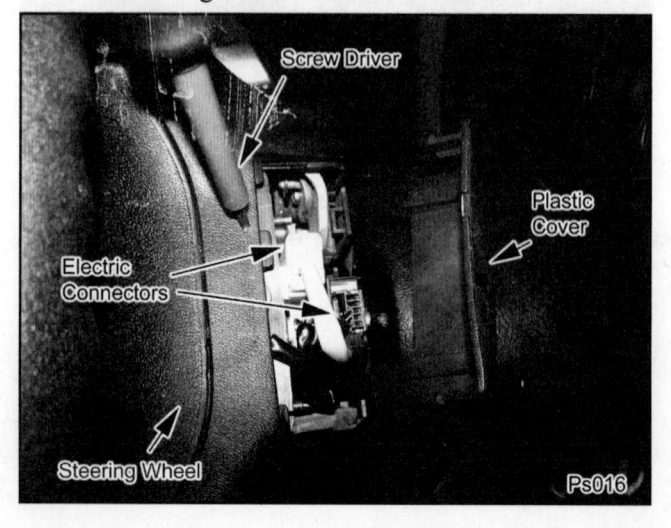
   c) On NM - NP models use a hexagonal bit socket (8mm x 75mm) to undo the mounting bolt and then remove the steering wheel and air bag module.
   Note: *Place the air bag module face up in a dry safe location.*
   d) To remove the air bag module undo the mounting nuts from the back of the steering wheel.
   e) Undo the mounting screws and electrical connectors for the clock spring and remove.

5. **Vehicles with SRS (NS):**
   a) On SRS vehicles remove the cover by inserting special tool (MB990784) or a thin screwdriver in to the small notch from underneath the steering wheel.
   b) Through the hole disconnect electrical connections for airbag module and the horn. 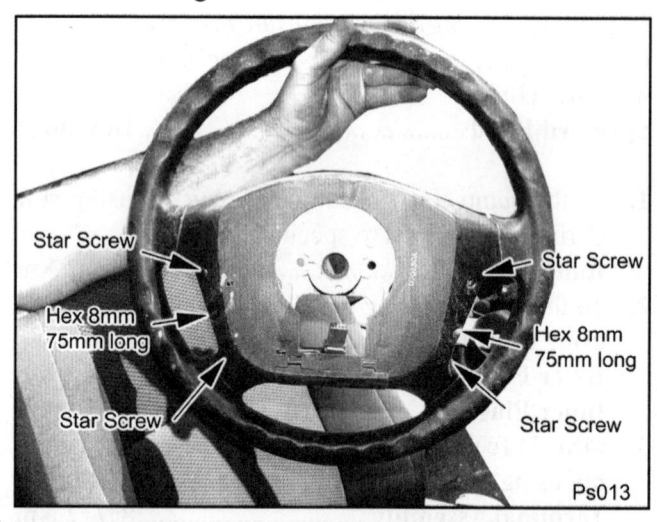
   c) From the back of the steering wheel remove the mounting screws for the air bag module.
   d) Remove the air bag module.
   e) Remove the steering wheel securing nut. Using a suitable steering wheel puller, remove the steering wheel.
   Note: *Damage can be done to the steering column shaft if a suitable puller is not used.*
   f) Undo the mounting screws and electrical connectors for the clock spring and remove.

Installation

1. **Vehicles with SRS (NM - NP):**
   a) Install the clock spring on the steering shaft. Fully turn the clock spring clockwise and then turn it anti-clockwise 3 times to align the mating marks.
   Clock Spring Screws...............0.69 +/- 0.15 Nm
   b) Install the air bag module to the steering wheel doing the nuts up to specification.
   Air Bag Module Nuts................3.09 +/- 0.4 Nm
   c) Install steering wheel and airbag module to steering column, then tighten retaining bolt to specification.

312

STEERING

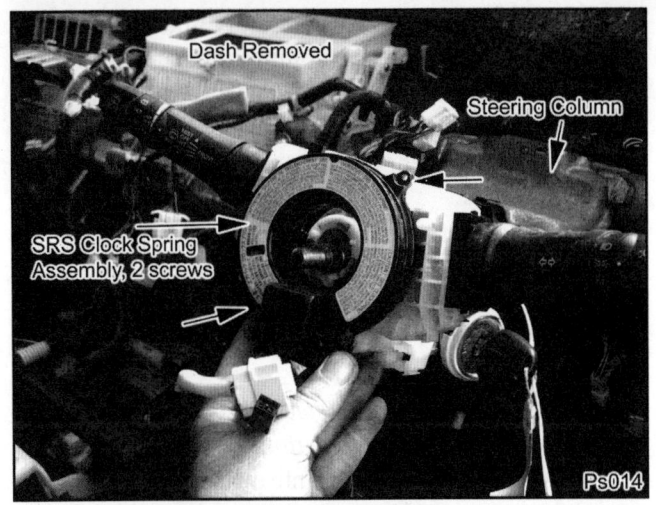

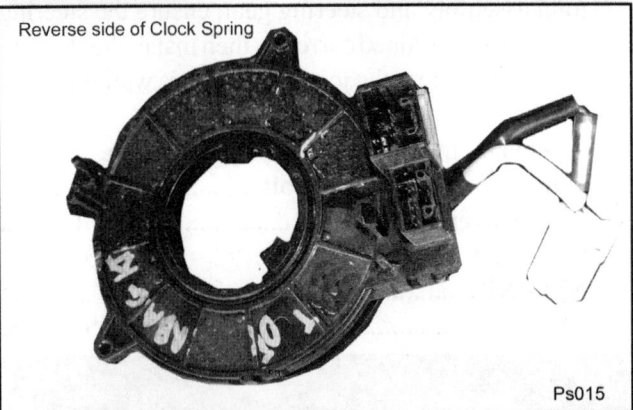

Photo captions:
- Dash Removed — Steering Column — SRS Clock Spring Assembly, 2 screws — Ps014
- Reverse side of Clock Spring — Ps015

Retaining Bolt .... **50 +/- 5 Nm**

d) Connect electrical connections for airbag module and horn, then press the lower cover into place.

2. **Vehicles with SRS (NS):**
   a) Install the clock spring on the steering shaft. Fully turn the clock spring clockwise and then turn it anti-clockwise 3 times to align the mating marks.
   Clock Spring Screws .... **0.69 +/- 0.15 Nm**
   b) Install the steering wheel to the steering column and do retaining nut up to specification.
   Steering Wheel Retaining Nut .... **41 +/- 8 Nm**
   c) Place air bag module onto steering wheel and do up the retaining screws.
   d) From underneath the steering wheel reconnect the air bag module and horn connectors.
   e) Replace the cover by pressing it into place.

3. **Vehicles without SRS:**
   a) Ensure steering is positioned straight ahead and fit the steering wheel.
   b) Install steering wheel retaining bolt, then tighten the retaining nut to specification.
   Steering Wheel Retaining Nut .... **41+/-8 Nm**
   c) Refit the horn pad doing up the bolt to specification.
   Horn Pad Retaining Bolt .... **2.5 +/- 0.5 Nm**

4. Check to make sure the steering wheel position is correct when the wheels are facing straight ahead.
5. Reconnect the negative battery terminal.

STEERING COLUMN

Steering Column Upper and Lower Cover
Removal
1. Remove steering wheel as described previously.
2. Remove the lower instrument cover as described in the body chapter.
3. Remove the screws securing the lower cover and remove lower steering column cover.
4. Lower the steering column to the lowest position then remove the top cover.

Installation
1. Replace the top cover.
2. Lift the column into position, and replace the lower steering column cover and tighten retaining screws. Make sure covers mesh together correctly and the tabs are all aligned.
3. Replace the lower instrument cover.
4. Replace the steering wheel as described previously.

Steering Column
Note: *Disconnect the negative battery terminal and allow to sit for at least 60 seconds before proceeding. Do not release the tilt lever until the shaft is reinstalled.*

Removal
1. From engine bay remove the air cleaner and intake duct to enable access to the steering knuckle joint.
2. Remove the lower cover panel from the instrument panel, refer to body/instrument chapter if required.
3. Remove the steering wheel as described previously.
4. Remove the lower and upper steering column covers as described earlier, then remove the harness protector.
5. Undo the screws holding the clock spring down and remove.
6. Remove the combination switch assembly retaining screws, disconnect electrical connection and remove

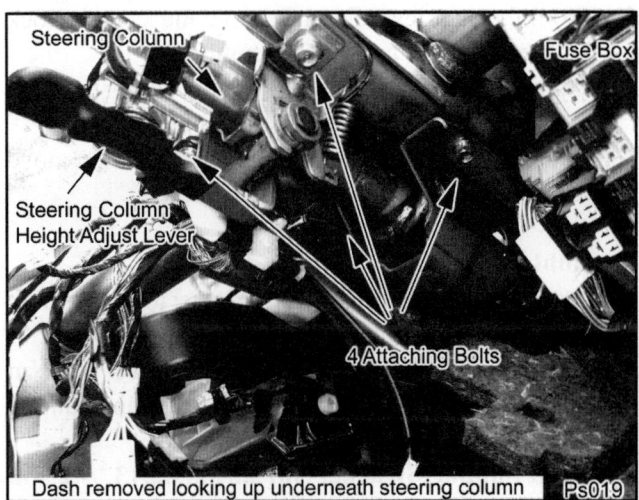

Photo caption: Steering Column — Fuse Box — Steering Column Height Adjust Lever — 4 Attaching Bolts — Dash removed looking up underneath steering column — Ps019

313

STEERING

switch assembly.
7. Remove the cover from the key interlock cable, then remove the key interlock cable. (auto transmissions)
8. Disconnect the brake pedal return spring if fitted, refer to brake chapter if required.
9. Remove the bolts securing the joint cover to the fire wall, then from the engine bay remove the bolt securing the joint assembly to the steering gear. Remove the bolts securing the joint assembly to the chassis rails.

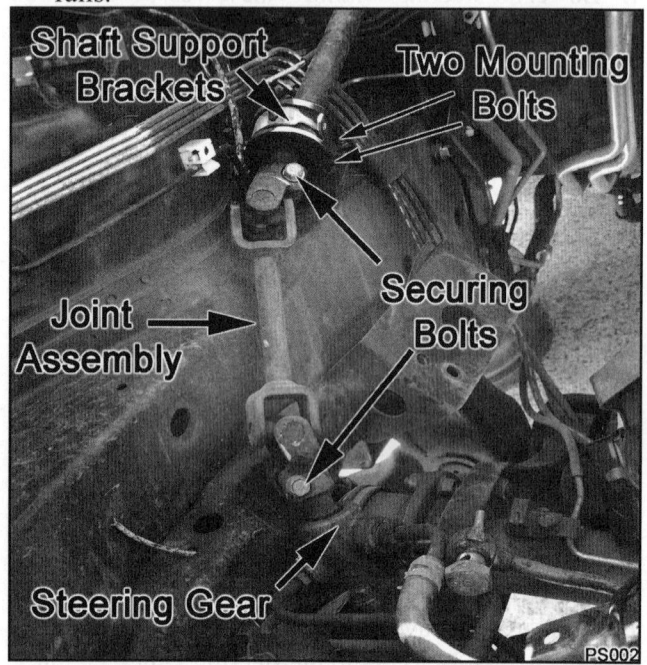

10. Carefully remove the steering column assembly from the vehicle.

Dismantle
1. Remove the retaining nut from the dynamic damper lower plate, then remove the lower plate and dynamic damper.
2. Drill a hole in the centre of the special bolt deep enough to install a tap, then use the tap to remove the special bolt.
3. From the steering column remove the steering lock bracket and lock cylinder assembly.
4. From the lower shaft remove the nut securing the shaft support brackets, then remove support brackets.
5. Loosen the joint assembly retaining bolt and remove the lower joint assembly from column.

Assembly
1. To the steering column install the lower joint assembly and tighten retaining bolt to specification.
   Joint Assembly Retaining Bolt............18 +/- 2 Nm
2. Install the shaft support brackets and tighten retaining nut to specification.
   Shaft Support Bracket Nut.................13 +/- 2 Nm

3. Install the steering lock assembly and lock bracket into position on steering column and partially tighten retaining bolts.
4. Ensure the steering lock assembly works correctly then tighten retaining bolts until the bolt heads twist off.
5. Install the steering dynamic damper and damper lower plate then tighten retaining bolt to specification.
   Dynamic Damper Retaining Nut........13 +/- 2 Nm

Installation
Note: Before installing the steering column make sure the tilt lever is in the lock position.
1. Install the steering column into the vehicle aligning the joint assembly and steering gear, ensure the steering column is positioned correctly then install the steering column bolts and the joint cover to fire wall retaining bolts.
2. Tighten all mounting bolts to specification.
   Joint to Steering Gear Bolt ....18 +/- 2 Nm
   Joint Cover to Fire Wall ....5 +/- 1.0 Nm
   Steering Column Bolts:
   NM - NP ....22 +/- 4 Nm
   NS ....12 +/- 2 Nm

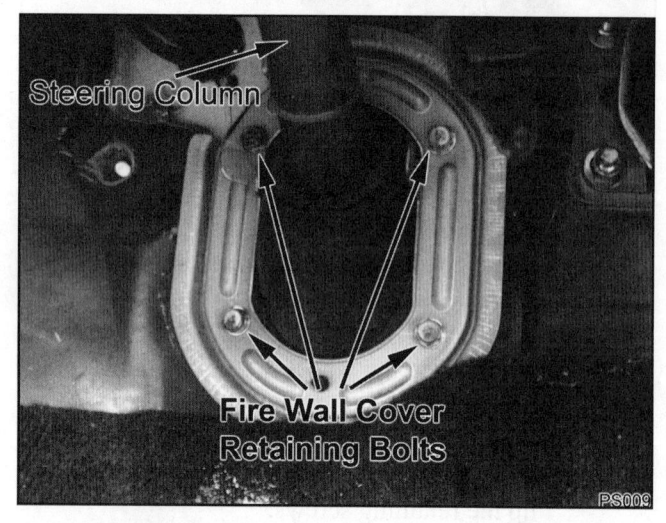

3. Reconnect the brake pedal return spring if fitted, refer to brake chapter if required.
4. Install the key interlock cable then install the cover.
5. Install the combination switch to steering column, connect electrical connection and tighten retaining screws, then install the harness protector.
6. Install the lower and upper steering column covers.
7. Install the steering wheel as described previously.
8. Install the lower instrument panel trim, refer to body chapter if required.
9. In the engine bay install the air cleaner and intake duct assembly.

PROBLEM DIAGNOSIS

Problem: Hard Steering
Possible Causes & Remedies:
Cause: Tyres incorrectly inflated.
Remedy: Inflate tyres to correct pressure.
Cause: Insufficient lubricant.
Remedy: Lubricate suspension & steering linkage.
Cause: Excessive caster.
Remedy: Check front wheel alignment.
Cause: Steering system joints worn.
Remedy: Replace steering system joints.
Cause: Lower arm ball joints worn.
Remedy: Replace lower arm ball joints.
Cause: Steering column sticking.
Remedy: Inspect steering column.
Cause: Rack & Pinion out of adjustment or broken.
Remedy: Adjust or repair steering gear.
Cause: Power steering belt loose.
Remedy: Adjust belt.
Cause: Fluid level in reservoir low.
Remedy: Check reservoir.
Cause: Power Steering unit faulty.
Remedy: Check power steering unit.

Power Steering Unit Checks
* Check fluid level.
* Loose drive belt.
* Drive belt slipping.
* High internal leakage.
* Insufficient pump pressure.
* Sticky flow control valve.
* Steering column to rack & pinion connection may not be correctly aligned.

Note: *If none of the above problems are found, carry out a pressure test as described in this chapter, for other possible causes such as:*
* Control valve problems.
* Pump pressure not as specified.
* Steering pump bypass of fluid.

Problem: Poor Return
Possible Causes & Remedies:
Cause: Tyres incorrectly inflated.
Remedy: Inflate tyres to correct pressure.
Cause: Insufficient lubricant.
Remedy: Lubricate suspension & steering linkage.
Cause: Wheel alignment incorrect.
Remedy: Check front wheel alignment.
Cause: Steering gear out of adjustment or broken.
Remedy: Adjust or repair steering gear.

Problem: Excessive Play
Possible Causes & Remedies:
Cause: Front wheel bearing worn.
Remedy: Replace front wheel bearing.
Cause: Main shaft yoke or intermediate shaft yoke worn.
Remedy: Replace main or intermediate shaft.
Cause: Lower arm ball joints worn.
Remedy: Replace lower arm ball joints.
Cause: Steering system joints worn.
Remedy: Replace steering system joints.
Cause: Rack & Pinion out of adjustment or broken.
Remedy: Adjust or repair steering gear.

Problem: Abnormal Noise !
Possible Causes & Remedies:
Cause: Steering linkage loose.
Remedy: Tighten steering linkage.
Cause: Steering system joints worn.
Remedy: Replace steering system joints.
Cause: Steering gear out of adjustment or broken.
Remedy: Adjust or repair steering gear.
Cause: Power Steering Pump Fluid Low.
Remedy: Top up fluid and check for fluid leakage.

Problem: Drive Belt Squeal
Possible Causes & Remedies:
Cause: Loose drive belt
Cause: Drive belt slipping
Cause: Drive belt badly worn
Cause: Drive belt has a glazed surface

Problem: Noise from Power Steering Pump
Possible Causes & Remedies:
Cause: High back-pressure.
Remedy: Blocked hose or faulty rack & pinion.
Cause: Scored pressure plate, thrust plate or rotor.
Remedy: Replace components.
Cause: Extreme wear of pump ring and vanes.
Remedy: Replace components.
Cause: Vanes not installed correctly.
Remedy: Reinstall vanes.

Problem: Discoloured Power Steering Fluid
Possible Causes & Remedies:
Cause: Power steering fluid has air mixed with it.
Remedy: Check pump for problem and repair.

Problem: Steering pump pressure not as specified.
Possible Causes & Remedies:
Cause: Pump has not been correctly assembled.

STEERING

Remedy: Reassemble pump.
Cause: Internal components of pump are extremely worn.
Remedy: Replace components.
Cause: Control valve problems.
Remedy: Repair control valve.
Cause: Pump pressure not as specified.
Remedy: Check and repair pump.
Cause: Steering pump internal bypass of fluid.
Remedy: Check and repair pump.

SPECIFICATIONS

POWER STEERING PUMP
Type .... Vane pump
Lubricant: - type: .... Dexron II ATF
Relief set pressure: NM - NP .... 8.8 MPa
                     NS 3800 .... 7.8 MPa
                     NS 3200 .... 8.8 MPa

Oil pump pressure:
- relief pressure
    NM - NP .... 8.3 - 9.0 MPa
    NS 3800 .... 7.8 - 8.3 MPa
    NS 3200 .... 8.5 - 9.0 MPa
- under no load
    NM - NP Petrol .... 0.34 MPa
    NM - NP Diesel .... 0.29 MPa
    NS .... 0.5 MPa
- Steering gear retention
    NM - NP .... 8.3 - 9.0 MPa
    NS 3800 .... 7.8 - 8.3 MPa
    NS 3200 .... 8.5 - 9.0 MPa

Power Steering Pressure Switch:
NM - NP 6G7, 4M41
    On - Off .... 1.5 - 2.0 MPa
    Off - On .... 1.5 - 2.0 MPa
NS 3800
    On - Off .... 1.2 or more MPa
    Off - On .... 1.65 - 2.0 MPa
NS 3200
    On - Off .... 0.5 - 2.0 MPa
    Off - On .... 1.5 - 2.0 MPa

Steering wheel free play:
    With engine running .... 0 - 30 mm
    With engine stopped .... 0 - 10 mm

Stationary steering effort:
    - All models .... 39.2 N or less
    - variation .... 5.9 N or less

Steering angle:
- Inner Wheel
    NM - NP .... 36°30' +/- 1°30'
    NS SWB .... 36°49' +/- 1°30'
    NS LWB .... 36°01' +/- 1°30'

- Outer Wheel (for reference)
    NM - NP .... 31°40'
    NS SWB .... 32°06'
    NS LWB .... 32°18'

Total pinion preload:
- All models .... 0.6 - 1.7 Nm
- Change in torque .... 0.4 Nm (or less)

Tie rod end ball joint turning torque
- NM - NP .... 0.49 - 2.45 Nm
- NS   0.5 - 5.1 Nm

Tie-rod swing resistance .... 11 - 35 N
Tie-rod swing torque .... 1.4 - 4.9 Nm

TORQUE SETTINGS

Power Steering Pump   Nm
Suction Connector .... 9.9 +/- 2.1
Pressure hose Bolt .... 57 +/- 7
Terminal Assembly .... 28 +/- 2
Oil pump cover .... 24 +/- 2
Oil pump Mounting Bolts:
    NM - NP .... 22 +/- 4
    NS .... 39 +/- 6

Rack & Pinion
Mounting bolts/nuts: NM - NP .... 69 +/- 9
Mounting Bolts:
    NS 3800 .... 117 +/- 17
    NS 3200 .... 82 +/- 12
Mounting Nuts:
    NS 3800 .... 82 +/- 12
    NS 3200 .... 117 +/- 17
Pinion housing attaching bolts .... 22 +/- 4
Tie rod end lock nut:
    NM - NP .... 71 +/- 7
    NS .... 93 +/- 15
Tie rod to knuckle attaching nut:
    NM - NP .... 39 +/- 5
    NS .... 47 +/- 13
Pressure hose/return tube flare nut .... 15 +/- 3
Fluid Pipe Bracket bolts .... 12 +/- 2

Steering Column
Steering wheel:
    NM - NP (without SRS) .... 41 +/- 8
    NM - NP (with SRS) .... 50 +/- 5
    NS .... 41 +/- 8
Air Bag Module: NM - NP .... 3.9 +/- 0.4
Clock Spring .... 0.69 +/- 0.15
Dynamic Damper Lower Plate:
    NM - NP .... 13 +/- 2
Steering Column Bolts .... 22 +/- 4
Shaft Support Brackets .... 13 +/- 2
Fire Wall Cover .... 5.0 +/- 1.0
Joint Assembly To Steering Rack .... 18 +/- 2

FRONT SUSPENSION, FRONT AXLE & DRIVE SHAFTS

Subject	Page	Subject	Page
General Information	318	**Front Hub & Knuckle Assembly**	324
Wheel Alignment	318	Removal	324
Visual Inspection	318	Disassembly	324
Camber	318	Inspect and Clean	324
Caster	318	Hub Rotation Starting Torque Check	324
Adjustment	318	Wheel Bearing Axial Play Check	324
Toe-In	319	Assembly	324
Adjustment	319	Installation	325
Front Suspension	320	**Front Drive Shaft**	325
Ball Joint Dust Cover Inspection	320	Removal	325
Stabilizer Bar	320	Disassembly	325
Removal	320	Inspection	326
Ball Joint Turning Torque Check	320	Assembly	326
Installation	320	Installation	326
Suspension Upper Arm	320	**Inner Shaft, Housing Tube**	326
Removal	320	Removal	326
Ball Joint Turning Torque Check	320	Disassembly	327
Installation	321	Assembly	327
Suspension Lower Arm	321	Installation	327
Removal	321	**Freewheel Clutch And Differential Carrier**	328
Ball Joint Turning Torque Check	321	Removal	328
Installation	321	**Freewheel Clutch Assembly**	328
Front Strut Assembly	322	Disassembly	328
Removal	322	Assembly	328
Disassembly	322	**Differential Carrier**	329
Inspection	322	Pre-disassembly Inspection	329
Assembly	322	Drive Gear Backlash Check	329
Installation	322	Drive Gear Tooth Contact Check	329
Front Axle Assembly	323	Drive Gear Run-out Check	329
Wheel Bearing Backlash Check	323	Differential Gear Backlash Check	329
Total Backlash Check	323	Disassembly	329
Gear Oil Level Check	323	Assembly	330
Solenoid Valve Operation Check	323	Installation	332
		Problem Diagnosis	332
		Specifications	334

FRONT SUSPENSION, AXLE & DRIVESHAFT ASSEMBLIES

GENERAL INFORMATION

The Mitsubishi Pajero uses a coil spring, double wishbone independent type suspension for the front of the vehicle. This type of suspension is rigid and has very little variation in roll centre height. A vacuum type freewheel clutch is used, it is switched between 2wd and 4wd by use of a solenoid valve and actuator. Vehicles fitted with ABS have a rotor that detects wheel speed press fitted to the U.J outer wheel.

WHEEL ALIGNMENT

VISUAL INSPECTION

It is necessary before any attempt is made to check camber, caster or toe-in, to carry out the following preliminary checks.

1. Check tyre and tyre mountings. Always check camber and toe-in at the mean run-out position on the tyre or rim.
2. Check and adjust tyre pressures.
3. Front wheel bearings should be correctly adjusted.
4. Lower control arm ball joints and inner bushes should be checked for wear.
5. Check steering gear mounting bolts for tightness and tie rod ball joints for wear.
6. The vehicle should be at curb weight (fuel tank full, without driver, passengers or luggage, etc).
7. Check for improperly operating front struts or rear shock absorbers.
8. Check for loose or missing stabilizer bar or tension rod attachments.

CAMBER

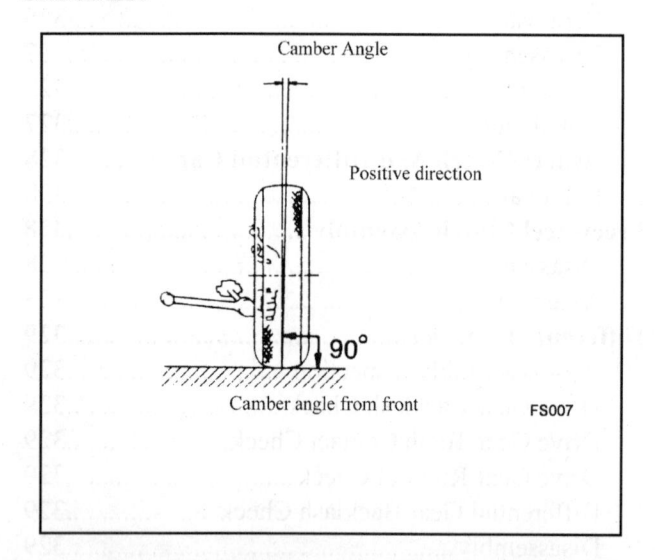

This is the angle that the top of the wheel leans in towards or away from the vehicle, when the wheel leans inwards at the top it is said to be negative camber.

CASTER

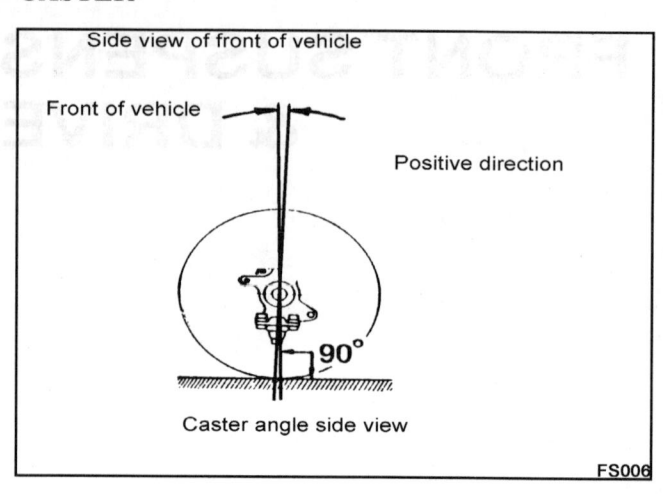

This refers to the tilting of the steering axis either forward or backward from the vertical (when viewed from the side of the vehicle). A backward tilt is said to be positive (+) and a forward tilt is said to negative (-).

ADJUSTMENT

1. Camber and caster adjustment is made by turning the lower arm camber adjusting bolt.

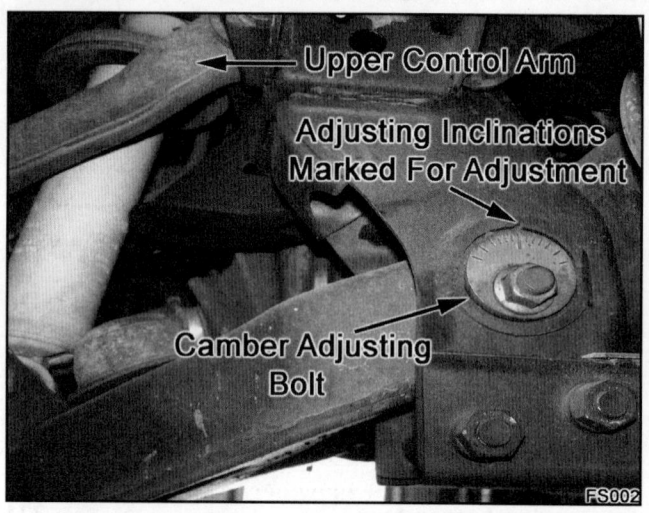

2. Refer to the following values and adjust the camber and caster.

   Camber Standard Value:
   NM - NP .... 0°30' +/- 0°30'
   NS - NT .... 0°00' +/- 0°30'
   (difference b/w wheels less than 30')

   Castor Standard Value:
   NM - NP .... 3°50' +/- 1°00'
   NS - NT (SWB) .... 3°39' +/- 1°00'
   NS - NT (LWB) .... 3°31' +/- 1°00'
   (difference b/w wheels less than 30')
   Kingpin Inclination .... 11°30'

3. After camber and caster adjustment has been made the toe adjustment should be made.

FRONT SUSPENSION, AXLE & DRIVESHAFT ASSEMBLIES

TOE-IN

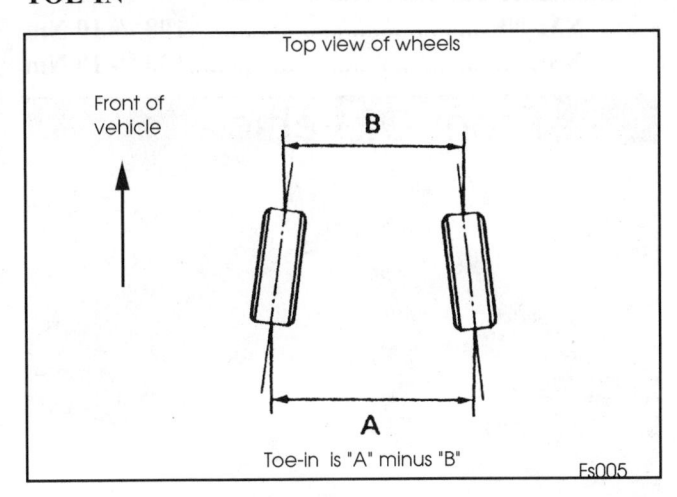

Top view of wheels

Toe-in is "A" minus "B"

This refers to the turning in of the wheels. The actual amount of toe-in is normally only a few millimetres. The purpose of a toe-in specification is to ensure parallel rolling of the wheels. Excessive toe-in or toe-out may increase tyre wear. A slight amount of positive toe-in, measured statically with the vehicle at rest, is required to offset the small deflections due to rolling resistance and brake applications which tend to turn the wheels outward.

ADJUSTMENT

Adjustment is achieved by winding the tie rods in or out, thus increasing or decreasing their length and thereby altering the toe-in setting.

1. Set steering gear and wheels in straight ahead position.
   Note: *If steering wheel is not in the right position it can be corrected when doing the adjustments.*
2. If the tie rods are to be re-used, a few checks need to be performed to check their condition.
   a) Using a ball joint removing tool remove from the tie rod from the control arm.
   b) Using a pre load socket measure the ball joint turning torque.
      Standard Value:
      - NM - NP .... 0.49 - 2.45 Nm
      - NS - NT .... 0.5 - 5.1 Nm
   c) Give the tie rod several hard swing then measure the swing resistance with a spring balance.
      Standard Value .... 1.4 - 4.9 Nm
   d) If any of the values are not meet, replace the tie rod before doing the toe-in adjustment.
   e) If replacing the tie rods the following distances will give you a good start when doing the toe-in adjustment. The distance is measured between the bellows end and the lock nut for the tie rod end.
      Standard Distance:
      - NM - NP .... 57 mm
      - NS - NT (SWB) .... 46 mm
      - NS - NT (LWB) .... 41 mm

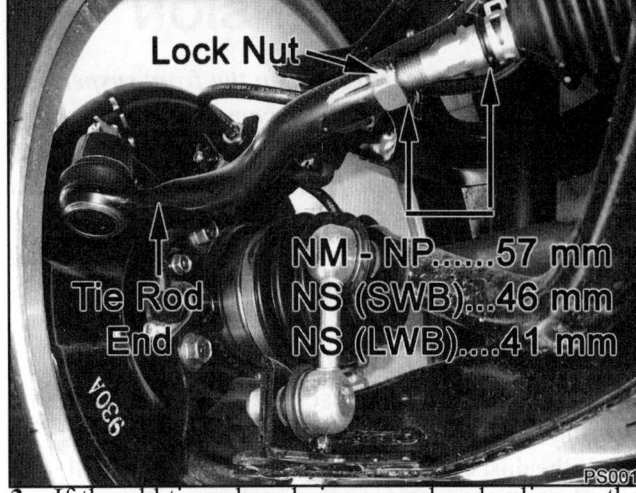

Lock Nut
Tie Rod End
NM - NP ..... 57 mm
NS (SWB) ... 46 mm
NS (LWB) .... 41 mm

3. If the old tie rod are being reused undo clips on the tie rod boots. Loosen tie rod lock nuts, then clean and lubricate threads that are exposed.
4. Turn each tie rod as required until the correct toe-in is obtained.
   Toe-In Standard Value:
   At centre of tyre tread:
   NM - NP .... 2.5 +/- 2.5 mm
   NS - NT .... 0 - 5 mm
   Toe angle (per wheel):
   NM - NP .... 0°05' +/- 05'
   NS - NT .... 0°00' - 0°12'
   Note: *During toe-in adjustment, ensure the steering wheel is held in the straight ahead position, also both tie rods will need adjusting equally to obtain the same reading both sides.*
5. When the correct reading has been obtained tighten tie rod lock nuts, with tie rod ends in alignment with their ball studs, then tighten outer tie rod boot clips securely, ensure boots are not distorted.
   Tie Rod Lock Nut:
   NM - NP .... 71 +/- 7 Nm
   NS - NT .... 93 +/- 15 Nm
6. Check steering angle by placing front wheels on a turning radius gauge.
   Steering Angle Standard Value:
   Inner wheels: NM - NP .... 36°30' +/- 1°30'
   NS - NT (SWB) .. 36°49' +/- 1°30'
   NS - NT (LWB) .. 36°01' +/- 1°30'
   Outer Wheels: NM - NP .... 31°40'
   NS - NT (SWB) .... 32°06'
   NS - NT (LWB) .... 32°18'
7. IF standard values are correct road test the vehicle, if not recheck toe angle again.

FRONT SUSPENSION

When any work is carried out on the front suspension components a few checks are recommended before any driving. The first one is to re-calibrate the steering wheel sensor refer steering chapter. Next is to check and adjust the wheel alignment. On models fitted with headlamp automatic levelling system the beam direction should be checked refer to the body chapter.

BALL JOINT DUST COVER INSPECTION

1. Check the ball joint dust covers by pressing with a finger and checking for cracks or damage.
2. If the dust cover is cracked or damaged the ball joint assembly should be replaced as a cracked or damaged dust cover may cause damage to the ball joint. If in doubt measure the ball joint in question turning torque.

STABILIZER BAR

Removal

1. Raise front of vehicle and support on safety stands, then remove the undercover from the vehicle.
2. Remove the stabilizer bar link to lower arm on each side.
3. Remove the bolts securing the stabilizer bar clamp to the cross member and remove stabilizer bar from the vehicle.
4. Remove the nut securing the link to the stabilizer bar.

Ball Joint Turning Torque Check

1. Shake the ball joint stud several times, then install the nut to the stud.
2. Using a preload socket and torque wrench check the turning torque of the ball joint.
   Standard Value: NM - NP .... 0.5 - 2.0 Nm
   NS - NT .... 4.9 - 19.6 Nm
3. If measured value exceeds the standard value replace the stabilizer link.
4. If measured value is lower than standard value, check to ensure ball joint turns smoothly and does not have excessive play. The ball joint can be used if checks are OK.

Installation

1. Install the stabilizer bar into position and position the bushes in the clamps as shown. The slit needs to face towards the rear of the vehicle.
2. Install and tighten the stabilizer bar clamp mounting bolts.
   Stabilizer Bar Clamp Bolts .... 44 +/- 10 Nm
3. Replace the stabilizer bar link to lower member and stabilizer bar, tighten retaining nuts to specification.

Stabilizer Bar Link Nuts:
NM-NP .... 108 +/- 10 Nm
NS .... 130 +/- 10 Nm

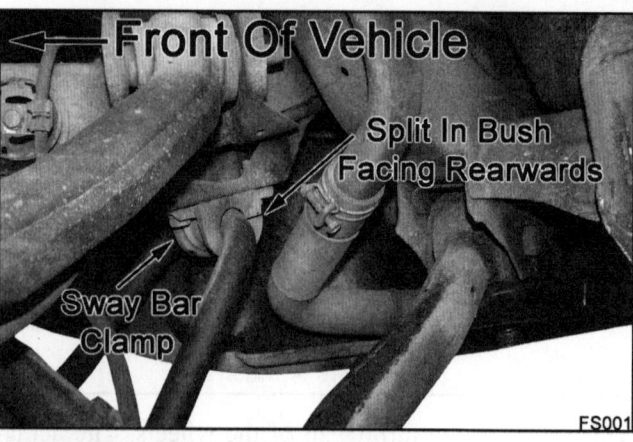

SUSPENSION UPPER ARM

Removal

1. Raise front of vehicle and support on safety stands.
2. Remove the front wheels and wheel speed sensor mounting brackets on models with ABS, and the clip retaining the brake hose. On models with headlamp automatic levelling system remove the connection to the upper arm.
3. Remove the upper arm to knuckle ball joint nut split pin. Do not fully remove the nut, use a ball joint splitter to break the hold of the ball joint. Then fully remove the nut.
4. Remove the upper control arm mounting bolts and nuts. Remove the control arm from vehicle. 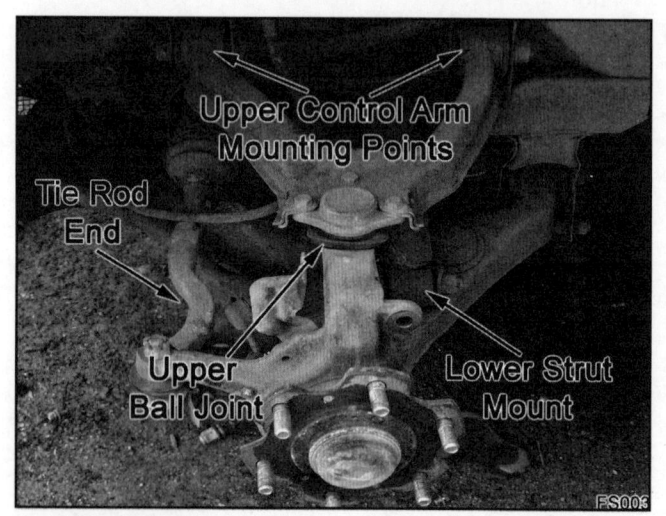
5. (If required) Remove the three bolts retaining the upper ball joint to the control arm and remove ball joint.

Ball Joint Turning Torque Check

1. Shake the ball joint stud several times, then install the nut to the stud.
2. Using a preload socket and torque wrench check the turning torque of the ball joint.

FRONT SUSPENSION, AXLE & DRIVESHAFT ASSEMBLIES

    Standard Value: NM - NP .... 0.4 - 2.5 Nm
                                  NS .... 0.4 - 5.6 Nm

3. If measured value exceeds the standard value replace the upper arm ball joint assembly.
4. If measured value is lower than standard value, check to ensure ball joint turns smoothly and does not have excessive play. Can be used if OK.

Installation
1. Install ball joint to upper control arm if removed and tighten retaining bolts to specification.
   Ball Joint to Upper Arm Bolts:
      NM - NP .... 30 +/- 4 Nm
      NS - NT .... 40 +/- 4 Nm
2. Install the upper arm assembly into position, then install the arm to frame bolts (do not fully tighten bolts).
3. Install the knuckle assembly to the upper arm ball joint, tighten retaining nut to specification then install new split pin.
   Upper Arm Ball Joint Nut:
      NM - NP .... 74 +/- 14 Nm
      NS - NT .... 75 +/- 15 Nm
4. Install the wheel speed sensor mounting brackets and the brake hose retaining clip.
5. On models equipped with headlamp automatic levelling system reinstall the connection to the upper arm.
   Mounting Nut .... 8.0 +/- 1.0 Nm
6. Lower vehicle and tighten the retaining nuts and bolts to specification with vehicle in unladen condition.
   Upper Arm to Frame Bolts:
      NM - NP .... 147 +/- 10 Nm
      NS - NT .... 108 +/- 12 Nm
7. Once the work is carried out the service procedures at the start of this chapter should carried out.

SUSPENSION LOWER ARM
Removal
1. Raise front of vehicle and support on safety stands, then remove the wheels. On vehicles fitted with headlamp automatic levelling system remove the connection to the upper arm.
2. Remove the skid and protection plates from under the front of the vehicle. Remove the front driveshafts, refer to Front Driveshaft removal section featured further in the chapter for assistance.
3. Remove the split pin and loosen the nut for the lower arm ball joint.
4. Remove the split pin from the tie rod end ball joint, then loosen the ball joint nut to the end of the thread.
5. Using a ball joint splitter tool separate the lower ball joint and tie rod end ball joint from the knuckle assembly. Then fully remove retaining nut.
6. Remove the bolts retaining the upper arm ball joint to the upper arm.
7. Remove knuckle assembly from vehicle.
8. Remove the lower strut retaining bolt, then remove the bump stopper if required.
9. Disconnect stabilizer link to lower arm assembly.
10. Before removing the lower arm mounting bolts place a mark on the adjuster bolt and frame, to help with re-assembly.

Ball Joint Turning Torque Check
1. Shake the ball joint stud several times, then install the nut to the stud.
2. Using a preload socket and torque wrench check the turning torque of the ball joint.
   Standard Value: NM - NP .... 0.3 - 4.5 Nm
                                   NS - NT .... 1.0 - 6.9 Nm
3. If measured value exceeds the standard value replace the upper arm ball joint assembly.
4. If measured value is lower than standard value, check to ensure ball joint turns smoothly and does not have excessive play. Can be used if OK.

Installation
Note: *The lower control arm to frame bolts/nuts and the lower shock absorber bolt/nut should not be tightened to specification until vehicle is lowered to the ground.*

1. Install the lower arm into position and install the arm to frame mounting bolts (Use the marks made on removal as a guide. Do not fully tighten). If the ball joint has been replaced do the nuts up to specified torque.
   Ball Joint Mounting Nuts:
      NM - NP .... 95 +/- 11 Nm
      NS - NT .... 125 +/- 25 Nm
2. Reconnect the stabilizer link to lower arm assembly.
   Stabilizer Bar Link Nut:
      NM - NP .... 108 +/- 10Nm
      NS - NT .... 130 +/- 10 Nm
3. Install the bump stopper. Then reconnect the lower shock absorber (do not fully tighten nut).
4. Fit the lower arm to knuckle assembly and tighten ball joint bolt to specification and install a new split pin.
   Lower Ball Joint Nut:
      NM - NP .... 147 +/- 29 Nm
      NS - NT .... 100 +/- 40 Nm
5. Fit the upper arm ball joint to the upper arm and tighten bolts to specification.
   Upper Ball Joint Mounting Bolts:
      NM - NP .... 30 +/- 4 Nm
      NS - NT .... 40 +/- 4 Nm

FRONT SUSPENSION, AXLE & DRIVESHAFT ASSEMBLIES

6. Fit the tie rod end to knuckle assembly and tighten ball joint bolt to specification and install a new split pin.
   Tie Rod Ball Joint Nut:
   NM - NP .... 39 +/- 4 Nm
   NS - NT .... 47 +/- 13 Nm
7. Install the front driveshaft, refer to Driveshaft Installation section for assistance. On models equipped with headlamp automatic levelling system reinstall the connection to the upper arm.
   Mounting Nut .... 8.0 +/- 1.0 Nm
8. Lower vehicle and tighten the lower control arm and strut nuts and bolts to specification with vehicle in unladen condition.
   Lower Arm to Frame Bolt/Nut:
   NM - NP .... 123 +/- 14 Nm
   NS - NT .... 145 +/- 10 Nm
   Lower Strut Bolt/Nut:
   NM - NP .... 162 +/- 14 Nm
   NS - NT .... 133 +/- 12 Nm
9. Replace the under cover and skid plate.
10. Once all work is carried out, the checks at the start of this chapter needs to be carried out.

FRONT STRUT ASSEMBLY

Removal
1. Raise front of vehicle and support on safety stands, then remove the wheels from the vehicle.
2. Remove the upper suspension arm assembly as described previously.
3. From the engine bay remove the battery and battery tray, reservoir tank and air cleaner, depending on which side you are working on.
4. From inside the engine bay remove the centre cap then remove the three upper strut assembly retaining nuts.
5. Remove the lower shock absorber mounting bolt and remove assembly from vehicle.

Disassembly
1. Compress the coil spring using a suitable spring compressor, then remove the strut assembly lock nut. To prevent the shaft from turning use a pair of multi-grips or shifter on the upper flat section above the thread.
   Note: It is not recommended to use a impact wrench as damage can be done to the strut assembly.
2. Slowly release the spring compressor and then separate the strut assembly components. First remove the seat, followed by the collar, upper bush, spring bracket assembly, upper pad, cup assembly, and helper rubber.
3. Remove the spring and lower pad. Keep parts in order to help when re-assembling unit.

Inspection
1. Check all rubber components for damage, wear and distortion.
2. Check springs for loss of tension, cracks, fractures and any other signs of deterioration.
3. Check the struts for leaking fluid.
   Important: *If a spring or strut needs to be replaced they should always be replaced in pairs and with ones of the same rating.*

Assembly
1. Install the lower pad, compress the coil spring using a suitable spring compressor. Place on the strut taking note of the stepped section for the coil end to sit in.
2. Carefully assemble the strut assembly components as shown. The helper rubber goes on next followed by the cup assembly, upper pad, spring bracket assembly. With the spring bracket assembly make sure to line up the indents on the upper pad with the bottom of the spring bracket.
3. Install the upper bush, collar and seat to the strut.
4. On the strut assembly loosely install the self locking nut, then release spring compressors and tighten the nut to specification. If reusing the old strut make sure to use a new locking nut.
   Strut Locking Nut: NM - NP .... 22 +/- 2 Nm
   NS - NT .... 25 +/- 5 Nm

Installation
1. Install the strut into the vehicle and support in position then install the strut insulator to body nuts, tighten to specification.
   Strut Assembly To Body Nuts .... 44 +/- 5 Nm
2. Install the lower arm to strut assembly bolt and partially tighten nut.
   Note: Do not fully tighten mounting nut until the vehicle is on the ground in unladen position.
3. In the engine bay install the air cleaner, reservoir tank, battery tray and battery depending which side you are working on.
4. Install the upper arm assembly as described previously.
5. Install the front wheels, tightening wheel nuts to specification, then remove safety stands and lower vehicle.
6. With the vehicle in the unladen position tighten lower strut nut and upper arm to specification.
   Lower Strut bolt/nut:
   NM - NP .... 162 +/- 14 Nm
   NS - NT .... 133 +/- 12 Nm
7. Once all work is done the notes at the start of the suspension chapter need to be performed.

FRONT AXLE ASSEMBLY

WHEEL BEARING BACKLASH CHECK

1. Jack up front of vehicle. Then place safety stands under the front body jacking points and remove wheels.
2. Remove the front brake caliper bracket attaching bolts, lift the caliper off the disc and tie the caliper out of the way. Do not leave the caliper hanging by the brake fluid hose, as this may damage the hose.
3. Remove the brake disc from the hub assembly.
4. Using a dial gauge move the hub in and out to measure movement, checking it is within specification.
   Wheel Bearing Backlash Limit......................0mm
6. If limit is exceeded, dismantle the hub assembly and inspect each component.
7. Replace the front hub assembly if the bearing is faulty.

FRONT AXLE TOTAL BACKLASH CHECK

1. a) On NM - NP models turn the ignition switch to OFF position and then place the transfer shift lever in the 2H position.
   Note: *Do not jack up the vehicle.*
   b) On NS - NT models turn the ignition switch to on position and then put transfer lever to 2H position. Turn the ignition switch to lock (off) position.
   Note: *Do not jack up the vehicle.*

2. Turn the propeller shaft clockwise until a click is heard, then turn the companion flange clockwise to remove all play.
3. Put mating marks on the companion flange and differential carrier.
4. Turn the companion flange anti-clockwise until all play is removed, place another mark on the differential carrier in line with the mark on the companion flange, then measure the difference in the mating marks.
   Front Axle Backlash Limit..........................11mm
5. If limit is exceeded inspect the following.
   - Final drive gear backlash
   - Differential gear backlash
   - Play in the splines of the side gears, drive shaft, inner shaft and drive flange.

FRONT AXLE GEAR OIL LEVEL CHECK

1. Remove the filler plug and inspect the height of oil, ensuring it is within specification.
   Oil Level not lower than 8mm from the bottom of the filler hole
2. If level is below limit top up with correct grade oil.
   Specified Oil.... Hypoid Gear GL-5, SAE90/W80
3. Replace the filler plug doing it up to specification.
   Front Axle Filler Plug........................50 +/- 10 Nm

SOLENOID VALVE OPERATION CHECK

1. From the solenoid valves remove the vacuum hoses (blue stripe, yellow stripe only), then disconnect the electrical connections.
2. To the disconnected port of solenoid valve A connect a hand pump and perform the following:

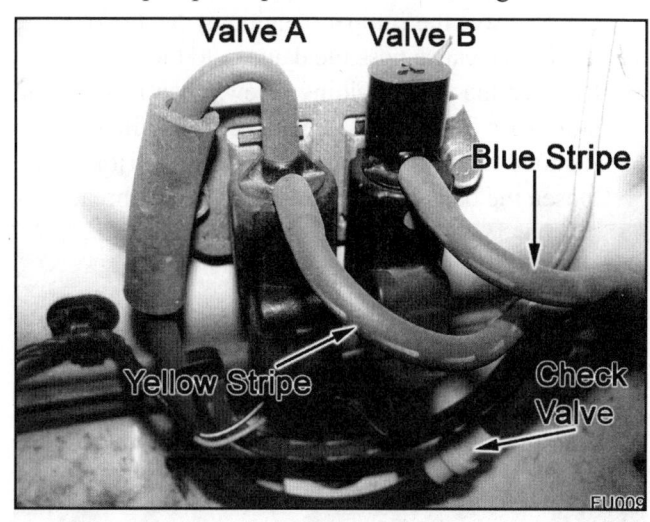

   a) Negative pressure does not develop when only the hand pump is operated.
   b) Apply battery voltage to valve A, negative pressure does not develop.
   c) Negative pressure is maintained when battery voltage is applied to solenoid valves A and B.

3. To disconnected port of solenoid valve B connect a hand pump, apply negative pressure and perform the following checks:

   a) Negative pressure is maintained when only hand pump is operated.
   b) Apply battery voltage to valve B, negative pressure disappears.
   c) Apply battery voltage to valve A, negative pressure disappears.

4. Measure solenoid valve resistance.
   Solenoid valve resistance.................36 - 46 Ohms

FRONT SUSPENSION, AXLE & DRIVESHAFT ASSEMBLIES

FRONT HUB & KNUCKLE ASSEMBLY
Removal
1. Jack up front of vehicle. Then place safety stands under the front body jacking points and remove wheels.
2. Remove the hub cap then remove the drive shaft nut split pin, castle nut and washer if fitted. On NS models there is a cover for the castle nut.
   Note: A special tool Mitsubishi part number MB990767 is used to stop the rotor from turning as the drive shaft nut is removed. Do not use the weight of the vehicle as damaged can be done to the bearing.
3. Remove the bracket for the brake hose and vehicle speed sensor, then remove the wheel speed sensor on vehicle fitted with ABS.
4. Remove the front brake caliper bracket attaching bolts, lift the calliper off the disc and tie it up out of the way. Do not leave the calliper hanging by the brake hose, as this can cause possible damage to the hose.
5. Remove the disc retaining screws then remove the brake disc followed by the dust cover if fitted.
6. Remove the split pin from the tie rod end ball joint, then loosen the ball joint nut to the end of the thread.

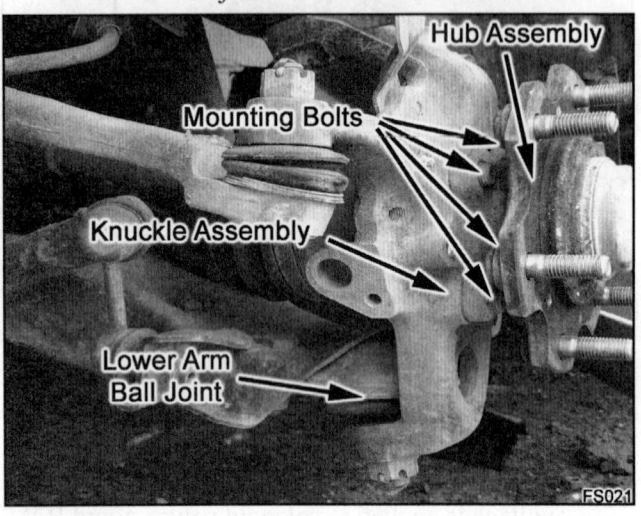

7. Using a ball joint splitter tool separate the tie rod ball joint from the knuckle assembly. Then fully remove retaining nut.
8. On vehicles fitted with headlamp automatic levelling system remove the connection to the upper arm.
9. Remove the split pin from the upper arm ball joint, then loosen the ball joint nut to the end of the thread.
10. Using a ball joint splitter tool separate the ball joint from the knuckle assembly. Then fully remove retaining nut.
11. Remove the split pin from the lower arm ball joint, then loosen the ball joint nut to the end of the thread.
12. Using a ball joint splitter tool separate the ball joint from the knuckle assembly. Then fully remove retaining nut.
13. Vehicle fitted with ABS remove the rotor protector, then remove the hub and knuckle assembly from the vehicle, making sure not to damage the thread on the drive shaft.

Disassembly
1. Remove the bolts retaining the front hub assembly to the knuckle and separate. On some models there is a dust cover and a front inner oil seal (LWB).

Inspect and Clean
1. Clean all components with a solvent solution and dry.
2. Inspect the knuckle assembly for damage and cracks.
3. Inspect the hub assembly for damage, cracks and worn drive shaft spline.
   Note: The hub assembly needs to be changed as a unit, the bearings are not interchangeable.

Hub Rotation Starting Torque Check
1. To the knuckle and hub assembly install the special Tool (MB990998) and tighten to specification.
   Specified Special Tool Tightening Torque:
   NM - NP .... 255 +/- 29 Nm
   NS - NT .... 220 +/- 10 Nm
   Note: Special tool is a Mitsubishi Tool. The tool is used to put pressure on the bearings in the hub to check rotation starting torque.
2. Using a preload socket and torque wrench check the starting torque.
   Hub Rotation Torque Limit:
   NM - NP .... 1.75 Nm or Less
   NS - NT (SWB) .... 3.0 Nm or Less
   NS - NT (LWB) .... 3.5 Nm or Less
3. Starting torque must be below the limit and should be smooth when rotating.

Wheel Bearing Axial Play Check
1. With the knuckle assembly mounted in a vice with the special tool installed as used in previous procedure, measure backlash using a dial gauge.
2. If limit value cannot be obtained when tighten to specification, inspect hub and knuckle assembly mounting bolt and replace hub assembly if no defects are found.
   Special Tool Tightening Torque:
   NM - NP .... 255 +/- 29 Nm
   NS - NT .... 220 +/- 10 Nm

Assembly
1. Install the front hub assembly to the knuckle assembly and tighten retaining bolts to specification.
   Knuckle to Hub Bolts:
   NM - NP .... 88 +/- 10 Nm
   NS - NT .... 90 +/- 10 Nm

FRONT SUSPENSION, AXLE & DRIVESHAFT ASSEMBLIES

2. On models with dust cover make sure to install the cover before doing up the retaining bolts.
3. On models with a front oil seal make sure to fit a new seal. The seal needs to have grease put around the inside of the seal where it contacts with the drive shaft before installing on vehicle.

Installation

1. Install the hub and knuckle assembly into position and install the rotor protector to ABS fitted vehicles.
2. Fit the lower arm to knuckle assembly and tighten ball joint bolt to specification and install a new split pin.
   Lower Ball Joint Nut:
   NM - NP..........................147 +/- 29 Nm
   NS - NT..........................100 +/- 40 Nm
3. Fit the upper arm to knuckle assembly and tighten ball joint bolt to specification and install a new split pin.
   Upper Ball Joint Nut:
   NM - NP..........................74 +/- 14 Nm
   NS - NT..........................75 +/- 15 Nm
4. Fit the tie rod end to knuckle assembly and tighten ball joint bolt to specification and install a new split pin.
   Tie Rod Ball Joint Nut:
   NM - NP..........................39 +/- 4 Nm
   NS - NT..........................47 +/- 13 Nm
5. Install the dust cover then install the brake disc tightening retaining bolts to specification,
   Dust Cover Bolts:
   NM - NP..........................8.9 +/- 1.9 Nm
   NS - NT..........................9.0 +/- 2.0 Nm
   Brake Disc Screws..........................5.0 +/- 1.0 Nm
6. Replace the front brake caliper and tighten retaining bolts to specification.
   Brake Caliper Bolts:
   NM - NP..........................113 +/- 10 Nm
   NS - NT..........................115 +/- 10 Nm
7. Install the wheel speed sensor to vehicles fitted with ABS, then install the bracket clamp for the brake hose.
   Wheel Speed Sensor..........................11 +/- 2 Nm
8. Install the drive shaft washer ensuring it is fitted the correct way (the smaller side facing out), then install a new castle nut and tighten to specification. On models fitted with a castle nut cover make sure to fit it correctly.
   Drive Shaft Nut:
   NM - NP..........................255 +/- 29 Nm
   NS - NT..........................220 +/- 10 Nm
9. Install a new drive shaft nut split pin, the install the hub cap into place so it sits flush.
10. Replace the wheels and lower vehicle.
11. The checks at the start of the chapter need to be done before driving the vehicle any great distance.

FRONT DRIVE SHAFT

Removal

1. For drive shaft removal refer to hub and knuckle assembly removal. Once hub and knuckle are removed go on to next step.
2. Drain the oil from the front differential.
3. **RHS** - Remove the nuts securing the drive shaft to the differential housing, then remove the driveshaft assembly.
4. **LHS** - Remove the cir-clip, then remove drive shaft from the vehicle being careful the drive shaft spline does not damage the oil seal.

Disassembly

1. Remove the large and small boot clamps, then remove the circlip and the D.O.J outer race.
2. From the drive shaft remove the snap ring with snap ring pliers then remove the inner race, cage and ball assembly.
3. Remove the D.O.J boot, firstly tape the shaft splines to prevent damage to the boot on removal.

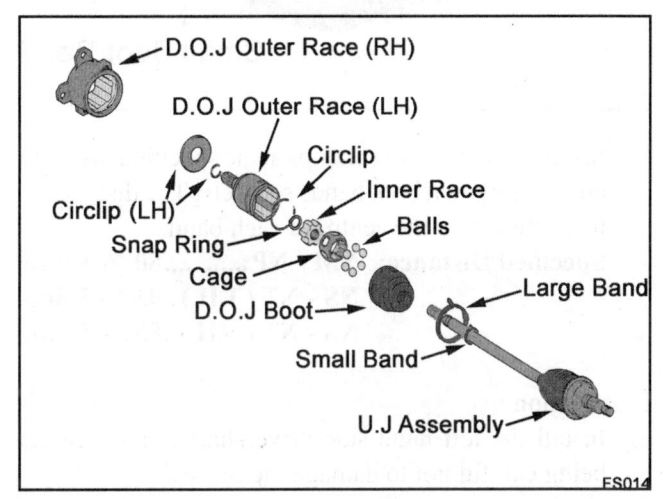

325

FRONT SUSPENSION, AXLE & DRIVESHAFT ASSEMBLIES

4. Remove the large and small U.J boot bands and then remove the U.J boot.
   Note: *Never disassemble the U.J assembly, only replace the boot if needed. The U.J assembly is a change over item.*

Inspection
1. Inspect the splines for wear.
2. Inspect boots for deterioration, tears and cracks.
3. Inspect joints for smooth operation and replace any components which are defective.

Assembly
Note: *Boot repair kits can be purchased from the dealer, new bands should be used on reassembly.*
1. Install the UJ boot onto the shaft.
2. Pack the UJ joint and boot with grease, and fully install the boot into position.
3. Install new bands and fasten the large and small UJ boot bands.
4. Install the D.O.J boot, firstly ensuring to tape the shaft splines to prevent damage to the boot.
5. Pack the inner race and ball assembly with specified grease (supplied in repair kit).
   Specified Grease: .... **Repair Kit Grease**
6. Install the inner race and ball assembly and secure with snap ring.
7. Install the D.O.J outer race, packed with specified grease (supplied in repair kit), then install the circlip.

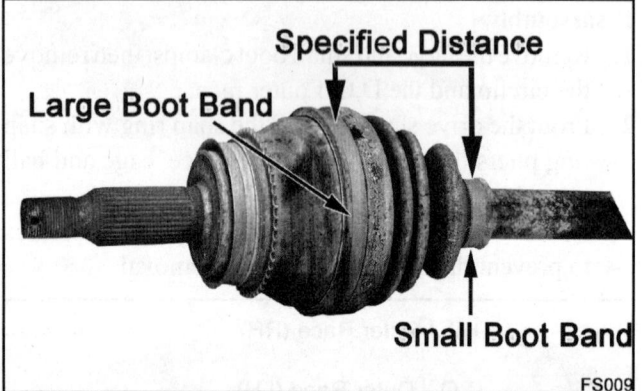

8. Install the D.O.J boot clamps at the specified distance and then tighten boot bands securely. The distance is measured from the centre of each band.
   Specified Distance: NM - NP .... 80 +/- 5 mm
   NS - NT (LH) .. 93 +/- 5 mm
   NS - NT (RH) .. 85 +/- 5 mm

Installation
1. Install the left hand side drive shaft to the vehicle being careful not to damage the oil seal.
2. On the right hand side install the shaft into place, then do up nuts to specification.
   RHS Drive Shaft Nuts To Housing .. 60 +/- 10 Nm
3. Fit the upper arm and lower arm to the knuckle assembly and tighten ball joints to specification and install new split pins.
4. Install the wheel speed sensor to vehicles fitted with ABS, then install the bracket clamp for the brake hose.
5. Install the drive shaft washer ensuring it is fitted the correct way, then install the nut and tighten to specification.
   Drive Shaft Nut: NM-NP .... 255 +/- 29 Nm
   NS - NT .... 220 +/- 10 Nm
6. Install the drive shaft nut split pin and hub cap.
7. Fit the tie rod end to knuckle assembly and tighten ball joint bolt to specification and install a new split pin.
8. Replace the front brake caliper and tighten retaining bolts to specification.
9. To the lower arm connect the shock absorber and stabilizer bar link. On models equipped with headlamp automatic levelling system reinstall the connection to the upper arm.
10. Fill up the differential with new gear oil as described earlier in the front axle assembly section.
11. Install the undercover protection plate under the front of the vehicle.
12. Replace the wheels and lower vehicle.
13. The checks at the start of the chapter will need to be done.

INNER SHAFT, HOUSING TUBE
Removal
1. Jack up front of vehicle. Then place safety stands under the front body jacking points and remove wheels.
2. Remove the skid and protection plates from under the front of the vehicle. The gear oil will need to be drained from differential assembly before commencing work.
3. Remove the right-hand drive shaft as described previously in this chapter.

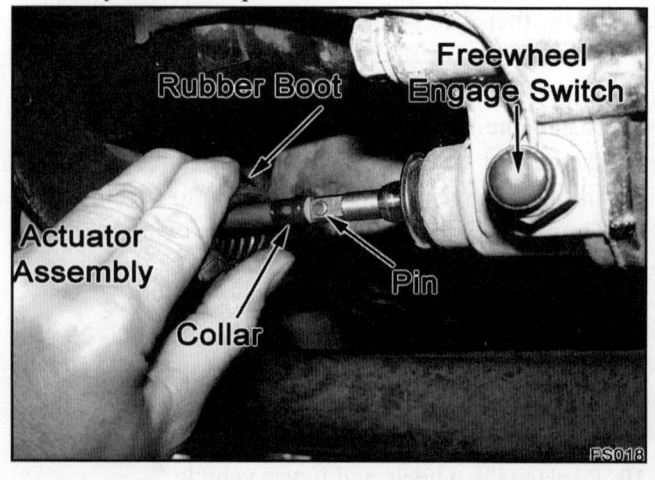

FRONT SUSPENSION, AXLE & DRIVESHAFT ASSEMBLIES

4. Remove the inner shaft from the differential carrier being careful not to damage the oil seal.
   Note: *A slide hammer and suitable adapter will be required to remove the shaft.*
5. Slide back the rubber boot and remove the collar and pin from the actuator assembly. Use a small punch to remove the pin. Then undo the bolts retaining the actuator and remove.
6. Remove the vacuum tank then disconnect and remove the free wheel engage switch assembly.
7. Using a floor jack and piece of wood support the differential carrier, then loosen the differential mounting insulator bolts.
8. Remove the bolts connecting the right hand differential mounting bracket to the housing tube and remove.

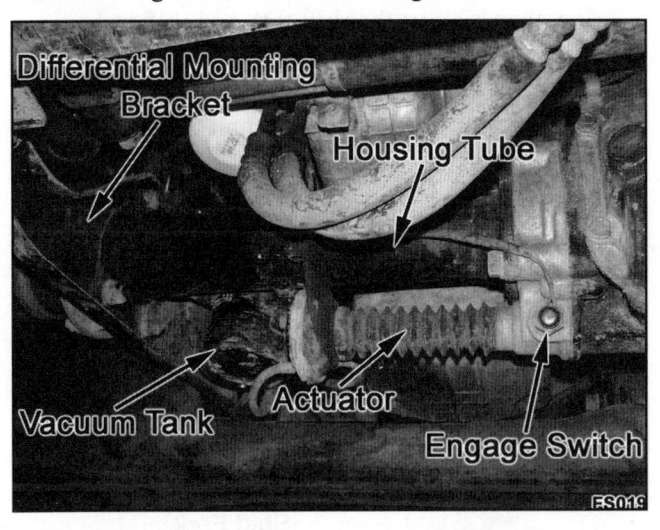

9. Remove the breather tube brackets then remove the housing tube assembly.

Disassembly

1. With the inner shaft removed, bend inward the outer perimeter of the dust cover by taping with a hammer so the bearing removal tool can grip on the bearing.
2. Install a bearing remover to the assembly and tighten until the tool touches the outer race.
3. Use a press to remove the bearing from the shaft.
4. Remove the dust seal from the end of the housing tube.

Assembly

1. Using an oil seal installer press the new dust seal onto the housing tube until it is sitting flush with the housing tube end face.
2. Install a new dust cover to the inner shaft using a steel pipe with the specified dimensions.
   Steel Pipe: - Length .... 50 mm
                    - Outside Diameter .... 75 mm
                    - Wall Thickness .... 4 mm
3. Press the bearing onto the inner shaft using a bearing installer and press.

Installation

1. Install the housing tube and tighten retaining bolts to the carrier housing.
   Housing Tube to Carrier Bolts:
   NM - NP .... 90 +/- 10 Nm
   NS - NT .... 93 +/- 12 Nm
2. Install the breather pipe and tighten pipe retaining bolts to specification.
   Breather pipe bolts .... 12 +/- 2 Nm
3. Install the differential mounting bracket to the housing tube and tighten retaining nuts/bolts to specification.
   Bracket to Housing Tube Nuts .... 89 +/- 9 Nm
4. Install the differential mounting insulator bolts and partially tighten.
   Note: *Do not fully tighten mounting bolts until the vehicle is on the ground in unladen position.*
5. Install the free wheel engage switch assembly tightening the switch to specification, then install the vacuum tank assembly.
   Free Wheel Engage switch:
   NM - NP .... 25 +/- 5 Nm
   Vacuum Tank Bolts:
   NM - NP .... 12 +/- 2 Nm
   NS - NT .... 11 +/- 2 Nm
6. Install the actuator assembly and tighten the mounting bolts to specification, then install the collar and pin to the actuator assembly.
   Actuator Bolts:
   NM - NP .... 17 +/- 3 Nm
   NS - NT .... 20 +/- 4 Nm
7. Install the cir-clip, then install the inner shaft, being careful not to damage the dust and oil seals.
8. Install the drive shaft as described previously, refill the differential with oil and then install wheels and lower vehicle.
9. Tighten the differential mounting insulator bolts to specification with the vehicle in unladen position.
   Differential Mounting Bolts:
   NM - NP .... 69 +/- 9 Nm
   NS - NT .... 80 +/- 10 Nm
   Note: *Do bolts up one at a time, going from one to the other in a clockwise direction.*
10. Install the skid and protection plates to under the front of the vehicle.

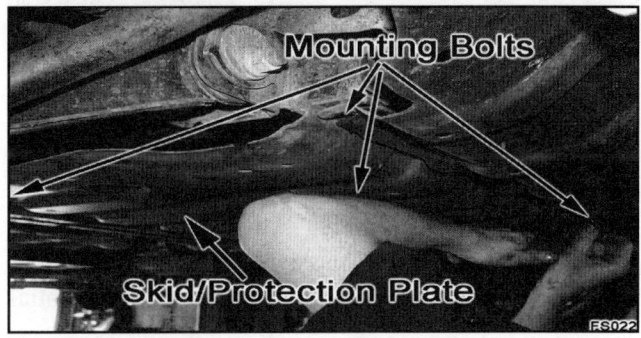

FRONT SUSPENSION, AXLE & DRIVESHAFT ASSEMBLIES

FREEWHEEL CLUTCH AND DIFFERENTIAL CARRIER
Removal

1. Jack up front of vehicle. Then place safety stands under the front body jacking points and remove wheels.
2. Remove the skid and protection plates from under the front of the vehicle.
3. Drain the gear oil then remove the drive shafts and inner shafts as described previously in this chapter.
4. Disconnect the front propeller shaft from the differential carrier, ensuring to first mark the relationship of the flanges for assembly and hang shaft from wire to prevent damage to joint and boot. 
5. Support the differential carrier assembly with a jack, then remove the through bolts securing the front of the differential mounting brackets.
6. Remove the bolts retaining the front frame and No.2 cross-member assembly. 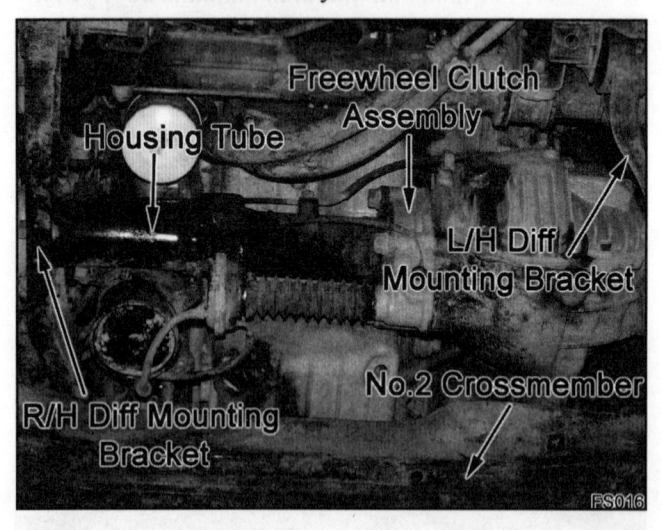
7. Disconnect the vacuum hose connections.
8. Remove the collar, then using an appropriate pin punch remove the pin from the freewheel engage switch.
9. Remove the switch assembly for the freewheel engagement.
10. Remove the bolts securing the housing tube assembly to the freewheel clutch assembly and any remaining bracket mounting bolts and remove the differential mounting bracket and housing tube assembly.
11. Remove the freewheel clutch assembly from the differential carrier then remove the LHS differential mounting bracket.
12. Carefully lower and remove the differential carrier assembly from the vehicle.
13. Remove the No. 2 crossmember assembly.

FREEWHEEL CLUTCH ASSEMBLY
Disassembly

1. Using a press and appropriate clamps, press the main shaft from the bearing being careful not to allow the main shaft to drop.
2. Remove the clutch sleeve followed by the spacer.
3. From the shift rod remove the spring pin and snap ring, then remove the shift fork and shift rod.
4. From the clutch housing remove the shift rod oil seal.
5. Using a press and steel plate press the clutch gear bearing from the clutch gear.
6. From the clutch housing remove the oil seal.

Assembly

1. Carefully install the oil seals to the clutch housing until they are flush with the surface being careful not to damage the seal. 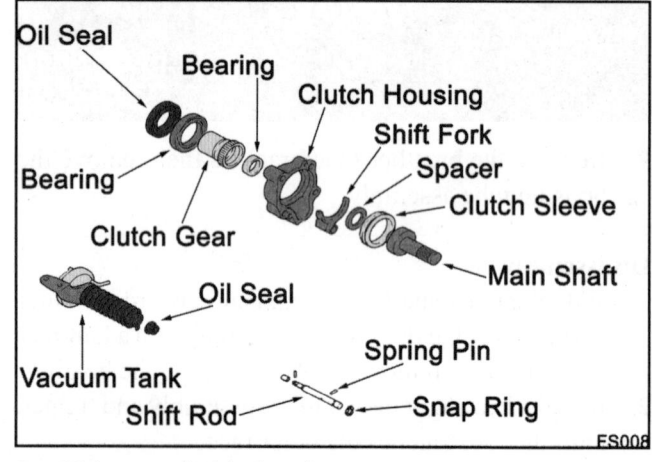
2. Using a suitable bearing press, press the bearing to the shoulder of the clutch gear.
4. Install the shift rod followed by the shift fork and snap ring.
5. Insert the spring pin from the chamfered side of the shift rod and tap into position.
6. Using a press, press the bearing to the shoulder of the main shaft.
7. Install the spacer and clutch sleeve, then install the main shaft assembly to the clutch housing.

DIFFERENTIAL CARRIER

PRE-DISASSEMBLY INSPECTION
From the differential housing remove the cover and gasket, then mount the assembly in a vice using appropriate mounting adaptor. Carry out the following procedures before disassembly of the unit.

DRIVE GEAR BACKLASH CHECK
1. With the drive pinion locked, use a dial gauge to measure the drive gear backlash in at least 4 places.
   Standard Drive Gear Backlash.....0.11 - 0.16 mm
2. If not within specification adjust backlash using the information in the assembly section later on in this chapter.

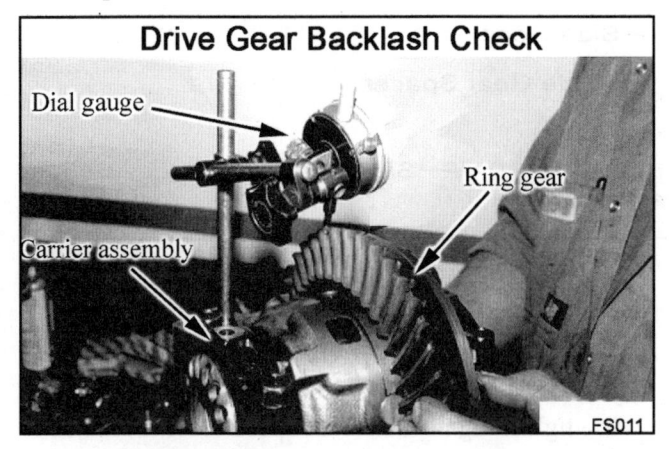

3. After adjustment has been carried out check the drive gear tooth contact.

DRIVE GEAR TOOTH CONTACT CHECK
1. Coat both sides of the drive gear teeth with an even coat of gear marking compound.
2. Insert the brass tool MB990939 between the differential carrier and case.
3. By hand rotate the companion flange one full revolution in each direction, while applying a load to the drive gear to achieve a revolution torque of approximately **2.5 - 3 Nm** to the drive pinion.
4. Inspect drive gear and drive pinion tooth contact pattern.

DRIVE GEAR RUN-OUT CHECK
1. Measure the run-out of the drive gear at the shoulder of the gear on the reverse side.
   Drive Gear Run-out Limit.......................0.05 mm
2. If limit value is exceeded inspect for foreign objects between the drive gear side and differential case, or loose installation bolts.

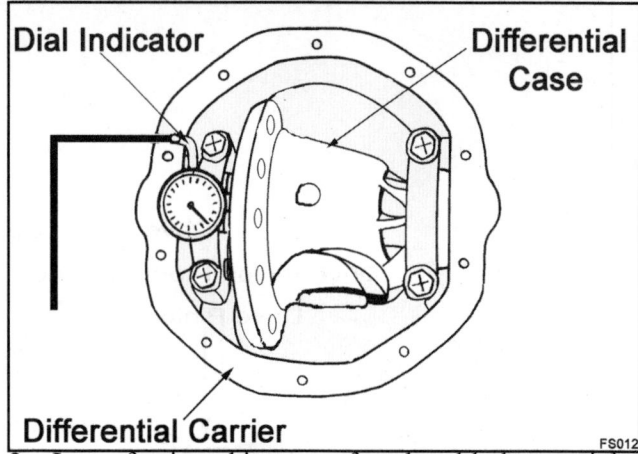

3. In no foreign objects are found and bolts are tight, reposition the drive gear and differential case and re-measure.
4. Replace the differential case or drive gear and pinion as a set if adjustment cannot be achieved.

DIFFERENTIAL GEAR BACKLASH CHECK
1. Use a wedge to lock the side gear, then using a dial indicator on the pinion gear measure the differential gear backlash.
2. Repeat for both pinion gears.
   Standard value:
   NM - NP ....0.0 - 0.076 mm
   NS - NT ....0.01 - 0.250 mm
   Limit..0.2 mm
3. If limit is exceeded use side gear thrust spacers to correct. If adjustment is not possible replace the side gear and pinion gear as a set.

DISASSEMBLY
Note: *Make sure to place all parts on the bench in the order of removal*
1. Ensure the assembly is mounted in a vice with the cover removed as described in the pre-disassembly inspection.
2. Undo the bolts of the bearing caps and carefully remove the differential case assembly, being careful not to drop the side bearing outer races.
3. Mount the differential case assembly securely in a vice.
4. From the case assembly remove the side bearing spacer and then remove the outer race.
   Note: *Keep spacers and outer bearing racers separated so they don't get mixed up during assembly.*
5. Using an appropriate puller carefully remove the side bearing inner race from the case assembly.
   Note: *There is two notches under the bearing for the claws of the bearing puller to locate.*
6. Mark with white out the relationship of the drive gear to differential case, then loosen the drive gear retaining bolts in a diagonal sequence and remove drive gear

FRONT SUSPENSION, AXLE & DRIVESHAFT ASSEMBLIES

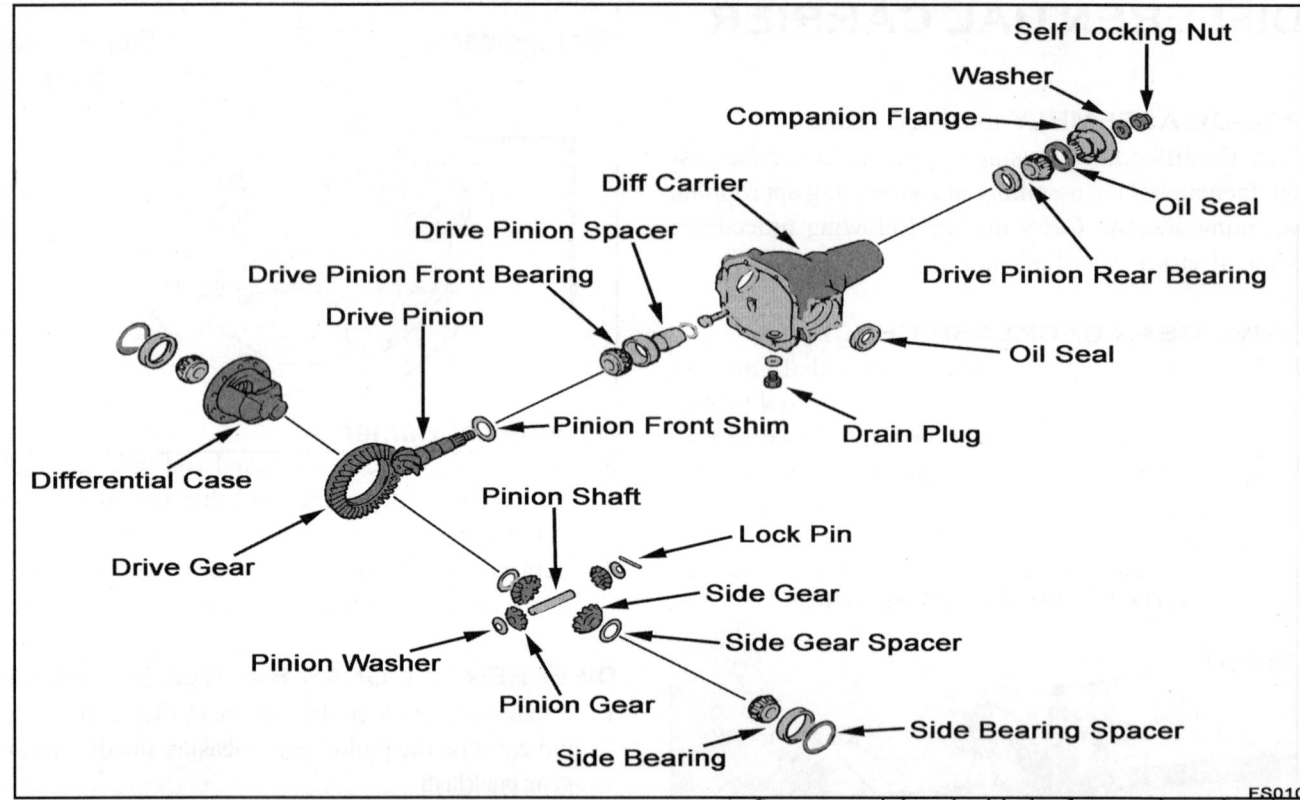

Exploded diagram of differential assembly showing: Self Locking Nut, Washer, Companion Flange, Diff Carrier, Drive Pinion Spacer, Drive Pinion Front Bearing, Drive Pinion, Oil Seal, Drive Pinion Rear Bearing, Oil Seal, Pinion Front Shim, Drain Plug, Differential Case, Drive Gear, Pinion Shaft, Lock Pin, Side Gear, Side Gear Spacer, Pinion Washer, Pinion Gear, Side Bearing, Side Bearing Spacer.

from assembly.

7. From the differential carrier remove the companion flange self-locking nut and washer, it will be necessary to hold the companion flange with an appropriate tool.
8. Mark the relationship of the drive pinion and companion flange, then using an appropriate puller remove the pinion assembly.
9. Remove the companion flange.
10. From the pinion assembly remove the drive pinion spacer and rear shim.
11. Using a bearing puller remove the drive pinion front bearing inner race, then remove the front shim from the drive pinion.
12. From the differential carrier remove the oil seal, drive pinion rear bearing inner race and outer race.
13. From the carrier assembly remove the drive pinion front bearing outer race, then remove the oil seal from the side of the carrier.
14. From the differential case remove the lock pin using a hammer and punch.
15. From differential case remove the pinion shaft, then remove the pinion gears and washers.
16. Remove the side gears and side gear spacers from the differential case.

ASSEMBLY

1. To the differential carrier install the side oil seal, then press fit the drive pinion front bearing outer race and the drive pinion rear bearing outer race.
2. Adjust the drive pinion height as follows:
   a) Set up special tool with the front and rear bearing inner races installed as shown in diagram, ensuring to coat the washer with multipurpose grease.
   Special tool MB990819
   b) Measure the turning torque of the drive pinion while tightening the nut of the special tool. Continue to tighten until the turning torque is to specification (without oil seal).
   Turning Torque .... 0.83 - 1.19 Nm
   c) Clean the side bearing hub, then install the special tools to the bearing hub of the carrier and install bearing caps.
   d) Measure the clearance between the special tools using a feeler gauge, and record reading as "A".
   Special tools MB991170, MB990819
   e) Remove the two special tools (*MB991170, MB990819*), then use a micrometer to measure the special tool in two positions. Record the readings as B & C.
   f) Install the bearing cap, then using a cylinder gauge and micrometer measure the inside diameter of the bearing cap and record reading as D.
   g) Using the below formula calculate the correct thickness of the drive pinion rear shim.
   E = A+B+C-(0.5D) - 100 mm
   h) To the drive pinion install the correct drive pinion shim/s and press in the drive pinion rear bearing inner race.
3. Adjust the drive pinion turning torque as follows:
   a) To the gear carrier install the drive pinion, drive pinion spacer, drive pinion rear shim, rear bear-

FRONT SUSPENSION, AXLE & DRIVESHAFT ASSEMBLIES

  ing inner race and companion shaft flange (do not install oil seal).
  b) Tighten the companion flange lock nut to specification.
  Companion flange .... 216 +/- 29 Nm
  c) Measure the drive pinion turning torque.
  Drive Pinion Turning Torque... 0.83 - 1.19 Nm
  d) If not within specification adjust preload by replacing the drive pinion front shim/s or drive pinion spacer.
  e) Remove companion flange and drive pinion, then insert drive pinion front bearing inner race to the carrier.
  f) Press fit the oil seal to the front of the carrier assembly, then install the drive pinion assembly and companion flange using aligning marks made on removal.
  g) Tighten the companion flange self locking nut to specification.
  Companion Flange Nut .... 216 +/- 29 Nm
  h) Measure the drive pinion turning torque.
  Drive Pinion Turning Torque:
  - no lubrication .... 0.93 - 1.28 Nm
  - gear oil applied .... 0.97 - 1.32 Nm
  i) If not within specification check the companion flange self locking nut is tightened to specification.
4. Adjust the differential gear backlash as follows:
  a) To the differential case install the side gears, side gear spacers, pinion gears and pinion washers.
  b) temporarily install the pinion shaft to the assembly, then lock the side gear by inserting a wedge between the side gear and pinion shaft.
  c) Using a dial indicator on the pinion gear measure the differential gear backlash.
  d) Repeat for both pinion gears.
  Standard value: NM - NP .... 0.0 - 0.076 mm
                      NS - NT .... 0.01 - 0.250 mm
  e) If limit is exceeded use side gear thrust spacers to correct. If adjustment is not possible replace the side gear and pinion gear as a set.
5. Align the lock pin holes of the pinion shaft with the holes of the case, then drive in the lock pin and stake pin in two places.
6. Ensure the drive gear retaining bolts and bolt hole threads are clean from old stud locking compound.
  Note: *If may be necessary to clean the hole threads using a M10 x 1.25 tap, carefully.*
7. To the differential case install the drive gear aligning marks made on removal, then install and tighten retaining bolts in a diagonal sequence.
  Drive Gear Bolts:
  NM - NP .... 83 +/- 5 Nm
  NS - NT .... 84 +/- 4 Nm

Note: *Apply stud locking compound to the bolt threads before installation.*
8. To the differential case install the side bearing inner races, then install the side gear outer race.
9. Adjust the drive gear backlash as follows:
  a) To the differential case assembly install the same size side bearing spacers (use thinner spacers than those removed), then mount the case assembly into the gear carrier.
  b) Push the case assembly to one side and using a feeler gauge measure the clearance between the gear carrier and the side bearing adjusting spacer.
  c) Measure the thickness of the side bearing adjusting spacers on one side and recheck measurement.
  d) Take the measurement of the spacers, add half the recorded clearance then add 0.05mm.
  e) Using this new thickness measurement, select two set of spacers and install one set to the drive pinion side and the other to the drive gear side.
  f) Install the side bearing adjusting spacers and differential case assembly to the carrier.
  g) Fit the side bearing adjusting spacers to the side bearing outer race by taping with special tool. *(Special tool MB990939)*
  h) Tighten the bearing cap after aligning the mating marks of the carrier and bearing cap.
  Bearing Caps:
  NM - NP .... Not Specified
  NS - NT .... 59 +/- 4 Nm
  i) With the drive pinion locked, use a dial gauge to measure the drive gear backlash in at least 4 places.
  Drive Gear Backlash .... 0.11 - 0.16 mm
  j) Adjust backlash by adjusting the spacers, refer to diagram.

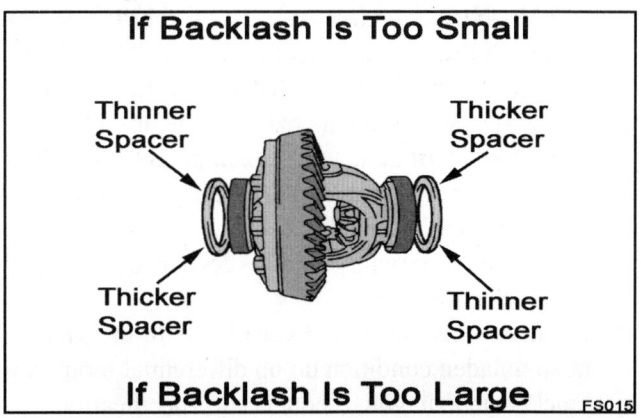

If Backlash Is Too Small
Thinner Spacer — Thicker Spacer
Thicker Spacer — Thinner Spacer
If Backlash Is Too Large

  k) Check the tooth contact of the drive gear and drive pinion and adjust as required.
  l) At the shoulder of the reverse side of the drive gear measure the drive gear run-out.
  Drive Gear Run-out Limit 0.05mm
  m) If limit is exceeded, reinstall changing the phase of the drive gear and differential case.

n) Re-measure, if adjustment is not possible replace the differential case or replace the side gear and pinion gear set.
10. To the differential carrier assembly install the cover using a new gasket, tightening bolts to specification.
    Rear Cover Bolts .... 18 +/- 3Nm
11. If removed install the drain and filler plugs to the assembly making sure to use new washers.
    Drain Plug .... 65 +/- 5Nm
    Filler Plug .... 50 +/- 10Nm

Installation

1. Carefully raise the differential carrier assembly into position under vehicle.
2. Install the freewheel clutch assembly to the differential carrier making sure to use a suitable sealant. Then install the LHS differential mounting bracket to the differential carrier and frame.
   Note: Do not do bolts of differential mounting brackets to specification until vehicle is on the ground in an unladen condition.
   Mounting Bracket To Differential ...... 89 +/- 9 Nm
3. Install the differential mounting bracket and housing tube assembly, tightening housing to clutch assembly bolts to specification.
   Housing Tube to Clutch Assembly .... 90 +/- 10 Nm
   Note: Do not do bolts of differential mounting brackets to specification until vehicle is on the ground in an unladen condition.
4. Install the freewheel engagement switch assembly.
5. Install the pin, then install the collar and reconnect the vacuum hoses.
6. Install the #2 cross-member assembly, tightening the mounting bolts to specification.
   Cross-member Mounting Bolts:
   NM - NP .... 128 +/- 9 Nm
   NS - NT .... 80 +/- 5 Nm
7. Connect the front propeller shaft to the differential carrier, ensuring to align the marks made on removal.
   Propeller Shaft .... 60 +/- 10 Nm
8. Install the inner shafts and drive shafts as described previously in this chapter.
9. Refill differential with gear oil as described previously in this chapter.
10. Install wheels and lower vehicle. With the vehicle in an unladen condition do up differential mounting brackets in a diagonal sequence to specification.
    Differential Mounting Bracket:
    NM - NP .... 69 +/- 9 Nm
    NS - NT .... 80 +/- 10 Nm
11. Install the skid and protection plates to the underside of the vehicle. The checks at the start of the chapter will need to be performed.

PROBLEM DIAGNOSIS

General

When diagnosing suspected front suspension problems, it should be remembered that steering, wheels and tyres all have an effect on front end performance.

Problem: Hard or heavy steering
Possible Causes and Remedies:
* Low or uneven tyre pressures.
* Steering gear or connections too tight or misaligned.
* Insufficient lubricant in steering gear.
* Excessive caster.
* Lower control arms or tension rods bent.
Remedy - Check front wheel alignment, check alignment or control arms and tension rods.
* Excessive toe-in. Remedy - Check and adjust toe-in.

Problem: Excessive play or looseness in steering
Possible Causes and Remedies:
* Steering gear or connections loose or worn.
Remedy - Adjust steering gear or install new components as necessary.
* Control arm ball joint loose or worn.
* Front wheel bearings incorrectly adjusted or worn.
Remedy - Adjust bearings or replace as necessary.
* Loose attachment of front suspension assembly to frame. Remedy - Check and tighten front suspension attaching nuts.

Problem: Erratic steering on brake application
Possible Causes and Remedies:
* Low or uneven tyre pressures.
* Excessive front brake disc run-out.
Remedy - Machine front brake discs.
* Oil soaked front brake pads.
Remedy - Replace brake pads, check & correct oil leak.
* Insufficient or uneven caster.
Remedy - Check front wheel alignment and adjust.
* Steering knuckle bent.
Remedy - Replace strut housing
* Excessive play in steering gear.
Remedy - Adjust steering gear or replace worn components as necessary.

Problem: Vehicle pulls to one side
Possible Causes and Remedies:
* Lower or uneven tyre pressures.
* Rear wheels not tracking with front wheels.
Remedy - Check alignment of rear wheels with front wheels and correct faults as necessary.

* Oil soaked front brake pads.
Remedy - Replace brake pads, check and correct cause of oil leakage.
* Toe-in incorrect.
* Incorrect or uneven caster or camber.
Remedy - Check wheel alignment and adjust as necessary.
* Rear axle assembly shifted.
Remedy - Check attaching bolts for looseness and control arm bushes for wear.
* Steering knuckle bent.
Remedy - Replace front strut housing.

Problem: Road shocks
Possible Causes and Remedies:
* Incorrect tyre pressures.
* Steering gear incorrectly adjusted.
* Front struts or rear shock absorbers operating incorrectly or unevenly, leaking fluid or inoperative.
Remedy - Check operation and replace components as necessary.
* Compression or rebound rubbers missing.
* Unbalanced wheels.
* Incorrect wheel alignment.
Remedy - Adjust.

Problem: Scuffed tyres
Possible Causes and Remedies:
* Toe-in incorrect.
* Tyres improperly inflated.
* Wheels or tyres out-of-true.
* Control arm ball joints worn.
Remedy - Replace worn ball joints.
* Uneven caster and camber. Remedy - Check front wheel alignment, adjust as necessary.
* Lower control arms or tension rods bent.
Remedy - Check alignment of control arms and tension rods. Replace components as necessary.
* Steering knuckle bent.
Remedy - Replace front strut housing.

Problem: Cupped tyres
Possible Causes and Remedies:
* Tyres improperly inflated.
* Wheels and tyres out of balance.
* Dragging brakes.
Remedy - Check for seizing of brake callipers.
* Control arm ball joints worn, or incorrectly adjusted or worn wheel bearings.
Remedy - Replace ball joints or bearings, adjust as required.
* Uneven caster.
Remedy - Check wheel alignment and adjust as necessary.

Problem: Front wheel shimmy
Possible Causes and Remedies:
* Low or uneven tyre pressures.
* Steering connections incorrectly adjusted or worn.
* Control arm ball joint or front wheel bearing loose or worn.
* Wheels and tyres out of balance.
* Wheels or tyres out-of-true.
* Incorrect or uneven caster or toe-in incorrect.
* Steering knuckle bent.
Remedy - Replace front strut housing.

Problem: Car wanders
Possible Causes and Remedies:
* Low or uneven tyre pressures.
* Steering gear or connections loose or worn.
Remedy - Test steering system for binding with front wheels off the ground.
* Control arm ball joints worn.
* Wheels toe-in too much to toe-out in straight ahead position.
Remedy - Adjust toe-in to specification.
* Incorrect or uneven caster.
Remedy - Replace front strut housing.
* Rear axle shifted.
Remedy - Check attaching bolts for looseness and control arm bushes for wear.
* Loose attachment of front suspension assembly to frame.
Remedy - Check and tighten attaching nuts.
* Incorrect front wheel bearing adjustment.

Problem: Vibration!
Possible Cause: Bent, damaged or abnormal wear of drive shaft.
Remedy: Replace drive shaft.
Possible Cause: Play in drive shaft and hub splines.
Remedy: Replace.
Possible Cause: Abnormal wear, play or seizure of wheel bearing.
Remedy: Replace wheel bearing.

Problem: Excessive Noise!
Possible Cause: Broken boot, grease leakage.
Remedy: Replace, re-pack grease.
Possible Cause: Bent, damaged or abnormal wear of drive shaft.
Remedy: Replace drive shaft.
Possible Cause: Play of drive shaft and hub spline.
Remedy: Replace.
Possible Cause: Malfunction of front suspension & steering.
Remedy: Adjust or replace.
Possible Cause: Loose wheel nuts.
Remedy: Tighten wheel nuts to specification.

FRONT SUSPENSION, AXLE & DRIVESHAFT ASSEMBLIES

SPECIFICATIONS

Wheel Alignment NM - NP
Camber	0°30' +/- 30'
Caster	3°50' +/- 1°
Toe-in (At centre of tyre tread)	2.5 +/- 2.5 mm
Toe-angle (Per wheel)	0°05' +/- 05'
Toe-out Angle on turns - (Inner wheel when outer wheel at 20°)	21°48'
Steering angle: - inner wheel	36°30' +/- 1°30'
- outer wheel	31°40'
Kingpin inclination	11°30'

Wheel Alignment NS - NT
Camber	0°00' +/- 0°30'
Caster (SWB)	3°39' +/- 1°00'
Caster (LWB)	3°31' +/- 1°00'
Toe-in (At centre of tyre tread)	0 - 5 mm
Toe-angle (Per Wheel)	0°00' - 0°12'
Steering Angle: - inner wheel (SWB)	36°49' +/- 1°30'
- inner wheel (LWB)	36°01' +/- 1°30'
Kingpin Inclination	11°30'

Ball Joint Starting Torque NM - NP
Upper Arm	0.4 - 2.5 Nm
Lower Arm	0.3 - 4.5 Nm
Stabilizer Bar	0.5 - 2.0 Nm

Ball Joint Starting Torque NS- NT
Upper Arm	0.4 - 5.6 Nm
Lower Arm	1.0 - 6.9 Nm
Stabilizer Bar	4.9 - 19.6 Nm

TORQUE SETTINGS

Description	Nm
Road Wheel Nuts	108 +/- 10
Upper Arm: NM - NP	147 +/- 10
NS - NT	108 +/- 12
Upper Ball Joint Mounting Bolt:	
NM - NP	30 +/- 4
NS - NT	40 +/- 4
Upper Ball Joint Nut	74 +/- 14
Upper Shock Absorber Mount	44 +/- 5
Lower Shock Absorber Mount:	
NM - NP	162 +/- 14
NS - NT	133 +/- 12
Shock Absorber Piston Nut:	
NM - NP	22 +/- 2
NS - NT	25 +/- 5
Lower Arm Mount: NM - NP	123 +/- 14
NS - NT	145 +/- 10
Lower Ball Joint Mounting Nut:	
NM - NP	95 +/- 11
NS - NT	125 +/- 25
Lower Ball Joint Nut: NM - NP	147 +/- 29
NS - NT	100 +/- 40
Tie Rod End: NM - NP	39 +/- 4
NS - NT	47 +/- 13
Tie Rod Lock Nut: NM - NP	71 +/- 7
NS - NT	93 +/- 15
Stabilizer Link To Stabilizer Bar:	
NM - NP	108 +/- 10
NS - NT	130 +/- 10
Stabilizer Mounting Clamp	44 +/- 10
Drive Shaft Nut: NM - NP	255 +/- 29
NS - NT	220 +/- 10
RH Drive Shaft To Front Axle Housing	60 +/- 10
Knuckle To Hub: NM - NP	88 +/- 10
NS - NT	90 +/- 10
Inner Shaft Housing Tube To Carrier	90 +/- 10
Breather Pipe Bolts	12 +/- 2
Vacuum Tank Bolts	12 +/- 2
Engage Switch	25 +/- 5
Diff Bracket To Axle Tube	89 +/- 9
Vacuum Actuator Mounting Bolts:	
NM - NP	17 +/- 3
NS - NT	20 +/- 4
Diff Mounting Bracket:	
NM - NP	69 +/- 9
NS - NT	80 +/- 10
Front Propeller Shaft Connection	60 +/- 10
No.2 Cross-member to Frame:	
NM - NP	128 +/- 9
NS - NT	80 +/- 5
Front Diff Cover Bolts	18 +/- 3
Filler Plug	50 +/- 10
Drain Plug	65 +/- 5
Companion Flange Nut	216 +/- 29
Diff Bearing Caps: NM - NP	Not Specified
NS - NT	59 +/- 4

REAR SUSPENSION, AXLE & DRIVE SHAFTS

Subject	Page
GENERAL INFORMATION	336
REAR WHEEL ALIGNMENT	336
Visual Inspection	336
Camber Adjustment	336
Toe-In Adjustment	336
SUSPENSION	337
Upper Arm Assembly	337
Removal	337
Ball Joint Turning Torque Check	337
Dust Cover Inspection	337
Installation	337
Shock Absorber	338
Removal	338
Installation	338
Coil Springs	338
Removal	338
Installation	338
Lower Arm Assembly	339
Removal	339
Installation	339
Stabilizer Bar Assembly	339
Removal	339
Link Ball Joint Turning Torque Check	339
Installation	339
Toe Control Arm Assembly	339
Removal	339
Ball Joint Turning Torque Check	340
Installation	340
Trailing Arm Assembly	340
Removal	340
Inspection	340
Installation	340
Drive Shaft	341
Removal	341
Disassembly	341
Assembly	341
Installation	341
REAR HUB ASSEMBLY	342
Wheel Bearing Axial End Play(On Vehicle)	342
Rear Axle Hub Assembly	342
Removal	342
Inspection	342
Wheel Bearing Rotation Starting Torque	342
Wheel Bearing Axial Play Check (off vehicle)	342
Installation	342
Knuckle Assembly	343
Removal	343
Installation	343

Subject	Page
PROPELLER SHAFTS	344
Front Propeller Shaft	344
Removal	344
Disassembly	344
Assembly	344
Installation	344
Rear Propeller Shaft	345
Inspection: CFRP Propeller Shaft	345
Removal	345
Disassembly	345
Installation	345
REAR AXLE ASSEMBLY	346
Rear Differential Lock	346
Rear Differential Lock Switch	346
Removal	346
Switch Check	346
Installation	346
Rear Differential Lock ECU	346
Removal	346
ECU Check	346
Installation	346
Rear Differential Lock Air Pump	347
Removal	347
Air Pump Check	347
Installation	347
Rear Differential Lock Detection Switch	347
Removal	347
Detection Switch Check	347
Installation	347
Differential Carrier	348
Removal	348
Installation	348
DIFFERENTIAL ASSEMBLY	349
Pre-disassembly Inspection	349
Drive Gear Backlash	349
Drive Gear Run-out	349
Differential Gear Backlash	349
Drive Gear Tooth Contact	349
Conventional Differential Carrier Disassembly	349
Conventional Differential Carrier Assembly	350
Rear Differential Lock With LSD Disassembly	351
Rear Differential Lock With LSD Assembly	352
SPECIFICATIONS	353
TORQUE SETTINGS	353

REAR SUSPENSION, AXLE & DRIVESHAFT ASSEMBLIES

GENERAL INFORMATION

A Multi-Link type double wishbone independent suspension is used on the rear. The wheels move independently of each other to try and contact the ground better without change in the posture of the wheels.

REAR WHEEL ALIGNMENT

Visual Inspection

It is necessary before any attempt is made to check wheel alignment to carry out the following preliminary checks:

1. Check tyre and mountings. Always check camber and toe-in at the mean run-out position on the tyre or rim.
2. Always adjust tyre pressures to recommendation.
3. Control arm bushes should be checked for wear.
4. The vehicle should be at curb weight, fuel tank full, without driver, passengers or luggage, etc.
5. Check for improperly operating rear shock absorbers.
6. Measure the wheel alignment with the vehicle parked on a level surface.

Camber Adjustment

Adjustment is achieved by turning the camber adjusting bolt on the lower arm as follows.

Camber Adjusting Bolt NM - NP:
 Left Wheel Turning Clockwise (-) Camber
 Right Wheel Turning Clockwise (+) Camber
Camber Adjusting Bolt NS:
 Left Wheel Turning Clockwise (+) Camber
 Right Wheel Turning Clockwise (-) Camber
 Camber: ....0°00' +/- 30'
 Difference b/w right & left ....less than 0°30'

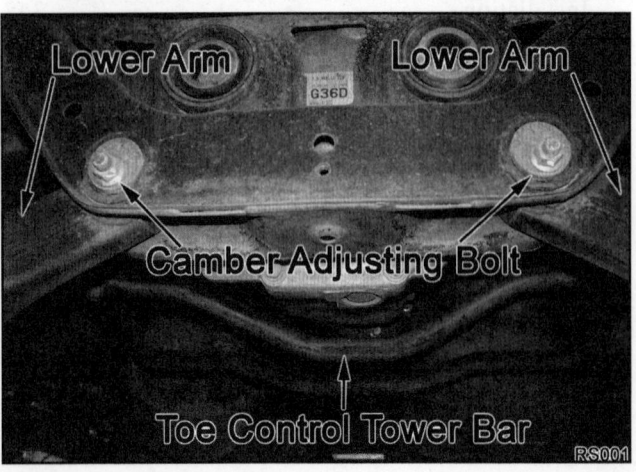

After adjustment is carried out toe-in should be adjusted.

Toe-In Adjustment

Adjustment is achieved by turning the toe control bolt as follows.

Toe Adjusting Bolt NM - NP:
 Left Wheel Turning Clockwise (-) Toe-In
 Right Wheel Turning Clockwise (+) Toe-In
Toe Adjusting Bolt NS:
 Left Wheel Turning Clockwise (+) Toe-In
 Right Wheel Turning Clockwise (-) Toe-In

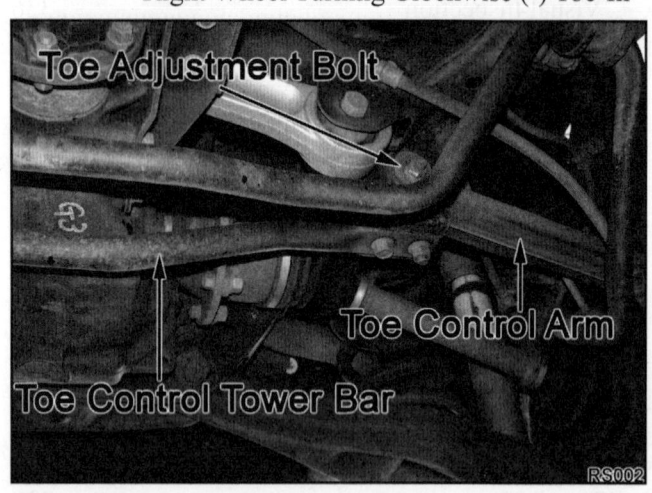

Toe-in Standard Value:
 At centre of tyre tread .... 3 +/- 3 mm
 Toe Angle (per wheel) NM - NP ....1°06' +/- 1°06'
 Toe Angle (per wheel) NS ....0°06' +/- 0°06'

Note: *After adjustment is carried out road test the vehicle.*

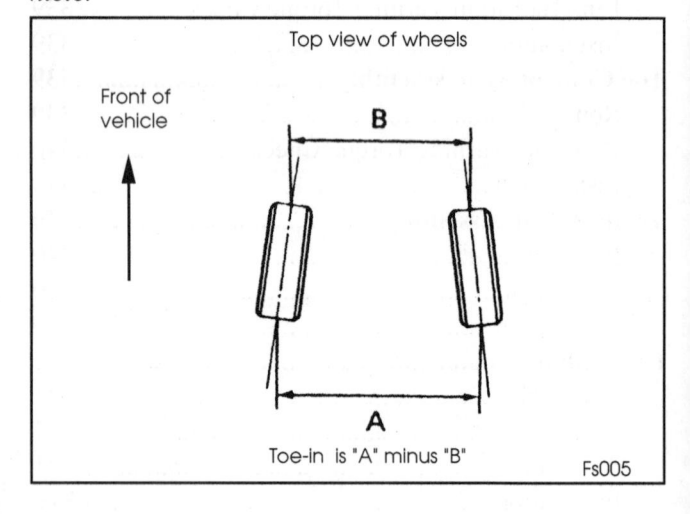

SUSPENSION

UPPER ARM ASSEMBLY
Removal
1. Jack up rear of vehicle. Then place safety stands under the rear body jacking points. Remove the wheels.
2. Drain the brake fluid, then remove the clip to free the brake hose. Disconnect the brake pipe connection. On vehicles fitted with headlamp auto levelling system remove the connection for the rear height sensor.
3. On vehicles fitted with ABS remove the two bolts securing the wheel speed sensor cable to the upper arm assembly.

4. From the upper arm assembly remove the bump stopper, then remove the stabilizer link to upper arm assembly nut.
5. Remove the split pin from the upper arm assembly ball joint, then loosen the ball joint nut to the end of the thread.
6. Using a ball joint splitter tool separate the ball joint from the knuckle assembly. Then fully remove retaining nut.
7. Separate the upper arm from the knuckle assembly
8. Remove the nuts/bolts securing the upper arm assembly to the frame then remove upper arm assembly from vehicle.
9. If required remove the nuts/bolts securing the ball joint to the upper arm assembly.

Ball Joint Turning Torque Check
1. Shake the ball joint stud several times, then install the nut to the stud.
2. Using a preload socket and torque wrench check the turning torque of the ball joint.
   Standard Value:
   NM - NP .... 0.5 - 3.0 Nm
   NS - NT .... 1.47 - 7.84 Nm
3. If measured value exceeds the standard value replace the upper control arm ball joint assembly.
4. If measured value is lower than standard value, check to ensure ball joint turns smoothly and does not have excessive play. Can be used if OK.

DUST COVER INSPECTION
1. Check the ball joint dust covers by pressing with a finger and checking for cracks or damage.
2. If the dust cover is cracked or damaged the ball joint assembly should be replaced as a cracked or damaged dust cover may cause damage to the ball joint.

Installation
1. If required install the ball joint to the upper arm assembly tightening retaining bolts to specification.
   Ball Joint to Upper Arm Nuts:
   NM - NP .... 98 +/- 12Nm
   NS - NT .... 82 +/- 12 Nm
2. Install upper arm assembly into position then install the upper arm to frame assembly retaining bolts, do not fully tighten nuts.

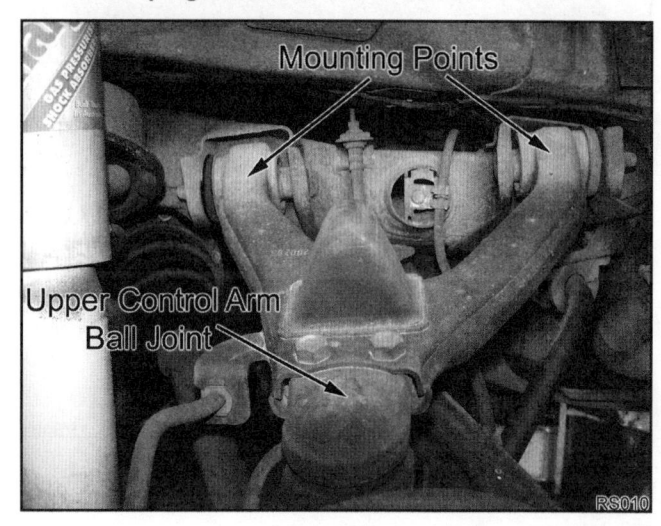

3. Fit the upper arm to knuckle assembly and tighten ball joint bolt to specification and install a new split pin.
   Ball Joint Nut: NM - NP .... 150 +/- 30Nm
   NS - NT .... 118 +/- 32 Nm
4. Reconnect the stabilizer link to upper arm assembly tighten nut to specification, then install the bump stopper to the upper arm assembly.
   Stabilizer Bar Link Nut:
   NM - NP .... 104 +/- 14Nm
   NS - NT .... 50 +/- 10 Nm
5. Vehicles fitted with ABS secure the cable for the wheel speed sensor to the upper arm assembly.
6. Replace the securing clip and reconnect the brake pipe, then fill and bleed the brake system.
   Brake Pipe Connection .... 15 +/- 2 Nm
7. On vehicles fitted with headlamp auto levelling system reconnect the rear height sensor.

REAR SUSPENSION, AXLE & DRIVESHAFT ASSEMBLIES

8. Once vehicle is back on the ground with the wheels fitted, fully tighten the upper control arm nuts. Check and adjust wheel alignment as required also check the direction of the low beam, adjust as necessary.

Upper Arm to Frame Nuts:
   NM - NP .... 167 +/- 10Nm
   NS - NT .... 124 +/- 18 Nm

SHOCK ABSORBER
Removal
1. Jack up rear of vehicle. Then place safety stands under the rear body jacking points. Remove the road wheels.
2. Remove the nut, washers and rubber bushes from the top mounting bracket for the shock absorber. Make sure to keep the removed parts in order to help with reassembly.
3. Remove the lower bolt attaching the shock absorber to lower arm assembly.

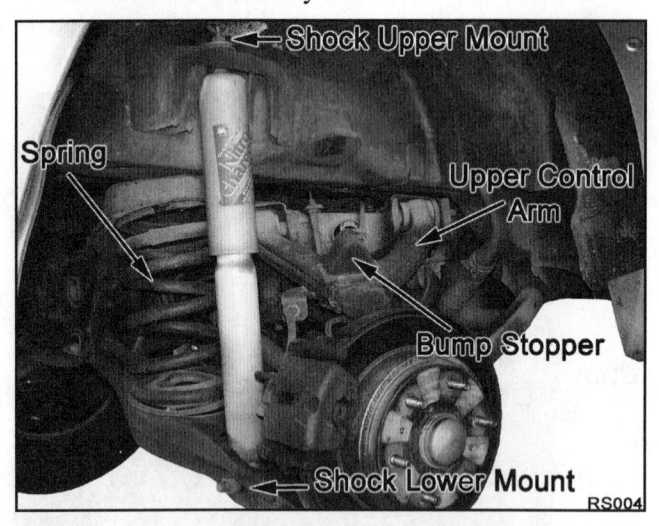

4. Remove shock absorber from vehicle.

Installation
1. Install the shock absorber into position then install the lower mounting bolt and washer (do not fully tighten nut).
2. Install the upper shock absorber retaining nut making sure to install the washers and collars in the opposite order of removal (do not fully tighten nut). It is recommended to use a new nut.
3. Lower vehicle and tighten the retaining nuts and bolts to specification with vehicle in unladen condition.

Shock Absorber Upper Nut:
   NM - NP .... 44 +/- 10 Nm
   NS - NT .... 30 +/- 5 Nm

Shock Absorber Lower Nut:
   NM - NP .... 152 +/- 25 Nm
   NS - NT .... 100 +/- 20 Nm

4. Check and adjust the wheel alignment as required

COIL SPRINGS
Removal
1. Jack up rear of vehicle, then place safety stands under the rear body jacking points. Remove the road wheels.
2. Remove the lower bolt attaching the shock absorber to lower arm assembly.
3. Using a floor jack and piece of wood, jack up the lower arm enough to take the pressure off the coil spring.
4. Remove the lower arm retaining bolt and slowly lower the jack to release the coil spring.
5. Remove the coil spring, then remove the upper and lower spring pads.

Installation
1. Install the upper and lower spring pads and coil spring into position ensuring the spring is correctly aligned. The identification mark on the spring should be located towards the bottom. The coil spring end should mount into the cavity of the pad.

2. Using a floor jack and piece of wood, jack up the lower arm to compress the coil spring.
3. Install the lower arm retaining bolt (do not fully tighten nut).
4. Install the shock absorber lower mounting bolt (do not fully tighten nut).
5. Lower vehicle and tighten the retaining nuts and bolts to specification with vehicle in unladen condition.

Lower Arm Mounting Nut:
   NM - NP .... 152 +/- 25 Nm
   NS - NT .... 145 +/- 10 Nm

Shock Absorber Lower Nut:
   NM - NP .... 152 +/- 25 Nm
   NS - NT .... 100 +/- 20 Nm

6. Check and adjust the wheel alignment as required

REAR SUSPENSION, AXLE & DRIVESHAFT ASSEMBLIES

LOWER ARM ASSEMBLY
Removal
1. Use the previous steps to remove the shock absorber and coil spring.
2. Place a mark the camber adjustment bolt, plate and frame to help with reassembly.
3. Remove the lower arm assembly from the vehicle.

Installation
1. Install lower arm assembly in to place, then install camber adjusting bolt using aligning position marks made on removal (do not fully tighten bolt).
2. Install the upper and lower spring pads and coil spring into position ensuring the spring is correctly aligned.
3. Using a floor jack and piece of wood, jack up the lower arm to compress coil spring.
4. Install the lower arm retaining bolt (do not fully tighten bolt).

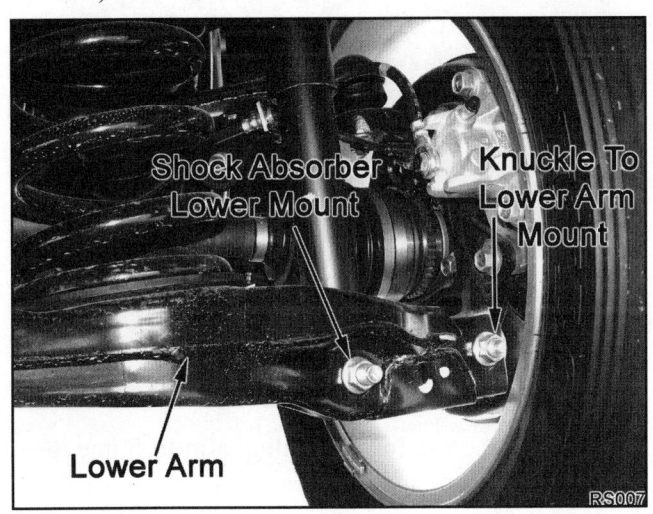

5. Install the shock absorber lower mounting bolt (do not fully tighten bolt). Install the upper nut and washers if removed (do not fully tighten).
6. Lower vehicle and tighten the retaining nuts and bolts to specification with vehicle in unladen condition.
   Lower Arm Mounting Nut:
   NM - NP .... 152 +/- 25 Nm
   NS - NT .... 145 +/- 10 Nm
   Note: For other specifications refer to previous procedures.
7. Check and adjust wheel alignment as required.

STABILIZER BAR ASSEMBLY
Removal
1. Jack up rear of vehicle. Then place safety stands under the rear body jacking points. Remove the wheels to make it easier.
2. Remove the nuts securing the stabilizer link assembly and remove stabilizer link from each side.
3. Remove the bolts securing the stabilizer clamps, then remove the clamps and bushing.
4. Remove the stabilizer bar assembly from vehicle.

Stabilizer Link Ball Joint Turning Torque Check
1. Shake the ball joint stud several times, then install the nut to the stud.
2. Using a preload socket and torque wrench check the turning torque of the ball joint.
   Standard Value: NM - NP .... 0.5 - 2.0 Nm
   NS - NT .... 4.9 - 19.6 Nm
3. If measured value exceeds the standard value replace the stabilizer link.
4. If measured value is lower than standard value, check to ensure ball joint turns smoothly and does not have excessive play. Can be used if OK.

Installation
1. Install the stabilizer bar into position ensuring the identification mark is facing the left side of the vehicle.
2. Install the bushes onto the stabilizer bar making sure the slit is facing towards the front of the vehicle. Install the clamps doing the bolts to specification. Before tightening, align the end of the mark with the end of the bush.
   Stabilizer Clamp Bolts .... 44 +/- 10 Nm

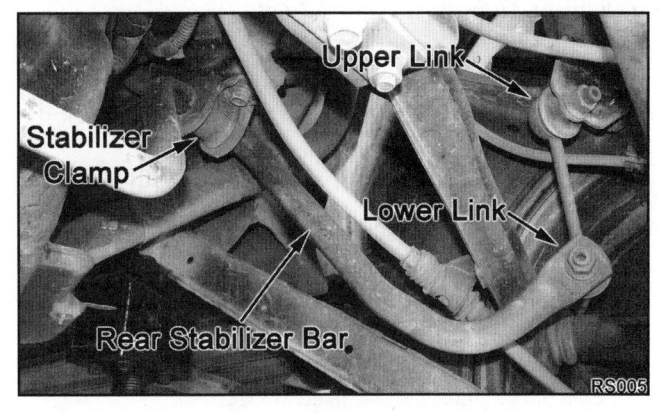

3. To each side of the stabilizer assembly install the stabilizer link assembly, tightening retaining nuts to specification.
   Stabilizer Link Nuts To Bar:
   NM - NP .... 104 +/- 14 Nm
   NS - NT .... 50 +/- 10 Nm
   Stabilizer Bar To Arm:
   NM - NP .... 104 +/- 14 Nm
   NS - NT .... 50 +/- 10 Nm

TOE CONTROL ARM ASSEMBLY
Removal
1. Jack up rear of vehicle. Then place safety stands under the rear body jacking points. Remove the wheels.

339

REAR SUSPENSION, AXLE & DRIVESHAFT ASSEMBLIES

2. Remove the bolt retaining the park brake cable to the control arm.
3. Remove the bolt and nut retaining the toe control tower bar.

4. Loosen the toe control arm ball joint bolt to the end of the thread, then using a ball joint splitter tool separate the ball joint from the knuckle assembly. Then fully remove retaining nut.
5. Mark the position of the toe adjustment bolt and bracket for reassembly.
6. Remove the toe adjustment bolt, then remove the toe control arm from vehicle.

Ball Joint Turning Torque Check
1. Shake the ball joint stud several times, then install the nut to the stud.
2. Using a preload socket and torque wrench check the turning torque of the ball joint.
   Standard Value: NM - NP .... 1.0 - 2.5 Nm
   NS - NT .... 0.67 - 3.9 Nm
3. If measured value exceeds the standard value replace the toe control arm ball joint assembly.
4. If measured value is lower than standard value, check to ensure ball joint turns smoothly and does not have excessive play, can be used if OK.

Installation
1. Install the toe control arm into position then install the toe adjustment bolt using marks made on removal as a guide. (Do not fully tighten bolt).
2. Install the ball joint to the knuckle assembly and tighten retaining nut to specification.
   Note: It is recommended to install a new retaining nut.
   Toe Control Arm Ball Joint Nut:
   NM - NP .... 67 +/- 7 Nm
   NS - NT .... 75 +/- 10 Nm
3. Install the toe control tower bar and tighten retaining bolt and nut to specification.
   Toe Control Tower Bar Bolt/Nut .... 46 +/- 8 Nm

4. Install the park brake cable into position and tighten bracket retaining bolt.
   NS - NT .... 11 +/- 2 Nm
5. Lower vehicle, replace the wheels and tighten the toe adjustment nut to specification.
   Toe Adjustment Bolt/Nut:
   NM - NP .... 123 +/- 15 Nm
   NS - NT .... 145 +/- 10 Nm
6. Check and adjust wheel alignment as required.

TRAILING ARM ASSEMBLY
Removal
1. Jack up rear of vehicle. Then place safety stands under the rear body jacking points. Remove the road wheels
2. Remove the bolt retaining the trailing arm to the knuckle assembly.

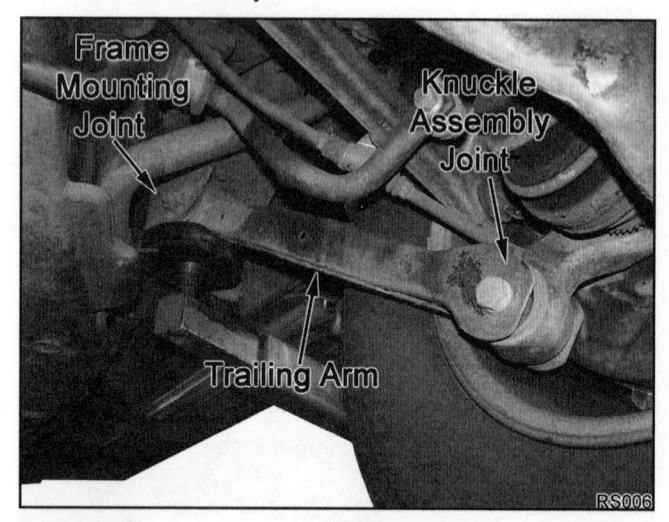

3. Remove the nut for the trailing arm to frame, then remove the bolt and stoppers.
4. Remove trailing arm from vehicle.

Inspection
1. Check arm for damage, deformation and replace if necessary.
2. If the bushes need to be replaced, a press and suitable adapter need to be used. Make sure the hollow parts of the bush are installed vertically to the arm, and protrude by the same amount both sides.

Installation
1. Install trailing arm into position, then install the arm to frame bolt, stoppers and retaining nut (do not fully tighten nut).
2. a) On NM - NP models install the bolt retaining the trailing arm to knuckle assembly and tighten to specification.
   Trailing Arm To Knuckle Bolt:
   NM - NP .... 231 +/- 34 Nm
   b) On NS models install the bolt retaining the trailing

REAR SUSPENSION, AXLE & DRIVESHAFT ASSEMBLIES

arm to the knuckle assembly, at this stage do not fully tighten nut.

3. a) On NM - NP models lower vehicle, replace the wheels and tighten the trailing arm to frame nut to specification with vehicle in unladen condition.
   Trailing Arm To Frame Nut:
   NM - NP .... 231 +/- 34 Nm
   b) On NS models lower vehicle, replace the wheels and tighten trailing arm to frame and trailing arm to the knuckle assembly to specification.
   Trailing Arm To Frame Nut:
   NS - NT .... 148 +/- 22 Nm
   Trailing Arm To Knuckle Bolt:
   NS - NT .... 148 +/- 22 Nm
4. Check and adjust wheel alignment as required.

Drive Shafts

Removal
1. Using a floor jack, jack up rear of vehicle, place safety stands under the rear body jacking points and remove wheels.
2. Remove the drive shaft nut cap, then remove the split pin and driveshaft nut and washer.
3. Remove the bolts and nuts securing the drive shaft and companion shaft assemblies.
4. Using a trolley jack and piece of wood under the lower control arm, compress the spring and remove the lower arm to knuckle bolt.
5. Remove the driveshaft assembly from the vehicle.

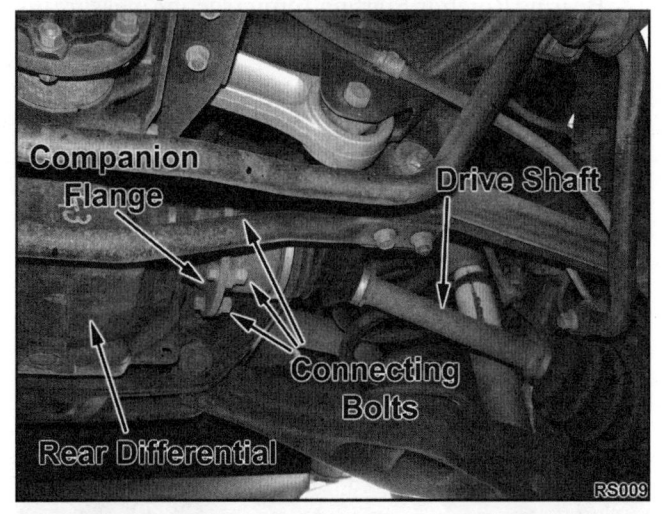

Disassembly
1. From the drive shaft assembly remove the large D.O.J boot band then remove the small boot band.
2. Remove the circlip, then remove the D.O.J outer race.
3. Remove the ball bearings from the D.O.J cage by levering out from the inside, then remove the cage.
4. Remove the snap ring then remove the inner race.
5. Remove the D.O.J boot, firstly tape the shaft splines to prevent damage to the boot on removal.
6. Remove the large and small B.J boot bands and then remove the B.J boot, firstly tape the shaft splines to prevent damage to the boot on removal.

Assembly
1. Tape the shaft splines to prevent damage to the boots on installation, then install the B.J boot followed by the D.O.J boot.
2. Fill the inside of the Joint and the BJ boot with specified grease, then install the B.J. boot bands.
   Specified Grease .... Repair Kit Grease
   Repair Kit Grease Amount 245g
   (135g inside joint, 110g inside boot)
3. Install the D.O.J cage to the drive shaft, then align the D.O.J inner race and shaft alignment marks and tap the inner race to press-fit into place on the shaft.
4. Install the snap ring, then install the ball bearings.
5. Fill the inside if the D.O.J outer race and the D.O.J boot with specified grease.
   Specified Grease .... Repair Kit Grease
   Repair Kit Grease Amount 295g
   (185g inside joint, 110g inside boot)
6. Install the D.O.J outer race and circlip then install the boot bands at the specified distance.
   Specified Distance:
   - 4M41 M/T .... 115 +/- 3mm
   - all except 4M41 M/T .... 110 +/- 3mm

   Note: Distance is measured from centre of large boot band to centre of small boot band.

Installation
1. Install the drive shaft into position in the vehicle, then carefully raise the lower control arm using the jack and block of wood.
2. Install the lower arm to knuckle bolt and tighten retaining nut to specification.
   Lower Arm to Knuckle Nut .... 152+/-25 Nm
3. Install the driveshaft to companion shaft assembly retaining bolts and tighten nuts to specification.
   Companion to Drive Shaft Nuts ...... 113+/-14 Nm
4. Install the washer, driveshaft retaining nut and tighten to specification, then install a new split pin and the dust cap.
   Driveshaft Nut .... 255+/-29Nm
5. Install wheels and lower vehicle to ground.

REAR HUB ASSEMBLY

Wheel Bearing Axial Play Check (On Vehicle)
1. Jack up rear of vehicle. Then place safety stands under the rear body jacking points and remove the wheels.
2. Remove the rear brake caliper and brake disc.
3. Using a dial gauge mounted against the hub surface check the bearing end play by moving the hub in the axial direction and checking dial reading.
   Bearing End Play (Limit)
   NM - NP .... 0.05 mm
   NS - NT .... 0 mm
   Hub Nut:
   NM - NP .... 255 +/- 29 Nm
   NS - NT .... 220 +/- 10 Nm

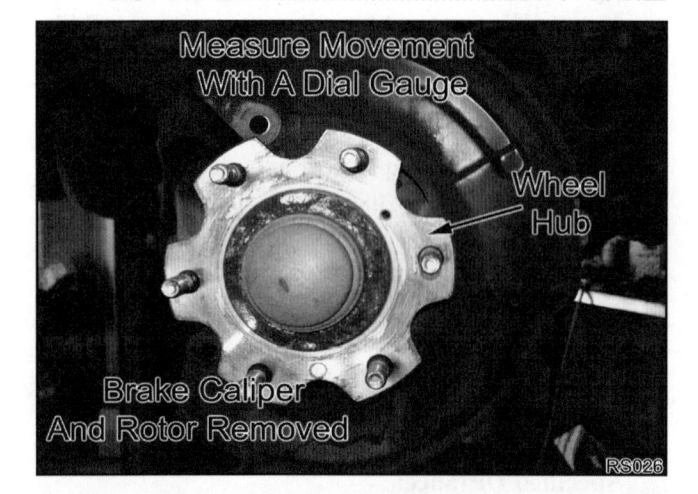

4. If end play is not within specification re-torque nut to specification and recheck. Replace the hub assembly if limits are exceeded.

Rear Axle Hub Assembly
Removal
1. Jack up rear of vehicle. Then place safety stands under the rear body jacking points and remove wheels.
2. Remove the hub cap, then remove the split pin and driveshaft nut.
3. Remove the rear brake caliper and suspend on a piece of wire, then remove the rear brake disc.
4. Remove the park brake shoe and lining assembly. Refer to brake chapter if required.
5. Remove the bolts/nuts securing the companion shaft and drive shaft connection.
6. Using a floor jack and piece of wood, jack up the lower arm to compress coil spring.
7. Remove the lower arm retaining bolt and slowly lower jack to release pressure on spring.
8. Remove the rear drive shaft assembly.
9. Remove the bolt securing the ABS rotor protect, then remove protector.
10. Remove the hub assembly retaining bolts and hub, then remove the backing plate.

Inspection
1. Inspect the rear hub for damage and wear.
2. Inspect the oil seal for damage and cracking.
3. Inspect rotor (ABS) for wear and damage.

Bearing Rotation Starting Torque (Off Vehicle)
1. Using Mitsubishi special tools (Hub Remover/installer) and Spacer, tighten rear hub assembly to the specified torque.
   Part No: MB991000 Spacer
              MB991017 Hub Remover/Installer
   Hub Nut: NM - NP .... 255 +/- 29 Nm
                NS - NT .... 220 +/- 10 Nm
2. Place hub into a vice using wooden blocks to avoid damage.
3. Measure wheel bearing rotation torque using a pre-load socket and torque wrench.
   Rotation Torque Limit:
   NM - NP .... 1.76 Nm
   NS - NT .... 3.0 Nm
4. Hub rotation starting torque should be under the limit value and show no signs of stickiness or roughness when turning hub assembly.

Wheel Bearing Axial Play Check (Off Vehicle)
1. Mount the hub in a vice using wooden blocks to secure it in place. Using special tools as described in Wheel Bearing Rotation Starting Torque section measure the bearing end play using a dial gauge.
   Bearing End Play (Limit)
   NM - NP .... 0.05 mm
   NS - NT .... 0 mm
2. If end play is not within specification re-torque nut to specification and recheck. Replace the hub assembly if limits are exceeded.

Installation
1. Install the backing plate, then install the hub assembly tightening retaining bolts to specification.
   Hub Assembly Retaining Bolts .... 81 +/- 6 Nm

REAR SUSPENSION, AXLE & DRIVESHAFT ASSEMBLIES

2. Install the ABS rotor protector then install the rear drive shaft assembly.
3. Using a floor jack and piece of wood, jack up the lower arm to compress the coil spring.
4. Install the lower arm retaining bolt tightening to specification, then slowly lower jack.
   Lower Arm Retaining Bolt/Nut ......152 +/- 25 Nm
5. Install the bolts/nuts securing the companion shaft and drive shaft connection, tightening to specification.
   Companion to Drive Shaft Nuts ..... 113 +/- 14 Nm

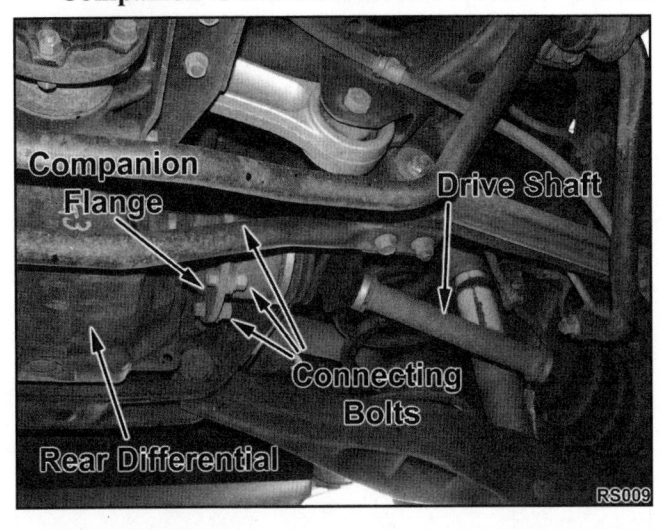

6. Install the park brake shoe and lining assembly. Refer to brake chapter if required.

7. Install the rear brake disc, then install the brake caliper tightening retaining bolts to specification.
   Brake Caliper Mounting Bolts..........88 +/- 10 Nm
8. Install the drive shaft washer and nut. Tighten retaining nut to specification.
   Drive Shaft Nut .... 255 +/- 29 Nm
9. Install the split pin to the drive shaft, then install the hub cap and speed sensor.
10. Adjust park brake assembly. Refer to brake chapter if required.

Knuckle Assembly
Removal
1. Jack up rear of vehicle. Then place safety stands under the rear body jacking points.
2. Remove the vehicle speed sensor.
3. Remove the rear hub assembly, brakes and drive shaft as described previously.
4. Remove the trailing arm, lower arm and toe control arm connector.

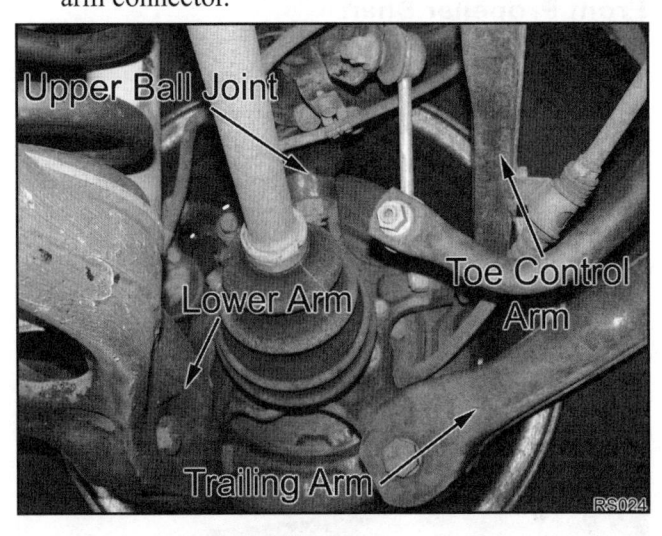

5. Disconnect the upper arm bolt joint and remove knuckle assembly.

Installation
1. To the knuckle assembly reconnect the upper arm ball joint and tighten retaining bolt to specification.
   Upper Arm Ball Joint Nut............... 150 +/- 30 Nm
2. Reconnect the trailing arm tightening retaining bolt to specification.
   Trailing Arm Bolt/Nut .... 231 +/- 34 Nm
3. Reconnect the toe control arm tighten nut to specification.
   Toe Control Arm Nut........................... 67 +/- 7 Nm
4. Install the rear hub assembly, drive shafts, brakes and ABS speed sensor as described earlier.
5. Adjust park brake assembly. Refer to brake chapter if required.

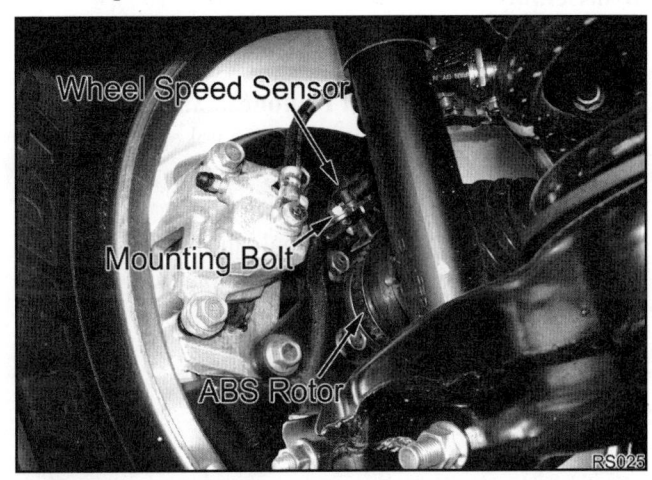

PROPELLER SHAFTS

Their was two different types of propeller shafts used for the front drive, one is a BJ type, the other is a UJ type. The rear shaft can be equipped with a carbon fibre reinforced plastic tube type. Caution should be taken when handling this type of propeller shaft. The shaft can be damaged easily.

Front Propeller Shaft
Removal
1. Ensure the transfer shift lever is set to "2H' range.
2. Raise the vehicle on a hoist or floor jack, ensuring to secure with safety stands if a floor jack is used.
3. Remove the transfer assembly drain plug and drain gear oil.
4. Mark the relationship of the propeller shaft with the mounting flanges, for installation purposes.
5. Remove the nuts/bolts securing the propeller shaft into place. Around the BJ assembly wrap a rag around the joint boot.
6. Carefully slide the propeller shaft from the transfer and plug with a bung or rag.
7. Fully remove propeller shaft from vehicle and place on clean work bench.

Disassembly
1. Before dismantling propeller shaft, check the runout.
   Front Propeller Shaft Runout.................. 0.5 mm
2. Place mating marks on the flange yoke and propeller shaft.
3. Remove grease nipple and snap ring.
4. Using a clamp press the journal cap inwards to remove the opposite side cap. Repeat on other journal cap to free the journal.

Assembly
1. Remove journal caps from journal, and place inside flange yoke.
2. With special tool MB990840 or clamp press in journal cap until snap ring groove can be completely seen.
   Note: *Do not tap in journal caps with a hammer or other tools as this can upset the balance of the shaft. Be sure to install journal caps straight as damage can be done to journal.*
3. Repeat this process with the other side cap.
4. Place journal inside propeller shaft making sure to align mating marks placed on shafts on disassembly.
5. Press fit other two journal caps, once this is done install the snap rings. Measure the clearance in the snap ring groove with a thickness gauge. Always use the same thickness snap ring on both sides.
   Standard Value "A"................................. 0-0.06m
6. If the standard value is not meet use other snap rings to adjust the clearance.

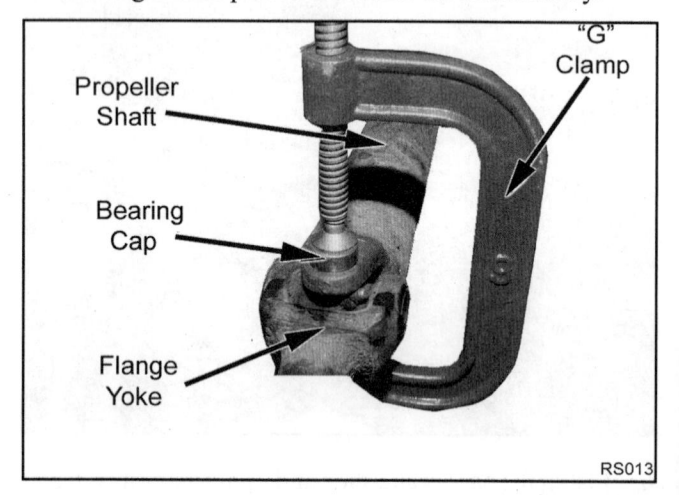

	Thickness mm	Identification Colour
Front Shaft	1.28	----
	1.31	Yellow
	1.34	Blue
	1.37	Purple
Rear Shaft	1.40	Brown

Installation
1. Install propeller shaft into transfer case aligning marks made on removal. Be careful not to damage the oil seal lips of the transfer case.
2. Install and tighten the propeller shaft retaining nuts/bolts to specification.
   Shaft to Differential Flange............... 60 +/- 10Nm
3. Ensure the drain plug has been tightened to specification. Using specified gear oil fill the transfer assembly until the oil level is level with the bottom of the filler hole, then tighten the filler plug to specification.
   Transfer Drain and Filler Plug........... 32 +/- 2Nm
   Hypoid Gear Oil -SAE 75W-90 or 75W-85 GL-4

REAR SUSPENSION, AXLE & DRIVESHAFT ASSEMBLIES

Rear Propeller Shaft

Inspection: CFRP (Carbon Fibre Reinforced Plastic) Propeller Shaft

1. If the propeller shaft tube is cracked, chipped or bent replace the propeller shaft.
2. Replace the propeller shaft if is has been dropped.
3. Care should be taken not to impact or damage the tube.
4. If cracks or peeling is found at the sealed section of the shaft, replace.
5. To prevent damage to the shaft during maintenance, wrap a rubber sheet (minimum thickness 10mm) around the propeller shaft tube.
6. Refer to diagram and measure the distances shown between the shaft and tube end. If not within specification replace shaft.
Distance "A" .... 0.2 - 0.5mm

Removal

1. Raise the vehicle on a hoist or floor jack, be sure to secure with safety stands if a floor jack is used.
2. Wrap a rubber sheet around the rear propeller shaft to prevent damage to shaft tube.
Rubber Sheet Minimum Thickness............10mm
3. Mark the relationship of the propeller shaft with the mounting flanges, for installation purposes.
4. Remove the nuts/bolts securing the propeller shaft to differential flange. Wrap a rag around the joint boot. 
5. Carefully slide the propeller shaft from the transmission and plug transmission with a bung or rag.
6. Fully remove propeller shaft from vehicle and place on clean work bench. Be careful not to drop the air breather which is located at the rear end of the shaft.

Disassembly

1. For the earlier vehicle fitted with universal joint type propeller shaft dismantling is the same as Front Propeller Shaft detailed earlier in the chapter. Only difference is the runout limit, which can be checked with a dial gauge.
Rear Propeller Shaft Runout 0.4mm
2. For the BJ type propeller shaft the unit is non-serviceable.

Installation

1. If reusing propeller shaft, install propeller shaft into vehicle using alignment marks made on removal. Ensure the shaft is positioned so that the marking on propeller shaft is as close as possible to the mark on the differential flange.
BJ type shaft .... within 30°
Universal joint type shaft .... within 45°
2. Install and tighten the propeller shaft retaining nuts/bolts to specification.
Shaft to Differential Flange............... 60 +/- 10 Nm
3. Remove the rubber sheet from the propeller shaft.
4. Check fluid level in transfer case and top up if needed.
5. Replace wheels and lower vehicle.

REAR AXLE ASSEMBLY

REAR DIFFERENTIAL LOCK

Rear Differential Lock Switch

Removal

Using a small flat blade screwdriver carefully lever the panel small from the centre console assembly. Disconnect the electrical connection and remove switch.

Switch Check

Switch Position		Continuity b/w Terminals
NM-NP	OFF	2 - 3
	ON	2 - 5
NS-NT	OFF	2 - 3
	ON	3 - 6

Installation

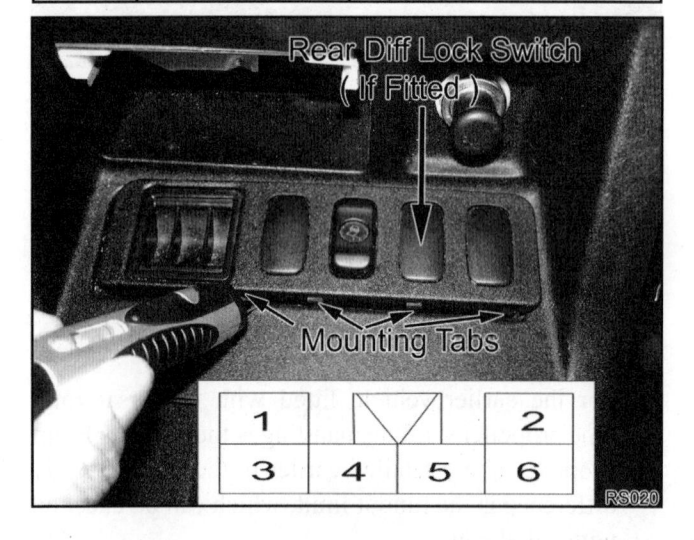

Reconnect electrical connection then install switch into position, pressing ensuring it clips into place. Install panel back into place making sure the tabs all line up.

Rear Differential Lock ECU

Removal

1. Remove the rear quarter trim panel, refer to body chapter if required.
2. Remove the nuts securing the ECU, then disconnect electrical connection and remove rear differential lock ECU from vehicle.

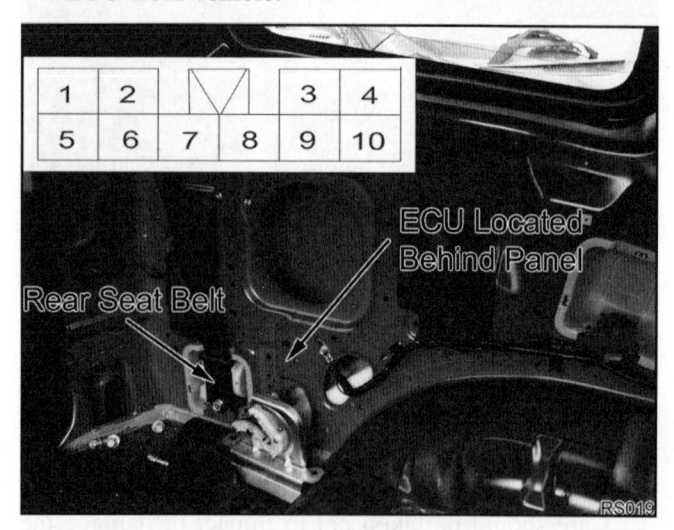

ECU Check

Note: *Refer to below table condition table.*

1. Measure terminal voltage under each condition.
2. With the ECU harness connected, measure the voltage between each terminal and the earth terminal (Terminal 6).

Installation

1. Position ECU into location and reconnect electrical connection.
2. Install and tighten retaining nuts to specification then install quarter trim panel.

Rear Differential Lock ECU .... 4.9 +/- 1 Nm

REAR DIFFERENTIAL LOCK ECU CHECK - CONDITION TABLE			
Terminal	Inspection Item	Condition		Terminal Voltage
1	Rear differential lock switch	Off side	Ignition switch: ON	When in Neutral	System Voltage
2	Vehicle speed read switch		Select 'D' or '1' and drive forward slowly	5 V
3	Ignition switch		Ignition switch	Off	0 V
				On	Battery Voltage
4	Rear differential lock air pump		Ignition switch: ON	When filling or holding	System Voltage
				When releasing	0 V
5			Ignition switch: ON	4WD	0 V
				2WD	System Voltage
8			Ignition switch: ON	Rear differential locked	0 V
				Rear differential free	System Voltage
9	Rear differential lock switch	On side	Ignition switch: ON	On side or Off side	0 V
10			Ignition switch: ON	Rear differential locked	0 V
				Rear differential free	System Voltage

REAR SUSPENSION, AXLE & DRIVESHAFT ASSEMBLIES

Rear Differential Lock Air Pump
Removal
1. Disconnect the hose and vapour hose from the air pump assembly.

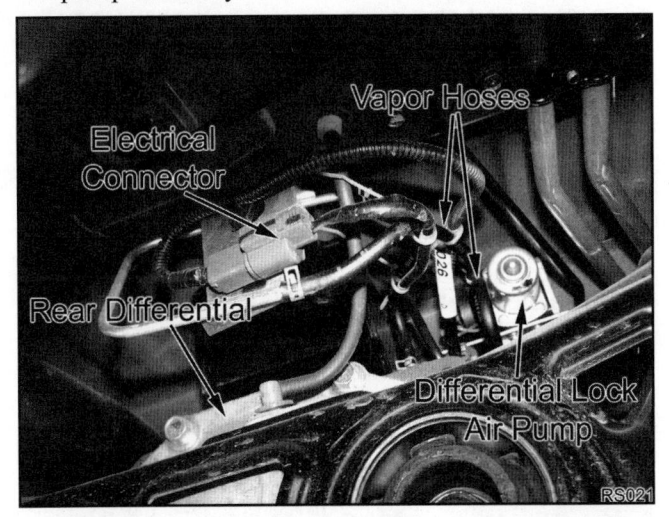

2. Remove the nipple, then remove the bolts securing the pump assembly and remove pump from vehicle.

Air Pump Check
1. Install air hose to differential.
2. To the air pump discharge outlet nozzle, via the air hose and T-joint, connect a pressure gauge.
3. To the air pump connector apply battery voltage, then measure the time from when the pump starts and stops. If pump stops within five seconds, the pressure switch inside the pump is normal.
4. Next 10-20 seconds after the pump has stopped measure the pressure.
   Standard Value.................................. 25 - 40 kPa
5. If pressure is within normal range the release valve inside the pump is normal.
6. Check to ensure the pump does not start to operate for approximately 5 minutes after it has stopped.
7. If all steps have proven to be normal the pump is fully operational.

Installation
1. Install the differential lock air pump assembly and tighten the mounting bolts to specification.
   Air Pump Bolts...................................... 12 +/-2 Nm
2. Install the nipple and vapour hose then install the hose to the assembly.

Rear Differential Lock Detection Switch
Removal
Disconnect the electrical connector then unscrew the switch from the Differential carrier.

Switch Check
1. To the switch connector, connect an ohmmeter between the two terminals.
2. Pull the detection switch rod, there should be continuity, and no continuity when the rod is returned to normal position.

Installation
Check condition of the gasket and renew if damaged. Screw switch back into place then reconnect the electrical connector.
Differential Lock Detection Switch .... 6 +/- 6Nm

Differential Carrier

Removal

1. Using a floor jack, raise the rear of the vehicle, then place safety stands under the rear body jacking points.
2. Remove the drain plug from the differential carrier and drain gear oil into a container.
3. Remove the wheels, then remove the rear speed sensor.
4. Mark the propeller shaft and carrier assembly alignment for assembly, then remove propeller shaft mounting bolts and suspend propeller shaft with wire from the body or ideally remove completely.(See Rear Propeller shaft removal)
5. Remove the rear brake caliper, disc and then remove the park brake shoe assembly. Refer to brakes chapter.
6. Remove the park brake cable retaining clip, then remove the park brake cable.
7. Remove the lower shock absorber mounting bolt, and then remove the trailing arm bolt.
8. Remove the mounting bolt for the lower arm, by using a jack and block of wood to take the pressure of the connection, then disconnect the toe control arm.
9. Carefully using a lever separate the drive shaft from the differential companion shaft and suspend the drive shaft using wire to prevent joint damage. Remove the harness connection and hoses for the rear differential lock if fitted.
10. Support differential carrier with a floor jack, then remove the differential carrier mounting bolts and remove carrier from vehicle. 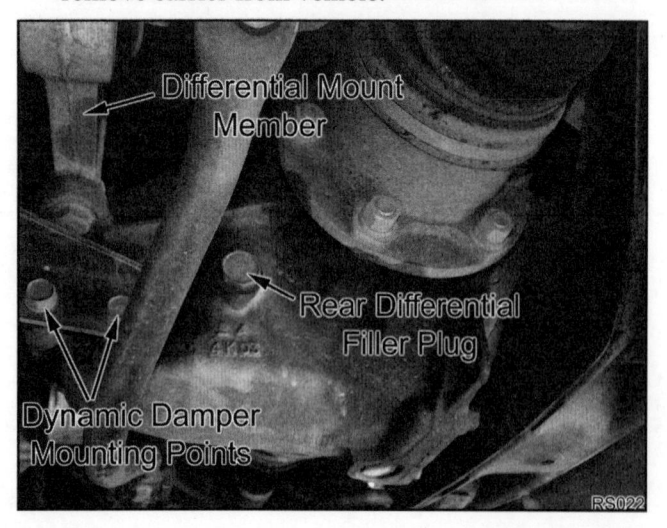
11. Remove the differential mounting bracket.

Installation

1. Install the differential mounting bracket, tighten retaining bolts to specification.
   Differential Mounting Bracket .... 152 +/- 25Nm
2. Raise the differential carrier into position using a floor jack, then install the differential carrier mounting bolts and tighten to specification. Do bolts up for the dynamic damper.
   Differential Carrier Bolts .... 152 +/- 25 Nm
   Dynamic Damper Bolts .... 83 +/- 12 Nm
3. Install the drive shafts to the companion shaft carriers.
   Drive Shaft Connection Bolts .... 113 +/- 14Nm
4. Install the propeller shaft, aligning the marks made on remove, then tighten retaining bolts to specification.
   Propeller shaft Mounting Nuts .... 60 +/- 10Nm
5. Reconnect the toe control arm tightening retaining nuts/bolts to specification. Install the lower arm bolts remembering to not fully tighten bolts until vehicle is lowered to the ground.
   Tow Control Arm .... 46 +/- 8Nm 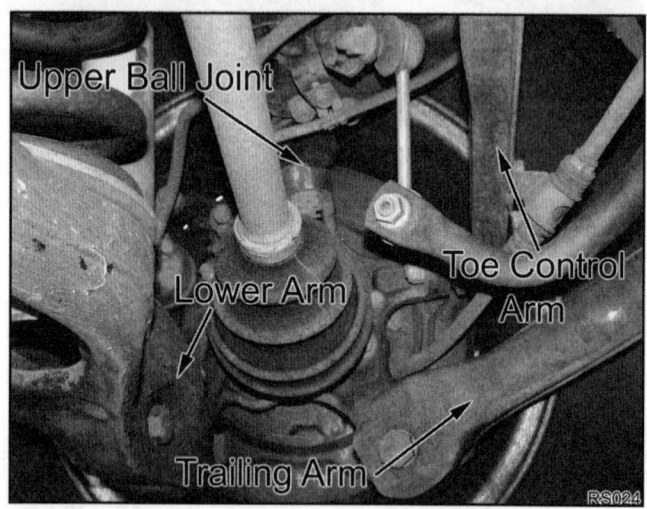
6. Install the trailing arm to knuckle doing nut up to specification.
   Trailing Arm Bolt/Nut .... 231 +/- 34 Nm
7. Reconnect the lower shock absorber and tighten retaining bolt/nut to specification.
   Lower Shock Absorber .... 152 +/- 25Nm
8. Reconnect the park brake cable and secure with retaining clip.
9. Install the park brake shoe assembly, brake disc and calliper. Refer to brakes chapter.
10. Connect the harness connector and hose for the rear differential lock. Then lower the vehicle.
11. Tighten the lower arm retaining nut to specification.
    Lower Arm Mounting Nut:
    NM - NP .... 152 +/- 25 Nm
    NS - NT .... 145 +/- 10 Nm
12. Adjust the park brake assembly, as outlined in brakes chapter.

DIFFERENTIAL ASSEMBLY

PRE-DISASSEMBLY INSPECTION

From the differential housing remove the cover and gasket then mount the assembly in a vice using appropriate mounting adaptor. Carry out the following procedures before disassembly of the unit.

DRIVE GEAR BACKLASH

1. With the drive pinion locked, use a dial gauge to measure the drive gear backlash in at least 4 places.
   Standard Drive Gear Backlash...... 0.13-0.18 mm
2. If not within specification adjust backlash.
3. After adjustment has been carried out check the gear tooth contact.

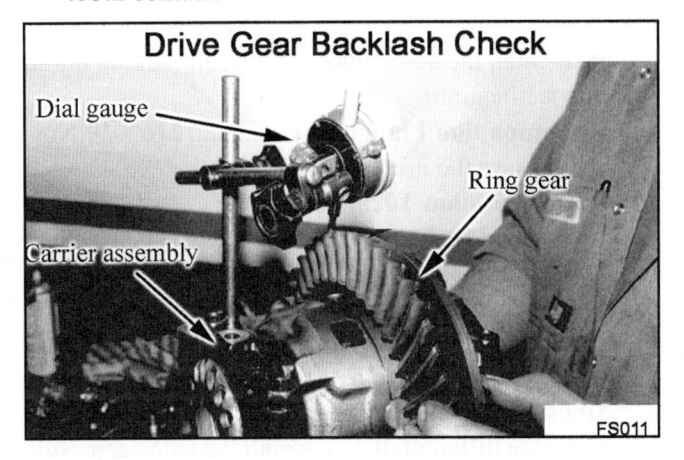

Drive Gear Backlash Check

DRIVE GEAR RUN-OUT

1. Measure the run-out of the drive gear at the shoulder of the gear on the reverse side.
   Drive Gear Run-out Limit .... 0.05 mm
2. If limit value is exceeded inspect for foreign objects between the drive gear side and differential case, or loose installation bolts.
3. In no foreign objects are found and bolts are tight, reposition the drive gear and differential case and re-measure.
4. Replace the differential case or drive gear and pinion as a set if adjustment cannot be achieved.

DIFFERENTIAL GEAR BACKLASH

1. Use a wedge to lock the side gear, then using a dial indicator on the pinion gear measure the differential gear backlash.
2. Repeat for both pinion gears.
   Standard value .... 0.0 - 0.076 mm
   Limit .... 0.2 mm
3. If limit is exceeded use side gear thrust spacers to correct. If adjustment is not possible replace the side gear and pinion gear as a set.

DRIVE GEAR TOOTH CONTACT

1. Coat both sides of the drive gear teeth with an even coat of gear marking compound.
2. Insert the brass tool between the differential carrier and case.
3. By hand rotate the companion flange one full revolution in each direction, while applying a load to the drive gear to achieve a revolution torque of approximately 2.5-3Nm to the drive pinion.
4. Inspect drive gear and drive pinion tooth contact pattern.

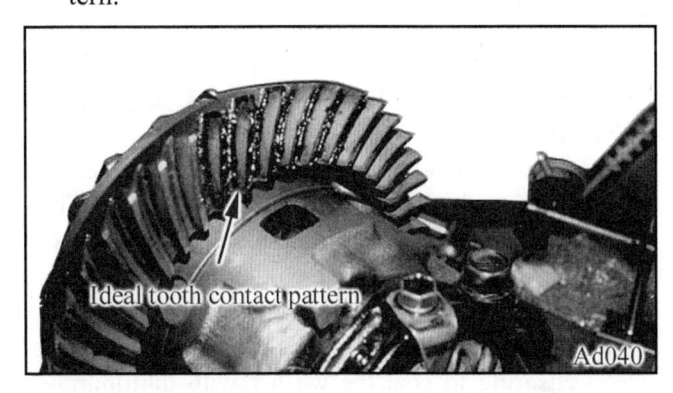

Ideal tooth contact pattern

CONVENTIONAL DIFFERENTIAL CARRIER DISASSEMBLY

1. Ensure the assembly is mounted in a vice with the cover removed as described in the pre-disassembly inspection.
2. From the differential carrier remove the bearing caps, then using the handle of a wooden hammer carefully remove the differential case assembly, being careful not to drop the side bearing outer races and shims.
3. From the case assembly remove the side bearing shims and the outer races.
4. Mount the differential case assembly securely in a vice.
5. Using an appropriate puller carefully remove the side bearing inner races from the case assembly.
6. Mark the relationship of the drive gear to differential case, then loosen the drive gear retaining bolts in a diagonal sequence and remove drive gear from assembly. With a suitable punch drive out the lock pin.
   Note: This step is the same with Limited Slip Differential. Do not disassemble LSD case assembly.
7. Now the shaft, gears, washers and spacers can be removed. Making sure to keep in order to help with assembly.
8. From the differential carrier remove the self-locking nut and washer, it will be necessary to hold the companion flange with an appropriate tool.
9. Mark the relationship of the drive pinion and companion flange, then using an appropriate puller remove the companion flange.

REAR SUSPENSION, AXLE & DRIVESHAFT ASSEMBLIES

10. Remove the drive pinion assembly.
11. From the pinion assembly remove the drive pinion spacer and rear shim.
12. Using a bearing puller remove the drive pinion rear bearing inner race, then remove the rear shim from the drive pinion.
13. From the differential carrier remove the oil seal, drive pinion front bearing inner race and outer race.
14. From the carrier assembly remove the drive pinion rear bearing outer race, then remove the oil seal's from the side of the carrier.

CONVENTIONAL DIFFERENTIAL CARRIER ASSEMBLY

1. To the differential carrier install the oil seal, where the companion shafts go in the side of the carrier. Then install the drive pinion front bearing outer race and the drive pinion rear bearing outer race.
2. Adjust the drive pinion height as follows:
   a) Set up the special tools as per their instructions, ensuring to coat the washer with multipurpose grease. Install drive pinion front and rear bearing inner races to the carrier.
   Special tool: MB990819, MB991169, MB99170
   b) Measure the turning torque of the drive pinion while tightening the nut of the special tool. Continue to tighten until the turning torque is to specification (without oil seal).
   Turning Torque .... 1.94-2.25 Nm
   c) Clean the side bearing hub, then install the special tool to the side bearing hub of the carrier and install bearing cap to the special tool.
   Special tool MB991534
   d) Measure the clearance between the special tools using a feeler gauge, and record reading as "A".
   e) Remove the two special tools (*MB991170, MB991169*), then use a micrometer to measure the special tool recording readings as "B" & "C".
   f) Install the bearing cap, then using a cylinder gauge and micrometer measure the inside diameter of the bearing cap and record reading as "D".
   g) Using the below formula calculate the correct thickness of the drive pinion rear shim.
   Shim Thickness =
   "A"+"B"+"C" - (0.5"D") - 86mm
   h) To the drive pinion install the correct drive pinion rear shim/s and press in the drive pinion rear bearing inner race.
3. Adjust the drive pinion turning torque as follows:
   a) To the gear carrier install the drive pinion, drive pinion spacer, drive pinion front shim, front bearing inner race and companion shaft flange (do not install oil seal).
   b) Tighten the companion flange to specification.
   Companion flange .... 216+/-29 Nm
   c) Measure the drive pinion turning torque.
   Drive Pinion Turning Torque .... 1.94-2.25 Nm
   d) If not within specification adjust preload by replacing the drive pinion front shim/s or drive pinion spacers. See Chart.

Height of Pinion Spacer (mm)	Identification Colour
52.50	Yellow
52.84	Red

   e) Remove companion flange and drive pinion, then insert drive pinion front bearing inner race to the carrier.
   f) Press fit the oil seal to the front of the carrier assembly, then install the drive pinion assembly and companion flange aligning marks made on removal.
   g) Tighten the companion flange self locking nut to specification.
   Companion Flange Nut .... 216+/-29 Nm
   h) Measure the drive pinion turning torque.
   Drive Pinion Turning Torque:
   - no lubrication .... 2.03-2.34 Nm
   - gear oil applied .... 2.10-2.40 Nm
   i) If not within specification check the companion flange self locking nut is tightened to specification and the oil seal is installed correctly.
4. Adjust the differential gear backlash as follows:
   a) To the differential case install the side gears, side gear spacers, pinion gears and pinion washers.
   b) Temporarily install the pinion shaft to the assembly, then lock the side gear by inserting a wedge between the side gear and pinion shaft.
   c) Using a dial indicator on the pinion gear measure the differential gear backlash.
   d) Repeat for both pinion gears.
   Standard value .... 0.0 - 0.076 mm
   Limit .... 0.2 mm
   e) If limit is exceeded use side gear thrust spacers to correct. If adjustment is not possible replace the side gear and pinion gear as a set.
5. Align the lock pin holes of the pinion shaft with the holes of the case, then drive in the lock pin and stake pin on both sides.
6. Ensure the drive gear retaining bolts and bolt hole threads are clean from old stud locking compound.
   Note: *If may be necessary to clean the hole threads using a M10 x 1.25 tap, carefully.*

REAR SUSPENSION, AXLE & DRIVESHAFT ASSEMBLIES

7. To the differential case install the drive gear aligning marks made on removal, then install and tighten retaining bolts in a diagonal sequence. When install the retaining bolts make sure to apply a small amount of stud locking compound.
   Drive Gear Bolts:
   6G72 .... 84 +/- 5 Nm
   4M4 and 6G74 .... 152 +/- 15 Nm
8. To the differential case install the side bearing inner race, then install the side gear outer race and shims.
9. Adjust the drive gear backlash as follows:
   a) To the differential case assembly install the side bearing spacers (thinner spacers than those removed), then mount the case assembly into the gear carrier.
   b) Push case assembly to one side and using a feeler gauge measure the clearance between the gear carrier and the side bearing adjusting spacer.
   c) Measure the thickness of the side bearing adjusting spacers on one side and record measurement.
   d) Take the measurement of the spacers, add half the recorded clearance then add 0.05mm.
   e) Using this new thickness measurements, select two pairs of spacers and install one pair to the drive pinion side and the other to the drive gear side.
   f) Install the side bearing adjusting spacers and differential case assembly to the carrier.
   g) Fit the side bearing adjusting spacers to the side bearing outer race by taping them.
   h) Tighten the bearing cap after aligning the mating marks of the carrier and bearing cap.
   Tightening Torque .... 74+/-5 Nm
   i) Use a dial gauge to measure the drive gear backlash in at least 4 places.
   Standard Drive Gear Backlash .0.13-0.18 mm
   j) Adjust backlash by adjusting the spacers, refer to diagram.

If Backlash Is Too Small
Thinner Spacer — Thicker Spacer
Thicker Spacer — Thinner Spacer
If Backlash Is Too Large

   k) Check the tooth contact of the drive gear and drive pinion and adjust as required.
   l) At the shoulder of the reverse side of the drive gear measure the drive gear run-out.
   Drive Gear Run-out Limit .... 0.05 mm
   m) If limit is exceeded, reinstall changing the position of the drive gear and differential case.
   n) Re-measure, if adjustment is not possible replace the differential case or replace the side gear and pinion gear set.
10. To the differential carrier assembly install the cover using a new gasket, tightening bolts to specification.
    Rear Cover Bolts .... 35 +/-5 Nm
11. If removed install the drain and filler plugs to the assembly.
    Drain Plug .... 63 +/-4 Nm
    Filler Plug .... 49 +/-9 Nm

REAR DIFFERENTIAL LOCK WITH LSD DISASSEMBLY

1. Ensure the assembly is mounted in a vice with the cover removed as described in the pre-disassembly inspection.
2. From the carrier remove the hoses that go to the air pump assembly.
3. From the differential carrier remove the bearing caps, then using the handle of a wooden hammer carefully remove the differential case assembly, being careful not to drop the side bearing outer races and shims. Now remove the actuator assembly and pressure plate.
4. From the case assembly remove the side bearing shims and the outer races.
5. Mount the differential case assembly securely in a vice.
6. Using an appropriate puller carefully remove the side bearing inner races from the case assembly.
7. Mark the relationship of the drive gear to differential case, then loosen the drive gear retaining bolts in a diagonal sequence and remove drive gear from assembly.
8. From the differential carrier remove the self-locking nut and washer, it will be necessary to hold the companion flange with an appropriate tool.
9. Mark the relationship of the drive pinion and companion flange, then using an appropriate puller remove the companion flange.
10. Remove the drive pinion assembly.
11. From the pinion assembly remove the drive pinion spacer and rear shim.
12. Using a bearing puller remove the drive pinion rear bearing inner race, then remove the rear shim from the drive pinion.
13. From the differential carrier remove the oil seal, drive pinion front bearing inner race and outer race.
14. From the carrier assembly remove the drive pinion rear bearing outer race, then remove the oil seal's from the side of the carrier.
15. Remove the differential lock position switch.

REAR DIFFERENTIAL LOCK WITH LSD ASSEMBLY

1. To the differential carrier install the oil seal, where the companion shafts go in the side of the carrier. Then install the drive pinion front bearing outer race and the drive pinion rear bearing outer race.
2. Install the differential lock position switch with a new gasket.
3. Adjust the drive pinion height as follows:
   a) Set up special tools ensuring to coat the washer with multipurpose grease. Install drive pinion front and rear bearing inner races to the carrier.
      Special tool: MB990819, MB991169, MB991770
   b) Measure the turning torque of the drive pinion while tightening the nut of the special tool. Continue to tighten until the turning torque is to specification (without oil seal).
      Turning Torque .... 1.94 - 2.25 Nm
   c) Clean the side bearing hub, then install the special tool to the side bearing hub of the carrier and install bearing cap to the special tool.
      Note: *Ensure notch and tools are firmly against side bearing hub.*
      Special tool MB991534
   d) Measure the clearance between the special tools using a feeler gauge, and record reading as "A".
   e) Remove the two special tools (*MB991170, MB991169*), then use a micrometer to measure the special tools and record readings as "B" & "C".
   f) Install the bearing cap, then using a cylinder gauge and micrometer measure the inside diameter of the bearing cap and record reading as "D".
   g) Using the below formula calculate the correct thickness of the drive pinion rear shim.
      Shim Thickness =
      "A"+"B"+"C" - (0.5"D") - 86mm
   h) To the drive pinion install the correct drive pinion rear shim/s and press in the drive pinion rear bearing inner race.
4. Adjust the drive pinion turning torque as follows:
   a) To the gear carrier install the drive pinion, drive pinion spacer, drive pinion front shim, front bearing inner race and companion shaft flange (do not install oil seal).
   b) Tighten the companion flange to specification.
      Companion flange .... 216 +/- 29 Nm
   c) Measure the drive pinion turning torque.
      Drive Pinion Turning Torque..1.94 - 2.25 Nm
   d) If not within specification adjust preload by replacing the drive pinion front shim/s or drive pinion spacers. See chart.

Height of Pinion Spacer (mm)	Identification Colour
52.50	Yellow
52.84	Red

   e) Remove companion flange and drive pinion, then insert drive pinion front bearing inner race to the carrier.
   f) Press fit the oil seal to the front of the carrier assembly, then install the drive pinion assembly and companion flange aligning marks made on removal.
   g) Tighten the companion flange self locking nut to specification.
      Companion Flange Nut .... 216 +/- 29 Nm
   h) Measure the drive pinion turning torque.
      Drive Pinion Turning Torque:
         - no lubrication..................... 2.03 - 2.34 Nm
         - gear oil applied .... 2.10 - 2.40 Nm
   i) If not within specification check the companion flange self locking nut is tightened to specification and the oil seal is installed correctly.
5. Adjust the differential gear backlash as follows:
   a) To the differential case install the side gears, side gear spacers, pinion gears and pinion washers.
   b) Temporarily install the pinion shaft to the assembly, then lock the side gear by inserting a wedge between the side gear and pinion shaft.
   c) Using a dial indicator on the pinion gear measure the differential gear backlash.
   d) Repeat for both pinion gears.
      Standard value .... 0.0 - 0.076 mm
      Limit... 0.2 mm
   e) If limit is exceeded use side gear thrust spacers to correct. If adjustment is not possible replace the side gear and pinion gear as a set.
6. Ensure the drive gear retaining bolts and bolt hole threads are clean from old stud locking compound.
   Note: *If may be necessary to clean the hole threads using a M10 x 1.25 tap, carefully.*
7. To the differential case install the drive gear aligning marks made on removal, then install and tighten retaining bolts in a diagonal sequence.
   Drive Gear Bolts
   (6G72)... 84 +/- 5 Nm
   (4M4, 6G74)..................................... 152 +/- 15 Nm
   Note: *Apply stud locking compound to the bolt threads before installation.*
8. Install the pressure plate and actuator assembly, torquing bolts to specifications.
   Pressure Plate Retaining Bolts.............. 5.8 +/- 2Nm
9. To the differential case install the side bearing inner race, then install the side gear outer race and shims.
10. Adjust the drive gear backlash as follows:
    a) To the differential case assembly install the side

bearing spacers (thinner spacers than those removed), then mount the case assembly into the gear carrier.

b) Push case assembly to one side and using a feeler gauge measure the clearance between the gear carrier and the side bearing adjusting spacer.

c) Measure the thickness of the side bearing adjusting spacers on one side and record measurement.

d) Take the measurement of the spacers, add half the recorded clearance then add 0.05mm.

e) Using this new thickness measurements, select two pairs of spacers and install one pair to the drive pinion side and the other to the drive gear side.

f) Install the side bearing adjusting spacers and differential case assembly to the carrier.

g) Fit the side bearing adjusting spacers to the side bearing outer race by taping them.

h) Tighten the bearing cap after aligning the mating marks of the carrier and bearing cap.
Tightening Torque............................74 +/- 5 Nm

i) Use a dial gauge to measure the drive gear backlash in at least 4 places.
Drive Gear Backlash ....0.13 - 0.18 mm

j) Adjust backlash by adjusting the spacers, refer to diagram.

If Backlash Is Too Small
Thinner Spacer — Thicker Spacer
Thicker Spacer — Thinner Spacer
If Backlash Is Too Large

k) Check the tooth contact of the drive gear and drive pinion and adjust as required.

l) At the shoulder of the reverse side of the drive gear measure the drive gear run-out.
Drive Gear Run-out Limit .... 0.05 mm

m) If limit is exceeded, reinstall changing the position of the drive gear and differential case.

n) Re-measure, if adjustment is not possible replace the differential case or replace the side gear and pinion gear set.

11. To the differential carrier assembly install the cover using a new gasket, tightening bolts to specification.
Rear Cover Bolts ....35 +/-5 Nm

12. If removed install the drain and filler plugs to the assembly. Install the air pipes and hose if removed.
Drain Plug............................63 +/- 4 Nm
Filler Plug ....49 +/- 9 Nm

SPECIFICATIONS

REAR SUSPENSION
Toe Control Arm ball joint turning torque ... 1.0-2.5 Nm
Upper Arm ball joint rotation torque .... 0.5-3.0 Nm
Stabilizer link ball joint turning torque .... 0.5-2.0 Nm

REAR WHEEL ALIGNMENT
Toe in .... 3 +/- 3 mm
Toe angle ....1°06' +/- 1°06'
Camber Standard Value .... 0° +/- 30'
    Difference b/w right & left ....less than 30'
Thrust angle ....0° +/- 9'

REAR AXLE
Wheel bearing axial play (limit) .... 0.05 mm
Rear Axle Total Backlash (limit) .... 5 mm
Wheel Bearing Turning Starting Torque .... 1.76 Nm

PROPELLER SHAFT
Front Limit .... 0.5 mm
Rear (Vehicles Without CFRP Shaft) .... 0.4 mm
Clearance b/w Rear Tube And Shaft (Vehicles With CFRP Shaft)...0.2-0.5 mm

TORQUE SETTINGS
Description	Nm
Upper Shock Absorber Nut	44 +/- 10
Lower Shock Absorber Nut	152 +/- 25
Lower Control Arm to Body	123 +/- 15
Lower Control Arm to Knuckle	152 +/- 25
Upper Control Arm Bolts	167 +/- 10
Upper Control Arm Ball Joint Bolt	150 +/- 30
Upper Control Arm Ball Joint Mounting	98 +/- 12
Stabiliser Bar Bracket Bolts	44 +/- 10
Stabiliser Link Nuts	104 +/- 14
Toe Control Adjustment Bolt/Nut	123 +/- 15
Toe Control Arm Ball Joint	67 +/- 7
Toe Control Tower Bar	46 +/- 8
Trailing Arm Nut	231 +/- 34
Trailing Arm To Knuckle	231 +/- 34
Knuckle To Lower Arm	152 +/- 25
Drive Shaft Nut	255 +/- 29
Propeller Shaft To Companion Shaft	113 +/- 14
Brake Caliper Retaining Bolts	88 +/- 10
Brake Backing Plate	81 +/- 6
Rear Diff Lock Switch	12 +/- 2
Rear Diff Lock Position Switch	36 +/- 6
Brake Pipe Connection	15 +/- 2
DOJ Assembly To Companion Shaft	113 +/- 14
Diff Carrier Mount	152 +/- 25
Dynamic Damper Bolts	83 +/- 12

BRAKE SYSTEM

Subject	Page
ROUTINE MAINTENANCE	355
Bleeding The Brake System	355
Checking Brake Lines and Hoses	356
Brake Pad Wear	356
Brake Roughness	356
Disc Brake Service Precautions	356
Burnishing Procedure	356
Measuring Brake Drag Force	357
BRAKE PEDAL	357
Brake Pedal Height	357
Brake Pedal Free Play	358
Brake Pedal Free Play (HBB Models)	358
Clearance Between Brake Pedal and Floor	358
Brake Pedal Assembly	358
Removal	358
Installation	358
Stop Lamp Switch Check	359
MASTER CYLINDER & BOOSTER (no ABS)	359
Operational Test	359
Check Valve Operation Check	359
Vacuum Leak Test	359
Master Cylinder Bleeding	359
Master Cylinder	359
Removal	359
Dismantle	360
Clean and Inspect	360
Assembly	360
Installation	360
Inspection of Brake Fluid Level Sensor	360
Brake Booster	360
Removal	360
Installation	360
HYDRAULIC BRAKE BOOSTER (HBB)	361
Power Supply Function & Operation Check	361
HBB System Air Bleeding	361
Removal	362
Dismantle	362
Clean and Inspect	362
Assembly	363
Installation	363

Subject	Page
LOAD SENSING PROPORTIONING VALVE	364
Spring Length Check & Adjustment	364
Function Test	364
Removal	364
Installation	364
FRONT BRAKE ASSEMBLY	365
Front Brake Caliper	365
Removal	365
Dismantle	365
Clean and Inspect	365
Assembly	365
Installation	365
Front Rotor	366
Removal	366
Inspection	366
Installation	366
Front Brake Pad	366
Removal	366
Installation	366
REAR BRAKE ASSEMBLY	367
Rear Brake Caliper	367
Removal	367
Dismantle	367
Inspection	368
Assemble	368
Installation	368
Rear Brake Pad	368
Removal	368
Installation	368
Rear Rotor	369
Removal	369
Inspection	369
Installation	369
PARK BRAKE	369
Park Brake Switch	369
Removal	369
Inspection	369
Installation	369
Check and Adjustment	369

BRAKE SYSTEM

Subject	Page
Lever Assembly	370
Removal	370
Installation	370
Park Brake Shoes	371
Removal	371
Inspection	371
Installation	371
Park Brake Cable	372
Removal	372
Installation	372
ABS COMPONENTS	372
Wheel Speed Sensor	372
Output Voltage Measurement	372
ABS VALVE RELAY CONTINUITY CHECK	373
SOLENOID VALVE CHECK	373
FRONT WHEEL SPEED SENSOR	373
Removal	373
Terminal Inspection	373
Insulation Check	374
Installation	374
REAR WHEEL SPEED SENSOR	374
Removal	374
Inspection	374
Insulation Check	374
Installation	374
ABS ECU	374
Removal	374
Installation	374
G-SENSOR	375
Removal	375
Installation	375
ASTC and ATC	375
ASTC-ECU and ATC-ECU	375
Removal	375
Installation	375
Initialization	375
HBB BUZZER	376
Removal	376
Installation	376
Deactivation of HBB Buzzer Operation Check	376
G and YAW RATE SENSOR	376
Removal	376
Installation	376
Initialization	376
STEERING WHEEL SENSOR	377
Removal	377
Installation	377
Initialization	377
SOLENOID VALVE CHECK	377
SPECIFICATIONS	378
TORQUE SETTINGS	378

ROUTINE MAINTENANCE

BLEEDING THE BRAKE SYSTEM

Bleeding Master Cylinder (empty master cylinder)
Fill the reserve tank with brake fluid, keeping the brake pedal depressed have a person place their finger over the master cylinder outlet.
Release brake pedal with master cylinder still closed. Repeat this process a number of times to fill the inside of the master cylinder.

Brake Line Bleeding

Clean dust grease and foreign matter from the brake bleeding valves on all four calipers.
At the rear left wheel prepare to start bleeding the brake system. Always bleed the caliper with the longest length of brake fluid pipe first, this is to help ensure there are no air trapped in the brake pipe system.
Place a ring spanner on the bleeder valve, then connect a clear plastic tube to the end of the bleeder valve, insert the other end of the plastic bleeder hose into a clean container half filled with clean brake fluid.

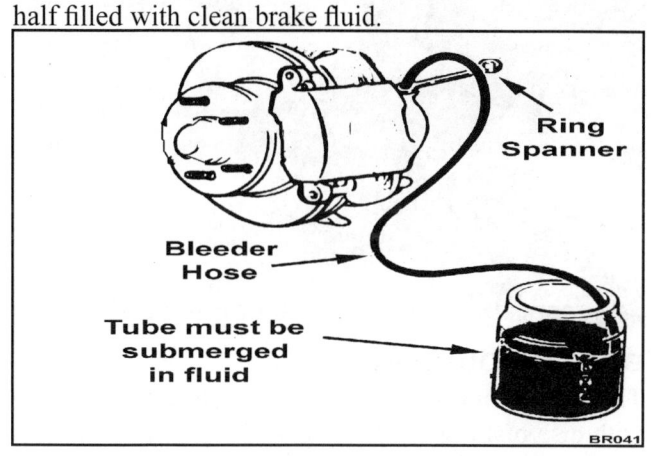

Have an assistant press the brake pedal 3 or 4 times and hold his foot on the pedal, this is pumping the brakes. After your assistant has pumped the brakes, with his/her foot still on the pedal, loosen the bleeder valve with the ring spanner approximately half a turn. This will allow fluid and air to pass out of the bleeder valve through the bleeder hose into the container with the brake fluid. When the assistants foot on the brake pedal has travelled to the floor, tighten the bleeder valve before the assistant allows the pedal to rise from the floor, otherwise old fluid and air will be sucked back into the brake system. Check the level of the master cylinder and keep topping it up with fluid otherwise air will enter the system.
Repeat above procedure (pumping the brakes) until all air has been released from the back left brake bleeder valve. Tighten the bleeder valve, remove the hose and spanner.
Repeat the bleeding procedure on the right front wheel, right rear wheel then left front wheel.

BRAKE SYSTEM

Check the level of the master cylinder.
Note: Do not use the old brake fluid to top up the master cylinder.

CHECKING BRAKE LINES and HOSES
Raise the vehicle, position on safety stands and remove rear wheels. Inspect braking disc, linings and caliper. Check all brake tube connection for possible leaks and flexible hoses for deterioration. Install new flexible hoses if required.

BRAKE PAD WEAR
If visual inspection thru the inspection port doesn't adequately determine condition of lining, a physical check is necessary. To check amount of lining wear, remove brake pad assemblies. Three thickness measurements with a micrometer should be taken across the centre of each pad assembly; one reading at each end and one in the centre.

Note: For wear limits refer to specification section at the end of this chapter.

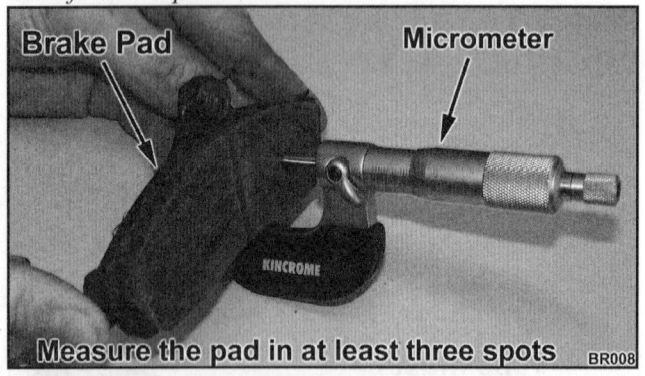

BRAKE ROUGHNESS
The most common cause of brake roughness (or chatter) with disc brake is excessive disc face run-out. This is easily checked with a dial indicator. If measurement is out of specification, disc must be resurfaced or replaced.

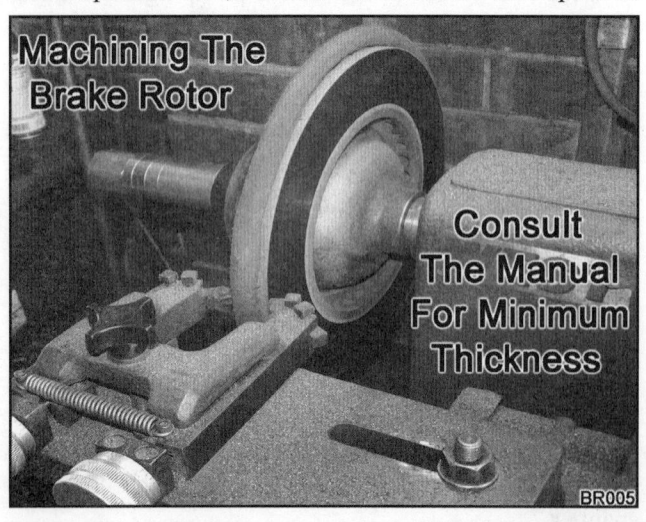

Other less prevalent causes of roughness can be the use of some type of nonstandard lining material and extreme abrasion of the disc faces. Vehicles which stand unused for periods of time in areas of high humidity or salt air may incur rust on the disc which could cause a temporary brake surge and roughness. Normally, however, this condition should correct itself after a short period of usage. If rust is severe enough, roughness will not clear up and the disc must be resurfaced or replaced.

Note: For wear limits refer to specification section at the end of this chapter.

DISC BRAKE SERVICE PRECAUTIONS
Grease and any foreign material must be kept off caliper assembly and surfaces of braking disc during service procedures. The braking disc and caliper should be handled, avoiding deformation of the disc and scratching or nicking of the pad linings.

If inspection reveals square sectioned caliper piston seal is worn or damaged, it should be replaced immediately. During removal and installation of a wheel and tyre assembly, use care not to strike the caliper.

Before moving vehicle after brake service work, obtain a firm brake pedal by using correct bleeding procedures. Dragging the brakes (common result of left foot application on vehicles with automatic transmission) should be avoided during vehicle operation.

As brake pad lining wears, reservoir level will go down. If fluid has been added between relines, then reservoir overflow may occur when piston is pushed back into new lining position. Overflow can be avoided by removing a small amount of fluid from reservoir.

Burnishing Procedure
The burnishing procedure should be done whenever new park brake shoes, rear brake rotors or when the brakes are not performing as well as they should.

1. Adjust the Park Brake Lever Stroke to specification.

   Lever Stroke :
   NM - NP ....5 - 7 notches @ 200N
   NS ....6 - 7 notches @ 200N

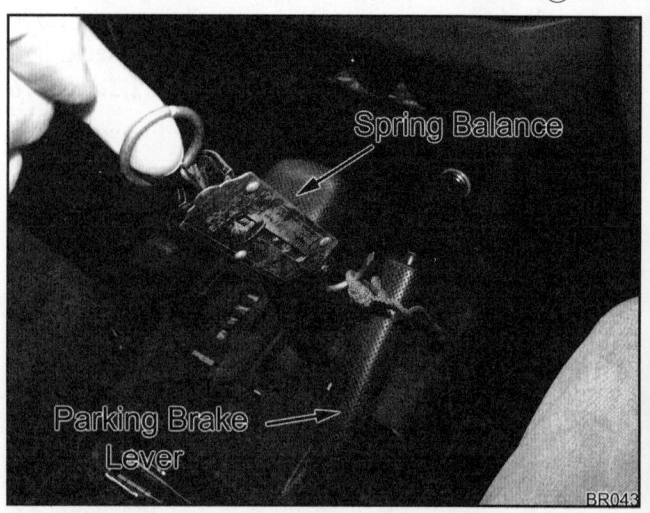

BRAKE SYSTEM

2. Pull on the parking brake lever with a force of approx. 100N. Drive the vehicle forward at a speed of 35-50km/h for 100m.
3. Come to a stop and release the brake lever, allow the brakes to cool for up to 10 minutes.
4. Repeat the steps **2** and **3** about four times.

MEASURING BRAKE DRAG FORCE

1. With the brake caliper assembly removed use a spring balance to measure the hub rotation resistance. To do this wrap a cord around the studs. Pulling in the direction the wheel would turn going forward. This is value **"A"**.
2. Install the brake caliper assembly. Start the engine and depress the pedal two or three times with firm force. Then stop the engine.
3. Rotate the rotor clockwise about 10 times.
4. Use a spring balance to measure the rotation resistance. This is value **"B"**.

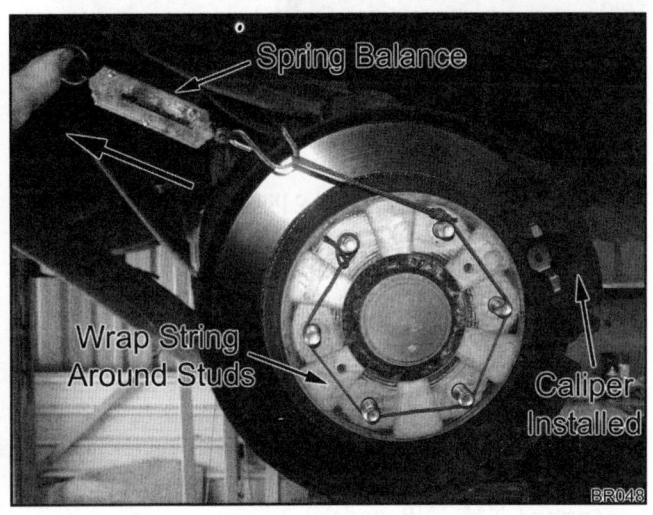

5. To calculate the drag force, calculate the difference between **"A"** and **"B"**.
   Standard Limit
   NM - NP Front .... 55 N
   NM - NP Rear .... 55 N
   NS Front .... 86 N
   NS Rear (SWB) .... 55 N
   NS Rear (LWB) .... 86 N
6. If the limit is exceeded the caliper may need to be overhauled as it may be binding, due to rust in the assembly bore.

BRAKE PEDAL

Brake Pedal Height
1. Fold the carpet back out of the way, then measure the brake pedal height as shown.
   Standard Value   - LHD .... 192 - 195 mm
                        - RHD .... 187 - 190 mm

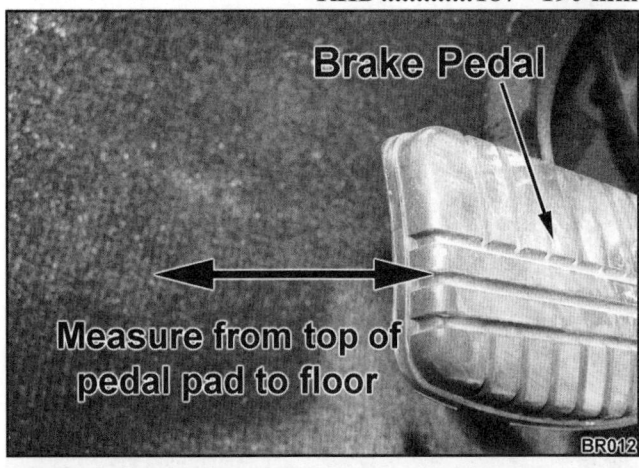

2. If brake pedal height is not within specification proceed to the next step.
3. Disconnect the electrical connector for the stop lamp switch, then loosen the stop lamp switch at least 1/4 turn anti-clockwise.
4. Remove the pin then adjust the clevis to obtain correct pedal height and reinstall the pin. On later model NS Pajero it is necessary to fully remove the brake pedal and support member. To adjust the pedal height turn the HBB clevis until the correct height is achieved. Then tighten pedal bolts.
   Pedal retaining bolts .... 12 +/- 2 Nm
5. Screw in the stop lamp switch until it contacts the stopper, then with the pedal held by hand at maximum height turn the stop lamp switch a further 1/4 turn clockwise.
6. Ensure the switch plunger to stopper is within specification, then reconnect the electrical connector.
   Plunger to Stopper Clearance .... 0.5 - 1.0 mm

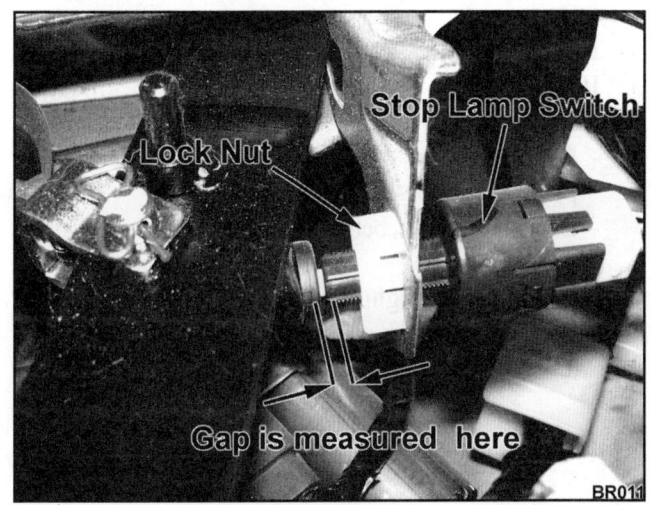

357

BRAKE SYSTEM

7. Check that brake light switch operates correctly, then return carpet into position.

Brake Pedal Free Play
1. With the ignition switch to the fully off position, pump the brake pedal until a hard pedal is obtained.
2. Press the pedal with your finger and measure the free play. The free play is the point from rest to where resistance is felt.
   Free Play .... 3 - 8 mm

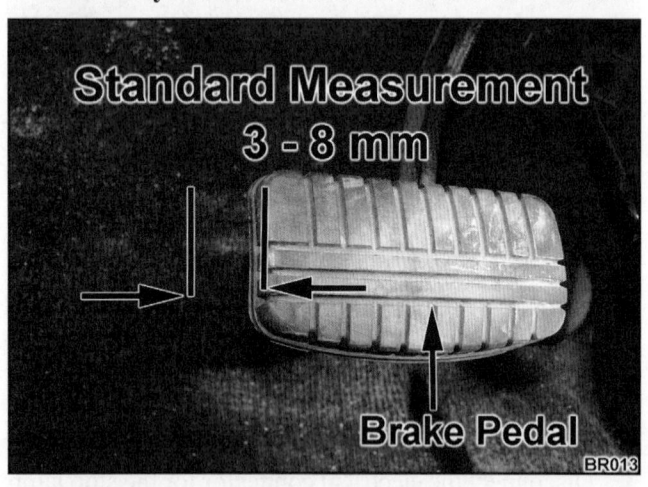

3. If brake pedal free play is not within specification check the following:
   - Excessive play between brake pedal and clevis pin.
   - Excessive play between clevis pin and booster operating rod.
   - Brake pedal height.
   - Stop lamp switch installation position.
4. Adjust or replace as required.

Brake Pedal Free Play (HBB Models)
1. Turn the ignition switch on and wait till the HBB accumulator pump motor stops. When the motor has stopped the accumulator is fully primed.
2. Press the pedal by hand and measure the free play. The free play is the point from rest to where resistance is felt.
   Free Play .... 3mm or Less
3. If brake pedal free play is not within specification check the following:
   - Excessive play between brake pedal and clevis pin.
   - Excessive play between clevis pin and booster operating rod.
   - Brake pedal height.
   - Stop lamp switch installation position.
4. Adjust or replace as required.

Clearance Between Brake Pedal & Floor
1. Fold the carpet back out of the way, then start the engine.
2. Depress the brake pedal with approximately **490 N** of force and measure the brake pedal to floor clearance as shown.
   Standard Value:
   NM - NP .... 90mm or more
   NS .... 80mm or more

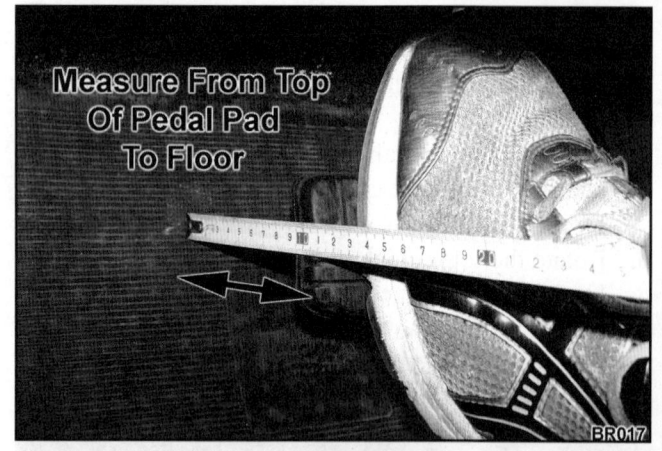

3. If brake pedal clearance is not to specification bleed the brake system to ensure air is not trapped in system. Also check to ensure brake pads do not need replacing.
4. When the checks are complete return the carpet to its position.

BRAKE PEDAL ASSEMBLY
Removal
1. Remove the instrument panel lower panel, refer to body chapter if required, then disconnect the return spring (NM - NP models).
2. Vehicles fitted with auto transmissions remove the split pin securing the shift lock cable and remove cable.
3. Disconnect the electrical connection from the stop lamp switch then remove the stop lamp switch assembly.
4. Remove the pedal stopper then remove the snap pin and the retaining pin from the pedal assembly.
5. On NS Models remove the guide bracket.
6. Remove the 4 mounting nuts from the brake booster, then remove the 2 upper brake pedal support retaining bolts from the vehicle.

Installation
1. Install the pedal support and pedal assembly into position and loosely install the mounting bolts and nuts.
2. Tighten the brake booster retaining nuts to specification, then tighten the pedal support retaining bolts to specification. On NS models install the guide bracket

BRAKE SYSTEM

to the pedal assembly.
Brake booster retaining nuts
  NM - NP ....14 +/- 3 Nm
  NS ....13 +/- 2 Nm
Pedal support retaining bolts: ....12 +/- 2 Nm
Guide bracket to body bolts................12 +/- 2 Nm
Guide bracket to pedal assembly........20 +/- 3 Nm

Note: Brake booster nuts must be tightened before pedal support bolts to obtain correct positioning.

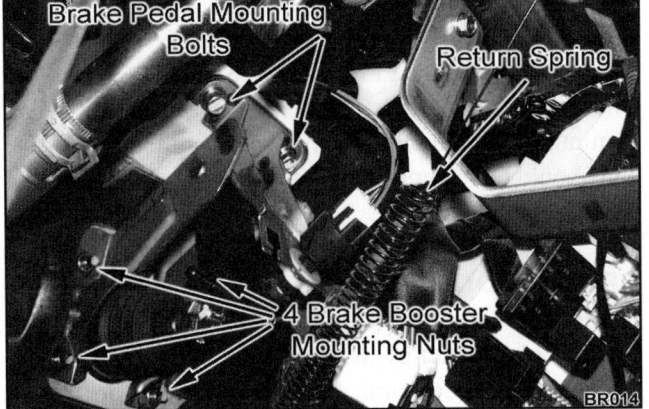

3. Install the pedal to booster push rod retaining pin, then install the retaining snap pin and the pedal stopper.
4. Install a new stop lamp switch adjuster, and stop lamp switch, then reconnect the electrical connection.
5. Vehicles fitted with an auto transmission install the shift lock cable and secure with split pin. On NM - NP models install the return spring.
6. Adjust the brake pedal as described previously, then check the stop lamp switch is operating correctly.
7. Install the instrument panel lower section.

Stop Lamp Switch
Check
1. On vehicles without auto cruise control connect a multimeter to the two terminals and measure the continuity. On vehicles with auto cruise control measure the continuity between terminal No. 1 and No. 2.
2. There should be no continuity when the plunger is pushed in, and continuity when it is released.

MASTER CYLINDER & BOOSTER - Vehicles without ABS

BRAKE BOOSTER OPERATION TEST
Operational Test
1. With the brake pedal depressed start the engine, if the pedal goes down slightly when the engine is started operation is normal.
2. With the engine running depress the brake pedal, now stop the engine. If the brake pedal height remains the same, the booster is okay.
3. If the tests fail, check the condition of the booster, vacuum hoses or check valve. Replace if needed.

CHECK VALVE OPERATION CHECK
1. Remove the vacuum hose, and attach a vacuum pump.
Note: The check valve should not be removed from the hose as they are one unit, and should be replaced as one.

Vacuum Pump Connection	Pressure
Brake Booster Side	Negative pressure is created and held
Intake Manifold Side	Negative pressure is not created

2. If the above pressures are not achieved the check valve as a unit will need to be replaced.

MASTER CYLINDER BLEEDING
Note: Two people are required for bleeding brake system. Bleeding the brake pipes will be easier if master cylinder has been bleed.
1. Press and hold down the brake pedal.
2. Fill the reservoir with brake fluid and cover the outlet port with your finger.
3. Release the brake pedal with the port still covered.
4. Repeat this procedure 3-4 times to fill master cylinder system with brake fluid.
5. Once the master cylinder is free from air bleed air from pipes/brake calipers are described earlier in the chapter.

MASTER CYLINDER
Removal
1. **LHD** vehicles disconnect and remove the battery.
   RHD vehicles remove air cleaner and air intake duct.
2. Disconnect electrical connector from brake fluid level sensor.
3. Disconnect brake lines from master cylinder and plug lines to prevent dirt from entering pipes.

BRAKE SYSTEM

4. Remove nuts securing the master cylinder to brake booster and remove master cylinder and bracket.
   Note: *Do not move brake booster push rod or press the brake pedal with master cylinder removed or reaction disc may become misaligned in booster.*

Dismantle

1. Remove reservoir retaining pin then remove the reservoir.
2. Remove the brake fluid level sensor and then remove the two reservoir seals.
3. Depress and hold the primary piston down, then using snap ring pliers remove the retaining snap ring.
4. From the main bore of the cylinder remove the piston guide, cylinder cup and plate.
5. Remove the primary and secondary piston assemblies from the master cylinder body.

Clean and Inspect

1. Wash master cylinder body, reservoir and cap in clean methylated spirits.
2. Wash all internal parts in brake fluid.
3. Check all recesses, openings and passages to ensure they are open and free of foreign matter.
4. Place all parts on a clean surface.
5. Inspect the master cylinder bores for signs of etching, pitting, scoring or rust. If in poor condition, replace the cylinder.
   Note: *Do not hone cylinder bore.*
6. When replacing cups, plastic retainers may be removed by cutting with a sharp knife or razor blade, ensuring that piston is not damaged in any way.

Assembly

Note: *Before assembly coat the cylinder bores and all internal parts with clean brake fluid. It is important to use new pistons, and rubbers when re-assembling master cylinder. Kits can be obtained from most auto shops*

1. Install the secondary piston assembly into master cylinder bore.
2. To the main bore of the cylinder install the primary piston assembly, then install the plate, cylinder cup and piston guide.
3. Compress the primary piston and install the snap ring ensuring it is fully seated into position.
4. Install the reservoir seals to the master cylinder body, then install the fluid level sensor.
5. Install the reservoir tank and secure in position with retaining pin.

Installation

1. Install master cylinder assembly onto brake booster using a new 'O' ring and take care not to disturb the brake booster push rod.

2. Install bracket and the master cylinder retaining nuts, tightening to specification.
   Master Cylinder to Brake Booster .....10 +/- 2 Nm
3. Unplug brake lines and master cylinder then securely reconnect brake lines to master cylinder.
   Brake Lines to Master Cylinder ....15 +/- 2 Nm
4. Reconnect electrical connector, then top up brake fluid and bleed the system as previously described.
5. **LHD** vehicles reconnect and install battery.
   RHD vehicles install air cleaner and duct.

Inspection Of Brake Fluid Level Sensor

Check the continuity of the sensor. Their should be no continuity when the float level is above the 'Min' mark and should have continuity when the float level is below the 'Minimum' mark.

BRAKE BOOSTER

Removal

1. Remove master cylinder as described previously.
2. Remove the vacuum hose from the booster check valve fitting.
3. In the cabin under dash panel, disconnect the booster push rod from the brake pedal by removing the retaining clip and clevis pin.
4. Remove the 4 brake booster to fire wall retaining nuts.

5. Remove the brake booster, sealer, insulator and spacer from vehicle.

Installation

1. Along with the seal, spacer and insulator install the booster assembly to the fire wall, by sliding the push rod and boot through the fire wall from the engine bay.
2. Install the booster securing nuts and tighten to specification.
   Booster Securing Nuts ....14 +/- 3 Nm

BRAKE SYSTEM

3. Attach the brake booster rod to the brake pedal then install the clevis pin and retaining clip.
4. Install the vacuum hose to the booster fitting.
5. The clearance between the brake booster push rod and the master cylinders primary piston when fitted together should as below.
   Standard Value:
   NM - NP 6G72 and 6G74.................0.5 - 0.9 mm
   NM - NP 4M40 and 4M41 ....0.8 - 1.2 mm

6. If not within specification adjust by turning the pushrod while holding the rod spline.
7. Install the master cylinder as described previously.
8. Bleed brakes as described earlier

HYDRAULIC BRAKE BOOSTER (HBB)

Power Supply System Function & Operation Check

1. Turn the ignition switch to the off position. Depressurise the power supply system by pressing the brake pedal at least forty times or until the pedal effort becomes hard.
2. Check to make sure the reservoir level is on the max mark. For safety chock the wheels and release the hand brake.
3. Turn the ignition on (do not start the engine) and measure the time it takes for the pump motor to stop.
   Standard Value............................. 20 - 80 seconds
4. Once the motor has stopped, start the engine and check the brake warning lamp is not turned on.
5. Stop the engine, and then turn the ignition switch on again

HBB SYSTEM AIR BLEEDING

Note: *Two people are required for bleeding brake system.*

If the reservoir has been drained due to the removal of the HBB system proceed with the following procedure.

1. Air bleeding from front brake system.
   a) Turn the ignition to the lock off position.
   b) Bleed front brake calipers by pumping the brake pedal.
2. Pump motor operation
   a) Turn the ignition to the on position and operate pump motor.
   b) With pump motor running free, depress the brake pedal 3-4 times to supply brake fluid into the pump motor.
3. Air bleeding from accumulator system
   a) After pump motor stops, depress the brake pedal 3-4 times.
   b) Observe fluid condition in reservoir, if fluid looks whitish wait a few minutes until it becomes clear.
   c) Repeat process until brake fluid remains clear.
4. Air bleeding from rear brake system
   a) With ignition turned on and brake pedal depressed bleed air from the rear calipers.
5. Air bleeding from power supply system.
   a) Turn the ignition to the lock off position.
   b) Press the brake pedal several times to depressurize the HBB system (brake pedal will become hard).
   c) Turn ignition to on position and quickly pump the brake pedal 20 times, check to ensure the pump motor stops.
   d) Turn the ignition to the lock off position then press

BRAKE SYSTEM

the brake pedal several times to depressurize the HBB system (brake pedal will become hard).

e) Turn ignition to on position and operate the pump motor, the motor should stop in about 25 seconds.

f) If pump motor does not stop repeat process to fully bleed air from power supply system.

6. Air bleeding from ABS system.
   a) Turn the ignition to the lock off position.
   b) Connect the M.U.T III to the diagnosis connector.
   c) Turn the ignition switch on, using the display menu select the following procedures.
   "ABS/ASC" to "Actuator Test" to "Air Bleeding (1)".

   Note: *If the "Air Bleeding (1)" procedure is carried out repeatedly, wait at least twenty seconds before moving on to the next procedure.*

   d) While the pedal is depressed and the ignition switch is on, carry out the actuator test "Air Bleeding (1)".
   e) Now with the pedal still depressed and ignition on select "Air Bleeding (2)".

7. Air bleeding from rear brake system (final stage)
   a) Bleed air from the rear calipers while the ignition is turned on and the pedal is depressed.

   Note: *Avoid letting the fluid in reservoir drop below the MIN mark as this can introduce air into the system.*

8. Air bleeding from front brake system (final stage). Turn the ignition switch on to operate the pump motor, pump the brake pedal until air is longer present.

9. Add brake fluid
   a) Turn the ignition to the lock off position. Press the brake pedal at least forty times or until the pedal becomes hard to push, this will depressurise the HBB system.
   b) Add specified brake fluid to the Max mark on the reservoir.

HYDRAULIC BRAKE BOOSTER (HBB)

Removal

1. With the ignition in the fully off position depressurise the system by pumping the brake pedal (minimum 40 times or until the pedal becomes hard to push).
2. **LHD** vehicles disconnect and remove the battery. **RHD** vehicles remove air intake cleaner housing and air intake duct.
3. Disconnect all electrical connections from brake booster system.
4. Drain brake fluid from system then disconnect brake lines from the hydraulic brake booster.
5. In the cabin under the dash panel, disconnect the booster push rod from the brake pedal by removing the retaining clip and clevis pin.

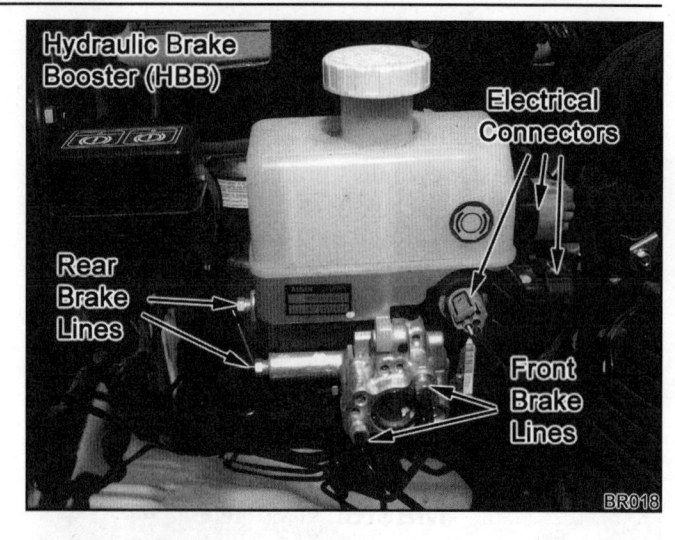

6. Remove the four retaining nuts holding the booster to the firewall.
7. Remove the hydraulic brake booster, seals, insulator (if fitted) and spacer from the vehicle.

Dismantle

1. Remove the three reservoir retaining screws and remove reservoir from assembly, then remove the sealing grommets.
2. From the pump motor remove the accumulator by unscrewing it, then remove the 'O' ring, spring and silencer tube.
3. From the pump motor remove the hose clamps retaining the hose and remove hose, then unscrew and remove the brake fluid tube.
4. Remove the screws securing the lead wire.
5. Remove the motor to bracket through bolt then from each side remove the washer, bushing and collar, then remove the pin.
6. Remove the mounting brackets from the hydraulic unit assembly and the pump motor.
7. From the push rod remove the clevis and nut then remove the boot and mount the unit in a vice using special mounting tool (MB991620).
8. Depress and push rod, and while holding in depressed position remove the retaining snap ring using a small screwdriver.
9. From the cylinder body squarely remove the power piston assembly and master cylinder piston assembly being careful not to damage the cylinder wall.

Clean and Inspect

1. Wash master cylinder body, reservoir and cap in clean methylated spirits.
2. Wash all internal parts in brake fluid.
3. Check all recesses, openings and passages to ensure they are open and free of foreign matter.
4. Place all parts on a clean surface.
5. Inspect the master cylinder bores for signs of etching,

BRAKE SYSTEM

pitting, scoring or rust. If in poor condition, replace the cylinder.

Note: *Do not hone cylinder bore.*

6. When replacing cups, plastic retainers may be removed by cutting with a sharp knife or razor blade, ensuring that piston is not damaged in any way.

Note: *Because special rubber compound is used, this master cylinder must be repaired using only the genuine kit. This kit includes new rubber components. Ensure all sections of the cylinder are repaired.*

Note: *The operating pressures of the proportioning valve are stamped on the front end of the cylinder and it is most important that, should a cylinder need replacing, an identical cylinder be used.*

Assembly

Note: *Before assembly coat the cylinder bores and piston assemblies with clean brake fluid.*

1. To the cylinder body install the master cylinder piston assembly and the power piston assembly.
2. Depress and push rod, and while holding in depressed position install the snap ring ensuring it is fully seated.
3. Install the boot to the assembly then to the push rod install the clevis tightening retaining nut to specification.
   Push Rod-Clevis Nut.......................25.5 +/- 5.1 Nm
4. To the hydraulics unit assembly and the pump motor install the mounting brackets and bushing.
   Mounting bracket (end) ....7.8 +/- 1.5 Nm
   Mounting bracket (centre) ....11.8 +/- 2.3 Nm
5. Install the pump motor into position then install the mounting bolt, followed by the washers, bushings and collars and pin.
   Mounting Bolt ....7.8 +/- 1.5 Nm
6. Install lead wire and tighten the retaining screws.
   Lead Wire Screws (side) ....3.0 +/- 0.5 Nm
   Lead Wire Screws (bottom) ....1.7 +/- 0.1 Nm
7. Install the tube to the pump motor then install the hose and secure with hose clamps.
   Tube Fittings..15.2 +/- 3 Nm
8. To the pump motor install the silencer tube, spring and 'O' ring then install the accumulator tightening to specification.
   Accumulator ....53.9 +/- 2.9 Nm
9. Install the reservoir mounting grommets into the main assembly then push the reservoir into the grommets, align the retaining screw holes and tighten retaining screws.
   Reservoir Retaining Screws ....1.7 +/- 0.3 Nm

Installation

1. Along with the seals, spacer and insulator (if fitted) install the booster assembly to the fire wall, by sliding the push rod and boot through the fire wall from the engine bay. It is recommended to install new seals.
2. Install the booster securing nuts and tighten to specification.
   Booster Securing Nuts
   NM - NP ....14 +/- 3 Nm
   NS ....13 +/- 2 Nm

3. Install the booster push rod to the brake pedal then install the clevis pin and retaining clip.
4. Reconnect the brake lines to the hydraulic brake booster, then reconnect all electrical connections.
5. LHD vehicles reconnect and install the battery. RHD vehicles install the air cleaner housing and air intake duct.

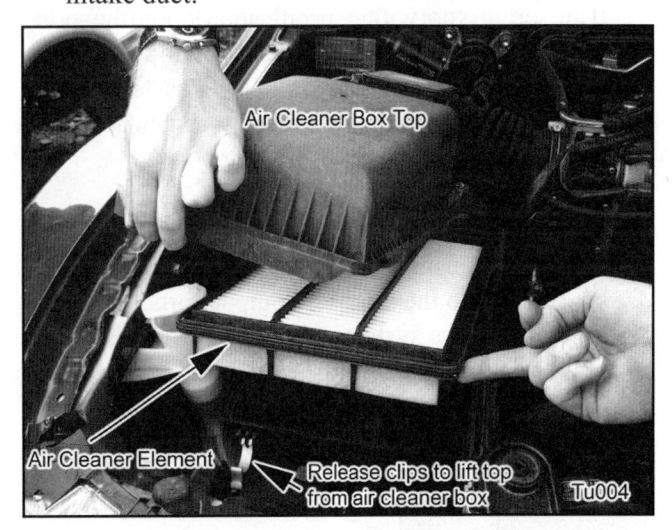

6. Refill and bleed brake system as described previously.
7. Adjust brake pedal as described previously.

363

LOAD SENSING PROPORTIONING VALVE (vehicles without ABS)

SPRING LENGTH CHECK & ADJUSTMENT
1. Have the vehicle parked on a level surface and in unladen condition. The vehicle should not be supported by axle stands.
2. Press the lever all the way to the proportioning valve side measure the spring length from end to end as shown in diagram.
   Standard Value.................................. 135 - 139 mm

3. If the spring is not within specification loosen the spring support mounting bolts, adjust support to achieve correct length making sure to hold lever as described in step 2 and tighten the bolt when the standard value is reached.

FUNCTION TEST
1. To the load sensing proportioning valve connect pressure gauges to the input and output ports.
2. Bleed the brake system referring to Brake Bleeding section in this chapter if needed.
3. Disconnect the spring from the support side.
4. Hold the spring parallel with the load sensing proportioning valve and pull to obtain length as shown in below table.

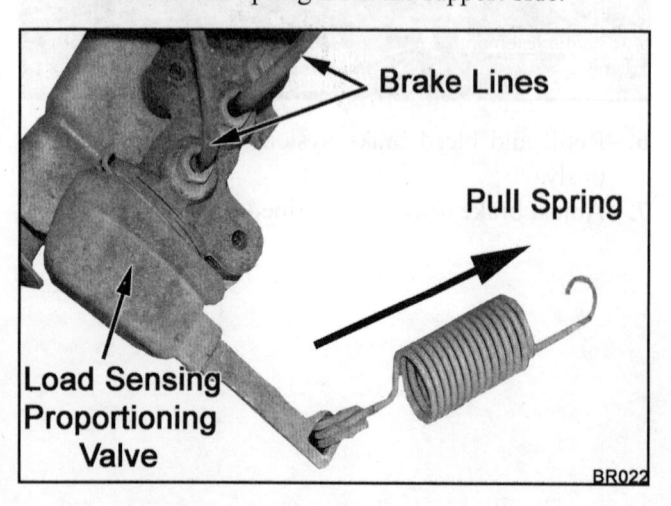

Vehicle in unladen condition	Spring Length mm	Input Fluid Pressure MPa	Output Fluid Pressure MPa
Short Wheelbase	133	9.8	4.9 - 5.9
Long Wheelbase	133	9.8	5.9 - 6.9

5. Check to ensure the pressures are within specification.
6. After checks have been carried out reconnect the spring and check the length is within the standard value. Remove the pressure gauges and bleed air from the system.

Removal
Note: *Be sure to drain the brake fluid from the system before removing the proportioning valve.*
1. Loosen the spring support retaining bolt, remove the load sensing spring. Remove the spring support if required.
2. Disconnect the brake lines and plug the ends of to prevent entry of foreign material.
3. Remove the bolts securing the load sensing proportioning valve and remove valve from vehicle.
4. Remove the bolts securing the mounting bracket assembly and remove bracket if required.

Installation
1. Install the mounting bracket into position and tighten retaining bolts, then install the valve into position and tightening retaining bolts.
2. Reconnect the brake lines ensuring to reconnect lines to the same ports they where removed from. Tighten brake lines to specification.
   Brake Lines..15 +/- 2 Nm
3. Install the load sensing spring, then install the spring support and lightly tighten retaining bolt.
4. Adjust load sensing spring length as described earlier in the chapter.
5. Top up brake fluid and bleed brake system as described previously.

FRONT BRAKE ASSEMBLY

FRONT BRAKE CALIPER
Removal
1. Raise vehicle, secure on jack stands and remove road wheels.
2. Place a drain tray beneath caliper assembly.
3. Loosen and remove brake hose to caliper attaching bolt. Separate bolt from hose and discard sealing washers.
4. Remove the two caliper attaching bolts and lift caliper assembly out over disc rotor.

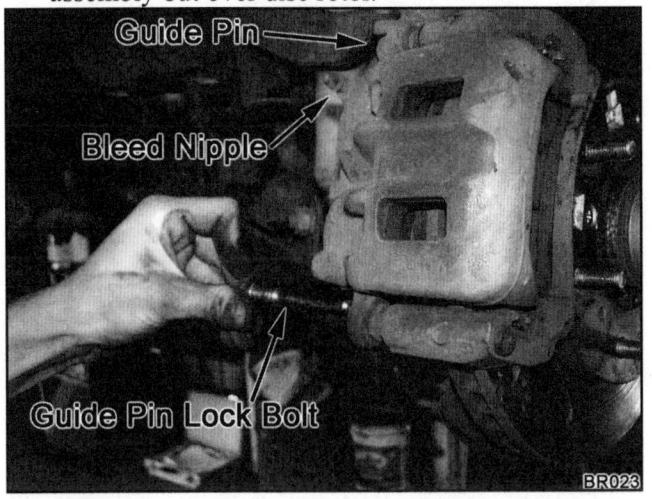

Dismantle
1. Remove guide pin and guide pin lock bolt.
2. Separate caliper housing from anchor plate and remove brake pads and shims.
3. Withdraw slide sleeves and boots from anchor plate. Separate boots.
4. Place a block of clean wood between caliper pistons and the opposite legs on housing and apply air pressure at brake hose inlet port to eject pistons.
   Caution: *Do not have your fingers inside of caliper when removing the pistons by this method.*
5. Remove rubber boot from pistons.
6. Remove seal from bore, using you finger, taking care not to damage bore or seal locating groove.
7. Remove bleeder screw.

Clean and Inspect
1. Wash all components of the caliper assembly in clean warm water to disperse the brake fluid.
2. Dry components with air blower or clean rag, ensuring all passage ways are clean and clear of blockages.
3. Once dried inspect all components for any wear and damage (scuffing, corrosion, pitting, scoring), if any is present the component will need replacing.
4. Inspect slides sleeves for corrosion. Replace if corroded.

Assembly
1. Lubricate cylinder bore and piston with specified brake fluid.
   Specified Brake Fluid .... Dot 4
2. Fit new seal into inner groove of bore. Ensure seal is not twisted and is fully seated in groove.
3. Install piston boot over end of pistons.
4. Position piston into caliper housing, seating boot into grove in caliper bore. Ensure boot flange is squarely and firmly seated in groove.
5. Push piston squarely into bore by hand until fully seated. Ensure piston boots are seated in piston/caliper bore grooves.
6. Lubricate slide sleeves with silicone type grease.
7. Reinstall slide sleeves in caliper housing, using new caliper housing to sleeve bolts. Use an open end spanner to hold hex section of guide pin when tightening bolts.
   Guide Pin Bolts: .... 88 Nm
   Note: *Do not reuse old bolts.*
8. Install new guide pin boots.
9. Assemble caliper housing and anchor plate together. Ensure guide pin boots are correctly located in guide pin and anchor plate grooves.
10. Install bleed screw, then brake pads as previously described.

Installation
Note: *Prior to installation of the caliper the brake drag force should be measured to make sure it is within the limits. The procedure is located at the start of this chapter*

1. Ensure anchor plate mounting surfaces are clean.
2. Press inner brake pad by hand or with a suitable tool to ensure piston is bottomed in bore.
3. Position caliper assembly over disc, insert retaining bolts and tighten to specification.
   Caliper Anchor Bolt NM - NP........... 113 +/- 9 Nm
   Caliper Mounting Bolt NS .... 115 +/- 10 Nm
4. Reconnect brake hose using new sealing washers.
   Brake Hose to Caliper .... 30 +/- 4 Nm
5. Bleed brake system as previously described.
6. Depress brake pedal several times to bring pads into position against disc.
7. Check level of fluid in master cylinder and top up if necessary
8. Install road wheels and lower vehicle.

BRAKE SYSTEM

FRONT ROTOR (Disc)
Removal
1. Remove the caliper assembly as described above. There is no need to disconnect the brake hose, if the caliper does not need to be pulled down. Place the caliper to a side, tie with string or support on a wire hook to front suspension, so the caliper is not supported on brake hose.

2. For re-assembly mark the position of the disc to hub, then remove the disc.
   Note: *If disc is difficult to remove, use two bolts in the holes as shown in Rear Rotor Removal section to assist with removal.*
   Bolt Size .... M8 x 1.25 mm

Inspection
Note: *The only repairs that can be performed is the rotor can be machined. If disc is under specification after it has been machined the disc will need to be replaced.*
Check disc surface for gouges and grooves, if excessive the pad life will be shortened, therefore machine to obtain a smooth surface.

Front Disc minimum thickness
NM - NP ....24.4 mm
NS (SWB)...................................24.4 mm
NS (LWB)...................................26.0 mm
Disc run-out All Models............................0.06 mm

Installation
1. Install the rotor on the hub using the alignment marks made on removal.
2. Install wheel nuts and tighten lightly against the rotor.
3. Check to ensure disc run-out is within specification.
   Disc Run-Out Specification......................0.06 mm
   Note: *If run-out is not to specification reposition the rotor on the hub, if this does not correct the disc run-out replace the disc/rotor.*
4. Replace the caliper assembly as previously described.

FRONT BRAKE PAD
Removal
Note: *The brake pads have wear indicators that make contact with the disc when the pads get to around 2mm in thickness, emitting a squealing sound to warn the driver to replace the pads.*

1. Remove one half of the fluid from the front section of the master cylinder reservoir. Do not remove the brake line or completely empty the reservoir or it will be necessary to bleed the hydraulic system. Discard the brake fluid.
   Note: *Brake fluid must be removed, this will prevent the reservoir overflowing when the caliper piston is forced in while replacing pads.*
2. Remove the wheels. Work on only one brake at a time. Pad assemblies must always be replaced as sets either front or rear.
3. Remove the lower mounting bolt which holds the caliper to the caliper frame, rotate the caliper up and away from the disc.

BRAKE SYSTEM

4. Lift the brake pads out of the caliper. If fitted remove the shims and clips.

Installation

Note: *Prior to installation of the caliper the brake drag force should be measured to make sure it is within the limits. The procedure is located at the start of this chapter*

1. Push the piston into the caliper bore, by hand if the caliper has been overhauled, or by using a suitable pad spreader. This is necessary to obtain enough clearance for the new pads and the caliper to fit over the rotor.

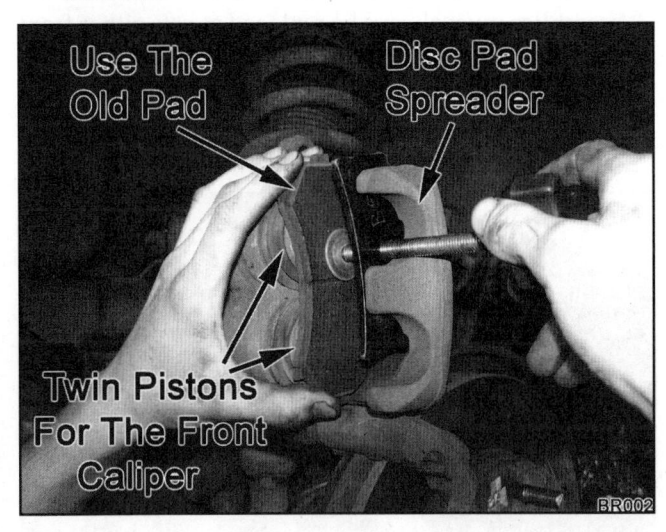

2. Locate the inboard pad in caliper first using the shim if fitted.
3. Slide the outboard pad into the caliper with the shim if fitted, install the clips if fitted.
4. Rotate the caliper back over the rotor until the caliper lower bolt hole aligns with the caliper frame.
5. Install caliper mounting bolt and torque to specification.
   Caliper Mounting Bolt NM - NP ..... 113 +/- 9 Nm
   Caliper Mounting Bolt NS .... 115 +/- 10 Nm
6. Replenish the brake fluid in the master cylinder. Pump the brake pedal several times to position the pad assemblies.
7. Check fluid level, install wheel and tighten wheel nuts to specification.
   Wheel Nuts .... 108 +/- 10 Nm
8. Road test the vehicle and make several light stops to seat the pads

REAR BRAKE ASSEMBLY

REAR BRAKE CALIPER

Removal

1. Raise vehicle, secure on jack stands and remove road wheels.
2. Place a drain tray beneath caliper assembly.
3. Loosen and remove brake hose to caliper attaching bolt. Separate bolt from hose and discard sealing washers.

4. Remove the two caliper attaching bolts and lift caliper assembly out over disc.

Dismantle

1. Remove guide and lock pins, also the bushing and boots for the pins.
2. Remove brake pads and separate caliper housing from caliper support.
3. Place a block of clean wood between caliper piston and opposite legs on housing and apply air pressure at brake hose inlet port to eject piston.
   Note: *Do not have your fingers inside of caliper when removing the piston by this method.*
4. Remove rubber boot from the bore.

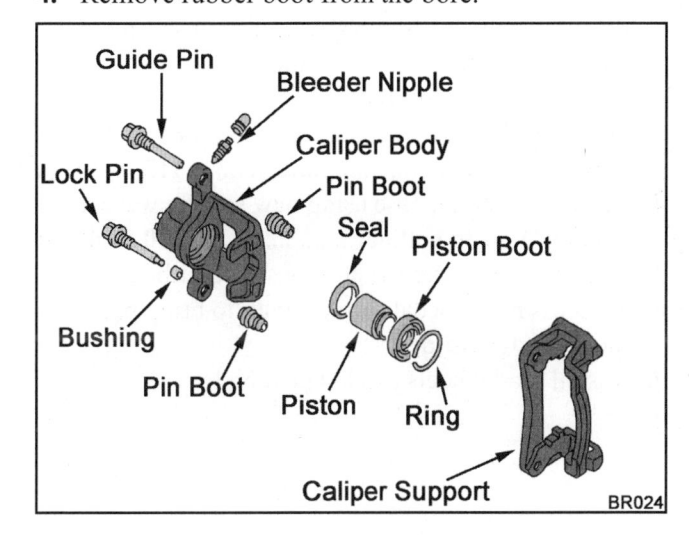

367

BRAKE SYSTEM

5. Remove seal from the bore, taking care not to damage the bore or seal locating groove.
6. Remove bleeder screw.

Inspection
1. Wash all components of the caliper assembly in clean warm water to disperse the brake fluid.
2. Dry components with air blower or clean rag, ensuring all passage ways are clean and clear of blockages.
3. Once dried inspect all components for any wear and damage (scuffing, corrosion, pitting, scoring), if any is present the component will need replacing.
4. Inspect guide and lock pins for corrosion. Replace if corroded.

Assemble
1. Lubricate cylinder bore and piston with clean brake fluid.
2. Fit new seal into inner groove of bore. Ensure seal is not twisted and is fully seated in groove.
3. Install piston boot over end of piston.
4. Position piston into caliper housing, seating boot into grove in caliper bore. Ensure boot flange is squarely and firmly seated in groove.
5. Push piston squarely into bore by hand until fully seated. Ensure piston boot is fully seated in piston and caliper bore grooves.
6. Install guide and lock pins using new boots. On the lock pin install the bushing. Tighten pins to specification.
   Guide/Lock Pins .... 44 +/- 5 Nm
7. Install bleed screw.

Installation
Note: *Prior to installation of the caliper the brake drag force should be measured to make sure it is within the limits. The procedure is located at the start of this chapter*
1. Ensure anchor plate mounting surfaces are clean.
2. Press inner brake pad by hand to ensure piston is bottomed in bore. Insert inner and outer pads.
3. Position caliper assembly over disc, insert retaining bolts and tighten to specification.
   Caliper Mounting Bolts
   NM - NP .... 88 +/- 10 Nm
   NS .... 113 +/- 9 Nm
4. Reconnect brake hose using new sealing washers.
   Brake Hose to Caliper .... 30 +/- 4 Nm
5. Bleed brake system as previously described.
6. Depress brake pedal several times to bring pads into position against disc.
7. Install road wheels and lower vehicle.

REAR BRAKE PAD
Removal
1. Remove one half of the fluid from the rear section of the master cylinder reservoir. Do not remove the brake line or completely empty the reservoir as it will be necessary to bleed the hydraulic system. Discard the brake fluid.
   Note: *Brake fluid should be removed to prevent the reservoir overflowing when the caliper piston is forced in while replacing pad.*
2. Raise vehicle, secure on jack stands and remove road wheels. Work on only one brake at a time. Pad assemblies must always be replaced as sets either front or rear.
3. Remove the lower and upper mounting bolts which holds the caliper to the caliper frame, using a screwdriver lever the caliper up and away from the disc.

4. Lift the brake pads out of the caliper.

Installation
1. Push piston into the caliper bore, by hand if the caliper has been overhauled, or by using a suitable pad spreader. This is necessary to obtain enough clearance for the new pads to fit over the rotor.
2. Locate the inboard pad in the caliper first.
3. Slide the outboard pad into the caliper.
4. Position caliper correctly over rotor and slide straight into position until caliper bolt holes align with their respective holes on the caliper support frame.
5. Install caliper mounting bolt and torque to specification.
   Caliper Mounting Bolts
   NM - NP .... 88 +/- 10 Nm
   NS .... 113 +/- 9 Nm
6. Replenish the brake fluid in the master cylinder. Pump the brake pedal several times to position the pad assemblies.
7. Check fluid level, install wheel and tighten wheel nuts to specification.

BRAKE SYSTEM

Wheel Nuts .... 108 +/- 10 Nm

8. Lightly pump the brake pedal several times to push the brake pads against the rotor, then road test the vehicle.

REAR ROTOR (Disc)
Removal
1. Remove caliper as described in earlier in this chapter.
2. Remove the rotor/disc assembly.
   Note: *If disc is difficult to remove, use two bolts in the holes as shown to assist with removal.*
   Bolt Size .... M8 x 1.25 mm

Inspection
Note: *The only repairs that can be performed is the rotor can be machined. If disc is under specification after it has been machined the disc will need to be replaced. Check disc surface for gouges and grooves, if excessive the pad life will be shortened, therefore machine to obtain a smooth surface.*

Rear Disc minimum thickness
NM - NP .... 20.4 mm
NS (SWB) .... 20.4 mm
NS (LWB) .... 16.0 mm
Disc run-out .... 0.06 mm

Installation
1. Replace rotor/disc to vehicle, then check disc run-out is within specification.
   Disc Run-out Specification .... 0.06 mm
   Note: *If run-out is not to specification reposition the rotor on the hub, if this does not correct the disc run-out replace the disc/rotor.*
2. Replace caliper as described in brake pad replacement (installation) previously in this chapter.

PARK BRAKE

PARK BRAKE SWITCH
Removal
1. Remove the cup holder and indicator panel as described in the Body Chapter.
2. Disconnect the electrical connector.
3. Remove the retaining bolt, and take out the park brake switch.

Inspection
1. Check for continuity between the park brake switch terminal and the switch mounting bolt. Do the checks with the switch still connected and in place.

Brake Lever Is Pulled	Continuity
Brake Lever Is Released	No Continuity

Installation
1. Install the switch and mounting bolt.
2. Reconnect the electrical connection.
3. Check to make sure the hand brake switch is functioning correctly using the above table.
4. Replace the indicator panel and cup holder

CHECK & ADJUSTMENT
1. Pull up the parking brake lever up with a force of 200N using a spring gauge and count the number of times it clicks through the notches.
   Lever Stroke NM - NP .... 5 - 7 notches @ 200N
   NS - NT .... 6 - 7 notches @ 200N
2. Adjust the park brake lever if not within specification as follows.
   Note: *If the console is still in place, remove the cup holder to gain access to the adjuster.*
   a) At the end of the rod loosen the adjusting nut, then jack up vehicle, place on safety stands and remove the rear wheels.
   b) Remove the adjustment hole plug on the brake

BRAKE SYSTEM

shoe backing plate. Use a flat blade screw driver to turn the adjuster to expand the shoes to a point where the disc rotor wont turn.

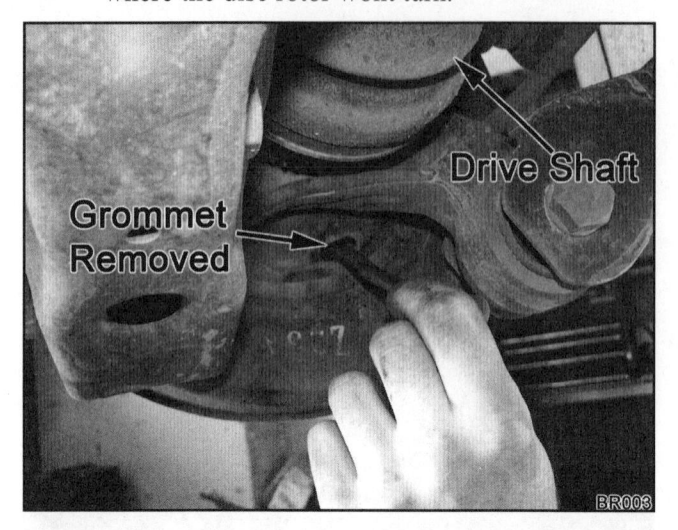

c) Now turn the adjuster in the opposite direction,
NM - NP .... 3 or 4 Notches
NS - NT (Short Wheel Base) .... 6 Notches
NS - NT (Long Wheel Base) .... 8 Notches

d) In the vehicle turn the adjusting nut until the parking brake lever is within specification. After these steps check to make sure there is no gap between the lever and adjusting nut.

e) Release parking brake then turn the rear wheels to ensure the brakes are not dragging.

PARK BRAKE LEVER ASSEMBLY
Removal
1. Remove the centre console from the vehicle referring to the body chapter if required.
2. Remove the bolts retaining the G sensor bracket, console bracket and then remove components. Take note of the bolt with an "E" stamped into it as this is the earth bolt and should be installed in the same position. 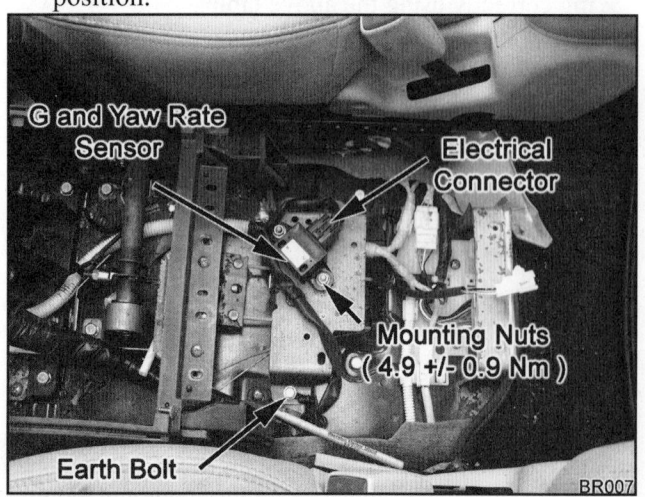
3. Release the adjusting nut from the hand brake cable rod, then disconnect the park brake cables from the lever assembly.
4. From the assembly remove the stay and bush, then remove the bolts securing the parking brake switch to the lever and remove switch.
5. Remove the bolts retaining the park brake lever assembly and remove assembly from vehicle.
6. Inspect lever ratchet for wear and damage.

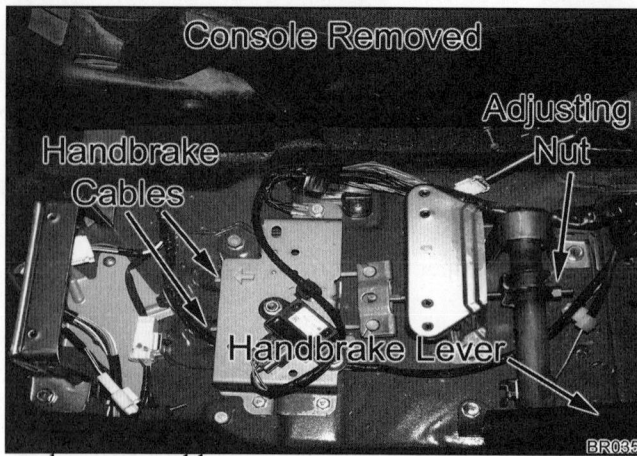

Installation
1. Coat the ratchet plate sliding parts, the ratchet pawl, also the bushing inner surface with multi-purpose grease.
2. To the lever assembly install the switch, stay and bush, then secure the parking brake lever assembly to the floor tightening retaining bolts.
Park Brake Lever .... 11 +/- 2 Nm
Park Brake Stay .... 11 +/- 2 Nm

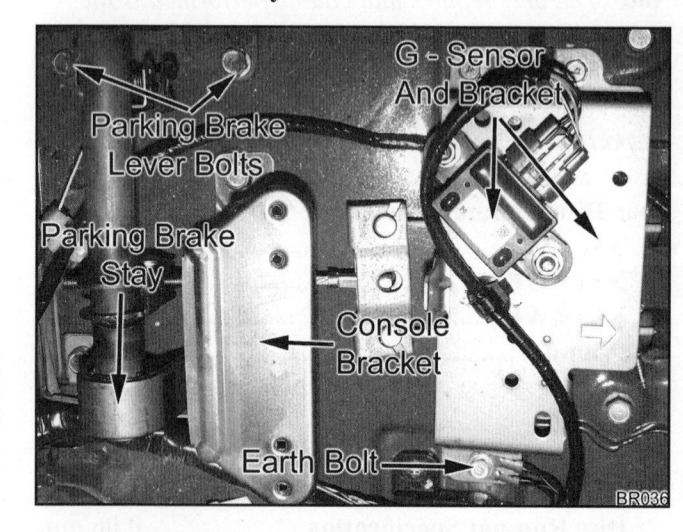

3. Reconnect the park brake cables, then install the adjusting nut and adjust until correct lever stroke is obtained.
Lever Stroke: NM - NP ...... 5 - 7 notches @ 200N
NS - NT .... 6 - 7 notches @ 200N
Note: *If needed see the section on Park Brake and Lever Check and Adjustment*
4. Install the centre console bracket and G sensor bracket.

370

G Sensor Bracket Bolts......................... 4.9 +/- 1 Nm
Earth Bolt .... 9.0 +/- 2 Nm

5. Install the centre console as described in body chapter.

PARK BRAKE SHOES

Note: *The burnishing procedure must be carried out when new shoes are fitted. See Routine Maintenance at the start of the chapter.*

Removal

1. Jack up the rear of the vehicle, support on axle stands and remove road wheels.
2. Remove the rear brake calipers without removing the hoses, tie the calipers away from rotors.
3. Remove the brake disc to expose the park brake shoes.
4. Next remove the shoe to anchor springs, adjuster wheel spring and adjuster assembly.

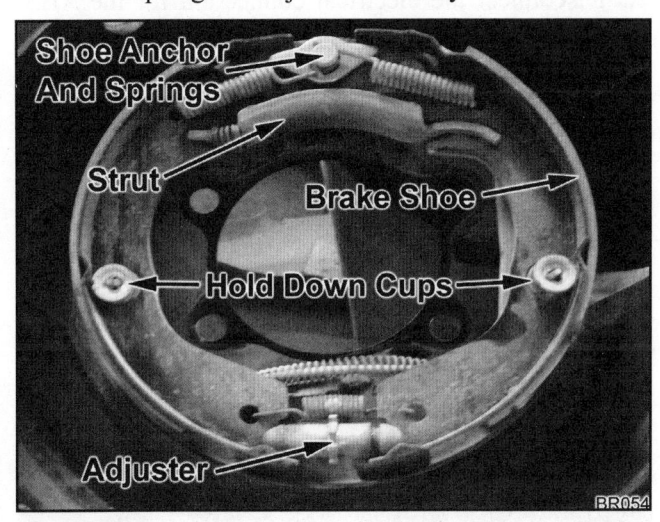

5. Remove the strut and strut to shoe spring.
6. Push down and turn the shoe hold down cup to release the pins. Take note of the order of removal of parts to help with installation.
7. Release the clip holding the park brake cable and remove. Now remove the brake shoes.

Inspection

1. At several locations measure the thickness of the brake lining, if not within specification replace brake shoe assembly on both sides.
   Brake lining Limit..1.0mm
2. Measure the inner diameter of the brake disc (drum) using a micrometer or dial indicator.
   Drum Diameter Limit
   NM - NP.. 200 mm
   NS Short Wheel Base................................. 200 mm
   NS Long Wheel Base................................ 211.0 mm
3. If disc is not within specification replace disc/drum assembly.

Installation

Note: *Before starting, lubricate the mounting points on the shoes where the adjuster and pivot mount. Also lubricate the threads on the adjuster.*

1. Before putting the shoe hold down pins through the backing plate make sure to put suitable sealant around the head of the pin to stop water from getting in to the brakes.
2. Install the shoes into position using the spring and cups, reinstalled the same as removal to hold shoes in place.
3. Place clip onto hand brake cable. Install the strut and spring.
4. Install the adjuster with the shoe adjusting bolt on the left hand wheel facing the rear of the vehicle. The right hand wheel has the bolt facing the front of the vehicle.
   Note: If the reverse is done, you will have to turn the adjuster assembly the opposite way to get it to open up for adjustment.
5. Install the adjusting wheel spring. Be careful installing the shoe to anchor springs. Make sure the spring with the paint mark is installed as per table.
   NM - NP .... **Towards Rear Of Vehicle**
   NS (SWB)................. **Towards Rear Of Vehicle**
   NS (LWB)................ **Towards Front Of Vehicle**
6. Next put the rear disc rotor in place and install the caliper.
   Caliper Retaining Bolts
   NM - NP............................. 88 +/- 10 Nm
   NS .... 113 +/- 10 Nm
7. Adjust the park brake lever stroke until the correct adjustment is obtained. If needed see appropriate section.
8. Install road wheels and lower vehicle.
9. Road test vehicle make sure to burnish the shoes as described at the start of the chapter.

BRAKE SYSTEM

PARK BRAKE CABLE
Removal
1. Remove the centre console as described in the body chapter.
2. From the end of the cable rod remove the adjusting nut and remove the cables from the lever assembly.
3. Remove the cable clamps for the parking brake cables, then remove the body sealing grommets.
4. Raise vehicle, secure on jack stands and remove wheels, then remove the caliper and support out of the way with a piece of wire to avoid damage to the brake hose.
5. Remove the disc/drum assembly then remove the hub and brake shoes as described earlier in the chapter.
6. From the actuator attached to the shoe and lining assembly remove the parking brake cable then release cable by removing the circlip on the back of the backing plate.
7. From underneath the vehicle remove all the cable retaining clamps and remove parking brake cables from vehicle.

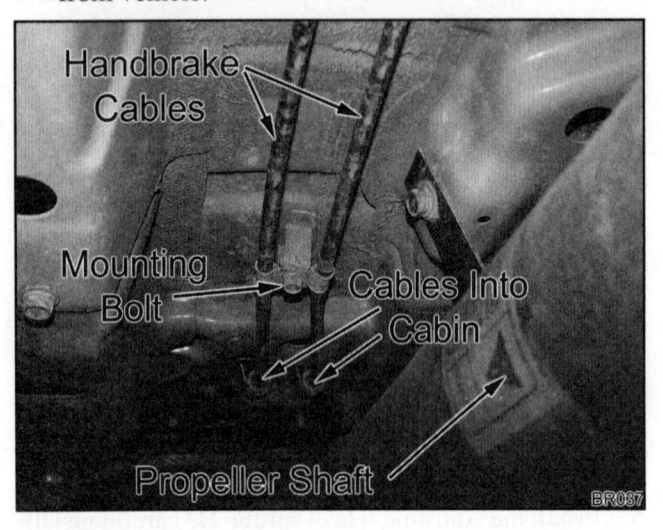

Installation
1. Install the parking brake cables into position on the vehicle and install cable retaining clamps to underside of vehicle. Do not fully tighten bolts yet.
2. Reconnect the cable to the actuator attached to the shoe and lining assembly then replace the circlip to the backing plate.
3. Install the hub and brake shoes as described in the park brake shoes installation section then install the disc assembly and install caliper.
4. Connect the cables to the park brake lever assembly and install adjusting nut just enough to hold on.
5. Inside the vehicle install the body grommets into place with the use of an appropriate sealant. Then install and tighten inside retaining clamps. Fully tighten under body cable clamps.

Underbody Brake Cable Bolts .... 11 +/- 2 Nm

6. Adjust the park brake lever stroke until the correct adjustment is obtained. If needed see appropriate section.

Lever Stroke: NM-NP .... 5-7 notches @ 200N
NS-NT .... 6-7 notches @ 200N

7. Install centre console as described in body chapter.

ABS COMPONENTS

WHEEL SPEED SENSOR
OUTPUT VOLTAGE MEASUREMENT

Note: The ABS-ECU is located in the centre console/dash assembly and has a blue connector. The Transfer-ECU looks the same but has a green connector and is located under the ABS-ECU.

1. Raise the vehicle, support on axle stands and release the parking brake.
2. Disconnect the electrical connection for the ABS-ECU and ensure to measure at the harness side of the connector.
3. Using a multimeter (AC/mV range) check the output voltage while rotating the wheel 1 turn.

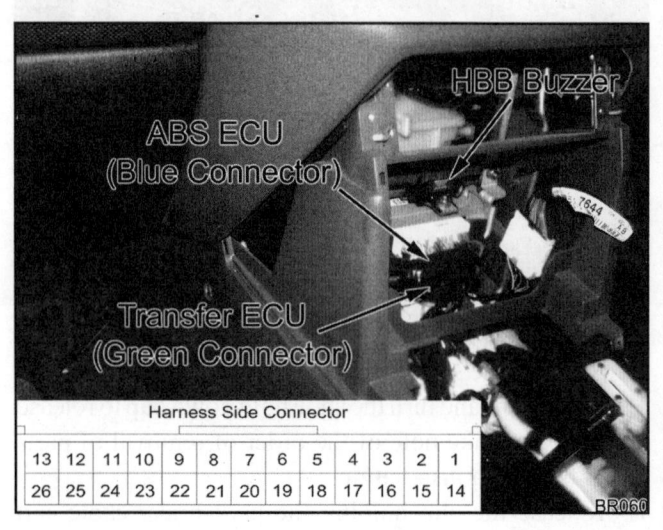

Wheel	Front Left	Front Right	Rear Left	Rear Right
Terminal	7	10	9	8
Terminal	20	23	22	21

Output Voltage .... 42 mV or more

4. If output voltage is lower than specification check the following and repair or replace as required.
   a) Excessive clearance between sensor pole and ABS rotor.

   Standard Gap NM - NP .... 0.9 mm

   b) Wheel speed sensor.

BRAKE SYSTEM

ABS VALVE RELAY CONTINUITY CHECK

Note: *On both petrol and diesel powered vehicles the ABS valve relay is situated near the battery.*

Check the continuity of the relay using the chart below. If found to be faulty replace relay.

Battery Voltage	Terminal Number				
	1	2	3	4	5
No Current Supplied	O——	——O			
		O——	——	——O	
Current Supplied	⊕——	——⊖			
		O——	——	——O

SOLENOID VALVE CHECK (HBB)

Measure the resistance between the terminals as listed in the following table.

Solenoid Valve (S.V.)	Terminals	Value (Ohms)
Control S.V. IN (FR)	19 - 34	4.75 - 5.25
Control S.V OUT (FR)	20 - 34	2.0 - 2.4
Control S.V IN (FL)	21 - 34	4.75 - 5.25
Control S.V OUT (FL)	22 - 34	2.0 - 2.4
Control S.V IN (RR)	15 - 34	4.75 - 5.25
Control S.V OUT (RR)	16 - 34	2.0 - 2.4
Control S.V IN (RL)	13 - 34	4.75 - 5.25
Control S.V OUT (RL)	14 - 34	2.0 - 2.4
Select S.V. (FR)	18 - 34	3.5 - 3.9
Select S.V. (FL)	17 - 34	3.5 - 3.9

FRONT WHEEL SPEED SENSOR

Removal

1. Jack up the front of the vehicle, support on axle stands and remove road wheels.
2. Remove the splash shield clips then disconnect electrical connection.
3. Remove the screws/bolts securing the speed sensor cable to vehicle. Remove the rotor protector. 
4. Remove the bolt securing the speed sensor and remove assembly from vehicle.

Note: *The ABS rotors are integrated with the driveshaft and cannot be disassembled. Be careful when removing the sensor as it can be damaged if it strikes the ABS rotor or other parts.*

Terminal Inspection

1. Inspect the pole piece of the sensor to ensure there is no build up of foreign material.

Note: *The sensors have magnets built into them and can attract small particles. This may interfere with the sensor detecting the wheel speed correctly.*

2. Inspect the cable of speed sensor to ensure it is good condition and there is no damage or breakage to the cable.

BRAKE SYSTEM

3. Measure the resistance of the speed sensor by installing a multimeter between the terminals. If not to specification replace speed sensor.
   Standard Value.............................. 1.0 - 1.5 kOhms
4. Inspect the teeth of the rotor to ensure they are not deformed or broken. Replace if necessary.

Insulation Check
1. With the wheel speed sensor removed, measure the resistance between terminal No. 1 and then No. 2 and the sensor body.
   NM - NP Resistance .... 100 k Ohms or more
   NS .... Circuit Open
2. Replace the sensor if not within specification.

Installation
1. Place sensor in position then install and tighten the retaining bolt.
   NS .... 11 +/- 2 Nm
2. Reconnect sensor electrical connection into loom and tighten the cable clamp retaining bolts. Replace the splash shield clips and bolts. Install the rotor protector.
   Retaining Bolts NS .... 11 +/- 2 Nm
3. Replace wheels and perform wheel speed sensor output voltage measurement check as shown earlier in the chapter.
4. Road test vehicle.

REAR WHEEL SPEED SENSOR
Removal
1. Jack up the rear of the vehicle, support on axle stands and remove road wheels.
2. Disconnect electrical connection. Remove the heat shield if fitted.
3. Remove the screws/bolts securing the speed sensor cable.
4. Remove the bolt securing the speed sensor and remove assembly from vehicle.

Inspection
1. Inspect the pole piece of the sensor to ensure the is no build up of foreign material.
2. Inspect cable of speed sensor to ensure good condition and no damage or breakage in cable.
3. Measure the resistance of the speed sensor by installing a multimeter between the terminals. If not to specification replace speed sensor.
   Standard Value.............................. 1.0 - 1.5 kOhms
4. Inspect the teeth of the rotor to ensure they are not deformed or broken. Replace if necessary.

Insulation Check
1. With the wheel speed sensor removed, measure the resistance between terminal No. 1 and No. 2 and the sensor body.
   NM - NP Resistance .... 100 kOhms or more
   NS .... Circuit Open
2. Replace the sensor if not within specification.

Installation
1. Place sensor in position then install and tighten the retaining bolt.
   Retaining Bolt.. 11 +/- 2 Nm
2. Reconnect sensor electrical connection into loom and tighten the cable clamp retaining bolts. Install the rotor protector if fitted.
   Retaining Bolts...................................... 11 +/- 2 Nm
3. Replace wheels and perform wheel speed sensor output voltage measurement check as shown earlier in the chapter.
4. Road test vehicle.

ABS ECU
Note: *The ABS ECU is located under the centre of the instrument panel.*

Removal
1. Remove the indicator panel and front panel from the instrument panel. Refer to body chapter for assistance.
2. Disconnect the electrical connections from the ABS ECU.
3. Remove the two nuts securing the ECU mounting bracket and remove assembly from instrument panel.
4. If required disconnect electrical connection for the HBB buzzer and remove.

Installation
1. Install the ECU assembly into position, then install the buzzer bracket into position remembering to reconnect electrical connection. If removed install the buzzer back onto the bracket.

BRAKE SYSTEM

2. Install and tighten the retaining nuts.
   Retaining Nuts.........................5 +/- 1 Nm
3. Install the front panel and indicator panel. Refer to body chapter for assistance.
4. Check ABS system operation.

G SENSOR
Removal
1. Remove the centre console from the vehicle, refer to body chapter for assistance.

2. Remove the nuts securing the G sensor into position, then disconnect electrical connection and remove G sensor from vehicle.
3. If required remove the G sensor bracket from the vehicle.

Installation
1. If removed install the G sensor bracket to vehicle and tighten retaining bolts to specification.
   G Sensor Bracket/Retaining Bolts..4.9 +/- 0.9 Nm
   Earth Bolt ....9 +/- 2 Nm
2. Install the G sensor into position and secure with the two retaining nuts, then reconnect electrical connection.

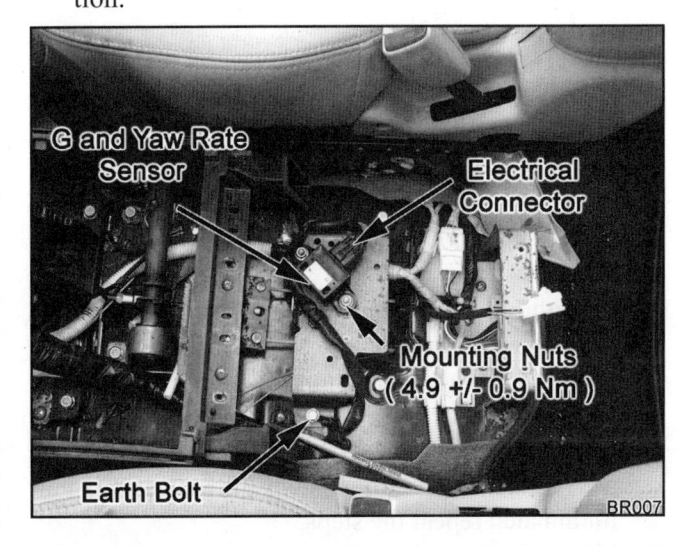

3. Install the centre console, refer to body chapter if required.

ACTIVE STABILITY (ASTC) & TRACTION CONTROL (ATC) - 2003 onwards

ASTC-ECU / ATC-ECU
Note: *The ECU's are located at the upper section of the floor console. There are two ECU's located in the same position, the upper one is the ASTC or ATC ECU and lower one is the Transfer ECU.*

Removal
1. Remove the indicator and front panel from the instrument panel. Refer to body chapter for assistance.
2. Disconnect the electrical connections from ABS ECU.
3. Remove the two nuts securing the ECU mounting bracket and remove assembly from instrument panel.
4. Disconnect electrical connection for the buzzer, then fully remove ECU from vehicle.

Installation
1. Install the ECU assembly into position, then install the buzzer into position remembering to reconnect electrical connection.
2. Install and tighten the two retaining nuts.
   Retaining Nuts.........................5 +/- 1 Nm
3. Install the front panel and indicator panel. Refer to body chapter for assistance.

Initialization
Note: *The initialization process has to be performed when the ECU is replaced with a new one. The ASTC OFF indicator is illuminated on the dash to warn that the ASTC ECU has not been initialized.*
Once the procedure has been done the HBB buzzer communication check will have to be deactivated. After the ECU has been replaced the HBB buzzer will sound for 5 seconds. See Deactivation of HBB Buzzer communication check later in the chapter.

375

BRAKE SYSTEM

1. Park the vehicle on a level surface. Turn the ignition off.
2. Connect the MUT-11, then turn the ignition to the on position.
3. Perform step No. 16 of the actuator test.
4. Quickly press the brake pedal using about 40 kgf. Check to see if the transfer lever can be put into all positions.
5. After doing this check to make sure the active stability control system off indicator has gone out. If not repeat the steps.
6. Turn the ignition switch off and disconnect the MUT-11.

HBB BUZZER
Removal
1. Remove the indicator and front panel from the instrument panel. Refer to body chapter for assistance.
2. Remove the nut securing the HBB buzzer.
3. Disconnect the electrical connector and remove the buzzer

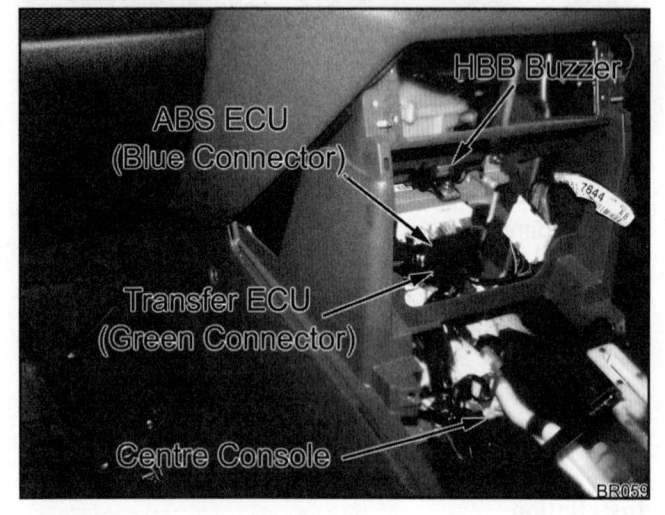

Installation
1. Install the HBB buzzer into position.
   Retaining nut............................5 +/-1 Nm
2. Reconnect the electrical connector.
3. Install the front panel and indicator panel. Refer to body chapter for assistance.

Deactivation of HBB Buzzer Operation Check
Note: *When the ignition is turned on next when the ASTC ecu is replaced the HBB buzzer will sound for 5 seconds. To deactivate the HBB buzzer operation check the following prucedure will need to be performed.*
1. Use MUT-11 to erase the HBB diagnostic code.
2. Drive the vehicle at speeds greater than 40 kmh.

G & YAW RATE SENSOR
Removal
1. Remove the centre console from the vehicle, refer to body chapter for assistance.
2. Remove the nuts securing the G sensor into position, then disconnect electrical connection and remove G sensor from vehicle.

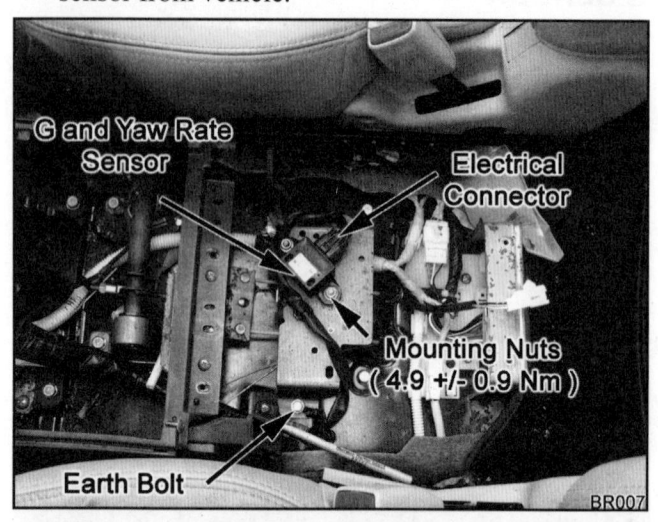

3. If required remove the G sensor bracket from the vehicle.

Installation
1. If removed install the G sensor bracket to vehicle and tighten retaining bolts to specification. Be sure to connect the earth lead to the earth bolt.
   G Sensor Bracket Bolts...................4.9 +/- 0.9 Nm
   Earth Bolt..............................9 +/- 2 Nm
2. Install the G sensor into position and secure with the two retaining nuts, then reconnect electrical connection.
   G Sensor Retaining Nuts................4.9 +/- 0.9 Nm
3. Install the centre console, refer to body chapter if required.

Initialization
Note: *When the G and Yaw rate sensor is replaced it has to be initialized as the learned neutral point has been erased. Follow the procedures in the next few steps.*
1. Place the vehicle on a flat surface.
2. Turn the ignition to the off position and connect the MUT-11.
3. Turn the ignition to the on position. Next turn the steering wheel to over 8° and then put the road wheels into a straight ahead position, this is called the neutral position.
4. Next perform item No. 16 of the actuator test. If the active stability control system off indicator is still illuminated repeat the steps.
5. If indicator is off, turn the ignition off and disconnect MUT-11.

BRAKE SYSTEM

STEERING WHEEL SENSOR

Note: *Extreme care should be taken when removing the steering wheel as injury can occur if the airbag deploys*

Removal

1. Remove the steering wheel, air bag module, clock spring, column switch. (see Steering Chapter)

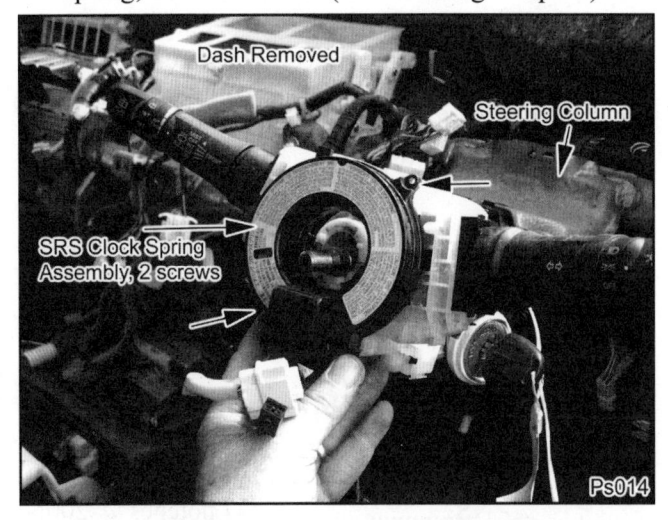

2. From the rear of the column switch undo and remove the three retaining screws holding the steering wheel sensor in place. Disconnect the electrical connector and remove the assembly.

Installation

1. Install the steering wheel sensor to the rear of the column switch.

2. Connect the electrical connector and install the assembly to the steering column.

3. Install the clock spring and airbag module refering to the steering chapter if needed.

INITIALIZATION

Note: *When the battery is disconnected the learned neutral position of the steering wheel sensor is erased, on the dash ASCS off indicator is illuminated. To reprogram the sensor the following procedure needs to be followed.*

1. Turn the steering wheel more than 8°.
2. Drive the vehicle in a straight line for at least one second at more than 35 km/h.
3. After this procedure the ASCS off indicator should not be illuminated anymore.

SOLENOID VALVE CHECK

Measure the resistance between the following solenoid valves and terminals.

Standard Value..3.5 - 3.9 Ohm

Solenoid Valve	Terminals
SA1	18 & 34
SA2	17 & 34
SA3	12 & 34
STR	11 & 34

377

BRAKE SYSTEM

SPECIFICATIONS

FRONT DISC BRAKES
Brake Pad Thickness - Standard:
- NM - NP .... 10.0 mm
- NS (SWB) .... 10.0 mm
- NS (LWB) .... 11.5 mm

Brake Pad Thickness - Minimum:
- NM-NP .... 2.0 mm
- NS (LWB) .... 2.0 mm
- NS (LWB) .... 2.0 mm

Braking Disc
Thickness - Standard:
- NM - NP .... 26.0 mm
- NS (SWB) .... 26.0 mm
- NS (LWB) .... 28.0 mm

Thickness - Minimum:
- NM - NP .... 24.4 mm
- NS (SWB) .... 24.4 mm
- NS (LWB) .... 26.0 mm

Maximum run-out allowable .... 0.06 mm
Disc Brake Drag Force:
- NM - NP .... 55 N
- NS .... 86 N

Front Hub Axial Play .... 0 mm

REAR DISC BRAKES
Brake Pad Thickness - Standard:
- NM - NP .... 10.0 mm
- NS .... 10.0 mm

Brake Pad Thickness - Minimum:
- NM - NP .... 2.0 mm
- NS .... 2.0 mm

Braking Disc
Thickness - Standard:
- NM - NP .... 22.0 mm
- NS (SWB) .... 22.0 mm
- NS (LWB) .... 18.0 mm

Thickness - Minimum:
- NM - NP .... 20.4 mm
- NS (SWB) .... 20.4 mm
- NS (LWB) .... 16.0 mm

Maximum run-out allowable .... 0.06 mm
Disc Brake Drag Force:
- NM - NP .... 55 N
- NS (SWB) .... 55 N
- NS (LWB) .... 86 N

Rear Hub Axial Play .... 0 mm

BRAKE PEDAL
Brake Pedal Height - Standard:
- NM - NP (LHD) .... 192-195 mm
- NM - NS (RHD) .... 187-190 mm

Brake Pedal Free Play - Standard
- NM - NP .... 3 - 8 mm
- NS .... 3 mm or less

Brake Pedal To Floor Clearance - Standard:
- NM - NP .... 90 mm or more
- NS (SWB) .... 85 mm or more
- NS (LWB) .... 80 mm or more

ABS
Speed Sensor .... Magnet coil type
Front Rotor Teeth NM - NP 50
Rear Rotor Teeth NM - NP 50
Gap Between Sensor And Rotor NM - NP .... 0.9 mm

PARK BRAKE SYSTEM
Lever Stroke - Standard:
- NM - NP .... 5-7 notches @ 200N
- NS .... 6-7 notches @ 200N

Maximum Inside Diameter Of Drum - Maximum:
- NM - NP .... 200.0 mm
- NS (SWB) .... 200.0 mm
- NS (LWB) .... 211.0 mm

Lining Thickness - Standard:
- NM - NP .... 3.0 mm
- NS (SWB) .... 3.0 mm
- NS (LWB) .... 4.0 mm

Lining Thickness Minimum .... 1 mm

TORQUE SETTINGS   NM
Brake Booster to Pedal Assembly Nuts NM ...... 14 +/- 3
Pedal Assembly NM - NP .... 12 +/- 2
Brake Lines to Master Cylinder .... 15 +/- 2
ECU Mounting Nuts .... 5 +/- 1
G Sensor and Yaw Rate Mounting Nut .... 4.9 +/- 0.9
Front Brake Hose to Caliper .... 30 +/- 4
Front Caliper Anchor Bolts NM - NP .... 113 +/- 9
    NS .... 115 +/- 10
Park Brake Lever Mounting Bolts .... 11 +/- 2
HBB Accumulator NM - NP .... 53.9 +/- 2.9
    NS .... 54 +/- 5
Standard Master Cylinder Mounting Nuts ...... 10 +/- 2
HBB Buzzer .... 5.0 +/- 1.0
Front Brake Bleed Nipple NM - NP .... 7.4 +/- 1.4
    NS .... 7.9 +/- 0.9
Front Brake Guide Pin and Lock Pin .... 88 +/- 5
Rear Brake Bleed Nipple .... 7.9 +/- 0.9
Rear Brake Guide Pin and Lock Pin .... 44 +/- 5
Proportioning Valve Brake Lines .... 15 +/- 2
Earth Bolt .... 9 +/- 2

BRAKE SYSTEM

ABS TERMINAL VOLTAGE CHECK CHART

Terminal #	Item	Inspection Conditions		Normal Condition
1	Front left control solenoid valve OUT	Ignition switch ON		System voltage
2	Rear right control solenoid valve OUT	Ignition switch ON		System voltage
3	Front left select solenoid valve			System voltage
4	G sensor input	Ignition switch ON		2.4 2.6 V
13	ABS-ECU power supply	Ignition switch ON		System voltage
		Ignition switch START		0 V
14	Front left control solenoid valve IN	Ignition switch ON		System voltage
15	Front left control solenoid valve IN	Ignition switch ON		System voltage
16	Front right select solenoid valve	Ignition switch ON		System voltage
18	G sensor earth	At all times		0.5 V or less
31	ABS-ECU power supply	Ignition switch ON		System voltage
		Ignition switch START		0 V
33	Rear differential lock switch	Ignition switch ON		System voltage
34	Stop lamp switch input	Ignition switch ON	Stop lamp switch ON	System voltage
			Stop lamp switch OFF	2 V or less
36	MUT-II	MUT-II is connected		Serial connection with MUT-II
		MUT-II is not connected		1 V or less
37	ABS valve relay output	Ignition switch ON	System abnormality is detected and relay is off	System Voltage
			Relay is on approx 1 second after engine starts	2 V or less
39	Brake warning lamp output	Ignition switch ON	Lamp is switched OFF	2 V or less
			Lamp is illuminated	System Voltage
40	Right left solenoid valve OUT	Ignition switch ON		System Voltage
41	Front right control solenoid valve OUT	Ignition switch ON		System Voltage
46	Centre diff lock switch input (super select 4WD-II)	Ignition switch ON	Transfer selector 2H, 4H	System voltage
			Transfer selector 4HLc, 4LLc	2 V or less
	4WD detection switch input (part time 4WD)	Ignition switch ON	Transfer selector 2H	System voltage
			Transfer selector 4H	2 V or less
47	Diagnosis select input	MUT-II connected		1 V or less
		MUT-II not connected		Approx 12 V
48	Valve relay monitor	Ignition switch ON		System voltage
50	ABS warning lamp output	Ignition switch ON	Lamp switched off	System voltage
			Lamp illuminated	2 V or less
51	Right left control solenoid valve IN	Ignition switch ON		System voltage
52	Front right control solenoid valve IN	Ignition switch ON		System voltage

ABS TERMINAL RESISTANCE & CONTINUITY CHECKS

Terminal #	Signal	Condition
7 - 20	Front left wheel speed sensor	1.0 - 1.5 kOhms
8 - 21	Rear right wheel speed sensor	1.0 - 1.5 kOhms
9 - 22	Rear left wheel speed sensor	1.0 - 1.5 kOhms
10 - 23	Front right wheel speed sensor	1.0 - 1.5 kOhms
Between terminal 12 & body earth	Earth	Continuity
Between terminal 25 & body earth	Earth	Continuity
Between terminal 26 & body earth	Earth	Continuity
Between terminal 42 & body earth	Earth	Continuity

FUEL TANK ASSEMBLY

(Tank, Fuel Pump & Gauge Unit)

Subject	Page
GENERAL INFORMATION	380
SERVICE OPERATIONS	381
Depressurising the fuel system - Petrol	381
Bleeding air from the fuel system	381
Fuel Tank - Petrol	381
Removal	381
Installation	382
Fuel Tank - Diesel	382
Removal	382
Installation	382
Fuel Gauge Unit	383
Removal	383
Resistance Values	383
Float Height	383
Installation	384
Fuel Pump Assembly - Petrol	384
Removal	384
Disassembly	384
Assembly	384
Installation	384
Fuel Filter Pipe Assembly - Diesel	385
Removal	385
Installation	385
Fuel Filter - Diesel	385
Removal	385
Disassembly	385
Assembly	385
Installation	385
Water Level Sensor Check	386
Fuel Line Heater Check	386
TORQUE SETTINGS	386

GENERAL INFORMATION

FUEL TANK
The fuel tank is located on the right hand side below the rear seat on long wheel base models, and under the drivers seat on short wheel base models. A plastic cover is used to protect the fuel tank from damage. A two way valve is incorporated to regulate fuel pressure inside the tank. On petrol models the high pressure pump is contained inside a module which includes the filter and a fuel pressure regulator.

Access to the fuel pump module and fuel level gauge is obtained from inside the cabin below the back seats under a series of inspection covers. This is done to seal the tank off from the passenger cabin.

FUEL INLET
The fuel filler cap is a "screw on" type with a (clicking) feature to lock. When installing the cap, screw it on until a click sound is heard, which indicates the cap is properly fitted. The valve assembly contains a valve which prevents fuel from flowing out the filler neck.

Note: Should a replacement cap be required, use only the cap specified for Pajero models. Use of an incorrect cap can cause malfunction of the emission control system.

FUEL TANK ASSEMBLY - tank, fuel pump, gauge unit

SERVICE OPERATIONS

DEPRESSURISING THE FUEL SYSTEM - Petrol

Before removing any of the fuel pipes the following procedure should be followed to prevent fuel spray.

1. Remove the fuel filler cap to release pressure in the tank.
2. The fuel pump relay needs to be removed.
   a) On NM - NP models the relay is situated in the engine compartment.

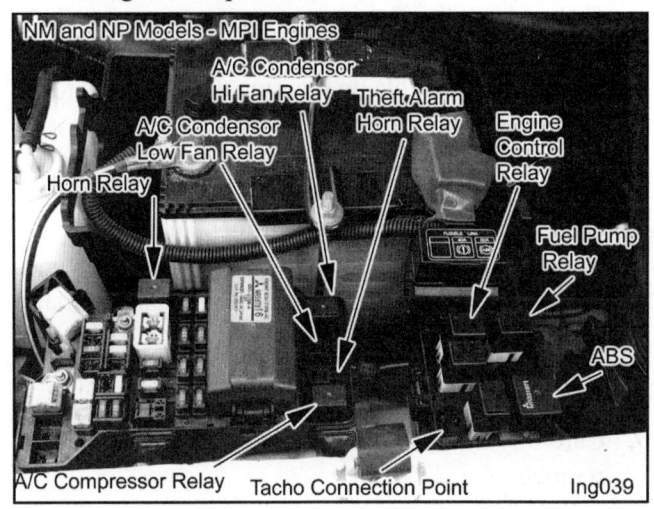

   b) On NS and NT models it is located in the fuse box under the steering wheel.

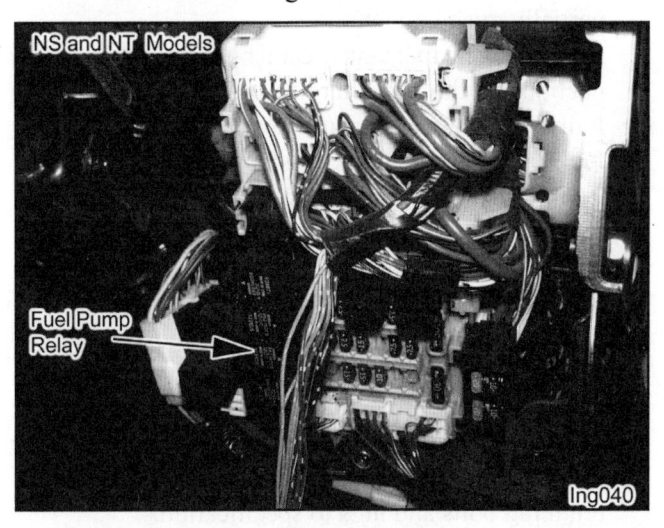

3. On NS and NT models remove the No. 2 fuel pump relay from the fuse panel.
4. Turn the ignition on and crank the engine for at least two seconds.
5. Turn the ignition off and reinstall the fuel pump relay.
6. The vehicle is now ready to be worked on.

BLEEDING AIR FROM FUEL SYSTEM - Diesel

Air needs to bleed from the fuel system after filter replacement, fuel nozzle disconnected, fuel injection pump removed and fuel lines replaced.

1. Loosen air bleeder screw at top of filter. Wrap a rag around the outside of the screw to prevent spillage of fuel.
2. Operate hand primer pump on top of fuel filter until all signs of air are removed, the pressure of the hand pump will increase.
3. Tighten air bleeder screw at top of filter.

   Air Bleeder Screw .... 6.0 +/- 1.0 Nm

FUEL TANK - Petrol
Removal

1. Drain the fuel tank and depressurize the fuel system.

   Note: Beware of distorting the fuel filler pipe deflector, with syphon hose.

2. Raise the rear of the vehicle and place on safety stands, then remove the centre transmission mount. On some models the stabilizer bar clamps will need to be removed so the bar can be moved out of the way.

   Note: Be careful not to damage the ball joint section of the stabilizer link.

3. Remove the nuts, bolts and plastic plugs securing the fuel tank protector and remove protector assembly from the vehicle.

4. Remove the hose clamp securing the filler hose to the tank then disconnect the filler hose.
5. Disconnect the fuel return, vapour and supply hoses, noting their correct location. Be careful as the supply hose is under pressure from the fuel pump. The high pressure hose has a double lock system. To remove push down on the connector to expose the lock tab, push the tab to release.
6. Support the fuel tank with a trolley jack ensuring to use a piece of wood to protect fuel tank.

FUEL TANK ASSEMBLY - tank, fuel pump, gauge unit

7. Remove the fuel tank retaining straps, then partially lower fuel tank.
8. Disconnect the fuel tank breather hose and electrical connections.
9. *Vehicles without canister:* Disconnect the two filler neck vapour hoses.
10. Carefully lower fuel tank assembly from vehicle and remove.

Installation
1. Install the fuel tank into position under vehicle and partially raise into position.
2. Reconnect the fuel tank breather hose and electrical connection.
3. *Vehicles without canister:* Reconnect the two filler neck vapour hoses.
4. Fully install fuel tank into position and tighten the fuel tank retaining strap nuts/bolts to specification.
   Fuel Tank Retaining Straps:
   NM - NP .... 26 +/- 4 Nm
   NS - NT .... 24 +/- 4 Nm
5. Reconnect the fuel return, vapour and supply hoses to their correct locations. On connection, the high pressure supply hose joint needs to be checked, there should be no more than 3mm of play
6. Reconnect the filler hose and tighten hose clamp.
7. Fill the fuel tank, checking for any leaks, then start vehicle to check operation of fuel pump.

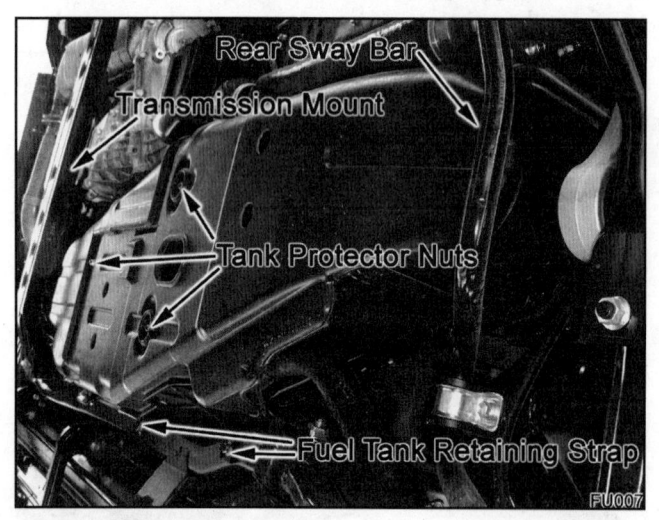

8. Install fuel tank protector into position and tighten retaining bolts and nuts to specification.
   Tank Protector NM - NP .... 26 +/- 4 Nm
   Tank Protector Bolts NS - NT .... 12 +/- 2 Nm
   Tank Protector Nuts NS - NT .... 5.0 +/- 1.0 Nm
9. Install the centre transmission mount (refer to transmission chapter if required), if moved place the stabilizer bar back into position and bolt clamps into place. Then remove safety stands and lower vehicle.

FUEL TANK - Diesel
Removal
1. Drain the fuel tank and depressurize the fuel system, refer to fuel chapter.
   Note: *Beware of distorting the fuel filler pipe deflector, with syphon hose.*
2. Raise the rear of the vehicle and place on safety stands, then remove the centre transmission mount. On some models the stabilizer bar clamps will need to be removed so the bar can be moved out of the way.
   Note: *Be careful not to damage the ball joint section of the stabilizer link.*
3. Remove the nuts, bolts and plastic plugs securing the fuel tank protector and remove protector assembly from the vehicle.
4. Remove the hose clamp securing the filler hose to the tank then disconnect the filler hose.
5. Disconnect the fuel return hose and main hose.
6. Support the fuel tank with a trolley jack ensuring to use a piece of wood to protect fuel tank.
7. Remove the fuel tank retaining strap or straps depending on the model you are working on, then partially lower fuel tank.
8. Disconnect the fuel tank breather hose, electrical connection and the two filler neck vapour hoses.
9. Carefully lower fuel tank assembly from vehicle and remove.

Installation
1. Install the fuel tank into position under vehicle and partially raise into position.
2. Reconnect the fuel tank breather hose, electrical connection and the two filler neck vapour hoses.
3. Fully install fuel tank into position and tighten the fuel tank retaining strap nuts/bolts to specification.
   Fuel Tank Retaining Straps:
   NM - NP .... 26 +/- 4 Nm
   NS - NT .... 24 +/- 2 Nm
4. Reconnect the fuel return hose and main hose.
5. Reconnect the filler hose and tighten hose clamp.
6. Fill the fuel tank, bleed air from the fuel lines. Checking for any leaks, then start vehicle to check operation of fuel supply system.
7. Install fuel tank protector into position and tighten retaining bolts and nuts to specification.
   Tank Protector NM - NP .... 26 +/- 4 Nm
   Tank Protector Bolts NS - NT .... 12 +/- 2 Nm
   Tank Protector Nuts NS - NT .... 5.0 +/- 1.0 Nm
8. Install the centre transmission mount (refer to transmission chapter if required), if moved place the stabilizer bar back into position and bolt clamps into place. Then remove safety stands and lower vehicle.

FUEL GAUGE UNIT -
Short and Long Wheelbase
Removal

1. On models fitted with dual a/c remove the rear heater grille from the floor.

2. a) On short wheel base models slide the right hand seat forward as far as possible, to gain access to the service hole in the carpet.
   b) On long wheel base models fold back and remove the right hand side second row of seats from the vehicle then remove the scuff plate and the seat belt outer anchor bolt. Remove the lower quarter trim panel screw and fold back the carpet to expose the cover.

3. Remove the service hole cover and the packing.

4. Disconnect the electrical wiring from the gauge unit.
   Note: *Use a small screwdriver to push down on the centre tab of the terminal to release*

5. Remove the gauge unit retaining nuts and remove unit from fuel tank assembly.
   Note: *Be careful removing gauge unit so as not to damage or bend the shaft.*

Inspection
Resistance Values

1. Measure the resistance between the fuel gauge unit terminal No.1 and earth terminal No.2 when the float is touching the stoppers in both the Full and Empty positions.

Float Position	Gauge Resistance
Full Position	3 +/- 0.6 Ohm
Empty Position	110 +/- 2.6 Ohm

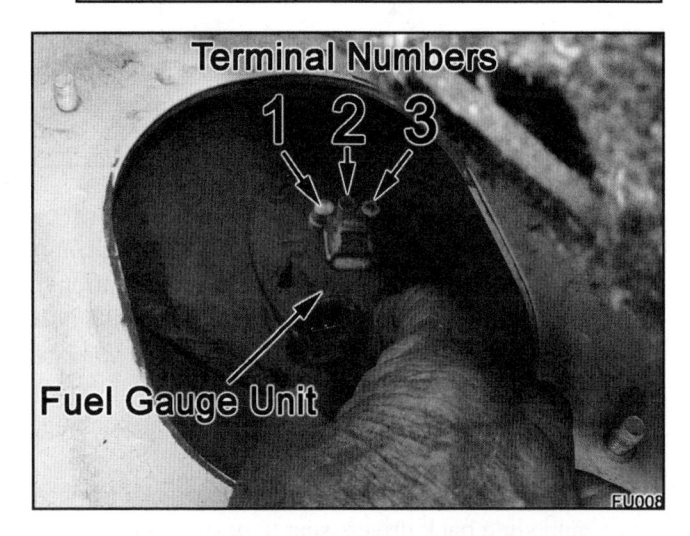

2. Check to ensure when the float is slowly moved between Full and Empty the resistance values change smoothly.

Float Height

1. Move the float to the full position, make sure the arm is contacting the stopper and measure from the centre of the float to the base of the unit. This is measurement "A", see diagram.

2. Next move the float to the empty position and measure from the centre of the float to the bottom of the unit. This is measurement "B". Check to make sure the heights are within specifications.

Float Position	Float Centre Height
Short Wheel Base	
Full "A"	11.9 +/- 3.0 mm
Empty "B"	195.2 +/- 3.0 mm
Long Wheel Base	
Full "A"	11.5 +/- 3.0 mm
Empty "B"	204.9 +/- 3.0 mm

3. If any check is not to specifications replace the fuel tank gauge unit.

FUEL TANK ASSEMBLY - tank, fuel pump, gauge unit

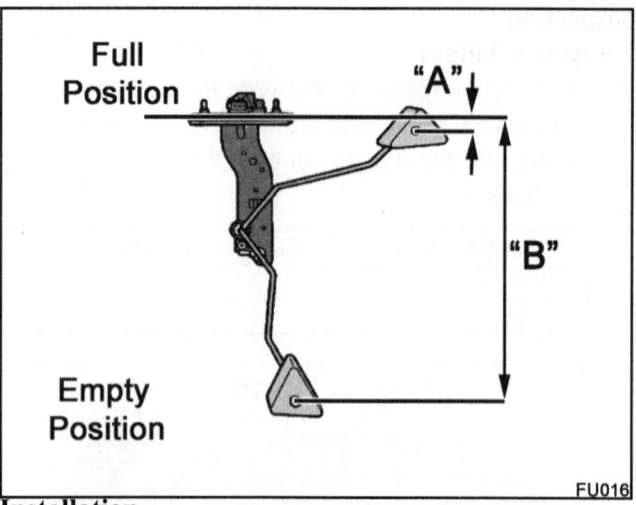

Installation

1. Clean mating surfaces of gauge unit and tank.
2. Install new seal to gauge unit then install unit into fuel tank tightening retaining nuts to specification.
   Gauge Unit Retaining Nuts .... 2.5 +/- 0.4 Nm
   Note: Caution should be taken not to bend or damage the float shaft on installation.
3. Reconnect electrical connection, then install packing, and service hole cover.
4. a) On short wheel base models return carpet into place and slide back drivers seat to normal position.
   b) On long wheel base models install the carpet then replace lower quarter trim panel screw. Replace the seat belt anchor bolt, tightening to specification, then install the scuff plate. Then install the second row of seats using the body chapter if needed.
   Seat Belt Anchor Bolt:
   NM - NP .... 44 +/- 10 Nm
   NS - NT .... 41 +/- 10 Nm
5. On models fitted with dual a/c install the rear heater grille.

FUEL PUMP ASSEMBLY (Petrol)

Removal

1. a) On SWB models remove the front scuff plate and the outer seat belt anchor bolt, then fold back carpet to access the service hole.
   b) On LWB models fold back the second row of seats.
2. Fold back the carpet to expose the service hole. Remove the bolts from the cover. Underneath is another access cover. Using a socket remove the nuts and pry the cover open.
3. Disconnect the electrical wiring from the fuel pump unit.
4. Disconnect the fuel suction, return hose, then disconnect the high pressure hose from the fuel pump unit. The high pressure hose has a double lock system. To remove push down on the connector to expose the lock tab, push the tab to release.
5. Remove the gauge unit retaining nuts, then remove the fuel pump unit from the tank.

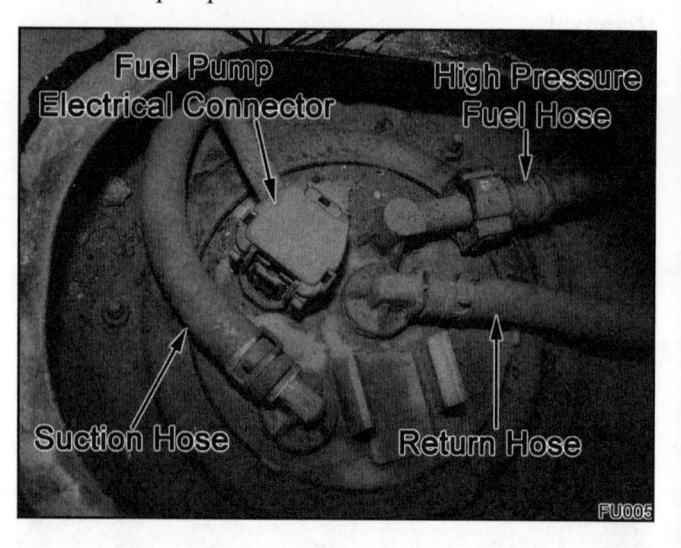

Disassembly

1. Remove the fuel pump bracket and cushion from the bottom of the fuel pump.
2. Remove the fuel pump, then remove the grommet and electrical harness.
3. From the high pressure filter assembly remove the housing then remove the cap and 'O-ring.
4. Remove the Assist pump and on GDI fuel vehicles remove the pressure regulator.

Assembly

1. Coat the 'O-ring and grommet with fuel before assembly. This will help to prevent them from damage. Place the O-ring and cap into the high pressure filter assembly.
2. On GDI fuel vehicles install the pressure regulator.
3. Install the Assist pump to the assembly.
4. To the high pressure filter assembly install the housing.
5. To the fuel pump install the grommet and electrical harness.
6. Install the cushion and bracket to the bottom of the fuel pump.

Installation

1. Clean mating surfaces of fuel pump assembly and tank.
2. Install fuel pump assembly into fuel tank, tightening retaining nuts to specification.
   Fuel Pump Retaining Nuts .... 2.5 +/- 0.4 Nm
3. Connect the tank suction hose, then connect the high pressure hose to the fuel pump unit.
4. Reconnect electrical connection, then install packing, and service hole cover.
5. Place the carpet back into position, then fold the second row of seats back into position.

FUEL FILTER PIPE ASSEMBLY (Diesel)
Removal
1. a) On short wheel base models remove the front scuff plate and the outer seat belt anchor bolt, then fold back carpet to access the service hole.
   b) On long wheel base models fold back the right hand side second row of seats then remove the service hole cover and packing.
2. Remove the cover from the service hole, then remove the packing.
3. Disconnect the tank return hose and tank main hose from the fuel filter unit.
   Note: *Mark the pipes on removal to help with installation.*
4. Remove the fuel filter pipe assembly retaining nuts, then remove the assembly from the tank. As the assembly is being withdrawn disconnect the suction pipe.

Installation
1. Clean mating surfaces of the filter assembly and tank.
2. Install a new filter to the assembly then install the unit into fuel tank, making sure to connect the suction pipe. Tighten retaining nuts to specification.
   Pump Retaining Nuts .... 2.5 +/- 0.4 Nm
3. Connect the tank return hose and main hose to the filter pipe assembly, using marks on removal as a guide.
4. Install packing, and the service hole cover.
5. a) On short wheel base models fold carpet back into position, then install the scuff plate and seat belt anchor bolt.
      Seat Belt Anchor Bolt:
      NM - NP .... 44 +/- 10 Nm
      NS - NT .... 41 +/- 10 Nm
   b) On long wheel base models fold the seats back into position.

FUEL FILTER (Diesel)

Removal
1. Where fitted remove the engine cover then disconnect the battery and remove the battery and battery tray.
2. Disconnect the fuel lines from the filter assembly, then disconnect the electrical connection for the water level sensor and fuel line heater.
3. Remove the bolts securing the filter assembly to the mounting bracket and remove assembly from vehicle.
4. If required remove filter mounting bracket.

Disassembly
1. From the fuel filter assembly remove the drain plug and O-ring where fitted. Remove the water level sensor.
2. Place the fuel filter pump in to a vice and using a filter wrench remove the filter cartridge.

Assembly
1. Clean the mounting surface on the filter pump side.
2. Install a new fuel filter cartridge and tighten to specification after the point where the gasket contacts the surface.
   Filter Cartridge:
   NM - NP .... 14 +/- 1 Nm
   NS - NT .... 3/4 to 1 turn or 17 +/- 2 Nm
3. Then install a new water level sensor and tighten to specification.
   Water Level Sensor:
   NM - NP .... 2.5 +/- 0.5 Nm
   NS - NT .... 4.9 +/- 0.4 Nm
4. Where fitted Install a new drain plug and O-ring and tighten to specification.
   Drain Plug .... 1.0 +/- 0.4 Nm

Installation
1. If removed reinstall the filter mounting bracket.
   Mounting Bracket Nuts .... 11 +/- 4 Nm
2. Install the fuel filter into position and tighten retaining bolts to specification.
   Filter mounting Bolts .... 11 +/- 4 Nm
3. Connect the fuel lines to the filter assembly, then

FUEL TANK ASSEMBLY - tank, fuel pump, gauge unit

connect the electrical connection for the water level sensor and fuel line heater.
4. Install the battery tray and battery.
5. Bleed air from the fuel lines as outlined at the start of this chapter. Start engine and check to ensure there are no leaks.
6. Install engine cover if equipped.

WATER LEVEL SENSOR CHECK

1. Connect a multimeter to the two terminals of the water level sensor connector.

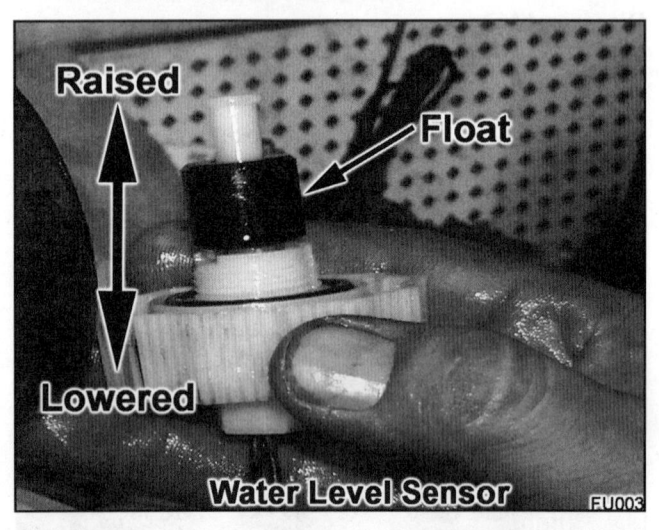

2. Raise the float and check to ensure there is continuity. There should be no continuity when float is lowered.
3. If faulty replace sensor.

FUEL LINE HEATER CHECK

1. Disconnect the electrical connector to the fuel line heater.
2. Plug the inlet port to stop it from leaking during the check. Connect a hand vacuum pump to the outlet port of the fuel filter pump.

3. Using a multimeter connected to the two terminals measure the resistance using the table as a guide when pressure is applied.

Pressure kPa	Continuity
- 31 +/- 5 or less	Yes
- 18 +/- 5	No

Note: *Lower the pressure gradually to prevent damage.*

4. If the above table is not achieved the fuel filter pump is defective and will need to be replaced.

SPECIFICATIONS

TORQUE SETTINGS   Nm
Fuel Tank Retaining Straps:
   NM - NP..26 +/- 4
   NS - NT...24 +/- 4
Fuel Tank Protector:
   NM - NP..26 +/- 4
   Bolts NS - NT..12 +/- 2
   Nuts NS - NT...5.0 +/- 1.0
Fuel Gauge Unit Retaining Nuts.....................2.5 +/- 0.4
Fuel Pump Retaining Nuts.............................2.5 +/- 0.4
Seat Belt Anchor Bolts:
   NM - NP..44 +/- 10
   NS - NT...41 +/- 10
Fuel Filter Mounting Bolts/Nuts........................11 +/- 4
Air Bleeder Screw...6.0 +/- 1.0
Filter Cartridge:
   NM - NP...14 +/- 1
   NS - NT.............................3/4 to 1 turn or 17 +/- 2
Water Level Sensor:
   NM - NP...2.5 +/- 0.5
   NS - NT...4.9 +/- 0.4
Drain Plug...1.0 +/- 0.4
Filter Mounting Bracket..11 +/- 4

386

BODY

Subject	Page
INSTRUMENT PANEL	388
Centre Console	388
Glove Compartment (Glove Box)	389
NM - NP	389
NS - NT	389
Instrument Cluster	389
Heater & A/C Controls	389
NM - NP	389
NS - NT	390
Rear Heater Controls	390
Dash (instrument) Panel Assembly	390
BACK DOOR (Tail Gate)	392
Internal Trim - Back door	392
Back Door Assembly	393
Lock Assembly - Back door	393
Lock Striker - Back door	394
Door Handle & Latch - Back door	394
Back Door External Handle Play	395
Back Door Internal Handle Play	395
Weather Strip Assembly - Back door	395
FRONT and REAR DOOR ASSEMBLIES	395
Front and Rear Doors	395
Lock Striker	396
Door Window Regulator Handle	396
Door Inner Trim Panel	396
Front	396
Rear	397
Front Door Lock Assembly	398
Rear Door Latch Assembly	399
Front Door Exterior Handle	399
Rear Door Exterior Handle	400
Interior Door Handle	400
Front Door Window Glass & Regulator	400
Rear Door Window Glass & Regulator	401
Door Window Glass Adjustment	402
Front & Rear Door Weather-strip	402
Door Belt Weather-strip & Moulding	402
Exterior Rear View Mirror - Electrical	402
Exterior Rear View Mirror Switch	402
Electric Retractable Mirror Control Unit	403
Electric Retractable Mirror Operation Check	403
STATIONARY GLASS	404
HEADLINING & TRIM	404
Rear Quarter Panel Trim	404
Headlining Assembly	404

Subject	Page
SEATS & SEAT BELTS	405
Front Bucket Seat Assembly	405
Head Restraint Assembly	405
Rear/Second Seat Assembly	406
Third Row Seat Assembly - Face to Face	406
Third Row Seat Assembly - Bench	406
Front Seat Belt Retractor & Buckle Assembly	407
Rear Seat Belt Retractor Assembly - SWB	408
Rear/2nd Seat Belt Retractor Assembly - LWB	408
Rear/3rd Seat Belt Retractor Assembly - LWB	408
SHEET METAL	409
Front Fender Assembly	409
Bonnet	409
Bonnet Latch	410
Bonnet Release Cable Assembly	410
BUMPER BARS & FRONT GRILLE	411
Front Grille (radiator)	411
NM - NP	411
NS - NT	411
Front Mud Guard	411
Rear Mud Guard	411
Splash Shield - Front	412
Engine Skid Plate & Under Covers	412
Front Bumper Bar	412
Rear Bumper Bar	413
2001-2006	413
2007-2008	413
Over Fender - Front (flares)	414
Over Fender - Rear (flares)	414
Side Steps	415
Roof Rails	415
Rear Deflector	415
WINDSCREEN WIPERS & WASHERS	415
Wiper Arm	415
Wiper Motor & Linkage	415
Wiper Motor Inspection	416
Rear Window Wiper Motor	416
Rear Wiper Motor Inspection	417
Wiper Blade Replacement	417
Washer Nozzle Adjustment	417
Headlamp Washer	417

INSTRUMENT PANEL

CENTRE CONSOLE

Removal

1. Disconnect the battery negative cable, as a safety procedure due to the SRS system.
2. Remove the park brake lever cover and the cup holder from the centre console by carefully levering out at the retaining clips (each side).
3. Remove the transfer shift and selector lever knobs, then remove the screws securing the indicator panel. 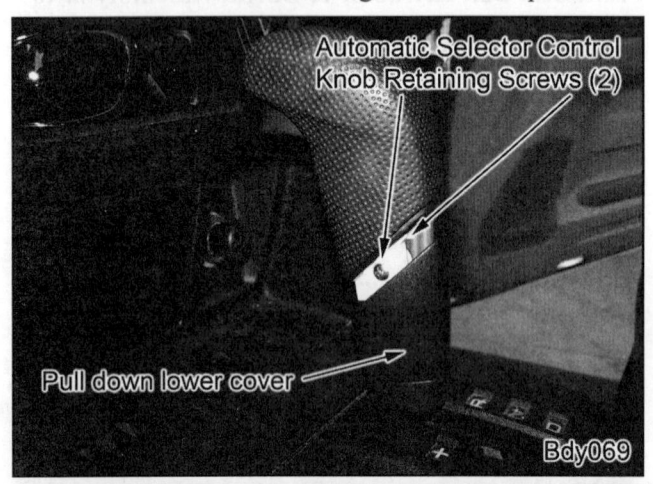 
4. Disconnect any electrical connections then remove the indicator panel.
5. Remove the shift lever cover (manual models), then remove the switch panel.
6. Remove the screws securing the lower centre panel, then partially remove the lower centre panel.
7. Disconnect the electrical connections, then fully remove panel from vehicle. 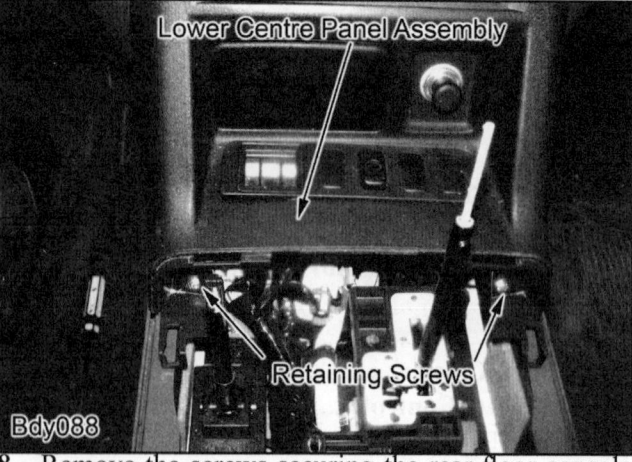
8. Remove the screws securing the rear floor console assembly and then remove the rear assembly from the vehicle. 
9. Remove the screws securing the front console assembly and then remove the front console assembly from the vehicle.

Note: *It may be necessary to remove the park brake lever to remove the front console assembly.*

Installation

1. Install the front console assembly into position and tighten the retaining screws.
2. Install the rear console assembly into position and tighten the retaining screws, then if removed install the park brake lever.

Note: *If park brake lever was removed, adjust lever as outlined in brakes chapter.*

3. Install the lower centre panel into place and tighten the retaining screws, then install the switch panel and shift lever cover on manual models.
4. Install the indicator panel reconnecting any electrical connections which may be present and tighten the panel retaining screws.
5. Install the transfer shift knob and the selector lever knob, then install the park brake lever cover and cup holder.
6. Reconnect the battery negative cable.

BODY - Instrument Panel

GLOVE COMPARTMENT - NM / NP
Removal
1. Open the main glove box assembly then rotate the glove box stopper from each side to release them.

2. Remove the glove box assembly from the instrument (dash) panel, the hinges are a press in pit to secure the base of the glove box.
3. Remove the two screws securing the upper glove box lock striker and remove the striker assembly.
4. Remove the screws securing the upper glove box assembly, then remove the glove box assembly from instrument (dash) panel.

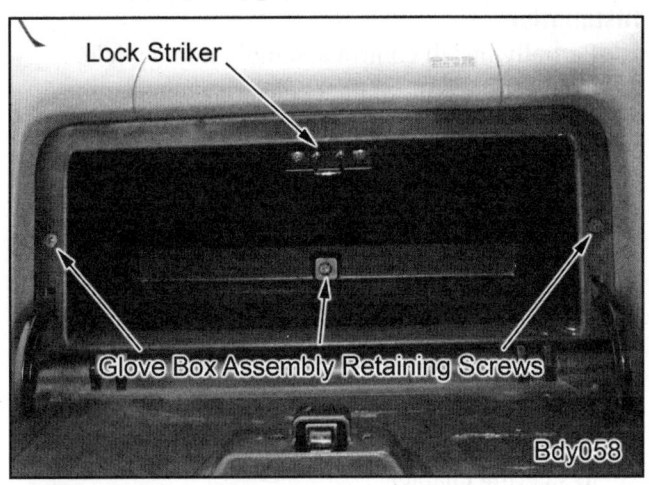

Installation
1. Install the upper glove box assembly into position and tighten the retaining screws.
2. Install the upper glove box assembly lock striker, and tighten retaining screws.
3. Install the main glove box assembly ensuring the hinges are pressed in fully to secure, then partially close glove box and install the stoppers on each side.

GLOVE COMPARTMENT - NS / NT
Removal
1. Remove the screws securing the passenger side lower cover and remove cover.
2. Open the glove box door then remove the screws securing the glove box assembly and remove the glove box assembly from the instrument (dash) panel.

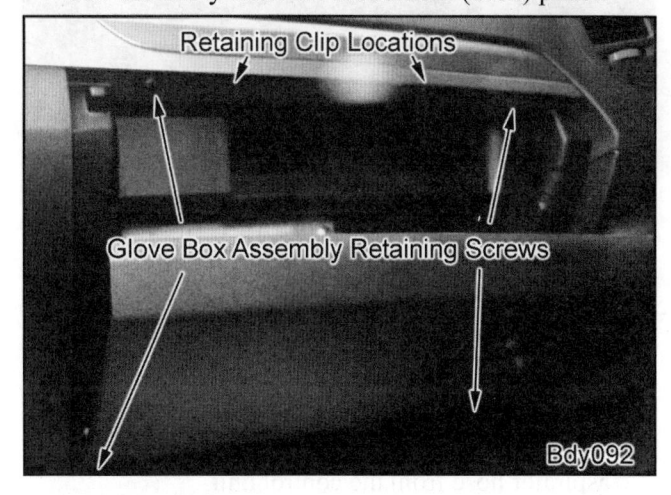

Installation
1. Install the glove box housing into position and secure with the retaining screws.
2. Install the passenger side lower trim cover into position and tighten retaining screws.
3. Check the alignment of the glove box door and ensure it opens and closes correctly.

INSTRUMENT CLUSTER
Refer to "Body Electrical" chapter for removal and installation procedures for the instrument cluster.

HEATER & A/C CONTROLS - NM/NP
Removal
1. Remove centre panel assembly by removing the two upper retaining screws, slide panel forward, disconnect any electrical connections and remove panel.

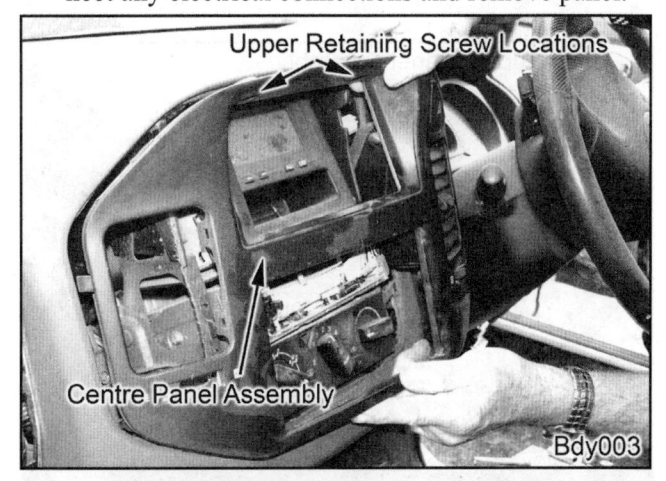

2. Remove the four screws securing the control unit to dash assembly and slide out control unit.
3. **Manual:** Disconnect the air selection control wire and outlet changeover damper cable control wire.

BODY - Instrument Panel

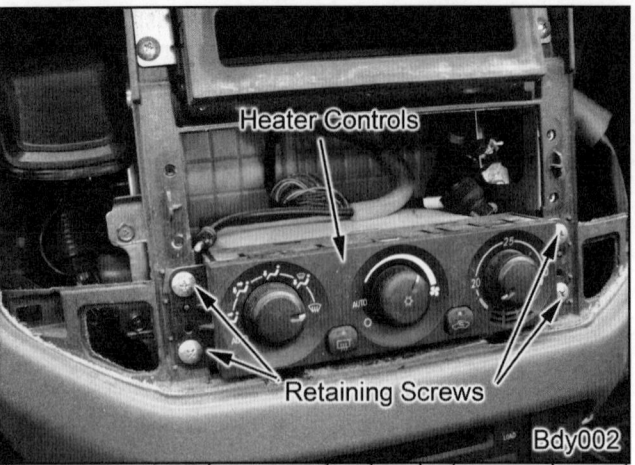

4. **Automatic:** Disconnect the electrical connection and aspirator hose from the control unit.
5. Fully remove unit from vehicle.

Installation
1. **Manual:** Connect the air selection control wire and outlet changeover damper cable control wire.
2. **Automatic:** Reconnect the electrical connection and aspirator hose.
3. Install control assembly into vehicle and tighten the four retaining screws.
4. Test the operation of the controls.
5. Replace the centre panel ensuring to reconnect any electrical connections then tighten the upper retaining screws.

HEATER & A/C CONTROLS - NS / NT
Removal
1. Remove the lower centre panel by gently prising out.

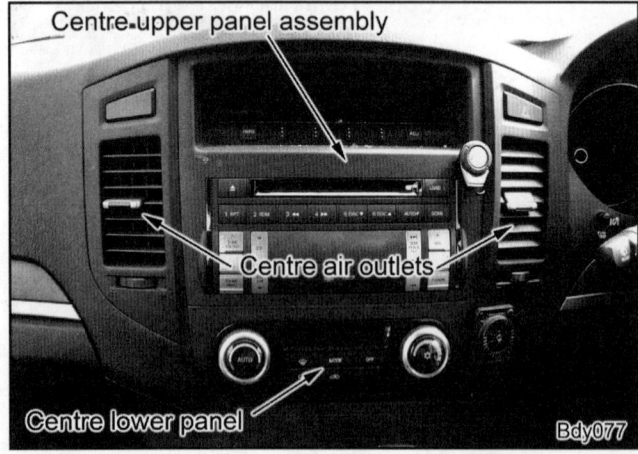

2. Remove the four screws securing the control and slide out control unit.
3. Disconnect and label the connections at the rear of the control unit, then fully remove unit from vehicle.

Install
1. Connect all connections to the rear on the control unit, then fully install unit and tighten retaining screws.

2. Replace the lower centre panel ensuring all retaining clips are properly secured, then test operation on heater controls.

REAR HEATER CONTROLS

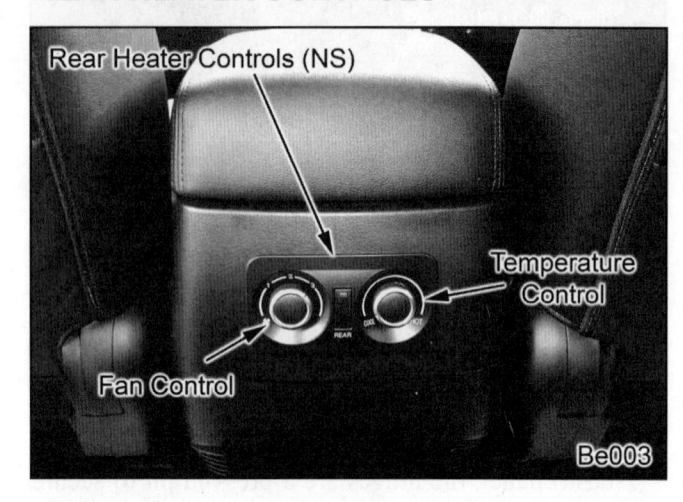

Removal
1. Remove the screws securing the control panel, then release retaining clips and partially remove panel.
2. Disconnect the control panel electrical connection and fully remove panel from vehicle.

Installation
1. Partially install control assembly into vehicle.
2. Connect the control panel electrical connection.
3. Install control panel into position and tighten retaining screws.
4. Test operation of controls.

INSTRUMENT (DASH) PANEL ASSEMBLY
Removal
1. Remove the centre console assembly as described previously.
2. Disconnect the battery negative cable then remove the steering column covers and steering wheel. Refer to steering chapter.
3. **NM/NP:** Remove the two screws securing the centre panel then remove the centre panel from the vehicle by gently prising out.
4. **NS/NT:** Remove the centre air outlets by gently prising out.
5. **NS/NT:** Remove the centre upper panel assembly by carefully levering at retaining clips, disconnect any electrical connections and remove panel.
6. **NS/NT:** Remove the lower centre panel by gently levering out.
7. Remove the screws securing the centre display unit, slide out unit disconnecting any electrical connections and remove assembly from vehicle.
8. Remove the screws securing the radio, slide radio out disconnecting electrical connections and aerial.

BODY - Instrument Panel

9. Remove the screws securing the heater controls, disconnect control wires and remove assembly.
10. Remove the glove box assembly as described previously in this chapter.
11. Disconnect the passenger side airbag module and also disconnect the photo sensor connector.
12. Remove the side cover from each end of the instrument panel.
13. From either end of the instrument panel remove the air outlet vent assemblies.

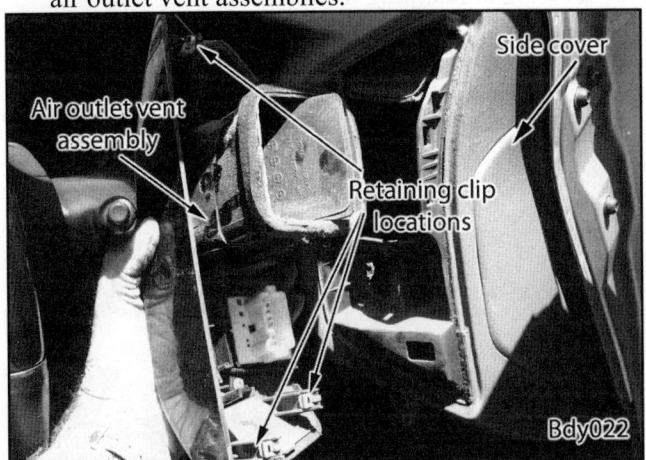

14. Remove the instrument cluster bezel and instrument cluster, referring to body electrical chapter for assistance if required.
15. Remove the release levers for the bonnet and the fuel door, then remove the screws securing the lower instrument panel and remove from vehicle.

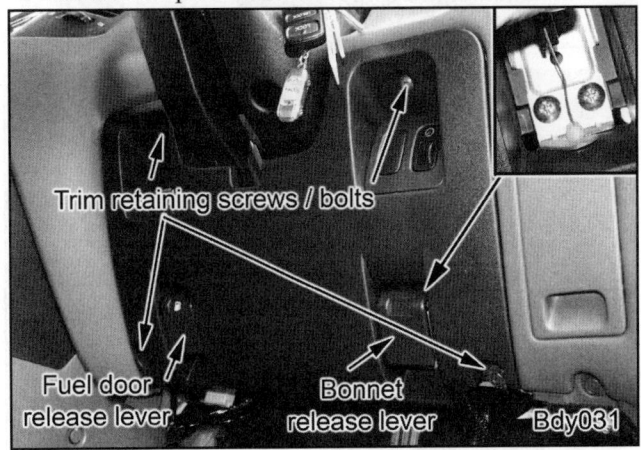

16. Remove the screws securing the lower steering column cover, then remove lower and upper column covers.
17. Remove the assist grips and front pillar trim panels.
18. Remove the stay brackets.
19. Remove the lower corner trim panels, then remove the instrument panel assembly retaining bolts and nuts.
20. Partially pull out the instrument panel and disconnect any electrical connections then carefully remove instrument panel assembly from vehicle.

Dismantle

1. Remove the screws securing the heater distribution duct to the instrument panel then remove duct.
2. Remove the screws securing the side and centre defroster ducts to the instrument panel and remove ducts.
3. From the instrument panel assembly remove the photo sensor.
4. Remove the passenger side air bag module from the instrument panel and store in a dry safe place.
5. Remove the glove box striker from the instrument panel then remove the centre reinforcement.
6. From the top of the instrument panel remove the defroster trim panel.

Assembly

1. To the top of the instrument panel install the defroster trim panel.
2. Install the glove box striker to the instrument panel then install the centre reinforcement.
3. Install the passenger side air bag module then install the photo sensor.
4. Install the side and centre defroster ducts to the instrument panel and tighten retaining screws.
5. Install the heater distribution duct to the instrument panel and tighten retaining screws.

Installation

1. Place instrument panel assembly into vehicle. At the rear of instrument panel, connect all applicable wiring connectors.
2. Fully install instrument panel and tighten the retaining bolts and nuts.
3. Install the lower corner trim panels, then install the stay brackets.
4. Install front pillar trim panels and the assist grips.
5. Install the steering column covers to the steering column and tighten lower cover retaining screws.
6. Install the lower instrument panel into position and tighten retaining screws, then install the bonnet and fuel door release levers.
7. Install the instrument cluster in position reconnecting all electrical connections then install the instrument cluster bezel.
8. To either end of the instrument panel install the air outlet vent assemblies and install the side cover to each end.
9. Connect the passenger side airbag module and also connect the photo sensor connector.
10. Install the glove box assembly as described previously in this chapter.
11. Install heater controls into position reconnecting control wires, then secure controls with retaining screws.

BODY - Back Door (Tail Gate)

12. Install radio assembly into position reconnecting electrical connections and aerial, then secure with retaining screws.
13. Install the centre display unit into position reconnecting electrical connections, then tighten retaining screws.
14. **NM/NP:** Install the centre panel into position reconnecting switch electrical connections and tighten the two retaining screws.
15. **NS/NT:** Install the lower centre panel ensuring retaining clips are properly engaged.
16. **NS/NT:** Replace the centre panel ensuring to reconnect any electrical connections and that all retaining clips are properly secured.
17. **NS/NT:** Install centre air outlets to the instrument panel.
18. Install the steering wheel, refer to "Steering Chapter" if required, then reconnect the battery negative cable.

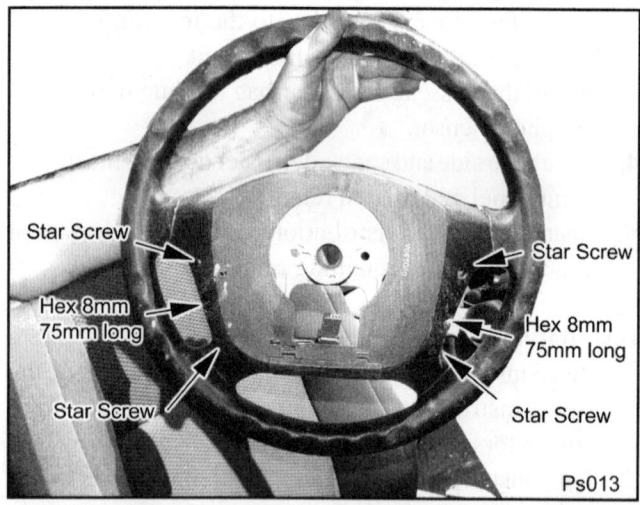

19. Install centre console assembly as described previously.
20. Check that all instrument panel switches, controls and gauges function correctly.

BACK DOOR (tailgate)

INTERNAL TRIM - BACK DOOR
Removal
1. Remove the high mount stop lamp, refer to "Body Electrical Chapter" for assistance.
2. Remove the screws securing the internal pull handle, then remove the upper trim from the door by carefully levering at retaining locations.

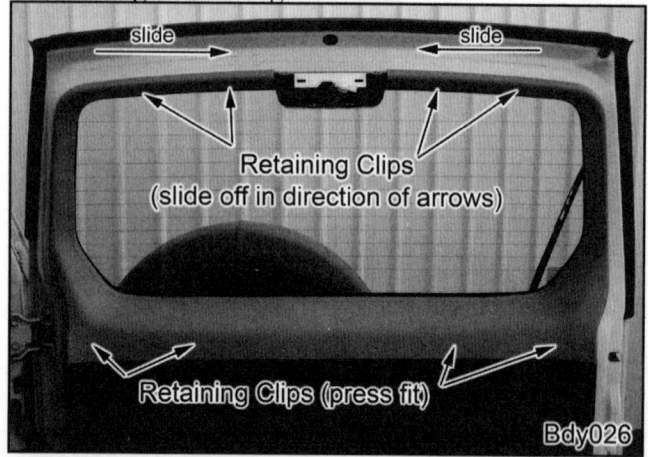

3. Remove the tool box assembly from the back door, then remove the lower trim panel by carefully levering at retainer locations.

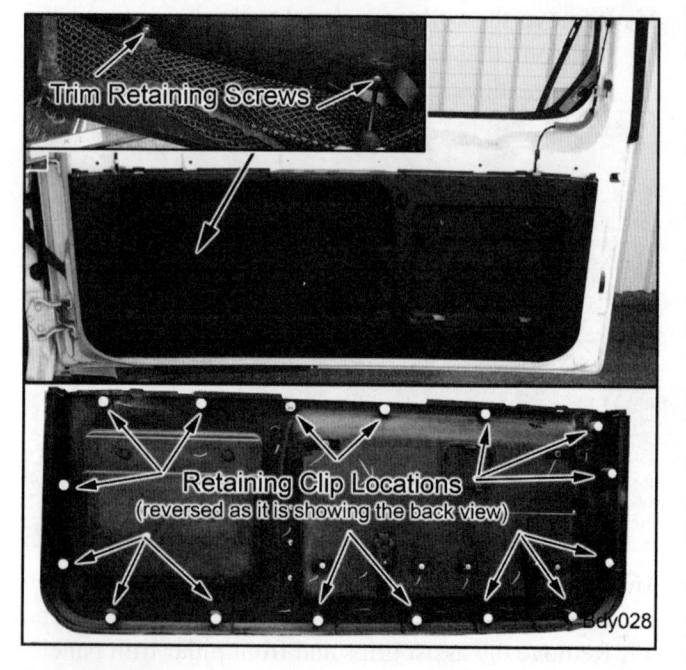

Installation
1. Install the lower trim panel, ensuring all retainers are properly secured, then install the tool box assembly to the rear door.
2. Install the upper trim panel, ensuring all retainers are properly secured, then install the internal pull handle.
3. Install the high mount stop lamp, referring to "Body Electrical Chapter" for assistance.

BACK DOOR ASSEMBLY
Removal
1. Remove the spare tyre and tyre carrier from the vehicle, refer to wheels chapter if required.
2. Remove the trim panel and waterproof film from the door assembly.
3. Disconnect the number plate lamps then remove the screws securing the number plate garnish and remove from vehicle.
4. Disconnect the electrical connections for the back door assembly.
5. Remove the screws securing the back door stopper then remove stopper.

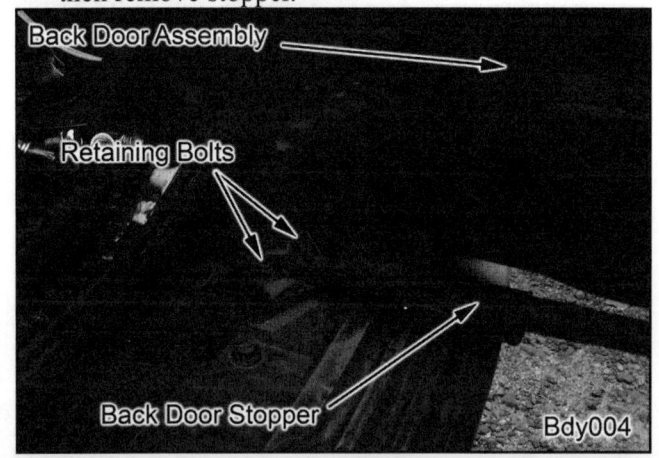

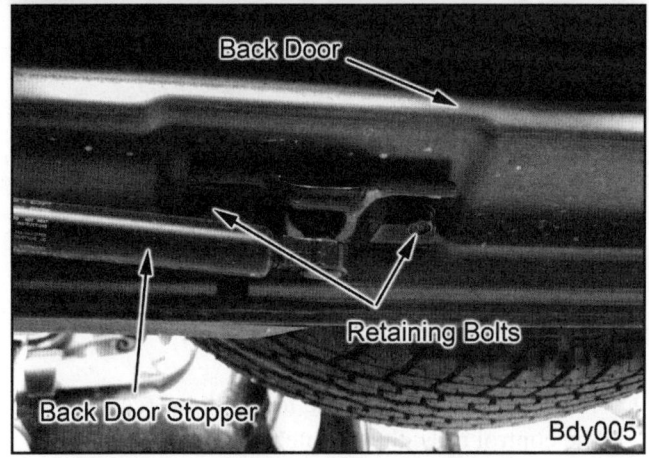

6. Mark the location of the hinges to body to assist in alignment on assembly.
7. Support the back door then remove the upper and lower hinge retaining bolts and remove door assembly.
   Note: *Be careful not to lose the adjustment shims from the hinge assemblies.*

Installation
1. Lubricate the tail gate hinge then position the tail gate into place, install the retaining bolts tightening to specification
   Back Door Hinge Bolts .... 21 Nm

2. Lubricate the back door stopper then install stopper tightening retaining bolts to specification.
   Stopper Retaining Bolts.............................. 18 Nm
3. Check alignment of door assembly, if alignment is not correct adjust using hinge shims and by adjusting the strikers.
4. Reconnect the electrical connections for the back door assembly.
5. Install the number plate garnish, tightening retaining screws/nuts, then connect the number plate lamps.
6. Install the spare tyre carrier and tyre to the vehicle, refer to wheels chapter if required.
7. Install the waterproof film and trim panel to the door assembly.

LOCK ASSEMBLY - BACK DOOR
Removal
1. Remove the back door inner trim panel, then carefully remove the inner waterproof cover.
2. Remove the licence plate lamp garnish.
3. Disconnect all control rods and electrical connections from the lock assembly, then remove the retaining screw from the inside of the door assembly.

4. Remove the three screws from the side of the door retaining the lock assembly and remove.

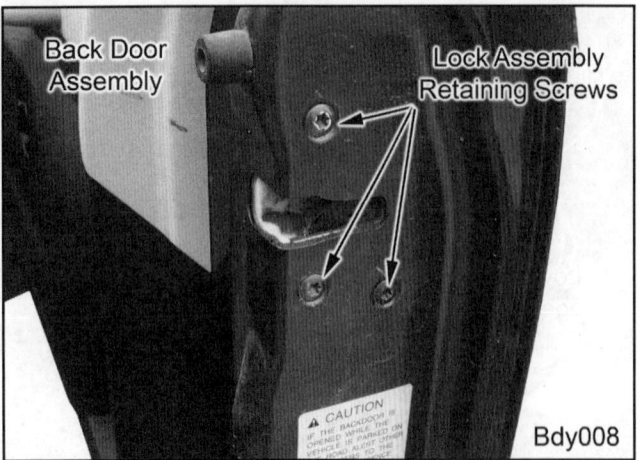

BODY - Back Door (Tail Gate)

5. Disconnect the control rod from the lock cylinder then remove the retaining clip from the lock cylinder and remove cylinder.

Installation

1. Install the cylinder lock into position and secure with retaining clip, then reconnect control rod.
2. Install lock assembly into position and tighten the four mounting screws.
3. Reconnect all control rods and electrical connections, then replace the trim panel.

LOCK STRIKER - BACK DOOR

The tail gate lock striker plate is secured by 2 bolts. These 2 bolts along with the striker shims provide the lock striker with horizontal, forward, rearward and side to side adjustment.

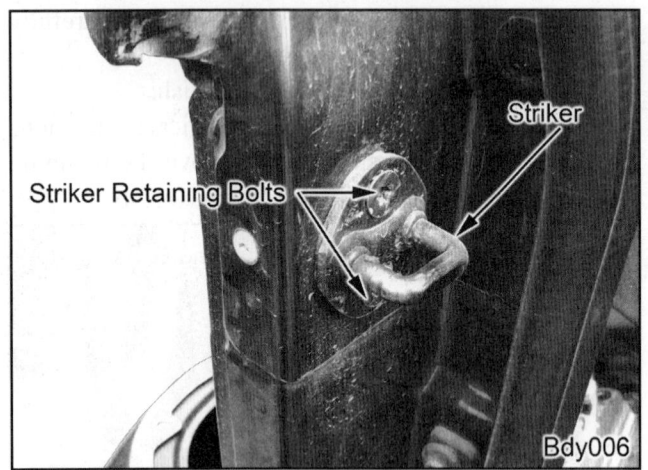

DOOR HANDLE & LATCH - BACK DOOR
Removal

1. Remove the internal trim from the door as described previously.
2. Remove the licence plate garnish, then disconnect the control rods from the outside handle and lock cylinder. 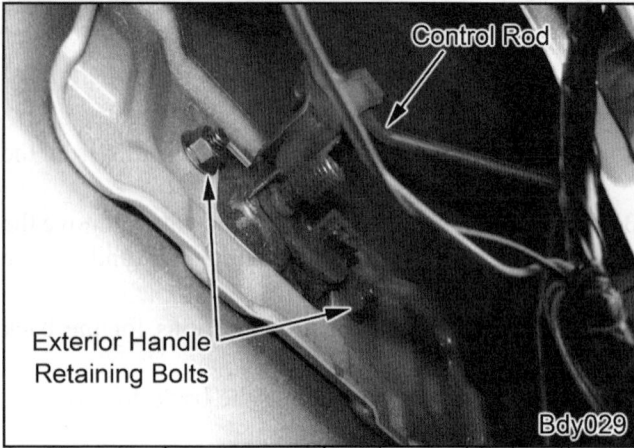
3. Remove the nuts securing the outside handle and remove handle from door assembly, then remove the lock cylinder retaining clip and remove cylinder from door. 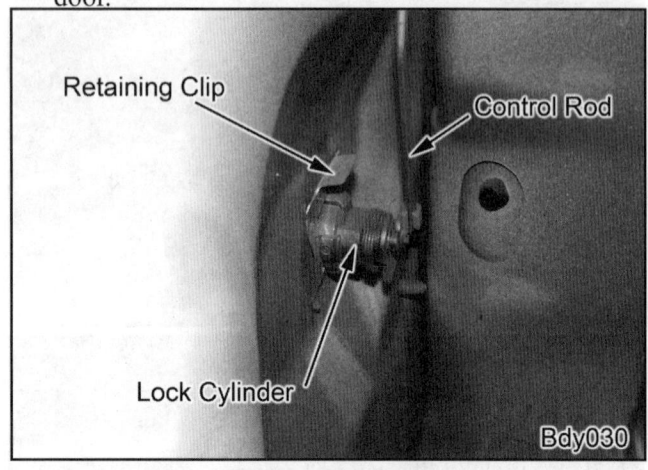
4. Disconnect the control rods and electrical connection from the lock assembly, then remove the three lock retaining bolts and remove assembly from door.
5. Remove the screws securing the internal handle, then release control rods and remove handle from door.

Installation

1. Install the internal handle to the door, reconnecting the control rods, then tighten retaining screws.
2. Install the lock assembly into the door and secure in place with the three retaining bolts, then reconnect the control rods and electrical connection.
   Lock Assembly Bolts.................................... 6 Nm
3. Install the lock cylinder and external handle to the door, reconnect the control rods, then install handle retaining nuts and lock cylinder retaining clip.
4. Install the licence plate garnish, then install the internal trim to the door as described previously.
5. Check the handle play for both inside and outside handles.

BACK DOOR EXTERNAL HANDLE PLAY
Inspection
1. Measure the play in the back door external handle and check to ensure it is within specification.
   External Handle Play .... 2.3 mm
2. If not to specification inspect the external handle and latch assembly, replace as required.

BACK DOOR INTERNAL HANDLE PLAY
Inspection
1. Measure the play in the back door internal handle and check to ensure is is within specification.
   Internal Handle Play .... 5.3 mm or less
2. If not to specification remove the rear door trim panel then adjust handle by the rod clip.

WEATHER STRIP ASSEMBLY - BACK DOOR OPENING
The one piece tail gate opening weather-strip is a rubber 'U' section fitted with an integral retaining system. It fits firmly over the upturned flange of the door opening.
NOTE: *When installing the weather-strip assembly, locate the longer side of the 'U' section on the outside of the tail gate opening upturned flange.*

WEATHER STRIP ASSEMBLY - BACK DOOR
The one piece back door weather-strip is secured by press fit retaining clips. Carefully lever retaining clips from door to remove weather-strip.

FRONT & REAR DOOR ASSEMBLIES (passenger)

FRONT & REAR DOORS
Removal
1. Remove the grommet for the electrical harness from the door pillar then withdraw connectors and disconnect.
2. Use a scribe or marker pen to mark the location of the hinges to the door and body to assist in assembly.
3. Remove the door check link retaining bolt.

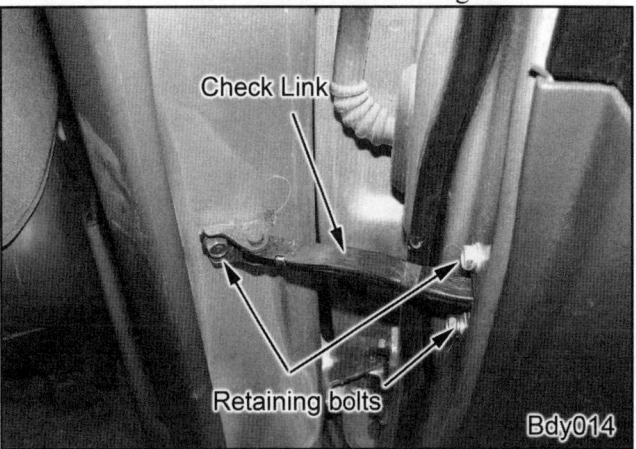

4. With the door supported remove the hinge to door mounting bolts and lift door from the vehicle.

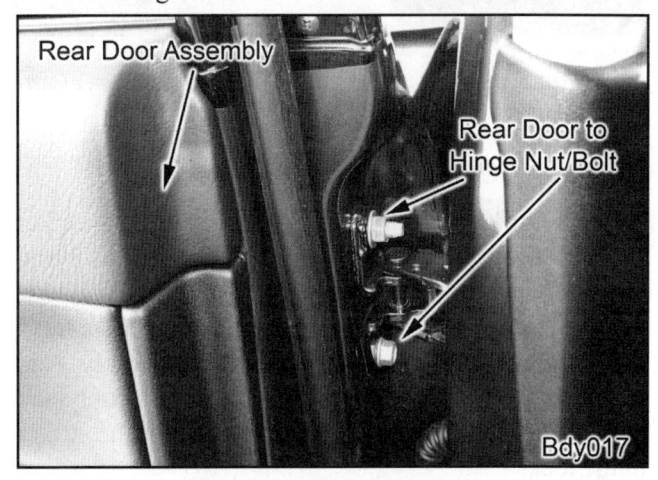

5. If hinges are damaged remove the bolts securing hinge to door and replace.

Installation
1. Install the door to the hinges using the alignment marks and install the retaining bolts.
2. Replace the door check link retaining bolt and cover, then reconnect electrical connections and check to ensure door is correctly aligned.

Adjust
Attention should be given to uniform margins and alignment between the door and surrounding parts when door

BODY - Front & Rear Door Assemblies

adjustments are being carried out.

Uniform margins and alignment of front and rear doors in relation to the body opening can be achieved by setting the appropriate door hinge.

Adjust hinges in conjunction with adjustment to lock striker to achieve an acceptable door closing effort with correct door lock to striker engagement.

LOCK STRIKER
Remove Or Adjust

1. Mark the striker position with a pencil or felt pen, this will help when installing the striker to its correct position.
2. Loosen or remove the two screws securing striker assembly.

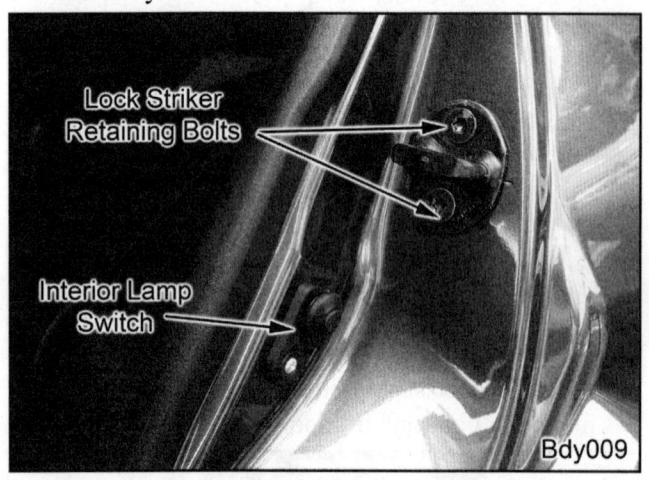

Note: Security torx bits are required for striker retaining bolts.

Installation

Align the striker assembly so that the bridge of the striker locates centrally in the lock fork as the door is being closed. Securely tighten the striker assembly.

Correct engagement can be achieved by vertical or horizontal adjustment of the door lock striker assembly. Add or delete spaces from between the striker assembly and body pillar to achieve correct engagement of the striker to the lock.

If a replacement door is being fitted, it is sound practise to remove the door lock striker assembly and allow the door to hang free on the hinges. Set the hinges as necessary to achieve correct alignment and uniform margins, then reinstall the striker and adjust.

DOOR WINDOW REGULATOR HANDLE
Removal

Using a flat tool or small screw driver release the regulator handle retaining clip and remove regulator handle.

Note: A strong cloth can also be used to release the retaining clip.

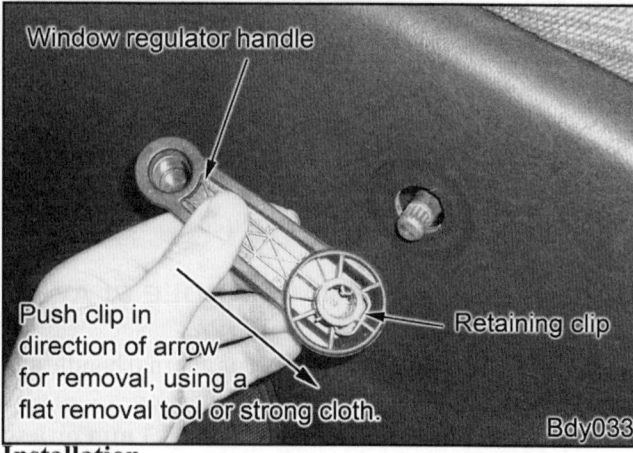

Installation

Place clip into position on back of regulator handle and press handle into position onto door assembly.

DOOR INNER TRIM PANEL - Front
Removal

1. Remove the window regulator handle as previously described (where fitted).
2. Vehicle fitted with power windows, remove the window switch panel by carefully levering out and disconnecting electrical connection. 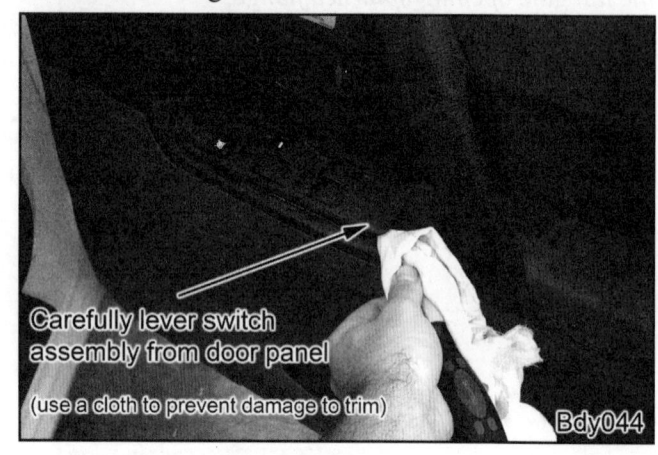
3. From the door remove the tweeter trim cover or delta cover.
4. Remove the screws securing the door lamp assembly then remove lamp assembly and disconnect electrical connection.
5. **NM/NP:** Remove the arm rest covers, then remove the screws from the bottom of the door pull handle.

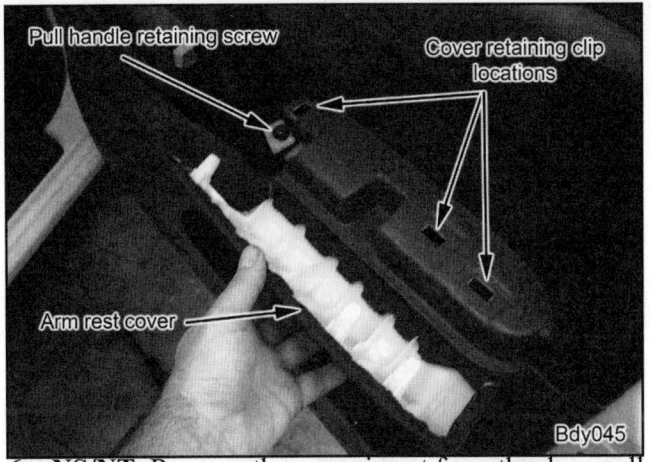

BODY - Front & Rear Door Assemblies

6. **NS/NT:** Remove the cover insert from the door pull handle, then remove the retaining screws.

7. Remove the trim retaining screws then carefully pull the trim panel away from the door releasing the retaining clips.

   Note: *Start at bottom of trim and work upwards.*

8. Disconnect any wiring connections which may be present.

9. Pull out the base of the door trim and lift trim panel upwards to remove.

10. Remove the bolts securing the arm rest brackets and remove brackets.

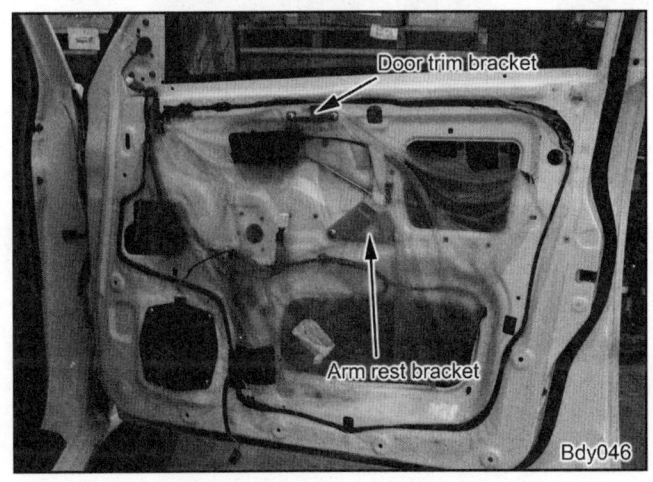

11. Peel back waterproof cover from door assembly.

Installation

1. Replace the waterproof cover into position securing with adhesive.
2. Replace the arm rest brackets and tighten bolts/screws.
3. Carefully position the door trim on to the door ensuring it is aligned correctly, reconnect any electrical connections then press the trim panel into position ensuring the retaining clips are fully secured.
4. **NM/NP:** Install the trim retaining screws then install the internal pull handle retaining screw and arm rest covers.
5. **NS/NT:** Install the trim retaining screws then install the retaining screws to the pull handle and press the insert into position.
6. Install the door lamp assembly reconnecting electrical connection, then tighten retaining screws.
7. Fit the tweeter trim cover or delta cover, then install the window regulator handle as previously described (where fitted).
8. Vehicle fitted with power windows, install the window switch panel.

DOOR INNER TRIM PANEL - Rear

Removal

1. Remove the window regulator handle as previously described (where fitted).
2. Vehicle fitted with power windows, remove the window switch panel by carefully levering out. 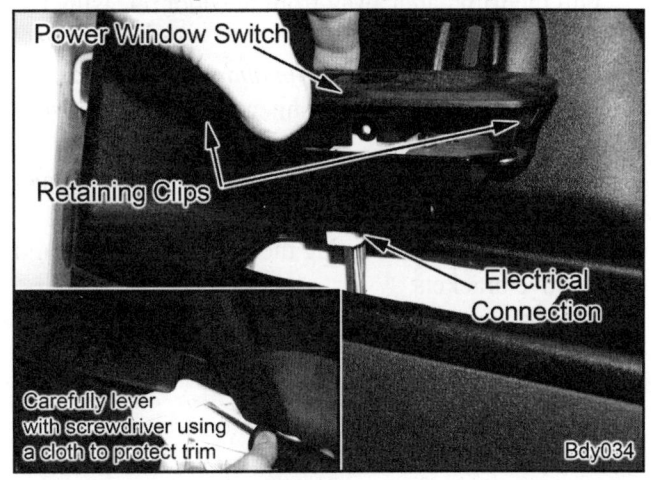
3. Remove the screws securing the door lamp assembly then remove lamp assembly and disconnect electrical connection.
4. **NM/NP:** Remove the arm rest covers, then remove the screws from the bottom of the door pull handle.

397

BODY - Front & Rear Door Assemblies

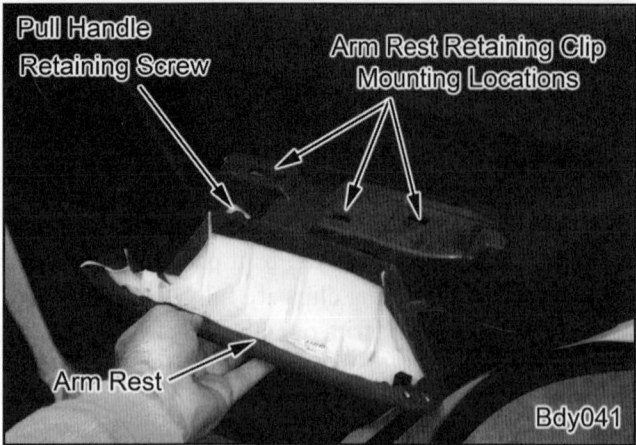

5. **NS/NT:** Remove the cover insert from the door pull handle, then remove the retaining screws.

6. Remove the trim retaining screws then carefully pull the trim panel away from the door releasing the retaining clips.
   Note: *Start at bottom of trim and work upwards.*
7. Disconnect any wiring connections which may be present.
8. Pull out the base of the door trim and lift trim panel upwards to remove.
9. Remove the bolts securing the arm rest brackets and remove brackets.
10. Peel back waterproof cover from door assembly.

Installation
1. Replace the waterproof cover into position securing with adhesive.
2. Replace the arm rest brackets and tighten screws.
3. Carefully position the door trim on to the door ensuring it is aligned correctly, reconnect any electrical connections then press the trim panel into position ensuring the retaining clips are fully secured.
4. **NM/NP:** Install the trim retaining screws then install the internal pull handle retaining screw and arm rest covers.
5. **NS/NT:** Install the trim retaining screws then install the retaining screws to the pull handle and press the insert into position.
6. Install the door lamp assembly reconnecting electrical connection, then tighten retaining screws.

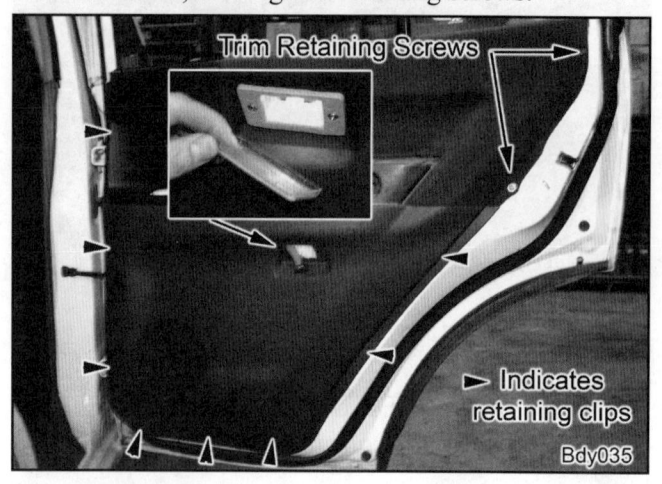

7. Install the window regulator handle as previously described (where fitted).
8. Vehicle fitted with power windows, install the window switch panel.

FRONT DOOR LOCK ASSEMBLY
Removal
1. Wind window glass up.
2. Remove door inner trim panel as described previously, then carefully peel off the water deflector from the door inner panel.
3. Disconnect the electrical connection for the lock assembly and lock cylinder (central locking vehicles).
4. Disconnect the control rod from the lock cylinder, remove the cylinder retaining clip and remove lock cylinder from door.

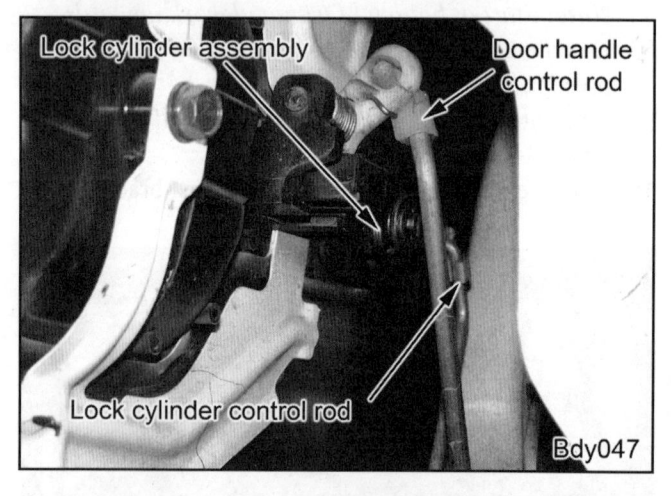

5. Remove the screws securing the rear lower sash and remove sash from the door.
6. Disconnect the lock assembly control rods, then remove the three lock assembly retaining screws and remove lock assembly from door.

398

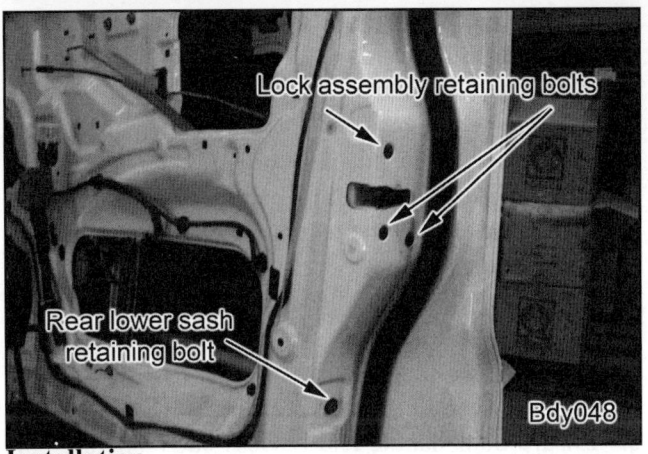

BODY - Front & Rear Door Assemblies

Installation

1. Lubricate frictional surfaces of the lock assembly with lithium grease.
2. Install the lock assembly to the door and tighten the retaining screws to specification.
   Lock assembly retaining screws .... 6 Nm
3. Install the lower rear sash into the door and tighten the retaining screws.
4. Install the lock cylinder into door and secure with retaining clip then reconnect control rod.
5. Reconnect the lock assembly control rods and electrical connections. 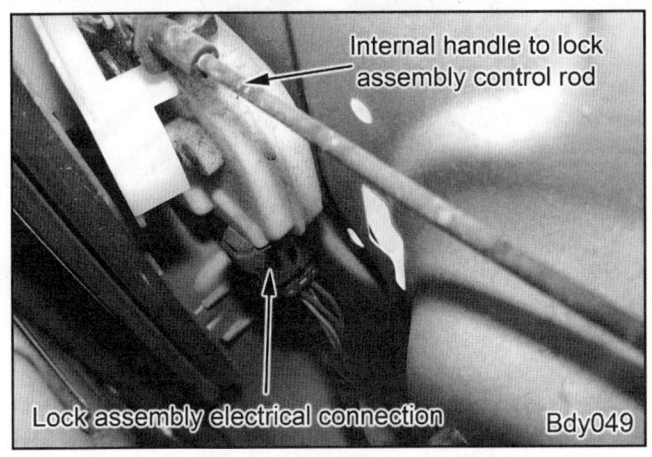
6. Check the handle play for the inside and outside handle and ensure they are within specification.
   Outside Handle............................... 2.0mm or less
   Inside Handle .... 5.3mm or less
7. Ensure door handle and keyless entry operate correctly then install waterproof cover, trim and components.

REAR DOOR LATCH ASSEMBLY

Removal

1. Wind window glass up.
2. Remove door inner trim panel as described previously, then carefully peel off the water deflector from the door inner panel.
3. Disconnect electrical connection, then disconnect the lock assembly control rods. 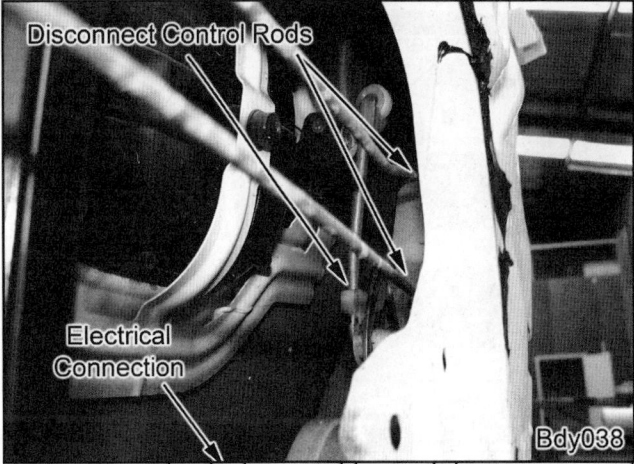
4. Remove the lock assembly retaining screws and remove lock assembly from door.

Installation

Note: *Lubricate frictional surfaces of the lock assembly with lithium grease.*

1. Install the lock assembly to the door and tighten the retaining screws to specification.
   Lock assembly retaining screws .... 6 Nm 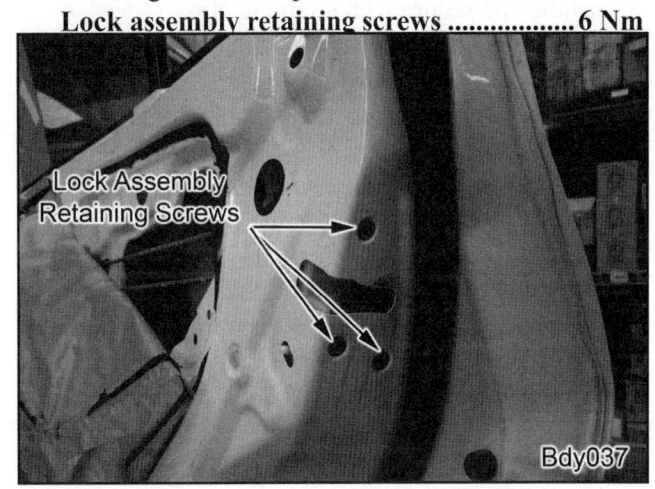
2. Reconnect the lock assembly control rods and electrical connection.
3. Check the handle play for the inside and outside handle and ensure they are within specification.
   Outside Handle............................... 1.7mm or less
   Inside Handle .... 5.3mm or less
4. Ensure door handle and keyless entry operate correctly then install waterproof cover, door trim and components.

FRONT DOOR EXTERIOR HANDLE

Removal

1. Wind window glass up.
2. Remove door inner trim panel as described previously, then carefully peel off the water deflector from the door inner panel.
3. From the outer door handle disconnect the lock and control rods.
4. Remove the bolts retaining exterior door handle.

399

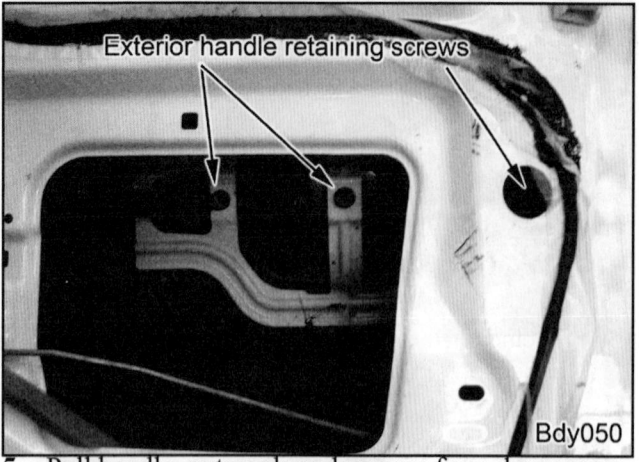

BODY - Front & Rear Door Assemblies

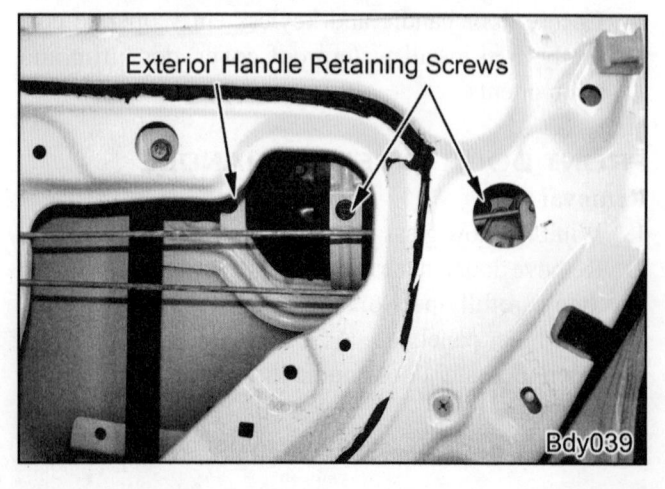

then remove the bolts retaining the door handle.
4. Pull handle outwards and remove from door.

Installation
1. Insert door handle into door assembly taking care not to damage the surrounding paint.
2. Install and tighten the retaining bolts for the exterior door handle.
3. To the outer door handle reconnect the control rod.
4. Check the handle play for the outside handle and ensure it is within specification.
   Outside Handle................................. 1.7mm or less
5. Ensure door handle and keyless entry operate correctly then install waterproof cover, door trim and components.

5. Pull handle outwards and remove from door assembly.
6. Where required remove the retaining clip securing the cylinder barrel to the exterior handle and remove cylinder from handle assembly.

INNER DOOR HANDLE
Removal
1. Remove the door inner trim panel as described previously.
2. Remove the inner door handle retaining screws, then disconnect the control rod.

Installation
1. If required replace cylinder barrel to exterior door handle and secure with retaining clip.
2. Insert door handle into door assembly taking care not to damage the surrounding paint.
3. Install and tighten the retaining bolts for the exterior door handle.
4. To outer door handle reconnect lock & control rod.
5. Check the handle play for the outside handle and ensure it is within specification.
   Outside Handle................................. 2.0mm or less
6. Ensure door handle and keyless entry operate correctly then install waterproof cover, door trim and components.

REAR DOOR EXTERIOR HANDLE
Removal
1. Wind window glass up.
2. Remove door inner trim panel as described previously, then carefully peel off the water deflector from the door inner panel.
3. From the outer door handle disconnect the control rod,

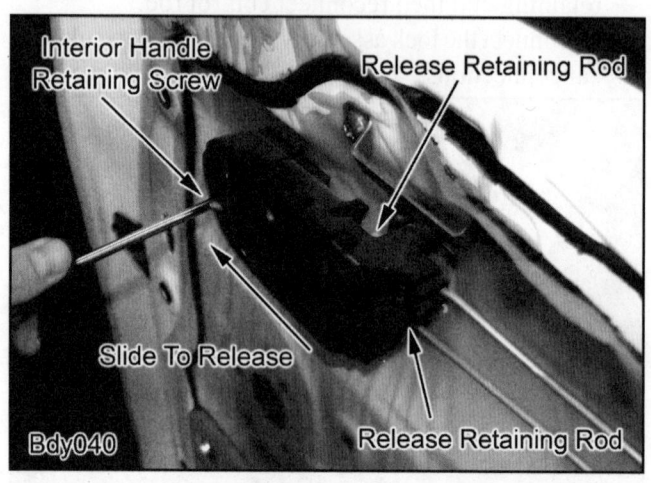

3. Slide the handle assembly detaching it from the door and remove.

Installation
1. Install the inner door handle into position and reconnect the control rod.
2. Check the handle play for the inside handle and ensure it is within specification.
   Inside Handle .... 5.3mm or less
3. Install and tighten the retaining screws, then install the inner trim panel as described previously.

FRONT DOOR GLASS & REGULATOR
Removal
1. Remove door inner trim panel as described previously, then carefully peel off the water deflector from the door inner panel.
2. Remove the screw securing the door belt line mould-

BODY - Front & Rear Door Assemblies

ing and remove moulding, then remove the glass run channel from the door assembly.

3. Remove the two glass retaining screws from the glass holders and carefully remove the glass panel from the door.

4. Disconnect the electrical connection for the power window regulator motor.
5. Remove the bolts securing the regulator and motor assembly and remove the assembly from the door.

Installation

1. a) Connect the electrical connection for the power window motor, then turn the ignition to ON.
   b) Press the up button for the power window motor to operate motor for 5-10 seconds to reset the limit switch inside the motor assembly.

   Note: *Do not operate the window motor again until the glass is fitted.*

2. Install the window regulator and power window motor assembly into the door and tighten retaining bolts.

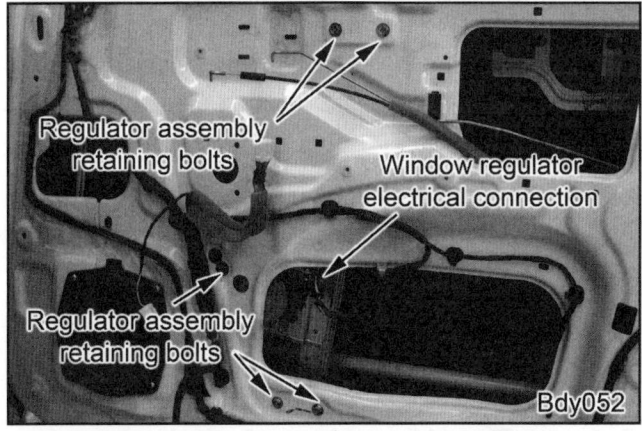

3. Install the window glass to the vehicle ensuring the glass holders are installed and tighten the glass retaining screws.
4. Press the control switch to fully close the window glass, then fully open the window glass to program the control unit.
5. Install the glass run channel to the door assembly, then install the door belt line moulding and tighten the retaining screw.
6. Adjust the window glass as outlined in this chapter, then install the dust cover, inner trim panel and accessories.

REAR DOOR GLASS & REGULATOR
Removal

1. Remove door inner trim panel as described previously, then carefully peel off the water deflector from the door inner panel.
2. Remove the screw securing the door belt line moulding and remove moulding, then remove the glass run channel from the door assembly.
3. Remove the screws securing the centre sash and remove the centre sash from door assembly.

   Note: *the sash upper retaining screw is located under the weather strip.*

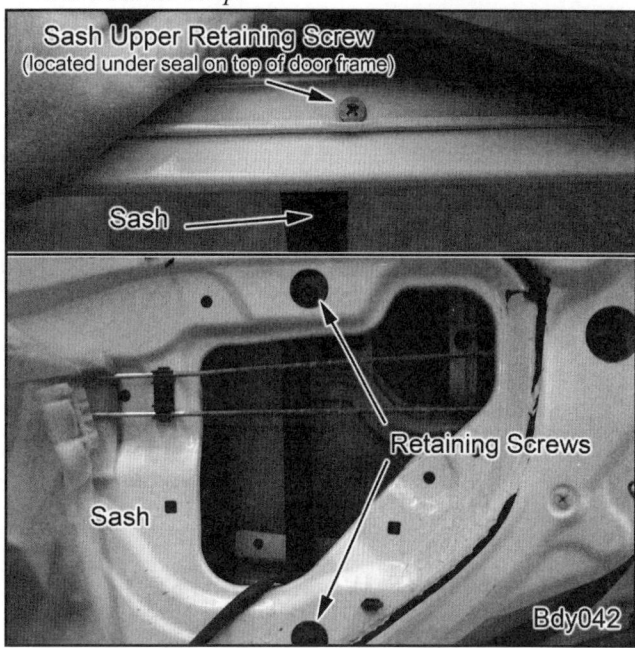

4. Remove the two glass retaining screws and carefully remove the glass panel from the door.
5. Disconnect the electrical connection for the power window regulator motor.
6. Remove the bolts securing the regulator and motor assembly and remove the assembly from the door.
7. If required remove the stationary glass assembly from the door.

Installation

1. If remove install the stationary glass weather-strip and glass to the door assembly.
2. a) Connect the electrical connection for the power window motor, then turn the ignition to ON.
   b) Press the up button for the power window motor to operate motor for 5-10 seconds to reset the limit switch inside the motor assembly.

   Note: *Do not operate the window motor again*

401

BODY - Front & Rear Door Assemblies

until the glass is fitted.

3. Install the regulator and motor assembly into position in the door and tighten the retaining screws.

4. Install the window glass to the vehicle ensuring the glass holders are installed and tighten the glass retaining screws.
5. Press the control switch to fully close the window glass, then fully open the window glass to program the control unit.
6. Install the centre sash assembly to the door and tighten the two retaining screws and ensure the door weather-strip is properly installed.
7. Install the glass run channel to the door assembly, then install the door belt line moulding and tighten the retaining screw.
8. Adjust the window glass as outlined in this chapter, then install the dust cover, inner trim panel and accessories.

DOOR WINDOW GLASS ADJUSTMENT

1. Remove the door trim and weather deflector from the door assembly.
2. Ensure the window glass is fully closed then loosen the glass mounting screws through the adjusting holes.
3. Lower the window glass slightly (3-5cm), then full close the window glass and tighten the retaining screws through the access holes.
4. Install the dust cover and inner trim panel to the door assembly and then check operation of window glass.

FRONT & REAR DOOR WEATHER-STRIP
Removal

Removing the weather-strip from the door by carefully prising the retaining lugs from the door.

Installation

Replace the weather-strip, pushing the retaining lugs on the weather-strip into the door.

DOOR BELT WEATHER-STRIP MOULDING
Removal

From the rear of the weather-strip remove the end retaining screw, then with the window fully lowered and using a wide blade screw driver, carefully prise the rear end of the weather-strip and moulding up off the door, working towards the front of the door, removing the assembly.

Installation

Locate door belt weather-strip and moulding assembly over the top of the door outer panel, then using the palm of your hand, firmly tap the assembly down, over door upper flange, then tighten the end retaining screw.

Exterior Rear View Mirror - Electrical
Removal

1. From the inside of the door remove the inner trim cover then remove the tweeter (where fitted).
2. Remove the three screws securing the mirror assembly to the door frame.
3. Lift the mirror assembly from the door frame, disconnect the electrical connection and fully remove mirror assembly.

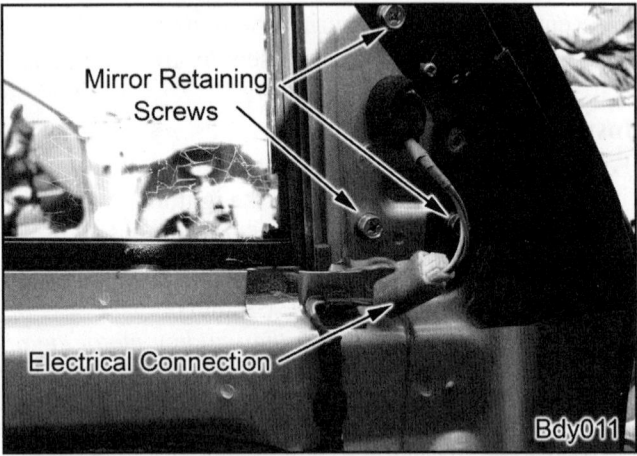

Installation

1. Reconnect the electrical connection to the mirror and position mirror into place on door assembly.
2. Tighten the retaining screws, then install the tweeter and trim cover.
3. Test operation of mirror and adjust to required position.

Exterior Rear View Mirror Switch
Removal

1. From the instrument panel, remove the drivers side air outlet assembly.
2. Disconnect the electrical connection for the mirror switch, then remove the switch assembly from the air outlet assembly.

BODY - Front & Rear Door Assemblies

Installation

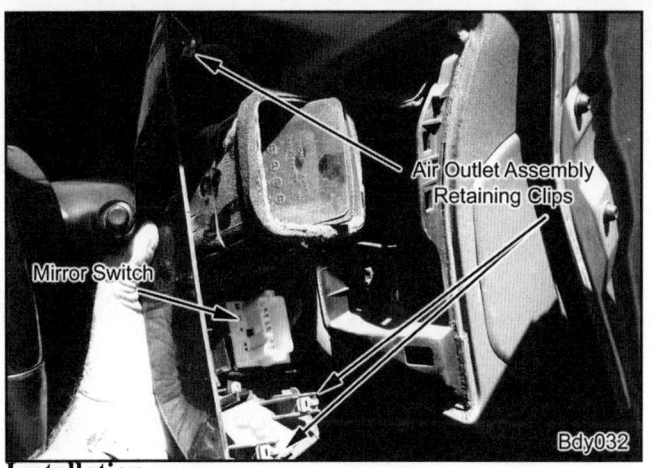

1. Install the switch to the air outlet assembly.
2. Reconnect electrical connection and install the air outlet assembly to the instrument panel.
3. Test operation of switch to ensure it works correctly.

Electric Retractable Mirror Control Unit
Removal

1. Remove the glove box assembly as described previously in this chapter, then remove the passenger side lower corner panel.
2. Remove the bolt securing the mirror control unit, then disconnect electrical connection and remove control unit.

Installation

1. Reconnect the electrical connection, then install control unit into position and tighten the retaining bolt.
   Control Unit Retaining Bolt.......................... 5 Nm
2. Install the passenger side lower corner trim, then install the glove box assembly as described previously.
3. Check the operation of the mirror assembly.

Electric Retractable Mirror Operation Check

Direction of Operation	Battery Connection Terminal	
	+ve	-ve
UP	3	5
DOWN	5	3
LEFT	5	4
RIGHT	4	5
RETURN or UNFOLD position to RETRACT position	1	2
RETRACT to RETURN position	2	1

Motor-Driven Remote Control Mirror Switch Continuity Check

Switch			Terminal No.	
			Left Side	Right Side
Adjustment Switch	Up		1-6	1-6
			9-11	3-9
	Down		6-9	1-3
			1-11	6-9
	Left		6-9	1-2
			1-10	6-9
	Right		1-6	1-6
			9-10	2-9
Retracting Switch (retract & return)			1-4	

STATIONARY GLASS

REPLACEMENT
Replacement of the windscreen and other fixed glass is recommended to be left to a windscreen specialist.

INTERIOR MIRROR - NM / NP
Removal
The mirror is attached to the mirror base by a spring. To remove mirror carefully push downward along window to remove mirror from base.

Installation
To install mirror slide mirror upwards onto mounting bracket until it si fully locked into position.

INTERIOR MIRROR - NS / NT
Removal
1. Release the claws on the side of the mirror base and pull mirror assembly forward.
2. Press in the second claw towards the mirror and slide the mirror assembly up off the mirror base.

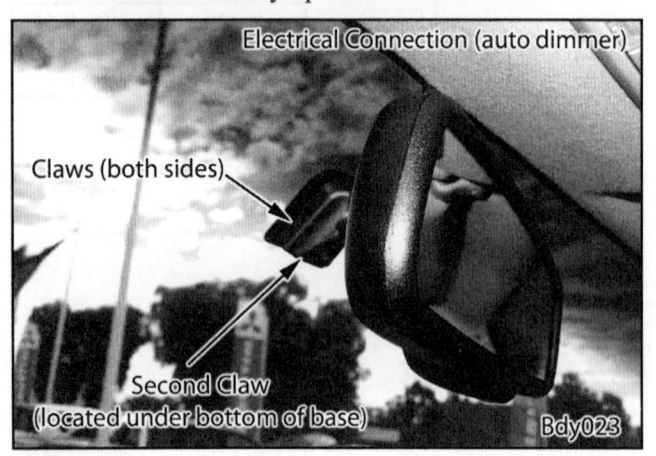

Installation
1. Installation is the reverse of the removal procedure.

Auto-Dimming Feature Test
1. With the ignition and mirror both turned on, use a black cloth to cover the light sensor on the back of the mirror.
2. Ensure light strikes the front sensor, simulating glare from vehicle behind you, the mirror should dim within 2 minutes when testing for the first time.
3. Replace the mirror if it does not dim.

HEADLINING AND INTERIOR TRIM

Clean hands are essential when working on interior trim.

REAR QUARTER PANEL TRIM
Removal
1. Remove the rear seats as described later in this chapter.
2. Remove the seat belt upper mounting bolts.
3. Remove the trim retainers securing the trim in position and partially remove trim.
4. Remove the screws securing the lower quarter panel trim into position.
5. Remove the lower trim panel from the vehicle, then remove the lower seat belt anchor bolt.
6. Feed the seat belt through the upper quarter trim panel and remove trim from vehicle.

Installation
1. Feed seat belt through the upper trim panel, then install and tighten the lower seat belt anchor bolt.
   Seat Belt Lower Anchor Bolt .... 44+/-10 Nm
2. Install the lower quarter panel into position and tighten the trim retaining screws.
3. Position the upper trim panel into place and secure with trim retainers.
4. Install the upper seat belt anchor bolt, tightening to specification, then install the rear seat assemblies.
   Seat Belt Upper Anchor Bolt............. 44+/-10 Nm
   Rear Seat Anchor Bolts .... 44 Nm

HEADLINING ASSEMBLY
Removal
1. Remove the sun visors, assist grips and interior lights.

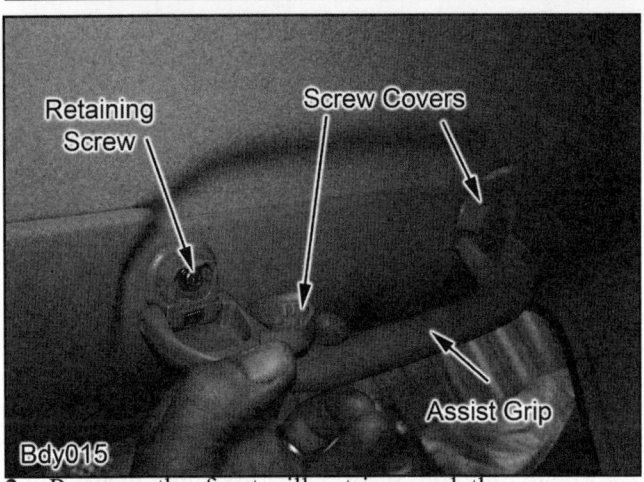

BODY - Seat & Seat Belts

[Figure Bdy015: Retaining Screw, Screw Covers, Assist Grip]

2. Remove the front pillar trims and the upper rear compartment trims and where fitted child restraint anchor points.
3. Remove the fasteners securing the headlining, then remove lining through rear of vehicle.

Installation

1. Position hood lining into vehicle through rear door of vehicle, then secure the headlining by inserting the fastener buttons into position.
2. Install the child restraint plugs, headlining trim and rear, centre and front pillar trims.
3. Replace the assist handles, interior lights and sun visors.
4. Clean the headlining of any marks that occurred during installation.

SEATS & SEAT BELTS

FRONT BUCKET SEAT ASSEMBLY
Removal

1. Remove the head rest from the seat assembly, then disconnect the electrical connection for the power seat controls and/or side airbag.
2. Remove the covers from over the retaining bolts and nuts, then remove the nuts and bolts retaining the seat into position.

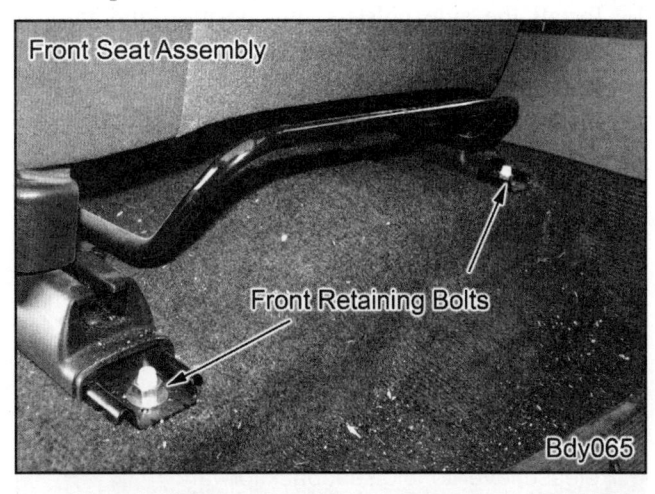

[Figure Bdy065: Front Seat Assembly, Front Retaining Bolts]

3. Remove the seat from the vehicle, then place seat assembly on a clean protected surface.

Installation

1. Install the seat assembly and loosely install the retaining bolts and nuts.
2. Once all nuts and bolts are installed, tighten to specification.
   Seat Retaining Bolts................................. 44 Nm
   Seat Retaining Nuts .... 30 Nm
3. Install the bolt and nut covers then reconnect the electrical connections.
4. Replace the head rest and test operation of seats.

HEAD RESTRAINT ASSEMBLY

Seat head restraints are retained by a press - release knob located in sleeves which are secured to the seat frame.

Removal

1. Press in the release knob to release the head restraint.
2. Remove the head restraint from the seat back.

Installation

Place the head restraint into position above the seat, and push the legs of the restraint down into the seat.

BODY - Seat & Seat Belts

REAR / SECOND SEAT ASSEMBLY
Removal - Short Wheelbase
1. Remove the head rest from the seats, then remove the covers from the seat retaining bolts.
2. Remove the bolts retaining the seat assembly to the vehicle then carefully remove the seat assembly from the vehicle.
3. Remove the seat hinge cover, then remove the bolts retaining the side bolster and remove side bolster.

Installation - Short Wheelbase
1. Install the side bolsters into position and tighten retaining bolts to specification.
   Bolster Assembly Bolts .... 44 Nm
2. Install the cover to the seat hinge.
3. Carefully install the rear seat assembly into position in the vehicle.
4. Install and tighten the retaining bolts to specification, then install the bolt covers.
   Seat assembly Mounting Bolts .... 44 Nm

Removal - Long Wheelbase
1. Remove the head rest from the seats, then fold the seat assembly forward into the raised position.

![Bdy066 - Release lever to fold seat back forward; Release lever to fold seat assembly upward]

2. Remove the covers from the seat retaining bolts.
3. Remove the bolts retaining the seat assembly to the vehicle then carefully remove the seat assembly from the vehicle.

![Bdy067 - Seat Assembly Folded Upwards; (press in to lower seat); Hinge Retaining Bolts]

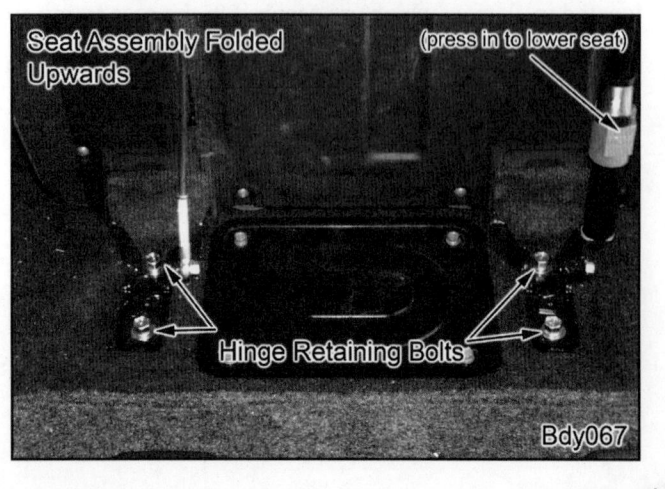

Installation - Long Wheelbase
1. Carefully install the rear seat assembly into position in the vehicle.
2. Install and tighten the retaining bolts to specification, then install the bolt covers.
   Seat assembly Mounting Bolts .... 44 Nm
3. Lower the seat assembly into position and ensure it locks into position.

THIRD ROW SEAT ASSEMBLY - Face to Face
Removal
1. Lower the seat down into position.
2. Remove the bolts securing seat assembly, then remove the seat assembly from the rear of the vehicle.

Installation
1. Install rear seat into position.
2. Install all the retaining bolts, then tighten retaining to specification.
   Seat Mounting Bolts .... 12 Nm

THIRD ROW SEAT ASSEMBLY - Bench
Removal
1. Remove the head rest from the seat assembly, then pull release lever and fold the seat assembly down.

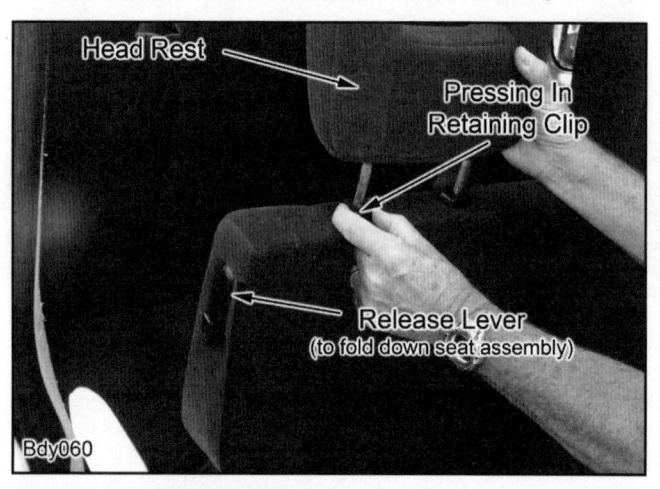

![Bdy060 - Head Rest; Pressing In Retaining Clip; Release Lever (to fold down seat assembly)]

2. With the seat assembly folded down pull the front release lever to release the front retaining clamps.
3. Pull the release handle at the back of the seat assembly and lift the seat from the vehicle mounting points.

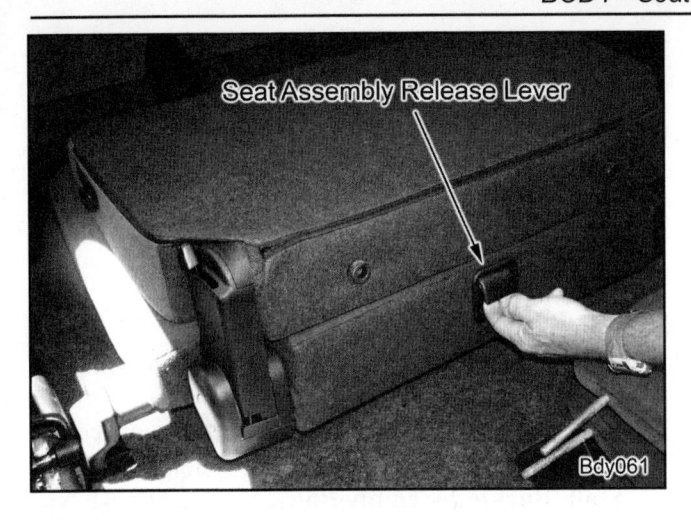

BODY - Seat & Seat Belts

Installation

1. Install seat assembly into the rear of the vehicle and ensure the rear and front mounting points are secured properly.
2. Fold the seat back upright into position and install the head rests to the seat assembly.

FRONT SEAT BELT RETRACTOR AND BUCKLE ASSEMBLY

Important: *If vehicle is fitted with pretensioner system, refer to the SRS section in the instrument chapter.*

Removal

1. Remove sash guide cover from bolt securing upper seat belt attachment to centre pillar, then remove the upper retaining bolt.
2. Remove the lower anchor bolt from the centre pillar, then remove the centre pillar trim panels (long wheelbase) or the lower quarter trim panel (short wheelbase). 
3. Remove the bolt retaining the seat belt retractor assembly and remove the seat belt assembly from the vehicle. 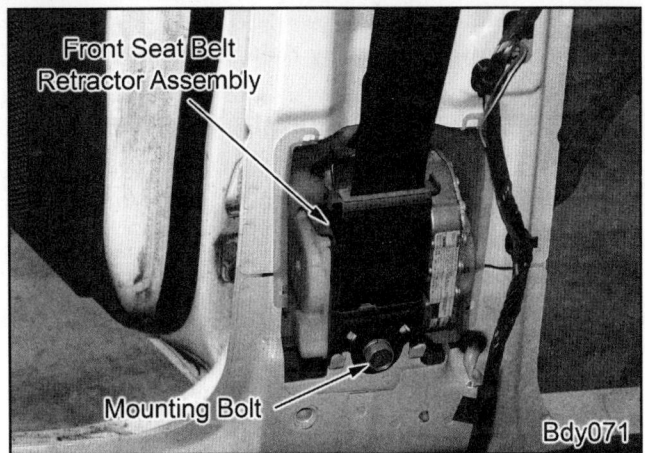
4. If required remove the front noise protector and the adjustable shoulder belt anchor.
5. From the inside of the seat assembly remove the inner seat belt stalk anchor bolt, then disconnect electrical connection and remove seat belt stalk.

Installation

When installing bolts ensure that the lower bolt threads are sealed with none hardening sealer and that all seat belt attaching bolts are tightened to specification.

1. To the inside of the seat assembly install the seat belt stalk and tighten the anchor bolt to specification, then connect the electrical connection.
   Seat Belt Stalk Bolt .... 44+/-10 Nm
2. If removed, install the front noise protector and the adjustable shoulder belt anchor.
   NM-NP: Shoulder Anchor Bolts .... 44+/-10 Nm
   NS-NT: Shoulder Anchor Bolts .... 41+/-10 Nm 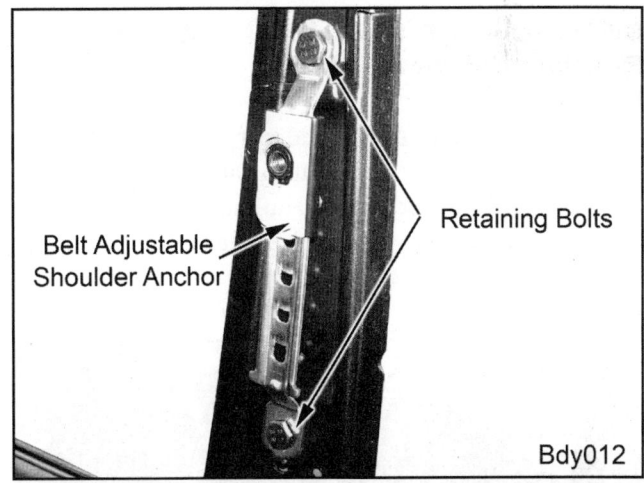
3. Install the seat belt retractor assembly into position and tighten the retaining bolt to specification.
   NM-NP: Retractor Assembly Bolt ... 44+/-10 Nm
   NS-NT: Retractor Assembly Bolt ... 41+/-10 Nm
4. Install the centre pillar trim panels (long wheelbase) or the lower quarter trim panel (short wheelbase).
5. Install the lower and upper anchor bolts to the centre pillar, tightening bolts to specification, then install

BODY - Seat & Seat Belts

the sash guide cover.
Upper/Lower Mounting Bolt .... 44+/-10 Nm

REAR SEAT BELT ASSEMBLY - SWB
Removal
1. Remove the rear seat assembly, then remove the quarter trim panel from the vehicle.
2. Remove sash guide cover from bolt securing upper seat belt attachment, then remove the upper retaining bolt.
3. Remove the belt lower anchor bolt, then remove the bolt retaining the seat belt retractor assembly and remove the seat belt assembly from the vehicle.
4. Remove the bolts securing the seat belt stalk/buckle assembly.

Installation
Note: *Ensure that bolt threads have sealer.*
1. Install the seat belt stalk/buckle assembly, tightening bolts to specification.
   Stalk/Buckle Assembly Bolts .... 44+/-10 Nm
2. Install the seat belt retractor assembly and tighten retaining bolt to specification, then install the lower anchor bolt.
   Retractor Assembly Bolt .... 44+/-10 Nm
   Belt Lower Anchor Bolt .... 44+/-10 Nm
3. Replace upper seat belt mount into position and tighten retaining bolt to specification, then install the quarter trim panel.
   Seat Belt Upper Attaching Bolts .... 44+/-10 Nm
4. Install rear seats as described previously.

SECOND/REAR SEAT BELT ASSEMBLY - Rear/Second Seat - LWB
Removal
1. Remove or fold forward the rear seat assembly, then remove the upper quarter trim panel (where fitted).
2. Remove the lower quarter trim panel from the vehicle and if fitted remove the sash guide cover from upper seat belt mount.

3. Remove the bolt securing the upper seat belt mount.
4. Remove the belt lower anchor bolt, then remove the bolt retaining the seat belt retractor assembly and remove the seat belt assembly from the vehicle.
5. Remove the bolts securing the seat belt stalk/buckle assembly and centre lap belt assembly.

Installation
Note: *Ensure that bolt threads are coated with appropriate sealer.*
1. Install the seat belt stalk/buckle assembly and centre lap belt, tightening bolts to specification.
   Stalk/Buckle Assembly Bolts .... 44+/-10 Nm
   Centre Lap Belt Bolts .... 44+/-10 Nm
2. Install the seat belt retractor assembly and tighten retaining bolt to specification, then install the lower anchor bolt.
   NM-NP:
       Retractor Assembly Bolt .... 44+/-10 Nm
       Belt Lower Anchor Bolt .... 44+/-10 Nm
   NS: **Retractor Assembly Bolt** .... 41+/-10 Nm
       Belt Lower Anchor Bolt .... 41+/-10 Nm
       Centre Retractor Assembly ...... 44+/-10 Nm
3. Replace upper seat belt mount into position and tighten retaining bolt to specification, then install the lower and upper quarter trim panels.
   NM-NP:
       Belt Upper Attaching Bolts ...... 44+/-10 Nm
   NS: **Belt Upper Attaching Bolts** ...... 41+/-10 Nm
4. Install rear seats as described previously in chapter.

REAR SEAT BELT RETRACTOR ASSEMBLY - Third Row Seat - LWB
Removal
1. Remove the rear seat assembly, then remove the lower quarter trim panel from the vehicle.
2. Remove the pillar duct and rear blower assembly.
3. Remove sash guide cover from upper seat belt attachment bolt, then remove the upper retaining bolt.
4. Remove the belt lower anchor bolt, then remove the

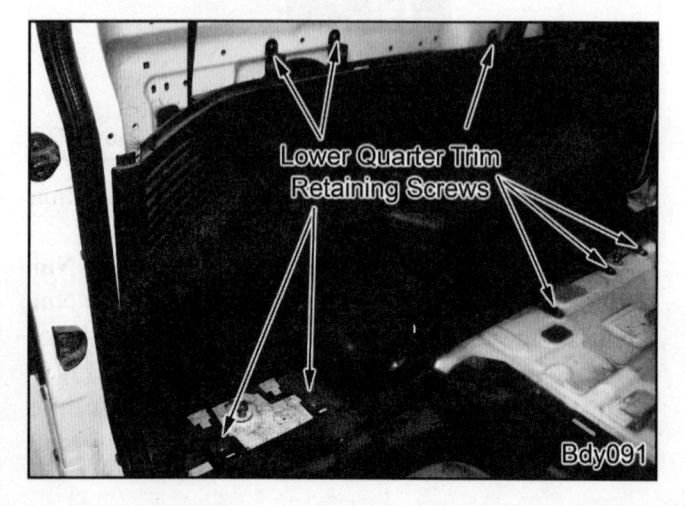

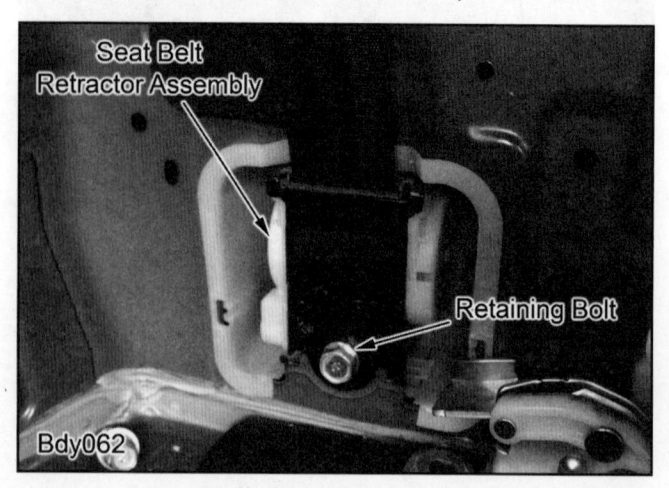

bolt retaining the seat belt retractor assembly and remove the seat belt assembly from the vehicle.
5. Remove the bolts securing the seat belt stalk/buckle assembly.

Installation
* Ensure that bolt threads are coated with appropriate sealer.
1. Install the seat belt stalk/buckle assembly, tightening bolts to specification.
   Stalk/Buckle Assembly Bolts............. 44+/-10 Nm
2. Install the seat belt retractor assembly and tighten retaining bolt to specification, then install the lower anchor bolt.
   NM-NP:
       Retractor Assembly Bolt .... 44+/-10 Nm
       Belt Lower Anchor Bolt .... 44+/-10 Nm
   NS: **Retractor Assembly Bolt .... 41+/-10 Nm**
       Belt Lower Anchor Bolt .... 41+/-10 Nm

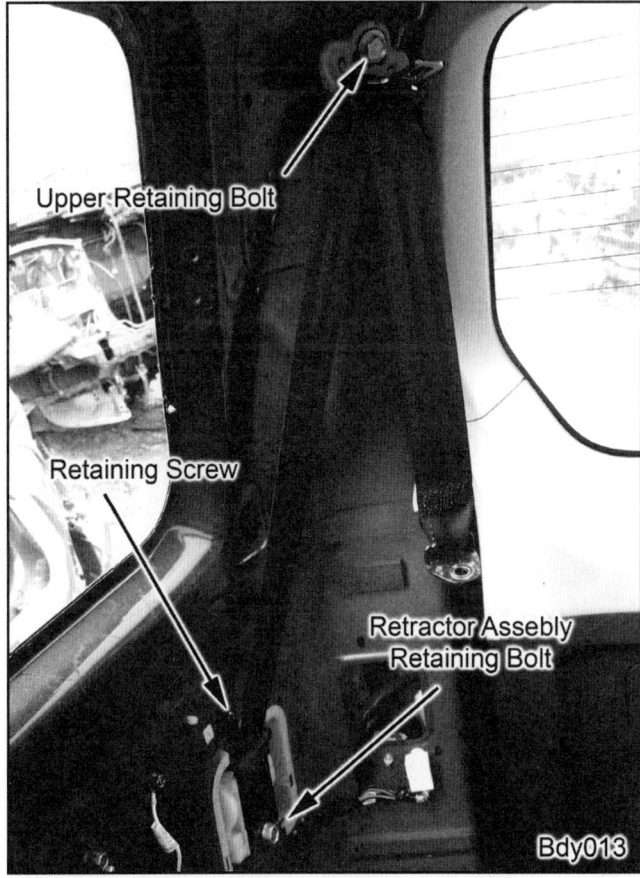

3. Replace upper seat belt mount into position and tighten retaining bolt to specification.
   NM-NP:
       Belt Upper Attaching Bolts ...... 44+/-10 Nm
       NS: **Belt Upper Attaching Bolts ...... 41+/-10 Nm**
4. Install the rear blower assembly and pillar duct, then install the lower quarter trim panel.
5. Install rear seats as described previously in chapter.

SHEET METAL

The bonnet lock release lever mounted beneath the right hand side of the instrument panel, controls the bonnet lock release spring. The bonnet, when released from the locked position, engages in a secondary safety catch which can be released by inserting fingers beneath the leading edge of the bonnet.

FRONT FENDER ASSEMBLY
Removal
1. Remove the front fender liners (splash shields) and the front bumper bar as described later in this chapter.
2. Remove the side turn indicator, by gently levering out with a flat blade screwdriver and disconnect electrical connection.
3. Remove the two rear and two lower rear fender retaining bolts.
4. Remove the front fender retaining bolt then remove the bolt and washer assemblies from along the top of the fender assembly (inside engine bay).
5. Carefully remove front fender from vehicle.

Installation
1. Place the front fender into position insert the bolt and washer assemblies to secure the fender.
2. Do not tighten the screws until the fender has been aligned so that it fits into the correct position with the other body panels.
3. Replace the fender lining (splash shields) and indicators.

BONNET
Removal
1. With the bonnet raised and supported, disconnect the hose for windscreen washer.
2. Pencil mark around the hinges on the bonnet, then remove the bolts securing the bonnet to the hinges as shown in diagram.
3. Remove the bonnet from the vehicle.

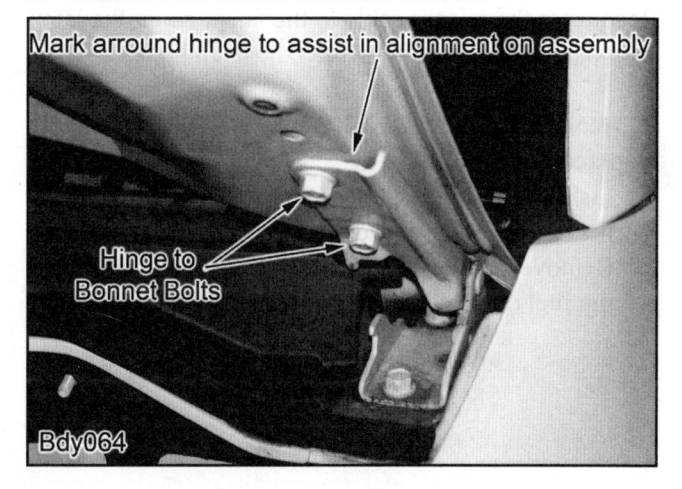

BODY - Sheet Metal

Installation
1. Position the bonnet into position aligning the pencil marks with the hinges.
2. Install the hinge to bonnet retaining bolts.
3. Adjust and tighten hinge retaining bolts.
   Hinge Retaining Bolts.............................. 22 Nm
4. Reconnect the windscreen washer hose.

Adjust
When adjusting the bonnet, uniform spacing and alignment between the bonnet and adjacent parts is important.

Slotted holes in the hinge arms provide horizontal adjustment, whilst floating anchor nuts mounted inside the bonnet inner panel, provide vertical adjustment for the rear end of the bonnet.

Vertical adjustment for the front of the bonnet is achieved by adjustment of the bonnet latch assembly and the bonnet buffers located on the front of the bonnet inner panel.

BONNET LATCH
Remove or Adjust
Raise and support the bonnet assembly. Slacken off the bonnet latch bolts. Remove the release cable from the latch and remove the bolts and latch. To adjust move the lock assembly to align with the striker.

It may be required to remove the trim panel to access latch assembly.

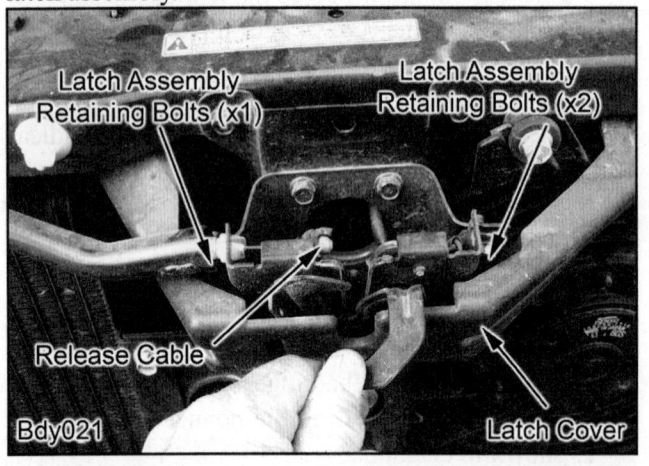

Installation
Reconnect the release cable to the latch. Align the latch with the lock striker and tighten the latch bolts.

BONNET RELEASE CABLE ASSEMBLY
Replacement
1. Inside the vehicle remove the two screws securing the bonnet release lever to the lower trim panel.
2. Remove the screws securing the lower trim panel and the fuel door release cable and remove lower trim. 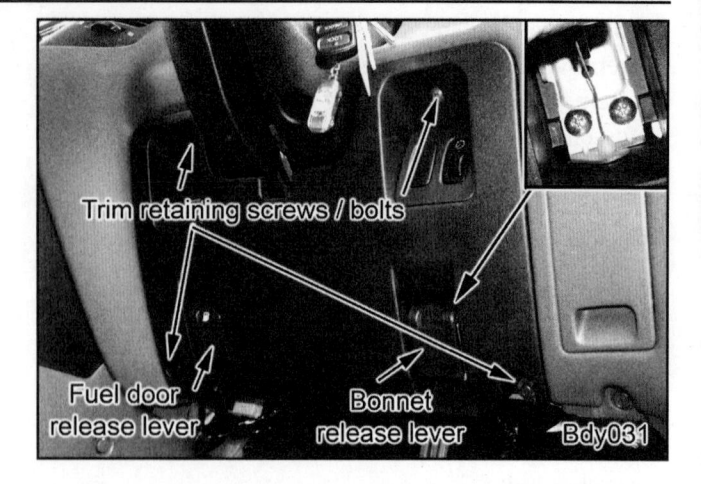
3. Remove the front grille from the vehicle.
4. Disconnect the release cable from the bonnet latch, then disconnect the cable from the retaining clips and pull the cable out of the vehicle from the interior.
5. Install new cable into vehicle from the interior of the vehicle, then reconnect cable to bonnet latch.
6. Install the lower trim panel, then install the bonnet release lever and tighten retaining screws.
7. Ensure cable is secured in all retaining clips then install the front grille.
8. Adjust and test operation of latch.

BUMPER BARS & GRILLE

RADIATOR GRILLE - NM/NP
Removal
1. With engine hood raised, remove the radiator cover retaining clips and then remove the radiator cover.
2. Use a screw driver to release the retaining clips by moving the black section of the clip in the direction of the arrows as shown. Gently pull out the grille assembly while removing clips.

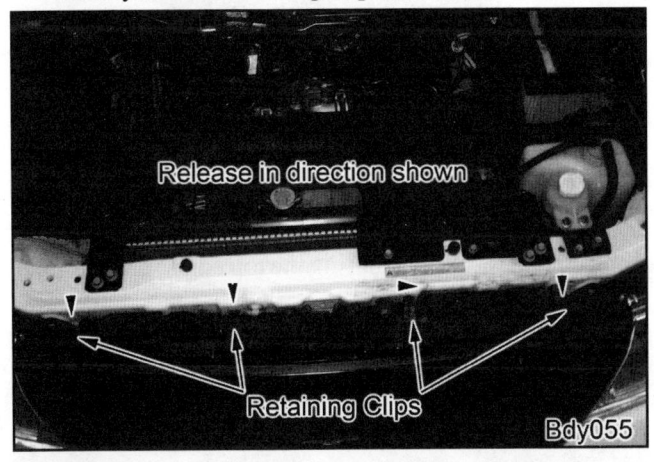

Installation
1. Install radiator grille into position and secure with retaining clips, then replace the radiator cover panel.

RADIATOR GRILLE - NS / NT
Removal
1. Use a screw driver to release the retaining clips by levering the centre section of the clip outwards, then remove the clips from the assembly.
2. Gently pull out the grille assembly releasing the remaining retaining clips and remove grille assembly from vehicle.

Installation
1. Install radiator grille into position and secure with retaining clips, pressing in the centre of the clip to secure.

FRONT MUD GUARD
Removal
Note: *Removal of the front wheel will make removal of the mud guard easier.*
1. Remove the bolts, screws and clips securing the front mud guard and then remove mudguard from vehicle.
2. Remove the bolt securing the mud guard bracket and remove bracket assembly.

Installation
1. Install the mud guard bracket into position and tighten the retaining bolt to specification.
   Mud Guard Bracket Retaining Bolt .... 4 Nm
2. Install the mud guard assembly into position, tighten retaining bolt to specification, then install the retaining screws and clips.
   Mud Guard Retaining Bolt .... 4 Nm

REAR MUD GUARD
Removal
Note: *Removal of the rear wheel will make removal of the mud guard easier.*
1. Remove the bolts and screws securing the rear mud guard and then remove the mudguard from vehicle.
2. Remove the bolts securing the mud guard protector and remove protector from vehicle.

BODY - Bumper & Grille

Installation
1. Install the protector to the vehicle and tighten the retaining bolts to specification.
   Mud Guard Retaining Bolt .... **4 Nm**
2. Install the mud guard assembly into position, tighten retaining bolt to specification, then install the retaining screws and clips.
   Mud Guard Retaining Bolt .... **4 Nm**

SPLASH SHIELD - Front
Removal
1. Raise the front of the vehicle, support on axle stands and remove front wheels.
2. If fitted remove mud guard as described previously.
3. Remove the retaining rivets and screws securing the splash shield to the inside of the front fender and bumper bar.
4. Remove splash shield from vehicle.

Installation
1. Install front splash shield into vehicle under front fender and secure with retaining rivets and screws.
2. Install the mud guards as described previously.
3. Install front wheels and lower vehicle.

ENGINE SKID PLATE & UNDER COVERS
Removal
1. Raise the front of the vehicle and secure on safety stands.
2. Remove the bolts securing the skid plate to the underside of the vehicle and then remove the skid plate.
3. Remove the bolts securing the front engine under cover and remove cover from the vehicle.
4. Remove the bolts securing the engine rear undercover and remove cover from underside of the vehicle.

Installation
1. Install the rear engine undercover into position and tighten the cover retaining bolts.
2. Install the engine front undercover into position and tighten the cover retaining bolts.
3. Install the skid plate into position and tighten the plate retaining bolts, then remove safety stands and lower vehicle.

FRONT BUMPER BAR
The removal and installation procedure is basically the same for all models. The number of retaining bolts/clips in each location may vary slightly.

Removal
1. Remove the front radiator grille and splash shield, then remove the screws securing the undercover panels and remove panels.
2. Remove the bolts securing the lower stay on each side of the bumper and remove lower stays. 
3. Where fitted disconnect the electrical connection for the front fog lamps (refer to lighting chapter).
4. Remove the bolts securing the top edge of the bumper assembly. 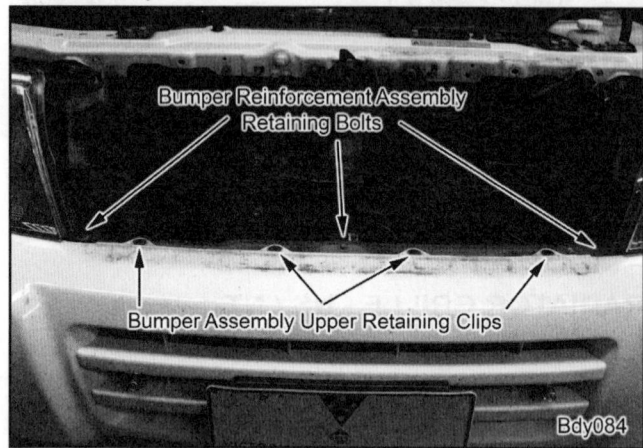
5. From bumper assembly remove the remaining lower mounting bolts/clips securing the bumper assembly and remove the bumper from the front of the vehicle. 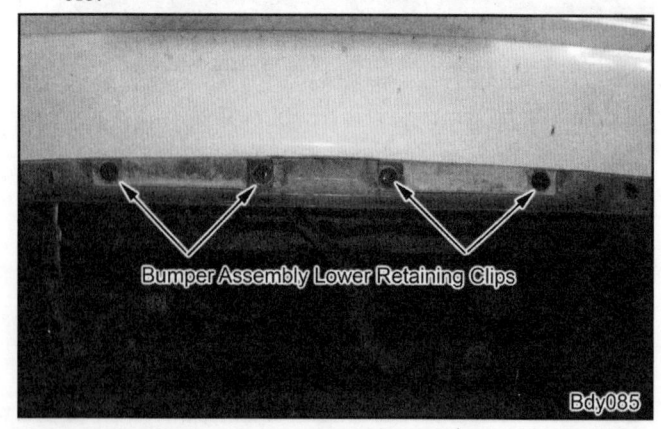
6. If required dismantle the front bumper assembly.

Installation
1. Assemble the front bumper assembly if dismantled.
2. Install front bumper bar assembly and support in posi-

BODY - Bumper & Grille

tion, while installing the mounting bolts and nuts.
3. Reconnect the fog lamps (where fitted), then install the lower stay to each side of the bumper bar and tighten retaining bolts.
4. Install the front radiator grille and splash shields, then install the undercover panels.

REAR BUMPER BAR 2001-2006
Removal
1. Remove the rear combination lamp, refer to "body electrical chapter" for assistance.
2. Jack up rear of vehicle, remove road wheels and then remove the rear mud guards as described previously.
3. **2001-2002 models:** Remove the bolts securing the bumper centre lower face and remove assembly.
4. **2003-2006 models:** Remove the lower bumper assembly mounting bolts.

5. From along the top edge of the bumper assembly remove the retaining bolts, then remove the side retaining bolts.
   Note: *Do not forget the bolt from the top corner under the wheel arch.*

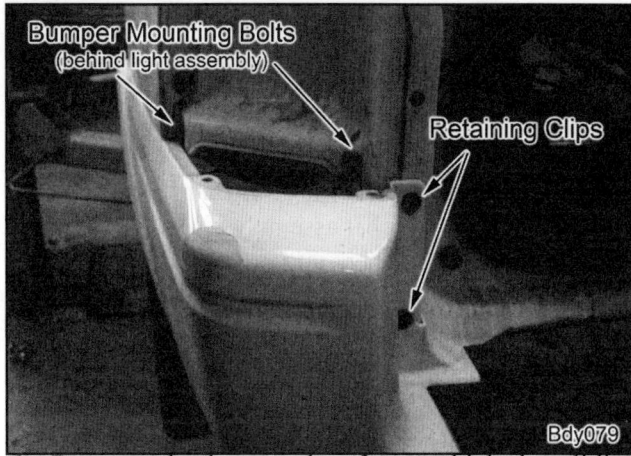

6. Remove the bumper bar from vehicle by sliding outwards and if required disassemble bumper bar assembly.

Installation
* Installation is reverse of the removal procedure.
1. Assemble bumper bar assembly if required.
2. Install rear bumper bar assembly into position and install retaining bolts and nuts.
3. Depending on model install the centre lower face assembly and tighten the retaining bolts or install the lower bumper mounting bolts and tighten.
4. Install the mud guards, then install the rear combination lamps.

REAR BUMPER BAR 2007-2008
Removal
1. Remove the rear combination lamp, refer to "body electrical chapter" for assistance.
2. Jack up rear of vehicle, remove road wheels and then remove the rear mud guards and splash shields as described previously.
3. Disconnect the electrical connection for the reversing sensors (where fitted).
4. Remove the bolts securing the rear bumper step and remove step.

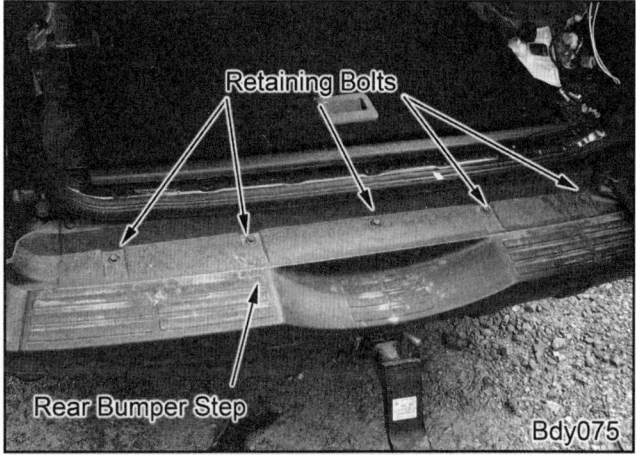

5. Remove the bolts securing the rear centre bumper and remove centre bumper assembly from vehicle.

413

BODY - Bumper & Grille

6. Remove the bolts securing the corner bumper and remove assembly from vehicle.
7. If required disassemble bumper bar assembly.

Installation
* Installation is reverse of the removal procedure.
1. Assemble bumper bar assembly if required.
2. Install corner bumpers into position and tighten retaining bolts, then install the centre bumper assembly into position and tighten retaining bolts.
3. Install the rear bumper step into position and tighten the retaining bolts, then reconnect the reversing sensor electrical connections.
4. Install the bumper bar inner wheel arch splash shields and mud guards, then install the rear combination lamp.

OVER FENDER - Front (flares)
Removal
1. Remove front mud guard as described previously.
2. Using a 4mm drill, drill out the centre of the rivets and remove rivets securing the flares.

3. Carefully pry out the over fender retainers, being carefully not to damage the over fender or the body and paintwork.
4. Remove the over fender pad, then carefully remove any remaining double sided tape on both the over fender and vehicle body.
5. Wipe the areas down with isopropyl alcohol to ensure a clean surface.

Installation
1. Wipe the tape application area down with isopropyl alcohol to ensure a clean surface, then to application surface apply the primer and allow to dry.
2. To the over fender install the pad ensuring the tape affixes correctly.
   Note: *If tape is not affixing properly in cold weather, heat the tape bonding surface to about 50ºC before affixing tape.*
3. Press the over fender assembly onto the body ensuring the retainers secure correctly and the pad is firmly secured.
4. Install new rivets to the over fenders, then replace the mud guards.

OVER FENDER - Rear (flares)
Removal
1. Remove rear mud guard as described previously.
2. Using a 4mm drill, drill out the centre of the rivets and remove rivets securing the flares.

3. Carefully pry out the over fender retainers, being carefully not to damage the over fender or the body and paintwork.
4. Remove the over fender pad, then remove the protector film from the vehicle body.
5. Carefully remove any remaining double sided tape on both the over fender and vehicle body.
6. Wipe the areas down with isopropyl alcohol to ensure a clean surface.

Installation
1. Wipe the protector film application area down with isopropyl alcohol to ensure a clean surface, then peel the backing paper from the film and carefully install film into position on vehicle.
2. Wipe the tape application area down with isopropyl alcohol to ensure a clean surface, then to application surface apply the primer and allow to dry.
3. To the over fender install the pad ensuring the tape affixes correctly.
   Note: *If tape is not affixing properly in cold weather, heat the bonding surface to about 50ºC before affixing tape.*
4. Press the over fender assembly onto the body ensuring the retainers secure correctly and the pad is firmly secured.
5. Install new rivets to the over fenders, then replace the mud guards.

SIDE STEPS
Removal
1. Disconnect the electrical wiring for those vehicles fitted with side step illumination, then have somebody support the side step.

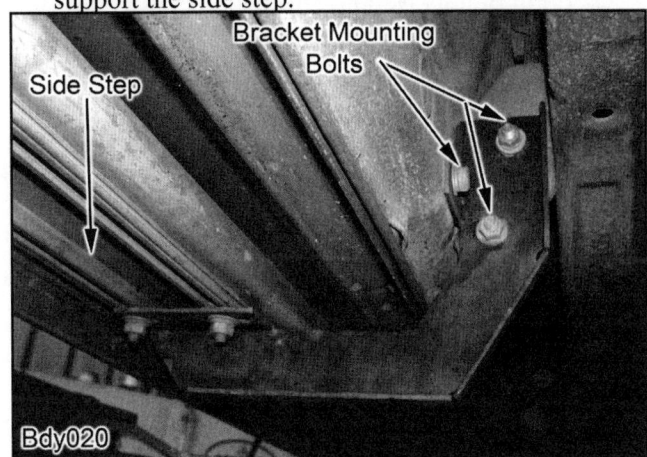

2. Remove the bolts securing the three mounting brackets to the underside of the vehicle and remove the step assembly from the vehicle.

Installation
1. Install the side step into position and secure with retaining bolts, tightening to specification.
   NM-NP models
   Mounting Bracket Bolts .... 12 Nm
   NS-NT models
   Front Mounting Bracket .... 60 Nm
   Centre Mounting Bracket .... 9 Nm
   Rear Mounting Bracket: A .... 60 Nm
   B .... 9 Nm
2. Reconnect electrical connection for the side step lamps.

ROOF RAILS
Removal
1. Remove the headlining as described previously in this chapter.
2. From inside the vehicle remove the nuts securing the roof rails.
3. Remove the roof rails and seals from the vehicle.

Installation
1. Install the roof rails into position ensuring to install all the seals, then tighten the retaining nuts.
2. Check to ensure there are no leaks around the mounting points, then install the headlining as described previously in this chapter.

REAR DEFLECTOR
Removal
1. From the top of the deflector assembly remove the covers from the screw locations.
2. Remove the retaining screws, then remove the rear deflector from the vehicle.

Installation
1. Install the rear deflector into position and tighten the retaining screws.
2. Replace the deflector covers to the screw locations.

WIPERS & WASHERS

WIPER ARM
Removal
1. Open bonnet then remove wiper arm retaining nut.

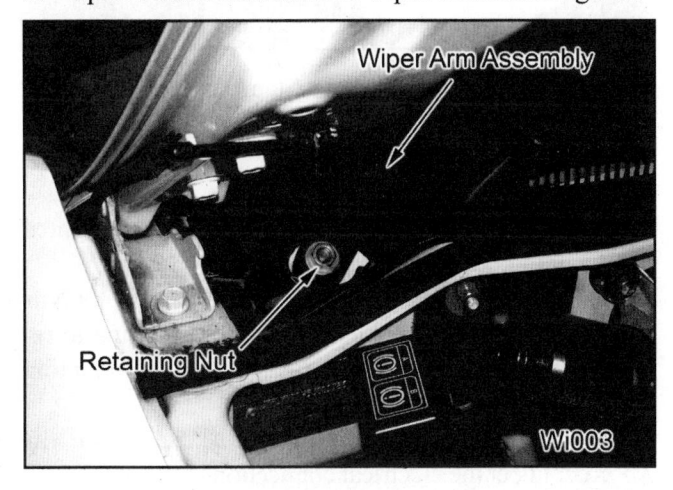

2. Place a screw driver under the arm with a cloth between the body and screwdriver to prevent damage to paint work. Gently lever the arm from the drive shaft and remove arm.
3. Remove wiper blade from arm if required.

Installation
1. Install the wiper blade onto the wiper arm.
2. Install wiper arm assembly onto spline so that the blade is positioned at the specified height from base of windscreen.
   Drivers Side .... 20 - 30mm
   Passenger Side .... 25 - 35mm
3. Press the arm onto the shaft ensuring the arm is fully seated on the shaft in the correct position.
4. Install attaching nut and tighten to specification.
   Wiper Arm Retaining Nut .... 13 Nm

WINDSHIELD WIPER MOTOR & LINKAGE
Removal
1. Remove the wiper arms as described previously.
2. Remove the screws securing the left and right trim panels and remove panels.
3. Disconnect the electrical connection from the wiper motor.

BODY - Wipers & Washers

4. Remove the bolts securing the wiper motor, then using a flat blade screwdriver leaver the motor from the wiper linkage and remove motor.

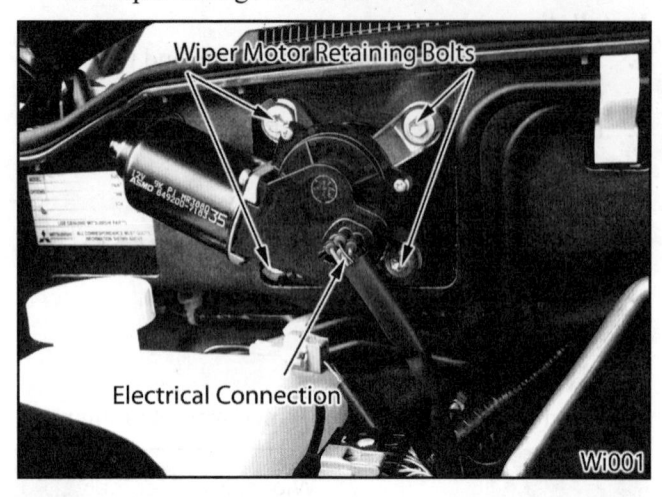

5. Remove the bolts securing the wiper linkage then remove the linkage from the vehicle.

Installation
1. Install the wiper linkage into vehicle and tighten retaining bolts to specification.
   Linkage Retaining Bolts .... 4.9 Nm
2. Install the wiper motor into position ensuring to reconnect the motor to linkage and tighten mounting bolts to specification.
   Wiper Motor Retaining Bolts .... 8.9 Nm
3. Reconnect the electrical connection to the wiper motor, then install the trim panels and the wiper arms as described previously.

WIPER MOTOR INSPECTION
When checking wiper motor the motor should be installed in position on vehicle and the electrical connection disconnected.

1. a) Connect a battery to the wiper motor for low and high speed as shown in table.

Speed	Battery (+ve) Terminal	Earth Terminal
Low	4	5
High	1	5
* Earth Battery Negative Terminal		

b) Test operation of wiper motor in both low and high speed.

2. a) Operate the wiper motor at low speed as shown in previous step, then disconnect the battery to stop wiper motor.
   b) Reconnect the battery using a jump wire.

Speed	Battery(+ve) Terminal	Earth Terminal	Jump Wire b/w terminals
Low	4	5	-
High	1	5	4 - 3
* Earth Battery Negative Terminal			

c) Check to ensure the wiper motor stops automatically in the correct position after is has been running at low speed.

REAR WINDOW WIPER MOTOR
Removal
1. Remove the wiper arm cover, then remove the retaining nut, wiper arm and grommet.

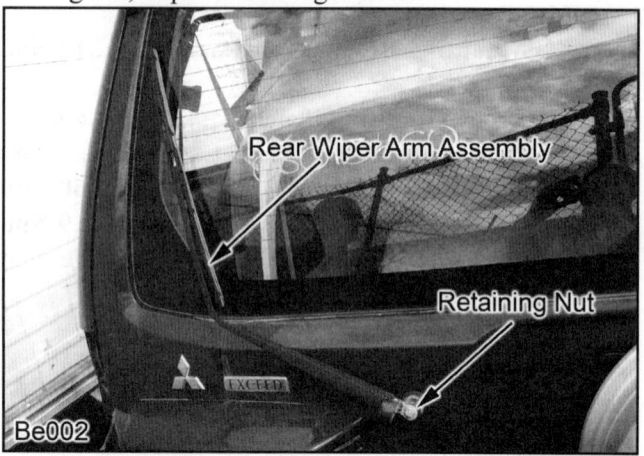

2. Open the tailgate then remove the tailgate trim panel as described previously in this chapter.
3. Disconnect the wiper motor electrical connection then remove the bolts securing the wiper motor and remove motor from vehicle.

Installation
1. Install the wiper motor into position, tighten retaining bolts to specification and reconnect the electrical connection.

BODY - Wipers & Washers

Image labels: Wiper Motor Retaining Bolts, Wiper Motor Electrical Connection, Wi002

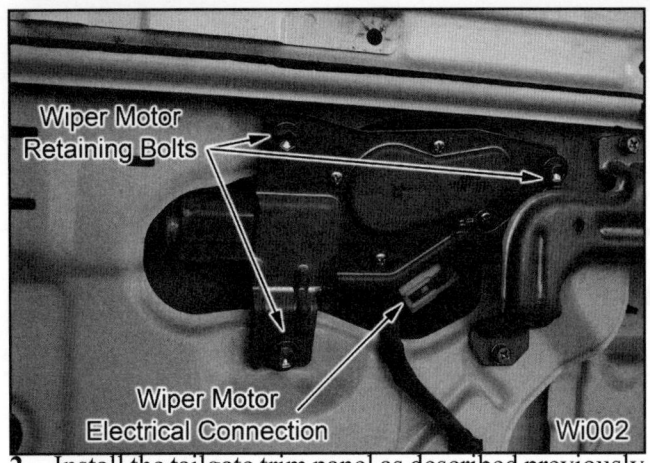

2. Install the tailgate trim panel as described previously in this chapter.
3. Install the grommet, then install the wiper arm so measurement from the base of the windscreen to the wiper arm is within specification.

   Measurement: - Driver Side.............25 +/- 5mm
   - Passenger Side.......30 +/- 5mm
4. Tighten retaining nut to specification and install wiper arm cover.

REAR WIPER MOTOR INSPECTION

When checking wiper motor the motor should be installed in position on vehicle and the electrical connection disconnected.

1. a) Connect a battery to the wiper motor with the positive connected to terminal #2 and negative connected to terminal #1.
   b) Test operation of wiper motor.
2. a) Operate the wiper motor as described previously then disconnect the battery to stop wiper motor.
   b) Reconnect the battery using a jump wire.

Battery(+ve) Terminal	Battery(-ve) Terminal	Jumper Wire b/w terminals
4	1	2 - 3

   c) Check to ensure wiper motor stops automatically in the correct position after is has been running.

REPLACE WIPER BLADES

Wiper insert rubbers deteriorate as a result of environmental conditions, such as atmospheric pollution and road grime, temperature extremes and natural ageing. It is therefore recommended that wiper inserts are replaced every twelve months or as required.

Wiper Blade Insert Assembly

1. Lift the blade away from the windscreen as far as it will go, so the wiper arm is held into position by its own spring tension.
2. Hold wiper blade and arm away from the glass to have access to the wiper blade.
3. Remove the retaining clip from the wiper and slide the old rubber blade out from the wiper assembly.
4. Slide the wiper insert assembly into position, install the metal retaining clip.
5. Install the wiper onto the wiper arm.

WINDSHIELD WASHER

Don't operate washer motor for more than 20 seconds continuously or when washer bottle is empty as motor or pump could be damaged.

Washer Liquid

Fill washer unit with either water or water and a small amount of detergent, this will help remove road grim such as oil and insects.

*Note: *Do not use too much detergent as this will obscure vision on the windscreen.*

Blocked Washer Nozzle

If the nozzles become blocked remove the hose from the back of the washer nozzle and use air pressure to blow the foreign matter from the nozzle. Reconnect the hose to the nozzle and test washer unit.

WASHER NOZZLE ADJUSTMENT

1. If adjustment is necessary use a metal wire or pin 1.0 mm or less in diameter inserted in nozzle hole, turn nozzle to direct spray at the desired angle.
2. If insufficient washer fluid is supplied check system for clogged, bent or crushed hoses.

HEADLAMP WASHER

The headlamp washer motor is mounted on the end of the windshield washer tank. An actuator is located at each headlight assembly.

HEADLAMP WASHER CHECK VALVE INSPECTION

Check the opening pressure of the check valve by applying pressure to the inlet valve.

Opening Pressure .... 78 kPa

HEADLAMP WASHER MOTOR INSPECTION

1. Disconnect the electrical connection from the motor, and ensure the washer tank is full.
2. Connect the positive battery terminal to terminal #1 and negative battery terminal to terminal #2.
3. Check to ensure the wash fluid has a strong spray while connected.

HEATER, AIR CONDITIONING & AUTOMATIC CLIMATE CONTROL

Subject	Page
GENERAL INFORMATION	419
Bleeding Air From The Heater Core	419
Refrigerant Circuit	419
Refrigerant Discharge/Recharge	419
A/C Refrigerant Line	419
Removal	419
Installation	420
Compressor	420
Removal	420
Disassembly	420
Reassembly	420
Oil Level Check	420
Magnetic Clutch Inspection (6G7)	421
Magnetic Clutch Inspection (4M40)	421
Magnetic Clutch Inspection (3200 & 3800)	421
Condenser Assembly & Condenser Fan	421
Removal	421
Condenser Inspection	421
Condenser Fan Inspection	421
Installation	421
Evaporator Assembly	422
Removal	422
Installation	422
Receiver Drier	422
Removal	422
Installation	422
Front Heater And Blower Assembly	422
Removal	422
Installation	423
Heater Unit Disassembly	423
Heater Unit Assembly	423
Clean Air Filter	424
Removal	424
Installation	424

Subject	Page
Blower Assembly	424
Disassembly	424
Reassembly	424
Heater and A/C Component Inspection	424
Front Blower Relay	424
Rear Blower Relay	425
Compressor Relay	425
Condenser Fan Relay Hi and Lo	425
Idle Up Operation - MPI	426
Idle Up Operation - 4M40	426
Idle Up Operation - 3800	426
Idle Up Operation - 3200	426
Idle Up Solenoid Valve - 4M40	426
Vacuum Actuator	427
Blower switch	427
Inside/Outside Air Changeover Switch	427
Inside/Outside Air Changeover Damper Motor	427
A/C Switch	428
Auto Comp. ECU & Air Thermo Sensor	428
Blower Motor	428
Blower Resistor	428
Lever Position Switch	428
Removal	428
Inspection	428
Installation	429
Air Outlet Changeover Damper Cable	429
Adjustment	429
Air Mix Damper Door Cable	429
Adjustment	429
Engine Coolant Temp Switch - 4M40	429
Inspection	429

HEATING, AIR CONDITIONING & AUTOMATIC CLIMATE CONTROL SYSTEM

Subject	Page
REAR HEATER AND AIR CONDITIONER	**430**
Rear Switch Assembly	**430**
Removal	430
Blower Switch Inspection	430
Rear Fan Switch Inspection	430
Temperature Adjustment Switch Inspection	430
Installation	430
Heater Unit and Blower Motor (Floor Console)	**430**
Removal	430
Disassembly	430
Reassembly	430
Installation	431
Component Check	**431**
Blower Motor	431
Resistor	431
PTC Heater	431
Relay	431
Heater Unit And Blower Motor (Quarter Trim)	**431**
Removal	431
Disassembly	431
Assembly	432
Installation	432
Component Check	**432**
Air Mix Damper Motor	432
Potentiometer	432
Expansion Valve (Magnet Valve)	432
Blower Motor	432
Resistor	432
AUTOMATIC CLIMATE CONTROL	**433**
PTC Heater, Switch and Relay (4M41)	**433**
Inspection	433
Switch Inspection	433
Relay Inspection	433
Idle Up Operation Check	**433**
6G7(GDI)	433
4M41	433
Blower Linear Controller Inspection	**433**
Air Mix Damper Motor Inspection	**433**
Potentiometer Inspection	**434**
Outlet Changeover Damper Motor Inspection	**434**
Heater Water Temperature Sensor	**434**
Inspection	434
Installation	434
Photo Sensor Inspection	**434**
Outside Air Temperature Sensor	**434**
Removal	434
Inspection	435
Installation	435
PROBLEM DIAGNOSIS	**435**
Automatic Climate Control	**436**

GENERAL INFORMATION

GENERAL INFORMATION
The following information provides basic service operations for the air conditioning system, including the compressor.

BLEEDING AIR FROM HEATER CORE
The heater core should bleed of air by having the heater turned to fully HOT with the engine operating, adding coolant as necessary. Always check coolant level after engine cools down to ensure it is at correct level

REFRIGERANT CIRCUIT
The major components of the system are a compressor, condenser, evaporator and a receiver drier.
The engine RPM is higher on air conditioned models so as not to drop to low at idle during system operation. When the ignition is turned off and the air conditioning has been operating, a faint sound of liquid flowing for 30-60 seconds maybe heard. This is the refrigerant in the system continuing to flow until high side and low side pressures equalize.

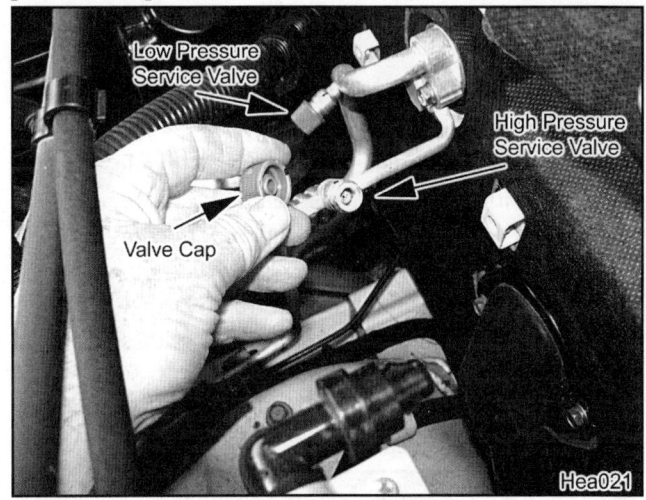

REFRIGERANT DISCHARGE/RECHARGE
Discharge
Discharge the refrigerant from A/C system following recommended EPA procedure, observing safety precautions.

Recharge
To check for leaks, evacuate and charge the refrigerant system following the recommended procedures and safety precautions.

REFRIGERANT (A/C) LINES
Removal
1. Discharge the refrigerant from A/C system following recommended EPA procedure, observing safety

precautions.
2. Remove the A/C lines using a backup spanner where required on each fitting.

Installation
1. Install new A/C line with protective caps removed.
2. Using new O-rings lubricated with clean refrigerant oil, connect the A/C line into the system. Use two wrenches when tightening the fittings to specification.
3. To check for leaks, evacuate and charge the refrigerant system following the recommended procedures and safety precautions.

COMPRESSOR

Note: Where a failure has occurred that may have resulted in foreign material in the system, the system must be flushed using Refrigerant R-12.

Note: All compressor removal and install operations, except belt replacement, can be performed only after the unit has been discharged.

Note: A port protection plate should be fitted to keep the compressor free from moisture and foreign material if it is necessary to store a serviced compressor.

Removal
1. Discharge the refrigerant from the system as described earlier in the chapter.
2. Remove the air intake duct from the vehicle. Release the tension from the drive belt and remove.
   Note: Place an arrow indicating the direction of rotation on the belt to help on installation.
3. Undo the mounting bolts and remove the discharge flexible hose and the suction flexible hose from the compressor.
   Note: Make sure to cover the hoses to prevent water from entering them.

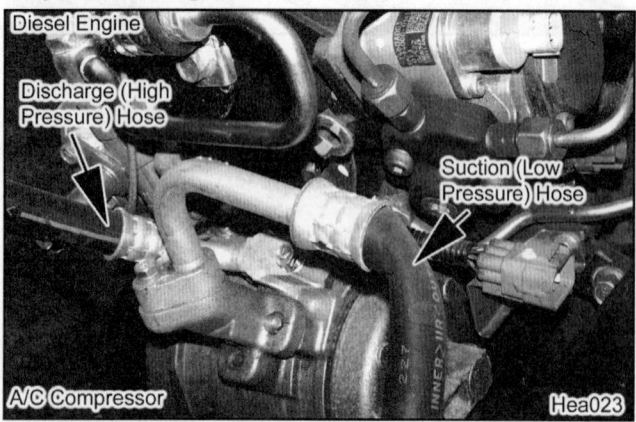

4. Remove the bolts securing the compressor to the mounting bracket.
   Note: When removing the compressor be careful not to spill the compressor oil.

Disassembly
1. Place the compressor in a suitable vice making sure not to damage the housing. Remove the lock sensor on the compressor if fitted (6G7).
2. Disconnect and remove the electrical connector.
3. Remove the armature by undoing the mounting bolt. Using snap ring pliers remove the snap ring holding the pulley in place.
4. Using snap ring pliers remove the snap ring securing the field core.
5. Next remove the washers from the front of the housing taking note of the order they come out.

Reassembly
1. Reinstall the washers/shims into the housing.
2. Align the compressor grove with the projection on the field core. Reinstall the holding snap ring making sure not to damage it by expanding it excessively.
3. Install the pulley/rotor next using a new snap ring to hold it in place.
4. Mount the armature to the compressor using the bolt to secure it.

Armature Mounting Bolt
NM - NP...13.5 +/- 2.7 Nm
NS ....18 +/- 3 Nm

5. After assembly the air gap needs to be checked. Using a dial gauge measure the movement of the armature when battery voltage is applied to the electrical terminal. See illustration on this page.
   Note: Use washers to adjust the air gap. They are available is three sizes 0.1mm, 0.3 mm, 0.5mm.

Air Gap .... 0.35-0.60 mm

6. If needed check level of oil in the compressor using the following procedure.

Oil Level Check
1. Drain oil from old compressor and measure amount of oil, this is "A" ml.
2. Use the following formula to work out how much oil to remove from the new compressor.
3. **NM - NP Pajero All Motors**
   Vehicles With Rear Cooler-
   140ml - "A"ml = Amount To Be Drained
   Vehicles Without Rear Cooler-
   120ml - "A"ml = Amount To Be Drained
   Note: The amounts 140ml and 120ml are the factory charged amount of oil in a new compressor.
   NS Pajero 3200 - 3800
   Vehicles With Rear Cooler-
   180ml - "A"ml = Amount To Be Drained
   Vehicles Without Rear Cooler-
   120ml - "A"ml = Amount To Be Drained
   Note: The amounts 180ml and 120ml are the factory charged amount of oil in a new compressor.

HEATING, AIR CONDITIONING & AUTOMATIC CLIMATE CONTROL SYSTEM

Magnetic Clutch (6G7)
Inspection
1. Remove the 3 pin electrical connector on the A/C compressor.
2. Connect battery (+) voltage to terminal No. 3 and battery negative (-ve) to compressor housing.
3. If a clicking sound is heard from the pulley and the armature making contact, then the magnetic clutch is okay.

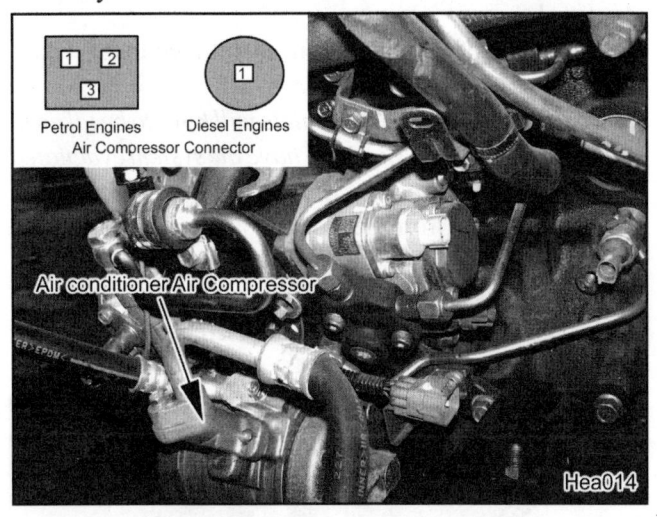

Magnetic Clutch (4M40)
Inspection
1. Remove the electrical connector to the A/C compressor.
2. Connect battery (+) voltage to the positive electrical connector on the compressor and the negative earth battery terminal directly to the compressor.
3. If a clicking sound is heard from the pulley and the armature making contact, then the magnetic clutch is okay.

Magnetic Clutch (3200 & 3800)
Inspection
1. Remove the electrical connector to the A/C compressor.
2. Connect battery (+) voltage to the positive electrical connector on the compressor and the negative earth battery terminal directly to the compressor. See illustration above.
3. If a clicking sound is heard from the pulley and the armature making contact, then the magnetic clutch is okay.

Installation
1. If removed bolt the compressor bracket to the engine. Place compressor into position and tighten bolts securing it into place.
2. Install the suction and discharge flexible hoses using new O-rings. Make sure to coat the pipe connections with A/C compressor oil where they connect with the compressor.
3. Install the drive belt on to the pulley using the arrow marked on removal as a guide and adjust tension as necessary. If needed refer to the Tune up and Maintenance Chapter.
   Note: Check the condition of the drive belt and replace if necessary.
4. Install the air intake duct to the vehicle.
5. The vehicle will need to be taken to a authorised service agent to have the A/C system recharged.

Condenser Assembly and Condenser Fan

Removal
1. Discharge the refrigerant system then remove the radiator and fan assembly.
2. Disconnect and cap both the inlet and outlet refrigerant lines.
3. Remove the bolts/nuts securing the condenser then carefully lift the condenser from the vehicle

Condenser Inspection
1. Inspect the condenser for crushed fins and blockage.
2. Inspect the pipe connections for damage.

Condenser Fan Inspection
To check the condenser fan, connect battery voltage directly to terminal No.1 and negative battery voltage to terminal No.2. The motor should run without any excess noise.

Installation
1. Install the condenser into the vehicle and secure with the retaining bolts/nuts.
2. Reconnect the refrigerant pipes to the condenser using new oil condenser line 'O-rings.
3. Install the radiator and cooling fan assembly, then evacuate and charge the system with refrigerant.

HEATING, AIR CONDITIONING & AUTOMATIC CLIMATE CONTROL SYSTEM

EVAPORATOR ASSEMBLY
Removal
1. Discharge refrigerant from air conditioning system then disconnect the pipes from the evaporator in the engine bay, also disconnect drain tube.
   Note: *Ensure to cap pipes to prevent entry of foreign material.*
2. Remove the centre console and dash panel as described in the body chapter, then remove the centre support.
3. Disconnect the evaporator unit electrical connections then remove the retaining bolts/nuts.
4. Remove the evaporator assembly from the vehicle, then release evaporator case clips and separate housing.
5. Inspect the evaporator fins and clean with compressed air if required.

Assembly
1. Assemble evaporator assembly and secure with retaining clips, then install evaporator unit into vehicle.
2. Tighten the unit retaining bolts/nuts and reconnect the evaporator unit electrical connections.
3. Install the centre support, dash panel and centre console as described in body chapter.
4. Reconnect the refrigerant pipes and drain tube, then evacuate and charge the system with refrigerant.

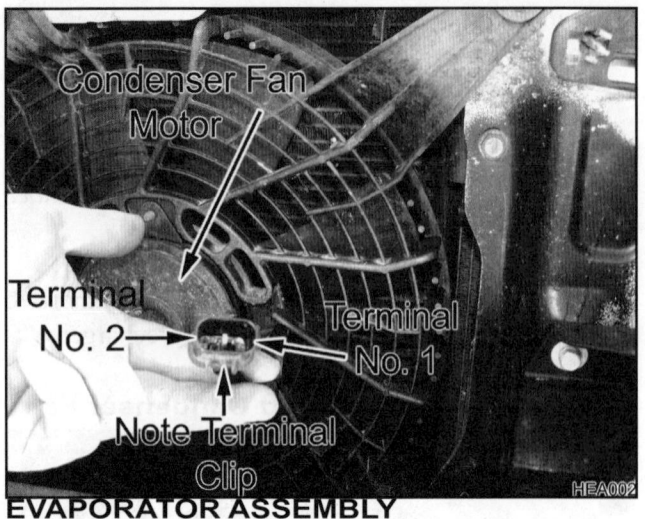

RECEIVER DRIER
Removal
1. Discharge refrigerant from air conditioning system.
2. Disconnect the refrigerant lines from the receiver drier, then disconnect the electrical connections.
   Note: *Ensure to cap pipes to prevent entry of foreign material.*
3. Remove the receiver drier mounting bolts/nuts and remove unit from vehicle.

Installation
1. Install receiver drier to vehicle and tighten retaining bolts/nuts.
2. Reconnect refrigerant lines ensuring to use new 'O-rings, then reconnect electrical connections.
3. Evacuate and charge the system with refrigerant.

FRONT HEATER AND BLOWER ASSEMBLY
Removal
1. Evacuate refrigerant system as outlined in this chapter.
   Note: *In most cases the vehicle will have to be taken to the dealer or a specialist to have the system evacuated and recharged, as specialist equipment is required.*
2. Drain coolant from the radiator by removing the lower radiator hose.
3. From inside engine bay disconnect the drain hose and heater hose connections, then disconnect the suction and liquid pipes.

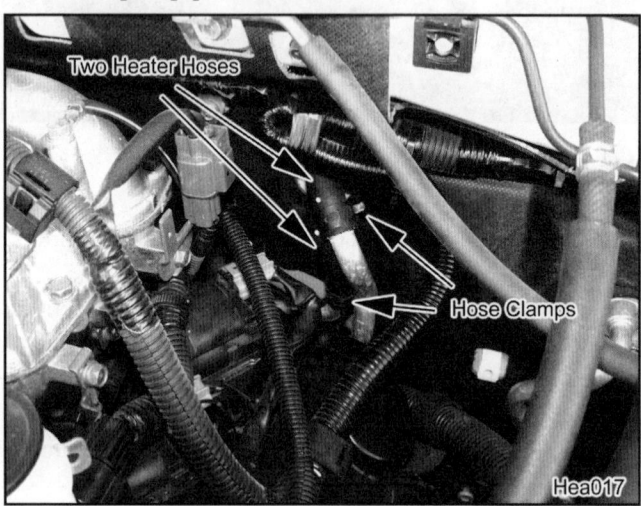

Note: Plug the hose connections for the suction and liquid pipes to prevent entry of foreign material. Ensure the plugs are air tight to prevent moisture from entering.

4. Remove the centre console and the dash panel as-

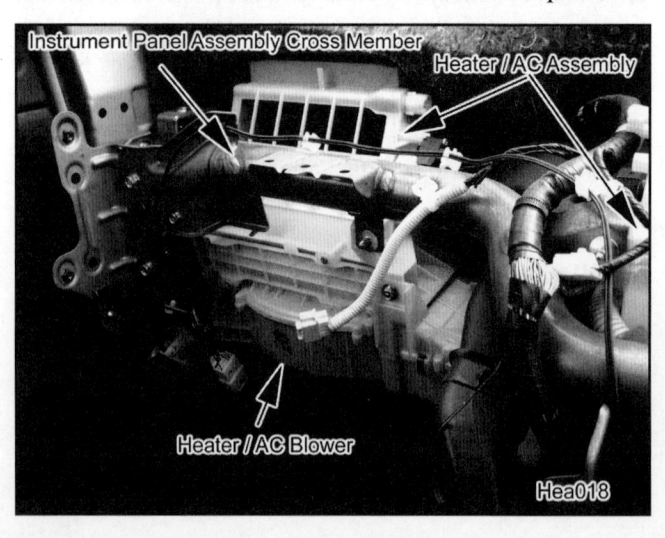

422

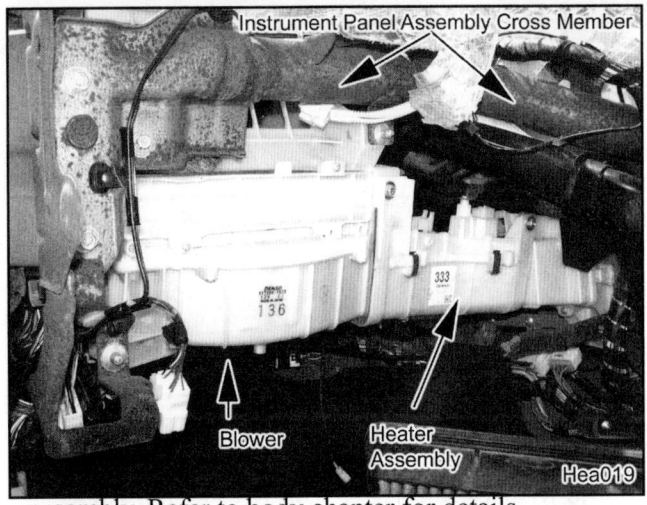

HEATING, AIR CONDITIONING & AUTOMATIC CLIMATE CONTROL SYSTEM

sembly. Refer to body chapter for details.
5. Disconnect the electrical connections, then remove the centre feet ducts.
6. Remove the bolts and nuts securing the instrument panel assembly cross-member and remove from vehicle.
7. Remove the bolts securing the flange bracket, then remove bracket.
8. Remove the screws/bolts securing the blower assembly, then remove the blower assembly from vehicle.
9. Remove the screws/bolts securing the main heater assembly and remove heater unit, disconnecting the drain hose. 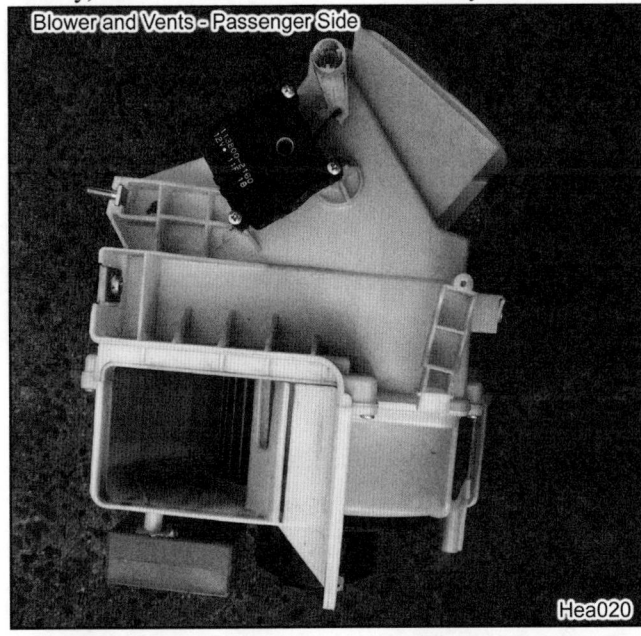

Installation
1. Install the main heater assembly into vehicle, connect the drain hose and secure with retaining screws/bolts.
2. Install the blower assembly to the vehicle and tighten retaining screws/bolts.
3. Install the flange bracket, tighten retaining bolts.
4. Install the instrument panel assembly cross-member and tighten retaining bolts and screws to the heater and blower units.
   Note: Ensure to replace rubber mounts/grommets with new ones on installation.
5. Install the centre foot ducts, then reconnect electrical connections.
6. Install the dash panel assembly and centre console. Refer to "Body" Chapter.
7. Inside the engine bay, reconnect the drain hose and heater hose connections, then connect high and low pressure pipes, ensuring new "O" rings are fitted.
8. Top up radiator with specified coolant then bleed the heater system of any air locks.
9. Check the operation of the heater.
10. Recharge system on vehicles with A/C.
    Note: In most case the vehicle will have to be taken to a specialist to have the system evacuated and recharged, as specialist equipment is required.

HEATER UNIT
Dismantle
1. From the heater unit remove the foot ducts retaining screws and then remove the foot ducts from the unit.
2. Remove the clip for the compressor-ECU and air thermo sensor, then remove the compressor-ECU and air thermo sensor assembly.
3. Remove the screws securing the resistor and remove resistor then where fitted remove the rear A/C control unit
4. Remove the screws securing the joint duct to the air duct sub assembly and remove joint duct.
5. Remove the screws securing the air duct sub-assembly and remove sub-assembly.
6. From the main heater unit remove the heater core.
7. Remove the front pipe assembly, then remove the expansion valve and pipe assembly.
8. From the heater unit case remove the evaporator.

Assemble
1. To the heater unit case install the evaporator.
2. Install the pipe assembly and expansion valve, then install the front pipe assembly, ensuring to use new 'O-rings.
3. Install the heater core to the heater unit assembly.
4. Install the air duct sub-assembly, tightening retaining screws, then install joint duct and tighten retaining screws.
5. Where fitted install the rear A/C control unit, then install the resistor.
6. Install the compressor-ECU and air thermo sensor, then install the compressor-ECU and air thermo sensor clip.
7. To the heater unit install the foot ducts and secure

423

HEATING, AIR CONDITIONING & AUTOMATIC CLIMATE CONTROL SYSTEM

with retaining screws.

CLEAN AIR FILTER
Removal
Remove the two screws securing the filter to the blower assembly. Remove the filter.

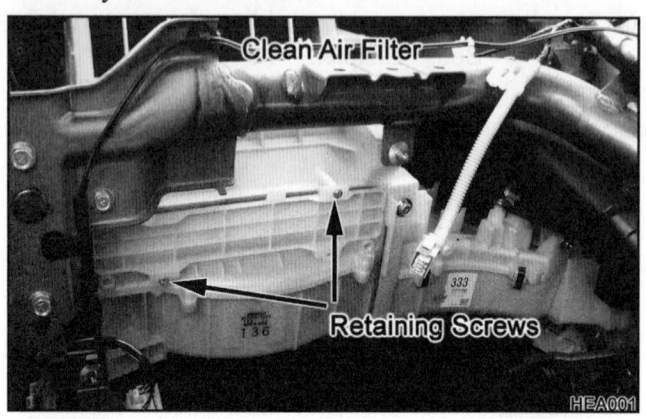

Installation
Secure the filter into the blower assembly doing the two screws up.

BLOWER ASSEMBLY
Removal
1. Remove the screws securing the blower motor to the case assembly and remove motor. 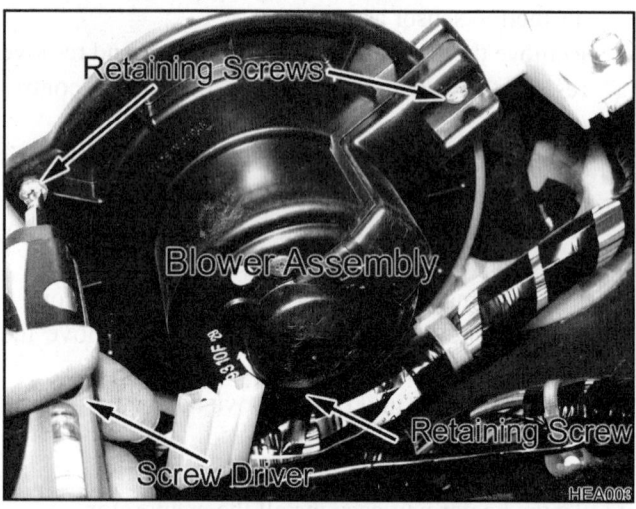
2. Where fitted remove the two screws securing the clean air filter to the case and remove filter element.
3. Remove the three screws securing the air changeover damper motor to the case and remove damper motor.

Installation
1. Fit the air changeover damper motor to the case and tighten retaining screws.
2. Where fitted install the air filter to the case and tighten retaining screws.
3. Install the blower motor to the case assembly and tighten retaining screws.

HEATER AND A/C COMPONENT CHECK

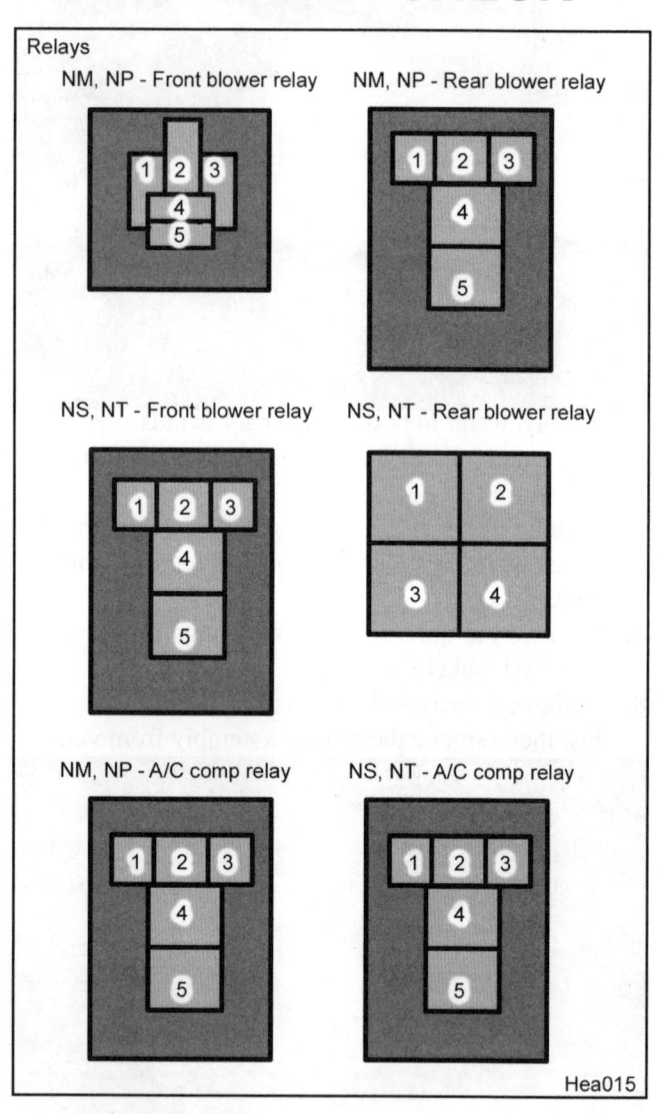

Relays

NM, NP - Front blower relay
NM, NP - Rear blower relay
NS, NT - Front blower relay
NS, NT - Rear blower relay
NM, NP - A/C comp relay
NS, NT - A/C comp relay

Front Blower Relay
Remove the relay from the fuse box and check the continuity between the terminals are as shown.

NM - NP

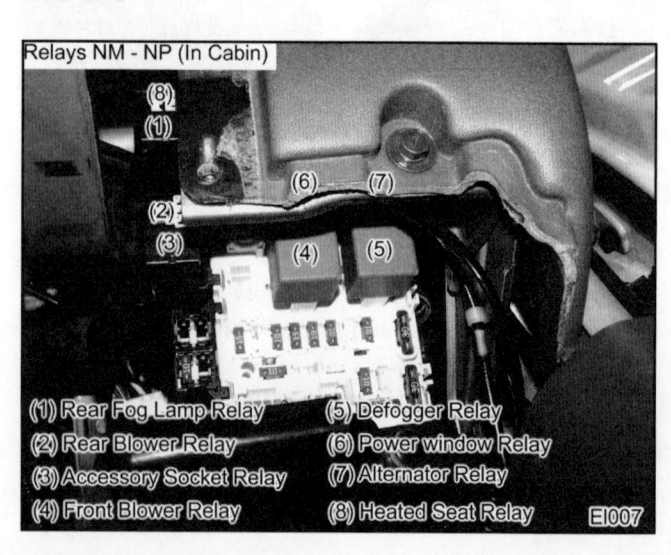

Relays NM - NP (In Cabin)
(1) Rear Fog Lamp Relay
(2) Rear Blower Relay
(3) Accessory Socket Relay
(4) Front Blower Relay
(5) Defogger Relay
(6) Power window Relay
(7) Alternator Relay
(8) Heated Seat Relay

424

HEATING, AIR CONDITIONING & AUTOMATIC CLIMATE CONTROL SYSTEM

NM, NP	Battery Voltage (applied to terminals) -ve	Battery Voltage (applied to terminals) +ve	Continuity b/w Terminals
Current Not Supplied	-	-	2 - 5
Current Supplied	3	1	

NS - NT

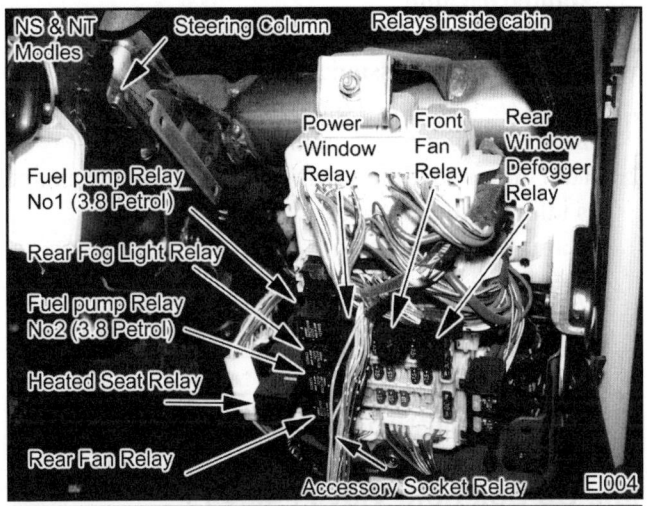 NS, NT	Battery Voltage (applied to terminals) -ve	Battery Voltage (applied to terminals) +ve	Continuity b/w Terminals
Current Not Supplied	-	-	-
Current Supplied	1	3	4 - 5

Rear Blower Relay

Remove the relay from the fuse box and check the continuity between the terminals are as shown.
See illustrations under Front Blower Relay

NM - NP

NM, NP	Battery Voltage (applied to terminals) -ve	Battery Voltage (applied to terminals) +ve	Continuity b/w Terminals
Current Not Supplied	-	-	1 - 3, 4 - 5
Current Supplied	3	1	

NS - NT

NS, NT	Battery Voltage (applied to terminals) -ve	Battery Voltage (applied to terminals) +ve	Continuity b/w Terminals
Current Not Supplied	-	-	-
Current Supplied	2	3	1 - 4

Compressor Relay

Remove the relay from the fuse box and check the continuity between the terminals are as shown.

NM - NP

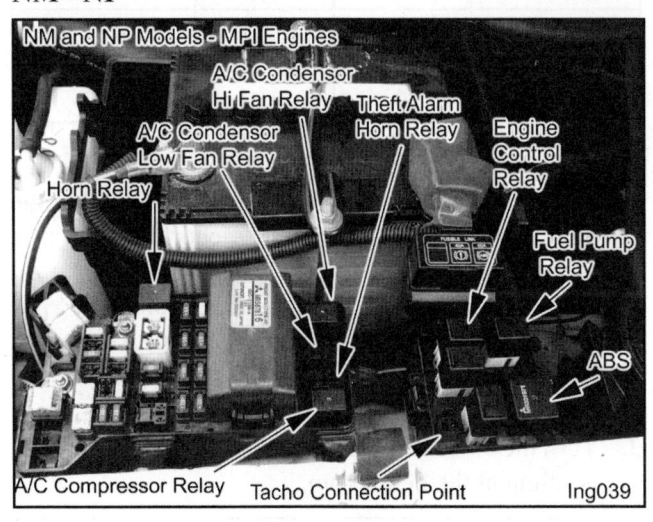

NS - NT

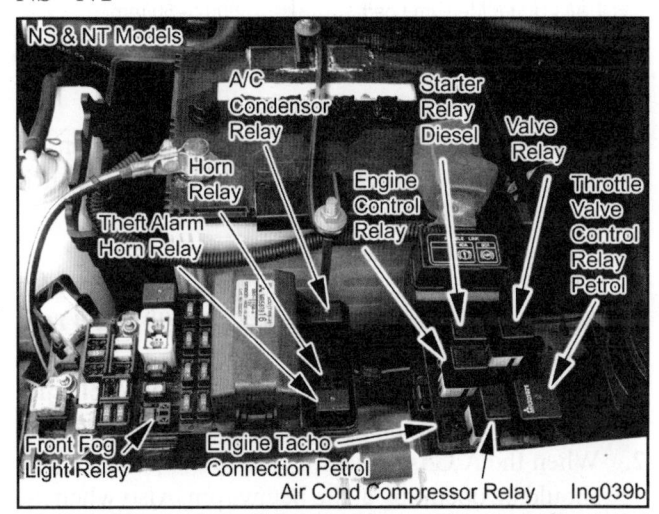

NM-NT	Battery Voltage (applied to terminals) -ve	Battery Voltage (applied to terminals) +ve	Continuity b/w Terminals
Current Not Supplied	-	-	1 - 3
Current Supplied	3	1	4 - 5

Condenser Fan Relay Hi and Lo

1. Remove the relays from the fuse box and check the continuity between the terminals are as shown.

See illustrations under Compressor Relay

425

HEATING, AIR CONDITIONING & AUTOMATIC CLIMATE CONTROL SYSTEM

NM - NT

NM-NT	Battery Voltage (applied to terminals) -ve	+ve	Continuity b/w Terminals
Current Not Supplied	-	-	1 - 3
Current Supplied	3	1	4 - 5

Idle Up Operation (6G7 MPI)

1. Park the vehicle out of the direct sunlight. Run the engine for at least two minutes checking that it is idling at
   NM - NP .... 700 +/- 50 rpm
   NS - NT .... 700 +/- 100 rpm
   Note: *The idle speed is controlled by the ISC system and should not be adjusted.*
2. Turn the air conditioner on and check that the engine is idling at the below rpm.

A/C Under Low Load	700 +/- 50 rpm
A/C Under Medium Load	800 +/- 50 rpm
A/C Under High Load	1000 +/- 50 rpm

Idle Up Operation (4M40)

1. Park the vehicle out of the direct sunlight. Run the engine for at least two minutes checking that it is idling at,
   Manual Transmission
   NM - NP .... 700 +/- 50 rpm
   NS .... 700 +/- 30 rpm
   Automatic Transmission
   NM - NP .... 750 +/- 50 rpm
   NS - NT .... 740 +/- 30 rpm
2. When the A/C is turned on and running the vehicle should be operating at the below rpm. Also when the heat is turned on to 32°C and with the blower on, the rpm should be achieved.
   Standard Value.............................. 950 +/-50 rpm
3. If the standard value is not achieved the idle speed will need to be adjusted as follows.
   a) Loosen nuts 1 and 2 and turn the adjuster for the actuator rod. Tighten nuts 1 and 2.
   b) Next remove the cap and loosen the locking nut. Adjust to the specified rpm by turning the adjusting screw.
   c) Tighten the locking nut and attach the cap.

Idle Up Operation (3800)

1. Park the vehicle out of the direct sunlight. Run the engine for at least two minutes checking that it is idling at,
   Standard Value............................. 700 +/- 100 rpm
   Note: *The idle speed is controlled by the ISC system and should not be adjusted.*
2. Turn the air conditioner on and check that the engine is idling at the below rpm.

A/C Under Low Load	700 +/- 50 rpm
A/C Under Medium Load	800 +/- 50 rpm
A/C Under High Load	1000 +/- 50 rpm

Idle Up Operation (3200)

1. Park the vehicle out of the direct sunlight. Run the engine for at least two minutes checking that it is idling at
   Standard Value
   Auto Transmission .... 740 +/- 30 rpm
   Manual Transmission .... 700 +/- 30 rpm
   Note: *The idle speed is controlled by the ISC system and should not be adjusted.*
2. Turn the air conditioner on and check that the engine is idling at the below rpm.
   Manual Transmission

A/C Under Low Load	700 +/- 50 rpm
A/C Under Medium Load	800 +/- 50 rpm
A/C Under High Load	1000 +/- 50 rpm

   Auto Transmission .... 1000 +/- 50 rpm

Idle Up Solenoid Valve (4M40)

1. Disconnect the vacuum hose (white stripes, yellow stripes) and the electrical connector from the solenoid valve. Place a mark on the hoses to help with replacing onto correct nipple
2. Connect a manual vacuum pump to the nipple (A) as indicated by the white stripe. Nipple (B) is the one with the yellow striped vacuum hose. Check for air tightness following the procedures in the chart below when battery voltage is applied and not applied.

Battery Voltage	Nipple B	Vacuum Condition
Applied to terminal "2"	Open	Vacuum Leaks From Nipple (B)
	Blocked With Finger #1	Vacuum Is Maintained
Not Applied	Open	Vacuum Is Maintained
	Blocked With Finger #2	Vacuum Is Maintained

#1- Vacuum can be felt.
#2- Vacuum can not be felt.

3. Next measure the resistance between the two terminals.
   Value .... *Approx. 40 Ohm*

HEATING, AIR CONDITIONING & AUTOMATIC CLIMATE CONTROL SYSTEM

Vacuum Actuator

1. Disconnect the yellow striped hose from the vacuum actuator. Connect a hand held vacuum pump to the nipple. The following values should be achieved.

Negative Pressure Applied	Actuator Rod Position
8 Kpa	Actuator Rod Starts To Contact
12 Kpa	Actuator Rod At Full Extension

2. Reconnect the Vacuum hose. Start the engine and let the engine idle.
3. With your finger cover the of the yellow striped hose and check for negative pressure when the A/C is turned off and on following the table below.

A/C Off/On	Negative Pressure At Hose End
Off	No
On	Yes

Blower Switch

1. Remove the A/C control panel assembly from the dash as described in the body chapter.
2. Check the continuity of the terminals on the blower switch following the steps below.

Switch Position	Terminal Number
0 (OFF)	
1 (LO)	3 and 5
2 (ML)	1 and 3
3 (MH)	3 and 6
4 (HI)	3 and 4

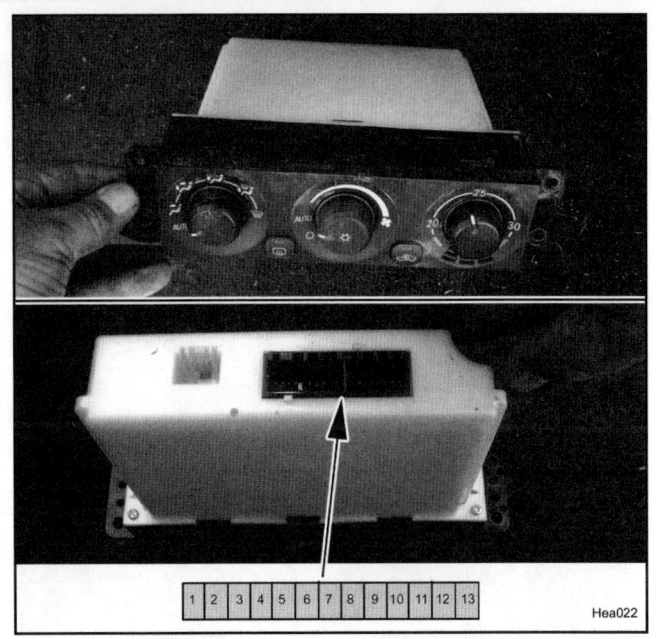

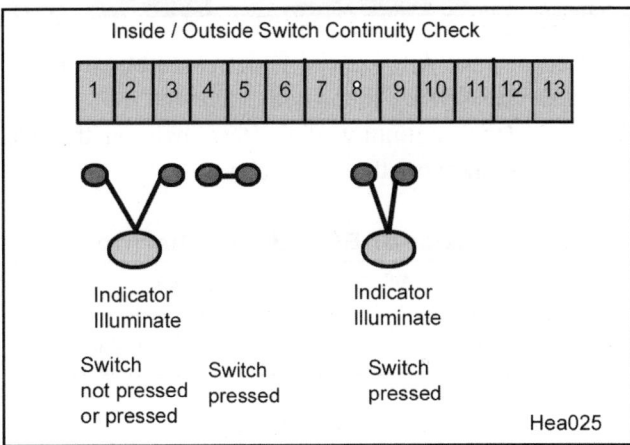

Inside/Outside Air Changeover Switch

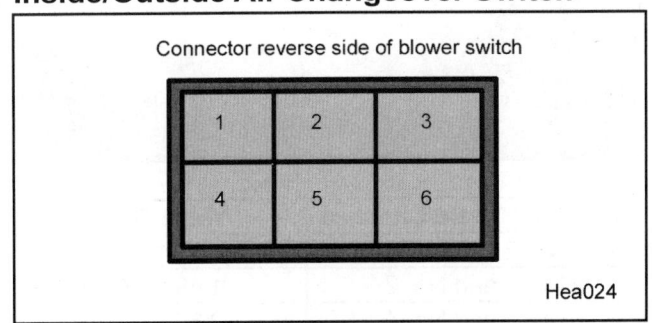

1. Remove the A/C control panel assembly from the dash as described in the body chapter.
2. Check the continuity of the terminals on the Inside/Outside Air Changeover switch following the steps below.

Inside/Outside Air Changeover Damper Motor

1. Disconnect the electrical terminal from the damper motor which is located on the side of the blower motor.
2. Connect battery voltage to the terminals following the table below.

Battery +ve	Battery -ve	Inside air	Outside air
Terminal 1	Terminal 3	Active	
Terminal 1	Terminal 2		Active

427

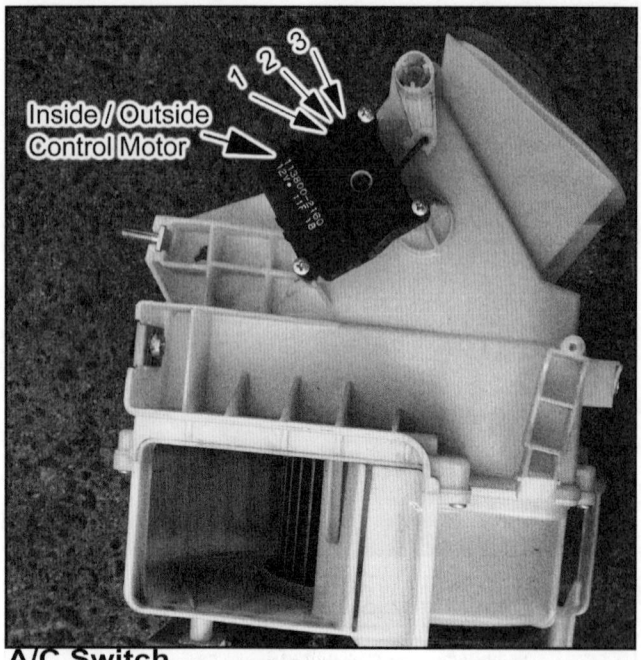

HEATING, AIR CONDITIONING & AUTOMATIC CLIMATE CONTROL SYSTEM

A/C Switch

1. Remove the A/C control panel assembly from the dash as described in the body chapter.
2. Check the continuity of the terminals on the A/C switch following the steps below.

Auto Compressor ECU & Air Thermo

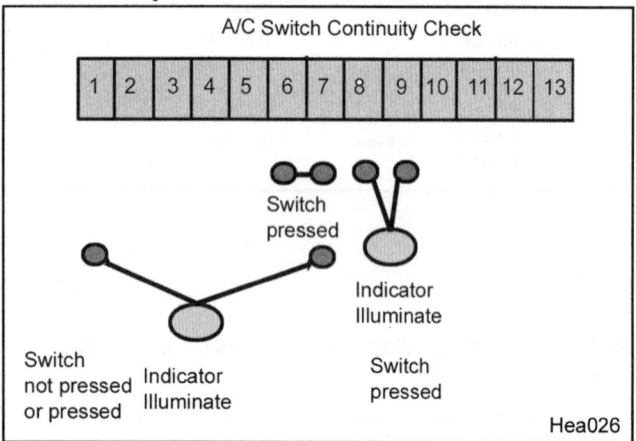

Sensor
Inspection

Measure the resistance between the terminals following the table below.

Note: The temperature should be within the shown range

| Resistance b/n the terminals ||
Temperature Deg C	Value kOhm
10	approx 2.9kOhms
20	approx 1.9kOhms
30	approx 1.3kOhms

Blower Motor

1. Disconnect the electrical terminal from the blower motor.
2. Connect battery voltage to the terminal as shown. The motor should run without any strange noises coming from the motor.

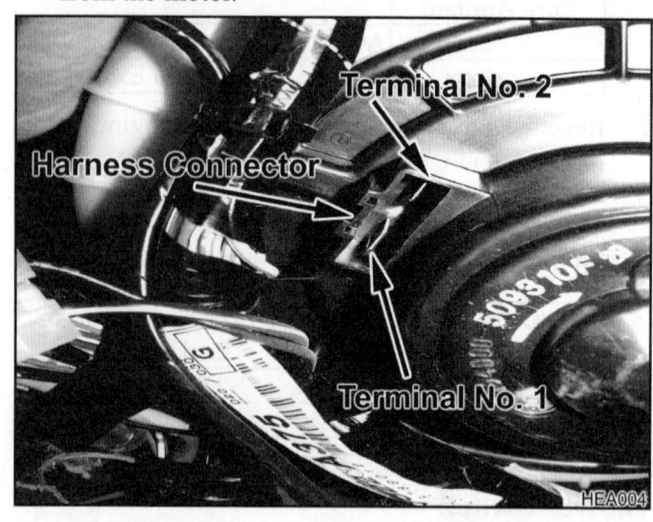

Blower Resistor

Disconnect the electrical connector from the resistor. Check resistance between the show terminal with a multimeter as shown in the table below.

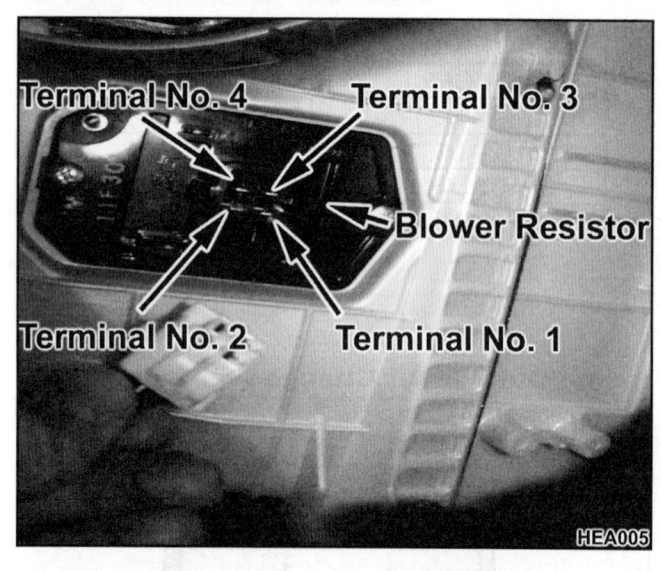

Terminals To Be Checked	Value Ohm
No. 2 and No. 3	2.79 +/- 7%
No. 1 and No. 2	1.49 +/- 7%
No. 2 and No. 4	0.39 +/- 7%

Lever Position Switch (4M40 Auto)
Removal

1. Disconnect the electrical connection.
2. Remove the two mounting screws.

Inspection

1. Connect a multi-meter to the lever position switch, one probe on terminal, the other probe on Lever Position

428

HEATING, AIR CONDITIONING & AUTOMATIC CLIMATE CONTROL SYSTEM

switch body.

2. Continuity should exist until the rod is gradually pushed 0.3mm past its free position

Installation

1. Check that the idle speed is within specification. Adjust if necessary referring to the engine chapter.
   Engine Idle Speed............................750+/-100rpm
2. Stop the engine, depress the accelerator pedal so the fuel injection pump is wide open.
3. Place the lever position switch into place doing the bolts up finger tight. Connect the electrical connector.
4. With the accelerator depressed, adjust the lever position switch so the rod is pushed in 4 +/- 0.5 mm from its free position.
5. Do the mounting bolts up tight.

Air Outlet Changeover Damper Cable
Adjustment

1. On the heater control panel set the dial to the DEF position.
2. Move the damper lever to the DEF position on the heater unit.
   Note: *Rotate the damper lever fully anti-clockwise.*

3. Connect the cable to the lever.

Air Mix Damper Door Cable
Adjustment

1. On the heater control panel set the dial to the fully hot position.
2. Move the air mix door lever to the MAX HOT position on the heater unit.
   Note: *Rotate the door lever fully clockwise.*

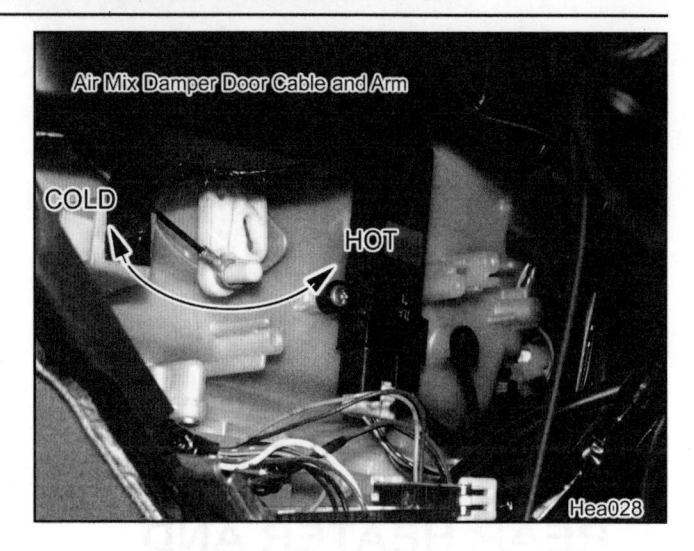

3. Connect the cable to the lever.

Engine Coolant Temp Switch (4M40)
Inspection

1. For the 4M40 engine there are two temperature switches, one is for A/C cut off, the other is for the control of the condenser fan.
2. Using a multimeter consult the table below to check the continuity of the switches.
   Note: *The switches will need to be heated to the temperatures shown in the table. Extreme care needs to be taken when dealing with hot liquids, do not heat switches any more than needed.*

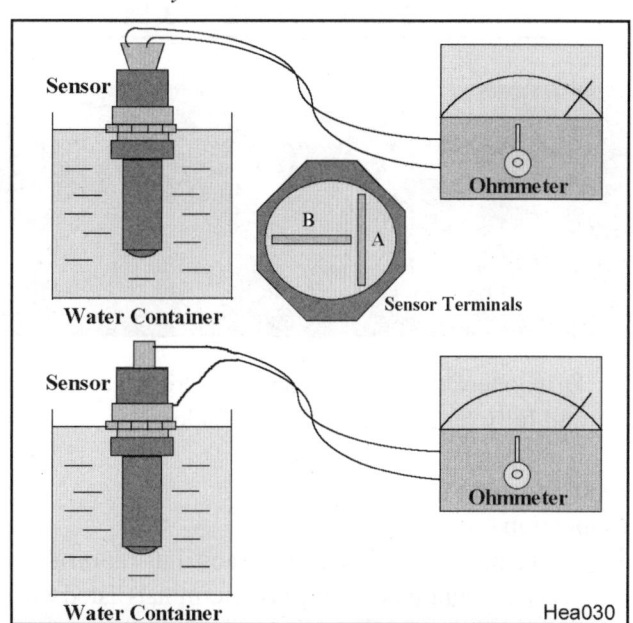

Engine Coolant Temp Switch	Temperature	Continuity
For A/C Cut Off	Less Than 108°C	Continuity
	More Than 115°C	No Continuity
For Condenser Fan	Less Than 97°C	No Continuity
	More Than 102°C	Continuity

429

HEATING, AIR CONDITIONING & AUTOMATIC CLIMATE CONTROL SYSTEM

REAR HEATER AND REAR COOLER

REAR SWITCH ASSEMBLY

Note: *The switch assembly layout changes between models but the pin configuration remains the same.*

Removal

1. Remove the screws securing the control panel, then release retaining clips and partially remove panel.
2. Disconnect the control panel electrical connection and fully remove panel from vehicle.

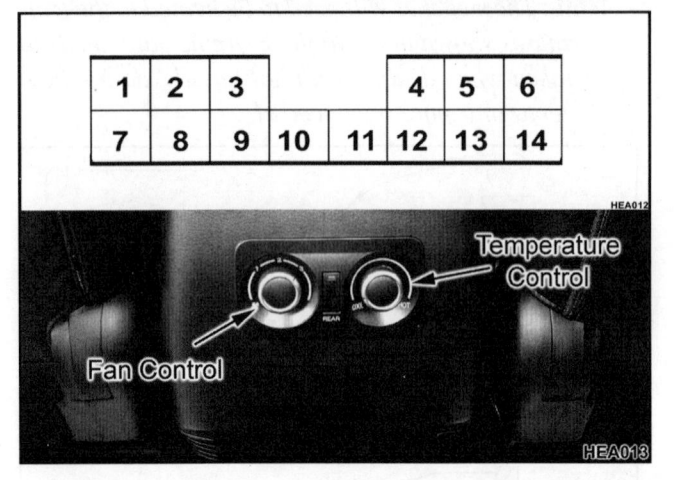

Rear Blower Switch
Inspection

1. Using the table on the next page and illustration above check the continuity between the terminals listed when the switch is turned.

Switch Position	Terminal Numbers
1	1 and 4
2	1 and 6
3	1 and 7

2. If faults are found, the switch is faulty and will need to be replaced or repaired.

Rear Fan Switch
Inspection

1. Toggle the rear fan switch on and off using the table below as a guide for checking.

See previous illustration for terminals.

Switch Position	Terminal Numbers	Specified Condition
Pressed	2 and 8	Continuity
Not Pressed	2 and 8	No Continuity

2. If the switch is found to be faulty repair or replace as required.

Temperature Adjusting Switch
Inspection

1. Using a multimeter check the resistance changes smoothly between the standard value.
   Standard Value.................................... 0 - 3 Kohm
   Check between terminals No. 3 and No. 5, also No. 5 and No. 13.
   See previous illustration for terminals.

2. If faults are found repair or replace as required.

Installation

1. Partially install control assembly into vehicle.
2. Connect the control panel electrical connection.
3. Install control panel into position and tighten retaining screws.
4. Test operation of controls.

HEATER UNIT AND BLOWER MOTOR (FLOOR CONSOLE)

Removal

1. Remove the centre console as described in body chapter.
2. Remove the upper bracket from each side of the assembly, then remove the assembly retaining bolts and remove heater unit from vehicle.

Dismantle

1. From the heater case remove the duct retaining screws and duct.
2. Remove the electrical connections, then remove the relay and resistor from the assembly.
3. From the assembly remove the heater core, then remove the blower fan and blower motor.

Assembly

1. Install the blower motor and fan assembly to the heater case and tighten retaining screws.
2. To the heater unit install the heater core, then install the resistor and tighten retaining screw.
3. Install the relay to the unit then install the electrical

HEATING, AIR CONDITIONING & AUTOMATIC CLIMATE CONTROL SYSTEM

connections.
4. To the heater case fit the duct and tighten retaining screws.

Installation
1. Install the heater unit into position in the vehicle, ensuring all ducts are properly connected.
2. Tighten heater unit retaining screws/bolts and then install the upper bracket to each side.
3. Install the centre console as described in body chapter.

COMPONENT CHECK
Blower Motor
1. Connect battery voltage to terminal No 3 and negative battery terminal to No 1 on the electrical connector.
2. When the blower motor runs check that there is not excessive noise.

RESISTOR
1. Using a multi-meter check the resistance between the terminals of the resistor using the table below.

Terminal Numbers	Standard Value Ohm
No. 1 and No. 6	4.9 +/- 7 %
No. 1 and No. 3	1.25 +/- 7 %

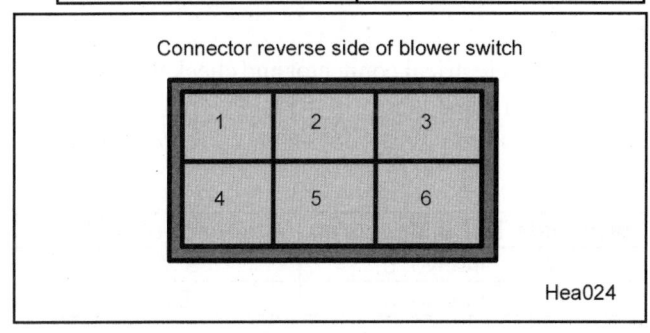

Connector reverse side of blower switch

Hea024

2. If the switch is found to be faulty repair or replace as required.

PTC HEATER
Remove the electrical connector and check that continuity exist between the terminal of the PTC heater using a multimeter.
Note: *If continuity does not exist check the condition of the electrical connector.*

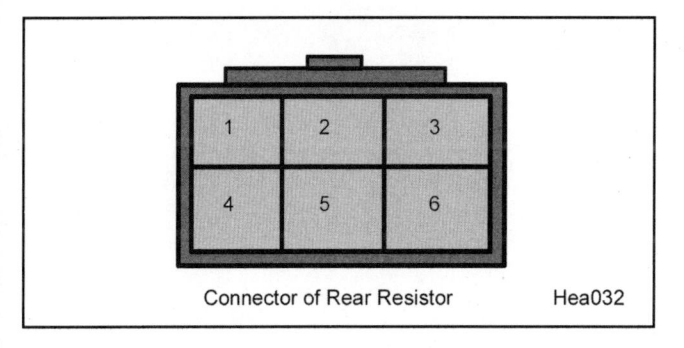

Connector of Rear Resistor   Hea032

RELAY
Disconnect the electrical connector and check the continuity of the relay using a multimeter. Refer to the table below.
Relay located in centre consul behind rear heater controls.

	Battery Voltage (applied to terminals)		Continuity b/w Terminals
	-ve	+ve	
Current Not Supplied	-	-	1 - 3
Current Supplied	3	1	2 - 5

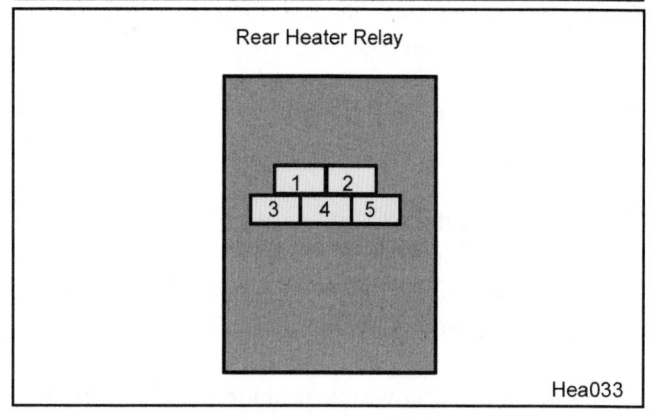

Rear Heater Relay

Hea033

HEATER UNIT AND BLOWER MOTOR (QUARTER TRIM)
Removal
1. Evacuate refrigerant system as outlined in this chapter.
   Note: *In most case the vehicle will have to be taken to a specialist to have the system evacuated and recharged, as specialist equipment is required.*
2. Drain the coolant from the cooling system then remove the rear mud guard, referring to body chapter if required.
3. Remove the four screws securing the heater cover and remove heater cover.
4. Disconnect the heater hose connections, then disconnect the suction & liquid pipes.
   Note: *Plug the hose connections for the suction and liquid pipes to prevent entry of foreign material, ensure the plugs are air tight to prevent moisture from entering.*
5. Remove the screws securing the heater unit in position then remove heater unit from vehicle.

Dismantle
1. Remove the tube accessory assembly and discard 'O-rings.
2. Remove the screws securing the heater cover, then remove the electrical harness.
3. Remove the screws securing the motor for the air mix damper and remove motor, then remove the air

HEATING, AIR CONDITIONING & AUTOMATIC CLIMATE CONTROL SYSTEM

thermo sensor.
4. Remove the heater core from the assembly, then remove the connector tube and expansion valve.
5. Remove the screws from the heater case, then separate heater case and remove evaporator.

Assembly
1. Install the evaporator into the heater case then tighten the heater case screws.
2. Install the expansion valve and connector tube to the case assembly, then install the heater core.
3. Install the air thermo sensor, then install the air mix damper motor and tighten retaining screws.
4. Install the electrical harness, then install the heater cover and tighten retaining screws.
5. Install the tube accessory assembly using new 'O-rings and tighten retaining screw.

Installation
1. Install the heater unit into position in the vehicle and tighten retaining screws.
2. Connect the heater hose connections, then reconnect the suction and liquid pipes, ensuring to use new 'O-rings.
3. Install the heater cover into position and tighten the four retaining screws, then install the rear mud guard.
4. Top up cooling system with specified coolant, then bleed the heater system of any air locks.
5. Check the operation of the heater.
6. Recharge system on vehicles with A/C.
   Note: *In most case the vehicle will have to be taken to a specialist to have the system evacuated and recharged, as specialist equipment is required.*

COMPONENT CHECK
Air Mix Damper Motor
Disconnect the electrical connector and apply battery voltage to the air mix damper motor using the table below as a guide.
Note: *When the control lever reaches its stopped position, disconnect the power otherwise the motor may be damaged.*

Terminal Number		Lever Position
1	2	
+	-	Cool Position
-	+	Hot Position

Air Mix Damper Motor Connector

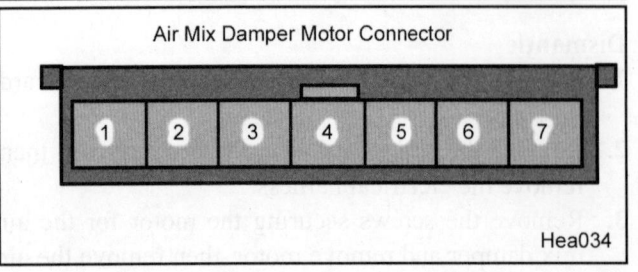

Hea034

Potentiometer
See illustration above
1. On NM - NP models the resistance needs to be checked between terminals No 1 and No 5, also No 3 and No 7 while power is being applied as described in the previous check.
2. On NS models only check terminals No 3 and No 5. The resistance value should change gradually within the standard value.
   Standard Value..................................1.2 - 4.8 kohm

Expansion Valve (Magnet Valve)
Disconnect the electrical connector and apply battery voltage to terminal number 1 of the expansion valve. Terminal number 2 needs to be earthed. When this is done an operating sound should be heard.

Blower Motor
1. a) On NM - NP models remove the electrical connector and apply battery voltage directly to terminal 1 and earth terminal 2.
   b) On NS models apply battery voltage to terminal No 1 and earth terminal No 3.
2. When the checks are done the motor should run without abnormal noise from within.

Resistor
Remove the electrical connector and check the ohm reading of the terminal below in the table.
Note: *If the readings are not achieved replace the resistor.*

Terminals To Be Measured	Standard ohm Value
No. 1 and No. 6	4.9 +/- 0.34
No. 1 and No. 3	2.15 +/- 0.15

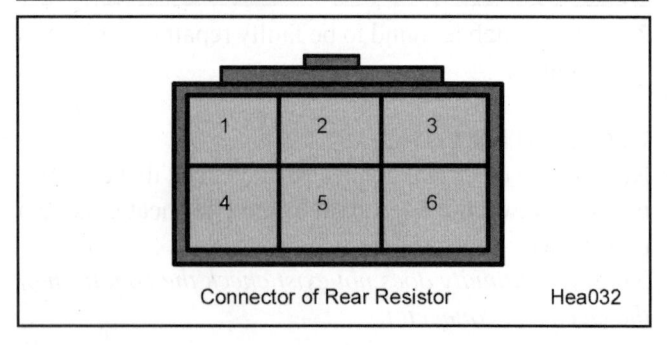

Connector of Rear Resistor   Hea032

432

AUTO CLIMATE CONTROL

DESCRIPTION & OPERATION

The control unit automatically controls the cabin temperature, the vehicle operator adjusts the temperature to the comfort level desired and the control system automatically adjusts to hold the temperature constant.

The automatic temperature control can also be overridden and used as a manual control unit similar to a standard vehicle.

PTC HEATER (4M41)
Inspection

Check that there is continuity between the two terminals with the connector disconnected. If no continuity exist the heater or wiring are faulty and will need to be replaced or repaired.

PTC HEATER SWITCH (4M41)
Inspection

1. Use a suitable tool covered with cloth to gently pry the heater switch out of the dash.
2. Remove the connector and use the table below to check the condition of the switch.
   Voltage at terminals 1,2 - 6 and 3 - 4 allowing indicator light to glow, with switch ON

PTC HEATER RELAY (4M41)
Inspection

Remove the relay from the vehicle and test its continuity using the table below as a guide. If faulty replace the relay.

Note: *The relay is located near the battery on 4M41 vehicles*

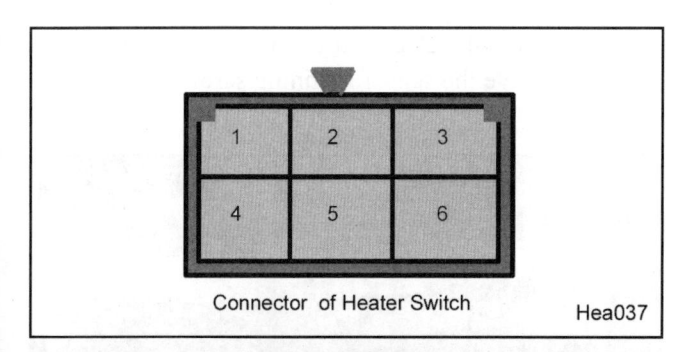

Connector of Heater Switch   Hea037

	Battery Voltage (applied to terminals)		Continuity b/w Terminals
	-ve	+ve	
Current Not Supplied	-	-	1 - 3
Current Supplied	3	1	2 - 5

IDLE UP OPERATION
Inspection (6G7 GDI)

1. Start the vehicle and let it idle for at least two minutes before checking it is idling at the recommended rate.
   Standard Idle Rate.......................... 600 +/- 50 rpm
   Note: *The idle speed is controlled by the ISC system and should not be adjusted.*
2. Turn the air conditioner on and run it as described below in the table. The rpm should be within specification.

A/C Under Low Load	700 +/- 50 rpm
A/C Under Medium Load	800 +/- 50 rpm
A/C Under High Load	1000 +/- 50 rpm

Inspection (4M41)

1. Start the vehicle and let it idle for at least two minutes before checking it is idling at the recommended rate.
   Standard Idle Rate.......................... 750 +/- 50 rpm
   Note: *If not adjust the idle rate, refer to the motor chapter.*
2. Turn the air conditioner on a check the idle rpm at the given conditions in the table below.

Air Conditioner Load	Engine rpm
A/C Under Low to Medium Load	800 +/- 50 rpm
A/C Under High Load	1000 +/- 50 rpm

BLOWER LINEAR CONTROLLER
Inspection

1. Turn on the ignition, leave the electrical connector connected.
2. Using a multimeter test the voltage at terminal No. 2 using the table below to check the results.

Blower Switch Position	Voltage At Terminal No2
Low Speed	4.0 V
Medium Speed	7.9 V
High Speed	13.7 V

AIR MIX DAMPER MOTOR
Inspection

1. Remove the electrical connector and apply battery voltage to the terminals in the table. Checking to make sure the motor lever turns the way as described in the table. If not replace motor.
   Note: *When the lever reaches its stopped position disconnect the battery voltage to ensure no damage is done to the motor.*

HEATING, AIR CONDITIONING & AUTOMATIC CLIMATE CONTROL SYSTEM

2. a) NM - NP Models

Terminal Number		Lever Position
1	2	
+	-	Hot Position
-	+	Cool Position

b) NS Models

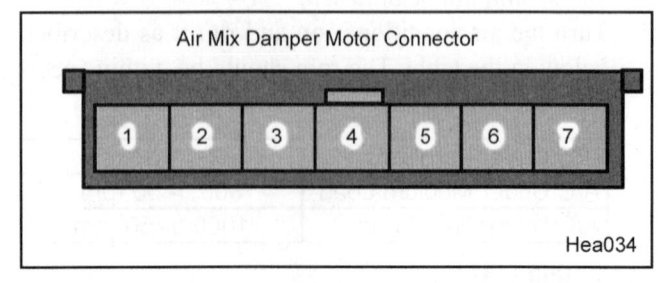

Air Mix Damper Motor Connector

Hea034

Terminal Number		Lever Position
1	2	
+	-	Cool Position
-	+	Hot Position

POTENTIOMETER
Inspection

1. a) On NM - NP models, while performing the checks on the air mix damper motor, use a multimeter on terminal numbers No. 3 and No. 5, also No. 3 and No. 7 to check the resistance.
   b) On NS models only check terminals No. 3 and No. 5.
   Note: *Check the resistance while the damper motor is changing from MAX. HOT to MAX. COOL position.*
2. The resistance reading should change gradually and be within these specification.
   Resistance: .... 0.96 - 5.76 Kohm

AIR OUTLET CHANGEOVER MOTOR
Inspection

Remove the electrical connector and apply battery voltage to the terminals in the table. Checking to make sure the damper lever turns the way as described in the table. If not replace motor.

Note: *When the lever reaches its stopped position disconnect the battery voltage to ensure no damage is done to the motor.*

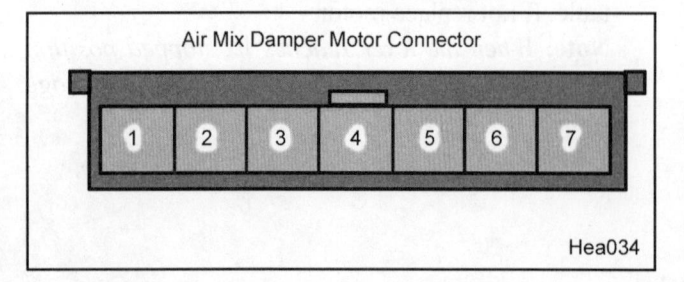

Air Mix Damper Motor Connector

Hea034

Battery Connection Terminal		Lever Operation
1	2	
+	-	Def Position
-	+	Face Position

HEATER WATER TEMPERATURE SENSOR
Inspection

Using a multimeter check the resistance between the electrical terminals using the chart below. The checks should be performed at more than two temperatures.

Resistance b/n the terminals	
Temperature Deg C	Value kOhm
20	approx 7Ohms
40	approx 3kOhms
60	approx 2kOhms

Installation

Install the temperature sensor into the mounting hole in the heater unit, using the clip to secure it.

PHOTO SENSOR

Located in the centre of the dash near the front windscreen.

Inspection

Cover the receiver section of the sensor with your hand to block out the sunlight. If the sensor is okay the blower motor should reduce its speed. If not replace the sensor making sure the motor is operating correctly. If needed refer to blower motor check earlier in the chapter.

OUTSIDE AIR TEMPERATURE SENSOR

Sensor located behind grille/front bumper near horn.
Removal

1. From the front bumper bar remove the lower under grille.
2. Disconnect the electrical connector from the sensor and remove the sensor retaining screw.

Outside Temperature Sensor Location

Hea036

434

Inspection

Disconnect the electrical connector and measure the resistance of the terminals using the below table as a guide. Take two or three readings at different temperatures. If the sensor is not within the range it will need to be replaced

Resistance b/n the terminals	
Temperature Deg C	Value kOhm
10	approx 3.5kOhms
20	approx 2.1kOhms
30	approx 1.5kOhms

Installation

1. Install the sensor into position and secure with retaining screw.
2. Reinstall the lower under grille to the front bumper.

PROBLEM DIAGNOSIS

Condition - Insufficient / No Heat or Demist

CAUSE: Low radiator coolant due to coolant leaks.
ACTION: Fill radiator if necessary, check for leaks.
CAUSE: Low radiator coolant due to engine over heating.
ACTION: Remove bugs, etc from radiator. Check for loose drive belt, sticking thermostat, incorrect ignition timing.
CAUSE: Plugged or partially plugged heater core.
ACTION: Clean and back-flush engine cooling system and heater core.

Condition - Too Much Heat

CAUSE: Loose or improperly adjusted control cables.
ACTION: Adjust as required.

AIR-CONDITIONER COMPRESSOR DIAGNOSIS

Problem: Oil Leaks

Remedy: Inspect for leaks.
Oil leaks do not necessarily indicate leaking refrigerant, check for oil leaks around the following components:
- Shaft seal, leak test area between clutch and compressor.
- Hose fittings.
- Compressor housing.

Thoroughly clean around compressor and components with detergent and hot water, starting detection procedures. Follow supplier instructions for the proper techniques to be used for 'ELECTRONIC' Leak Detectors.

Another useful test is a soap bubble test. Apply a soapy mixture around all joints or possible leak areas, start air conditioner and turn on to high operation, check for bubbles. If bubbles are found at any section or joint where the soapy solution was applied it will indicate a leak requiring repair.

Problem: Bearing Noise

Remedy: Carry out the following procedure: Remove belt. Disengage clutch. Rotate rotor pulley by hand. Listen for bearing noise. Feel for hard spots. If excessive, repair or replace compressor.

* All compressors have operating noise, this should not be mistaken for a faulty compressor.

Problem: Suspect bearing or seal failure.

Remedy: Discharge the system, disengage clutch, rotate front plate by hand. While rotating, if severe rough spots or 'catches' are felt, repair or replace the compressor.

Problem: Compressor noise.

Remedy: Visual inspection of:
Broken or loose bolts at compressor and engine fixing points - replace and/or torque bolts to specifications.
Broken bracket and/or compressor body mounting - replace broken component.
Oil level - insufficient oil can cause unusual noise.
Drive belt not at correct tension.
Generator bearing noisy - replace.
Water pump bearing noisy - replace.
Loose engine mounting bolts - re-torque.
Low refrigerant charge. Low charge can be determined by low suction pressure together with low head pressure.

AUTOMATIC CLIMATE CONTROL

* Before carrying out diagnostic procedures ensure the air ducts are not blocked or become disengaged.
* Also ensure connectors are disconnected when checking components.

Automatic Air-conditioning Service Diagnosis Chart

#	Condition	Possible Cause	Solution
1	When car is running air-conditioner does not operate	Power circuit harness open-circuited	Repair or replace harness
		Control panel defective	Replace control panel
		Air-conditioner control unit defective	Replace air-conditioner control unit
		Engine coolant temperature switch defective	Replace coolant temperature switch
2	Interior temperature does not increase (no warm air)	Room-temperature sensor input circuit defective	Replace defective parts
		Air mix damper potentiometer input circuit defective	
		Air mix damper drive motor defective	Replace air mix damper drive motor
		Air mix damper drive motor lever and air mix damper engagement incorrect	Correctly engage
		Air mix damper sticking	Correct air mix damper
		Harness open-circuited b/w air mix damper drive motor and a/c control unit	Replace or repair harness
		Control panel defective	Replace control unit
		Air conditioner control unit defective	Replace air conditioner control unit
3	Interior temperature does not decrease (no cold air)	Room-temperature sensor input circuit defective	Replace defective parts
		Outside-air-temperature sensor input circuit defective	
		Air thermo sensor input circuit defective	
		Refrigerant-temperature sensor input circuit defective	
		Air mix damper potentiometer input circuit defective	
		Photo sensor defective	Replace photo sensor
		Air mix damper drive motor defective	Replace air mix damper drive motor
		Air mix damper drive motor lever and air mix damper engagement incorrect	Correctly engage
		Air mix damper sticking	Correct air mix damper
		Harness open-circuited b/w air mix damper drive motor and a/c control unit	Replace or repair harness
		Harness open-circuited b/w photo sensor and a/c control unit	
		Air conditioner compressor relay defective	Replace relay
		Water-temperature sensor defective	Replace water-temperature sensor
		Refrigerant leak	Repair and recharge system
		Air inlet sensor defective	Replace air inlet sensor
		Magnetic clutch defective	Replace magnetic clutch
		Belt lock controller defective	Replace belt lock controller
		Control panel defective	Replace control panel
		Air conditioner control unit defective	Replace air conditioner control unit
4	Blower motor does not rotate	Blower motor defective	Replace blower motor
		Thermal fuse blown (inside power transistor)	Replace power transistor
		Heater relay defective	Replace heater relay
		Harness open-circuited b/w fuse and heater relay	Replace or repair harness
		Harness open-circuited b/w heater relay and blower motor	
		Harness open-circuited b/w power transistor and a/c control unit	
		Control panel defective	Replace control panel
		Air conditioner control unit defective	Replace air conditioner control unit
5	Blower motor does not stop rotating	Blower motor defective	Replace power relay
		Harness short-circuited b/w blower motor relay and power transistor air conditioner control unit	Replace or repair harness
		Control panel defective	Replace control panel
		Air conditioner control unit defective	Replace air conditioner control unit
6	Inside/outside air selector damper does not operate	Inside/outside air selector drive motor defective	Replace inside/outside air selector drive motor
		Inside/outside air selector drive motor and inside/outside air selector damper engagement incorrect	Correctly engage
		Inside/outside air selector damper malfunction	Correct inside/outside air selector damper
		Harness open-circuited b/w inside/outside air selector motor & a/c control unit	Replace or repair harness
		Control panel defective	Replace control panel
		Air conditioner control unit defective	Replace air conditioner control unit
7	Outside selector damper does not operate	Outlet selector damper potentiometer input circuit defective	Replace defective parts
		Outlet selector drive motor defective	Replace outlet selector drive motor
		Outlet selector drive motor and outlet selector damper engagement incorrect	Correctly engage
		DEF, FACE and FOOT damper malfunctioning	Correct DEF, FACE and FOOT damper
		Harness open-circuited b/w outlet selector motor & control unit	Replace or repair harness
		Control panel defective	Replace control panel
		Air conditioner control unit defective	Replace air conditioner control unit
8	When air conditioner is activated condenser fan does not operate	Condenser fan motor relay defective	Replace power relay
		Water temperature switch defective	Replace water temperature switch
		Condenser fan motor defective	Replace condenser fan motor

HEATING, AIR CONDITIONING & AUTOMATIC CLIMATE CONTROL SYSTEM

Automatic Air-Conditioning Inspection Chart

Inspection Point	Inspection Check	Condition - Normal	Condition - Abnormal	Possible Cause	Solution
Room-temperature sensor	Room temperature at 25°C, measure sensor resistance	Approx 1.7 kOhms	Deviates largely from approx 1.7 kOhms	Room temperature sensor defective	Replace room temperature sensor
	Room temperature at 25°C, measure voltage across terminal 15 of a/c control unit and ground	Approx 2.7-3.1 V	—	Harness open-circuited b/w room-temperature sensor and a/c control unit	Repair or replace harness
		—	Outside approx 2.7-3.1 V	A/C control unit connector has poor connection or a/c control unit defective	Fix connector connection or replace control unit
Outside-air-temperature sensor	Ambient temperature at 25°C, measure sensor resistance	Approx 1.5 kOhms	Deviates largely from approx 1.5 kOhms	Outside-air sensor defective	Replace outside-air-temperature sensor
	Ambient temperature at 25°C, measure voltage across terminal 6 of a/c control unit and ground	Approx 2.6-3.1 V	—	Harness open-circuited b/w outside-air-temperature sensor and a/c control unit	Repair or replace harness
		—	Outside approx 2.6-3.1 V	A/C control unit connector has poor connection or a/c control unit defective	Fix connector connection or replace control unit
Water temperature sensor	Water temperature b/w 22.5°C & 30.5°C, measure sensor resistance	Approx 4-5.6 kOhms	Deviates largely from approx 4-5.6 kOhms	Water-temperature sensor defective	Replace water-temperature sensor
	Water temperature b/w 22.5°C & 30.5°C, measure voltage across terminal 3 of a/c control unit and ground	Approx 2.4-3.2 V	—	Harness open-circuited b/w water-temperature sensor and a/c control unit	Repair or replace harness
		—	Deviates largely from approx 2.4-3.2 V	A/C control unit connector has poor connection or a/c control unit defective	Fix connector connection or replace control unit
Air thermo sensor	Sensors sensing temperature is 25°C, measure sensor resistance	Approx 1.5 kOhms	Deviates largely from approx 1.5 kOhms	Air thermo sensor defective	Replace air thermo sensor
	Sensors sensing temperature is 25°C, measure voltage across terminal 14 of a/c control unit and ground	Approx 2.6-3.1 V	—	Harness open-circuited b/w air thermo sensor and a/c control unit	Repair or replace harness
		—	Outside approx 2.6-3.1 V	A/C control unit connector has poor connection or a/c control unit defective	Fix connector connection or replace control unit
Air mix damper potentiometer				Air mix damper potentiometer defective	Replace air mix damper potentiometer
	Potentiometer at MAX COOL position, measure voltage across terminal 3 of a/c control unit and ground	Approx 0.9-1.1 V	—	Harness open-circuited b/w air mix damper potentiometer and a/c control unit	Repair or replace harness
		—	Outside approx 0.9-1.1 V	A/C control unit connector has poor connection or a/c control unit defective	Fix connector connection or replace control unit
Outlet selector damper potentiometer				Outlet selector damper potentiometer defective	Replace outlet selector damper potentiometer
	Potentiometer in FACE position, measure voltage across terminal 3 of a/c control unit and ground	Approx 3.8-4.2 V	—	Harness open-circuited b/w outlet selector damper potentiometer and a/c control unit	Repair or replace harness
		—	Outside approx 3.8-4.2 V	A/C control unit connector has poor connection or a/c control unit defective	Fix connector connection or replace control unit

BODY ELECTRICAL

(instruments, lights, cruise control etc.)

Subject	Page
SERVICE OPERATIONS	439
Instrument Cluster	439
Removal	439
Installation	440
Service Reminder - NS/NT	440
Cancel service Reminder Warning	440
How to Set Schedule	440
Tachometer Check	440
Combination Switch (column switch)	440
Switch Removal	440
Inspection	441
Switch Installation	441
Switch Body Removal	441
Switch Body Installation	441
Clock, RV Meter & Centre Display	441
Removal	441
Installation	441
RADIO - STEREO SYSTEM	442
Radio Cassette Unit - NM/NP	442
CD Changer - NM/NP	442
Radio Cassette Unit - NS/NT	442
Door Speakers	443
Front Speaker - NS/NT	443
Front Tweeters	443
Rear Tweeters	443
Rear Speakers - Short Wheel Base	443
Rear Speakers - Long Wheel Base	444
Amplifier	444
Sub-Woofer	444
Manual Antenna	444
Power Antenna	444
Glass Antenna	444
SWITCHES & COMPONENTS	445
Speedometer Sensor	445
Speed Alarm ECU	445
Removal/Installation	445
ECU Terminal Voltage Inspection	445
Power Window Switches	445

Subject	Page
Ignition Switch & Immobilizer	445
Ignition Switch Continuity Check	446
Immobilizer ECU - Diesel	446
Key Pad Battery Replacement	446
Keypad Programming	446
Theft Alarm System	446
Theft Alarm Horn Relay Check	446
Theft Alarm Horn	447
Installation	447
Accessory Socket	447
Reversing Sensor - NS/NT	447
Reversing Sensor ECU - NS/NT	447
SRS - AIRBAGS	448
Service Precautions	448
Drivers Airbag (front)	448
Passenger Airbag (front)	448
Side Airbag	448
Front Impact Sensors	448
Side Impact Sensors	449
SRS - ECU	449
Seat Belts With Pretensioner - Front	450
Removal/Installation	450
Pre-installation procedure	450
Inspection Chart & Codes	450
HORN ASSEMBLY	451
Removal	451
Relay Continuity Check	451
Installation	451
Horn Actuator	451
CRUISE CONTROL SYSTEM	451
Component Testing - NM/NP	451
Component Testing - NS/NT	451
Cruise Control Switch - Steering Wheel	452
Removal	452
Switch Resistance	452
Installation	452
Stop Lamp Switch Inspection	452

BODY ELECTRICAL - Service Procedures

Subject	Page
Inhibitor Switch Inspection	452
Clutch Pedal Switch Inspection	452
Throttle Position Switch	453
Electric Vacuum Pump	453
Inspection	453
Removal	453
Installation	453
Vacuum Actuator	453
Cruise Control ECU	453
Removal	453
Installation	453
LIGHTS & SWITCHES	454
Headlight Globe Replacement - NM/NP	454
Standard Type	454
Discharge Type	454
Headlight Globe Replacement - NS/NT	454
Headlamp Assembly - All	454
Headlamp Automatic Levelling Motor Test	455
Headlamp Automatic Levelling ECU	455
Headlamp Automatic Levelling Height Sensors	455
Front Height Sensor	455
Rear Height Sensor	455
Adjust Headlight Pattern	455
Front Fog Lamps (2001-2002)	456
Removal/Installation	456
Adjustment	456
Front Fog Lamps (2003 onwards)	456
Removal/Installation	456
Adjustment	457
Side Turn Signal Lamp	457
Door Mirror Side Turn Signal Lamp	457
Licence Plate Lamp Globe Replacement	457
Rear Combination Lamp	458
Globe Replacement	458
Removal	458
Installation	458
Rear Lamp (in bumper)	458
Globe Replacement	458
Removal	458
Installation	459
High Mount Stop Lamp	459
Side Step Illumination	459
Side Step Illumination - ECU	459
Interior Lamp	459
Interior Lamp Switch	460
Photo Sensor	460
Stop Lamp Switch	460
Fog Lamp Switch	460
Hazard Light Switch	460
SPECIFICATIONS	461

SERVICE OPERATIONS

INSTRUMENT CLUSTER
Removal

1. Lower the steering column to its lowest setting.
2. **NM-NP:** Remove the screws securing the instrument cluster facia, then remove the facia assembly.

NS-NT: Remove the instrument cluster facia by carefully releasing the facia retaining clips.

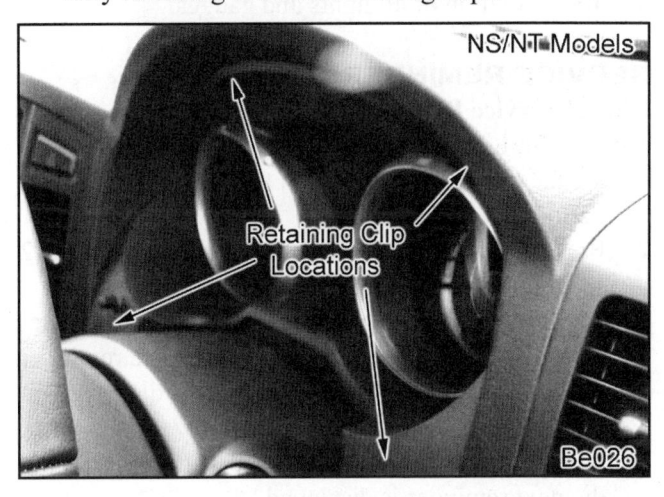

3. Remove the screws securing the instrument cluster, then partially remove instrument cluster from vehicle.

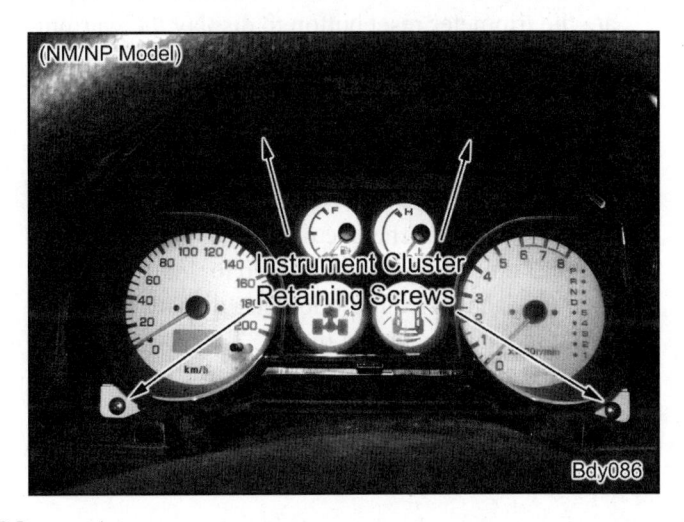

BODY ELECTRICAL - Service Procedures

NS Model

Bdy072

4. Disconnect electrical wiring harness and remove instrument cluster from vehicle.

Installation
1. Partially install instrument cluster and reconnect electrical wiring harness.
2. Fully install the instrument cluster into position and tighten the retaining screws.
3. Install the instrument facia into position and tighten the retaining screws.
4. Test operation of all lights and gauges.

SERVICE REMINDER - NS / NT
Cancel Service Reminder Warning
1. Turn the ignition switch to the Off position, then operate the tripmeter reset button to display the warning period on the odometer.
2. Press and hold the reset button for longer than 1.2 seconds, the service reminder indicator flashes.
3. With the reminder indicator flashing press the tripmeter reset switch for less than 1.2 seconds. The reminder indicator is turned ON and "CLEAR is displayed on the odometer display for 3 seconds.
4. After "CLEAR" is displayed the warning period to the next reminder is displayed.

How To Set Schedule
1. Turn the ignition switch to the Off position, then operate the tripmeter reset button to display the warning period on the odometer.
2. Press and the reset button 3 times ensuring to hold for longer than 1.2 seconds each time. The reminder indicator is turned ON and the current schedule is displayed.
3. With the current schedule displayed, press the reset button 3 times ensuring not to hold for longer than 1.2 seconds each time. The odometer display is shifted to the schedule selection mode.
4. Pressing the tripmeter reset button for less than 1.2 seconds changes the schedule. Pressing the switch for longer than 1.2 seconds sets the schedule.

TACHOMETER CHECK
1. Connect a engine tachometer to the engine speed detection terminal as shown.

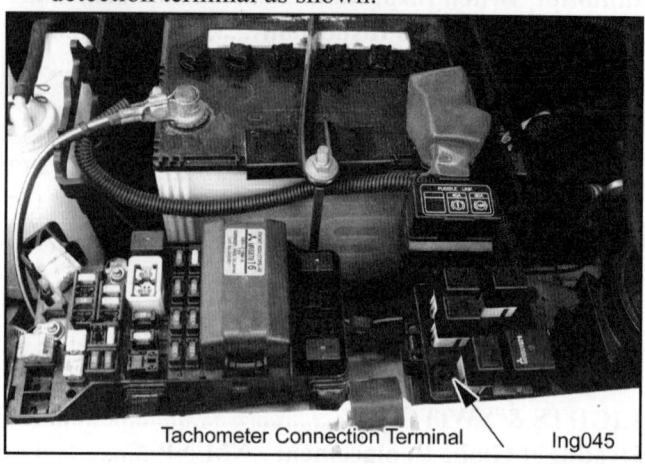

Ing045

2. Compare the engine tachometer reading with the vehicle tachometer reading and ensure display errors are within specification.

Engine Speed RPM		Display Error RPM
700		+/- 120
2,000	Petrol	+225/- 175
	Diesel	+/- 175
3,000	Petrol	+300/- 75
	Diesel	+/- 225
4,000	Petrol	+375/- 225
	Diesel	+/- 300
4,750	Diesel	+/- 260
5,000	Petrol	+425/- 225
6,000	Petrol	+475/- 225

COMBINATION SWITCH (Column switch)
Operates the headlights, turn signal and wipers.

Removal
1. Lower the steering column to the lowest position then remove the screws securing the column covers.
2. Release the retaining clip and remove the wiper/washer switch.
3. Release the retaining clip and remove the lighting switch.

Be016

BODY ELECTRICAL - Service Procedures

Inspection

1. Check the lighting switch continuity, refer to the following table.

Switch Position	Continuity b/w Terminals
Off	-
Tail gate lamps	3 - 7
Headlamps	3 - 6
Passing lamps	3 - 8
Dimmer	3 - 9
Turn-signal lamp (R)	3 - 10
Turn-signal lamp (L)	3 - 11

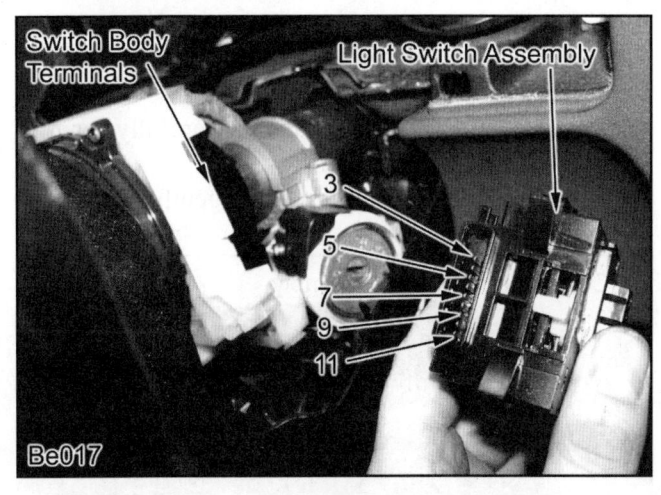

2. Switch Body (column) continuity check.
   With the lighting switch and the wiper/washer switch removed from the switch base, check that continuity exists between the corresponding terminals on either side of the switch body from terminals 3 to 11.
   i.e. Continuity b/w terminal 3 on each side of the switch. Then check continuity b/w #4 terminals, and continue this process to #11 terminals.

Installation

1. Press the lighting switch into position ensuring the retaining clips engage correctly.
2. Press the wiper/washer switch into position ensuring the retaining clips engage correctly.
3. Install the steering column covers.

Switch Body Removal

1. Remove the airbag module, steering wheel and clock spring, referring to the Steering Chapter for assistance.
2. Remove the screws securing the column covers, then remove the column covers.
3. Disconnect the combination switch electrical connection and release the harness retainers.
4. Remove the switch assembly retaining screws, then remove the combination switch body from the steering column.

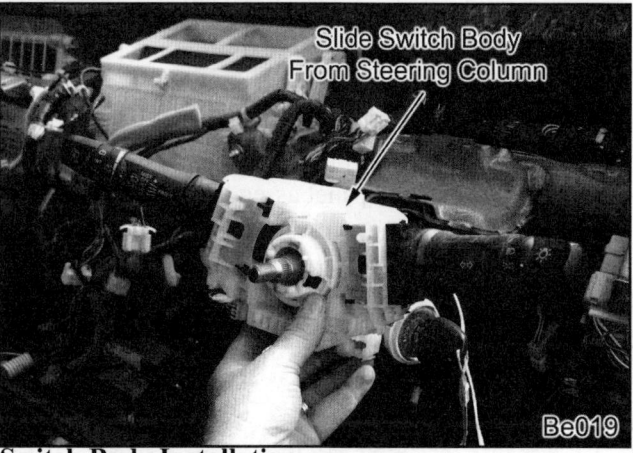

Switch Body Installation

1. Install the combination switch into position and tighten the retaining screws.
2. Correctly position the wiring loom, secure with harness retainers and reconnect to switch assembly.
3. Install the steering column covers, clock spring, steering wheel and air bag module as described in the steering chapter.

CLOCK, RV METER & CENTRE DISPLAY

Removal

1. Remove the two screws from the top of the centre panel then remove panel from vehicle, disconnecting any electrical connections.
2. Remove the screws retaining the clock assembly, then slide out clock and disconnect electrical connections.
3. Remove the screws retaining the centre display/RV meter, then slide out unit and disconnect electrical connections.
4. If required remove the mounting brackets from the display unit.

Installation

1. In required fit the mounting brackets to the centre display/RV meter unit.
2. Connect electrical connections to the display unit, then slide into position and tighten retaining screws.
3. Connect electrical connections to the clock then slide into position, install and tighten retaining screws.
4. Install the centre panel into position ensuring all retaining clips are properly engaged, then install and tighten the two retaining screws.

RADIO - STEREO SYSTEM

RADIO CASSETTE UNIT - NM/NP
Removal
1. Remove the centre panel assembly by removing the two upper retaining screws, slide panel forward, disconnect electrical connections and remove panel.

2. Remove the four mounting screws from the bracket.
3. Pull radio/cassette unit out sufficiently to access electrical connectors at rear of radio/cassette unit.
4. Disconnect electrical connectors and antenna connector and remove unit from vehicle.

Installation
1. Connect electrical connectors and antenna connector to rear of radio/cassette. Install radio/cassette.
2. Install the four mounting screws to the bracket.

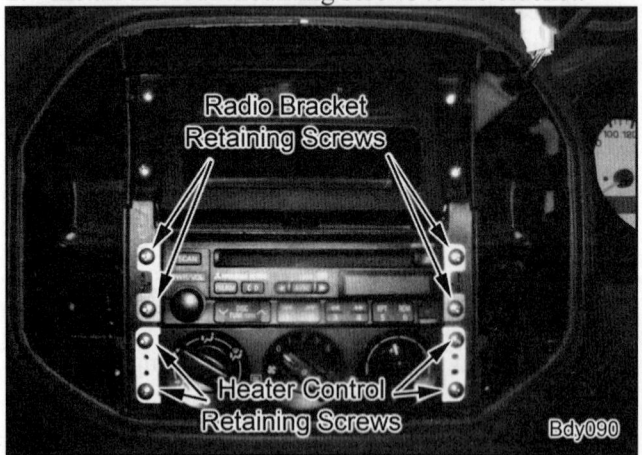

3. Replace the centre panel ensuring to reconnect any electrical connections then tighten the upper retaining screws.
4. Test operation of the radio/cassette unit.

CD AUTO CHANGER - NM/NP
Removal
1. Remove the lower centre panel assembly, refer to body chapter if required.
2. Remove the four mounting bracket screws.
3. Pull CD changer unit out sufficiently to access electrical connections at rear of unit.
4. Disconnect electrical connections and remove unit from vehicle.

Installation
1. Connect electrical connections and install CD changer unit into position and tighten the retaining screws.
2. Replace the lower centre panel, refer to body chapter if required.
3. Test operation of CD changer unit.

RADIO/STEREO UNIT - NS / NT
Removal
1. Remove the centre lower panel by carefully levering out to release retaining clips.
2. Remove the centre air outlets by gently prising out as shown in diagram.

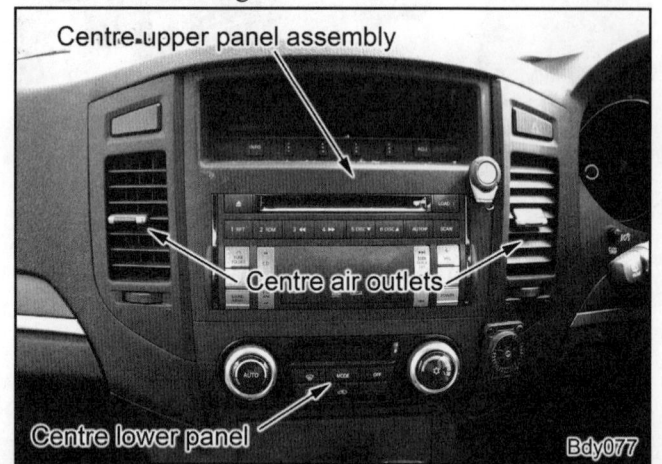

3. Remove the centre upper panel assembly by carefully levering at retaining clips, disconnect any electrical connections and remove panel.
4. Remove the radio/stereo unit retaining screws, pull stereo unit out sufficiently to access electrical connectors at rear of unit.
5. Disconnect electrical connectors and antenna connector and remove unit from vehicle.

BODY ELECTRICAL - Stereo System

Installation

1. Connect electrical connectors and antenna connector to rear of radio/stereo and slide unit into position.
2. Install and tighten the unit mounting screws, then install the centre upper panel assembly.
3. Install the centre air outlets and lower centre panel to the instrument panel, then test the operation of the stereo unit.

DOOR SPEAKERS
Removal

1. Remove the door trim panel, refer to body chapter.
2. Remove the speaker retaining screws securing the speaker to the inner door panel. 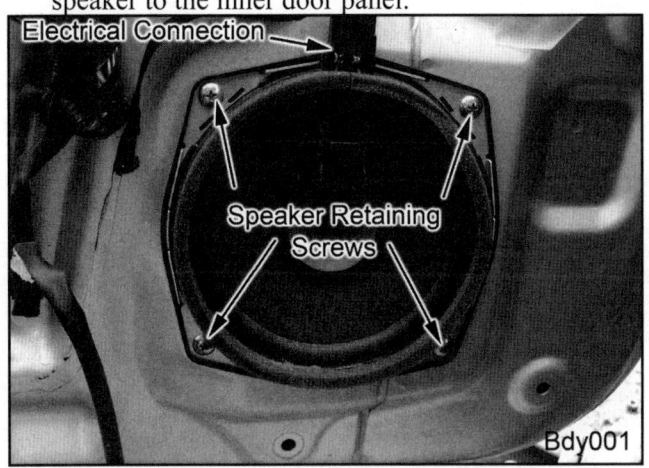
3. Disconnect the electrical connection and remove speaker.

Installation

1. Install the speaker into position and reconnect the electrical connections.
2. Tighten the speaker retaining screws then replace the door trim panel as described in body chapter.

FRONT SPEAKER - NS / NT
Removal

1. Remove the front speaker garnish by gently prying from the centre top of the instrument panel.
2. Remove the screws retaining the speaker bracket, disconnect the electrical connection and fully remove speaker assembly.
3. If required remove the screws securing the speaker to the speaker bracket separate speaker from bracket.

Installation

1. Install speaker to speaker bracket and tighten retaining screws.
2. Reconnect speaker electrical connection and position assembly into place, tightening retaining screws.
3. Press the speaker garnish into position by hand and then test operation of the speaker to ensure it works correctly.

FRONT TWEETERS
Removal

1. Remove the delta inner cover by carefully levering with a screwdriver. 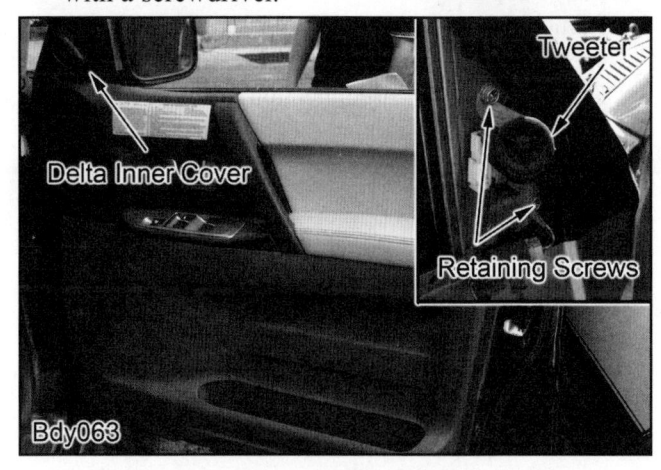
2. Remove screws securing the speaker, then disconnect the electrical connection and remove speaker.

Installation

1. Replace the speakers into position and reconnect the electrical connections.
2. Tighten retaining screws and press the delta cover into position.

REAR TWEETERS
Removal

1. Remove the rear door trim, referring to body chapter for assistance.
2. From the back of the door trim panel remove the tweeter bracket, then remove the tweeter from trim.

Installation

1. Install the tweeter into position and secure with retaining bracket.
2. Install door trim as described in body chapter, then text operation of speaker.

REAR SPEAKERS - Short Wheelbase
Removal

1. Remove the rear quarter lower trim panel as described in the body chapter.
2. Remove the speaker retaining screws securing the speaker to the rear quarter panel, then disconnect the electrical connection and remove speaker.

Installation

1. Install the speaker into position reconnecting the electrical connections.
2. Tighten the speaker retaining screws then replace the rear quarter trim panel as described in body chapter.

BODY ELECTRICAL - Stereo System

REAR SPEAKERS - Long Wheelbase
Removal
1. Remove the rear door trim panel as described in the body chapter.
2. Remove the speaker retaining screws securing the speaker to the inner door panel.
3. Disconnect electrical connection and remove speaker, then remove the speaker bracket retaining screws and bracket if required.

Installation
1. If removed install speaker bracket to door assembly and tighten retaining screws.
2. Install the speaker into position and reconnect the electrical connections.
3. Tighten the speaker retaining screws then replace the door trim panel as described in body chapter.

AMPLIFIER
Removal
1. Remove the lower rear quarter trim panel from the left hand side, then remove the rear speaker box assembly.
2. Remove the screws securing the amplifier, then disconnect electrical connections and remove amplifier.
3. If required, remove the screws securing the amplifier bracket and remove bracket from vehicle.

Installation
1. Install the amplifier bracket into location and tighten the retaining screws.
2. Reconnect electrical connection to amplifier, then install amplifier and tighten retaining screws.
3. Install the rear speaker box, then install the lower quarter trim panel.

SUB-WOOFER
Removal
1. Remove the lower quarter trim panel from the left hand side.
2. Remove the screws securing the speaker to the speaker box, disconnect electrical connection and fully remove speaker from vehicle.
3. If required remove the speaker box from the rear quarter panel.

Installation
1. If removed, install the speaker box to the rear quarter panel.
2. Reconnect the speaker electrical connection, then install speaker into position and tighten retaining screws.
3. Install the lower quarter trim panel and test to ensure speaker operates correctly.

MANUAL ANTENNA / AERIAL
Removal
1. Remove the scuff plate and cowl trim panel retaining screws, then remove scuff plate and panel.
2. Remove centre facia panel, refer to body chapter.
3. Remove radio unit and disconnect antenna cable.
4. Release the antenna cable retaining tape, then remove antenna retaining screws.
5. Remove the antenna and cable from pillar.

Installation
Installation is the reverse of the removal procedure. Ensure antenna cable is routed correctly.

POWER ANTENNA / AERIAL
Removal
1. Remove the passenger side kick panel, then disconnect the aerial lead.
2. From the end of the aerial mast, remove the retaining nut and base.
3. Raise the vehicle and secure on safety stands then remove the passenger side front wheel.
4. Remove the screws securing the mud flap and splash shield to the underside of the mudguard and then remove splashshield from vehicle.
5. Prise the sealing grommet from the inner guard then withdraw the aerial lead.
6. Disconnect electrical connection for the antenna.
7. While supporting the antenna unit remove the assembly retaining bolts/nuts then carefully remove unit from vehicle.

Installation
1. Install the aerial assembly into position, ensuring it is fully installed against the mudguard.
2. Install and tighten the assembly retaining bolts/nuts, then to the aerial mast install then base and tighten the chrome retaining nut.
3. Connect the electrical connection for the power antenna, then feed the aerial lead into the vehicle install the sealing grommet.
   Note: *It may be necessary to apply a small amount of sealant to the grommet to prevent water leaks.*
4. Install the splash shield and mud flap into position and tighten retaining screws, then install the wheel and lower vehicle to ground.
5. Inside the vehicle reconnect he aerial lead, then install the kick panel.
6. Check operation of power antenna to ensure it is working correctly.

GLASS ANTENNA
Glass antenna is incorporated into the rear quarter windows.

COMPONENTS & SWITCHES

SPEEDOMETER SENSOR

Removal
1. Raise vehicle and support on axle stands.
2. Disconnect electrical connection from vehicle speed sensor, then remove retaining bolt.
3. Remove vehicle speed sensor from vehicle.

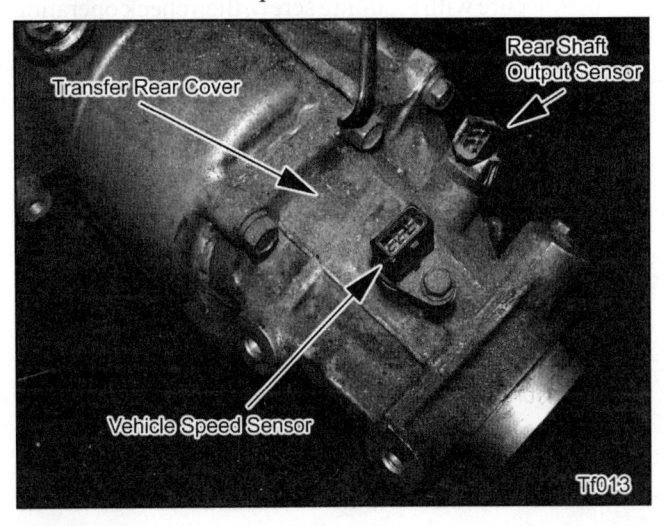

Inspection
1. Raise the rear of the vehicle and secure on jack stands.
2. Disconnect the vehicle speed sensor electrical connection.
3. Connect a 3-10 kOhm resistance to the speed sensor.
4. Using a multimeter check the change in voltage between terminals 2 and 3 when turning the propeller shaft.
   Correct reading .... 4 pulses per rotation
5. Reconnect electrical connection and lower vehicle.

Installation
1. Install vehicle speed sensor and tighten retaining bolt.
2. Reconnect electrical connection and lower vehicle.
3. Drive vehicle to test operation of speedometer.

SPEED ALARM ECU
Note: *Limited Vehicles are equiped with speed alarm ECU. This information is only valid for limited vehicles.*

Removal
1. Remove the drivers side lower instrument panel, refer to body chapter in required.
2. Remove the nut securing the speed alarm ECU, disconnect electrical connection and remove ECU.

Installation
1. Reconnect electrical connection and install ECU into position and tighten retaining nut to specification.
   Speed Alarm ECU Nut 5Nm
2. Install the lower instrument panel trim, referring to body chapter if required.

ECU Terminal Voltage Inspection

Terminal	Item	Condition	Value
1	Ignition switch (IG1) power supply	Ignition switch: Lock (Off)	0V
		Ignition switch: On	Battery Voltage
4	Speed sensor signal input	Vehicle being driven	0-12V (pulse signal)
8	Earth	At all times	0V

POWER WINDOW SWITCHES

Removal
1. From the arm rest use a screwdriver to carefully pry the switch panel out.
2. Disconnect the electrical connections and remove the switch assembly.

Installation
1. Reconnect the electrical connections to the switch assembly.
2. Press into position in the arm rest.

IGNITION SWITCH & IMMOBILIZER

Removal
1. Remove the steering wheel as described in the steering chapter.
2. Remove instrument panel lower cover and then remove the lower and upper steering column covers.
3. Remove the combination switch, refer to steering chapter if required.
4. Insert the key in the steering lock cylinder and turn to ACC position.
5. Using a small phillips screwdriver push the lock pin inwards and pull out the lock cylinder.

BODY ELECTRICAL - Components & Switches

6. Remove the ignition switch and the key reminder switch.
7. **Petrol** - Remove the screw securing the Immobilizer-ECU and remove assembly.

Installation
1. **Petrol** - Install the Immobilizer-ECU and tighten the retaining screw.
2. Install ignition switch and the key reminder switch.
3. Insert new lock cylinder into assembly and ensure locking pin engages.
4. Install the combination switch, then reconnect electrical connections.
5. Install steering column upper and lower covers, then install the lower instrument panel lower cover.
6. Install steering wheel as described in steering chapter.

IGNITION SWITCH CONTINUITY CHECK
Disconnect the ignition switch connector and check for continuity using the following table.

Switch Position	Continuity b/w Terminals
LOCK	
ACC	1 - 6
ON	1 - 2 - 4 - 6
START	1 - 2 - 5

Ignition Switch Connector
(for testing do not remove from vehicle) Be021

IMMOBILIZER ECU - DIESEL
The immobilizer for the diesel vehicles (4M40) is located behind the lower centre panel and centre console on the drivers side.

Removal
1. Remove the lower centre panel and front section of the centre console, refer to body chapter for assistance.
2. Disconnect the electrical connector from the immobilizer-ECU, then remove the ECU assembly.

Installation
1. Install the ECU into position, then reconnect the electrical connection.

2. Install the instrument panel centre lower panel and front centre console, referring to body chapter id required.

KEY PAD
Battery Replacement
1. Remove the screw securing the key pad, then gently separate the key pad.
2. Remove old battery and install new battery.
3. Carefully assemble the ensuring the O-ring is in place then secure with retaining screw, then check operation of each switch.

KEY PAD PROGRAMMING
Once teach mode is entered all existing codes will be deleted. Ensure you have all keypad which are to programmed for use on the vehicle.
1. Insert the ignition key in the ignition switch, then connect terminal 1 of the diagnostic connector to earth.
2. Within 10 seconds press the hazard switch 6 times.
   * *The doors will lock and unlock once after pressing the hazard switch 6 times and the system will switch to recognition mode.*
3. Press the transmitter lock or unlock switch then press another 2 times within 10 seconds to register the code. After registration the doors will be locked and unlocked automatically.
4. The same procedure should be used for additional transmitters within 1 minute of the first transmitter registration.
5. The teach mode will be terminated if any of the following occur.
   a) The ignition key is removed.
   b) One minute after registration mode started.
   c) 4 remote's/keys have been taught to the module.
   d) Earth is released.

THEFT ALARM SYSTEM
Theft Alarm Horn Relay Continuity Check
Refer to diagram for location of theft alarm horn relay.

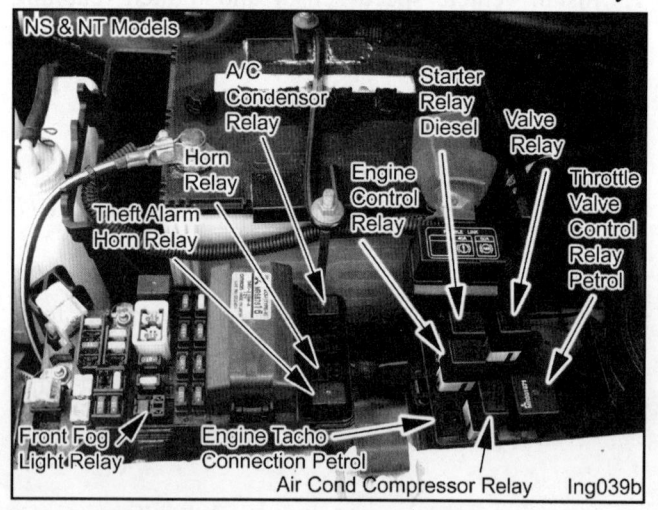

NS & NT Models
A/C Condensor Relay, Starter Relay Diesel, Valve Relay, Horn Relay, Engine Control Relay, Throttle Valve Control Relay Petrol, Theft Alarm Horn Relay, Front Fog Light Relay, Engine Tacho Connection Petrol, Air Cond Compressor Relay Ing039b

446

BODY ELECTRICAL - Components & Switches

Switch Position	Battery Voltage (applied to terminals) -ve	Battery Voltage (applied to terminals) +ve	Continuity b/w Terminals
Current Not Supplied	-	-	1 - 3
Current Supplied	3	1	4 - 5

Theft Alarm Horn
Removal

Disconnect the electrical connection for the horn, then remove the assembly retaining bolts

Installation

Install horn into position, tighten retaining bolts and reconnect electrical connection.

ACCESSORY SOCKET
Relay Continuity Check

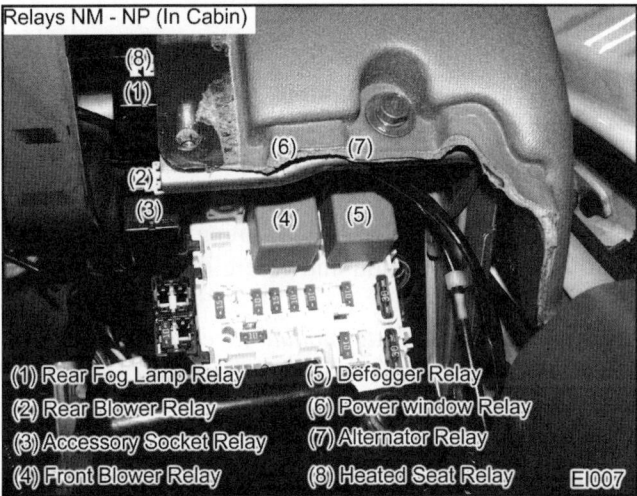

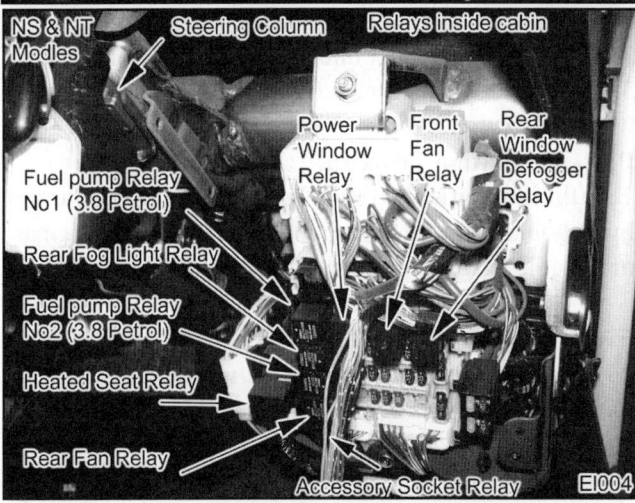

Relays NM - NP (In Cabin)
(1) Rear Fog Lamp Relay
(2) Rear Blower Relay
(3) Accessory Socket Relay
(4) Front Blower Relay
(5) Defogger Relay
(6) Power window Relay
(7) Alternator Relay
(8) Heated Seat Relay

NS & NT Models - Relays inside cabin
- Fuel pump Relay No1 (3.8 Petrol)
- Rear Fog Light Relay
- Fuel pump Relay No2 (3.8 Petrol)
- Heated Seat Relay
- Rear Fan Relay
- Power Window Relay
- Front Fan Relay
- Rear Window Defogger Relay
- Accessory Socket Relay

Switch Position	Battery Voltage (applied to terminals) -ve	Battery Voltage (applied to terminals) +ve	Continuity b/w Terminals
Current Not Supplied	-	-	1 - 3
Current Supplied	1	3	4 - 5

REVERSING SENSOR - NS
Removal

Release the retaining claws on the reverse sensor and remove sensor from bumper assembly or license plate garnish. Disconnect electrical connection and fully remove sensor.

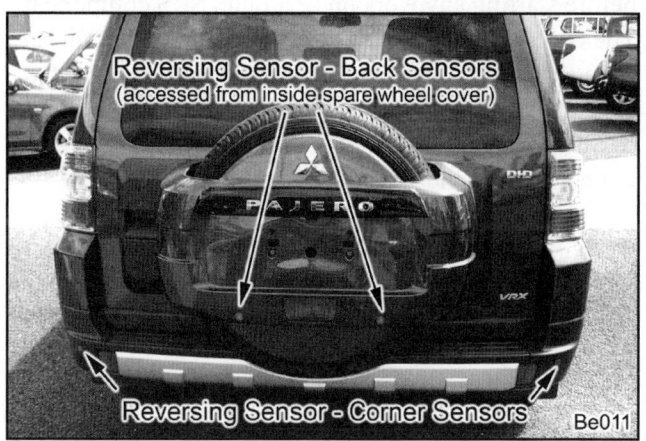

Reversing Sensor - Back Sensors (accessed from inside spare wheel cover)
Reversing Sensor - Corner Sensors

Installation

Reconnect electrical connection to the sensor assembly, then press the sensor into position ensure the retaining claws are properly secured.

REVERSING SENSOR ECU - NS / NT
Removal

1. Remove the glove box assembly, referring to the body chapter if required.
2. Remove the screws securing the sensor-ECU then disconnect the electrical connection and remove ECU assembly.

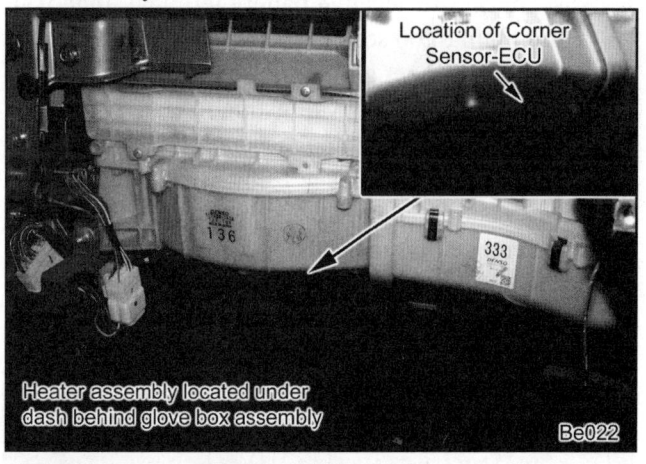

Location of Corner Sensor-ECU
Heater assembly located under dash behind glove box assembly

Installation

1. Connect electrical connection, then fully install sensor-ECU and tighten retaining screws.
2. Install the glove box assembly, referring to the body chapter if required.

447

SRS - Supplemental Restraint System

SERVICE PRECAUTIONS

* Ensure to disconnect battery and wait at least 60 seconds before starting any work on or around SRS components. The system maintains enough voltage to deploy the air bags for a short time after the power has been disconnected.

* After servicing any of the SRS system, check the warning lamp to ensure the system is functioning correctly.

* If baking a vehicle after painting, ensure to remove the SRS ECU, airbag module, clock spring and pretensioner seat belts as these components should not be subject to heat over 93°C.

* Never attempt to repair SRS system components, if any components are faulty they should be replaced.

* Do not use electrical test equipment on or near SRS airbag components unless specifically instructed to do so.

DRIVERS AIRBAG (front)

For removal and installation of the drivers side airbag refer to the steering chapter as this is interlinked with the steering wheel removal.

PASSENGER AIRBAG (front)

Removal

1. Disconnect the negative battery terminal, then wait a minimum of 60 seconds before continuing.
2. Remove the upper glove box and glove box, refer to body chapter for removal instructions.
3. Remove the bolt securing the air bag side plate, slide plate down and disengage from airbag module.
4. Remove the bolts and nuts securing the air bag module then remove the side plate.
5. Disconnect electrical connection from the airbag.
6. Pull on the dash panel as shown and carefully remove the airbag module from the vehicle.

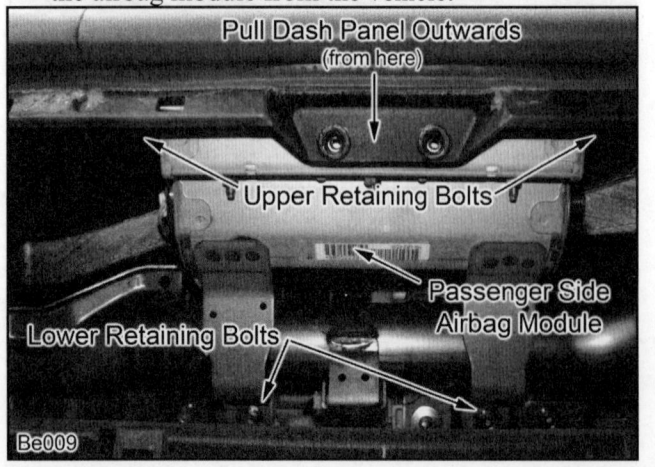

Note: *Place air bag module face up in a dry safe location.*

Installation

1. Connect airbag module electrical connection then install module into position in vehicle and tighten the lower retaining bolts and upper retaining nuts.
2. Install the airbag side plate into position and tighten retaining bolts.
3. Install glove box and upper glove box assemblies. Refer to body chapter if required.
4. Reconnect battery negative cable.
5. Turn the ignition key to the ON position. The SRS warning light should illuminate for about 7 seconds and then remain off for at least 5 seconds once ignition is turned off.

SIDE AIRBAG (seat)

Removal

1. Disconnect the negative battery terminal from the battery, then wait a minimum of 60 seconds before continuing.
2. Remove the back panel assembly from the rear of the seat back.
3. Remove the Airbag module retaining screw, disconnect electrical connection and carefully remove module from seat.

Note: *Place air bag module face up in a dry safe location.*

Installation

1. Install airbag module into position, reconnect electrical connection and secure with retaining nut.
2. Replace back panel into position on back of seat.
3. Reconnect battery negative cable.

Post-Installation Procedure

Turn the ignition key to the ON position. The SRS warning light should illuminate for about 7 seconds and then remain of for at least 5 seconds once ignition is turned off.

FRONT IMPACT SENSORS

* *Vehicles are fitted with 2 front sensors, the sensors are located on the headlight support panel.*

Removal

1. Disconnect the negative battery terminal from the battery, then wait a minimum of 60 seconds before continuing.
2. Remove the radiator reservoir bottle.
3. Disconnect the sensor electrical connections.
4. Remove the two screws securing the sensor and remove sensor from vehicle.

BODY ELECTRICAL - SRS

Inspection

1. Inspect the sensor for any signs of dents, cracks or deformation also check for any signs of rust.
2. Replace the sensor with a new one if any of the above have been found.
3. Check for short or open circuit between front impact sensor terminals.
   Short Circuit.................................. 1 Ohm or less
   Open Circuit........................... 1 MOhm or more
4. If short or open circuit is found replace the sensor.
5. Check continuity between terminal and bracket, id continuity exists replace the sensor.

Installation

1. Install the front impact sensors into position and tighten retaining bolts to specification.
   Sensor Retaining Bolts.............................. 4.9 Nm
2. Replace the radiator reservoir bottle, and reconnect the negative battery terminal.
3. Turn the ignition key to the ON position. The SRS warning light should illuminate for about 7 seconds and then remain of for at least 5 seconds once ignition is turned off.

SIDE IMPACT SENSORS

Removal

1. Disconnect the negative battery terminal from the battery, then wait a minimum of 60 seconds before continuing.
2. Remove the front seat belt and pillar trim panel, refer to body chapter if required.
3. Remove noise protector from inside of the pillar, then remove the nuts securing the sensor into position.
4. Disconnect the sensor electrical connection and remove the side impact sensor from the centre pillar.

Inspection

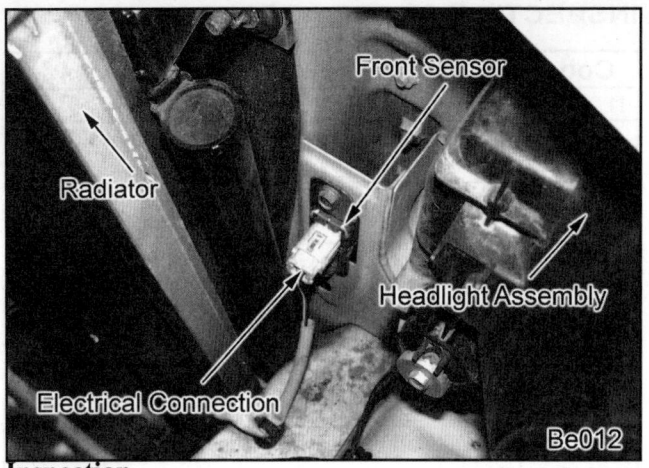

1. Inspect the sensor for any signs of dents, cracks or deformation also check for any signs of rust.
2. Inspect the connector and terminals for damage and any signs of deformation.
3. Inspect the centre pillar/quarter panel for any signs of rust or deformation.
4. Replace the sensor with a new one if any of the above have been found.

Installation

1. Reconnect electrical connection to the impact sensor, then position sensor into place in the centre pillar.
2. Install the front impact sensor retaining nuts and tighten to specification, ensuring the sensor is properly installed.
   Sensor Retaining Nuts .... 4.9 Nm
3. Install the noise protector then install the seat belt and centre pillar trim panel. Refer to Body Chapter if required.
4. Connect the negative battery terminal.
5. Turn the ignition key to the ON position. The SRS warning light should illuminate for about 7 seconds and then remain of for at least 5 seconds once ignition is turned off.

SRS ECU

Removal

1. Turn the ignition key to the lock position then disconnect the negative battery terminal from the battery and wait a minimum of 60 seconds before continuing.
2. Remove the centre console assembly. Refer to body chapter for assistance.
3. Disconnect the electrical connections from the transfer-ECU, then remove retaining nuts and remove the transfer-ECU from the vehicle.
4. Disconnect the electrical connections from the connector bracket then remove the bracket assembly from the vehicle.
5. Disconnect the electrical connections from the SRS-ECU, then remove retaining bolts and remove the ECU from the vehicle.

Inspection

1. Inspect the ECU for any signs of dents, cracks or deformation.
2. Inspect the connector and terminals for damage and any signs of deformation.
3. Replace the ECU with a new one if any of the above have been found.

Installation

1. Install the SRS ECU into the vehicle and tighten retaining bolts to specification, then reconnect electrical connections.
   SRS ECU Retaining Bolts .... 4.9 Nm
2. Install the connector bracket and reconnect electrical connections.
3. Install the transfer-ECU, tighten retaining nuts to

BODY ELECTRICAL - SRS

specification then reconnect electrical connections.

Engine ECU retaining screws .... 4.9 Nm

4. Install the centre console assembly. Refer to "Body Chapter" if required.
5. Reconnect negative battery terminal.
6. Turn the ignition key to the ON position. The SRS warning light should illuminate for about 7 seconds and then remain of for at least 5 seconds once ignition is turned off.

SEAT BELTS With PRETENSIONER - FRONT

Removal

1. Disconnect the negative battery terminal from the battery, then wait a minimum of 60 seconds before continuing.
2. Remove sash guide cover from the bolt securing upper seat belt attachment to centre pillar, then remove the upper retaining bolt.
3. Remove the lower anchor bolt from the centre pillar, then remove the centre pillar trim panels (long wheelbase) or the lower quarter trim panel (short wheelbase).
4. Remove the bolt retaining the seat belt retractor assembly and remove seat belt assembly from vehicle.

Installation

1. Perform post-installation inspection before continuing.
   a) Connect the negative battery terminal, then connect the MUT-II to the diagnostic connector.
   b) Turn the ignition key to the ON position, read the diagnostic code.
   Note: *Code should display system is OK except for an open in the pretensioner circuit.*
   c) Turn the ignition switch to OFF position, disconnect the MUT-II and negative battery terminal.
   Important: *Wait a minimum of 60 seconds after the battery has been disconnected.*
2. Install the seat belt retractor assembly into position and tighten the retaining bolts to specification.
   Retractor Assembly Bolts .... 44+/-10 Nm
3. Install the centre pillar trim panels (long wheelbase) or the lower quarter trim panel (short wheelbase).
4. Install the lower and upper anchor bolts to the centre pillar, tightening bolts to specification, then install the sash guide cover.
5. Reconnect negative battery terminal., then perform the pre-installation procedure.

Post-Installation Procedure

Turn the ignition key to the ON position. The SRS warning light should illuminate for about 7 seconds and then goes out.

INSPECTION CHART / CODES

Code	Diagnosis / Fault Item
11, 12, 13	Front impact sensor system
14	Front impact analog G-sensor system inside SRS-ECU
15, 16	Front impact safing G-sensor system inside SRS-ECU
17	Side impact safing G-sensor system inside SRS-ECU
21*2, 22*2, 61, 62	Drivers airbag module (squib) system
24*2, 25*2, 64, 65	Passenger's airbag module (squib) system
31, 32	DC-DC converter system inside SRS-ECU
34*1	Connector lock system
35	SRS-ECU (deployed air bag) system
41*1	Power circuit system (fuse #6 circuit)
42*1	Power circuit system (fuse #8 circuit)
43*1	SRS warning lamp drive circuit system — Lamp does not illuminate / Lamp does not go out/off
44*1	SRS warning lamp drive circuit system
45	Internal circuit system of non-volatile memory (EEPROM) inside SRS-ECU
51, 52	Drivers airbag module (squib) system
54, 55	Passenger's airbag module (squib) system
71*2, 72*2, 75, 76	Side air bag module (R.H) (squib) system
73, 74	Side air bag module (R.H) (squib) system
79, 93	Side impact sensor (L.H) communication system
81*2, 82*2, 85, 86	Side air bag module (L.H) (squib) system
83, 84	Side air bag module (L.H) (squib ignition drive circuit) system
89, 96	Side impact sensor (R.H) communication system
91*1	Side impact sensor (L.H) power supply circuit system
92	Analog G-sensor system inside side impact sensor
94*1	Side impact sensor (R.H) power supply circuit
95	Analog G-sensor system inside side impact sensor (R.H)

NOTES:

*1 - When troubles are corrected, the warning lamp will go out with diagnosis history automatically erased.

*2 - If vehicle condition returns to normal the diagnosis code will automatically be erased and warning lamp will return to normal.

If vehicle has a flat/low battery codes 41 and 42 will be displayed, check battery condition.

BODY ELECTRICAL - Horn / Cruise Control

HORN ASSEMBLY

Removal

1. Remove front grille assembly, referring to the body chapter for assistance if required.
2. Disconnect electrical connector from the horn. Unscrew attaching bolts and remove horn assemblies from the vehicle.

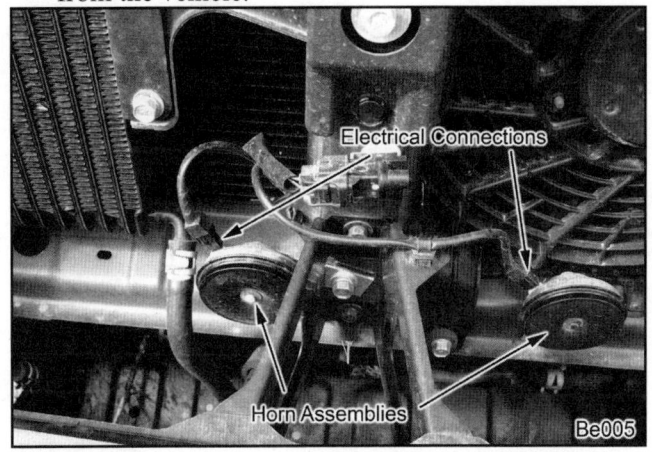

Horn Relay Continuity Check

Switch Position	Battery Voltage (applied to terminals) -ve	Battery Voltage (applied to terminals) +ve	Continuity b/w Terminals
Current Not Supplied	-	-	1 - 3
Current Supplied	1	3	4 - 5

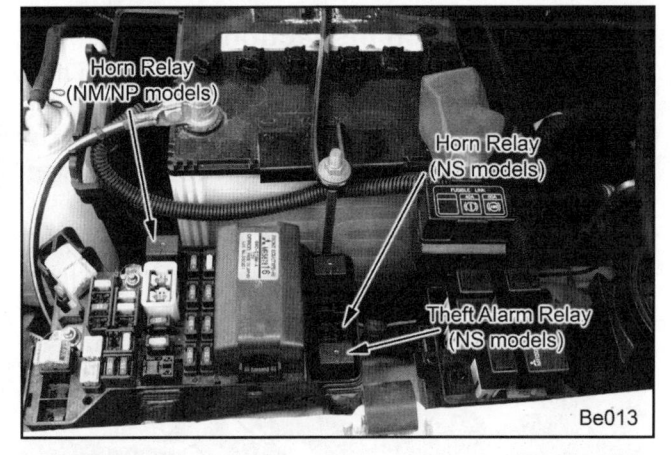

Installation

1. Install the horn assembly into position and tighten the retaining bolt.
2. Reconnect electrical connections to the horn and test horn operates correctly.
3. Install front grille assembly, ensuring all retaining clips are properly secured.

HORN ACTUATOR

The horn actuator is located in the centre of the steering wheel. To sound the horn the centre of the steering wheel is pushed in towards the steering column.

CRUISE CONTROL

COMPONENT TESTING (NM-NP)

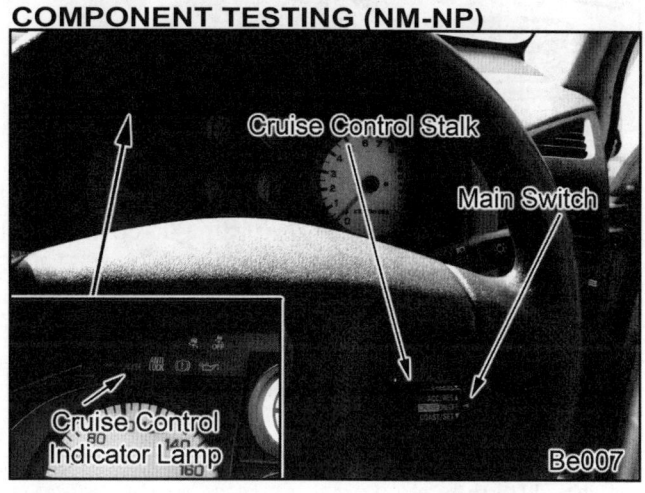

Switch - Set

1. Drive the vehicle at a legal speed within the range of 40 - 110km/h.
2. Turn on the main control switch then flick the stalk control switch downwards to set speed.
3. When the lever switch is released check to ensure a constant speed is maintained.

Switch - Acceleration Reset

1. Set the desired speed as described previously.
2. Switch the stalk control switch upwards, the speed should increase while the switch is held on.
3. Release switch and the speed should remain at the speed the vehicle was when the switch was released.

Switch - Deceleration Set

1. Set the desired speed as described previously.
2. Switch the stalk control switch downwards, the speed should decrease while the switch is held on.
3. Release switch and the speed should remain at the speed the vehicle was at when the switch was released.

Switch - Cancel & Return Set

1. Set the desired speed as described previously.
2. a) Switch the stalk control switch towards driver, the cruise should cancel and the vehicle decelerate.
   b) Depress the brake pedal then release, the cruise should cancel and the vehicle decelerate.
   c) Depress the clutch pedal then release, the cruise should cancel and the vehicle decelerate.
   d) Selector lever is moved to "N" range, the cruise should cancel and the vehicle decelerate.
3. At a speed higher than 40km/h flick the stalk control switch upwards, the speed should increase to the set vehicle speed before cruise was cancelled.
4. With the cruise control set as described previously turn off the main switch. The cruise should cancel and the vehicle decelerate.

COMPONENT TESTING (NS / NT)

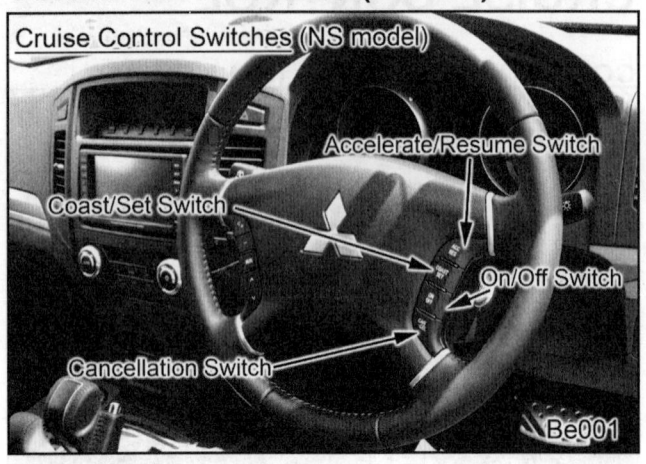

Cruise Control Switches (NS model)

Switch - Set
1. Drive the vehicle at a legal speed within the range of 40 - 110km/h.
2. Turn on the main control switch then press the set switch to set speed.
3. Then check to ensure a constant speed is maintained.

Switch - Acceleration Reset
1. Set the desired speed as described previously.
2. Press the "Acc/Res" switch, the speed should increase while the switch is held on.
3. Release the switch and the speed should remain at the speed the vehicle was at when the switch was released.

Switch - Deceleration Set
1. Set the desired speed as described previously.
2. Press the "Coast/Set" switch, the speed should decrease while the switch is held on.
3. Release the switch and the speed should remain at the speed the vehicle was at when the switch was released.

Switch - Cancel & Return Set
1. Set the desired speed as described previously.
2. a) Press the cancel switch, the cruise should cancel and the vehicle decelerate.
   b) Depress the brake pedal then release, the cruise should cancel and the vehicle decelerate.
   c) Depress the clutch pedal then release, the cruise should cancel and the vehicle decelerate.
3. At a speed higher than 40km/h press the "Acc/Res" switch, the speed should increase to the set vehicle speed before cruise was cancelled.
4. With the cruise control set as described previously turn off the main switch. The cruise should cancel and the vehicle decelerate.

Cruise Control Switch - Steering Wheel
Removal
1. Remove the horn pad/airbag module as described in the steering chapter.
2. Remove the screw securing the control switch, disconnect electrical connection and fully remove switch from vehicle.

Switch Resistance
Measure resistance of the control switch between the terminals when the switch is in the Set position, then measure resistance in the Resume and Cancel positions as well.

Switch Resistance:		
Switch State	**Terminals**	**Resistance**
Main Switch Off		0 Ohm
Main Switch On	1 & 2	3.9 kOhm
Cancel switch On	2 & 3	0.0 Ohm
Resume switch On	2 & 3	910 Ohm
Set switch On	2 & 3	220 Ohm

Installation
1. Reconnect electrical connection to control switch and install switch into position.
2. Tighten the control switch retaining screw, then replace the horn pad/airbag module.
3. Test operation of cruise control to ensure switch is operating correctly.

Stop Lamp Switch Inspection
Disconnect the connector for the stop lamp switch then operate the brake pedal and check the continuity between terminals.

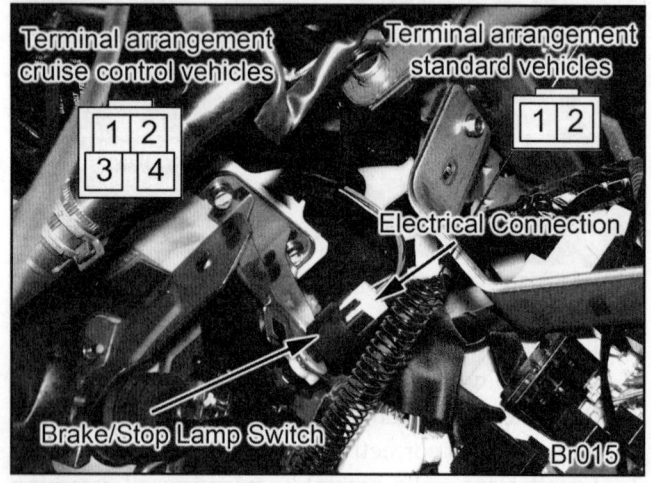

Inhibitor Switch Inspection (safety/neutral switch)
Refer to the "Automatic Transmission Chapter" for inspection procedures for the inhibitor switch.

Clutch Pedal Switch Inspection
Refer to the "Clutch Chapter" for inspection procedure for clutch pedal position switch.

BODY ELECTRICAL - Cruise Control

Throttle Position Switch Inspection

Refer to the "Ignition, Fuel & Emission Chapter" or "Glow, Fuel & Emission Chapter" for inspection procedures for throttle position switch.

Electric Vacuum Pump
Inspection

1. From the electric vacuum pump disconnect the vacuum hose and to the vacuum pump connect a vacuum gauge.
2. Disconnect the electrical connection for the vacuum pump.
3. To the battery positive terminal connect switch terminal 1 and to the negative battery terminal connect switch terminal #2, #3 & #4.
4. Vacuum gauge should show a reading of 27kPa or more.
5. a) Disconnect terminal #4. Leave terminal #1, #2 & #3 connected. The vacuum should be maintained.
   b) Disconnect terminal 2 and leave terminals #1 & #3 connected. The vacuum should read 0 kPa.
6. a) Disconnect terminal 4 and leave terminals #1, #2 & #3 connected. Vacuum should be maintained.
   b) Disconnect terminal #3 and leave terminals #1 & #2 connected. The vacuum should read 0 kPa.

Removal

1. Disconnect the electrical connectors from the vacuum pump, then disconnect the vacuum hose.
2. Remove the bolts securing the vacuum pump mounting bracket to the vehicle and then remove assembly. 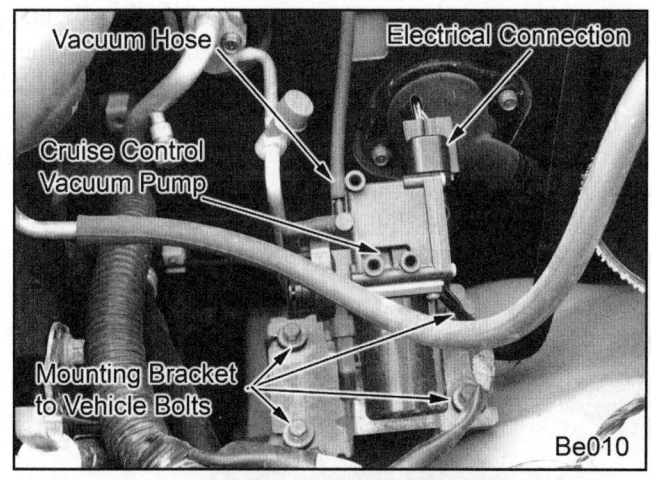
3. Remove the mounting screws/bolts securing the vacuum pump to the mounting bracket and seperate.

Installation

1. Install the mounting bracket to vacuum pump and tighten the retaining screws.
2. Install the vacuum pump assembly to vehicle and tighten the retaining bolts securely.
   Mounting Bracket Bolts/Nuts .... 14 Nm

3. Reconnect electrical connection and vacuum hose.

Vacuum Actuator
Inspection

1. From the vacuum actuator disconnect the vacuum hose and to the actuator connect a hand pump.
2. Check to ensure that when vacuum is applied the throttle lever operates and vacuum is kept.

Cruise Control ECU

NM Models have a separate cruise control ECU which is located behind the engine-ECU. The NP/NS models are controlled by the engine-ECU.

Removal

1. From the passenger side of the vehicle, remove the side cowl trim panel (kick panel).
2. Disconnect the electrical connections for the engine-ECU, then remove mounting bolts and remove engine-ECU from vehicle. 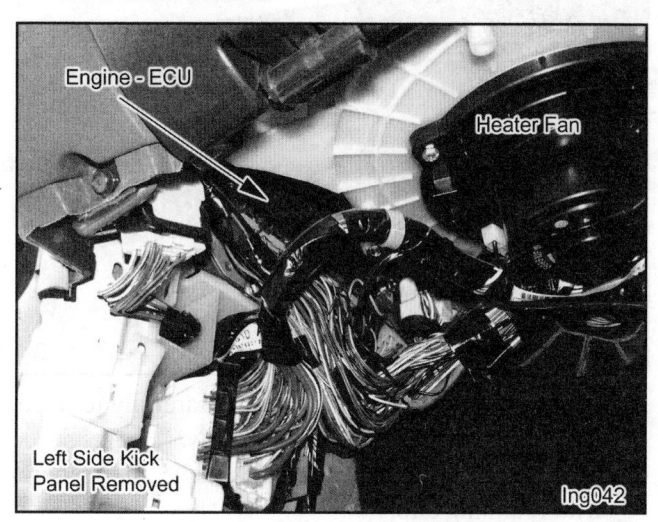
3. **NM models:** Disconnect the electrical connections for the cruise control-ECU, then remove mounting nut and remove from vehicle.
4. If required remove the bolt securing the mounting bracket and remove bracket.

Installation

1. If removed install ECU mounting bracket and tighten bolts to specification.
   ECU Mounting Bracket Bolt .... 5 Nm
2. **NM models:** Install the cruise control-ECU into position, tighten mounting nut to specification and connect the electrical connections.
   ECU Mounting Nut .... 5 Nm
3. Install the engine-ECU into position, tightening the mounting bolts to specification then connect the electrical connections.
   Engine-ECU Mounting Bolts .... 5 Nm
4. Replace the side cowl trim panel (kick panel).

BODY ELECTRICAL - Lighting

LIGHTS & SWITCHES

HEADLIGHT GLOBE REPLACEMENT - NM/NP

Caution: *Never hold bulb with bare hands, dirty gloves, etc, or premature bulb failure will occur. If the glass surface is dirty, be sure to clean it with alcohol, and install after air drying thoroughly.*

Note: *If removing right-hand side headlight globe remove the air cleaner case. If removing left-hand side headlight Globe remove the ABS valve relay.*

Replacement - Standard Headlamp

1. Disconnect the electrical connection for the headlight.
2. Remove dust cap from rear of headlamp assembly. 
3. Depress the bulb retaining clip and carefully remove the bulb from the headlight assembly.
4. Replace bulb with one of same wattage, then secure with retaining clip.
5. Install dust cap, reconnect the electrical connection.
6. Check lamp operation.

Replacement - Discharge Headlamp

1. Disconnect the electrical connection for the headlight assembly.
2. Remove the cover from the headlamp assembly, cover is secured using security screws.
3. Depress the bulb retaining clip and carefully remove the bulb from the headlight assembly.
4. Replace bulb with one of same wattage, then secure with retaining clip.
5. Securely fit the connector, then install the lamp cover and reconnect the assembly electrical connection.
6. Check lamp operation.

HEADLIGHT GLOBE REPLACEMENT - NS

1. Unscrew the headlamp bulb socket cover from the rear of the lamp assembly.
2. Disconnect the electrical connection for the headlight, then turn the igniter to remove. 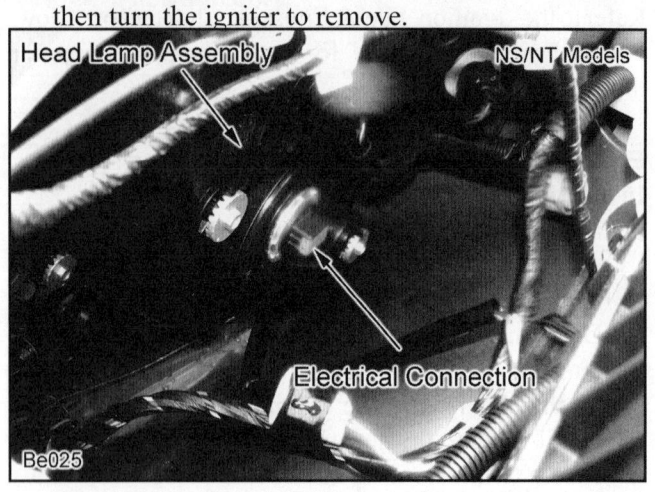
3. Release the bulb retaining clip and carefully remove the bulb from the headlight assembly.
4. Replace bulb with one of same wattage, then secure with retaining clip.
5. Turn igniter to ensure it is secured properly then reconnect electrical connection.
6. Install and tighten the headlamp bulb socket cover and then test operation of lights.
   CAUTION: *Never hold bulb with bare hands, dirty gloves, etc, or premature bulb failure will occur. If the glass surface is dirty, be sure to clean it with alcohol, and install after air drying thoroughly.*

HEADLAMP ASSEMBLY - ALL

Removal

1. Depress locking tab on headlamp wiring harness connectors and separate connectors from headlight.
2. Remove the front radiator grille as described in the body chapter, then remove front splash shield.
3. Remove the retaining screw from behind front splash shield.
4. Remove the three headlight assembly retaining screws, then remove headlight assembly.

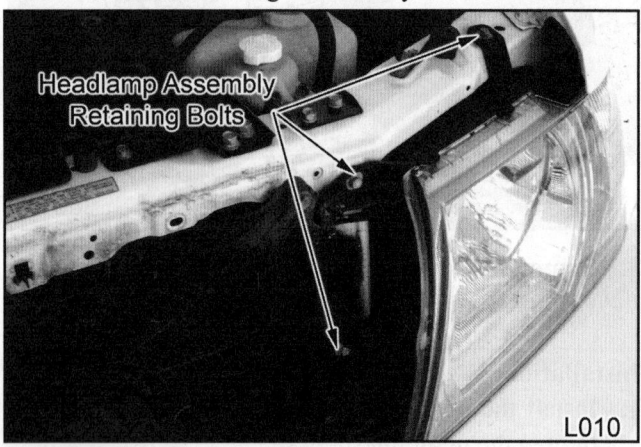

Installation

1. Position the headlight assembly into position and tighten the retaining screws and nut.

2. Install the front splash shield, then install the radiator grille as described in body chapter.
3. Reconnect the headlight electrical connection.
4. Check operation of headlamp and turn signal lamps.
5. Check headlamp aim.

HEADLAMP AUTOMATIC LEVELLING MOTOR TEST

1. Earth terminal #1 of the diagnostic connector.
2. Turn on the ignition switch, followed by the headlamp switch.
3. Check that headlamp levelling operates downwards for 1.5 seconds.
   Note: *When headlamp is facing downwards at start of test it will remain facing downwards.*
4. Check that the headlamp levelling operates upwards for 3 seconds.

HEADLAMP AUTOMATIC LEVELLING ECU
Removal
1. Remove the front side panel from the centre console to gain assess to ECU.
2. From the underside of the heater unit remove the connector bracket, then cut the insulation pad to gain access to the ECU mounting screws.
3. Disconnect the ECU then remove the retaining screws and lift unit from vehicle.

Installation
1. Install the ECU assembly into position, tighten retaining screws and reconnect electrical connection.
2. Using a good quality tape repair the cut in the insulation pad, then install the connector bracket.
3. Install the front side panel to the centre console.

HEADLAMP AUTOMATIC LEVELLING HEIGHT SENSORS
Front Height Sensor
The front height sensor is located on the front suspension system.

Removal
1. Disconnect the electrical connector from the sensor.
2. Remove the bolts securing the height sensor to the vehicle.

Installation
1. Install the height sensor into position and tighten the retaining bolts, then reconnect the electrical connection.
   Height Sensor Bolts..................................23 Nm
2. Check the headlight aiming is adjusted correctly.

Rear Height Sensor
The rear height sensor is located on the rear suspension system.

Removal
1. Disconnect the electrical connection from the sensor, then remove the bolts securing the height sensor to the vehicle.
2. Remove the nut/bolt securing the height sensor bracket to the vehicle.

Installation
1. Install the height bracket and tighten retaining nut/bolt to specification.
   Height Sensor Bracket Nut/Bolts..............23 Nm
2. Install the height sensor into position and tighten the retaining bolts to specification, then reconnect the electrical connection.
   Height Sensor Bolts..................................23 Nm
3. Check the headlight aiming is adjusted correctly.

ADJUST HEADLIGHT PATTERN
Always adjust headlight pattern according to the state laws and regulations.

Before adjusting headlight take note of the following procedure:
1. Ensure tyres are inflated correctly.
2. Clean headlight lenses.
3. Check the vehicle is positioned on a level floor.
4. Bounce vehicle to ensure it is at normal height.
5. Place sufficient weight in vehicle to simulate full load conditions (1 litre of fuel = 0.72 kg).

ADJUSTMENT
Adjusting screws are located on the headlamp assembly as shown. Adjustment is made by turning the adjustment screws using a screwdriver.

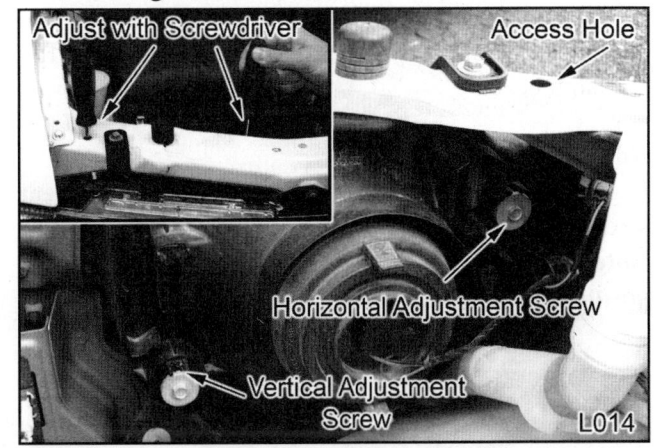

Vertical: Adjust vertically by turning the inside adjustment screw.

Horizontal: Adjust horizontally by turning the outside adjustment screw.

BODY ELECTRICAL - Lighting

USING A WALL
1. Manufacture an aiming target on a light coloured wall.
2. With vehicle up against wall, align vehicle centre line with centre line of screen.
3. With vehicle up against wall, mark head light height and centre of light lens on wall.
4. Place vehicle 3.5 meters in front of screen ensuring the vehicle is aligned with vehicle centre line mark on screen.
5. Switch headlights onto low beam and adjust head lamps to achieve correct alignment.
   a) Adjust inboard adjuster to achieve correct vertical beam height.
   b) Adjust outboard adjuster to centralize beam.

FRONT FOG LAMPS (2001-2002)
* The fog lamp assembly needs to be removed for globe replacement.

Removal
1. From the fog lamp remove the fog lamp bezel by uncoupling.
2. From the lamp assembly remove the two retaining screws then partially remove the lamp assembly.
3. Disconnect the electrical connections, then fully remove lamp assembly from vehicle.
4. If required remove the fog lamp mounting bracket by removing the retaining screws from the back side of the front bumper.

Installation
1. If removed install the fog lamp mounting bracket and tighten retaining screws.
2. Inspect the globe to ensure it is in good working order and not blown, then reconnect electrical connections and install lamp assembly into position.
3. Install and tighten lamp assembly retaining screws, then adjust lamps.
4. Once fog lamp adjustment is correct, install the fog lamp bezel.

Adjust
Fog light adjustment is achieved by turning the adjustment screw located on the outer side of the light assembly.
Note: *Only vertical adjustment is possible. Horizontal position is fixed.*

FRONT FOG LAMPS (2003 onwards)
* The fog lamp assembly needs to be removed for globe replacement.

Removal
1. Remove the front fender splash shield, refer to body chapter for assistance. 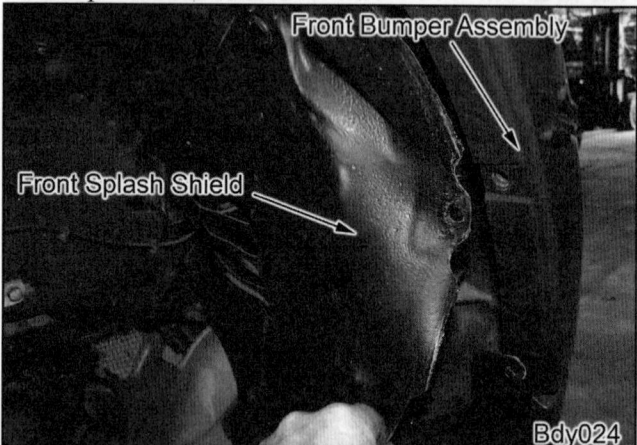
2. From the back of the lamp assembly remove the three retaining screws. 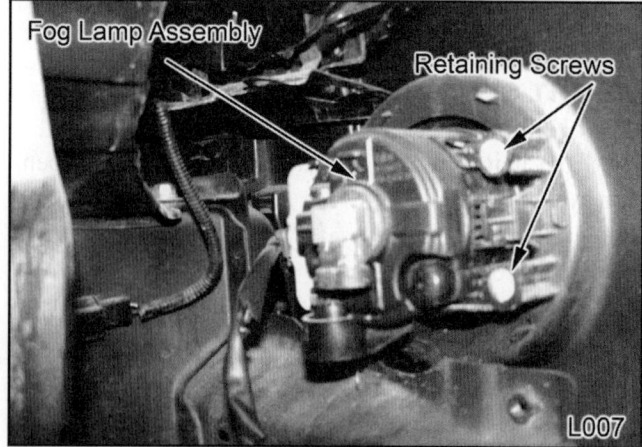
3. Disconnect the electrical connection, then fully remove lamp assembly from vehicle.

Installation
1. Inspect the globe to ensure it is in good working order and not blown, then reconnect electrical connections

BODY ELECTRICAL - Lighting

and install lamp assembly into position.
2. Install and tighten lamp assembly retaining screws, then install the front fender splash shield.
3. Check and adjust the lamp alignment.

Adjust
Fog light adjustment is achieved by turning the adjustment screw located under the light assembly.
Note: *Only vertical adjustment is possible. Horizontal position is fixed.*

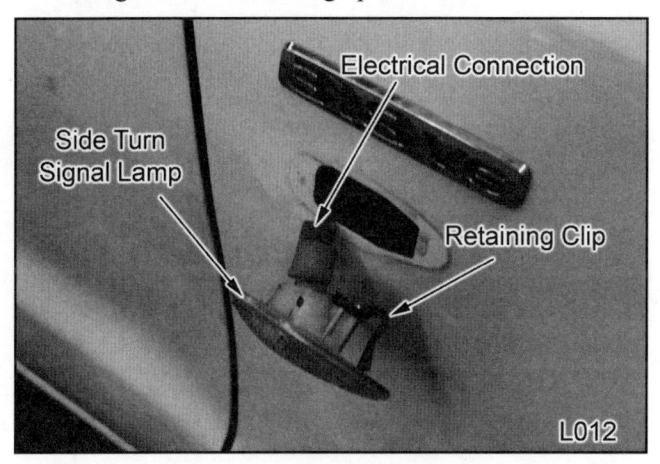

2. Remove the lamp assembly from the front fender and disconnect electrical connection.
3. Replace globe with one of same wattage.

Installation
1. Connect the wiring connector then slide lamp assembly into position ensuring retaining clip engages correctly.
2. Test operation of light.

DOOR MIRROR SIDE TURN SIGNAL LAMP
Removal
1. Remove the mirror glass from the mirror assembly.
   a) Gently press the top of the mirror with your hands to tilt upwards.
   b) Apply protective tape to a flat blade screwdriver, then carefully release the lower mirror retainer using the screwdriver.
   c) Release the top section of the mirror glass and gentle pull glass assembly from mirror.
   Note: *Electrical connection will need to be disconnected on vehicles with heated mirrors.*
2. From the mirror assembly remove the rear cover, then remove lamp assembly retaining screws.
3. Replace globe with one of same wattage.

Installation
1. Install lamp assembly into position in mirror, reconnect electrical connection and tighten retaining screws.
2. Install rear cover to the mirror assembly and test operation of lamp.
3. Gently press the mirror glass into position, ensuring the retainers are securely engaged.
   Note: *Vehicle with heated mirrors, reconnect the electrical connection before installing glass.*
4. Test operation of mirror.

SIDE TURN SIGNAL LAMPS
Removal
1. Using an appropriate tool carefully disengage the lamp assembly retaining clip from the front fender, taking care not to damage paintwork.

LICENCE PLATE LAMP
Bulb Replacement
1. Remove the screws securing the lamp assembly, then remove assembly from vehicle.

BODY ELECTRICAL - Lighting

2. From the lamp assembly remove globe holder then remove globe and replace with one of the same wattage.
3. Replace globe holder into assembly then install into position reconnecting electrical connections.
4. Tighten the light assembly retaining screws.

REAR COMBINATION LAMP
Bulb Replacement

1. Open the rear door to gain access to the lamp retaining screws, then remove the screws securing the lamp assembly to the rear of the vehicle.

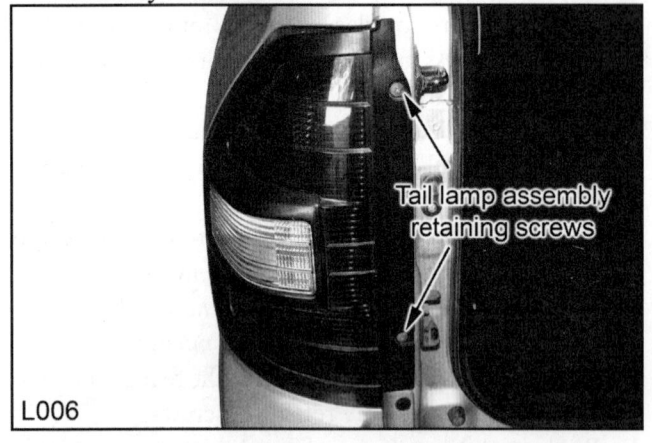

L006

2. Lift the lamp assembly away from the vehicle then remove the bulb holder from the rear of the lamp assembly by turning anti-clockwise.

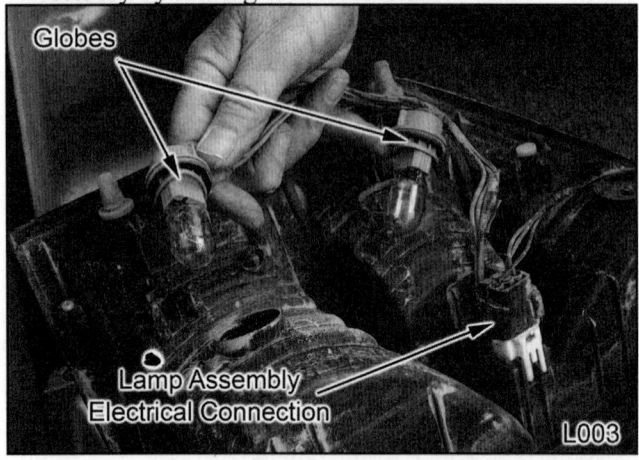

L003

3. Replace globe with one of same wattage then install bulb holder into position.
4. Reinstall lamp assembly and tighten retaining screws.

Removal

1. Open the rear door to gain access to the lamp retaining screws, then remove the screws securing the lamp assembly to the rear of the vehicle.
2. Lift the lamp assembly away from the vehicle disconnect the electrical connection and remove lamp assembly from vehicle.

Installation

1. Reconnect the electrical connection, then install the lamp assembly into position and tighten the retaining nuts.

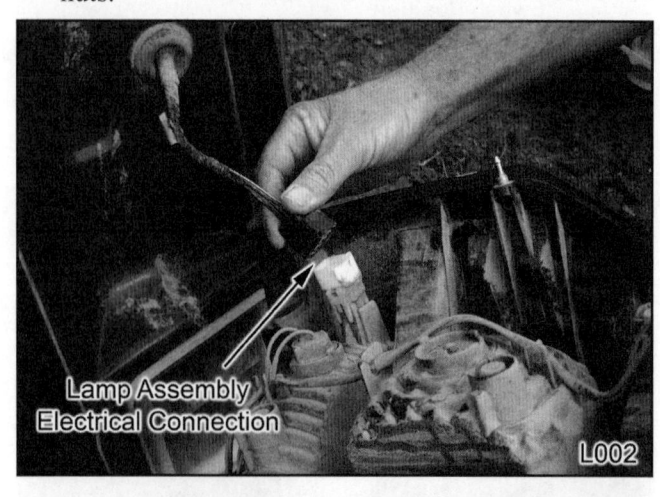

L002

2. Test operation of lamps to ensure all lights are working correctly.

REAR LAMP (in bumper)
Bulb Replacement

1. Raise the rear of the vehicle to gain access to the back of the lamp assembly from the underside of the rear bumper.
2. Remove the bulb holder from the rear of the lamp assembly by turning anti-clockwise.

L011

3. Replace globe with one of same wattage then install bulb holder into position.

Removal

1. Remove the two retaining screws from the rear lamp assembly and lift lamp assembly from rear bumper.
2. Disconnect the electrical connection and remove lamp assembly from vehicle.

BODY ELECTRICAL - Lighting

Installation
1. Reconnect electrical connection, then install the lamp assembly into position and tighten retaining screws.
2. Test operation of lamps to ensure all lights are working correctly.

HIGH MOUNT STOP LAMP
Bulb Replacement
1. Open rear door/tailgate then remove the lamp cover, it may be necessary to remove cover retaining screws (depending on model).
2. From the lamp assembly remove the bulbs, if required remove the screws securing the lamp assembly and remove assembly. 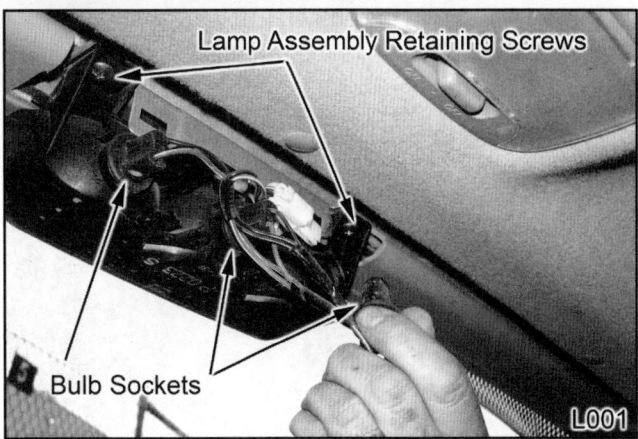
3. Install assembly if removed, tighten retaining screws then replace bulbs with one of same wattage.
4. Replace lamp cover and tighten retaining screws.

SIDE STEP ILLUMINATION LAMPS
Globe Replacement
1. From the underside of the step remove the screws securing the lamp bracket, then remove bracket assembly.
2. Remove the globe socket from the lamp assembly and replace globe with one of same wattage.
3. Install globe socket to the lamp assembly then install into position and tighten bracket retaining bolts to specification.

Lamp Bracket Bolts .... 5 Nm

SIDE STEP ILLUMINATION ECU
Removal
1. Remove the drivers side lower instrument panel, refer to body chapter for assistance.
2. Remove the side step ECU retaining bolt, then disconnect electrical connection and remove ECU assembly.

Installation
1. Reconnect the ECU electrical connection, then position the ECU into place and tighten the retaining bolt to specification.

Side Step Lamp ECU Bolt .... 5 Nm

2. Install the lower instrument panel, referring to body chapter if required.

INTERIOR LAMP
Replace globe
1. Remove the lens from the light assembly by carefully prising the lens from the assembly with a small screwdriver.
2. Remove globe and replace with one of same wattage.
3. Replace lens by pushing in, ensuring the lens clips into position properly.

BODY ELECTRICAL - Lighting

INTERIOR LAMP SWITCH

This photograph illustrates the installation of the interior lamp switch, fitted on all doors, on all models.

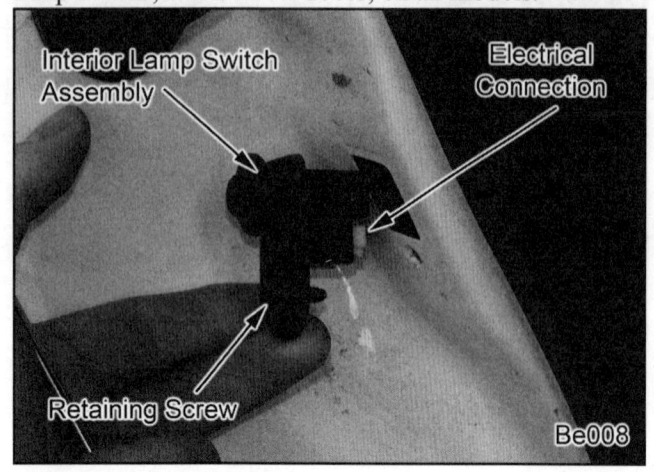

PHOTO SENSOR
Removal

1. Remove the clock and centre display assembly or RV meter from the instrument panel, refer to body chapter.
2. From the centre top of the instrument panel remove the photo sensor cover.
3. Through the front of the instrument panel pull out the photo sensor harness with the sensor attached.
4. Disconnect photo sensor from harness.

Installation

1. Feed photo sensor harness through mounting hole in the top of the instrument panel.
2. Connect the photo sensor to the electrical harness, then install photo sensor into position in the top of the instrument panel.
3. To the centre top of the instrument panel install the photo sensor cover.
4. Install clock and centre display assembly or RV meter to the instrument panel, refer to body chapter.

Sensor Check

1. During daylight hours ensure the lamp switch is in the auto position then cover the sensor and ensure the headlamps illuminate.
2. Replace the photo sensor if the headlights do not illuminate.
   Note: *Ensure it is a sunny day when testing sensor.*

STOP LAMP SWITCH
Replacement

1. The switch is located under the dash on the brake pedal mounting bracket.
2. Refer to the "Brakes Chapter" for removal and installation instructions or refer to "Cruise Control" section of this chapter.

FOG LAMP SWITCH
Removal

1. Using a fine blade screwdriver which has the blade protected by a rag, carefully lever the switch from the instrument panel.
2. Disconnect the electrical connector and fully remove switch.

Installation

1. Connect electrical connector to the switch assembly, then press the switch assembly into position in instrument panel, ensuring switch is securely seated.

Fog Lamp Switch Continuity Inspection

Switch Position	Continuity b/w Terminals	
	Front	Rear
OFF	-	-
ON	1 - 2	5 - 6

HAZARD LIGHT SWITCH
Removal

1. **NM/NP:** Remove the centre panel from the instrument panel, then remove the two screws securing the switch bracket.

2. **NS/NT:** Remove the drivers side centre air outlet by gently prising out, then remove the two screws securing the switch bracket.
3. Remove the switch bracket and switch assembly from centre panel.

Installation

1. Install the switch to the centre panel or centre air outlet, secure in place with the bracket and tighten retaining screws.
2. Install centre panel or centre air outlet to the instrument panel, then test operation of switch.

Hazard Light Switch Continuity Inspection

Switch Position	Continuity b/w Terminals
OFF	-
ON	1 - 2

SPECIFICATIONS

Speedometer
Tolerance:
- @ 20 km/h .... 18-23 km/h
- @ 40 km/h .... 37-45 km/h
- @ 80 km/h .... 75-88 km/h
- @ 120 km/h .... 113-132 km/h
- @ 160 km/h .... 150-176 km/h

Needle Swing @ 35km/h or above .... +/-3

Tachometer
Tolerance (rpm):
- 700 rpm - petrol .... +/- 120
- - diesel .... +/- 120
- 2000 rpm - petrol .... -175 / +225
- - diesel .... +/- 175
- 3000 rpm - petrol .... -175 / +300
- - diesel .... +/- 225
- 4000 rpm - petrol .... -225 / +375
- - diesel .... +/- 300
- 4750 rpm - diesel .... +/- 260
- 5000 rpm - petrol .... -225 / +425
- 6000 rpm - petrol .... -225 / +475

Fuel Gauge Unit
Resistance:

Gauge Position	Resistance
Full	3 Ohms
Empty	110 Ohms

Float Height:

Gauge Position	Height (centre)
Full	11.9 mm
Empty	195.2 mm

Temperature Sender Unit
Test resistance @ 70°C .... 104 +/- 13.5 Ohms

BULB SPECIFICATIONS

NM - NP Models — Watt
- Standard Headlamp
  - High-beam (H9) 60
  - Low-beam (H11) 55
  - Position lamp 5
  - Front turn signal 21
- Fog Lamps
  - Front 51
  - Rear 21
- Side turn-signal lamps - Fender 5
- Side Step Lamps 5
- Approach Lamp 5
- Rear Combination Lamp
  - Stop/tail 21/5
  - Buck-up 21
  - Turn-signal 21
- High mounted stop lamp .... 16 / 18
- Licence Plate Lamp 5
- Interior lamps
  - Room & Personal lamps 7.5
  - Door lamps 5
  - Rear Personal lamps 8
- Luggage compartment lamp 8

NS/NT Models — Watt
- Standard Headlamp
  - High-beam (H9) 60
  - Low-beam (H11) 55
  - Position lamp 5
  - Front turn signal 21
- Discharge Headlamp
  - High-beam (H9) 65
  - Low-beam (discharge) 35
  - Position lamp 5
  - Front turn signal 21
- Fog Lamps
  - Front 55
  - Rear 21
- Side turn-signal lamps
  - Fender 5
  - Mirror .... LED
- Approach Lamp 5
- Rear Combination Lamp
  - Stop/tail 21/5
  - Buck-up 21
  - Turn-signal 21
- High mounted stop lamp 18
- Licence Plate Lamp 5
- Interior lamps
  - Front lamp (x2) 8
  - Personal lamp 8
- Luggage compartment lamp 8
- Glove box illumination lamp 1.4
- Ceiling Lamp .... LED
- Foot Lamp .... LED
- Ignition Key Cylinder 1.5
- Door Lamp 3.4
- Vanity Mirror Lamp 3

BODY ELECTRICAL - Specifications

COMBINATION METER (INSTRUMENT CLUSTER) SERVICE SPECIFICATIONS

Item			Standard Value	Limit
Speedometer indication range (km/h)	@ 20 km/h		18-23	-
	@ 40 km/h		37-45	-
	@ 80 km/h		75-88	-
	@ 120 km/h		113-132	-
	@ 160 km/h		150-176	-
Speedometer needle swing (km/h) when driving at 35km/h +			-	+/-3
Tachometer indication error (r/min)	Engine speed 700 r/min		+/-120	-
	Engine speed 2000 r/min	Petrol	-175+225	-
		Diesel	+/-75	-
	Engine speed 3000 r/min	Petrol	-175+300	-
		Diesel	+225	-
	Engine speed 4000 r/min	Petrol	-225+375	-
		Diesel	+300	-
	Engine speed 4,750 rpm (diesel)		+260	-
	Engine speed 5,000 rpm (petrol)		-225+425	-
	Engine speed 6,000 rpm (petrol)		-225+475	-
Engine coolant temp gauge unit standard resistance value (ohms)			104+/-13.5	-
Combination meter internal resistance value (measured at connector D-38 & D-40)	62-11 (ignition power supply - earth)		1+ MOhms	-
	62-25 (ignition power supply - earth)		1+ MOhms	-
	62-63 (ignition power supply - fuel gauge)		1+ MOhms	-
	62-64 (ignition power supply - coolant temp)		1+ MOhms	-
	63-11 (fuel gauge - earth)		180 Ohms	
	63-25 (fuel gauge - earth)		180 Ohms	
	64-11 (coolant temp gauge - earth)		210 Ohms	
	64-25 (coolant temp gauge - earth)		210 Ohms	
	67-11 (battery power supply - earth)		1+ MOhms	
	67-25 (battery power supply - earth)		1+ MOhms	
	67-63 (battery power supply - fuel gauge)		1+ MOhms	
	67-64 (battery power supply - coolant temp gauge)		1+ MOhms	

COMBINATION METER (INSTRUMENT CLUSTER) INTERNAL RESISTANCE VALUE CHECK

Terminal No's.	Terminal Names	Resistance
62 - 11	Ignition Power Supply - Earth	1+ MOhms
62 - 25	Ignition Power Supply - Earth	1+ MOhms
62 - 63	Ignition Power Supply - Fuel Gauge	1+ MOhms
62 - 64	Ignition Power Supply - Coolant Temp Gauge	1+ MOhms
63 - 11	Fuel Gauge - Earth	180 Ohms
63 - 25	Fuel Gauge - Earth	180 Ohms
64 - 11	Coolant Temp Gauge - Earth	210 Ohms
64 - 25	Coolant Temp Gauge - Earth	210 Ohms
67 - 11	Battery Power Supply - Earth	1+ MOhms
67 - 25	Battery Power Supply - Earth	1+ MOhms
67 - 63	Battery Power Supply - Fuel Gauge	1+ MOhms
67 - 64	Battery Power Supply - Coolant Temp Gauge	1+ MOhms

DIAGNOSTICS

Description	Page
GENERAL INFORMATION	464
Diagnostic Connector	464
Reading Diagnostics Codes	464
Using warning light	464
Using voltmeter	464
Erasing Diagnostic Codes	464
MPI (SOHC) DIAGNOSTICS	465
MPI 3.5 & 3.8 Engines Pre 2004	465
Fuel System	465
Reading Diagnostic Codes	465
Fuel System Diagnostic Codes	466
Fuel System Inspection Procedures	467
Terminal Voltage Check	468
Terminal Resistance & Continuity Check	469
MPI 3.8L (SOHC) DIAGNOSTICS	471
Fuel System	471
Fuel System Diagnostic Codes	471
Sensor Inspection Values	473
Terminal Voltage Check	476
Terminal Resistance & Continuity Check	478
GDI (DOHC) DIAGNOSTICS	481
Fuel System	481
Reading Diagnostic Codes	481
Fuel System Diagnostic Codes	481
GDI Inspection Values	482
Terminal Voltage Check	484
Terminal Resistance & Continuity Check	485
4M41 3.2 Diesel (DOHC) DIAGNOSTICS	488
Fuel System	488
Reading Diagnostic Codes	488
Fuel System Diagnostic Codes	489

Description	Page
Fuel System Inspection Procedures	490
Sensor Inspection Values	491
Terminal Voltage Check	492
4M41 3.2 Diesel (DOHC) COMMON RAIL FUEL SYSTEM 2008 On DIAGNOSTICS	495
Fuel System Diagnostic Codes	495
Terminal Voltage Check	496
Terminal Resistance & Continuity Check	500
Cruise Control Diagnostics	502
Reading Diagnostic Codes	502
Cruise Control Diagnostic Codes	502
Inspection Procedures	502
Auto Transmission Diagnostics	503
Reading Diagnostic Codes	503
Cruise Control Diagnostic Codes	504
Inspection Procedures	505
Automatic Climate Control Diagnostics	507
Service Diagnostic Chart	507
Inspection Chart	507
ABS Diagnostics	508
Reading Diagnostic Codes	508
Inspection Procedures	508
Diagnostic Trouble Codes	509
SRS Diagnostics	510
Reading Diagnostic Codes	510
Inspection Procedures	510
Diagnostic Trouble Codes	511

DIAGNOSTIC INFORMATION & TROUBLESHOOTING

General Information

The diagnostic results can be read using a "MUT II" or a diagnostic tool compatible with Mitsubishi vehicles. In some circumstances the warning light for the particular system can be used in conjunction with the earthing out the No1 terminal of diagnostic connector.

Diagnostic Connector.

The diagnostic connector is located under the lower dash trim, in front of the driver as shown.

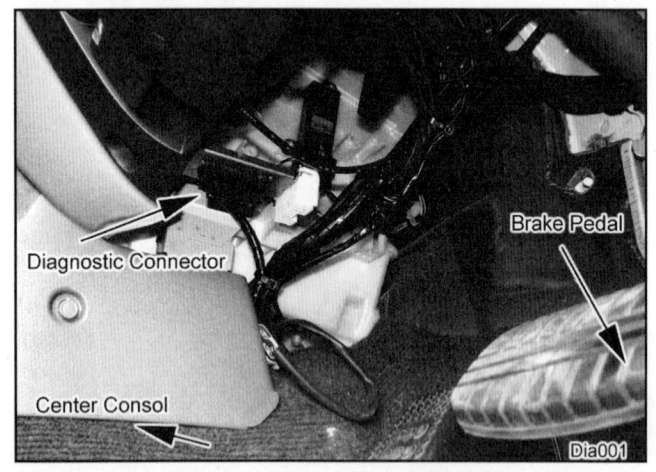

Reading Diagnostic Codes - Using a Warning Light

Systems that can use the warning light for reading diagnostic codes.

System	Warning Light
Automatic Transmission	Neutral position light
ABS	ABS warning light
SS4 II	4WD warning light
Brake system	Brake warning light

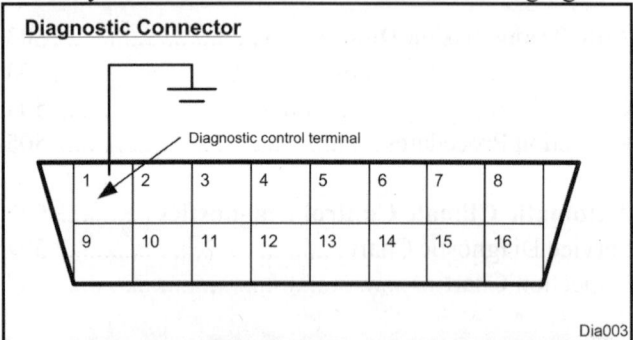

1. Use an electrical wire and terminal probe to earth out the No1 terminal, refer to diagram.
2. Turn on the ignition and read the diagnosis output pattern of the particular warning light for the system that has the faults, record results.
3. Refer to the diagnostic chart and repair all faults as required.
4. Turn the ignition off, then disconnect the battery negative terminal for at least 10 seconds.
5. Reconnect battery, turn on ignition and recheck diagnostic output to ensure normal output code appears.

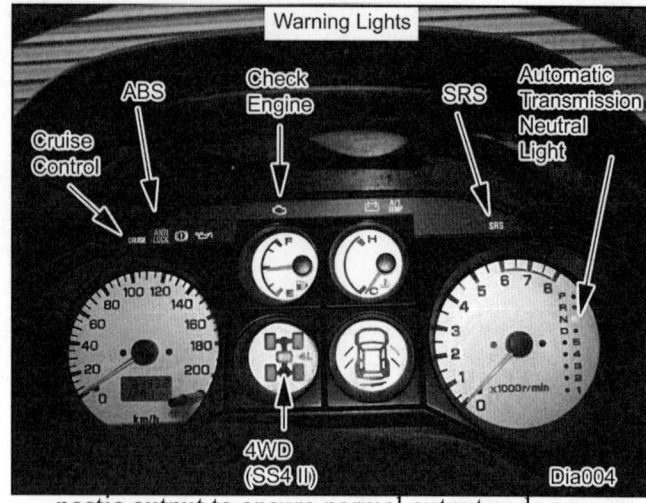

Reading Diagnostic Codes - with voltmeter

1. To the diagnostic connector, connect a voltmeter to the self diagnostic output terminal No9 and the earth terminals Nos4 & 5, refer to diagram.
2. Turn on the ignition and read the diagnosis output pattern from the voltmeter as the voltage alters and record results.
3. Refer to the diagnostic chart and repair all faults as required. 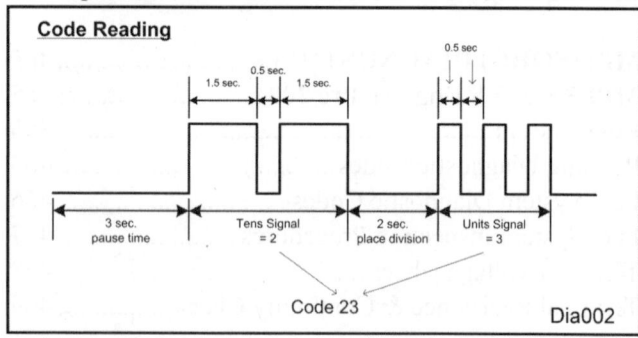
4. Turn the ignition off, then disconnect the battery negative terminal for at least 10 seconds.
5. Reconnect battery, turn on ignition and recheck diagnostic output to ensure normal output code appears.

Erasing Diagnostic Codes
Cutting Power

1. Turn the ignition off, then disconnect the battery negative terminal for at least 10 seconds.
2. Reconnect battery, turn on ignition and recheck diagnostic output to ensure normal output code appears.
3. Start the engine and allow the engine to warm, idle engine for approx 15 minutes.

MUT II or similar Diagnostic Tool.

1. Turn the ignition off.
2. Connect the diagnostic tool to diagnostic connector.
3. Turn ignition ON and operate the diagnostic tool as per instructions supplied with the tool.

464

MPI (SOHC) Diagnostics

MPI 3.5 and 3.8 Engines Pre 2004

FUEL SYSTEM

The diagnostic results can be read using a MUT II Mitsubishi diagnostic tool an after market diagnostic code reading tool.

Also diagnostic results can be read using a the engine warning lamp.

Reading Diagnostic Codes
Using Indicator Light

1. Earth the diagnostic control terminal (terminal 1) of the diagnostic connector. 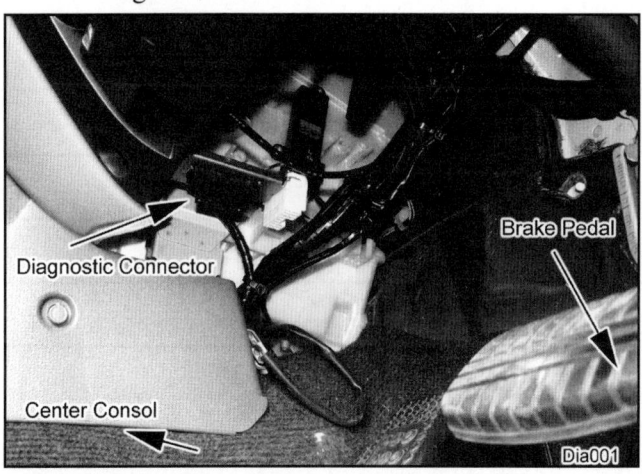 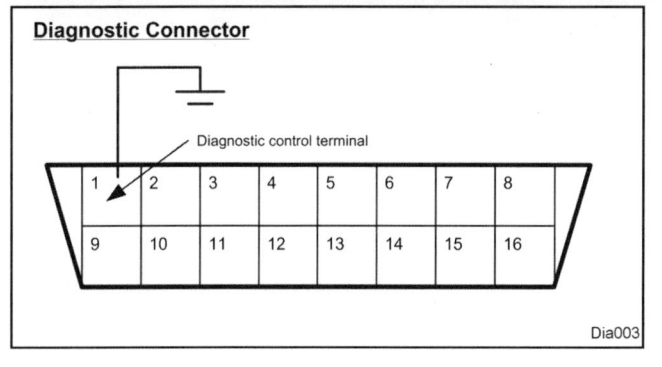
2. Turn on the ignition.
3. Read the diagnosis output pattern from the engine warning lamp and record results.
4. Refer to the diagnostic chart and repair all faults as required.
5. To delete/reset codes disconnect the battery negative cable for at least 10 seconds, reconnect battery warm up engine and idle for atl east 10 minutes.

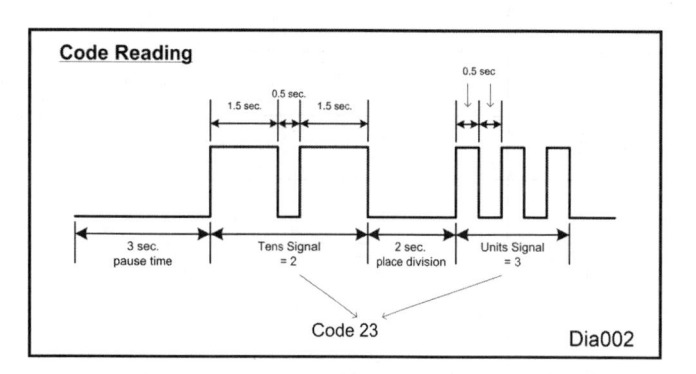

Fuel System Diagnostic Trouble Codes - Using Warning Lamp

Diagnostic Code	Inspection Item
11	Oxygen sensor system
12	Air flow sensor system
13	Intake air temperature sensor system
14	Throttle position sensor system
21	Engine coolant temperature sensor system
22	Crank angle sensor system
23	Top dead centre sensor system
24	Vehicle speed sensor system
25	Barometric pressure sensor system
41	Injector system
44	Ignition coil & power transistor unit system – Cylinders 1 and 4
52	Ignition coil & power transistor unit system – Cylinders 2 and 5
53	Ignition coil & power transistor unit system – Cylinders 3 and 6
54	Imobiliser system

DIAGNOSTIC INFORMATION & TROUBLESHOOTING

FUEL SYSTEM – INSPECTION PROCEDURES

Code #11 – Oxygen Sensor System
Probable Cause:
- Malfunction of oxygen sensor
- Malfunction of wiring harness or connector
- Malfunction of Engine ECU

Code #12 – Air Flow Sensor System
Probable Cause:
- Malfunction of air flow sensor
- Malfunction of wiring harness or connector
- Malfunction of Engine ECU

Code #13 – Intake Air Temperature Sensor System
Probable Cause:
- Malfunction of intake air temperature sensor
- Malfunction of wiring harness or connector
- Malfunction of Engine ECU

Code #14 – Throttle Position Sensor System
Probable Cause:
- Malfunction of throttle sensor or incorrect adjustment
- Malfunction of wiring harness or connector
- Malfunction of Engine ECU

Code #21 – Engine Coolant Temperature Sensor System
Probable Cause:
- Malfunction of engine coolant temperature sensor
- Malfunction of connector
- Malfunction of Engine ECU

Code #22 – Crank Angle Sensor System
Probable Cause:
- Malfunction of crank angle sensor
- Malfunction of wiring harness or connector
- Malfunction of Engine ECU

Code #23 – Top Dead Sensor System (Camshaft position sensor)
Probable Cause:
- Malfunction of crank angle sensor
- Malfunction of wiring harness or connector
- Malfunction of Engine ECU

Code #24 – Vehicle Speed Sensor System
Probable Cause:
- Malfunction of vehicle speed sensor
- Malfunction of wiring harness or connector
- Malfunction of Engine ECU

Code #25 – Barometric Pressure Sensor System
Probable Cause:
- Malfunction of vehicle speed sensor
- Malfunction of wiring harness or connector
- Malfunction of Engine ECU

Code #41 – Injector System
Probable Cause:
- Short circuit to earth of the diagnosis control line
- Malfunction of wiring harness or connector
- Malfunction of Engine ECU

Code #44 – Ignition Coil & Power Transistor Unit System–Cylinders 1 & 4
Probable Cause:
- Malfunction of ignition coil
- Malfunction of wiring harness or connector
- Malfunction of power transistor unit
- Malfunction of Engine ECU

Code #52 – Ignition Coil & Power Transistor Unit System–Cylinders 2 & 5
Probable Cause:
- Malfunction of ignition coil
- Malfunction of wiring harness or connector
- Malfunction of power transistor unit
- Malfunction of Engine ECU

Code #53 – Ignition Coil & Power Transistor Unit System–Cylinders 3 & 6
Probable Cause:
- Malfunction of ignition coil
- Malfunction of wiring harness or connector
- Malfunction of power transistor unit
- Malfunction of Engine ECU

Code #54 – Immobiliser System
Probable Cause:
- ID code confusion
- ID code does not match
- Malfunction of wiring harness or connector
- Malfunction of Engine ECU
- Malfunction of immobiliser ECU

CHECK AT THE ENGINE-ECU
Terminal Voltage Check Chart

Caution: *Short-circuiting the +ve probe between a connector terminal and ground could damage the vehicle wiring, sensor and Engine-ECU.*

1. Ensure the ignition switch is turned to OFF and wait at least 3 seconds.
2. Refer to the check chart and measure the voltage for each of the terminals of the Engine-ECU connector.
3. If reading is not to specification, check the corresponding sensor, actuator and related wiring. Repair or replace as required.
4. After repair recheck voltage to ensure problem has been corrected.
5. Use a long pointy narrow probe attached to multimeter ends, so it can be inserted into the back of the connector terminals.

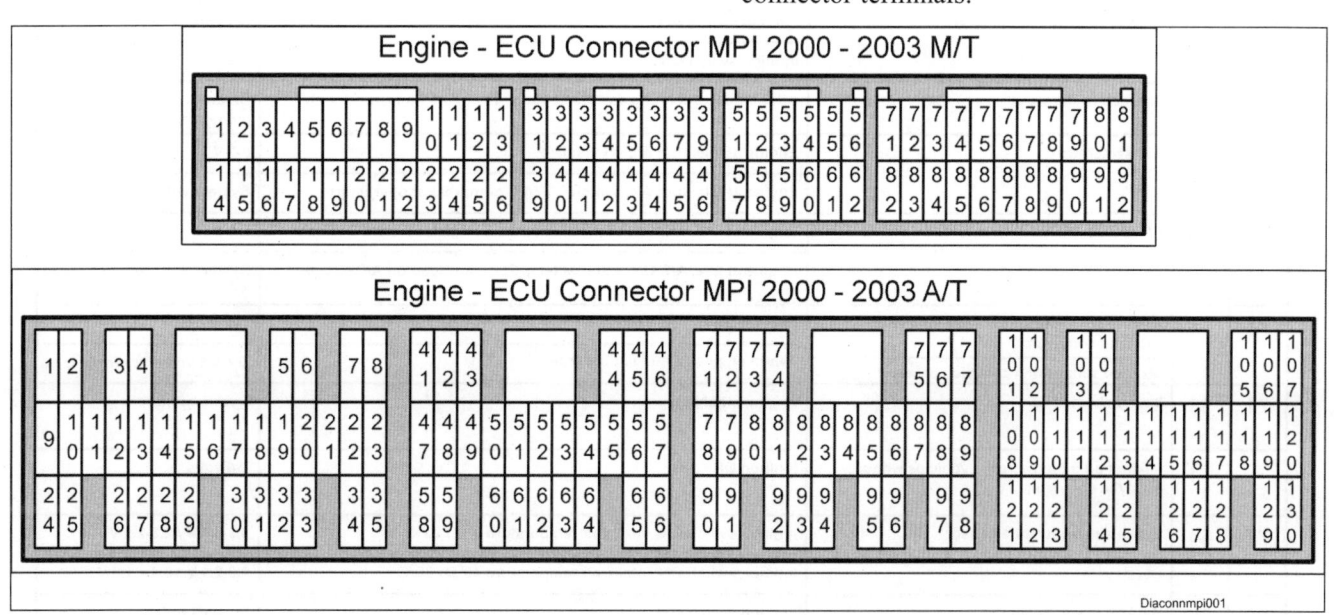

Engine - ECU Connector MPI 2000 - 2003 M/T

Engine - ECU Connector MPI 2000 - 2003 A/T

Engine ECU – Terminal Voltage Check Chart MPI – 2000 – 2003

Terminal (V6) Man	Terminal (V6) Auto	Circuit Name	Inspection Requirements	Normal Condition
1	1	Injector #1	Engine idling at operating temperature, suddenly depress the accelerator pedal (slightly)	11-14 V drops momentarily
14	9	Injector #2		
2	24	Injector #3		
15	2	Injector #4		
3	10	Injector #5		
16	25	Injector #6		
4	14	Stepper motor coil (A1)	Shortly after warmed up engine is started	Changes repeatedly between System Voltage and 0-3 V
17	28	Stepper motor coil (A2)		
5	15	Stepper motor coil (B1)		
18	29	Stepper motor coil (B2)		
8	20	A/C relay for vehicles in Australia and South Africa	Engine at idle, A/C switched from OFF to ON (A/C compressor operating)	System voltage or momentarily 6V to 0-3V
10	11	Power transistor unit - A	Engine at 3000rpm	0.3 – 3.0 V
12	41	Power supply	Ignition switch ON	System Voltage
25	47			
19	19	Volume air flow sensor reset signal	Engine at idle	0-1 V
			Engine at 3000rpm	6-9 V
11	12	Power transistor unit - B	Engine at 3000rpm	0.3 – 3.0 V
23	13	Power transistor unit - C	Engine at 3000rpm	0.3 – 3.0 V
21	18	Fan motor relay	Radiator fan not operating (coolant temp less than 90°C)	System voltage
			Radiator fan operating at low speed (coolant temp 90°C - 105°C)	0-3 V
22	21	Fuel pump relay vehicles in Australia and South Africa	Ignition switch ON	System voltage
			Engine at idle	0-3 V
24	34	Purge Control for vehicles with catalytic converter	Engine at 3000rpm, while warming up engine	0-3 V
36	22	Engine warning lamp	Ignition switch Off to ON	0-3 V to 9-13 V (after several seconds)
37	52	Power steering fluid pressure switch	After idling, steering wheel stationary	System voltage
			After idling, steering wheel turned	0-3 V
38	49	Control relay (power supply)	Ignition switch OFF	System voltage
			Ignition switch ON	0-3 V
44	44	Antilock Brake signal	After engine operating as vehicle ready to depart – speed 0-10kph	Battery voltage, then 0-3V momentarily
45	83	A/C switch No1	Engine at idle, turn A/C switch OFF	0-3 V
			Engine at idle, turn A/C switch ON (A/C compressor operating)	System voltage
57	61	A/C switch No2	Engine at idle, A/C ON, external temp 25 C. high load on A/C to cool	0-3 V
			Engine at idle, A/C ON, external temp 25 C. low load on A/C to cool	System voltage
76	--	Mixture adjusting screw – vehicles with catalytic converter	Ignition ON	1-4 volts
		Oxygen sensor with catalyic converter	Warm engine running at 2500rpm	0 – 0.8 volts flickering
71	58	Ignition switch-ST	Engine cranking	8 volts or more
--	71	Mixture adjusting screw – vehicles without catalytic converter	Ignition ON	1-4 volts
72	64	Intake air temperature sensor	Ignition switch ON, intake air temperature 0°C / 20°C	3.2-3.8 V / 2.3-2.9 V
			Ignition switch ON, intake air temperature 40°C / 80°C	1.5-2.1 V / 0.4 – 1.0 V
80	66	Backup power supply	Ignition switch OFF	System voltage
81	46	Sensor supply voltage	Ignition switch ON	4.5 – 5.5 V
82	98	Ignition switch - IG	Ignition switch ON	System voltage

DIAGNOSTIC INFORMATION & TROUBLESHOOTING

Terminal Resistance & Continuity Checks

Caution: *If checks are performed on the wrong terminals damage could be caused to the vehicle wiring, sensor and Engine-ECU.*

1. Ensure the ignition switch is turned to OFF, then disconnect the Engine-ECU connector.
2. Refer to the check chart and measure the resistance and check for continuity between the terminals of the Engine-ECU connector, harness-side.
3. If reading is not to specification, check the corresponding sensor, actuator and related wiring. Repair or replace as required.
4. After repair recheck to ensure problem has been corrected.

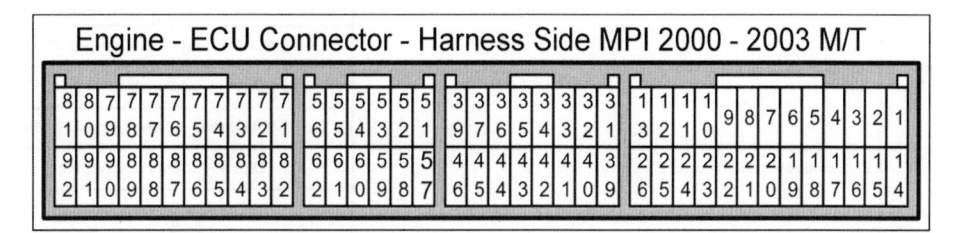

469

DIAGNOSTIC INFORMATION & TROUBLESHOOTING

Engine ECU – Terminal Resistance & Continuity Checks - MPI - 2000 - 2003

diaecumpi002

Terminal (Manual / Tran)	Terminal (Automatic/Tran)	Inspection Item	Terminal Voltage
1-12	1-41	Injector #1	13 - 16 Ohms @ 20°C
14-12	9-41	Injector #2	13 - 16 Ohms @ 20°C
2-12	24-41	Injector #3	13 - 16 Ohms @ 20°C
15-12	2-41	Injector #4	13 - 16 Ohms @ 20°C
3-12	10-41	Injector #5	13 - 16 Ohms @ 20°C
16-12	25-41	Injector #6	13 - 16 Ohms @ 20°C
4-12	14-41	Stepper motor coil (A1)	28 - 33 Ohms @ 20°C
17-12	28-41	Stepper motor coil (A2)	28 - 33 Ohms @ 20°C
5-12	15-41	Stepper motor coil (B1)	28 - 33 Ohms @ 20°C
18-12	29-41	Stepper motor coil (B2)	28 - 33 Ohms @ 20°C
6-12	6-41	EGR control solenoid valve	34 - 44 Ohms @ 20°C
24-12	34-41	Purge control solenoid valve	34 - 44 Ohms @ 20°C
13-body earth	42-body earth	Engine ECU earth	0 Ohms (continuity)
26-body earth	48-body earth	Engine ECU earth	0 Ohms (continuity)
72-92	64-57	Intake air temperature sensor	5.3 – 6.7 kOhms – intake air temp @ 0°C
			2.3 – 3.0 kOhms – intake air temp @ 20°C
			1.0 – 1.5 kOhms – intake air temp @ 40°C
			0.30 – 0.42 kOhms – intake air temp @ 80°C
83-92	44-57	Engine coolant temperature sensor	5.1 – 6.5 kOhms – engine coolant temp @ 0°C
			2.1 – 2.7 kOhms – engine coolant temp @ 20°C
			0.9 – 1.3 kOhms – engine coolant temp @ 40°C
			0.26 – 0.36 kOhms – engine coolant temp @ 80°C
87-92	79-57	Idle position switch	Continuity – throttle valve idle position
			No Continuity – throttle valve slightly open

MPI 3.8 litre (SOHC) Diagnostics

MPI 3.8 CONTROL

* Before carrying out diagnostic procedures ensure the air ducts are not blocked or become disengaged.
* Also ensure connectors are disconnected when checking components.

Note: *Pre MPI 3.8 2004 vehicles check with codes for the MPI 3.5 engine.*

FUEL SYSTEM

The diagnostic results can be read using a MUTII Mitsubishi diagnostic tool an after market diagnostic code reading tool.

Codes below introduced in 2004.
* Codes below with an * were introduced in 2005.
# Codes below with a # were introduced in 2006.
+ Codes below with a + were introduced in 2008.
As new codes are introduced, a similar code may be dropped off the system.

FUEL and IGNITION CODES	
Code	Sensor and sensor circuit
P0100	Air Flow Sensor (AFS)
P0102+	Air Flow Sensor (AFS) low input
P0103+	Air Flow Sensor (AFS) high input
P0105	Barometric Pressure
P0107+	Manifold absolute pressure low input
P0108+	Manifold absolute pressure high input
P0110	Intake air temperature sensor
P0112+	Intake air temperature sensor low input
P0113+	Intake air temperature sensor high input
P0115	Engine coolant temperature sensor
P0117+	Engine coolant temperature low input
P0118+	Engine coolant temperature high input
P0122	Throttle Position Sensor circuit low input
P0123	Throttle Position Sensor circuit high input
P0125+	Coolant temperature to low for closed loop fuel control
P0130 #	Right bank oxygen sensor (front)
P0131+	Right bank oxygen sensor heater (front) low voltage
P0132+	Right bank oxygen sensor heater (front) high voltage
P0133+	Right bank oxygen sensor heater (front) slow signal
P0134+	Right bank oxygen sensor heater (front) no signal received
P0135 #	Right bank oxygen sensor heater (front)
P0136 #	Right bank oxygen sensor (rear)
P0137+	Right bank oxygen sensor heater (rear) low voltage
P0138+	Right bank oxygen sensor heater (rear) high voltage
P0141 #	Right bank oxygen sensor heater (rear)
P0150 #	Left bank oxygen sensor (front)
P0151+	Left bank oxygen sensor heater (front) low voltage
P0152+	Left bank oxygen sensor heater (front) high voltage
P0153+	Left bank oxygen sensor heater (front) slow signal
P0154+	Left bank oxygen sensor heater (front) no signal received
P0155#	Left bank oxygen sensor heater (front)
P0156#	Left bank oxygen sensor (rear)
P0157+	Left bank oxygen sensor heater (rear) low voltage
P0158+	Left bank oxygen sensor heater (rear) high voltage
P0161 #	Left bank oxygen sensor heater (rear)

DIAGNOSTIC INFORMATION & TROUBLESHOOTING

FUEL and IGNITION CODES	
P0170 #	Abnormal fuel system (Right bank)
P0171 +	Abnormal fuel system (Right bank) lean
P0172 +	Abnormal fuel system (Right bank) rich
P0173 #	Abnormal fuel system (Left bank)
P0174 +	Abnormal fuel system (Left bank) lean
P0175 +	Abnormal fuel system (Left bank) rich
P0201	No.1 injector
P0202	No.2 injector
P0203	No.3 injector
P0204	No.4 injector
P0205	No.5 injector
P0206	No.6 injector
P0222	Throttle position sensor low input
P0223	Throttle position sensor high input
P0325	Detonation sensor
P0300 *	Ignition and Power Transistor
P0301#	No.1 cylinder misfire detected
P0302#	No.2 cylinder misfire detected
P0303#	No.3 cylinder misfire detected
P0304#	No.4 cylinder misfire detected
P0305#	No.5 cylinder misfire detected
P0306#	No.6 cylinder misfire detected
P0325+	Detonation sensor
P0335	Crank angle sensor
P0340	Camshaft position sensor
P0403#	EGR control solenoid valve system
P0421#	Catalyst malfunction (Right bank)
P0431#	Catalyst malfunction (Left bank)
P0443#	Purge control solenoid valve
P0500	Vehicle speed sensor // A/T DTC29
P0505#	Idle speed control (ISC) system
P0513+	Immobilizer problem
P0551#	Power steering fluid pressure switch
P0603+	EEPROM problem
P0606	Powertrain control module main processor malfunction
P0622+	Alternator problem at FR connector
P0638	Throttle valve control servo circuit range/performance problem
P0642	Throttle position sensor power supply
P0657	Throttle valve control servo relay circuit malfunction
P0660+	Variable induction control solenoid valve system
P1021+	Oil feed control valve system
P1601	Communication malfunction
P1602 *	Communication malfunction
P1603+	Battery power backup problem
P1610	Immobilizer
P2100	Throttle valve control servo circuit (open)
P2101	Throttle valve control servo magneto malfunction (short)

FUEL and IGNITION CODES	
P2102	Throttle valve control servo circuit (shorted low)
P2103	Throttle valve control servo circuit (shorted high
P2108	Throttle valve control servo processor malfunction
P2121	Accelerator pedal position sensor (main) circuit problem
P2122	Accelerator pedal position sensor (main) circuit low input
P2123	Accelerator pedal position sensor (main) circuit high input
P2126	Accelerator pedal position sensor (sub) circuit problem
P2127	Accelerator pedal position sensor (sub) circuit low input
P2128	Accelerator pedal position sensor (sub) circuit high input
P2135	Throttle position sensor (main and sub) range/performance problem
P2138	Accelerator pedal position sensor (main and sub) range/performance problem
P2228+	Barometric pressure signal low input
P2229+	Barometric pressure signal high input

DIAGNOSTIC INFORMATION & TROUBLESHOOTING

MPI 3.8 (SOHC) Sensor Inspection Values

Problem Code	Sensor	Condition		Whats Normal
P0100	Air flow sensor	- Engine coolant temperature: 80 95 deg C	Idling	22 – 48 Hz
		- All lights and accessories OFF	2,500 rpm	60 – 100 Hz
		- Transmission in "P"	Racing	Frequency increases as rpm increases
P0105	Barometric pressure sensor	Ignition switch: ON	At altitude of 0 m	101 kPa
			At altitude of 600 m	95 kPa
			At altitude of 1200 m	88 kPa
			At altitude of 1800 m	81 kPa
P0110	Intake air temperature sensor	Ignition switch: ON or with engine running	When intake air temperature is −20 deg C	−20 deg C
			Intake air temperature is 0 deg C	0 deg C
			Intake air is 20 deg C	20 deg C
			Intake air is 40 deg C	40 deg C
P0115	Engine coolant temperature sensor	Ignition switch: ON or with engine running	Engine coolant temperature is −20 deg C	−20 deg C
			Engine coolant temperature is 0 deg C	0 deg C
			Engine coolant temperature is 20 deg C	20 deg C
			Engine coolant temperature is 40 deg C	40 deg C
P0122 P0123	Throttle position sensor (main) - Disconnect throttle valve control servo, delete DTC code after this test.	Ignition switch ON, engine stopped. Remove intake air tube at throttle body. Disconnect throttle position sensor connector, then connect terminals 1, 2, 3 and 4 with special tool MB991348.	Close the throttle valve with a finger fully.	200 – 800 mV
			Open the throttle valve with a finger fully.	3,800 – 4,900 mV
		No load		450 – 1,000 mV
		A/C switch: "OFF" to "ON" A/C switch: "OFF" Shift lever "N" to D"		Voltage rises
P0122 P0123	Throttle position sensor (main) mid opening learning value	Ignition switch: ON		500 – 2,000 mV
P0130#	Right bank oxygen sensor - front	Warming up engine	High rpm then let accelerator off	200 mV or less
			Race engine	600 – 1,000 mV
			Idling engine	Voltage fluctuates b/n 400 mv or less and 600–1,000mV
			Engine 2500 rpm	
P0136#	Right bank oxygen sensor - rear	Engine previously warmed up	Race engine	0 & 600–1,000mV alternate.

473

MPI 3.8 (SOHC) Sensor Inspection Values c'ntd

Problem Code	Sensor	Condition		Whats Normal
P0150#	Left bank oxygen sensor - front	Warming up engine	High rpm then let accelerator off	200 mV or less
			Race engine	600 – 1,000 mV
			Idling engine	Voltage fluctuates b/n 400mv or less and 600–1,000mV
			Engine 2500 rpm	
P0156#	Left bank oxygen sensor - rear	Engine previously warmed up	Race engine	0 & 600–1,000mV alternate.
P0201	Injector 1 cut off	Engine, warm, idling. Stop fuel to each injector in turn to see if affects idle		Rough idle
P0202	Injector 2 cut off			
P0203	Injector 3 cut off			
P0204	Injector 4 cut off			
P0205	Injector 5 cut off			
P0206	Injector 6 cut off			
P0222 P0223	Throttle position sensor (sub)	Ignition switch ON, engine stopped. Remove intake air tube at throttle body. Disconnect throttle position sensor connector, then connect terminals 1, 2, 3 and 4 with special tool MB991348.	Close the throttle valve with a finger fully.	200 – 800 mV
			Open the throttle valve with a finger fully.	3,800 – 4,900 mV
P0335	Crank angle sensor	- Engine: Cranking - Tachometer connected	Compare the tachometer with the MUT-II reading	Identical
		- Engine: Idling - Idle position switch ON - Within 6 minutes after engine started, engine coolant temp at 80 deg C	When engine coolant temperature is −20 deg C	1,250 – 1,450 rpm
			Engine coolant temp 0° C	1,100 – 1,300 rpm
			Engine coolant temp 20°C	1,000 – 1,200 rpm
			Engine coolant temp 40°C	900 – 1,100 rpm
			Engine coolant temp 80°C	550 – 650 rpm
P0403#	EGR Control solenoid valve	Solenoid valve turns On and Off	Turn ignition On	Solenoid valve clicks
P0443#	Purge Control solenoid valve	Solenoid valve turns On and Off	Turn ignition On	Solenoid valve clicks
P0551#	Power steering fluid pressure switch	Engine idling	Steering wheel stationary	Off
			Steering wheel turning	On
P1221 P2122 P2123	Accelerator pedal position sensor (main)	Ignition switch: ON	Release the accelerator pedal	905 – 1,165 mV
			Depress accelerator pedal gradually	Increases
			Accelerator full depressed	4,035 mV or more
P1226 P2127 P2128	Accelerator pedal position sensor (sub)	Ignition switch: ON	Release the accelerator pedal	905 – 1,165 mV
			Depress accelerator pedal gradually	Increases
			Accelerator full depressed	4,035 mV or more

MPI 3.8 (SOHC) Sensor Inspection Values c'ntd

Problem Code	Sensor	Condition		Whats Normal
------	Ignition coils and power transistor (ignition advance value)	- Engine: After having warmed up - Timing light is set. (The timing light is set in order to check ignition timing) - Within six minutes after engine starting	Idling	2 – 27 deg BTDC
			2,500 rpm	27 – 47 deg BTDC

CHECK AT THE ENGINE-ECU
Terminal Voltage Check Chart

Caution: *Short-circuiting the +ve probe between a connector terminal and ground could damage the vehicle wiring, sensor and Engine-ECU.*

1. Ensure the ignition switch is turned to OFF and wait at least 3 seconds.
2. Refer to the check chart and measure the voltage for each of the terminals of the Engine-ECU connector.
3. If reading is not to specification, check the corresponding sensor, actuator and related wiring. Repair or replace as required.
4. After repair recheck voltage to ensure problem has been corrected.
5. Use a long pointy narrow probe attached to multimeter ends, so it can be inserted into the back of the connector terminals.

Engine A/Trans - ECU Connector Terminals - MPI 3.8 2004 on

EngineECU3.82004

Engine ECU – Terminal Voltage Check Chart MPI – 2004 on

diaecumpi006a

Terminal	Circuit Name	Inspection Requirements	Normal Condition
1	Injector #1	Engine idling at operating temperature, suddenly depress the accelerator pedal (slightly)	11-14 V drops momentarily
5	Injector #2		
14	Injector #3		
21	Injector #4		
2	Injector #5		
6	Injector #6		
31	Ignition Coil No1 & 4 -Ignition power transistor	Engine 3000 rpm	0-3 V
35	Ignition Coil No2 & 5 -Ignition power transistor		
44	Ignition Coil No3 & 6 -Ignition power transistor		
79	Vehicle Speed Sensor	Ignition ON / Slowly push vehicle forward	0 - System voltage, alternates between above
70	Crank Angle Sensor	Engine cranking / Engine idling	0.4 – 4.0 V / 1.5 – 2.5 V
34	Power supply	Ignition switch ON	System Voltage
43			
37	Volume air flow sensor reset signal	Engine at idle	0-1 V
		Engine at 3000rpm	6-9 V
71	Camshaft position sensor	Engine cranking / Engine idling	0.4 – 3.0 V / 0.5 – 0.2 V
87	Tachometer signal	Engine at 3000rpm	0.3 – 3.0 V
17	Fan motor relay	Radiator fan not operating (coolant temp less than 90°C)	System voltage
		Radiator fan operating at low speed (coolant temp 90°C - 105°C)	0-3 V
8	Fuel pump relay vehicles in Australia and South Africa	Ignition switch ON	System voltage
		Engine at idle	0-3 V
23	Purge Control for vehicles with catalytic converter	Engine at 3000rpm, while warming up engine	Approx 9 V
7	Engine warning lamp	Ignition switch Off to ON	0-3 V to 9-13 V (after several seconds)
47	Power steering fluid pressure switch	After idling, steering wheel stationary	System voltage
		After idling, steering wheel turned	1 V or less
57	Control relay (power supply)	Ignition switch OFF	System voltage
		Ignition switch ON	1 V or less
44	Antilock Brake signal	After engine operating as vehicle ready to depart – speed 0-10kph	Battery voltage, then 0-3V momentarily
16	A/C Relay	Engine at idle, turn A/C switch OFF	0-3 V
		Engine at idle, turn A/C switch ON (A/C compressor operating)	System voltage
69	A/C switch	Engine at idle, A/C ON, external temp 25 C. high load on A/C to cool	0-3 V
78		Engine at idle, A/C ON, external temp 25 C. low load on A/C to cool	System voltage
108	Oxygen sensor veh's w/out catalytic converter	Ignition ON	1-4 volts
	Mixture adjusting screw – vehicles catalytic converter	Warm engine running at 2500rpm	0 – 0.8 volts flickering
51	Ignition switch-ST	Engine cranking	8 volts or more

Engine ECU – Terminal Voltage Check Chart MPI – 2004 on

Terminal	Circuit Name	Inspection Requirements	Normal Condition
108	Mixture adjusting screw – vehicles without catalytic converter	Ignition ON	1-4 volts
99	Intake air temperature sensor	Ignition switch ON, intake air temperature 0°C / 20°C	3.2-3.8 V / 2.3-2.9 V
		Ignition switch ON, intake air temperature 40°C / 80°C	1.5-2.1 V / 0.4 – 1.0 V
58	Backup power supply	Ignition switch OFF	System voltage
97	Sensor supply voltage	Ignition switch ON	4.5 – 5.5 V
50	Ignition switch - IG	Ignition switch ON	System voltage
100	Barometric Pressure sensor	Ignition switch ON, Altitude 0 meters / 600 meters	3.7- 4.3 V / 3.4 - 4.0 V
		Ignition switch ON, Altitude 1200 meters / 1800 meters	3.2-3.8 V / 2.9 – 3.5 V
63	Air Flow Sensor	Engine Idling	2.2 – 3.2 volts
		Engine operating at 2500rpm min	
4	Variable induction control valve	Engine Idling	1 V or less
		Engine operating at 4000rpm min	System voltage
15	Throttle Valve Control Servo Relay	Ignition ON	System voltage
		Ignition OFF	1 V or less
38	Accelerator pedal position switch	Ignition ON – Closed throttle	0 – 1 V
		Ignition ON – Slightly open throttle	4 V or more
107	Accelerator pedal position sensor (sub)	Ignition ON – Accelerator pedal released	0.905 – 1.165 V
		Ignition ON – Accelerator pedal push down	4.035 V or more
114	Accelerator pedal position sensor (main)	Ignition ON – Accelerator pedal released	0.905 – 1.165 V
		Ignition ON – Accelerator pedal push down	4.035 V or more
113	Throttle Position Sensor (sub) Remove air intake from throttle body, disconnect throttle position sensor, use MUT-II connect terminals 1,2,3&4. Ignition ON	Close throttle valve with finger	2.2-2.8 V
		Fully open throttle valve with finger	3.8 – 4.9 V
92	Accelerator pedal sensor power supply - main	Ignition Switch ON	4.5 – 5.5 V
106	Throttle position sensor power supply - main	Ignition Switch ON	4.5 – 5.5 V
108	Oxygen Sensor Heater	Engine warming up – 2500rpm	0 – 0.8 V alternates
115	Throttle Position Sensor (main) Remove air intake from throttle body, disconnect throttle position sensor, use MUT-II connect terminals 1,2,3&4. Ignition ON	Close throttle valve with finger	0.2-0.8 V
		Fully open throttle valve with finger	3.8 – 4.9 V
133	Throttle Control Servo (+ve)	Ignition ON – Accelerator fully open to fully closed	Decreases slightly 2 V under battery volts
141	Throttle Control Servo (- ve)	Ignition ON – Accelerator fully open to fully closed	Decreases slightly 2 V under battery volts
20	EGR control solenoid – except Taiwan	Ignition ON	System voltage
		Engine idling, suddenly push down accelerator pedal	System volts, temp drop

DIAGNOSTIC INFORMATION & TROUBLESHOOTING

Engine ECU – Terminal Voltage Check Chart MPI – 2006 additions

diaecumpi006c

Terminal	Circuit Name	Inspection Requirements	Normal Condition
10	Oxygen sensor heater, front left bank	Engine Idling, warming up – 15 seconds idling time	9 to 11 volts
		Engine racing to 4000rpm	9-11V then system voltage
18	Oxygen sensor heater, rear left bank	Engine Idling, warming up – 15 seconds idling time	1 V or less
		Engine racing to 4000rpm	System voltage
24	Oxygen sensor heater, rear right bank	Engine Idling, warming up – 15 seconds idling time	1 V or less
		Engine racing to 4000rpm	System voltage
25	Oxygen sensor heater, front right bank	Engine Idling, warming up – 15 seconds idling time	9 to 11 volts
		Engine racing to 4000rpm	9-11V then system voltage
108	Oxygen sensor, front left bank	Engine warming up at 2500rpm	Alternates b/n 0 – 0.8 Volts
109	Oxygen sensor, front right bank	Engine warming up at 2500rpm	Alternates b/n 0 – 0.8 Volts
116	Oxygen sensor, rear left bank	- Engine warming up - Engine racing	- 0 to 0.6-1 volts - Alternates
117	Oxygen sensor, rear right bank	- Engine warming up - Engine racing	- 0 to 0.6-1 volts - Alternates

Terminal Resistance & Continuity Checks

Caution: *If checks are performed on the wrong terminals damage could be caused to the vehicle wiring, sensor and Engine-ECU.*

1. Ensure the ignition switch is turned to OFF, then disconnect the Engine-ECU connector.
2. Refer to the check chart and measure the resistance and check for continuity between the terminals of the Engine-ECU connector, harness-side.
3. If reading is not to specification, check the corresponding sensor, actuator and related wiring. Repair or replace as required.
4. After repair recheck to ensure problem has been corrected.

Engine - ECU Connector Harness - MPI 3.8 2004 on

Engine ECUHarn382004

DIAGNOSTIC INFORMATION & TROUBLESHOOTING

Engine ECU – Terminal Resistance & Continuity Checks - MPI - 2004 to 2008
diaecumpi007

Terminal	Inspection Item	Terminal Voltage
1 - 34	Injector #1	13 - 16 Ohms @ 20°C
5 - 34	Injector #2	13 - 16 Ohms @ 20°C
14 - 34	Injector #3	13 - 16 Ohms @ 20°C
21 - 34	Injector #4	13 - 16 Ohms @ 20°C
2 - 34	Injector #5	13 - 16 Ohms @ 20°C
25 - 34	Injector #6	13 - 16 Ohms @ 20°C
3 - 34	EGR Valve - Stepper motor coil (A1) [Taiwan only]	20 - 24 Ohms @ 20°C
12 - 34	EGR Valve - Stepper motor coil (A2) [Taiwan only]	20 - 24 Ohms @ 20°C
19 - 34	EGR Valve - Stepper motor coil (B1) [Taiwan only]	20 - 24 Ohms @ 20°C
26 - 34	EGR Valve - Stepper motor coil (B2) [Taiwan only]	20 - 24 Ohms @ 20°C
20 - 34	EGR control solenoid valve [Vehicles except for Taiwan]	36 - 44 Ohms @ 20°C
23 - 34	Purge control solenoid valve [Vehicles with catalytic converter]	30 - 34 Ohms @ 20°C
33-body earth	Engine – A/T - ECU earth	0 Ohms (continuity)
42-body earth	Engine – A/T - ECU earth	0 Ohms (continuity)
99 - 96	Intake air temperature sensor	5.3 – 6.7 kOhms – intake air temp @ 0°C
		2.3 – 3.0 kOhms – intake air temp @ 20°C
		1.0 – 1.5 kOhms – intake air temp @ 40°C
		0.30 – 0.42 kOhms – intake air temp @ 80°C
98 - 96	Engine coolant temperature sensor	5.1 – 6.5 kOhms – engine coolant temp @ 0°C
		2.1 – 2.7 kOhms – engine coolant temp @ 20°C
		0.9 – 1.3 kOhms – engine coolant temp @ 40°C
		0.26 – 0.36 kOhms – engine coolant temp @ 80°C
10 - 34	Oxygen sensor Heater [Vehicles except for Taiwan] Oxygen sensor front left bank [Taiwan only]	4.5 – 8.0 Ohms @ 20°C
25 - 34	Oxygen sensor front right bank [Taiwan only]	4.5 – 8.0 Ohms @ 20°C
24 - 34	Oxygen Sensor rear right bank [Taiwan only]	11 - 18 Ohms @ 20°C
18 - 34	Oxygen Sensor rear left bank [Taiwan only]	11 - 18 Ohms @ 20°C
4 - 34	Variable Induction control valve	29 - 35 Ohms @ 20°C
144-bodyearth	Engine – A/Trans – ECU earth	Continuity (0 Ohms)
145-bodyearth		
133 - 141	Throttle Valve control servo	0.3 - 100 Ohms @ 20°C

Engine ECU – Terminal Resistance & Continuity Checks - MPI - 2006 to 2008
diaecumpi007

Terminal	Inspection Item	Terminal Voltage
10 - 34	Oxygen sensor front left bank	4.5 – 8.0 Ohms @ 20°C
25 - 34	Oxygen sensor front right bank	4.5 – 8.0 Ohms @ 20°C
24 - 34	Oxygen Sensor rear right bank	11 - 18 Ohms @ 20°C
18 - 34	Oxygen Sensor rear left bank	11 - 18 Ohms @ 20°C

Engine ECU – Terminal Resistance & Continuity Checks - MPI - 2008 On

diaecumpi008

Terminal	Inspection Item	Terminal Voltage
1 - 34	Injector #1	10.5 – 13.5 Ohms @ 20°C
5 - 34	Injector #2	10.5 – 13.5 Ohms @ 20°C
14 - 34	Injector #3	10.5 – 13.5 Ohms @ 20°C
21 - 34	Injector #4	10.5 – 13.5 Ohms @ 20°C
2 - 34	Injector #5	10.5 – 13.5 Ohms @ 20°C
6 - 34	Injector #6	10.5 – 13.5 Ohms @ 20°C
3 - 34	EGR Valve - Stepper motor coil (A1) [Taiwan only]	20 - 24 Ohms @ 20°C
12 - 34	EGR Valve - Stepper motor coil (A2) [Taiwan only]	20 - 24 Ohms @ 20°C
19 - 34	EGR Valve - Stepper motor coil (B1) [Taiwan only]	20 - 24 Ohms @ 20°C
26 - 34	EGR Valve - Stepper motor coil (B2) [Taiwan only]	20 - 24 Ohms @ 20°C
20 - 34	EGR control solenoid valve [Vehicles except for Taiwan]	36 - 44 Ohms @ 20°C
23 - 34	Purge control solenoid valve	22 - 26 Ohms @ 20°C
33-body earth	Engine – A/T - ECU earth	0 Ohms (continuity) (2 Ohms or less)
42-body earth	Engine – A/T - ECU earth	0 Ohms (continuity) (2 Ohms or less)
99 - 96	Intake air temperature sensor	5.3 – 6.7 kOhms – intake air temp @ 0°C
		2.3 – 3.0 kOhms – intake air temp @ 20°C
		1.0 – 1.5 kOhms – intake air temp @ 40°C
		0.30 – 0.42 kOhms – intake air temp @ 80°C
98 - 96	Engine coolant temperature sensor	5.1 – 6.5 kOhms – engine coolant temp @ 0°C
		2.1 – 2.7 kOhms – engine coolant temp @ 20°C
		0.9 – 1.3 kOhms – engine coolant temp @ 40°C
		0.26 – 0.36 kOhms – engine coolant temp @ 80°C
10 - 34	Oxygen sensor front left bank	4.5 – 8.0 Ohms @ 20°C
25 - 34	Oxygen sensor front right bank	4.5 – 8.0 Ohms @ 20°C
24 - 34	Oxygen Sensor rear right bank	11 - 18 Ohms @ 20°C
18 - 34	Oxygen Sensor rear left bank	11 - 18 Ohms @ 20°C
4 - 34	Variable Induction control valve	29 - 35 Ohms @ 20°C
144-bodyearth	Engine – A/Trans – ECU earth	Continuity (0 Ohms)
145-bodyearth		
133 - 141	Throttle Valve control servo	0.3 - 100 Ohms @ 20°C

GDI (DOHC) Diagnostics

GDI (DOHC) - CONTROL

* Before carrying out diagnostic procedures ensure the air ducts are not blocked or become disengaged.
* Also ensure connectors are disconnected when checking components.

FUEL SYSTEM

The diagnostic results can be read using a MUT-II Mitsubishi diagnostic tool an after market diagnostic code reading tool.
Also diagnostic results can be read using a the engine warning lamp.

Reading Diagnostic Codes
Using Indicator Light

1. Earth the diagnostic control terminal (terminal 1) of the diagnostic connector.
2. Turn on the ignition.
3. Read the diagnosis output pattern from the engine warning lamp and record results.
4. Refer to the diagnostic chart and repair all faults as required.
5. To delete/reset codes disconnect the battery negative cable for at least 10 seconds, reconnect battery warm up engine and idle for at least 10 minutes.

FUEL and IGNITION CODES	
Code	Sensor and sensor circuit
P0100	Air Flow Sensor (AFS)
P0105	Barometric pressure sensor
P0110	Intake air temperature sensor
P0115	Engine coolant temperature sensor
P0120	Throttle Position Sensor 1 (TPS1)
P0130	Oxygen sensor (right bank)
P0135	Oxygen sensor heater (right bank)
P0150	Oxygen sensor (left bank)
P0155	Oxygen sensor heater (left bank)
P0170	Abnormal fuel system (right bank)
P0173	Abnormal fuel system (left bank)
P0190	Abnormal fuel - fuel block, air, etc.
P0201	No.1 injector
P0202	No.2 injector
P0203	No.3 injector
P0204	No.4 injector
P0205	No.5 injector
P0206	No.6 injector
P0220	Accelerator Pedal Position Sensor 1 (APS1)
P0225	Throttle Position Sensor 2 (TPS2)
P0300	Ignition coil (power transistor)
P0325	Detonation sensor
P0335	Crank angle sensor
P0340	Camshaft position sensor
P0403	EGR valve
P0425	Catalyst temperature sensor
P0443	Purge control solenoid valve
P0500	Vehicle speed sensor
P1200	Injector driver
P1220	Electronic-controlled throttle valve
P1221	Throttle valve position feedback
P1222	Throttle control servo
P1223	Communication line with throttle valve controller
P1225	Accelerator Pedal Position Sensor 2 (APS2)
P1226	Throttle valve controller
P1500	Alternator FR terminal
P1610	Immobilizer

GDI Sensor Inspection Values

Problem Code	Sensor	Condition		Whats Normal
P0100	Air flow sensor	- Engine coolant temperature: 80 95 deg C - All lights and accessories OFF - Transmission in "P"	Idling	22 - 48 Hz
			2,500 rpm	60 - 100 Hz
			Racing	Frequency increases as rpm increases
P0100	Air flow sensor reset signal	Engine: After having warmed up	Idling	ON
			3000 rpm	OFF
P0105	Barometric pressure sensor	Ignition switch: ON	At altitude of 0 m	101 kPa
			At altitude of 600 m	95 kPa
			At altitude of 1200 m	88 kPa
			At altitude of 1800 m	81 kPa
P0110	Intake air temperature sensor	Ignition switch: ON or with engine running	When intake air temp is −20°C	−20°C
			Intake air temperature is 0°C	0°C
			Intake air is 20°C	20°C
			Intake air is 40°C	40°C
P0115	Engine coolant temperature sensor	Ignition switch: ON or with engine running	Engine coolant temperature is −20°C	−20°C
			Engine coolant temperature is 0 °C	0°C
			Engine coolant temperature is 20°C	20°C
			Engine coolant temperature is 40°C	40°C
P0120	Throttle position sensor (1st channel)	Engine warmed up Ignition switch: ON (engine stopped)	Release the accelerator pedal.	400 - 800 mV
			Depress the accelerator pedal gradually.	Increases in response to the pedal depression stroke.
			Depress the accelerator pedal gradually.	4,200 - 4,800 mV
		Engine: Idling after warming UP	No load	450 - 1,000 mV
			A/C switch: OFF - ON	Increases by 100 to 600 mV
			Transmission: P to D range	Increases by 0 - 200 mV.
P0130	Oxygen sensor (right)	Engine warmed up, air/fuel mixture is made leaner when decelerating, and is made richer when racing.	When at 4,000 r/min, engine is decelerated	200 mV or less
			Rev the engine suddenly.	600 - 1,000 mV
P0150	Oxygen sensor (left)	Engine warmed up, The oxygen sensor signal is used to check the air/fuel mixture ratio, and control condition by the engine ECU.	Idling (after six minutes)	400 mV or less
			2,500 r/min	600 - 1,000 mV (changes)
P0170	Learned value (right bank)	Warm engine, no load, 2500 rpm		−10 - 10%
P0170	Feed back (right bank)	Warm engine, no load, 2500 rpm		−25 - 25%
P0173	Learned value (left bank)	Warm engine, no load, 2500 rpm		−10 - 10%
P0173	Feed back (left bank)	Warm engine, no load, 2500 rpm		−25 - 25%

GDI Sensor Inspection Values (c'ntd)

Problem Code	Sensor	Condition		What's Normal
P0190	Fuel pressure sensor	- Engine coolant temperature: 80-95°C - All lights and accessories OFF - Transmission in "P"	Engine: Cranking	2 MPa or more
			Engine: Idling	4.0 – 6.9 MPa
P0220	Accelerator pedal position sensor	Ignition switch: ON	Release the accelerator pedal.	985 – 1085 mV
			Depress the accelerator pedal gradually.	Voltage increases as pedal is depressed.
			Depress the accelerator pedal fully.	4,000 mV or more
P0225	Throttle position sensor (2nd channel)	- Engine: After having warmed up - Ignition ON, engine not running	Release the accelerator pedal.	4,000 mV or more
			Depress the accelerator pedal gradually.	Voltage decreases as pedal is depressed.
			Depress the accelerator pedal fully.	400 – 600 mV
P0300	Ignition advance value	- Engine: After having warmed up - Timing light is set. (The timing light is set in order to check ignition timing) - Within six minutes after engine starting	Idling	7 – 23 deg BTDC
			2,500 rpm	15 – 35 deg BTDC
P0335	Crank angle sensor	- Engine: Cranking - Tachometer connected	Compare the tachometer with the MUT-II reading	Identical
		- Engine: Idling - Idle position switch ON - Within 6 minutes after engine started, engine coolant temp at 80 deg C	When engine coolant temperature is −20 deg C	1,250 – 1,450 rpm
			Engine coolant temp 0° C	1,100 – 1,300 rpm
			Engine coolant temp 20° C	1,000 – 1,200 rpm
			Engine coolant temp 40° C	900 – 1,100 rpm
			Engine coolant temp 80° C	550 – 650 rpm
P0403	EGR valve	- Engine coolant temperature 80−95deg C - All lights and accessories OFF - Transmission in "P"	Idling	2 – 20 STEP
			2,500 r/min	0 – 10 STEP
P0500	Vehicle speed sensor	Driving at 40 km/h		Approx. 40km/h
P1200	Injector drive time at:	Cranking engine at 250 rpm	Engine coolant temp 0° C	120 – 160ms
			When engine coolant temperature 20 deg C	70 – 90 ms
			When engine coolant temperature 80 deg C	20 – 35 ms
		- Engine coolant temp 80−95deg C - All lights and accessories OFF - Trans in "P" - 6 minutes after starting engine	Idling	Increases
			2,500 r/min	7 – 23 deg BTDC
			When engine is suddenly raced	15 – 35 deg BTDC
P1225	Accelerator pedal position sensor (2nd channel)	Ignition switch: ON	Release the accelerator pedal	985 – 1,085 mV
			Depress accelerator pedal	Increases
			Accelerator full depressed	4,000 mV or more

DIAGNOSTIC INFORMATION & TROUBLESHOOTING

CHECK AT THE ENGINE-ECU
Terminal Voltage Check Chart
Caution: *Short-circuiting the +ve probe between a connector terminal and ground could damage the vehicle wiring, sensor and Engine-ECU.*

1. Ensure the ignition switch is turned to OFF and wait at least 3 seconds.
2. Refer to the check chart and measure the voltage for each of the terminals of the Engine-ECU connector.
3. If reading is not to specification, check the corresponding sensor, actuator and related wiring. Repair or replace as required.
4. After repair recheck voltage to ensure problem has been corrected.
5. Use a long pointy narrow probe attached to multimeter ends, so it can be inserted into the back of the connector terminals.

GDI (DOHC) Engine - ECU Connector (A/T)

484

Engine ECU – Terminal Voltage Check Chart GDI – 2000 on

diaecuGDI001a

Terminal	Circuit Name	Inspection Requirements	Normal Condition
1	Injector #1	Engine idling at operating temperature, suddenly depress the accelerator pedal (slightly)	9-13 V drops momentarily
9	Injector #2		
24	Injector #3		
2	Injector #4		
10	Injector #5		
25	Injector #6		
80	Vehicle Speed Sensor	Ignition ON / Slowly push vehicle forward	0 - System voltage, alternates between above
45	Crank Angle Sensor	Engine cranking / Engine idling	0.4 – 4.0 V / 1.5 – 2.5 V
41	Power supply	Ignition switch ON	System Voltage
47			
19	Volume air flow sensor reset signal	Engine at idle	0-1 V
		Engine at 3000rpm	6-9 V
56	Camshaft position sensor	Engine cranking / Engine idling	0.4 – 3.0 V / 0.5 – 0.2 V
87	Tachometer signal	Engine at 3000rpm	0.3 – 3.0 V
18	Condensor fan motor relay	Condensor fan not operating	System voltage
		Condensor fan operating	0-3 V
21	Fuel pump relay	Ignition switch ON	System voltage
		Engine at idle	0-3 V
34	Purge Control for vehicles with catalytic converter	Engine at 3000rpm, while warming up engine	Approx 9 V
22	Engine warning lamp	Ignition switch Off to ON	0-3 V to 9-13 V (after several seconds)
52	Power steering fluid pressure switch	After idling, steering wheel stationary	System voltage
		After idling, steering wheel turned	0 - 3 V
49	Control relay (power supply)	Ignition switch OFF	0-3 voltage
		Ignition switch ON	System voltage
20	A/C Relay	Engine at idle, turn A/C switch OFF	System voltage
		Engine at idle, turn A/C switch ON (A/C compressor operating)	Initially 6 V, then 0 – 3 V
58	Ignition switch-ST	Engine cranking	8 volts or more
11	Ignition Coil #1	Engine operating at 3000 rpm	0.3 – 3.0 V
31	Ignition Coil #2		
13	Ignition Coil #3		
30	Ignition Coil #4		
12	Ignition Coil #5		
32	Ignition Coil #6		

Engine ECU – Terminal Voltage Check Chart GDI – 2000 on

Terminal	Circuit Name	Inspection Requirements	Normal Condition
46	Apply power supply volts to accelerator pedal position sensor – terminal 1	Ignition ON	4.5 – 5.5 volts
64	Intake air temperature sensor	Ignition switch ON, intake air temperature 0°C / 20°C	3.2-3.8 V / 2.3-2.9 V
		Ignition switch ON, intake air temperature 40°C / 80°C	1.5-2.1 V / 0.4 – 1.0 V
66	Backup power supply	Ignition switch OFF	System voltage
87	Sensor supply voltage	Ignition switch ON	4.5 – 5.5 V
98	Ignition switch - IG	Ignition switch ON	System voltage
55	Barometric Pressure sensor	Ignition switch ON, Altitude 0 meters / 600 meters	3.7- 4.3 V / 3.4 - 4.0 V
		Ignition switch ON, Altitude 1200 meters / 1800 meters	3.2-3.8 V / 2.9 – 3.5 V
65	Air Flow Sensor	Engine Idling	2.2 – 3.2 volts
		Engine operating at 2500rpm min	
6	Injector driver relay	Ignition ON	0 – 0.1 voltage
		Ignition OFF	0.5 – 1.0 volts
14	Throttle Valve Control Servo Relay	Ignition ON	0 – 0.1 voltage
		Ignition OFF	1 V or less
79	Accelerator pedal position switch	Ignition ON – Closed throttle	0 – 1 V
		Ignition ON – Slightly open throttle	4 V or more
3	Oxygen Sensor Heater - left	Engine - ON	0 – 3 volts
		Engine running at 5000 rpm	System voltage
4	Oxygen Sensor Heater - right	Engine - ON	0 – 3 volts
		Engine running at 5000 rpm	System voltage
23	GDI ECO indication light	Engine - idling	0 – 3 volts
		Engine – quickly rev engine	System volts
51	EGR valve - A	Turn ignition switch from OFF to ON	Flicker between 5-8 V for 3 seconds
53	EGR valve - B	Turn ignition switch from OFF to ON	Flicker between 5-8 V for 3 seconds
60	EGR valve - C	Turn ignition switch from OFF to ON	Flicker between 5-8 V for 3 seconds
115	Throttle Position Sensor (main) Remove air intake from throttle body, disconnect throttle position sensor, use MUT-II connect terminals 1,2,3&4. Ignition ON	Close throttle valve with finger	0.2-0.8 V
		Fully open throttle valve with finger	3.8 – 4.9 V
62	EGR valve - D	Turn ignition switch from OFF to ON	Flicker between 5-8 V for 3 seconds
63	Injector open circuit check	Engine for idling to 4000 rpm gradually	Decreases slightly 0.7 V under 4.5-5 volts
123	Stop light switch	Push brake pedal down	System voltage
		Release brake pedal	0 – 3 Volts

Engine ECU – Terminal Voltage Check Chart GDI – 2000 on

Terminal	Circuit Name	Inspection Requirements	Normal Condition
43	Engine Ignition signal	Engine at 3000 rpm	0.3 – 3.0 volts
44	Engine coolant temperature sensor	Ignition switch ON, intake air temperature 0°C / 20°C	3.2-3.8 V / 2.3-2.9 V
		Ignition switch ON, intake air temperature 40°C / 80°C	1.5-2.1 V / 0.4 – 1.0 V
71	Oxygen sensor - left	Warm engine at 2500 rpm	Flickers between 0V - 0.8 V
72	Oxygen sensor - right	Warm engine at 2500 rpm	Flickers between 0V - 0.8 V
93	Fuel Pressure Sensor	Engine Idling	0.3 – 4.7 volts
78	Throttle position sensor 2	Ignition switch ON, release accelerator pedal	4.0 volts or higher
		Ignition switch ON, depress accelerator pedal	0.4 – 0.6 volts
83	Air Flow Sensor	Engine Idling – A/C OFF	0 - 3 volts
		Engine Idling – A/C ON – compressor operating	System voltage
86	Parking lights	Park light switch ON	System voltage
		Park light switch OFF	0 – 3 volts
95	Accelerator pedal position sensor 1	Ignition ON – release accelerator pedal	0.985 – 1.085 volts
		Ignition ON – depress accelerator pedal	4 V or higher

4M41 3.2 Diesel (DOHC) Diagnostics

FUEL SYSTEM

The diagnostic results can be read using a MUT-II Mitsubishi diagnostic tool an after market diagnostic code reading tool.
Also diagnostic results can be read using a the engine warning lamp.

Reading Diagnostic Codes
Using Indicator Light
1. Earth the diagnostic control terminal (terminal 1) of the diagnostic connector.
2. Turn on the ignition.
3. Read the diagnosis output pattern from the engine warning lamp and record results.
4. Refer to the diagnostic chart and repair all faults as required.
5. To delete/reset codes disconnect the battery negative cable for at least 10 seconds, reconnect battery warm up engine and idle for atl east 10 minutes.

DIESEL 3.2 DOHC Fuel System Diagnostic Trouble Codes - Using Warning Lamp 2000-08

Diagnostic Code	Inspection Item
11	Accelerator pedal position sensor system
12	Boost pressure system
13	Barometric pressure sensor located in the ECU
14	Fuel temperature sensor system
15	Engine coolant temp sensor system
16	Boost air temp sensor system
17	Vehicle speed sensor system
18	Engine speed sensor system – backup system
21	Engine speed sensor system – main system
23	Idle switch system – located in accelerator pedal position sensor
25	Timer piston position sensor system – sub system
26	Control sleeve position sensor
27	Accelerator pedal position sensor system – sub system
41	Main throttle solenoid valve system
43	Timing control valve system
46	Injection correction ROM system
48	GE Actuator system – located in the center of the control sleeve position sensor
49	Over boost – turbo waste gate fault
54	Immobilizer system

3.2 DOHC DIESEL FUEL SYSTEM – INSPECTION PROCEDURES 2001-2008 Diacod32D002

Code #11 – Accelerator Pedal Position Sensor System
Probable Cause: Malfunction of accelerator pedal sensor
Malfunction of wiring harness or connector
Malfunction of Engine ECU

Code #12 – Boost Pressure Sensor System
Probable Cause: Malfunction of boost pressure sensor
Malfunction of wiring harness or connector
Malfunction of Engine ECU

Code #13 – Barometric Pressure Sensor System
Probable Cause: Malfunction of barometric pressure sensor
Malfunction of wiring harness or connector
Malfunction of Engine ECU

Code #14 – Fuel Temperature Sensor System
Probable Cause: Malfunction of fuel temperature sensor
Malfunction of wiring harness or connector
Malfunction of Engine ECU

Code #15 – Engine Coolant Temperature Sensor System
Probable Cause: Malfunction of engine coolant temperature sensor
Malfunction of wiring harness or connector
Malfunction of Engine ECU

Code #16 – Boost Air Temperature Sensor System
Probable Cause: Malfunction of boost air temperature sensor
Malfunction of wiring harness or connector
Malfunction of Engine ECU

Code #17 – Vehicle Speed Sensor System
Probable Cause: Malfunction of vehicle speed sensor
Malfunction of wiring harness or connector
Malfunction of Engine ECU

Code #18 – Engine Speed Sensor System – Back-up System
Probable Cause: Malfunction of engine speed sensor and or back-up system
Malfunction of wiring harness or connector
Malfunction of Engine ECU

Code #21 – Engine Speed Sensor System
Probable Cause: Malfunction of engine speed sensor
Malfunction of wiring harness or connector
Malfunction of Engine ECU

Code #23 – Idle Switch Sensor System
Probable Cause: Malfunction of idle speed sensor and / or accelerator pedal sensor
Malfunction of wiring harness or connector
Malfunction of Engine ECU

Code #25 – Timer Piston Position Sensor System
Probable Cause: Malfunction of timer piston position sensor
Malfunction of wiring harness or connector
Malfunction of Engine ECU

Code #26 – Control Sleeve Position Sensor System
Probable Cause: Malfunction of control sleeve position sensor
Malfunction of wiring harness or connector
Malfunction of Engine ECU

Code #27 – Accelerator Pedal Position Sensor System
Probable Cause: Malfunction of accelerator pedal position sensor
Malfunction of wiring harness or connector
Malfunction of Engine ECU

Code #41 – Main Throttle Solenoid Valve System
Probable Cause: Malfunction of main throttle solenoid valve sensor
Malfunction of wiring harness or connector
Malfunction of Engine ECU

Code #43 – Timing Control Valve Sensor System
Probable Cause: Malfunction of timing control valve sensor
Malfunction of wiring harness or connector
Malfunction of Engine ECU

Code #46 – Injector ROM System
Probable Cause: Malfunction of injection ROM system
Malfunction of wiring harness or connector
Malfunction of Engine ECU

Code #48 – GE Actuator System
Probable Cause: Malfunction of GE actuator – inside control sleeve position sensor
Malfunction of wiring harness or connector
Malfunction of Engine ECU

Code #49 – Over Boost System
Probable Cause: Malfunction of turbo waste gate
Malfunction of wiring harness or connector
Malfunction of Engine ECU

Code #54 – Immobiliser System
Probable Cause: ID code confusion
ID code does not match
Malfunction of wiring harness or connector
Malfunction of Engine ECU
Malfunction of immobiliser ECU

3.2 (DOHC) Diesel Sensor Inspection Values 2001-2008

Problem Code	Sensor	Condition		Whats Normal
11	Accelerator pedal position sensor	Ignition switch: ON	Accelerator pedal released	0.9 - 1.1 V
			Accelerator pedal fully down	4.1 volts plus
12	Boost pressure sensor	- Ignition ON - Warm engine - Lights, fan, radio etc OFF - Transmission in P	At altitude of 0 m	101 kPa
			At altitude of 600 m	95 kPa
			At altitude of 1200 m	88 kPa
			At altitude of 1800 m	81 kPa
			Idle engine	81-109 kPa
			Race engine suddenly	Increases
13	Barometric pressure sensor	Ignition ON	At altitude of 0 m	101 kPa
			At altitude of 600 m	95 kPa
			At altitude of 1200 m	88 kPa
			At altitude of 1800 m	81 kPa
14	Fuel temperature sensor	Ignition switch: ON or with engine running	When intake fuel temperature is −20 deg C	−20 deg C
			Intake fuel temperature is 0 deg C	0 deg C
			Intake fuel is 20 deg C	20 deg C
			Intake fuel is 40 deg C	40 deg C
15	Engine coolant temperature sensor	Ignition switch: ON or with engine running	Engine coolant temperature is −20 deg C	−20 deg C
			Engine coolant temperature is 0 deg C	0 deg C
			Engine coolant temperature is 20 deg C	20 deg C
			Engine coolant temperature is 40 deg C	40 deg C
16	Boost air temperature	Ignition switch: ON or with engine running	Intake air temperature is −20 deg C	−20 deg C
			Intake air temperature is 0 deg C	0 deg C
			Intake air temperature is 20 deg C	20 deg C
			Intake air temperature is 40 deg C	40 deg C
17	Vehicle speed sensor	Read speed on MUT II		Speed should match MUT II
18	Engine speed sensor (rpm) back-up	Engine cranking	Read rpm on MUT II	RPM should match MUT II
		Engine idling	Read rpm on MUT II	RPM should match MUT II
21	Engine speed sensor (rpm)	Engine cranking	Read rpm on MUT II	RPM should match MUT II
		Engine idling	Read rpm on MUT II	RPM should match MUT II

3.2 (DOHC) Diesel Sensor Inspection Values 2001-2008

Problem Code	Sensor	Condition		Whats Normal
23	Idle switch	Ignition ON	Accelerator pedal released	0 - 1 V
		Engine idling	Accelerator pedal slightly depressed	RPM should match MUT II
25 or 43	Timing control valve - % of opening degree	Ignition ON	Idling	0%
			2500 rpm	35 - 45%
			High idle	20 - 30%
26	Control sleeve position	Warm engine	Idling	1.535 - 1.735V
			2500 rpm	slightly decreased
			High idle	1.884 - 2.084V
26 or 48	GE Actuator	Warm engine	Idling	0%
			2500 rpm	35 - 45%
			High idle	20 - 30%

CHECK AT THE ENGINE-ECU
Terminal Voltage Check Chart
Caution: *Short-circuiting the +ve probe between a connector terminal and ground could damage the vehicle wiring, sensor and Engine-ECU.*

1. Ensure the ignition switch is turned to OFF and wait at least 3 seconds.
2. Refer to the check chart and measure the voltage for each of the terminals of the Engine-ECU connector.
3. If reading is not to specification, check the corresponding sensor, actuator and related wiring. Repair or replace as required.
4. After repair recheck voltage to ensure problem has been corrected.
5. Use a long pointy narrow probe attached to multimeter ends, so it can be inserted into the back of the connector terminals.

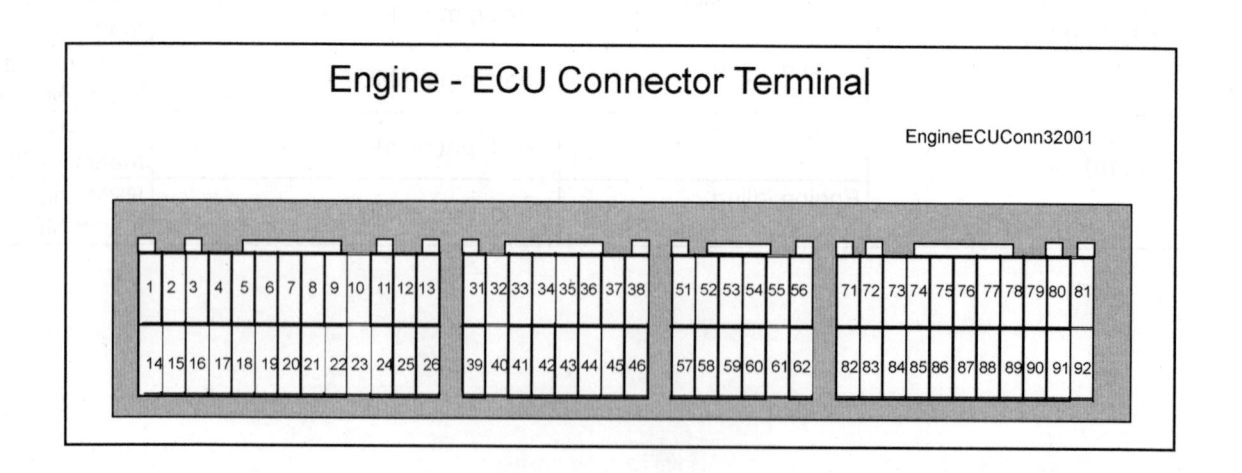

Engine - ECU Connector Terminal

EngineECUConn32001

1	2	3	4	5	6	7	8	9	10	11	12	13		31	32	33	34	35	36	37	38		51	52	53	54	55	56		71	72	73	74	75	76	77	78	79	80	81
14	15	16	17	18	19	20	21	22	23	24	25	26		39	40	41	42	43	44	45	46		57	58	59	60	61	62		82	83	84	85	86	87	88	89	90	91	92

Engine ECU - Terminal Voltage Check Chart 3.2 Diesel DOHC - 2001-2008

Terminal	Circuit Name	Inspection Requirements		What's Normal
1	GE Actuator	Ignition ON		9 volts or higher
2	Fuel Cut Solenoid	Ignition key from OFF to Start		0 - 1 volt
		Engine from idling to stopped		System volts
3	Timing Control Valve	Ignition switch ON		11 volts or higher
4	Glow Light	Engine coolant at running temperature Turn ignition key from OFF to ON		0 -1 volts
5	EGR control solenoid valve No2	Ignition key from OFF to ON		0 -1 volts
7	Condenser Fan Relay	Condenser fan operating		0 - 1volts
8	Engine warning light	Ignition key from OFF to ON		0 -1 volts then go to system voltage
9	PTC heater relay	Engine coolant at running temperature Heating switch ON, Air Con max with blower fan ON		0 - 1 volts
14	Main throttle solenoid valve	Ignition ON		System voltage
		Warm engine, idle engine then race engine		0 - 1 volts
16	Glow plug relay	Cool engine temperature Ignition key from OFF to ON		0 - 1 volts
18	Sub throttle solenoid valve	Engine idling		System voltage
		Engine from idle to stop		0 - 1 volts
21	Air Con relay	Air Con switch ON		0 - 1 volts
31	Idle switch	Ignition switch ON	Accelerator pedal released	0 - 1 volts
			Accelerator pedal slightly down	4 volts plus
32	Air Con swith	Air Con operating (compressor)		System voltage
35	Power steering fluid pressure switch	Warm engine idling	Turning steering wheel	0 - 1 volts
36	Selector switch - between A/T and M/T	Ignition switch ON		0 - 1 volts
37	Inhibitor switch	Ignition switch ON	Gear selector lever in either P or N	0 - 1 volts
			Gear selector lever in either R, D, 2 or L	System volts
39	Stop light switch	Ignition ON, Press brake pedal down		System voltage
40	Brake switch	Ignition ON, Press brake pedal down		0 - 1volts
46	Control relay	Ignition switch ON		0 - 3 volts
		Ignition from ON to OFF in approx 8 seconds		System volts
51	Engine rpm sensor - backup	Engine idling		1.5 - 2.5 volts
55	Accelerator position sensor	Ignition ON	Accelerator pedal released	0.6 - 1.0 volts
			Accelerator pedal fully pressed down	4.4 - 4.6 volts
71	Ignition Switch - ST	Turn key to start	Engine cranking	8 volts plus
73	Control sleeve position sensor	Ignition key ON		2.0 - 4.0 volts
74				2.2 - 2.7 volts
75				2.0 - 4.0 volts

Engine ECU - Terminal Voltage Check Chart 3.2 Diesel DOHC - 2001-2008

Terminal	Circuit Name	Inspection Requirements		What's Normal
76	Timer piston position sensor	Ignition key ON		2.0 - 4.0 volts
77				2.2 - 2.7 volts
78				2.0 - 4.0 volts
80	Power supply- backup	Ignition key OFF		System voltage
82	Ignition Switch - IG	Ignition key ON		System voltage
83	Engine coolant temperature sensor	Ignition key ON	Eng coolant temp 0 deg C	3.4 - 4.5 volts
			Eng coolant temp 20 deg C	2.6 - 3.6 volts
			Eng coolant temp 40 deg C	1.8 - 2.5 volts
			Eng coolant temp 80 deg C	0.7 - 1.7 volts
84	Accelerator pedal position sensor (main)	Ignition key ON	Accelerator pedal released	0.6 - 1.0 volts
			Accelerator pedal fully down	4.4 - 4.6 volts
85	Boost pressure sensor	Ignition key ON (760mmHg)		1.2 - 1.6 volts
86	Vehicle speed sensor	Ignition key ON Move vehicle forward		0 volts to 5 volts alternating
87	Engine fuel temperature sensor	Ignition key ON	Fuel temp 0 deg C	3.2 - 3.6 volts
			Fuel temp 20 deg C	2.3 - 2.7 volts
			Fuel temp 40 deg C	1.4 - 1.8 volts
			Fuel temp 80 deg C	0.4 - 0.8 volts
88	Boost air temperature	Ignition key ON	Air temp 0 deg C	3.2 - 3.8 volts
			Air temp 20 deg C	2.3 - 2.9 volts
			Air temp 40 deg C	1.5 - 2.1 volts
			Air temp 80 deg C	0.4 - 1.0 volts
89	Engine speed sensor, rpm	Engine idling		1.5 - 2.5 volts
91	Neutral switch	Ignition key ON	Gear selector lever in either P or N	0 - 1 volts
			Gear selector lever in either R, D, 2 or L	System voltage

3.2 Diesel DOHC Common Rail Fuel System 2008 on

* Before carrying out diagnostic procedures ensure the air ducts are not blocked or become disengaged.
* Also ensure connectors are disconnected when checking components.

The diagnostic results can be read using a MUT-II Mitsubishi diagnostic tool an after market diagnostic code reading tool.

Codes below introduced in 2008 with common rail fuel system.

\multicolumn{2}{c}{FUEL and IGNITION CODES}
Code	Sensor and sensor circuit
P0016	Crank angle senor / camshaft sensor problem
P0047	Variable geometry control solenoid valve (AT) low input
P0048	Variable geometry control solenoid valve (AT) high input
P0072	Air intake control solenoid No2 valve circuit low input
P0073	Air intake control solenoid No2 valve circuit high input
P0088	Common rail pressure problem
P0089	Suction control valve stuck
P0093	Fuel leak problem (reducing fuel pressure)
P0102	Air Flow Sensor (AFS) low input
P0103	Air Flow Sensor (AFS) high input
P0106	Manifold absolute pressure range problem
P0107	Manifold absolute pressure low input
P0108	Manifold absolute pressure high input
P0112	Intake air temperature sensor low input
P0113	Intake air temperature sensor high input
P0117	Engine coolant temperature low input
P0118	Engine coolant temperature high input
P0122	Throttle Position Sensor circuit low input
P0123	Throttle Position Sensor circuit high input
P0182	Fuel temperature sensor low input
P0183	Fuel temperature sensor high input
P0191	Common Rail pressure range problem
P0192	Common Rail pressure low input
P0193	Common Rail pressure high input
P0201	No.1 injector
P0202	No.2 injector
P0203	No.3 injector
P0204	No.4 injector
P0234	Turbocharger over boost situation
P0299	Turbocharger under boost situation
P0301	No.1 cylinder no injection
P0302	No.2 cylinder no injection

\multicolumn{2}{c}{FUEL and IGNITION CODES}
P0303	No.3 cylinder no injection
P0304	No.4 cylinder no injection
P0335	Crank angle sensor
P0336	Crank angle sensor range problem
P0340	Camshaft position sensor
P0341	Camshaft position sensor range problem
P0403	EGR control solenoid valve DC motor
P0405	EGR control solenoid valve low input
P0406	EGR control solenoid valve high input
P0420	Catalyst malfunction
P0427	Exhaust gas sensor No2 circuit low input
P0428	Exhaust gas sensor No2 circuit high input
P0472	Exhaust absolute pressure sensor circuit low input
P0473	Exhaust absolute pressure sensor circuit high input
P0502	Vehicle speed sensor low input
P0513	Immobilizer problem
P0545	Exhaust gas sensor No1 circuit low input
P0546	Exhaust gas sensor No1 circuit high input
P0551	Power steering fluid pressure switch
P0603	EEPROM problem
P0604	Random access memory (ram) malfunction
P0605	Read only memory (flash) malfunction
P0606	Engine ECU module main processor malfunction
P0607	Engine ECU module sub processor malfunction
P0628	Suction control valve open
P0629	Suction control valve battery short
P0630	Chassis number not programmed
P0638	Throttle valve control servo circuit range/performance problem (possible stuck)
P0642	Analog sensor ref voltage No1 low
P0643	Analog sensor ref voltage No1 high
P0652	Analog sensor ref voltage No2 low
P0653	Analog sensor ref voltage No2 high
P1203	Capacitor insufficient charging
P1204	Capacitor over charging
P1272	Pressure limiter malfunction
P1273	Supply pump low flow
P1274	Supply pump problem
P1275	Supply pump exchange
P1298	Variable geometry turbo system - high pressure
P1299	Variable geometry turbo system - low pressure
P1427	Exhaust gas (DPF) temp sensor No3 circuit low input
P1428	Exhaust gas (DPF) temp sensor No3 circuit high input

DIAGNOSTIC INFORMATION & TROUBLESHOOTING

FUEL and IGNITION CODES

Code	Description
P1474	Exhaust differential pressure sensor ambient temp sensor circuit low input
P1475	Exhaust differential pressure sensor ambient temp sensor circuit high input
P1497	DPF system malfunction
P1498	Excessive PM accumulated in DPF
P1499	Unusual high DPF temperature
P1625	Injection quality compensation valve error
P1626	Injection quality compensation valve not coding
P2009	Swirl control solenoid valve low input
P2010	Swirl control solenoid valve high input
P2118	Throttle valve control motor current malfunction
P2122	Accelerator pedal position sensor (main) circuit low input
P2123	Accelerator pedal position sensor (main) circuit high input
P2127	Accelerator pedal position sensor (sub) circuit low input
P2128	Accelerator pedal position sensor (sub) circuit high input
P2138	Accelerator pedal position sensor (main and sub) range/performance problem
P2146	Injectors cylinders 1 & 4 circuit open
P2147	Injector common circuit earth short
P2148	Injector common circuit positive short
P2149	Injectors cylinders 2 & 3 circuit open
P2228	Barometric pressure signal low input
P2229	Barometric pressure signal high input

CHECK AT THE ENGINE-ECU
Terminal Voltage Check Chart

Caution: *Short-circuiting the +ve probe between a connector terminal and ground could damage the vehicle wiring, sensor and Engine-ECU.*

1. Ensure the ignition switch is turned to OFF and wait at least 3 seconds.
2. Refer to the check chart and measure the voltage for each of the terminals of the Engine-ECU connector.
3. If reading is not to specification, check the corresponding sensor, actuator and related wiring. Repair or replace as required.
4. After repair recheck voltage to ensure problem has been corrected.
5. Use a long pointy narrow probe attached to multimeter ends, so it can be inserted into the back of the connector terminals.

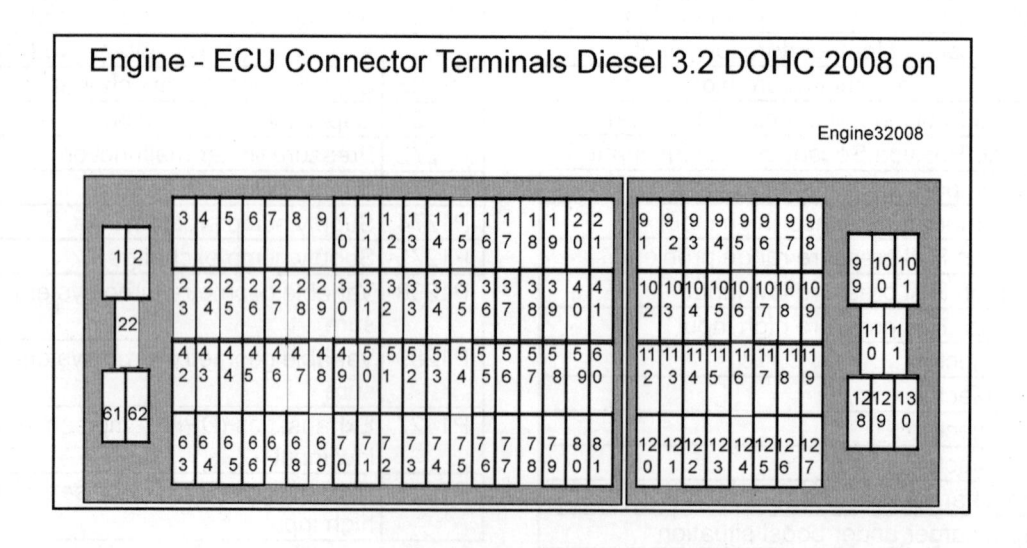

Engine - ECU Connector Terminals Diesel 3.2 DOHC 2008 on

Engine32008

DIAGNOSTIC INFORMATION & TROUBLESHOOTING

Engine ECU - Terminal Voltage Check Chart 3.2 Diesel DOHC - 2001-2008

Terminal	Circuit Name	Inspection Requirements		What's Normal
10	Swirl control solenoid	Ignition switch ON		System voltage
		Warm engine 4000 rpm		Decreasing voltage
13	Air Con load signal	Warm engine idling Air Con switch ON	Compressor clutch not engaged	1 volt or less
			Compressor clutch engaged	Alternating b/n 1 volt and system volts
14	Select rail switch - M/T	Ignition ON	Gear lever - 2nd, 4th or Reverse	System voltage
			Gear lever - 1st, 3rd or 4th	1 volt or less
15	Air Con switch	Warm engine idling	Air Con switch OFF	1 volt or less
			Air Con switch ON compressor operating	System voltage
16	3rd and 4th rail switch - M/T	Ignition ON	Gear lever - 3rd or 4th	System voltage
			Gear lever - other than 3rd or 4th	1 volt or less
17	Suction control valve +ve	Engine idling		5-6 volts
		Engine accelerating		Decreases
19	EGR motor +ve	Warm engine idling		1-3 volts
		Warm engine at 3500 rpm		1 volt or less
20	EGR motor -ve	Warm engine idling		1-3 volts
		Warm engine at 3500 rpm		1 volt or less
21	Variable geometry solenoid control valve	Ignition ON		System voltage
		Engine accelerating		Changes according to travel of accelerator pedal
29	Glow plug relay	Ignition OFF to ON	Cool engine	1 volt to system voltage after several seconds
			Warm Engine	System voltage
39	Condenser fan relay	Ignition ON	A/C OFF Engine coolant less than 95 deg C	System voltage
			A/C ON Vehicle speed under 60 kph	1 volt or less
40	Air Con relay	Warm engine idling	Air Con OFF	System voltage
			Air Con ON compressor no operating	System voltage
			Air Con ON compressor operating	1 volt or less
44	Exhaust differential pressure sensor ambient air temperature sensor (A/T)	Ignition ON	Ambient air temp -20° C	4.0-4.6 volts
			Ambient air temp 0° C	3.1-3.7 volts
			Ambient air temp 20° C	2.1-2.7 volts
			Ambient air temp 40° C	1.2-1.8 volts
			Ambient air temp 60° C	0.6-1.2 volts
			Ambient air temp 80° C	0.2-0.8 volts
46	Exhaust differential pressure sensor (A/T)	Disconnect pressure hoses to exhaust differential pressure sensor Ignition ON	Hose nipples left open	1 volt or less
			Apply air pressure hand pump to one of the nipples	Voltage changes according to pressure

Engine ECU - Terminal Voltage Check Chart 3.2 Diesel DOHC - 2001-2008

Terminal	Circuit Name	Inspection Requirements		What's Normal
47	Exhaust gas temperature sensor No2	Warm engine idling	Catalyst temp 200° C	4.0-4.6 volts
			Catalyst temp 400° C	2.4-3.0 volts
			Catalyst temp 600° C	1.2-1.8 volts
			Catalyst temp 800° C	0.5-1.1 volts
48	Exhaust gas temperature sensor No1	Warm engine idling	Exhaust temp 200° C	4.0-4.6 volts
			Exhaust temp 400° C	2.4-3.0 volts
			Exhaust temp 600° C	1.2-1.8 volts
			Exhaust temp 800° C	0.5-1.1 volts
49	Air intake temperature sensor No1	Ignition ON	Air temp -20° C	4.0-4.6 volts
			Air temp 0° C	3.1-3.7 volts
			Air temp 20° C	2.1-2.7 volts
			Air temp 40° C	1.2-1.8 volts
			Air temp 60° C	0.6-1.2 volts
			Air temp 80° C	0.2-0.8 volts
50	Air flow sensor	Engine rpm gradually increasing		Voltage gradually increasing
51	EGR position sensor	Warm engine idling		2.0 volts plus
		Warm engine 3500 rpm		1.5 volts or less
52	Manifold absolute pressure sensor	Ignition ON		0.7-1.2 volts
		Engine rpm increasing		Voltage increases
53	Engine coolant temperature sensor	Ignition ON	Coolant temp -20° C	4.4-4.9 volts
			Coolant temp 0° C	4.4-4.6 volts
			Coolant temp 20° C	3.3-3.9 volts
			Coolant temp 40° C	2.4-3.0 volts
			Coolant temp 60° C	1.5-2.1 volts
			Coolant temp 80° C	0.9-1.5 volts
54	Fuel temperature sensor	Ignition ON	Fuel temp -20° C	3.9-4.5 volts
			Fuel temp 0° C	3.1-3.7 volts
			Fuel temp 20° C	2.1-2.7 volts
			Fuel temp 40° C	1.2-1.8 volts
			Fuel temp 60° C	0.6-1.2 volts
			Fuel temp 80° C	0.2-0.8 volts
56	Rail pressure sensor	Warm engine idling		1.15-1.75 volts
57	Camshaft position sensor	Engine cranking		2.0-4.9 volts
		Engine idling		3.5-4.5 volts
58	Crank angle sensor	Engine cranking		1.5-4.5 volts
		Engine idling		2.5-3.5 volts
59	Camshaft position sensor power supply	Ignition ON		4.9-5.1 volts
60	Crankangle sensor power supply	Ignition ON		4.9-5.1 volts
63	Exhaust absolute pressure sensor	Ignition ON. Remove hoses to each exhaust differential pressure nipple	Apply pressure 60 kPa	1.8-2.0 volts
			Apply pressure 100 kPa	2.5-2.7 volts
			Apply pressure 150 kPa	3.5-3.7 volts
			Apply pressure 200 kPa	4.4-4.6 volts
65	Air intake temperature sensor No2	Ignition ON	Air temp -20° C	4.0-4.6 volts
			Air temp 0° C	3.1-3.7 volts
			Air temp 20° C	2.1-2.7 volts
			Air temp 40° C	1.2-1.8 volts
			Air temp 60° C	0.6-1.2 volts
			Air temp 80° C	0.2-0.8 volts
80	Sensor power	Ignition ON		4.9-5.1 volts

DIAGNOSTIC INFORMATION & TROUBLESHOOTING

Engine ECU - Terminal Voltage Check Chart 3.2 Diesel DOHC - 2001-2008

Terminal	Circuit Name	Inspection Requirements		What's Normal
81	Rail pressure sensor power	Ignition ON		4.9-5.1 volts
92	Ignition switch - IG	Ignition ON		System voltage
96	Power steering fluid switch	Engine idling	Steering wheel not moving	System voltage
			Moving steering wheel	1.0 volts or less
99	Battery	Ignition ON		System voltage
100				
101	Battery back up	Ignition ON		System voltage
103	Ignition switch - ST	Engine cranking		System voltage
104	1st & 2nd rail switch M/T	Ignition ON	Gear lever - 1st or 2nd	System voltage
			Gear lever - Except 1st or 2nd	1 volt or less
105	Reverse light switch	Ignition ON	Gear lever - Reverse	System voltage
			Gear lever - Except reverse	1 volt or less
106	Exhaust gas (DPF) temperature sensor No3	Warm engine idling	DPF temp 200° C	4.0-4.6 volts
			DPF temp 400° C	2.4-3.0 volts
			DPF temp 600° C	1.2-1.8 volts
			DPF temp 800° C	0.5-1.1 volts
109	Engine control relay	Ignition lock OFF		System voltage
		Ignition ON		1 volt or less
111	Throttle valve control servo -ve	Engine idling then stopped		Voltage change temporarily
112	Accelerator pedal position sensor sub power supply	Ignition ON		4.9-5.1 volts
113	Accelerator pedal position sensor sub	Ignition ON	Accelerator pedal released	0.2-0.8 volts
			Accelerator pedal fully depressed	2.0 volts plus
119	Vehicle speed sensor	Ignition ON Move vehicle froward		Alternating 0-5 volts
120	Accelerator pedal position sensor main power supply	Ignition ON		4.9-5.1 volts
121	Accelerator pedal position sensor main	Ignition ON	Accelerator pedal released	0.7-1.3 volts
			Accelerator pedal fully depressed	4.0 volts plus
124	Throttle position sensor	Air intake tube removed from throttle body Disconnect throttle body electrical connector, use Mitsubishi tool MB991658 or similar to bridge terminals 1, 2 & 4 of connector Ignition ON	Close throttle body valve by hand	0.3-0.7 volts
			Open fully throttle body valve by hand	4.0 volts plus
130	Throttle valve control servo +ve	Engine idling then stopped		Voltage changes for a short time

Terminal Resistance & Continuity Checks

Caution: *If checks are performed on the wrong terminals damage could be caused to the vehicle wiring, sensor and Engine-ECU.*

1. Ensure the ignition switch is turned to OFF, then disconnect the Engine-ECU connector.
2. Refer to the check chart and measure the resistance and check for continuity between the terminals of the Engine-ECU connector, harness-side.
3. If reading is not to specification, check the corresponding sensor, actuator and related wiring. Repair or replace as required.
4. After repair recheck to ensure problem has been corrected.

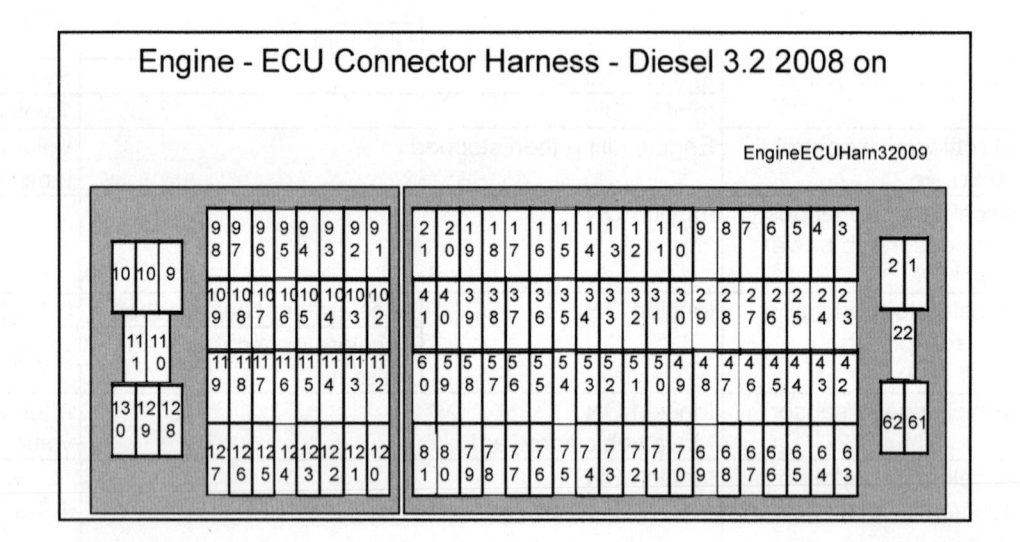

Engine - ECU Connector Harness - Diesel 3.2 2008 on

EngineECUHarn32009

ECU Terminal Resistance and Continuity Check - 3.2 Diesel DOHC - 2001-2008

Terminals	Inspection Circuit	What's normal
10-99	Swirl control solenoid valve	29-35 ohms @ 20° C
17-37	Suction control valve	Approx 2.1 ohms @ 20° C
21-99	Variable geometry control solenoid valve. A/T	10-14 ohms @ 20° C
22-body earth	Engine-ECU earth	Continuity (2 ohms or less)
61-body earth		
44-99	Exhaust differential pressure sensor ambient air temperature sensor. A/T	11-20 ohms @ -20° C
		4.5-7.0 kohms @ 0° C
		2.0-2.9 kohms @ 20° C
		0.98-1.4 kohms @ 40° C
		0.48-0.75 kohms @ 60° C
		0.25-0.45 kohms @ 80° C
47-48	Exhaust gas temperature sensor No2	120-560 kohms @ 20° C
48-69	Exhaust gas temperature sensor No1. A/T	120-560 kohms @ 20° C
49-70	Air intake temperature No1 sensor	13-17 kohms @ -20° C
		5.4-6.6 kohms @ 0° C
		2.3-3.0 kohms @ 20° C
		1.0-1.5 kohms @ 40° C
		0.56-0.76 kohms @ 60° C
		0.31-0.43 kohms @ 80° C
53-74	Engine coolant temperature sensor	14-17 kohms @ -20° C
		5.1-6.5 kohms @ 0° C
		2.1-2.7 kohms @ 20° C
		0.9-1.3 kohms @ 40° C
		0.48-0.68 kohms @ 60° C
		0.26-0.36 kohms @ 80° C
54-75	Fuel temperature sensor	2.0-3.0 kohms @ 20° C
65-75	Air intake temperature No2 sensor	13-18 kohms @ -20° C
		5.1-6.9 kohms @ 0° C
		2.0-3.0 kohms @ 20° C
		0.9-1.5 kohms @ 40° C
		0.40-0.78 kohms @ 60° C
		0.23-0.42 kohms @ 80° C
106-107	Exhaust gas temperature sensor No3 - DPF temp	120-560 kohms @ 20° C
111-130	Throttle valve servo	0.3-100 kohms @ 20° C

DIAGNOSTIC INFORMATION & TROUBLESHOOTING

CRUISE CONTROL

READING DIAGNOSTIC CODES
Using Indicator Light - 2000 to 2005 Models
1. Turn ignition switch ON, turn cruise control resume switch ON within 1 second
2. Read the diagnosis output pattern from the cruise control indicator lamp and record results.
3. Refer to the diagnostic chart and repair all faults as required.

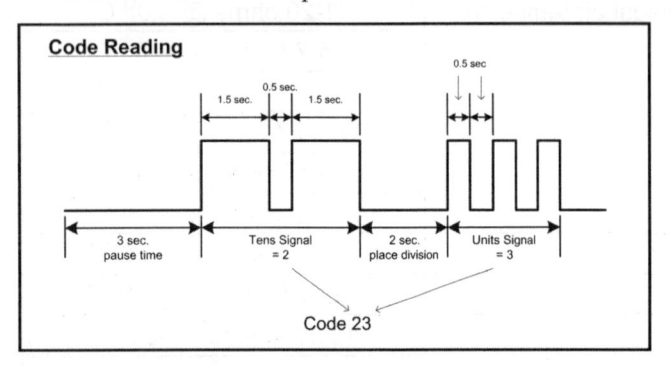

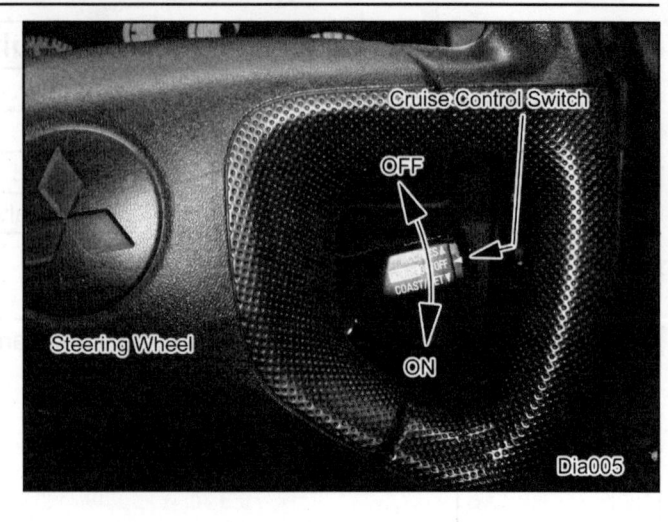

Cruise Control Diagnostic Trouble Codes 2000-2005

Diagnostic Code	Diagnostic Item	Self Diagnostic Output Pattern
0	Normal State (no diagnostic code output)	
11	Electric vacuum pump drive system	
12	Vehicle speed sensor system	
14	Electric vacuum pump power supply system	
15	Cruise control switch	
16	Cruise control ECU	
17	Throttle position sensor system	

Cruise Control Diagnostic Trouble Codes 2005 on

Diagnostic Code	Diagnostic Item	Self Diagnostic Output Pattern
15	Auto-cruise control switch system	
21	Cancel latch signal system	
22	Stop light switch system	

CRUISE CONTROL – INSPECTION PROCEDURES

Code #11 – Electric Vacuum Pump Output System
Probable Cause:
- Electric vacuum pump fault
- Stop lamp switch malfunction
- Wiring harness or connector fault
- Cruise control ECU fault

Code #12 – Vehicle Speed Signal System
Probable Cause:
- Vehicle speed sensor fault
- Wiring harness or connector fault
- Cruise control ECU fault

Code #14 – Electric Vacuum Pump Power Supply System
Probable Cause:
- Stop lamp switch fault
- Wiring harness or connector fault
- Cruise control ECU fault

Code #15 – Cruise Control Switch
Probable Cause: Cruise control switch fault

Code #16 – Cruise Control ECU
Probable Cause: Cruise control ECU fault

Code #17 – Throttle Position Sensor System
Probable Cause:
- Throttle position sensor fault
- Wiring harness or connector fault
- Cruise control ECU fault

DIAGNOSTIC INFORMATION & TROUBLESHOOTING

AUTO TRANSMISSION

The Neutral range light in the instrument cluster is used to diagnose automatic transmission faults and to retrieve diagnostic codes.

If the lamp is flashing at a rate of once per second (1Hz) there is a problem with the auto transmission system. Retrieve diagnostic codes.

If the lamp is flashing at a rate of 2 flashes per second (2Hz) it indicates the auto transmission fluid temperature is too high. Stop the vehicle and wait until the lamp switches off.

Reading Diagnostic Codes - Using 'N' Lamp

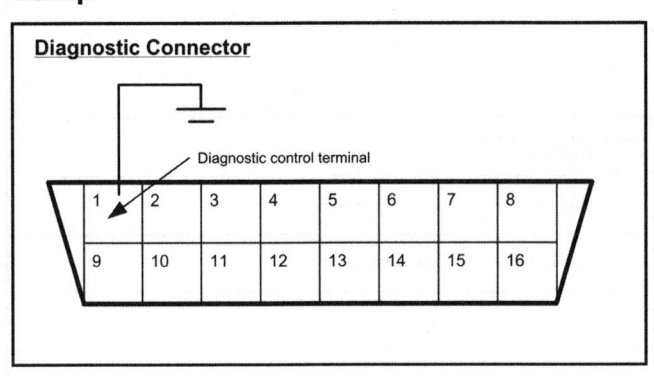

1. Earth the diagnostic control terminal (terminal 1) of the diagnostic connector.

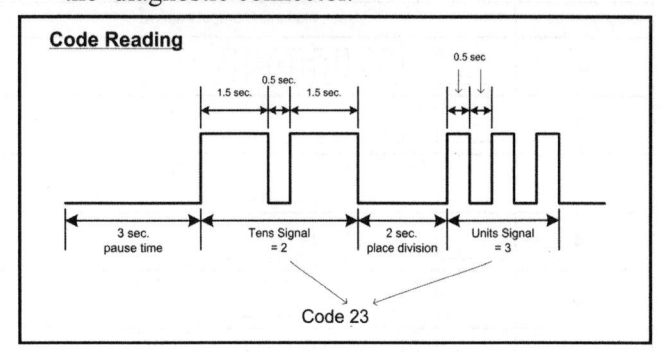

2. Turn on the ignition and read the diagnosis output pattern from the N range lamp and record results.
3. Refer to the diagnostic chart and repair all faults as required.
4. Turn the ignition off, then disconnect the battery negative terminal for at least 10 seconds to erase codes.

Automatic Transmission Diagnostic Codes

Codes listed starting with NM build 2000, as additional codes added they have been identified.
   ** 2004
   # 2006
   * 2008.

DIAGNOSTIC INFORMATION & TROUBLESHOOTING

Auto Transmission Diagnostic Trouble Codes

Auto Tran NM-NS

Diagnostic Code	Self Diagnostic Output Pattern	Inspection Item
0		Normal state (no diagnostic code output)
11		Throttle position sensor system short circuit
12		Throttle position sensor system open circuit
14		Throttle position sensor incorrect adjustment
15		A/T Oil temperature sensor system open circuit
16		A/T Oil temperature sensor system short circuit
21		Crank angle sensor system open circuit (6G7*) Engine Speed (4M41) Revolution (4M40)
22		Input shaft speed sensor system short/open circuit
23 24 * & 25 *		Output shaft speed sensor system short/open circuit
26		Stop light switch system short/open circuit, except 4M40
27 #		Inhibitor switch system open circuit
28 # 29 **		Inhibitor switch system short circuit / Vehicle Speed Sensor
31		Low and reverse solenoid valve system short/open circuit
32		Underdrive solenoid valve system short/open circuit
33		Second solenoid valve system short/open circuit
34		Overdrive solenoid valve system short/open circuit
35		RED solenoid valve system
36		Damper clutch solenoid valve system short/open circuit
41		1st Gear incorrect ratio
42		2nd Gear incorrect ratio
43		3rd Gear incorrect ratio
44		4th Gear incorrect ratio
45		5th Gear incorrect ratio
46		Reverse Gear incorrect ratio
51		Abnormal communication with engine-ECU, except 4M40
52		Damper clutch solenoid system defective
53		Damper clutch solenoid system lock-up stuck on
54		A/T control relay system short circuit to ground/open circuit
13 *		A/T control relay system contact point melted or sticking
56		N range light system short circuit to ground
61 **		Malfunction of A/T-ECU, M-ATC, M-ASTC or ASTC

DIAGNOSTIC INFORMATION & TROUBLESHOOTING

AUTOMATIC TRANSMISSION – DIAGNOSTIC CODE INSPECTION PROCEDURES
Auto Tran InspecPro

Code #11, 12, 14 – Throttle Position Sensor System
Probable Cause:
- Malfunction of the throttle position sensor
- Malfunction of connector
- Malfunction of Engine A/T-ECU

Code #15 – Oil Temperature Sensor System
Probable Cause:
- Faulty oil temperature sensor
- Malfunction of connector
- Malfunction of Engine A/T-ECU

Code #21 – Crank Angle Sensor System
Probable Cause:
- Malfunction of the crank angle sensor
- Malfunction of connector
- Malfunction of Engine A/T-ECU

Code #22 – Input Shaft Speed Sensor System
Probable Cause:
- Malfunction of the input shaft speed sensor
- Malfunction of the underdrive clutch retainer
- Malfunction of connector
- Malfunction of Engine A/T-ECU

Code #23 – Output Shaft Speed Sensor System
Probable Cause:
- Malfunction of the output shaft speed sensor
- Malfunction of the transfer drive gear or driven gear
- Malfunction of connector
- Malfunction of Engine A/T-ECU

Code #26 – Stop Light Switch System
Probable Cause:
- Malfunction of the stop light switch
- Malfunction of connector
- Malfunction of Engine A/T-ECU

Code #27, 28 – Inhibitor Switch System
Probable Cause:
- Malfunction of the inhibitor switch
- Malfunction of the ignition switch
- Malfunction of connector
- Malfunction of Engine A/T-ECU

Code #31 – Low & Reverse Solenoid Valve System
Code #32 – Underdrive Solenoid Valve System
Code #33 – Second Solenoid Valve System
Code #34 – Overdrive Solenoid Valve System
Code #35 – RED Solenoid Valve System
Probable Cause:
- Malfunction of solenoid valve
- Malfunction of connector
- Malfunction of Engine A/T-ECU

Code #36, 52, 53 – Damper Clutch Solenoid System
Probable Cause:
- Malfunction of the damper clutch solenoid
- Malfunction of connector
- Malfunction of Engine A/T-ECU

Code #41 – 1st Gear Incorrect Ratio
Probable Cause:
- Malfunction of the input shaft speed sensor
- Malfunction of the output shaft speed sensor
- Malfunction of the underdrive clutch retainer
- Malfunction of the transfer drive gear or driven gear
- Malfunction of the low & reverse brake system
- Malfunction of underdrive clutch system
- Noise Generated

Code #42 – 2nd Gear Incorrect Ratio
Probable Cause:
- Malfunction of the input shaft speed sensor
- Malfunction of the output shaft speed sensor
- Malfunction of the underdrive clutch retainer
- Malfunction of the transfer drive gear or driven gear
- Malfunction of the second brake system
- Malfunction of underdrive clutch system
- Noise Generated

Code #43 – 3rd Gear Incorrect Ratio
Probable Cause:
- Malfunction of the input shaft speed sensor
- Malfunction of the output shaft speed sensor
- Malfunction of the underdrive clutch retainer
- Malfunction of the transfer drive gear or driven gear
- Malfunction of the underdrive clutch system
- Malfunction of overdrive clutch system
- Noise Generated

Code #44 – 4th Gear Incorrect Ratio
Probable Cause:
- Malfunction of the input shaft speed sensor
- Malfunction of the output shaft speed sensor
- Malfunction of the underdrive clutch retainer
- Malfunction of the transfer drive gear or driven gear
- Malfunction of the second brake system
- Malfunction of overdrive clutch system
- Noise Generated

Code #45 – 5th Gear Incorrect Ratio
Probable Cause:
- Malfunction of the input shaft speed sensor
- Malfunction of the output shaft speed sensor
- Malfunction of the underdrive clutch retainer
- Malfunction of the direct planetary carrier
- Malfunction of the second brake system
- Malfunction of overdrive clutch system
- Malfunction of DIR clutch system
- Noise Generated

Code #46 – Reverse Gear Incorrect Ratio
Probable Cause:
- Malfunction of the input shaft speed sensor
- Malfunction of the output shaft speed sensor
- Malfunction of the underdrive clutch retainer
- Malfunction of the transfer drive gear or driven gear
- Malfunction of the low & reverse brake system
- Malfunction of the reverse clutch system
- Noise Generated

Code #51 – Abnormal communication with Engine A/T-ECU
Probable Cause:
- Malfunction of Engine A/T-ECU

Code #13 – A/T Control Relay System
Probable Cause:
- Malfunction of the A/T control relay
- Malfunction of Connector
- Malfunction of Engine A/T-ECU

Code #56 – N Range Light System
Probable Cause:
- Malfunction of Connector
- Malfunction of Engine A/T-ECU

Code #61 – Malfunction of Engine A/T-ECU
Probable Cause:
- Malfunction of Engine A/T-ECU, M-ATC, M-ASTC or ASTC

AUTOMATIC TRANSMISSION – FAULT INSPECTION PROCEDURES

Auto Tran FaultInspect

Unable to start
Probable Cause: * Faulty engine system * Faulty torque converter

Vehicle won't move forward
Probable Cause: * Inadequate line pressure * Faulty UD solenoid valve
* Faulty UD clutch * Faulty valve body

Vehicle won't move backward
Probable Cause: * Inadequate reverse clutch pressure * Inadequate LR brake pressure
* Faulty LR solenoid valve * Faulty reverse clutch
* Faulty LR brake * Faulty valve body

Vehicle won't move forward or backward
Probable Cause: * Inadequate line pressure * Faulty power train component
* Faulty oil pump * Faulty valve body

Engine stalls during shifting
Probable Cause: * Faulty engine system * Faulty DCC solenoid valve
* Faulty valve body * Faulty torque converter

Shock during shift from N to D (large time lag)
Probable Cause: * Inadequate UD clutch pressure * Faulty UD clutch
* Faulty valve body * Faulty idle switch

Shock during shift from N to R (large time lag)
Probable Cause: * Inadequate reverse clutch pressure * Inadequate LR brake pressure
* Faulty LR solenoid valve * Faulty reverse clutch
* Faulty LR brake * Faulty valve body
* Faulty idle switch

Shock during shift from N to D and N to R (large time lag)
Probable Cause: * Inadequate line pressure * Faulty oil pump
* Faulty valve body

Shock, higher transmission than engine revolutions
Probable Cause: * Inadequate line pressure * Faulty solenoid valves
* Faulty oil pump * Faulty valve body
* Faulty brakes/clutches

All shift points incorrect
Probable Cause: * Faulty output shaft speed sensor * Faulty throttle position sensor
* Inadequate line pressure * Faulty solenoid valves
* Faulty valve body * Faulty A/T-ECU

Some shift points incorrect
Probable Cause: * Faulty valve body

No diagnostic code output (no shift)
Probable Cause: * Faulty Inhibitor switch * Faulty A/T-ECU

Poor acceleration
Probable Cause: * Faulty engine system * Faulty brakes/clutches

Vibration
Probable Cause: * Abnormal damper clutch pressure * Malfunction of engine system
* Malfunction of damper clutch control * Malfunction of valve body
* Malfunction of torque converter solenoid valve

Inhibitor switch system
Probable Cause: * Faulty inhibitor switch * Faulty ignition switch
* Faulty connector * Faulty A/T-ECU

May be defects with idle switch circuit or A/T-ECU
Probable Cause: * Faulty idle switch * Faulty connector
* Faulty A/T-ECU

Dual pressure switch system
Probable Cause: * Faulty duel pressure switch * Faulty A/C system
* Faulty connector * Faulty A/T-ECU

Vehicle speed sensor system
Probable Cause: * Faulty vehicle speed sensor * Faulty connector
* Faulty A/T-ECU

Automatic cruise ECU system
Probable Cause: * Faulty connector * Faulty A/T-ECU
* Faulty automatic cruise ECU

Vehicle speed sensor system
Probable Cause: * Malfunction of vehicle speed sensor * Faulty connector
* Faulty A/T-ECU

Automatic Transmission Control - ECU Connector (4cyl)

1	2	3	4	5	6	7	8	9	10	11	12	13
14	15	16	17	18	19	20	21	22	23	24	25	26

31	32	33	34	35	36	37	38
39	40	41	42	43	44	45	46

51	52	53	54	55	56	57	58	59	60	61
62	63	64	65	66	67	68	69	70	71	72

AUTOMATIC CLIMATE CONTROL

* Before carrying out diagnostic procedures ensure the air ducts are not blocked or become disengaged.
* Also ensure connectors are disconnected when checking components.

The diagnostic results can be read using a MUT II Mitsubishi diagnostic tool an after market diagnostic code reading tool.

Automatic Climate Control Diagnostic Trouble Codes 2000-2008

Diagnostic Code	Diagnostic Item
0	Normal State
11	Passenger compartment temperature sensor (open circuit)
12	Passenger compartment temperature sensor (short circuit)
13	Outside air temperature sensor system (open circuit)
14	Outside air temperature sensor system (short circuit)
15	Heater water temperature sensor system (open circuit)
16	Heater water temperature sensor system (short circuit)
21	Air thermo sensor system (open circuit)
22	Air thermo sensor system (short circuit)
31	Potentiometer system for air mix damper motor
32	Potentiometer system for mode selector damper motor

AUTOMATIC AIR CONDITIONING – INSPECTION PROCEDURES

Code #11 – Passenger Compartment Temperature Sensor Open Circuit
Probable Cause: Passenger compartment temperature sensor fault
Wiring harness or connector fault
A/C-ECU fault

Code #12 – Passenger Compartment Temperature Sensor Short Circuit
Probable Cause: Passenger compartment temperature sensor fault
Wiring harness or connector fault
A/C-ECU fault

Code #13 – Outside Air Temperature Sensor System Open Circuit
Probable Cause: Outside air temperature sensor fault
Wiring harness or connector fault
A/C-ECU fault

Code #14 – Outside Air Temperature Sensor System Short Circuit
Probable Cause: Outside air temperature sensor fault
Wiring harness or connector fault
A/C-ECU fault

Code #15 – Heater Water Temperature Sensor System Open Circuit
Probable Cause: Heater water temperature sensor fault
Wiring harness or connector fault
A/C-ECU fault

Code #16 – Heater Water Temperature Sensor System Short Circuit
Probable Cause: Heater water temperature sensor fault
Wiring harness or connector fault
A/C-ECU fault

Code #21 – Air Thermo Sensor System Open Circuit
Probable Cause: Air thermo sensor fault
Wiring harness or connector fault
A/C-ECU fault

Code #22 – Air Thermo Sensor System Short Circuit
Probable Cause: Air thermo sensor fault
Wiring harness or connector fault
A/C-ECU fault

Code #31 – Potentiometer System For Air Mix Damper
Probable Cause: Air mix damper potentiometer fault
Wiring harness or connector fault
A/C-ECU fault

Code #32 – Potentiometer System For Mode Selector Damper
Probable Cause: Mode selector damper potentiometer fault
Wiring harness or connector fault
A/C-ECU fault

DIAGNOSTIC INFORMATION & TROUBLESHOOTING

ABS SYSTEM

Before carrying out diagnostic procedures ensure the air ducts are not blocked or become disengaged.
* Also ensure connectors are disconnected when checking components.

Code Diagnostic Reading - Using warning lamp

1. Earth the diagnostic control terminal (terminal 1) of the diagnostic connector.
2. Turn on the ignition and read the diagnosis output pattern from the ABS warning lamp and record results.
3. Refer to the diagnostic chart and repair all faults as required.
4. Turn the ignition off, then disconnect the battery negative terminal for at least 10 seconds to erase codes.

Diagnostic Connector

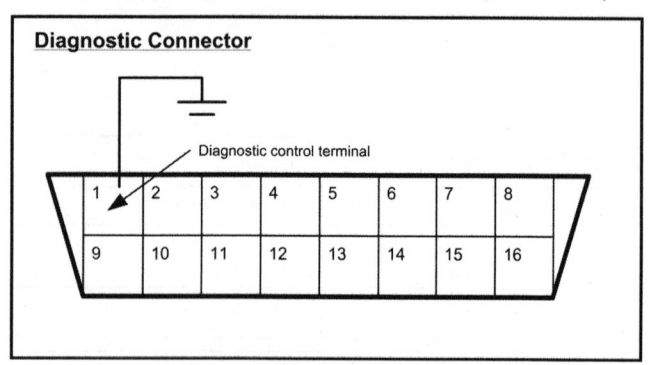

Code Reading

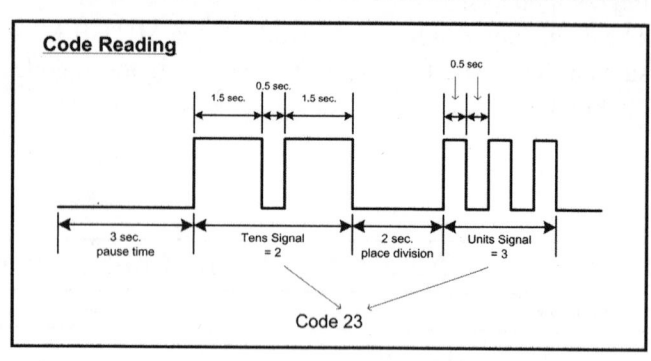

ABS – INSPECTION PROCEDURES

ABS InspectPro

Code #11, 12, 13, 14 – Wheel Speed Sensor Open Circuit
Probable Cause:
  Malfunction of wheel speed sensor (open circuit)
  Malfunction of wiring harness or connector
  Malfunction of ABS-ECU

Code #15 – Wheel Speed Sensor - Abnormal Output Signal
(other than an open or short circuit)
Probable Cause:
  Improper installation of wheel speed sensor
  Malfunction of wheel speed sensor
  Damaged Rotor
  Wheel bearing worn or loose
  Malfunction of wiring harness or connector
  Malfunction of ABS-ECU

Code #16 – Power Supply System
Probable Cause:
  Malfunction of wiring harness or connector
  Malfunction of battery or alternator
  Malfunction of ABS-ECU

Code #21, 22, 23, 24 – Wheel Speed Sensor Short Circuit
Probable Cause:
  Malfunction of wheel speed sensor
  Malfunction of wiring harness
  Malfunction of ABS-ECU

Code #32 – G Sensor
Probable Cause:
  Malfunction of G sensor
  Malfunction of wiring harness or connector
  Malfunction of ABS-ECU

Code #33 – Stop Light Switch System
Probable Cause:
  Malfunction of stop light switch
  Malfunction of wiring harness or connector
  Malfunction of ABS-ECU

Code #41, 42, 43, 44 – Solenoid Valve (inlet)
Probable Cause:
  Malfunction of hydraulic unit
  Malfunction of wiring harness
  Malfunction of ABS-ECU

Code #45, 46, 47, 48 – Solenoid Valve (outlet)
Probable Cause:
  Malfunction of hydraulic unit
  Malfunction of wiring harness
  Malfunction of ABS-ECU

Code #51 – Valve Relay
Probable Cause:
  Malfunction of ABS valve relay
  Malfunction of wiring harness or connector
  Malfunction of hydraulic unit
  Malfunction of ABS-ECU

Code #53 – Motor Relay, Motor
Probable Cause:
  Malfunction of ABS motor relay
  Malfunction of wiring harness or connector
  Malfunction of hydraulic unit
  Malfunction of ABS-ECU

Code #63 – ABS-ECU
Probable Cause:
  Malfunction of wiring harness or connector
  Malfunction of ABS-ECU

DIAGNOSTIC INFORMATION & TROUBLESHOOTING

ABS Diagnostic Trouble Codes - Using Warning Lamp

ABS codes

Diagnostic Code	Inspection Item	Conditions
0	Normal State	
11	Front right wheel speed sensor	B, C
12	Front left wheel speed sensor	B, C
13	Rear right wheel speed sensor	B, C
14	Rear left wheel speed sensor	B, C
15	Wheel speed sensor output signal abnormal	A, B
16	Power supply system	A, B, C
21	Front right wheel speed sensor	B, C
22	Front left wheel speed sensor	B, C
23	Rear right wheel speed sensor	B, C
24	Rear left wheel speed sensor	B, C
25 #	Incorrect tyre size	A, B, C
26	Center differential lock switch	B, C
27	Rear differential lock switch	B, C
31 *	Ignition switch(IG2) for 2004 / ASTU-ECU power supply fro 2008 on	A, B, C
32	G sensor (AWD)	A, B, C
33 #	Stop light switch	A, B, C
34 #	CAN communication	A, B, C
35 #	Engine system fault	A, B, C
36 #	Engine – ECU communication fault	A, B, C
37 #	A/T system fault	A, B, C
38	Stop light switch system 2000 / A/t-ECU communication fault 2004	B, C
41	Front right solenoid valve (inlet)	B, C
42	Front left solenoid valve (inlet)	B, C
43	Rear right solenoid valve (inlet)	B, C
44	Rear left solenoid valve (inlet)	B, C
45	Front right solenoid valve (outlet)	B, C
46	Front left solenoid valve (outlet)	B, C
47	Rear right solenoid valve (outlet)	B, C
48	Rear left solenoid valve (outlet)	B, C
51 / 52	Valve relay	A, B, C
53	Pump Motor fault	A, B, C
54 *	Motor Relay System	A, B, C
55 *	Pump Motor System	A, B, C
56 *	Pressure Switch System – low pressure	B, C
57 *	Accumulator system – motor operating to long or accumulator pressure to low	B, C
58 *	ASTC-ECU system	A, B, C
63	ABS-ECU	A, B, C

Conditions:
A: During system check immediately after starting
B: While ABS control is not operating while driving
C: While ABS control is operating

DIAGNOSTIC INFORMATION & TROUBLESHOOTING

SRS SYSTEM

We strongly recommend any maintenance or troubleshooting of the SRS system only be carried out by a qualified person, as serious injury may result from improper service or maintenance.

Code Diagnostic Reading - Using warning lamp

1. Earth the diagnostic control terminal (terminal 1) of the diagnostic connector.
2. Turn on the ignition and read the diagnosis output pattern from the SRS warning lamp and record results.
3. Refer to the diagnostic chart and repair all faults as required.
4. Turn the ignition off, then disconnect the battery negative terminal for at least 10 seconds to erase codes.

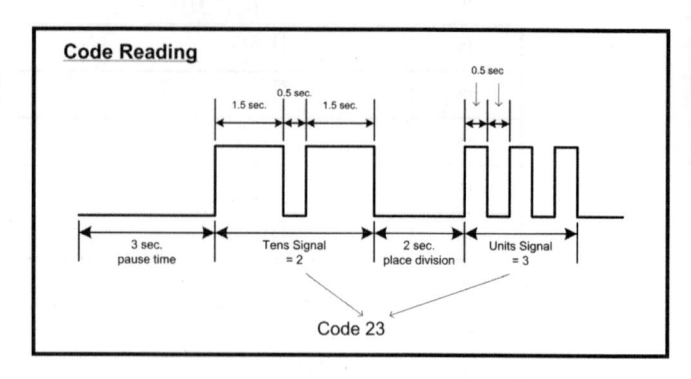

Code Reading

(Diagram showing pulse pattern: 3 sec. pause time, Tens Signal = 2 (1.5 sec. pulses with 0.5 sec. gaps), 2 sec. place division, Units Signal = 3. Code 23)

SRS – INSPECTION PROCEDURES 2000-2008
SRS InspectPro

Code #14 – SRS-ECU Front Impact Analog G-Sensor System
Probable Cause: Malfunction of SRS ECU

Code #15, 16 – SRS-ECU Front Impact Saving G-Sensor System
Probable Cause: Malfunction of SRS ECU

Code #17 – SRS-ECU Side Impact Saving G-Sensor System
Probable Cause: Malfunction of SRS ECU

Code #21 – Steering Wheel Airbag Module (squib) System
Probable Cause: Clock spring fault – short
Malfunction of wiring harness or connector
Steering wheel airbag module (squib) fault – short
Malfunction of Engine ECU

Code #22 – Steering Wheel Airbag Module (squib) System
Probable Cause: Clock spring fault – open circuit
Malfunction of wiring harness or connector
Steering wheel airbag module (squib) fault – open circuit
Malfunction of Engine ECU

Code #61 – Steering Wheel Airbag Module (squib) System
Probable Cause: Power supply short in steering wheel airbag module (squib) harness
Malfunction of Engine ECU

Code #62 – Steering Wheel Airbag Module (squib) System
Probable Cause: Short to ground in steering wheel airbag module (squib) harness
Malfunction of Engine ECU

Code #24 – Passenger Side Airbag Module (squib) System
Probable Cause: Malfunction of wiring harness or connector
Passenger side airbag module (squib) fault – short
Malfunction of Engine ECU

Code #25 – Passenger Side Airbag Module (squib) System
Probable Cause: Malfunction of wiring harness or connector
Passenger side airbag module (squib) fault – open circuit
Malfunction of Engine ECU

Code #64 – Passenger Side Airbag Module (squib) System
Probable Cause: Power supply short in passenger side airbag module (squib) harness
Malfunction of Engine ECU

Code #65 – Passenger Side Airbag Module (squib) System
Probable Cause: Short to ground in passenger side airbag module (squib) harness
Malfunction of Engine ECU

Code #26 – Drivers Seat Belt Pre-tensioner (squib) System
Probable Cause: Malfunction of wiring harness or connector
Drivers seat belt pre-tensioner (squib) circuit fault – short circuit
Malfunction of Engine ECU

Code #27 – Drivers Seat Belt Pre-tensioner (squib) System
Probable Cause: Malfunction of wiring harness or connector
Drivers seat belt pre-tensioner (squib) circuit fault – open circuit
Malfunction of Engine ECU

Code #28 – Front Passenger Seat Belt Pre-tensioner (squib) System
Probable Cause: Malfunction of wiring harness or connector
Passengers seat belt pre-tensioner (squib) circuit fault – short circuit
Malfunction of Engine ECU

Code #29 – Front Passenger Seat Belt Pre-tensioner (squib) System
Probable Cause: Malfunction of wiring harness or connector
Passenger seat belt pre-tensioner (squib) circuit fault – open circuit
Malfunction of Engine ECU

Code #31, 32 – DC-DC Converter System In SRS-ECU
Probable Cause: Malfunction of SRS ECU

Code #34 – Connector Lock System
Probable Cause: Malfunction of connector
Malfunction of SRS ECU

Code #35 – SRS-ECU System – Airbag Triggered
Probable Cause: Malfunction of SRS ECU

Code #41 – IG1 (A) Power Supply Circuit System
Probable Cause: Malfunction of wiring harness or connector
Malfunction of SRS ECU

Code #42 – IG1 (B) Power Supply Circuit System
Probable Cause: Malfunction of wiring harness or connector
Malfunction of SRS ECU

Code #43 – SRS Warning Lamp Driving Circuit System (lamp does not illuminate)
Probable Cause: Blown Globe
Malfunction of wiring harness or connector
Malfunction of SRS ECU
Instrument cluster fault

Code #43 – SRS Warning Lamp Driving Circuit System (lamp does not go out)
Probable Cause: Malfunction of wiring harness or connector
Malfunction of SRS ECU
Instrument cluster fault

Code #44 – SRS Warning Lamp Drive Circuit System
Probable Cause: Malfunction of wiring harness or connector
Malfunction of SRS ECU

Code #45 – SRS-ECU Non-volatile Memory
Probable Cause: Malfunction of SRS ECU

Code #51, 52 – Steering Wheel Airbag Module (squib) System
Probable Cause: Malfunction of SRS ECU

Code #54, 55 – Passenger Side Airbag Module (squib) System
Probable Cause: Malfunction of SRS ECU

Code #73, 74 – R.H. Side Airbag Module (squib) System
Probable Cause: Malfunction of SRS ECU

Code #83, 84 – L.H. Side Airbag Module (squib) System
Probable Cause: Malfunction of SRS ECU

Code #56, 57, 58, 59 – System Inside SRS-ECU
Probable Cause: Malfunction of SRS ECU

Code #71, 72, 75, 76 – R.H. Side Airbag Module (squib) System
Probable Cause: Malfunction of wiring harness or connector
Malfunction of R.H. side air bag module (squib)
Malfunction of SRS ECU

Code #79, 93 – L.H. Side Impact Sensor Communication System
Probable Cause: Malfunction of wiring harness or connector
Malfunction of L.H. side side impact sensor
Malfunction of SRS ECU

Code #81, 82, 85, 86 – L.H. Side Airbag Module (squib) System
Probable Cause: Malfunction of wiring harness or connector
Malfunction of L.H. side air bag module (squib)
Malfunction of SRS ECU

Code #89, 96 – R.H. Side Impact Sensor Communication System
Probable Cause: Malfunction of wiring harness or connector
Malfunction of R.H. side side impact sensor
Malfunction of SRS ECU

Code #91 – L.H. Side Impact Sensor Power Supply Circuit System
Probable Cause: Malfunction of wiring harness or connector
Malfunction of L.H. side impact sensor
Malfunction of SRS ECU

Code #92, 95 – Side Impact Sensor System
Probable Cause: Malfunction of R.H. side impact sensor
Malfunction of L.H. side impact sensor

Code #94 – R.H. Side Impact Sensor Power Supply Circuit System
Probable Cause: Malfunction of wiring harness or connector
Malfunction of R.H. side side impact sensor
Malfunction of SRS ECU

DIAGNOSTIC INFORMATION & TROUBLESHOOTING

SRS Diagnostic Trouble Codes 2000-2008

SRS codes A

Diagnostic Code	Inspection Item
11	SRS – ECU front impact sensor system
12	SRS – ECU front impact sensor system
13	SRS – ECU front impact sensor system
14	SRS-ECU front impact analog G-sensor system
15	SRS-ECU front impact safing G-sensor system
16	SRS-ECU front impact safing G-sensor system
17	SRS-ECU side impact safing G-sensor system
21	Steering wheel airbag module (squib) system
22	Steering wheel airbag module (squib) system
24	Front Passenger side airbag module (squib) system
25	Front Passenger side airbag module (squib) system
26	Driver's side pre-tensioner (squib) system
27	Driver's side pre-tensioner (squib) system
28	Front passengers side pre-tensioner (squib) system
29	Front passengers side pre-tensioner (squib) system
31	DC-DC Converter system in SRS-ECU
32	DC-DC Converter system in SRS-ECU
34	Connector lock system
35	SRS-ECU system – airbag triggered/deployed
41	IG1 (A) Power supply circuit system (fuse #6)
42	IG1 (B) Power supply circuit system (fuse #8)
43	SRS warning lamp driving circuit system (light does not illuminate/ does not go out)
44	SRS warning lamp driving circuit system
45	Internal Circuit system of non-volatile memory (EEPROM)
51	Driver's air bag module (squib) system
52	Driver's air bag module (squib) system
54	Passenger side airbag module (squib) system
55	Passenger side airbag module (squib) system
56	Driver's side pre-tensioner (squib ignition driving circuit) system
57	Driver's side pre-tensioner (squib ignition driving circuit) system
58	Passenger side pre-tensioner (squib ignition driving circuit) system
59	Passenger side pre-tensioner (squib ignition driving circuit) system

DIAGNOSTIC INFORMATION & TROUBLESHOOTING

SRS Diagnostic Trouble Codes 2000-2008

SRS codes B

Diagnostic Code	Self Diagnostic Output Pattern	Inspection Item
61		Steering wheel airbag module (squib) system
62		Steering wheel airbag module (squib) system
64		Front passenger side airbag module (squib) system
65		Front passenger side airbag module (squib) system
66		Driver's side pre-tensioner (squib) system
67		Driver's side pre-tensioner (squib) system
68		Passenger side pre-tensioner (squib) system
69		Passenger side pre-tensioner (squib) system
71		Side air bag module (R.H.) (squib) system
72		Side air bag module (R.H.) (squib) system
73		Side air bag module (R.H.) (squib) system
74		Side air bag module (R.H.) (squib) system
75		Side air bag module (R.H.) (squib) system
76		Side air bag module (R.H.) (squib) system
79		Side impact sensor (L.H.) communication system
81		Side air bag module (L.H.) (squib) system
82		Side air bag module (L.H.) (squib) system
83		Side air bag module (L.H.) (squib ignition drive circuit) system
84		Side air bag module (L.H.) (squib ignition drive circuit) system
85		Side air bag module (L.H.) (squib) system
86		Side air bag module (L.H.) (squib) system
89		Side impact sensor (R.H.) communication system
91		Side impact sensor (L.H.) power supply circuit system
92		Analog G-sensor system inside side impact sensor
93		Side impact sensor (L.H.) communication system
94		Side impact sensor (L.H.) communication system
95		Analog G-sensor system inside side impact sensor (R.H.)
96		Side impact sensor (R.H.) communication system

ELECTRICAL SYSTEM & WIRING DIAGRAMS

Description	Page
Fuses and Relays	513
Wire Colour Chart	515
ELECTRICAL DIAGRAMS	**515**
MPI 6G72 Engine Control System	515
MPI 6G75 Engine Control System	516
MPI Charging & Ignition System	517
GDI Charging & Ignition System	517
GDI Engine Control System	518
Diesel Charging System	519
4M41 Engine Control System	519
4M40 Engine Control System	520
4 Speed Automatic Transmission	520
INVECS-II 5A/T Automatic Transmission	521
Cruise Control	521
Automatic Air Conditioning System	522
Manual Air Conditioning System	522
Headlights & Levelling System	523
Warning Lights	523
Hazard Lights & Indicators	524
Reverse, Stop, Tail & Fog Lights	524
Interior & Side Step Lights	525
Vanity Mirror, Door & Glove Box Lighting	525
Central Locking & Keyless Entry	526
Supplemental Restraint System	526
Horn, Cigarette Lighter, Clock & Acc. Socket	526
Power Windows	527
Power Seat	527
Basic Radio	527
Audio System	527
Windscreen Wipers & Electric Mirrors	528
Power Mirrors	528

FUSES & RELAYS

The main fuse panels are located below the instrument panel on the outer side of the steering column. Access to the junction block fuse panel is gained by lifting the panel door on the driver's side of the dash and pulling outwards.

The engine bay centralised junction block is located near the battery.

* Refer to photos on the following pages

Fuses

Fuses are multicoloured to easily identify the fuse capacity. The fuse capacity is also printed on the fuse.

Fuses are identified by the fuse block cover label showing which circuit they belong to, as an example "wipers".

Inspection of fuses is achieved by removing the suspected fuse and examining the element in the fuse for a break.

* Always replace blown fuses with fuses of the same rating, if another fuse failure occurs, the circuit must be checked to find the fault, once the fault has been corrected replace the fuse, with the correct rating.

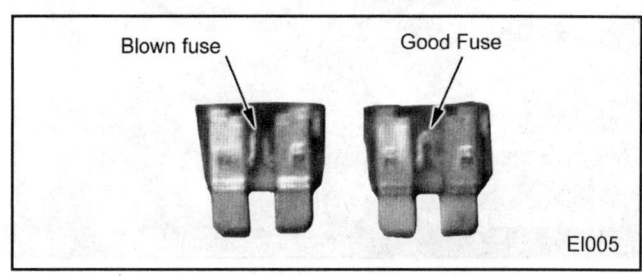

Electrical System - Fuses & Relays

Main Cabin Fuse Panel

Fuses NM - NP (In Cabin)

- Rear Window Wiper - 15A
- Blank
- Radio - 10A
- Cigarette Lighter - 15A
- Relay - 10A
- Gauges - 10A
- Engine Control - 20A
- Reversing Lights - 10A
- Heated Seat - 20A
- Heated Door Mirror - 10A
- Rear Window Demister - 30A
- Heater - 30A
- ABS - 10A
- Sunroof - 20A
- Spare
- Rear Fog Lights - 10A
- Central Door Locks - 20A
- Spare

EI006

Relays NM - NP (In Cabin)

(1) Rear Fog Lamp Relay
(2) Rear Blower Relay
(3) Accessory Socket Relay
(4) Front Blower Relay
(5) Defogger Relay
(6) Power window Relay
(7) Alternator Relay
(8) Heated Seat Relay

EI007

NS & NT Modles — Relays inside cabin

- Steering Column
- Fuel pump Relay No1 (3.8 Petrol)
- Rear Fog Light Relay
- Fuel pump Relay No2 (3.8 Petrol)
- Heated Seat Relay
- Rear Fan Relay
- Power Window Relay
- Front Fan Relay
- Rear Window Defogger Relay
- Accessory Socket Relay

EI004

Engine Bay Fuse Panel

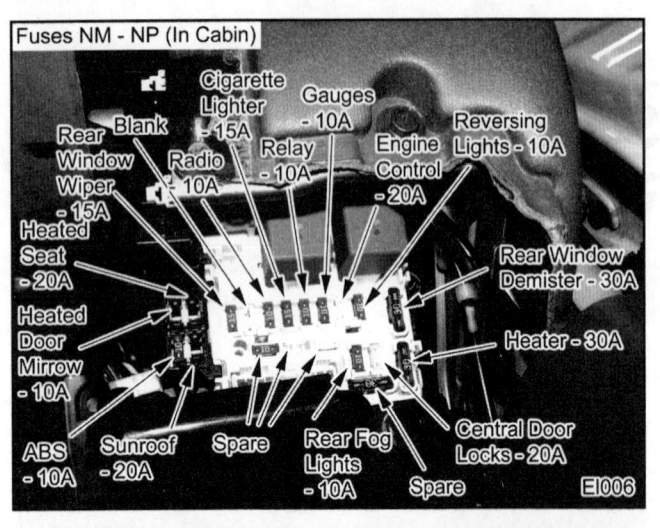

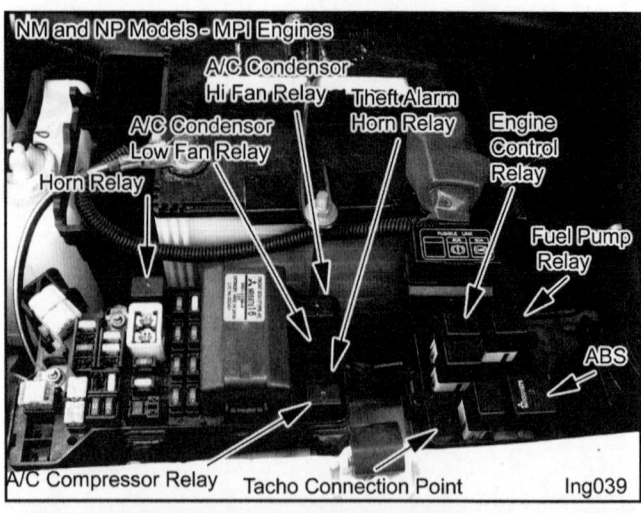

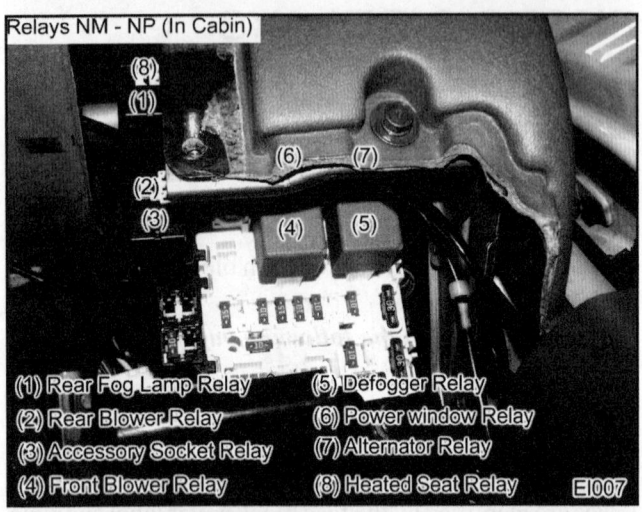

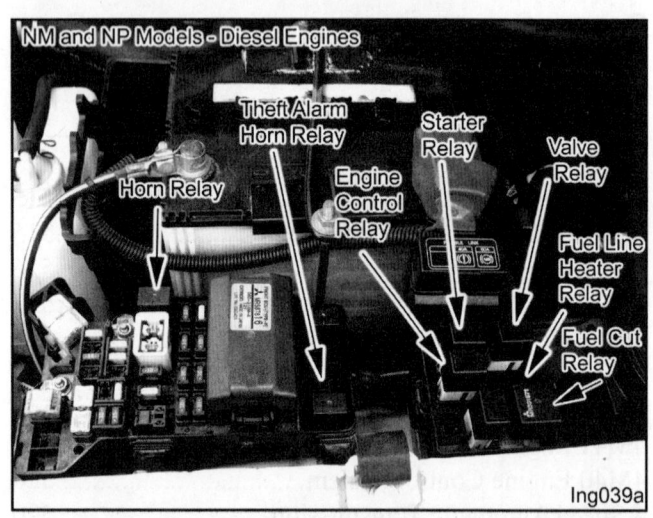

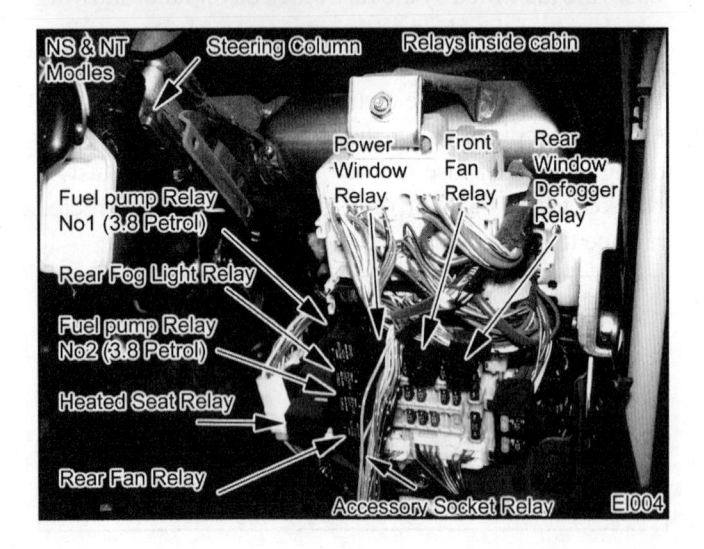

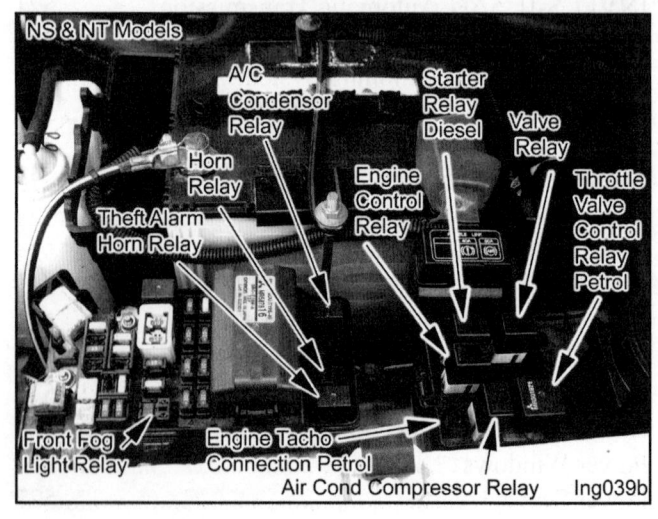

NM and NP Models - MPI Engines

- A/C Condensor Hi Fan Relay
- A/C Condensor Low Fan Relay
- Theft Alarm Horn Relay
- Horn Relay
- Engine Control Relay
- Fuel Pump Relay
- ABS
- A/C Compressor Relay
- Tacho Connection Point

Ing039

NM and NP Models - Diesel Engines

- Theft Alarm Horn Relay
- Starter Relay
- Valve Relay
- Horn Relay
- Engine Control Relay
- Fuel Line Heater Relay
- Fuel Cut Relay

Ing039a

NS & NT Models

- A/C Condensor Relay
- Starter Relay Diesel
- Valve Relay
- Horn Relay
- Theft Alarm Horn Relay
- Engine Control Relay
- Throttle Valve Control Relay Petrol
- Front Fog Light Relay
- Engine Tacho Connection Petrol
- Air Cond Compressor Relay

Ing039b

514

WIRING DIAGRAMS

Wire Colour Chart

All wiring diagrams use a colour coding system to help identify the correct wires or circuit. The coding system uses alphabetical characters to help identify each wire correctly.

Code	Colour	Code	Colour
Bk	Black	Pk	Pink
Bl	Blue	O	Orange
Sb	Sky Blue (light blue)	Y	Yellow
Br	Brown	V	Violet
Gr	Green	R	Red
Gy	Grey	W	White
Lg	Light Green		

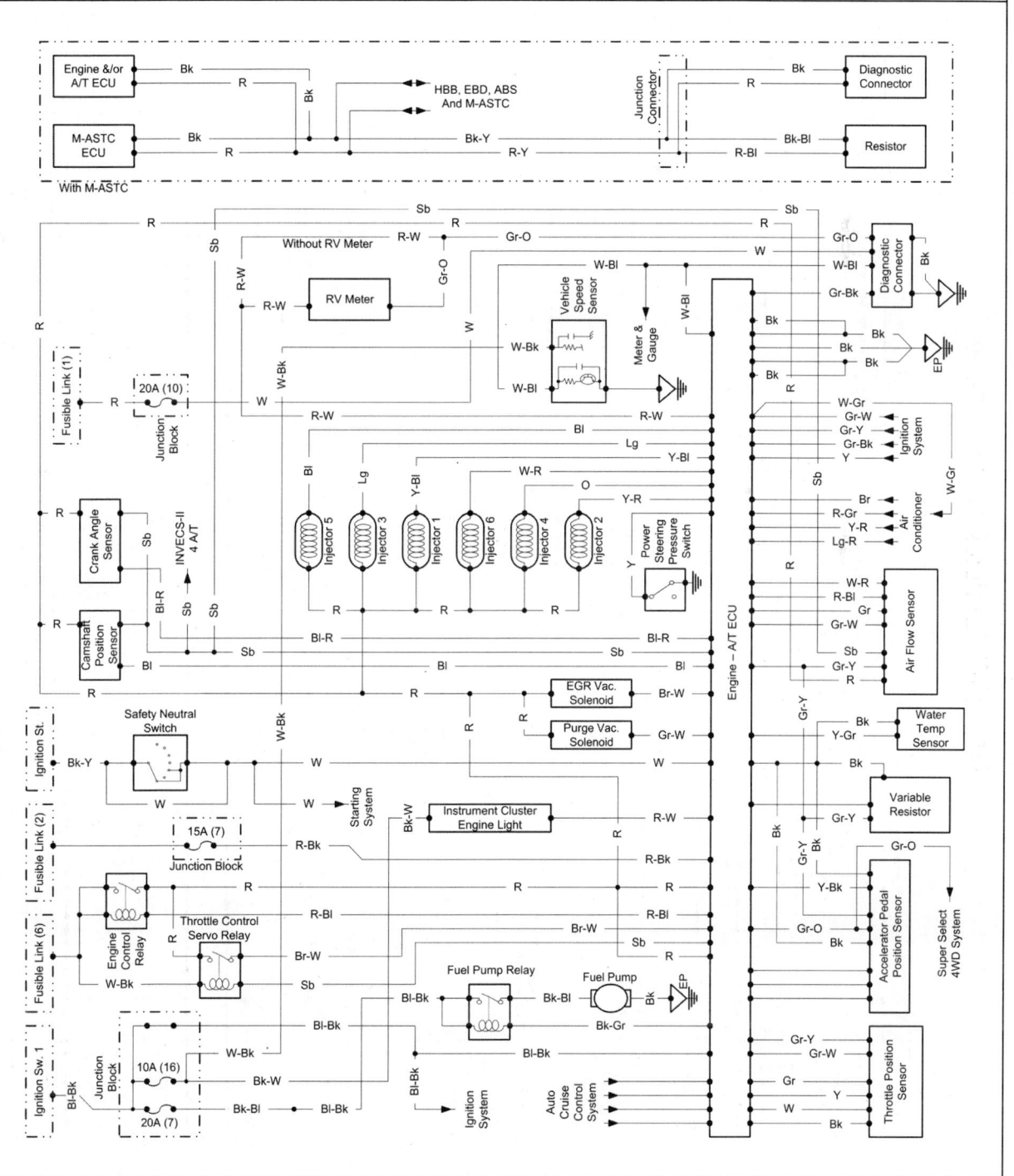

MPI 6G72 Engine Control System

515

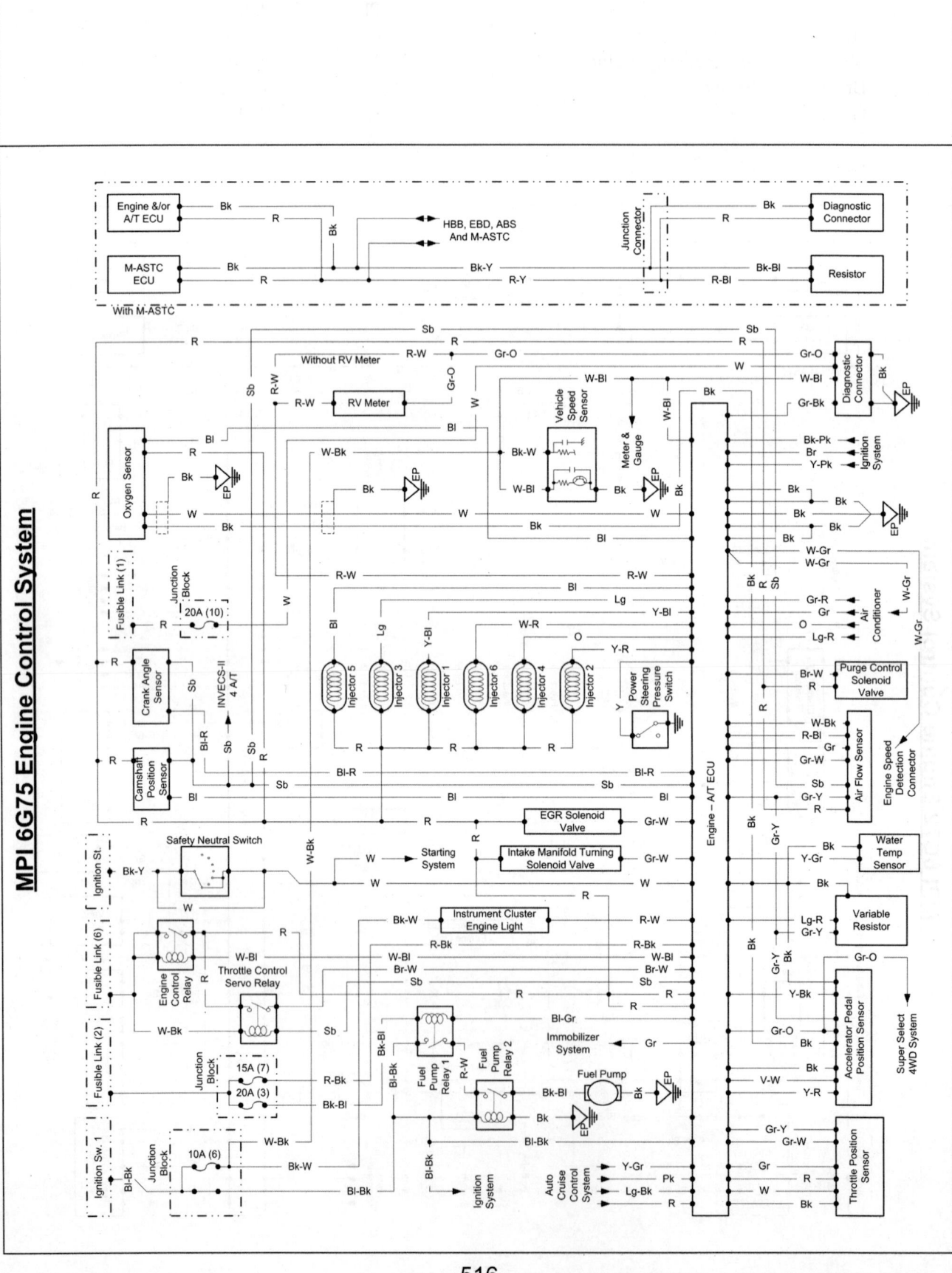

WIRING DIAGRAMS

516

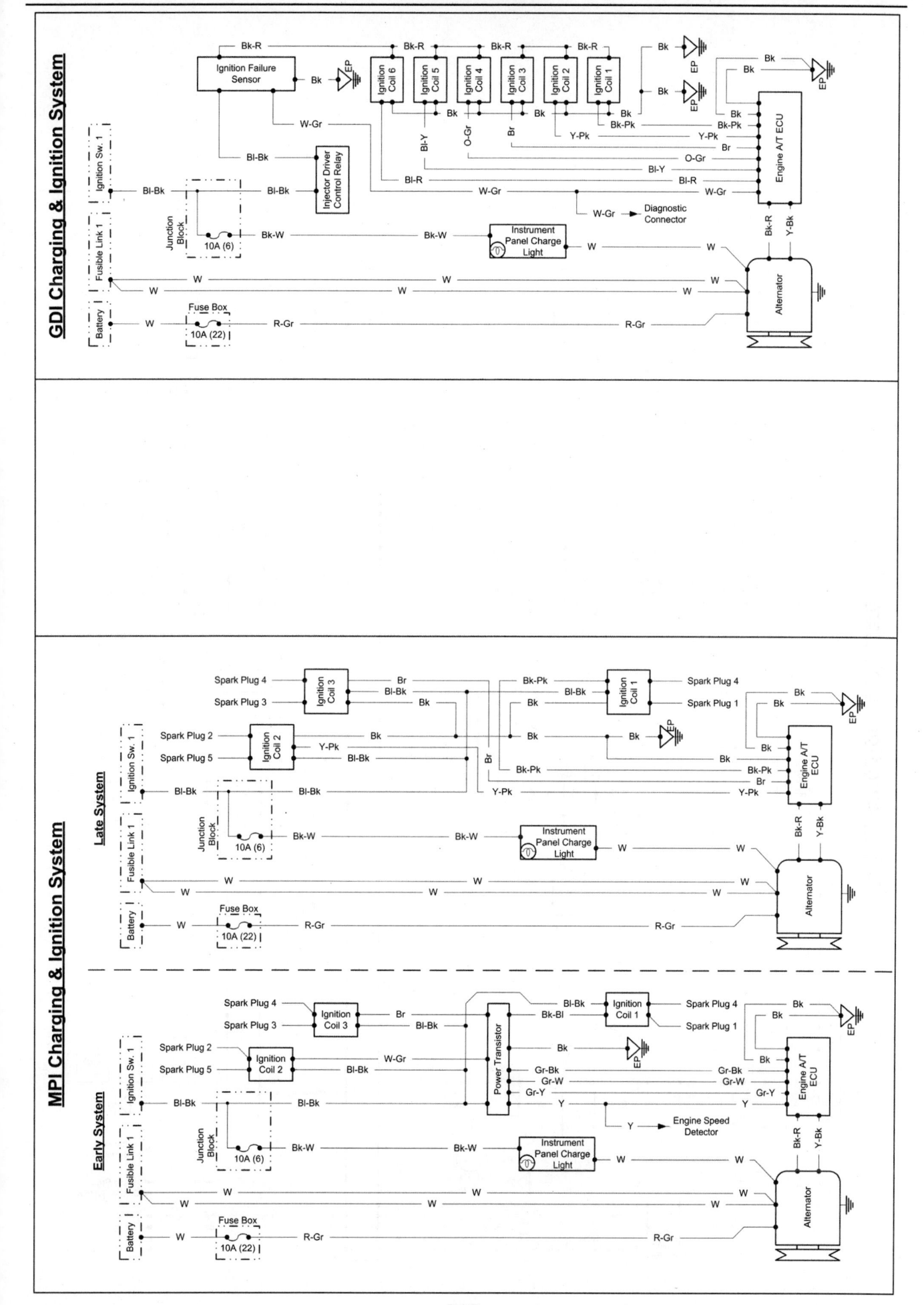

WIRING DIAGRAMS

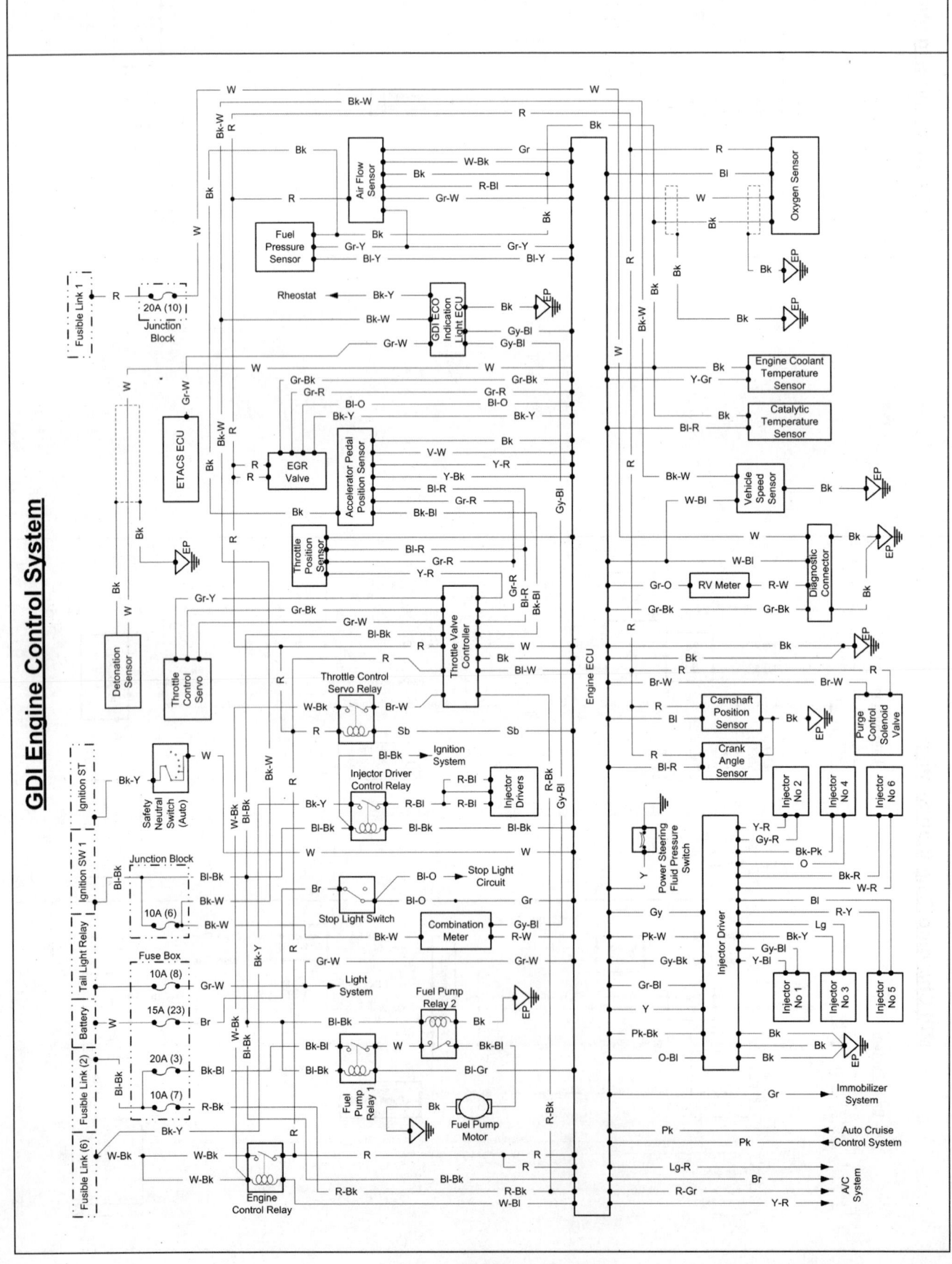

WIRING DIAGRAMS

GDI Engine Control System

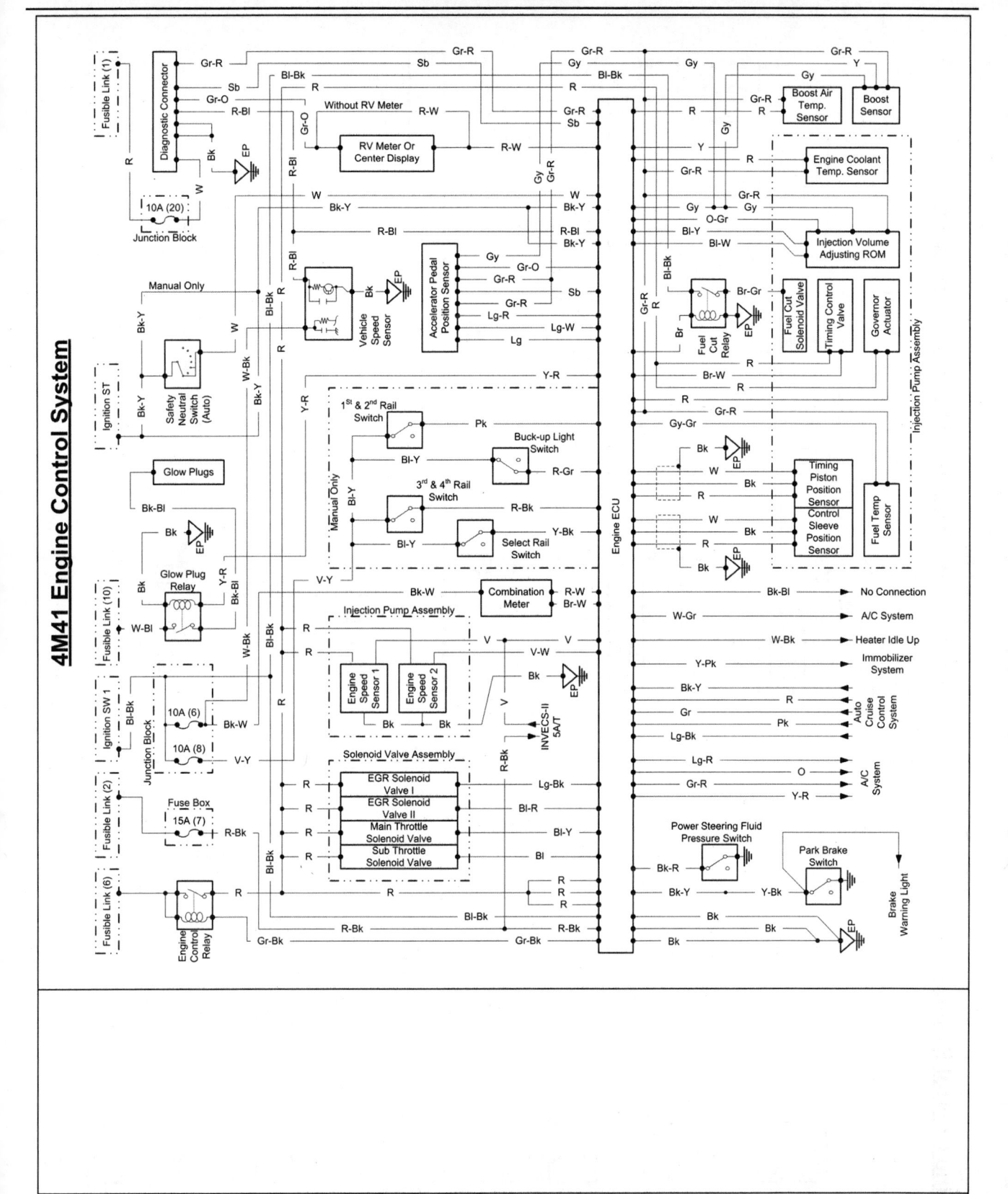

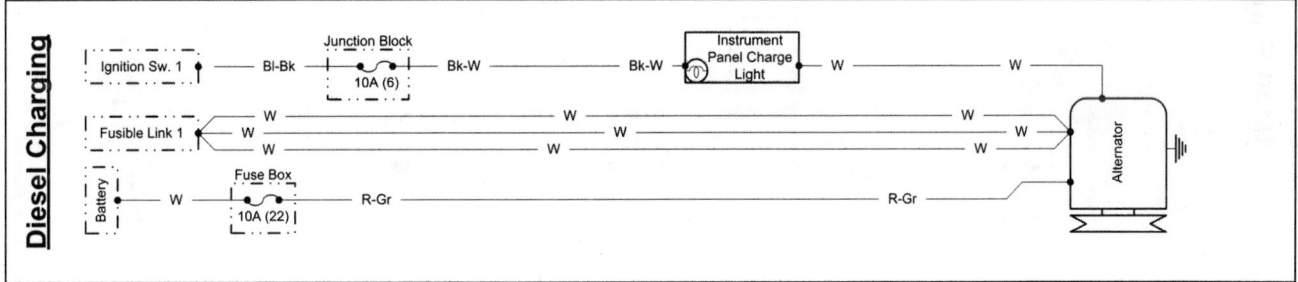

WIRING DIAGRAMS

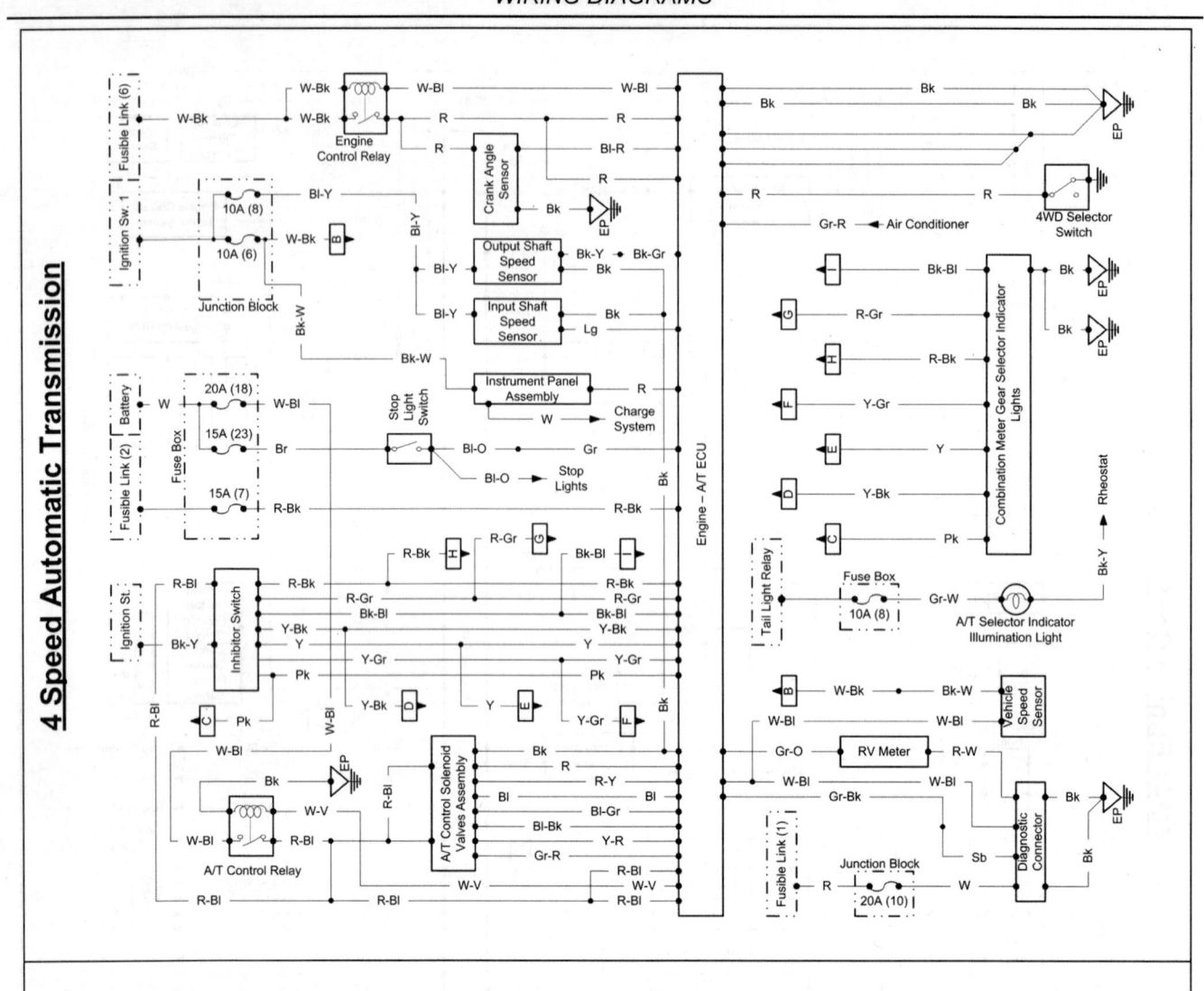

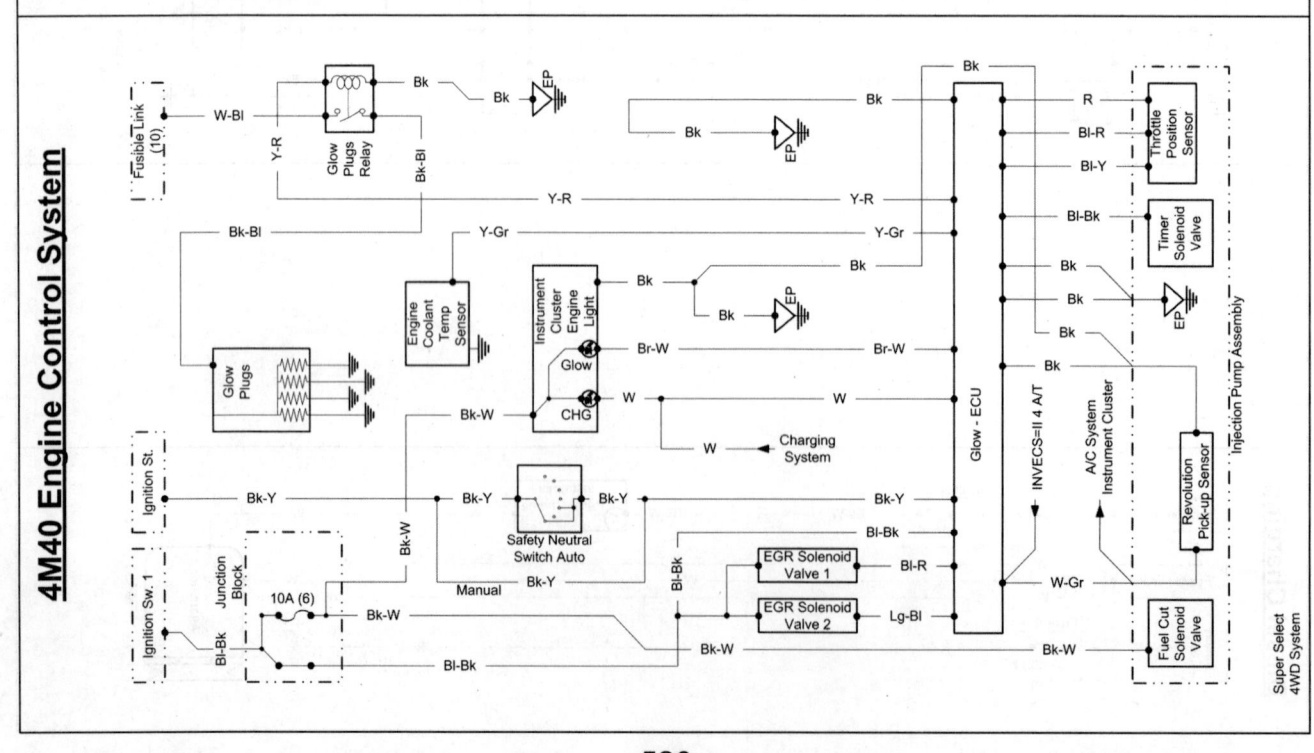

WIRING DIAGRAMS

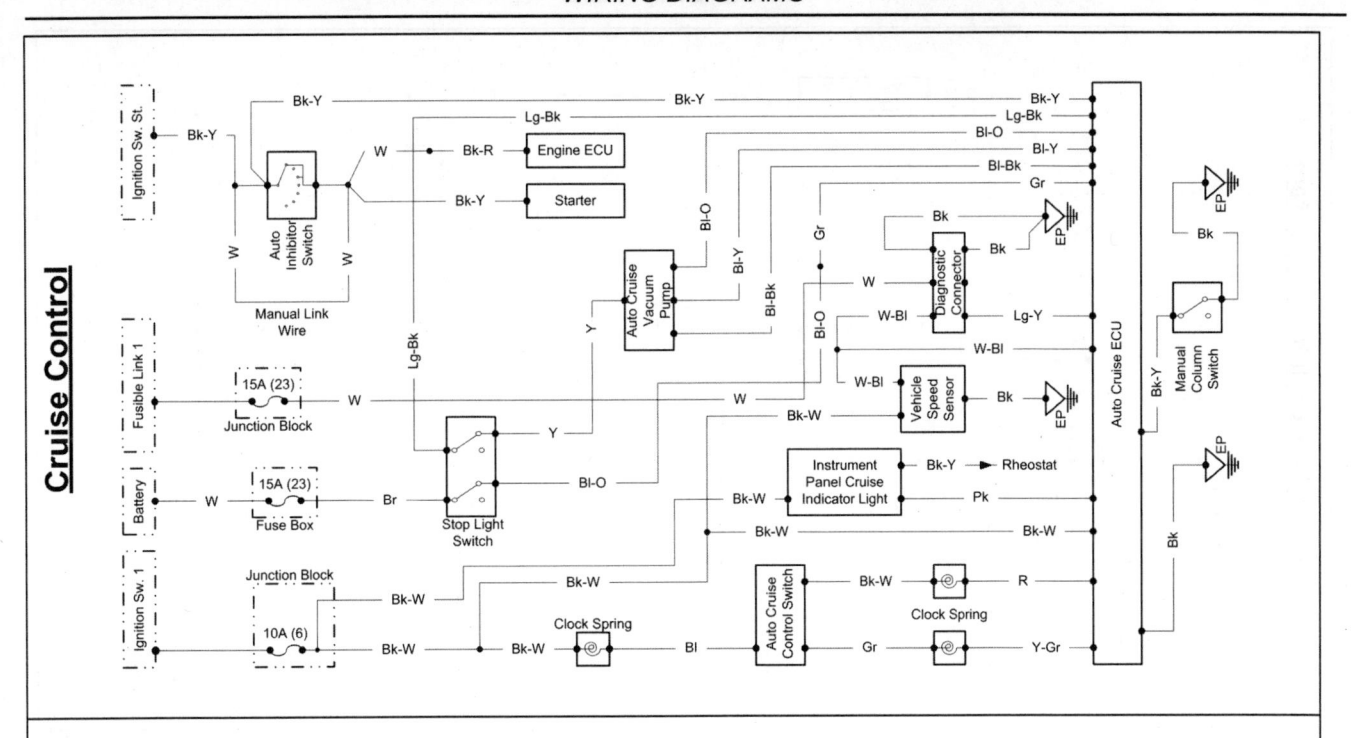

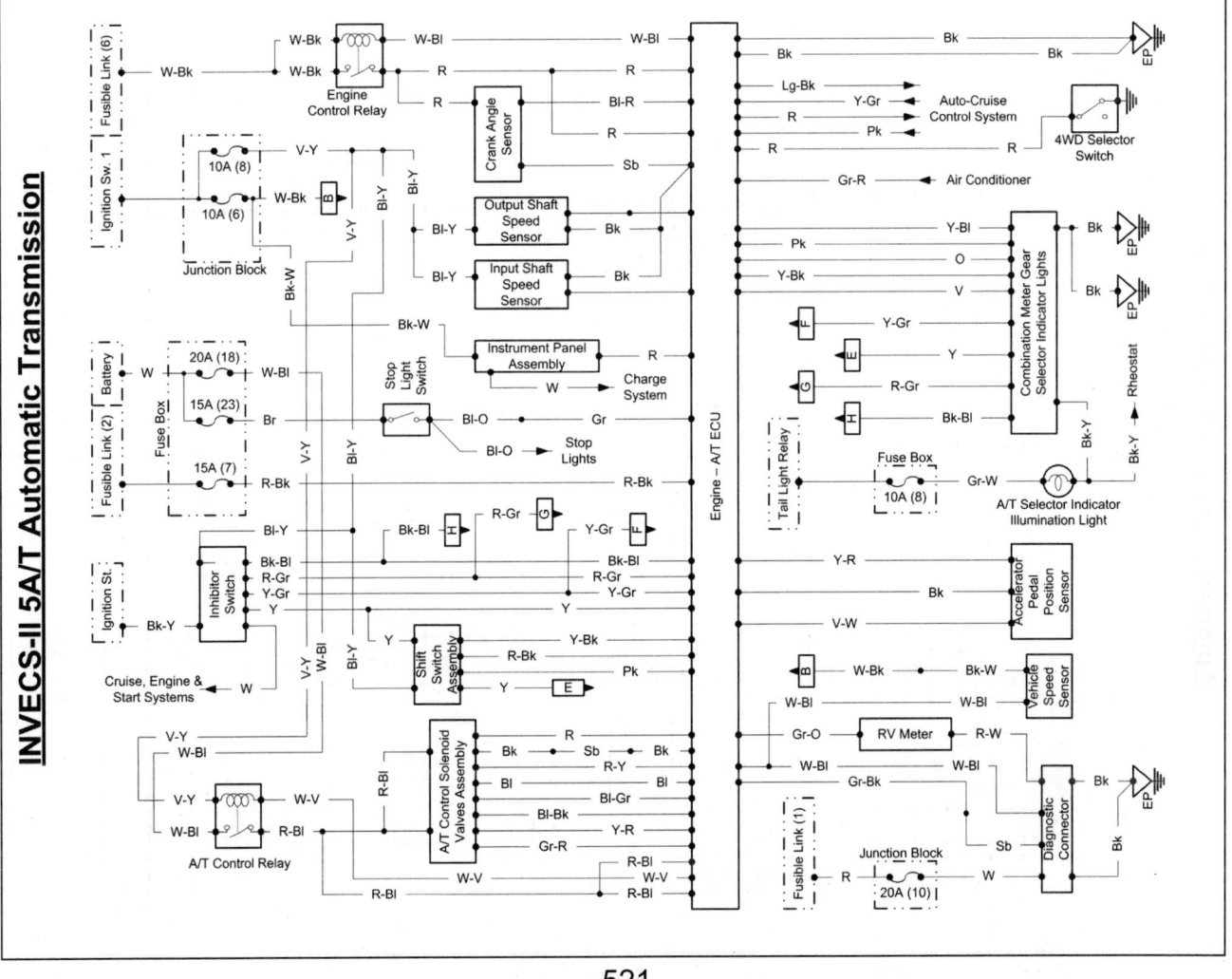

WIRING DIAGRAMS

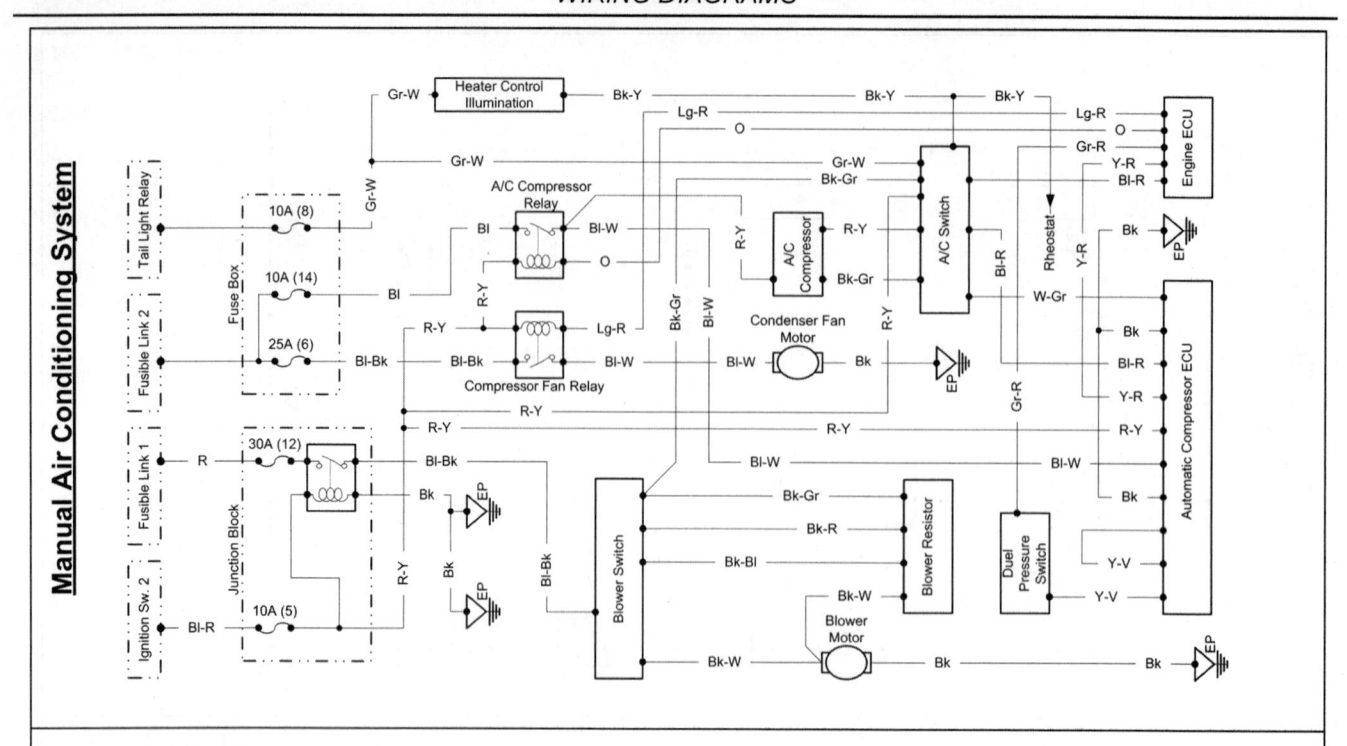

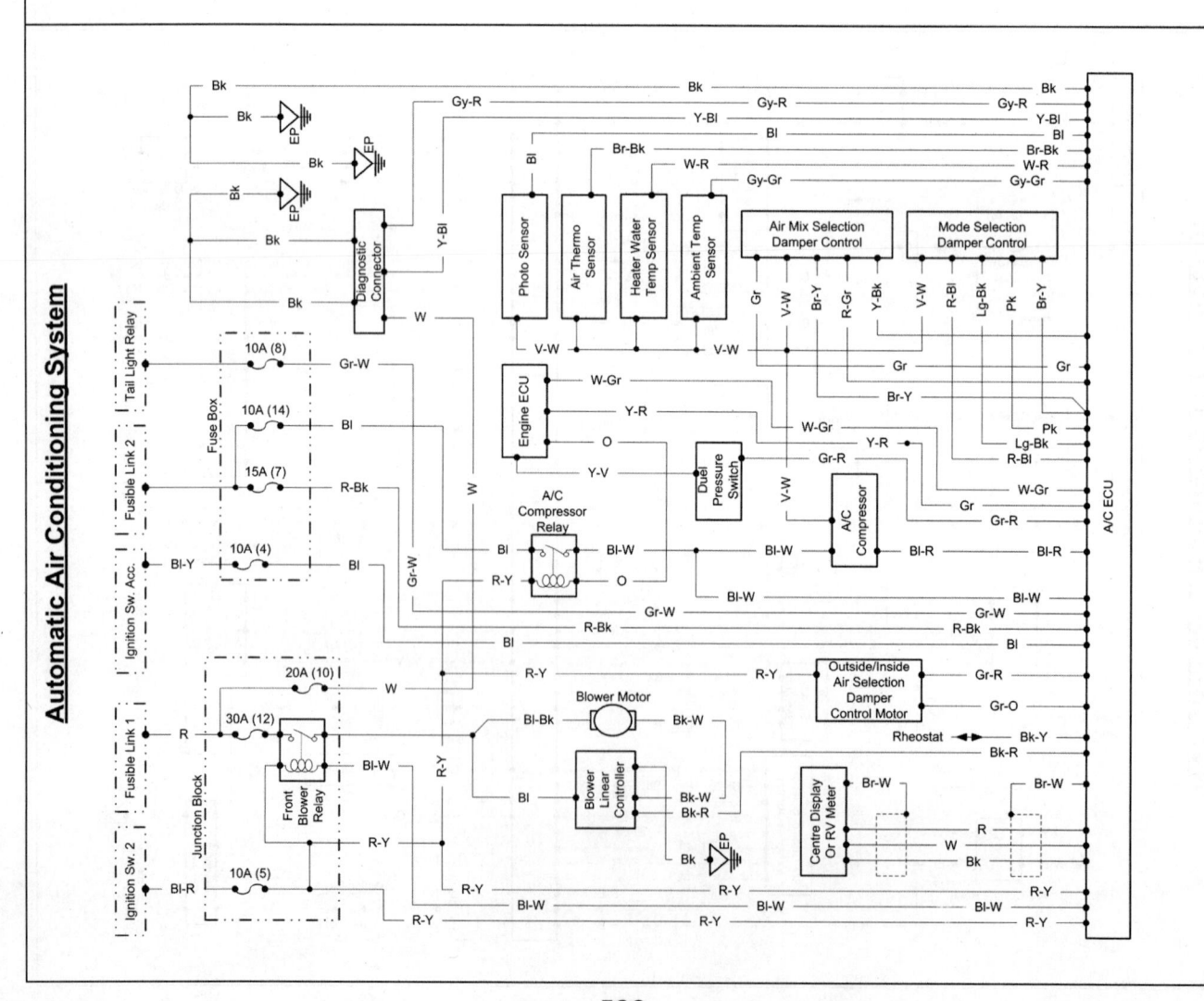

WIRING DIAGRAMS

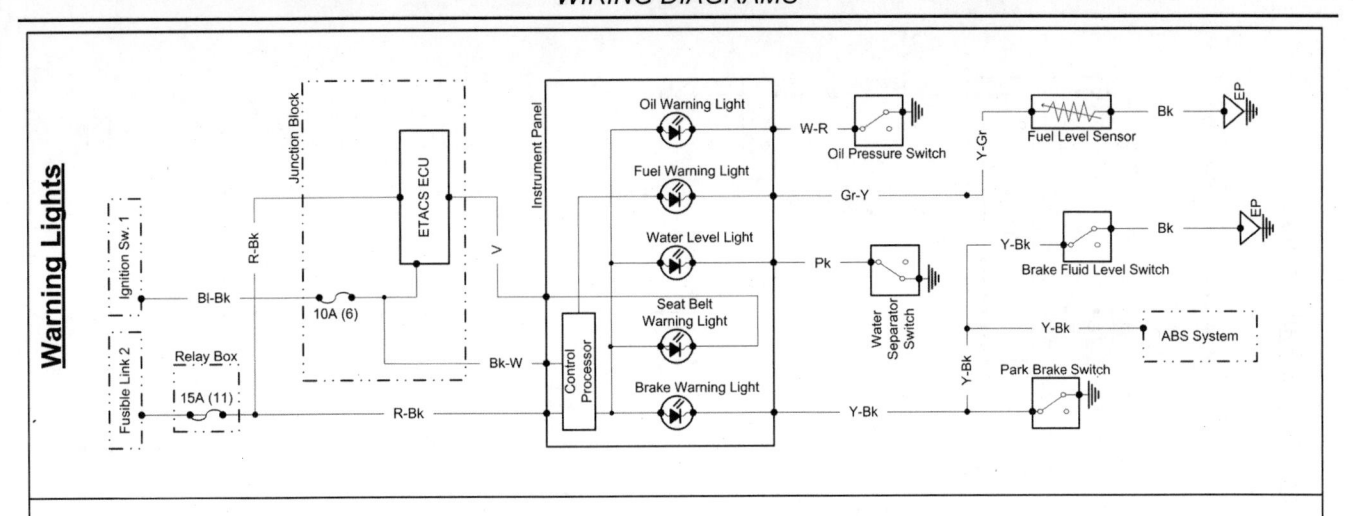

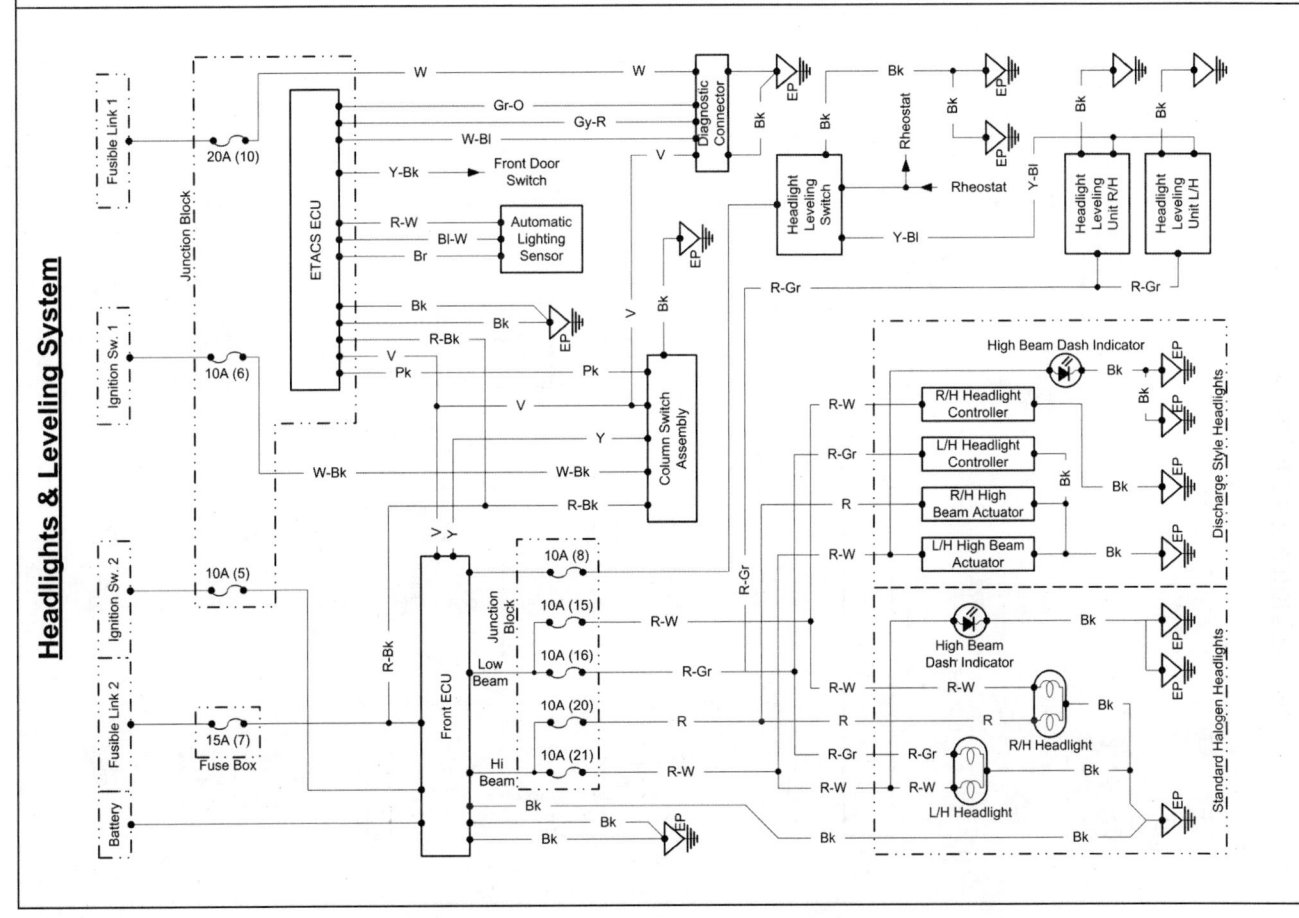

WIRING DIAGRAMS

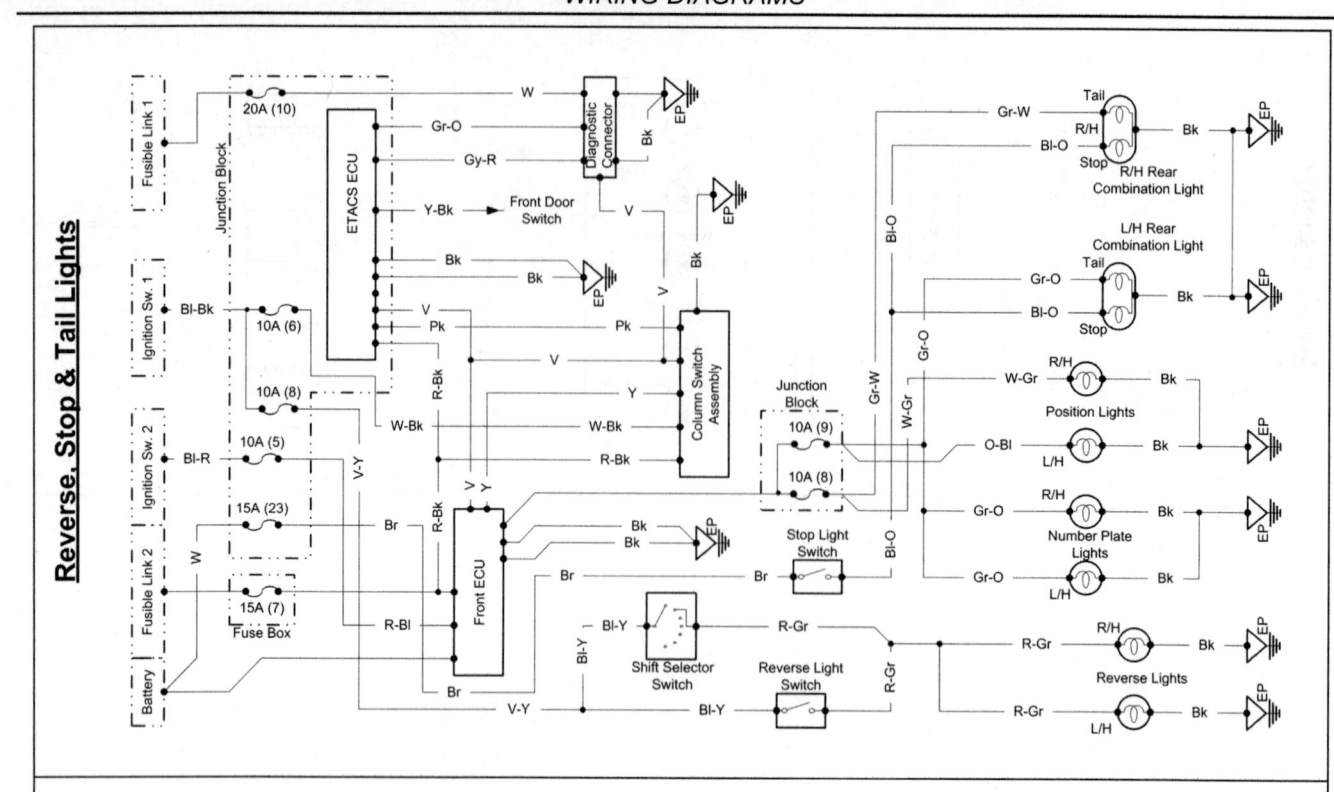

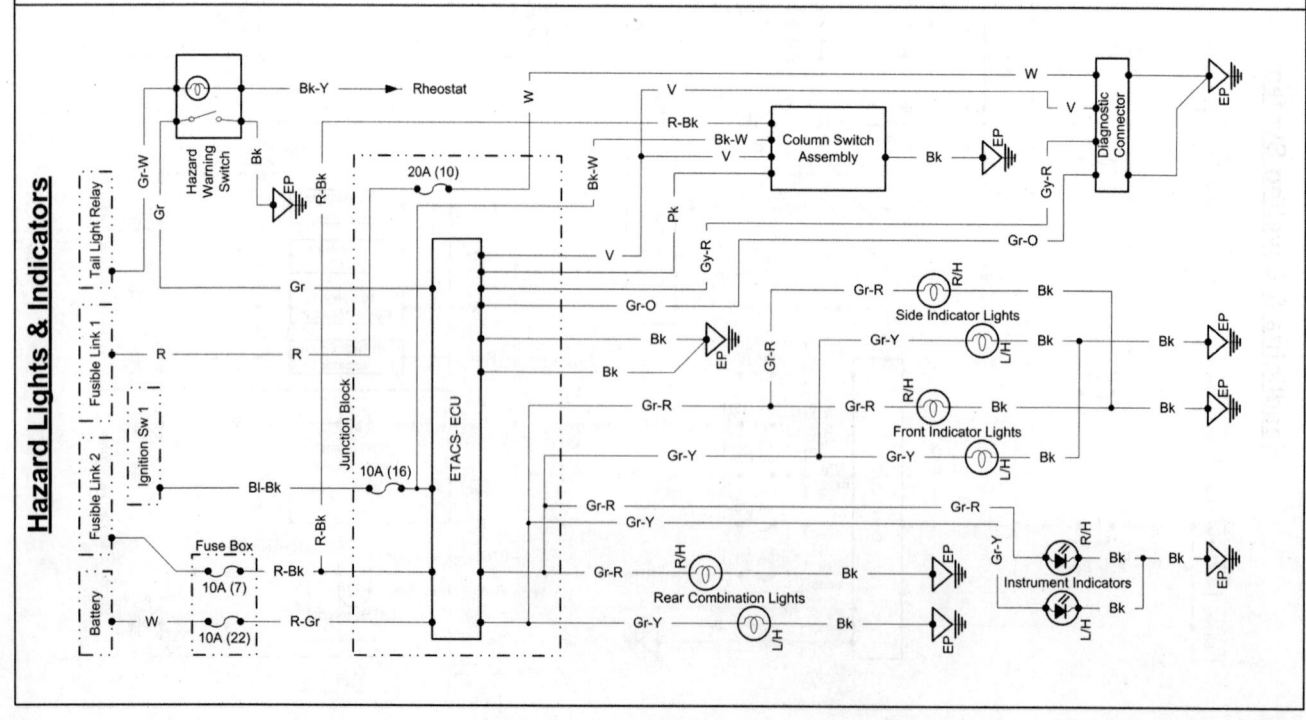

WIRING DIAGRAMS

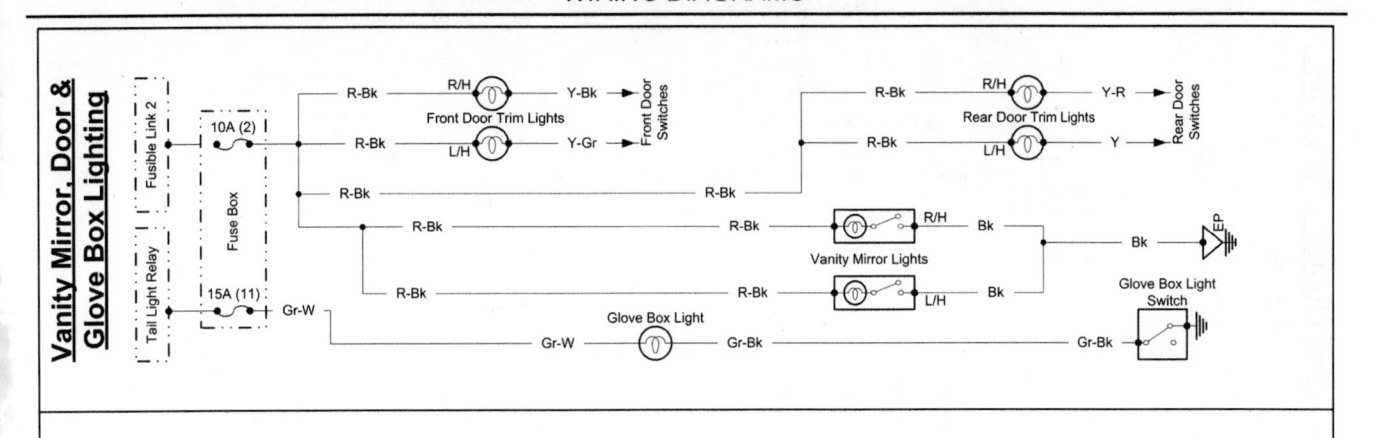

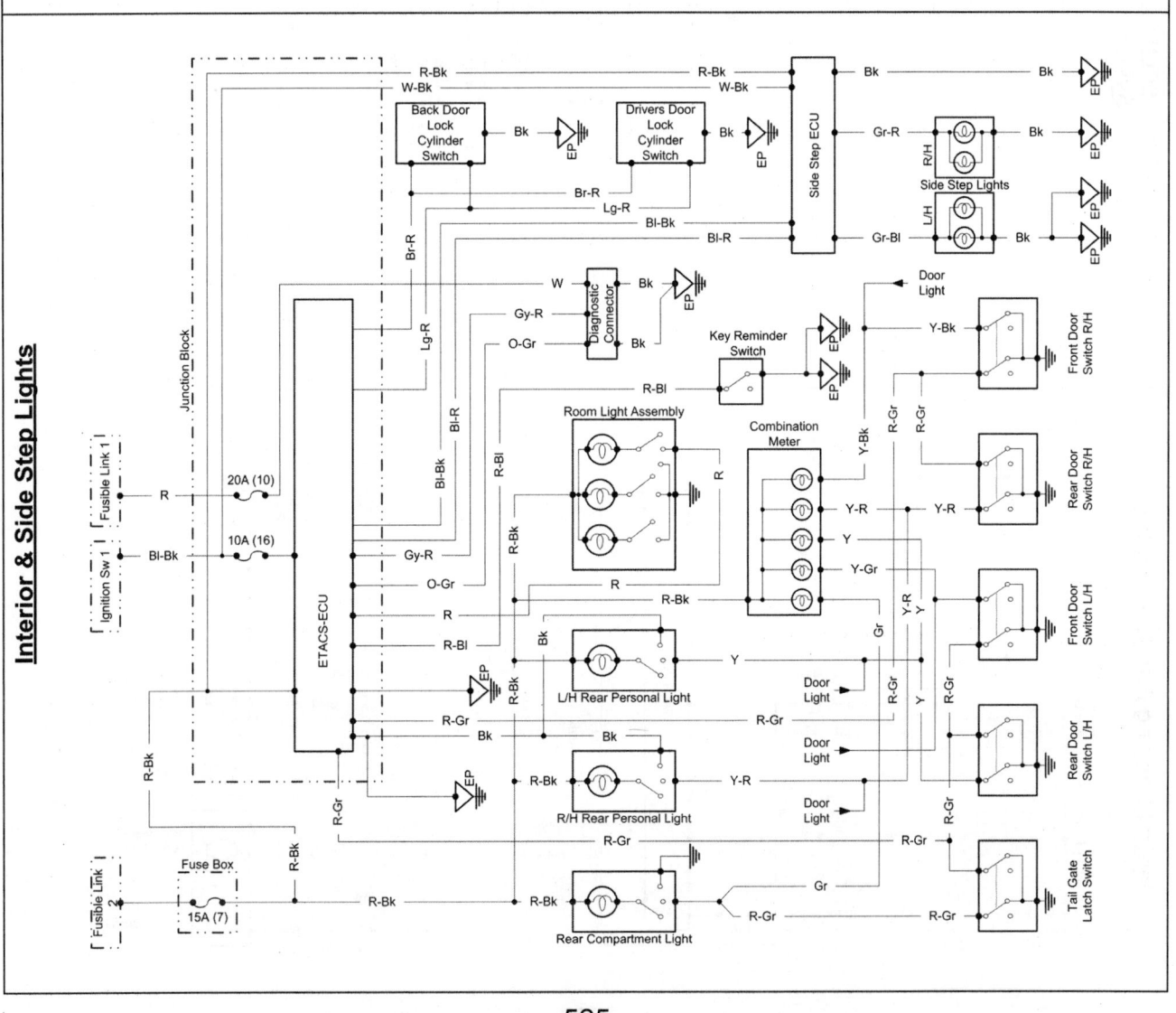

WIRING DIAGRAMS

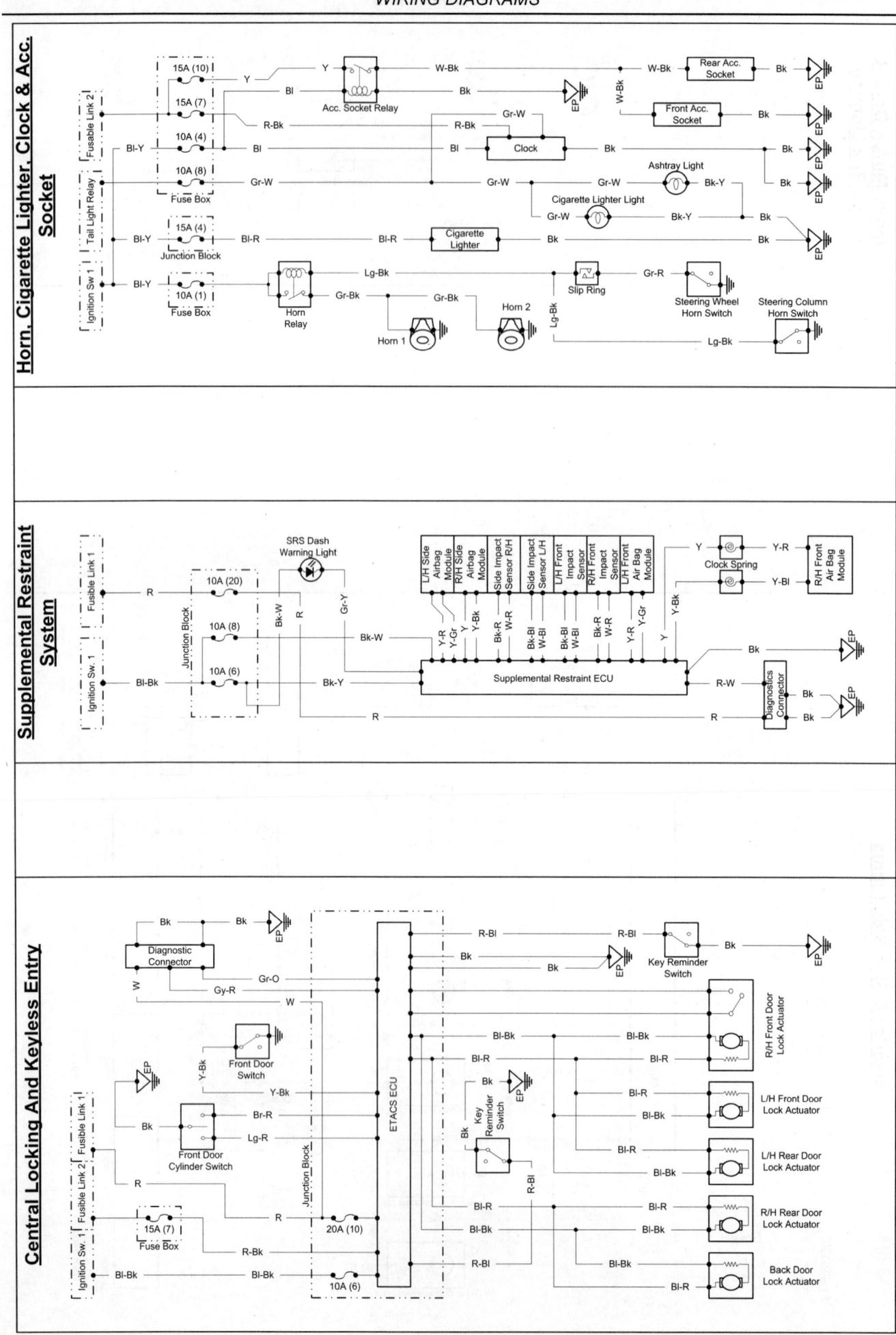

WIRING DIAGRAMS

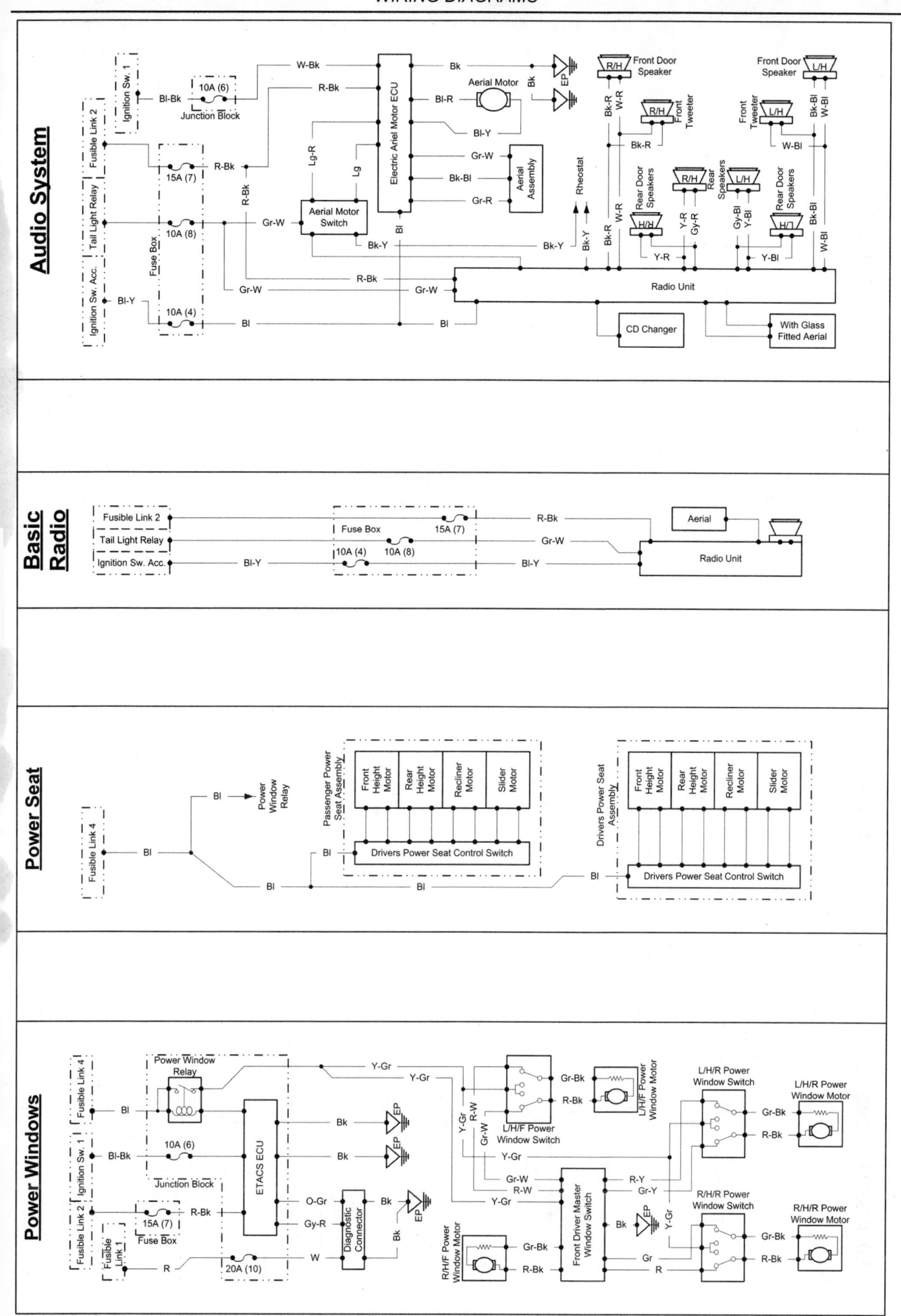

WIRING DIAGRAMS

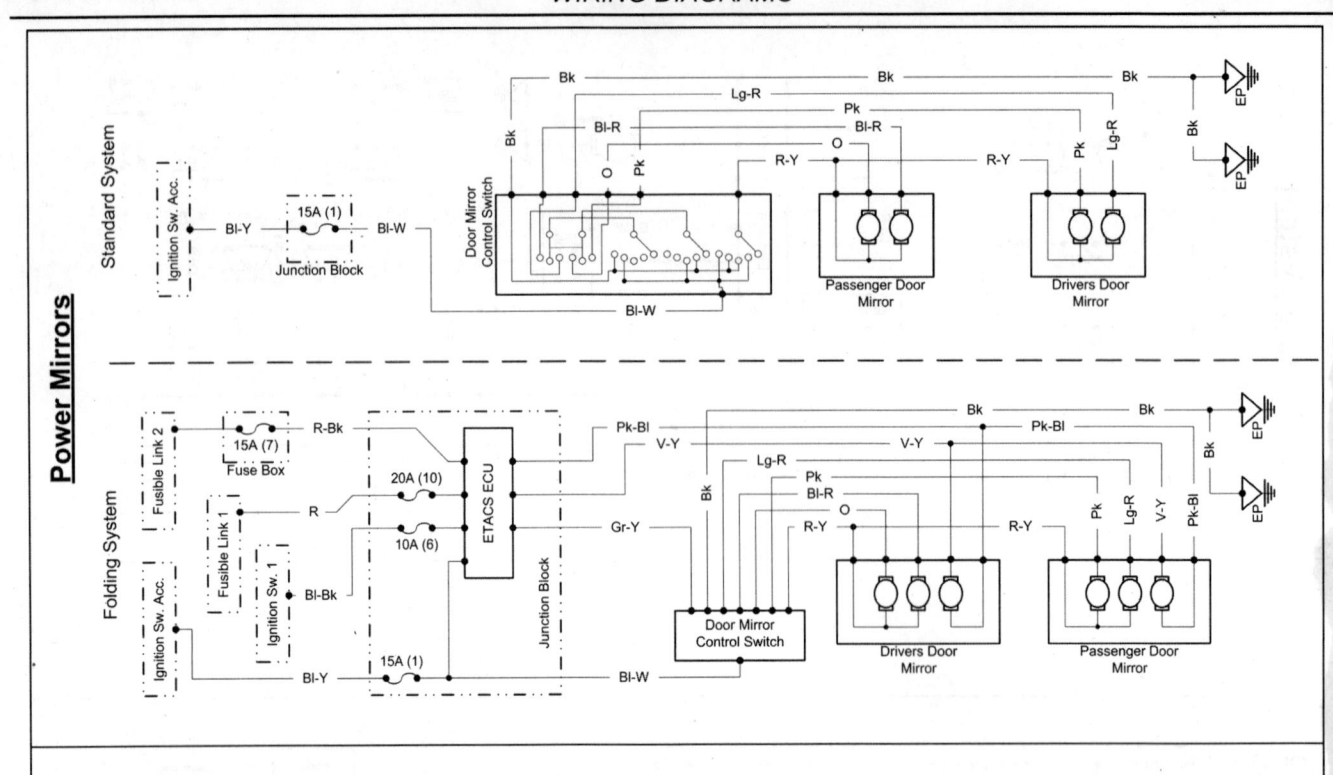

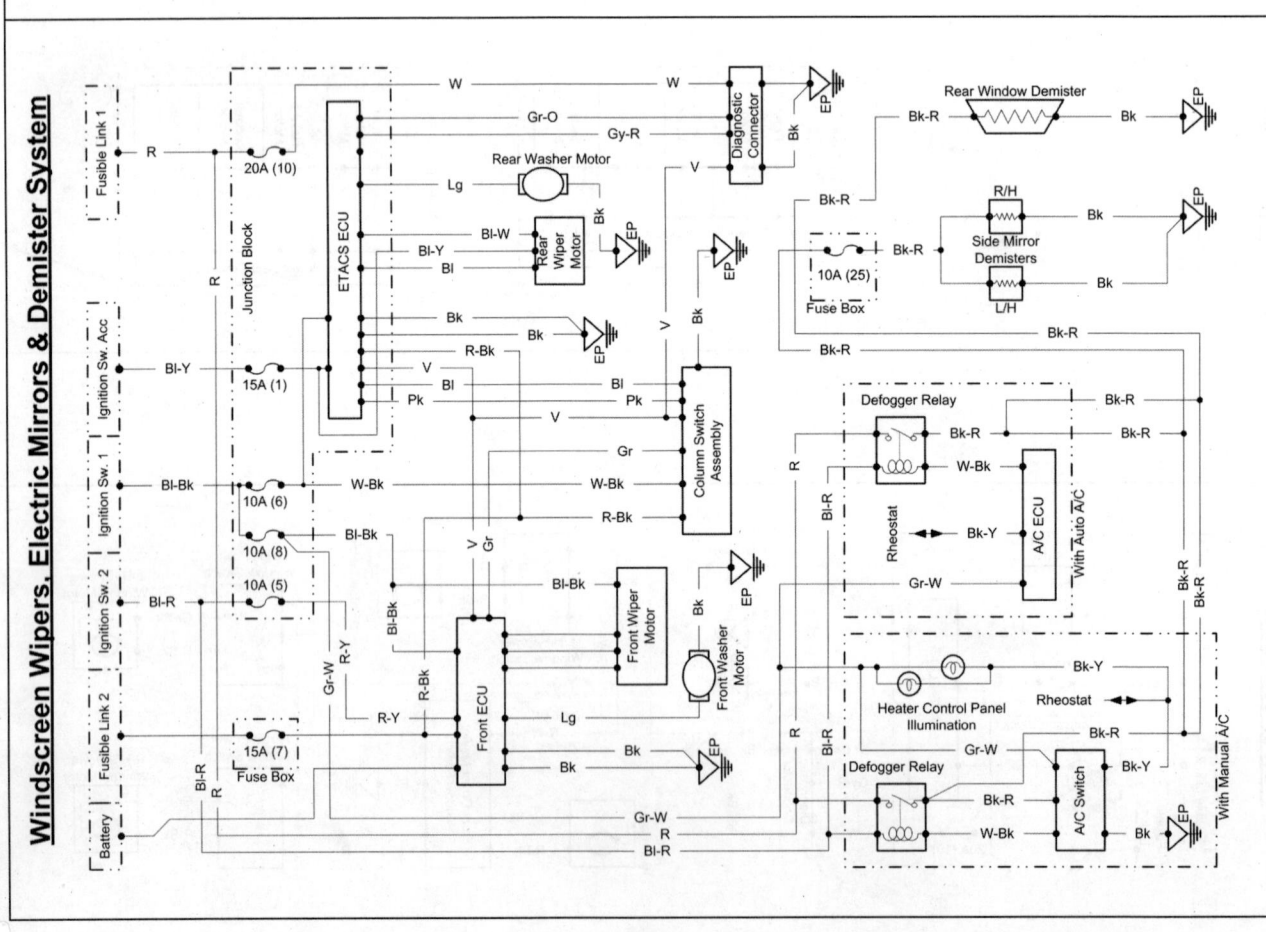

WIRING DIAGRAMS